THE OXFORD HANDBOOK OF

THE HISTORICAL BOOKS OF THE HEBREW BIBLE

THE OXFORD HANDBOOK OF

THE HISTORICAL BOOKS OF THE HEBREW BIBLE

Edited by
BRAD E. KELLE
and
BRENT A. STRAWN

OXFORD
UNIVERSITY PRESS

Oxford University Press is a department of the University of Oxford. It furthers
the University's objective of excellence in research, scholarship, and education
by publishing worldwide. Oxford is a registered trade mark of Oxford University
Press in the UK and certain other countries.

Published in the United States of America by Oxford University Press
198 Madison Avenue, New York, NY 10016, United States of America.

© Oxford University Press 2020

All rights reserved. No part of this publication may be reproduced, stored in
a retrieval system, or transmitted, in any form or by any means, without the
prior permission in writing of Oxford University Press, or as expressly permitted
by law, by license, or under terms agreed with the appropriate reproduction
rights organization. Inquiries concerning reproduction outside the scope of the
above should be sent to the Rights Department, Oxford University Press, at the
address above.

You must not circulate this work in any other form
and you must impose this same condition on any acquirer.

Library of Congress Cataloging-in-Publication Data
Names: Kelle, Brad E., 1973- editor. | Strawn, Brent A., editor.
Title: The Oxford handbook of the historical books of the Hebrew Bible /
edited by Brad E. Kelle and Brent A. Strawn.
Description: New York, NY, United States of America : Oxford University
Press, 2020.
Identifiers: LCCN 2020018914 (print) | LCCN 2020018915 (ebook) | ISBN
9780190261160 (hardback) | ISBN 9780190074111 (epub)
Subjects: LCSH: Bible. Historical Books–Criticism, interpretation, etc.
Classification: LCC BS1205.52 .O94 2020 (print) | LCC BS1205.52 (ebook) |
DDC 222/.06–dc23
LC record available at https://lccn.loc.gov/2020018914
LC ebook record available at https://lccn.loc.gov/2020018915

1 3 5 7 9 8 6 4 2

Printed by Sheridan Books, Inc., United States of America

Editorial Preface

Our initial discussions about this volume stretch back at least six, if not seven years, and so we are thankful, at the end of a long process, for the help and support we have received along the way, especially from the staff of Oxford University Press and our friend and editor Steve Wiggins. Our thanks also go to Caleb Strawn, who prepared the indices. Of course our deepest debts go to the contributors for their fine work and their patience during the slow process of bringing this large project to completion.

Although we took great editorial care during the review process, the reader will note some inconsistencies—a few of which, at least, are present by design. We have not, for instance, regularized all translations, whether of biblical or non-biblical texts. Similarly, we have not always provided versification differences across Hebrew, Greek, and English editions of the Bible. We have not always regularized the spelling of the divine name *Yhwh*, though our own preference was to devocalize it. We also did not require contributors to use "Hebrew Bible" rather than "Old Testament." In all of these cases—and similar ones—we have deferred to the individual preferences of the contributors. Additionally, in the case of some essays, original scripts were required; in most others, we have opted for transliteration so as to make the essays accessible to those who don't read the original languages. Again, these inconsistencies are often by design; at the least they are not naive. We hope that whatever discomfort readers may experience upon encountering such discrepancies will pale in comparison to the insight afforded by the contributions contained herein.

Finally, in a large reference work such as this one, with so many different contributors, some degree of overlap is to be expected and is, in fact, unavoidable. One will notice, for example, that several essays touch on compositional theories and debates regarding the Deuteronomistic History or the books of Chronicles and Ezra-Nehemiah, with several others rehearsing the vexed tradition history of Ezra in its various ancient versions. Here again we have chosen not to eliminate such overlap, but have preferred to let it stand. We deem this a matter of scholarly integrity: letting each contributor have her or his say. Yet we also deemed it helpful, both pedagogically and interpretively: repetition is, after all, a useful method in teaching and learning; it is also the case that a number of the biblical books treated here abound in it!

Brad E. Kelle, Point Loma Nazarene University, San Diego, CA
Brent A. Strawn, Duke University, Durham, NC

Contents

List of Abbreviations   xi
List of Contributors   xix

    Introduction   1
    Brad E. Kelle and Brent A. Strawn

PART I CONTEXTS: SOURCES, HISTORY, TEXTS

1. Historiography and History Writing in the Ancient World   7
   Richard D. Nelson

2. Assyrian and Babylonian Sources   20
   Martti Nissinen

3. Achaemenid Political History and Sources   34
   Amélie Kuhrt

4. Text-Critical Issues with Samuel and Kings   50
   Julio Trebolle Barrera and Eugene Ulrich

5. Text-Critical Issues in Ezra-Nehemiah and 1 Esdras   64
   Lisbeth S. Fried

6. Early Israel's Origins, Settlement, and Ethnogenesis   79
   Ann E. Killebrew

7. Israelite State Formation and Early Monarchy in History and Biblical Historiography   94
   Walter Dietrich

8. The Later Monarchy in History and Biblical Historiography   109
   Paul S. Evans

9. New Perspectives on the Exile in Light of Cuneiform Texts   130
   Laurie Pearce

10. New Perspectives on the Return from Exile and Persian-Period
    Yehud   147
    MARY JOAN WINN LEITH

PART II CONTENT: THEMES, CONCEPTS, ISSUES

11. Israelite and Judean Society and Economy   173
    ROGER S. NAM

12. Politics and Kingship in the Historical Books, with Attention
    to the Role of Political Theory in Interpretation   187
    GEOFFREY PARSONS MILLER

13. The Distinctive Roles of the Prophets in the Deuteronomistic
    History and the Chronicler's History   201
    MARVIN A. SWEENEY

14. The Various Roles of Women in the Historical Books   214
    MERCEDES L. GARCÍA BACHMANN

15. Exogamy and Divorce in Ezra and Nehemiah   228
    HERBERT R. MARBURY

16. Yahwistic Religion in the Assyrian and Babylonian Periods   241
    RICHARD S. HESS

17. Yahwistic Religion in the Persian Period   254
    MELODY D. KNOWLES

18. A Theological Comparison of the Deuteronomistic History
    and Chronicles   266
    MATTHEW J. LYNCH

19. Divine and Human Violence in the Historical Books   284
    DOUGLAS S. EARL

PART III APPROACHES: COMPOSITION, SYNTHESIS, THEORY

20. The So-called Deuteronomistic History and Its Theories
    of Composition   303
    THOMAS RÖMER

21. Reading the Historical Books as Part of the Primary History 323
RICHARD S. BRIGGS

22. Synchronic Readings of Joshua-Kings 339
SERGE FROLOV

23. The Rise and Fall of the So-called Chronicler's History and the Current Study of the Composition of Chronicles, Ezra, and Nehemiah 353
RALPH W. KLEIN

24. 1 Esdras: Structure, Composition, and Significance 367
KRISTIN DE TROYER

25. Synthetic and Literary Readings of Chronicles and Ezra-Nehemiah 379
STEVEN J. SCHWEITZER

26. The Role of Orality and Textuality, Folklore and Scribalism in the Historical Books 393
SUSAN NIDITCH

27. Feminist and Postcolonial Readings of the Historical Books 406
CAMERON B. R. HOWARD

28. The Deuteronomistic History as Literature of Trauma 421
DAVID JANZEN

PART IV RECEPTION: LITERATURE, TRADITIONS, FIGURES

29. Joshua in Reception History 437
ZEV I. FARBER

30. Deborah in Reception History 452
JOY A. SCHROEDER

31. Samson in Reception History 466
KELLY J. MURPHY

32. Saul in Reception History 483
BARBARA GREEN

33. David in Reception History — 496
DOMINIK MARKL

34. Solomon in Reception History — 511
SARA M. KOENIG

35. Ezra and Nehemiah in Reception History — 526
ARMIN SIEDLECKI

36. The Historical Books in the New Testament — 537
STEVE MOYISE

Ancient Sources Index — 549
Author Index — 577

LIST OF ABBREVIATIONS

AASF	Annales Academiae Scientiarum Fennicae
AASFSerB	Annales Academia Scientiarum Fennica. Series B
AB	Anchor Bible
ABS	Archaeology and Biblical Studies
AcadBib	Academia Biblica
ADOG	Abhandlungen der deutschen Orientgesellschaft
AfO	*Archiv für Orientforschung*
AIL	Ancient Israel and Its Literature
AJA	*American Journal of Archaeology*
AJS Review	*The Journal of the Association for Jewish Studies*
ALW	*Archiv für Liturgiewissenschaft*
ANEM	Ancient Near Eastern Monographs
ANET	*Ancient Near Eastern Texts Relating to the Old Testament*. Edited by J. B. Pritchard. 3rd ed. Princeton, 1969
AOAT	Alter Orient und Altes Testament
AoF	*Altorientalische Forschungen*
AOTC	Abingdon Old Testament Commentary
ARTA	*Achaemenid Research on Texts and Archaeology*
ATM	Altes Testament und Moderne
AYB	Anchor Yale Bible
AYBRL	Anchor Yale Biblical Research Library
BA	*Biblical Archaeology*
BaAr	Babylonische Archive
BAR	*Biblical Archaeology Review*
BASOR	*Bulletin of the American Schools of Oriental Research*
BBB	Bonner Biblische Beiträge
BBET	Beiträge zur biblischen Exegese und Theologie
BBFC	British Board of Film Classification
BEATAJ	Beiträge zur Erforschung des Alten Testaments und des antiken Judentum

BETL	Bibliotheca Ephemeridum Theologicarum Lovaniensium
BHS	Biblia Hebraica Stuttgartensia
Bib	Biblica
BibInt	Biblical Interpretation
BiOr	Bibliotheca Orientalis
BJS	Biblical and Judaic Studies
BR	Bible Review
BThSt	Biblisch-theologische Studien
BTS	Biblical Tools and Studies
BWANT	Beiträge zur Wissenschaft vom Alten (und Neuen) Testament
BZABR	Beihefte für altorientalische und biblische Rechtsgeschichte
BZAW	Beihefte zur Zeitschrift für die alttestamentliche Wissenschaft
CAH	The Cambridge Ancient History
CAH IV	J. Boardman, N. G. L. Hammond, D. M. Lewis, and M. Ostwald, eds., *The Cambridge Ancient History*, Vol. IV: *Persia, Greece and the Western Mediterranean c.525 to 479 BC* (2nd ed.; Cambridge: Cambridge University Press, 1988)
CAH VI	D. M. Lewis, J. Boardman, S. Hornblower and M. Ostwald, eds., *The Cambridge Ancient History*, Vol. VI: *The Fourth Century B.C.* (2nd ed.; Cambridge: Cambridge University Press, 1994)
CBOT	Coniectanea Biblica: OT Series
CBQ	Catholic Biblical Quarterly
CCR	Critical Research in Religion
CCWJCW	Cambridge Commentaries on Writings of the Jewish and Christian World 200 BC to AD 200
CDAFI	Cahiers de la Délégation Française en Iran
CHANE	Culture and History of the Ancient Near East
COS	The Context of Scripture
CS	Cistercian Studies
CSCO	Corpus Scriptorum Christianorum Orientalium
CUSAS	Cornell University Studies in Assyriology and Sumerology
DDD^2	*Dictionary of Deities and Demons in the Bible.* 2nd rev. ed. Edited by Karel van der Toorn. Grand Rapids: Eerdmans, 1999
DJD	Discoveries in the Judaean Desert
DSD	Dead Sea Discoveries
Dtr	The Deuteronomistic History

EBR	*Encyclopedia of the Bible and Its Reception*
EJL	Early Judaism and Its Literature
EncJud	Encyclopedia Judaica. Edited by Fred Skolnik and Michael Berenbaum. 2nd ed. 22 vols. New York: Macmillan, 2007 [orig. 1972]
ErIsr	*Eretz-Israel*
ET	English translation(s)
FAT	Forschungen zum Alten Testament
FC	The Fathers of the Church
FCB	Feminist Companion to the Bible
FGrH	Felix Jacoby, *Die Fragmente der griechischen Historiker*. Berlin, Leiden: Brill 1923–58
fin	end
FOTL	The Forms of the Old Testament Literature
FRLANT	Forschungen zur Religion und Literatur des Alten und Neuen Testaments
GMTR	Guides to the Mesopotamian Textual Record
HAT	Handbuch zum Alten Testament
HBM	Hebrew Bible Monographs
HBS	Herders biblische Studien
HCOT	Historical Commentary on the Old Testament
HDB	*Harvard Divinity Bulletin*
HdO	Handbuch der Orientalistik
HeBAI	*Hebrew Bible and Ancient Israel*
HSM	Harvard Semitic Monographs
HThKAT	Herders theologischer Kommentar zum Alten Testament
HTR	*Harvard Theological Review*
HUCA	Hebrew Union College Annual
ICC	International Critical Commentary
IDBSup	*Intepreter's Dictionary of the Bible, Supplementary Volume*
IEJ	*Israel Exploration Journal*
init	beginning
IrAnt	*Iranica Antiqua*
IrAntSupp	Iranica Antiqua Supplement
ISBL	Indiana Studies in Biblical Literature
JA	*Journal Asiatique*

JANEH	*Journal of Ancient Near Eastern History*
JANER	*Journal of Ancient Near Eastern Religions*
JANES	*Journal of the Ancient Near Eastern Society*
JAOS	*Journal of the American Oriental Society*
JBL	*Journal of Biblical Literature*
JBR	*Journal of Biblical Reception*
JCS	*Journal of Cuneiform Studies*
JEA	*Journal of Egyptian Archaeology*
JECS	*Journal of Early Christian Studies*
JHS	*Journal of Hebrew Scriptures*
JJS	*Journal of Jewish Studies*
JNES	*Journal of Near Eastern Studies*
JQR	*Jewish Quarterly Review*
JSJ	*Journal for the Study of Judaism*
JSJSup	Supplements to the Journal for the Study of Judaism
JSNTSup	Journal for the Study of the New Testament Supplement Series
JSOT	*Journal for the Study of the Old Testament*
JSOTSup	Journal for the Study of the Old Testament Supplement Series
JSP	*Journal for the Study of the Pseudepigrapha*
JTI	*Journal for Theological Interpretation*
JTISup	Journal for Theological Interpretation, Supplements
JTS	*Journal of Theological Studies*
KJV	King James Version
LAI	Library of Ancient Israel
LAOS	Leipziger Altorientalische Studien
LCI	*Lexikon der christlichen Ikonographie*
LHBOTS	Library of Hebrew Bible/Old Testament Studies
LSTS	Library of Second Temple Studies
LXX	Septuagint
LXX^{Acx}	Alexandrian and related manuscripts (c and x) of the LXX
LXX^L	Lucianic/Antiochene text of the LXX
LXX^{N++}	manuscript N and related LXX manuscripts
LXX^O	Hexapla
MT	Masoretic Text

NABU	*Nouvelles assyriologiques brèves et utilitaires*
NCB	New Century Bible
NEA	*Near Eastern Archaeology*
NICOT	The New International Commentary on the Old Testament
NIV	New International Version
NJB	New Jerusalem Bible
NPNF	*The Nicene and Post-Nicene Fathers*
NRSV	New Revised Standard Version
OBO	Orbis Biblicus et Orientalis
OBT	Overtures to Biblical Theology
OED	*Oxford English Dictionary*
OG	Old Greek
OG^B	Vaticanus
OIS	Oriental Institute Seminars
OL	Old Latin
OLA	Orientalia Lovaniensia Analecta
OLZ	*Orientalistische Literaturzeitschrift*
Or	*Orientalia*
OrAnt	*Oriens Antiquus*
OrNS	*Orientalia (NS)*
OTL	Old Testament Library
OTS	Oudtestamentische Studien
PEQ	*Palestine Exploration Quarterly*
PFES	Publications of the Finnish Exegetical Society
PIHANS	Publications de l'Institut historique-archéologique néerlandais de Stamboul
PRS	*Perspectives in Religious Studies*
PTMS	Pittsburgh Theological Monograph Series
PTSD	Posttraumatic Stress Disorder
RA	*Revue d'assyriologie et d'archéologie orientale*
RÉA	*Revue des Études Anciennes*
REB	Revised English Bible
RGTC	Répertoire géographique des textes cunéiformes
RHPR	*Revue d'histoire et de philosophie religieuses*

RIMA	The Royal Inscriptions of Mesopotamia, Assyrian Periods
RINAP	Royal Inscriptions of the Neo-Assyrian Period
RlA	*Reallexikon der Assyriologie und Vorderasiatischen Archäologie*
SAA	State Archives of Assyria
SAAB	*State Archives of Assyria Bulletin*
SAAS	State Archives of Assyria Studies
SAOC	Studies in Ancient Oriental Civilizations
SBA.AT	Stuttgarter Biblische Aufsatzbände. Alten Testament
SBL	Society of Biblical Literature
SBLABS	Society of Biblical Literature Archaeology and Biblical Studies
SBLDS	Society of Biblical Literature Dissertation Series
SBLEJL	Society of Biblical Literature Early Judaism and Its Literature
SBLMS	Society of Biblical Literature Monograph Series
SBLSCS	Society of Biblical Literature Septuagint and Cognate Studies
SBLWAW	Society of Biblical Literature Writings from the Ancient World
SBR	Studies in the Bible and Its Reception
SBS	Stuttgarter Bibelstudien
SBT	Studies in Biblical Theology
SCS	Septuagint and Cognate Studies
Sem	*Semeia*
SemeiaSt	Semeia Studies
SHANE	Studies in the History of the Ancient Near East
SHCANE	Studies in the History and Culture of the Ancient Near East
SJOT	*Scandinavian Journal of the Old Testament*
SNT	Supplements to Novum Testamentum
SOTSMS	Society for Old Testament Studies Monograph Series
STR	Studies in Theology and Religion
TA	*Tel Aviv*
TAD	Bezalel Porten and Ada Yardeni, eds., *Textbook of Aramaic Documents from Ancient Egypt* (4 vols.; Jerusalem: Hebrew University, 1986–99)
TB	Theologische Bücherei: Neudrucke und Berichte aus dem 20. Jahrhundert
TCS	Texts from Cuneiform Sources
TF	Theologie und Frieden
Transeu	*Transeuphratène*

TSAJ	*Texte und Studien zum antiken Judentum*
TSO	Texte und Studen zur Orientalistik
TTH	Translated Texts for Historians
UF	*Ugarit Forschungen*
VT	*Vetus Testamentum*
VTSup	Supplements to Vetus Testamentum
WAWSup	Writings from the Ancient World Supplement Series
WBC	Word Biblical Commentary
WMANT	*Wissenschaftliche Monographien zum Alten und Neuen Testament*
WO	*Die Welt des Orients*
WVDOG	Wissenschaftliche Veröffentlichungen der deutschen Orient-Gesellschaft
WZKM	*Wiener Zeitschrift für die Kunde des Morgenlandes*
YNER	Yale Near Eastern Researches
ZA	*Zeitschrift für Assyriologie*
ZABR	*Zeitschrift für altorientalische und biblische Rechtsgeschichte*
ZAW	*Zeitschrift für die alttestamentliche Wissenschaft*
ZDPV	*Zeitschrift des deutschen Palästina-Vereins*
α′	Aquila, recension of the LXX
θ′	Theodotion, recension of the LXX
σ′	Symmachus, recension of the LXX

List of Contributors

Richard S. Briggs Lecturer in Old Testament, Director of Biblical Studies St. John's College, Durham University

Kristin De Troyer Professor of Old Testament Biblical Studies at Universität Salzburg

Walter Dietrich Professor Emeritus of Old Testament Studies at Universität Bern

Douglas S. Earl author of *The Joshua Delusion?: Rethinking Genocide in the Bible*, Durham University

Paul S. Evans Associate Professor of Old Testament at McMaster Divinity College, McMaster University

Zev I. Farber Fellow and Editor at Project TABS, TheTorah.com

Lisbeth S. Fried Visiting Scholar at the University of Michigan

Serge Frolov Professor of Religious Studies at Southern Methodist University

Mercedes L. García Bachmann Director of the Instituto para la Pastoral Contextual, Iglesia Evangélica Luterana Unida, Argentina-Uruguay

Barbara Green Professor of Biblical Studies at the Dominican School of Philosophy and Theology

Richard S. Hess Distinguished Professor of Old Testament at Denver Seminary

Cameron B. R. Howard Associate Professor of Old Testament at Luther Seminary

David Janzen Associate Professor of Hebrew Bible/Old Testament in the Department of Theology and Religion at Durham University

Brad E. Kelle Professor of Old Testament and Hebrew at Point Loma Nazarene University

Ann E. Killebrew Associate Professor of Classics and Ancient Mediterranean Studies, Jewish Studies, and Anthropology at Pennsylvania State University

Ralph W. Klein Christ Seminary-Seminex professor of Old Testament at the Lutheran School of Theology at Chicago

Melody D. Knowles Associate Professor of Old Testament at Virginia Theological Seminary

Sara M. Koenig Associate Professor of Biblical Studies at Seattle Pacific University

Amélie Kuhrt Professor Emeritus of Ancient Near Eastern History at University College London

Mary Joan Winn Leith Professor of Religious Studies at Stonehill College

Matthew J. Lynch Assistant Professor of Old Testament at Regent College

Herbert R. Marbury Associate Professor of Hebrew Bible at The Divinity School, Vanderbilt University

Dominik Markl Professor of Exegesis of the Old Testament at the Pontifical Biblical Institute

Geoffrey Parsons Miller Stuyvesant P. Comfort Professor of Law at New York University School of Law

Steve Moyise Professor of New Testament at St. Hild College

Kelly J. Murphy Associate Professor of Philosophy and Religion at Central Michigan University

Roger S. Nam Professor of Hebrew Bible Emory University

Richard D. Nelson W. J. A. Power Professor of Biblical Hebrew and Old Testament at Southern Methodist University

Susan Niditch Samuel Green Professor of Religion at Amherst College

Martti Nissinen Reader and Professor in Old Testament Studies at University of Helsinki

Laurie Pearce Lecturer in Akkadian, Assyriology, and Cuneiform at University of California, Berkeley

Thomas Römer Professor at the Collège de France

Joy A. Schroeder Professor of Religion at Capital University

Steven J. Schweitzer Academic Dean and Professor at Bethany Theological Seminary

Armin Siedlecki Head of Cataloging and Rare Book Cataloger at Emory University

Brent A. Strawn Professor of Old Testament and Professor of Law at Duke University

Marvin A. Sweeney Professor of the Hebrew Bible at Claremont School of Theology

Julio Trebolle Barrera Professor Emeritus of the Department of Hebrew and Aramean Studies at the Complutense University of Madrid

Eugene Ulrich Professor Emeritus of Hebrew Scripture and Theology in the Department of Theology at the University of Notre Dame

INTRODUCTION

BRAD E. KELLE AND BRENT A. STRAWN

THE category "Historical Books of the Hebrew Bible" is hardly a self-evident one for at least two reasons. First, the Hebrew Bible proper knows of no such category. In the Hebrew Bible, the compositions that are considered "Historical Books" fall into either the Former Prophets (Joshua, Judges, 1–2 Samuel, 1–2 Kings) or the Writings (Ruth, 1–2 Chronicles, Ezra-Nehemiah, Esther). To be sure, a four-part division of the biblical compositions found in the now tripartite Hebrew Bible has ancient roots: the idea of "historical books" and "poetic books" existing alongside Pentateuch and Prophets (the latter more narrowly circumscribed) appears to go back to certain traditions (and manuscripts) in the Greek translation known as the Septuagint. Whatever the case, "Historical Books" is not native to the Hebrew Bible.

The second problem with a category of "Historical Books" is that it is potentially misleading with regard to other compositions, on the one hand—are those "*non*-historical" books?—and, on the other, with reference to contemporary historiography. Whatever the "Historical Books" are, it is certainly not the latter. Scholars debate, often sharply, if, let alone how far, these compositions reflect ancient history as that can be known and reconstructed using the tools, methods, and sources available to historians today. If there is any current scholarly agreement on these controverted issues, it is typically that the "Historical Books" are not particularly or especially "historical"—not, at least, by contemporary canons. Then, too, there is the general (and correlate) agreement that these books are often more about religion and theology, even ideology, than they are about history per se—and this despite the fact that many of these books do have significant intersections with ancient history as known and reconstructed today.

These caveats duly entered, the present handbook is nevertheless (and for various reasons) dedicated to the Historical Books, though not comprehensively—and this, again, for two reasons. For one, to offer something exhaustive with reference to these books would be impossible. Each is too rich, with the history of their interpretation too vast, to attempt any such thing for any one of these books, let alone all of them. The current volume thus pursues an *essential*, not exhaustive approach to covering the Historical Books. Toward that end, the essays gathered here make contact with the following crucial nodes:

- *Contexts*: Sources, History, Texts;
- *Content*: Themes, Concepts, Issues;

- *Approaches*: Composition, Synthesis, Theory; and
- *Reception*: Literature, Traditions, Figures.

While far from comprehensive, it is hoped that these nodes permit thorough and representative coverage of most, though certainly not all, of what should be included in a handbook such as this one.

The second reason why the current handbook is not comprehensive has to do with the rather notable exceptions of extensive treatments of either Ruth or Esther, both of which fall in the third part of the Hebrew canon. This omission is not a failure of editorial oversight in terms of design, neither is it the result of a delinquent contributor or two (or more!) to deliver their articles on time. Instead, it goes back to the initial design of the present handbook alongside other Oxford volumes in planning, production, or already in print. The current volume was originally to be focused only on the Deuteronomistic History—the Former Prophets of the Hebrew Bible: Joshua through Kings—but, at the Press's request, Chronicles and Ezra-Nehemiah were included. There are good reasons for including these books with the others (which is in part how the "Historical Books" category was birthed), but the current configuration nevertheless leaves two important compositions undiscussed. While this is a lamentable situation, it remains true that Ruth and Esther are important enough—and for several reasons—that they deserve more extensive treatment than could be offered here. We hope, therefore, that both books will receive the attention each is due in another Oxford Handbook soon.

This volume, like so many others these days, will likely be accessed by many readers in electronic form. Electronic formats permit certain types of metadata that print versions do not. That includes abstracts and key words for search purposes. Given these factors, we have decided not to overview each of the essays in this introduction. There are a large number of essays, after all, and interested readers will no doubt find what they are looking for without a brief sentence or two from the editors. Instead, we would like to offer a bit more insight into how the volume was designed and what we learned in the process of editing the collection.

First, then, with reference to *design*, in addition to the four nodes already mentioned above, we asked all of the contributors to write their essays with two main guiding questions in mind: "What does the topic/area/issue you are writing on have to do with the Historical Books?" and "How does this topic/area/issue help readers better interpret the Historical Books?" Answering the first question would seem the easier of the two, especially when the essay in question is included in a reference work devoted to the Historical Books, but the inclusion of the second—indeed the combination of the two questions together—makes, we believe, each essay of maximum benefit to readers who are not interested solely in *information* but also *interpretation*.

Second, the editorial process has revealed to us several trends in the study of the Historical Books. Astute readers will notice these trends for themselves—they are evident, we believe, already in the Table of Contents—but the trends are especially apparent at the larger, book level and few indeed are the readers who read reference works cover to cover. Since the editorial task requires such reading (and rereading), it is worth highlighting a few of the trends and themes that we noticed in editing the collection.

The most important trend or theme, perhaps unsurprisingly, is *diversity*, which is felt on many levels and worked out in different ways throughout the volume. For one thing, compositional theories and approaches have now advanced well beyond the parameters provided by older hypotheses around, say, the Deuteronomistic History, on the one hand, or the so-called Chronicler's History, on the other. Those theories have long been debated and discussed, of course, but the diversity of approaches that now marks the field means that questions that had previously been governed, if not constrained, by those theories may now be investigated anew and with vigor. Assessment of rhetorical function and effect, analysis of literary styles within these books, and so forth are all open game—again—in a way that they have not been in previous generations of scholarship. So it is that readers will find plenty of discussion of traditional theories and newer updates to the same, and of the textual traditions themselves, which give rise to compositional analyses; but readers will also find approaches that move in entirely different ways altogether, whether those are by attending to synchronic, literary, theoretical, or reception aspects of the texts at hand.

Another way diversity is felt is in how any one particular thematic node is engaged. So, for example, essays under "Contexts" (Part I) run the gamut from text-critical issues (the ground context, as it were, for the Historical Books) to the nature of ancient historiography, Israel's ethnogenesis, state formation and development, consideration of ancient Near Eastern texts, and so forth. Similarly, the topics covered under "Content" (Part II) range widely so as to include society and economy, political theory, violence studies, and the roles and portrayals of women—usually with heavy interdisciplinary engagement. So also with "Approaches" (Part III): diachronic analyses are treated extensively here alongside synchronic/synthetic ones. But beyond this typical dyad, there are also essays on orality, feminism and postcolonialism, and trauma theory. On the face of it, the essays that go under the rubric "Reception" (Part IV) may seem more pro forma, titled, as they are, "X in Reception History." While these titles may be formulaic, here again the essays are quite diverse in representing a panoply of options when it comes to gathering, assessing, and interpreting the manifold—dare one say, diverse—ways the biblical texts have been received over the centuries and now.

We would be remiss if we did not observe that the diversity of the present collection is no doubt the happy result of the diversity of the contributors themselves. Readers will find here a mixture of emerging and established scholars, of different religious background (and levels of adherence), and of different gender and ethnicity. The authors of the essays that follow come from teaching colleges to "R1" research universities; some teach only undergraduates, others teach only graduate students; some teach in confessional institutions that train students for ministry of various kinds, while others teach exclusively in secular institutions. We hope that readers will not only benefit but delight in the range of perspectives offered here as we have.

PART I
CONTEXTS: SOURCES, HISTORY, TEXTS

CHAPTER 1

HISTORIOGRAPHY AND HISTORY WRITING IN THE ANCIENT WORLD

RICHARD D. NELSON

1.1 ON RECOGNIZING (AND DEFINING) HISTORIOGRAPHY

DISTINGUISHING historiography from other genres of literary composition from the ancient world is a form-critical task. It would be a procedural error to begin with a definition of historiography, perhaps one derived from the classical world or modern historiographic practice, and then ask whether a given text from Israel or the wider ancient world corresponds to that genre label. Genres are not realities outside the social world in which they function and should not be treated as real entities that exist apart from their heuristic value in interpreting specific texts. *Historiography* is thus a useful taxonomic category that can negotiate similarities among texts that reflect common characteristics but not something that can be defined once and for all. The term *historiography* highlights, instead, the similar usage and purposes of certain texts in the institutions and social behaviors of various cultures, even though they diverge in geography and time.

The idea that there is a predetermined, correct definition of history writing that can be delineated a priori has led to numerous, but ultimately pointless controversies about the presence of historiography in the Hebrew Bible. Instead, one should begin by observing that texts deriving from societies in the ancient west Asian and Mediterranean world evidence similarities in character and intention and functioned in relationship to comparable social institutions and situations. Insofar as those texts match up with the classical Greek and modern category *historiography*, we may use the term without apology. Correspondences among texts originating from cultures as diverse as the Hittites, Assyrians, Babylonians, and Greeks stem both from cultural diffusion (in some cases) and from the circumstance that similar recurring social situations (for example, identity formation and definition, kingship, warfare, and scribal activity) naturally generated texts with similar formats and intentions. Because they were sponsored and produced by educated elites and directed toward elite audiences, ancient historiographic texts characteristically sought to support the status quo of temple and king. Formation and preservation of a unifying identity through a fixation of cultural memory was also an important goal, especially when that identity was under threat.

Fundamental elements of history writing are evidenced in various texts from the ancient world, as well as in the historical books of the Hebrew Bible. Written history tends to take the form of a narrative that seeks to coordinate and explain past events that its authors believe to have actually taken place. These events and their interrelationships are at least in part derived from sources—texts certainly, but also oral and anecdotal resources. Incidents are recounted and interpreted to serve the contemporary interests and needs of the culture to which a historiographic text is addressed. In other words, history writers seek to discover meaning in past events and to communicate this significance to an audience. In order to make disparate events understandable and meaningful, historians communicate them through organizing templates—which may be chronological, thematic, or causative in nature—or through matters relating to narrative plot.

Historiographic texts intend to explain the past and not just chronicle it. They seek to render the past intelligible and meaningful to end users. Those who write (and read) history do so out of a conviction that what has taken place was not merely a purposeless sequence of events, but that some sort of pattern or significance may be discovered in the past. Historiography presents unique past events as representative of general laws or uniformities: the gods protect the temple, the king is victorious with divine support, actions rebound upon those who perform them, and so forth. Because ancient historiography reported both human and divine actions, ancient causative explanations included the presumed desires, purposes, convictions, and emotions of both human rulers and the gods, something that remained true of historiography up until the Enlightenment.

This focus on significant individuals (whether divine or human) is one facet of a larger issue—namely, that ancient history does not meet the accepted criteria of modern historians, who profess to strive for objectivity, empiricism, and dispassionate method. A great chasm yawns between the worldview of biblical historiographers and that of the modern historian at this point. Geography, environmental conditions, technological change, economics, and social factors are central to the causation model of modern historiography. More recently, themes such as race, class, ethnicity, gender, colonialism, and climate change have come to the fore. All of these are largely absent in ancient historiography, but three factors, especially, alienate modern historians from their ancient counterparts: reliance on divine causation, naive and uncritical acceptance of sources, and lack of concern for facticity.

First, in the ancient world divine forces were often set forth as causative explanations. Theology as an explanatory device is utterly opposed by the philosophical basis of modern history writing, although moral explanations and ethical evaluations remain important. This means that modern historians must reformat biblical texts into non-theistic judgments and statements, something that makes the historical books of the Bible seem non-historiographic to many. However, interpretations of ancient texts cannot transcend the social and ideological location of either the text's original milieu or that of the present-day interpreter. Both must somehow be held together in focus.

Second, biblical authors and editors engaged in a less suspicious and more credulous assessment of traditions and other sources they worked with than is characteristic of contemporary historians. Folktales, tomb and sanctuary traditions, prophetic legends, and the like were treated with the same respect as written lists, administrative documents, and archived letters. At the same time, biblical historiographers regularly modified, corrected, expanded, and recast the sources they inherited, as is clear from a comparison of Chronicles and Kings. Sometimes traces of views embedded in a source that were contrary to those of the later writer were retained. This tendency may be seen in neutral evaluations of non-centralized altars in material from Deuteronomistic authors or anti-monarchic sentiments retained in a pro-monarchic final form.

Third, ancients do not seem to have been focused on facticity in the same way as or to the same extent that we are. What is reported to have occurred was important to them, not in sense of what happened precisely, but because of a conviction that the events that their (oral and written) sources reported led to who they were and how they got into their present situation. Ancient scribes were perfectly capable of setting side by side statements that we now deem incompatible or contradictory. The decisive question is to what degree biblical historians simply invented material or intentionally mischaracterized what they thought their sources told them. Because we lack the rich cross-check controls for biblical history that are often available for Egyptian and Mesopotamian events and reigns, this is a difficult question to answer in some cases. However, balanced consideration of materials within the historical books indicate that their authors mostly related the past as they thought it had happened—or at least as it *should* have happened given the reality structures of their culture. Once again, they thought they were portraying real events and real people. At the same time, it is clear that some materials in the historical books represent authorial constructions, analogous to the practice of Thucydides, for example, who put invented but appropriate speeches into the mouths of historical persons. Obvious examples are Josh. 23, 1 Sam. 12, 1 Kgs. 8, and the prophetic and royal speeches in Chronicles. Nevertheless, from a genre standpoint, even history writing that is thoroughly biased and even largely wrong is not quite the same thing as full-blown fiction. History writers intend to write about reality because they have access to sources and seek to keep faith with them.

1.2 Historiography in the Ancient World

Comparative examples from other ancient west Asian and Mediterranean cultures provide helpful exemplars. The Hittites were remarkable for producing texts of a historiographic nature (*COS* 1.72–77: 182–204). The earliest extant is the Proclamation of Anitta, produced for a royal purpose but not limited to material about the king. The assertion of royal accomplishments by Suppiluliuma I, the larger literary complex of his son Mursili II in which each year of his reign is documented, and a tablet of Suppiluliuma II recounting his conquests along with those of his father are historiographic in the fullest sense. The Proclamation of Telipinu consists of summaries of anarchy experienced under previous royal figures and the story of his own succession to the throne, intended to introduce a promulgation of succession rules. Hattusili III offered a religious defense of his usurpation in a manner that may be compared to narratives recounting David's accession. Remarkably, Hittite texts sometimes offer evidence to support or challenge the truth of some statements. Certain texts refer to letters and even take readers into the enemy camp. Although these materials are distant in both time and geography from Israel, they illustrate the cultural and political role that historiography can play in a similar social system.

One must look to Mesopotamia for direct cultural influences that led Israel to write history. Israel and Judah were caught up into the neo-Assyrian political orbit from the mid-ninth century on, and Babylon remained the dominant cultural center for biblical literature after Assyria passed from the scene. Mesopotamian civilization was marked by a consciousness of being heir to an extended past and preserved old canonical texts through scribal recopying. This practice meant that scribes could conceive of a future audience for their labors. Babylonia scribes wrote about the king as patron of religion and one who promoted activities for the common good. In contrast, Assyrian scribes promoted the king's military glory as an instrument of divine will.

Comparative Mesopotamian materials consist of inscriptions, chronographic or annalistic texts, and, as close parallels to biblical examples, literary historiographic texts. Inscriptions began as commemorations of building endeavors, relating to a temple, perhaps, or a canal, that were addressed to the gods. Later, longer inscriptions concerning royal achievements were addressed to the public. Assyrians produced a special genre of inscriptions in the form of annals, year by year descriptions of military campaigns.

Not quite falling into the category of historiography is the genre of king list. Rosters of kings stating the length of their reigns were created and preserved in order to facilitate dating legal documents and to legitimate an orderly succession of rulers. Examples survive from Assyria (*ANET*, 564–66; *COS* 1.135: 463–65) and Babylon (*ANET*, 271–72; *COS* 1.134: 461–63). There is also a synchronistic list for both nations (*ANET*, 272–74) that in some ways corresponds to the way the biblical book of Kings traces the parallel histories of the two Yahwistic kingdoms. King lists are also extant from Egypt (Turin Canon; *COS* 1.37D: 71–73), Ugarit (*COS* 1.104: 356–57), and Ammon (*COS* 2.25: 139–40).

The Assyrian Eponym Chronicle tied events and campaigns to a chronographic system based on the two-year tenure of a specific governmental official, citing one significant event per year. This does not quite fall into the genre of historiography in that the discrete events mentioned do not form a narrative nor are the meanings of events explored (*COS* 1.136: 465–66).

Of particular interest for our understanding of scribal technique in the realm of historiography are monumental inscriptions of the Assyrian kings. These are characterized as annals (already mentioned above), and summary inscriptions, which condensed and telescoped royal exploits in order to fit limited space, categorizing them by geography or political importance rather than chronology. Both chronicled royal accomplishments with a propagandistic spin. These inscriptions sometimes reveal a process of successive editorial and recensional development from one example to the next. For example, the Monolith Inscription of Shalmaneser III (dated 853–852 BCE) covered years 1–6 of his reign. A second example repeats years 1–6 and then updates matters up to year 18. A third example from 828–827 BCE carries events down to year 31, summarizing, modifying, and shortening earlier texts in the process (*ANET*, 277–81; *COS* 2.113A–F: 261–71). Like biblical historiographical texts such texts evidence an ideological purpose and reflect editorial change over time.

The Babylonian Weidner Chronicle, composed around 1150 BCE, is historiography of a literary nature. It reflects a schematic pattern and a presumption that events can be explained on the basis of divine causation. In a somewhat propagandistic fashion, it describes how kings who neglected the Marduk cult at Esagila came to a bad end (*COS* 1.138: 468–70).

A useful comparison to biblical historiography can be made with an Assyrian text called the Synchronistic History. This text covers a period from the fifteenth century up to the start of the eighth century and reports on military engagements triggered by alleged Babylonian incursions into Assyrian territory. Divided into ruled-off panels, each section deals with an Assyrian king and his Babylonian contemporary or contemporaries. Linguistic parallels to extant inscriptions show clearly that the author used monuments of the Assyrian kings concerned as source documents. Assyrian superiority is emphasized at every turn, even to the point of distorting facts known from other sources. The text insists, for example, that Babylon was defeated even when it is clear that such was not the case. This document was composed to support Assyrian morale in a period of national crisis. It has a theological color in that the god Assur intervenes to defeat Babylon.

A long series of tablets collectively known as the Babylonian Chronicle reports on events and successive dynasties in chronological order with a royal focus. The series is made up of linked texts that cover events from Nabu-nasir (747–734) to Seleucus II (246–226). The text only reports on selected years, however. Reigns are marked off by lines and regnal date formulas at the start and end of each section. The emphasis is on royal succession and the fate of divine images (*ANET*, 301–307; *COS* 1.137: 467–468). In contrast to the Synchronistic History, the Babylonian Chronicle appears somewhat more objective in that defeats of Babylonian kings are recorded without comment.

Mesopotamian literary works narrate past events for ideological purposes. The Curse of Agade (beginning of the second millennium) is a didactic tale that describes how Naram-Sin committed impious acts and consequently caused the gods to destroy the Akkadian Empire, analogous of the role played by Manasseh in Kings (*ANET*, 646–51). The Old Babylonian Legend of Naram-Sin, copied in several versions for about 1500 years, was composed to revive interest in divination by extispicy rather than astrology. Royal autobiographies, such as those of Adda-Guppi, mother of Nabonidus (*ANET*, 560–62; *COS* 1.147: 477–78) and Idrimi king of Alalakh (*ANET*, 557–60; *COS* 1.148: 479–80), are also of a literary nature, but still represent a species of historiography in which intervention of the gods and communications from them provide explanations for past events. Like the book of Kings, the Verse Account of Nabonidus (*ANET*, 312–15) blames the fall of the neo-Babylonian kingdom on that king's cultic and religious apostasy from the proper cult.

Geographically and culturally closer to Judah and Israel are inscriptions sponsored by local kings of Syria-Palestine. The stela of Mesha king of Moab (*ANET*, 320–21; *COS* 2.23: 138–39) evidences a theology and culture of warfare similar to that reflected in Joshua. A memorial inscription of Kulamuwa (*ANET*, 654–55; *COS* 2.30: 147–48) shows the scribal technique of chiasm common in the Hebrew Bible: A *the past*, B *foreign affairs*, B' *domestic affairs*, A' *the future*. The stela of Zakur of Hamath (*ANET*, 655–66; *COS* 2.35: 155) illustrates the role of the divine in royal affairs. Zakur was besieged by the king of Damascus and his allies. Like Hezekiah and Ahaz, he received an oracle of salvation from the god Ba'lshamayn: "do not be afraid," and context makes it clear that he was delivered. The Tel Dan stela, perhaps commissioned by Hazael of Damascus, asserts that the god Hadad made him king and celebrates success over the kings of Israel and Judah (*COS* 2.39: 161–62). In contrast, it is striking that no royal inscriptions have been found from either Judah or Israel. A limestone fragment from Samaria with one legible word provides evidence that Israel's kings did authorize inscriptions but none have survived. An eighth-century ostracon from Arad may be a copy or draft of a royal inscription: "I became king in... gather strength and... king of Egypt" (*COS* 3.43M: 85). In that it lacks any reference to a king and was not freely accessible, the Siloam Inscription (*ANET*, 321; *COS* 2.28: 145–46) cannot be considered an official royal production.

The Persians had a native tradition of oral narrative about the past, some of which has been preserved in Zoroastrian scripture (Avesta). At the same time, the Achaemenid Empire continued the Mesopotamian historiographic tradition. The Cyrus Cylinder (*ANET*, 315–16; *COS* 2.124: 314–16) and the Bisitun Inscription of Darius I, copies of which were sent throughout the realm, recounted events to demonstrate that Persian kings were divinely appointed and were patrons of order and justice. Babylonian scribes continued the tradition of king lists, bringing them down through time as far as the Seleucids. There is corroborating evidence for royal decrees (see, e.g., Ezra 6:1–2; Esth. 2:23; 6:1–2) and daybooks. (Herodotus describes the scribes of Xerxes during the Battle of Salamis, *Histories* 8.90.) A shift to writing on perishable materials instead of clay tablets no doubt led to the loss of much historiographic material.

Western thought tends to view questions of historiography through the lens of the classical Greeks of the fifth century, considerably later than Mesopotamian or even early Israelite endeavors. Hecataeus of Miletus critiqued folk narratives based on their inherent irrationality. Herodotus encountered oral stories and cultural information through contacts with informants and his own travels, recording them as *historiai* (inquiries and knowledge obtained from them). He sometimes incorporated translations of Persian documentary sources. He was critical of received tradition and of other writers, discussed the biases of sources and weighed their comparative value, and reasoned on the basis of probability. Divine or moral causation is sometimes adduced. Herodotus was able to fashion an overarching story out of a vast array of information, a narrative recounting Persian imperial growth and the interaction of comparative political systems. Thucydides focused on the protracted Peloponnesian War, its causes, the motives of its central characters, and its consequences. His narration is dramatic and rhetorical, told often from an omniscient point of view. He insisted on high evidential standards and avoided supernatural causation. In the third century, the Babylonian Berossus and the Egyptian Manetho sought to convey their national history in a positive way to a Hellenistic audience.

1.3 Sources in the Historical Books

Historiography entails the employment of sources. However, unlike modern historians, biblical authors rarely if ever critically evaluated their sources. Oral traditions and written documents were taken at face value. The historical books fall short of our contemporary standards for history writing because sources were reproduced, recast, and expanded, but not weighed. Yet the writers generally seem to have represented their sources accurately. The story of Israel's past would have been well known, so authors of biblical historiography must have felt compelled to (re)tell that story in an acceptable way. The same would be true of widely circulated folktales. Certain written sources, too, may have been available to contemporary readers (see 1 Kgs. 11:41; 14:19, 29).

Oral sources included burial traditions, sanctuary legends, prophetic tales and miracle stories, and folktales about heroes. There is evidence that Israel esteemed the supposed burial sites of ancestors and heroes. These seem to have been the goal of pilgrimages, and narrative traditions were developed and preserved there. Examples include Joseph's grave at Shechem (Josh. 24:30, 32) and that of Rachel in Benjamin (1 Sam. 10:2). It is likely that heroic stories about Gideon (Judg. 8:32), Jephthah (12:7), Samson (16:31), and Abner (2 Sam. 3:32; 4:12) were recounted at their respective tombs. Saul's memory was sustained near a (sacred?) tree at Jabesh-gilead (1 Sam. 31:11–13) and at Gibeah (2 Sam. 21:12–14), the latter of which is significantly identified as Gibeah *of Saul* (1 Sam. 11:4; Isa. 10:29, etc.). A miracle of Elisha was associated with his grave (2 Kgs. 13:20–21). It is explicitly said that the story of the altar of Bethel and the two prophets was retold at their gravesite (1 Kgs. 13:30–31; 2 Kgs. 23:16–18).

Traditions were also likely repeated at famous landmarks: stone cairns in the Valley of Achor and outside the ruined gates of Ai (Josh. 7:26; 8:29), the Rock of Oreb (Judg. 7:25: Isa. 10:26), or Absalom's monument outside Jerusalem (2 Sam. 18:18). A hill, a hollow, and a spring, all in the neighborhood of Lehi, played a role in the preservation and transmission of a tale about Samson's heroics (Judg. 15:19). Important water sources performed the same function: two pools near Debir (Judg. 1:15), the spring of Harod (Judg. 7:1, 4–7), and the pool at Gibeon (2 Sam. 2:12–32). Stories about Saul were connected with two rocky outcrops (1 Sam. 14:4–5), a prominent tree in Gibeah (1 Sam. 14:2; 22:6), and a monument at Carmel in Judah (1 Sam. 15:12). Elements of the David tradition were linked to Keilah, Horesh, the Rock of Escape, and the hill of Hachilah (1 Sam. 23:1–29; 26:1, 3). The historical books also used sanctuary foundation legends as a source of tradition. Examples are Bochim (Judg. 1:1–5), Orphah (6:11–24), and Jerusalem (2 Sam. 24).

Prophetic legends were intended to glorify the prophetic office and instill confidence in prophetic oracles. Prophets were to be respected (2 Kgs. 8:1–15) and obeyed (1 Kgs. 17:10–16; 2 Kgs. 5:10–14), perhaps even feared (2 Kgs. 1:9–15; 2:23–24). Such stories were transmitted orally within prophetic circles and to the general population (e.g., 2 Kgs. 8:4). The book of Kings incorporates legends about Ahijah (1 Kgs. 11:29–39; 14:1–18), Shemaiah (12:21–24), Micaiah (22:1–28), as well as numerous anonymous prophets (1 Kgs. 20:1–43). Similar tales appear in 1 Kgs. 13 and 2 Kgs. 18–20. Legends about Elijah and Elisha make up most of 1 Kgs. 17:1–2 Kgs. 8:15. In some of these prophetic legends, the royal protagonist was anonymous, identified as only as *the king of Israel* (see 1 Kgs. 20, 22; 2 Kgs. 3, 5, 6). This lack of specific royal referent is evidently what led to the Syrian Wars (1 Kgs. 20, 22; 2 Kgs. 6:24–7:20) being placed into what seems to be the wrong time period, that is, into the reigns of Ahab and Jehoram rather than during the subsequent Jehu dynasty.

The historical books also utilized poems and songs as historiographic data. The most substantial example is the Song of Deborah (Judg. 5). Perhaps preserved at the inter-tribal sanctuary on Mount Tabor, its archaic language and the non-standard tribal structure it reflects point to an early date, perhaps in the late pre-monarchic period or in the early days of the northern monarchy. Three songs for which the author cites a written source are Josh. 10:12–13; 2 Sam. 1:18–27; and 1 Kgs. 8:12–13 (LXX). Proverbs or aphorisms are cited in Judg.

8:2, 21; 1 Sam. 10:11–12; 19:24; 2 Sam. 5:8; and 1 Kgs. 20:11. A pre-existing parabolic fable about foolish choices or presumptuous pride is applied to kingship in Judg. 9:7–20.

The historical books used written sources, some ostensibly of an administrative or archival character. The existence of a scribal culture and of sources of an official nature, at least in the later Judahite monarchy, is confirmed by the abundance of seals of official persons and impressions of them on clay (bullae)—from now-perished papyrus documents—revealed by archaeology. It is inconceivable that the book of Kings could have been so accurate about the sequence and tenure of native kings and their relations with other nations without reliance on trustworthy sources. Kings reports correctly about Omri. It describes Mesha and his revolt with reasonable accuracy and rightly understands the Hazael/Ben-hadad/Rezin royal succession in Damascus. Mesopotamian texts synchronize Shalmaneser III with Ahab and Jehu. They witness that Hazael usurped the throne of Damascus from Adad-idri (the Ben-hadad of 2 Kgs. 8:7–15). Kings properly coordinates Adad-nirari III with Jehoash of Samaria and Tiglath-pileser III with Ahaz of Judah—and then with Menahem, Pekah, and Hoshea of Israel. Sennacherib was indeed an adversary of Hezekiah. Kings puts Merodach-baladan into the right timeframe. Arda-Mullissi, Sennacherib's assassin, is corrupted into the Hebrew form Adrammelech in 2 Kgs. 19:37. Manasseh in reality did follow a compliance policy and was a loyal vassal of Assyria.

In Joshua, scholars have recognized that the list preserved in Josh. 15:20–62 and 18:21–28 describes administrative districts into which the kingdom of Judah was organized in the period of Josiah. In fact, it can be demonstrated that the Benjaminite district outlined in 18:21–24 represents territory incorporated by Josiah into Judah from the vanquished kingdom of Israel. Reliable sources may stand behind the rest of Joshua's tribal geography in chapters 15–19, which is a mixture of city lists and boundary descriptions. In its present form this material represents a scribal construction with an ideological purpose. So also the list of Levitical cities in Joshua 20 is an artificial creation based on materials taken elsewhere from Joshua.

A pre-existing list of so-called minor judges was used by the author of Judges (Judg. 10:1–5; 12:7–15). From it was taken the notion of a series of leaders who "judged Israel" and a chronology of their succession. These six clan ancestors or heroes form an uninterrupted sequence of leadership marked by peace, prosperity, and positive family life. It was previously postulated that Judges 1 went back to an early, so-called negative settlement list. However, it is now clear that this chapter was composed, at least in part, by using material taken from the geographical materials in Joshua so as to create a bridge between the end of Joshua and the beginning of Judges.

The book of Samuel incorporates two versions of a roster of Davidic officials (2 Sam. 8:16–18; 20:23–26). If authentic, these would indicate that David had a sophisticated structure of royal administration, which is highly unlikely. In reality, these lists appear to have been derived from the list of Solomon's officials in 1 Kgs. 4:2–6. The list of David's elite warriors (2 Sam. 23:8–39) appears to be a late scribal compilation of information from oral hero tales. A similar source text recounts the exploits of four giant-slayers (2 Sam. 21:15–22). Both were intended to glorify David.

The list of Solomon's officials in 1 Kgs. 4:7–19 is usually misunderstood as a description of twelve administrative districts. Closer inspection shows it to be a roster of representatives or agents who acted for Solomon's interests in cities and within tribes that fell into his sphere of influence, but were not actually under his direct control. This explains the absence of Judah from the roster. The list is most likely a genuine survival from a Solomonic polity that joined Jerusalem and its agricultural territory to tribal Judah. The list of court officials reproduced in 1 Kgs. 4:2–6 shows several indications of authenticity.

Kings cites two extensive sources for the period after Solomon, the Book of the Chronicles of the Kings of Judah and the Book of the Chronicles of the Kings of Israel. Admittedly, alluding to these documents is a literary strategy intended to validate the reliability of what is reported. However, the balance of probability indicates that they were based on genuine archival sources. These works were not official annals or archives, but literary in nature and purportedly available to readers. The author of Kings used material from them to compose the summary citations that conclude the reigns of most of the kings of Judah and Israel. It is notable that these summaries are ideologically neutral and do not reflect the Deuteronomistic theology of the final author (with the exception of 2 Kgs. 21:17, "the sins he committed"). Seven of these summary citations refer to information said to be reported more fully in the source document: notable royal exploits and power (Baasha, 1 Kgs. 16:5; Omri, v. 27), palace intrigue (Zimri, v. 20); building projects (Ahab, 22:39), military actions (Jehoshaphat, 22:45), and the pool and conduit of Hezekiah (2 Kgs. 20:20). Because Kings does not elaborate further on these topics, the references are hardly authorial inventions (contrast the fictional source citations of the Chronicler). It is reasonable to conclude moreover that other materials have been quarried from these two documents: campaigns and generalship (1 Kgs. 14:19; 15:23; 16:5, 27; 22:45; 2 Kgs. 10:34; 13:8, 12; 14:15, 28; 20:20), construction (1 Kgs. 15:23; 22:39), and uprisings (1 Kgs. 16:20; 2 Kgs. 15:15).

For the parallel chronologies of Judah and Israel, Kings apparently had access (perhaps through the two chronicles documents) to an Israel King List and a Judah King List. These were used to compose notices that open and close the narratives about each king. At a minimum, these king lists would have preserved the names of each king in succession and the length of his reign. Two separate king lists are indicated by a regular difference in word order. The formula for Judah, using the Hebrew word order, is *x years reigned [name] in Jerusalem*, while for Israel the length of the reign comes after the verb. Separate lists are also indicated in that material about the kings' mothers and ages at accession are given for Judah only. The opening and closing notices also report capital city, burial (often), and succession. Because these data are firmly linked with the length of reign notices, they were most likely also derived from the king lists. Frequent references to royal burial suggests a cult memorializing former kings. (One might compare the Ugaritic King List, which was used in a royal mortuary cult.)

Other material in the book of Kings could also go back to archival or inscriptional sources. Menahem's tribute sounds as though it is from a chronicle (2 Kgs. 15:19–20) and is confirmed by an Assyrian source. Written sources most likely lie behind events dated by a king's regnal year (1 Kgs. 14:25–28; 2 Kgs. 12:7 [ET v. 6]; 17:5–6; 18:9–12 and 13–15), reports of conspiracies (2 Kgs. 15:10, 14, 25, 30; 21:23), and lists of items and persons. Sources almost certainly lie behind military reports featuring the verbs *go up, besiege, fight,* and *capture* (2 Kgs. 12:18–19 [ET vv. 17–18] 16:6–9; 24:10–17) and building reports using *build* or *make* (1 Kgs. 7:2–8; 12:25; 15:17, 22; 16:24, 34; 2 Kgs. 14:22). Scholars often propose the existence of a document reporting on the assets of the Jerusalem temple that could lie behind 1 Kgs. 14:26 (Shishak); 15:18 plus adjoining verses; 2 Kgs. 12:19 [ET 18] along with surrounding material;

14:14; 16:8; 18:15; and 24:13. This could explain the partial correspondence between 2 Kgs. 18:15 and Assyrian sources itemizing gold tribute paid by Hezekiah.

In summary, written sources may be realistically postulated for certain narratives in Kings about battles, building projects, notable acts, usurpations, and temple-related matters. This is even more certain for data about age at accession and reign length. However, it is not always possible to distinguish between actual records and literary imitations of such records by an author with scribal training.

First Chronicles 1–9 incorporates genealogies from a variety of sources to bridge from creation (Adam) to the death of Saul. These were not simply duplicated, but reflect the Chronicler's commitment to the so-called doctrine of retribution (1 Chr. 5:1, 25–26; 10:13–14) and interest in the organization of temple personnel (6:31–48; 9:17–34). They witness to a venerable tradition of clan structures and notable ancestors that often coordinates with material in books composed earlier. Rehoboam's fortifications (2 Chr. 11:5–12) and other accurate details not found in Kings (blocking up Gihon, 32:30; Carchemish, 35:20) were probably also taken from source material.

Ezra-Nehemiah quotes several sources. Some of these appear fictitious, but others seem to be genuine. The latter category includes inventories (Ezra 1:9–11; 8:26–27) and rosters (8:1–14; 10:18–43; Neh. 3:1–32; 9:38–10:27; 11:3–24, 25–36; 12:1–26). The duplicated list of returnees (Ezra 2:1–70 and Neh. 7:7–72a) appears to be a census or tax roll. Ezra incorporates texts and letters purporting to be official documents. Ezra 1:2–4 is fictitious, but accurately reflects Cyrus's policy, while a memorandum reproduced in 6:3–5 covers some of the same ground and appears to be genuine. Ezra 4:6–23 brings together three apparently genuine communications, but places them in an inappropriate setting. The context refers to the Zerubbabel's start on building the temple, but the quoted documents have to do with opposition to the fortification of Jerusalem in the time of Xerxes I (v. 6) and Artaxerxes I (vv. 7–23). Ezra 5:6–17 purports to be a letter from Tattenai governor of Beyond the River to Darius I in regard to rebuilding the temple. Ezra 6:3–5 is supposedly a memorandum of a decree by Cyrus authorizing and funding this, and Ezra 6:6–12 claims to be a decree from Darius permitting temple construction to proceed. Ezra 7:12–26 is a partially authentic letter of Artaxerxes commissioning Ezra's mission.

In addition to what appear to be administrative or archival sources, pre-existing narrative works of a literary nature were incorporated into the historical books. For example, Joshua employed a pre-deuteronomistic conquest narrative using the reactions of fearful enemy kings (Josh. 2:9–10; 5:1; 9:1–2; 10:1–2; 11:1) and the figure of Joshua to systematize individual stories into a unified, pan-Israel subjugation of Canaan. An Ark Narrative traces the divinely guided itinerary of the ark up to its installation in Jerusalem (1 Sam. 4:1–7:2, 2 Sam. 6:1–19). The Rise of David offsets the decline of Saul with David's ascent from shepherd boy to shepherd king (1 Sam. 16:14–2 Sam. 5:12; note 1 Sam. 16:19 and 2 Sam. 5:2). Most scholars recognize the existence of a highly entertaining and sophisticated Court History (2 Sam. 9–20; 1 Kgs. 1–2), but its starting point and purpose remain a matter of controversy. It seems intended to defuse the dogged hostility of Benjaminites still loyal to the house of Saul and insists that Solomon was David's legitimate heir even at the expense of David's reputation. A collection of narratives, lists, and poetry in 2 Sam. 21–24 is structured as a chiasm. This compilation is enclosed by narratives of famine and plague, each resolved when "God heeded supplications for the land" (NRSV; 2 Sam. 21:14 and 24:25).

Kings cites the book of the Acts of Solomon as a source for what it reports in 1 Kgs. 3–11. This work reported on "all that he did as well as his wisdom" (11:41) and thus appears to have included building activities, lists of officials, and folktales extolling Solomon's insight. An Elijah-Elisha cycle intertwines prophetic legends about these two figures, linking them together by means of parallel stories and a transfer of authority and mission (1 Kgs. 17–2 Kgs. 10; note 1 Kgs. 19:15–17 and 2 Kgs. 2:13–14). In part this compilation was aimed at supporting the pro-Yhwh usurpation of Jehu. Chronicles used Samuel and Kings (in a non-MT text form) and Psalms. A source commonly known as the Memoirs of Nehemiah underlies Neh. 1–7; 11:1–2; 12:31–43; and 13:4–31. This is a first-person account and defense of his public service, addressed to God. It is similar in purpose and format to the Egyptian tomb inscriptions of royal officials (ANET, 233–34; COS 2.1: 5–7).

1.4 Communicating Significance and Meaning

The historical books are historiography because their goal was to make the events they reported intelligible and meaningful. They did this in ways still common to historians. First, interpretation was effected *through organization*. The past was systematized and links between events were established. Biblical writers sometimes followed a chronological scheme, most obviously in Judges and Kings. Alternatively, they focused on important themes or mapped out repeated patterns. Joshua is organized by a pattern featuring divine command and the fear of enemy kings. A cyclical pattern of apostasy and deliverance is used by Judges to explain the changes in Israel's fortunes. The Rise of David contrasts David's increasing success with Saul's simultaneous collapse. Analogies, too, could unify and organize. Kings parallels quarreling mothers (1 Kgs. 3:16–28; 2 Kgs. 6:26–33) and visitors received with wisdom or folly (1 Kgs. 10:1–13; 2 Kgs. 20:12–19). Chronicles brackets David's involvement with the temple by his prayers in 1 Chr. 17:16–27 and 29:10–19. Calls for repentance by Abijah (2 Chr. 13:4–12) and Hezekiah (30:6–9) enclose the story of the divided kingdom.

Often it is the *basic structure of narrative plot* as it moves from problem to resolution that organizes material to generate meaning. This can be effective, because narrative invites readers into the world of the story and its interpretive terms. The reader of 2 Samuel, summoned into the narrative problem of the future of David's throne—brought into focus by the childlessness of Michal (2 Sam. 6:23) and the disability of Mephibosheth (2 Sam. 9:13)—follows the narrator though all the vicious and violent complications of David's family life. In the end, when the product of David's alliance with Bathsheba becomes king, the reader is convinced that Yhwh's will has been done (2 Sam. 12:24; 1 Kgs. 2:12, 46).

Secondly, biblical historiographers created meaning by selecting certain events and people from a wider range of data. The momentous effects of the campaign of Pharaoh Shishak, as demonstrated by archaeology, are passed over in favor of its consequences for the temple furnishings (1 Kgs. 14:25–28). Kings shows its particular interests when it portrays Omri, arguably Israel's most important ruler, in a mere eight verses (1 Kgs. 16:21–28). In describing Ahab, Kings takes no notice of the crucial battle of Qarqar and instead focuses on religious failings. Chronicles bypasses almost everything about the kings of Israel unless their presence is required to report on Judah. It also chooses to ignore negative items about David.

Tracing causation provided a third approach to interpretation. Old Testament historiography sometimes adduces psychological (1 Kgs. 1:6), social (1 Kgs. 12:4), or geo-political (Judg. 18:27–28; 2 Kgs. 17:4) causative factors. However, the passions, commitments, and purposes of Yhwh are presented as the primary cause for what takes place. The foremost example of this is the assertion that the catastrophe that befell Judah was caused by Yhwh's reaction to Manasseh's misdeeds committed decades earlier (2 Kgs. 21:10–15; 23:26–27; 24:3–4).

A fourth tactic was simply to provide *direct, explicit statements about the significance of events*. This is the case with the cyclical evaluative structure of Judges and the long editorial in 2 Kgs. 17. Significance is often revealed through prophetic declarations (Judg. 6:7–10; 1 Sam. 2:27–36; 1 Kgs. 13:1–3; 2 Kgs. 22:15–20) or unmediated divine speech (Judg. 10:11–14; 2 Kgs. 23:27). Kings is patterned on the explicitly stated judgments that most kings did evil, a few did good, and Hezekiah and Josiah were unparalleled in their virtue. Sometimes speeches are placed in the mouths of characters. In the case of Josh. 1 and 23, 1 Sam. 12, 2 Sam. 7, and 1 Kgs. 8, these speeches interpret events and prepare readers for what is to come. The author of Chronicles also composed speeches and prayers in which main characters evaluate events. Examples are 1 Chr. 22:7–16; 28:2–21; 29:1–5, 10–19 (David); 2 Chr. 13:4–12 (Abijah); and 30:6–9 (Josiah). The prayers in Ezra 9 and Nehemiah 9 lay out the threatening consequences of the nation's situation before God.

The purpose of biblical historiography was to narrate the past as the authors understood it to have happened in order to create faith in the religious establishment, authenticate a certain social and political system, and generate a sense of common ethnic identity. Biblical historians sought to claim Israel's ancestral lands in the face of opposition (Joshua), urged loyalty to Yhwh (Judges), legitimated the dynasty of David (Samuel), and tried to explain defeat and exile (Kings). Chronicles communicated a message of legitimate identity and encouragement, and Ezra-Nehemiah added to this a call for community purity.

In spite of continuing and sometimes strident skepticism, a legitimate history of the Yahwistic people of ancient Israel/Palestine and their later diaspora can indeed be written. Modern historians should not be lured by the Bible's theologically driven narrative into writing a faith-based account, something intellectually incoherent by contemporary canons of historiography. Nor should a nationalistic approach be followed, given the ethical dangers involved. Rather, the best history will critically weigh the sources behind the historical books and coordinate that material with data from outside sources and archaeology.

Bibliography

Amit, Yairah. 1999. *History and Ideology: An Introduction to Historiography in the Hebrew Bible*. Translated by Yael Lotan. Sheffield: Sheffield Academic Press.
Brettler, Marc Z. 1995. *The Creation of History in Ancient Israel*. London: Routledge.
Davies, Philip R. 2008. *Memories of Ancient Israel: An Introduction to Biblical History—Ancient and Modern*. Louisville, KY: Westminster John Knox.

Emerton, John A. 2006. "The Kingdoms of Judah and Israel and Ancient Hebrew History Writing." In S. E. Fassberg and A. Hurvitz, eds., *Biblical Hebrew in Its Northwest Semitic Setting: Typological and Historical Perspectives.* Leiden: Brill, 33–49.

Gilmour, Rachelle. 2011. *Representing the Past: A Literary Analysis of Narrative Historiography in the Book of Samuel.* VTSup 143. Leiden: Brill.

Glassner, Jean-Jacques. 2004. *Mesopotamian Chronicles.* SBLWAW 19. Atlanta: SBL.

Grayson, A. Kirk. 2000. *Assyrian and Babylonian Chronicles.* Winona Lake, IN: Eisenbrauns.

Güterbock, Hans. 1984. "Hittite Historiography: A Survey." In Hayim Tadmor and Moshe Weinfeld, eds., *History, Historiography and Interpretation: Studies in Biblical and Cuneiform Languages.* Jerusalem: Magnes, 21–35.

Hoffner, Harry A. 1980. "Histories and Historians of the Ancient Near East: The Hittites." *Or* 49: 283–332.

Kofoed, Jens B. 2005. *Text and History: Historiography and the Study of the Biblical Text.* Winona Lake, IN: Eisenbrauns.

Mayes, A. D. H. 2002. "Historiography in the Old Testament." In John Barton, ed., *The Biblical World*, Volume 1. London: Routledge, 65–87.

Nelson, Richard D. 2014. *Historical Roots of the Old Testament (1200–63 BCE).* Biblical Encyclopedia 13. Atlanta: SBL.

Parker, Simon B. 1997. *Stories in Scripture and Inscriptions: Comparative Studies on Narratives in Northwest Semitic Inscriptions and the Hebrew Bible.* New York: Oxford University Press.

Van Seters, John. 1983. *In Search of History: Historiography in the Ancient World and the Origins of Biblical History.* New Haven, CT: Yale University Press.

CHAPTER 2

ASSYRIAN AND BABYLONIAN SOURCES

MARTTI NISSINEN

The narrative of the historical books of the Hebrew Bible runs from the period of the Early Iron Age through the Persian period, that is, roughly, from the twelfth through the fourth centuries BCE. The time-span of the pertinent Assyrian and Babylonian sources is much shorter. Sources predating the Neo-Assyrian period do not mention Israel or Judah, nor does the biblical narrative refer to Assyrian and Babylonian history prior to the ninth century BCE. It is only with the emergence of Assyria as an empire that southern Levantine polities enter the Assyrian historical records. The expansion of the Assyrian empire towards the West began with the campaigns of Assurnasirpal II (883–859 BCE), and the incorporation large parts of the Levant into the Assyrian provincial administration eventually took place under Tiglath-pileser III (745–727 BCE). The area remained under Assyrian control until the end of the Assyrian empire.

Babylonian history reflected by the historical books of the Hebrew Bible is related to the invasions of Jerusalem in 597 and 586 BCE by the Babylonian king Nebuchadnezzar II (605–562 BCE) and the subsequent deportation of a considerable number of Judeans to Babylonia. These events have left traces even in Babylonian sources which, unlike the Hebrew Bible, also yield some historical information concerning the life of the Judean community in Babylonia in the sixth and fifth centuries BCE.

2.1 Israel and Judah in Assyrian Records

The first non-biblical historical source recognizing the kingdom of Israel as a political entity is the inscription on the Kurkh Monolith, containing the account of Shalmaneser III (858–824 BCE) of the battle of Qarqar by the river Orontes in the year 853 BCE (RIMA 3 A.0.102.2; Grayson 1996: 13–24). Shalmaneser claims to have defeated twelve kings from Syria and Phoenicia, and among them is Ahab, king of Israel (*Aḫabbu Sirʾalāia*), the second king of the Omride dynasty (ca. 873–851 BCE; cf. 1 Kgs. 16:29–22:20). The anti-Assyrian coalition of kings, of whom seven are named, was led by Hadad-ezer (*Adda-idri*) of

Damascus and Irḫulenu of Hamath. Ahab is said to have lent 2,000 chariots and 10,000 soldiers to the military force of the alliance. The Hebrew Bible does not know this event. The only king of Damascus associated with Ahab is Ben-Hadad, whose identity vis-à-vis Hadad-ezer is debated. Some scholars have equated Hadad-ezer with Ben-Hadad (e.g., Younger 2016: 580–91), while others (e.g., Lipiński 2000: 397) argue that the problem is due to the editorial history of the narratives in 1 Kgs. 20 and 22 actually reflecting events in the late ninth century.

In his inscription concerning the campaign of his eighteenth year (841 BCE; RIMA 3 A.0.102.10; Grayson 1996: 51–56), Shalmaneser III reports to have marched as far as the mountains of Hauran, locking up Hazael, Hadad-ezer's successor, in Damascus and receiving tribute from Ba'al-manzer of Tyre, and Jehu, "son of Omri" (*Iāūa mār Ḫumrî*). Other inscriptions reporting the same event (RIMA 3 A.0.102.2 and 12; Grayson 1996: 44–48, 59–61) add even the Sidonians to the tributaries. An epigraph on Shalmaneser's Black Obelisk specifies the tribute of Jehu, son of Omri (RIMA 3 A.0.102.88; Grayson 1996: 149), the most noteworthy of the many precious items being the staff (*ḫuṭārtu*), a symbol of royal authority, the delivery of which symbolizes subjugation to the great king. Indeed, the obelisk depicts Jehu kissing the ground before the feet of the Assyrian king while paying his tribute to him. However, Jehu's tribute is not mentioned in the Hebrew Bible. Moreover, that Jehu is called son of Omri runs contrary to 2 Kgs. 9, according to which Jehu revolted and killed Jehoram, his Omride predecessor. The designation *mār Ḫumrî* either indicates that the Assyrians saw Jehu as a descendant of the Omride dynasty, or that this was simply the Assyrian designation of the kings of the country called *Bīt Ḫumrî*.

The next king of Israel mentioned in Assyrian records is Joash (ca. 836–796 BCE), mentioned in the inscription on the royal stela discovered at Tell el-Rimaḥ and commemorating the campaign of Adad-nirari III (810–783 BCE) to the Levant (RIMA 3 A.0.104.7; Grayson 1996: 211). According to the inscription, the king marched all the way to the Mediterranean Sea and subdued "the entire lands of Amurru and Ḫatti," receiving tribute from Mari' of Damascus and Joash of Samaria (*Iū'āsu Samerināia*), as well as from Tyre and Sidon. In another inscription referring to the same event (RIMA 3 A.0.104.8; Grayson 1996: 212–13), Adad-nirari III lists "the land of Ḫumrî" among the names of several areas he claims to have conquered. A special section is devoted to the confinement of Mari', king of Damascus, and his huge tribute to the Assyrian king, which indicates how important the conquest of Damascus was from the Assyrian perspective.

Adad-nirari's campaign to the Levant is likely to have happened in the year 796 BCE, which means that Mari', king of Damascus, must be identical with the above-mentioned Ben-Hadad. In the Hebrew Bible, 2 Kgs. 13:25 describes the confrontation between Joash and Ben-Hadad (see Younger 2016: 632–40) without mentioning Joash's tribute to the Assyrian king but relating instead how Joash defeated Ben-Hadad three times, recovering the towns his father Jehoahaz had lost to the Aramean king. Nothing of this is known from other sources, but one can plausibly think that Israel, in spite of paying the tribute to Assyria, profited from the weakened position of Damascus (Weippert 1992).

Assyrian sources between Adad-nirari III and Tiglath-pileser III do not mention Israel or Judah, nor do they refer to any events narrated in 2 Kgs. 14, notably the extension of Israel's borders by Jeroboam II to Lebo-Hamath (2 Kgs. 14:25), a place identified with Tell Qaṣr Lebwe (Akk. Labʿu) at the sources of Orontes river (Na'aman 1997: 421). If this note reflects historical circumstances, the expansion of the kingdom of Israel as far as the northern part of the Beqaa Valley does not seem to have provoked a counter-reaction of Assyria. This could not have been the case if Jeroboam had annexed Damascus and Hamath to his kingdom, as the problematic sentence in 2 Kgs. 14:28b seems to claim (for the problems of interpretation, see Younger 2016: 490–92). Even though Syria-Palestine was not yet annexed to the Assyrian Empire, the kings following Adad-nirari did not leave the Assyrian interests unattended in the area (Bagg 2011: 211–13). Thus, Shalmaneser IV (781–772 BCE) received tribute from Ḫadianu of Damascus (RIMA 3 A.0.105.1; Grayson 1996: 240); Aššur-dan III (771–754 BCE) marched to Ḫatarikka and Arpad (Eponym Chronicle; Millard 1994: 42); and Aššur-nirari V (753–746 BCE) concluded a treaty with Mati'-il of Arpad (SAA 2 2; Parpola and Watanabe 1988: 8–13).

It was only under Tiglath-pileser III that Assyria developed into a full-scale empire. He reorganized the provincial structure of Assyria and arranged a regular series of military campaigns, as the result of which large parts of northern and central Syria were incorporated into the Assyrian provincial system and Assyrian control was consolidated in the entire Levant (Bagg 2011: 213–26). The military and political activities of Tiglath-pileser are recorded in his several inscriptions, in which even kings of Israel and Judah are mentioned.

According to the biblical narrative, "Pul [i.e., Tiglath-pileser], king of Assyria, marched against the country," and Menahem, king of Israel, gave him a thousand talents of silver "so that he might help him confirm his hold on the royal power" (2 Kgs. 15:19–20). The tribute of Menahem the Samarian (*Meniḫimme Samerināia*) is mentioned in two inscriptions of Tiglath-pileser, together with the payment of several Syrian, Tabalean, Phoenician, and Arabian rulers (RINAP 1 14/15 and 35; Tadmor and Yamada 2011: 45–49, 81–87). It has often been assumed that this happened in 738 BCE when the Syrian cities of Arpad, Kullani, and Ḫatarikka (Hadrach) were annexed as Assyrian provinces, but there are some problems in the sources with regard to this dating (for different views, see Loretz and Mayer 1990). These inscriptions do not say that Tiglath-pileser invaded the area of Israel by that time. A few years later, however, he marched to the Wadi of Egypt (*naḫal Muṣri*/Wadi el-Arish), conquering the city of Gaza in 734 BCE. This campaign was prompted by an anti-Assyrian alliance initiated by Rezin (Akk. *Raḫiānu*, Aram. *Raḍyān*), the king of Damascus, and joined by many kingdoms including Tyre, Israel, Gaza, Ashkelon, and the Arabs. The war culminated in a two-year siege of Damascus, which was finally taken and annexed in 732 BCE and most of the Levant was brought under direct control of Assyria. The kingdom of Israel (*Bīt Ḫumria*) was not formally annexed to Assyria, but its area was reduced to consist of little more than the capital city of Samaria, and a considerable number of the population was deported. This is recorded both by the Hebrew Bible (2 Kgs. 15:29–30; 1 Chr. 5:26) and the inscriptions of Tiglath-pileser (RINAP 1 21/22, 44, 49; Tadmor and Yamada 2011: 61–63, 111–12, 129–33). Both sources agree that Pekah (*Paqaḫu*), king of Israel, was either killed or overthrown and replaced by Hoshea (*Awsēa'*). According to 2 Kgs. 15:30, Pekah was killed by Hoshea who conspired against him. The Assyrian sources do not mention this; instead, Tiglath-pileser claims to have himself installed Hoshea who seems to have been obliged to pay obeisance to him in the Babylonian city of Sarrabanu (RINAP 1 42, 44, 49; Tadmor and Yamada 2011: 105–107, 111–12, 129–33).

Compared to Israel, the kingdom of Judah was a much less significant actor on the political scene of the eighth century BCE. The political and military activity of Tiglath-pileser did not leave Judah untouched; however, Judah did not suffer from the Assyrian policy but, rather, profited from it. The first king of Judah to appear in the Assyrian records is Ahaz (*Iaū-ḫazi*)[1] mentioned in a long list of tributary kings from the year 729 BCE (RINAP 1 47; Tadmor and Yamada 2011: 116–25). Ahaz had not joined the anti-Assyrian coalition, whereby he, in spite of the harsh condemnation of his policy in the biblical narrative, saved Judah from the fate of the kingdom of Israel and many other neighbouring states. The Assyrian sources do not mention the attack of Rezin and Pekah against Judah, the so-called "Syro-Ephraimite War," known only from 2 Kgs. 16:5 and Isa. 7:1–9. If this war took place, it may be interpreted as an act of hostility towards Ahaz who refused to join the anti-Assyrian alliance (Na'aman 2008: 62–64). Another biblical narrative without counterpart in Assyrian records is the journey of Ahaz to Damascus where he, according to 2 Kgs. 16:10, met Tiglath-pileser in person.

No historical inscriptions of Tiglath-pileser's follower, Shalmaneser V (726–722 BCE) have been preserved, and the case of the fall of Samaria in 722 BCE is confusing because of the discrepancy about who actually conquered the city. According to the Babylonian Chronicle it was Shalmaneser who conquered Samaria (Grayson 1975: 73), whereas Sargon II in his inscriptions claims to have done it himself (Ann. 10–17; Fuchs 1994). The small cuneiform fragment discovered in Samaria may have originally belonged to a stela commemorating the conquest, but the preserved text reveals no names (Samaria 4; Horowitz, Oshima and Sanders 2018: 119). The Hebrew Bible adds to the confusion by stating that Shalmaneser besieged Samaria for three years (2 Kgs. 18:9–10), but without stating clearly which of the two kings is referred to as "king of Assyria" in 2 Kgs. 17:5–6, 24–27; 18:11. Probably the biblical writer had no exact knowledge of what exactly happened in these tumultous years. Perhaps two events are merged together here: the conquest of Samaria by Shalmaneser in 722 BCE, and the renewed capture of Samaria by Sargon in 720 BCE (Tadmor 1958; cf. Becking 1992; Younger 1999; for different views, see Na'aman 1990); or perhaps Sargon simply takes the credit of Shalmaneser's conquest for himself (Frahm 2019: 84–85).

Whatever the actual chain of events in Samaria around 722–720 BCE was, these events led to the annexation of Samaria to the Assyrian Empire as a province. There is also evidence of mass deportations of inhabitants of the former kingdom of Israel to Assyria. Both Sargon's inscriptions and the Hebrew Bible refer to deportations of Israelites, resulting in a number of Hebrew names in Neo-Assyrian documents from different parts of the empire, including Halah (*Ḫalaḫḫu*), Gozan (*Guzāna*), Dur-Katlimmu, and what may be identified as the "cities of the Medes" mentioned in 2 Kgs. 17:6; 18:11 (Becking 1992: 61–93; 2002; Younger 1998; Oded 2000); a part of this population may have been deported already by Tiglath-pileser. The majority of the deportees probably ended up as farmers, soldiers, and construction workers, such as the Samarians provided for work in Dur-šarruken (SAA 15 280; Fuchs and Parpola 2001: 176–77). Some of them, however, appear to have been well established in the Assyrian civil administration; in Gozan, for instance, the governor's official Palṭi-iau and the chief of accounts Neri-iau are accused of crimes against the king, and the same letter knows Ḫalbišu the Samarian whose title is broken away but who probably also belongs to the civil administration (SAA 16 63; Luukko and Van Buylaere 2002: 58–62). People were deported also to Samaria from other parts of the empire. The Assyrian sources do not mention people brought to Samaria from Babylonia (thus 2 Kgs. 17:24), but the annals of Sargon mention certain Arab tribes who resettled in Samaria (Fuchs 1994: 110; for further evidence of Assyrian deportations to Samaria, see Na'aman and Zadok 2000).

The kingdom of Judah appears seldom in the sources from the time of Sargon. It is never mentioned in the royal inscriptions of this period, save the historically unverifiable title of Sargon in the Juniper Palace Text, "subduer of the land of Judah, which lies far away" (Winckler 1889, Taf. 48, line 8; Frahm 2019: 66–67.). A letter to Sargon mentions emissaries from Egypt, Gaza, Judah, Moab, and Ammon entering Calah with their tribute (SAA 1 110; Parpola 1987: 92–93). Both the tribute and the absence of military activities indicate peaceful relations between Judah and Assyria. The royal tomb excavated at Nimrud in 1988–89 revealed two female bodies together with inscribed objects belonging to Iabâ, the queen of Tiglath-pileser, and Atalia, the queen of Sargon. These women have been interpreted as Judeans (Dalley 1998; 2004), but the Hebrew origin of the names is not certain (Younger 2002).

Political circumstances in the Levant stabilized under the reign of Sargon, and even the rule of his son Sennacherib (705–681 BCE) did not bring about substantial changes. The most significant event was Sennacherib's campaign in 701 BCE, reported in his inscriptions (RINAP 3 4; Grayson and Novotny 2012: 60–69; cf. Cogan 2014). The purpose of his extensive military action was to quell a revolt of several Syrian and Palestinian rulers, including Hezekiah of Judah (*Ḫazaqi-iāu Iaudāia*). Sennacherib attacked Sidon and continued to Philistia, after which he marched to Judah. He says to have invaded forty-six fortified cities and deported no less than 200,150 people from Judah. Interestingly, the capture of Lachish, the second city of the kingdom of Judah, is not mentioned in the inscription; instead, it was depicted on the wall reliefs of Sennacherib's Southwest palace in Nineveh, giving a pictorial interpretation of an Assyrian artist—rather than an eyewitness report—of the event (Uehlinger 2007: 211–19). Archaeological evidence both in Lachish and in other sites testifies to the devastation of large areas of Judah (Young 2012: 62–66; Ussishkin 2014). Hezekiah, however, refused to capitulate and, even though he eventually had no other choice but submit to Sennacherib and pay a heavy tribute to him, Judah retained restricted independence as a vassal state of Assyria.

The conquest of the Judean cities and the tribute Hezekiah paid to Sennacherib are recorded both in Assyrian inscriptions and in the biblical narrative (2 Kgs. 18:13–16). According to 2 Kgs. 18:14, the Assyrian king demanded of Hezekiah three hundred talents of silver and thirty talents of gold, while Sennacherib reports to have received from him eight hundred talents of silver and thirty talents of gold together with furniture, textiles, and different kinds of equipment, and also his daughters, palace women, and male and female singers. The same amount of gold in both sources may indicate that the earliest writer of the biblical narrative had access to contemporary records. More problematic is the alleged siege of Jerusalem related in 2 Kgs. 18:17–19:36//Isa. 36–39 (cf. 2 Chr. 32:1–23), ending with a miraculous defeat of the Assyrian army caused by the angel of the Lord. Sennacherib claims to have confined Hezekiah in Jerusalem, his royal city, "like a bird in a cage," to have set up blockades against Hezekiah, and made him "dread exiting his city gate." This account is traditionally understood to refer to the siege of Jerusalem (e.g., Gallagher 1999: 133–35). Many scholars, however, interpret it as denoting a blockade which required only a minor military operation, setting up fortifications to control people's movements rather than a full-scale siege (e.g., Mayer 2003; Knauf 2003; Ussishkin 2014). Whatever the scale of the military operation was, Jerusalem was saved. While the biblical narrative laconically states that Sennacherib "left, went home, and lived at Nineveh" (2 Kgs. 19:36), the Assyrian inscription says that Hezekiah sent a mounted messenger to Sennacherib to deliver the tribute and to do obeisance. It is probable that Hezekiah's agreement to pay tribute gave the Assyrian king enough reason to end his military operations against Judah.

The biblical text continues with a sentence concerning the death of Sennacherib. According to 2 Kgs. 19:37//Isa. 37:38, Sennacherib's sons Adrammelech and Sharezer killed him with the sword when he was worshipping in the house of his god Nisroch (probably the temple of Ninurta in Calah; Uehlinger 1999), and escaped into the land of Ararat. The murder of Sennacherib is mentioned in a Babylonian chronicle, according to which he was killed by his son in a rebellion (Chr. 1 iii 34–35; Grayson 1975: 81). The son is not named and no further circumstances are recorded. Esarhaddon tells how his brothers "went out of their minds and did everything that is displeasing to the gods and mankind" (RINAP 4 1; Leichty 2011: 12), but he does not directly claim that his brothers actually killed their father. This has given rise to the idea that Esarhaddon himself was involved in the murder of Sennacherib (e.g., Knapp 2015: 317–25). However, the biblical account can be confirmed by cuneiform records, according to which the murderer of Sennacherib indeed was his eldest son Arda-mullissi (Heb. ʿAdrammelek). He had been replaced as the crown prince of Assyria by his younger brother Esarhaddon and, therefore, tried to capture the throne by means of a civil war (Parpola 1980). Even Assyrian prophecies accompanying Esarhaddon's rise to power indicate that the brothers were two, and that they fled "up to the mountain" (SAA 9 1.8; 3.3; Parpola 1997: 9, 23–24; cf. Nissinen 1998: 14–30).

The Assyrian Empire was at its height under the rule of Esarhaddon (681–669 BCE) and his son Assurbanipal (668–627 BCE). The Assyrian sources from this long period have surprisingly little to report on anything regarding the kingdom of Judah. Esarhaddon was active in the West, but mostly because of political pressure in northern Syria and Tabal. He passed through southern Levant on his way to Egypt in 671 BCE, and some fragments of royal stelae found at Qaqun and Ben Shemen may be parts of a stela erected by Esarhaddon on this occasion (Horowitz and Oshima 2006: 45, 111; Cogan 2008). Judah is not mentioned in the inscriptions concerning the Egyptian campaign and was apparently not affected by it. Instead, Judah seems to have remained a loyal vassal state of Assyria throughout the reigns of Esarhaddon and Assurbanipal. No incidents related to Judah are mentioned in the Assyrian sources from his time. The very sparse appearances of Judah in Assyrian sources may indicate a lack of conflicts due to the loyalty of the kings of Judah to their political overlords. This was also the period when the Assyrian cultural influence on Judah was at its height.

Both Esarhaddon and Assurbanipal mention Manasseh, king of Judah (*Menasê/Minsê šar Iaudī*) in their inscriptions. Esarhaddon lists Manasseh among twenty-two kings from the Levant and Cyprus who contributed to the extension of the Nineveh arsenal (RINAP 4 1 and 5; Leichty 2011: 23, 46). Assurbanipal mentions him on the occasion of his Egyptian campaign in the year 667 BCE as one of the kings who gave him tribute and military support. The list is virtually identical to the list of Esarhaddon, but not necessarily copied from it, since the names of the kings of Arwad, Samsimurunna, and Ammon are different (Prism C ii 27; Novotny and Jeffers 2018: 116). The long reign of Manasseh in Jerusalem covers the entire reign of Esarhaddon and almost two-thirds of the reign of Assurbanipal, but the Hebrew Bible has not much to say about these two Assyrian kings. Neither of the two are mentioned in the biblical accounts of the reign of Manasseh (2 Kgs. 21:1–18; 2 Chr. 33:1–20), even though one could assume that the religious renewals condemned by the biblical writers were at least partly inspired by political circumstances. Amon and Josiah, the successors of Manasseh, are never mentioned in the Assyrian texts.

Esarhaddon is mentioned in the Hebrew Bible only as the successor of Sennacherib after his murder (2 Kgs. 19:37//Isa. 37:38, cf. Tob. 1:21–22). In addition, the Samaritans who wanted to contribute to the rebuilding of the temple say that they had been sacrificing to God "ever since the days of King Esarhaddon of Assyria who brought us here" (Ezra 4:2). The somewhat mysterious prediction of Isa. 7:8, "Within sixty-five years Ephraim will be shattered, no longer a people," has been interpreted as a reference to this deportation, roughly corresponding to the time between the alleged date of the prophecy and the latter part of Esarhaddon's reign. There are no Assyrian records of such a deportation which, theoretically, could have happened, for instance, during Esarhaddon's campaign to the West in 676 BCE.

The only biblical reference to Assurbanipal is found in Ezra 4:7–11, listing the people and nations "whom the great and noble Osnappar deported and settled in the cities of Samaria and in the rest of the province Beyond the River" as the senders of the letter to King Artaxerxes opposing the rebuilding of Jerusalem. In addition, the "king of Assyria" whose army took Manasseh captive and brought him to Babylon (2 Chr. 33:11) would logically be Assurbanipal; however, the Chronicler's account of the time of Manasseh in 2 Chr. 33:1–20 is a theological interpretation no longer based on historical records.

2.2 Judah and Judeans in Babylonian Sources

Babylonian sources pertaining to the events narrated in the historical books of the Hebrew Bible can be divided into three groups: (1) the neo-Babylonian Chronicles; (2) the palace archives of Nebuchadnezzar II; and (3) miscellaneous administrative and economic texts documenting the activity of Judean people living in Babylonia in the sixth and fifth centuries BCE (see Pearce 2016).

2.2.1 Neo-Babylonian Chronicles

Royal inscriptions similar to the Assyrian texts discussed above have not been preserved from Babylonia. Instead, the Babylonian Chronicles are the best available historiographic sources from the time of Nabû-naṣir (757–734 BCE) to the Seleucid period. Even Neo-Assyrian kings are mentioned in the earlier chronicles (e.g., in the cases of the conquest of Samaria and the murder of Sennacherib; see above pp. 23–24). Only one of the Babylonian chronicles covering the early reign of Nebuchadnezzar relates to events in Judah (Chronicle 5; Grayson 1975: 99–102). The section concerning his seventh year says that Nebuchadnezzar encamped against "the city of Judah" (*āl-Iāḫūdu*), which can only mean Jerusalem, and captured the city on the second day of the month Adar (March 16, 597 BCE). According to the chronicle, the Babylonian king seized the king of Judah (Jehoiachin), appointed a king of his own choice (Zedekiah), and took a vast tribute. Several biblical texts refer to Nebuchadnezzar's invasion of Jerusalem, the replacing of King Jehoiachin by Zedekiah, and the booty that was carried to Babylonia (2 Kgs. 24:10–17; 2 Chr. 36:9–10; cf. Jer. 22:24–27). Several problems in the textual history of these passages make it difficult to reconstruct the historical events from the biblical accounts (Pakkala 2006). There is no doubt, however, that the biblical and Babylonian texts refer to the same event. The final defeat of Jerusalem in 586 BCE is not recorded in the Babylonian chronicles, because the last extant chronicle breaks after Nebuchadnezzar's eleventh year (594/3 BCE). Apart from biblical texts (2 Kgs. 25:1–21; 2 Chr. 36:11–21; Jer. 39:1–10), the destruction and its aftermath is identifiable in the archeological record (Lipschits 2005: 36–126; Valkama 2010).

2.2.2 Palace Archives of Nebuchadnezzar II

The palace archives of Nebuchadnezzar II comprise ca. 350 tablets, of which only thirteen have been fully or partially published (Pedersén 2005). The available material comprises tablets from the years 601–577 BCE, recording the delivery and distribution of foods and other properties to various people living in Babylon. The best known of these tablets are the four partially published ration lists, one of which is datable to the thirteenth year of Nebuchadnezzar (591 BCE; Weidner 1939; Alstola 2020: 58–78). These texts concern the distribution of sesame oil to certain groups and individuals often of foreign origin, such as Philistia, Phoenicia, Elam, Egypt, Asia Minor, Greece, and even Judah. The most prominent of the Judeans receiving oil rations is Jehoiachin (*Ia'ūkin/Ia'kin/Iakūkinu*), king of Judah, and his five sons. Moreover, a group of eight Judeans is mentioned in the ration lists, and the palace archive knows Judean courtiers (*ša rēš šarri*) and three persons with Yahwistic names (Qana-Yama, Samak-Yama, and Šalam-Yama; see Pedersén 2005: 269).

The number of people of foreign origin in the palace archive of Babylon is probably due to the forced migrations in the early sixth century. Among the deportees there were different kinds of professionals employed by the royal palace, including Judean ones. Members of foreign royalty were held hostage in Babylon, not only from Judah but also from Ashkelon and, possibly, Lydia. The foreign nobles seem to have lived under the aegis of the Babylonian king, not in a hard confinement but enjoying a limited freedom. These circumstances are probably reflected by 2 Kgs. 25:27–30, which tells about the release of Jehoiachin from imprisonment by Amel-Marduk (Evil-merodach), Nebuchadnezzar's successor. The biblical passage says that in the thirty-seventh year of Jehoiachin's exile (ca. 561 BCE) the Babylonian king "spoke kindly to him, and gave him a seat above the other seats of the kings who were with him in Babylon," giving him a regular allowance for the rest of his life. This narrative presupposes, however, that before this, the Judean king was indeed in confinement wearing prison clothes, which is difficult to reconcile with the Babylonian records. The narrative is not merely a historical note but has literary affinities with, for instance, the Joseph story in Genesis (Chan 2013). Contrasting Jehoiachin's imprisonment with his amnesty is probably written to inspire the audience's confidence in a better future, perhaps also in the continuation of Jehoiachin's dynastic line (Pakkala 2006: 452).

2.2.3 Administrative and Economic Texts

Hundreds of miscellaneous administrative and economic texts from Babylonia informing on the Judeans in Babylonia and/or with relevance to biblical texts have become scholarly knowledge only recently. The earliest of these tablets derives from Sippar, dating to 595 BCE (Jursa 2008). It records the delivery of 1.5 minas of gold belonging to Nabû-šarrussu-ukin, the chief eunuch (*rab ša-rēši*), to the temple of Esagila in Babylon. There are good grounds to identify this person with the chief eunuch (*rab-sārîs*) Nebo-sarsekim who, according to one of the narratives related to the final destruction of Jerusalem, belonged to the high command of the Babylonian army when Jerusalem was taken (Jer. 39:3).

Other texts pertain especially to the Judean population in Babylonia, identifiable by their Yahwistic names (Zadok 2002; 2014). A group of six tablets originates from Sippar and dates to the second half of the sixth century BCE (Bloch 2014; Alstola 2017b). People who feature in these texts include descendants of Ariḫ, a family of Judean royal merchants who were well-integrated members of the local business community. Two of the tablets are marriage agreements demonstrating that one of Ariḫ's granddaughters married into a Babylonian family.

The Murašû archive was excavated in Nippur already in 1893 and partially published between 1898 and 1912, but the publication of the entire archive, comprising some 730 texts, took another century (Stolper 1985; Donbaz and Stolper 1997). All the documents in this archive focus on the business of the Murašû in Nippur and its environs in the second half of the fifth century BCE. The Murašû were agricultural entrepreneurs who acted as middlemen between landowners and subsistence farmers. They had been granted land owned by royal aristocracy and high officials and were obliged to pay taxes and perform military and corvée services in exchange. The archive consists of economic and legal texts documenting credit granting and agricultural management. People taking part in such transactions often worked for the land-for-service sector, and many of them seem to belong to communities of foreigners settled in the Nippur countryside. A fair number of Judeans appear in these documents, typically belonging to the class of subsistence farmers cultivating modest plots of land, but some of them had even larger holdings indicating a higher socioeconomic position (Alstola 2020: 164–222).

The most recent corpus consists of more than 200 Babylonian tablets, 113 of which have been published thus far (Joannès and Lemaire 1996; 1999; Abraham 2005/6; 2007; Pearce and Wunsch 2015; for the rest, see Wunsch forthcoming). The texts derive originally from places called Al-Yahudu, Bit-Našar, and Bit-Abi-Râm situated in the countryside near the city of Nippur between the Tigris river and the southern marshlands. The place name Al-Yahudu, "Judahtown," denotes the origin of its inhabitants; Bit-Našar was to be found in its vicinity. The texts date from the period between 572 and 477 BCE and, even though their original findspot is unknown, are likely to have belonged to a single corpus.

Like the tablets belonging to the Murašû archive, the texts from Al-Yahudu and surroundings bear witness to the contribution of Judeans to the land-for-service system. The documents include a considerable number of Judean names identifiable by the Yahwistic theophorical element (Pearce and Wunsch 2015: 10–29). The Judeans appear predominantly as subsistence farmers whose economical transactions are mostly tax payments and credit operations related to agriculture. Most Judeans do not occupy higher-level positions of the society, since they were not free to alienate their landholdings; a few of them, however, are attested as officials such as tax-summoners (*dēkû*). Two individuals of Judean descent stand out because of their long-term economical activity and independent businesses in the region: Aḫiqam, a rent farmer who owned a brewing enterprise in Babylon, and Aḫiqar, who granted credit to landholders to help them to pay their taxes (Alstola 2020: 102–63).

Of the administrative tablets discussed above, only the palace archive and the Murašû archive have a provenanced findspot. The tablets mentioning the descendants of Ariḫ originate from early, badly documented excavations in Sippar, and the entire corpus of tablets from the environs of Al-Yahudu is unprovenanced. This notwithstanding, they are doubtless genuine artifacts that document important aspects of the life of the descendants of the Judean deportees over several generations from neo-Babylonian to Achaemenid times. The Judeans belong roughly to three social groups: the royal elite in the earliest documents, the merchants doing business in different parts of Babylonia, and the subsistence farmers in Al-Yahudu and surroundings. Generally, the Judeans appear as not very wealthy but not extremely poor either. They seem to be integrated into the economic institutions of the Babylonian society, yet forming communities composed of largely their fellow Judeans (Wunsch 2013; Pearce 2014).

2.3 THE SIGNIFICANCE OF THE ASSYRIAN AND BABYLONIAN SOURCES

The Assyrian sources relevant to the history of the kingdoms of Israel and Judah cover the period between the mid-ninth and mid-seventh centuries BCE, thus pertaining to the period narrated in 1 Kgs. 16 to 2 Kgs. 21. The Assyrian source material consists overwhelmingly of royal inscriptions mentioning military events related to kings of Israel (Ahab, Jehu, Joash, Menahem, Pekah, Hoshea) and Judah (Ahaz, Hezekiah, Manasseh). The Assyrian and biblical accounts of these events agree in the basic structure of the unfolding of historical events, even though some episodes mentioned in the Assyrian sources are not known from the biblical texts and vice versa. Both ways, the historical information is embedded in a thoroughly ideological narrative. In the Assyrian royal inscriptions, the implied speaker is the king who gives an account of his own deeds—not primarily to his own citizens but to his gods, representing the Assyrian royal theology. In the Hebrew Bible, the historical narrative in 2 Kings belongs to a multi-layered composition, representing (post-)deuteronomistic theologies and written with the main purpose of explaining the reason of the destruction of Jerusalem. Hence, the presentation of the achievements of Assyrian and Israelite or Judean kings is heavily dependent on the genre and purpose of writing, which in the case of Assyria tends to emphasize the king's military and political merits, while the Hebrew Bible judges each king mainly with regard to the orthodoxy of their worship. The agreements between the Assyrian and biblical narratives make it probable, however, that the writers of 2 Kings had source-based knowledge of past events, and the recurring references to the annals of the kings of Israel and Judah (e.g., 1 Kgs. 14:19, 29) probably refer to such sources (Grabbe 2017: 21–28).

The significance of the Babylonian administrative tablets lies somewhat paradoxically in things about which the biblical texts have little to say. Apart from confirming the conquest of Jerusalem in 597 BCE and the forced migration of the Judeans including King Jehoiachin and his entourage, the Babylonian texts have virtually no direct connections to any events and persons mentioned in the Hebrew Bible. Instead, they increase our knowledge of circumstances not discernible from the biblical texts—namely, the social environment and living conditions of the Judean population in a certain part of Babylonia in the sixth to fifth centuries BCE. The persistence of the use of Yahwistic names indicates the will of the community to maintain their Judean identity, but the sources do not yield much information on the religion of the Judeans, neither do they include any hints at the return of some members of the Judean community to their homeland.

Note

1. An inscription of Tiglath-pileser (RINAP 1 13/31; Tadmor and Yamada 2011: 42–44, 76) mentions a king called *Azrī-Iāu*. This person was formerly, but mistakenly, identified with Azariah/Uzziah, king of Judah, the grandfather of Ahaz. The assumption was based on an incorrect join of a fragmentary tablet to the inscription, producing the reading "Azriyau of Yaudi"; however, such a text has never actually existed. The name mentioned in the inscription may refer to the king of Ḫatarikka (thus Na'aman 1995).

Bibliography

Abraham, Kathleen. 2005/6. "West Semitic and Judean Brides in Cuneiform Sources from the Sixth Century BCE: New Evidence from a Marriage Contract from Al-Yahudu." *AfO* 51: 198–219.

Abraham, Kathleen. 2007. "An Inheritance Division among Judeans in Babylonia from the Early Persian Period." In Meir Lubetski, ed., *New Seals and Inscriptions, Hebrew, Idumean, and Cuneiform*. HBM 8. Sheffield: Sheffield Phoenix, 206–21.

Alstola, Tero. 2017b. "Judean Merchants in Babylonia and Their Participation in Long-Distance Trade". *WO* 47: 25–51.

Alstola, Tero. 2020. *Judeans in Babylonia: A Study of Deportees in the Sixth and Fifth Centuries BCE.* CHANE 109. Leiden: Brill.

Bagg, Ariel. 2011. *Die Assyrer und das Westland*. OLA 216. Leuven: Peeters.

Becking, Bob. 1992. *The Fall of Samaria: An Historical and Archaeological Study*. SHANE 2. Leiden: Brill.

Becking, Bob. 2002. "West Semites at Tell Šēḫ Ḥamad: Evidence for the Israelite Exile?" In Ulrich H Hübner and Ernst Axel Knauf, eds., *Kein Land für sich allein: Studien zum Kulturkontakt in Kanaan, Israel/Palästina und Ebirnâri für Manfred Weippert zum 65. Geburtstag*. OBO 186. Freiburg: Universitätsverlag and Göttingen: Vandenhoeck & Ruprecht, 153–66.

Bloch, Yigal. 2014. "Judeans in Sippar and Susa during the First Century of the Babylonian Exile: Assimilation and Perseverance under Neo-Babylonian and Achaemenid Rule." *JANEH* 1: 119–72.

Chan, Michael J. 2013. "Joseph and Jehoiachin: On the Edge of Exodus". *ZAW* 125: 566–77.

Cogan, Mordechai. 2008. "The Assyrian Stela Fragment from Bet Shemen." In Mordechai Cogan and Dan'el Kahn, eds., *Treasures on Camels' Humps: Historical and Literary Studies from the Ancient Near East Presented to Israel Eph'al*. Jerusalem: Magnes Press, 66–69.

Cogan, Mordechai. 2014. "Cross-examining the Assyrian Witnesses to Sennacherib's Third Campaign: Assessing the Limits of Historical Reconstruction." In Isaac Kalimi and Seth Richardson, eds., *Sennacherib at the Gates of Jerusalem: Story, History and Historiography*. CHANE 71. Leiden: Brill, 51–74.

Dalley, Stephanie. 1998. "Yabâ and Atalya and the Foreign Policy of Late Assyrian Kings." *SAAB* 12: 83–98.

Dalley, Stephanie. 2004. "Recent Evidence from Assyrian Sources for Judaean History from Uzziah to Manasseh." *JSOT* 28: 387–401.

Donbaz, Veysel and Matthew W. Stolper. 1997. *Istanbul Murašû Texts*. PIHANS 79. Istanbul: Nederlands Historisch-Archeologisch Instituut te Istanbul.

Frahm, Eckart. 2019. "Samaria, Hamath, and Assyria's Conquests in the Levant in the Late 720s BCE: The Testimony of Sargon II's Inscriptions." In Shuichi Hasegawa, Christoph Levin, and Karen Radner, eds., *The Last Days of the Kingdom of Israel*. BZAW 511. Berlin: de Gruyter, 55–86.

Fuchs, Andreas. 1994. *Die Inschriften Sargons II. aus Khorsabad*. Göttingen: Cuvillier.

Fuchs, Andreas and Simo Parpola. 2001. *The Correspondence of Sargon II, Part III: Letters from Babylonia and the Eastern Provinces*. SAA 15. Helsinki: Helsinki University Press.

Gallagher, William R. 1999. *Sennacherib's Campaign to Judah: New Studies.* SHCANE 18. Leiden: Brill.
Grabbe, Lester L. 2017. *1 & 2 Kings: History and Story in Ancient Israel.* London: Bloomsbury.
Grayson, A. Kirk. 1975. *Assyrian and Babylonian Chronicles.* TCS 1. Locust Valley, NY: Augustin.
Grayson, A. Kirk. 1996. *The Royal Inscriptions of Mesopotamia, Assyrian Periods 3: Assyrian Rulers of the Early First Millennium BC II (858—745 BC).* RIMA 3. Toronto: University of Toronto Press.
Grayson, A. Kirk and Jamie Novotny. 2012. *The Royal Inscriptions of Sennacherib, King of Assyria (704-681 BC), Part 1.* RINAP 3/1. Winona Lake, IN: Eisenbrauns.
Horowitz, Wayne, Takayoshi Osima, and Seth L. Sanders. 2018. *Cuneiform in Canaan: The Next Generation.* 2nd ed. University Park, PA: Eisenbrauns.
Joannès, Francis and André Lemaire. 1996. "Contrats babyloniens d'époque achéménide du Bît-abî Râm avec une épigraphie araméenne." *RA* 90: 41–60.
Joannès, Francis and André Lemaire. 1999. "Trois tablettes cunéiformes à l'onomastique ouest-sémitique (Collection Sh. Moussaieff)." *Transeuphratène* 17: 17–34.
Jursa, Michael. 2008. "Nabû-šarrūssu-ukīn, *rab ša-rēši*, und 'Nebusarsekim' (Jer 39:3)." *NABU* 2008/1: 9–10.
Knapp, Andrew. 2015. *Royal Apologetic in the Ancient Near East.* WAWSup 4. Atlanta: SBL.
Knauf, Ernst Axel. 2003. "701: Sennacherib at the Berezina". In Lester L. Grabbe, ed., *"Like a Bird in a Cage": The Invasion of Sennacherib in 701 BCE.* JSOTSup 363. Sheffield: Sheffield Academic Press, 141–49.
Leichty, Erle. 2011. *The Royal Inscriptions of Esarhaddon, King of Assyria (680-669 BC).* RINAP 4. Winona Lake, IN: Eisenbrauns.
Lipiński, Edward. 2000. *The Aramaeans: Their Ancient History, Culture, Religion.* OLA 100. Leuven: Peeters.
Lipschits, Oded. 2005. *The Fall and Rise of Jerusalem: Judah under Babylonian Rule.* Winona Lake, IN: Eisenbrauns.
Loretz, Oswald and Walter Mayer. 1990. "Pūlu-Tiglatpileser III. und Menahem von Israel nach assyrischen Quellen und 2 Kön 15, 19–20." *UF* 22: 221–31.
Luukko, Mikko and Greta Van Buylaere. 2002. *The Political Correspondence of Esarhaddon.* SAA 16. Helsinki: Helsinki University Press.
Mayer, Walter. 2003. "Sennacherib's Campaign of 701 BCE: The Assyrian View". In Lester L. Grabbe, ed., *"Like a Bird in a Cage": The Invasion of Sennacherib in 701 BCE.* JSOTSup 363. Sheffield: Sheffield Academic Press, 168–200.
Millard, Alan. 1994. *The Eponyms of the Neo-Assyrian Empire: 910-612 BC.* SAAS 2. Helsinki: Helsinki University Press.
Na'aman, Nadav. 1990. "The Historical Background of the Fall of Samaria (720 BC)." *Bib* 71: 206–25.
Na'aman, Nadav. 1995. "Tiglath-Pileser III's Campaigns against Tyre and Israel (734-732 B.C.E.)." *Tel Aviv* 22: 268–78.
Na'aman, Nadav. 1997. "Lebo-hamath, Ṣubat-hamath and the Northern Boundary of the Land of Canaan." *UF* 31: 417–41.
Na'aman, Nadav. 2008. "Let Other Kingdoms Struggle with the Great Powers—You, Judah, Pay the Tribute and Hope for the Best: The Foreign Policy of the Kings of Judah in the Ninth–Eighth Centuries BCE." In Raymond Cohen and Raymond Westbrook, eds., *Isaiah's Vision of Peace in Biblical and Modern International Relations: Swords into Plowshares.* New York: Palgrave Macmillan, 55–73.
Na'aman, Nadav and Ran Zadok. 2000. "Assyrian Deportations to the Province of Samerina in the Light of Two Cuneiform Tablets from Tel Hadid." *TA* 27: 159–88.
Nissinen, Martti. 1998. *References to Prophecy in Neo-Assyrian Sources.* SAAS 7. Helsinki: The Neo-Assyrian Text Corpus Project.
Nissinen, Martti. 2018. *The Royal Inscriptions of Ashurbanipal (668-631 BC), Aššur-etel-ilāni (630-627 BC), and Sîn-šarra-iškun (626-612), Kings of Assyria, Part 1.* RINAP 5/1. University Park, PA: Eisenbrauns.

Novotny, Jamie and Joshua Jeffers. 2018. *The Royal Inscriptions of Ashurbanipal (668–631 BC), Aššur-etel-ilāni (630–627 BC), and Sîn-šarra-iškun (626–612), Kings of Assyria, Part 1*. RINAP 5/1. University Park, PA: Eisenbrauns, 116.

Oded, Bustenay. 2000. "The Settlements of the Israelite and Judaean Exiles in Mesopotamia in the 8th–6th Centuries BCE." In Gershom Galil and Moshe Weinfeld, eds., *Studies in Historical Geography and Biblical Historiography Presented to Zecharia Kallai*. VTSup 81. Leiden: Brill, 91–103.

Pakkala, Juha. 2006. "Zedekiah's Fate and the Dynastic Succession." *JBL* 125: 443–52.

Parpola, Simo. 1980. "The Murderer of Sennacherib." In Bendt Alster, ed., *Death in Mesopotamia*. Mesopotamia 8. Copenhagen: Akademisk, 161–70.

Parpola, Simo. 1987. *The Correspondence of Sargon II, Part I: Letters from Assyria and the West*. SAA 1. Helsinki: Helsinki University Press.

Parpola, Simo. 1997. *Assyrian Prophecies*. SAA 9. Helsinki: Helsinki University Press.

Parpola, Simo and Kazuko Watanabe. 1988. *Neo-Assyrian Treaties and Loyalty Oaths*. SAA 2. Helsinki: Helsinki University Press.

Pearce, Laurie E. 2014. "Continuity and Normality in Sources Relating to the Judean Exile." *HeBAI* 3: 163–84.

Pearce, Laurie E. 2016. "Cuneiform Sources for Judeans in Babylonia in the Neo-Babylonian and Achaemenid Periods: An Overview." *Religion Compass* 10: 230–43.

Pearce, Laurie E. and Cornelia Wunsch. 2015. *Documents of Judean Exiles and West Semites in Babylonia in the Collection of David Sofer*. CUSAS 28. Bethesda, MD: CDL Press.

Pedersén, Olof. 2005. *Archive und Bibliotheken in Babylon: Die Tontafeln der Grabung Robert Koldeweys 1899–1917*. ADOG 25. Saarbrücken: Saarländische Druckerei und Verlag.

Stolper, Matthew W. 1985. *Entrepreneurs and Empire: The Murašû Archive, the Murašû Firm, and the Persian Rule in Babylonia*. PIHANS 54. Istanbul: Nederlands Historisch-Archaeologisch Instituut te Istanbul.

Tadmor, Hayim. 1958. "The Campaigns of Sargon II of Aššur: A Chronological-Historical Study." *JCS* 12: 22–40, 77–100.

Tadmor, Hayim and Shigeo Yamada. 2011. *The Royal Inscriptions of Tiglath-Pileser III (744–727 BC) and Shalmaneser V (726–722 BC), Kings of Assyria*. RINAP 1. Winona Lake, IN: Eisenbrauns.

Uehlinger, Christoph. 1999. "Nisroch." DDD^2: 630–32.

Uehlinger, Christoph. 2007. "Neither Eyewitnesses, nor Windows to the Past, but Valuable Testimony in Its Own Right." In H. G. M. Williamson, ed., *Understanding the History of Ancient Israel*. Proceedings of the British Academy 143. Oxford: Oxford University Press, 173–228.

Ussishkin, David. 2014. "Sennacherib's Campaign to Judah: The Archaeological Perspective with Emphasis on Lachish and Jerusalem." In Isaac Kalimi and Seth Richardson, eds., *Sennacherib at the Gates of Jerusalem: Story, History and Historiography*. CHANE 71. Leiden: Brill, 75–104.

Valkama, Kirsi. 2010. "What Do Archaeological Remains Reveal of the Settlements in Judah during the Mid-Sixth Century BCE?" In Ehud Ben Zvi and Christoph Levin, eds., *The Concept of Exile in Ancient Israel and Its Historical Contexts*. BZAW 404. Berlin: de Gruyter, 39–59.

Weidner, Ernst F. 1939. "Jojachin, König von Juda, in Babylonischen Keilschrifttexten." In *Mélanges syriens offerts à Monsieur René Dussaud par ses amis et ses élèves*, Vol. 2. Bibliothèque archéologique et historique 30. Paris: Geuthner, 923–35.

Weippert, Manfred. 1992. "Die Feldzüge Adadnararis III. nach Syrien: Voraussetzungen, Verlauf, Folgen." *ZDPV* 108: 42–67.

Winckler, Hugo. 1889. *Die Keilschrifttexte Sargons nach den Papierabklatschen und Originalen, Vol. 2: Texte*. Leipzig: Eduard Pfeiffer.

Wunsch, Cornelia. 2013. "Glimpses on the Lives of Deportees in Rural Babylonia." In Angelika Berlejung and Michael P. Streck, eds., *Arameans, Chaldeans, and Arabs in Babylonia and Palestine in the First Millennium BC*. LAOS 3. Wiesbaden: Harrassowitz, 247–60.

Wunsch, Cornelia. Forthcoming. *Judeans by the Waters of Babylon: New Historical Evidence in Cuneiform Sources from Rural Babylonia*. BaAr 6. Dresden: ISLET.

Young, Robb Andrew. 2012. *Hezekiah in History and Tradition*. VTSup 155. Leiden: Brill.
Younger, K. Lawson. 1998. "The Deportations of the Israelites." *JBL* 117: 201–27.
Younger, K. Lawson. 1999. "The Fall of Samaria in Light of Recent Research." *CBQ* 61: 461–82.
Younger, K. Lawson. 2002. "Yahweh at Ashkelon and Calah? Yahwistic Names in Neo-Assyrian," *VT* 52: 207–18.
Younger, K. Lawson. 2016. *A Political History of the Arameans: From Their Origins to the End of Their Polities*. ABS 13. Atlanta: SBL.
Zadok, Ran. 2002. *The Earliest Diaspora: Israelites and Judeans in Pre-Hellenistic Mesopotamia*. Publications of the Diaspora Research Institute 151. Tel Aviv: The Diaspora Research Institute, Tel Aviv University.
Zadok, Ran. 2014. "Judeans in Babylonia: Updating the Dossier." In Uri Gabbay and Shai Secunda, eds., *Encounters by the Rivers of Babylon: Scholarly Conversations between Jews, Iranians, and Babylonians in Antiquity*. TSAJ 160. Tübingen: Mohr Siebeck, 109–29.

CHAPTER 3

ACHAEMENID POLITICAL HISTORY AND SOURCES

AMÉLIE KUHRT

The Achaemenid Empire is the earliest of the great Iranian empires (ca. 550–330 BC). The name derives from the legendary founder of its ruling dynasty, Achaemenes, which was also the name of the royal clan (Herodotus *Hist.* 1.125), members of which ruled the empire for over two hundred years. It was the largest empire the world had yet seen, spanning the territory from the Hellespont to north India, including Egypt and extending to Central Asia up to the frontiers of modern Kazakhstan. Unlike earlier and later periods, no contemporary political entity of even remotely comparable size capable of challenging it existed along its frontiers, until the development of Macedonian power under Philip II.

Before Cyrus's conquests in 550, the Persians are barely attested in the world of the Middle East. Archaeological and written evidence suggests that until the mid-seventh century BC, they consisted of pastoral groups located in the region of modern Fars (Old Persian *Parsa*; see Miroschedji 1985; Sumner 1994), which had previously formed part of the important, though poorly known and still surviving, kingdom of Elam (Anshan), centered now in Susa (Carter and Stolper 1984; Potts 1999). A linguistically related people, the Medes, located further north in the Zagros and around modern Hamadan (ancient Ecbatana), appear more prominently in the eighth to sixth centuries BC, since they had (as a result of their relationship to the Assyrian Empire to the west) begun to coalesce into a state and made some moves towards territorial expansion (Brown 1986; Sancisi-Weerdenburg 1988; Lanfranchi et al. 2003). This may, indeed, have put pressure on Parsa and provoked the relatively rapid emergence of a Persian state there. Under its kings Cyrus II and Cambyses II (559–522) this developing polity incorporated, through conquest and in the space of less than thirty years, the large, highly developed empires and states of western Asia: the great neo-Babylonian Empire (heir to Assyria), Egypt, Lydia, and Elam, as well as Media and Central Asia to the north and east (Briant 2002: 107–38). Elam, Mesopotamia, and Egypt in particular contributed to the emerging formulation of the Persian imagery of power (Root 1979; Alvarez-Mon and Garrison 2011). This can be particularly clearly seen in the Achaemenid royal monuments and iconography, although these traditions were fundamentally and deliberately reshaped in the process of adoption and adaptation. Despite serious upheavals experienced by the empire as a result of this incredibly rapid expansion, it survived (Briant 2002: 107–38; Kuhrt 2007: 135–77) and, indeed, expanded when Darius I (522–486) added the Indus Valley to the empire. Although his and his son's attempt to add territory in Europe failed to impose lasting direct control there, the empire suffered little territorial loss. By Xerxes's reign (486–465), we can describe it as a "mature" and stable state (Briant 2002: 139–61; 515–68; Kuhrt 2007: 181–309). There continued, of course, to be chronic problems of control mainly along the frontiers: the best known are Persian interactions with Greeks along the Aegean seaboard. More serious was the temporary loss of Egypt between ca. 400 and 343. Before further discussion of Achaemenid political history is possible, the sources for reconstructing that history should be delineated.

3.1 Sources

The sources for understanding the empire present us with difficulties, not so much because they are sparse, but because they are extremely disparate and exist in a number of different languages and forms providing a range of perspectives (see, in general, Kuhrt 2007: 1–15). Before excavation and decipherment of the early eastern scripts, the Achaemenid empire was primarily known through classical authors and the Old Testament/ Hebrew Bible.

3.1.1 Classical Writers

The most important classical source is the Greek historian Herodotus, who wrote in the later fifth century BC. As his aim was to celebrate the victories won by Greeks over Persians between 490–478, his valuable information is limited, chronologically, to the early period of the empire. Although Herodotus gives us a sense of the broad geographical sweep of the empire, he treated the imperial regions very superficially, apart from Egypt and the northwestern frontier area (i.e., western Turkey). Later classical writers, aside from the "Alexander historians" (such as Arrian *Anabasis*, Quintus Curtius Rufus, Diodorus xvii, Plutarch's *Life of Alexander*), generally exhibit similar geo-political limitations. One exception is the early fourth-century author Ctesias, a doctor at the Achaemenid court who wrote a substantial history of Persia. Unfortunately, his work only survives in a heavily epitomized version made by the ninth-century Byzantine patriarch, Photius (see Lenfant 2004). Because of the fascination exercised by the wealth and power of the Persian ruler, many classical writers tend to focus on tales of court corruption and intrigue. As a result, the image of the empire to be gleaned from these sources is lopsided, presenting a picture of weakness.

3.1.2 The Old Testament

From the Old Testament (or Hebrew Bible) come the influential depictions of the Persian kings as restorers of the Jerusalem temple and supporters of the Yhwh cult (Ezra-Nehemiah; Chronicles 36). This depiction alone is responsible for the mistaken notion of the unique policy of Achaemenid religious tolerance (Kuhrt 2008). A Persian court story, comparable in some respects to the classical tales, is represented by Esther (Momigliano 1977). While not biblical, Josephus's image of the Persian empire echoes the Old Testament version (*Ant.* 11.1–8i) and likely reflects Jewish tradition.

3.1.3 Sources in the Old Persian Script

The pool of sources deepened when the Old Persian script was deciphered in the nineteenth century. Even so, the surviving texts are largely in the form of monumental royal inscriptions (Kent 1953; Lecoq 1996; Schmitt 1991; 2000) which were intended to reflect the unchanging majesty of Persian power (the one exception is Darius I's inscription at Bisotun). They are thus not (so far, at least) directly informative on political changes or administrative structures.[1]

3.1.4 Documents in Other Languages

For further illumination, recourse must be made to other sources including: Babylonian (Kuhrt 1988; Stolper 1994b), Egyptian (e.g., Posener 1936; Perrot et al. 1974; Chauveau 1996; 2003; 2008; Martin 1996; Smith and Martin 2009), Aramaic (Grelot 1972; Metzger et al. 1979; Segal 1983; Lemaire 1996; 2015; Eph'al and Naveh 1996; Porten and Yardeni 1986–99; 2014; Dušek 2007; Naveh and Shaked 2012), and Elamite (Cameron 1948; Hallock 1969; 1978). The last mentioned languages are exceptionally significant in providing an insight into the intricacies of the Persian bureaucracy (Henkelman 2008: 65–179; Briant, Henkelman, and Stolper 2008). Aramaic, which had been widely used in the Near East prior to the Persian conquest, was adopted by the régime as the most widely used administrative language (it was used, alongside Elamite, in the administration at Persepolis; see Azzoni 2008). Its widespread use is now dramatically illustrated by the parchments and tallies from Bactria-Sogdiana, the majority dating from Artaxerxes III to Alexander III ("the Great"; Naveh and Shaked 2012). They show, unmistakably, that this area was tightly held by the Achaemenids down to the very end of the empire's existence (Shaked 2004).

3.1.5 Archaeological Exploration

The area of the empire has been excavated unevenly (see, in general, Briant and Boucharlat 2005). Most attention has been paid to the great royal centers of Pasargadae (Stronach 1978; Gondet et al. 2012), Persepolis (Schmidt 1953–57; Tilia 1972–78; Callieri 2007), and Susa (Boucharlat 1990; Harper et al. 1992: 215–52). But recently the Achaemenid levels of long-occupied sites in conquered territories such as Sardis in Lydia (Dusinberre 2003), the Levant (see Stern 1982 and the journal *Transeuphratène*), and Central Asia (Francfort 1988; Briant 1984) are being examined more closely. One problem is that a number of sites known to have been important in the period are now covered by extensive modern towns making excavation difficult. This is true of Arbela (modern Erbil in north Iraq), Damascus, and Ecbatana (modern Hamadan).

3.2 Imperial Government and Administration

Considered together, the various sources described above cast important light on imperial government and administration, revealing information about the empire's satraps and subjects, regional variation, and central control—each of which is taken up in order in what follows.

3.2.1 Satraps and Subjects

The immense imperial territories were divided into provinces, generally called by the Iranian-derived term, satrapies. Each province was extensive, and each was governed by a "satrap" (governor) who was virtually always a Persian or Iranian noble resident in the satrapal capital. The satrapal center was in many cases identical with the old capital of the original political units conquered. Modifications to this system were introduced, although not all at the same time but in response to particular circumstances. Early in Xerxes's reign, for instance, the area that had formed the neo-Babylonian empire was divided into two new satrapies: "Beyond the River," west of the Euphrates and stretching down to the Egyptian frontier, and Babylonia, the whole of Mesopotamia (Stolper 1989).

The satrapal capital functioned as the administrative center of the governor. It is here that tax was collected and stored (or sent on), satrapal archives were kept, petitions sent, and royal orders and edicts received. Each satrapal capital contained a palace, used by the satrap himself and also maintained for the king who moved around his realm (Briant 1988). Physical evidence of such a palace, partly decorated in a Persian style, has been found at Babylon (Haerinck 1997; Vallat 1989; Gasche 2010: 446–63). Satrapal residences in the provinces are also attested at Memphis, Daskyleion (north-west Turkey), Sardis, Ecbatana, and Bactra (modern Balkh). In addition, there were fortified storehouses dotted throughout the provinces and their subdivisions (Grelot 1972: 310–12). In the Persian heartlands (Fars, Elam) were the major royal centers, such as the old city of Susa, which was completely rebuilt in a typically Persian style, and the new, spectacular foundations of Pasargadae and Persepolis. The satrap himself was, within his satrapy, in control of military affairs, such as general mobilization for war and public works, and the garrisons which served to protect the population as well as maintain order in the province. He also controlled its administrative and financial affairs to ensure the province's continued productivity (Klinkott 2005).

3.2.2 Regional Variation

Despite the unification of so many different areas under the imperial umbrella, there were regional variation in administration. The transhumant populations of the great Zagros mountain chain, for example, were never integrated into the provincial structure. The productive potential of this group was slight and topography made military campaigns difficult; in addition, this highly mobile population was hard to pin down. Hence the

Persians and these scattered mountain dwellers arrived at a *modus vivendi*. The Persian king regularly presented the local leaders with gifts, creating and renewing a mutually profitable alliance. This allowed the king to draw on their manpower when needed: the tribes helped to secure routes through the mountains, supplied the administration with additional livestock (Henkelman 2005), and their goodwill reduced the incidence of raids on nearby adjacent settled communities (Briant 1982: 57–112).

Arab groups on the empire's fringe enjoyed another kind of relationship with the central authority. In return for help with finding safe routes through the desert and organizing the lucrative caravan trade which ran from the southern tip of the peninsula to Palestinian ports, such as Persian-controlled Gaza, they paid no tax but instead presented the king with a regular "gift" of incense, creating a mutually beneficial relationship. Again, Arab contingents are attested serving in the Achaemenid armies (Briant 1982: 113–79). Other important frontier-groups were the nomadic Scythians living in the steppes beyond the Oxus. How precisely the Persian authority managed relations with them is unknown, but they certainly supplied warriors to the Persian army, particularly as marines (Dandamaev 1979), which again suggests that a reciprocal arrangement had been set up (Briant 1982: 181–234). The populations in the Caucasus seem to have reached a similar agreement (see Herodotus *Hist.* 3.97), while relations with the factitious Greeks illustrate some of the recurring problems that had to be dealt with.

Various provinces, too, reflect differences in the style of imposition of Persian control, indicative of local factors with which the authorities had to deal. Egypt, for example, retained its own very characteristic culture, especially in the realm of artistic expression and production, in styles of architecture and in its belief system, which traditionally assigned a special divine role to the king. As a result, from Cambyses on, Persian kings were hailed as pharaohs, represented as such, and given a pharaonic-style titulary (see Posener 1936: 1–87; Perrot et al. 1974: 181–83; see also Wasmuth 2017). In Babylonia, too, the Persian king acted in accordance with local royal ideology. The king was expected to build and maintain temples and city walls, confirm the protected status of certain cities, ensure that rituals were performed, authorize divine offerings, and support important ceremonies. At no point were the essential ingredients for carrying out these crucial rituals dismantled by the Persians (Kuhrt 2014), but inevitably there were major changes. In Egypt, the office of "God's Wife of Amun," which was very important for the previous five hundred years or so, disappeared, while in Babylonia elite families who had been in control of temple offices were replaced by new officials (see Waerzeggers 2003/4) perhaps in the wake of revolts in 484. At the same time, it is clear that both regions were home to a variegated mass of peoples, including Greeks, Carians, Syrians, Bactrians, and Jews. The latter group is particularly well documented by texts found on Elephantine Island in the extreme south of Egypt (see Porten 1968) and by recent evidence for the existence of a "Town of the Judaeans" in Babylonia (see Stökl and Waerzeggers 2015).

Furthermore, within each satrapy, local conditions varied from place to place because a diversity of political units could all form part of one overall satrapy. To cite just one instance: in the province "Beyond the River," a place such as Jerusalem, within the district of Yehud, retained its sacred laws, its priestly hierarchy, and was governed by Jews (Avigad 1976: 30–36). Meanwhile, neighbouring Samaria was administered by the local family of Sanballat (Dušek 2007); the Phoenician cities continued under the control of local rulers (Betlyon 1980; Elayi 1989); and Ammon, east of the Jordan, formed a provincial subdivision under a local governor (Herr 1992). In the course of the fourth century, the Negev region was organized as the province of Idumaea (Lemaire 2006: 416–19). So, while all these divergent entities were answerable to the Persian satrap in Damascus, internally they lived according to their diverse local customs.

This is borne out by what is known (so far) of legal regulations in the empire—once again, local customs were the rule, although they could be overridden, if need be, by the king's "word" or "law" (Old Persian *data*). This came in the form of decrees issued in response to specific situations. The hypothesis put forward in the 1980s by Frei (1984; elaborated in 1996) that the Achaemenids developed a unique legal instrument or "code" ("the law of the king"; see Ezra 7:26) for managing their diverse subjects which was applied across the empire has not found many supporters. One reason is that the examples Frei depended on to validate his thesis do not bear him out, especially as the prime instance—the "Gadatas Letter" from Magnesia in western Turkey (Briant 2017: 128–66)—is very probably a forgery dating to the time of the Roman Empire (Watts 2001; Kuhrt 2001), leaving Ezra (whose authenticity is much disputed) as the only possibly witness for Frei's theory.

One aim of Frei's thesis was to explain the supposedly unprecedented tolerance of other religions displayed by the Persian regime (see the arguments against this marshalled in van der Spek 2014), which might be linked to their own belief system. The question of Persian religion in the Achaemenid period has been, and continues to be, a hotly debated topic. The only reliable guide must be the contemporary evidence, which consists of the terse Old Persian royal inscriptions, on the one hand, and the Elamite administrative texts from Persepolis, on the other. While the Old Persian inscriptions name only Auramazda, later adding Anahita and Mithra, the "other gods" or "all the gods" are regularly, albeit anonymously, referred to, showing that a multiplicity of gods was worshipped. The Persepolis administrative texts make it clear that the government in Fars issued provisions for a whole range of deities, both Iranian and Elamite in origin, which were used in regular daily and monthly rites (many Elamite in origin), as well as offerings made at the tombs of royalty and for public festive occasions (Henkelman 2003; 2008; 2011). At present, judging from the quantities supplied, it looks very much as though the most important deity at the time was the old Elamite god Humban, which would suggest that the prominence of the Iranian Auramazda (who received lower quantities) in the inscriptions reflects the fact that he was the god of the king. What is important to note here is that it was *only* gods local to the Fars region who were in receipt of such official provisions: the cults of the many foreign peoples living and working in Fars were ignored by the regime—that is, these people were free to perform their own cults, but received no state funding to support them. It is this exclusive combination of old Elamite cults and those of Iranian origin which formed the religion of the Persians at this time.

3.2.3 Central Control

Variation in patterns of rule does not indicate imperial weakness (see Henkelman 2017). The varieties of political relationship and domination should rather be seen as a positive element, which made central government more elastic and sensitive in its response to local needs and conditions, while maintaining strong overall control for its own benefit (Briant

2017: 43–73). Notably, the empire endured for over two hundred years, experiencing within that time only one serious loss, Egypt, which had seceded by 400/399. It was regained in 343, however, so even its loss proved not to be permanent. Moreover, from Darius I on, the grip of the Achaemenid family on the throne was never broken: despite repeated violent struggles for the succession, its hold of the kingship was never effectively challenged. Aside from the secession of Egypt, and chronic problems in frontier-regions, such as the Aegean sea-board, all serious revolts from ca. 480 onwards, with the exception of Egypt, took place within the Persian power structure itself and centered on struggles at court for the throne. This is to say that these struggles did not threaten the coherence of the empire but turned, instead, on who should rule it.

Despite local variations in the form of Persian rule, control of the various provinces by the satraps was extremely effective. The rule of exclusively appointing Persians/Iranians to these high positions seems generally to have been the norm, reinforced by Iranians always holding the highest military commands and the most important posts in the provinces. At the same time, members of the central authority developed close links with local elites in various areas of the empire, which could lead to the recruitment of members from such groups to powerful governmental positions—a practice that was particularly noticeable in the empire's later phases (Hornblower 1982; Stolper 1987). There are also indications of intermarriage: Persian nobles married women from the families of local dynasts (see Herodotus *Hist.* 5.21; Xenophon *Hellenica* 4.1.607; Mathiesen et al. 1995), and local dignitaries or soldiers, who had particularly distinguished themselves, are attested receiving a wife from a high-ranking Persian family (Herodotus *Hist.* 6.41). Particularly interesting is the chance information that the secondary wives of the kings themselves could be non-Persian, and in certain circumstances their sons might succeed to the throne, as in the case of Darius II (Ctesias *FGrH* 688 F15). Thus, while power was carefully restricted to an exclusive group made up of Persian aristocrats, this group could, and did, recruit selected members of the subject populations, so that the governing elite established a system of kinship ties and local alliances that reached right into the various subject populations and helped to root its power at local level to create an identity of interest. Persian dignitaries also developed links with local cults (Kuhrt 2007: 865–69; Briant 2017: 77–98).

Lower down the social scale, local peoples, soldiers, and deportees were allocated land parcels that carried with them the obligation to perform specified military duties when required. The parcels could be identified according to the kind of service demanded (Stolper 1985; 1994): "bow-land" for archers, "horse-land" for cavalry, and "chariot-land" presumably relating to chariot-teams and equipment. Clearly, the aim of assigning such "fief-holdings" was intended to fulfill imperial army requirements and occupy the imperial lands. Just as clearly, the surviving sources reveal that, after the empire's formative phase, general conscriptions were relatively infrequent and routine needs were often fulfilled by mercenaries or garrisons, so that at times the obligations associated with land holding were discharged in the form of a silver tax. Did that weaken the strength of the Persian armies? Enough evidence survives to show that the names of the original grantees and the expected military service associated with the grant were kept on satrapal army registers (Stolper 1977). Since the grants could not be sold, when a demand came to supply, say, a cavalry-soldier, and the descendant of the grantee was not in a position to carry this out, he was obliged to supply and equip a substitute to perform the service on his behalf (Ebeling 1952; Stolper 1985). There is thus no reason to suppose that the empire was over-dependent on hired mercenaries and incapable of raising an army throughout its existence when necessary—a fact shown clearly during Alexander's invasion (Briant 2002: 783–800). What is less clear, and still debated, is how the state labor requirements were met. It is likely, and the evidence is growing, that conscription for this was organized on the same (or, at least, similar) basis as army service and groups of such conscripted soldiers were sent to where particular construction projects needed the extra manpower (Briant 2002: 429–39).

The empire's far-flung territories were connected by a complex road system. Herodotus (*Hist.* 5.52–54) describes part of it between Sardis and Susa, but the Elamite documents show that it was much more extensive, linking all the main centers of the empire and guarded by a series of posting stations, which held supplies of fresh horses, fodder, and food for travellers. Entitlement to draw on these supplies was obtained by written authorization issued to individuals by the king, members of the court, and satraps (Hallock 1969: 365–440 Q texts; Graf 1994; Briant 2002: 357–77; Kuhrt 2007: 730–62). They were extensively used, not simply by the king, royal retinue, and army-contingents, but also for the speedy communication between king and satrapal authorities—the famous Persian express service, attested in the Persepolis texts and lyrically evoked by both Herodotus (*Hist.* 8.98) and Xenophon (*Cyropaedia* 8.617–18)—and to facilitate the journeys of personal servants of Persian nobles engaged in looking after their landed estates. The clearest illustration is a document issued by the satrap of Egypt, then perhaps in Babylon or Susa, to permit the manager of his Egyptian estates to travel, together with three other servants, to Egypt and draw supplies at posting stations along the way (Porten and Yardeni 1986: 114–16 no. A6.9). The Aramaic documents from Bactria, dating to the very end of the empire's existence, testify to the continued functioning of this system through into Alexander's time. He would have depended on it heavily as he progressed along the main imperial routes.

Persian-held estates were located throughout the empire, including Central Asia (Briant 1985). While some of the highest-ranking owners held such properties simultaneously in several different regions and were thus, perforce, absentee landholders, others were firmly and permanently settled on their estates with their families. The estates included a fortified dwelling, and it is clear from several accounts that they were guarded by soldiers, and included holders of military fiefs who could be used to fend off attacks or, conversely, levied by the owner in response to larger military threats. The estates within the provinces thus served to spread the Persian presence and military control throughout the empire (Xenophon *Anabasis* 7.8; Stolper 1985; 1994a).

The king himself (and members of the royal family) also possessed such domains from Lydia to Samarkand, carefully laid out and cultivated; these are the royal *paradeisoi* ("paradises") including formal gardens, parks, game reserves, orchards, livestock, and arable fields. Keeping and extending land under production was a prime royal concern in order to ensure and safeguard an adequate agricultural base and the concomitant creation of state-wealth. Irrigation projects, both the extension of existing ones and the installation of new ones, were particularly fostered by the Persian rulers: in Babylonia the intricate canal system was managed by crown agents; the local Bactrian water systems were maintained; a *qanat* system was fostered in northern Iran, with this typically Iranian form of water distribution introduced in one of the Egyptian oases (Briant 2001; Wuttman 2001). The most striking landscape transformation is attested in Fars where it has been established archaeologically that in the four to five hundred years preceding the emergence of the Achaemenid state the area was sparsely settled, with virtually no large urban centers and a prevailing pastoral mode of land exploitation, but, by the end of the empire, the region was seen as a veritable Garden of Eden: densely settled, agriculturally rich, and well watered (see, e.g., Diodorus 19.21.2–4). The hard reality of this change has been established, not only by excavation of the palatial centers of Pasargadae and Persepolis, but also by surveys in the region, which chart the sudden and massive increase of settlements in the Achaemenid period including cities, large and smaller towns, and villages (Sumner 1986).

3.3 The King and Royal Ideology

At the apex of the empire stood the king, who regularly proclaimed himself as king of kings and ruler on this earth, set up as such by the great god Auramazda as part of his bountiful creation. The king also stressed that he was an Iranian and a Persian, a member of the Achaemenid family, ideally directly descended from his predecessor.

3.3.1 Succession and Coronation

The king usually chose his successor from among his sons and seems generally to have been expected to choose the eldest. But this was not an unalterable rule; he could, and did, if political considerations so dictated, select a younger son to the position of crown-prince (Kent 1953; Schmitt 2000: 81–85—XPf). Failing "legitimate" offspring (by which presumably the sons of primary wives are meant), the sons of secondary wives called "bastards" in the classical sources had the next best claim to succeed; this, too, happened on occasion (Ctesias FGrH 688 F15). Conversely, husbands of royal daughters—that is, royal sons-in-law—seem never to have been able to claim the throne, although their offspring could become eligible failing male royal children. The matrimonial policies of the Achaemenids were thus carefully guarded as the marriage of royal daughters to members of the aristocracy could lead to another family laying claim to the throne. This potential threat to the Achaemenid monopoly of power led at times to the practice of endogamy, in order to safeguard dynastic integrity (Sancisi-Weerdenburg 1983a).

On the king's death, it fell to the legitimate successor to convey the body in an elaborately decorated hearse to Persepolis for burial in the rock-cut tombs at, and near, Persepolis, which, from Darius I on, never varied in their pattern and decoration. This great ceremonial progress provided a major public spectacle, in which the successor was displayed to his future subjects. It seems likely that the "royal fires" associated with the "living king" were extinguished on the ruler's demise (Briant 1991; 2002: 916); certainly a period of public mourning was enjoined on all. The Persepolis texts make it clear that a centrally funded cult was maintained around the king's tombs, as well as those of other members of the royal family (Henkelman 2003).

The coronation of the king took place in Pasargadae, the royal center laid out by Cyrus the Great. Here the prospective king went through an initiation ritual: he was dressed in the garments of Cyrus before his rise to the kingship, ate bitter herbs, and drank sour milk (Plutarch *Artaxerxes* 3). Although the ritual is not fully understood, it clearly evoked the origins of the dynasty and connected the new king directly with the founder of the empire. Only after this was the king adorned with the royal insignia and revealed to the people in his crowned, royal glory (Sancisi-Weerdenburg 1983b).

3.3.2 The Dynamics of Absolute Power

Emphasis is placed in several inscriptions and stories on the king's military valour and physical prowess. He underwent a special education, shared by other aristocratic sons: young boys were taken from their parents at age five and subjected to tough training for twenty years in military and survival skills, as well as being instructed in Persian myths and legends by the magi (Strabo 15.3.18). Learning "to tell the truth" was another aspect of this training, though the precise meaning of this phrase is uncertain (Sancisi-Weerdenburg 1993). A likely interpretation is that it related to the concept of loyalty to the king, who himself was empowered to uphold the god-given order since he was conceived as holding the throne as a grant from Auramazda. This "truth" was expressed through total obedience, actively promoting the king's personal wellbeing and guarding him from physical and political dangers. Individuals who had particularly distinguished themselves in this respect could be raised in rank by royal favor, which was marked by royal "gifts" of special dress, elaborate ornaments, a horse "that had been ridden by the king" (cf. Esth. 6:8–11), sometimes the revenues of an estate, the right of salutation with a royal kiss, and/or even marriage to a royal daughter (Sancisi-Weerdenburg 1989; Briant 2002: 302–31; Brosius 1996). This system of royal rewards resulted in the emergence of a royally created aristocracy, superimposed on the ranks of the older aristocratic families, effectively limiting their privileges and forcing them to compete with the newer nobility to maintain their position (Briant 2002: 331–38). All thus became the king's "servants" (Old Persian *bandaka*).

All this demonstrates the absolute power of the king, who was not subject to legal restrictions, but who was himself the upholder and embodiment of what was right and just, encapsulated in the Persian concept of *arta*, commonly translated "truth" (see Kellens 1995). In this role he represented a dignified and vigorous moral force, rewarding the "good" and opposing all that might threaten this divine order and unleash the forces of moral and political chaos (the "lie" = Old Persian *drauga*; see, e.g., Kent 1953; Schmitt 1991: 50–51—DB I 30–35). This royal message was expressed visually by the widely diffused image on the central authority's seals, which showed a kingly hero masterfully restraining a rampant wild animal or monster (Garrison and Root 2002), and verbally in the statement of royal virtues found in two exemplars of a royal inscription composed in the name of two Persian kings, Darius I and Xerxes (see Schmitt 2000: 33–44—DNb, 88–95—XPl), both of which ended with an exhortation to communicate it to others.

The central motif here is the king's qualities as a just ruler: Auramazda has equipped the ruler with the insight and ability to distinguish right from wrong, which enables him to be the guarantor of justice and maintainer of the social order. He can do this because he does not react unthinkingly and is able to control his temper; as a result the king metes out reward and punishment fairly, and only after consideration of each case. He judges services rendered according to individual potential, and is ever ready to reward loyalty. Following on this ethical image come the physical qualities which give him the sheer bodily strength to campaign, conquer, and maintain control. In these, too, he excels, so that the two aspects confirm the fact that he is fitted to exercise kingship as already affirmed by his god Auramazda, to whom he is closely linked, because (as this and other inscriptions show) he is part of Auramazda's bountiful creation and plan for human happiness. It is, therefore, the duty of all subjects to support and obey the king and spread abroad his excellent qualities.

That this inscription reflects widely known and high ideals of Persian kingship is shown, first, by the fact that we have the text written in the names of two different kings—that is, it is not a personal statement, but a generic one; second, by the fact that it was inscribed on different types of monuments;[2] third, by the fact that part of the text was written in Aramaic on a late fifth-century papyrus found in the tiny Jewish garrison at Elephantine. Echoes of it are also found in the Greek writer Xenophon (e.g., *Anabasis* 1.9). In sum, this inscription powerfully conveys an ideology of legitimate power effectively diffused through the empire.

Persian Kings

Teispes (of Anshan) ca. 650–620
Cyrus I (son) ca. 620–590
Cambyses I (son) ca. 590–559
Cyrus II "the Great" (son) 559–530
Cambyses II (son) 530–522
Bardiya (brother) 522
Darius I (son of Hystaspes, grandson of Arsames, descendant of Achaemenes) 522–486
Xerxes I (son) 486–465
Artaxerxes I (son) 465–424/3
Xerxes II and Sogdianus (sons) 424/3
Darius II (brother) 423–405
Artaxerxes II (son) 405–359
Artaxerxes III (son) 359–338
Artaxerxes (Arses) IV (son) 338–336
Darius III (second cousin) 336–330

NOTES

1. For the fragmentary administrative text in Old Persian found among the Persepolis Fortification tablets, see *ARTA* 2007 no. 001 (www.achemenet.com/ressources-en-ligne).
2. DNb is one of two texts inscribed on the tomb of Darius I; XPl was found out of context, but was obviously intended to serve a non-funerary function.

Bibliography

Álvarez-Mon, Javier and M. B. Garrison, eds. 2011. *Elam and Persia*. Winona Lake, IN: Eisenbrauns.

Avigad, Nahman. 1976. *Bullae and Seals from a Post-Exilic Judaean Archive*. Qedem 4. Jerusalem: Hebrew University of Jerusalem.

Azzoni, Annalisa. 2008. "The Bowman MS and the Aramaic tablets." In P. Briant, W. Henkelman, and M. W. Stolper, eds., *L'archive des Fortifications de Persépolis: État des questions et perspectives de recherches*. Persika 12. Paris: de Boccard, 253–74.

Betlyon, John W. 1980. *The Coinage and Mints of Phoenicia: The Pre-Alexandrine Period*. HSM 26. Chico, CA: Scholars Press.

Boucharlat, Rémy. 1990. "Suse et la Susiane à l'époque achéménide: données archéologiques." In H. Sancisi-Weerdenburg and A. Kuhrt, eds., *Achaemenid History* IV: *Centre and Periphery*. eideLn: Netherlands Institute for the Near East, 149–75.

Briant, Pierre. 1982. *État et pasteurs au Moyen-Orient ancient*. Collection Production Pastorale et Société. Cambridge: Cambridge University Press.

Briant, Pierre. 1984. *L'Asie Centrale et les royaumes proche-orientaux du premier millénaire (c.VIIIe–IVe siècles avant notre ère)*. Recherches sur les Civilisations 42. Paris: Éditions Recherches sur les Civilisations.

Briant, Pierre. 1985. "Dons de terres et de villes: l'Asie Mineure dans le contexte achéménide." *RÉA* 87: 53–71.

Briant, Pierre. 1987. "Pouvoir central et polycentrisme culturel dans l'empire achéménide." In H. Sancisi-Weerdenburg, ed., *Achaemenid History* I: *Sources, Structures, Synthesis*. Leiden: Netherlands Institute for the Near East, 1–31.

Briant, Pierre. 1988. "Le nomadisme du grand roi." *IrAnt* 23: 253–73.

Briant, Pierre. 1991. "Le roi est mort: vive le roi! Remarques sur les rites et rituels de succession chez les Achéménides." In J. Kellens, ed., *La religion iranienne à l'époque achéménide: Actes du Colloque de Liège, 11 décembre 1987*. IrAntSup 5. Gent: Iranica Antiqua, 1–11.

Briant, Pierre. 2002. *From Cyrus to Alexander: History of the Persian Empire*. Winona Lake, IN: Eisenbrauns. (French original 1996.)

Briant, Pierre. 2017. *Kings, Countries, Peoples: Selected Studies on the Achaemenid Empire*. Ories et Occidens 26. Stuttgart: Franz Steiner.

Briant, Pierre, ed. 2001. *Irrigation et drainage dans l'antiquité: qanats et canalisations souterraines en Iran, en Égypte et en Grèce*. Persika 2. Paris: Thotm Editions.

Briant, Pierre and Rémy Boucharlat, eds. 2005. *L'Archéologie de l'Empire Achéménide: nouvelles recherches*. Persika 6. Paris: de Boccard.

Briant, Pierre, W. Henkelman, and M. W. Stolper, eds. 2008. *L'archive des Fortifications de Persépolis: État des questions et perspectives de recherches*. Persika 12. Paris: de Boccard.

Brosius, M. 1996. *Women in Ancient Persia (559–531 BC)*. Oxford Classical Monographs. Oxford: Oxford University Press.

Brown, S. C. 1986. "Media and Secondary State Formation in the Neo-Assyrian Zagros: An Anthropological Approach to an Assyriological Problem." *JCS* 38: 107–19.

Callieri, Pierfrancesco. 2007. *L'archéologie du Fars à l'époque hellénistique*. Persika 11. Paris: de Boccard.

Cameron, George G. 1948. *Persepolis Treasury Tablets*. Oriental Institute Publications 65. Chicago: University of Chicago Press.

Carter, Elizabeth and M. W. Stolper. 1984. *Elam: Surveys of Political History and Archaeology*. Berkeley, CA: University of California Press.

Chauveau, M. 2008. "Les archives démotiques d'époque perse: à propos des archives démotiques d'Ayn Manawir." In P. Briant, W. Henkelman, and M. W. Stolper, eds., *L'archive des Fortifications de Persépolis: État des questions et perspectives de recherches*. Paris: de Boccard, 513–24.

Dandamaev, M. A. 1979. "Data of the Babylonian Documents from the 6th to the 5th Centuries B.C. on the Sakas." In János Harmatta, ed., *Prolegomena to the Sources on the History of Pre-Islamic Central Asia*. Budapest: Akadémiai Kiadó, 95–109.

Dušek, Jan. 2007. *Les manuscripts araméens du Wadi Daliyeh et la Samarie vers 450–332 av. J.C.* Leiden: Brill.

Dusinberre, Elsbeth. 2003. *Aspects of Empire in Achaemenid Sardis*. Cambridge: Cambridge University Press.

Ebeling, Erich. 1952. "Die Rüstung eines babylonischen Panzerreiters nach einem Vertrag aus der Zeit Dareios II." *ZA* 50: 203–14.

Elayi, Josette. 1989. *Sidon: cite autonome de l'empire perse*. Paris: Gabalda.

Eph'al, Israel and Jacob Naveh. 1996. *Aramaic Ostraca of the Fourth Century BC from Idumaea*. Jerusalem: Magness.

Francfort, H.-P. 1988. "Central Asia and Eastern Iran." In J. Boardman, N. G. L. Hammond, D. M. Lewis, and M. Ostwald, eds., *Cambridge Ancient History*, Vol. IV: *Persia, Greece and the Western Mediterranean c. 525 to 479*. 2nd ed. Cambridge: Cambridge University Press, 165–93.

Frei, Peter and Klaus Koch. 1984. *Reichsidee und Reichsorganisation im Perserreich*. OBO 55. Freiburg: Universitätsverlag Frieburg Schweiz. (2nd ed. = 1996.)

Garrison, Mark B. and Margaret Cool Root. 2001. *Seals on the Persepolis Fortification Tablets* I: *Images of Heroic Encounter*. 2 vols. Chicago: University of Chicago Press.

Gasche, Hermann. 2010. "Les palais perses achéménides de Babylone." In Jean Perrot, ed., *Le Palais de Darius à Suse: une residence royale sur la route de Persépolis à Babylone*. Paris: Presse de l'Université Parsi-Sorbonne, 446–43.

Gondet, Sébastien, Benech, C., and R. Boucharlat. 2012. "Organisation et aménagement de l'espace à Pasargades: reconnaissances archéologiques de surfaces, 2003–2008." *ARTA* 2012.003 (www.achemenet.com/ressources-en-ligne).

Graf, David. 1994. "The Persian Royal Road System." In H. Sancisi-Weerdenburg, A. Kuhrt, and Margaret Cool Root, eds., *Achaemenid History* VIII: *Continuity and Change*. Leiden: Netherlands Institute for the Near East, 167–89.

Grelot, Pierre. 1972. *Documents araméens d'Égypte*. Littératures Anciennes du Proche-Orient. Paris: Les Éditions du Cerf.

Haerinck, Ernest. 1997. "Babylonia under Achaemenid Rule." In J. Curtis, ed., *Mesopotamia and Iran in the Persian Period*. London: British Museum Press, 26–34.

Hallock, Richard T. 1969. *Persepolis Fortification Tablets*. Oriental Institute Publications 92. Chicago: University of Chicago Press.

Hallock, Richard T. 1978. "Selected Fortification Texts." *CDAFI* 8: 109–36.

Harper, Prudence, J. Aruz, and F. Tallon, eds. 1992. *The Royal City of Susa: Ancient Near Eastern Treasures in the Louvre*. New York: Metropolitan Museum of Art. (Rev. French ed., 1994, Paris: Musée de Louvre.)

Henkelman, Wouter F. M. 2003. "An Elamite Memorial: The *sumar* of Cambyses and Hystaspes." In W. Henkelman and A. Kuhrt, eds., *A Persian Perspective: Essays in Memory of Heleen Sancisi-Weerdenburg*. Achaemenid History XIII. Leiden: Netherlands Institute for the Near East, 101–72.

Henkelman, Wouter F. M. 2005. "Animal Sacrifice and 'External' Exchange in the Persepolis Fortification Tablets." In H. Baker and M. Jursa, eds., *Approaching the Babylonian Economy*. AOAT 330. Münster: Ugarit-Verlag, 137–65.

Henkelman, Wouter F. M. 2008. *The Other Gods Who Are: Studies in Elamite-Iranian Acculturaltion Based on the Persepolis Fortification Texts*. Achaemenid History XIV. Leiden: Netherlands Institute for the Near East.

Henkelman, Wouter F. M. 2011. "Parnakka's Feast: šip in Pārsa and Elam." In J. Alvarez-Mon and M. B. Garrison, eds., *Elam and Persia*. Winona Lake, IN: Eisenbrauns, 89–166.

Henkelman, Wouter F. M. 2017. "Imperial Signature and Imperial Paradigm: Achaemenid Administrative Structure and System across and beyond the Iranian Plateau." In B. Jacobs,

W. F. M. Henkelman, and M. W. Stolper, eds., *The Administration of the Achaemenid Empire: Tracing the Imperial Signature*. Wiesbaden: Harrassowitz, 245–56.

Herr, L. G. 1992. "Two Stamped Jar Impressions from the Persian Province of Ammon from Tell el-'Umeiri." *Annals of the Department of Antiquities, Jordan* 36: 163–66.

Hornblower, Simon. 1982. *Mausolus*. Oxford: Oxford University Press.

Kellens, J. 1995. "L'âme entre le cadavre et le paradis." *JA* 283: 19–56.

Kent, Roland G. 1953. *Old Persian: Grammar, Texts, Lexicon*. 2nd ed. New Haven: American Oriental Society.

Klinkott, Hilmar. 2005. *Der Satrap: Ein achaimenidischer Amtsträger und seine Handlunsspielräume*. Oikumene, Studien zur Weltgeschichte 1. Frankfurt-am-Main: Verlag Antike.

Kuhrt, Amélie. 1988. "Babylonia." in J. Boardman, N. G. L. Hammond, D. M. Lewis, and M. Ostwald, eds., *The Cambridge Ancient History IV: Persia, Greece and the Western Mediterranean c.525 to 479 BC*. 2nd ed. Cambridge: Cambridge University Press, 112–38.

Kuhrt, Amélie. 2001. "The Persian Kings and Their Subjects: A Unique Relationship?" *OLZ* 96.2: 165–73.

Kuhrt, Amélie. 2007. *The Persian Empire: A Corpus of Sources from the Achaemenid Period*. 2 vols. London: Routledge.

Kuhrt, Amélie. 2008. "The Problem of Achaemenid 'Religious Policy.'" In B. Groneberg and H. Spieckermann, eds., *Die Welt der Götterbilder*, 117–42. Berlin: de Gruyter.

Kuhrt, Amélie. 2014. "Reassessing the Reign of Xerxes in the Light of New Evidence." In M. Kozuh, W. F. M. Henkelman, C. Jones, and C. Woods, eds., *Extraction and Control: Studies in Honor of Matthew W. Stolper*. Chicago: University of Chicago Press, 163–70.

Lanfranchi, Giovanni, Michael Roaf, and Robert Rollinger, eds. 2003. *Continuity of Empires(?): Assyria, Media, Persia*. History of the Ancient Near East Monographs 5. Padua: Editrice e Liberia.

Lecoq, Pierre. 1997. *Les inscriptions de la Perse achéménide*. Paris: Gallimard.

Lemaire, André. 1996. *Nouvelles inscriptions araméennes d'Idumée au Musée d'Israël*. Supplément 3 á Transeuphratène. Paris: Gabalda.

Lemaire, André. 2006. "La Transeuphratène en transition (c. 350–300)." In Pierre Briant and F. Joannès, eds., *La transition entre l'empire achéménide et les royaumes hellénistiques (vers 350-300 avant J.-C.)*. Persika 9. Paris: de Boccard, 405–41.

Lemaire, André. 2015. *Levantine Epigraphy and History in the Achaemenid Period (539-322 BCE)*. Oxford: Oxford University Press.

Lenfant, Dominique. 2004. *Ctésias de Cnide: La Perse; L'Inde; autres fragments*. Paris: Les Belles Lettres.

Martin, Carey. 1996. "Letters and Report." In B. Porten, *The Elephantine Papyri in English: Three Millennia of Cross-cultural Continuity and Change*. Documenta et Monumenta Orientalis Antiqui 22. Atlanta: SBL, 276–384.

Mathiesen, Ian, E. Bettles, S. Davies, and H. S. Smith. 1995. "A Stela of the Persian Period." *JEA* 81: 23–41.

Metzger, Henri, et al. 1979. *Fouilles de Xanthos VI: La stèle trilingue du Létôon*. Paris: Libraire C. Klincksieck.

Miroschedji, Pierre de. 1985. "La fin du royaume d'Anshan et de Suse et la naissance de l'empire perse." *ZA* 75: 265–306.

Momigliano, A. D. 1977. *Essays in Ancient and Modern Historiography*. Oxford: Oxford University Press.

Naveh, Joseph and Shaul Shaked. 2012. *Aramaic Documents from Ancient Bactria (Fourth Century BCE) from the Khalili Collection*. London: The Khalili Family Trust.

Perrot, Jean et al. 1974. *Recherches dans le secteur este du tépé de l'Apadana CDAFI* 4. Paris: Association Paléorient.

Porten, Bezalel. 1968. *Archives from Elephantine: The Life of an Ancient Jewish Military Colony*. Berkeley, CA: University of California Press.

Porten, Bezalel and Ada Yardeni. 1986–99. *Textbook of Aramaic Documents from Ancient Egypt.* 4 vols. Jerusalem: University of California Press.

Porten, Bezalel and Ada Yardeni. 2014. *Textbook of Aramaic Ostraca from Idumaea,* Vol. 1: *Dossiers 1–10: 401 Commodity Chits.* Winona Lake, IN: Eisenbrauns.

Posener, Georges. 1936. *La première domination perse en Égypte.* Bibliothèque d'Études 11. Cairo: Institut Français d'Archéologie Orientale.

Potts, Daniel. 1999. *The Archaeology of Elam: Formation and Transformation of an Ancient Iranian State.* Cambridge World Archaeology. Cambridge: Cambridge University Press.

Root, Margaret Cool. 1979. *The King and Kingship in Achaemenid Art: Essays on the Creation of an Iconography of Empire.* Acta Iranica 19. Leiden: Brill.

Sancisi-Weerdenburg, Heleen. 1983a. "Exit Atossa: Images of Women in Greek Historiography on Persia." In A. Cameron and A. Kuhrt, eds., *Images of Women in Antiquity.* London: Croom Helm, 20–33. (Rev. ed., London: Routledge, 1993.)

Sancisi-Weerdenburg, Heleen. 1983b. "The Zendan and the Kabah." In H. Koch and D. N. Mackenzie, eds., *Kunst, Kultur und Geschichte der Achämenidenzeit und ihr Fortleben.* Berlin: Dietrich Reimer, 145–51.

Sancisi-Weerdenburg, Heleen. 1988. "Was There Ever a Median Empire?" In A. Kuhrt and H. Sancisi-Weerdenburg, eds., *Achaemenid History* III: *Method and Theory.* Leiden: Netherlands Institute for the Near East, 197–212.

Sancisi-Weerdenburg, Heleen. 1989. "Gifts in the Persian Empire." In Pierre Briant and C. Herrenschmidt, eds., *Le tribut dans l'empire achéménide.* Actes de la Table Ronde de Paris, 12–13 décembre 1986. Travaux de l'Institut d'Études Iraniennes de l'Université de la Sorbonne Nouvelle 13. Louvain: Peeters, 129–45.

Sancisi-Weerdenburg, Heleen. 1993. "Political Concepts in Old Persian Inscriptions." In K. Raaflaub, ed., *Anfänge politischen Denkes in der Antike: Die nahöstlichen Kulturen und die Griechen.* Schriften des Historischen Kollegs Kolloquien 24. Oldenburg: de Gruyter, 145–63.

Schmidt, Erich F. 1953–70. *Persepolis* I–III. Oriental Institute Publications 68–70. Chicago: University of Chicago Press.

Schmitt, Rüdiger. 1991. *The Bisitun Inscription of Darius the Great: Old Persian Text.* Corpus Inscriptionum Iranicarum I/1, 1. London: School of Oriental and African Studies.

Schmitt, Rüdiger. 2000. *The Old Persian Inscriptions of Naqsh-i Rustam and Persepolis.* Corpus Inscriptionum Iranicarum I/1, 2. London: School of Oriental and African Studies.

Segal, Judah B. 1983. *Aramaic Texts from North Saqqâra with Some Fragments in Phoenician.* EES Excavations at North Saqqara, Documentary Series 4. London: Egypt Exploration Society.

Shaked, Shaul. 2004. *Le satrape de Bactriane et son gouverneur: documents araméens du IV s.av.notre ère provenant de Bactriane.* Persika 4. Paris: de Boccard.

Smith, Harry S. and Carey Martin. 2009. "Demotic Papyri from North Saqqara: Certainly or Possibly of Achaemenid Date." In Pierre Briant and M. Chauveau, eds., *Organisation des pouvoirs et contacts culturels dans les pays de l'empire achéménide.* Persika 14. Paris: de Boccard, 23–78.

Stern, Ephraim. 1982. *The Material Culture of the Land of the Bible in the Persian Period, 538–332 BC.* Warminster: Aris and Philipps.

Stökl, Jonathan and C. Waerzeggers, eds. 2015. *Exile and Return: The Babylonian Context.* BZAW 478. Berlin: de Gruyter.

Stolper, Matthew W. 1977. "Three Iranian Loanwords in Late Babylonian Texts." In L. D. Levine and T. C. Young, eds., *Mountains and Lowlands.* Bibliotheca Mesopotamica 7. Malibu, CA: Undena, 251–66.

Stolper, Matthew W. 1985. *Entrepreneurs and Empire: The Murasu Archive, the Murasu Firm and Persian Rule in Babylonia.* Leiden: Netherlands Institute for the Near East.

Stolper, Matthew W. 1987. "Belšunu the Satrap." In F. Rochberg-Halton, ed., *Language, Literature and History: Philological and Historical Studies Presented to Erica Reiner.* New Haven: American Oriental Society, 389–402.

Stolper, Matthew W. 1989. "The Governor of Babylon and Across-the-River in 486 BC." *JNES* 48: 283–305.

Stolper, Matthew W. 1994a. "Militärkolonisten." In *RlA* 8/3–4: 205–207.

Stolper, Matthew W. 1994b. "Mesopotamia, 482–330 B.C." In David Lewis, John Boardman, Simon Hornblower, and Martin Ostwald, eds., *The Cambridge Ancient History* VI: *The Fourth Century* BC. 2nd ed. Cambridge: Cambridge University Press, 234–60.

Stronach, David. 1978. *Pasargadae*. Oxford: Oxford University Press.

Sumner, W. 1986. "Achaemenid Settlement in the Persepolis Plain." *AJA* 90: 3–31.

Tilia, Ann B. 1972–78. *Studies and Restorations at Persepolis and Other Sites in Fars*. Reports and Memoirs 16 and 18. Rome: Instituto Medio ed Estremo Oriente.

Vallat, F. 1989. "Le palais d'Artaxerxès II." *CDAFI* 10: 171–80.

Van der Spek, Robartus J. 2014. "Cyrus the Great, Exiles and Foreign Gods: A Comparison of Assyrian and Persian Policies on Subject Nations." In M. Kozuh, W. F. M. Henkelman, C. Jones, and C. Woods, eds., *Extraction and Control: Studies in Honor of Matthew W. Stolper*. SAOC 68. Chicago: University of Chicago Press, 233–64.

Waerzeggers, Caroline. 2003/4. "The Babylonian Revolts against Xerxes and the 'End of Archives.'" *AfO* 50: 150–78.

Wasmuth, Melanie. 2017. *Ägypto-persische Herrscher- und Herrschaftspräsentation in der Achämenidenzeit*. Oriens et Occidens 27. Stuttgart: Franz Steiner.

Waters, Matthew. 2014. *Ancient Persia: A Concise History of the Achaemenid Empire, 550–330 BCE*. Cambridge: Cambridge University Press.

Watts, James W., ed. 2001. *Persia and Torah: The Theory of Imperial Authorization of the Pentateuch*. Atlanta: SBL.

Wiesehöfer, Josef. 1993. *Das Antike Persien: von 550 v.Chr.bis 650 n.Chr*. Zurich: Artemis. (English ed: *Ancient Persia*, London: Tauris, 1996; 2nd ed. 2001.)

Wuttman, M. 2001. "Les qanâts de 'Ayn-Manâwir (oasis de Kharga, Égypte)." In Pierre Briant, ed., *Irrigation et drainage dans l'antiquité: qanats et canalisations souterraines en Iran, en Égytpe et en Grèce*. Persika 2. Paris: Thotm Edtions, 109–36.

CHAPTER 4

TEXT-CRITICAL ISSUES WITH SAMUEL AND KINGS

JULIO TREBOLLE BARRERA
AND EUGENE ULRICH

It is important for any kind of interpretive analysis of a biblical book to know the character of the various textual witnesses for that book. A major lesson that the Qumran manuscripts have taught us is that the Masoretic Text (MT) is not "*the* text of Samuel–Kings," it is just *one* text among others. The MT is a very important text, since it is the only complete text in Hebrew, but the fragmentary Qumran manuscripts and the ancient translations, especially the Septuagint (LXX) and the Old Latin (OL), but the other versions as well, are also highly important and are to be evaluated on an egalitarian basis. Each witness has "original" as well as secondary readings, readings that are to be preferred alongside those that are erroneous. Thus, all major witnesses must be analyzed for each reading on which any one wishes to base any analysis, argument, or conclusion. In the late twentieth century a tendency toward a minimalist view of the historicity of the biblical books surfaced. But whether one has a maximal or minimal view of the historicity of these compositions, or whether one seeks a traditional exegetical or a theological understanding, one must begin any interpretive analysis with a sound text reconstructed from the witnesses to the text as it has been transmitted (and received) in its various forms.

The text is developmental: it grew in different ways at different times by different authors/editors/scribes. Thus, there are different layers to the text, different sources (introducing therefore the possibility of inconsistent or contradictory views). Some parts of the text may be truly historical, others ideological or religiously motivated. If one wishes to use Samuel–Kings for historical purposes, one should seek the earliest ("original") reading. If one wishes to use the text for reception-history purposes, one should seek the later or more developed readings. Exegetes, commentators, and theologians would presumably wish to seek and appreciate both the "original" level as well as any and all subsequent levels of the text for full exposition. No one text will contain all of the earliest readings or all of the latest; full textual analysis is essential to discover early and secondary readings for every verse, every sentence, even every word.

As an example, consider a scholar presenting a conference paper on Jeremiah's message to the exiles. The audience might correctly have expected the paper to be at least somewhat historical: "This is what Jeremiah said to the exiles," presumably near the turn of the sixth century BCE. But let's say the basis used for the scholar's argument was solely the MT of Jeremiah. The specific passages used by the speaker were taken only from the MT, and most of these were from sections of the Hebrew text that are not present in the LXX of Jeremiah. According to many Jeremiah scholars, however, these sections were not originally part of the book of Jeremiah but are later additions that were not part of the message that the historical Jeremiah originally spoke to the early sixth-century exiles. In this way, one can see that the scholar's paper was flawed from the very start.

4.1 SAMUEL

4.1.1 Manuscript Evidence

With regard to the book of Samuel there is a wealth of textual evidence especially from the Qumran scrolls, the various Greek and Latin traditions, and the *Antiquities* of Josephus. Due to its size, 4QSam^a (the first Samuel scroll from Cave 4 at Qumran) teaches us much about the history of the text. Although "only just under fifteen percent of the text of Samuel is extant on the leather fragments," 4QSam^a is still "the most extensively preserved of the biblical manuscripts from Cave 4" (Cross et al. 2005: 3) and the fourth most extensively preserved of the entire corpus of scriptural scrolls.[1] Since it is so well preserved, it is a potentially rich candidate for providing a comparative view of the character of the MT, for confirming the fidelity of the Old Greek (OG) translation, and for helping distinguish the OG from the subsequent recensions of the Greek transmission process.

In addition to the manuscripts of Samuel and Kings, the *Antiquities* of Josephus can be studied as a text-critical indicator as well as a historical source for many readings. In the case of Samuel, Josephus used texts that antedated the destruction of the temple. He relates in his *Vita* (417–18) that Titus allowed him to take some "sacred books" from the temple. The fact that his narrative often agrees with 4QSam^a or the LXX indicates that Josephus's text of Samuel was probably among those taken from the temple.

It will be helpful to differentiate four different levels of variation in manuscripts: (1) variant literary editions, (2) isolated insertions, (3) individual textual variants, and (4) orthographic differences. These operate on different levels of textual history and transmission; the types of variation on each separate level do not affect the other levels, and so conclusions concerning one level may seem not to agree with conclusions concerning another level.

4.1.1.1 Possible Variant Literary Editions of the Book of Samuel

Although several scholars find variant literary editions in Samuel, the only passage that has gained wide acceptance in this regard is 1 Sam. 17–18, the story of David and Goliath. There are clearly different text families (4QSam^a-OG-OL-Josephus vs. MT-Targum-Peshitta), but all the witnesses attest a single literary edition for the book of Samuel.

4.1.1.2 Isolated Insertions

For scriptural manuscripts scribes usually attempted to copy as accurately as possible the text before them. On occasion, however, a "junior partner in the creative process" would insert into the traditional text a new idea or passage that he considered important. This could be a clarification, a "footnote" or additional detail, a parallel passage from another source, a customary saying or liturgical community response, or a pious or apocalyptic thought.

Sometimes the insertion is merely a learned identification, such as seen in 2 Sam. 6:2:[2]

(a) 2 Sam. 6:2 (DJD 17:123)
4QSam[a] Chr   בעלה היא קר[ית יערים אשר] ליהו֯ה
MT   מבעלי > יהודה

Here, a scribe has simply added a kind of "footnote," identifying the place Baale-judah (MT) as Kiriath-jearim (cf. Josh. 15:9; 1 Chr. 13:6).

First Sam. 2:22 presents an interesting example in which 4QSam[a] adds an insertion early in the verse and MT adds another at the end, while neither has the other's insertion:

(b) 1 Sam. 2:22[init] (DJD 17:39)
4QSam[a]   ²²ועלי זקן מאד בן תשעים שנה [ושמונה שנים] וישמע
MT LXX   ²²ועלי זקן מאד > וישמע

Into the MT/LXX's short statement that "Eli was very old and heard ...," 4QSam[a] inserts Eli's age as "ninety[-eight years]," borrowing information that all other texts report at 1 Sam. 4:15.

(c) 1 Sam. 2:22[fin] (DJD 17:39-47)
4QSam[a] OG   ²³ו[יאמר] > [לבני ישר]אל]
MT LXX[O]   לכל ישראל ואת אשר ישכבון את הנשים
הצבאות פתח אהל מועד ²³ויאמר

In this example, the MT, followed by the Hexapla (LXX[O]), inserts into the short text of 4QSam[a] and OG a different addition at the end of 2:22 concerning the sin of Eli's sons—namely, that "they used to lie with the women who served at the entrance to the tent of meeting."

(d) 2 Sam. 8:7 (DJD 17:132)
4QSam[a] LXX   [ירוש]ל[ים] גם] [אותם ל[קח אחר שושק מלך
מצרים בעל[ותו אל י]רושלים בימי רחבעם בן שלו[מה
MT > ירושלם:

This reading is an intentional addition, incorporating a later, related historical detail from the time of King Rehoboam (cf. 1 Kgs. 14:25-26 and 1 Chr. 18:8), that Shishak took away the golden shields when he came up to Jerusalem. It is the first of a pair of insertions and, though the scroll is not preserved for the second, it probably contained the other as well, since no extant manuscript has the first insertion while lacking the second. The OG, LXX[L], OL, and Josephus (Ant. 7.104–106) contain the insertions, whereas the MT lacks them.

Examples like these demonstrate that different scribes added different insertions into different manuscripts, including into MT.

4.1.1.3 *Individual Textual Variants*

In contrast to larger intentional insertions, all manuscripts contain small individual variants, such as errors, clarifications, revisions, and alternate views.

(a) 1 Sam. 1:23 (DJD 17:31)
   4QSam^a [יקם יהו]ה היוצא מפיך
   MT   יקם יהוה את דברו
   OG   στήσαι κύριος τὸ ἐξελθὸν ἐκ τοῦ στόματός σου

Elkanah's response to Hannah, "may the LORD confirm what has issued from your mouth," as in 4QSam^a and OG is probably the original text. The MT tradition has revised toward Deuteronomistic theology which emphasized the prophecy-fulfillment theme: "may the LORD confirm his word." Thus, if one is seeking the earliest form of the text, the 4QSam^a reading should be chosen; if one is seeking the more developed theological meaning, MT should be chosen.

(b) 1 Sam. 17:4 (DJD 17:78)
   4QSam^a [גבהו א]רבע [א]מות חרת
   MT LXX^{Acx} σ'   גבהו שש אמות וזרת
   OG   ὕψος αὐτοῦ τεσσάρων πήχεων καὶ σπιθαμῆς

4QSam^a and the OG list Goliath's height at four cubits and a span; some Greek manuscripts (LXX^{N++}) raise the four cubits to five, while the MT, followed by the Hexaplaric tradition (LXX^{Acx} σ'), raises the number to six. Since traditions tend to become more exaggerated as they develop, 4QSam^a probably retains the earlier text, and it is supported by Josephus (*Ant.* 6.171), who often agrees with a Greek text in the 4QSam^a-OG tradition.

(c) 1 Sam. 20:32 (DJD 17:230)
   (no Hebrew preserved)   [שאול למה]
   OG^B τῷ Σαουλ Ἵνα τί
   4QSam^b [שאול] אביו ויאמר למה
   LXX^L τῷ Σαουλ πατρὶ αὐτοῦ καὶ εἶπεν Ἵνα τί
   MT   שאול אביו ויאמר אליו למה
   LXX^O τῷ Σαουλ πατρὶ αὐτοῦ καὶ εἶπεν πρὸς αὐτὸν Ἵνα τί

This set of readings gives us a glimpse of the developmental nature of the text over time. The OG translation as in Vaticanus (OG^B) preserves the original, short but clear, reading, "(Jonathan answered) Saul: Why...?" though no Hebrew manuscript still shows this original reading. The 4QSam^b tradition shows the clarifying addition "(Jonathan answered) Saul *his father, and said*: Why...?," and the Lucianic Greek (LXX^L) follows 4QSam^b. The MT goes further, reading "(Jonathan answered) Saul his father, and said *to him*: Why...?," and the Hexaplaric Greek (LXX^O) follows MT.

4.1.1.4 *Orthographic Differences*

As the Hebrew language developed through the Second Temple period, vowel letters were increasingly added to the consonantal text to aid in pronunciation and interpretation. The orthography of the Samuel texts (and parallel texts in Chronicles) shows a mild progression from early, shorter forms to longer, fuller spellings. 4QSam^b is one of the earliest scrolls recovered and presents a consistently short spelling, and MT Samuel is generally similar. MT Chronicles occasionally shows a longer form than MT Samuel. 4QSam^a in turn often has longer forms, and 4QSam^c usually has yet longer forms.[3] There are, of course, some exceptions to these general tendencies, but some characteristic examples are as follows:

4QSamᵇ	אלהי	כל	כי	לא	דוד	אפד
MT-Sam	אלהי	כל	כי	לא	דוד	אפוד
MT-Chr	אלהי	כל	כי	לא	דויד	אפוד
4QSamᵃ	אלוהי	כול	כיא/כי	לוא/לא	דויד	אפוד
4QSamᶜ	אלוהי	כול	כיא	לוא	—	—

4.1.2 Assessment of Textual Evidence

There is more historical information in Kings than in Samuel, but the textual evidence must still be examined for the successful attainment or rejection of any historical information. It will be helpful to analyze two possible examples.

First, 2 Sam. 5:4–5 may or may not necessarily be an accurate historical datum, but it presents itself as such, similar to data encountered in Kings. The two verses appear in the MT, supported by the form of the LXX that the preserved Greek tradition transmits. The verses are not, however, in 4QSamᵃ, OL, Josephus (*Ant.* 7.54, 61, 65), or the parallel in 1 Chr. 11:3–4. The fact that the OL lacks the verses virtually confirms that the OG—like 4QSamᵃ, Josephus, and Chronicles—also lacked the verses (see Trebolle 1984). Second Samuel 5:1–3 narrates the anointing of David as king, and 5:6–10 narrates his capture of Jerusalem. The interspersed chronological notice is not integral to the context and seems rather to be an unnecessary chronological parenthesis or footnote. The point is that the earlier text did not contain that "historical" information, and that it was added at some (possibly much) later time in the late Second Temple period. If that is the case, how historically reliable would the information be? On the positive side, it is possible that, even though the information was inserted late into the text of Samuel, it may contain accurate information known from elsewhere, such as 1 Kgs. 2:11.

Second, in the transition from 1 Sam. 10 to 11, the MT concludes chapter 10 with the unusual reaction of Saul to his maligners who brought him no gifts: "but he was like one who is deaf" (ויהי כמחריש). It then moves immediately to Nahash the Ammonite's campaign against Jabesh-gilead. But the MT does not identify Nahash with his title—the normal designation is "X, king of Y"—nor does it say why Nahash would be attacking Jabesh-gilead. 4QSamᵃ, however, is quite different. It, jointly with the MT, concludes chapter 10 with the maligners who brought Saul no gifts. But it then adds a three-and-a-half line paragraph which begins with the expected identification, "Nahash, king of the Ammonites," and describes his cruel maiming of the Gadites and Reubenites in Transjordan, which provides the motive for the escape of seven thousand men to Jabesh-gilead. It then continues with a routine chronological introduction, "About a month later" (ויהי כמו חדש), which is probably the correct form of MT's unusual (and thus likely corrupt) ויהי כמחריש. The narrative smoothly follows with Nahash's campaign against Jabesh-gilead. 4QSamᵃ is the only biblical manuscript which contains this longer narrative. The preserved LXX tradition agrees with the MT in lacking the paragraph, though it agrees with the scroll against the MT since it contains "About a month later" (καὶ ἐγενήθη ὡς μετὰ μῆνα = ויהי כמו חדש). Highly important evidence is provided by Josephus (*Ant.* 6.67–69), who, significantly, also recounts the longer 4QSamᵃ narrative with the same details in the same order.

Scholars judge the two versions differently. Some consider the scroll's (and Josephus's) longer text as original, due to the routine literary pattern and the logical explanation of why

Nahash attacked Jabesh-gilead. Others consider the short text (as in the MT) as original with the paragraph in 4QSam^a as a later "midrashic" addition precisely to explain the abrupt narrative of Nahash's attack on Jabesh-gilead. If one were writing a military history of ancient Israel, it would be necessary to analyze the narrative in 4QSam^a–Josephus and decide whether or not to include Nahash's subjugation and mutilation of the Gadites and Reubenites as an historical event, or exclude it as a later literary insertion.

Analogously, if one wished to understand sacrificial practices in the late pre-monarchic era, one would have to consider the following two passages.

(a) 1 Sam. 1:24 (DJD 17:31–33)
4QSam^a [בפר בן]בקר משלש ולחם
MT LXX^{Acx} σ' בפרים שלשה
OG ἐν μόσχῳ τρετίζοντι καὶ ἄρτοις = בפר משלש ולחם*

Was one three-year-old bull offered, as in 4QSam^a and OG (for the addition of בן בקר see Lev. 16:3; 2 Chr. 13:9), or three bulls, as in MT? Was bread included, or not?

(b) 1 Sam. 1:25 (DJD 17:31–33)
4QSam^a [וי]שחט []
MT LXX^L וישחטו
OG καὶ ἔσφαξεν ὁ πατὴρ αὐτοῦ

Who offered the sacrifice? MT has the plural, implicitly indicating that both Hannah and Elkanah offered the sacrifice. 4QSam^a and the OG have the singular: the OG specifies "his father" Elkanah, while 4QSam^a does not preserve the following words which may or may not have included "his father." Stanley Walters proposed that the Greek "intends to exclude Anna from participation in the cult" (1988: 404). That proposal, however, seems stretched: 4QSam^a already has the Hebrew basis for the singular in the Greek. The words ὁ πατὴρ αὐτοῦ could be a scribal insertion (cf. the insertion in 1 Sam. 20:32 above). And though the birth of Samuel is the more important theme of the chapter, the larger narrative frame is Elkanah's yearly pilgrimage to offer sacrifice at Shiloh (1 Sam. 1:3; 2:11). Finally, note that in 1 Sam. 2:11 Hannah is not mentioned when Elkanah (singular) goes home, though she surely went home with him.

In sum, the MT has many preferred readings, but it also has inadvertent errors and intentional small and large additions, just as the Samuel scrolls from Qumran and the LXX also have preferable readings but also contain errors and small and large additions. Thus, reliable historical, exegetical, theological, or reception-historical analyses require the establishment of a sound text and text-history; to arrive at the same requires an examination of all the principal witnesses on an egalitarian basis.

4.2 Kings

4.2.1 Manuscript Evidence

There is little Hebrew manuscript evidence for the text of Kings beyond the MT and the parallels in Chronicles. Among the Qumran Scrolls, Kings survives in only three very fragmentary manuscripts. (1) 5QKgs has seven fragments, only one of which has connected text—a couple of words at the beginnings of twelve lines—but does not attest any variants. (2) 6QpapKgs has forty fragments, but only two have connected text, and there are no significant variants. (3) 4QKgs has eight fragments, only two of which are of modest size. The orthography of 4QKgs, as of 4QSam^a, is moderately fuller than that of MT. Only one of its fragments displays a meaningful variant (see Trebolle 1995: 177): at 1 Kgs. 8:16 it correctly preserves a line (in brackets below) lost from MT through homoioteleuton (underlined below), but preserved partially in LXX and fully in 2 Chr. 6:5–6:...I had not chosen a city...in which to build a house that <u>my name might be there</u>; [and I chose no one as ruler...; but I have chosen Jerusalem that <u>my name might be there</u>,] and I have chosen David....

Notwithstanding the paucity of preserved Hebrew evidence, the LXX and its presumed *Vorlage* together with its versions, when compared with the MT, highlight numerous significant developments in the MT. To understand the interrelationships of the Hebrew and Greek texts, it is helpful to know that the LXX manuscripts contain different types of text. The OG was translated from a Hebrew *Vorlage* which was quite different from the MT at many points.

The base text for 1 Kgs. 2:12–21:29 [43] is OG. In the *Kaige* sections, 1 Kgs. 1:1–2:11 and 1 Kgs. 22:1–2 Kgs. 25:30, the majority Greek tradition, with Codex Vaticanus (LXX^B) leading the way, does not transmit the OG text of the second century BCE. It rather presents the text of the *Kaige*-Theodotionic recension, from shortly before or after the turn of the era. The OG text of these sections is preserved in the pre-Lucianic level of the Antiochene text (LXX^L), the OL, the pre-Hexaplaric level of the Armenian and Georgian versions, Josephus, and the parallel readings of Chronicles. The late Lucianic level of the Antiochene textual tradition (LXX^L) added Hexaplaric readings to an OG base. Many of the Hexaplaric readings attributed to the Lucianic recension were introduced later in its textual tradition and not in all the manuscripts. Most of them, and the more important ones, are found only in manuscript e$_2$, the most hexaplaric.

4.2.2 The Textual Growth of Kings: Additions and Double Readings

The history of the biblical text demonstrates the progressive eclipsing by the Masoretic text of other ancient Hebrew texts, particularly the one underlying the Septuagint. Consequently, the history of the LXX and its secondary versions is that of the progressive revision of their texts to adapt them to the MT. This process of revision, which starts with the *Kaige*-Th recension and culminates with the Hexaplaric one, entailed mainly the addition of Masoretic readings to the old shorter texts of the LXX and the daughter versions.

In this way, first, the *Kaige*-Th revision replaced OG readings with readings closer to the proto-MT, resulting in the text transmitted in LXX^B, as in 2 Kgs. 17:2 (below). Second, *Kaige*- Theodotionic readings became part of the Antiochene text, creating typical double readings in the Lucianic manuscripts boc$_2$e$_2$ (LXX^L = pre-Lucianic + *Kaige*-Theodotionic), as in 2 Kgs. 2:23 and 3:20 (below). Third, Hexaplaric additions supplemented the short OG text with *pluses* from the proto-MT (LXX^O). The following scheme gives an idea of an even more complex textual history:

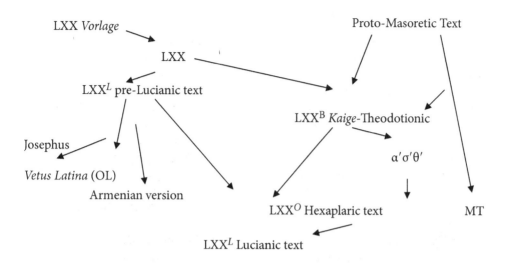

4.2.3 The Hexaplaric Additions

The Hexaplaric additions in the Greek text provide empirical evidence of interpolations in the proto-MT. Harry Orlinsky was correct: "wherever the Masoretic text has an excess over the LXX, it is most frequently the former that underwent expansion in post-LXX days, rather than a case of contraction in the latter" (1939–40: 40). For example, in 1 Kgs. 6, between verses 10 and 15, there is a theological passage (1 Kgs. 6:11–14) made of Deuteronomistic and Priestly phraseology that is strange in the context and absent from OG and Josephus (*Ant.* 8.70); it is an insertion (in italics below) in the proto-MT and Hexaplaric text:

> ¹⁰He built the structure... timbers of cedar.
>
> ¹¹*Now the word of the LORD came to Solomon,* ¹²*"Concerning this house that you are building, if you will walk in my statutes...* ¹³*I will dwell among... my people Israel...."*
>
> ¹⁵He lined the walls... with boards of cedar....

On a larger scale, the long literary unit about Jeroboam in MT and LXX^O 1 Kgs. 14:1–20 is not found in the LXX there. Rather, (the *Vorlage* of) the OG has a version of the story differently told in 1 Kgs. 12:24g–n (see below).

The extent of a Hexaplaric addition (in italics below) helps to recognize the exact length of the corresponding Hebrew addition, frequently introduced by means of a resumptive repetition (underlined below). In the list at 1 Kgs. 4:13 the rather obvious insertion (in italics) in MT and LXX^O, lacking in OG, shows the growth of the text from the older Greek *Vorlage* to the secondary MT:

> Ben Geber, in Ramoth-<u>Gilead</u>
> *he had the villages of Jair son of Manasseh, which are in <u>Gilead</u>*
> and the region of Argob in Bashan.

Some other cases from the non-*Kaige* section of the Greek text, 1 Kgs. 2:12–21:43, are 1 Kgs. 6:5; 6:18–19; 7:30–32; 7:38 and LXX 8:65.

4.2.4 The Antiochene Text

In the Antiochene text (LXX^L), study of variants, additions, omissions, and double readings helps determine the OG and its Hebrew *Vorlage*, which was quite different from the MT at many points.

At LXX 1 Kgs. 2:46–47 LXX^L (boc₂e₂) preserves the OG that ignores the interpolation present in the parallel passage of MT 5:4 (4:24 NRSV) and transmitted also by the B text in 2:46–47: "<u>west of the River</u>, [*from Tiphsah even to Gaza, over all the kings* <u>west of the River</u>.]" "West of the River" reveals the Mesopotamian perspective of a postexilic insertion.

At 2 Kgs. 17:2, LXX^L παρα πάντας τοὺς γενομένους (OL *prae omnes qui fuerunt*), "compared with all who were before," transmits the OG reading (מכל אשר היו). The *Kaige* recension replaced this OG reading with a more literal translation of the MT: the LXX^B reads πλὴν οὐχ ὡς οἱ βασιλεῖς Ισραηλ οἳ ἦσαν (MT רק לא כמלכי ישראל אשר היו) "yet not like the kings of Israel who were before him."

At 1 Kgs. 22:32 in the *Kaige* section, the plus of the Lucianic (LXX^L) text καὶ Κύριος ἔσωσεν αὐτόν ("and the Lord helped him") is often considered an "addition" to the majority Greek text, but the parallel passage of 2 Chr. 18:31 offers the corresponding Hebrew ויהוה עזרו. Chronicles transmits here a Hebrew text of Kings akin to the OG *Vorlage* reflected by the pre-Lucianic text and the OL. The reading may be an "addition," but it was already in the Hebrew *Vorlage* of the OG.

4.2.5 The Kaige-Theodotionic Readings

The Kaige-Theodotionic readings, when compared with the pre-Lucianic and OG, make it easier to recognize variants and double readings in the Hebrew textual tradition: At 2 Kgs. 2:23 the LXX^L double reading καὶ ἐλίθαζον αὐτόν (OL *et lapidabant illum*) καὶ κατέπαιζον αὐτοῦ, "and they threw stones at him and they mocked him," is made of the OG reading "and they threw stones at him" (ויסקלו) plus the *Kaige*-Theodotionic "and they mocked him" (MT ויתקלסו). The two readings reflect different groups of consonants: λιθάζω = סקל *pi'el*, "to stone," (cf. 2 Sam. 16:6) in OG and καταπαίζω = קלס *hitpa'el*, "to mock," (2 Kgs. 2:23) in MT.

At 2 Kgs. 3:20 LXX^L and OL offer a conflate reading ἐξ ὁδοῦ τῆς ἐρήμου Σουρ ἐξ Εδωμ (*de via eremi Sur ex Edom*), made of OG ἐξ ὁδοῦ τῆς ἐρήμου Σουρ, "from the way of the wilderness of Sour" (cf. 3:8 MT דרך מדבר אדום, L ὁδὸν ἐρήμου Εδωμ) and *Kaige*-Theodotionic ἐξ ὁδοῦ Εδωμ that follows MT's מדרך אדום, "from the way of Edom." This too is possibly a confusion of letters: מדרך אדום > מדרך סאור, and ἐρήμου may have been added to help identify the unfamiliar סאור.

In 2 Kgs. 9:37 the conflate reading of LXX^L ὥστε μὴ εἰπεῖν Αὕτη Ιεζαβελ καὶ οὐκ ἔσται ὁ λέγων Οἴμμοι (OL *et non est qui dicat: Vae mihi!*) is made of the *Kaige*-Theodotionic reading that follows MT's אשר לא יאמרו זאת איזבל, "so that no one can say, 'This is Jezebel,'" and the pre-Lucianic or OG "there will not be anyone saying, 'Woe is me!'" (ולא יהיה האמר אהה).

4.2.6 The Name and the Deuteronomist

Additions and variants linked with the "Name" of Yahweh and insertions in Deuteronomistic wording are especially significant: see the examples at 1 Kgs. 8:16//2 Chr. 6:5–6 ("that my name might be there") and 1 Kgs. 6:11–14 ("Now the word of the LORD came to Solomon") already discussed above.

Again at 1 Kgs. 8:41–42 the MT adds an insertion not in the OG (though *BHS* does not note its absence in OG). The MT insertion is enclosed by a resumptive repetition (underlined below):

> [41]When a <u>foreigner…comes</u>
>
> *from a distant land because of your name,* [42]*—for they shall hear of your great name, your mighty hand, and your outstretched arm—when a <u>foreigner comes</u>]*
>
> and prays toward this house….

First Kgs. 3:14 is an insertion with nomistic Deuteronmisic phraseology. Some consider v. 13b as well as v. 14 part of the Dtr addition, but the resumptive repetition in MT of "your days" (underlined below; note that LXX^O and OL have "your days" in v. 13b, although LXX^B lacks it) delimits the addition to v. 14 (in italics):

> [13b]so that there will not be any among the kings like you all <u>your days</u>
>
> [14]*And if you walk in my ways, to keep my statutes and commandments, as your father David walked, then I will lengthen <u>your days</u>.*

At 1 Kgs. 8:29 the longer LXX text preserves better than MT and 2 Chr. 6:20 (MT-LXX) the resumptive repetition (underlined) that encloses the addition (italicized) related to the "Name" and the Jerusalem temple:

> that your eyes may be open toward this house <u>day and night</u>
>
> *<u>this place</u> of which you said, "My Name shall be there," that you may heed the prayer that your servant prays toward <u>this place day and night</u>.*

In 2 Kgs. 21:2–9 the OL attests the OG whose Hebrew original differs from the reworked proto-MT edition. The present LXX (LXX^{BL}) text follows the *Kaige*-Theodotionic revision akin to MT, but the OL attests among other variants that it lacked the text (italicized) enclosed by the resumptive repetition (underlined).

> <u>He built altars</u>
>
> *in the house of the LORD, of which the LORD had said, "In Jerusalem I will put my name." <u>He built altars</u>*
>
> in the two courts of the house of the LORD.

4.2.7 The Process of Edition

The MT presents frequent cases of repetition and double readings that allow us to recognize the developing process of the formation of the text. See the example at 1 Kgs. 8:41–42 "when a foreigner comes" above. Alleged haplographies of LXX are rather interpolations in the proto-MT introduced by means of resumptive repetitions.

At 1 Kgs. 15:5–6 the LXX preserves the text free of additions, but an obvious insertion is added in MT (in italics), signaled by the resumptive repetition (underlined):

> [5]Because David…<u>all the days of his life</u>.
>
> *except in the matter of Uriah the Hittite.* [6]*The war begun between Rehoboam and Jeroboam continued <u>all the days of his life</u>.*
>
> [7]The rest of the acts….

At 1 Kgs. 12:24a the OG preserves the short original, whereas MT LXX^O introduces into the parallel at 1 Kgs. 14:21 an insertion (in italics), lacking in OG there:

> [Rehoboam]... reigned twelve (seventeen MT) years in Jerusalem,
>
> *the city that the* LORD *had chosen out of all the tribes of Israel, to put his name there.*
>
> and his mother's name was Naamah....

First Kings 16:11-12 displays another interpolation in MT (against *BHS*):

> He killed all the house of Baasha
>
> *he did not leave him a single male of his kindred or his friends.* ¹²*Zimri destroyed* all *the house of Baasha.*

The verb "killed" (MT נכה, OG regularly ἐπάταξεν) is usual in the expression (cf. 1 Kgs. 15:29), while the use of "destroyed" (שמד, ἐξέτριψεν hexaplaric), strange in the context, indicates the secondary character of the repetition. Moreover, the secondary character of v. 12 is confirmed by the prophecy-fulfillment motif, "according to the word of the LORD," referring back to vv. 2-4.

4.2.8 Variant Literary Editions of the Books of Kings

The MT and LXX of Kings exhibit variant literary editions characterized by numerous transpositions. Many of the interpolations discussed above combine to illustrate the process that resulted in the different editions.

The two versions of the stories about Jeroboam and Rehoboam, represented by the OG *Vorlage* 1 Kgs. 12:24a-z and by MT 1 Kgs. 11:40-14:22 belong to different editions of the book. These editions differ mainly in the order of the literary units in 1 Kgs. 2-11 and consequently in the chronological order of events of Solomon's reign. Needless to say, critical study of the variant narratives is essential for sound judgment regarding the history and depiction of Solomon's reign.

Again, the literary units about Hiram's activities and the construction of Solomon's temple and palace (1 Kgs. 5:15-9:14), present both in Kings (MT and LXX) and Chronicles, constitute the central body of 1 Kings 3-10. Before and after these common materials LXX and MT contain several elements placed in different locations:

MT 3:1b in LXX post 5:14;   MT 6:38b = LXX 2:35c^b;
5:1a in LXX post 10:26;   7:1-12 in LXX post 7:51;
5:2-4 in LXX post 5:8;   9:15-22 in LXX post 10:22;
5:5 cf. LXX 2:46g^b;   9:23 cf. LXX 2:35h;
5:6 = LXX 10:26;   9:24a in LXX post 9:9 (cf. 2:35f);
5:31-32a in LXX post 6:1;   9:24b = LXX 2:35f;
6:37-38a in LXX post 5:31-32a;   9:25 = LXX 2:35g.

In contrast to the verses found in different loci in the MT and LXX, there are pluses in the MT absent from LXX: 1 Kgs. 3:1a; 4:20; 5:5, 6; 6:1b; 6:11-14; 6:38b; 9:23; 9:24b; and 9:25. Much of the transposed material in MT and LXX, as well as the additions of MT absent from LXX, are found in the so-called supplements of LXX in 1 Kgs. 2:35a-o and 2:46a-l.

In 2 Kings the prophetic narratives about Elijah-Elisha of 2 Kgs. 2:1–25 and 13:14–21 stand outside any regnal frame, violating the compositional rule of the book, according to which any literary unit must be included between the initial and concluding formulae of the reign with which it synchronizes. Similarly, the unit 1 Kgs. 16:21–22, placed outside the regnal formulae of Zimri and Omri, is probably an interpolation related to the chronological system of Kings as differently attested in MT and LXX.

When literary units that make up the composition are transposed, or when one is introduced inside the other, textual variants pile up at the junctures of those units; their text undergoes an adaptation in the boundaries between the two. This explains the variants between MT and LXX in the formulation of synchronisms at the points where the Elijah-Elisha stories were inserted into the "synchronic history," as in 1 Kgs. 16:29; 22:41; 22:52; 2 Kgs. 1:17 and 3:1.

4.2.9 Parallels of Kings in Chronicles, Isaiah, and Jeremiah

The comparative study of the parallel texts in Chronicles, Isaiah, and Jeremiah also contributes to the study of the editing process of Kings.

Chronicles has many significant agreements with the OG of Kings, such as the clause of LXX 1 Kgs. 2:46d ᾠκοδόμησεν τὴν Θερμαι ἐν τῇ ἐρήμῳ, in agreement with 2 Chr. 8:4, ויבן את תדמר במדבר, against MT 1 Kgs. 9:15b, 17–18 (cf. LXX). LXX Kings is based on a Hebrew text that did not know the influence of Chronicles such as the glosses of MT 1 Kgs. 8:1–6 taken from 2 Chr. 5:2–7. Chronicles reflects a literary form of Kings prior to the present MT and LXX editions of Kings.

Isaiah 8 and 2 Kings 20 tell two versions of the same episode, variant editions of the same basic story. Though much is the same, a few distinctive features are added in Isaiah 8 but many more are added in the longer version in 2 Kings 20. Additions in 2 Kings 20 specify the place where Isaiah received the word of the LORD (v. 4), add that Hezekiah is "the prince of my people," promise that he will be healed and go up to the house of the Lord on the third day (v. 5), and command that a lump of figs should be applied for recovery (v. 6). Moreover, in Isaiah 8, the prophet *announces* the sign, "This is the sign.... I will make the shadow turn back.... So the sun turned back" (Isa. 8:7–8). In contrast, in Kings, Hezekiah *asks* (2 Kgs. 20:8), "What shall be the sign..." and specifies (alluding to v. 5) "...that I shall be healed and go to the house of the LORD on the third day?" Kings also inserts a dialogue, lacking in Isaiah 8: the prophet asks Hezekiah, "shall [the shadow] retreat ten intervals?" (2 Kgs. 20:9), and Hezekiah retorts, "It is normal for the shadow to lengthen...; let it retreat ten intervals" (v. 10).

In 2 Kings 25//Jeremiah 52 the OG of Jeremiah represents the oldest attainable textual layer, which did not know Jer. 52:2–3, 15 and also partially 52:7, 18–19, 27. MT Jeremiah 52 constitutes the more developed and late textual form, which juxtaposes readings of 2 Kings and materials specific to the textual tradition of the book of Jeremiah.

4.3 CONCLUSION

To sum up, the study of the composition, redaction, and editing of Samuel and Kings, as well as the study of the history of the Israelite monarchy—and of its chronology in particular—simply cannot succeed without analysis of the textual history of these books.

The Samuel scrolls from Qumran and the LXX exhibit preferable readings in contrast to the MT, but they also contain errors and small and large additions. The MT also has many preferred readings, but it also has inadvertent errors and intentional small and large additions.

An Old Hebrew edition of Kings, translated in the Old Greek, was replaced by a more developed and authorized edition represented by the (proto-)Masoretic text. Similarly, the OG was progressively replaced by the *kaige*-Theodotionc and the Hexaplaric recensions that reflect in Greek the previous growth of the Hebrew text. With the history of the Hebrew text thus well mapped, other historical, literary, or theological study can proceed successfully.

Notes

1. Abegg (2010: 2:25) reports that of the more than 94,000 extant words in the corpus of the preserved biblical scrolls, 4QSam^a ranks fourth with 3,656 words, almost 4% of the preserved biblical material.
2. For this and all of the following examples, the DJD reference is provided. The texts in question can also be found collected in Ulrich (2010).
3. Fuller descriptions of the orthography of 4QSam^a and 4QSam^b can be found in Cross et al. 2005: 5–15, 220–21; for 4QSam^c see ibid.: 250–51.

Bibliography

Abegg, Martin Jr. 2010. "Linguistic Profile of the Isaiah Scrolls." In Eugene Ulrich and Peter W. Flint, eds. *Qumran Cave 1: II The Isaiah Scrolls*. DJD 32, Part 2. Oxford: Clarendon, 25–41.
Abegg, Martin Jr., Peter Flint, and Eugene Ulrich. 1999. *The Dead Sea Scrolls Bible: The Oldest Known Bible Translated for the First Time into English*. San Francisco: HarperSanFrancisco.
Aejmelaeus, Anneli. 2007. *On the Trail of the Septuagint Translators*. 2nd ed. Leuven: Peeters.
Ausloos, Hans, Bénédicte Lemmelijn, and Julio Trebolle Barrera, eds. 2012. *After Qumran: Old and Modern Editions of the Biblical Texts—The Historical Books*. BETL 246. Leuven: Peeters.
Cross, Frank Moore, Donald W. Parry, Richard J. Saley, and Eugene Ulrich, eds. 2005. *Qumran Cave 4.XII: 1–2 Samuel*. DJD 17. Oxford: Clarendon Press.
Fernández Marcos, N. and J. R. Busto Saiz. 1992. *El texto antioqueno de la Biblia griega II 1–2 Reyes*. Madrid: Consejo Superior de Investigaciones Científicas.
Fernández Marcos, Natalio. 2000. *The Septuagint in Context: Introduction to the Greek Versions of the Bible*. Translated by W. G. E. Watson. Leiden: Brill.
Hugo, Philippe and Adrian Schenker, eds. 2010. *Archaeology of the Books of Samuel: The Entangling of the Textual and Literary History*. VTS 132. Leiden: Brill.
Hugo, Philippe and Adrian Schenker. 2017. "Textual History of Kings." In Armin Lange and Emanuel Tov, eds., *The Textual History of the Hebrew Bible*, 1B: 310–318. 3 vols. Leiden: Brill.
McCarter, P. Kyle, Jr. 1986. *Textual Criticism: Recovering the Text of the Hebrew Bible*. Philadelphia: Fortress Press.
Moreno Hernández, A. 1992. *Las glosas marginales de* Vetus latina *en las biblias vulgatas españolas*. Madrid: Consejo Superior de Investigaciones Científicas.
Orlinsky, Harry M. 1939–40. "The Kings-Isaiah Recensions of the Hezekiah Story." *JQR* 30: 33–49.
Schenker, Adrian. 2004. *Älteste Textgeschichte der Königsbücher. Die hebräische Vorlage der ursprünglichen Septuaginta als älteste Textform der Königsbücher*. Fribourg: Academic Press. Göttingen: Vandenhoeck & Ruprecht.

Talshir, Zipora. 1993. *The Alternative Story: 3 Kingdoms 12:24 A-Z*. Jerusalem Biblical Studies 6. Jerusalem: Simor.

Talshir, Zipora. 2014. "The Relationship between Sam-MT, 4QSam^a, and Chr and the Case of 2 Sam 24." In Kristin De Troyer et al., eds., *In the Footsteps of Sherlock Holmes: Studies in the Biblical Text in Honour of Anneli Aejmelaeus*. CBET 72. Leuven: Peeters, 273-98.

Torijano Morales, Pablo. 2017. "Vetus Latina: Samuel-Kings." In Armin Lange and Emanuel Tov, eds., *The Textual History of the Hebrew Bible*. 3 vols. Leiden: Brill, 1B:400-403.

Tov, Emanuel. 2012. *Textual Criticism of the Hebrew Bible*. 3rd ed. Minneapolis: Fortress.

Tov, Emanuel. 2015. *The Text-Critical Use of the Septuagint in Biblical Research*. 3rd ed. Winona Lake, IN: Eisenbrauns.

Trebolle Barrera, Julio. 1984. "From the 'Old Latin' through the 'Old Greek' to the 'Old Hebrew' (2 Kings 10:23-35)." *Textus* 11: 17-36.

Trebolle Barrera, Julio. 1995. "54. 4QKgs." In Eugene Ulrich et al., eds., *Qumran Cave 4.IX: Deuteronomy, Joshua, Judges, Kings*. DJD 14. Oxford: Clarendon, 171-83.

Trebolle Barrera, Julio. 1998. *The Jewish Bible and the Christian Bible: An Introduction to the History of the Bible*. Leiden: Brill and Grand Rapids: Eerdmans.

Trebolle Barrera, Julio. 2010. "Textual Criticism and The Composition History of Samuel: Connections between Pericopes in 1 Samuel 1-4." In P. Hugo and A. Schenker, eds., *Archaeology of the Books of Samuel: The Entangling of the Textual and Literary History*. VTSup 132. Leiden: Brill, 261-85.

Trebolle Barrera, Julio. 2012. "Textual Criticism and the Literary Structure and Composition of 1-2 Kings / 3-4 Reigns: The Different Sequence of Literary Units in MT and LXX." In Siegfried Kreuzer et al., eds., *Die Septuaginta: Entstehung, Sprache, Geschichte*. Tübingen: Mohr Siebeck, 55-78.

Trebolle Barrera, Julio. 2017. "Vetus Latina." In Armin Lange and Emanuel Tov, eds., *The Textual History of the Bible*, vol. 1B. Leiden: Brill, 207a-11b and 660a-665a.

Ulrich, Eugene. 1978. *The Qumran Text of Samuel and Josephus*. HSM 19. Missoula, MT: Scholars Press.

Ulrich, Eugene. 2001. "The Developmental Composition of the Book of Isaiah: Light from 1QIsa^a on Additions in the MT." *DSD* 8: 288-305.

Ulrich, Eugene. 2012. "The Old Latin, Mount Gerizim, and 4QJosh^a." In Andrés Piquer Otero and Pablo Torijano Morales, eds., *Textual Criticism and Dead Sea Scrolls Studies in Honour of Julio Trebolle Barrera: Florilegium Complutense*. JSJSup 157. Leiden: Brill, 361-75.

Ulrich, Eugene. 2012. "David, the Plague, and the Angel: 2 Samuel 24 Revisited." In H. Ausloos, B. Lemmelijn, and J. Trebolle Barrera, eds., *After Qumran: Old and Modern Editions of the Biblical Texts—The Historical Books*. BETL 246. Leuven: Peeters, 63-79.

Ulrich, Eugene. 2015. *The Dead Sea Scrolls and the Developmental Composition of the Bible*. VTSup 169. Leiden: Brill.

Ulrich, Eugene, ed. 2010. *Biblical Qumran Scrolls: Transcriptions and Textual Variants*. VTSup 134. Leiden: Brill.

Walters, Stanley D. 1988. "Hannah and Anna: The Greek and Hebrew Texts of 1 Samuel 1." *JBL* 107: 385-412.

CHAPTER 5

TEXT-CRITICAL ISSUES IN EZRA-NEHEMIAH AND 1 ESDRAS

LISBETH S. FRIED

EZRA, Nehemiah, and 1 Esdras are the three narrative books of the Bible that portray the period of the Judeans' return to Judah and Jerusalem under the Persians. They tell the story not only of the return to Judah, but also of the enduring faithfulness of Israel's God, YHWH, who resurrected Israel from the dead and returned her to life in her land (Ezra 3:11, cf. Ezek. 37:1–13; Holmgren 1987). Ezra 1–6 tells the story of how God led the Judeans back to resettle Judah and to rebuild their temple in Jerusalem after nearly fifty years of exile in Babylon. It concludes with a celebration of the temple's dedication in the sixth year of Darius (Ezra 6:15–18). Ezra 7–10 shifts to the story of the installation of the Torah in Judah (Rothenbusch 2012: 47). Ezra, a priest and scribe of the law of Moses, arrives in Jerusalem in the seventh year of King Artaxerxes with a mandate to establish Torah law in Judah (Ezra 7). As part of this effort he brings about a mass divorce of the people from their foreign wives and so purifies the community of foreign influences (Ezra 9–10). The story of Ezra continues in Nehemiah 8 when Ezra reads the torah to the assembled population.

The story of Nehemiah follows Ezra 10 immediately, on the same page of the torah scroll, without a break. It tells the tale of Nehemiah's arrival in Jerusalem as the Persian governor of Judah in the twentieth year of King Artaxerxes of Persia. Nehemiah rebuilds and rededicates Jerusalem's city walls (Neh. 2–6; 12:27–43), establishing within them the rightful population, having already been purified of their foreign wives by Ezra (Ezra 10). The center and climax of the Ezra-Nehemiah story is the covenant renewal ceremony (Nehemiah 8–10) in which Ezra reads the Torah of Moses to the assembled populace in Jerusalem. The people respond to the reading by reaffirming their allegiance to the Law, to their temple, and to their God. Nehemiah 13 is a coda which ends Ezra-Nehemiah (Eskenazi 1988: 6). It looks back on the main body of the work and creates a sense of balance among the various themes of the book—law and temple.

The Apocryphal Greek text, 1 Esdras, is so called because in the Septuagint it precedes 2 Esdras, the literal translation of Ezra-Nehemiah. Second Esdras is part of the reason that Ezra and Nehemiah are considered one book. The thirteen chapters currently assigned to

Nehemiah in English Bibles are simply chapters 11–23 in 2 Esdras. First Esdras, by way of contrast, is basically the book of Ezra-Nehemiah, but with several differences. To begin with, canonical Ezra-Nehemiah and 2 Esdras include the story of Nehemiah, a story entirely omitted from 1 Esdras. Second, the story of Ezra-Nehemiah (and 2 Esdras) begins with the last two verses of Chronicles, whereas 1 Esdras begins with the entire last two chapters of Chronicles. Third, the story of Zerubbabel's return to Judah and the chapter containing the correspondence with King Artaxerxes have exchanged positions in the two versions. Fourth, 1 Esdras contains a story of King Darius and his three bodyguards which is not present either in canonical Ezra-Nehemiah or 2 Esdras. Finally, 1 Esdras includes the story of Ezra reading the law to the assembled populace, even though in the canonical text it appears only in Nehemiah 8. In spite of these differences, Ezra-Nehemiah and 1 Esdras tell the story of Ezra in nearly identical language. Indeed, the language and stories are so similar that it is clear that the two versions are not independent. One has copied the story of Ezra from the other, or both have copied from a third source. Their several differences however raise the *text-critical* issue of the original form(s) of the text and the *historical-critical* issue of whether these text-critical differences should prevent us from using these books to understand the history of the early Persian period in Judah. The texts used of the two Greek versions have been prepared by Robert Hanhart based primarily on the text of MS *Vaticanus* (Hanhart 1974, 1993).

5.1 Ancient Witnesses to the Text of Ezra-Nehemiah

The Hebrew text of Ezra-Nehemiah employed in most translations of the Bible is the Masoretic Text (MT), now available in the *Biblia Hebraica Quinta* (BHQ). The MT is traditionally understood as the agreement between three Tiberian manuscripts: the Leningrad Codex (manuscript EPB, I B 19a of the Russian National Library, St. Petersburg, dated to 1008 CE); Sassoon 1053, a tenth-century manuscript, housed in the National Library of Israel; and manuscript 1753 of the Cambridge University Library (see Marcus 2006: x, 8*). The last manuscript is Yemenite, but is very close to the Leningrad Codex. In fact, the three manuscripts differ only slightly, and only orthographically, with regard to spelling of certain words. Unfortunately, about one-third of Ezra-Nehemiah in the Sassoon manuscript is lost, and parts of the existing text are damaged and difficult to read (Marcus 2006: 8*). All three manuscripts place Ezra-Nehemiah last among the biblical books, and all three have Daniel preceding it. This text of Ezra-Nehemiah is the text presented in *BHQ*.

Prior to 1947 there were no Hebrew manuscripts earlier than these of the medieval period. In 1947, however, manuscripts were found in the caves above the Dead Sea: the so-called Dead Sea Scrolls, which date to the second–first century BCE. Other manuscripts were found in the ruins of the Herodian fortress on Masada (which date to before 73 CE), and in other caves of the Judean desert (copied before 135 CE). Among the fragments at Qumran were several of Ezra (Ulrich 1992: 291–93; Z. Talshir 2003: 213–18) but so far none of Nehemiah. These manuscripts contain Ezra 4:2–6 (= 1 Esdr. 5:66–70), Ezra 4:9–11 (no 1 Esdras parallel), Ezra 5:17–6:5 (= 1 Esdr. 6:20–25). Except for orthographic differences, the manuscripts of Ezra found at Qumran differ little from the consonantal text of the Leningrad Codex. In spite of the care in which these texts were preserved and copied, the Masoretes, who are credited with preserving the Masoretic text, record no less than fifty-three differences between what is written in the text and what was read or pronounced orally (*Kethib-Qere* differences). In these instances, the Masoretes note that what is written in the body of the text (the *Kethib*) is not to be read; instead, the *Qere*, which they have written in the margin, is to be read instead. These differences appear to reflect early textual variations or scribal corrections that have been maintained over the millennia.

In addition to the two Greek versions of Ezra-Nehemiah (1 and 2 Esdras), the *Peshitta*, maintained by the Syrian church, contains a translation into Syriac of the proto-MT of Ezra-Nehemiah (an online edition is at: cal.huc.edu). Although its origin is not known, the original translation was likely completed in the first or second centuries CE essentially as a literal translation of the Hebrew. The earliest extant manuscripts are from the end of the sixth or the beginning of the seventh centuries CE, however (Balzaretti 2013: 35, n. 16).

There are also two Latin translations: the *Old Latin* (see the apparatus of Hanhart 1993) and the *Vulgate* (Gasquet 1987). Both are extremely literal translations of the Hebrew (Marcus 2006: 11*). The Latin editions refer to canonical Ezra as 1 Esdras, canonical Nehemiah as 2 Esdras, and label Greek 1 Esdras as 3 Esdras. The separation of Ezra and Nehemiah into two books stems from the Vulgate.

Since the manuscripts of these Greek and Latin translations are older than the medieval copies of the Hebrew that we possess (but not older than the fragments from the Judean desert), it is possible to use them to reconstruct the original Hebrew text that lay behind them. This hypothetical original is called the *Vorlage* of the translation in question.

5.2 LOCATION OF EZRA-NEHEMIAH IN THE CANON

In the LXX and Vulgate, Ezra-Nehemiah follows Chronicles immediately, reflecting an early Babylonian Talmudic tradition that the former is a direct continuation of the latter. (This is also the order followed in most Christian Bibles.) In the Hebrew Bible, however, these two books are not always connected. The Aleppo and Leningrad Codices, for example, follow the Palestinian tradition in which Chronicles is placed first among the Writings (Kethubim) and Ezra-Nehemiah last in that section and last in the Bible, in what D. N. Freedman called an "envelope construction" (personal communication). Freedman suggested that the repetition of the end of Chronicles in the beginning of Ezra acts as an *inclusio*, indicating that the intervening books are to be read as a unit. In the Babylonian Talmud's list of the biblical books (see *b. B. Bat.* 14b), the books are placed next to each other, with Ezra-Nehemiah unexpectedly preceding Chronicles, setting Chronicles as the last book in the Hebrew Bible. (This is the order followed in most Hebrew Bibles today). Placing Chronicles last allows the Bible to end with Cyrus's command to go up to Jerusalem and rebuild the temple (2 Chr. 36:23) which, for the readers of the Talmud, had most recently been destroyed by Rome.

5.3 Textual History of Ezra-Nehemiah

5.3.1 Chronicles and Ezra–Nehemiah: Not One Book, Not One Author

Beginning with Zunz (1832: 13–36), many commentators have concluded that Ezra-Nehemiah was originally a continuation of the books of Chronicles and was written by the same author, whom they call the Chronicler (e.g., Batten 1913; Rudolph 1949; Freedman 1961: 436–42; Haran 1986: 18–20; Blenkinsopp 1988; Z. Talshir 1986: 39–61; D. Talshir 1988: 165–93). They emphasize that the last few verses of 2 Chronicles are repeated in the first few verses of Ezra, forming a catch-phrase. They also point out that the Greek 1 Esdras contains all of 2 Chronicles 35–36 and continues directly on to the story of Ezra-Nehemiah with no break and no repetition of verses, and therefore posit that 1 Esdras expresses the original form of Ezra. Torrey (1970) deviated from this consensus slightly in that he suggested that the Chronicler wrote Chronicles and continued with 1 Esdras (not Ezra), ending with Ezra's reading the law, but that this author was not responsible for the rest of Nehemiah. Other scholars maintain that Chronicles and Ezra-Nehemiah was originally one book by one author because of the many linguistic features—approximately 140—that they share (see Curtis and Madsen 1910; Driver 1913; Williamson 1977; cf. Torrey 1986). However, these similarities should be attributed to the nature of the specific language stratum used— late biblical Hebrew—rather than to a single author (Williamson 1977: 37–59).

Japhet settled the issue, however, when she showed that the linguistic forms that the Chronicler alters in his sources from Samuel and Kings are unchanged in the Nehemiah memoir, proving that the Chronicler could not have been the one who incorporated Nehemiah's memoir into the book of Ezra-Nehemiah (Japhet 1968: 330–71). The Chronicler could not be the author of Ezra-Nehemiah therefore, and Chronicles-Ezra-Nehemiah cannot be considered one long book but at least two books, if not three.

5.3.2 Ezra-Nehemiah: One Book, but Not One Author

The book of Chronicles is no longer read as part of Ezra or Nehemiah, but are Ezra and Nehemiah one book or two? As discussed above, the earliest evidence points to Ezra-Nehemiah's acceptance as one book, called simply Ezra. The Septuagint (LXX) labels Ezra-Nehemiah as one book (2 Esdras). Dated by scholars to the second-first centuries BCE, it is a literal Greek translation of both Ezra and Nehemiah (see Z. Talshir, 1999; 2001). The Talmud (*b. Bab. Bat.* 14b and 15a) also lists Ezra and Nehemiah as a single book, and finally, the Masoretes total the words of both Ezra-Nehemiah together (685), counting the middle of the text at Neh. 3:32, not at the end of Ezra.

Although according to earliest tradition Ezra and Nehemiah formed one book, scholars have questioned whether they were written originally as one book or as two. Several ancient authors mention Nehemiah but do not appear to know Ezra (i.e., Sir. 49:12–13; 2 Macc. 1:18,

20–36), and 1 Esdras knows Ezra but does not seem to know Nehemiah. Furthermore, Josephus's story of Ezra (*Ant.* 11.1–158) is based on 1 Esdras, and he does not begin his story of Nehemiah until after narrating Ezra's death (*Ant.* 11.158).

The current story of Ezra-Nehemiah must be seen as one book, however. Ezra arrives in Jerusalem in order to teach "statutes and ordinances in Israel" (Ezra 7:10; NRSV), yet the story of his doing so, of his teaching the law to the assembled populace, is not told until Nehemiah 8. Moreover, the book of Nehemiah begins: "The [following are the] words of Nehemiah son of Hacaliah: 'In the month of Chislev, in the twentieth year, while I was in Susa the capital, one of my brothers, Hanani, came [to me]'" (Neh. 1:1–2; NRSV). The twentieth year refers to the twentieth year of the reign of a king, but we are not told which king. Presumably, the reader is to think it is the same King Artaxerxes who was the king in the previous four chapters: Ezra 7–10 (Min 2004: 25–26).

Even though the final product must be read as one book, Ezra-Nehemiah includes the works of several independent authors and editors that have now been completely and complexly intertwined (VanderKam 1992: 55–75; Kraemer 1993: 73–92; Becking 1998: 40–61).

5.3.3 When Was Ezra-Nehemiah Written?

Given that Ezra-Nehemiah now forms one book, we can ask when its final form was achieved. Although the dates of its individual components must be determined separately, determining the date of its final redaction must account for Neh. 12:22, and one name in the verse, Yaddua. The verse lists the last four priests of the Persian Empire, up to "Darius the Persian" (i.e., Darius III), as Eliyashib, Yoiada (Yehoiada), Yoḥanan (Yehoḥanan), and Yaddua. This list of the last four priests in Neh. 12.22 is complete to 330 BCE and the conquest of Alexander the Great (Fried 2003a; VanderKam 2004: 44–99). Further, many of the sites listed as belonging to Judah in Nehemiah 11 did not belong to Judah under the Persians, but only as a result of the Maccabean conquest (Fulton 2015; Finkelstein 2018). Ezra-Nehemiah, therefore, was not finalized until the period of the Maccabees. Constituent elements that went into the book as we now have it would, of course, be earlier.

5.3.4 The Final Date of 1 Esdras

The story of King Darius and his three bodyguards in 1 Esdras, not present in either canonical Ezra-Nehemiah or 2 Esdras, allows us to date the final version of that book. In 1 Esdr. 3:7 we read that the winner of the debate among the guards will be called "kinsman (Greek *syggenēs*) of the king." This title was first introduced in the Egyptian court by Ptolemy II Philadelphus (238–246 BCE) as the highest level of titles bestowed upon a courtier (Harvey 2011: 179–81). Indeed, the list of officials in 1 Esdras 3 is a rank ordered list of Egyptian Hellenistic honorific titles. These facts establish a locale in Egypt, and a *terminus a quo* of Ptolemy II, for the composition of the book. If, however, the story of the bodyguards is a late addition, then it provides the date only of the final redaction of 1 Esdras, not the entire composition.

5.3.5 Ezra-Nehemiah's Transmission History

The key to understanding Ezra-Nehemiah's transmission history may lie in the lists of returnees in Ezra 2 and Nehemiah 7 (Williamson 1983: 1–30; 1985: xxxiii–xxxv; Gunneweg 1985: 53; Pakkala 2004: 137–44). These lists are virtually identical except for varieties in spelling. Since it is not likely that the same author would repeat two lists verbatim in a single composition, the presence of these identical lists must be explained. The most likely explanation is that we have at least two separate authors. Indeed, there are only three ways to account for the identical lists in Ezra 2 and Nehemiah 7: (1) the author of Ezra 2 copied the list from Nehemiah 7; (2) the author of Nehemiah 7 copied the list from Ezra 2; or (3) they each copied their list independently from a third source.

The solution lies in the fact that both lists end with a nearly identical narrative verse: the notice that when the seventh month arrived and the people Israel were settled in their towns, they gathered as one in Jerusalem:

> When the seventh month arrived—the Israelites being in their towns—the entire people assembled as one in Jerusalem. (Ezra 3:1)
>
> When the seventh month arrived—the Israelites being in their towns—the entire people assembled as one in the square before the Water Gate. (Neh. 7:72–8:1)

The intent of these verses is to link the population as a whole (as described in the preceding lists in Ezra 2 and Nehemiah 7, respectively) to the narrative that follows. Ezra 3, however, follows with an account of a private ceremony with only Zerubbabel and his kin and Jeshua and his kin setting up the temple's sacrificial altar. The linking verse of Ezra 3:1 has thus no meaning in its larger context. Nehemiah 8, in contrast, follows this linking verse with the story of Ezra reading the law to the entire gathered populace. Since only the story of the law-reading involves the entire population, the linking verse must be original to Nehemiah 8, not to Ezra 3 (Fried 2008: 75–97). Therefore, the author of Ezra 2 must have copied the list with its linking verse from Nehemiah 8; it cannot be the other way, nor is it possible that they each copied from an independent third source.

There must have been at least two authors of Ezra-Nehemiah as we now have it, therefore: an earlier one who compiled the list of returnees (Nehemiah 7) and who followed it in his text by the story of Ezra's law-reading ceremony (Nehemiah 8), and a later author who included the same list as the list of returnees in Ezra 2. The later author prefaced the story of Ezra-Nehemiah which he received with an account of the return to Judah and the rebuilding and dedication of the temple. This later writer who created the final form of the text was likely a priest. He interpreted the construction of the city wall and the people's recommitment to the Torah described in the book of Nehemiah as a consequence of the rebuilt House of God.

The transmission history of Ezra-Nehemiah can be further deduced from the text of Ben Sira who likely wrote between 198 and 195 BCE (Askin, in press). In his encomium of the fathers (Ben Sira 44–49), Ben Sira praises the well-known men of the Hebrew Bible, beginning with Adam and culminating with Zerubbabel, Jeshua, and Nehemiah. In Ben Sira 49:11, he praises Zerubbabel as the signet ring on God's right hand, quoting Hag. 2:23.

In 49:12, he refers to Jeshua son of Jozadak, who rebuilt the temple and the altar, described in Ezra 1–6. Finally, in 49:13, he refers to Nehemiah:

> The memory of Nehemiah also is lasting; he raised our fallen walls, and set up gates and bars, and rebuilt our ruined houses.

Ben Sira thus knows Ezra 1–6 and the story of the rebuilt temple, and he knows the story of Nehemiah rebuilding Jerusalem's city walls, but it seems that he does not know of anyone named Ezra. Had he known of Ezra bringing the Mosaic law to Jerusalem as told in Ezra 7:1–10 and of his reading it to the people as told in Nehemiah 8, he certainly would have included it (for the long history of the discussion of Ben Sira's omission of Ezra, see Piwowar 2011: 105–31, and the many articles cited therein). There would have been no reason for Ben Sira to omit Ezra if he had known about him. We must assume that Ezra 7–10 and Nehemiah 8 had not yet been written by the time of Ben Sira, and that Ezra 1–6 (which he did know) and the story of Nehemiah (which he also knew) had most likely not yet been combined into one book. The stories of the temple's rebuilding and of Nehemiah's rebuilding Jerusalem's city wall apparently existed initially as two separate stories. The story of Nehemiah's building the wall likely originally included only Nehemiah 2, 4–6, and 12:27–43—i.e., the story of Nehemiah asking to go to Jerusalem to repair the wall, the actual wall-building along with the friction that surrounded it, and the dedication ceremony. The story of Ezra bringing and reading the torah and the rest of Nehemiah must all have been added later. It is also likely that the torah-reading was initially placed immediately after the story of the wall's dedication. Only the story of the wall's dedication can explain why the people had all spontaneously gathered in Jerusalem (Ezra 3:1; Neh. 7:73–8:1). Only the story of the wall's dedication can further explain the location of the torah-reading. During the dedication, Ezra leads a procession which circumambulates the wall toward the north (Neh. 12:33, 36), and Nehemiah leads a second procession which circumambulates the wall toward the south (Neh. 12:38). The two processions meet inside the temple (12:40)—the first procession, the one led by Ezra, entering it through the Water Gate on the East (12:37). The story of the torah-reading very likely immediately followed. The people have assembled in Jerusalem for the wall's dedication, they have watched the two processions, and have watched Ezra enter the temple through the Water Gate. They now call out to him to come out and read the torah to them, perhaps the torah scroll that he had been carrying. The story of the law-reading was eventually moved and placed between the wall's completion (Neh. 6:15) and the wall's dedication (12:27–43), perhaps to put the torah in the center of the rebuilt city (Fried 2008). As a result, however, the people's gathering in Jerusalem and the location of the torah-reading before the water gate are completely unmotivated.

This story of the law-reading likely stems from the period of the final redaction of Ezra-Nehemiah—the time of the Maccabees. Besides the fact that it is unknown to Ben Sira, we know that other passages in Ezra-Nehemiah are also that late. For example, Neh. 11:25–36 lists towns and villages of Judah and Benjamin, yet, we know that they were annexed to Judah not by the Persians, but only under the Maccabees (Rudolph 1948; Fulton 2015; Finkelstein 2018). This town list demonstrates that sections were added to Ezra-Nehemiah in piece-meal fashion. The date of the translation into Greek provides a *terminus ante quem*.

The book Ezra-Nehemiah was completed when an author in the Maccabean period wrote the story of Ezra (Ezra 7–10) and the story of his reading the law (Neh. 8). This author added the penitential prayer (Neh. 9) and a pre-existing temple-association document (Neh. 10) to create a covenant-renewal ceremony (Fried 2005). He placed these three chapters (Neh. 8–10) after the verse noting the wall's completion (Neh. 6:15) but before the chapter detailing the wall's dedication (Neh. 12:27–43). He thus sandwiched the law-reading between the story of the wall's completion and its dedication. He then prefaced it all with the pre-existing story of the rebuilt and rededicated temple.

5.4 Ezra-Nehemiah vs. 1 Esdras

5.4.1 Which Was Written First: Ezra-Nehemiah or 1 Esdras?

Understanding the transmission history of 1 Esdras involves discerning whether its author knew the story of Nehemiah and decided not to include it, or whether he did not know it. Does the book of Nehemiah contain an expansion of 1 Esdr. 9:37–55 (the law-reading ceremony) or was the latter excerpted from Nehemiah 8? Ezra-Nehemiah (and 1 Esdras) contains a number of documents which are (at base) authentic. These include: the second temple's original building inscription (embedded within passages of Ezra 1–6; see Fried 2003b; 2010: 319–38; 2015: 18–32); the letter from Tattenai to Darius I inquiring about the temple building project in Jerusalem (Ezra 5:7b–17; 1 Esdr. 6:8–22; Fried 2015: 253–55) and Darius's response to it (Ezra 6:6–12; 1 Esdr. 6:24–34; see Fried 2015: 265–76); the letter from Rehum to Artaxerxes I and Artaxerxes's response regarding concerns over rebuilding Jerusalem's city wall (Ezra 4:11b–22; 1 Esdr. 2:17–29; see Fried 2012; 2015: 223–28); the letter from Artaxerxes II to Ezra appointing him as the "King's Eye or Ear" in Beyond-the-River (Ezra 7:12–26; 1 Esdr. 8:9–24; see Fried 2015: 311–34; 2017); the list of builders of Jerusalem's city wall (Nehemiah 3; see Fried forthcoming); and the second temple's Association Agreement, the 'Amānā (Neh. 10:1–39 [ET Neh. 9:38–10:39]; see Fried 2005: 75–93).

These documents made it possible for the biblical authors to construct their story about the return to Judah and rebuilding the temple. Although the order of events differs between Ezra-Nehemiah and 1 Esdras, the wording is so similar that it is clear that one is a revision of the other; they are not independent. The issue for exegetes is which came first: Ezra-Nehemiah or 1 Esdras? It must be concluded that Ezra-Nehemiah is earlier. To begin with, authentic documents common to both Ezra and 1 Esdras provide for the return to Jerusalem under Cyrus and Sheshbazzar and permission to begin temple-rebuilding at that time (see Ezra 1–4; 1 Esdr. 2:1–15). Ezra places the temple and altar rebuilding and their interruption in the time of Cyrus through Artaxerxes (Ezra 1–4), and the resumption of work on the temple in the second year of Darius. First Esdras, like Ezra, reports a beginning of work on the city walls and the temple in the time of Cyrus (1 Esdr. 2:1–15) as well as its stoppage in the reign of Cyrus (through Artaxerxes) until the second year of Darius (1 Esdr. 2:16–30). It then inserts a story of a competition among three bodyguards for Darius's favor (1 Esdr. 3:1–5:3), a second return to Judah under Darius (1 Esdr. 5:4–46), a second rebuilding at that time (1 Esdr. 5:47–65), and a second stoppage of the work under Darius (1 Esdr.

5:66–73). None of these latter are in Ezra-Nehemiah. According to Ezra-Nehemiah, this second stoppage lasted "as long as King Cyrus lived," not "as long as Darius lived" (1 Esdr. 5:73), which indicates that there was originally only one stoppage and that it occurred in the reign of Cyrus, not Darius. This admission reveals a dislocation and repetition of events due to the insertion of the story of the three bodyguards, and that the original textual sequence is closer to what we find preserved in Ezra-Nehemiah.

Schenker, however, has argued for the originality of 1 Esdras because (among other reasons) it reports that the people weep when they see the completed temple (1 Esdr. 5:60), whereas in Ezra 3:12 they weep when they see its foundations being built (Schenker 2011; see also Böhler 1997; 2003: 35–50; also Schenker 1991: 218–48). Schenker maintains that it is far more likely that people would be disappointed when they see the poverty of the finished temple than merely when they see only its small foundations. The weeping, however, belongs to a prescribed lamentation or *kalû* ritual that continues as long as temple foundations are being built, until the *maḥritu* brick, the brick taken from the old temple, is inserted into the walls of the new one (Thureau-Dangin 1921; Fried 2003b; 2015: 184–87). The lamentation ritual ends when this brick is inserted in the temple wall, which would have been before the walls were paneled and the building completed. It is likely that the author of 1 Esdras, writing in Egypt in the Ptolemaic period, did not understand this Babylonian lamentation ritual although it continued to be practiced in Babylon and evidently also in Judah into Seleucid times. He therefore assumed the temple was being mourned for its small size, rather than that a prescribed ritual was being portrayed. This too suggests that the text of Ezra is the original version, not 1 Esdras.

5.4.2 Did the Author of 1 Esdras Know the Story of Nehemiah?

The story of Ezra was likely written before that of 1 Esdras, but did the version of Ezra-Nehemiah that the author of 1 Esdras knew include the story of Nehemiah and did the author of 1 Esdras purposely omit it? The answer to this question must be yes: the author of 1 Esdras exhibits knowledge of Nehemiah in at least two ways. First, 1 Esdr. 5:40 includes the name of Nehemiah. Indeed, we may compare this verse with its parallels in Ezra 2:63, 2 Esdr. 2:63, and Neh. 7:65.

1 Esdras 5:40 and Parallels

1 Esdr. 5:40	And *Nehemiah and Attharias* [Greek *Neemias kai Attharias*] told them that they were not to share in the holy things until the high priest should arise wearing explanation and truth.
Ezra 2:63	And *Hattirshata'* said to them that they were not to eat from the most holy food, until a priest stands with Urim and Thummim.
2 Esdr. 2:63	And *Hatesatha* [Greek *Athersatha*] spoke to them so that they would not eat from the holy of holies until a priest should arise for the things that enlighten and the things that are flawless.
Neh. 7:65	And *Hattirshata'* said to them that they were not to eat of the most holy food, until a priest stands with Urim and Thummim.

Of these verses, only the author of 1 Esdr. 5:40 has associated Nehemiah with Hattirshata'; the association is not made in the parallel passages. How then does the author of 1 Esdras come to make this association? Where does he learn it? The association is explicit only in the book of Nehemiah, and indeed it is explicit in the heading of one of the primary documents upon which the book Ezra-Nehemiah is based: the 'Amānā (see Fried 2005).

> Because of all this we cut an 'Amānā and write it, and upon the seals are our commanders, our Levites, and our priests, and on the seals is Nehemiah Hattirshata' ben Hacaliah, and Zedekiah. (Neh. 10:1–2; ET 9:38–10:1)

If the name "Nehemiah Hattirshata' ben Hacaliah" is indeed original to what is likely an authentic document, then this must be the source of the association, and consequently the source of 1 Esdr. 5:40. The author of 1 Esdras either knew Nehemiah 10 as an independent document, or he knew the book of Nehemiah as it is presently constituted.

The association of Nehemiah with the name Hattirshata' also appears in Neh. 8:9, the scene in which Ezra reads the law to the assembled populace. Once again, a comparison of the versions is revealing.

The Law-Reading: Neh. 8:9 and Parallels

Neh. 8:9	And *Nehemiah, that is Hattirshata'*, *and Ezra* the priest and scribe, said...
2 Esdr. 18:9	And *Nehemiah and Ezra* [Greek *Neemias kai Esdras*] the priest and scribe said
1 Esdr. 9:49	And *Attharates* said to *Ezra*, the chief priest and reader

The association of Nehemiah and Hattirshata', present in Neh. 8:9, is absent in both 2 Esdras and in 1 Esdras, the former reading only Nehemiah and the latter reading only Attharates (the Greek form of Hattirshata'). It seems clear, however, that both 2 Esdr. 18:9 and 1 Esdr. 9:49 know either Neh. 8:9 or 10:2, or both, where the association is explicit. It is impossible to account for these variations otherwise. It may be that the author of 1 Esdras was familiar with the 'Amānā as a separate document, however, and did not know the book of Nehemiah as a whole. Thus he may have known that Nehemiah was also called Hattirshata', but nothing else. It should be pointed out that although most commentaries translate Hattirshata' as "the governor," that translation is no longer accepted. The word is no longer viewed as a title, but as the common Persian personal name "Happy through [the god] Attar" (Benveniste 1966: 120; Zadok 2012: 160–61; Tuplin 2013: 615, n. 3; Lemaire 2015: 104–105; Tavernier, personal communication, 2/8/2016).

This leads directly to, and is connected with, the second reason demonstrating that 1 Esdras knows the book of Nehemiah: the story of the law-reading. Indeed, both 1 Esdras and Ezra-Nehemiah contain the story of Ezra's reading the law to the assembled population (1 Esdr. 9:37–55; Neh. 8:1–12). The text-critical issue here is its original position. That is, did it originally appear as it does in 1 Esdras, immediately after the mass divorce? Or, did it originally follow the story of the wall building and moved by 1 Esdras secondarily when he excised the story of Nehemiah?

Beginning with Torrey (1970: 253–55), many scholars have argued that Nehemiah 8 originally appeared between Ezra 8 and Ezra 9, although this is not its position in 1 Esdras (see Rudolph 1949: 143; Clines 1984: 180–81; Williamson 1985: xxx; Blenkinsopp 1988: 44; Pakkala 2004; 2006: 17–24). Torrey complains that in Ezra-Nehemiah, Ezra arrives in the seventh year of Artaxerxes to teach and administer the law (Ezra 7:10, 14, 25), but he does not perform those tasks until thirteen years later, in Artaxerxes's twentieth year (Nehemiah 8). In Ezra 9, officials approach Ezra to inform him that the people have transgressed, implying that the law was already known to them, and so Ezra must have taught it. Yet, according to the present narrative in Ezra-Nehemiah, this teaching does not occur until more than a decade later. Hence Torrey thinks that Neh. 7:70–8:18, the story of the law-reading proper, must have originally appeared at the end of Ezra 8. When Nehemiah 8 is inserted after Ezra 8, Ezra arrives on the first day of the fifth month (Ezra 7:9) and reads the law on the first day of the seventh month (Neh. 8:2)—only two months later. The mass divorce then begins three months after that, on the first day of the tenth month (Ezra 10:16).

This is not the order of things found in 1 Esdras either, however: in that book the divorce also precedes the law-reading (1 Esdras 9). The order "divorce → law-reading" suggests that there is nothing in the torah that provides a blanket prohibition of intermarriage; therefore, the law-reading could not and did not motivate the officials' complaint. One can read the entire torah and never conclude that all foreign marriages are prohibited. Furthermore, neither the officials who approach Ezra nor Ezra himself in his prayer refer to a written law code. Ezra's prayer to God refers to Judeans' having "abandoned your (i.e., Yhwh's) commandments that you (Yhwh) commanded *by the hand of your servants the prophets*" (Ezra 9:10–11; 1 Esdr. 8:82; emphasis added). This is a reference to an oral tradition, not to a written law code, and especially not to a law code that had just been read. In fact, there is no evidence that the authors of Ezra 7–10 or 1 Esdr. 1–9:36 knew anything of a written code of law.

To be sure, a written law code is what is read in Neh. 8 and in 1 Esdr. 9:37–55, but in neither case is the reading motivated; in both accounts it seems to stem from a spontaneous gathering in Jerusalem in the seventh month. Originally, however, the law-reading likely followed the dedication of the wall (now in Neh. 12:27–43). The people have all gathered in Jerusalem for the wall's dedication ceremony. During it, they see Ezra carrying the torah and they watch him carry it into the temple precincts through the Water Gate. Thus, they assemble in front of that same gate and ask him to come out and read it to them, which he does (Neh. 8).

That the author of the first-person account in Nehemiah did not write the story of the law-reading is clear, however, from the way the dates are cited. In the first-person account (Neh. 1:1; 2:1; and 6:15), the months are cited by name (Kislev, Nisan, Elul), but in Neh. 8, in the law-reading, the month is cited only by ordinal number: it is "the seventh month." This is the way months are cited in the story of Ezra and in 1 Esdras (Ezra 7:8, 9 = 1 Esdr. 8:6; Ezra 8:31 = 1 Esdr. 8:61; Ezra 10:9 = 1 Esdr. 9:5; Ezra 10:16, 17 = 1 Esdr. 9:16, 17). The story of Ezra's reading the law is a late insertion into the story of Nehemiah, likely by the author of Ezra 7:1–10, the author who states that Ezra came to "teach the statutes and ordinances in Israel."

Yet the story of the law-reading was not written by the author of Ezra 7:27–10:44 either. This is shown by the choice of the Hebrew root *'āsap*, "to assemble" (see J. L. Wright 2004: 327). The word used for "assembled" in Neh. 8:1 is based on this root and is used twice more in the same pericope (Neh. 8:13, 9:1). It appears only once in all of Ezra 7–10 (at 9:4), and this is in the prayer, also a later insertion. The word used most commonly in Ezra 7–8 and 10 for gathering or assembling is based on the Hebrew root *qābaṣ*, and it is used five times in this section (Ezra 7:28, 8:15, 10:1, 7, 9). It seems unlikely that the author of the original story in Ezra 7:28–10:44, who uses *qābaṣ* quite consistently would employ *'āsap* in the story of the law-reading in Nehemiah 8 and the prayer in Ezra 9—and in these texts alone. The author of Ezra 7:25–10:44 cannot be the author of Nehemiah 8, therefore (so also Rendtorff 1984: 165–84; 1999: 89–91; VanderKam 1992). The story of the law-reading must have been written by the author of Ezra 7:1–10. Ezra comes to Jerusalem to teach the torah in Israel (Ezra 7:10), and then in Nehemiah, after the people have gathered for the wall's dedication, he is shown doing just that. Consequently, the author of 1 Esdras must have lifted the story of the law-reading from its original location in Nehemiah and added it to his text to make a fitting conclusion to his book which begins with Josiah's celebrating the Passover (1 Esdras 1). He purposely omitted the rest of Nehemiah's story.

5.5 Implications of the Text-Critical Results for Interpreting the History of the Early Persian Period in Judah

Text-critical evaluation of the documents embedded in the text of Ezra-Nehemiah (see above) allow us to confirm their authenticity and so to understand better the history of Judah and the Judeans under the Persians. The second temple's building inscription which is at the base of Ezra 1–6 confirms an exile and a return to Judah and Jerusalem from Babylon in 538 BCE, the first year of Cyrus as king of Babylon. It also confirms that temple-building was begun at that time. The authentic letter from Tattenai, the vice-satrap of Beyond-the-River, to Darius in the second year of that king (Ezra 5:6–17; Fried 2015: 253–55), along with the king's response (Ezra 6:1–5; Fried 2015: 263–64), indicate that Tattenai inspected the temple in Darius's second year (520 BCE), receiving confirmation at that time that construction of the temple could continue; the letter also confirms that the temple was completed in Adar of Darius's sixth year (516 BCE) (Fried 2003b; 2010).

The letter from Rehum, vice-satrap of Beyond-the-River, to Artaxerxes I (Ezra 4:11–16) indicates concern about a city wall being built around Jerusalem in the reign of that king. Thus, it is Nehemiah's wall to which an objection is being raised. It is not likely that progress on the wall was actually stopped, however, since rather than reporting a stoppage, Nehemiah states that the wall was completed in only fifty-two days (Neh. 6:15). Archaeologists disagree about whether Jerusalem's city wall was actually repaired in the fifth century. They have found remnants of the original eighth-century city wall, but it is impossible to know if the stones that they have found had been from an eighth-century wall that was destroyed in the sixth century and subsequently repaired in the fifth or if it had never been repaired at all.

Finally, the letter from Artaxerxes II to Ezra indicates that a person by that name was appointed as the "King's Eye" in the satrapy Beyond-the-River. Text-critical evaluation allows us to confirm that he brought release from taxes and corvée labor to the priesthood of the Jerusalem temple (Fried 2017; 2015: 311–34). Text-critical evaluation allows us to recognize that this Ezra never instituted a law code, nor a mass divorce, nor did he ever read the torah to the assembled populace (Fried 2014: 8–27). Text-critical evaluation allows us to confirm that the historical Ezra was a high-ranking Persian official. Nevertheless, the story of his bringing the torah from Babylon to Judah and reading it to the assembled population is a fabrication conceived by an anonymous author during the Maccabean period. Further work must explore the question of why obedience to a written law code was so important under the Maccabees, and to whom it would have been important.

Bibliography

Askin, Lindsey. In Press. "Beyond Encomium or Eulogy: The Role of Simon the High Priest in Ben Sira." *Journal of Ancient Judaism*.

Balzaretti, Claudio. 2013. *The Syriac Version of Ezra-Nehemiah: Manuscripts and Editions, Translation Technique and Its Use in Textual Criticism*. Translated by Michael Tait. Rome: Pontifical Biblical Institute.

Batten, Loring W. 1913. *A Critical and Exegetical Commentary on the Books of Ezra and Nehemiah*. ICC. Edinburgh: T&T Clark.

Becking, Bob. 1998. "Ezra's Re-enactment of the Exile." In Lester L. Grabbe, ed., *Leading Captivity Captive: "The Exile" as History and Ideology*, 40–61. JSOTSup 278. Sheffield: Sheffield Academic Press.

Benveniste, Émile. 1966. *Titres et Noms Propres en Iranien Ancien*. Paris: C. Klincksieck.

Blenkinsopp, Joseph. 1988. *Ezra-Nehemiah: A Commentary*. OTL. Philadelphia: Westminster Press.

Böhler, Dieter. 1997. *Die Heilige Stadt in Esdras a und Esra-Nehemia: Zwei Konzeptionen der Wiederherstellung Israel*. OBO 158. Göttingen: Vandenhoeck & Ruprecht.

Böhler, Dieter. 2003. "On the Relationship between Textual and Literary Criticism: The Two Recensions of the Book of Ezra: Ezra-Neh (MT) and 1 Esdras (LXX)." In Adrian Schenker ed., *The Earliest Text of the Hebrew Bible: The Relationship Between the Masoretic Text and the Hebrew Base of the Septuagint Reconsidered*, 35–50. SCS 52. Atlanta: SBL.

Clines, David J. A. 1984. *Ezra, Nehemiah, Esther*. NCB Commentary. Grand Rapids: Eerdmans, 1984.

Curtis, Edward Lewis and Albert Alonzo Madsen. 1910. *A Critical and Exegetical Commentary on the Books of Chronicles*. ICC. Edinburgh: T&T Clark.

Driver, Samuel R. 1913. *An Introduction to the Literature of the Old Testament*. Edinburgh: T&T Clark.

Eskenazi, Tamara Cohn. 1988. *In an Age of Prose: A Literary Approach to Ezra-Nehemiah*. Atlanta: Scholars Press.

Finkelstein, Israel. 2018. *Hasmonean Realities behind Ezra, Nehemiah, and Chronicles*. AIL 34. Atlanta: SBL.

Freedman, David Noel. 1961. "The Chronicler's Purpose." *CBQ* 23: 436–42.

Fried, Lisbeth S. 2003a. "A Silver Coin of Yohanan Hakkôhen." *Transeuphratène* 26: 65–85 and Pls. II–V.

Fried, Lisbeth S. 2003b. "The Land Lay Desolate: Conquest and Restoration in the Ancient Near East." In Oded Lipschits and Joseph Blenkinsopp, eds., *Judah and the Judeans in the Neo-Babylonian Period*. Winona Lake, IN: Eisenbrauns, 21–54.

Fried, Lisbeth S. 2005. "A Greek Religious Association in Second Temple Judah? A Comment on Nehemiah 10." *Transeuphratène* 30: 75–93.

Fried, Lisbeth S. 2008. "Who Wrote Ezra-Nehemiah—and Why Did They?" In Mark J. Boda and Paul L. Redditt, eds., *Unity and Disunity in Ezra-Nehemiah: Redaction, Rhetoric, and Reader*. HBM 17. Sheffield: Phoenix, 75–97.

Fried, Lisbeth S. 2010. "Temple Building in Ezra-Nehemiah." In Mark J. Boda and J. R. Novotny, eds., *From the Foundations to the Crenellations: Essays on Temple Building in the Ancient Near East and Hebrew Bible*. AOAT 366. Münster: Ugarit-Verlag, 319–38.

Fried, Lisbeth S. 2012. "The Artaxerxes Correspondence of Ezra 4, Nehemiah's Wall, and Persian Provincial Administration." In A. M. Maeir, Jodi Magness, and Lawrence H. Schiffman, eds., *"Go Out and Study the Land" (Judges 18:2): Archaeological, Historical and Textual Studies in Honor of Hanan Eshel*, 35–58. JSJSup 148. Leiden: Brill.

Fried, Lisbeth S. 2014. *Ezra and the Law in History and Tradition*. Studies on Personalities of the Old Testament. Columbia, SC: University of South Carolina Press.

Fried, Lisbeth S. 2015. *Ezra: A Commentary*. Sheffield Phoenix Critical Commentary Series. Sheffield: Sheffield Phoenix Press.

Fried, Lisbeth S. 2017. "Artaxerxes' Letter and the Mission of Ezra—*noch einmal*." In Robert M. Kerr, Robert Miller II, and Philip C. Schmitz, eds., *"His Words Soar above Him": Biblical and Northwest Semitic Studies Presented to Charles R. Krahmalkov*, 31–44. Ann Arbor, MI.

Fried, Lisbeth S. forthcoming. *Nehemiah: A New Translation with Introduction and Commentary*. Sheffield: Sheffield Phoenix.

Fulton, Deirdre N. 2015. *Reconsidering Nehemiah's Judah*. FAT S2 80. Tübingen: Mohr Siebeck.

Gasquet, Francis A. 1987. *Ezrae, Tobiae, Iudith*. Biblia sacra iuxta Latinam Vulgatam versionem ad codicum fidem 8. Rome: Libreria Editrice Vaticana.

Gunneweg, A. H. J. 1985. *Esra*. Kommentar zum alten Testament. Gütersloh: Gütersloher Verlagshaus Mohn.

Hanhart, Robert. 1974. *Esdrae Liber I*. Septuaginta 8/1. Göttingen: Vandenhoeck & Ruprecht.

Hanhart, Robert. 1993. *Esdrae Liber II*. Septuaginta 8/2. Göttingen: Vandenhoeck & Ruprecht.

Haran, Menahem. 1986. "Explaining the Identical Lines at the End of Chronicles and the Beginning of Ezra." *BR* 2.3: 18–20.

Harvey Jr., P. B. 2011. "Darius' Court and the Guardsmen's Debate: Hellenistic Greek Elements in 1 Esdras." In Lisbeth S. Fried, ed., *Was 1 Esdras First? An Investigation into the Nature and Priority of First Esdras*. Ancient Israel and Its Literature 7. Atlanta: SBL, 179–90.

Holmgren, Fredrick C. 1987. *Israel Alive Again: A Commentary on the Books of Ezra and Nehemiah*. Grand Rapids: Eerdmans.

Japhet, Sara. 1968. "The Supposed Common Authorship of Chronicles and Ezra-Nehemiah Investigated Anew." *VT* 18: 330–71.

Kraemer, D. 1993. "On the Relationship of the Books of Ezra and Nehemiah." *JSOT* 59: 73–92.

Lemaire, André. 2015. "Atarshamain." In Eric Orlin, Lisbeth S. Fried, Jennifer W. Knust, Michael L. Satlow, and Michael E. Pregil, eds. *The Routledge Encyclopedia of Ancient Mediterranean Religions*. New York: Routledge, 104–105.

Marcus, David. 2006. *Ezra and Nehemiah*. BHQ 20. Eds. Adrian Schenker et al. Stuttgart: Deutsche Bibelgesellschaft.

Min, Kyung-Jin. 2004. *The Levitical Authorship of Ezra-Nehemiah*. JSOTSup 409. London: T&T Clark.

Pakkala, Juha. 2004. *Ezra the Scribe: The Development of Ezra 7–10 and Nehemiah 8*. BZAW 347. Berlin: de Gruyter.

Pakkala, Juha. 2006. "The Original Independence of the Ezra Story in Ezra 7–10 and Nehemiah 8." *BN* 129: 17–24.

Piwowar, Andrzej. 2011. "Dlaczego Syrach Pominal Ezdrasza w Pochwale Ojców (Syr 44–50)?" *The Biblical Annals* 1: 105–31.

Rendtorff, Rolf. 1984. "Esra und das 'Gesetz.'" *ZAW* 96: 165–84.

Rendtorff, Rolf. 1984. 1999. "Noch Einmal: Esra und das 'Gesetz.'" *ZAW* 111: 89–91.

Rothenbusch, Ralf. 2012. *"...Abgesondert zur Tora Gottes hin": Ethnisch-Religiöse Identitäten im Esra/Nehemiabuch*. HBS 70. Freiburg: Herder.

Rudolph, Wilhelm. 1949. *Esra und Nehemia Samt 3. Esra*. Tübingen: Mohr.

Schenker, Adrian. 1991. "La Relation d'Esdras A' au Texte Massorétique d'Esdras-Néhémie." In G. J. Norton and S. Pisano, eds., *Tradition of the Text: Studies Offered to Dominique Barthélemy in Celebration of His 70th Birthday*. OBO 109. Freiburg: Universitätsverlag and Göttingen: Vandenhoeck & Ruprecht, 218–48.

Schenker, Adrian. 2011. "The Relationship between Ezra-Nehemiah and 1 Esdras." In Lisbeth S. Fried, ed., *Was 1 Esdras First? An Investigation into the Nature and Priority of First Esdras*, 45–58. Ancient Israel and Its Literature 7. Atlanta: SBL.

Talshir, David. 1988. "A Reinvestigation of the Linguistic Relationship between Chronicles and Ezra-Nehemiah." *VT* 38: 165–93.

Talshir, Zipora. 1986. "The Chronicler and the Composition of 1 Esdras." *CBQ* 48: 39–61.

Talshir, Zipora. 1999. *1 Esdras: From Origin to Translation*. Atlanta: SBL.

Talshir, Zipora. 2001. *1 Esdras: A Text Critical Commentary*. Atlanta: SBL.

Talshir, Zipora. 2013. "Fragments of the Book of Ezra at Qumran." *Megillot* 1: 213–18.

Thureau-Dangin, F. 1921. *Rituels Accadiens*. Paris: Leroux.

Torrey, C. C. 1970. *Ezra Studies*. Repr. ed. New York: Ktav.

Torrey, C. C. 1986. *The Composition and Historical Value of Ezra-Nehemiah*. BZAW 2. Giessen: J. Ricker.

Tuplin, Christopher. 2013. "Serving the Satrap: Lower Rank Officials Viewed through Greek and Aramaic Sources." In Bruno Jacobs, Matthew Stolper, and Wouter F. M. Henkelman, eds. *Die Verwaltung Im Achämenidenreich/Administration in the Achaemenid Empire*. Classica et Orientalia 17. Wiesbaden: Harrassowitz Verlag, 613–76.

Ulrich, Eugene. 1992. "4QEzra–4Q117." In Eugene Ulrich et al., eds. *Qumran Cave 4.XI: Psalms to Chronicles*. DJD 16. Oxford: Clarendon, 291–93.

VanderKam, James C. 1992. "Ezra-Nehemiah or Ezra and Nehemiah?" In E. Ulrich, J. W. Wright, R. P. Carroll, and P. R. Davies, eds., *Priests, Prophets and Scribes: Essays on the Formation and Heritage of Second Temple Judaism in Honour of Joseph Blenkinsopp*. JSOTSup 149. Sheffield: Sheffield Academic Press, 55–75.

VanderKam, James C. 2004. *From Joshua to Caiaphas: High Priests after the Exile*. Minneapolis: Fortress Press.

Williamson, Hugh G. M. 1977. *Israel in the Books of Chronicles*. Cambridge: Cambridge University Press.

Williamson, Hugh G. M. 1983. "The Composition of Ezra i–vi." *JTS* 34: 1–30.

Williamson, Hugh G. M. 1985. *Ezra, Nehemiah*. WBC 16. Waco, TX: Word.

Wright, Jacob L. 2004. *Rebuilding Identity: The Nehemiah-Memoir and Its Earliest Readers*. BZAW 348. Berlin: de Gruyter.

Zadok, Ran. 2012. "Some Issues in Ezra-Nehemiah." In Isaac Kalimi, ed. *New Perspectives on Ezra-Nehemiah: History and Historiography, Text, Literature and Interpretation*. Winona Lake, IN: Eisenbrauns, 151–81.

Zunz, Leopold. 1832. "Dibre Hajamim oder die Bücher der Chronik." In *Die Gottesdienstliche Vorträge der Juden: Historisch Entwickelt*. Frankfort: J. Kaufmann, 13–36.

CHAPTER 6

EARLY ISRAEL'S ORIGINS, SETTLEMENT, AND ETHNOGENESIS

ANN E. KILLEBREW

IN the Hebrew Bible, God's covenant and promise of the Land of Canaan as Abraham's and his descendants' eternal inheritance mark the emergence of the people of Israel (Gen. 17:7–8). But before Abraham's progeny can take possession of the promised land, they embark on a detour to Egypt as recounted in Genesis 37–50. Abraham's grandson Jacob (whom God renames "Israel," Gen. 32:28) witnesses his favorite son Joseph's sale into slavery, orchestrated by jealous brothers. The saga, which continues with Joseph's subsequent rise to a position of power and the migration of Joseph's brothers to Egypt during a time of famine, serves as a literary bridge to one of the central themes of Israel's emergence—their ensuing enslavement in Egypt and escape to freedom as described in the book of Exodus. The books of Joshua and Judges continue to tell the story of how the twelve tribes, or "sons" of Israel, after four decades of desert wanderings, conquer the Land of Canaan and settle there. For millennia, this story was taken for granted as a reliable account of the genesis of Israel as a people in its land. However, with the advent of eighteenth- and nineteenth-century post-Enlightenment methods of text criticism and the discovery of contemporary ancient Near Eastern texts and cultures, the historical reliability of the biblical text came into question. Aided by an ever-growing body of archaeological evidence, our understanding of early Israel has been transformed during the past century. This essay will review the theories of Israel's emergence that have been advanced by critical scholarship, beginning with a critique of the two schools of thought developed during the first half of the twentieth century that use the Exodus story and the books of Joshua and Judges as their starting point. Subsequently, two additional models, utilizing sociological, anthropological, and archaeological approaches, attempted to write a secular history of early Israel largely independent of the biblical account. The essay concludes with recent efforts to reconcile the biblical, extrabiblical textual, and archaeological primary sources, considered together with contemporary sociological and anthropological models to reconstruct Israel's ethnogenesis.

6.1 PRELUDE TO ISRAEL'S EMERGENCE: OUT OF EGYPT

Any attempt to reconstruct the emergence of early Israel must begin with the exodus story. As recounted in the books of Exodus, Leviticus, Numbers, and Deuteronomy, the genesis of Israel entailed enslavement, followed by a miraculous mass exodus from Egypt under the leadership of Moses, a forty-year sojourn in the desert, and the eventual arrival to the promised land, Canaan. In the Torah, the exodus from Egypt and the desert experience were crucial and transformative experiences that led to a unifying ideology centered on the worship of Yhwh and the creation of an Israelite identity. Efforts to reconstruct the history of Israel beginning with this foundation story, or origin myth, and the supernatural events associated with the escape from Egypt have proven to be one of the most challenging scholarly endeavors concerning Israel's past (see the edited volume by Levy, Schneider, and Propp 2015 for an extensive treatment of the exodus from a variety of perspectives).

The lack of any direct reference to Israel's enslavement or escape in New Kingdom Egyptian sources raises questions regarding the historicity of the biblical account (Redford 1987; 1992: 408–22; Redmount 2001 and bibliography there; but see Hoffmeier [1997; 2015] who presents evidence supporting a New Kingdom Egypt background for the exodus). Suggestions for dating the exodus story, based on internal biblical chronology (e.g., 1 Kgs. 6:1) or coinciding with New Kingdom Egypt's imperial control over Canaan,[1] range from the sixteenth through thirteenth centuries BCE. However, pinpointing a moment in time for the exodus remains inconclusive due to inconsistencies between the biblical account and the contemporary textual and archaeological evidence (see, e.g., Dever 2003: 7–18; Geraty 2015 for summaries and additional bibliography). These incongruities have led others to advocate a first-millennium BCE date for the saga's composition, long after the timeline presented in the Hebrew Bible (see, e.g., Grabbe 2014), with some suggesting that it represents a literary work devoid of historical value (Lemche 1998: 44–61).

Although there is no direct evidence to support the Bible's contention that the descendants of the sons of Israel were among those enslaved in Egypt, foreign slavery is well known in New Kingdom texts and reliefs, corresponding to a period when Late Bronze Age Canaan was under Egyptian imperial domination (see Killebrew 2005: 51–92 and Morris 2005 for an overview of New Kingdom Egyptian imperialism and its impact on Canaan). Prisoners of war captured during frequent Egyptian military campaigns to the Levant were a particularly rich source of Canaanite slaves. Already in the fifteenth century BCE, Thutmose III boasts of transporting large numbers of human booty, including men, women, and children, to Egypt in his annals inscribed on the walls of the Temple of Amun at Karnak. Campaigns to Canaan and the forced migration of captives increased in frequency during the Nineteenth and Twentieth Dynasties. Later Ramesside-period texts reflect the growing economic dependency on slave labor in the public and private domain. Most toiled on agricultural, industrial, domestic, and public works projects in Egypt, especially as part of temple endowments, or as coerced labor providing support for New Kingdom imperialistic endeavors in Canaan. However, a few ascended to positions of authority, serving as priests or high-ranking administrative officials. While attempted escapes must have been common, only one specific account of runaway slaves is preserved. Papyrus Anastasi V, attributed to the late Nineteenth Dynasty (ca. 1200 BCE), describes an unsuccessful attempt to capture two fleeing slaves. Following the decline of the New Kingdom empire and its withdrawal from Egyptian-administered lands during the twelfth century BCE, the practice of foreign enslavement is rare (for a summary of slavery in pharaonic Egypt, see Loprieno 1997; 2012; see also Redford 1992: 221–27; Hendel 2001: 604–8; 2015; Redmount 2001: 72–76; Na'aman 2005, 2011; Killebrew 2017 regarding slavery in the context of the biblical exodus).

In view of the silence of the Egyptian texts and the lack of archaeological evidence of a mass escape of slaves from Egypt, it is not surprising that attempts to prove the historicity of the exodus story have floundered. While the primary theme of the exodus story—bondage in Egypt and escape to freedom—could only have been possible during the Nineteenth and Twentieth Dynasties when domination and enslavement of Canaan's population reached its peak, other aspects of this saga and subsequent sojourn in the desert do not appear to reflect one historical context but rather a layering of numerous historical events spanning centuries.[2]

Approaches that consider the role of cultural memory or mnemohistory with forced migration and refugee studies have been especially effective in understanding the formation of the exodus saga, so central to the theme of Israel's emergence, as representing numerous "exoduses" of runaway Semitic slaves that over time coalesced into a single event. In narratives of modern forced migrations and displacement, personal memories that incorporate ideology, religion, and myth merge to create a powerful collective identity and memory of a homeland and quest to return (see most recently Hendel 2015; Killebrew 2017). A collective memory of dramatic escapes from slavery must have especially resonated in Canaan and other regions that suffered under New Kingdom domination, especially during the thirteenth and early twelfth centuries BCE. It represents the merging of many experiences of displacement, slavery, and escape—a common feature of forced migration accounts—into a shared narrative that served as the national epic for ancient Israel. Regardless of the circumstances of the Torah's composition and the historical value of events described in the first five books of the Hebrew Bible, the exodus story of escape from slavery and arrival to the promised land is the single most important unifying theme in Israel's past. It remains until today a powerful symbol of freedom's triumph over oppression.

6.2 The Biblical Account of the Emergence of Israel in Joshua and Judges: Conquest and Settlement

The Israelites' forty-year journey through the Sinai wilderness and Transjordan culminates in the final chapter of the Torah (Deut. 34) with the promised land in sight and Moses's death at Mount Nebo. The Israelites, united under the leadership of Joshua, are now poised to enter Canaan. The books of Joshua and Judges narrate their conquest and settlement of their inheritance. Joshua and Judges are part of the "Former Prophets," the second division of the books of the Hebrew Bible, which present a prophetical history of God's interactions with the people of Israel, beginning with Joshua's conquest through the Babylonian exile. The book of Joshua comprises two sections. The first twelve chapters deal with the conquest of Canaan and annihilation of its inhabitants by a second generation of Israelites born to those who escaped Egypt. This section commences with the miraculous crossing of the Jordan River, followed by entry into the land (Josh. 1–5), and a blitzkrieg conquest of Canaan. Beginning with Jericho (Josh. 6), Joshua and the people conduct three lightning campaigns through the center of the land (Ai, Bethel, construction of an altar on Mount Ebal: Josh. 7–9), to the south (Gibeon, Libnah, Lachish, Hebron, Debir, Makkedah, and Eglon: Josh. 10), and lastly the north, culminating in the conflagration of Hazor (Josh. 11), the "head of all those kingdoms" (Josh. 11:10). The biblical book's second half deals with apportionments. It describes the land's territorial division among the tribes (Josh. 13–21), concluding with the renewal of the covenant, Joshua's death at the age of 110, and his burial in the land of "his inheritance" (Josh. 22–24).

However, in the following book of Judges, it is clear already in the first chapter that Israelite control of Canaan is far from complete. In contrast to the portrayal of Joshua's conquest of Canaan as linear and invincible, Judges presents the settlement of the land by a politically decentralized tribal confederation that is fragmented, poorly equipped, and often at odds with one another. Instead of a well-organized united military campaign, the actions of the Israelite tribes resemble guerilla warfare in their efforts to complete the conquest and consolidate control of the land. Throughout Judges, Israel continues a cycle of disobedience to God, oppression, repentance, and delivery from oppression by a judge.

Since the nineteenth century, many biblical scholars have considered the books of Joshua and Judges part of the Deuteronomist History (DH). According to this view, the books of Joshua through 2 Kings were composed with reference to the book of Deuteronomy. These books, including Deuteronomy, formed what became known as the DH. In the mid-twentieth century, M. Noth (1991) developed the theory further. He proposed that the books associated with the DH were redacted by an individual during the exilic period, whom he referred to as the "Deuteronomist" (Dtr), and thus were composed following the Babylonian destruction of Jerusalem. More recent scholarship has moved away from Noth's single-author theory, pointing out the diversity of styles that suggests two or more redactions of the DH with multiple stages of composition, which likely span the reign of Hezekiah through the postexilic period. Others challenge the notion of a DH altogether and propose to examine the redaction history of each book individually (see Knoppers and Greer 2010 for an overview and extensive bibliography). What is clear even to the cursory reader is that these books reflect an editorial splicing of a variety of narrative materials.

6.2.1 Book of Joshua and the Conquest of the Land

As aptly characterized by J. G. McConville and S. N. Williams, the crossing of the Jordan River by Joshua and the Israelites is a "threshold, marking the passage of a people without a land to a people with a land" (2010: 1) who thereby fulfill God's promise to Abraham. From the biblical perspective, the conquest of Canaan is a logical act when considered in the context of Israel's cultural conflict with the Canaanites over the promised land, as presaged in Gen. 13:7 and Deut. 20:16, 18. Although the literary style of Joshua is historiography, the stories and geographical lists serve both nationalistic and theological purposes with a central theme of faithfulness to Yhwh. Thus, attempts to identify diachronic patterns and assign historical contexts to the literary layers of the Joshua story have proven difficult (see, e.g., Nelson 1997: 1–24; McConville and Williams 2010: 1–12). Some, including J. Van Seters (1990) and N. Na'aman (1994), discern similarities with Neo-Assyrian campaign reports that they propose served as models for the Joshua conquest narrative. Others, such as R. Alter (2013: 5–6), propose that the Joshua story is a cultural, rather than an historical, memory presenting a national myth of a chosen "people that dwells apart" (Num. 23:9). In this approach, Joshua's military successes should be understood as signaling Yhwh's intervention in history, rather than actual identifiable events, illustrating the deuteronomistic view of historical causation that Israel conquers and prevails when it is loyal to God. The three miraculous victories at Jericho (Josh. 6), Ai (Josh. 7–8), and Gibeon (Josh. 9–10) demonstrate that God will intercede in history as a divine warrior to support Israel. On the other hand, analyses of the rhetorical structuring of the conquest account (Younger 2008) and the role of sites such as Gilgal, Shechem, and Shiloh, which were not significant places during the late monarchy or exilic periods (McConville 2001: 159), suggest that the book of Joshua may preserve some real memories of Israel's early days in Canaan.

6.2.2 Unified Conquest Model

Attempts to identify Joshua's conquest in the archaeological record have been equally challenging, although early archaeologists invoked the archaeological record in support of the biblical narrative. Based on his dating of Israel's conquest of Canaan to the end of the Late Bronze Age, W. F. Albright (1935, 1939) attributed late thirteenth-century BCE destruction layers at sites such as Tell Beit Mirsim (erroneously identified as Debir), Beitin (biblical Bethel), and Lachish to Joshua's actions. Joined by G. E. Wright and J. Bright, and later by Y. Yadin (1982), who pointed to a thirteenth-century destruction layer at his excavations at Hazor, this view came to be known as the "unified military conquest" model. It considered the account in the book of Joshua as an historically accurate portrayal of Israel's arrival in Canaan.

Hazor's mid-thirteenth-century massive conflagration provides the most convincing archaeological evidence in support of the historicity of the book of Joshua. Though it is unclear who is responsible for the destruction of Hazor, both Y. Yadin and his successor as excavator of Hazor, A. Ben-Tor (2013), attribute Hazor's demise to conquest by the Israelites.[3] However, with the notable exceptions of Hazor and the discovery of an Iron I (twelfth–eleventh century BCE) altar on Mount Ebal (Zertal 1986–87), the unified conquest theory finds little historical or archaeological support. Excavations reveal that many places mentioned in the Joshua account, including Ai and Jericho, the site of the most famous battle, were unoccupied (and thus could not have been conquered) during the thirteenth century, casting doubt on the entire conquest story (see, e.g., Dever 2003: 54–71 for a summary).[4] Both these external discrepancies between the conquest account and the archaeological evidence as well as the internal biblical contradictions likely reflect the passage of time between Israel's proto-historical period and the actual composition of the texts (see, e.g., Na'aman 1994: 222–27 for a detailed discussion). Although a few elements of the conquest narrative suggest an authentic historical component, consensus exists that, whatever its sources (either oral and/or written), the conquest account as narrated is historically problematic and should be treated with caution.

6.2.3 Book of Judges: Settlement of the Land

The following book, Judges, offers an alternative account of early Israel's history and the settlement of the tribes. It depicts Israelite rural settlement in the hill country of Canaan as gradual and fraught with difficulties. Contrary to the claim in Josh. 11:16–23 that Canaan had been conquered and the land allocated to the twelve tribes, already in the opening line of the book of Judges it is apparent that the Canaanites and Philistines occupying the lowlands were still groups to be reckoned with. The "judges" were charismatic individuals who led Israel during this transitional period that chronologically links the conquest and the rise of the monarchy. These judges are presented as warrior chiefs, epic heroes, champions, or social bandits who rescue the people of Israel from apostasy and military defeat. They are often anointed by divine blessing and are responsible for both the administration of justice and governing. Of the thirteen leaders mentioned in the book of Judges, six are featured: Ehud (Judg. 3), Deborah (Judg. 4–5), Gideon (Judg. 6–8), Abimelech (Judg. 9, a non-judge), Jephthah (Judg. 11–12), and Samson (Judg. 13–16). The book of Judges culminates with two additional stories that portray a period of chaos, conflict, and anarchy: the migration of Dan to the north (Judg. 17–18) and the rape and murder perpetrated by the men of Gibeah with the resulting punishment (Judg. 19–21; see, e.g., Hackett 2001; Matthews 2004: 3–36; and Niditch 2008: 1–13 for detailed commentaries on the book of Judges and additional bibliography).

Scholars traditionally have given more historical credence to the Judges account, in part because critical analyses of the book point to early source materials, some of which are believed to date to the pre-monarchical period. The Song of Deborah (Judg. 5), dated by many to the twelfth–eleventh century BCE, is considered among the earliest texts in the Hebrew Bible and has been characterized as a self-portrait of pre-monarchic Israel (see, e.g., Echols 2008: 44–63). What both Joshua and Judges share is the insistence that the Israelites were outsiders, a non-indigenous group that was distinct from the Canaanites. This idea was fully adopted by scholars who championed the conquest theory but also by others who formulated a peaceful infiltration model to explain Israel's emergence.

6.2.4 Peaceful Infiltration Model

Albrecht Alt (1967), a leading German Protestant theologian during the period between the two world wars, first proposed the peaceful infiltration model. In contrast to a united military conquest, this theory combines the biblical account in Judges with toponymy, second-millennium Near Eastern texts, ethnographic analogy to the Bedouin seminomadic lifestyle, and archaeological discoveries, an approach that Alt hoped would move beyond the limits of literary criticism to reconstruct the early history of Israel. Martin Noth, Alt's student, and later Y. Aharoni, M. Kochavi, A. Zertal, A. Rainey, and others developed the theory further. In this scenario, nonindigenous seminomads originating in the desert regions wintered in the Transjordanian desert and summered in the highlands outside the control of Egypt, in areas not populated by permanent settlements. In the process, they developed symbiotic relations with the inhabitants of Late Bronze Age villages and cities. Eventually, they began to settle down, building villages in the sparsely populated hill country and gradually expanding into the more fertile regions, which occasionally resulted in violent confrontations with the lowland peoples. Archaeological surveys in the central hill country that documented the dramatic increase in small rural settlements during the twelfth and eleventh centuries BCE provide some of the strongest support for this model (see Finkelstein 1988: 302–6 and Dever 2017: 194–210 for discussion and bibliography).

It has been tempting to identify these pastoralists with various groups mentioned in Near Eastern texts. Albrecht Alt and others argued that the early Hebrews belonged to the ethnically defined ʿapiru of Near Eastern texts, though today this term is considered to refer to a social class rather than an ethnic entity (see Killebrew 2014 for a detailed discussion and bibliography). Manfred Weippert and A. Rainey dispute the association with the ʿapiru, rather identifying the pastoralists with the *shasu* mentioned in Egyptian texts (see Rainey 1995 for a detailed discussion). According to this view, overpopulation and dwindling economic resources forced them to settle in permanent villages in the highland regions and Transjordan. Archaeologically, the close cultural contacts between the region of the central hill country in Cisjordan and regions in Transjordan (especially the territory of Reuben in Moab) may reflect the biblical traditions that indicate the close connection of several Israelite tribes in western Palestine with those on the eastern side of the Jordan River (see Herr 1998 for a discussion and bibliography).

6.3 Extra-Biblical Textual Sources: The Egyptian Evidence

Although the Bible served as the starting point for both the conquest and peaceful infiltration models that adopted the biblical perspective of the Israelites as outsiders, the earliest and most significant textual evidence relevant to Israel's emergence appears on the late thirteenth-century BCE victory stela of Merneptah (ca. 1213–1203 BCE), a Nineteenth Dynasty Pharaoh and the thirteenth son of Ramesses II. The Merneptah Stela (or "Israel Stela") reveals that an entity known as Israel already resided in Canaan at the end of the thirteenth century, challenging the biblical account of Israel as an external group, which arrived either as conquerors or infiltrators. This indisputable reference to "Israel" forms a cornerstone to all theories that propose the largely indigenous origins of biblical Israel. Two copies of this text exist—one placed in Merneptah's mortuary temple and the second in the temple of Karnak. Included in the last three lines (26–28) of Merneptah's poetic version of his victory over the Libyans is an account of his Year 5 campaign to Canaan. In line 27, a set of hieroglyphs appear, accompanied by the determinative for people in the plural form that most Egyptologists translate as Israel (*ysry3r/l*) referring to a people, not a place, who were annihilated during Pharaoh's campaign (see Lichtheim 1976: 73–78 for a translation and description of their context). Although doubts have been raised regarding the historicity of Merneptah's campaign, the mention of Israel in Canaan already in the thirteenth century supports a Canaanite origin for this group, seemingly contradicting biblical claims. What remains uncertain is if the Israel in the Merneptah Stela can be directly associated with the biblical Israel. Other questions include the location of Merneptah's Israel. Based on the structure of the hymnic-poetic unit and the order of the inscription's toponyms, most scholars place Israel as residing generally in the highlands, either in Cisjordan (as the majority propose) or Transjordan. What remains undisputed is that it is the only late second-millennium BCE primary source mentioning Israel as a collective entity that may be contemporary with the period of Israel's ethnogenesis (see Hasel 2008 for a detailed discussion).

It has been suggested that Merneptah's Israel may also be depicted in four battle scenes incised on the western wall of Karnak's "Cour de la Cachette." Traditionally assigned to Ramesses II, three of the reliefs depict the conquest of three fortified Canaanite city-states. Ashkelon is specifically mentioned, but the names of the other two cities are not indicated. The fourth, badly damaged, scene depicts a battle in a hilly environment that lacks any indication of a fortified city and is directed against a foe that is portrayed as Canaanite. Based on a comparison with the campaign described in the Israel Stela, F. J. Yurco proposes that these reliefs should be attributed to Merneptah, suggesting that the two unnamed sites in the relief should be associated with Gezer and Yeno'am, which appear as conquered cities of Merneptah's Year 5 campaign to the Levant (see, e.g., Stager 1985; Yurco 1997 for his most detailed treatment of the topic). In Yurco's view, the Canaanites depicted in the fourth scene should be identified with the same Israel mentioned in the Merneptah Stela. If this reassignment to Merneptah is correct, we have a second possible reference to "Israel," one in which the people are represented as Canaanites. Although this is an attractive suggestion, not all Egyptologists accept the reattribution of these battle scenes to Merneptah (see, e.g., Redford 1986).

6.4 BEYOND THE BIBLICAL ACCOUNT: ISRAEL'S CANAANITE ORIGINS

The picture gleaned from the Egyptian sources is supported by results of archaeological surveys in the southern Levant. These document dramatic shifts in Iron I settlement patterns, especially in the central hill country, and, together with the excavation results of several of these small Iron I rural villages, demonstrate that several key aspects of Iron I hill-country material culture continued Late Bronze Age traditions. This is best illustrated by the ceramic assemblage of these hill-country hamlets, which developed directly out of the Canaanite pottery tradition (see, e.g., Killebrew 2005: 177–81). This observation, together with aspects of religious continuity with earlier Canaanite practices evident in the Hebrew Bible (see, e.g., Smith 2002) and Iron I hill-country cultic practices (Killebrew 2006: 571–72), casts doubt on the theory of a largely external origin of the Iron I villagers.[5] In addition, evolutionary models of nomadism as an intermediary stage between hunter-gatherer societies and settled agriculturalists have also been discounted. Recent ethnographic and archaeological studies demonstrate more complex nomadic-sedentary interactions over the millennia in the ancient Near East (see, e.g., Bar-Yosef and Khazanov 1992 and Szuchman 2009 for detailed discussions).

Beginning in the 1960s, sociological and anthropological analyses of the biblical account also inspired new interpretations of the emergence of Israel (see, e.g., Lemche 1985). Attempts to write a secular history of Israel's emergence include the social revolution and pastoral Canaanites models of the origins and evolution of early Israel. During the late twentieth century, scholars such as P. R. Davies and others, often referred to as "minimalists" or "revisionists," even challenged the existence of an ancient Israel, claiming that political or religious motivations lead biblical scholars to accept most of the Bible's description of Israel's origins (see, e.g., Davies 1992; Whitelam 1996; but see Dever 2010 for a rebuttal). What remains undisputable is the appearance of an entity known to the Egyptians as "Israel," which resided in Canaan already in the late thirteenth century BCE.

6.4.1 Social Revolution Model

Rejecting Albright's and Alt's biblically based theories of external origins, another school of thought proposes that the origins of Israel can be traced to a conflict between the Canaanite elite and a dissatisfied indigenous peasant class. George E. Mendenhall (1962, 1973) first developed this theory in 1962, maintaining that Israel originated from the "exodus" of discontented native peasant groups from lowland city-states to the hill country during the final chaotic decades of the Late Bronze Age that heralded the demise of this interconnected age of internationalism, collapse of the Hittite Empire, and decline of New Kingdom Egypt (for a summary and extensive bibliography regarding the end of the Late Bronze Age see Cline 2014). Mendenhall associated this disaffected group with the *'apiru*, a sociopolitical group mentioned in Late Bronze Age Near Eastern texts, who were united by a shared religious ideology or covenant. Building on Marxist theory to explain the phenomenon described by Mendenhall, N. K. Gottwald (1979) took this theory a step further, claiming that the emergence of Israel was the result of a violent class struggle between the rural peasantry and the urban elite classes of Canaanite society. In this view, the hill country and other marginal areas of Canaan, underpopulated during the Late Bronze Age, served as their refuge. Although this sociologically based approach to Late Bronze Age society has been discredited by biblical scholars and archaeologists who note its lack of basis in the biblical account and primary textual and material culture evidence (see, e.g., Halpern 1983: 47–106; Finkelstein 1988: 306–14), in recent years this theory has been revived, especially in relation to Hazor (see, e.g., Zuckerman 2007 who attributes Hazor's destruction to a disaffected Canaanite underclass).

6.4.2 Pastoral Canaanite Model

This theory, developed by I. Finkelstein (1994), examines the emergence of ancient Israel from a long-term perspective. Although this approach is often presented as a variation of the peaceful infiltration theory, it differs significantly in its understanding of early Israel as emerging from Canaan. As such, it deserves particular attention, especially as the biblical text is regarded only as a secondary source. Based on evidence from archaeological surveys and excavation data, ecological, geographical, and environmental factors, ethnoarchaeological case studies, and Turkish land use records, this school of thought stresses the indigenous pastoral origins of the hill country villagers over a mainly external source of the seminomadic "peaceful infiltrators" (Finkelstein 1988). Regional survey results, especially from the West Bank and Galilee, convincingly demonstrate a marked increase in the number of agricultural villages in the biblical heartland of Israel's settlement, thus transforming the social and cultural landscape of Canaan during the twelfth and eleventh centuries BCE. Considered in its longer-term historical context, according to Finkelstein this phenomenon is not unique. Rather, it represents the "cyclic settlement and demographic processes that characterized the hill-country in the third-second millennia BCE" resulting from a "long process that started with the destruction of the urban culture of the Bronze Age and the uprooting of large population groups in vast areas, and the subsequent settlement of various pastoral and uprooted groups and individuals in the highlands of Canaan" (Finkelstein and Na'aman 1994: 15). Against this theory, however, it has been pointed out that ethnographic studies indicate there is seldom such a clear-cut division between pastoral and agricultural activities. Instead, the same individuals in rural societies usually engaged in both endeavors (Bienkowski and van der Steen 2001). Others find no evidence for the development of the round or oval Iron I village plans out of Bedouin tent arrangements, an assumption that forms a key component of Finkelstein's theory (see, e.g., Saidel 2008; see also Dever 2017: 194–210 for a detailed critique and relevant bibliography).

6.5 THE ETHNOGENESIS OF ISRAEL: THE BIBLICAL ACCOUNT AND BEYOND

What emerges from the discussion above is that no single theory satisfactorily takes into account all of the evidence, both biblical and extrabiblical, to reconstruct the emergence of early Israel. A fifth approach, which I have termed the mixed multitude theory, interprets the biblical and archaeological evidence as reflecting a non-homogeneous, multifaceted, and complex process of Israelite formation and crystallization. While this complexity and the mixed origins of early Israel have been noted and emphasized by a number of scholars, most have identified themselves as supporting one or another of the four major schools of thought outlined above.[6]

6.5.1 The Mixed Multitude Theory

Derived from the biblical description of the Israelites as a "mixed multitude" in Exod. 12:38, this term is used here as a metaphor to characterize the process of Israelite ethnogenesis, or a coming together of peoples from diverse backgrounds into a single tribal group which shares a belief in a common descent and ideology as explored by H. Wolfram (1997) in his classic work on early medieval Germanic origins. In this view, identity was not a result solely of genetic descent, rather it formed around small groups of charismatic leaders—or in the case of early Israel, judges—who united people by a common tradition (see Killebrew 2006: 566–72 for a detailed description, presentation of the evidence relevant to early Israel, and extensive bibliography). This theory considers the mention of a people named Israel in the Merneptah Stela as its starting point. Second, the mixed multitude theory incorporates the ever-growing body of archaeological evidence that points to both continuity (aspects of the ceramic assemblage and cultic practices) and discontinuity (settlement patterns, demography, economy, social structure, and political organization) in the Iron I material culture and settlement patterns in the central-hill country (see Finkelstein 1988: 235–92;

Faust 2006; Killebrew 2006; Dever 2017: 119–247). Lastly, ethnogenesis, or the process of the formation of group identity, based on both the biblical account and contemporary studies of ethnicity, provides the narrative and theoretical framework for this approach.

Key to our understanding of Israel's emergence are features that are considered to be binding components of group formation and identity. These can include an empowering narrative of shared experiences, woven into an epic account of primordial deeds, miracles, and genealogies (see, e.g., Erickson 2003). In the case of Israel's prehistory, its enduring epic narrative, the Bible, recounts the journey from slavery to salvation in a land promised to them by the Israelite God, Yhwh. The central theme of Israel's ethnogenesis is the saga of their unique relationship as the chosen people of Yhwh. The worship of Israel's God formed the core ideology of ancient Israel and Judah and is still an essential component of Jewish identity. Ancient Israel's mixed multitude is defined here as a collection of loosely organized and largely indigenous, tribal, and kin-based groups whose porous borders permitted penetration by smaller numbers from external groups (Parkinson 2002). Although it is impossible to reconstruct with certainty the protohistory of Israel's origins, it most likely comprised diverse elements of Late Bronze Age society, namely, the rural Canaanite population, displaced peasants and pastoralists, and lawless 'apiru and shasu. Fugitive or runaway Semitic slaves from New Kingdom Egypt may have joined this mixed multitude. Nonindigenous groups mentioned in the biblical narrative, including Midianites, Kenites, and Amalekites, may also have been part of this mixed multitude. New Kingdom Egypt's decline and eventual retreat from Canaan undoubtedly was one of the major contributing factors in Canaan's return to a more fragmented kinship-based tribal society and Israel's subsequent ethnogenesis.

Attempts to locate Israel's ethnogenesis in the small Iron I villages in the hill country and marginal regions ultimately go back to the biblical narrative, in particular the tradition that situates their initial settlement in these regions as recounted in the books of Joshua and Judges. Despite their complex history of composition and the purpose of these texts, they do appear to preserve some authentic memories from the late second millennium, as noted above. Corroborating evidence is found in the archaeological record that documents noteworthy changes in twelfth- and eleventh-century BCE settlement patterns and in the distinct material culture that characterizes the central highland regions on both sides of the Jordan. At the same time, aspects of the ceramic repertoire, notably its utilitarian function and mode of production at these small hill-country hamlets, distinguish it from Iron I pottery assemblages from sites in the lowlands and seem to demarcate a social "boundary" that may reflect group identity (Killebrew 2003).

Utilizing the full arsenal of sources available, including the archaeological evidence, a cautious and critical reading of the biblical texts, the appearance of the word "Israel" as a people in the Israel (Merneptah) Stela, and theoretical models, it is possible to begin to delineate social and material-culture boundaries that define the peoples who emerged during this period between the collapse of the Late Bronze Age empires (ca. 1200 BCE) and the reemergence of regional kingdoms (ca. tenth/ninth century BCE), including those of Israel and Judah. When considered in its larger eastern Mediterranean context, the process of Israelite ethnogenesis is not unique. Similar processes of breakdown and fragmentation were occurring simultaneously throughout the region during the final centuries of the second millennium, a societal transformation that formed the foundations of both the biblical and classical worlds.

Notes

1. Military campaigns to Canaan were a regular feature of New Kingdom Egyptian imperial policy in the Levant, culminating in the implementation of formal administrative imperialism in Canaan. This is best expressed in the construction of Egyptian residences and fortresses at several sites in Canaan, e.g., Beth Shean, Tel Mor, and Deir el-Balah, during the thirteenth and first half of the twelfth centuries BCE. See Hasel 1998; Killebrew 2005: 51–92; and Morris 2005 for a summary of the archaeological and textual evidence.
2. The chronological layering of the Torah is especially evident in the geographical place names and sites that appear in the exodus story, which clearly reflect later historical realities. See, e.g., Grabbe 2014: esp. 70–80; Bietak 2015; Finkelstein 2015; and Dever 2017: 119–91 for a detailed discussion of the textual and archaeological evidence and extensive bibliography.
3. But compare Zuckerman (2007), who suggests the city's destruction resulted from an uprising of the local population against the ruling classes.
4. Bienkowski (1986) provides a detailed publication of Late Bronze Age remains from Garstang's and Kenyon's excavations at Jericho. The site was unoccupied during the thirteenth and twelfth centuries BCE, while only a very modest unwalled settlement dating to the fourteenth century BCE could be identified archaeologically.
5. Although it should be noted that other features, such as settlement type and distribution, demography, economy, social structure, and political organization, mark a departure from Late Bronze Canaanite culture (see, e.g., Dever 2017: 211–13).
6. This approach to the emergence of Israel is mentioned briefly or referred indirectly to in several earlier studies on this topic. Stager (1985: 61*) defines ancient Israel during the period of Judges as a loose confederation of tribes based in the central highlands. Finkelstein and Na'aman (1994: 13–15) state that there were groups of other origin as well. Bright (2000: 134) also stresses the complexity of early Israel's origins, pointing out that they were by no means all descendants of Jacob but, rather, included in their midst a "mixed multitude" or "rabble." Dever (2017: 226–27) refers to early Israel as a "motley crew."

Bibliography

Albright, W. F. 1935. "Archaeology and the Date of the Hebrew Conquest of Palestine." *BASOR* 58: 11–18.

Albright, W. F. 1939. "The Israelite Conquest of Canaan in Light of Archaeology." *BASOR* 74: 11–23.

Alt, A. 1967. "The Settlement of the Israelite Tribes in Palestine." In *Essays on Old Testament History and Religion.* Garden City, NY: Doubleday, 172–221.

Alter, R. 2013. *Ancient Israel. The Former Prophets: Joshua, Judges, Samuel, and Kings. A Translation with Commentary.* New York: W. W. Norton and Company.

Bar-Yosef, O. and A. M. Khazanov, eds. 1992. *Pastoralism in the Levant: Archaeological Materials in Anthropological Perspectives.* Monographs in World Archaeology 10. Madison, WI: Prehistory Press.

Ben-Tor, A. 2013. "Who Destroyed Canaanite Hazor?" *BAR* 39.4: 28–36, 58–59.

Bienkowski, P. 1986. *Jericho in the Late Bronze Age.* Warminster, Wiltshire, UK: Aris & Phillips.

Bienkowski, P. and E. van der Steen. 2001. "Tribes, Trade, and Towns: A New Framework for the Late Iron Age in Southern Jordan and the Negev." *BASOR* 323: 21–47.

Bietak, M. 2015. "On the Historicity of the Exodus: What Egyptology Today Can Contribute to Assessing the Biblical Account of the Sojourn in Egypt." In T. E. Levy, T. Schneider, and W. H. C. Propp, eds., *Israel's Exodus in Transdisciplinary Perspective: Text, Archaeology, Culture, and Geoscience*. Quantitative Methods in the Humanities and Social Sciences. Cham, Switzerland: Springer, 17–37.

Bright, J. 2000. *A History of Israel*. 4th ed. Louisville, KY: Westminster.

Cline, E. H. 2014. *1177 BC: The Year Civilization Collapsed*. Princeton: Princeton University Press.

Davies, P. R. 1992. *In Search of "Ancient Israel."* JSOTSup 148. Sheffield: Sheffield Academic Press.

Dever, W. G. 2003. *Who Were the Early Israelites and Where Did They Come From?* Grand Rapids, MI: Eerdmans.

Dever, W. G. 2010. "Merenptah's 'Israel,' the Bible's, and Ours." In J. D. Schloen, ed. *Exploring the Longue Duree: Essays in Honor of Lawrence E. Stager*. Winona Lake, IN: Eisenbrauns, 89–96.

Dever, W. G. 2017. *Beyond the Texts: An Archaeological Portrait of Ancient Israel and Judah*. Atlanta: SBL.

Echols, C. L. 2008. *"Tell Me, O Muse": The Song of Deborah (Judges 5) in the Light of Heroic Poetry*. LHBOTS 487. New York: T&T Clark.

Erickson, K. C. 2003. "'They Will Come From the Other Side of the Sea': Prophecy, Ethnogenesis, and Agency in Yaqui Narrative." *Journal of American Folklore* 116: 465–82.

Faust, A. 2006. *Israel's Ethnogenesis: Settlement, Interaction, Expansion and Resistance*. Approaches to Anthropological Archaeology. London: Equinox.

Finkelstein, I. 1988. *The Archaeology of the Israelite Settlement*. Jerusalem: Israel Exploration Society.

Finkelstein, I. 1994. "The Emergence of Israel: A Phase in the Cyclic History of Canaan in the Third and Second Millennia BCE." In I. Finkelstein and N. Na'aman, eds., *From Nomadism to Monarchy: Archaeological and Historical Aspects of Early Israel*. Jerusalem: Israel Exploration Society, 150–78.

Finkelstein, I. 2015. "The Wilderness Narrative and Itineraries and the Evolution of the Exodus Tradition." In T. E. Levy, T. Schneider, and W. H. C. Propp, eds., *Israel's Exodus in Transdisciplinary Perspective: Text, Archaeology, Culture, and Geoscience*. Quantitative Methods in the Humanities and Social Sciences. Cham, Switzerland: Springer, 39–53.

Finkelstein, I. and N. Na'aman. 1994. "Introduction: From Nomadism to Monarchy—the State of Research in 1992." In I. Finkelstein and N. Na'aman, eds., *From Nomadism to Monarchy: Archaeological and Historical Aspects of Early Israel*. Jerusalem: Israel Exploration Society, 9–17.

Geraty, L. T. 2015. "Exodus Dates and Theories." In T. E. Levy, T. Schneider, and W. H. C. Propp, eds., *Israel's Exodus in Transdisciplinary Perspective: Text, Archaeology, Culture, and Geoscience*. Quantitative Methods in the Humanities and Social Sciences. Cham, Switzerland: Springer, 55–64.

Gottwald, N. K. 1979. *The Tribes of Yahweh: A Sociology of the Religion of Liberated Israel, 1250–1050*. Maryknoll, NY: Orbis.

Grabbe, L. L. 2014. "Exodus and History." In T. Dozeman, C. A. Evans, and J. N. Lohr, eds., *The Book of Exodus: Composition, Reception, and Interpretation*. VTSup 164. Leiden: Brill, 61–87.

Hackett, J. A. 2001. "'There Was No King in Israel': The Era of the Judges." In M. D. Coogan, ed., *The Oxford History of the Biblical World*. New York: Oxford University Press, 132–64.

Halpern, B. 1983. *The Emergence of Israel in Canaan*. Chico, CA: Scholars Press.

Hasel, M. G. 1998. *Domination and Resistance: Egyptian Military Activity in the Southern Levant, ca. 1300–1185 BC*. Probleme der Ägyptologie 11. Leiden: Brill.

Hasel, M. G. 2008. "Merenptah's Reference to Israel: Critical Issues for the Origin of Israel." In R. S. Hess, G. A. Klingbeil, and P. J. Ray Jr., eds., *Critical Issues in Early Israelite History*. Winona Lake, IN: Eisenbrauns, 47–59.

Hendel, R. 2001. "The Exodus in Biblical Memory." *JBL* 120: 601–22.

Hendel, R. 2015. "The Exodus as Cultural Memory: Egyptian Bondage and the Song of the Sea." In T. E. Levy, T. Schneider, and W. H. C. Propp, eds., *Israel's Exodus in Transdisciplinary Perspective: Text, Archaeology, Culture, and Geoscience*. Quantitative Methods in the Humanities and Social Sciences. Cham, Switzerland: Springer, 65–77.

Herr, L. G. 1998. "Tell el-'Umayri and the Madaba Plains Region during the Late Bronze-Iron I Transition." In S. Gitin, M. Mazar, and E. Stern, eds., *Mediterranean Peoples in Transition: Thirteenth to Early Tenth Centuries BCE*. Jerusalem: Israel Exploration Society, 252–64.

Hoffmeier, J. K. 1997. *Israel in Egypt: The Evidence for the Authenticity of the Exodus.* New York: Oxford University Press.

Hoffmeier, J. K. 2015. "Egyptologists and the Israelite Exodus from Egypt." In T. E. Levy, T. Schneider, and W. H. C. Propp, eds., *Israel's Exodus in Transdisciplinary Perspective: Text, Archaeology, Culture, and Geoscience.* Quantitative Methods in the Humanities and Social Sciences. Cham, Switzerland: Springer, 197–208.

Killebrew, A. E. 2003. "The Southern Levant during the 13th–12th Centuries BCE: The Archaeology of Social Boundaries." In B. Fischer, H Genz, É. Jean, and K. Koroğlu, eds., *Identifying Changes: The Transition from Bronze to Iron Ages in Anatolia and Its Neighbouring Regions. Proceedings of the International Workshop, Istanbul, November 8–9, 2002.* Istanbul: Türk Eskiçağ Bilimleri Enstitüsü, 117–26.

Killebrew, A. E. 2005. *Biblical Peoples and Ethnicity: An Archaeological Study of Egyptians, Canaanites, Philistines, and Early Israel, 1300–1100 BCE.* SBLABS 9. Atlanta: SBL.

Killebrew, A. E. 2006. "The Emergence of Ancient Israel: The Social Boundaries of a 'Mixed Multitude' in Canaan." In A. M. Maeir and P. de Miroschedji, eds.,*"I Will Speak the Riddles of Ancient Times": Archaeological and Historical Studies in Honor of Amihai Mazar on the Occasion of His Sixtieth Birthday.* Vol. 2. Winona Lake, IN: Eisenbrauns, 555–72.

Killebrew, A. E. 2014. "Hybridity, Hapiru, and the Archaeology of Ethnicity in Second Millennium BCE Western Asia." In J. McInerney, ed., *A Companion to Ethnicity in the Ancient Mediterranean.* Blackwell Companions to the Ancient World. Malden, MA: Wiley Blackwell, 142–57.

Killebrew, A. E. 2017. "'Out of the Land of Egypt, Out of the House of Slavery...' (Exodus 20:2): Forced Migration, Slavery, and the Emergence of Israel." In O. Lipschits, Y. Gadot, and M. J. Adams, eds., *Rethinking Israel: Studies in the History and Archaeology of Ancient Israel in Honor of Israel Finkelstein.* Winona Lake, IN: Eisenbrauns, 151–58.

Knoppers, G. N. and J. S. Greer. 2010. "Deuteronomistic History." In C. R. Matthews, *Oxford Bibliographies: Biblical Studies.* http://www.oxfordbibliographies.com/view/document/obo-9780195393361/obo-9780195393361-0028.xml (accessed January 1, 2018).

Lemche, N. P. 1985. *Early Israel: Anthropological and Historical Studies on the Israelite Society before the Monarchy.* VTSup 37. Leiden: Brill.

Lemche, N. P. 1998. *Prelude to Israel's Past: Background and Beginnings of Israelite History and Identity.* Translated by E. F. Maniscalco. Peabody, MA: Hendrickson.

Levy, T. E., T. Schneider, and W. H. C. Propp, eds. 2015. *Israel's Exodus in Transdisciplinary Perspective: Text, Archaeology, Culture, and Geoscience.* Quantitative Methods in the Humanities and Social Sciences. Cham, Switzerland: Springer.

Lichtheim, M. 1976. *Ancient Egyptian Literature: A Book of Readings.* Vol. 2: *The New Kingdom.* Berkeley, CA: University of California Press.

Loprieno, A. 1997. "Slaves." In S. Donadoni, ed., *The Egyptians.* Chicago: University of Chicago Press, 185–219.

Loprieno, A. 2012. "Slavery and Servitude." In E. Frood and W. Wendrich, eds., *UCLA Encyclopedia of Egyptology.* http://escholarship.org/uc/item/8mx2073f (accessed January 5, 2018).

Matthews, V. H. 2004. *Judges and Ruth.* Cambridge: Cambridge University Press.

McConville, J. G. 2001. "Joshua." In J. Barton and J. Muddiman, eds., *The Oxford Bible Commentary*, Oxford: Oxford University Press, 158–76.

McConville, J. G. and S. N. Williams. 2010. *Joshua.* Two Horizons Old Testament Commentary. Grand Rapids: Eerdmans.

Mendenhall, G. E. 1962. "The Hebrew Conquest of Palestine." *BA* 25: 66–87.

Mendenhall, G. E. 1973. *The Tenth Generation: The Origins of the Biblical Tradition.* Baltimore: Johns Hopkins University Press.

Morris, E. 2005. *The Architecture of Imperialism: Military Bases and the Evolution of Foreign Policy in Egypt's New Kingdom.* Probleme der Ägyptologie 22. Leiden: Brill.

Na'aman, N. 1994. "The 'Conquest of Canaan' in the Book of Joshua and in History." In I. Finkelstein and N. Na'aman, eds., *From Nomadism to Monarchy: Archaeological and Historical Aspects of Early Israel*. Jerusalem: Israel Exploration Society, 218–81.

Na'aman, N. 2005. "Pharaonic Lands in the Jezreel Valley in the Late Bronze Age." In *Canaan in the Second Millennium BCE: Collected Essays*. Vol. 2. Winona Lake, IN: Eisenbrauns, 232–41.

Na'aman, N. 2011. "The Exodus Story: Between Historical Memory and Historiographical Composition." *JANER* 11: 39–69.

Nelson, R. D. 1997. *Joshua: A Commentary*. OTL. Louisville: Westminster John Knox.

Niditch, S. 2008. *Judges: A Commentary*. OTL. Louisville: Westminster John Knox.

Noth, M. 1991. *The Deuteronomistic History*. 2nd ed. JSOTSup 15. Sheffield, UK: Sheffield Academic Press.

Parkinson, W. A., ed. 2002. *The Archaeology of Tribal Societies*. Archaeological Series 15. Ann Arbor: International Monographs in Prehistory.

Rainey, A. F. 1995. "Unruly Elements in Late Bronze Canaanite Society." In D. Wright, D. Pearson, D. N. Freedman, and A. Hurvitz, eds., *Pomegranates and Golden Bells: Studies in Biblical, Jewish, and Near Eastern Ritual, Law, and Literature in Honor of Jacob Milgrom*. Winona Lake, IN: Eisenbrauns, 481–96.

Redford, D. B. 1986. "The Ashkelon Relief at Karnak and the Israel Stela." *IEJ* 36: 188–200.

Redford, D. B. 1987. "An Egyptological Perspective on the Exodus Narrative." In A. F. Rainey, ed., *Egypt, Israel, Sinai: Archaeological and Historical Relationships in the Biblical Period*. Tel Aviv University Kaplan Project on the History of Israel and Egypt. Tel Aviv: Tel Aviv University, 137–61.

Redford, D. B. 1992. *Egypt, Canaan, and Israel in Ancient Times*. Princeton: Princeton University Press.

Redmount, C. 2001. "Bitter Lives: Israel in and out of Egypt." In M. D. Coogan, ed., *The Oxford History of the Biblical World*. New York: Oxford University Press, 58–89.

Saidel, B. A. 2008. "The Bedouin Tent: An Ethno-Archaeological Portal to Antiquity or a Modern Construct?" In H. Barnard and W. Wendrich, eds., *The Archaeology of Mobility: Old World and New World Nomadism*. Los Angeles: University of California Press, 465–86.

Smith, M. S. 2002. *The Early History of God: Yahweh and the Other Deities in Ancient Israel*. Biblical Resource Series. Grand Rapids, MI: Eerdmans.

Stager, L. 1985. "Merenptah, Israel, and Sea Peoples: New Light on an Old Relief." *ErIsr* 18:56*–64*.

Szuchman, J., ed. 2009. *Nomads, Tribes, and the State in the Ancient Near East: Cross-Disciplinary Perspectives*. Oriental Institute Seminars No. 5. Chicago: Oriental Institute of the University of Chicago.

Van Seters, J. 1990. "Joshua's Campaign of Canaan and Near Eastern Historiography." *SJOT* 4/2: 1–12.

Whitelam, K. W. 1996. *The Invention of Ancient Israel: The Silencing of Palestinian History*. New York: Routlege.

Wolfram, H. 1997. *The Roman Empire and Its Germanic Peoples*. Translated by T. Dunlap. Berkeley: University of California Press.

Yadin, Y. 1982. "Is the Biblical Account of the Israelite Conquest of Canaan Historically Reliable?" *BAR* 8/2: 16–23.

Younger, Jr., K. L. 2008. "The Rhetorical Structuring of the Joshua Conquest Narratives." In R. S. Hess, G. A. Klingbeil, and P. J. Ray, eds., *Critical Issues in Early Israelite History*. Winona Lake, IN: Eisenbrauns, 3–32.

Yurco, F. J. 1997. "Merenptah's Canaanite Campaign and Israel's Origins." In E. S. Frerichs and L. H. Lesko, eds., *Exodus: The Egyptian Evidence*. Winona Lake, IN: Eisenbrauns, 27–55.

Zertal, A. 1986–87. "An Early Iron Age Cultic Site on Mt. Ebal: Exavation Seasons 1982-1987: Preliminary Report." *TA* 13-14: 105–65.

Zuckerman, S. 2007. "Anatomy of a Destruction: Crisis Architecture, Termination Rituals and the Fall of Canaanite Hazor." *Journal of Mediterranean Archaeology* 20: 3–32.

CHAPTER 7

ISRAELITE STATE FORMATION AND EARLY MONARCHY IN HISTORY AND BIBLICAL HISTORIOGRAPHY

WALTER DIETRICH

7.1 THE BIBLICAL HISTORIOGRAPHY

No fewer than six of the Hebrew Bible's Historical Books tell of the formation of the state in Israel and its early kingship: Judges, the two books of Samuel, 1 Kings, and the two books of Chronicles.[1] Thus this theme is given unusually broad treatment in Israel's historical writing. The time of the first kings was apparently of great significance in the sensibilities and memory of Israel. We can see from the texts that Israel struggled with the step from a decentralized tribal society to a centrally governed state. There was resistance; a number of attempts and initiatives were required before it was realized; and after it was achieved there were still efforts to reverse what had been done.

7.1.1 The Sources

Factually, the Bible is our only source for Israel's early royal period. This has allowed (hyper-)critical exegetes and historians to regard this historical epoch as pure fiction, a dream of former grandeur. The three kings of the period—Saul, David, and Solomon—have also been declared to be mythical figures.[2]

We will see that these scholars have overshot the mark. There may be other reasons for the lack of extra-biblical confirmation of the biblical account. First, the land of Israel (and Judah) was of little importance, either geopolitically or economically, in the ancient Near Eastern world. It was not at either of the significant poles of the so-called Fertile Crescent, nor did it lie on the eastern Mediterranean coast that was so central to international commerce. Instead, it occupied an inland territory in the southern Levant, a place with a meager ecological endowment. This hill country with its lack of rain could not sustain a large population and it was difficult to accumulate a surplus that would foster political and economic development. Second, the people of Israel were latecomers among the peoples of the ancient Near East. We first encounter an ethnic group with that name on the Merneptah stela (ca. 1200 BCE). The Bible pictures Israel as a people who had entered or forced their way (Joshua) into the land from elsewhere. In reality, they may have left the relatively populous river valleys and coastal plains of Canaan in the early Iron Age (ca. 1200–1000 BCE) and settled in the nearly empty hill country of Palestine. But poor hill farmers do not develop a high culture; the ability to read and write was surely a rare exception. That changed with the rise of the kingship, but only slowly.

So it is really no surprise that there are no written sources outside the Bible for the founding of the Israelite state. The only (partial) exception is a stela made for the Aramaean king Hazael (ca. 845–800 BCE) and erected in Dan, on the border between Aram-Damascus and Israel. On it he boasts of having killed a king of Israel and one from the "house of David." Although the stela is damaged at the crucial point, the names of the two kings can be reconstructed: Joram (of Israel, 850–845 BCE) and Ahaziah (of Judah, 845 BCE). That is a relatively early attestation to the existence of two states in the land, one of which ostensibly traced its identity back to a certain "David."[3] According to the Bible, the Israelite king Joram was the fourth member of the Omri dynasty, before which there had been another, the Jeroboam dynasty, also numbering four kings. If we add up the regnal periods given in biblical texts of the two dynasties we arrive at an early royal period in the tenth century.

We can look only to the biblical witness to tell us what may have happened in Israel and Judah in the tenth century. That must be done carefully and critically. What we have before us are neither the products of pure fantasy nor absolutely reliable historical accounts, but something in between. The biblical authors were certainly interested in history, but they were not subject to the (modern) ideal of historical objectivity. In what follows, we will apply this premise to the various biblical books that give an account of the early royal period.

7.1.2 The Books of Chronicles

The latest of the relevant sources is Chronicles, which was composed in the late Persian or early Hellenistic period, that is, in the fourth or third century BCE, and thus about three-quarters of a millennium after the early royal period. The two books give accounts of differing length about the first three kings. David is the subject of eighteen chapters (1 Chr. 11–29) and Solomon of nine (2 Chr. 1–9), while only one is about Saul (1 Chr. 10). This lets us conclude something about the authors' intention: they were Judeans, or Jews, who set themselves sharply apart from the Samarians or Samaritans in the region of the former northern kingdom of Israel. For the authors, the beginnings of the Judahite dynasty of David were important, but not those of the (proto-)Israelite king Saul.

The Chroniclers found their sources in the questionable historical sections of the books of Samuel and Kings (perhaps not necessarily in the version that now exists in the Hebrew Bible). They omitted a great deal that was not to their liking and added some things so as to give events the desired direction and interpretation. Of the approximately seventeen chapters of 1 Samuel that deal with Saul, they adopted only the one about his death (1 Sam. 31), adding a summary assessment according to which his fate was well deserved (1 Chr. 10:13–14). In the depiction of David, Chronicles agrees with the books of Samuel, for example, in the account of the transportation of the Ark to Jerusalem (1 Chr. 13; 15; cf. 2 Sam. 6), the dynastic predictions of the prophet Nathan (1 Chr. 17; cf. 2 Sam. 7), the lists of David's wars and victories (1 Chr. 18; cf. 2 Sam. 8), and the story of the discovery of the future place where the temple was to be built (1 Chr. 21; cf. 2 Sam. 24). But a great deal is left out—everything, one senses, that seems less advantageous to David, such as his convoluted and obstacle-ridden rise (1 Sam. 16–2 Sam. 4) and the bloody conflicts within his family and his nation (2 Sam. 11–20). On the other hand, some things are added: nearly half the space devoted to David in Chronicles shows him preparing for the building of the temple and the establishment of its worship (1 Chr. 21–29); there is practically nothing about this in the books of Samuel. The Solomon of Chronicles is essentially nothing but the builder of the temple. Six chapters are devoted to that activity (2 Chr. 2–7), while the others deal primarily with his wisdom and his wealth (2 Chr. 1; 9), which he needed for his sacred task. In contrast, Chronicles omits his thoroughly murky seizure of power as depicted in 1 Kgs. 1–2 and his lack of fidelity to Yhwh according to 1 Kgs. 11.

Chronicles shows the rule of David and of Solomon as well as the worship of the temple flowering in the early royal period. At the time they were written, Jerusalem was ruled by a hierocracy, though it was subject to foreign kings. Thus the early royal period appears as a springtime of the temple community—but under their own rulers!

7.1.3 The Book of Judges

The book of Judges deals not with the early royal period but with a time before it, a period of preparation for the introduction of the kingship. The major central section of the book (chs. 3–16) tells how charismatic leaders rescued Israel from the attacks of foreign enemies. Scattered throughout are lists of so-called minor judges who apparently had the duty of maintaining an orderly community life during times of peace (10:1–5; 12:8–15). It seems that kings were not needed then! Israel's community life is pictured as egalitarian and anti-totalitarian, segmented and opposed to centralization—and on the whole as functioning very well.

The implicit anti-monarchical tendency of Judges becomes explicit in the story of Abimelech (ch. 9), a man who established a kingdom in central Palestine through treachery and violence, threw the whole region into misery by his boundless ambition, and finally lost his own life. This account includes the fable of Jotham (9:8–15). Jotham, the youngest brother of Abimelech, survives his brother's massacre of the whole family and, standing on a mountain, proclaims a beautifully composed but bitterly angry speech about monarchy: the trees wanted to choose a king to rule over them, but only the thornbush, the most unworthy and unpleasant of all, was willing. The uselessness and even the perilousness of royal rule could not be addressed with greater sarcasm.

Even earlier in Judges, kingship was rejected for religious reasons. After Gideon, one of the great "saviors," has brilliantly defeated the thieving nomadic tribe of the Midianites, the "men of Israel" offer him the title of king, but he refuses on the ground that he does not wish to be king, for Yhwh ought to be Israel's king (8:22–23). That is surprising in the extreme. Nowhere in the entire ancient Near East did faith in divine kings prevent the installation of human kings; on the contrary, rulers on earth worked hand in hand with those in heaven. There was no ancient Near Eastern king who did not believe and proclaim that he was called by a divinity, if possible adopted or even begotten by the god. But according to Gideon, Israel is to be a theocracy, not a monarchy. Scholars are agreed that these maxims do not come from an early period, especially not a pre-monarchical era, but from a later, post-state time. A theologian and redactor of the so-called deuteronomistic school wanted to dissuade his readers from any idea of restoring the monarchy and to instill the notion of a theocracy or hierocracy. If Gideon, who had liberated Israel so grandly, had strictly refused the kingship, how could anyone seek it now, when Judah was subjected to foreign powers?

There are, however, some directly contrary tendencies in Judges according to which the time of the judges *had* to result in a royal period. The hero Samson (chs. 14–16), while he was in possession of superhuman strength, was a hot-headed hoodlum and a dubious womanizer. His end is characteristic of him: when the Philistines capture him, he pulls a great number of them down to death with him. Should such a man be head of Israel?

In the so-called appendix to Judges (chs. 17–21), the situation is even worse. Here the tribal society of Israel goes off the rails cultically, morally, politically, and militarily. People worship an idol in place of God. A gang rape leads to a fratricidal war, which in turn leads to the kidnapping of women. The anarchic chaos is confirmed again and again by the notice that there was no king and each person did as he or she willed (see 17:6; 18:1; 19:1, 25). Anyone reading that would wish for a king, in whose time no such gruesome things would happen any more. These pro-monarchical expressions are also the work of a deuteronomistic redactor, but one who regarded the kingship not as anti-God but as a blessed institution. Evidently, there were contrary points of view among the deuteronomists regarding kingship and statehood.

7.1.4 The Books of Samuel

The books of Samuel deal primarily with the first two kings of Israel, Saul and David, and with the man who is supposed to have anointed both of them, Samuel.

Everything starts with Samuel. He functions as one—the last!—of the "minor judges" from the book of Judges. In the border region between the tribes of Ephraim and Benjamin he rotates from place to place to dispense justice, probably in matters the village community cannot resolve for itself "in the gate" (1 Sam. 7:15; cf. Amos 5:15). It is not altogether clear from the previous narratives how Samuel arrived at his position. According to the narrative in 1 Samuel, he inherited it from the priestly line of Eli, which served the shrine at Shiloh but whose members lost their lives and offices along with the Ark, which had been entrusted to them (1 Sam. 2–4). Samuel was not Eli's son, but the son of an Ephraimite named Elkanah and his wife Hannah. She had long remained childless, and when, through a miracle, she bore a son, she named him "Samuel," supposedly because she had "asked" God so urgently. However, the Hebrew verb *š'l*, "ask,"—a key word in 1 Sam. 1—sounds much more like *Sha'ul* (Saul) than *Shemu'el* (Samuel). Hence, the face of the future King Saul is already visible in the face of the newborn Samuel. When Hannah, fulfilling her vow, gives the child back to God—that is, to the sanctuary at Shiloh—the career of Samuel, the king-maker, begins (1 Sam. 1).

After Samuel has risen to the rank of something like a people's tribune, the people themselves come to him and demand that he install a king over them (1 Sam. 8). Samuel reacts negatively, as does God. But then God tells Samuel to give in to the people's desire—although not before having warned them (in a magnificently satirical speech about the rights of the king in 1 Sam. 8:11–17) about the insatiable nature of kingship. Here again, anti-monarchical tones appear, followed immediately, however, by pro-monarchical ones. God, we learn, has brought Saul to Samuel (1 Sam. 9:1–10:16) and in a casting of lots has steered the lot toward Saul (1 Sam. 10:17–27). God has also helped Saul to achieve a convincing victory over the aggressive Ammonites from east of the Jordan (1 Sam. 11). If any of the three etiologies for Saul's becoming king comes close to historical reality, it is this one. At any rate, the text presents to our eyes the figure of a tall (1 Sam. 9:2; 10:23), modest (1 Sam. 9:21; 10:21–22), charismatic (1 Sam. 11:6–8) man, beloved of God and the people, who is destined to form the tribal society of Israel into a unified nation.

The primary sources that seem to have been shaped into the depiction of the rise and rule of Saul are two collections of popular tales, one about him and Samuel, the other about him and David. The first, important parts of which we have already mentioned, closed with a summary about Saul's family and his victorious wars (1 Sam. 14:47–52). The second began earlier, with the almost fairytale story of how the young Saul once went out to look for his father's strayed asses and came back as YHWH's anointed (1 Sam. 9:1–10:16). It continued with the account of the first great battle against the Philistines (1 Sam. 13–14). There Saul was originally depicted as a shining hero, but now he is eclipsed by his son Jonathan. Since the latter was later to become David's closest friend, an anti-Saul tendency already shows itself here; it becomes still more obvious in an insertion according to which Saul clashed bitterly with his "discoverer," Samuel (1 Sam. 13:7–15). This is repeated, even more drastically, when Samuel demands a war of total destruction against the nomadic Amalekites and Saul does not pursue it ruthlessly enough (1 Sam. 15). The biblical authors try desperately to find black marks on Saul's character, but they are only partially successful; in essence, the first king of Israel remains a tragic figure. Saul's decline is connected with the rise of David, who appears on the stage in 1 Samuel 16. At the beginning, Saul favors him and even becomes his father-in-law, but increasingly he appears as his opponent and persecutor. The fates of the two remain painfully entwined for a long time before the agonizing entanglement is resolved in David's favor, and Saul falls by the wayside.

Earlier scholars typically regarded the major text complex that tells of all this as an independent "History of David's Rise," but the posited source had no clear beginning or end. The start of David's career is interwoven with the story of Saul, and stories about Saul's descendants continue throughout 2 Samuel and even into 1 Kings (2 Sam. 9; 16:1–14; 19:17–31; 1 Kgs. 1:8; 2:8–9, 36–46). It seems better to posit a variety of narrative collections rather than a single "History of David's Rise." These collections would have been—probably much later—compiled into an overarching narrative and shaped into the first part of the biblical biography of David. In essence, two narrative cycles are thus combined: the one about David, Saul, and the Saulides we have already discussed (extending from 1 Sam. 9 to 1 Kgs. 2), and another about the adventures of the young David: first at Saul's side, serving him as musician and armor-bearer, then as a freebooter in the Judean desert and vassal of the Philistine prince of Gath, and finally as king, first of Judah, with his residence in Hebron, then of Israel too, with a new residence in Jerusalem (*1 Sam. 16–2 Sam. 5). In both narrative collections the relationship between David and Saul is an important theme; in both the preference is for David, yet neither shows him as flawlessly good or Saul as completely bad. Even at this early level of biblical historiography, we can observe a remarkable ability to create subtle descriptions of characters and events.

For a long time, the second part of David's biography was regarded as an originally independent "Succession History." But it is much the same here as in the case of the "History of David's Rise": in this case the ending is clear (1 Kgs. 2), but the beginning is not, nor is the theme of "royal succession" present throughout. In my view there are two highly dramatic and accomplished literary novellas combined in 2 Sam. 11–1 Kgs. 2. One is about Solomon's birth and his seizure of power (*2 Sam. 11–12 + *1 Kgs. 1–2), and the other is primarily about the relationship between David and his oppositional son, Absalom (*2 Sam. 13–20). This double novella is preceded by a mosaic of smaller source fragments: the transfer of the Ark to Jerusalem (2 Sam. 6), Nathan's prophecy (*2 Sam. 7), a summary of David's wars and victories (2 Sam. 8), an excerpt from the narrative cycle about the house of Saul concerning Saul's grandson Meribaal (2 Sam. 9), and a story of the war against the Ammonites (*2 Sam. 10 + 12:26–31). (I leave aside here the so-called appendix in 2 Sam. 21–24, which combines older information about David with newer lyrics).

The author who created this composition, as well as the other about the young David, and brought the two together into a biography was a historiographer of the first order—a historian steeped in the sources, a careful redactor, a gifted writer, and a profound theologian. I call him the "Court Narrator" because he must have worked in the sphere of the royal court at Jerusalem (otherwise he would not have had access to so many sources). Because he is also concerned with the fate of Saul and the northern tribes he may well have been influenced by the fall of the Northern Kingdom of Israel (in 722 BCE) and the massive flight of people from northern Israel to Judah. He wants to show his contemporaries the early royal period as a model for a community life that, while not without conflicts, enabled Judeans and Israelites to thrive together.

The Court Narrator not only selected and arranged older materials; in shaping the overall picture he also applied his own coloring at many points. Thus, for example, the story of David's anointing by Samuel (1 Sam. 16:1–13) is entirely his composition. Above all, he is the author of many dialogues he places on the lips of figures in the narrative in order to bring the action to life and interpret it (most impressively in 1 Sam. 20; 24; 25; 26; 27; 2 Sam. 1; 14; 17; 18; 1 Kgs. 2). Above all, it was this author who made the books of Samuel a major contribution to world literature.

7.1.5 First Kings

Three quarters of the forty-seven chapters in 1–2 Kings cover a period of three and a half centuries and tell of more than three dozen kings, but the first quarter (1 Kgs. 1–11) tells of only a single king who ruled not even half a century. The weight given to Solomon likely results from the combination of several factors—his historical significance as David's first successor, the state of the sources, which provide an unusual quantity of material about him, and an especially vivid imaginary picture of him in later times.

Two particular sources contributed to the portrayal of Solomon: the David and Bathsheba novella in 1 Kgs. 1–2 (at the conclusion of the David narrative) and a "Book of the Acts of Solomon" mentioned in 1 Kgs. 11:41, which probably formed the basis for 1 Kgs. 3–11. The first source is relatively old, its original form not far removed from the events surrounding Solomon's ascent to power. It tells, with precise information and a critical undertone, how Adonijah projects himself as the successor to David, now grown senile; how he assembles his own party of notables and officials, principally from the Judean countryside; how, suddenly, a Jerusalem-city party is activated around Solomon as the prophet Nathan and Solomon's mother, Bathsheba, intervene with the old king on behalf of Solomon; how David then in fact orders the coronation of Solomon; and how the leaders of Adonijah's party lose heart and Solomon eliminates them, one after the other, until the kingship is "established in his hand" (1 Kgs. 2:46). It all sounds quite realistic, and it is anything but flattering to Solomon—especially if we consider a number of somewhat mitigating additions (some from a deuteronomistic hand, some from that of the Court Narrator). The truth may well have been more disturbing than the current text reveals: it is possible that David was simply shunted aside in a coup.

A completely different Solomon takes the stage in 1 Kgs. 3. Here he is modest, pious, graced by God, and above all, wise. When God appears to him in a dream and grants him a wish, he decides on wisdom as the highest good, and he is immediately promised it—along with many other things (1 Kgs. 3:4–15). In the very next story, the one about the famous "Judgment of Solomon" (3:16–28), he is able to demonstrate the wisdom with which he is endowed (though this is a floating narrative that appears at various places in the world's cultures and hence is not historically attached to Solomon). The subsequent laudatory stories about Solomon's wisdom and wealth (*1 Kgs. 5; 9–10) are apparently intended to paint a glowing portrait of this king, showing him as predestined to build the Jerusalem temple (1 Kgs. *6–7). For that same purpose, he is shown establishing the governmental system that helps him to generate his wealth (1 Kgs. 4). This is probably the main content of the "Book of the Acts of Solomon." It may have been the Court Narrator who thus gave his work a placative conclusion.

Deuteronomistic (and sometimes still later) authors added to the pericope on the building of the temple Solomon's prayer at its consecration and a subsequent divine appearance (1 Kgs. *8; 9:1–6), as well as the conclusion to the story of Solomon (1 Kgs. 11). On the one hand, they stylized him as the one who prays for and before Israel; on the other hand, they sought to relativize his brilliance as a ruler to some degree. With similar intent, deuteronomistic authors inserted a passage in the Mosaic law in which future kings are warned against Solomonic-type luxury and enjoined to remain true to the Torah (Deut. 17:14–20). Similarly, the sarcastic "Right of Kings" Samuel presents to the people (1 Sam. 8:11–17) is a warning against the Solomonic-type of kingship.

7.2 THE HISTORY

We have seen that the biblical depiction of the formation of the state is not an objective historical account but one that mixes fact and fiction. That is understandable; after all, the early royal period offered outstanding opportunities for demonstrating and measuring the advantages and dangers of royal rule. The advantages lay in a unified and powerful outward stance and increased stability and prosperity within. The dangers came from the great degree of power and possible misuse of it by the monarch, aggravated social dissonance, and a relativizing of religious values. But if the introduction of the monarchy was unavoidable, there were still a number of very different ways in which it could be exercised. That, too, could be vividly demonstrated in the history of the first three kings. We must lay all that aside if we want to obtain the most objective and historically correct image possible of the formation of the state and the characters and achievements of the first kings. In this sense, we have to distinguish between fact and fiction, between memory and interpretation. Besides exegetical criticism, we should apply other approaches—namely, historical scholarship in general, archaeology, ancient Near Eastern studies, and cultural anthropology.

7.2.1 Conditions of State Formation

Scholars long regarded it as a settled conclusion that a state was established in Israel primarily because the tribes were forced to unite in the face of external pressure—namely, from the eastward expansion of the Philistines. That picture is too narrow. Complex processes like those under debate here usually require multi-causal rather than mono-causal explanations. First, we should consider that monarchy was a long-established form of political organization in the Levant—for example, in the Canaanite city-kingdoms or among the Phoenicians—and thus was available to the Israelites as a model. It is scarcely accidental that in the tenth (and ninth) centuries territorial states were established not only in Israel and Judah but also in Syria and the lands east of the Jordan. Apparently the time was ripe for them. An acephalic tribal system may at first glance seem an attractive alternative to the contemporary monarchical systems; it was certainly appealing in a decentralized structure of settlements scattered over a broad highland with many hills and isolated valleys. But several factors called for an overarching set of rules and a form of organization that extended over a number of regions: (1) populations grew and became more concentrated (according to archaeological findings there was a positive avalanche of new village settlements in the hill country of Palestine in the twelfth and eleventh centuries); (2) the inhabited and cultivated portions became increasingly connected; (3) more and more commercial (and marital!) contacts extended beyond the borders of villages and clans; (4) the society became more differentiated (with some villages remaining poor, others flourishing; with some small farmers becoming big ones, and with wealthy owners of large flocks crowding small shepherds); (5) an economy originally devoted only to survival was increasingly segregated by tasks and crafts (cattle breeding versus caring for flocks of small animals, cultivation of wine grapes and olives alongside farm fields, craftspersons here, farmers there); and (6) distant commercial relationships and resulting multi-local networks of paths and roads were created. If in fact an overarching organization emerged, it was bound in turn to upset the neighbors (such as the Philistines and those east of the Jordan) and cause them to adopt preventative or invasive countermeasures, which in turn brought the tribes in the hill country into a tighter alliance, even militarily. Thus one thing led to another, and in the end, as a consequence, to the Israelite (and Judahite) territorial state.

This development can be traced quite clearly in the older biblical sources. There are indications of the preliminary stages of political and military unification in the tales of savior figures and lists of judges in the book of Judges. As judge, Samuel acted beyond the tribal boundaries of Ephraim and Benjamin and supposedly even gained a victory over the Philistines (1 Sam. 7). It is entirely possible that such a man used his reputation and influence to install the first king (1 Sam. 10; on the other hand, his having anointed the second as well, as told in 1 Sam. 16:1–13, is altogether improbable). But another picture is likewise plausible: that the tribal warriors elevated their leader on their shields after a victory (1 Sam. 11; here the figure of Samuel has been inserted secondarily at 11:12–14). We are not able to gain a clearer picture of the first step to statehood. More perceptible, however, is how the progress from the first to the second king, and thence to the third, came about, and how in the process the forms of rule were altered and the kingship was stabilized.

7.2.2 The Kingdom of Saul

No matter how misty his individual contours remain, King Saul is not a mythical figure. Had he not existed, he would never have been invented. In the first place, in his remarkably ambivalent relationship with Samuel, the man of God, and in his ultimate failure, he is no mythically enlightened superman. In the second place, as predecessor and counter-pole to David, so celebrated in tradition, he is more of an annoyance than a *desideratum*.

Saul's kingdom was still very close to being a tribal structure. He was emphatically a Benjaminite (1 Sam. 9:1; 10:20), and he was a farmer: supposedly the "Spirit" had to seize him from behind the plow and set him at the head of the army (1 Sam. 11:5). Afterward he recruited his military leaders from Benjamin (1 Sam. 22:7). Members of his family had the top ranks in his hierarchy: son, son-in-law, cousin (1 Sam. 20:25). No one can build a state out of a single family, and besides, Saul's tribe, Benjamin, was a small one (1 Sam. 9:21). Hence his personal power center was weak—and that may indeed have been a reason for making him king.

This king was markedly dependent on the loyalty of the tribes. He could not or would not set up state structures. There is no indication of royal administration or a state apparatus for compelling obedience. Nowhere is it said that he could have summoned the tribes for war against their will or that he collected taxes. We read only of "presents" that were brought to him (1 Sam. 10:3–4)—or that some refused to bring (1 Sam. 10:27). If there was a royal decree issued at his installation (something hinted at in 1 Sam. 10:25), it must have established the rights of his subjects more than those of the king.

Israel's economic situation was precarious when Saul entered into office. The people of the hill villages, already poor, were also under the thumb of the Philistines, who evidently could take from the land whatever they wanted (1 Sam. 13:17–18; see also 23:1). Moreover, they appear to have guaranteed themselves a monopoly on the production and upkeep of iron farming tools; production of weapons was completely banned (1 Sam. 13:19–22). So in case of war, it could happen that Saul's "Hebrews" (a name for social underdogs: cf. e.g., Gen. 39:17; Exod. 1:15; 2:6–7; 1 Sam. 14:11) deserted *en masse* (1 Sam. 13:4–7).

Apparently Saul attempted to create a measure of freedom of action, both economically and militarily. Coming from a well-to-do farming family, he accumulated additional land

and fields, either by clearing new areas, acquiring those that had been abandoned, or conquering territories at the borders of his realm (2 Sam. 21:2; 4:2–3). In this way he accumulated a royal treasury from which he covered his own modest expenses and was able to reward deserving fighters (cf. 1 Sam. 21:8; 22:7; 2 Sam. 9:7, 9; 16:4; 19:30).

Evidently Saul found the tribal summons to war too difficult and unreliable, so he established a troop of mercenaries (1 Sam. 14:52) who were available to him at all times and were unswervingly loyal—unless there were those among them who pursued their own plans, not agreeable to Saul. One such was David, whom Saul tried to bind to himself as his armor-bearer and even his son-in-law, and who nevertheless became his most serious opponent.

It is unclear how long Saul's rule endured. The number of years has been omitted or was no longer remembered at a later time (1 Sam. 13:1). However, the wealth of memories of him indicates a reign that was not all too brief. Certainly he never achieved control over all Israel and Judah. His sphere of influence was limited to the hill country of central Palestine, with a bulge into transjordanian Gilead (cf. 1 Sam. 11; 31:11–13; 2 Sam. 2:9). He had no residence worthy of the name. The thesis sometimes proposed, that he elevated Gibeon—already a handsome Canaanite city—to that status cannot be proven, nor can the proposal that the newly discovered fortified town of Qeiyafa, southwest of Jerusalem, was his foundation. Saul probably lived all his life in his hometown of Gibeah (Tell el-Ful), but larger architectural structures found there cannot be verified as being Saul's fortress or palace.

It seems that Saul always remained a farmer at heart. Perhaps it would be better to style him "chief" rather than "king." At the same time, he did attempt to establish a dynasty. According to the common law of inheritance, his firstborn would have been his natural successor. It cannot firmly be established whether Jonathan really was David's dearest friend and declined his inheritance in favor of David (thus 1 Sam. 18:1–4; 20; 23:14–18). In any case, Jonathan and some of his brothers fell alongside their father in a battle against the Philistines near the northern border of their territory (1 Sam. 31). Saul's surviving son, Ishbaal, received his father's inheritance, but he died soon after at the hands of assassins who thought they were doing David a favor (2 Sam. 2–4). Thus the Saulide kingdom was quickly extinguished, while that of David flourished. (The recently offered hypothesis that the one who brought down the Saulide kingdom was Pharaoh Shoshenq I and not the Philistines—or David—is unlikely.)[4]

7.2.3 The Kingdom of David

David appears on the historical stage as a crass interloper. The biblical authors do everything they can to explain and justify his utterly unbelievable career, but they are unable to conceal the fact that he was, ultimately, a usurper. Born the youngest son of a small farmer in Bethlehem (Judah was not part of Saul's kingdom), he joined Saul's mercenaries in his young manhood, was quickly found to be especially gifted, but roused the mistrust of his lord and thus withdrew from his hostility into his Judahite homeland. There he survived as the head of a group of bandits (something that was possible in the tenth century thanks to the sparse population and lack of any kind of public order). Then, together with his militia, he entered the service of the ruler of Gath (a Philistine city that was important only at that time), receiving the town of Ziklag in the Negev as his fiefdom and using it as a base for raiding the neighborhood and finally as a springboard for his return to Judah—more precisely, to Hebron, where he had himself named king of Judah. He thereby destabilized Saulide Israel to the extent he could. After the royal house there was destroyed, he also was made king of Israel and chose Jerusalem, a city lying between the two parts of the kingdom, as capital of the double monarchy he had thus created. (This is the solid core of the account in 1 Sam. 16–2 Sam. 5. The hypothesis that the motif of a Judean kingship of David was secondary in the texts and that he became in reality first, and even only, king of Israel is hard to believe.[5] The same is the case with the supposition that Saul's and Ishbaal's reigns lasted long enough to be removed directly by Jeroboam I without an interlude of a United Kingdom governed by David and Solomon.)[6]

David appears to have been skilled from the outset in the art of networking. While he was in Saul's service, he made himself popular with everyone. As a militia leader, he drew people on the borders of society to him (1 Sam. 22:1–2) and shaped them into a troop who would go through fire for him (cf. 2 Sam. 21:15–22; 23:8–38). As commandant of the city of Ziklag, he had good relations both with the Philistines (1 Sam. 27) and with the Judeans (1 Sam. 30:26–30). As king, he maintained and cultivated a great many and different connections: with both parts of the kingdom, with individual cities and tribes, with clans and interest groups, with local lords and neighboring kings, with divisions of the army and their leaders, with a variety of wives (together with their families of origin) and sons (including their adherents).

David's rule seems not to have functioned in the same way everywhere. In Judah and Jerusalem he could on the whole do as he chose, but he had to make a treaty with Israel that probably fixed the rights of the king to collect taxes and require the service of soldiers while also establishing the rights of the tribes to consultation and some degree of self-government. He does not seem to have conquered Jerusalem militarily but to have seized it without bloodshed and in some sense to have ruled it as his own possession (2 Sam. 5:6–9). He installed important religious (2 Sam. 6) and politico-military (2 Sam. 8:16–18; 20:23–26) institutions there that served to cement the realm together.

As for the borders of David's kingdom, we find the following: he forced the eastern neighbors (Ammon, Moab, Edom) into a kind of colonial status (though he treated them each differently). Those in the north (several Aramean chiefdoms), he kept within their borders. With the regions to the west (Philistia, Phoenicia), he maintained a kind of hands-off coexistence. The core of his kingdom extended "from Dan to Beersheba" (2 Sam. 3:10; 17:11; 24:15; see also 1 Kgs. 5:5)—that is, from the Lebanon to the Negev. It included the Galilean tribes Saul had not yet incorporated as well as the plains and cities of Canaan. Thus David was ruler not of a great, but of a middle-level realm.[7]

As much as David was master of the art of compromise and juggling, he struck hard when he saw a threat to his interests. People who damaged his reputation or stood in his way were removed (1 Sam. 27; 2 Sam. 1; 4; 11) and rebellions were ruthlessly put down (2 Sam. 15–18; 20). And yet his lack of squeamishness and scruples were mixed with tentativeness and even tenderness (e.g., 2 Sam. 3; 12; 13; 19). The attribution of these features to David was probably not without basis in reality. Apparently, he was a character of unusual complexity. He was remembered later not only as a fighter and conqueror but also as someone persecuted and threatened. It is no accident that out of the biblical literature many psalms were attributed to him, and more of them are laments and petitions than songs of thanksgiving and victory.

It appears that David lived to a ripe old age. There is no way of saying whether he reigned a full four decades, as asserted in 2 Sam. 5:4 and 1 Kgs. 2:11. In any case, the span of his life, as its fundamental features are plausibly painted for us, was extraordinarily eventful: a rise over many obstacles from farm boy to king, the construction of a complicated state system, innumerable battles and wars, the creation of a large family (with numerous wives, chosen not least from a diplomatic point of view, and at least sixteen often difficult and over-ambitious sons), and finally aging and a more or less voluntary withdrawal from power. The multiple ups and downs of that life, the astonishing successes and profound calamities, the mixture of happiness and tragedy, the attractive and repulsive traits of his character, the love and enmity of his contemporaries—all these made David an icon not only of Jewish and Christian literature but of the arts in every form.

7.2.4 The Kingdom of Solomon

Solomon was able to draw directly from what his father had created. Very few innovations and no expansive activities at all are attributed to him. Nevertheless, he built a handsome temple and an even more lavish palace complex in the capital city (1 Kgs. 6–7), and he may have established one or another minor administrative center. He subdivided the administration of the double kingdom somewhat more, and in northern Israel he created a provincial system for levying provisions and labor (1 Kgs. 4:1–19). It is not impossible that he integrated the northern and southern parts of the kingdom more firmly within the network of Near Eastern mercantile connections and drew from it additional resources for a state budget that was relatively opulent in comparison to that of David's time, and certainly to that of Saul.

But on the whole, Solomon's rule was much less magnificent and brilliant than the Bible depicts it. Under him, Israel remained what it had been under David—a middle-level power that under his leadership already began to show signs of declining coherence within and a retreat from dominance without (1 Kgs. 11). It was long thought that Solomon could be shown, by means of archaeological investigation, to have been the great builder he is portrayed to have been especially in 1 Kgs. 9:17–19, but that has been called into question. That he equipped his buildings with unheard-of luxuries, that he and his household consumed hecatombs of cattle and tons of other foods annually, that he had a harem of one thousand wives, that he made Israel a center of international commerce dominating the whole Levant from Egypt to the Euphrates, that he equipped and sent out whole fleets of oversea ships, and above all that he had more wisdom than anyone else—all that is legend.[8] The greater part of the biblical account of Solomon is intended to create the impression that his time was Israel's golden age.

What one can concede is that it was a time of peace. We do not hear of a single war conducted by Solomon. Though he may have been less of a political genius than his father, he did understand how to keep his inheritance intact. Immediately after the end of his reign (supposedly again lasting forty years according to 1 Kgs. 11:42), the double monarchy broke apart (1 Kgs. 12), and thereafter Israel and Judah went their separate ways.

7.3 Conclusion

The biblical picture of the formation of the state and the early kingship in Israel is neither complete nor historically accurate at every point. From today's perspective it is especially evident that the Bible does not bring social-political aspects to the fore so much as theological ones. What was God's attitude toward the monarchy? The answer: God was not especially fond of it, but wanted neither to deny his people its advantages nor to protect them against its disadvantages. And what was God's opinion of the first three kings? The answer: God's hand was at work in the installation of all three, but not all of them were equally close to God. Saul was the man of God's choice, and yet it almost seems as if God made a mistake with him and quickly let him drop. God held immovably to David, in success but also in failures and missteps. As for Solomon, in the beginning God favored him and gave him much success, but in the end he proved a disappointment. In all this, the biblical presentation never descends to the level of propaganda; it always retains its subtlety, never losing contact with historical reality. It portrays the early royal period as a time when important switches were thrown and when the basis was laid for the half-millennium in which Israel and Judah enjoyed more or less political independence (and, beyond that, for repeated blossoming of messianic expectations). But in the context of the whole history of Israel, extending over several thousand years, kingship with political independence remains only a single episode and a marginal phenomenon.

Notes

1. I wish to thank Linda Maloney for her excellent translation of my German written text.
2. For an extended discussion with examples, see Moore and Kelle 2011.
3. That the label, "house of David" does not mean a state but only a kinship group, as recently assumed by Leonard-Fleckman 2016, is improbable.
4. For this hypothesis, see Finkelstein and Silberman 2006.
5. Against Leonard-Fleckman 2016: 182–87.
6. So Finkelstein 2013.
7. Cf. Mazar's (2006: 268) statement, "Thus we may envision a talented leader such as David, who was charismatic, manipulative, and adept at intertribal affairs; combine this with the use of a small but competent military and the absence of a significant external force to intervene, and we have a man who may have been able to gain considerable political and military power in his time and place."
8. The last-mentioned aspect was especially influential as no fewer than four wisdom books—Proverbs, Qoheleth, Song of Songs, and Wisdom of Solomon—were attributed to him.

Bibliography

Abadie, Philippe. 2011. *Des héros peu ordinaires: Théologie et histoire dans le livre des Juges*. Lectio Divina 243. Paris: Cerf.
Alt, Albrecht. 1964. "Die Staatenbildung der Israeliten in Palästina." In Albrecht Alt, *Kleine Schriften zur Geschichte des Volkes Israel*, vol. 2. 3rd ed. Munich: Beck, 1–65.

Bezzel, Hannes. 2015. *Saul.* FAT 97. Tübingen: Mohr Siebeck.
Brenner, Athalya, ed. 1993. *A Feminist Companion to Judges.* FCB 4. Sheffield: Sheffield Academic Press.
Brenner, Athalya, ed. 1994. *A Feminist Companion to Samuel and Kings.* FCB 5. Sheffield: Sheffield Academic Press.
Brettler, Marc Zvi. 1995. *The Creation of History in Ancient Israel.* London: Routledge.
Dever, William G. 2017. *Beyond the Texts. An Archaeological Portrait of Ancient Israel and Judah.* Atlanta: SBL.
Dietrich, Walter. 2007. *The Early Monarchy in Israel: The Tenth Century BCE.* Translated by Joachim Vette. Biblical Encyclopedia 3. Atlanta: SBL.
Dietrich, Walter. 2016. *David: Der Herrscher mit der Harfe.* 2nd ed. Biblische Gestalten 14. Leipzig: Evangelische Verlagsanstalt (orig. 2006).
Dietrich, Walter, Cynthia Edenburg, and Philippe Hugo, eds. 2016. *The Books of Samuel: Stories—History—Reception History.* BETL 284. Leuven: Peeters.
Ehrlich, Carl S. and Marsha C. White, eds. 2006. *Saul in Story and Tradition.* FAT 47. Tübingen: Mohr Siebeck.
Faust, Abraham. 2019. " 'The Inhabitants of Philistia.' On the Identity of the Iron I Settlers in the Periphery of the Philistine Heartland." PEQ 151, 105–33.
Finkelstein, Israel. 2013. *The Forgotten Kingdom: The Archaeology and History of Northern Israel.* ANEM 5. Atlanta: SBL.
Finkelstein, Israel and Neil A. Silberman. 2006. *David and Solomon: In Search of the Bible's Sacred Kings and the Roots of the Western Tradition.* New York: Simon & Schuster.
Fokkelman, Jan P. 1981–93. *Narrative Art and Poetry in the Books of Samuel.* 4 vols. Assen: Van Gorcum.
Galil, Gershon et al., eds. 2012. *The Ancient Near East in the 12th–10th Centuries BCE.* AOAT 392. Münster: Ugarit-Verlag.
Gilmour, Rachelle. 2011. *Representing the Past: A Literary Analysis of Narrative Historiography in the Book of Samuel.* VTSup 143. Leiden: Brill.
Grabbe, Lester L., ed. 2010. *Israel in Transition: From Late Bronze II to Iron IIA (c. 1250–850 BCE)*, vol. 2: *The Texts.* LHBOTS 521. New York: T&T Clark.
Grabbe, Lester L. 2016. "The Mighty Men of Israel: 1–2 Samuel and Historicity." In Walter Dietrich, Cynthia Edenburg, and Philippe Hugo, eds., *The Books of Samuel: Stories—History—Reception History.* BETL 284. Leuven: Peeters, 83–104.
Graham, M. Patrick et al., eds. 1997. *The Chronicler as Historian.* JSOTSup 238. Sheffield: Sheffield Academic Press.
Gunn, David M. 1978. *The Story of King David: Genre and Interpretation.* JSOTSup 6. Sheffield: Sheffield Academic Press.
Gunn, David M. 1980. *The Fate of King Saul.* JSOTSup 14. Sheffield: JSOT Press.
Halpern, Baruch. 2001. *David's Secret Demons: Messiah, Murderer, Traitor, King.* Grand Rapids: Eerdmans.
Handy, Lowell K., ed. 1997. *The Age of Solomon: Scholarship at the Turn of the Millennium.* SHANE 11. Leiden and New York: Brill.
Hentschel, Georg. 2003. *Saul: Schuld, Reue und Tragik eines "Gesalbten."* Biblische Gestalten 7. Leipzig: Evangelische Verlagsanstalt.
Japhet, Sara. 1997. *The Ideology of the Book of Chronicles and Its Place in Biblical Thought.* 2nd ed. BEATAJ 9. Frankfurt a. M.: Peter Lang.
Kessler, Rainer. 2007. *Samuel: Priester und Richter, Königsmacher und Prophet.* Biblische Gestalten 18. Leipzig: Evangelische Verlagsanstalt.
Kessler, Rainer, Walter Sommerfeld, and Leslie Tramontini, eds. 2016. *State Formation and State Decline in the Near and Middle East.* Wiesbaden: Harrassowitz.
Kipfer, Sara. 2015. *Der bedrohte David: Eine exegetische und rezeptionsgeschichtliche Studie zu 1 Sam 16–1 Kön 2.* SBR 3. Berlin and Boston: de Gruyter.

Kratz, Reinhard G. 2000. *Die Komposition der erzählenden Bücher des Alten Testaments*. Göttingen: Vandenhoeck & Ruprecht.

Lee, Kaung Jae. 2017. *Symbole für Herrschaft und Königtum in den Erzählungen von Saul und David*. BWANT 210. Stuttgart: Kohlhammer.

Leonard-Fleckman, Mahri. 2016. *The House of David: Between Political Formation and Literary Revision*. Minneapolis: Fortress.

Mazar, Amihai. 2006. "Jerusalem in the 10th Century B.C.E.: The Glass Half Full." In Yairah Amit et al., eds., *Essays on Ancient Israel in Its Near Eastern Context: A Tribute to Nadav Na'aman*. Winona Lake, IN: Eisenbrauns, 255–72.

McKenzie, Steven L. 2000. *King David: A Biography*. New York: Oxford University Press.

Moore, Megan Bishop and Brad E. Kelle. 2011. *Biblical History and Israel's Past: The Changing Study of the Bible and History*. Grand Rapids: Eerdmans.

Müller, Reinhard. 2004. *Königtum und Gottesherrschaft*. FAT 2/3. Tübingen: Mohr Siebeck.

Na'aman, Nadav. 2006. *Ancient Israel's History and Historiography: The First Temple Period*. Collected Essays. Vol. 3. Winona Lake, IN: Eisenbrauns.

Noth, Martin. 1991. *The Deuteronomistic History*. 2nd ed. JSOTSup 15. Sheffield: Sheffield Academic Press.

Sæbø, Magne, Peter Machinist, and Jean Louis Ska, eds. 2015. *Hebrew Bible/Old Testament: The History of Its Interpretation*, Vol. 3: *From Modernism to Post-Modernism*. Göttingen: Vandenhoeck & Ruprecht.

Scherer, Andreas. 2005. *Überlieferungen von Religion und Krieg: Exegetische und religionsgeschichtliche Untersuchungen zu Richter 3–8 und verwandten Texten*. WMANT 105. Neukirchen-Vluyn: Neukirchener Verlag.

Van Seters, John. 2009. *The Biblical Saga of King David*. Winona Lake, IN: Eisenbrauns.

Vaughn, Andrew G. and Ann E. Killebrew, eds. 2003. *Jerusalem in Bible and Archaeology: The First Temple Period*. Leiden and Boston: Brill.

Veijola, Timo. 1975. *Die ewige Dynastie: David und die Entstehung seiner Dynastie nach der deuteronomistischen Darstellung*. AASF.B 193. Helsinki: Suomalainen Tiedeakatemia.

Veijola, Timo. 1977. *Das Königtum in der Beurteilung der deuteronomistischen Historiographie: Eine redaktionsgeschichtliche Untersuchung*. AASF.B 198. Helsinki: Suomalainen Tiedeakatemia.

Vermeylen, Jacques. 2000. *La loi du plus fort: Histoire de la redaction des récits davidiques de 1 Samuel 8 a 1 Rois 2*. BETL 154. Leuven: Peeters.

Wälchli, Stefan. 1999. *Der weise König Salomo*. BWANT 141. Stuttgart: Kohlhammer.

Weinberg, Joel P. 1992. *The Citizen-Temple Community*. JSOTSup 151. Sheffield: Sheffield Academic Press.

Willi, Thomas. 1972. *Die Chronik als Auslegung: Untersuchungen zur literarischen Gestaltung der historischen Überlieferung Israels*. FRLANT 106. Göttingen: Vandenhoeck & Ruprecht.

Wolpe, David. 2014. *David: The Divided Heart*. Jewish Lives. New Haven, CT and London: Yale University Press.

Wright, Jacob L. 2014. *David, King of Israel, and Caleb in Biblical Memory*. Cambridge: Cambridge University Press.

Zachary, Thomas. 2016. "Debating the United Monarchy: Let's See How Far Wi've Come." BTB 46, 59–69.

CHAPTER 8

THE LATER MONARCHY IN HISTORY AND BIBLICAL HISTORIOGRAPHY

PAUL S. EVANS

ACCOUNTS of the reigns of Hezekiah, Manasseh, and Josiah are found in both the books of Kings and Chronicles. Our understanding of their reigns is greatly illuminated by the wealth of archaeological and epigraphic evidence available from that time period. Archaeological surveys help us better assess the breadth and status of their kingdoms, and ancient inscriptions fill in gaps in our understanding of the political and international events of that era. At the same time, correlating this extrabiblical material with that of the historical books often leads to difficult questions and reassessments of Judah's history during this period. The majority of historical issues related to their reigns are tied up with our understanding of the actions of the neo-Assyrian Empire, with its great expansion and dominance of Syria-Palestine, and then its decline and eventual collapse. This chapter will focus on historical issues that affect the way we understand these biblical kings and the biblical books in which their accounts are found.

8.1 THE FALL OF SAMARIA

One of the key historical events in this period is the fall of Samaria to the Assyrians. According to the account in 2 Kings, the last king of northern Israel, Hoshea, initially submitted to Assyria when Shalmaneser attacked (2 Kgs. 17:3), but then withheld tribute and sought out support from Egypt (2 Kgs. 17:4). The Hebrew Bible lists "King So" as the Egyptian monarch to whom Hoshea appealed; however, no such monarch is known from other sources. Some have suggested that "So" could be a hypocoristicon of Osorkon IV (Kitchen 1986: 373–76, 551–52), while others suggest that "So" was a geographical location rendering "Sais," where King Tefnakht, the founder of the Twenty-fourth Dynasty, had his capital (Redford 1992: 346; Younger 2002: 290). In response to Hoshea's treachery the Assyrians took Hoshea prisoner (2 Kgs. 17:4) and mounted a full-scale invasion (2 Kgs. 17:5), laying siege to Samaria for three years. In Hoshea's ninth year (ca. 722 BCE) Samaria fell (2 Kgs. 17:6; 18:10).

Biblical and deuterocanonical sources all ascribe the capture of Samaria to Shalmaneser (2 Kgs. 17:3; 18:9; Tob. 1:2, 13, 15; 2 Esdr. 13:40), as does the Babylonian Chronicle (Grayson 1975: 5:73; Younger 1999: 466; Kelle and Bishop Moore 2006: 662). While there are no extant inscriptions from Shalmaneser in this regard, eight extant inscriptions of his successor, Sargon II, claim that he captured Samaria (see *COS* 2.118A: 293–94; 2.118D: 295–96; 2.118E: 296–97), making a definitive reconstruction problematic.

Several different reconstructions have been suggested given the available evidence. Some have suggested that all three sources (biblical, Babylonian, and Assyrian) refer to different campaigns against Samaria (Hayes and Kuan 1991: 180), first by Shalmaneser, then by Sargon. This view places the first siege of Samaria (referenced in the Babylonian Chronicle) in Shalmaneser's second regnal year (ca. 725 BCE) and views it as distinct from the siege of Samaria mentioned in the Hebrew Bible (Hayes and Kuan 1991: 180). The second siege of Samaria (as recorded in the Hebrew Bible) would then be dated to 724 BCE (not reflected in extrabiblical texts) and seen as lasting three years. Either shortly before or after the end of this siege, Shalmaneser died (722/1)—evidently of natural causes (Younger 1999: 468 n. 28). With the death of the king, the army may have withdrawn, leaving matters in Samaria "unsettled" (Hayes and Kuan 1991: 180). His successor, Sargon, experienced trouble on the homefront in his first year, with local rebellion against his regency. This internal unrest, it is suggested, proved a perfect pretext for renewed rebellion in the west. Therefore, in Sargon's second regnal year (ca. 720 BCE), the third siege of Samaria occurred as he campaigned to the west and forcefully put down all rebellion. In this final submission, northern Israel lost all independence and was annexed into an Assyrian province. A more simplified version of events has Shalmaneser conquering Samaria in 722 BCE (as in biblical texts and the Babylonian Chronicle), then Sargon returning in 720 BCE to do so again, and exile the population.

Against these reconstructions, it seems unlikely that following a three-year siege and conquest by Shalmaneser (ca. 722 BCE), Samaria could muster forces to rebel after only about a year and a half, requiring another siege by Sargon (720 BCE). Furthermore, Sargon was a usurper to the throne and his accession was plagued by internal revolts (Tadmor 1981: 27) and an early defeat in conflict with Babylon and Elam (ca. 720 BCE), making it unlikely he could campaign again in the west within the same year (Park 2012: 100). What is more, the Assur charter places the internal unrest as taking place *after* Sargon's campaign to the west (*COS* 2.118C). This timeline also fits with Sargon's exiling six thousand "guilty" Assyrian soldiers to Hamath (Borowski Stela) for their role in the internal revolt. Given that Hamath was only captured in Sargon's campaign to the west, the internal unrest must have been *after* his capture of Samaria (Park 2012). Thus, 720 BCE is too late in his reign for the siege of Samaria. Furthermore, some Assyrian texts from Sargon locate the conquest of Samaria "at the beginning of [Sargon's] royal rule" (*ANET* 284). Archaeological evidence is also somewhat problematic for a multiple conquest theory. Excavators of Samaria have found fewer signs of destruction compared to other sites that suffered destruction by the Assyrians (Avigad 1993: 1300–1310; Park 2012: 100).

The biblical description of the event, while naming Shalmaneser, otherwise agrees most closely with Sargon's inscriptions. In congruence with biblical claims (2 Kgs. 17:5–6), Sargon II claims to have made mass deportations (*COS* 2.295–96). Furthermore, the five nationalities mentioned in 2 Kgs. 17:24 from where new peoples were brought by Assyria to replace the Israelite deportees match Mesopotamian locations which Sargon conquered in his reign (Barrick 1996: 632–36). Furthermore, some Israelite exiles were deported to Halah (2 Kgs. 17:6). This was the district where Sargon was building his new capital city of Dūr-Šarrukin, which was built by prisoners of war—probably some of them Israelites (Younger 2002: 298).

In all likelihood then, the siege and conquest of Samaria under Sargon only happened once. Under Shalmaneser, Sargon likely led the army on the campaign as Assyrian prince (a common Assyrian practice). Shalmaneser died either during the three-year siege of Samaria or shortly thereafter. After taking Samaria and quelling the rebellion in the west (including Hamath), Sargon returned home to usurp the throne, leading to the internal revolts, and his exiling the "guilty" Assyrian soldiers who revolted to recently conquered Hamath. Sargon's first campaign as king, then, was not against the west, but against Babylon and Elam (ca. 720 BCE), though it was not a successful one. Sargon eventually defeated Elam but not until 710 BCE. Sargon's scribes likely attributed the successful campaign against the west (though carried out under the aegis of his predecessor) to the beginning of the usurper Sargon's reign to bolster his legitimacy.

8.2 THE ASHDOD REVOLT

Shortly after the fall of Samaria, rebellion again stirred in the western regions. Ashdod, one of the five great cities of the Philistines, led a rebellion against Assyria, supported by Egypt. Assyria put down the rebellion ca. 712 or 711 BCE. Assyrian texts suggest that Sargon himself led the punitive campaign, though biblical evidence has the high ranking Assyrian Tartan leading the army (Isa. 20:1). While the historical books of the Hebrew Bible do not mention the Ashdod revolt, it is mentioned in the brief narrative in Isaiah 20 where Isaiah is told to walk barefoot and naked for three years (v. 2)—that is, appearing as a prisoner of war—as a sign of what will happen to the Egyptians and Ethiopians on whom the rebels relied (vv. 3–6). Nothing is said in the passage, however, of whether Judah was involved in the rebellion. Presumably, Isaiah is called to perform his sign action to dissuade Judah from such participation.

One Assyrian text explicitly mentions Judah in the context of the Ashdod rebellion. It reads:

> Then [to] the rulers of Palestine (*Pi-lii-te*), Judah (*Ia-u-di*), Ed[om], Moab (and) those who live (on islands) and bring tribute [and] *tāmartu*-gifts to my lord Ashur—[he spread] countless evil lies to alienate (them) from me. (*ANET* 287)

Is not clear whether the countries listed here actually participated in the rebellion. In the aftermath of the rebellion, Sargon claims to have captured "Ashdod, Gath, Asdudimmu"

(*ANET* 286) and "reorganized" these cities, making them Assyrian provinces. Furthermore, Sargon boasts of threatening Egypt for their part in the rebellion, resulting in the pharaoh extraditing the rebel king of Ashdod to Sargon, as well as giving him horses (*ANET* 286). Yet no such reprisal or posturing is mentioned in regards to Judah.

Seeing as the prophet Isaiah explicitly argued against such participation (ch. 20), it seems likely that his lobbying was effective and that Hezekiah did not throw in with Ashdod at this time (Miller and Hayes 1986: 351). This would be consistent with the portrayal of Hezekiah in the historical books as being on good terms with the prophet Isaiah (contra Ahaz, his father, who defied the prophet; cf. Isa. 7).

8.3 HEZEKIAH'S FOURTEENTH YEAR

One of the most debated issues surrounding Hezekiah's reign is the reference to Sennacherib's invasion of 701 BCE occurring in Hezekiah's fourteenth year (2 Kgs. 18:13), which contradicts the statement in 2 Kgs. 18:9–10 that Hezekiah was in his sixth year when Samaria fell to Assyria in 722 BCE.

In order to solve the problem, some have suggested that 2 Kgs. 18:13–16 originally referred to the revolt of Ashdod that dates ca. 712 BCE (Jenkins 1976; Becking 2003). Against this view, Sennacherib is explicitly named as king in 2 Kgs. 18:13–16, and his base of operations is said to be Lachish, the same as in the following story (18:17; 19:8). What is more, conquering Lachish was a source of significant boasting for Sennacherib, with a relief depicting the event decorating his palace wall (Uehlinger 2003), making it unlikely that Sargon had captured it previously. Finally, Hezekiah's tribute payment in 2 Kgs. 18:13–16 coheres remarkably with the amount recorded in Sennacherib's annals with both recording the payment of 30 talents of gold. While Kings records 300 talents of silver, Sennacherib's annals appear to claim 800 talents of silver were paid. The discrepancy between the amounts of silver, however, has been adequately explained by understanding the number 800 in Sennacherib's inscription (*ANET* 288) as referring not only to the silver but the weight of the total amount of different goods listed in inscription (Mayer 1995: 360–63; 2003: 183).

A simpler solution to Hezekiah's fourteenth year would be to emend the text from Hezekiah's "14th" year to his "24th" year, which would make Hezekiah take the throne in 725 BCE—a better fit with the dating of the fall of Samaria. Of course, no textual witnesses support this emendation, leading most to reject the proposal. Alternatively, a plausible literary solution to the problem suggests that the reference to the fourteenth year was an invention of a later compiler who arrived at it by subtracting the fifteen-year-extension of Hezekiah's life in 2 Kgs. 20:6 from Hezekiah's twenty-nine-year reign. However, most studies conclude that the reference in 2 Kgs. 18:13 is from archival material and not the work of a later compiler (Cogan and Tadmor 1988: 228; Grabbe 2003: 319;).

Probably the proposal most likely to solve the issue is one that accounts for years of co-regencies of Judahite kings (Thiele 1951). Egyptian evidence shows the practice of co-regencies (joint rule) of father and son was intended to secure the succession of the dynasty, and co-regencies may have been the norm in Judah since Athaliah nearly destroyed the Davidic dynasty (2 Kgs. 11:1) (Na'aman 1986: 91). If so, Hezekiah's accession to the throne in Hoshea's third year (2 Kgs. 18:1) refers to when his co-regency with his father Ahaz began. The later synchronization with Hoshea's reign (2 Kgs. 18:9–10) continues to reflect his co-regency. However, the twenty-nine years ascribed to Hezekiah in 2 Kgs. 18:2 covered only Hezekiah's time as sole ruler (Na'aman 1986: 89), as did the reference to Hezekiah's fourteenth year in 2 Kgs. 18:13. Thus, the dates for Hezekiah's sole reign were ca. 715–686 BCE.

8.4 THE ASSYRIAN INVASION OF JUDAH (701 BCE)

As we have seen in Hezekiah's early reign, he did not join the many anti-Assyrian rebellions that occurred around him (Miller and Hayes 1986: 351). Following Sargon II's subjugation of the Ashdod revolt, there appear to have been some years devoid of military conflict with Assyria. Biblical sources attribute to Hezekiah an extensive religious reform during this time that centralized worship (cf. 2 Kgs. 18:3–8; 2 Chr. 29–31) and consolidated both religious and political authority in Jerusalem (Halpern 1991: 11–107). Archaeologically, there is little sign of a drastic change in the religious practices of Judah during this time, or the iconoclasm suggested in biblical sources (e.g., 2 Kgs. 18:4). Some find archaeological evidence at Arad (stratum IX) of a temple that was destroyed not by military invasion but by deliberate dismantling to be evidence of Hezekiah's religious reform (Herzog 1997: 175) though others are not convinced (Na'aman 1995: 184–85).

On the other hand, an ample amount of archaeological evidence seems to support Hezekiah's economic buildup and the centralization of power in Jerusalem. Judahite expansion can be archaeologically seen in the many new settlements in the Shephelah that appeared early in Hezekiah's reign, suggesting growing economic and civil power (Vaughn 1999: 22–27). The buildup is also seen in sites in the central hill country and the Negeb (Vaughn 1999: 32–79) and in the expansion of Jerusalem during this time (Cogan 1998: 246; Finkelstein and Silberman 2001: 243). Finally, more than 1,700 jars with *lmlk* or "belonging to the king" stamped on their handles have been found in ancient Judah and date to the reign of Hezekiah specifically (Ussishkin 1988: 50–53). These jars appear to be evidence of Hezekiah's advanced preparation for an Assyrian attack (Na'aman 1979: 73–76, 85–86; cf. Rainey 1982: 57–62 and Vaughn 1999: 167).

Given the relative prosperity of Judah during this time, the reason for Hezekiah's rebellion is debated. There is little doubt that the leading motivation to rebel against Assyria was the burden of being a vassal, with the exorbitant tribute draining the economy and negatively affecting the quality of life for the people of Judah. These problems, however, were not new in Hezekiah's regency. More likely, changes in Assyria led the Judahite king to believe that the time for rebellion was ripe and that chances of success were substantial.

With Sargon's new capital city Dūr-Šarrukin completed six years after quelling the Ashdod revolt, Sargon compelled the kings of the west, probably including Hezekiah (Gallagher 1999: 268), to attend its dedication. The building of the city had required forced labor from prisoners of war and from vassal states, and there is evidence that the extensive building projects put significant strain on the Assyrian Empire. An inscription of Sennacherib speaks of Assyrian kings exhausting "every workman" and using "up the oil, wax and wool" (Gallagher 1999: 266). Other texts talk of previous kings—possibly Sargon—cutting down trees for his projects till no trees were left. Two extant letters to Sargon explicitly talk about a shortage of soldiers (Parpola 1987: 115–16 no. 143). There is also evidence of extensive shortages of straw (required both for feeding horses and for making bricks) under Sargon. Correspondence to the king also indicated that Sargon was losing control of southern Babylonia (Gallagher 1999: 266). While the vassal kings visiting Dūr-Šarrukin were no doubt impressed with Sargon's new capital city, it is possible their visit to the heart of the empire also resulted in their picking up hints of such weaknesses that were hurting the empire.

When Sargon was killed in battle against Anatolia about a year later, it sent shock waves through the empire. After his son, Sennacherib, took the throne, Sargon's new capital city was abandoned (Tadmor, Landsberger, and Parpola 1989: 28–29), and the new king inquired of the gods about "Sargon's sin" that may have led to his untimely death (Tadmor, Landsberger, and Parpola 1989: 9–24; Younger 2002: 319). The unsettling aftermath in Assyria emboldened Assyrian enemies to make their move.

The first to do so was Babylon. While Sargon II was the official king of Babylon from 709 BCE onwards until his death (Brinkman 1964: 22), Sennacherib lost the Babylonian throne when Marduk-zakir-shumi took it in 704 BCE. A month later Merodach-baladan took the throne from Marduk-zakir-shumi and assembled a coalition of Elamites and others against Assyria (*ANET* 272). This rebellion completely occupied Sennacherib at the beginning of his reign (*Babylonian Chronicle* ii 12–23) and prevented him from campaigning against the rebels in the west for some time.

Biblical sources clearly suggest that Hezekiah had ties with Merodach-baladan (2 Kgs. 20:12), and it seems likely their rebellions were somewhat coordinated (2 Kgs. 18:7). With the failure of the Babylonian rebellion in late 704 BCE, if he had not already done so, Hezekiah probably began preparations for an Assyrian invasion. Biblical sources tell us that Hezekiah restructured the army (2 Chr. 32:6) and fortified the walls of Jerusalem (2 Chr. 32:5). Archaeological excavations have found part of a fortified wall on the western hill of Jerusalem approximately twenty feet thick, as well as a fortified wall at Lachish dating to Hezekiah's time (Finkelstein and Silberman 2001: 255–57).

Biblical sources also indicate that part of his preparation was rerouting Jerusalem's water supply in preparation for a siege (2 Chr. 32:3–4; cf. 2 Kgs. 20:20), which appears to be verified archaeologically by the so-called Siloam Tunnel. Originally discovered in 1838, the discovery in 1880 of an inscription in the tunnel brought the tunnel's importance to the fore. While some have attempted to date the tunnel to a later period (Rogerson and Davies 1996), a broad consensus dates it to Hezekiah's time and associates it with Hezekiah's preparations for an Assyrian assault on Jerusalem (Hackett 1997). This was a massive project that had to have begun well in advance rather than being undertaken on the eve of the Assyrian campaign (contra the sense in 2 Chr. 32:2).

Hezekiah's exact role in the anti-Assyrian coalition has been debated. The rebellion in the west included at least Sidon, Ashkelon, Ekron, and Egypt, and many studies have asserted that Hezekiah was the leader of the western rebellion (Vogt 1986: 6–9; Na'aman

1991b: 94; Redford 1992: 351; Gallagher 1999: 110–12, 263–74). Several pieces of evidence may point to Hezekiah's leadership role in the rebellion: (1) Hezekiah's contact with Merodach-baladan (2 Kgs. 20); (2) Hezekiah's aggression against Philistia (understood as attempts to bring them into the anti-Assyrian coalition); (3) the fact that Padi, the pro-Assyrian king of Ekron, was given to Hezekiah as prisoner; and (4) Hezekiah's alliance with Egypt.

The evidence, however, is inconclusive, and it is not clear that Hezekiah played the central role in the western rebellion. First, Hezekiah's contact with Merodach-baladan does not show Hezekiah was the ring-leader, just that he was a rebel. Second, Hezekiah's actions against the Philistines could be understood as mainly attempts at state expansion (against Judah's long-time enemy). Third, Sennacherib portrays the Ekronites deposing Padi of their own volition (*ANET* 287), and Hezekiah's role in imprisoning him need not show him as their leader, but as co-conspirator in the rebellion. Finally, it is unclear whether Hezekiah sought out an alliance with Egypt. Sennacherib's annals clearly attribute the call to Egypt to the people of Ekron (*ANET* 287) and the Egyptian force engaged in battle to defend Philistia, not Judah (which makes sense given Philistine proximity to Egypt). While the Rabshakeh (2 Kgs. 18:20–21) accuses Hezekiah of reliance on Egypt (claiming that Egypt is unreliable), the context is clearly a hostile Assyrian figure attempting to dissuade the Jerusalem population from following their king. The prophet Isaiah agreed with the Rabshakeh about the unreliability of Egypt (Isa. 30:6–7). Given Hezekiah's adherence to the prophet's words elsewhere (2 Kgs. 19; 20), it is possible such prophetic rhetoric could have successfully influenced the king in this regard.

In sum, there is no clear evidence that Hezekiah did, in fact, rely on Egypt in his rebellion (Gallagher 1999: 274; Seitz 1991: 71–81). Biblical sources instead suggest Hezekiah was not trusting in a coalition to succeed, though no doubt biblical texts are theologically skewed to present Hezekiah as relying solely on Yhwh for success. Of course, Hezekiah's preparations for an Assyrian invasion are also recorded in biblical sources (e.g., 2 Chr. 20:2–6), so his reliance on God did not preclude his other plans for surviving an Assyrian assault.

The invasion of Sennacherib is recorded in three biblical texts (2 Kgs. 18–19; Isa. 36–37; 2 Chr. 32) and numerous Assyrian texts, and a significant amount of archaeological remains are relevant to a historical reconstruction. While the main outline of events is obvious, several issues are the subject of intense debate and disagreement among scholars.

All agree that Sennacherib's invasion devastated Judah. Both biblical and extrabiblical texts detail massive destruction of Judahite cities (*ANET* 288; 2 Kgs. 18:13). Sennacherib further claims to have taken 200,105 captives (*ANET* 288), though the number is clearly too high to be accurate (Knauf 2003: 146). Possibly the number reflects the count of all live booty (animals included) from the entire campaign and not just from Judah (Mayer 2003: 182).

Archaeological evidence clearly supports this devastation as well. Excavations have shown the extensive damage suffered by the city of Lachish, with a burn layer dating to 701 BCE (Ussishkin 1982). The Shephelah suffered the worst, with archaeological estimates suggesting its population dropped by two-thirds after the invasion (Finkelstein and Silberman 2001: 264).

Attempts to explain the account in Kings have frequently suggested that it is a compilation of three sources (Stade 1886; Childs 1967). The first source (Account A) explained the withdrawal of the Assyrian army due to Hezekiah's payment (2 Kgs. 18:13–16). The second source (Account B1) explained the withdrawal of the Assyrian army as due to Sennacherib hearing a report of an Egyptian threat (2 Kgs. 18:17–19a, 36–37). The third source (Account B2) explained the Assyrian withdrawal as due to an angelic attack that decimated Sennacherib's army. Based on these source critical delineations, some even suggested that the putative sources reflect two different campaigns of Sennacherib against Hezekiah, though no Assyrian evidence for such a campaign exists. According to this view, Account A reflects the 701 BCE campaign, while the B accounts reflect a later (otherwise unknown) campaign in 688 BCE. Initially, the mention of Tirhakah (2 Kgs. 19:9) was thought to necessitate a second campaign because it was thought he was only a boy in 701 BCE. Later work on Egyptian chronology, however, revealed that Tirhakah was a prince of around 20 years old in 701 BCE and could have campaigned into Palestine (Millard 1985: 63; Kitchen 1986: 386; Redford 1992: 353). In sum, the two-campaign theory has been rejected by a significant consensus, based as it is on speculative source-critical delineations and unsupported by any Assyrian texts. Recent study has also undermined the source-critical delineations significantly (Person 1997; Evans 2009).

According to the account in Kings, when Sennacherib was at Lachish, Hezekiah initially offered a conditional surrender (2 Kgs. 18:14). Hezekiah says in the imperative, "turn back from me" (2 Kgs. 18:14), implying the payment offered was to secure an Assyrian withdrawal from Judahite territory (Gallagher 1999: 256). If Hezekiah's demands were met, then Hezekiah could remain on the throne and Judah would not be annexed into an Assyrian state. With the sending of the Assyrian emissaries to demand the total surrender of Jerusalem (2 Kgs. 19:17), it would appear that Hezekiah's conditional surrender was initially rejected. However, the listing of Hezekiah's payment at the end of Sennacherib's account in his annals suggests that it was eventually accepted. It was likely initially rejected because the Assyrian goal was the deposing of Hezekiah and the installation of a pro-Assyrian king (or possibly the annexation of Judah into an Assyrian state).

While Hezekiah's initial offer of payment for withdrawal was rejected, remarkably, no siege of Jerusalem occurred as a result. The report of a "heavy force" (2 Kgs. 18:17) visiting Jerusalem appears to refer to an Assyrian military detachment that accompanied the Assyrian messengers rather than a besieging army. In the biblical sources, no siege language appears in the narrative, except where Isaiah prophesies (2 Kgs. 19:32) that there will be no siege (Evans 2009: 161–62). The likely reason that scholars have often read a siege into the biblical account is due to Sennacherib's famous statement that "[Hezekiah] Himself I made a prisoner in Jerusalem, his royal residence, like a bird in a cage" (*ANET* 288). Recent work, however, has questioned whether this claim implies an actual siege of the city. In Sennacherib's annals, when describing the siege of the fortified cities of Judah, the description is much more elaborate (*COS* 2.119E: 305). If Jerusalem was besieged, one would expect more elaborate descriptions of siege warfare concerning Jerusalem. Many studies have now concluded that Sennacherib did not put Jerusalem to siege (Tadmor 1985; Kooij 1986; Mayer 1995; Grabbe 2003a, 2003b; Evans 2009) and no archaeological evidence for such a siege has been found (Ussishkin 2006: 352).

The most debated part of the reconstruction of Sennacherib's campaign against Judah surrounds how the campaign concluded. Second Kings purports that losses suffered by the Assyrian army resulted in Sennacherib's withdrawal (2 Kgs. 19:35) and contradict the Assyrian annals, which describe the campaign as an unmitigated victory. Although victory is claimed by both sides, the fact that Hezekiah remained on the throne suggests that the Assyrian campaign did not go quite as planned.

A hint at the events that led to Sennacherib's withdrawal may be seen in the account in Kings where an Egyptian force appears to be instrumental in the Assyrian withdrawal from Jerusalem (2 Kgs. 19:9). When Sennacherib hears of the Egyptian threat, Sennacherib no longer approaches Jerusalem or sends an army, but merely sends messengers with letters (2 Kgs. 19:14), probably gathering his army for the Egyptian attack.

The presence of an Egyptian force in Palestine is also attested in Sennacherib's annals, though it is portrayed as a dismal failure (COS 2.119B: 303). Of course, the extent of success achieved by the Egyptians need not imply a complete victory when viewed from a Judahite perspective. In fact, all that may have been needed by Judah was a distraction to delay the military action against their capital. The Egyptian expedition may have allowed Hezekiah to hold out long enough that Sennacherib could no longer move against Jerusalem. Besides which, as several scholars have pointed out, the language used in Sennacherib's annals to describe the defeat of the Egyptians may hint that it was "far from a glorious victory" for Sennacherib (Eph'al 1983: 98; Knauf 2003: 147).

It is also possible that Sennacherib suffered more than a loss of time in his battle with the Egyptians. Herodotus gives an account of an Egyptian victory over Sennacherib (Herodotus *Hist.* 2.141). Through a detailed literary analysis, Grabbe has demonstrated the independence of the Herodotus text (Grabbe 2003a: 119–40, esp. 136–37; similarly Kahn 2014: 28; contra Strawn 2006). While it is true that Herodotus does not locate this Assyrian defeat near Jerusalem, neither does the account in 2 Kings. In the account in 2 Kings, the last we hear of Sennacherib before the angelic assault (19:35) is Sennacherib learning of Tirhakah's approach and leaving his base of operations at Lachish (2 Kgs. 19:8), implying that the Assyrian king was about to fight the Egyptians. In other words, in 2 Kgs. 19 when Assyria suffers defeat (the angel), Sennacherib is engaged with the Egyptians. It seems likely that the Assyrian setback that occurred in conflict with the Egyptians was interpreted by the Judahites as an act of Yhwh. Without an attempt to correlate this text with the biblical one in detail (e.g., that both refer to a plague), the fact that a tradition of an Assyrian defeat under mysterious circumstance is referred to in two different accounts coming from two disparate groups may indicate it is a genuine historical memory.[1]

One of the biggest questions surrounding the Assyrian invasion of 701 BCE concerns whether Hezekiah's rebellion proved utterly disastrous or somewhat successful. Some state unequivocally that the Assyrian campaign was completely successful (Na'aman 2005a: 112) and that "Sennacherib fully achieved his goals" (Finkelstein and Silberman 2001: 264). However, if we were to judge Sennacherib's aims by the speeches of the Rabshakeh in 2 Kgs. 18:19–35, or by Assyrian treatment of other rebels, the Assyrian goals were not met. The Rabshakeh speaks of a long siege of Jerusalem (18:27) and the deportation of its inhabitants (18:32), neither of which were accomplished. Assyrian policy was usually to depose rebel rulers and to place a new pro-Assyrian king on the throne (e.g., COS 2.119B: 302–303; COS 2.119A: 300–302), yet Hezekiah remained king in Judah.

Reconstructions emphasize the destruction suffered by Judah in the wake of Sennacherib's invasion (Finkelstein 1994; Stern 2001: 142). In his annals, Sennacherib claims to have redistributed parts of Hezekiah's territory and put them under Philistine control (*ANET* 288). The extent of this loss of territory is unclear, however, as Hezekiah had expanded his kingdom at Philistia's expense (2 Kgs. 18:8) so that some of the territory put under Philistine control could have been more of a restoration of Philistine territory rather than the loss of Judahite territory proper (Gallagher 1999: 110). What is more, epigraphic evidence from Judahite sites suggests that the areas in question (e.g., Tel Arad, Khirbet Beit Lei) did not become Philistine territory (Becking 2003: 69).

While it is undeniable that the Assyrians devastated the Shephelah, the deplorable state of Judah after Sennacherib's withdrawal saw rapid improvement. After the invasion, Jerusalem was a city with no rivals, since most other comparably sized cities had been destroyed (Tatum 1991: 141–42). Settlements once again increased, with new towns and growth in rural areas (Tatum 1991: 142; Finkelstein 1994: 174–80). The entire country was not devastated by Sennacherib, as some areas show signs of prosperous existence both before and after the 701 BCE invasion (Ofer 2001). Jerusalem itself expanded significantly, possibly due to the immigration from the Shephelah after the invasion (Broshi 1974; Grabbe 2005: 83).

All this to say that archaeological evidence does not suggest that Judah's territory was limited to the area around Jerusalem after the Assyrian invasion (Becking 2003: 69). Evidently Jerusalem continued to control the countryside (Weippert 1988: 559–681). It seems likely that Hezekiah's payment, grudgingly accepted by Sennacherib after his setback with the Egyptians, could have resulted in the Judahite king gaining control of his country again. Thus, Hezekiah's bold rebellion paid off in some ways. Archaeological excavations show Judah enjoying a time of "rebuilding and relative prosperity" after Sennacherib's withdrawal (Stern 2001: 163), with the rebuilding taking place rapidly following 701 BCE (Stern 2001: 130–31). The return to prosperity occurred early in the seventh century (Finkelstein and Silberman 2001: 265–69). While many place the time of recovery and prosperity in Manasseh's reign, dates for Hezekiah's reign suggested above would actually place much of this progress still within Hezekiah's tenure.

In sum, Hezekiah's rebellion was a calculated risk, the results of which were mixed. While there was clear devastation in the wake of Sennacherib's assault, with the Assyrian withdrawal and failure to take Jerusalem, Jerusalem was left with no local rivals and Judah was poised to prosper. Whether things in Judah improved after 701 BCE vis-à-vis conditions prior to the rebellion seems unlikely. Psychologically, however, it is possible that there was a perceived improvement and optimism since Judah had survived the worst Assyria could throw at them. Such optimism is captured in the biblical accounts, and their preservation must account for something of this nature.

8.5 MANASSEH

The accession of Manasseh to the throne began a period with marked differences from his father Hezekiah. While Hezekiah was renown for his cultic fidelity to Yhwh, Manasseh embraced the worship of other gods (2 Kgs. 21:1–9). Even so, Manasseh reigns the longest of any other Judahite king—fifty-five years.

Following Sennacherib's invasion, Judah was in a rebuilding mode with the majority of the growth and prosperity occurring under Manasseh. Archaeological evidence points to a somewhat peaceful period during Manasseh's tenure. During Manasseh's regency, the Assyrian Empire reached the pinnacle of its imperial power and expansion. Though Sennacherib never again campaigned in the west, his son, Esarhaddon, led multiple assaults. He campaigned against Tyre, Sidon, and Cyprus around 679 BCE (Miller and Hayes 1986: 366), twice invaded Egypt, first unsuccessfully (though not acknowledged in Assyrian sources, but only in the Babylonian Chronicle; see *ANET* 302) in 673 BCE, then defeating their king, Tirhakah, in 671 BCE (*ANET* 293).

When Esarhaddon returned to Egypt two years later to put down Tirhakah's rebellion, he fell ill on route to Egypt and died, leaving it for his son, Ashurbanipal, to finish the job in 664 BCE. Ashurbanipal removed the anti-Assyrian Cushite dynasty and installed the Saite Dynasty. The Assyrians withdrew from Egypt ca. 655 with Psammeticus I on the throne, who proved an Assyrian ally during his reign (Sweeney 2007: 429). Not long after this, a Babylonian revolt led by Shamash Shum-ukin, the king of Babylon (and elder brother of Ashurbanipal), challenged Ashurbanipal ca. 652–648 BCE. Ashurbanipal put down the revolt, killing his brother in the process (Kuhrt 1995: II.587–89).

Being a relatively unimportant king in the big picture, Manasseh is mentioned only twice in extant Assyrian texts despite his lengthy reign. He is listed along with other vassal kings who transported construction materials to Nineveh for Esarhaddon (*ANET* 291), and later is said to have sent troops to aid in Ashurbanipal's Egyptian campaign (*ANET* 294). These texts suggest that Manasseh was a loyal vassal of Assyria (i.e., he complied with Assyrian demands).

Manasseh is reviled in both 2 Kgs. 21 and 2 Chr. 33 for his worship of foreign gods, a portrait which could also fit with his apparent fidelity to Assyria. Some have argued that Manasseh's cultic innovations were adoptions of "elements of the Assyrian state religion" (Noth 1958: 272) and there is speculation that it was Assyrian policy that Assyria required vassal states to worship Assyrian deities (Spieckermann 1982). Others have countered that there is no Assyrian evidence to support the thesis (McKay 1973). Cogan further refined this position, finding a distinction between vassal states and territories annexed by Assyria. In the former, he found "no evidence of imposition upon or interference with native cults" (Cogan 1993: 403). He concluded that since Judah was a vassal state (not annexed into the empire), Manasseh's cultic innovations were voluntary and not imposed on him by his suzerain (Cogan 1974: 113). Nevertheless, though not forced to do so, it is possible that a vassal king might have felt it politically expedient to incorporate the worship of Assyrian deities (Bright 2000: 276, 312). Of course, the biblical texts do not state that Manasseh worshipped foreign gods in order to please Assyria, so the theory, while cogent, remains speculative.

As is well known, the Manasseh account in Chronicles diverges from the portrait in 2 Kings, as it recounts a story of Manasseh's being brought by the Assyrians in chains to Babylon (2 Chr. 33:11). As noted above, although the Assyrians campaigned to the west under Esarhaddon and Ashurbanipal, no direct action against Judah is recorded. In Chronicles, when Manasseh was in "distress" (while being brought in chains?), he repents and seeks God (2 Chr. 33:12–13), who then restores him to the throne. The reformed king then undertakes Yahwistic reforms and constructs an outer wall in Jerusalem (2 Chr. 33:14–16).

Many scholars dismiss the historicity of the Chronicler's Manasseh story as created to reconcile Manasseh's lengthy reign with his wicked behavior (Wellhausen 1973: 206–207).[2] The silence in the book of Kings on Manasseh's being dragged to Babylon in chains is also seen as problematic, especially since the punishment of Manasseh would fit with the Deuteronomist's paradigm of punishment for covenant breaking (Stavrakopoulou 2004: 113–14). Further, the fact Manasseh is taken to Babylon, instead of the Assyrian capital of Nineveh, has suggested to many that Manasseh in Chronicles is meant to foreshadow Israel's experience of exile to Babylon and subsequent restoration (Mosis 1973: 192–94; North 1974; Ackroyd 1977: 2–32).

Despite these objections, the Babylonian revolt against Ashurbanipal in 648 BCE provides a reasonable context for Manasseh's deportation to Babylon. Though no extant Assyrian text records it, it seems reasonable to posit Manasseh being summoned to Babylon, as Ashurbanipal would have been in Babylon putting down the rebellion and dealing with the traitors (*ANET* 298–300; Evans 1980: 167–68). The Assyrian king may have summoned Manasseh "to ascertain and guarantee his loyalty" to Assyria (Sweeney 2005b: 271).[3] After all, Manasseh's father, Hezekiah, was a notorious rebel who was in league with Babylon. It seems likely, then, that Ashurbanipal might suspect Judah of siding with Babylon again. While we have no Assyrian texts stating such, Judah's later actions under Josiah (see below) wherein he marched against Egypt in support of Babylon, suggest that Judahite-Babylonian ties went deep (Sweeney 2001: 208–33).

Alternatively, Manasseh, like his father before him, may have found the Babylonian rebellion an opportunity to rebel against his overlord. Assyrian antipathy spread in Syria-Palestine during this time, and Edom, Moab, and other Assyrian vassals were overrun by Arabs (McKay 1973: 25). After crushing the Babylonian revolt, Assyria eventually punished the Arab tribes in the west who had sided with Babylon, taking them prisoner (Brinkman 1970: III.2:382–83). This Assyrian activity in Syria-Palestine may also be supported by Ezra 4:9–10, which talks of Ashurbanipal ("Osnappar" in Aramaic) resettling Babylonians and other conquered peoples there (Williamson 1982: 392; Kelly 2002: 142). If Manasseh did rebel against Ashurbanipal, the Assyrian reprisal against western rebels could be the context in which Manasseh was dragged in chains to Babylon. It may also explain the Deuteronomist's silence on Manasseh's rebellion. Since he had praised Hezekiah's rebellion (2 Kgs. 18:7), recounting Manasseh's rebellion would have detracted from the otherwise completely negative portrayal of the monarch in 2 Kings. Furthermore, having Manasseh punished in his story may have undermined the monarch's role in Kings as the one whose sins merited the exile (2 Kgs. 23:26–27; 24:3).

The pardoning and restoration of Manasseh also fits with our knowledge of Ashurbanipal's practice. Ashurbanipal took Necho I prisoner to Nineveh after his rebellion, but then reinstated him as king in Egypt (*ANET* 246). Ashurbanipal was similarly lenient to the king of Tyre (*ANET* 296). Therefore, his reinstating Manasseh after bringing him to Babylon would not be exceptional (Oded 1977: 455–56; Kelly 2002: 142).

The fact that the Chronicler gives Assyria a continued dominant role for the period of Manasseh (contra his *Vorlage* which does not mention Assyrian intervention after Hezekiah's rebellion) could suggest reliance on another source for his story (Keulen 1996: 214). Furthermore, the Chronicler's account of Manasseh's building a wall in Jerusalem (not mentioned in 2 Kings) may also suggest a different source, as such a wall, dated to this time, has been excavated near the Gihon on the eastern slope of Jerusalem (Kenyon 1974: 144–47; Bahat 1981; Kelly 2002: 144).

Manasseh's religious reform described in Chronicles is minimal, with his removing foreign gods from the temple and its immediate vicinity (2 Chr. 33:15; cf. 33:4–5). Of course, 2 Kings explicitly presents Josiah as destroying the altars Manasseh had put in the temple (2 Kgs. 23:12), which contradicts the Chronicler's account of Manasseh doing so himself.

Manasseh died ca. 644 BCE, and his son Amon succeeded him, though he reigned for only two years before he was assassinated (2 Kgs. 21:23–24; 2 Chr. 33:24) in what may have been a coup (Hobbs 1985: 310). The biblical texts do not give any reason for his assassination though some have speculated it was borne of pro-Egyptian (Malamat 1953: 82–102; 1975: 126) or anti-Assyrian circles (Hayes and Hooker 1988: 82). Regardless of the motivation for Amon's assassination, "the people of the land," who were supporters of the Davidic dynasty (cf. 2 Kgs. 11:14–18), killed the assassins and installed Josiah as king.

8.6 JOSIAH

Josiah came to the throne in 640 BCE and reigned until his death at the hands of Pharaoh Necho II ca. 609 BCE. Many studies have concluded that Josiah was a strong ruler who exerted his influence in the vacuum left by the Assyrian retreat from the west by expanding his nation's territory. The most important historical issue of the reign of Josiah is the weakening and collapse of the Assyrian Empire (Kuhrt 1995: II.540–46). Ever since withdrawing from Egypt ca. 655 BCE, Assyria struggled with persistent challenges to their north, which weakened their hold in other areas of the empire (Miller and Hayes 1986: 383). Near the time that Ashurbanipal died (ca. 630 BCE), Babylon again challenged Assyrian hegemony with Nabopolassar taking the Babylonian throne ca. 625 BCE and beginning a rebellion that would lead to the fall of the Assyrian capital of Nineveh in 612 BCE.

During this time, Josiah may have exerted some independence from his suzerain, as the timing of his reforms suggests. According to 2 Chr. 32:4, Josiah began religious reforms in his twelfth year, which would be ca. 628 BCE—not long after the death of the Assyrian king Ashurbanipal ca. 630 BCE (Sweeney 2005a: 579). Furthermore, Josiah's reform of the temple began in his eighteenth year (2 Kgs. 22:3; 2 Chr. 34:8) ca. 622 BCE, which is only one year after the end of the long civil war (626–623 BCE) in Assyria between the Assyrian king Sin-shar-sihkun and his general. This war "had a serious effect on the Assyrian position both in the west and in the south-east" (Na'aman 1991a: 263). Assyrian weakness likely enabled Josiah to carry out his reforms so thoroughly (Na'aman 2005b: 214) and rededicate the temple to Yhwh alone.

The account in 2 Kgs. 22–23 presents Josiah as fulfilling the Davidic ideal and as the most righteous king since David. Similarly, 2 Chr. 34–35 present Josiah positively. The reason for this glowing assessment of Josiah is his cultic fidelity to Yhwh and his iconoclastic religious reformation that reversed the idolatrous policies of his grandfather, Manasseh. Like Hezekiah, Josiah centralized worship in Jerusalem and destroyed the high places throughout the land. What is more, Josiah is said to have even reformed worship in parts of the old northern kingdom of Israel, destroying sanctuaries in Bethel and Samaria (2 Kgs. 23:15–20).

Archaeological evidence for the religious reform of Josiah is minimal. Some have pointed to the many Yahwistic names that appear in epigraphic evidence from this period, clearly divergent in respect to theophoric elements in names among Judah's neighbors (e.g., Ammon) (Hess 2007: 269–74, 350). However, equating the use of Yahwistic names with exclusive worship of Yhwh has been questioned due to the fact that Yahwistic names predominate throughout Israel's entire monarchic history (Zevit 2001: 586–609). Glyptic evidence from Judah from the eighth to sixth centuries BCE shows a move away from iconic and deity-related designs of seals (Uehlinger 2005: 295). Furthermore, in comparison with the prevalence of Egyptian cultic symbolism evident elsewhere in Syria-Palestine at the time, Judah appears not to have participated in the trend, which fits with Josiah's presentation in the Hebrew Bible (Uehlinger 2005: 295).

Of course, in the ancient world a cult reform includes economic and political motivations and consequences, so part of the historical debate concerns Josiah's putative political and territorial expansion. Some suggest that Josiah's reforms were part of his territorial expansion made possible by the void left behind by Assyria's withdrawal and the northern area's inability to compete with Josiah, given the mass deportation they suffered and the lack of national cohesion among those who had been settled there. Thus Josiah's regency is usually thought to be one of expansion and independence (Soggin 1985: 257; Bright 2000: 316). Studies along these lines suggest that Josiah annexed territory in the north (e.g., Samaria) and west (e.g., Megiddo), perhaps even subjecting the new territory to his cultic reform (Ginsberg 1950: 362; Cross 1973: 283; Malamat 1974: 271; Aharoni 1979: 309–10). Thus, under Josiah, Judah became the dominant state in Syria-Palestine.

The biblical texts themselves do not clearly present Josiah as establishing hegemony over Syria-Palestine (Kelle 2014: 374), though some may imply territorial gains. Josiah did destroy religious shrines beyond Judah's boundaries in the north (2 Kgs. 23:15, 19; 2 Chr. 34:6, 33), and the Chronicler tells us that northerners (2 Chr. 34:9) were monetary contributors to the repair of the temple and celebrated the Passover with Judah (2 Chr. 35:17–18). Furthermore, Josiah's attempt to block Necho II could imply Josiah's perceived hegemony, though this is not clear (see below).

Several pieces of extra-biblical evidence are marshaled to support the thesis of Josiah's expansion. Evidence of bullae from Josiah's time suggests that northern towns may have been paying taxes to Jerusalem during this time (Matthews 2002: 88). A massive fortress at Megiddo, constructed during this period, is sometimes understood to be Josiah's strategic outpost in the north. Meṣad Ḥashavyahu, a fortress in northern Philistia, was found to contain ostraca written in Hebrew, including Hebrew names with Yahwistic theophoric elements (Naveh 1977). This epigraphic evidence suggests to many that the inhabitants of the fortress were Judahite, and that Josiah had the fortress built after taking over the coast (Miller and Hayes 1986: 389). Several southern cities (e.g., Arad, Kadesh-Barnea, Haseva) were fortified during this period as well (Finkelstein and Silberman 2001: 348–49). A text at the fortress of Arad orders the Judahite commander of the fortress, Elyashib, to transfer supplies to a group called "Kittim," usually understood to be Greek mercenaries (Lemaire 1977: 159–61, 229–30, 233). Thus, some suggest that the Judahite army was employing Greek mercenaries (Aharoni 1981: 12–13).

Others have argued against this reconstruction suggesting that the evidence has been misinterpreted. First, no epigraphic or material evidence in the excavations of the Megiddo fortress links it to Josiah, though the fortress has no Egyptian finds either (Finkelstein and Silberman 2001: 350). Epigraphic evidence from the fort at Meṣad Ḥashavyahu does show that it had a Judahite commander. The ostraca, however, indicate not only the presence of Judahites but also Greeks, perhaps indicating the fort was Egyptian since they were known to have Greeks in their service (Na'aman 2005b: 220–21). Herodotus records that the Egyptians took Ashdod during this time (Herodotus *Hist.* 2.157), which would suggest their dominance in the area, though no archaeological evidence verifies this. Egyptian artifacts have also been recovered in Syria-Palestine near Arvad, though their significance is unclear (Schipper 2010: 200–29). Further, the Greek mercenaries mentioned in the ostraca at Arad (noted above) may be understood as serving in the Egyptian rather than the Judahite army, so that the Judahite commander of the fortress was forced to supply them due to Judah's subjugation to Egypt (Na'aman 2005b: 223). Clearly, the evidence is inconclusive and can be interpreted in different ways. The inscriptions indicate Judahite control (as the commander is Judahite), though possibly in service to the Egyptians.

In the end, we do not know exactly how Assyrian rule broke down in Syria-Palestine or to what degree and at what point it was replaced by Egyptian rule (Albertz 2005: 42). Positing a seamless transition from Assyria to Egypt seems unlikely, and biblical texts about Josiah could evince somewhat of a vacuum (even if brief) that the Judahite king exploited to his advantage. Even those who think that the domination of Syria-Palestine passed from Assyria to Egypt uninterrupted admit that Egypt's interests were mainly on the coastline (Finkelstein and Silberman 2001: 283), making Judah's vassalage to Egypt nominal. As Na'aman writes "Judah enjoyed a considerable measure of independence despite being formally subordinate to Egypt" (Na'aman 2005b: 231). The biblical texts clearly evince Egyptian dominance following Josiah's death as the pharaoh deposes Josiah's successor and installs a puppet king on the throne (2 Kgs. 23:30–34). While Josiah clearly expanded his kingdom, his extended rule was likely limited to areas where Egyptian interests were low and would not result in a military response from the pharaoh.

The extent of Josiah's expansion may be connected to his ambiguous death recorded in Hebrew Bible texts, as his acts of annexation could have been viewed by Egypt as acts of aggression. Josiah's death occurred in the context of the end of the Assyrian Empire. After the fall of the important Assyrian city of Ashur at the hand of the Medes in 614 BCE, Babylon allied with the Medes and together in 612 BCE they destroyed the Assyrian capital city of Nineveh. The Assyrian king was killed and the new king moved westward to Haran with what was left of his army. Around 610 BCE Pharaoh Necho II led his army to support the new Assyrian king Ashur-uballit II at Haran against the Babylonian-Median coalition. According to the account in 2 Chr. 35:20–27, Josiah went out to oppose the pharaoh at this time. The account in 2 Kings simply states that Josiah went to "meet" Necho, but upon meeting him, the pharaoh killed him (2 Kgs. 23:29). It could be that the Kings account was purposefully vague in order to preserve Josiah's spotless record as Judah's most righteous king (thus making his death tragic), while Chronicles more accurately recounts Josiah's intentions to oppose the Egyptians. If the Chronicler's account of Josiah militarily opposing Necho is accurate, it could support the reconstruction that understands Josiah expanding Judah and exerting some hegemony in the area—even though this was not enough to stop the king of Egypt.[4]

Despite Josiah's efforts, Necho eventually reached Haran to support the Assyrians, but the Egyptian-Assyrian coalition was repulsed by the Babylonian-Median coalition (though some have argued that Josiah did delay the Egyptians enough to mitigate their success in supporting Assyria [Sweeney 2005a]). The Egyptian-Assyrian forces regrouped and counterattacked a year later but were roundly defeated, essentially ending the Assyrian Empire. Thus, the fall of the last Judahite king of any substance coincided with the fall of Judah's longtime enemy, Assyria.

Notes

1. Based on the structural similarities of the stories in Herodotus's account and 2 Kgs. 18–19, Strawn asserts that the former account is based on an oral version of the latter (Strawn 2006), though he does not offer a plausible scenario wherein the Kings account could have been communicated to the Egyptian priests (who were Herodotus's source). While anything is possible, a simpler explanation is that both rely on a historical memory of a defeat of Sennacherib in his 701 BCE campaign.
2. Williamson (1982: 389) points out, however, that the Chronicler makes nothing of the length of Manasseh's reign in his account, so "it is unlikely to have been amongst the Chronicler's dominant concerns."
3. Williamson (1982: 392) suggested that Manasseh may have been summoned to Babylon earlier in 672 when vassals were gathered to swear allegience to "safeguard the succession from Esarhaddon to Assurbanipal."
4. Kelle notes that Herodotus (*Hist.* 2.159.2) references opposition to Necho near Gaza, which could support the idea of Josiah opposing the pharaoh as well but concludes that it is speculative (Kelle 2014: 378).

Bibliography

Ackroyd, Peter R. 1977. "The Chronicler as Exegete." *JSOT* 2: 2–32.
Aharoni, Yohanan. 1979. *The Land of the Bible: A Historical Geography*. 2nd ed. Philadelphia: Westminster Press.
Aharoni, Yohanan. 1981. *Arad Inscriptions*. Judahite Desert Studies. Jerusalem: Israel Exploration Society.
Albertz, Rainer. 2005. "Why a Reform Like Josiah's Must Have Happened." In Lester L. Grabbe, ed., *Good Kings and Bad Kings: The Kingdom of Judah in the Seventh Century BCE*. LHBOTS 393. London: T&T Clark, 27–46.
Albright, William Foxwell. 1932. *The Excavation of Tell Beit Mirsim*. 3 vols. The Annual of the American Schools of Oriental Research. New Haven, CT: American Schools of Oriental Research.
Arnold, Bill T. 2005. "Hezekiah." In Bill T. Arnold and H. G. M. Williamson, eds., *Dictionary of the Old Testament Historical Books*. Downers Grove, IL: InterVarsity, 406–13.
Arnold, Bill T. 2006. "The Neo-Babylonian Chronicle Series." In Mark W. Chavalas, ed., *The Ancient Near East: Historical Sources in Translation*. Malden, MA: Blackwell, 407–26.
Avigad, Nahman. 1993. "Samaria." In Ephraim Stern, ed., *The New Encyclopedia of Archaeological Excavations in the Holy Land*. New York: Hendrickson, 1300–1310.
Bahat, Dan. 1981. "The Wall of Manasseh in Jerusalem." *IEJ* 31: 235–36.
Barrick, W. Boyd. 1996. "On the Meaning of bêt-habbamôt and batê-habbamôt and the Composition of the Kings History." *JBL* 115: 621–42.

Becking, Bob. 2003. "Chronology: A Skeleton without Flesh? Sennacherib's Campaign as a Case-Study." In Lester L. Grabbe, ed., *"Like a Bird in a Cage": The Invasion of Sennacherib in 701 BCE*. LHBOTS 363. London: Sheffield Academic Press, 46–72.

Beit-Arieh, Itzhaq, ed. 1999. *Tel 'Ira: A Stronghold in the Biblical Negev*. Monograph Series of the Institute of Archaeology, Tel Aviv University 15. Tel Aviv: Emery and Claire Yass Publications in Archaeology of the Institute of Archaeology, Tel Aviv University.

Bright, John. 2000. *A History of Israel*. 4th ed. Louisville, KY: Westminster John Knox.

Brinkman, J. A. 1964. "Merodach Baladan II." In R. D. Biggs and J. A. Brinkman, eds., *Studies Presented to A. Leo Oppenheim*. Chicago: University of Chicago Press, 6–53.

Brinkman, J. A. 1970. "The Great Rebellion (652–648 B.C.) and Its Aftermath: Ashurbanipal versus Shamash-shuma-ukin and His Allies." In I. E. S. Edwards, C. J. Gadd, N. G. L. Hammond, and E. Sollberger, eds., *CAH* II. London: Cambridge University Press, 53–60.

Broshi, Magen. 1974. "Expansion of Jerusalem in the Reigns of Hezekiah and Manasseh." *IEJ* 24: 21–26.

Campbell Jr., E. 1998. "A Land Divided: Judah and Israel from the Death of Solomon to the Fall of Samaria." In M. Coogan, ed., *The Oxford History of the Biblical World*. Oxford: Oxford University Press, 206–41.

Childs, Brevard S. 1967. *Isaiah and the Assyrian Crisis*. SBT 3. London: SCM.

Cogan, Mordechai. 1974. *Imperialism and Religion*. Missoula, MT: Scholars Press.

Cogan, Mordechai. 1993. "Judah Under Assyrian Hegemony: A Reexamination of Imperialism and Religion." *Journal of Biblical Literature* 112: 403–14.

Cogan, Mordechai. 1998. "Into Exile: From the Assyrian Conquest of Israel to the Fall of Babylon." In M. Coogan, ed., *The Oxford History of the Biblical World*. Oxford: Oxford University Press, 247–75.

Cogan, Mordechai and Hayim Tadmor. 1988. *II Kings*. AB 11. Garden City: Doubleday.

Cross, Frank Moore. 1973. *Canaanite Myth and Hebrew Epic: Essays in the History of the Religion of Israel*. Cambridge, MA: Harvard University Press.

Dalley, Stephanie. 2004. "Recent Evidence from Assyrian Sources for Judaean History from Uzziah to Manasseh." *JSOT* 28: 387–401.

Day, John. 1992. "The Problem of 'So, King of Egypt' in 2 Kings XVII:4." *VT* 42: 289–301.

Eph'al, Israel. 1983. "On Warfare and Military Control in the Ancient Near Eastern Empires: A Research Outline." In Moshe Weinfeld and Hayim Tadmor, eds., *History, Historiography and Interpretation: Studies in Biblical and Cuneiform Literatures*. Jerusalem: Magnes, 88–106.

Evans, Carl D. 1980. "Judah's Foreign Policy from Hezekiah to Josiah." In Carl D. Evans, William W. Hallo, and John B. White, eds., *Scripture in Context: Essays on the Comparative Method*. Pittsburgh: Pickwick, 157–78.

Evans, Paul S. 2009. *The Invasion of Sennacherib in the Book of Kings: A Source-Critical and Rhetorical Study of 2 Kings 18–19*. VTSup 125. Leiden: Brill.

Finkelstein, Israel. 1994. "The Archaeology of the Days of Manasseh." In Michael D. Coogan, Cheryl J. Exum, and Lawrence E. Stager, eds., *Scripture and Other Artifacts: Essays on the Bible and Archaeology in Honor of Philip J. King*. Louisville, KY: Westminster John Knox, 169–87.

Finkelstein, Israel and Nadav Na'aman. 2004. "The Judahite Shephelah in the Late 8th and Early 7th Centuries BCE." *TA* 31: 60–79.

Finkelstein, Israel and Neil Asher Silberman. 2001. *The Bible Unearthed: Archaeology's New Vision of Ancient Israel and the Origin of Its Sacred Texts*. New York: Touchstone.

Gallagher, William R. 1999. *Sennacherib's Campaign to Judah: New Studies*. SHCANE 18. Leiden; Boston: Brill.

Ginsberg, Harold Lewis. 1950. "Judah and the Transjordan States from 734 to 582 B.C.E." In S. Lieberman, ed., *Alexander Marx Jubilee Volume*. New York: The Jewish Theological Seminary of America, 347–68.

Grabbe, Lester L. 2003a. "Of Mice and Dead Men: Herodotus 2.141 and Sennacherib's Campaign in 701 BCE." In Lester L. Grabbe, ed., *"Like a Bird in a Cage": The Invasion of Sennacherib in 701 BCE*. LHBOTS 363. London: Sheffield Academic Press, 119–40.

Grabbe, Lester L. 2003b. "Reflections on the Discussion." In Lester L. Grabbe, ed., *"Like a Bird in a Cage": The Invasion of Sennacherib in 701 BCE*. LHBOTS 363. London: Sheffield Academic Press, 308–23.

Grabbe, Lester L. 2005. "The Kingdom of Judah from Sennacherib's Invasion to the Fall of Jerusalem: If We Had Only the Bible...." In Lester L. Grabbe, ed., *Good Kings and Bad Kings: The Kingdom of Judah in the Seventh Century BCE*. LHBOTS 393. London: T&T Clark, 78–122.

Grayson, Albert Kirk. 1975. *Assyrian and Babylonian Chronicles*. TCS. Locust Valley, NY: J. J. Augustin.

Hackett, Jo Ann. 1997. "Defusing Pseudo-Scholarship: The Siloam Inscription Ain't Hasmonean." *BAR* 23: 41–50, 68.

Hallo, William W. 1960. "From Qarqar to Carchemish: Assyria and Israel in the Light of New Discoveries." *Biblical Archaeologist* 23:34–61.

Halpern, Baruch. 1991. "Jerusalem and the Lineages in the Seventh Century BCE: Kinship and the Rise of Individual Moral Liability." In B. Halper and D. W. Hobson, eds., *Law and Ideology in Monarchic Israel*. Sheffield: JSOT Press, 11–107.

Hayes, John H. and Jeffrey K. Kuan. 1991. "The Final Years of Samaria (730–720 BC)." *Bib* 72: 153–81.

Hayes, John H. and Paul K. Hooker. 1988. *A New Chronology for the Kings of Israel and Judah and Its Implications for Biblical History and Literature*. Atlanta: John Knox.

Herzog, Z. 1997. "Arad: Iron Age Period." In E. M. Meyers, ed., *The Oxford Encyclopedia of Archaeology in the Near East*. Oxford: Oxford University Press, 174–76.

Hess, Richard S. 2007. *Israelite Religions: An Archaeological and Biblical Survey*. Grand Rapids: Baker Academic.

Hobbs, T. R. 1985. *2 Kings*. WBC 13. Waco, TX: Word Books.

Hurowitz, Victor. 1992. *I Have Built You an Exalted House: Temple Building in the Bible in Light of Mesopotamian and Northwest Semitic Writings*. JSOTSup 115. Sheffield: JSOT Press.

Jenkins, A. K. 1976. "Hezekiah's Fourteenth Year: A New Interpretation of 2 Kings 18:13–19:37." *VT* 26: 284–98.

Kahn, Dan'el. 2014. "The War of Sennacherib against Egypt as Described in Herodotus II 141." *Journal of Ancient Egyptian Interconnections* 6: 22–33.

Kelle, Brad E. 2014. "Judah in the Seventh Century: From the Aftermath of Sennacherib's Invasion to the Beginning of Jehoiakim's Rebellion." In Bill T. Arnold and Richard S. Hess, eds., *Ancient Israel's History: An Introduction to Issues and Sources*. Grand Rapids: Baker Academic, 350–82.

Kelle, Brad E. and Megan Bishop Moore, eds. 2006. *Israel's Prophets and Israel's Past: Essays on the Relationship of Prophetic Texts and Israelite History in Honor of John H. Hayes*. LHBOTS 446. New York: T&T Clark.

Kelly, Brian. 2002. "Manasseh in the Books of Kings and Chronicles (2 Kings 21:1–18; 2 Chron 33:1–20)." In V. Philips Long, David W. Baker, and Gordon J. Wenham, eds., *Windows into Old Testament History: Evidence, Argument, and the Crisis of "Biblical Israel."* Grand Rapids: Eerdmans, 131–46.

Kenyon, Kathleen M. 1974. *Digging up Jerusalem*. New York: Praeger.

Keulen, P. S. F. van. 1996. *Manasseh through the Eyes of the Deuteronomists: The Manasseh Account (2 Kings 21:1–18) and the Final Chapters of the Deuteronomistic History*. OTS 38. Leiden: Brill.

Kitchen, Kenneth A. 1986. *The Third Intermediate Period in Egypt (1100–650 B.C.)*. 2nd ed. Warminster: Aris & Phillips.

Knauf, Ernst Axel. 2003. "Sennacherib at the Berezina." In Lester L. Grabbe, ed., *"Like a Bird in a Cage": The Invasion of Sennacherib in 701 BCE*. LHBOTS 363. London: Sheffield Academic Press, 141–49.

Kooij, Arie van der. 1986. "Das assyrische Heer vor den Mauern Jerusalems im Jahr 701 v. Chr." *ZDPV* 102: 93–109.

Kuhrt, Amélie. 1995. *The Ancient Near East: c. 3000–330 BC*. 2 vols. Routledge History of the Ancient World. London and New York: Routledge.

Lemaire, André. 1977. *Inscriptions hébraïques I: Les Ostraca, Littératures anciennes du Proche-Orien.* Paris: Cerf.

Malamat, Abraham. 1953. "The Historical Background of the Assassination of Amon, King of Judah." *IEJ* 3: 26–29.

Malamat, Abraham. 1974. "Josiah's Bid for Armageddon: The Judahite-Egyptian Encounter in 609 BC." *Journal of the Ancient Near Eastern Society of Columbia University* 5 *(The Gaster Festschrift)*, 267–79.

Malamat, Abraham. 1975. "The Twilight of Judah: In the Egyptian-Babylonian Maelstrom." In Luis Alonso Schökel, ed., *Congress Volume: Edinburgh 1974.* Leiden: Brill, 123–45.

Matthews, Victor H. 2002. *A Brief History of Ancient Israel.* Louisville, KY: Westminster John Knox.

Mayer, Walter. 1995. *Politik und Kriegskunst der Assyrer.* Munster: Ugarit.

Mayer, Walter. 2003. "Sennacherib's Campaign of 701 BCE: The Assyrian View." In Lester L. Grabbe, ed., *"Like a Bird in a Cage": The Invasion of Sennacherib in 701 BCE.* LHBOTS 363. London: Sheffield Academic Press, 168–200.

McKay, J. W. 1973. *Religion in Judah under the Assyrians.* SBT 2/26. London: SCM Press.

Milgrom, Jacob. 1998. "The Nature and Extent of Idolatry in Eighth-Seventh Century Judah." *Hebrew Union College Annual* 69: 1–13.

Millard, Alan R. 1985. "Sennacherib's Attack on Hezekiah." *Tyndale Bulletin* 36: 61–77.

Miller, J. Maxwell and John H. Hayes. 1986. *A History of Ancient Israel and Judah.* 1st ed. Philadelphia: Westminster.

Mosis, Rudolf. 1973. *Untersuchungen zur Theologie des chronistischen Geschichtswerkes.* Freiburger Theologische Studien 92. Freiburg: Herder.

Na'aman, Nadav. 1979. "Sennacherib's Campaign to Judah and the Date of the lmlk Stamps." *VT* 29: 61–86.

Na'aman, Nadav. 1986. "Historical and Chronological Notes on the Kingdoms of Israel and Judah in the 8th Century BC." *VT* 36: 71–92.

Na'aman, Nadav. 1990. "The Historical Background to the Conquest of Samaria (720 BC)." *Biblica* 71: 206–25.

Na'aman, Nadav. 1991a. "Chronology and History in the Late Assyrian Empire (631–619 B.C.)." *ZA* 81: 243–67.

Na'aman, Nadav. 1991b. "Forced Participation in Alliances in the Course of the Assyrian Campaigns to the West." In Mordechai Cogan and Israel Eph'al, eds., *Ah, Assyria... Studies in Assyrian History and Ancient Near Eastern Historiography Presented to Hayim Tadmor.* Jerusalem: Magnes Press, 80–98.

Na'aman, Nadav. 1995. "The Debated Historicity of Hezekiah's Reform in the Light of Historical and Archaeological Research." *ZAW* 107: 179–95.

Na'aman, Nadav. 2005a. *Ancient Israel and Its Neighbors: Interactions and Counteractions.* Winona Lake, IN: Eisenbrauns.

Na'aman, Nadav. 2005b. "Josiah and the Kingdom of Judah." In Lester L. Grabbe, ed., *Good Kings and Bad Kings: The Kingdom of Judah in the Seventh Century BCE.* LHBOTS 393. London: T&T Clark, 189–247.

Naveh, J. 1977. "Meṣad Ḥashavyahu." In Michael Avi-Yonah, ed., *Encyclopedia of Archaeological Excavations in the Holy Land.* Jerusalem: Israel Exploration Society and Carta.

North, Robert Grady. 1974. "Does Archaeology Prove Chronicles Sources?" In H. H. Bream, R. D. Heim, and C. A. Moore, eds., *A Light Unto My Path: Old Testament Studies in Honor of Jacob M. Myers.* Philadelphia: Temple University Press, 375–401.

Noth, Martin. 1935. "Studien zu den historisch-geographischen Dokumenten des Josuabuches." *Zeitschrift des deutschen Palästina-Vereins* 58: 185–255.

Noth, Martin. 1958. *The History of Israel.* London: A. & C. Black.

Oded, Bustenay. 1977. "Judah and the Exile." In John H. Hayes and J. Maxwell Miller, eds., *Israelite and Judaean History.* Philadelphia: Westminster, 435–88.

Ofer, Avi. 2001. "The Monarchic Period in the Judaean Highland: A Spatial Overview." In Amihay Mazar, ed., *Studies in the Archaeology of the Iron Age in Israel and Jordan*. Sheffield: Sheffield Academic Press, 14-37.

Olmstead, A. T. 1908. *Western Asia in the Days of Sargon of Assyria, 722-705 B.C.: A Study in Oriental History*. Cornell Studies in History and Political Science 2. New York: Holt.

Park, Sung Jin. 2012. "A New Historical Reconstruction of the Fall of Samaria." *Bib* 93: 98-106.

Parpola, Simo. 1987. *The Correspondence of Sargon II, Part I*. SAA 1. Helsinki: Helsinki University Press.

Person, Raymond F. 1997. *The Kings-Isaiah and Kings-Jeremiah Recensions*. BZAW 252. Berlin: de Gruyter.

Rainey, Anson F. 1982. "Wine from the Royal Vineyards." *BASOR* 245: 57-62.

Rainey, Anson F. and R. Steven Notley. 2006. *The Sacred Bridge: Carta's Atlas of the Biblical World*. Jerusalem: Carta.

Redford, Donald B. 1992. *Egypt, Canaan, and Israel in Ancient Times*. Princeton: Princeton University Press.

Rogerson, John and Philip R. Davies. 1996. "Was the Siloam Tunnel Built by Hezekiah?" *Biblical Archaeologist* 59: 138-49.

Rosenbaum, Jonathan. 1979. "Hezekiah's Reform and the Deuteronomistic Tradition." *HTR* 72: 23-43.

Schipper, Bernd U. 2010. "Egypt and the Kingdom of Judah under Josiah and Jehoiakim." *TA* 37: 200-29.

Seitz, Christopher R. 1991. *Zion's Final Destiny: The Development of the Book of Isaiah: A Reassessment of Isaiah 36-39*. Minneapolis: Fortress.

Seitz, Christopher R. 1993. "Account A and the Annals of Sennacherib: A Reassessment." *JSOT* 58: 47-57.

Soggin, J. Alberto. 1985. *A History of Ancient Israel*. Philadelphia: Westminster.

Spalinger, Anthony. 1974. "Assurbanipal and Egypt: A Source Study." *JAOS* 94: 316-28.

Spalinger, Anthony. 1976. "Psammetichus, King of Egypt I." *Journal of the American Research Center in Egypt* 13:133-147.

Spieckermann, Hermann. 1982. *Juda unter Assur in der Sargonidenzeit*. FRLANT 129. Göttingen: Vandenhoeck and Ruprecht.

Stade, B. 1886. "Miscellen: Anmerkungen zu 2 Kö. 15-21." *ZAW* 6: 156-89.

Starkey, J. L. 1937. "Excavations at Tell ed Duweir: The Wellcome Marston Archaeological Research Expedition to the Near East." *PEQ* 69: 228-41.

Stavrakopoulou, Francesca. 2004. *King Manasseh and Child Sacrifice: Biblical Distortions of Historical Realities*. Berlin: de Gruyter.

Stern, Ephraim. 2001. *Archaeology of the Land of the Bible*. Volume II: *The Assyrian, Babylonian, and Persian Periods, 732-332 BCE*. Anchor Bible Reference Library. New York: Doubleday.

Strawn, Brent A. 2006. "Herodotus' History 2.141 and the Deliverance of Jerusalem: On Parallels, Sources, and Histories of Ancient Israel." In Brad E. Kelle and Megan Bishop Moore, eds., *Israel's Prophets and Israel's Past: Essays on the Relationship of Prophetic Texts and Israelite History in Honor of John H. Hayes*. LHBOTS 446. New York: T&T Clark, 210-38.

Sweeney, Marvin A. 2001. *King Josiah of Judah: The Lost Messiah of Israel*. Oxford: Oxford University Press.

Sweeney, Marvin A. 2005a. "Josiah." In Bill T. Arnold and H. G. M. Williamson, eds., *Dictionary of the Old Testament Historical Books*. Downers Grove, IL: InterVarsity, 575-80.

Sweeney, Marvin A. 2005b. "King Manasseh of Judah and the Problem of Theodicy in the Deuteronomistic History." In Lester L. Grabbe, ed., *Good Kings and Bad Kings: The Kingdom of Judah in the Seventh Century BCE*. LHBOTS 393. New York: T&T Clark, 264-78.

Sweeney, Marvin A. 2007. *I & II Kings: A Commentary*. OTL. Louisville, KY: Westminster John Knox.

Tadmor, Hayim. 1981. "History and Ideology in the Assyrian Royal Inscriptions." In Frederick Mario Fales, ed., *Assyrian Royal Inscriptions: New Horizons in Literary, Ideological, and Historical Analysis*. Rome: Istituto per l'Oriente, 13-33.

Tadmor, Hayim. 1985. "Sennacherib's Campaign to Judah: Historical and Historiographical Considerations." *Zion* 50: 65–80.

Tadmor, Hayim, B. Landsberger, and Asko Parpola. 1989. "The Sin of Sargon and Sennacherib's Last Will." *SAAB* 3: 3–51.

Tatum, Lynn. 1991. "King Manasseh and the Royal Fortress at Horvat 'Uza." *The Biblical Archaeologist* 54: 136–45.

Thiele, Edwin R. 1951. *Mysterious Numbers of the Hebrew Kings: A Reconstruction of the Chronology of the Kingdoms of Israel and Judah.* Chicago: University of Chicago Press.

Uehlinger, Christoph. 2003. "Clio in a World of Pictures: Another Look at the Lachish Reliefs from Sennacherib's Southwest Palace at Nineveh." In Lester L. Grabbe, ed., *"Like a Bird in a Cage": The Invasion of Sennacherib in 701 BCE.* LHBOTS 363. London: Sheffield Academic Press, 221–305.

Uehlinger, Christoph. 2005. "Was There a Cult Reform under King Josiah?: The Case for a Well-Grounded Minimum." In Lester L. Grabbe, ed., *Good Kings and Bad Kings: The Kingdom of Judah in the Seventh Century BCE.* LHBOTS 393. London: T&T Clark, 279–316.

Ussishkin, David. 1982. *The Conquest of Lachish by Sennacherib.* Publications of the Institute of Archaeology 6. Tel Aviv: Tel Aviv University, Institute of Archaeology.

Ussishkin, David. 1983. "Excavations at Tel Lachish 1978–1983: Second Preliminary Report." *TA* 23: 97–175, pls. 13–43.

Ussishkin, David. 1988. "The Destruction of Lachish by Sennacherib and the Dating of the Royal Judahite Storage Jars." *TA* 4: 28–60.

Ussishkin, David. 2006. "Sennacherib's Campaign to Philistia and Judah: Ekron, Lachish, and Jerusalem." In Yairah Amit, Ehud Ben Zvi, Israel Finkelstein, and Oded Lipschits, eds., *Essays on Ancient Israel in Its Near Eastern Context: A Tribute to Nadav Na'aman.* Winona Lake, IN: Eisenbrauns, 339–58.

Vaughn, Andrew G. 1999. *Theology, History, and Archaeology in the Chronicler's Account of Hezekiah.* SBLABS. Atlanta: Scholars Press.

Vogt, Ernst. 1986. *Der Aufstand Hiskias und die Belagerung Jerusalems 701 v. Chr.* Rome: Biblical Institute.

Weippert, Helga. 1988. *Palästina in vorhellenistischer Zeit: Handbuch der Archäologie, II.* Munich: C H Beck.

Wellhausen, Julius. 1973. *Prolegomena to the History of Israel.* Gloucester, MA: Peter Smith.

Williamson, H. G. M. 1982. *1 and 2 Chronicles.* New Century Bible Commentary. Grand Rapids: Eerdmans.

Yadin, Yigael. 1976. "Beer-Sheba: The High Place Destroyed by King Josiah." *BASOR* 222: 5–17.

Younger, K. Lawson, Jr. 1999. "The Fall of Samaria in Light of Recent Research." *CBQ* 61: 461–82.

Younger, K. Lawson, Jr. 2002. "Recent Study on Sargon II, King of Assyria: Implications for Biblical Studies." In Mark W. Chavalas and K. Lawson Younger, Jr., eds., *Mesopotamia and the Bible: Comparative Explorations.* JSOTSup 341. Grand Rapids; London: Baker Academic; Sheffield Academic Press, 288–329.

Zevit, Ziony. 2001. *The Religions of Ancient Israel: A Synthesis of Parallactic Approaches.* New York: Continuum.

CHAPTER 9

NEW PERSPECTIVES ON THE EXILE IN LIGHT OF CUNEIFORM TEXTS

LAURIE PEARCE

9.1 INTRODUCTION

ACADEMIC interest in the Exile is commensurate with its role as a catalyst to the formation of a nascent Jewish identity. Matters of content, compositional history, and theological agenda in the relevant biblical texts compound the challenges of preparing an essay dedicated to new assessments of the Exile in a volume devoted to the Old Testament Historical Books. The richness of Exile studies is evident from the scope of volumes such as Rainer Albertz's comprehensive *Israel in Exile* (Albertz 2003), which surveys the broad historical backgrounds and major literature groups of the Exilic period, and Jon Berquist's *Approaching Yehud* (Berquist 2007), which addresses a variety of features and approaches to the province in the Persian era. Study of the Exile has traditionally been supported with contributions from the disciplines of Assyriology, Semitic epigraphy, and archaeology. New sources, methodological innovations, and theoretical approaches promise continuity in this ongoing relationship, even as the pace of Exile scholarship has quickened. With the appearance of new sources (e.g., Pearce and Wunsch 2014), and the reassessment of others, the understanding of the Exile continues to evolve (see Kelle, Ames, and Wright 2011).

With a nod to the philological foundation of biblical scholarship, the present survey focuses on the cuneiform and alphabetic extrabiblical texts relevant to the study of the Exile. Indeed, the need for integration of the diverse sources has been flagged as a desideratum from the beginning of the current floruit of Exile studies. Here, focus will be placed on the economic and administrative cuneiform output produced under the neo-Babylonian and Achaemenid kings from the late seventh until the first third of the fifth centuries BCE, a period now referenced in Assyriology as "the long sixth century"—a neologism coined with obvious reference to Braudel's "long sixteenth century" (Jursa 2010: v). The continuity that characterizes the categories and content of the cuneiform sources supports exploration of the social and economic status of the Judeans as exiles, returnees, and members of the Golah. Thus, this survey aims to consider evidence in harmony with Berquist's claim that an understanding of the economics is critical to understanding the society and literature of the period and the place of Yehud as a site of ethnic definition (Berquist 2007: 3–4). Of necessity, some topics current in the scholarship of the Exile (e.g., the sociologically driven study of forced migration, and matters of cult, ritual, and theology) will not be included, as the available cuneiform sources contribute little or nothing to their explication. With full cognizance of the limitations of the term *exile* in assessing the experience and records of all Judeans whose lives were impacted by the Babylonian conquests and their aftermath (Middlemas 2009), it is hoped we may give voice to the ancients' experiences.

9.2 READING OLD SOURCES WITH NEW EYES

Extrabiblical sources relevant to the study of the Exile have been known for more than a century; others have more recently come to light. A recent summary describes cuneiform evidence that originated in both palace and administrative sectors (Pearce 2016a), and thus, here, the sources need be mentioned by name only: the Nebuchadnezzar Prism (titled *Hofkalendar* in most secondary literature); the Chronicle of Early Years of Nebuchadnezzar; the Cyrus cylinder; the Weidner Ration lists; administrative and legal texts from Sippar, Susa, and Neirab; the Murašû archive from Nippur; and, notably and most recently, the āl-Yāḫūdu and Bīt Našar texts (Pearce and Wunsch 2014), a corpus of approximately one hundred texts that confirm the presence of Judeans and other deportee and non-native populations on the Babylonian landscape from the earliest days of the Exile. Comprising diverse media and scripts, the well-populated category of alphabetic extrabiblical sources relevant to the study of the Exile includes Aramaic ostraca, stamped jar handles, Aramaic epigraphs on cuneiform documents, and papyri. Unfortunately, no summary description of them all exists in a convenient, accessible publication. Because those corpora stand outside the present author's areas of expertise, they are only referenced here. We consider the old documents with fresh perspectives applicable to the following categories: chronology and historiography, economic and political history, identity, and intellectual contact.

9.3 CHRONOLOGY AND HISTORIOGRAPHY

The broad outline of the periods of Exile, Return, and Golah are well known, yet inconsistencies remain that challenge the alignment of biblical and Judean chronologies (Albertz 2003: 81). While the āl-Yāḫūdu texts do not change those contours, as might be hoped from a newly published corpus of texts that refers so specifically to members of the exilic population, they do fill in the ~150 year gap in extrabiblical documentation of the history of the Judean experience from the 597 BCE deportation of Jehoiachin (roughly reflected in the cuneiform ration lists from Babylon [Weidner 1939]) to the witness lists of the Murašû documents (454–405 BCE) in which the first identification of Judeans in the cuneiform corpus was made on the basis of their diagnostic Yahwistic names. Neither the beginning nor the closing date of the āl-Yāḫūdu corpus—572 BCE (year 33 of Nebuchadnezzar's reign) and 477 BCE (Xerxes's ninth year), respectively—carries significance for the history of the Exile per se. But early assessments of the social and economic status of the Judeans at āl-Yāḫūdu depict a scenario of nearly immediate Judean integration into the social and economic life of the Babylonian heartland, as well as of a trajectory of their experiences comparable to that of other deportee and native population groups (Abraham 2005; 2007; Pearce 2006; 2015; 2011; Lambert 2007; Magdalene and Wunsch 2011; Wunsch 2013; Bloch 2014). These sources support new as well as revised approaches to understanding the Judeans' experiences and the Exile.

The presence of Judeans at āl-Yāḫūdu attests to the existence of an ongoing community in the Babylonian countryside, even as the walls of Jerusalem are being rebuilt and important changes are taking place in the organization of urban economic structures in the Achaemenid Empire. The comprehensive investigation of the economy of the neo-Babylonian and Achaemenid Empires depends upon the tens of thousands of texts from temple and private archives, particularly at Borsippa and Sippar (Jursa and Baker 2005; Jursa 2010). Notably, the dates of the latest āl-Yāḫūdu texts extend beyond an important chronological turning point in the history and geographic distribution of cuneiform archives in the Persian Empire. In his second year, Xerxes displaced the old urban elites in the northern Babylonian cities, home to the major temple complexes, whereupon the production of administrative archives in those contexts ceased (Stolper 1999; Waerzeggers 2003; Oelsner 2007; Kuhrt 2014). That no such action was taken in the heartland's southern urban centers or in the rural environments throughout Mesopotamia is evident from the continuity in documentation from these locales. As āl-Yāḫūdu is presumed to have been situated in a triangle that extends east (and largely south) of Nippur, the continued documentation of the Judean experience is not unexpected. Known evidence for Judeans living in the northern urban centers of Borsippa, Sippar, Babylon, and the Achaemenid capital Susa (Zadok 2002; Jursa 2007; Bloch 2014) predates the end of the archives. Throughout these sources, Judeans appear in contexts where it is clear they enjoyed contact with members of the higher ranks of the administration, but they would not have been admitted to the ranks of the closed, hereditary society of the urban elite. While the disappearance of the urban archives from the documentation is a consequence of Xerxes's purge, it is a loss for the study of the Exile, for those cities, with their temples and schools, were loci of intellectual activity and exchange.

9.4 ECONOMIC AND POLITICAL HISTORY

The trajectory of current research into the social, economic, and political history of the Exile followed closely on the debunking of the so-called myth of the empty land (Barstad 1996; 2003; Emerton 1998; Lipschits 2004; 2011; Middlemas 2009; Levin and Ben Zvi 2010). The seeming continuity in the archaeological record of Judah in the transition from the neo-Babylonian to Achaemenid periods, paralleled by continuity in the documentary record of the economies of their eponymous empires, are being explored through a variety of approaches that accommodate the notion of a long sixth-century (Miller, Ben Zvi, and

Knoppers 2015), although its impact on the study of the Exile has yet to be fully realized. In part, ongoing compartmentalizing of the study of Mesopotamian and Levantine economic and social structures, reflected in the omission of Assyriology from a list of cognate disciplines that may contribute to the study of agrarian economies (Miller 2015: 3), plagues some—but not all (e.g., Fried 2015)—research efforts, even those that aim to be inter- or cross-disciplinary. Perhaps the reluctance to abandon such divisions is reflected in the enduring appeal of the theoretical construct of *center/core* and *periphery*. In spite of its origin as an outgrowth of World Systems Theory (Wallerstein 1974) in the field of economics, this construct enjoys currency as a heuristic in biblical studies (Ben Zvi and Levin 2016), where it is applied frequently to label dualities or polarities perceived in literary and theological approaches to the text. As we turn to consider how the notion of core/periphery may be productively applied to the study of the Exile, it is worth drawing attention to the notion of contested peripheries (Berquist 1995; Cline 2000) and to promote its inclusion along with many other theoretical models applied to the study of the Exile (Miller 2015).

Recent examinations of long-known as well as newly excavated neo-Babylonian royal inscriptions offer new perspectives on the genre (described in Da Riva 2008) that invite review of the notion of core/periphery as it applies to the neo-Babylonian and, by extension, the Achaemenid Empire. Da Riva addresses the role of the paired monumental inscriptions at Wadi esh-Sharbin (Wadi Brisa) in Lebanon (Da Riva 2010; 2012a; 2012b; 2014). These inscriptions continued the Assyrian iconographic program, even as they promoted Babylonian imperial values. In connection with the latter, the inscriptions are physical representations or markers of the boundaries and contours of the neo-Babylonian Empire, and reinforce notions previously promoted about the relationship of the crown to its conquered territories or countries (Vanderhooft 1999; Jursa 2010: 60–61; Albertz 2012).

Babylonian royal monuments recently excavated in Jordan and Saudi Arabia (Eichmann, Schaudig, and Hausleiter 2006; Hausleiter and Schaudig 2015) fill in details of the enigmatic ten-year sojourn in Tayma of the neo-Babylonian king Nabonidus (Beaulieu 1995; 2007) and establish economic as well as ideological reasons for the journey. The iconography of local deities depicted on the al-Ḥāʾiṭ stela (Hausleiter and Schaudig 2015) speaks in favor of a degree of Babylonian (or at least Nabonidus's) openness to other conceptual systems and suggests the existence of some degree of a comprehensive, inclusive Babylonian self-understanding. This openness supports the cuneiform archival evidence of ways and means that facilitated Judean integration into Babylonian culture. In view of the picture that is emerging of an empire with broad understanding of its physical boundaries and a degree of official cultural inclusiveness in dealing with populations in its distant reaches, the appropriateness of the core/periphery model for describing Judah's relationship to Babylonia may now require reassessment (Pearce 2016b) or refinements in the vocabulary of the model (Parker 2006).

As the corpus of extrabiblical evidence for the presence of Judeans in the Babylonian heartland has expanded, scholars have looked for possible contributions to identifying the processes and locations of intellectual contact between Judeans and Babylonians. It is in this area that innovative approaches to the āl-Yāḫūdu texts in their larger context are beginning to be productive. Building on Liverani's suggestion that the Babylonian Chronicles served as a model for the biblical books of Chronicles, Waerzeggers has applied principles of social network analysis to suggest an environment in which Judean descendants of the exiled population could have interacted with individuals who had access to the copyists, places of text storage, and the texts of the Babylonian Chronicles themselves (Waerzeggers 2014a). She posited a likely candidate for this cultural interlocutor: a Babylonian merchant (Marduk-rēmanni) active in the early years of Persian rule (Waerzeggers 2014a; 2014b), whose physical and social mobility brought him into contact with all geographic regions and social sectors of the empire, and who, through his priestly heritage, had access to the temple archives where chronicle texts were produced and/or stored. The speculative nature of this suggestion, which Waerzeggers explicitly acknowledges, integrates established social science tools, methodologies, and best practices into humanities research.

In addition to supporting the positing of persons responsible for the transmission of Babylonian culture to the Judean inhabitants of the heartland, cuneiform administrative documents may offer hints at the geographic locus of the process as well. Texts from the reign of Xerxes and the environs of Nippur (Zadok 1985: 373; Joannès and Lemaire 1996: no. 7; Zilberg, Pearce, and Jursa 2019) reference the canal Nār-Kabaru, surely identifiable as the Chebar river along which Ezekiel prophesied in the Exile's early days. The Kabaru waterway (which extended from the Babylon region south toward Nippur and then east toward Elam [Tolini 2011: 56–72]) already figured in Cyrus's hydraulic program (Tolini 2011: 43) and could have served as a conduit for transmission and transport of intellectual capital as well as of economic products. Thus, the possibility of contact between Ezekiel or his like and Babylonian businessmen and administrative officials along the Kabaru waterway should be expected, perhaps even on a regular basis, in the form of business trips from the heartland to the capital. Although documentation is lacking, it is likely that the community of Judean officials attested at Susa (Bloch 2014), the Judean royal merchants at Sippar (Jursa 2007; Bloch 2014), and possibly others whose existence is not yet known, maintained contact—if they did not, in fact, travel back and forth to visit or conduct business—with their confrères and Babylonian colleagues throughout the empire.

9.5 IDENTITY

In the past two decades, the themes of identity and ethnicity, with notable focus on Israel and Judah, have received their share of attention in the study of the ancient world (Sparks 1998; Grosby 2002; 2007; 2009; Knoppers 2009; Knoppers and Ristau 2009; Liss and Oeming 2010; Southwood 2012; Siapkas 2014). Rooted in anthropological theory, the study of ethnicity/identity depends on individual or group reports of perceived differences or otherness. Barth categorized these differences as reflections of genealogical characteristics; cultural traits such as language, religion, customs, and shared history; and, inherited phenotypical characteristics (Barth 1969). More generally, Sparks views common ancestry as marker of identity and approaches identity as a concept of sociocultural integration, a tool for sociocultural delimitation, and a model for explaining origins of other peoples (Sparks 1998). These multiple approaches produce diverse understandings of the textual and material culture records of interpersonal and inter-institutional engagements. Furthermore, efforts at teasing out a person's or a people's identity are complicated by the lack of living human witnesses. In the cuneiform record, the study of identity/ethnicity has focused heavily on data in Assyrian sources, as reflected in the textual, archaeological, and iconographic record (Collon 2005; Brown 2008). Through words and images, annals and palace inscriptions document an interest in and concern with the diverse peoples and places with which the Assyrian kings and empire came into contact. Babylonian royal inscriptions and chronicles do not share such concerns, and thus the locus of the exploration of identity shifts from the corpus of monumental and royal texts to administrative and archival ones.

9.5.1 Ethnicity and Identity in the Administrative Record

Gentilics (*nisbe*) offer the most accessible point of entry for study of ethnicity/identity of individuals who are so identified, or whose names are so modified. The linguistic composition of personal names and patronymics provides another. Both kinds of evidence, abundant in the Babylonian cuneiform sources, are accessible to modern researchers of the Exile largely through Ran Zadok's studies. In addition to comprehensive collections focused specifically on data relevant to the Exile and the Judean experience (Zadok 1977; 1979; 1985; 1988; 2002), Zadok's bibliography treating the full range of linguistic, onomastic, and geographic evidence for population groups across the landscape of the neo-Babylonian and Achaemenid Empires provides a foundation for study of identity in the ancient Near East. Although comprehensive narratives that account for the diverse population with which the exiles and returnees interacted remain to be written, it is clear that the onomastic evidence from names and gentilics augments assessments of the demography of the Exile.

9.5.2 Onomastics and Identity

Archaeologists know that pots are not people; historians and linguists acknowledge that text is not language. Evaluations of onomastics and identity in the larger contexts of the communities in which the textual evidence was produced show that the linguistic background of a person's name indeed may not represent the language he/she spoke, or even provide a full picture of the family background. Many factors, including the hope of assimilating or "fitting in," impact the assignment and choice of personal names. Nonetheless, the linguistic background of personal names remains the most accessible and frequently applied external identity marker in the cuneiform sources. In addition, alphabetic inscriptions on ostraca, papyri, and neo-Babylonian bricks contribute to the discussion of identity, as they document interactions between persons across the multilingual environments of the Babylonian and Achaemenid Empires.

Among the more intriguing alphabetic sources relevant to the assessment of identity in the Exile is a group of neo-Babylonian bricks from Babylon (maximally dated to the full reigns of Nebuchadnezzar through Nabonidus, 604–539 BCE), stamped with standard royal inscriptions and accompanied by Babylonian and West Semitic personal names in Aramaic script (Sass and Marzahn 2010). The function of these marks remains unclear (Fales 2011: 610), but they are surely reflective of the linguistic and ethnic character of the period in which the Exile occurred. Although the letters of the script and the impressions themselves are remarkably legible, the direction in which the writing was to be read is not always maintained or evident. There exists a good number of examples in which a name must be read left-to-right, and other impressions yield unknown names regardless of the direction in which the letters are read. The corpus editors maintain that while some names can be identified securely as Babylonian or West Semitic, the ambiguities associated with the identification of the direction of writing complicates the carrying out of an ethnolinguistic analysis of the forty-two securely identifiable individual names (Sass and Marzahn 2010: 127, 174–75). Equally intriguing is the question of the identity and social standing of the men named in these inscriptions. If the names are understood as those of construction supervisors or high officials responsible for specific phases of construction, it is difficult to reconcile the lack of patronymics or titles expected to be associated with such individuals. Moreover, two-thirds of the identifiable names are Akkadian, even though they are stamped in the Aramaic script. The inclusion of the alphabetic script on the bricks used in the construction of the edifices that expressed the might of the Babylonian kings is but one noteworthy example of the spread of Aramaic that had begun at least in the eighth century BCE (Beaulieu 2006).

The distinctive marking of ethnic identity may be instigated either by the ethnic group itself or by the population against which it stands out. The cuneiform records that preserve names of Judeans were not produced by members of the Judean community, but by Babylonian administrative officials. The lack of any individual being identified as Judean though use of a gentilic suggests that such marking was of little consequence to the imperial organization (Pearce 2011; 2015). On the other hand, it appears that some Judeans self-identified, at least insofar as their ongoing use of names constructed with the distinctive Yahwistic theophoric element is taken as a marker of the same. While the intentionality of such a choice may be presumed in light of the near abandonment of Yahwistic names in the genealogical tree of the family of Judean royal merchants (Jursa 2007; Bloch 2014), it is impossible to confirm that any particular aspect of Judean identity, beyond connection with family traditions, was reflected in those names. In the assessment of Judean identity, we would do well to heed the caution expressed in a recent study of emerging Arab identity: "The search for instances of the word 'Arab' is in part an onomastic exercise, the pitfalls of which have been noted.... But Arab identity can only have been meaningful at the point when people began to call themselves Arabs and recognized their mutual connections..., so we need to find instances of the name 'Arab', and we can overstep the shortcomings of rigid onomastic analysis by undertaking close consideration of our sources' historical and discursive contexts" (Webb 2016: 20 n. 47).

Less frequently attested than personal names, gentilics are more informative and more reliable markers of ethnicity/identity, as they preserve the name of a place with which the individual is associated. They may provide an attribute of otherness, upon which any definition of ethnicity depends, although it remains impossible to determine whether the gentilic was included in the documentation at the behest of the individual or of the scribe. In either case, the motivation for its inclusion cannot be determined. In the date formulas of two of the āl-Yāḫūdu texts, the first attestations in the administrative corpus of cuneiform renderings of the gentilic Judean appear. Thus, the Babylonian scribes (of CUSAS 28: 1 [572 BCE] and BaAr 6: 1 [566 BCE], years 33 and 38 of Nebuchadnezzar, respectively) preserved the place of origin of a significant component of the population of that particular town: ālu ša ᴸᵘ́yāḫūdāia, the "town of the Judeans." When, less than a dozen years later, the Babylonian scribes replaced the gentilic-toponym with ᵁʳᵘYāḫūdu ("[the city] Judah," the Babylonian name or metonym for Jerusalem), they minimized emphasis on the origin (and thus, the otherness) of the town's primary population. While the names of such mirror towns—deportee settlements named for the population's place of origin (Eph'al 1978; Dandamaev 2004; Tolini 2011)—evoked places conquered in Nebuchadnezzar's Levantine campaigns, the general lack of the gentilic in the toponyms suggests a focus on geography rather than ethnicity. This focus might correlate with tracking economic obligations and outputs of defeated and deported regions, cities, or kingdoms.

The diverse linguistic background of the personal names attested at āl-Yāḫūdu and Bīt Našar (discussed in Pearce and Wunsch 2014: 31–94) finds parallels in the comprehensive corpus of alphabetic textual sources. The degree of linguistic mixing in the inventory of theophoric and predicative elements in personal names of the Idumean ostraca reflects "a blending of cultures in an environment of apparently minimal ethnic boundaries" (Stern 2007: 208). Although these texts originate primarily in the fourth century, subsequent to the time with which this essay is concerned, Stern's observation of the apparent ease with which persons from different languages (and, presumably, cultural backgrounds) interacted challenges Barth's contention that "boundaries exist despite the fact that groups interact both socially and economically and in fact ethnic distinctions can exist not due to any lack of interaction but many times as a result of it" (Barth 1969: 9–13; Stern 2007: 213).

9.5.3 Exile and Return

In this brief section, the notion of exile and return, which usually refers to Judeans who returned from Babylonia to their ancestral home, refers to the experience of another group attested in a different corpus of cuneiform texts—the only other documentation of a population to have been displaced to Babylon and to have returned to its place of origin, a journey comparable in some ways to that of the Judeans. The twenty-seven texts excavated in the Syrian city of Neirab, now a southern suburb of Aleppo, span the reigns of Neriglissar (560–556 BCE) to Darius (521–486 BCE) and thus mirror the chronological contexts of the āl-Yaḫūdu texts (Dhorme 1928; Fales 1973; Eph'al 1978; Oelsner 1989; Cagni 1990; Timm 1995; Tolini 2014; 2015). Although a minority opinion (summarized in Cagni 1990) held that the Neirab texts were written in Syria, most scholars maintained—and it has now been demonstrated (Tolini 2015)—that the documents were composed near Nippur, in the mirror town Neirab that lay proximate to other deportee settlements and were carried back with the Nusku-gabbē family when it returned to Syria. A recent study extends the previous knowledge of the family and archive by investigating the geographic context of the interactions of the family members (Tolini 2015). It establishes the presence of a son of Nusku-gabbē in four neighboring settlements in the Babylonian heartland. In combination with the paleographic study of the five Aramaic epigraphs, which resemble those on tablets written in Babylonia, there remains no doubt that the texts were produced in Babylonia. Not unlike Judeans who perpetuated their reverence of Yahweh, members of this family maintained a connection to the deity, the moon god, whose cult was prevalent in their Syrian homeland, by promoting the name of that deity (Babylonian Sîn and West Semitic Nusku) as the theophoric element in personal names.

Parallels between the documentation of the Judean and Neirabean communities suggest the existence of a widespread pattern of imperial treatment of deportees and a general lack of marking them as "other." However, there is an important difference between the corpora that influences our understanding of the nature of the returning population. The Neirab documents show Nusku-gabbē and sons to have been civic and financial leaders among the Neirab deportee population, providing financial support in the form of loans to members of their own community. The texts also demonstrate that over time, the Nusku-gabbē family members enjoyed increasingly greater social standing and economic influence as well as geographic mobility. For a family that originally held a high social rank in their homeland, the motivation to return could be explained as a desire to resume their previous social position as their exilic conditions in the Mesopotamian heartland changed (Tolini 2015: 77–83). Notably lacking, however, is a comparable corpus of cuneiform evidence from an excavated Judean geographic context. As Judean returnees are presumed largely to have been members of the priestly class or other high social standing, and as Judean priests would not have been admitted to the exclusive Babylonian priesthood or cultic precincts, their absence from the cuneiform sources is not surprising. The standing of Judeans documented in the āl-Yāḫūdu and Murašû sources ranged from tenant farmers to mid-level entrepreneurs; in the Sippar texts, they appear as royal merchants; and at Susa, as palace attendants. All of these are royal dependents, and not the rank of those Judeans who returned. Although it is impossible to know how hereditary members of the Judahite priesthood were situated in Babylonian society, it is unlikely to have been in capacities where carrying documentation of their business activities back to Judah would have conferred or reinforced their standing upon their return.

9.5.4 Marriage

Cuneiform evidence from marriage documents concerning Judean brides in Mesopotamia will surely contribute to understanding the experiences of those who return and inform research into the issue of the crisis concerning the marriage of foreign wives in Ezra and Nehemiah (Southwood 2012), an issue that speaks to the heart of the matter of identity. Three documents record marriages of or transactions related to a Judean bride (Abraham 2005; 2015; Jursa 2007; Bloch 2014). They adhere to the standard pattern of the genre in the neo-Babylonian corpus (Roth 1989), and deviations from the norms can be explained as idiosyncratic variants, specific to conditions of particular marriages (Abraham 2005; 2015). Of particular interest for the relationship of the cuneiform evidence to the matter of the foreign wives is the pair of documents related to the marriage of a Judean bride named Kaššaya, daughter of Amušê, who was married to a Babylonian: Guzānu, son of Kiribtu, descendant of Ararru, whose family name ("Miller") situates him among the urban elite (Wunsch 2014). This information would suggest that Kaššaya "married up." The fact that such an intermarriage occurred is not in and of itself exceptional; of the forty-odd examples of neo-Babylonian marriage documents, a handful document unions between a Babylonian groom and a West Semitic or Egyptian bride (no known examples exist of a contract between a foreign groom and a Babylonian bride). However, social or financial reverses in the groom's family are usually the motivation for intermarriage; the value of a dowry from a foreign wife outweighed the constraints of the relatively closed Babylonian society that would have argued against such an arrangement. The implications of these texts and the socio-economic background of the Babylonian contexts of marriage remain to be explored insofar as they bear on the dilemma Ezra and Nehemiah confronted (Abraham 2005; 2015; Frevel 2011; Southwood 2012; Wolak 2012).

9.6 INTELLECTUAL CONTACT

Thus far, we have focused on the contribution of cuneiform evidence to assessing aspects of the social and economic context of the Exile. The form and content of the administrative texts that have informed the preceding discussion do not suggest their relevance for identifying the intellectual environment in which the Exile was situated and which nurtured nascent Jewish identity and writings. However, the connections have long been recognized, and the documentation produced in both cuneiform and alphabetic scripts increasingly has been considered in the context of the multilingual worlds of the Babylonian and Achaemenid Empires. The intersection of the administrative and intellectual realms occurs in the scribal schools and curricula. One need think only of the standing of the literary figures Ezra and Daniel, who, as officers in the Persian government, were undoubtedly trained in the scribal chancellery (Schniedewind 2006: 139). There exist numerous approaches to and perspectives on the role of the scribal school and curriculum in the cuneiform and alphabetic worlds, and much information is available about them (Tinney 1998; Gesche 2001; Veldhuis 2003).

While explicit evidence for schools and curricula in the training of West Semitic alphabetic scribes is lacking, there is a general consensus that they existed (Lemaire 1981; Rollston 2016: 93). One of the many challenges posed by the absence of data on the schools is the formulation of appropriate and answerable questions to guide and advance the research. To that end, socio-linguistics, which depends on strong textual foundations to discern aspects of the social environment responsible for the production of the sources, may provide a useful context, particularly for unraveling the knotty relationship between writing, language, and identity (Schniedewind 2006; 2013). One recent study considers the expanding roles of scribes among the Judeans and other West Semitic groups in the Levant and western Asia and raises the question of whether the scribes viewed scripts and their graphic technologies as markers of "ethnic self-consciousness" (Vanderhooft 2011: 529–30).

One exceptional incised epigraph on a recently published cuneiform document (CUSAS 28: 10) provides a rare piece of evidence for evaluating the role of script in linguistic and identity marking. Alphabetic epigraphs, inked onto or incised into cuneiform tablets, bridge boundaries of script and language. They are well attested in the Murašû corpus and were the first evidence recovered for the identification of Judeans in the Mesopotamian heartland (Clay 1912). Another small number of alphabetic epigraphs appear on the āl-Yāḫūdu and related texts (CUSAS 28: 10, 37, 40, 41, 42, 52, 53, 71, 103). Like the Murašû epigraphs, all but one were written in Aramaic script. The epigraph incised in the left edge of CUSAS 28: 10, dated to the sixth year of the reign of Nabonidus (550 BCE), presents the letters Š-L-M-Y-H in paleo-Hebrew letters. The scribe of this tablet, as do all scribes of the āl-Yāḫūdu texts, bears a good Babylonian name and patronymic. While it is plausible that some scribes—in addition to those who bear the professional designation *sepīru*, meaning, alphabetic scribe (Bloch 2018)—may have received training in the Aramaic script, it is unlikely that this singular example of Hebrew paleography on cuneiform was the product of such a hand. The mid-sixth-century date of the text places the epigraph at the very end of the period of classical Hebrew and of the use of the paleo-Hebrew script until its revival for purposes of antiquarianism and legitimation in the Hellenistic and Roman periods (Schniedewind 2006: 140). As the use of Hebrew script is unattested in Mesopotamia in this period, it is necessary to consider the possibility that Šalam-Yāma added the epigraph himself (or drew it for a dexterous Babylonian scribe to copy). In either case, it is a unique piece of evidence for Hebrew literacy as the classical chapter in the language's history is drawing to a close, and another contribution to the discussion of the identity of the population at āl-Yāḫūdu and the other southern Mesopotamian towns populated by deportees.

9.6.1 Transmission of Babylonian Ideas

These examples demonstrate concretely the existence of language contact between Judeans and Babylonians. Such contact could have been nurtured in the scribal school and curriculum where it may have contributed to the spread of intellectual ideas. This setting was the likely locus for the transmission of those aspects and features of Babylonian literature that appear in biblical or later Jewish texts. The appearance in quick sequence of two conference volumes dedicated to Babylonian-Judean cultural contact (Gabbay and Secunda 2014; Stökl and Waerzeggers 2015)—the first of which is concerned exclusively with matters of intellectual interchange—attests to current interest in the problem.

Above, reference was made to the possibility that one route of transmission of features of the Babylonian Chronicles occurred when there was contact between a Judean and a Babylonian businessman who had access to the temple library in a city known for the production of Chronicle texts. It was also suggested that the Kabaru canal was a conduit along which knowledge, or its proponents, traveled with the commodities and personnel of trade. In the case of the latter, the association of the place with Ezekiel seems unavoidable, as his prophecies took place at the homophonous Chebar river.

The book of Ezekiel has long been recognized as being replete with references to Babylonian culture (e.g., Greenberg 1983). Two recent studies rehearse previous scholarship and add substantial new insights to Ezekiel's debt to Babylonian literary tradition. David Vanderhooft invokes theoretical scholarship on acculturation and concludes that Ezekiel's acculturation was an instrument through which the prophet could effectively criticize his Judean contemporaries (Vanderhooft 2014: 104). Jonathan Stökl (2015) considers the relevant text corpora from the level of phonology and lexicography to the advanced stages of the scribal curriculum. In a third study, Abraham Winitzer (Winitzer 2014) explores similarities between the book of Ezekiel and the literature of the Babylonian intelligentsia, particularly the renowned Gilgamesh Epic. These studies all presume a high degree of literacy among the Judeans, and, even more, a mastery of the highest levels of the Babylonian school curriculum. The task would not have been impossible, as the neo-Babylonian school curriculum could be mastered in six years, and advanced study could proceed thereafter (Stökl 2015: 231).

9.7 Perspective and Prospective

This brief essay has presented a number of scenarios in which extrabiblical evidence bears on the Exile. The cuneiform texts augment the understanding of chronology, identity, intellectual transmission, and social and economic standing. However, they are devoid of information that would provide a Babylonian perspective on the topics of forced exile and migration (Ahn 2010) and of religious diversity (Stavrakopoulou and Barton 2010). As the contributions of new evidence are harmonized with research in biblical studies and integrated with social science methods, a fuller picture of the Exile will come into focus. Answers to questions of Judean identity and the development of the nascent Judaism of the Second Temple period are closer at hand.

Bibliography

Abraham, Kathleen. 2005. "West Semitic and Judean Brides in Cuneiform Sources from the Sixth Century BCE. New Evidence from a Marriage Contract from Āl-Yahudu." *AfO* 51: 198–219.

Abraham, Kathleen. 2007. "An Inheritance Division among Judeans in Babylonia from the Early Persian Period." In Meir Lubetski, ed., *New Seals and Inscriptions, Hebrew, Idumean, and Cuneiform*. Sheffield: Sheffield Phoenix Press, 206–21.

Abraham, Kathleen. 2015. "Negotiating Marriage in Multicultural Babylonia: An Example from the Judean Community in Āl-Yāhūdu." In Jonathan Stökl and Caroline Waerzeggers, eds., *Exile and Return: The Babylonian Context*. BZAW 478. Berlin: de Gruyter, 33–57.

Ahn, John J. 2010. *Exile as Forced Migrations: A Sociological, Literary, and Theological Approach on the Displacement and Resettlement of the Southern Kingdom of Judah*. BZAW 417. Berlin: de Gruyter.

Albertz, Rainer. 2003. *Israel in Exile: The History and Literature of the Sixth Century B.C.E.* Studies in Biblical Literature 3; Biblische Enzyklopaedie 7. Atlanta: SBL.

Albertz, Rainer. 2012. "More and Less than a Myth: Reality and Significance of Exile for the Political, Social, and Religious History of Judah." In John J. Ahn and Jill Anne Middlemas, eds., *By the Irrigation Canals of Babylon: Approaches to the Study of the Exile*. LHBOTS 526. London: T&T Clark, 20–33.

Barstad, Hans. 1996. *The Myth of the Empty Land: A Study in the History and Archaeology of Judah During the "Exilic" Period*. Symbolae Osloenses Fasc. Supplement 28. Oslo: Scandinavian University Press.

Barstad, Hans. 2003. "After the 'Myth of the Empty Land': Major Challenges in the Study of Neo-Babylonian Judah." In Oded Lipschits and Joseph Blenkinsopp, eds., *Judah and the Judeans in the Neo-Babylonian Period*. Winona Lake, IN: Eisenbrauns, 3–20.

Barth, Fredrik, ed. 1969. *Ethnic Groups and Boundaries. The Social Organization of Culture Difference (Results of a Symposium Held at the University of Bergen, 23rd to 26th February 1967)*. Bergen: Universitetsforlaget.

Beaulieu, Paul-Alain. 1995. "King Nabonidus and the Neo-Babylonian Empire." In Jack Sasson, et al., eds., *Civilizations of the Ancient Near East*. New York: Charles Scribners Sons, 969–79.

Beaulieu, Paul-Alain. 2006. "Official and Vernacular Languages: The Shifting Sands of Imperial and Cultural Identities in First-Millennium B.C. Mesopotamia." In Seth L. Sanders, ed., *Margins of Writing, Origins of Cultures*. OIS 2. Chicago: The Oriental Institute, 187–216.

Beaulieu, Paul-Alain. 2007. "Nabonidus the Mad King." In Marlies Heinz and Marian Feldman, eds., *Representations of Political Power: Case Histories from Times of Change and Dissolving Order in the Ancient Near East*. Winona Lake, IN: Eisenbrauns, 137–66.

Ben Zvi, Ehud and Christoph Levin, eds. 2016. *Centres and Peripheries in the Early Second Temple Period*. FAT 108. Tübingen: Mohr Siebeck.

Berquist, Jon L. 1995. "The Shifting Frontier: The Achaemenid Empire's Treatment of Western Colonies." *Journal of World-Systems Research* 1: 71–90.

Berquist, Jon L. 2007. *Approaching Yehud: New Approaches to the Study of the Persian Period*. SemeiaSt 50. Atlanta: SBL.

Bloch, Yigal. 2014. "Judeans in Sippar and Susa during the First Century of the Babylonian Exile: Assimilation and Perseverance under Neo-Babylonian and Achaemenid Rule." *JANEH* 1: 119–72.

Bloch, Yigal. 2018. *Alphabet Scribes in the Land of Cuneiform. Sēpiru Professionals in the Neo-Babylonian and Achaemenid Periods*. Piscataway, NJ: Gorgias.

Brown, Brian A. 2008. "Monumentalizing Identities: North Syrian Urbanism, 1200–800 BCE." Ph.D. diss., Berkeley: University of California, Berkeley.

Cagni, L. 1990. "Considérations sur les textes babyloniens de Neirab près d'Alep." *Transeuphratène* 2: 169–85.

Clay, Albert. 1912. *Business Documents of Murashu Sons of Nippur Dated in the Reign of Darius II*. PBS II/1. Philadelphia: University Museum [of the University of Pennsylvania].

Cline, Eric H. 2000. "'Contested Peripheries' in World Systems Theory: Megiddo and the Jezreel Valley as a Test Case*." *Journal of World-Systems Research* 6: 7–16.

Collon, Dominique. 2005. "Examples of Ethnic Diversity on Assyrian Reliefs." In Wilfred van. Soldt, D. Kalvelagen, and D. Katz, eds., *Ethnicity in Ancient Mesopotamia: Papers Read at the 48th Rencontre Assyriologique Internationale Leiden, 1–4 July 2002*. PIHANS 102. Leiden: Nederlands Instituut voor het Nabije Oosten, 66–77.

Da Riva, Rocío. 2008. *The Neo-Babylonian Royal Inscriptions*. GMTR 4. Münster: Ugarit-Verlag.

Da Riva, Rocío. 2010. "A Lion in the Cedar Forest. International Politics and Pictorial Self-Representations of Nebuchadnezzar II (605–562 BC)." In Jordi Vidal, ed., *Studies on War in the Ancient Near East: Collected Essays on Military History*. AOAT 372. Münster: Ugarit-Verlag, 165–91.

Da Riva, Rocío. 2012a. "BM 67405 and the Cross-Country Walls of Nebuchadnezzar II." In Gregorio del Olmo Lete, Jordi Vidal, and Nicolas Wyatt, eds., *The Perfumes of Seven Tamarisks: Studies in Honour of Wilfred G. E. Watson*. AOAT 394. Münster: Ugarit-Verlag, 15–18.

Da Riva, Rocío. 2012b. *The Twin Inscriptions of Nebuchadnezzar at Brisa (Wadi Esh-Sharbin, Lebanon): A Historical and Philological Study*. AfO Beih. 32. Vienna: Institut für Orientalistik der Universität Wien.

Da Riva, Rocío. 2014. "Nebuchadnezzar II's Prism (EŞ 7834): A New Edition." *ZA* 103: 196–229.

Dandamaev, M. A. 2004. "Twin Towns and Ethnic Minorities in First-Millennium Babylonia." In Robert Rollinger, Christoph Ulf, and Kordula Schnegg, eds., *Commerce and Monetary Systems in the Ancient World: Means of Transmission and Cultural Interaction: Proceedings of the Fifth Annual Symposium of the Assyrian and Babylonian Intellectual Heritage Project, Held in Innsbruck, Austria, October 3rd–8th 2002*. Melammu Symposia 5. Oriens et occidens 6. Stuttgart: Franz Steiner Verlag, 138–51.

Dhorme, Édouard. 1928. "Les tablettes babyloniennes de Neirab." *RA* 25: 53–82.

Eichmann, Ricardo, Hanspeter Schaudig, and Arnulf Hausleiter. 2006. "Archaeology and Epigraphy at Tayma (Saudi Arabia)." *Arabian Archaeology & Epigraphy* 17: 163–76.

Emerton, J. 1998. "Review of The Myth of the Empty Land: A Study in the History and Archaeology of Judah during the 'Exilic' Period." *VT* 48: 121.

Eph'al, Israel. 1978. "The Western Minorities in Babylonia in the 6th–5th Centuries B.C.: Maintenance and Cohesion." *OrNS* 47: 74–90.

Fales, Frederick Mario. 1973. "Remarks on the Neirab Texts." *OrAnt* 12: 131–42.

Fales, Frederick Mario. 2011. "Review of: SASS, B., MARZAHN, J.—Aramaic and Figural Stamp Impressions on Bricks of the Sixth Century B.C. from Babylon. (Wissenschaftliche Veröffentlichungen der deutschen Orient-Gesellschaft 127). Verlag Otto Harrassowitz, Wiesbaden, 2010." *BiOr* 68: 606–11.

Frevel, Christian. 2011. *Mixed Marriages: Intermarriage and Group Identity in the Second Temple Period*. New York: T&T Clark.

Fried, Lisbeth S. 2015. "Exploitation of Depopulated Land in Achaemenid Judah." In Marvin Lloyd Miller, Ehud Ben Zvi, and Gary N. Knoppers, eds., *The Economy of Ancient Judah in Its Historical Context*. Winona Lake, IN: Eisenbrauns, 151–64.

Gabbay, Uri and Shai Secunda, eds. 2014. *Encounters by the Rivers of Babylon: Scholarly Conversations between Jews, Iranians, and Babylonians in Antiquity*. TSAJ 160. Tübingen: Mohr Siebeck.

Gesche, Petra. 2001. *Schulunterricht in Babylonien im ersten Jahrtausend v. Chr.* AOAT 275. Münster: Ugarit-Verlag.

Greenberg, Moshe. 1983. *Ezekiel 1–20: A New Translation with Introduction and Commentary*. AB 22. Garden City, NY: Doubleday.

Grosby, Steven. 2002. *Biblical Ideas of Nationality: Ancient and Modern*. Winona Lake, IN: Eisenbrauns.

Grosby, Steven. 2007. *Nationalism and Ethnosymbolism: History, Culture and Ethnicity in the Formation of Nations*. Edinburgh: Edinburgh University Press.

Grosby, Steven. 2009. "Kinship, Territory, and the Nation in the Historiography of Ancient Israel." *ZAW* 105: 3–18.

Hausleiter, Arnulf and Hanspeter Schaudig. 2015. "Rock Relief and Cuneiform Inscription of King Nabonidus at Al-Ḥā'iṭ (Province of Ḥā'il, Saudi Arabia), Ancient Fadak/Padakku." *Zeitschrift für Orient-Archäologie* 8.

Joannès, Francis and André Lemaire. 1996. "Contrats babyloniens d'époque achéménide du Bît-Abî Râm avec une épigraphie araméenne." *RA* 90: 41–60.

Jursa, Michael. 2007. "Eine Familie von Königskaufleuten judäischer Herkunft." *NABU* 2007–22.

Jursa, Michael, ed. 2010. *Aspects of the Economic History of Babylonia in the First Millennium BC: Economic Geography, Economic Mentalities, Agriculture, the Use of Money and the Problem of Economic Growth*. AOAT 377. Münster: Ugarit-Verlag.

Jursa, Michael and Heather Baker, eds. 2005. *Approaching the Babylonian Economy: Proceedings of the START Project Symposium Held in Vienna, 1–3 July 2004*. AOAT 330. Münster: Ugarit-Verlag.

Kelle, Brad E., Frank Ritchel Ames, and Jacob L. Wright, eds. 2011. *Interpreting Exile: Displacement and Deportation in Biblical and Modern Contexts*. AIL 10. Atlanta: SBL.

Knoppers, Gary N. 2009. "Ethnicity, Geneaology, Geography, and Change: The Judean Communities of Babylon and Jerusalem in the Story of Ezra." In Gary N. Knoppers and Kenneth A. Ristau, eds., *Community Identity in Judean Historiography: Biblical and Comparative Perspectives*. Winona Lake, IN: Eisenbrauns, 147–71.

Knoppers, Gary N. and Kenneth A. Ristau, eds. 2009. *Community Identity in Judean Historiography: Biblical and Comparative Perspectives*. Winona Lake, IN: Eisenbrauns.

Kuhrt, Amélie. 2014. "Reassessing the Reign of Xerxes in the Light of New Evidence." In Michael Kozuh, Wouter Henkelman, Charles E. Jones, and Christopher Woods, eds., *Extraction and Control: Studies in Honor of Matthew W. Stolper*. SAOC 68. Chicago: The Oriental Institute, 163–70.

Lambert, W. G. 2007. "A Document from a Community of Exiles in Babylonia." In Meir Lubetski, ed., *New Seals and Inscriptions, Hebrew, Idumean, and Cuneiform*. Hebrew Bible Monographs 8. Sheffield: Sheffield Phoenix Press, 201–205.

Lemaire, André. 1981. *Les écoles et la formation de la Bible dans l'ancien Israël*. OBO 39. Fribourg: Editions universitaires.

Levin, Christoph and Ehud Ben Zvi, eds. 2010. *The Concept of Exile in Ancient Israel and Its Historical Contexts*. BZAW 404. Berlin: de Gruyter.

Lipschits, Oded. 2004. "The Rural Settlement in Judah in the Sixth Century B.C.E.: A Rejoinder." *PEQ* 136: 99–107.

Lipschits, Oded. 2011. "Shedding New Light on the Dark Years of the 'Exilic Period': New Studies, Further Elucidation, and Some Questions Regarding the Archaeology of Judah as an 'Empty Land.'" In Brad E. Kelle, Frank Ritchel Ames, and Jacob L. Wright, eds., *Interpreting Exile: Displacement and Deportation in Biblical and Modern Contexts*. AIL 10. Atlanta: SBL, 57–90.

Liss, Hanna and Manfred Oeming, eds. 2010. *Literary Construction of Identity in the Ancient World. Proceedings of a Conference, Literary Fiction and the Construction of Identity in Ancient Literatures: Options and Limits of Modern Literary Approaches in the Exegesis of Ancient Texts, Heidelberg, July 10–13, 2006*. Winona Lake, IN: Eisenbrauns.

Magdalene, F. Rachel and Cornelia Wunsch. 2011. "Slavery Between Judah and Babylon: The Exilic Experience." In Laura Culbertson, ed., *Slaves and Households in the Near East*. OIS 7. Chicago: The Oriental Institute, 113–34.

Middlemas, Jill A. 2009. "Going Beyond the Myth of the Empty Land: A Reassessment of the Early Persian Period." In Gary N. Knoppers, Lester L. Grabbe, and Deirdre N. Fulton, eds., *Exile and Restoration Revisited: Essays on the Babylonian and Persian Periods in Memory of Peter R. Ackroyd*. London: T&T Clark, 174–94.

Miller, Marvin Lloyd. 2015. "Cultivating Curiosity: Methods and Models for Understanding Ancient Economies." In Marvin Lloyd Miller, Ehud Ben Zvi, and Gary N. Knoppers, eds., *The Economy of Ancient Judah in Its Historical Context*. Winona Lake, IN: Eisenbrauns, 3–23.

Miller, Marvin Lloyd, Ehud Ben Zvi, and Gary N Knoppers, eds. 2015. *The Economy of Ancient Judah in Its Historical Context*. Winona Lake, IN: Eisenbrauns.

Oelsner, Joachim. 1989. "Weitere Bemerkungen zu den Neirab-Urkunden." *AoF* 16: 68–77.

Oelsner, Joachim. 2007. "Das zweite Regierungsjahr des Xerxes (484/3 v.Chr.) in Babylonien." In Markus Köhbach, eds., *Festschrift für Hermann Hunger: Zum 65. Geburtstag gewidmet von seinen Freunden, Kollegen und Schülern*. WZKM 97. Vienna: Selbstverl. des Inst. für Orientalistik, 289–303.

Parker, Bradley J. 2006. "Toward an Understanding of Borderland Processes." *American Antiquity* 71: 77–100.

Pearce, Laurie E. 2006. "New Evidence for Judeans in Babylonia." In Oded Lipschits and Manfred Oeming, eds., *Judah and the Judeans in the Persian Period*. Winona Lake, IN: Eisenbrauns, 399–411.

Pearce, Laurie E. 2011. "'Judean': A Special Status in Neo-Babylonian and Achemenid Babylonia?" In Oded Lipschits, G. N. Knoppers, and Manfred Oeming, eds., *Judah and the Judeans in the Achaemenid Period: Negotiating Identity in an International Context*. Winona Lake, IN: Eisenbrauns, 267–77.

Pearce, Laurie E. 2015. "Identifying Judeans and Judean Identity in the Babylonian Evidence." In Jonathan Stökl and Caroline Waerzeggers, eds., *Exile and Return: The Babylonian Context*. BZAW 478. Berlin: de Gruyter, 7–23.

Pearce, Laurie E. 2016a. "Cuneiform Sources for Judeans in Babylonia in the Neo-Babylonian and Achaemenid Periods: An Overview." *Religion Compass* 10/9: 230–43.

Pearce, Laurie E. 2016b. "Looking for Judeans in Babylonia's Core and Periphery." In Ehud Ben Zvi and Christoph Levin, eds., *Centres and Peripheries in the Early Second Temple Period*. FAT 108. Tübingen: Mohr Siebeck, 43–64.

Pearce, Laurie E. and Cornelia Wunsch. 2014. *Documents of Judean Exiles and West Semites in Babylonia in the Collection of David Sofer*. CUSAS 28. Bethesda: CDL Press.

Rollston, Christopher. 2006. "Scribal Education in Ancient Israel: The Old Hebrew Epigraphic Evidence." *BASOR* 344: 47–74.

Rollston, Christopher. 2016. "Scribal Curriculum during the First Temple Period: Epigraphic Hebrew and Biblical Evidence." In Brian B. Schmidt, ed., *Contextualizing Israel's Sacred Writings: Ancient Literacy, Orality, and Literary Production*. AIL 22. Atlanta: SBL, 71–101.

Roth, Martha Tobi. 1989. *Babylonian Marriage Agreements: 7th–3rd Centuries BC*. AOAT 222. Kevelaer: Neukirchen-Vluyn.
Sass, Benjamin and Joachim Marzahn. 2010. *Aramaic and Figural Stamp Impressions on Bricks of the Sixth Century BC from Babylon*. WVDOG 127. Wiesbaden: Harrassowitz.
Schniedewind, William M. 2006. "Aramaic, the Death of Written Hebrew, and Language Shift in the Persian Period." In Seth L. Sanders, ed., *Margins of Writing, Origins of Cultures*. OIS 2. Chicago: The Oriental Institute, 141–51.
Schniedewind, William M. 2013. *A Social History of Hebrew: Its Origins through the Rabbinic Period*. New Haven: Yale University Press.
Siapkas, Johannes. 2014. "Ancient Ethnicity and Modern Identity." In Jeremy McInerney, ed., *A Companion to Ethnicity in the Ancient Mediterranean*. Oxford: Wiley-Blackwell, 66–81.
Southwood, Katherine E. 2012. *Ethnicity and the Mixed Marriage Crisis in Ezra 9–10: An Anthropological Approach*. Oxford Theological Monographs. Oxford: Oxford University Press.
Sparks, Kenton L. 1998. *Ethnicity and Identity in Ancient Israel: Prolegomena to the Study of Ethnic Sentiments and Their Expression in the Hebrew Bible*. Winona Lake, IN: Eisenbrauns.
Stavrakopoulou, Francesca and John Barton, eds. 2010. *Religious Diversity in Ancient Israel and Judah*. London: T&T Clark.
Stern, Ian. 2007. "The Population of Persian-Period Idumea According to the Ostraca: A Study of Ethnic Boundaries and Ethnogenesis." In Yigal Levin, ed., *A Time of Change: Judah and Its Neighbours in the Persian and Early Hellenistic Periods*. London: T&T Clark, 205–38.
Stökl, Jonathan. 2015. "'A Youth without Blemish, Handsome, Proficient in All Wisdom, Knowledgeable and Intelligent': Ezekiel's Access to Babylonian Culture." In Jonathan Stökl and Caroline Waerzeggers, eds., *Exile and Return: The Babylonian Context*. BZAW 478. Berlin: de Gruyter, 223–52.
Stökl, Jonathan and Caroline Waerzeggers, eds. 2015. *Exile and Return: The Babylonian Context*. BZAW 478. Berlin: de Gruyter.
Stolper, Matthew. 1999. "Late Achaemenid Babylonian Chronology—A. Xerxes-Artaxerxes I." *NABU* 1999–2006.
Timm, Stefan. 1995. "Die Bedeutung des spätbabylonischen Texte aus Nêrab für die Rückher des Judäer aus dem Exil." In Manfred Weippert and Stefan Timm, eds., *Meilenstein: Festgabe für Herbert Donner zum 16. Februar 1995*. Ägypten und Altes Testament 30. Wiesbaden: Harrassowitz, 276–88.
Tinney, Steve. 1998. "Texts, Tablets, and Teaching." *Expedition* 40.2: 40.
Tolini, Gauthier. 2011. "La Babylonie et l'Iran. Les relations d'une province avec le coeur de l'empire achéménide (539–331 avant nôtre ère)." Ph.D. diss., Paris: Université Paris I—Panthéon-Sorbonne.
Tolini, Gauthier. 2014. "Le rôle de la famille de Nusku-Gabbe au sein de la communauté de Neirab*." In Lionel Marti, ed., *La Famille dans le Proche-Orient ancien: réalités, symbolismes et images. Proceedings of the 55th Rencontre Assyriologique Internationale, Paris, July 6–9, 2009*. Winona Lake, IN: Eisenbrauns, 591–98.
Tolini, Gauthier. 2015. "From Syria to Babylon and Back: The Neirab Archive." In Jonathan Stökl and Caroline Waerzeggers, eds., *Exile and Return: The Babylonian Context*. BZAW 478. Berlin: de Gruyter, 58–93.
Vanderhooft, David. 1999. *The Neo-Babylonian Empire and Babylon in the Latter Prophets*. HSM 59. Atlanta: Scholars Press.
Vanderhooft, David. 2011. "'el-medînâ ûmedînâ kiktābāh: Scribes and Scripts in Yehud and in Achaemenid Transeuphratene." In Oded Lipschits, Gary N. Knoppers, and Manfred Oeming, eds., *Judah and the Judeans in the Achaemenid Period: Negotiating Identity in an International Context of the Neo-Babylonian Period*. Winona Lake, IN: Eisenbrauns, 529–44.
Vanderhooft, David. 2014. "Ezekiel in and on Babylon." In Josette Elayi and Jean-Marie Durand, eds., *Bible et Proche-Orient. Mélanges André Lemaire III (Transeuphratène 46)*. Transeuphratène 46. Paris, 99–119.

Veldhuis, Niek. 2003. "On the Curriculum of the Neo-Babylonian School." *JAOS* 123: 627–33.

Waerzeggers, Caroline. 2003. "The Babylonian Revolts against Xerxes and the 'End of Archives'." *AfO* 50: 150–73.

Waerzeggers, Caroline. 2014a. "Locating Contact in the Babylonian Exile: Some Reflections on Tracing Judean-Babylonian Encounters in Cuneiform Texts." In Uri Gabbay and Shai Secunda, eds., *Encounters by the Rivers of Babylon: Scholarly Conversations between Jews, Iranians, and Babylonians in Antiquity*. TSAJ 160. Tübingen: Mohr Siebeck, 131–46.

Waerzeggers, Caroline. 2014b. "Social Network Analysis of Cuneiform Archives: A New Approach." In H. D. Baker and Michael Jursa, eds., *Documentary Sources in Ancient Near Eastern and Greco-Roman Economic History: Methodology and Practice*. Oxford: Oxbow Books, 207–33.

Wallerstein, Immanuel. 1974. "The Rise and Future Demise of the World Capitalist System: Concepts for Comparative Analysis." *Comparative Studies in Society and History* 16: 387–415.

Webb, Peter. 2016. *Imagining the Arabs: Arab Identity and the Rise of Islam*. Edinburgh: Edinburgh University Press.

Weidner, Ernst. 1939. "Jojachin, König von Juda, in babylonischen Keilschrifttexten." In *Mélanges Syriens offerts à M. René Dussaud*. Paris: Paul Geunther, 923–35.

Winitzer, Abraham. 2014. "Assyriology and Jewish Studies in Tel Aviv: Ezekiel among the Babylonian Literati." In Uri Gabbay and Shai Secunda, eds., *Encounters by the Rivers of Babylon: Scholarly Conversations Between Jews, Iranians, and Babylonians in Antiquity*. TSAJ 160. Tübingen: Mohr Siebeck, 163–216.

Wolak, Arthur J. 2012. "Ezra's Radical Solution to Judean Assimilation." *Jewish Bible Quarterly* 40: 93–104.

Wunsch, Cornelia. 2013. "Glimpses on the Lives of Deportees in Rural Babylonia." In Angelika Berlejung and Michael P. Streck, eds., *Arameans, Chaldeans, and Arabs in Babylonia and Palestine in the First Millennium B.C.* LAOS 3. Wiesbaden: Harrassowitz Verlag, 247–60.

Wunsch, Cornelia. 2014. "Babylonische Familiennamen." In Manfred Krebernik and Hans Neumann, eds., *Babylonien und seine Nachbarn in neu- und spätbabylonischer Zeit: wissenschaftliches Kolloquium aus Anlass des 75. Geburtstags von Joachim Oelsner, Jena, 2. und 3. März 2007*. AOAT 369. Münster: Ugarit-Verlag, 289–314.

Zadok, Ran. 1977. *On West Semites in Babylonia during the Chaldean and Achaemenian Periods: An Onomastic Study*. Jerusalem: H. J. & Z. Wanaarta.

Zadok, Ran. 1979. *The Jews in Babylonia during the Chaldean and Achaemenian Periods According to the Babylonian Sources*. Studies in the History of the Jewish People and the Land of Israel. Monograph Series vol. 3. Haifa: University of Haifa.

Zadok, Ran. 1985. *Geographical Names According to New- and Late-Babylonian Texts*. RGTC 8. Wiesbaden: L. Reichert.

Zadok, Ran. 1988. *The Pre-Hellenistic Israelite Anthroponymy and Prosopography*. OLA 28. Leuven: Peeters.

Zadok, Ran. 2002. *The Earliest Diaspora: Israelites and Judeans in Pre-Hellenistic Mesopotamia*. Pirsume Ha-Makhon Le-Ḥeker Ha-Tefutsot 151. Tel Aviv: Diaspora Research Institute Tel Aviv University.

Zilberg, Peter, Laurie Pearce, and Michael Jursa. 2019. "Zababa-šar-uṣur and the Town on the Kabar Canal." *RA* 113: 165–169.

CHAPTER 10

NEW PERSPECTIVES ON THE RETURN FROM EXILE AND PERSIAN-PERIOD YEHUD

MARY JOAN WINN LEITH

FROM 550–332 BCE, the Achaemenids ruled over a vast territory that extended from Anatolia and Egypt across western Asia to northern India and Central Asia (Cook 1983; Briant 2002; Wiesehöfer 2006; Waters 2014). The Achaemenids are the same Persians who invaded Greece in the fifth century BCE, even sacking the Athenian Acropolis before their defeat at the Battle of Marathon. From a biblical perspective, however, the Persian period begins in 539 BCE, when King Cyrus the Great toppled the neo-Babylonian empire by capturing its capital, Babylon. Thus ended the approximately half century of enforced exile for the Judeans deported to Babylon in 586 BCE after the fall of Jerusalem to Nebuchadnezzar II. According to Ezra 1:3 (cf. 2 Chr. 36), Cyrus issued a royal edict that the exiled Judeans could return to Jerusalem in Judah and rebuild the house of the LORD.

No longer exiles, Judeans could choose to return to their homeland, a Persian province (Yehud) in the ten-province Persian satrapy of *Abar-nahara* ("Beyond the River"), or could remain where they had put down several generations of roots: Ezra's Babylonian lineage, for example, went back six or seven generations (Knoppers 2011). In their combined twenty-three chapters, Ezra and its companion book, Nehemiah, report on Judeans who returned (Williamson 1987; Blenkinsopp 1988). In their present canonical configuration, Ezra and Nehemiah may have been edited by the same hand(s) (Boda and Reddit 2008). Regardless of that, they share a similar (but not identical) exclusivistic rhetoric in their account of the trials and triumphs of the returnee *Golah* (exile) community as it endeavored to reestablish life in Yehud centering on the Jerusalem Temple. Haggai and Zechariah provide incidental references to Judean leaders mentioned in Ezra-Nehemiah: the Persian-appointed governor, Zerubbabel, and Joshua, the priest. These two prophetic books also mention efforts to rebuild the Temple (Meyers and Meyers 1987; 1998). Esther is also set in the Persian period and its depiction of the Persian court and bureaucracy rings true on many points, though the book belongs to the genre of historical fiction and as such falls outside the category of "Historical Book" proper (note that it is found in the Writings section of the Hebrew canon). Similarly, Daniel's account of exilic life is fictional and composed later than Esther. Three other prophetic works, Third Isaiah (Isaiah 56–66), Malachi, and Joel come from the Persian period but the nature of their language typically eschews explicit historical references.

Until the last quarter of the twentieth century, biblical scholars largely ignored the Persian period, not unlike biblical archaeologists who routinely dug down through Persian period layers (not to mention Islamic levels) to reach Iron Age strata where they hoped to uncover evidence they thought most pertinent to the bulk of the biblical narrative. Notably, attitudes began to change with Stern's groundbreaking study of Persian-period material culture (Stern 1982). Since then, much more has been learned about imperial policies and ideology in relation to Persia's subject peoples, including Yehud and its neighbors. A better understanding of the social and cultural mechanisms by which individuals and communities drew the attention and patronage of Persian authorities has been brought to bear on the activities described in Ezra-Nehemiah (Briant 2002; Fitzpatrick-McKinley 2015; Granerød 2016) and on the history of the Pentateuch during this time (Watts 2001; Knoppers and Levinson 2007; Dozeman et al. 2011).

In light of the storied Persian road and postal system, Judah had more access to the wider world than ever before, despite being a small province in a world empire. Its citizens could communicate with other Yahwistic communities in nearby Samaria, Ammon, and Idumaea, or even further away in Egypt, Babylonia, or Persia. Each of these communities, living within the larger context of an international empire, considered themselves heirs to ancient Israel's religious traditions, and scholars are much more likely today to view the various forms of Yahwism they practiced as branches of one tree. This cosmopolitan and self-consciously antiquarian climate (Ska 2007; Granerød 2016) nurtured the development of the canonical Pentateuch—and likely much else in the Hebrew Bible. Much in the Bible predates the Persian period, but scribal editors collected and revised preexilic texts while composing new material.

New data from archaeological surveys, excavations, and, sadly, from looted artifacts purchased on the antiquities market have advanced knowledge of the Persian period in its local and international aspects (Stern 2001; Grabbe 2004; Betlyon 2005; Pearce and Wunsch 2014; Lemaire 2015). Archaeological discoveries since the 1970s have demonstrated that preexilic Israelite religion was not yet monotheistic and that strictly monotheistic Yahwism gained adherents in the Persian period (Gnuse 1997; Smith 2002; Albertz and Becking 2003). Not surprisingly then, the last few decades have witnessed reassessments of old certainties and new questions about the history, religion, and culture of the people who worshiped Yhwh in the sixth through late fourth centuries BCE.

10.1 Exile and After: Curating Identity

After 586 and the fall of Jerusalem, Judeans—whether exiles in Babylonia, refugees in Egypt, or survivors in Judah—had suffered the loss of their city, their king, their temple, and their accustomed way of life. They experienced the end of a traditional religious orientation based on close association between the ruling dynasty and the priesthood. Judeans suffered the very real, if intangible, shame and stigma associated across the ancient Near East with exile from one's land, a fate akin to identity erasure. Perhaps the Bible's silence about exilic life in the Diaspora is a reflex of that; it certainly reflects an almost exclusive historiographic focus on "life in the land" (Knoppers 2011), even as Ezekiel 37's story of the dry bones speaks to this *erasure-as-death* in exile. The temple's destruction also carried with it a common assumption that the tutelary deity had been defeated or had departed, leaving human survivors in a psychic limbo. Elite exiles from Judah who were unwilling to assimilate into Babylonian culture had to find new ways of conceiving their religious, cultural, and political identity as minority subjects of non-native kings—first Babylonian, then Persian (Berquist 2006). Embracing a narrative of divine punishment, purification, and redemption as articulated by prophets like Jeremiah and Ezekiel, the *Golah* community developed new modes of piety and worship as they went about curating their heritage—their cultural traditions and memories—whether in oral or written form. Begun in earnest in the exilic period, this process characterized the Persian period and thereafter, eventually culminating in the production of the canonical scriptures of Judaism and Christianity.

"Curating," a concept borrowed from museum studies, provides a helpful model for imagining the complicated process that faced the Judean exiles and, subsequently, the *Golah* returnees as they went about selecting, prioritizing, preserving, managing, and interpreting their native traditions. In essence, the Hebrew Bible as a whole can be understood as a centuries-long curating project with one possible high point in the Persian period when the Torah/Pentateuch approached its final form. (It should be stressed that the concept of "canon," a fixed collection of authoritative texts, does not predate the first century CE; see Barton 1986). In the Persian period, even as daily sacrifice to Yhwh resumed on the altar of the rebuilt Jerusalem Temple, Yahwism began the long shift to a new religious orientation based on authoritative writings and controlled by expert interpreters (Knoppers and Levinson 2007; van der Toorn 2007; Schmidt 2012; Edelman 2014; Stern 2015). How these two very different styles of religiosity evolved and interacted over the same time is the subject of ongoing investigation.

The "curating" model functions in tandem with the interpretive analogy frequently drawn between studying the Bible and excavating an archaeological site or *tell*. Just as a *tell* consists of layers (strata) of human occupation accumulated over time with each stratum preserving artifacts from a different time period, so too the Bible consists of textual layers from different eras. While the attempt to date biblical texts remains a key task in biblical studies, equally important is the awareness that the contents of the Bible, unlike archaeological artifacts found in situ, were not preserved randomly. The Bible contains texts, such as the putative Priestly document, that show signs of having been written and edited by elites with political authority, many of whom were or had access to scribes. Other "curators" appear to have re-worked older prophetic texts (Barton 1986) to address concerns of their own time.

Because they narrate events of the Persian period from a distinct ideological bias, Ezra and Nehemiah provide a useful starting point for thinking about the curatorial process which is perhaps more transparent here than in any other biblical books. Ezra and

Nehemiah are historical in the sense that they narrate events in the Persian period that the author(s) intended the reader to accept as factual, an impression strengthened by the absence of overtly miraculous or visionary episodes. At the same time, alert readers will note Ezra-Nehemiah's many indicators of redactional layering, among them contradictory census and boundary lists, confusing chronologies, the anachronistic appearance of Ezra and Nehemiah together in Nehemiah 8, and may also be aware of significant differences between the Masoretic Text and other versions (Wright 2004; 2007; Japhet 2006).

Equally "curated" are the transcriptions of purportedly official imperial documents, beginning with Cyrus's decree in Ezra 1:2–4, including letters (and a transcript of the Cyrus decree) in Aramaic, which was the diplomatic language of the Persian imperial chancellery. Nehemiah 8 (considered by some to be a Hellenistic addition), when Ezra reads from the "book of the Law of Moses," may be viewed as another instance of curation, and on several different levels. On the one hand, the missions of Ezra and Nehemiah do not otherwise overlap, so this episode involving Ezra seems out of place in Nehemiah, with Nehemiah's name inserted artificially in verse 9. On the other hand, within the storyline itself, the written text of the Law of Moses (perhaps a version of the Pentateuch?) is curated before our eyes: the narrator emphasizes that Ezra's audience consisted of attentive "men and the women and those who could understand" (Neh. 8:3), but the text of the law does not stand on its own; rather, it is the Levites' oral interpretation that "gave the sense, so that the people understood the reading" (Neh. 8:8) (see Stern 2015).

10.2 MASTER NARRATIVES

In addition to demonstrating the curatorial process involved in identity-building, Ezra-Nehemiah's "master narrative," considered from a hermeneutic of suspicion, helps to identify problematic assumptions and subtexts regarding Persian-period Yahwism. Many biblical scholars still take for granted the dominant claim of the Hebrew Bible that in the Persian period authentic Yahwistic cult only took place in Yehud, an assertion well established for the preexilic period thanks to the Deuteronomistic History's "Judah-centrism." Somewhat ironically, one of the most important series of publications devoted to reassessing biblical religion in the exilic and Persian periods mentions "Judah and the Judeans" in all its titles—and this despite the fact that its authors have consistently drawn attention to Yahwism *outside* Yehud/Judah (Lipschits and Blenkinsopp 2003; Lipschits and Oeming 2006; Lipschits, Knoppers, and Albertz 2007; Lipschits and Vanderhooft 2011). Hence, as reported in Ezra-Nehemiah, exiled Judeans did indeed return in the Persian period, but the archaeological record contradicts the high numbers reported by Ezra-Nehemiah. The reference in this chapter's title to Yehud, then, should not be read as implying that the only Yahwists of historical or religious relevance to the history of the Bible—or to the Jewish and Christian heirs of the biblical tradition—were the repatriated *Golah* community.

From the standpoint of Ezra-Nehemiah, *Golah* returnees are represented as the only legitimate political and religious community in Jerusalem or Yehud, demanding strict endogamy (marriage within one's group); any man with a non-*Golah* wife (Ezra 10's "foreign woman") or a wife from Ashdod, Ammon, or Moab (Nehemiah 13) was to divorce her. Yet two other books that are likely contemporary with Ezra-Nehemiah—namely, Ruth and Jonah, take a far more inclusive view of acceptable Yhwh-worshipers. Intriguingly, neither Ruth nor Jonah mentions Jerusalem or the Temple which together comprise the ideological core of Ezra-Nehemiah. Yet Ruth is an ancestress of the Temple-building dynasty of David, and Deuteronomistic law (part of the Pentateuch) may function as an organizing principle for the author of Ruth (Berman 2007). In another Persian-period text, 1–2 Chronicles, no topics matter more than Jerusalem and the Temple, but Chronicles' vision of restored postexilic Israel includes the people of both northern Israel (Persian Shomron/Samaria) and Judah (see Williamson 1977; 1982; Japhet 1983; 1989; 1993; Knoppers 2007). The exclusive claims of Ezra-Nehemiah, such as its mention of "holy seed" (Ezra 9:2) should therefore be understood as political and rhetorical rather than historical (Grabbe 2015). The archaeological record suggests that returnees, never very large in number, were quickly absorbed by the majority non-exiled Judean population (Grabbe 2004; Lipschits 2011). Equally salient to Yahwism in the Persian period are discoveries related to Yahwist groups *beyond* Judah/Yehud: in neighboring Shomron/Samaria; in Idumaea to the south; east across the Jordan in Ammon; in Egypt; and, of course, Mesopotamia.

Also lurking unstated behind the title of the present essay are the problematic terms, "Judaism" and "Jew," which have been intentionally avoided because of their complicated and time-bound aspects (Davies 2011; Boyarin 2011). "Judaism" does not make an appearance as a collective term of any sort before the Hellenistic era when it appears for the first time in 2 Maccabees, a Jewish composition of the late second century BCE written in Greek. What 2 Maccabees means by "Judaism" is debated, but no apparent earlier equivalent can be identified in ancient sources about Israel (see Boyarin 2011). A "Jew" in the Persian period was someone living in, or with acknowledged roots in, Judah/Yehud. The term carried no primary religious connotation. Because "Jew" became a religious label in later centuries, however, it is not surprising that a religious meaning has been anachronistically read back into Ezra-Nehemiah and Esther, the three books where the term appears most frequently (Berquist 2006). Even in Ezra-Nehemiah the word "Jew" is best understood in a geographic/ethnic, not religious, sense. Neh. 1:2 refers to "the Jews that survived, those who had escaped the captivity," indicating that non-*Golah* returnees are also "Jews." Simply put, communities of Yhwh worshipers lived throughout the Persian Empire and if we designate them as "Jews" we do so advisedly, for lack of a better term. Expressions like "early Judaism(s)" that tries to account for the variety evident on the ground are inappropriate because "Judaism(s)" is inappropriate for the periods in question. At this point students of biblical religion in the Persian period confront a terminological and methodological quandary reminiscent of the variety of "Christianities" in the first Christian centuries when not all Jesus worship looked like what became creedal Christianity, even though all variations merit attention in the quest for a more accurate understanding of developing Christian belief. In the same way, in the Persian period, all of the various Yhwh-worshipping groups merit consideration as heirs of ancient Israelite religion and culture and as potential contributors to its subsequent growth and development.

10.3 YEHUD: DECIPHERING THE "EMPTY LAND"

In biblical studies, the phrase, "Empty Land," refers to the description in 2 Kgs. 24–25, Jer. 52, and 2 Chr. 36:20–21 of the desolate condition of Judah in the wake of the Babylonian wars and the destruction of Jerusalem in 586 BCE. 2 Kgs. 24:14, for example, reports that the Babylonians "carried away all Jerusalem, all the officials, all the warriors, ten thousand captives, all the artisans and the smiths; no one remained, except the poorest people of the land." In truth, biblical accounts of the exilic period have as little to say about Judean life in exile as about the life of those Judeans who remained on the land, as if both groups had become a kind of "non-people." That point granted, the land was far from empty, given the continued presence of some Judeans in it after the deportations and throughout the exile. Symbolically, however, lacking both king and temple, Judah *was* empty, as the mourners complain in Lam. 5:1–8.

The biblical trope of an empty land after 586 BCE implies that the *Golah* returnees of Ezra-Nehemiah displaced no local Judeans. Perhaps not surprisingly, for a number of years this topic became entangled, even in scholarly circles, in allegations of partisanship regarding modern Israelis and Palestinians (Oded 2003). Critics accused empty land advocates of aligning themselves with the State of Israel which had imitated the *Golah* returnees in Ezra-Nehemiah by confiscating "ancestral" lands from "illegitimate" interlopers. Those who argued that the land had never been empty were suspected of sympathizing with the Palestinians whose circumstances were equated with non-exiled Judeans. Archaeological data, however, clearly indicate ongoing occupation in Yehud under Babylonian rule by a small but far from negligible population of Judeans who escaped the fate of exile (Grabbe 2004; Lipschits 2011). Jerusalem may have been in ruins, but as evidenced by archaeological surveys and excavations, Judeans continued to live in Judah after 586 (see Barstad 1996; Lipschits 2004; 2005; 2011; Faust 2012; Gadot 2015). Ezra 4 reports that when the returnees attempted to rebuild the Jerusalem Temple, they faced opposition from locals who are described as "adversaries of Judah and Benjamin" and "the people of the land" (*'am hā'āreṣ*). Much ink has been spilled in an attempt to identify these opponents more precisely (Fried 2006; Thames 2011), yet it now appears that Ezra-Nehemiah's picture of division between the returnees and long-term Yehud residents is rhetorical rather than an actual picture of the early Achaemenid situation in Yehud (Williamson 1998; Bedford 2001; Grabbe 2015).

Undoubtedly, the Assyrian deportations from Judah by Sennacherib in 701 followed by the Babylonian wars, more deportations, drought, disease, and starvation severely depleted the Judean population after 586, perhaps by 70 to 90 percent (Carter 1999; Lipschits 2003; Faust 2012). Urban sites came to an end, but rural settlements in parts of Judah show continuity from the sixth century into the Persian period (Carter 1999; Lipschitz 2011; Gadot 2015). By the fifth century and the ensuing *pax Persica*, trade in grapes and olives cultivated in the vineyards and groves of the Yehud countryside became key to economic recovery. Just north of Jerusalem, the territory of Benjamin was left almost untouched by the Babylonians, and the Benjaminite town of Mizpah (*Tel en-Nasbeh*) replaced Jerusalem as provincial capital under the Babylonians and possibly also for a time under the Persians (Grabbe 2004; Lipschits 2011).

Drawing definitive provincial borders for Yehud or any of its neighboring provinces in the Persian period has proven difficult, however, with proposals based on differing criteria and presuppositions as well as on disputed textual and material data (Stern 1982; Carter 1999; Betlyon 2005); the boundary lists in Ezra 2 and Nehemiah 7 disagree, for example. Topography probably influenced boundaries, but so did political factors (Grabbe 2004). Yehud's eastern boundary was almost surely the Jordan River and the Dead Sea, probably including Jericho. To the north the territory reached Lower Beth-Horon, and the dividing line on the west was probably at the Shephelah: Yehud apparently did not include Gezer, Lachish, or Azekah. The southern border between Yehud and Idumaea extended beyond Beth-Zur but how far is unclear; that border may have advanced and receded according to political factors (Grabbe 2004; Betlyon 2005).

It has been suggested that by its proximity to oft-rebelling Egypt and to valuable southern trade routes, Judah's strategic value within the Persian Empire increased Persia's investment in the territory's administration and southern border. This historical framework has generated a remarkable array of theories: the reason for Artaxerxes's sponsorship of Nehemiah, the explanation for a possible build-up of southern fortresses, even the motivation for the creation of the Pentateuch and especially for the Exodus story (Hoglund 1992; Betlyon 2004; Fantalkin and Tal 2012). These proposals remain more or less speculative and must be subjected to future exploration.

After the loss of the Temple in 586, Judeans remaining in the land may have moved their cultic center slightly north to Mizpah, the seat of the Babylonian governor, or to Bethel. Bethel had been one of the primary northern Israelite shrines but the tribal territory of Benjamin came under Judean control in the Assyrian-dominated early seventh century, and Bethel was continuously occupied until the fall of Babylon (Finkelstein and Avitz-Singer 2009). Some have speculated that the Pentateuch might have been compiled at Bethel (Blenkinsopp 1998; Knauf 2006; Davies 2007; but see Fleming 2012; Nihan 2007). By the late sixth century, however, Jerusalem's temple had been restored and its sacrificial cult re-established. Jerusalem again became a religious center, a pilgrimage destination (Knowles 2006), and Persian Yehud's only city. Nevertheless, for most of the Persian period, Jerusalem occupied only about twelve acres, restricted to the ancient City of David (atop the narrow north-south spine of Jerusalem's eastern hill, the Ophel) and the Temple Mount. Its population over most of the Persian period has been estimated at around 1,500 inhabitants (Carter 1999; Lipschits 2009).

Any future consideration of Jerusalem's status in the Persian period will have to take into account the site of Ramat Rahel, which was situated on a prominent summit four kilometers south of Jerusalem where excavations have revealed a monumental architectural complex in use from the Assyrian through the Persian period (Lipschits, Gadot, Arubas, and Oeming 2011). The site has raised new questions about the Persian administration of Yehud and the function of Jerusalem (Lipschits, Gadot, and Dafna 2012). The Bible is mute with regard to Ramat Rahel, and with its ancient name unknown (Lipschits, Gadot, Arubas, and Oeming 2011) the discoveries there have been a surprise. The hundreds of stamped jar handles found on the site suggest that Ramat Rahel was a production and tax-collecting center starting at least under the Babylonians and continuing on an even greater scale

Table 1 Governors of Yehud

Based on biblical and epigraphic sources, the following is a list of the known (or possible) governors of Yehud and their approximate dates (after Fitzpatrick-McKinley 2015).
Sheshbazzar (ca. 530s)
Zerubbabel (ca. 520)
Elnathan (510–490)*
Yeho'ezer (490–470/45?)*
Ahzai (470?)*
Nehemiah (445–432)
Bagohi (late fifth century)
Hezekiah (ca. 350–330)

*The inscriptions in question read "governor," with no mention of Yehud

through much of the Persian period (Lipschits and Vanderhooft 2011). With the abandonment of Mizpah, the excavators reason, the palatial complex at Ramat Raḥel became the seat of the governors of Yehud, whether Judean or Persian (Table 1). Also surprising within the palace grounds was discovery of a pleasure garden with water features and a wide variety of ornamental plants and trees including exotics such as the citron and Persian walnut (Lipschits 2012). Traditionally, ancient Near Eastern rulers cultivated luxurious gardens that proclaimed the king's power of conspicuous consumption and royal control of nature (Stronach 1990; Foster 1998). A key component of Persian royal establishments, gardens (or, more literally, "paradises"; Greek *paradeisos* from Iranian *pairidaeza*), were associated with the Persian rulers, satraps, and their elite emulators across the empire (Briant 2002; Boucharlat 2009).

The presence of a palatial stronghold complete with formal gardens almost in plain sight of Jerusalem seriously calls into question the likelihood that Jerusalem was the seat of the Persian-appointed governor. It is telling that the closest contemporary counterpart to Ramat Raḥel's palace and *paradeisos* is found in the city of Shomron/Samaria, the seat of Samaria's provincial governor, one of those being Sanballat, Nehemiah's adversary. Very probably, the "former governors" Nehemiah criticizes for the "heavy burdens on the people" (Neh. 5:15) occupied the Ramat Raḥel complex. As governor, Nehemiah himself may have commuted from Ramat Raḥel to supervise the repairs to Jerusalem's walls, then returned to enjoy the *paradeisos* with the "one hundred fifty people, Jews and officials, beside those who came to us from the nations around us" who ate at his table (Neh. 5:17).

With regard to territorial governors under the Persians, a considerable debate has raged over whether, before Nehemiah's arrival in 445 BCE, Yehud was administered on behalf of the Persians by the Governor of Samaria or was assigned its own governor. In light of the Samarian officials' authoritative tone in their disputes with the temple-builders, Yehud's more prosperous and populous northern neighbor was likely understood to exercise official authority over Yehud. The textual evidence is ambiguous, however, and our understanding of Persian local administration remains incomplete, even in better documented territories. Different configurations of provincial and para-provincial authorities can be found across the Persian Empire, even within a single province at different times (Grabbe 2004;

Fitzpatrick-McKinley 2015). Both possibilities have merit, therefore, with momentum gaining in the direction of Yehudian independence from Samaria (Carter 1999; Briant 2002; Grabbe 2004). The fact that the administrative complex at Ramat Raḥel was continuously in use for most of this time period would seem to tip the balance in favor of an independent Governor of Yehud from early in the Persian period (Table 1). At the same time, throughout the Persian period, Yehud remained a poor, rural territory, especially in comparison to Samaria and the Phoenician-controlled coast. Alliances between elites from Yehud and Shomron would be to Yehud's advantage and probably occurred much more often than implied by the single report of the high-level marriage between the son of the Judean high priest and the daughter of Sanballat, the Governor of Samaria (Neh. 13:28). Determining how such alliances might affect the governance of Yehud in the seventy-odd years between Zerubbabel and Nehemiah requires further study.

10.4 A PROVINCE OF PERSIA

As subject territories in the vast Persian Empire, Yehud and its neighbors were not colonies in the modern sense; the Persians did not maintain the "rhetoric of an aggressive, post-Enlightenment civilizing mission intended to correct and change [their subjects'] affect and identity" or "create particular moralities" (Katchadourian 2016: xxx; Comaroff and Comaroff 1997). Persian rulers were swift with harsh measures against rebellious or uncooperative subjects, but they had no interest in spreading "Persian civilization" (Briant 2002). A recent argument that the Persians rejected rule by indigenous elites (Fried 2004) has usefully corrected an uncritical picture of "tolerant" Persians, but for the most part has not affected the longstanding view that as long as their orders were obeyed, the Persians enlisted local elites alongside Persian military and bureaucratic officials as governors and imperial overseers (Fitzpatrick-McKinley 2015). The Achaemenid Persians formulated a distinctive program of imperial verbal and visual propaganda (Root 1979), but outside of the Persian heartland, pure "court style" imagery was mediated through local artisans and native iconographic traditions (Uehlinger 1999; Boardman 2000; Dusinberre 2003). Persia's propaganda was adjusted according to the traditional royal imagery and language of its subject peoples (Root 1979; Lincoln 2012; Schulte 2016). In the Cyrus Cylinder, for example, Cyrus the Persian is the liberator of Babylon, champion of Markduk (Babylon's patron deity), and restorer of Marduk's temples and priesthood (Kuhrt 1983). In Egypt, the Persian king is Pharaoh (Briant 2002). The Judean prophet known as Second Isaiah announces in exile that it is Yhwh who has stirred up Cyrus, awarding him the ancient Davidic title of Messiah (anointed one) (Isa. 45:1). No clear examples have surfaced in Judah, but in Samaria some typical Persian imagery appears alongside a remarkable variety of other images on fourth-century seals and coins (Uehlinger 1999; Leith 1997; 2000; 2014). Whether and how these images relate to local assertions of or resistance to imperial power is difficult to determine.

The tone of Persian visual propaganda differed from that of Assyria and Babylon by celebrating the ideal of co-operation by all the king's subjects in the king's heroic efforts to ensure "happiness for humankind" (Root 1979; Lincoln 2012). These claims should not be interpreted as "tolerance of diversity." Rather, where apparent tolerance of diversity appears, it should be recognized as the consequence of an imperial strategy to ensure that the king of Persia had the same thing as his Assyrian and Babylonian predecessors: uninterrupted delivery of tribute into the royal treasury. Disempowering local elites who generally controlled trade in their areas would be counterproductive. By adapting to local conditions the Persians could better control regions, peoples, and their resources (Fitzpatrick-McKinley 2015).

From the local perspective, power—and, thus, wealth—depended on alliances between elite families, and was balanced and tempered by any special access a local elite had to Persian officials higher up the administrative food chain (Fitzpatrick-McKinley 2015). As Persian subjects, all local elites maneuvered to arrange matters for their own benefit, sometimes independently and at other times harnessing the influence of and/or acting as imperial officers. Ezra-Nehemiah provides examples of these modes of power relations. On the one hand, by their arrival in Jerusalem, the *Golah* returnees had upset arrangements among local elites who in turn set about protecting the economic status quo with an appeal to imperial officials (Ezra 4–5). On the other hand, when Nehemiah's efforts in Jerusalem interfered with arrangements between Persian-sponsored local officials from Samaria and Ammon and an Arab tribal area, Nehemiah's sponsorship and financial backing by Artaxerxes himself was his trump card.

The various transcripts of official documents in Ezra-Nehemiah are hardly archival records, but they do align in many respects with Persian royal rhetoric, and so actual imperial documents probably lie behind them (Grabbe 2004; Schulte 2016). These documents' role in the narratives of Ezra-Nehemiah, moreover, accurately conveys trajectories of local power struggles within the Persian Empire (Fitzpatrick-McKinley 2015). The proto-Pentateuch, if it may be equated with Ezra's "Book of the law of Moses" or "Law of God" (Nehemiah 8), should also be contextualized in local rather than the empire-wide terms suggested by Frei (2001; Watts 2001). The Persian king sponsored local religious initiatives on an ad hoc basis and local "codifiers" sought the sanction of Persian king to capitalize on the advantages of royal support. This support could be rhetorically framed in terms of traditional ancient Near Eastern royal ideology in the manner of the Code of Hammurabi. Law codes assured their subjects that the king and deity could ensure justice—that is, order, fertility, and peace in the land (Abusch 1985). These laws, however, were not civil law codes in the modern sense, and there is no evidence that legal cases involving Yahwists anywhere in the Persian period were settled on the basis of Pentateuchal law. The public act of codifying and promulgating legal traditions functioned as a "coded" or symbolic activity by which the promulgators asserted (and legitimated) their natural right to local power.

10.5 THE INTERNATIONAL PERSPECTIVE: A SPECTRUM OF YAHWISMS

As noted above, the terms "Jew" and "Judaism" are misleading in any discussion of Yahwism in the Persian period. Especially given the era's remarkable communication infrastructure and existing evidence for interactions between Yhwh-worshiping communities across the Persian Empire, Yahwism should instead be imagined in terms of a spectrum of traditions operating within an international context. In the absence of any defined orthodoxy, simply because a community worshiped Yhwh in its own way outside Yehud does not mean it should be considered heterodox, much less pagan (the diversity of the early Christian landscape is again instructive here). In Jerusalem, the cradle of Jewish monotheism, clay figurines recovered from Persian-period levels may indicate that Yahwism was still not strictly monotheistic (Lipschits 2009; de Hulster 2012; cf. Fredriksen 2004). Even a concept like "sectarianism" is misleading in the context of the sixth–fourth centuries BCE when different communities pursued and sometimes—but not always—contested the legacy of "Classical Israel." For example, the Yahwism practiced in Samaria in the Persian period was not sectarian but one of the varieties of Yahwism, including Yahwism in Yehud, that characterized this period (see further below). The legacy of Classical Israel was maintained even as it evolved across the Yahwistic world, and the mechanisms by which the Yahwistic traditions of one community could have affected communities elsewhere remain elusive (Cogan 2013; Gabbay and Secunda 2014; Zadok 2015; Granerød 2016). Were elites, wherever they lived, the only influential voice or did "bottom-up" popular traditions also affect and effect Yahwist religious evolution? How and why did Purim, a non-Jewish festival of eastern origin absorbed by Yahwist communities of the Diaspora, eventually join the Jewish calendar? The imagery and even words used in the canonical text of Ezekiel have strong affinities to Babylonian learned scribal traditions (Winitzer 2014) as does, to a lesser extent, the Pentateuchal Priestly source: who were the intended readers of such sophisticated compositions? How and why did they eventually become authoritative in Yehud?

10.6 Other Temples, Other Yahwists: Elephantine, Idumaea, Ammon (?)

By the late sixth century the Jerusalem Temple had been rebuilt, if on a modest scale. Most of the biblical texts related to the Persian period assume or assert the dominant Deuteronomistic view that the only legitimate Yhwh sanctuary was the Jerusalem Temple. Nevertheless, Yhwh temples or shrines are documented outside Yehud in Idumaea, Samaria, and Egypt. Others have been suggested for Ammon (Ji 1998) and Babylon. The Deuteronomist master narrative, what Granerød (2016) calls "canonized presuppositions," has prevented a more clear-eyed and inclusive investigative approach to the Yahwistic diversity in the Persian period. Any Yahwistic practice that does not conform to the master narrative is still too often dismissed as tainted by foreign influences (Leith 2014).

The best-documented Yahwist community in the Persian period is the "Judean garrison" (*hyl' yhwdy'*) at Elephantine in Upper Egypt (Granerød 2015; 2016). When, how, and whence this community of mercenaries and their families arrived in Egypt is unclear but they had lived there since sometime in the second half of the sixth century. Whereas the Bible's descriptions of Yahwism in the Persian period are chronologically compromised and hardly disinterested, the extraordinary papyri and ostraca from Elephantine document the Judean community there as the best extant, historically verifiable example of Persian period Yahwism (Granerød 2016: 339).

Elephantine Yahwism is both familiar and strange. In 407 BCE community leaders at Elephantine petitioned not just Bagohi, Governor of Yehud, but also the sons of Sanballat, Governor of Shomron/Samaria, for support in rebuilding their Temple of Yhwh after Egyptians sacked it in 410. The letter cites an earlier petition that had also been addressed to priests in Jerusalem. The same archive also contains a memorandum of the joint statement of approval sent back to Elephantine by Governor Bagohi and one Delaiah of Samaria (now Governor?) and the draft of a letter from the Elephantine Judeans to an official, possibly the Satrap of Egypt, outlining their intentions for the rebuilt temple. This set of documents alone allows the following observations pertinent to the complicated picture of Persian-period Yahwism:

- Elephantine's religious leaders sought the support of Persian government officials as well as Jerusalem priests in their petition to rebuild their temple.
- They take for granted a religious kinship with Yahwists in both Judea and Samaria; both classical Israelite homelands were appealed to with no clear indication that one was more authoritative than the other.
- Grain and incense sacrifices would be resumed if the Elephantine temple were rebuilt, but animal sacrifices would cease, perhaps suggesting deference to the centrality of Jerusalem (Knowles 2006). Yet the Elephantine Judeans did not seem to feel that their petition compromised the status of the Jerusalem Temple.
- Multiple Yahwist communities communicated among themselves.
- Elephantine maintained ancestral ties with the classical Israelite homelands, with members traveling there and back.

It also seems clear that the Elephantine "Judeans" were not monotheists. Their documented oaths, as among Yahwists in Mesopotamia (see below), included West Semitic deities like Anatyahu and Ḥerem and the Egyptian Sati (Granerød 2016). Also of relevance to the "development of Yahwism" are indications that the soldiers and their families celebrated the Sabbath and the Passover. At the same time, however, since Passover and Unleavened Bread seem still to be separate festivals, the Exodus story may not yet have been associated with the Passover, and the Sabbath may not yet have been celebrated on the seventh day (Kratz 2007; Lemaire 2013). Finally, Elephantine Yahwism seems unaware of any sacred texts (Granerød 2016), although admittedly, existing evidence is based on randomly preserved, often fragmentary documents.

In Idumaea, Yehud's neighbor to the south, a single ostracon (inscribed potsherd) from a huge corpus of recently discovered Aramaic ostraca from the second half of the fourth century mentions a temple of Yahô (the Judean form of Yhwh) along with a temple of the Arabian goddess al-'Uzza (Becking 2008; Lemaire 2013). The variety of ethnicities attested to by the many names on the ostraca—including Arabic, Edomite, Aramaic, Egyptian, and Yahwistic/Judean (six percent)—suggests a peacefully existing multiethnic society (Kloner and Stern 2007; Lemaire 2013). Direct proximity to Yehud probably allowed Judeans to travel easily between territories (for trade?) and perhaps to worship in both Idumaea and Jerusalem.

A similar mix of peoples—Persians and other West Semites in addition to Judeans—has been proposed for Ammonite Tel al-Mazar on the basis of a single fifth–fourth-century ostracon (Becking 2008). In the fifth century, one of Nehemiah's adversaries with special privileges inside the Jerusalem Temple was the Ammonite, Tobiah (Nehemiah 13), who shares a Yahwistic name with a prominent Ammonite family of the Hellenistic period. New pottery evidence at 'Iraq al-Amir, the seat of the Hellenistic Tobiads and a possible Hellenistic-era Yhwh shrine, shows that the site was occupied in the Persian period (Ji 1998). This raises the possibility that the Persian-period Tobiah might have maintained a Yhwh shrine in his time as well. His presence in the Jerusalem Temple could also signify that he had some claim to Israelite identity on terms Nehemiah contested (Knoppers 2013).

10.7 No Longer Samaritans: Shomron/ Samaria in the Persian Period

The last two decades have seen a profound transformation in approach to the study of Shomron/Samaria (the city and the province) in the Persian period (Pummer 2007; 2016b; Knoppers 2013). The polemical power of 2 Kgs. 17's peroration on the fall of the Northern Kingdom has been tempered by archaeology and via scrutiny of the biblical record (Knoppers 2013). Yahwists in Persian-period Samaria were neither foreigners nor a breakaway group but for the most part descendants of northern Israelites. By the Persian period, imported Assyrian populations—who are somewhat elusive in the archaeological record (Knoppers 2013)—had fully assimilated. (It should be noted that the "ten lost tribes of Israel" story motif only appeared after the end of the Second Temple Period; see Barmash, 2005). In the 1960s James Purvis established that the text types underlying both the Samaritan and Jewish versions of the Pentateuch were the same and could not have diverged before the first century BCE (Purvis 1968). In other words, Samaria and Judea shared the same Pentateuch. If the "Samaritan Schism" belongs to the Hellenistic period, "Samarian" should be the preferred term with reference to the territory of the old northern kingdom before the first century BCE. If the Pentateuch did reach its final form in the Persian period, then Yahwists from both north and south cooperated in its formulation (Nihan 2007; Pummer 2007; 2016b). Deuteronomy 12's apparent reluctance to name Jerusalem in its cultic centralization law would make sense if the Pentateuch were a "compromise document" (Nihan 2007).

The religion and culture of northern Israel were not wiped out by the Assyrian invasions or by Babylon rule. Galilee and Gilead (in the Transjordan) suffered serious devastation, but surviving settlements in the core tribal areas of Ephraim and Manasseh show continuity in material culture from before the arrival of the Assyrians into the Persian period (Zertal 2003; 2004; 2008). Evidence for elite Assyrian presence in selected sites, such as the city of Samaria that survived as the provincial capital, appears alongside indigenous Israelite material culture. Unlike the Babylonians, the Assyrians deported Israelites selectively, leaving many still on the land (Knoppers 2013). Northern Israelite Yahwism continued to evolve as a living tradition among a population aware of its cultural inheritance (Leith 1997; Knoppers 2013). The Chronicler takes for granted that Yhwh should be worshiped in

> **Table 2 Governors of Shomron/Samaria (fifth–fourth centuries)**
>
> Based on Nehemiah and epigraphic evidence (Samaria Papyri, Elephantine Papyri, Samarian seals, and coins), the following is a possible list of governors of Shomron/Samaria (after Eshel 2007):
> Sanballat I, "the Horonite" (mid-fifth century)
> Delaiah (late fifth/early fourth century)
> Shelemaiah (early fourth century)
> Sanballat II (first half of fourth century)
> Yeshua/Yeshaiah (first half of fourth century)
> Hananiah (mid-fourth century)
> Sanballat III (?) (second half of fourth century)

Jerusalem alone, but the Chronicler's definition of "all Israel" takes for granted the inclusion of the northern populations. Nehemiah himself seems to accept that Sanballat and Tobiah worshipped Yhwh as he did and complains about their supporters in Yehud (Knoppers 2013). Samaria's governors (Table 2) were Yahwists (Eshel 2007). Nor is there any evidence that Persian authorities stirred up rivalry between Yehud and Shomron. The northern population's continuous "Israelite" identity is particularly striking in the predominance of Yahwistic names recorded in the fourth-century Samaria Papyri (Gropp 2001; Dušek 2007) and in the traditionally northern biblical names on post-Persian period inscriptional material from the shrine at Gerizim (Knoppers 2010). Some of the images on the wide variety of fourth-century Samarian coin issues directly mimic Achaemenid "Court Style" propaganda iconography, but others show remarkable continuity with pre-exilic Israelite traditions (Leith 2000; 2014). The presence of the preexilic royal name Jeroboam on Samarian coins also points toward an "Israelite" identity (Leith 2014).

Evidence for how and where Samarian Yahwists worshiped in the Persian period is problematic, however. Excavations on Mount Gerizim, the holy mountain of the later Samaritans, have confirmed the fifth-century construction of what was probably a temple there (Magen 2007; 2010) where, on the basis of inscriptional evidence, sacrifices probably took place (Pummer 2016a). The existence of earlier Yhwh shrines in Shomron/Samaria cannot be confirmed, although one may have been located in the city of Samaria, perhaps originating in the pre-conquest period (Eshel 1994; Niehr 1997). Wherever it was that the northern Yhwh priests presided, they claimed the same Aaronid line of descent as the priests in Jerusalem. The two priestly establishments differed in many respects, but they were at least periodically in communication and they intermarried. Scribes from both territories also used the same script to write the same language. It is even possible that in the Persian period, northern scribal circles had a hand in collecting and editing biblical texts other than the Pentateuch. The two provinces were not the same, to be sure, with Samaria wealthier by far and far more open to foreign influences (Leith 1997; Cornelius 2011), but each acknowledged a common Israelite inheritance. As late as the 160s BCE, the "Jewish" author of 2 Macc. 6:2 condemns equally the profanation of both the Jerusalem and Gerizim temples by Antiochus IV. Knoppers stresses the substantial and persistent links between the neighboring areas that continued into the Common Era despite the escalation of hostilities (Knoppers 2013).

10.8 JUDEANS IN EXILE AND AFTER

As noted earlier, once the release of exiled King Jehoiachin is announced in 2 Kgs. 25 (cf. 2 Chr. 36), the Bible contains only scattered bits of information about life in the diaspora: names of a few Mesopotamian and Persian towns inhabited by exiles; a note about Judean elders acting in some leadership capacity; maybe a Yhwh shrine in Casiphia; the very occasional opportunity for an exile to accumulate wealth (Knoppers 2011). Ezra-Nehemiah and Esther indicate that the exiles, like deracinated groups everywhere, clung to their identity by cultivating and maintaining careful genealogies, by pursuing pious activities like prayer and fasting that did not depend on a sanctuary, and by reinterpreting purity rules for life away from the Temple. The Babylonian diaspora community should be recognized as the returnees' sponsor and driving force, and the two would have kept in close touch. Yehud was a backwater of the Achaemenid Empire, whereas Babylon and Susa were at its heart. *Golah* returnees depended on the diaspora communities for financial support and leadership, and diaspora groups in turn cultivated patronage advantages for their communities through elite Persian officials as close as possible to the throne. Some level of royal patronage was necessary to recapitalize the Jerusalem Temple, to authorize Ezra's mission (if that is not fictive), and to facilitate Nehemiah's wall-building—a project that is equal parts mythic, defensive (Cogan 2006), and politically sensitive. It is educative, therefore, to consider which community— *Golah* or diaspora—was the center and which the periphery (Knoppers 2011).

Additional data on diaspora life comes from cuneiform sources (Stolper 1985; Younger 2003; Cogan 2013; Pearce and Wunsch 2014; Pearce 2015; 2016; Zadok 2015). Beyond the well-known Babylonian ration list that names the exiled king Jehoiachin and his family, Israelite and Judean names (they are hard to differentiate) have been gleaned from individual tablets. Most exiles pursued humble or modest professions, although a few Judeans achieved positions at the Persian court according to early fifth-century texts from Susa. Two corpora of tablets, however, provide more detailed information about the lives and professions of "ordinary exiles." These are the Al-Yahudu ("Judah-town") tablets of the sixth century that first came to notice in 1999 (Pearce and Wunsch 2014; Pearce 2015; 2016), and the Murašu tablets from the second half of the fifth century, excavated in the late nineteenth century (Stolper 1985).

Al-Yahudu, somewhere south of Borsippa, appears to have been one of a series of new or formerly abandoned settlements where the Babylonians assigned newly arrived foreign deportees to expand local agricultural production. The forty-four tablets date from around 560 to 477 BCE, thus from the Babylonian into the Achaemenid periods. More than two hundred individuals with Yahwistic names are mentioned in what are mostly promissory notes related to grain transactions. These exilic families seem to have lived in an ethnically uniform town, working in agriculture as dependents of the king (Pearce 2011). A very few of the Judeans served as low-level officials.

The Murašu tablets record the extensive transactions around Nippur of the entrepreneurial Murašu family. Some eighty names have been identified as diaspora Judeans among the 2,200 ethnically diverse personal names that are preserved in the texts. The Judeans in these tablets were slightly more prosperous than those at al-Yahudu: they are small property holders, petty officials, or simply witnesses. They appear no more or less

"Babylonian" than the other ethnic groups represented in the archive or at al-Yahudu. The term "Jew" (Judean) never appears, and bearers of the Judean names often gave their children Babylonian names. Little is known about their religious life, although they seem to have avoided doing business on the Sabbath (Stolper 1985).

Neither group of tablets contains information related to religious life in the diaspora beyond the existence of Yahwistic names. The general impression is that whatever their religious practices, these populations had largely assimilated into Babylonian society. Even a Babylonian-era marriage contract from al-Yahudu involving Judeans (or West Semites) follows the standard Babylonian legal format (Abraham 2005). Persian-era evidence of the Babylonian diaspora communities whose elites had the wealth, political influence, and religious capital to sponsor and guide the returnee community in Yehud has thus far proved elusive. Jewish tradition links these elites with the Babylonian rabbis who compiled the Talmud some thousand years later, but barring new evidence, that link remains conjectural (Gabbay and Secunda 2014).

10.9 Persianisms among the Yahwists

Finally, Persia's imperial presence and propaganda could not help but affect the religious perspective of its Yahwistic subjects. The iconographic turn in biblical studies led by the Othmar Keel and his students in Fribourg (Switzerland) has made itself felt in recent work on Persian period materials. For example, Mitchell has called attention to parallels between Old Persian inscriptions and creation language in Zechariah 12 and Isaiah 42. The archer motif in Zechariah 9 may be derived from Persian gold darics (coins) showing the Persian Hero/King as an archer (Bonfiglio 2015). A recent analysis of Isaiah 60 has argued that Third Isaiah adapted Persian royal iconography as expressed in the Persepolis Apadana procession reliefs to apply, not to the Persian king, but to Yhwh and Jerusalem (Strawn 2007). These biblical texts focus on Yehud and Jerusalem's Temple, which, as has been emphasized, cut a very modest figure on the stage of the Persian Empire. Even so, the biblical authors reveal a literary sophistication out of all proportion to the modest status of their subject. Like Nehemiah's walls, these texts can be viewed as a metaphor for the international resonances felt by Yahwists across the Persian Empire. When Nehemiah boasts in his memoir that he successfully withstood the forces of his enemies to complete the walls of Jerusalem, he surely was familiar with the theme, if not the actual text, of Darius's Susa Inscription (Lincoln 2012): "By the Wise Lord's will, much handiwork that previously was not in place, that I made in place. In Susa, a wall had fallen down as a result of its old age. Formerly it was unrepaired. I made another wall [that will endure] from that time into the future."

Bibliography

Abraham, Kathleen. 2012. "The Reconstruction of Jewish Communities in the Persian Empire: The Al-Yahudi Clay Tablets." In David Yerushalmi, ed., *Light and Shadows: The Story of Iranian Jews*. Los Angeles: Fowler Museum at UCLA; Tel Aviv: Beit Hatfutsot, Museum of the Jewish People, 265–261 (*sic*/Hebrew pagination).

Abraham, Kathleen. 2015. "Negotiating Marriage in Multicultural Babylonia: An Example from the Judean Community in Al-Yahudi." In Jonathan Stökl and Caroline Waerzeggers, eds., *Exile and Return: The Babylonian Context*. Berlin/Boston: de Gruyter, 33–57.

Abusch, Tzvi. 1985. "Hammurabi." In Paul J. Achtemeier et al., eds., *Harper's Bible Dictionary*. San Francisco: Harper and Row, 370–71.

Albertz, Rainer. 2003. *Israel in Exile: The History and Literature of the Sixth Century B.C.E.* Atlanta: SBL.

Albertz, Rainer and Bob Becking, eds. 2003. *Yahwism after the Exile: Perspectives on Israelite Religion in the Persian Era: Papers Read at the First Meeting of the European Association for Biblical Studies, Utrecht, 6–9 August 2000*. Assen: Van Gorcum.

Altmann, Peter. 2016. *Economics in Persian-Period Biblical Texts*. Tübingen: Mohr Siebeck.

Barag, Dan. 1993. "Bagoas and the Coinage of Judea." In Tony Hackens et al., eds., *Proceedings of the XIth International Numismatic Congress, Brussels, Sept. 8–13th, 1991, Vol. I*. Louvain le Neuve, 261–65.

Barmash, Pamela. 2005. "At the Nexus of History and Memory: The Ten Lost Tribes." *American Jewish Studies Review* 29.2: 207–36.

Barstad, Hans M. 1996. *The Myth of the Empty Land: A Study in the History and Archaeology of Judah during the "Exilic" Period*. Symbolae Osloenses Fasciculus Suppletorius 28. Oslo: Scandinavian University Press.

Barton, John. 1986. *Oracles of God: Perceptions of Ancient Prophecy in Israel after the Exile*. London: Darton, Longman & Todd.

Becking, Bob. 2008. "Temples across the Border and the Communal Boundaries within Yahwistic Yehud." *Transeuphratène* 35: 39–54.

Bedford, Peter R. 2001. *Temple Restoration in Early Achaemenid Judah*. JSJSup 65. Leiden: Brill.

Berman, Joshua. 2007. "Ancient Hermeneutics and the Legal Structure of the Book of Ruth." *ZAW* 119: 22–38.

Berquist, Jon L. 2006. "Constructions of Identity in Postcolonial Yehud." In Oded Lipschits and Manfred Oeming, eds., *Judah and the Judeans in the Persian Period*. Winona Lake, IN: Eisenbrauns, 53–66.

Betlyon, John. 2005. "A People Transformed: Palestine in the Persian Period," *NEA* 68: 4–58.

Blenkinsopp, Joseph. 1988. *Ezra-Nehemiah: A Commentary*. OTL. Philadelphia: Westminster Press.

Blenkinsopp, Joseph. 1998. "The Judaean Priesthood during the Neo-Babylonian and Achaemenid Periods: A Hypothetical Reconstruction." *CBQ* 60: 25–43.

Boardman, John. 2000. *Persia and the West*. London: Thames and Hudson.

Boda, Mark J. and Paul L. Reddit, eds. 2008. *Unity and Disunity in Ezra-Nehemiah: Redaction, Rhetoric, and Reader*. Sheffield: Sheffield Phoenix.

Bonfiglio, Ryan P. 2015. "Divine Warrior or Persian King? The Archer Metaphor in Zechariah 9." In Izaak de Hulster, Brent A. Strawn, and Ryan P. Bonfiglio, eds., *Iconographic Exegesis of the Hebrew Bible/Old Testament: An Introduction to its Method and Practice*. Göttingen: Vandenhoeck & Ruprecht, 227–41.

Boucharlat, René. 2009. "The 'Paradise' of Cyrus at Pasargadae, the Core of the Royal Ostentation." In J. Ganzert and J. Wolschke-Bulmahn, eds., *Bau- und Gartenkulture zwischen "Orient" und "Okzident"*. Munich: Martin Meidenbauer, 47–64.

Boyarin, Daniel. 2011. Review of Philip R. Davies, *On the Origins of Judaism*. *Review of Biblical Literature*, online at: https://www.bookreviews.org/bookdetail.asp?TitleId=8176.

Briant, Pierre. 2002. *From Cyrus to Alexander: A History of the Persian Empire*. Translated by Peter T. Daniels. Winona Lake, IN: Eisenbrauns.

Cogan, Mordechai. 2006. "Raising the Walls of Jerusalem (Nehemiah 3:1–32): The View from Dur-Sharrukin." *IEJ* 56: 84–95.

Cogan, Mordechai. 2013. *Bound for Exile: Israelites and Judeans under Imperial Yoke, Documents from Assyria and Babylonia*. Jerusalem: Carta.

Comaroff, John L. and Jean Comaroff. 1997. *Of Revelation and Revolution*, Volume 2: *The Dialectics of Modernity on a South African Frontier*. Chicago: Chicago University Press.

Cook, J. M. 1983. *The Persian Empire*. London: Dent.

Cornelius, Izak. 2011. "A Tale of Two Cities: The Visual Imagery of Yehud and Samaria, and Identity/Self-Understanding in Persian-period Palestine." In Louis Jonker, ed., *Texts, Contexts and Readings in Postexilic Literature*. Tübingen: Mohr Siebeck, 213–37.

Cross, Frank Moore, Jr. 1966. "Aspects of Samaritan and Jewish History in Late Persian and Hellenistic Times." *HTR* 59: 201–11.

Davies, Philip R. 2007. "The Trouble with Benjamin." In Robert Rezetko, Timothy H. Lim, and W. Brian Aucker, eds., *Reflection and Refraction: Studies in Biblical Historiography in Honour of A. Graeme Auld*. Leiden: Brill, 93–111.

Davies, Philip R. 2011. *On the Origins of Judaism*. London: Equinox.

Davies, Philip R. 2016. "Monotheism, Empire, and the Cult(s) of Yehud in the Persian Period." In Diana Edelman, Anne Fitzpatrick-McKinley, Philippe Gillaume, eds. *Religion in the Achaemenid Persian Empire: Emerging Judaism and Trends*. Tübingen: Mohr Siebeck, 24–35.

de Hulster, Isaak J. 2012. "Figurines from Persian Period Jerusalem?" *ZAW* 124: 73–88.

Dozeman, Thomas B., Konrad Schmid, and Baruch J. Schwartz, eds. 2011. *The Pentateuch: International Perspectives on Current Research*. Tübingen: Mohr Siebeck.

Dušek, Jan. 2007. *Les manuscript araméens du Wadi Daliyeh et la Samarie vers 450–332 av. J.-C.* Leiden: Brill.

Dusinberre, Elspeth. 2003. *Aspects of Empire in Achaemenid Sardis*. Cambridge: Cambridge University Press.

Edelman, Diana V., ed. 2014. *Deuteronomy-Kings as Emerging Authoritative Books: A Conversation*. Atlanta: SBL.

Edelman, Diana, Anne Fitzpatrick-McKinley, and Philippe Gillaume, eds. 2016. *Religion in the Achaemenid Persian Empire: Emerging Judaism and Trends*. Tübingen: Mohr Siebeck.

Epha'al, Israel. 1998. "Changes in Palestine during the Persian Period in Light of Epigraphic Sources." *IEJ* 48: 106–19.

Eshel, Hanan. 1994. "The Samaritan Temple on Mt. Gerizim and the Historical Research." *Beit Mikra* 39: 141–55. (Hebrew)

Eshel, Hanan. 2007. "The Governors of Samaria in the Fifth and Fourth Centuries, B.C.E." In Oded Lipschits, Gary N. Knoppers, and Rainer Albertz, eds., *Judah and the Judeans in the Fourth Century BCE*. Winona Lake, IN: Eisenbrauns, 223–34.

Fantalkin, Alexander and Oren Tal. 2012. "Judah and Its Neighbors in the Fourth Century BCE: A Time of Major Transformation." In Johannes Ro, ed., *From Judah to Judaea: Socio-Economic Structure and Processes in the Persian Period*. Sheffield: Sheffield Phoenix Press, 134–96.

Faust, Avraham. 2007. "Settlement Dynamics and Demographic Fluctuations in Judah from the Late Iron Age to the Hellenistic Period and the Archaeology of Persian-Period Yehud." In Y. Levin, ed., *A Time of Change: Judah and Its Neighbours During the Persian and Early Hellenistic Periods*. London: Continuum, 23–51.

Faust, Avraham. 2012. *Judah in the Neo-Babylonian Period: The Archaeology of Desolation*. Atlanta: SBL.

Finkelstein, Israel. 2008. "Jerusalem in the Persian (and Early Hellenistic) Period and the Wall of Nehemiah." *JSOT* 32: 501–20.

Finkelstein, Israel and Lily Avitz-Singer. 2009. "Reevaluating Bethel." *ZDPV* 125: 33–48.

Finkelstein, Israel and Yitzak Magen, eds. 1993. *Archaeological Survey of the Hill Country of Benjamin*. Jerusalem: Israel Antiquities Authority.

Fitzpatrick-McKinley, Anne. 2015. *Empire, Power and Indigenous Elites: A Case Study of the Nehemiah Memoir*. Leiden: Brill.

Fleming, Daniel E. 2012. *The Legacy of Israel in Judah's Bible: History, Politics, and the Reinscribing of Tradition*. Cambridge: Cambridge University Press.

Foster, Karen Polinger. 1998. "Gardens of Eden: Exotic Flora and Fauna in the Ancient Near East." In Jeff Albert et al., eds., *Transformations of Middle Eastern Natural Environments: Legacies and Lessons*. New Haven: Yale University Press, 320–29.

Fredriksen, Paula. 2004. Review of Larry W. Hurtado, *Lord Jesus Christ: Devotion to Jesus in Earliest Christianity*. *JECS* 12: 537–41.

Frei, Peter. 2001. "Persian Imperial Authorization: A Summary." In James W. Watts, *Persia and Torah: The Theory of Imperial Authorization of the Pentateuch*. Atlanta: SBL, 5–40.

Fried, Lisbeth. 2004. *The Priest and the Great King: Temple-Palace Relations in the Persian Empire*. BJS 10. Winona Lake, IN: Eisenbrauns.

Fried, Lisbeth. 2006. "The 'am ha'areṣ in Ezra 4:4 and Persian Imperial Administration." In Oded Lipschits and Manfred Oeming, eds., *Judah and the Judeans in the Persian Period*. Winona Lake, IN: Eisenbrauns, 123–45.

Friedman, Richard E. "From Egypt to Egypt: Dtr^1 and Dtr^2." In Baruch Halpern and Jon Levinson, eds., *Traditions in Transformation: Turning Points in Biblical Faith*. Winona Lake, IN: Eisenbrauns, 168–92.

Gabbay, Uri and Shai Secunda, eds. 2014. *Encounters by the Rivers of Babylon: Scholarly Conversations between Jews, Iranians, and Babylonians in Antiquity*. Tübingen: Mohr Siebeck.

Gadot, Yuval. 2015. "In the Valley of the King: Jerusalem's Rural Hinterland in the 8th-4th Centuries BCE." *TA* 42: 3–26.

Gnuse, R. K. 1997. *No Other Gods: Emergent Monotheism in Israel*. Sheffield: Sheffield Academic Press.

Grabbe, Lester L. 2004. *A History of the Jews and Judaism in the Second Temple Period*, Vol. 1: *Yehud: A History of the Persian Province of Judah*. London: T&T Clark.

Grabbe, Lester L. 2015. "The Reality of the Return: The Biblical Picture versus Historical Reconstruction." In Jonathan Stökl and Caroline Waerzeggers, eds., *Exile and Return: The Babylonian Context*. Berlin/Boston: de Gruyter, 292–307.

Granerød, Gard. 2015. "The Former and the Future Temple of YHW in Elephantine: A Traditio-historical Case Study of Ancient Near Eastern Antiquarianism." *ZAW* 127: 63–77.

Granerød, Gard. 2016. *Dimensions of Yahwism in the Persian Period: Studies in the Religion and Society of the Judaean Community at Elephantine*. Berlin/Boston: de Gruyter.

Gropp, Douglas. 2001. *Wadi Daliyeh II: The Samaria Papyri from Wadi Daliyeh*. DJD 28. Oxford: Oxford University Press.

Japhet, Sara. 1983. "The People and the Land in the Restoration Period." In G. Strecker, ed., *Das Land Israel in biblischer Zeit*. Göttingen Theologische Arbeiten 25. Göttingen: Vandenhoeck & Ruprecht, 103–25.

Japhet, Sara. 1993. *I & II Chronicles: A Commentary*. OTL. Louisville, KY: Westminster John Knox.

Japhet, Sara. 1997. *The Ideology of the Book of Chronicles and Its Place in Biblical Thought*. 2nd ed. New York: Peter Lang.

Japhet, Sara. 1993. *I & II Chronicles: A Commentary*. OTL. Louisville, KY: Westminster John Knox.

Ji, Chang-Ho C. 1998. "A New Look at the Tobiads in 'Iraq al-Amir." *Liber Annus* 48: 417–440.

Khatchadourian, Lori. 2016. *Imperial Matter: Ancient Persia and the Archaeology of Empires*. Oakland, CA: University of California Press.

Kloner, Amos and Ian Stern. 2007. "Idumea and the Late Persian Period (Fourth Century BCE)." In Oded Lipschits, Gary N. Knoppers, and Rainer Albertz, eds., *Judah and the Judeans in the Fourth Century BCE*. Winona Lake, IN: Eisenbrauns, 139–44.

Knauf, Ernst A. 2006. "Bethel: The Israelite Impact on Judean Language and Literature." In Oded Lipschits and Manfred Oeming, eds., *Judah and the Judeans in the Persian Period*. Winona Lake, IN: Eisenbrauns, 291–349.

Knoppers, Gary. *I Chronicles*. AB. Garden City, NY: Doubleday, 2004.

Knoppers, Gary. 2007. "Nehemiah and Sanballat: The Enemy Without or Within?" In Oded Lipschits, Gary N. Knoppers, and Rainer Albertz, eds., *Judah and the Judeans in the Fourth Century BCE*. Winona Lake, IN: Eisenbrauns, 305–31.

Knoppers, Gary. 2010. "Aspects of Samaria's Religious Culture during the Early Hellenistic Period." In Philip R. Davies and Diana V. Edelman, eds., *The Historian and the Bible*. New York and London: T&T Clark, 159-74.

Knoppers, Gary. 2011. "Exile, Return and Diaspora: Expatriates and Repatriates in Late Biblical Literature." In Louis Jonker, ed., *Texts, Contexts and Readings in Postexilic Literature*. FAT 2/53. Tübingen: Mohr Siebeck, 29-61.

Knoppers, Gary. 2013. *Jews and Samaritans: The Origins and History of Their Early Relations*. Oxford: Oxford University Press.

Knoppers, Gary. 2015. "The Construction of Judean Diasporic Identity in Ezra-Nehemiah." *JHS* 15: 1-29.

Knoppers, Gary R. and Bernard M. Levinson, eds. 2007. *The Pentateuch as Torah: New Models for Understanding Its Promulgation and Acceptance*. Winona Lake, IN: Eisenbrauns.

Knowles, Melody. 2006. *Centrality Practiced: Jerusalem in the Religious Practice of Yehud and the Diaspora in the Persian Period*. ABS. Atlanta: Scholars Press.

Kratz, Reinhard G. 2006. "Temple and Torah: Reflections on the Legal Status of the Pentateuch between Elephantine and Qumran." In Gary N. Knoppers and Bernard M. Levinson, eds., *The Pentateuch as Torah: New Models for Understanding Its Promulgation and Acceptance*. Winona Lake IN: Eisenbrauns, 77-103.

Kuhrt, Amélie. 1983. "The Cyrus Cylinder and Achaemenid Imperial Policy." *JSOT* 25: 83-97.

Kuhrt, Amélie. 2009. *The Persian Empire: A Corpus of Sources from the Achaemenid Period*. London: Routledge.

Leith, Mary Joan Winn. 1997. *The Wadi Daliyeh Seal Impressions*. DJD 24. Oxford: Oxford University Press.

Leith, Mary Joan Winn. 2000. "Seals and Coins in Persian Period Samaria: Setting the Scene for Early 'Judaisms?'" In Lawrence H. Schiffman, Emanuel Tov, and James C. VanderKam, eds. *The Dead Sea Scrolls Fifty Years after Their Discovery*. Jerusalem: Israel Exploration Society, 691-707.

Leith, Mary Joan Winn. 2014. "Religious Continuity in Samaria/Israel: Numismatic Evidence." In Christian Frevel, Katharina Pyschny, Izak Cornelius, eds., *A "Religious Revolution" in Yehûd? The Material Culture of the Persian Period as a Test Case*. OBO 267. Fribourg: Academic Press and Göttingen: Vandenhoeck & Ruprecht, 267-304.

Lemaire, André. 2004. "Nouveau temple de Yahô." In Matthias Augustin and Hermann Michael Niemann, eds., *"Basel und Bibel": Collected Communications to the XVIIth Congress of the International Organizations for the Study of the Old Testament, Basel 2001*. Frankfurt am Main: Lang, 265-73.

Lemaire, André. 2015. *Levantine Epigraphy and History in the Achaemenid Period (539-332 BCE)*. Oxford: Oxford University Press.

Lincoln, Bruce. 2012. *"Happiness for Mankind": Achaemenian Religion and the Imperial Project*. Leuven: Peeters.

Lipschits, Oded. 2003. "Demographic Changes in Judah between the Seventh and the Fifth Centuries B.C.E." In Oded Lipschits and Joseph Blenkinsopp, eds., *Judah and the Judeans in the Neo-Babylonian Period*. Winona Lake, IN: Eisenbrauns, 323-76.

Lipschits, Oded. 2004. "The Rural Settlement in Judah in the 6th Century B.C.E. A Rejoinder." *PEQ* 136: 99-107.

Lipschits, Oded. 2005. *The Fall and Rise of Jerusalem: Judah under Babylonian Rule*. Winona Lake, IN: Eisenbrauns.

Lipschits, Oded. 2009. "Persian Period Finds from Jerusalem: Facts and Interpretations." *JHS* 9. Online at http://www.jhsonline.org/Articles/article_122.pdf.

Lipschits, Oded. 2011. "Persian-Period Judah: A New Perspective." In Louis Jonker, ed., *Texts, Contexts and Readings in Postexilic Literature*. FAT 2/53. Tübingen: Mohr Siebeck, 187-211.

Lipschits, Oded and Joseph Blenkinsopp, eds. 2003. *Judah and the Judeans in the Neo-Babylonian Period*. Winona Lake, IN: Eisenbrauns.

Lipschits, Oded and Manfred Oeming, eds. 2006. *Judah and the Judeans in the Persian Period.* Winona Lake, IN: Eisenbrauns.

Lipschits, Oded and David Vanderhooft. 2011. *The Yehud Stamp Impressions: A Corpus of Inscribed Impressions from the Persian and Hellenistic Periods in Judah.* Winona Lake, IN: Eisenbrauns.

Lipschits, Oded, Gary N. Knoppers, and Rainer Albertz, eds. 2007. *Judah and the Judeans in the Fourth Century BCE.* Winona Lake, IN: Eisenbrauns.

Lipschits, Oded, Gary N. Knoppers, Manfred Oeming, eds. 2011. *Judah and the Judeans in the Achaemenid Period: Negotiating Identity in an International Context.* Winona Lake, IN: Eisenbrauns.

Lipschits, Oded, Yuval Gadot, and Dafna Langgut. 2012. "The Riddle of Ramat Raḥel during the Babylonian and Persian Periods: The Archaeology of a Royal Persian Edifice." *Transeuphratène* 41: 57–79.

Lipschits, Oded, Yuval Gadot, Benjamin Arubas, and Manfred Oeming. 2011. "Palace and Village, Paradise and Oblivion: Unraveling the Riddles of Ramat Raḥel." *NEA* 74: 1–49.

Magen, Yitzak. 2007. "The Dating of the First Phase of the Samaritan Temple on Mount Gerizim in Light of the Archaeological Evidence." In Oded Lipschits, Gary N. Knoppers, Rainer Albertz, eds., *Judah and the Judeans in the Fourth Century BCE.* Winona Lake, IN: Eisenbrauns, 157–211.

Magen, Yitzak. 2010. "Bells, Pendants, Snakes and Stones: A Samaritan Temple to the Lord on Mt. Gerizim." *BAR* 36.6: 24–36.

McKenzie, Steven L. 2004. *1–2 Chronicles.* Nashville: Abingdon.

Meyers, Carol L. and Eric M. Meyers. 1987. *Haggai, Zechariah 1–8.* AB. Garden City, NY: Doubleday.

Meyers, Carol L. and Eric M. Meyers. 1998. *Zechariah 9–11.* AYB. New Haven: Yale University Press.

Niehr, Herbert. 1997. "In Search of Yhwh's Cult Statue in the First Temple." In Karel van der Toorn, ed., *The Image and the Book: Iconic Cults, Aniconism, and the Rise of Book Religion in Israel and the Ancient Near East.* Leuven: Peeters, 73–95.

Nihan, Christophe. 2007. "The Torah between Samaria and Judah: Shechem and Gerizim in Deuteronomy and Joshua." in Gary R. Knoppers and Bernard M. Levinson, eds., *The Pentateuch as Torah New Models for Understanding its Promulgation and Acceptance.* Winona Lake, IN: Eisenbrauns, 187–223.

Oded, B. 2003. "Where Is the 'Myth of the Empty Land' to Be Found? History versus Myth." In Oded Lipschits and Joseph Blenkinsopp, eds., *Judah and the Judeans in the Neo-Babylonian Period.* Winona Lake, IN: Eisenbrauns, 55–89.

Pearce, Laurie E. 2015. "Identifying Judeans and Judean Identity in the Babylonian Evidence." In Jonathan Stökl and Caroline Waerzeggers, eds., *Exile and Return: The Babylonian Context.* Berlin/Boston: de Gruyter, 7–32.

Pearce, Laurie E. 2016. "How Bad Was the Babylonian Exile?" *BAR* 42.5: 48–54.

Pearce, Laurie E. and Cornelia Wunsch. 2014. *Documents of Judean Exiles and West Semites in Babylonia in the Collection of David Sofer.* Bethesda, MD: CDL Press.

Pummer, Reinhard. 2007. "The Samaritans and Their Pentateuch." In Gary N. Knoppers and Bernard M. Levinson, eds., *The Pentateuch as Torah: New Models for Understanding Its Promulgation and Acceptance.* Winona Lake IN: Eisenbrauns, 237–69.

Pummer, Reinhard. 2016a. "Was There an Altar or a Temple in the Sacred Precinct on Mt. Gerizim?" *JSFJ* 47: 1–21.

Pummer, Reinhard. 2016b. *The Samaritans: A Profile.* Grand Rapids: Eerdmans.

Porten, Bezalel and Ada Yardeni. 1986–99. *Textbook of Aramaic Documents from Ancient Egypt.* 4 vols. Jerusalem: Hebrew University of Jerusalem.

Purvis, James D. 1968. *The Samaritan Pentateuch and the Origin of the Samaritan Sect.* Cambridge, MA: Harvard University Press.

Root, Margaret Cool. 1979. *King and Kingship in Achaemenid Art: Essays on the Creation of an Iconography of Empire.* Leiden: Brill.

Schulte, Lucas. 2016. *"My Shepherd, Though You Do Not Know Me": The Persian Royal Propaganda Model in the Nehemiah Memoir.* Leuven: Peeters.

Ska, Jean-Louis. 2007. "From History Writing to Library Building: The End of History and the Birth of the Book." In Gary R. Knoppers and Bernard M. Levinson, eds., *The Pentateuch as Torah New Models for Understanding Its Promulgation and Acceptance*. Winona Lake, IN: Eisenbrauns, 145–69.

Smith, Mark S. 2002. *The Early History of God: Yahweh and the Other Deities in Ancient Israel*. 2nd ed. Grand Rapids: Eerdmans.

Stern, Elsie. 2015. "Royal Letter and Torah Scrolls: The Place of Ezra-Nehemiah in Scholarly Narratives of Scripturalization." In Brian B. Schmidt, ed., *Contextualizing Israel's Sacred Writings: Ancient Literacy, Orality and Literary Production*. Atlanta: Scholars Press, 239–62.

Stern, Ephraim. 1982. *Material Culture of the Land of the Bible in the Persian Period 538–323 BC*. Wiltshire/Jerusalem: Aris & Phillips/Israel Exploration Society.

Stern, Ephraim. 2001. *Archaeology of the Land of the Bible*, Volume 2: *The Assyrian, Babylonian, and Persian Periods (732–332 BCE)*. New York: Doubleday.

Stern, Ephraim. 2009. "A Persian-period Hoard of Bullae from Samaria." In J. David Schloen, ed., *Exploring the Longue Durée: Essays in Honor of Lawrence E. Stager*. Winona Lake, IN: Eisenbrauns, 421–38.

Strawn, Brent A. 2007. "'A World Under Control': Isaiah 60 and the Apadana Reliefs from Persepolis." In Jon L. Berquist, ed., *Approaching Yehud: New Approaches to the Study of the Persian Period*. Atlanta: SBL, 85–116.

Stolper, Matthew. 1985. *Entrepreneurs and Empire: The Murašu Archive, the Murašu Firm, and Persian Rule in Babylonia*. Leiden: Uitgaven van het Nederlands Historisch-Archaeologisch Instituut te Istanbul.

Stronach, David. 1990. "The Garden as a Political Statement: Some Case Studies from the First Millennium B.C." *Bulletin of the Asia Institute* 4: 171–80.

Thames, John Tracy Jr. 2011. "A New Discussion of the Meaning of the Phrase, 'am ha'areṣ in the Hebrew Bible." *Literature* 130: 109–25.

Van der Toorn, Karel. 2007. *Scribal Culture and the Making of the Hebrew Bible*. Cambridge, MA: Harvard University Press.

Uehlinger, Christoph. 1999. "'Powerful Persianisms' in Glyptic Iconography of Persian Period Palestine." In Bob Becking and Marjo C. A. Korpel, eds., *The Crisis of Israelite Religion: Transformation of Religious Tradition in Exilic and Post-Exilic Times*. Leiden/Boston: Brill, 134–82.

Waters, Matt. 2014. *Ancient Persia: A Concise History of the Achaemenid Empire*. New York: Cambridge University Press.

Waerzeggers, Caroline. 2014. "Locating Contact in the Babylonian Exile: Some Reflections on Tracing Judean-Babylonian Encounters in Cuneiform Texts." In Uri Gabbay and Shai Secunda, eds., *Encounters by the Rivers of Babylon: Scholarly Conversations between Jews, Iranians, and Babylonians in Antiquity*. Tübingen: Mohr Siebeck, 131–46.

Watts, James W. 2001. *Persia and Torah: The Theory of Imperial Authorization of the Pentateuch*. Atlanta: SBL.

Wiesehöfer, Josef. 2006. *Ancient Persia from 550 BC to 650 AD*. Translated by Azizeh Azodi. London: Tauris.

Williamson, Hugh G. M. 1977. *Israel in the Books of Chronicles*. Cambridge: Cambridge University Press.

Williamson, Hugh G. M. 1982. *I and II Chronicles*. New Century Bible Commentary. Grand Rapids: Eerdmans.

Williamson, Hugh G. M. 1987. *Ezra and Nehemiah*. Sheffield: JSOT Press.

Williamson, Hugh G. M. 1998. "Judah and the Jews." In M. Brosius and A. Kuhrt, eds., *Studies in Persian History: Essays in Memory of David M. Lewis*. Leiden: Nederlands, Instituut voor het Nabije Oosten, 145–63.

Winitzer, Abraham. 2014. "Assyriology and Jewish Studies in Tel-Aviv: Ezekiel among the Babylonian literati." In Uri Gabbay and Shai Secunda, eds., *Encounters by the Rivers of Babylon: Scholarly Conversations between Jews, Iranians, and Babylonians in Antiquity*. Tübingen: Mohr Siebeck, 163–216.

Wright, Jacob L. 2004. *Rebuilding Identity: The Nehemiah-Memoir and Its Earliest Readers*. BZAW 348. New York, NY: de Gruyter.

Wright, Jacob L. 2007. "A New Model for the Composition of Ezra-Nehemiah." In Gary N. Knoppers and Rainer Albertz, eds., *Judah and the Judeans in the Fourth Century BCE*. Winona Lake, IN: Eisenbrauns, 333–49.

Younger, K. L., Jr. 2003. "Israelites in Exile." *BAR* 29.6: 36–45, 65–66.

Zadok, Ran. 2015. "West Semitic Groups in the Nippur Region between c. 750 and 330 B.C.E." In Jonathan Stokl and Caroline Waerzeggers, eds., *Exile and Return: The Babylonian Context*. Berlin/Boston: de Gruyter, 94–156.

Zertal, Adam. 1999. "The Province of Samaria during the Persian and Hellenistic Periods." In Y. Avishur and R. Deutsch eds., *Michael: Historical, Epigraphical and Biblical Studies in Honor of Professor Michael Heltzer*. Tel Aviv: Archaeological Center Publications, 75*–98*. (Hebrew)

Zertal, Adam. 2003. "The Province of Samaria (Assyrian *Samerina*) in the Late Iron Age (Iron Age III)." In Oded Lipschits and Joseph Blenkinsopp, eds., *Judah and the Judeans in the Neo-Babylonian Period*. Winona Lake, IN: Eisenbrauns, 2003, 377–412.

Zertal, Adam. 2004. *The Manasseh Hill Country Survey*, Vol. 1: *The Shechem Syncline*. CHANE 21/2. Leiden: Brill.

Zertal, Adam. 2008. *The Manasseh Hill Country Survey*, Vol. 2: *The Eastern Valleys and the Fringes of the Desert*. CHANE 21/2. Leiden: Brill.

PART II

CONTENT: THEMES, CONCEPTS, ISSUES

CHAPTER 11

ISRAELITE AND JUDEAN SOCIETY AND ECONOMY

ROGER S. NAM

11.1 Introduction

THE historical books of the Hebrew Bible describe a chronological period that spans many centuries, from the conquest of Canaan to settlement, monarchy, division, exile, and return. Although the historical books primarily devote themselves to a theological interest, the very task of depicting and illustrating history necessitates certain assumptions regarding the society and economy, and these assumptions are largely unstated. This essay begins with a review of the dominant theoretical approaches to ancient economies in order to better frame the analysis and to serve as a methodological control. These theories then lead to describing the nature of the primary sources for reconstructing the society and economy: biblical texts, extrabiblical texts, and archaeology. The main body of the essay follows the chronology within the historical books from Joshua to Esther. Of course, the delineations are neither clean nor simplistic in terms of assigning biblical books entirely to their purported historical periods, as these texts are composite collections, influenced by editing and ideological bias. At the same time, these biblical books may still reflect certain historical realities, particularly since the social and economic systems were part of the compilers' subconscious worldview, and less subject to ideological revision compared to religious ideologies. The overarching thesis of this essay is that the historical books indicate both complex and dynamic economic worlds, including periods of subsistence and specialization, limited trade, forced centralization, and both resistance and capitulation to larger empires.

11.2 Theories and Sources

Critical studies on biblical economics remains at a relatively nascent stage. Because economic values are often simultaneously axiomatic and subconscious, it is hard to imagine societal life outside of one's own social frame. For example, how does society function without the tool of money as a medium of exchange? What is the seasonal rhythm of a patriarchal household? What is the nature of agrarian life, whether subsistence-based or collective? How can a disenfranchised kin-group survive, or even thrive, when caught in the orbit of greater empires? Each of these situations were fundamental aspects of economic life for many in ancient Israel and Judah. Consequently, one must step back from modern, and often capitalistic, economic assumptions and think through ways that the ancient economy functioned. In doing so, ancient historians have turned to different economic theories to frame understandings of ancient society as well as to catalyze imagination on distinctly unfamiliar societies.

Most biblical scholarship on the historical books assumes formalism, that is, an economic understanding in line with Adam Smith and general notions of Western capitalism in that an "invisible hand" controlled the market effectively and independently of any central regulations. For formalists, equilibriums deeply align to the self-interest within human nature, and therefore formalist principles of supply and demand are universal in all economies except for pure subsistence societies. For these reasons, formalists would see the ancient economy through values and methods roughly analogous to modern Western economies, only at a much smaller scale. Within the historical books, one may look at the long-distance trade of Solomon with the Phoenician city-state of Tyre (1 Kgs. 5:15–32) as an example of such formalist exchange in which Israel gets access to cedars in exchange for their own grain surpluses. Israel needed the massive timber of cedar to build their own palatial architecture. Tyre lacked a hinterland to provide basic food supplies for their own population. Both parties hold to their competitive advantage in acquiring products that were not accessible within their own natural resources. Therefore, formalism supports an economy based on mutually symbiotic exchanges that are primarily utilitarian with little regard for social relations.

As a response to the nearly axiomatic understanding of a universal capitalism, some ancient economists challenged formalist assumptions by drawing on the growing fields of cultural anthropology. Ethnographic observations revealed that non-Western societies could follow complex economic systems without the use of currency. These so-called substantivist economies revolved around a different set of economic values, namely, duties and obligation, beliefs and magic, social ambitions and vanities. Karl Polanyi (1944) had the single greatest influence in articulating a substantivist understanding of ancient economies, arguing that economic transactions of the ancient world were deeply socially embedded, and, therefore, disanalogous to the economies of today. Economic exchange may have had some competitive advantage, but such motivations were secondary to the social impact of exchange. For example, the substantivist may look at the aforementioned long-distance exchange between Solomon and Tyre and determine that the exchange has much more of a social impact. Although both parties economically derive utilitarian benefits from the exchange, the establishment of a more formal relationship between Israel and Tyre was the core motivation for the trade. This deeper relationship later manifests with the political marriage between Israel and Phoenicia and the resulting syncretistic practices that arise among the Israelites.

In addition to formalists and substantivists, scholars applied other interpretive theories to the ancient economies. Karl Marx theorized a grand progression of class struggle along a dialogical continuum, and such an approach continues to this day with modifications.

Norman Gottwald's seminal volume, *The Tribes of Yahweh* (1979), applies a Marxist paradigm to the settlement of Israel, but largely emphasizes the social formation of an inchoate state, rather than focusing on the economic aspect. Regardless of one's feelings for Gottwald's conclusions, he rightly emphasizes the role of kinship as a social unit. Other Marxist advocates draw from particular subsets of Marxist theory, whether emphasizing the means of production (or Asiatic Mode of Production; cf. Wittfogel 1944), the center-periphery imbalances (or World-Systems Theory associated with Wallerstein 2004, though see critique by Altmann 2016: 26; Nam 2012: 40–42), or approaches to economic instability (or Regulation Theory, cf. Boer 2015). Max Weber (1952) provides an additional alternative to capitalism. Weber rejected the universalism of formalist economics, but insisted that each economy adheres to a particular set of ideal types, and for the ancient world patrimonialism was the ideal type for economic life. In a patrimonial system, the centralized government organized itself along the model of a household with the most powerful person (emperor or king) in the role of the chief patriarch. Such a system fostered a shared identity and thus loyalty towards this fictive kinship. This patrimonial concept could be embedded within smaller organizational units such as the tribe or clan. Weber argued that the concept of patrimonial loyalty was much more effective than coercion.

In retrospect of these somewhat contentious debates, an increasing number of approaches recognize the multiplicity of economic perspectives as a more effective method for capturing the complexity of ancient economies. Theoretical assumptions need to be explicit. Not only must scholars refrain from importing modern (and often capitalist) assumptions in interpretation, they must also not be seduced by singular economic theories. As social-scientific tools are less empirical and more heuristic, one must not be on either extreme but look to an assortment of models in analysis of the ancient society and economy.

The economic theories provide a starting point, but these theoretical approaches require sources, specifically biblical texts, extrabiblical texts, and archaeology. In this study of the economy and society of Israel and Judah, we can begin with the actual historical books of the Hebrew Bible. The texts begin with the entry to the promised land in the early Iron Age I (1200–1000 BCE), then move to the settlement and period of the judges, the rise of the united monarchy, the subsequent division, the Babylonian exile, the return to Jerusalem, and the rebuilding of the Second Temple during the Persian period (515 BCE). Within this broad chronological scope, critical scholarship has universally recognized that the historical books betray complex layers of textual development. Broadly, one can assume that major portions of these texts were compiled and edited through the prism of exile and later. More significantly, these texts do not intend to present a purely historical account, but rather a theological explanation of the events of the past. Despite these limitations, the historical books provide a starting point to create a clearer picture of the economic and social worlds that these texts inhabit. In addition to biblical texts, extrabiblical sources help to supplement and even supplant biblical descriptions. Extrabiblical sources span a rich assortment of genres, such as economic archives, legal cases, epistolary texts, graffiti, tribute lists, votive offerings, and royal inscriptions. Whereas biblical scholars most famously refer to such extrabiblical texts for parallel studies of passages, such as Genesis and ancient Near Eastern cosmologies, or the confirmation of certain biblical figures like Jehu (Black Obelisk), the vast majority of extrabiblical texts are actually economic in nature. Finally, archaeology serves as an additional, constantly expanding source for our reconstructive efforts. The advent of "new archaeology" of the 1970s utilized more mature social models to build reconstructions rather than the mere recovery of "pure" data. The study of archaeology is vast and overwhelming, but this article will look to broad segments of evidence to observe long-range patterns of continuity and discontinuity, as well as both regional and chronological peculiarities. All of these sources are subject to interpretation, and controversy sometimes attends the interpretation of their form and significance in reconstructing Israelite and Judean society and economy.

11.3 PRE-MONARCHICAL SOCIETY AND ECONOMY: JOSHUA, JUDGES, AND RUTH

The historical books begin the settlement of God's people into the Land of Canaan with the divine command, "And now, arise and cross this Jordan, you and all this people, to the land which I am giving to them, to the Israelites. Every place, upon which the sole of your foot will tread, I will give it to you" (Josh. 1:2–3). Chronologically, Joshua covers a narrow period at the beginning of Iron Age I (1200–1000 BCE), and Judges takes place throughout this period before the transition to monarchy. Martin Noth (1991) argued that both Joshua and Judges form part of a lengthier integrated tradition of the Deuteronomistic History (Deuteronomy to 2 Kings, hereafter DH). For some scholars, the first major textualization of the DH takes place in the preexilic time, as early as the eighth century BCE. At the other extreme, several scholars place the writing of the DH primarily during the Persian period, a full five hundred years after the events of Iron Age I. Regardless of the textual origins, Joshua and Judges purport to reflect the economic and social settings of Iron Age I.

Joshua emphasizes the theme of the acquisition and subsequent allotment of the promised land as the culmination of the patriarchal covenants (Gen. 12:7; cf. 15:7; 17:8). This promise later expands through constant reference to the frequently repeated phrase "land flowing with milk and honey" (Josh. 5:6; cf. Exod. 3:8; Deut. 31:20) to describe the economic quality of this land. Even the moniker of "Canaan" imported some sense of economic bounty as the toponymic descriptor of Canaan has etymological origins in the idea of "trading/importing." The topography of Israel befits the idea of material blessing. Although the total area is quite narrow, Israel and Judah contain a remarkably diverse topography with drastic changes in elevation, rainfall, soil types, and vegetation from region to region. Generally, the northern lands have a much stronger agricultural potential with large valleys, relatively heavy rainfall, and moderate topographical features. In addition, the north had access to premium trade routes. In contrast, the Judean hills had roughly half the rainfall, harsher land formations, and consequently saw much less settlement activity until the monarchical periods. These topographical differences undergird much of the tribal society of the settlement, but especially the political histories of northern Israel and southern Judah. In the agrarian world of the historical books, land was the single most dominant resource available.

Without strong centralization in the wake of the Late Bronze Age destructions, Joshua and Judges assume a modest economic system and localized leadership. Joshua highlights the importance of kinship by allocating the promised land according to tribe. Passages like Josh. 7:16–18 may hint at the inner workings of tribal society, with distinct subsets of larger tribes and smaller clans. In reality, tribal strength varied, often times emerging collectively as a response to an externalized threat. For example, the Philistines often were an instrument to catalyze a degree of tribal loyalty. These threats were economic in motivation, whether as a short-term raid in desire of more possessions, or the longer-term encroachments upon the promised land. In line with the rest of the DH, obedience to God is the lynchpin for receiving or losing such economic blessings.

This emphasis on tribal kinship in Joshua and Judges leads to major repercussions on the social and economic life. Economic systems of localized tribal leadership were much more modest when compared to the preceding empires of the Late Bronze Age. Archaeologically, the southern Levant witnessed major contraction in both number of sites and overall population in comparison to the massive city-states of the Bronze Age. Sites were largely unfortified and the population was fragmented and de-urbanized. Many of these settlements were not directly on major travel routes, suggesting vulnerability to the dangers of banditry in the wake of a decentralized authority. The land was widely divided, thus economic systems were divided as well. All this suggests that the period of the Judges may reflect a time of less formalized/official economies. Evidence for international trade essentially disappeared, with only minor exceptions near the end of this period with Phoenician and limited Cypriot vessels. Instead of trade, kinship groups largely relied on a subsistence economy with diversified crops and a limited capacity for storage. Though falling outside of the Iron Age I period, the tenth-century Gezer Calendar attests to such subsistence strategies. This limestone text references an agricultural schedule that includes at least six different crops. Such a diverse agrarian schedule contrasts with the highly specialized planning of later periods, such as eighth-century Samaria or seventh-century Ekron. The ending chapters of Judges give a negative assessment of this localized tribal leadership with the phrase "in those days, there was no king and everyone did what was right in their own eyes" (Judg. 17:16; 21:25). The explicit reasons are moral failures and external threats, though the economic vulnerabilities also contributed to a movement towards a unified monarchy.

The book of Ruth stands at a distinct place in the preexilic historical books. Although many scholars place the origins of the book of Ruth in the postexilic period, its explicit origins are set in the "days of the Judges" (Ruth 1:1). Within the decentralized social structure of Iron Age I, Ruth presents an insightful look at family kinship. The central figure of Ruth stands as the most disenfranchised person in a deeply patrilineal society like the ancient Near East: female, widowed, foreigner, lacking any economic assets. Despite the admonition to return to Moab, Ruth displays loving-kindness to her mother-in-law and journeys with her. The story intends to show the grace of God given to Ruth through others, but it also implicitly confirms the harshness of life for the marginalized. Ruth does receive favor, but it is primarily not through her agency, except through her sexuality. Instead, she is forced to rely on the kindness of Boaz and the villagers. Eventually, the story ends with a Levirate marriage and the redemption of Ruth through marriage to Boaz.

Immediately with the marriage, Ruth then regains power through her new husband: property, kids, and grafting into Israel through her lineage.

The book of Ruth centers on a single foreign widow, though it spurs additional consideration of the role of women in this period. With the notable exceptions of Deborah and Sisera and others, the books of Joshua and Judges revolve primarily around male figures. Of course, women are essential to any social group, though the extent to which this is true is difficult to ascertain. But for the subsistence strategies of Iron Age I, ethnographic examples can help to illustrate different roles. Carol Meyers (2005) notes a difference between authority (based on cultural legitimacy) and power (based on ability) and suggests that the Iron Age I subsistence economy gave power to women. Because of the importance of labor required for survival in a subsistence society, gender lines were largely blurred, and Meyers postulates that gender hierarchy may have been functionally non-existent. This Iron Age I tribal society would soon transition to a very different economic society with advent of monarchy for Israel as well as neighboring lands.

11.4 Society and Economy during the Transition to Monarchy: 1 and 2 Samuel

The books of 1 and 2 Samuel thematically cover this societal shift from the tribal governance of the Judges to monarchical rule, beginning with Saul, who transitions Israel as both the final judge and the first king. Not surprisingly, the relationship of the biblical portrayal to historical reality of Israel's state formation is the subject of continued and spirited debate. The biblical claim of the establishment of a centralized monarchy at the inception of Iron Age II (1000–586 BCE) may have some merit in the archaeological record. Many sites in the early Iron Age IIA (1000–840/830 BCE) period began to build fortifications and clusters of villages. In the Upper and Lower Galilee, several Iron I settlements vanished and at least some of them were supplanted by larger fortified sites in Iron Age IIA. Samaria and Ephraim show similar patterns. Judah sees consolidation from unwalled Iron I villages to fortified centers in the early Iron Age II throughout its territory including Jerusalem and its surrounding Judean Hills, the Shephelah, coastal plain, and the Negev. Much of this urbanization took place in peripheral areas of the hill country that presumably protected against Philistine encroachment. Centralized planning is not restricted to large-scale architecture. For example, the settlements of the central Negev highlands appear to follow a concerted scheme to create an enclosure to regulate the passing trade routes. These settlements suggest a more centralized authority, spatially organized into districts reflected in 1 Kgs. 4:7–19. Traditionally, archaeologists have turned to common structural designs that demonstrate a degree of uniformity, primarily the six-chambered gates of Megiddo, Hazor, and Gezer (cf. 1 Kgs. 9:15), as indications of a centralized monarchy. With the unified monarchy, Israel moved toward a centralized organization with a complex social structure. The monarchy regulated the distribution of the factors of production, most notably land and labor. In order to create surpluses to support a bureaucratic class, specializations emerged in contrast to the diversified labor systems of the Iron Age I subsistence economies. The patterns of labor for such a society may be reflected in 1 Sam. 8:11–17 with references to multiple professions and stratified social classes in the context of the negative assessment of monarchy.

More recently, different groups of scholars have challenged the historicity of the united monarchy as described in biblical traditions. Drawing on anthropological studies of chiefdom societies, Robert Coote and Keith Whitelam (1987) describe a much more moderate understanding of the early Iron Age IIA period, declaring it a chiefdom and not a monarchy. Under this view, the development to state formation did not occur until later than the tenth century. This chiefdom model found allied support from a branch of archaeology, namely, the proponents of the so-called low chronology. Israel Finkelstein (Finkelstein and Mazar 2007) argues that the stratigraphy of the gates of Megiddo, Hazor, and Gezer should be down-dated to the ninth century. In the absence of any fixed anchor for the early Iron Age II period, Finkelstein and his adherents contend for a low chronology in that these gates do not belong to any united monarchy, but they ascribe the building activity and the centralization to rulers like the Omrides. For these interpreters, the regional chiefdom had two primary characteristics. First, such a social organization relied on distinguished social rank, with the chief as the highest rank. This chief had to organize economic networks and group identity, often using religion as a tool. Second, social organization was regionally defined. Economic decisions no longer revolved around the subsistence strategies of the kinship-based household, as they did in Iron Age I, but along larger regional organization. Chiefs needed to effectively control resources of labor and land to execute more efficient defense and agrarian strategies such as terracing. Regional chiefdoms also relied on greater interregional trade.

Overall, more Levantine archaeologists subscribe to the high chronology, which supports a relatively positive assessment of the historicity of the biblical description of the early monarchy—namely, that a single royal house actually did consolidate land and that many of the traditional Iron Age IIA structures legitimately are products of a centralized royal building plan. Regardless, the Iron Age IIA brought the advent of a more deliberate centralization program and a major shift in the economic and social organization. This visible shift in social organization from regional tribal leadership (Iron Age I) to a more centralized decision making, whether monarchical or chiefdom, had major repercussions on economy and society. The inability of outside empires to effectively penetrate the region spawned opportunities for significant trade. As a result, this increased economic activity naturally generated parallel developments. The increased productivity through more collective agriculture and trade naturally resulted in more developed public architecture: royal residences, enclosures, cultic places, and fortifications. The central authority needed to implement means for collection of various goods and labor as well as some system of bureaucracy. Agricultural specialization and increased trade required greater storage capacities, resulting in the appearance of massive silos and tripartite buildings at multiple sites. But one must be careful not to overstate stratification. The early Iron Age II period often associated with the united monarchy undoubtedly saw a general pattern of political centralization. But it was modest compared with later years as Israel split into northern and southern kingdoms.

11.5 SOCIETY AND ECONOMY AND THE KINGDOMS OF ISRAEL AND JUDAH: 1 AND 2 KINGS

After the end of Solomon's reign, the united monarchy split into the northern kingdom of Israel and southern kingdom of Judah along tribal lines. Understanding the difference between the two states is crucial for interpreting the portrayal of the divided monarchy. Northern Israel had significantly more advanced and structured economic systems. This befits much of the historical geography of northern Israel in comparison to the south. They had many more natural resources and agricultural potential. They also controlled strategic land routes such as the Megiddo Pass, which overlooked the Carmel ridge serving as a major passage between Mesopotamia and Egypt. Northern Israel enjoyed a much more robust economy as exhibited by multiple lines of material culture evidence. The capital of Samaria in Iron Age IIB contained a large collection of Phoenician-style decorated ivories. The Samaria Ostraca indicate a distribution list of luxury products to a cabal, strategically spaced around the city. The pottery vessels evidence significant trade via the Phoenician city-states, particularly Tyre. This economic thriving was surely one of the major reasons for the political turmoil of the northern kingdom, and thus informs a critical reading of 1 and 2 Kings. First, the economic advantages of the north present it as a naturally more desirable target for both internal usurpation of power and colonization from outside polities. Second, the economic thriving of the northern kingdom highlights some of the social commentary against the stratification that comes with economic growth. The critique against the privileged is most pronounced in Amos and Hosea, but it certainly has a parallel in the prophetic narratives of Elijah and Elisha, particularly in their own polemic against the wealthy.

Similar to the northern kingdom, Judah continued to transition towards greater urbanization in terms of settlement size and the growing sophistication of the architecture, though at a much more modest rate. Defense systems were improved both in fortifications as well as intricate water storage systems. Major storage facilities were also a defensive strategy against military siege. With the external threat of the Assyrians, both text and material culture point to a broad centralization, at least on the macro level. One of the most telling signs of centralization is the spatial distribution of the *lmlk* ("for the king") seals on large storage vessels, suggesting a royal collection during the late eighth century, presumably in preparation for defense against an oncoming Assyrian invasion. In addition, from the eighth century, writing begins to flourish, indicating a growing administrative branch and development into a more complex political economy. Specifically, much of these material signs point to centralization in line with the nature of economic activity. From a biblical perspective, the centralization was an effort to purge the country from syncretistic idolatrous practices. But the economic effect was the movement of economic power from a regional level to a central level, empowering the Judean monarchy to prepare better its defenses from outside invasion.

Although the economy had advanced, the period of the divided kingdom continued to have a socially embedded economy. Kinship, whether fictive or genetic, dominated the social world. Most of the portrayals of economic activity are examples of reciprocal or symmetrical exchange in order to foster new social ties and maintain older ones. One prime example is the exchange between Solomon and Sheba (1 Kgs. 10). In this exchange, Sheba and her retinue travel far and engage Solomon in a test of wisdom. Only upon Solomon's successful passing of the test does Sheba give Solomon a generous assortment of luxurious gifts of gold, spices, precious stone, and imported wood (1 Kgs. 10:10–11). In response, Solomon gives back, "all that she desired" (1 Kgs. 10:13). Interestingly, no mention is made of any sort of negotiation towards price equilibrium, a hallmark of supply and demand exchange. Rather, the two participants of the exchange seem to engage in mutual praise and one-upping each other's generosity. Although such gifts may have some economic utility, such motivations are secondary to the reinforcement of a social connection. These gifts were done between both elite (1 Kgs. 5:15–32; 2 Kgs. 20:12–15) and non-elite (1 Kgs. 14:1–3) and often across social levels for both empowering the disenfranchised (1 Kgs. 17:8–15; 2 Kgs. 4:1–7) and subverting authority (1 Kgs. 13:1–10; 2 Kgs. 5:8–27; 8:7–11). Non-elite gifting does not leave much in the archaeological evidence, but one can observe the arrangements of the domestic residences in deliberate clusters. This spatial arrangement suggests that social bonds dictated economic life, which surely included reciprocity among kin. Such gifting was an integral part of ancient Near Eastern societies (substantivism), though the degree to which it permeated Israel and Judah remains under discussion.

In addition to reciprocity, 1 and 2 Kings show significant levels of asymmetrical redistribution as well. Redistribution is the movement of goods from the periphery to an authoritative center, then the redistribution of these goods, often in a different form, to the people. Like reciprocity, the movements of economy redistribution are socially embedded. But because of the asymmetrical nature, redistribution is not necessarily egalitarian, but based on a locus of authority that enforces the redistribution through either political or social coercion. For example, Solomon gathered foodstuffs (1 Kgs. 4:7), labor (1 Kgs. 5:27–32), and livestock for sacrifice (1 Kgs. 8:62–63). These goods then get redistributed in the form of a glorious palace and sustenance of the bureaucratic and priestly groups. Because of the emphasis on asymmetry, redistributive exchange potentially works well with some of the core-periphery approaches associated with Wallerstein (2004). From 1 Kgs. 9, the centralization efforts are deemed as oppressive, and eventually create a schism in the kingdom.

Although reciprocity and redistribution appear to serve as the dominant modes of exchange, some aspects of market economy arise. In 1 Kgs. 20:34, Ahab wins concessions to set up markets in Damascus. While under siege, the economy of Samaria sees hyperinflation to the diminishing supply and demand (2 Kgs. 6:24–25). One of the most blatant examples of market exchange occurs in 2 Kgs. 4:1–7: Elisha meets a destitute foreign widow, restores her empty jars with oil, and commands her to "go outside (to the market?) and pay your debts." Although the passage focuses on the aspect of prophetic provision for the destitute, the mechanism of the exchange clearly points to some degree of market orientation. The foreign widow had no assets, no kinship ties, and yet Elisha presumes that she has access to a market where she can exchange oil to fulfill debt obligations. The oil functions as a medium of exchange even in the absence of any social connection. These infrequent examples, however, cannot determine the nature of these exchange mechanisms against one another. The economies of Israel and Judah were complex and varied. There was growing stratification and deeper complexities. At the same time, preexilic Israel and Judah had relative independence, and their economies organically grew, keeping sight of a shared economy under regional variation and aspects of common worship, as well as duties to the monarchy. All of this would change in the aftermath of the destruction of Jerusalem.

11.6 Society and Economy and the Babylonian Exile: The Exilic Editions of the Deuteronomistic History

Though it stands as the single most transformative event in the society and economy of Judah, the historical books devote merely a single chapter (2 Kgs. 25) to the sacking of Jerusalem. The traumatic destruction of both the temple and the Davidic line, and the ensuing forced migrations, whether as prisoners or refugees, overturned the traditional kin-based social structures. In the reality of the temple ruins, the Judeans were forced to reinterpret the self-proclaimed identity as God's people now that they lost independence and were subjects of another empire.

As often the case with military invasion, the Jerusalem capitulation reversed the economic booms of the preexilic world, resulting in a depressed economy of subsistence and abandonment. The scope of this disaster in the historical books matches well with the limited understanding of the destruction. Because of the relatively short reign of the Babylonian Empire and the lack of distinction between the Babylonian and ensuing Persian period in the archaeological record, the sources for reconstructing Babylonian-period economy and society are modest. But a few broad strokes can be surmised. The Babylonian period shows a sharp break in continuity throughout the southern Levant, including Judah. In addition to the surroundings of Jerusalem (including Jerusalem itself), Ramat Rahel, and Beth Shemesh, destruction layers appear in Philistia, the Northern Coast, Lachish, the Shephelah, and the Beer-sheva valley. Most of these sites do not have any Babylonian remains, suggesting widescale abandonment. The only major places of continuity are in Central Samaria and Mizpah, which likely served as a Babylonian administrative center. Excavations also point to an abrupt stoppage of significant trade. Overall, archaeology presents a fairly compelling picture of widescale destruction and abandonment in comparison to the preexilic period, though archaeologists differ as to the extent of such destruction with population decline estimates from 90 percent to 70 percent (Faust 2012). It is important to point out a minority of scholars advocate that the actual destruction of the Babylonian invasion was much more moderate than reported in biblical texts. These scholars advocate that the biblical texts represent a small portion of the Judeans, or even in some cases, that the Babylonian destruction was a fabrication by elite scribal literati, attempting to create an identity through a collective memory. But this is a minority view, as the material culture and biblical texts carry a similar tone of destruction and devastation, and the economic life struggled in the wake of the Babylonian destruction.

Not only did the exile devastate the economy, but it also devastated the kinship systems that undergirded social organization. The forced migrations wiped out the kin-based systems. Family units contracted from the extended kin to the nuclear family. Many of these peoples were deported to Babylonia or they fled as refugees. In response to this displacement, life in exile quickly rebounded for some of these refugees. Though the actual exile event was surely traumatic, several scholars suggest a benign existence for exiles in Babylonia. Many of the exiles lived in designated spaces for exiled communities with relative independence. Two particular collections richly illustrate the lives of these exiles, the Al-Yehuda Tablets (Pearce and Wunsch 2014) and the Murashu Archives. Both hint at a relative normalcy of family life, agricultural production, labor opportunities, and even some economic thriving. This matches some of the biblical depictions of exiles' ability to purchase land and raise families (Jer. 29). In addition to Babylon, some of the socially displaced also made their way to Egypt, negotiating a space between their own Jewish identity, with worship and affinities to Jerusalem, and the need to assimilate. Overall, the limited evidence suggests relative freedom under a larger political hegemony. One can reasonably ascertain that the economic and social world of the Babylonian Empire was initially chaotic as fitting a refugee experience, but over the years these refugees potentially began a path towards assimilation and normalcy for a colonized state. The picture of such a state becomes more clear with the advent of the Persian Empire.

11.7 Economy and Society and the Persian Period: 1 and 2 Chronicles, Ezra-Nehemiah, Esther, and Postexilic Redactions of the Deuteronomistic History

The end of the Babylonian period marked the beginning of a profound shift in the economy and society of Judah. Ezra-Nehemiah picks up from the exile event that closes both 2 Kings and 2 Chronicles. Although the people return to Jerusalem, they will remain a subjugated people. The opening verses of Ezra-Nehemiah acknowledge the Persian king Cyrus as the leader of the society and economy, as he sanctions the return of the exiles to Jerusalem. Theologically, this verse sets the stage for a discourse that centers on the proper worship of Yhwh while underneath Persian imperial hegemony. From an economic perspective, the repatriation under Persian rule begins a profound change. The area of Judah became an extension of the Persian Empire, within the satrapy "Beyond the River." This followed the known strategy of the Achaemenid Empire to establish political control, security, and the collection of royal and satrapal taxes.

As mentioned, the demarcation between the Babylonian and Persian periods is nearly impossible to delineate, not just in archaeology, but even in the neo-Babylonian archives. This reveals that the early Persian Empire was likely marked by continuity with its predecessors in terms of the administration of the empire. Archaeologically, the impact of the Babylonian destruction remained evident through the Persian period. Even traditionally large sites, such as Jerusalem and Shechem, remained small rural towns during this period. With the lack of resources on Persian Judah (or Yehud), Ezra-Nehemiah serves as a main source. According to the narrative, the people returned and rebuilt the Jerusalem temple with provisions from the Persian Empire. In return, Ezra-Nehemiah espouses a robust centralization program focusing on the proper temple worship. In addition, some of the epistolary texts in the middle of the narrative suggest that the Judeans had major in-kind and precious metal taxes that regularly went to the Persian Empire. Within the text, economics function as a central dynamic to undergird broader theological themes. For example, the donations to the temple constitute an act of identity formation under the worship of Yhwh. On an international level, the Judeans are an agent in the movement of goods/taxes to and from the Persian Empire (Ezra 4:17). Nehemiah continues this theme of economic centralization by portraying the Persian king as magnanimous provider, but also addressing the role of the elite within Judah for the disenfranchised (Neh. 5:1–18) and the function of the Levites and temple servants (Neh. 13:4–22).

Whereas Ezra-Nehemiah describes the repatriation, Chronicles reinforces the notion of a colonized and socially disembedded economy. Chronicles can indirectly present an interesting perspective on the economics of the Persian period, particularly if one compares parallel economic texts with the older source of Samuel/Kings. Two perspective emerge, the first of which portrays exchange as less socially embedded and more utilitarian. One of the prominent examples is the tendency for Chronicles to inflate the numbers from earlier sources. For example, the payment for the threshing floor of Ornan the Jebusite rises from 50 shekels in 2 Sam. 24:24 to 600 shekels in 1 Chr. 21:25. This increase does not align to any hyperinflation, but rather reflects a consistent theme of directing resources to the temple. Independent Chronicles materials have similar themes of abundance such as David's call to mass donations from the peoples (1 Chr. 29:6–9). In the second perspective, Chronicles contains some of the few references to coinage, specifically the Daric, which is unique to Chronicles (1 Chr. 29:7), Ezra (2:69; 8:27), and Nehemiah (7:70–72). Although the development of coinage may have multiple functions (market functions, taxation), in the contexts of the Bible, coinage always supports the donation to the center through the means of cultic materials.

The book of Esther, though explicitly set in the Persian period, is likely a compilation that has at least some Hellenistic influence. Esther follows a subgenre of "court tales" in which a foreigner comes to power in a foreign court (see also the Joseph narrative and Daniel). This subgenre naturally found appeal in the Babylonian and Persian periods when Judeans had to make sense of their own theology in the midst of a vast empire. Although the names in Esther have no historical confirmation, and the figure of Mordecai is surely anachronistic, the book does present some assumptions of royal family life that are plausible and consistent with Persian governance. It is clear that the Persian royal family has control and has subjugated the Judeans so that their very existence is dependent on the imperial powers.

Though the assumption is not without opponents, many scholars also generally assign priestly materials to a postexilic layer. The P layer is consistent in keeping a temple ideology as a tool for centralization. Naturally, most of the studies on P center on the theological assertions for holiness, divine transcendence, and proper worship. In line with the traditional priestly emphasis on worship (especially the tabernacle narratives of Exodus), P brings an emphasis on the economic contributions of the priestly people towards the tabernacle construction (Exod. 25; 28:21–29; 30:12–13; 35:4, 20–29; 36:3–7; Altmann 2016: 192–95). This emphasis aligns with the people's donations to the temple in Ezra. The redaction of Josh. 20:6, traditionally assigned to P, can illustrate this emphasis in two ways. First, the cities of refuge in Joshua give the priestly circles a level of judicial authority. Second, the multiple references to the "congregation" place the religious community as transcendent over the tribes in economic priority.

11.8 Summary and Conclusions

The vast chronological period from conquest to repatriation reveals a rich and complex economic world. The multiple social contexts necessitate an awareness of the these shifts as Israel developed into a nation and then fell into disarray in the orbit of greater empires. With dialogue between textual studies and archaeology, as well as the use of economic theories as a control, one can gain a firmer understanding of the ancient social and economic worlds that undergird the historical books. Continued investigation will yield more sophisticated understandings of Israelite and Judean society and economy, and, in turn, lead to deeper readings of the biblical texts.

Bibliography

Adams, Samuel L. 2014. *Social and Economic Life in Second Temple Judea*. Louisville, KY: Westminster John Knox.
Altmann, Peter. 2016. *Economics in Persian-Period Biblical Texts: Their Interactions with Economic Developments in the Persian Period and Earlier Biblical Traditions*. FAT 109. Tübingen: Mohr Siebeck.
Boer, Roland. 2015. *The Sacred Economy of Ancient Israel*. Louisville, KY: Westminster John Knox.
Coote, Robert and Keith Whitelam. 1987. *The Emergence of Early Israel in Historical Perspective*. Ann Arbor: Almond Press.
Faust, Avraham. 2012. *Judah in the Neo-Babylonian Period: The Archaeology of Desolation*. Atlanta: SBL.
Finkelstein, Israel and Amihai Mazar. 2007. *The Quest for the Historical Israel: Debating Archaeology and the History of Early Israel*. Atlanta: SBL.
Finley, Moses. 1985. *The Ancient Economy*. 2nd ed. London: Hogarth.
Gottwald, Norman. 1979. *The Tribes of Yahweh: A Sociology of the Religion of Liberated Israel 1250–1050 BCE*. Maryville: Orbis.
Katz, Hayah. 2008. *A Land of Grain and Wine... A Land of Olive Oil and Honey: The Economy of the Kingdom of Judah*. Jerusalem: Yad Ben-Zvi Press.
Meyers, Carol L. 2005. *Households and Holiness: The Religious Culture of Israelite Women*. Minneapolis: Fortress.
Murphy, Catherine M. 2002. *Wealth in the Dead Sea Scrolls and in the Qumran Community*. Leiden: Brill.
Nam, Roger. 2012. *Portrayals of Economic Exchange in the Book of Kings*. Leiden: Brill.
Noth, Martin. 1991. *The Deuteronomistic History*. Sheffield: JSOT Press.

Pearce, Laurie E. and Cornelia Wunsch. 2014. *Documents of Judean Exiles and West Semites in Babylonia in the Collection of David Sofer*. Bethesda: CDL Press.

Polanyi, Karl. 1944. *The Great Transformation: The Political and Economic Origins of Our Time*. Boston: Beacon Press.

Wallerstein, Immanuel. 2004. *World-Systems Analysis: An Introduction*. Durham: Duke University Press.

Weber, Max. 1952. *Ancient Judaism*. Translated by H. H. Gerth and D. Martindale. New York: Free Press.

Wittfogel, Karl. 1944. *Oriental Despotism: A Comparative Study of Total Power*. New Haven, CT: Yale University Press.

CHAPTER 12

POLITICS AND KINGSHIP IN THE HISTORICAL BOOKS, WITH ATTENTION TO THE ROLE OF POLITICAL THEORY IN INTERPRETATION

GEOFFREY PARSONS MILLER

This chapter explores the idea that the Bible's historical narratives address issues of political theory. The chapter first examines the question of what political theory is and why the historical books may be seen as embodying political-theoretical ideas. The chapter then considers the Bible's analyses of the following topics: anarchy, obligation and sovereignty, distributive justice, and the comparative analysis of governmental design.

12.1 Political Theory

We begin with a basic issue: what is "political theory"? The concept refers to ideas about the nature, scope, and legitimacy of government. Political theory is theoretical in the sense that it asks questions at a general level—not just evaluating the merits of particular governments and political leaders, but rather formulating questions and proposing answers that apply to a range of governments in different social and historical contexts. Political theory is political in the sense that it looks at issues pertaining to government and law. It is not concerned with matters such as religion, ethics, social practices, or aesthetics except insofar as these topics intersect with issues of law and government. Political theory, in this sense, is roughly synonymous with "political philosophy," but is a better term for our subject because it does not come freighted with the idea that the abstract analysis of government and law originated in ancient Greece.

There is no doubt that the Bible contains examples of political theory in the sense used here. Deuteronomy contains injunctions about the obligations of kings of Israel (Deut. 17:15–20); Judges describes the condition of the people when "there was no king in Israel" (Judg. 21:25); and the books of Samuel and Kings describe the history of the kings of Israel and Judah along with pungent judgments as to whether their reigns found favor in the eyes of God. The poetic and wisdom books, too, contains examples of political thought: Psalms praises kings who dispense justice and refrain from oppression (e.g., Pss. 99:4; 105:14) and Proverbs offers advice for Israel's rulers (e.g., Prov. 14:35; 16:12–14). At several points the Bible offers more extended analysis of political issues: Samuel's warning about the dangers of kings is one example (1 Sam. 8:11–17); Jotham's parable of the trees is another (Judg. 9:7–15).

These instances of political thought, however, do not add up to the sort of developed political theory of the sort we have inherited from ancient Greece. The Bible does not, as Plato does in the *Republic*, take up a question of political theory (e.g., the nature of justice), develop the topic through logical analysis, and propose an answer framed at a level of abstraction that is not contingent on any particular political or cultural setting. One searches in vain for discursive analysis of the classic issues in political theory: what is the basis of obligation? what is justice? what are the proper means for allocating the social surplus? what is the best form of government? what is the justification for war? what limits the prerogative of rulers? These and other questions receive no explicit treatment in Scripture. One might conclude, based on such a search, that while the Bible is occasionally curious about political *questions*, it does not develop a political *theory*.

12.2 Narrative and Political Theory in the Historical Books

Those who seek a political theory in the Bible's historical books need to abandon the idea that a political philosophy must take the form of self-identified, abstract analysis of the sort Western culture has inherited from Plato and Aristotle. Instead, the political theory of the Bible, if it exists, is found in its *narratives*: the stories of Israelite kings and heroes that form such a large and familiar part of the Bible's text.

It may appear odd to embody ideas about government and law in narratives. To derive abstract ideas from a narrative, the expositor must supply an interpretive lens or kind of codebook that associates items in the narrative with the idea being explored. The process is inherently complex and also ambiguous because the lens or code in question must be constructed in the process of interpretation. The approach of Greek political thought, which provides explicit definitions and clear signals about the nature of the topic under consideration, might appear to be a superior method for exploring political ideas.

Despite these potential shortcomings of narratives, this form of discourse also offers benefits as a medium for conveying abstract concepts. Narratives convey ideas in a form that is easy to remember and to pass on to others. This would have been an advantage in a society in which literacy was far from universal and where media for recording written words were expensive. Even as literacy became more widespread in ancient Israel, the narrative form could have been retained as a holdover from times when abstract ideas, if they were to be preserved at all, would have been recorded and transmitted in oral form.

A second advantage of narratives is their artistic quality. The beauty and vibrancy of well-constructed narratives enhances their communicative force relative to discursive analysis. The Bible's stories of patriarchs, judges, and kings probably had greater impact on the day-to-day lives and thoughts of ordinary people than did the dry discourses of Plato and Aristotle.

Narratives also offer resources for validation. Greek philosophy used the metric of rationality—a principle expressed in the Socratic dialogues in which a person is brought by the force of reason to accept the validity of certain conclusions and to reject others. Narratives can draw on reason, but they also have access to other strategies for authenticating their message including etiology, etymology, embeddedness in ritual, and references to familiar matters from popular culture.

Finally, and perhaps most importantly, narratives are a flexible means for framing abstract ideas in simplified models of human society. By selecting the characters and the setting in which figures interact, a narrative can isolate a question under consideration and focus attention on its resolution. Narratives are in fact used in this way in a variety of present-day intellectual disciplines. Even the seemingly mathematically precise discipline of economics uses narratives: as Nobel laureate Robert Lucas observed, economists are "storytellers, operating much of the time in worlds of make-believe.... It is the only way we have found to think seriously about reality."[1] The narratives of the historical books arguably do the same thing when they address issues of political theory.

12.3 Previous Scholarship on the Bible and Political Theory

Do the biblical narratives in fact contain a political theory of the sort described above? Scholars have debated this issue and offered different answers. The following discussion highlights contributions to this debate but should not be taken as being in derogation of other valuable work, some of which is cited in the bibliography below.

Michael Walzer (2013) recognizes that political ideas are present in the historical books, but disputes the proposition that these ideas cohere into a general theory. His skepticism on this score comes from several considerations: perceived inconsistencies in basic concepts (e.g., the unconditional nature of the Abrahamic covenant versus the conditional nature of the covenant at Sinai), the diversity of the Bible's legal materials and their embeddedness in the narratives of Israel's history, the omnipresent role of Israel's God, and the proposition that kingship in Israel was a foreign import never firmly embedded in that society's political culture.

Thomas Pangle's (2003) meditation on the Book of Genesis offers a different form of skepticism. Pangle explores with great sensitivity the connections between political theory, which he traces to the ancient Greeks, and faith-based wisdom drawn from the Bible and its interpreters. Although Pangle finds areas of overlap between these two, his analysis valorizes the notion that philosophy and faith are incommensurable: philosophy is the province of the Greeks; religious faith and revelation is the province of the Bible (see Strauss 1979).

Other commentators see a broader scope for political theory. Bernard Levinson's insightful studies of the Book of Deuteronomy stress ways in which that text articulates and validates ideas familiar to political theory today, such as the ideal of the rule of law and the principle of separate and divided powers (Levinson 1997; 2006; 2008). Joshua Berman's impressive work (2008) argues that the Bible broke from its cultural and historical setting by articulating principles of social equality and human rights—principles that resonate with values widely shared in today's world.

Several commentators have gone further in promoting the contribution of the Bible as political theory. In my own work I have presented the Bible's Primary History as containing a comprehensive set of ideas about political obligation and governmental design (Miller 2011). In my judgment, the biblical narratives from Genesis to 2 Kings systematically address questions central to later political thought: obligation, anarchy, patriarchy, leadership, consent of the governed, revelation as a source of authority, jurisprudence, sovereignty, distributive justice, and the comparative analysis of political institutions.

Yoram Hazony (2012), in a similar vein, argues that the Bible is and should be treated as a foundational text in the Western tradition of political theory—a text that should be celebrated as a masterpiece of political philosophy, just as it has long been revered from a religiously observant point of view. While not breaking wholly from Straussian premises, Hazony argues that the Bible addresses many issues fundamental to political theory including such matters as the necessity of government, the advantages and disadvantages of anarchy, the best form of political organization, the obligations of rulers, the necessary conditions for a just society, the dangers of oppressive government, and the proper relationship between the citizen and the state.

The debate over the Bible's place in political theory continues. It appears that scholarly opinion is beginning to swing towards the view that biblical texts do explore topics of interest to Western political thought, and that they do so in an intelligent and deliberate way. Whether and to what extent the Bible's political ideas can be counted as a contribution that can rival the Greeks in scope and sophistication remains an open question, but not one outside the range of credible analysis. The following discussion presents ideas about political theory that an interpreter open to this line of thinking might derive from the Bible's historical narratives.

12.4 ANARCHY, OBLIGATION, AND SOVEREIGNTY

The Book of Joshua takes up the analysis of political theory in mid-stream. Earlier texts, especially Genesis and Exodus, provide a rich source of insight into basic questions of political theory—questions that have already been addressed by the time the Bible gets to Israel's history in the Promised Land. A brief description of the political ideas developed in the Pentateuch is therefore useful as background to understanding political ideas in the historical books.

The story of the Garden of Eden explores the issue of political obligation—when and why citizens are required to obey their political leaders—as well as the topic of how political obligation is breached. The antediluvian "Dark Age" stories investigate the topic of anarchy: they ask whether human beings can develop the institutions of a good and decent life in the absence of government and law—the answer to that question is "no." Beginning with the story of Noah and the Flood, the Bible turns to the topic of patriarchal authority, offering a nuanced account of power relationships within families and clans. Exodus turns to the topic of political authority—power exercised over persons unrelated by kinship. The Bible provides models of political organization—nomadism, dependency, slavery, and nationhood—and concludes that nationhood trumps the other alternatives. Exodus then begins the Bible's investigation of three basic attributes of nationhood identified in later political thought: *self-governance, legal institutions,* and *control over territory.*

The narratives of Moses in Egypt explore the issue of self-governance. The stories of Israel's encounter with its God at Mount Sinai examine the second basic attribute of nationhood, domestic legal institutions. The Sinai narratives insightfully distinguish the categories of legal rules recognized in later political theory: a basic commitment to joining together as a nation, a rule of recognition that identifies norms as legally binding, constitutional rules that set the framework of fundamental law, standards for the effective organization of government, and ordinary legislation. The narratives of Mount Sinai also provide the Bible with its principal setting for exploring fundamental aspects of political authority. The Bible recognizes revelation as a source of obligation but also addresses its potential for upsetting existing arrangements. The Bible also offers a sophisticated account of consent as a basis for authority. Remarkably, the Sinai narratives establish knowledge conditions for valid consent that closely resemble those found in the social contract theories of Hobbes (1985), Locke (2003), Rousseau (1762), and Rawls (1971).

In the Book of Joshua, the Bible turns to the third and final attributes of nationhood: control over territory. The Bible seeks to establish Israel's unclouded title to the Promised Land, and in the process draws on essentially all the theories of property rights that have been recognized in later jurisprudence. The Bible develops the theory of an *original grant of title* to Abraham and the *passage of that title in an unbroken chain* to Abraham's descendants at the time of Joshua and beyond. A different theory supports Israelite title based on the idea that *God promised the land to the Israelites if they kept their covenant with him* and delivered on that promise when they (partially) performed their part of the bargain. The Book of Joshua develops the idea of *right of conquest*: the Israelites' acquisition of territory in a just war gives them the right to displace the prior inhabitants and take possession of the land (the Bible's theory of title by right of conquest has resonances in later Western philosophy in the theories of Hugo Grotius (1925) and Emmerich de Vattel (1883). Still another theory suggests that Abraham acquired title to the Promised Land by *prior appropriation*, much as explorers of a later age claimed title for their sponsors by planting a flag on newly discovered lands. The prior appropriation theory is suggested in Gen. 13:14–17, where God tells Abraham to "Go, walk through the length and breadth of the land, for I am giving it to you." In the case of certain properties within the Promised Land, the Bible supports Israelite title with *a theory of voluntary transfer*: this is the case, for example, with the narrative of Abraham's purchase of the cave in Machpelah as a tomb for his wife (Gen. 23:7–9). Finally, the Bible asserts that *non-Israelites who remained in the land ceded sovereignty* when they entered into a treaty submitting to Israelite domination (Josh. 9:3-23). These various theories—conquest, appropriation, grant, promise, purchase, and submission—provide a compendium of legal arguments for Israel's title to the Promised Land vis-à-vis non-Israelite indigenous groups.

12.5 DISTRIBUTIVE JUSTICE

The Joshua narratives also provide the Bible with an opportunity to explore the topic of distributive justice. When people become politically organized, they generate a social surplus: more wealth is created than would be the case if people simply acted on their own. The problem is how the surplus should be allocated. The Bible addresses the issue in the narratives of the distribution of the Promised Land among tribes and individuals.

One important factor for distributive justice is the principle of rewarding claimants based on the merit of their contributions. The tribes of Reuben and Gad make a deal with Moses under which they will receive lands east of the Jordan River if they participate in the war of conquest in the west (Num. 32:1-24; see also Deut. 3:12-20). They perform their part of the bargain and receive the requested lands in exchange (Josh. 4:12; 22:3). Caleb, likewise, receives an inheritance in the hill country of Judah, including the city of Hebron, as a reward for extraordinary service in spying out the land at Kadesh-Barnea (Josh. 14:6-14; see also Numbers 13; 14:24; 32:12; Deut. 1:36). Joshua receives a special grant in the territory of Ephraim as a reward for extraordinary leadership (Josh. 19:49-50).

A different merit-based principle of allocation concerns the commitment of the recipient to make productive use of the resource in the future. Charitable foundations in today's world award grants based on an analysis of which applicants will do most to further the foundation's objectives. The Bible also recognizes a forward-looking principle of merit: Joshua allocates forests to Ephraim and Manasseh based on their commitment to put the lands to productive use: "Clear it, and its farthest limits will be yours" (Josh. 17:18). Something of the same principle is at work in Joshua's decision not to allocate a contiguous territory to the Levites. Instead of a single parcel of land, they receive towns and pasture-lands scattered throughout Israel, together with Joshua's promise that the priesthood will be their inheritance. As a partial substitute for not receiving a contiguous territory, the Levites get a lucrative franchise to perform religious services for the Israelite people.

In addition to rewarding a commitment to develop resources, Joshua's grant to Ephraim and Manasseh recognizes the principle of distributing the surplus to those who need it the most. Ephraim and Manasseh complain that as half-tribes of Joseph they have received only one allotment to share between them, even though they have each grown in population to rival full-fledged tribes. Joshua agrees and gives them extra land (Josh. 17:14-18).

These special grants reflect considerations of distributive justice applicable to particular individuals or groups. For everyone else, the Bible recognizes that properties that cannot be subdivided should be distributed by a form of lottery. The Bible's emphasis on procedural fairness as a principle of distributive justice is echoed in institutions of the present-day world: examples include the tossing of a coin to decide which team gets the ball to begin play and the strategy of allowing one person to cut the cake and the other to select which piece he desires (see Brams 1980). The fairness of the distribution by lottery only works, however, if the lottery is fair: the dice cannot be loaded. The Bible emphasizes the fairness of the lottery that distributes the Promised Land by enlisting Joshua to carry it out. Having already received his inheritance, Joshua has no interest in the outcome other than that it be fair to all. Joshua's judgments on this score are likely to be respected because he has already proven himself to be a great national leader with unimpeachable integrity. The Bible's treatment of distributive justice, in summary, suggests that no single principle dominates in all circumstances, and that a variety of equitable factors should be considered when a social surplus is distributed among competing claimants—including preserving procedural fairness, rewarding merit, protecting reasonable expectations, allocating resources to productive users, and distributing assets in proportion to need.

An initial distribution of resources, even if grounded on reasons of fairness and equity, will not necessarily be viewed as legitimate if the outcomes are grossly unequal. If people feel resentment *ex post* about the portion they receive, the result may be a reduced willingness to engage in cooperative behavior in the future. This issue is present in every system for distributing a social surplus but is particularly acute when land is in issue, since unlike fungible resources, land cannot be indefinitely subdivided. The great American political philosopher John Rawls puts the problem as follows, "however attractive a conception of justice might be on other grounds, it is seriously defective if the principles of moral psychology are such that it fails to engender in human beings the requisite desire to act upon it" (1971: 455).

The narrative of the covenant at Shechem recognizes and deals with this problem of *ex post* dissatisfaction. Shortly before his death, Joshua assembles the tribes of Israel and offers them a surprising option: "If serving the LORD seems undesirable to you, then choose for yourselves this day whom you will serve, whether the gods your ancestors served beyond the Euphrates, or the gods of the Amorites, in whose land you are living" (Josh. 24:15). In other words, the Israelites are given the opportunity to back out of covenants previously made. The Israelites respond by unanimously reaffirming their commitment to serve the God of Israel (Josh. 24:16–18). The covenant at Shechem deals with the problem of *ex post* dissatisfaction because at the time the Israelites enter into this agreement, they have full knowledge of the nature of their inheritance in the Promised Land. The matter is especially salient to them because they have just received their allotments. In prior covenants, the Bible shields the human counterparties from knowledge about their endowments—a veil of ignorance that works to ensure the *ex ante* fairness of the agreement being made. In the case of the covenant at Shechem, the Bible dispenses with the veil of ignorance in order to assure the *ex post* fairness of the distribution of the Promised Land which Joshua carries out pursuant to authority of prior covenants.

12.6 Political Organization

A final issue concerns the comparative analysis of political organization at the national level. The Bible offers four examples of national political organization and systematically compares their advantages and disadvantages.

The Israelites are first organized in a form of military rule during the war of conquest under Joshua and afterwards remain temporarily in this form of organization following their acquisition of the Promised Land. The Bible recognizes advantages in this form of organization: the Israelites are united in a common cause and do not conspicuously turn to other gods during this period. But military rule also involves a subordination of individual autonomy and private life that is inconsistent with a peacetime environment. Joshua commendably dissolves his military government and returns the country to civilian rule.

The period that ensures is described in the Book of Judges. Modern biblical scholarship has romanticized this period, viewing it as reflecting an idealized period of religious purity uninfected by government or politics, and also as a period reflecting desirable attributes of equality, freedom, and liberation. A review of the texts suggests, however, that the Bible adopts a more nuanced view.

The Israelites during the period of the judges are portrayed as organizing themselves into a confederacy of tribes subject to a baseline set of legal rights and duties. Tribes may not partition religious observances, must provide assistance to one another to defend against foreign aggression, must be allowed to participate in defensive battles and to share in the spoils of victory, must respect property rights and freedom of movement, and must extradite members of their community who commit egregious offenses. The tribal confederacy was supported by three political institutions. The national judicial function was carried out by a judge who was authorized to resolve questions of national importance brought to him or her by members of the confederacy. These military leaders arose in times of crisis to lead Israel; their office was limited in duration to that period. The popular assembly of all the tribes met in times of national crisis to consider matters involving the welfare of Israel as a nation.

The Bible presents a mixed assessment of this tribal confederacy. Israelites under the judges enjoyed freedom and fluid social boundaries and no kings were around to oppress, tax, or extract forced labor. Overall, however, the Bible's assessment of confederacy is negative. The confederacy was not ordained, approved, or inspired by God: it was a creation of human beings and therefore subject to the weakness and instability that comes when decisions are made without God's input or approval. And its political institutions were too weak to deliver the benefits of prosperity or national security. Because there was "no king in Israel," everyone did whatever seemed right in their own eyes (Judg. 17:6; 21:25; cf. 18:1; 19:1)—a condition of radical freedom, but also one without much capacity to maintain social order.

The Bible illustrates the weaknesses of the confederacy by pointing to numerous ways in which this form of national government failed to deliver the goods. The judicial authority was passive, lacking the power to enforce its judgments. Military leaders had to persuade the tribes to cooperate for mutual self-help, something people are naturally disinclined to do (Judg. 4:5–6). The popular assembly was also of limited value: it was an unusual event, probably only occurring once or twice in an average person's lifetime, and even if it occurred, it often resulted in a failure to take decisive action. The delegates to the assembly called in response to the outrage at Gibeah all swear that "none of us will go home. No, not one of us will return to his house" (Judg. 20:8). Although this vow reflects a commitment to do something in the particular instance, it also recognizes that many popular assemblies end inconclusively with the attendees simply returning to their homes with no action taken.

The tribal confederacy did not prevent apostasy: the Israelites, unconstrained by strong institutions of national government, repeatedly turned to other gods during this period. Neither did it protect commerce: in the episode of Deborah and Barak, the Canaanites capture the plain of Jezreel and extract oppressive tolls, resulting in a severe disruption of trade: "the highways were abandoned; travelers took to winding paths" (Judg. 5:6). The confederacy also failed to protect productive economic activities: when the Midianites descend on the land, their depredations "so impoverished the Israelites that they cried out to the Lord for help" (Judg. 6:6). The confederacy performed no better when it came to assuring national security: Israel is oppressed during this period by nearly all of its neighbors, including the Arameans (Judg. 3:7–11), Moabites (Judg. 3:12–30), Canaanites (Judg. 4–5), Midianites (Judg. 6–8), Ammonites (Judg. 10:6–12:6), and Philistines (Judg. 13–16). While in each case Israel ends up rescued by a heroic judge, these rescues would not have been needed if the Israelites had not been oppressed in the first place. Worst of all, the confederacy did not assure domestic tranquility. A civil war between Benjamin and the rest of Israel results in twenty-five thousand casualties for Benjamin alone (Judg. 20:46). In an earlier episode, forty-two thousand Ephraimites die for having the temerity to suggest that Gilead was not a full-fledged tribe (Judg. 12:1–6).

The Bible's analysis of the shortcomings of the tribal confederacy as a form of national government parallels the analysis found in the American *Federalist Papers*, which also presents a thoughtful analysis of the defects of confederacy as a form of government. Like the *Federalist Papers*, the Book of Judges critiques the confederate form of government in order to lay the groundwork for a more positive assessment of stronger forms of national government.

The Bible next discusses a third form of national government: theocratic rule, defined as governance by God's chosen representative on earth. Samuel, although described as a judge, does not fit the model of the judges of the Israelite confederacy. He is a theocratic ruler whose authority in office is founded and whose decisions are made on the basis of religious rather than political or military considerations. The Bible presents a nuanced assessment of the advantages and disadvantages of theocratic rule. If it could be administered faithfully, it would be an ideal form of government, hearkening back to the direct rule by God in the Garden of Eden. But theocratic rule is also subject to significant shortcomings: the theocratic ruler may not actually govern according to God's will, the form of government is poorly suited to establish durable institutions of effective governance, it fails to protect national security, and it deals poorly with the problem of succession. In the case of the latter point, one may observe how Samuel appointed his two sons as judges, who subsequently corrupted the office (1 Sam. 8:1–3). The Bible codes its misgivings about theocratic rule in the facts that God never requires it as a system of government for Israel and that it is the people (not God) who rise up to demand that Samuel appoint a king to lead them.

The fourth and final system assessed in the historical books is that of monarchy. The Bible presents a nuanced but generally favorable view of monarchy as a form of national government. Arguments for monarchy are found in the reasons the elders of Israel provide to Samuel in support of their request that he appoint a king over them: "Behold, you are old and your sons do not walk in your ways; now appoint a king to lead us, such as all the other nations have" (1 Sam. 8:5). And later: "We want a king over us. Then we will be like all the other nations, with a king to lead us and go out before us and fight our battles" (1 Sam. 8:19–20). Coded here are a number of arguments in favor of monarchy. First, the institution of monarchy deals with the problem of succession that plagues theocratic rule. Even though an unworthy son might become king, that person would need to operate within legal, political, and bureaucratic structures that limit their range of action. The Bible recognizes no such checks in the case of theocratic rule. Second, the elders ask for a king "to lead us." The people want a stronger, more pro-active executive than the sort of leaders they have experienced under confederacy or theocratic rule. Third, the elders want a king to "fight our battles." That is, they want a standing army to protect their national security, something that confederacy and theocratic rule had failed to deliver. Finally, the people want a king "like all the other nations have." This request can be criticized theologically on the ground that the Israelites want to abandon the feature that made them different from other groups. In context, however, the wish to be like other nations makes good sense. If Israel's neighbors are all led by kings, then Israel would be placed in jeopardy if it did not so the same, since the sustained military power that surrounding kings could deploy would threaten to overwhelm Israel's own, comparatively weak defensive capacities.

The Bible is not oblivious to the dangers of powerful central government. In a variant of Acton's adage that "power corrupts and absolute power corrupts absolutely," the Bible observes that kings tend to abuse their powers. Samuel warns that kings will take cherished things away from citizens and use them for their own advantage (1 Sam. 8:11–17). Once kings have been placed in office, moreover, they relentlessly hold on to power. Even if the people tire of royal rule and wish to return to an earlier form of government, their wishes are unlikely to be answered. As Samuel puts it: "When [the king imposes excessive burdens on you,] you will cry out for relief from the king you have chosen, but the LORD will not answer you in that day" (1 Sam. 8:18).

The Bible's solution to monarchical overreaching is to impose limitations on the powers of kings. Some of these are hortatory: they encourage kings to act in desirable ways but do not expressly mandate that they do so. The figures of David, Solomon, and Josiah, in particular, offer a compendium of attributes to be desired in a monarch of Israel—what Shakespeare called the "king-becoming graces." Yet at least the first two of these monarchs were also subject to conspicuous shortcomings—illustrating the point, repeatedly emphasized in the historical books, that no earthly form of rule is likely to be perfect.

In addition to non-legal constraints on royal action, the Bible sets forth a set of constitutional requirements. Kings are subject to the general rules applicable to the public as a whole (Deut. 17:19–20). They must "fear the Lord and serve and obey him and [must] not rebel against his commands" (1 Sam. 12:14–15). When kings do behave in oppressive ways, the Bible rebukes them. Even a king as favored as David is criticized for his scandalous behavior in the matter of Bathsheba (2 Sam. 11:27b). Less favored monarchs receive even sharper rebuke, as illustrated in the Bible's condemnation of Ahab for expropriating Naboth's vineyard (1 Kgs. 21:17–19).

The Bible also imposes more specific obligations on Israel's kings. They must obey the constitution that Samuel writes down and entrusts for safekeeping to the religious authorities (1 Sam. 10:25). They may not acquire too many horses, take too many wives, or accumulate too much wealth (Deut. 17:16–17). Each new king must "write for himself on a scroll a copy of this law" (Deut. 17:18). Succession is subject to constitutional constraints:

candidates for the office must be approved by the religious authorities (Deut. 17:15), although there is little evidence that priests often used this power in the history of ancient Israel.

The topic of the Bible's attitude towards monarchy has been much discussed by scholars, with many adopting the view that the Bible contains an "anti-monarchical" theme critical of this form of government. Discussions of anti-monarchial ideas in the Bible, however, should clarify the nature of the criticism being expressed in a given biblical text. There is no doubt that many passages in the historical books criticize particular kings. These texts are not critiques of monarchy as a system of government per se, however; instead, they are assessments of specific individuals who happened to hold the office and failed to live up to its requirements.

While a few biblical texts appear to offer more general critiques of monarchy as a system of government, in context these need not be read as rejecting the institution as a whole. The Gideon narratives in Judges 8–9 describe how Gideon rebuffs the people's request that he establish himself as a dynastic ruler over Israel. The text is not hostile to monarchy, however. Gideon's reason for rejecting the people's invitation is that he wants to set himself up as a theocratic ruler, a decision that has catastrophic consequences: "all Israel prostituted themselves by worshipping [Gideon's ephod] there, and it became a snare to Gideon and his family" (Judg. 8:27). In the next stage of the Gideon narrative, Jotham offers a parable in which he warns the Shechemites against crowning Abimelech as king. The trees gather to select a king, and when the olive, the fig, and the vine have turned down the position, they offer it to the thorn bush, which replies, "If you really want to anoint me king over you, come and take refuge in my shade; but if not, then let fire come out of the thorn bush and consume the cedars of Lebanon!" (Judg. 9:15). Jotham doesn't offer the story as a critique of kingship as an institution, but rather as a warning about selecting a king who assumes the position through treachery: Abimelech, the candidate for king of Shechem, murdered most of his brothers. The thorn bush, unlike the fig, the olive, or the vine, doesn't provide food for humans to eat, but in the context of the fable it does provide something of value: governance. The parable warns that once a king has been crowned, he will not leave office readily, but this is not a fundamental objection to monarchy so much as a word of caution that the decision to appoint a king is a momentous action that should not be undertaken without careful consideration of the consequences (cf. Deut. 17:14–20, specifying checks and balances in the selection of Israel's kings).

The biblical text that most famously codes what appear to be anti-monarchical ideas is 1 Sam. 8, in which Samuel warns the Israelites of all bad things that a king may do to them if they opt for that form of government. God, however, does not oppose monarchy in this passage. On the contrary, he instructs a reluctant Samuel to listen to the people's petition and to give them a king if they really want one. That the people go ahead and demand a king, even after receiving Samuel's warning, indicates that they truly desire the benefits that monarchy can provide.

To be sure, this interpretation of the historical books as being favorably disposed towards monarchy is not irrefutable. These texts frequently depict kings (and queens) acting in foolish or sinful ways. Even great kings such as David and Solomon fall into error and others less great do much worse. But under monarchy an Israelite polity does exist as a self-governing nation for a very long time. And, although this small country is eventually swept away by geopolitical forces beyond its control, its track record of survival is impressive when compared with the experience of many other nations in that region during the same time frame.

12.7 Conclusion

The foregoing discussion has investigated a strong form of the thesis that the historical books of the Bible contain an impressive political theory—one that rivals in sophistication the ideas put forward in Greece by Plato, Aristotle, and others, and that may have been written hundreds of years earlier. The concept of the Bible as political theory is not, of course, in derogation of its value as a spiritual document which, for believers, is an embodiment of the word of God. Yoram Hazony's recent study (2012) reminds us that there is no necessary inconsistency between the spiritual and the political-theoretical aspects of biblical texts. Once the idea of the incommensurability of the Bible and political theory is abandoned, a pathway is opened for an analysis that can enhance and deepen our understanding of this fundamental text of Western culture.

Note

1. Robert Lucas, Jr. "What Economists Do" (1998); online at: http://homepage.ntu.edu.tw/~mjlin/lucas.pdf.

Bibliography

Berman, Joshua. 2008. *Created Equal: How the Bible Broke with Ancient Political Thought*. Oxford: Oxford University Press.
Brams, Steven J. 1980. *Biblical Games: Game Theory and the Hebrew Bible*. Cambridge: MIT Press.
Brettler, Mark Zvi. 1989. "The Book of Judges: Literature as Politics." *JBL* 108: 395–418.
Buber, Martin. 1967. *Kingship of God*. New York: Harper & Row.
Coote, Robert B. 1990. *Power, Politics and the Making of the Bible: An Introduction*. Minneapolis: Fortress.
de Vattel, Emmerich. 1883. *The Law of Nations*. Philadelphia: T. and J. W. Johnson and Co. First published 1758.
Elazar, Daniel J. 1995. *Covenant and Polity in Biblical Israel: Biblical Foundations and Jewish Expressions*. Covenant Tradition in Politics 1. New Brunswick, NJ: Transaction Publishers.
Elazar, Daniel J. 1980. "The Political Theory of Covenant: Biblical Origins and Modern Developments." *Publius* 10.4: 3–30.
Gottwald, Norman. 2001. *The Politics of Ancient Israel*. LAI. Louisville, KY: Westminster John Knox Press.
Grotius, Hugo. 1925. *The Rights of War and Peace*. Translated by Frances W. Kelley. Indianapolis: Bobbs Merrill. First published 1625.
Hazony, Yoram. 2012. *The Philosophy of Hebrew Scripture*. Cambridge: Cambridge University Press.
Hobbes, Thomas. 1985. *Leviathan*. Edited by C. B. McPherson. London: Penguin. First published 1651.

Leuchter, Mark. 2005. "A King Like All the Nations: The Composition of I Sam 8, 11–18." *ZAW* 117: 543–58.
Levinson, Bernard M. 1997. *Deuteronomy and the Hermeneutics of Legal Innovation*. New York: Oxford University Press.
Levinson, Bernard M. 2000. "The Covenant at Mount Sinai: The Argument of Revelation." In Michael Walzer, Menachem Lorderbaum, and Noam J. Zohar, eds., *The Jewish Political Tradition*, Vol. 1: *Authority*. New Haven, CT: Yale University Press, 23–27.
Levinson, Bernard M. 2001. "The Reconceptualization of Kingship in Deuteronomy and the Deuteronomistic History's Transformation of Torah." *VT* 51: 511–34.
Levinson, Bernard M. 2006. "The First Constitution: Rethinking the Origins of the Rule of Law and Separation of Powers in Light of Deuteronomy." *Cardozo Law Review* 27: 1853–88.
Levinson, Bernard M. 2008. *Legal Revision and Religious Renewal in Ancient Israel*. Cambridge: Cambridge University Press.
Levinson, Bernard M. 2010. "The Bible's Break with Ancient Political Thought to Promote Equality: 'It Ain't Necessarily So.'" *JTS* 61: 685–94.
Locke, John. 2003. *Two Treatises of Government and a Letter Concerning Toleration*. New Haven, CT: Yale University Press. First published 1690.
McCarthy, Dennis J. 1964. "Three Covenants in Genesis." *CBQ* 26: 179–89.
Mendenhall, George. 1973. *The Tenth Generation: The Origins of the Biblical Tradition*. Baltimore: Johns Hopkins University Press.
Mettinger, Tryggve. 1976. *King and Messiah: The Civil and Sacral Legitimation of the Israelite Kings*. Lund: Gleerup.
Miller, Geoffrey P. 2011. *The Ways of a King: Legal and Political Ideas in the Bible*. Göttingen: Vandenhoeck & Ruprecht.
Miller, Geoffrey P. 2016. "The Kingdom of God in Samuel." In Diana Edelman and Ehud Ben Zvi, eds., *Leadership, Social Memory, and Judean Discourse in the 5th–2nd Centuries BCE*. Worlds of the Ancient Near East and Mediterranean Series. Sheffield: Equinox, 77–87.
Morgenstern, Mira. 2009. *Conceiving a Nation: The Development of Political Discourse in the Hebrew Bible*. University Park, PA: Penn State University Press.
Muilenberg, James. 1959. "The Form and Structure of the Covenantal Formulations." *VT* 9: 347–65.
Pangle, Thomas L. 2003. *Political Philosophy and the God of Abraham*. Baltimore: Johns Hopkins University Press.
Porter, J. R. 1963. *Moses and Monarchy: A Study in the Biblical Tradition of Moses*. Oxford: Blackwell.
Rawls, John. 1971. *A Theory of Justice*. Cambridge: Harvard University Press.
Rosenberg, J. 1986. *King and Kin: Political Allegory in the Hebrew Bible*. Bloomington: Indiana University Press.
Rousseau, Jean Jacques. 1762. *The Social Contract: Or, Principles of Political Right*. Translated by D. G. H. Cole. Swan Sonnenschein and Co.
Sherman, Phillip. 2013. "Is There a Political Theory in the Hebrew Bible?" *Marginalia*. February 28, 2013. Online at https://marginalia.lareviewofbooks.org/phillip-sherman-on-in-gods-shadow-by-michael-walzer/.
Strauss, Leo. 1979. "The Mutual Influence of Theology and Philosophy." *Independent Journal of Philosophy* 3: 111–18.
Talmon, Shemaryahu. 1980. "The Biblical Idea of Statehood." In G. Rendsburg et al. eds., *The Bible World: Essays in Honor of Cyrus H. Gordon*. New York: Ktav, 239–48.
Walzer, Michael. 1985. *Exodus and Revolution*. New York: Basic Books.
Walzer, Michael. 2012. *In God's Shadow: Politics in the Hebrew Bible*: New Haven, CT: Yale University Press.
Wells, Bruce and Raymond Westbrook. 2009. *Everyday Law in Biblical Israel: An Introduction*. Louisville, KY: Westminster John Knox.
Whitelam, Keith W. 1989. "Israelite Kingship: The Royal Ideology and Its Opponents." In R. E. Clements, ed., *The World of Ancient Israel*. Cambridge: Cambridge University Press, 119–40.

Whitelam, Keith W. 1979. *The Just King: Monarchical Judicial Authority in Ancient Israel.* JSOTSup 12. Sheffield: JSOT Press.

Whitelam, Keith W. 1986. "The Symbols of Power: Aspects of Royal Propaganda in the United Monarchy." *BA* 49: 166–73.

Wildavsky, Aaron. 1984. *The Nursing Father: Moses as a Political Leader.* Tuscaloosa: University of Alabama Press.

Wilson, Robert R. 1983. "Enforcing the Covenant: The Mechanisms of Judicial Authority in Early Israel." In Herbert B. Huffmon, Frank A. Spina, and Alberto R. W. Green, eds., *The Quest for the Kingdom of God: Studies in Honor of George E. Mendenhall.* Winona Lake, IN: Eisenbrauns, 59–75.

CHAPTER 13

THE DISTINCTIVE ROLES OF THE PROPHETS IN THE DEUTERONOMISTIC HISTORY AND THE CHRONICLER'S HISTORY

MARVIN A. SWEENEY

13.1 INTRODUCTION

ALTHOUGH both the Deuteronomistic and Chronicler's Histories have been the subjects of extensive discussion in recent years, scholars have not adequately explained the roles of the prophets in either of these works.[1] The reasons are two-fold. For most of the twentieth century, scholars focused especially on the Deuteronomistic History (DtrH) because it was viewed to be historically more reliable and because the Chronicler's History (ChrH) was deemed to be historically unreliable due its priestly theological viewpoint.[2] Recognition that the DtrH also has its own distinctive theological and historiographical viewpoints prompted scholars to pay greater attention to the ChrH as well as to the DtrH, but such increased attention has initiated a debate on the literary-historical relationship between the two works. Most scholars have followed Noth in positing that the DtrH is a tradition-historical or redactional composition that employed many earlier works, including narratives concerning the prophets, whereas the ChrH is derived from the DtrH and other works. Interpreters recognize that the DtrH and the ChrH have distinctive presentations of Israel's and Judah's history, including the presentations of the prophets that functioned within that history.

This article examines the distinctive roles of the prophets in the DtrH and ChrH. It posits that the prophets are especially associated with leadership in the DtrH, beginning with prophetic figures such as Joshua, Deborah, and Samuel, who functioned as leaders in Israel, and continuing with the prophetic figures who played major roles in establishing and critiquing the various dynasties that came to power and ruled both Israel and Judah. It further posits that prophets play a key role in establishing and critiquing the house of David in the ChrH. But the prophets function primarily in the ChrH to explain the significance of their subjects and the reasons why they so frequently suffered either blessing or judgment for their conduct in relation to Yhwh and the Jerusalem temple.

13.2 PROPHETS IN THE DEUTERONOMISTIC HISTORY

Modern critical research begins with Martin Noth's ground-breaking study, *Überlieferungsgeschichtlichestudien*, which posits that the Former Prophets, viz., Joshua, Judges, Samuel, and Kings, are the product of an overarching tradition-historical composition which he calls the Deuteronomistic History (Noth 1981; German originals 1943; 1957). Noth maintains that the composers of this work functioned as both authors and editors who pulled together a wide assortment of earlier traditions concerning various aspects of Israel's and Judah's history from the time of the conquest of the land under Joshua through the aftermath of the loss of the land in the Babylonian exile. The resulting historical composition employed the theological principles of the book of Deuteronomy to evaluate the course of Israel's history and to explain why Israel lost the land. The DtrH argued that Yhwh had granted the land to Israel on the condition that the nation would obey deuteronomic law, but the historical presentation in Joshua, Judges, Samuel, and Kings was designed to demonstrate that Israel had violated Yhwh's laws throughout its history and suffered the loss of the land and Babylonian exile in keeping with the blessings and curses in Deuteronomy 28–30. Major figures, such as Joshua (Josh. 24), Samuel (1 Sam. 8), and the anonymous DtrH author (2 Kgs. 17), articulated DtrH viewpoints throughout the work.

Subsequent scholarship has focused especially on redaction-critical models to explain the composition of the work. Rudolf Smend (1971: 494–509) distinguished two exilic-period compositional layers in the work, a basic deuteronomistic *Grundschrift* that laid out the basic history (DtrG) and a nomistic redaction that highlighted concern with deuteronomic law (DtrN). Walter Dietrich (1972) built on Smend's work by positing a prophetic redaction that emphasized the role of the prophets in articulating the theological premises of the work (DtrP). The so-called "Smend-Dietrich Hypothesis" is problematic, however, because the twenty-four-year window for the composition of three layers is improbable and unable to give full expression to the historiographical principles of the work. Dietrich's work is largely formal and limited to Kings.

North American scholarship has been far more successful at positing the historiographical viewpoint of the DtrH beyond simple reliance on the theological principles of Deuteronomy. Frank Moore Cross (1973: 274–89) pointed to the contrasting concerns with the northern Israelite and Davidic monarchies throughout the work by demonstrating DtrH's disenchantment with the reign of Jeroboam ben Nebat, the first king of the northern kingdom of Israel following its revolt against the house of David. The DtrH charges that Jeroboam initiated idolatrous worship in northern Israel by erecting golden calves in the sanctuaries at Beth El and Dan, and it explains the destruction of northern Israel in 2 Kgs. 17 as a result of idolatry by all of the kings of Israel who followed the example of Jeroboam. Cross posited that an earlier edition of the DtrH pointed to King Josiah of Judah as the righteous monarch of the Davidic line who would adhere to Yhwh's Torah, restore the sanctity of the Jerusalem temple as the one sanctuary for the worship of Yhwh in the land, and reunite northern Israel and southern Judah to form an ideal Davidic kingdom that would finally achieve the ideals outlined in Deuteronomy. But Josiah's early death at the hands of Pharaoh Necho of Egypt derailed Josiah's reforms and required a second edition of the work that would account for the decline of the nation and its ultimate destruction by the Babylonian Empire.

Other models have also emerged. Antony Campbell and Mark O'Brien (2000) posit a Prophetic Record in the books of Samuel and Kings, which point to the roles played by prophets in the establishment of the northern kingdom of Israel from the reigns of Saul ben Kish through Jeroboam ben Joash.[3] Baruch Halpern and David Vanderhooft (1991) have argued for a Hezekian edition of the DtrH, and the present writer (Sweeney 2007: 1–32) has argued for even earlier editions going back to Solomon's history. Nevertheless, questions are beginning to rise concerning Noth's hypothesis insofar as scholars doubt its adequacy to explain the composition of the highly diverse material now found in Joshua, Judges, Samuel, and Kings.[4] One aspect of this concern is the role of the prophets in the DtrH. Although prophets appear throughout the work, beginning with Joshua himself, no one has yet been able to explain the role of the prophets in the DtrH as a whole as scholars have focused instead on individual prophetic figures or circles.[5]

Prophets play a key role in the DtrH beginning with Joshua and concluding with Huldah. Prior to the establishment of the various monarchies that ruled Israel and Judah, Ephraimite prophets, such as Joshua, Deborah, and Samuel, frequently served as the leaders of the nation. They also played constituent roles in the formation of the monarchies, such as Samuel in relation to the houses of Saul and David, Nathan in relation to the house of David and the line of Solomon, and Ahijah in relation to the houses of Jeroboam ben Nebat and Baasha ben Ahijah. Others served as severe critics of the monarchies and other forms of leadership. Examples include the anonymous prophet who condemned the priestly house of Eli, the Judean man of G-d who condemned Jeroboam's altar at Beth El, and Elijah who announced the destruction of Ahab's house. In some cases, prophets also gave sage advice to the kings and would-be leaders, such as Shemaiah, who advised Rehoboam against attacking the rebellious northern tribes, Micaiah ben Imlah, who warned Ahab of his impending doom, and Huldah, who informed Josiah that he would be granted a peaceful death so that he would not witness the demise of his kingdom. Altogether, prophets in the DtrH serve initially as Yhwh's agents for ruling the people, but subsequently serve in the founding and sustaining of the dynastic houses as well as their critics when they fail.

Joshua ben Nun is the first of the prophets to rule Israel on behalf of Yhwh. Although Joshua is never labelled as a prophet, a number of features point to his prophetic status.[6] He is the successor to Moses who is portrayed throughout the Bible as a prophet of Yhwh. He is filled with the spirit of wisdom because Moses laid his hands upon him (Num. 27:18–20; Deut. 34:9). Joshua is called "the servant of Yhwh" like Moses (Josh. 24:29). Josh. 20:1 employs the same form as that employed for Moses to indicate Yhwh's address to Joshua, "And Yhwh spoke to Joshua, saying." Finally, Joshua's farewell address to Israel begins in

Josh. 24:2 with the classic prophetic messenger formula, "Thus says Yhwh, the G-d of Israel." Joshua is an ideal leader of Israel who adheres to the Torah of Yhwh given to Israel through Moses. Richard Nelson (1997: 21–22) has noted this role in his comparative analysis of Joshua and King Josiah ben Amon of Judah, who arguably stands as the ideal monarch of the house of Judah and as the monarch who served as the focal point for the so-called Josianic edition of the DtrH.

The second major prophetic figure in the DtrH is Deborah, the wife of Lapidoth, who serves as a leader of Israel during the period of the Judges, following the conquest of Canaan. Like Joshua, she is an Ephraimite. In addition to her role as prophet, she serves as a judge in Israel, deciding cases of law under the Palm Tree of Deborah between Ramah and Beth El in the hill country of Ephraim. She summons Barak ben Abinoam of the tribe of Naphtali to lead Israel together with her in battle against the forces of King Jabin of Hazor, whose army is commanded by Sisera. Deborah functions in a role like that of Miriam, the sister of Moses, who is also designated as a prophet in the pentateuchal narratives. Like Miriam, Deborah leads the people in song following Israel's victory over Jabin and Sisera by Mount Tabor, the waters of Megiddo, and the Wadi Kishon. Although Deborah and Barak win the battle, Deborah does not emerge as the idealized leader of Israel like Joshua. She is part of a sequence of six major judges of Israel, who show a progressive decline in the leadership of the nation that demonstrates the inadequacy of the northern tribes to rule themselves, culminating in the rape and murder of the Levite's concubine at Gibeah in Judg. 19–21 (see Sweeney 2001: 110–24). Deborah is unable to unite all of the tribes of Israel in battle against Jabin and Sisera and curses several tribal groups for failing to join the battle. The portrayal of the decline of Israel under the rule of northern judges serves the interests of the Hezekian and Josianic redactions of the DtrH that pointed respectively to Hezekiah and Josiah as the ideal monarchs of the Davidic line who would overcome the shortcomings of the northern kings of Israel.

The brief reference to the anonymous prophet of Yhwh in the account of the judge Gideon in Judg. 6:7–10 serves as a means to warn Israel against engaging in foreign worship. This is particularly pertinent at the outset of the narrative, insofar as Gideon, also known by the Canaanite name, Jerubaal, "may Baal be magnified," destroyed his father's altar to Baal at the beginning of the story. But even after defeating Midian, Amalek, and the Kedemites, Gideon reverts to his Canaanite inclinations. At the close of the narrative, he declined an offer of kingship, but he manufactured an ephod, which became an object of idolatrous worship in Israel. Insofar as Gideon is from the tribe of Manasseh, the Gideon narrative serves as part of the critique of northern Israelite rule in the book of Judges that forms part of the Hezekian and Josianic editions of the DtrH.

Samuel is the last of the prophetic leaders in the DtrH, and he is also the transitional figure who brings about the institution of kingship in the nation, including both the house of Saul and the house of David. He is the son of Elkanah ben Jeroham of the tribe of Ephraim. Samuel also serves as a priest, insofar as he is the firstborn son of his mother, Hannah, who deposited him in the Shiloh sanctuary after he was weaned to be raised and educated under the tutelage of the high priest, Eli, in keeping with early northern Israelite practice in which the firstborn sons of women were dedicated to the service of Yhwh (Sweeney 2011). Samuel's designation as a prophet in 1 Sam. 3 appears to constitute a form of priestly ordination; he sleeps by the Ark of the Covenant in the Holy of Holies of the

Shiloh sanctuary and has a vision from Yhwh that defined his role as a prophet of Yhwh. A key element in the Samuel narratives is the inadequacy of the priestly house of Eli, which is communicated to Samuel in his inaugural vision and by an anonymous prophet who announces judgment against the house of Eli in 1 Sam. 2:27–36. Campbell and O'Brien (2000) argue convincingly that the Samuel narratives form the first elements of their so-called Prophetic Record.

The end of Samuel's rule and pressure from the Philistines necessitates the institution of kingship in Israel, and Samuel serves as the prophetic figure who inaugurates the house of Saul as the first dynasty of ancient Israel. Noth (1981) and others maintain that the account of the inauguration of the monarchy in 1 Sam. 8–12 is the product of the DtrH, which took up positive accounts of Saul's selection as king in 1 Sam. 9:1–10:16 and 11 and framed them with critical discussion of the monarchy and of Saul in 1 Sam. 8; 10:17–27; and 12. Indeed, Saul is condemned twice for violating Yhwh's will in 1 Sam. 13–14, where he oversteps his bounds by offering sacrifice prior to battle against the Philistines, and again in 1 Sam. 15, where he fails to fulfill Yhwh's instructions to eradicate the Amalekites and loses his kingship as a result.

Samuel, fearing for his life because of Saul's wrath, is compelled to find a replacement in the form of David ben Jesse in 1 Sam. 16. First Sam. 16–31 are devoted to recounting David's rise to kingship and Saul's unsuccessful attempts to kill or control as David's reputation grows among the people. Saul emerges as a tragic figure who is unable to control David or defeat the Philistines, and he dies in battle as a suicide at Mount Gilboa in a failed attempt to protect Beth Shemesh from the Philistine attack. Samuel's dead spirit is conjured by the medium at Endor in a futile attempt to secure sound advice from the deceased prophet in 1 Sam. 28. But Samuel is only able to tell Saul that he will soon join him in Sheol.

The prophet, Nathan, emerges as the key figure in the establishment of David's dynasty at the conclusion of the History of David's Rise in 2 Sam. 1–8 (Sweeney 2001: 93–124). It is clear throughout the narrative that David rises to power as a member of the house of Saul due to his marriage to Saul's daughter, Michal. But when David refuses to have relations with her after she criticizes his conduct while bringing the Ark of the Covenant to Jerusalem in 2 Sam. 6, it also becomes clear that Saul's descendants will never again sit on the throne of Israel. Nathan therefore becomes the prophet who announces Yhwh's eternal covenant with David to build for him a house, i.e., a dynasty, so that his sons will rule over Israel forever. But the so-called Succession Narrative or Court History in 2 Sam. 9–20 and 1 Kgs. 1–2 demonstrates that David is an inadequate father and this failing threatens his kingship when his sons commit murder, revolt against him, and vie for power to succeed him on his throne. Insofar as the narrative points to David's adulterous affair with Bathsheba and his role in the murder of her husband, Uriah, as the root cause of his family troubles in 2 Sam. 10–12, Nathan then takes on a different role as the prophet who holds David to account for his crimes. David repents of his sins, but his conduct remains a blemish on the future of the dynasty. Nathan again plays a key role at the end of David's life when it is time to choose his successor. David's older sons are dead, but Adonijah, the son of his wife Haggit, and Solomon, the son of his wife Bathsheba, are left to compete for the throne. Although Adonijah presumes that he is David's choice, Nathan prompts Bathsheba to convince David that he in fact had designated her son, Solomon, as his successor, and Nathan confirms her story to complete the ruse. Nathan therefore sets the future course of the house of David by insuring that the Jerusalem-based faction of the house will control the throne with Solomon as king. The questions raised concerning the circumstances of Solomon's birth and selection as king serve both the interests of the Prophetic Record, insofar as they aid in discrediting Judean rule over Israel, and the Josianic edition of the DtrH, insofar as they aid in portraying Solomon as a king who introduces idolatry due to his many marriages with foreign women.

The prophet, Ahijah the Shilonite, plays the key role in the transition from Solomon's reign to those of Jeroboam ben Nebat of the northern kingdom of Israel and Rehoboam ben Solomon of the southern kingdom of Judah.[7] First Kgs. 11:26-39 recounts how Ahijah met Jeroboam, who at the time served as Solomon's officer in charge of the forced labor of the house of Joseph, to anoint him as the next king of Israel. The narrative is careful to specify that Jeroboam would rule only over the ten tribes of the north whereas Rehoboam would continue to rule in Jerusalem in keeping with Yhwh's promise of an eternal dynasty to David. The present form of the narrative serves the interests of the Josianic edition of the DtrH by portraying Yhwh's choice of Jeroboam as a consequence of Solomon's idolatry. Josiah would later correct this issue by dismantling the idolatrous installations of Solomon and the other kings of Judah and Israel during the course of his reforms. But the identification of Jeroboam as an Ephraimite in charge of the forced labor of the house of Joseph indicates its origins in the so-called Prophetic Record insofar as it points to Solomon's pharaonic oppressive rule of the northern Israelite tribes as the cause for Yhwh's decision to anoint Jeroboam.

Ahijah also plays an important role in the condemnation of Jeroboam's dynasty. When Jeroboam's son, Abijah, fell ill, 2 Kgs. 14:1-18 reports that Jeroboam's wife visited Ahijah in an attempt to heal her son. Nevertheless, the blind prophet recognized her and declared that Abijah would not survive due to Jeroboam's idolatry. Such a charge indicates that this narrative serves as part of the Josianic DtrH. It also builds upon the earlier narrative in 1 Kgs. 13 concerning the anonymous Man of G-d from Judah who condemned Jeroboam as he officiated at the Beth El altar and claimed that Josiah would one day destroy the site. The ensuing encounter with the lying prophet from Beth El then provides the background for the account of Josiah's destruction of the Beth El altar by defiling it with the remains of the two prophets who were buried there (2 Kgs. 23:15-18).

The prophet, Shemaiah, likewise plays a role in the transition from Solomon's to Rehoboam's rule insofar as he advises Rehoboam not to go to war with northern Israel following the revolt (1 Kgs. 12:21-24). Because the cause of the revolt in 1 Kgs. 12:1-24 is Rehoboam's decision to continue the oppressive rule of his father over the north, it would appear that this narrative also originated in the Prophetic Record.

The role of the prophet, Jehu ben Hanani, in condemning the house of Baasha appears to be the product of the Josianic DtrH. Baasha had assassinated Jeroboam's son, Nadab, and Baasha's son, Elah, would likewise succumb to assassination by Zimri in keeping with Jehu's word (1 Kgs. 16:1-14). Zimri would fall in turn to Omri, who would build Samaria as Israel's new capital and found one of the best-known dynasties of northern Israel.

The Elijah-Elisha narratives in 1 Kgs. 17-2 Kgs. 14 portray the two prophets as the key figures in the fall of the house of Omri and the rise of the house of Jehu. The Elijah-Elisha narratives were likely composed independently to account for Jehu's revolt against the house of Omri, but they would have been worked into the Prophetic Record/Jehu Dynastic

History to point to the rise of the house of Jehu, especially the reign of Jeroboam ben Joash, as the culmination of Yhwh's efforts to realize a safe and secure Israelite kingdom like that of Solomon (2 Kgs. 14:23–29). Elijah appears as a prophet like Moses who represents Yhwh in competition with Baal to be recognized as the true G-d of Israel much as Moses represented Yhwh against Pharaoh. Elijah thereby represents Yhwh as the true G-d of creation and nature, viz., he is supported by creation in the Wadi Kerith (1 Kgs. 17:2–6), he provides food for the Zarephath widow and her son in Phoenicia (1 Kgs. 17:7–16), he brings the widow's son back to life (1 Kgs. 17:17–24), and he demonstrates Yhwh to be the true G-d of rain and fertility instead of Baal by winning the contest against the prophets of Baal and Asherah at Mount Carmel (1 Kgs. 18). When he is forced to flee for his life because Jezebel, the Phoenician wife of King Ahab ben Omri, intends to kill him and the other prophets of Yhwh, he flees to Mount Horeb where Yhwh is revealed to him as "the sound of absolute silence" rather than any particular manifestation of the created world. Here, Yhwh commands Elijah to anoint Hazael as king of Aram, Jehu as king of Israel, and Elisha as his successor.

Elijah goes on to condemn Ahab for the murder of Naboth (1 Kgs. 21) and Ahab's son, Ahaziah, for turning to the Philistine god, Beelzebub (2 Kgs. 2). Other prophets are also involved, including the anonymous prophets in 1 Kgs. 20—one who granted Ahab victory over Ben Hadad and another who condemned him for allowing Ben Hadad to live—and Micaiah ben Imlah in 1 Kgs. 21 who predicted Ahab's death in battle at Ramot Gilead.

When Elijah ascended to heaven in a fiery chariot, he left his hairy mantle for Elisha who used it to request double the power of his predecessor from Yhwh. Elisha is a powerful figure: he purified the drinking water of Jericho, he called bears out of the woods to kill the boys who insulted him, he resurrected the dead son of the Shunnamite woman, and he anointed Hazael as king of Aram. But most importantly, he sent a messenger to anoint Jehu ben Nimshi, a general in the Omride army fighting the Arameans as Ramot Gilead, as Yhwh's chosen king of Israel. Jehu then assassinated King Joram ben Ahab, Joram's mother, Jezebel, and the supporters of the house of Omri in a coup that saw the establishment of the new ruling house of Jehu. Although the dynasty began on a rather weak basis, Jehu's grandson, Joash ben Jehoahaz, restored Israel's power, and his great-grandson Jeroboam ben Joash ruled over a kingdom that would rival Solomon's.

The account of the fall of the northern kingdom of Israel in 2 Kgs. 17 makes a brief reference to the prophets who warned Israel concerning the consequences of Jeroboam's alleged idolatry. Such an account serves the interests of both the Hezekian and the Josianic editions of the DtrH insofar as it justifies the fall of the northern kingdom by charging all of the northern monarchs with following in the sins of Jeroboam. Such a charge would then stand in contrast with righteous Davidic monarchs, such as Hezekiah and Josiah, who kept Judah safe by adhering to Yhwh's expectations.

The prophet Isaiah plays a key role in the account of Hezekiah's reign in 2 Kgs. 18–20, which includes narratives concerning Sennacherib's siege of Jerusalem, Hezekiah's illness, and Hezekiah's reception of a Babylonian embassy in preparation for his 705–701 BCE revolt against the Assyrian Empire (see Sweeney 2007: 397–424 and 1996: 454–511). Isaiah condemned the Assyrians in the first instance, saw to the healing of Hezekiah in the second, and condemned Hezekiah in the third, noting that his sons would someday be exiled to Babylon. This narrative block also appears in Isaiah 36–39 where it concludes the so-called

First Isaiah materials. Although the narratives are nearly the same, there are subtle differences between the two, viz., Isaiah 36–39 presents a largely idealized Hezekiah, whereas subtle differences in 2 Kgs. 18–20 leave Hezekiah's actions and statements open to question. The present idealized form in Isaiah 36–39 appears to be a revised version of the current 2 Kgs. 18–20 narrative that was designed to contrast Hezekiah with the flawed character of King Ahaz in Isaiah 7–9. First Kgs. 18–20 serves the interests of both the final exilic form of the DtrH as well as the Josianic edition. The condemnation of Hezekiah in 2 Kgs. 20:12–19 anticipates the Babylonian exile in the exilic edition of the DtrH, and the flawed character of Hezekiah throughout the narrative paves the way for the idealized Josiah in the Josianic edition of the DtrH.

The condemnation of King Manasseh ben Hezekiah of Judah in 2 Kgs. 21:1–18 is attributed to Yhwh's prophets in v. 10 (see Sweeney 2007: 424–32 and 2001: 52–63). Insofar as the future destruction of Jerusalem and the Babylonian exile is the consequence of Manasseh's evil actions, this account of his reign serves the interests of the exilic edition of the DtrH.

The account of King Josiah's reign in 2 Kgs. 22:1–23:30 gives a special place to the prophet, Huldah, wife of Shallum ben Tiqvah ben Harhas (see Sweeney 2007: 434–50 and 2001: 40–51). She informed Josiah in 2 Kgs. 22:11–20 that because of his righteousness Yhwh would grant him the mercy of an early death in peace so that he would not see the judgment that Yhwh would bring on Jerusalem and Judah for their failure to observe Yhwh's Torah. This narrative clearly builds upon the condemnation of Manasseh in 2 Kgs. 21:1–18, as well as Elijah's word of mercy to King Ahab of Israel in 1 Kgs. 21:27–29 when he repented for his role in the murder of Naboth. The Huldah narrative serves the purposes of the exilic edition of the DtrH by explaining that the ideal Josiah must die despite his righteousness due to the sins of Manasseh and his other predecessors.

13.3 PROPHETS IN THE CHRONICLER'S HISTORY

Noth's work is also foundational for the study of the Chronicler's History (ChrH). Noth (1987) maintained that the ChrH was a priestly historical work that included Ezra-Nehemiah and drew on earlier sources, such as the DtrH, the pentateuch, the psalms, and other materials in its presentation of Israel's history. Later interpreters, such as Japhet (1993), McKenzie (2004), Klein (2006), and Knoppers (2003), recognize that Ezra-Nehemiah is a separate work that was later combined with Chronicles by means of an introduction to the building of the Second Temple in Ezra 1–6 that takes up and extends the account of Cyrus's decree in 2 Chr. 36:22–23. Most interpreters view the ChrH as a fourth-century historical work that begins its presentation with the genealogy of Adam insofar as it focuses on the Jerusalem temple as the capstone and holy center of creation. Contrary to the DtrH, the ChrH pays little attention to the northern kingdom of Israel and its dynasties. Rather, the ChrH focuses especially on David, Solomon, and the rest of the house of David as the founder, builder, and guardians of the temple. Although the narrative concludes with the destruction of the Jerusalem temple as in the DtrH, the ChrH differs by closing with an account of Cyrus's decree to allow Jews to return to Jerusalem to rebuild the temple. Such a conclusion points to the centrality of the Jerusalem temple in the historiographical agenda of the ChrH, but it leaves open questions concerning the future role of the house of David.

The ChrH frequently serves as a corrective to the DtrH by eliminating or revising material to fit its own theological agenda. Indeed, the ChrH views the Levitical singers of the temple as the heirs of the prophets (Petersen 1977: 55–87). In addition to its foci on the temple and the house of David, the ChrH has a distinctive theological viewpoint concerning retribution that differs markedly from the DtrH. The DtrH explains disasters in Israel's and Judah's histories as the result of wrongdoing by the kings and the people from prior generations, such as Jeroboam ben Nebat and Manasseh ben Hezekiah. The ChrH, however, holds the kings and people accountable for their own wrongdoing and punishment. Manasseh commits grievous sins during his early years, but becomes a righteous monarch when he repents of his wrongdoing after having been dragged in chains to Babylon by the king of Assyria. King Josiah ben Amon of Judah is the ideal monarch of the house of David in the DtrH who is granted an early death so that he will not see the destruction of Jerusalem and the exile of his people. But the ChrH holds him accountable for his own death when he is accused by Pharaoh Necho of Egypt for acting against the will of Yhwh in 2 Chr. 35:20–25. Second Chr. 36:14 makes it clear that the Jerusalem temple was destroyed because the officers of the priests and the people defiled the temple in their own time.

In keeping with the theological outlook of the ChrH, the prophets in the narrative critique or commend the nation or the house of David for various actions during the course of Israel's history.[8] In some cases, the ChrH corrects the presentation of the prophets (e.g., Samuel and his father Elkanah are identified as Levites in 1 Chr. 6:1–15, esp. vv. 12–13, whereas 1 Sam. 1:1 identifies Elkanah as an Ephraimite). The ChrH includes no major account of Samuel; he appears elsewhere only in 1 Chr. 29:29, where the ChrH advises the reader that the other details of David's reign appear in the accounts of David, Nathan, and Gad. Many of the prophets associated with the foundation or demise of the northern dynasties in the DtrH are absent in the ChrH, and other prophets, otherwise unknown in the DtrH, appear in the ChrH to serve its theological purposes.

The first major prophetic narrative of the ChrH appears in 1 Chr. 17, which presents an account of Yhwh's promise of an eternal dynasty to David by the prophet, Nathan. The narrative includes the same tension between David's desire to build a house for Yhwh and Yhwh's intention to build a house for David as in the DtrH, but the ChrH presents a more compact and esthetically ordered account of Nathan's interaction with David. Whereas 2 Sam. 7:12–16 promises that David's house and kingship shall be secure forever (v. 16), 1 Chr. 17:10b–14 promises only that Yhwh will secure the throne of David's son, i.e., Solomon (v. 14). First Chronicles does not promise David a secure dynasty forever; it only promises that the throne of his son will be secure forever. Such a move resolves the tension in the DtrH between the eternal dynastic promise of 2 Sam. 7 and the qualified promises mentioned in 1 Kgs. 2:1–4; 8:15–26; and 9:1–9, which maintain that subsequent Davidic kings must observe Yhwh's commandments to secure their rule. The ChrH includes versions of these statements in 1 Chr. 28:1–8; 2 Chr. 6:3–17; and 7:17–22, but there is no conflict with Nathan's promise of eternal kingship for David's son in 1 Chr. 17:1–14. The account of Nathan's condemnation of David for his affair with Bathsheba and his role in the murder of Uriah the Hittite in 2 Sam. 12 does not appear in the ChrH because

David does not commit these crimes in the ChrH. Nor does Nathan play a role in the intrigue that brought Solomon to the throne in 1 Kgs. 1 because David forthrightly announces that Yhwh chose Solomon as his successor in 1 Chr. 29. Although David has blood on his hands as a warrior, he is idealized in the ChrH as the king who planned the Jerusalem temple and assigned the task of building it to his son, Solomon, in 1 Chr. 28:1–8.

Otherwise, the prophet Gad plays a similar role in the DtrH and ChrH in the selection of the threshing floor of Ornan/Araunah as the site for the future temple in 2 Sam. 24 and 1 Chr. 21. Gad is also mentioned as the author of a Chronicle in 1 Chr. 29:29, and together with Nathan, Gad is identified in 2 Chr. 29:25 as one of the authorities for David's decision to station the Levites in the temple with musical instruments in accordance with the words of the prophets.

Solomon has little to do with the prophets in the ChrH. There is no account of his encounter with Ahijah the Shilonite as in 1 Kgs. 11:26–40. Second Chr. 9:29 advises the reader to seek further information on Solomon's reign in the accounts of the prophets Nathan and Ahijah the Shilonite, as well as information on Jeroboam ben Nebat in the account of Iddo the seer. Second Chr. 10:15 refers to Yhwh's promise of kingship through the prophet, Ahijah the Shilonite, but no such encounter appears in the ChrH.

The encounter between King Rehoboam ben Solomon and the prophet Shemaiah is markedly different in the DtrH and the ChrH. Following northern Israel's revolt in 1 Kgs. 12:21–24, Shemaiah counsels Rehoboam not to take up arms in an attempt to force Israel to return to Davidic rule. But in 2 Chr. 12:1–12, Jeroboam and northern Israel are not the issue. Instead, Shemaiah counsels Rehoboam not to resist Pharaoh Shishak of Egypt (cf. 1 Kgs. 14:25–28). When Rehoboam heeded Shemaiah's warning, Yhwh made sure that Shishak did not destroy Judah entirely. According to 2 Chr. 12:15, the deeds of Rehoboam were recorded in the Chronicles of the prophet Shemaiah and Iddo the Seer, and 2 Chr. 13:22 reports that the deeds of Rehoboam's son, Abijah (Abijam in 1 Kgs. 15:1–8), were recorded in the Midrash of Iddo the Seer.

Like his grandfather, Rehoboam, King Asa ben Abijah was counselled by a prophet, identified as Azariah ben Oded in 2 Chr. 15:1–7 and simply as Oded in 2 Chr. 15:8–15, to seek G-d to ensure the security of nation. Asa is judged to be righteous in both 2 Chr. 14–15 and 1 Kgs. 15:9–24, but the ChrH narrative explains Asa's righteousness as his response to Azaraiah ben Oded. Second Chr. 16:7–10 qualifies the account of Asa's reign by presenting his condemnation by Hanani the Seer for his reliance on Aram. Asa arrested Hanani and afflicted some of his people. The ChrH explains the foot ailment that Asa suffered in his later years as a result of his failure to turn to G-d (2 Chr. 16:12; contra 1 Kgs. 15:23).

Although the major Elijah-Elisha narratives of 1 Kgs. 17–2 Kgs. 13 do not appear in the ChrH, their colleagues are quite active. Micaiah ben Imlah appears in 2 Chr. 18 in a narrative quite similar to 1 Kgs. 22:1–40. In both instances, Micaiah foretells Ahab's death in battle and he discloses that Yhwh sent a lying spirit to Ahab to ensure that the Israelite king would meet his demise. But Ahab's ally, King Jehoshaphat ben Asa, escaped the battle with his life. The prophet, Jehu ben Hanani, who had condemned the northern Israelite king Baasha ben Ahijah for following in the sins of Jeroboam in 1 Kgs. 16:1–4, likewise condemns Jehoshaphat in 2 Chr. 19:1–3 for giving aid to the evil King Ahab. But Jehu ben Hanani also declares that there is good in Jehoshaphat insofar as he purged the land from idolatrous installations and sought G-d. When Jehoshaphat prayed to G-d for support when attacked by the Moabites, Ammonites, and Arameans, the prophet, Jehaziel ben

Zechariah ben Benaiah ben Jehiel ben Mattaniah the Levite of the sons of Asaph, counselled Jehoshaphat and all Judah to obey Yhwh, who would give Jehoshaphat victory in 2 Chr. 20:1–30. When Jehoshaphat allied with King Ahaziah ben Ahab of Israel in 2 Chr. 20:35–37 to pursue trade in the Red Sea, the prophet Eliezer ben Dodavahu of Mareshah condemned him. Jehoshaphat's son, King Jehoram of Judah, was born as a result of Jehoshaphat's marriage to Athaliah bat Omri of Israel, also identified as Ahab's sister. When Jehoram slaughtered his brothers and their supporters to secure his hold on the throne in 2 Chr. 21, the prophet Elijah wrote him a letter stating that Yhwh would condemn him with bowel disease for following in the practices of the house of Ahab rather than those of his father, Jehoshaphat, and grandfather, Asa.

Prophets continued to be active in later times as well in the ChrH. When King Joash ben Ahaziah abandoned Yhwh and the temple to pursue foreign worship in 2 Chr. 24:17–27, the prophet Zechariah ben Jehoiada, the son of the priest who had saved Joash's life and placed him on the throne when his grandmother, Athaliah, seized power, condemned him for his actions. Joash put Zechariah to death, and so Yhwh ensured that the Arameans would defeat Judah. In this manner, the ChrH explains why Judah was invaded and why Joash was assassinated by his courtiers in bed (cf. 2 Kgs. 12). King Amaziah ben Jehoash, who would be assassinated for his failed attempt to revolt against northern Israel, was repeatedly condemned by the prophets for his behavior. When he assembled his army to join his northern Israelite overlord in battle, a man of G-d exhorted him to abandon the alliance and turn to G-d instead, which led to his victory over Edom in 2 Chr. 25:5–13. When Amaziah worshipped the gods of the Edomites, another prophet condemned him in 2 Chr. 25:14–28. But Amaziah threatened the prophet with death if he did not remain silent and proceeded to revolt against King Jehoash ben Jehoahaz ben Jehu of Israel. The result was a disaster, and Amaziah was eventually assassinated. Amaziah's son Uzziah was initially righteous during the time of Zechariah, an expert in the visions of G-d, which led to his many victories over enemies in 2 Chr. 26:1–15. But when Uzziah grew arrogant, he desecrated the temple by entering it to offer incense, a duty reserved only for priests. The ChrH thereby explains why Uzziah was stricken with leprosy (2 Chr. 26:16–23). Uzziah's grandson, King Ahaz ben Jotham of Judah, is portrayed as an idolatrous king throughout 2 Chr. 28, which resulted in his defeats at the hands of both Aram and Israel. The prophet Oded rebuked the northern Israelites for their treatment of Judean captives in vv. 9–21, which prompted the Israelites to take proper care of their Judean prisoners and return them to their homeland. Ahaz continued in his worship of foreign gods and suffered the consequences for doing so.

Prophets play important roles in the last stages of the ChrH as well. Although Isaiah ben Amoz figures prominently in 2 Kgs. 18–20 (cf. Isaiah 36–39) in the DtrH Hezekiah narratives, he receives only limited mention in the ChrH when he prays together with King Hezekiah of Judah in 2 Chr. 32:20 to deliver Judah from the Assyrians. The ChrH account thereby eliminates the problem of how Isaiah, who was not a priest, could be in the temple when Hezekiah appealed to him for assistance, and it removes Isaiah's references to the Babylonian exile. The ChrH Hezekiah narrative ends with a notice in 2 Chr. 32:32 that the other events of Hezekiah's life appear in the "Vision of Isaiah ben Amoz the Prophet," apparently a reference to the Book of Isaiah, and the Book of the Kings of Israel and Judah.

The prophet, Huldah, wife of Shallum ben Tokhath ben Hasrah, plays a similar role in the ChrH account of Josiah's reign as she does in the DtrH account. Upon discovering the book of Torah in the temple, Josiah ordered his officers to consult Yhwh. In both 2 Chr. 34:22–28 and 2 Kgs. 22:14–20, Huldah speaks about the coming punishment of Jerusalem because the people abandoned Yhwh for other gods. But she also commends Josiah's piety and declares that he will die in peace without having to witness the coming destruction. The ChrH account of Josiah's reign differs from the DtrH account by portraying Josiah as responsible for his own death. When he meets Pharaoh Necho at Megiddo, Necho speaks on behalf of G-d to charge Josiah with disobedience in 2 Chr. 35:20–24, and Josiah dies when he goes to battle against the Egyptians. The narrative in 2 Kgs. 23:29–30 simply states that Necho killed Josiah at Megiddo. Second Chr. 35:25 adds a note that the prophet Jeremiah composed laments on behalf of Josiah that were still done "until this day."

Jeremiah plays a role in the ChrH account of Jerusalem's destruction as well. Zedekiah refused to humble himself before Jeremiah and rebelled against Nebuchadnezzar, thereby violating his oath before G-d according to 2 Chr. 36:11–13. Second Chr. 36:14–21 follows with a notice that the officers of the priests and the people defiled the temple of Yhwh. The passage further recounts how Yhwh had sent prophets to warn the people and notes how they taunted the prophets, prompting Yhwh to bring the Babylonian king to kill the people in the temple and destroy it in fulfillment of the words of Jeremiah.

Second Chr. 36:22–23 concludes the ChrH with a notice of Cyrus's decree that exiled Jews might return to Jerusalem to rebuild the temple. Cyrus's decree comes at the behest of Yhwh after the words of Jeremiah were fulfilled.

13.4 CONCLUSION

Although prophets play key roles in both the DtrH and the ChrH, their roles differ markedly. The DtrH portrays prophets as the early leaders of Israel and the key figures in the foundation and dissolution of the various dynasties of both Israel and Judah. Insofar as the ChrH focuses on the temple and the house of David, it is less interested in the dynasties and focuses more on the prophets' interaction with the various monarchs, condemning them when they are wrong and blessing them when they are right.

NOTES

1. For discussion of the Deuteronomistic History, see Sweeney 2001; 2007: 1–32; Römer 2005. For the Chronicler's History, see Japhet 1993: 1–49; Knoppers 2003: 47–137; Klein 2006: 1–50.
2. See Moore and Kelle 2011.
3. See the present writer's revision of this hypothesis to form the Jehu Dynastic History (Sweeney 2007: 26–30).
4. e.g., Römer 2005: 35–43.
5. See, e.g., Jacobs and Person 2013: 187–99.
6. Aharoni 2007: 265–66.
7. For discussion of the following texts from Kings, see esp. Sweeney 2007.
8. For discussion of the prophets in the ChrH, see esp. Schniedewind 1995 and Micheel 1983.

Bibliography

Aharoni, Yohanan. 1972. "Joshua." *EncJud* 10: 265–66.
Campbell, Antony F. and Mark A. O'Brien. 2000. *Unfolding the Deuteronomistic History: Origins, Upgrades, Present Text*. Minneapolis: Fortress.
Cross, Frank M., Jr. 1973. "The Themes of the Book of Kings and the Structure of the Deuteronomistic History." In *Canaanite Myth and Hebrew Epic*. Cambridge, MA: Harvard University Press, 274–89.
Dietrich, Walter. 1972. *Prophetie und Geschichte*. FRLANT 108. Göttingen: Vandenhoeck & Ruprecht.
Halpern, Baruch and David Vanderhooft. 1991. "The Editions of Kings in the 7th–6th Centuries," *HUCA* 62: 179–244.
Jacobs, Mignon R. and Raymond F. Person, Jr., eds. 2013. *Israelite Prophecy and the Deuteronomistic History: Portrait, Reality, and the Formation of a History*. SBL AIL. Atlanta: SBL.
Japhet, Sarah. 1993. *1 and 2 Chronicles: A Commentary*. OTL. Louisville, KY: Westminster John Knox.
Klein, Ralph W. 2006. *1 Chronicles: A Commentary*. Hermeneia. Minneapolis: Fortress.
Knoppers, Gary N. 2003. *1 Chronicles 1–9*. AB 12. New York: Doubleday.
McKenzie, Steven L. 2004. *1–2 Chronicles*. AOTC. Nashville: Abingdon.
Micheel, Rosemarie. 1983. *Die Seher- und Prophetenüberlieferungen in der Chronik*. BBET 18. Frankfurt am Main: Peter Lang.
Moore, Megan Bishop and Brad E. Kelle. 2011. *Biblical History and Israel's Past: The Changing Study of the Bible and History*. Grand Rapids: Eerdmans.
Nelson, Richard D. 1997. *Joshua: A Commentary*. OTL. Louisville, KY: Westminster John Knox.
Noth, Martin. 1981. *The Deuteronomistic History*. JSOTSup 15. Sheffield: JSOT Press.
Noth, Martin. 1987. *The Chronicler's History*. JSOTSup 50. Sheffield: JSOT Press.
Petersen, David L. 1977. *Late Israelite Prophecy: Studies in the Deutero-prophetic Literature and in Chronicles*. Missoula, MT: Scholars Press.
Römer, Thomas C. 2005. *The So-Called Deuteronomistic History: A Sociological, Historical and Literary Introduction*. London and New York: T&T Clark.
Schniedewind, William M. 1995. *The Word of G-d in Transition: From Prophet to Exegete in the Second Temple Period*. JSOTSup 197. Sheffield: JSOT Press.
Smend, Rudolph. 1971. "Die Gesetz und Völker. Ein Beitrag zum deuteronomistischen Redaktionsgeschichte." In H. W. Wolff et al., eds., *Probleme Biblischer Theologie*. Fest., G. von Rad. Munich: Chr. Kaiser, 494–509.
Sweeney, Marvin A. 1996. *Isaiah 1–39, with an Introduction to Prophetic Literature*. FOTL 16. Grand Rapids: Eerdmans.
Sweeney, Marvin A. 2001. *King Josiah of Judah: The Lost Messiah of Israel*. Oxford and New York: Oxford University Press.
Sweeney, Marvin A. 2007. *1 and 2 Kings: A Commentary*. OTL. Louisville, KY: Westminster John Knox.
Sweeney, Marvin A. 2011. "Samuel's Institutional Identity in the Deuteronomistic History." In L. Grabbe and M. Nissinen, eds., *Constructs of History in the Former and Latter Prophets and Other Texts*. SBL ANEM. Atlanta: SBL, 165–74.

CHAPTER 14

THE VARIOUS ROLES OF WOMEN IN THE HISTORICAL BOOKS

MERCEDES L. GARCÍA BACHMANN

How do the portrayals of women and their various roles in the historical books of the Hebrew Bible contribute to a larger understanding of both these books and the struggles and realities of women's lives in past and present contexts? Were we to map the women present in the historical books, Judges-Kings would be ranked positively in quantitative terms. A qualitative examination in terms of difference in status between women and men of similar categories (such as queens over against kings), or in terms of violence, tells us about a world in which women are perceived as both needed and sometimes respected and loved, but also feared and oppressed. In this article, I have chosen a few themes and characters to indicate some paths for further study, hardly enough for the richness of these books.

14.1 How to Become a Woman: Female Identity in the Historical Books

First, it should be noted that defining "woman" is no simple task, particularly when there is recognition (even if partial and still wanting) that many people identify themselves in categories other than male or female and rightly expect respect for their own identity. Furthermore, "woman" in the singular easily leads into essentialist and hegemonic statements, ignoring the differences that age, race, class, education, family configurations, religions, and other factors create among women. Still, the question remains as to how to look at this category, besides simply identifying those mentioned by a feminine pronoun, names typically considered feminine (which, however, do not always hold true), and identifications of "sister, daughter, wife, or mother of."

As part of their mutual encouragement before fighting Yhwh, the (uncircumcised) Philistines cheer each other: "Make yourselves strong and become males, O Philistines, lest you are slaves of the Hebrews...you become males and fight!" (1 Sam. 4:9, cf. Samson forced to perform traditional female work in Judg. 16:21). Thus, paraphrasing Simone de Beauvoir: A male is not born but becomes one by war and in freedom (Stone 2006: 204). While war turns feeble people into men, there is no similar biblical definition of woman.

How does one come to be considered a woman according to these books, then? I do not know any direct answer to this question. At least marriage and motherhood, particularly of sons, were important in a woman's life in the historical books. Marriage is too complex an issue to be thoroughly discussed here. Part of its complexity is that we do not have a lexicon that would confirm our suppositions—for instance, that the term *pîlegeš* meant a wife of secondary status (judging from several texts, she was unfree). Also adding to this complexity is the different social conditions affecting women, as the following few examples will show. Judges starts with Achsah, given by her father in marriage to whomever conquered the city (see below), and it ends with two terrible stories about a *pîlegeš* gang-raped and dismembered and six hundred young women taken by Benjaminites against their own and their families' will to produce offspring (Judges 19–21). These women's fates vary as much as day and night, even though they were all attached to a man through some relationship involving cohabitation and sex.

Women married to a ruler walked the tight rope of their husband's fate. David's execution of all but one of Saul's remaining male offspring shows the painful fate of being married to a (fallen) ruler. But stories such as Michal's and Bathsheba's also depict the painful fate of being married to a reigning ruler from whom they did not have much freedom. Huldah the prophetess is identified through her husband and their neighborhood's residence, but he plays no role in her prophetic ministry. And a final story to grasp the diversity of situations related to marriage is that of Ezra's and Nehemiah's ejection of the non-Judean wives and children (Ezra 9–10; Nehemiah 13). These examples show that marriage could give a woman an honorable status (Achsah), serve as an identity marker (Huldah), be her nightmare (the dismembered concubine), or be a source of disruption (for the divorced couple and the children in Ezra-Nehemiah).

As to child-bearing as a component of a woman's identity, many stories could be mentioned, such as the unnamed woman presented as Eli's daughter-in-law who gives birth, names her son, Ichabod ("Where is [Yhwh's] glory?"), and dies while her attendants encourage her with the fact that she bore a son (1 Sam. 4:21). Often good and bad mothers are pitted against each other for pedagogical effects (1 Sam. 1–2; 1 Kgs. 3). And there is also at least one symbolic "mother in Israel," Deborah, contrasted in Judges 5 to Sisera's mother, who is mocked for comforting herself, covering his delay (he lies dead in Jael's tent, but she does not know this) by imagining him and his soldiers getting scarfs for the women and women for themselves as war spoil.

14.2 WOMEN AND WAR

Women are much more than wives and mothers in the historical books. They are slaves, prostitutes, midwives, childcare providers, messengers, queens, ad hoc murderers of enemies, builders of cities and walls, cooks, diviners, prophetesses, and judges, among others (García Bachmann 2013). One of the primary other contexts concerns women and war.

Throughout all the historical books, conflicts happen with the Canaanite population, the people of the land, the Samaritans, the empires that conquered them, and among internal Israelite groups. In contexts of war, women are robbed of agency and are often taken as a labor force, as wombs (see Deut. 21:10–14; Judg. 5:30), or as sexual trophies. We do not know to what extent women took an active part in war. Deborah seems to have been more engaged than just encouraging warriors (Judges 4–5), and the wise woman of Abel-Beth-Maacah acts as the city's commander (2 Sam. 20). There are other forms of political participation besides the battlefield (even though there probably were women on the battlefield, at least to cook for the soldiers and care for the wounded and dying ones; but there is no record of their contributions). Ilse Müllner (1998: 117–18) includes singing and playing music as another way for women to be subjects and not objects of war. While Miriam leads the singing and dancing as soon as Israel crosses the Reed Sea (Exodus 15), it is in the historical books where we find some of the best examples of this art: Deborah's song (Judges 5); Jephthah's daughter coming out to meet her father after his military victory (Judg. 11:34); the annual festival offered in her memory (Judg. 11:40); the girls from Shiloh singing in the vineyards (Judg. 21:21); Hannah's song (1 Sam. 2:1–10); the women praising David over against Saul (1 Sam. 18:6–10); and the singing men and women lamenting over Josiah's death "to this day" (2 Chr. 35:25; cf. Jer. 9:16). Even though two elegies and a psalm are attributed to David (2 Sam. 1:19–27; 3:33; 22:1–23:7), it has long been shown that singing, including mock, religious, and war songs, was part of women's responsibilities in ancient Israel.

14.3 WOMEN AND LAND IN JOSHUA AND JUDGES

Access to land was important for Israelite males, because it meant livelihood (although some men made their living otherwise), belonging to a family and tribe, and being remembered after death, as five daughters argue: "Why should the name of our father be taken away from his clan because he had no son? Give to us a possession among our father's brothers" (Num. 27:4 NRSV; all translations mine unless otherwise noted). In the Hebrew Bible, women's relationship to land is almost always mediated by male kin, even in the case of daughters inheriting in their father's name (Numbers 36). There is one Shunamite woman who seems to be the exception to this mediated relationship to the land (2 Kgs. 4:8–13; 8:1–6). Mothers are the vehicles to transfer the land to their children. However, it is noteworthy that the only seven named women in the book of Joshua (Rahab, Achsah, Mahlah, Noah, Hoglah, Milcah, and Tirzah) intend to warrant land for themselves and their family, but no children are mentioned in these stories. Although the theme of conquest runs through the book and it has been used to support colonial claims, there is a counter-message: Israel's identity hangs especially on obedience to God. Thus seen, the first woman we meet in Joshua 2—a Canaanite of a suspicious sexuality (Hebrew *zônâ*), a prostituted or a single woman in charge of the local tavern—opens the way for non-Israelites. Rahab, her family, and "all (things and people) belonging to her" (6:25) saved their lives by her deal with the Israelites. As a prostitute, men would think her body did not belong to her (see Josh. 2:3); as the Deuteronomist's spokeswoman, her voice is colonized.

Even so, she is a model of a shrewd and active seeker of security (*šālôm*): "Men may fight the battles, but women certainly share in the victimization" (Fewell 1992: 64).

If belonging to Israel meant choosing Yhwh (as Rahab did but Achan did not; see Joshua 2; 7), then females should be as much part of the community as males: gender does not determine faithfulness. However, faithfulness to Yhwh alone is tied to other criteria in Joshua, such as being circumcised (5:1–9) and getting a portion in the tribes' allotment (chapters 13–22)—criteria that bar most women from participation. Five youngsters are singled out as exceptions to this latter criterion: Mahlah, Noah, Hoglah, Milcah, and Tirzah, daughters of unknown mother and of Zelophehad, defunct in the wilderness. They are mentioned by name every time their story is recalled (Num. 27 and 36; Josh. 17:3). Being named in a world where most women are anonymous is already exceptional. They are also worthy of notice by embodying the struggles unprotected people (orphans) had to go through even when their cause had been pronounced right by none other than Yhwh (Num. 27:7).

In Judges 1, the Israelites conquer Debir, with Achsah, the daughter of Caleb, offered as prize-wife to its conqueror (see Josh. 15:16–17). Achsah may be a token of how women are exchanged between men in the biblical world (and ours!), but she is also outspoken and able to request from her father another piece of land, one with wells. One possible translation of her request is "Give me a present, for you have given me away as Negeb-land, so give me springs of water" (JPS).

Throughout Judges we encounter some named women (Achsah, Deborah, Jael, Delilah) and also unnamed subjects of diverse actions (e.g., one kills Abimelech with her grinding stone, one founds a family sanctuary with her silver). But we also encounter several women who are objects of violent acts: one is burnt by her enraged countrymen, one is gang-raped and dismembered, and six hundred teenagers are abducted to repopulate Benjamin. Several women and children were also killed whenever a city was conquered, a fate unfortunately not restricted to Judges (see Judg. 1; 2 Chr. 28:8; in the context of war, there are other sad stories, such as Absalom's rape of David's concubines in 2 Sam. 16:21 or two mothers facing their children's death by siege in 2 Kgs. 6:26–31). Violence against women in Judges seems to be more blatant than in other books; or is it only that here violence is made explicit, dispelled, and denounced, while in Joshua (for instance) it is omitted? The contemporary question whether there are, in fact, more femicides today than in previous eras or whether femicides are simply better known today prompts me to suspect that violence has been there all along and it surfaces in varied ways throughout the historical books.

14.4 WOMEN IN 1–2 SAMUEL

Violence against women did not end with the election of a king. The books of 1–2 Samuel may be read as a theo-political story (Stone 2006: 195) around three male characters—Samuel, Saul, and David, with Jonathan and Michal, Saul's children who loved David, instrumental to his safety and promotion to kingship. But women provide several turning points in these books. The first one is Hannah's conception of a son, Samuel, offered to Yhwh in response to her prayer that she may conceive (1 Sam. 1–2). Hannah belongs to a patriarchal family in which her husband Elkanah's other wife provoked her for her barrenness, perhaps because she was Elkanah's favorite wife.

Another turning point is Saul's death together with three of his sons in battle with the Philistines (1 Sam. 31). No wife of Saul or mother of his children is recorded, only his *pîlegeš*, always identified as Rizpah, the daughter of Aiah. She is first mentioned in a quarrel between Ishbaal and Abner, who had had sex with her (2 Sam. 3:7, no consent from her is recorded). Other deaths will severely affect her lineage. A drought during David's kingship is explained as a blood guilt unpaid for by Saul (2 Sam. 21). Her two sons and five from Saul's oldest daughter Merab are killed. Rizpah is able only to mourn, watching over the bodies until David gives them their due burial. This sad story shows how much women and children were tied to the *paterfamilias*'s fate, independently of their own behavior or status.

Another turning point, one that will affect David and his whole family, occurs when David stayed in Jerusalem while Joab, his servants, and all Israel were fighting for him (2 Sam. 11). He saw Bathsheba, the daughter of Eliam, the wife of Uriah the Hittite, wanted her, and had her brought to him. Since the story is well known, here I will only reflect on its effects on women. This is not a story of love but rape. A woman summoned by a king powerful enough to have her husband, a renowned soldier, killed with premeditation had no say in being brought to the king's bed. Like most women in the Bible of whom it is said that they were taken for sex, we do not learn about her feelings. We read that she mourned her husband killed by David (2 Sam. 11:26) and, since according to 2 Sam. 12:24 David comforted her after their firstborn's death, the narrator suggests she mourned the child as well. Bathsheba is the object of several actions: taken to David's room, made pregnant, made a widow, made a wife, and perhaps made a queen mother before she becomes, with the prophet Nathan, a subject in making Solomon king (1 Kgs. 1–2).

David's double crime signals the beginning of his downfall, as Nathan clearly announces. The main problem with this punishment is that those to suffer directly for his murder and adultery are his wives, sons, and daughters: "the sword shall never depart from your house" (2 Sam. 12:10). Particularly in what concerns women's share in David's punishment, his daughter Tamar was raped by Amnon, her half-brother (2 Sam. 13), who in turn was killed by Absalom, her brother (from the same mother, Maacah the daughter of Talmai king of Geshur). Absalom will later rebel against David, who will then flee Jerusalem leaving ten of his secondary wives (*pîlegeš*) in the palace to see whether Absalom would rape them as a way of claiming the throne (which Absalom does in 2 Sam. 16:22). Absalom was killed and David mourned him. We do not hear how Absalom's and Tamar's mother, and Amnon's mother, felt about their children being involved in rape and murder.

14.5 WOMEN WHO RULE

In terms of gender analysis, it is important not only to record which types of women appear in a certain text, but also what is said and left unsaid about them. It matters that in narratives where kingship plays such a fundamental role in the life of Yhwh and the people, there is recognition, even if biased, of queens alongside kings. In this sense, recording a king's mother's name on most summaries of Judah's rulers in the books of Kings shows they mattered to the recorders. Ideologically, however, political rule belongs to males. Hebrew terminology provides a clue on that principle: in the Hebrew Bible the only ones deserving the title of *malkâ* are the queen of Sheba and Esther, while the corresponding masculine *melek* is extremely common. This is a subtle way of denying the role of queens in Israel or Judah. Another clue is how positive contributions of queen mothers (for whom the texts use "his mother" or the title *gĕbîrâ*) are taken for granted (that is, ignored) and only those with wrong religious affiliations are mentioned as bad influences on their children (e.g., Athaliah, the daughter of Omri on Ahaziah in 2 Chr. 22:3) or as causes for their demise (e.g., Maacah in 1 Kgs. 15:13). Kings are evaluated according to their connivance or rejection of the Deuteronomist's religious program and more fathers than mothers are blamed as bad role models, but unlike any queen mother, faithful kings (e.g., Josiah) receive explicit praise.

One additional clue to evaluate the historical books' stance on women and kingship may be taken from the way in which they praise or punish women seizing power. The stories of queens Athaliah and Jezebel are telling. Athaliah is presented as a ruthless power seeker, who did not hesitate in trying to kill any male contender to the Judean throne. She was a "foreigner," an Omride (from Israel, not Judah) widow of a king. However, the text itself gives us clues to doubt this portrait, even though it was produced by the group who killed her and accessed the throne after her, led by the priest Jehoiada who installed young Jehoash (2 Kgs. 12:2). Athaliah must have been smart and must have been backed by a party, since she stayed in power six years after her family had been murdered by Jehu (2 Kgs. 10). It is also doubtful that the child Jehoash would have survived, had she wanted to kill rather than protect him (Lee 1999: 142).

The other queen portrayed as abominable and promiscuous is Jezebel, a Sidonian princess married to Ahab of Israel (1 Kgs. 16). As long as her role as queen is assessed only in deuteronomistic religious terms, her allegiance to Baal and Asherah always puts her on the wrong side. She had a strong personality and a way of understanding political power that clashed with that of the conservative Yahwists like Elijah, and she was powerful enough to make him flee. The stories about her, particularly about her death, were written much later than the Omride rule, but served the redactors to set a warning (another one!) against a foreign influential woman.

On the other hand, a queen like the one from Sheba, who tests Solomon on his wisdom and pronounces, "blessed are all your men (or people? Is *'ănāšêkā* intended as inclusive?) and blessed are your servants who stand in front of you," is rewarded with remembrance, even if anonymous (1 Kgs. 10:8; 2 Chr. 9:7). Is that due perhaps to the fact that she did not become part of Solomon's harem, but returned home? For even Solomon's main wife, an Egyptian princess, is anonymous and mute (and, according to 2 Chr. 8:11, may not share the same compounds with Yhwh; see Jonker 2016).

14.6 WOMEN REWRITTEN IN CHRONICLES AND EZRA-NEHEMIAH

One way to exercise violence against women is to ignore contributions we make, and most of the historical books are guilty of this bias. In this section, we will see how Chronicles,

Ezra, and Nehemiah deal with women. Roland Boer calls the books of 1-2 Chronicles "one of the first men-only utopias" (Boer 2006: 251). One may infer from such utopia that their ideal world was one without women, or that they wanted to believe reality is simpler if we are all alike. One thing is clear: the writers belonged to a distinct group (scribes, priests) from a particular gender (males) within a holy people (Israel) devoted to a unique Deity (Yhwh). In order to be that special, they needed several instances of separateness from those prevented from belonging—be it for their sex or gender (women and males with certain permanent physical characteristics), their ethnic affiliation (non-Israelites and Israelites from other tribes than the Levites), their religious allegiance (qĕdēšîm and other heterodox worshippers), or some other reason. Was this a case of overcompensation at a time when the temple was no longer the magnificent institution it had formerly been and religious officers no longer enjoyed a strong political influence on their rulers? There are clues, such as the controversy over marriage to foreign women, Nehemiah's quick reference to antagonistic prophetic voices, and other books such as Ruth, indicating that not everyone bowed happily to scribal teaching or political decisions in the late Persian period. It is to be celebrated that Nehemiah singles out a female prophet together with two prominent citizens among his opponents (6:14), for he lets us know there were recognized women prophets in postexilic Yehud.

What factors created this "men-only utopia" depicted in Chronicles, Ezra, and Nehemiah? One contributing factor is the selection of subject matters. The writers' interest in wars, succession to the throne, and temple order are not unique to them; history often neglects class, women, children, arts, village life, and other topics. In a literary world where the rule was that only men inherited the land, went to war, ruled Judah, and performed as priests (and only those able among them)—and in a world where these subject matters are the ones worthy of being recorded—there is not much room for women. Still, Chronicles includes some exceptions, such as Sheshan's fourteen generations stemming from his daughter, whom he marries to his Egyptian slave (1 Chr. 2:34; see Labahn and Ben Zvi 2003 and Ben Zvi 2014 on Chronicles's otherness), or Heman's daughters, temple singers, and perhaps, considering Jeremiah's association to prophecy and to singing, also women prophets (2 Chr. 35:25).

Women's agency, even in their most traditional gender role of mother, is denied most of them in the genealogy that opens 1 Chronicles. Its first four verses consist of no less than twelve generations, but nobody would realize that unless they read the corresponding stories of beginnings: from Adam to "the sons of Japheth" (1 Chr. 1:1–5) there is only a list of male names with no added information. We know, however, that "Adam, Seth, Enosh," for instance, actually indicates the fuller account given in Genesis: "the first human male (and his wife) had a son whose name was Seth, who had a son (again, by the agency of a woman, whose name was) Enosh," and so forth (Gen. 4:25–5:11). Using the formula "the son of PN," implicitly recognizes a mother and a father, except in certain myths. However, neither the "mother of all living" (Gen. 3:20) nor most mothers are recognized in Chronicles. A serious case of neglect of women occurs in 1 Chr. 1:11, 13, 18, where fathers give birth to their sons (hiphil of the verb *yld* has been replaced by its qal; see Mitchell 2012: 186).

One key to a feminist interpretation of the biblical books is to ask about absences. By focusing on Judah alone, Chronicles leaves out several women, such as Hannah, Rizpah, the court advisers, the widows and other poor encountered by Elijah and Elisha—or even

Elijah's contest with Jezebel, the foreign wife of Ahab. On the other hand, the texts expand on Rehoboam's women, his affection for one of his wives, and his having more than double the number of daughters than sons (1 Chr. 11:18–21; Laffey 1992: 112–15). And since David is an almost ideal king, affairs with women that might darken his image (his rape of Bathsheba and murder of Uriah and Amnon's rape of Tamar) are passed over. David's patriarchal power over his whole family is visible in how Solomon is treated. After David's forty years as king, Solomon is no longer a child when he succeeds him; nevertheless, he has no personal agency, is told what to do, given the building plans and the builders (1 Chr. 22:5–19), and is chosen king (apparently, by David and the assembly; see 29:20). This message is important in what it does to women and subordinated men by ignoring and not fostering personal agency, unless validated by the *paterfamilias*.

The books of Ezra and Nehemiah make a very fruitful case study on the question of how the historical books help or hinder processes of gender justice and respect for every human being. A quick reading leads to a very restricted picture of women's contributions to postexilic Yehud. Not one woman speaks in Ezra-Nehemiah. This is particularly telling, given evidence from the region under Persian rule that women could inherit land (even if they had brothers or sons), initiate divorce, and buy and sell property. Mothers' contribution in teaching children their native language is seen as cause for expulsion from the community (Neh. 13:23–24). For Ezra and his officials, the cause for the same action is religious: "The people of Israel, the priests, and the Levites have not separated themselves from the peoples of the lands according to their abominations" (Ezra 9:1–2 NRSV). In the same verse, they speak of themselves as "the holy seed," showing a religious worldview with a strong interest in social and ethnic factors. What is at stake is not only the orthodoxy of a faith, but a community with a strong identity based on the temple, city, and written law.

Certain women were included in this community. Neh. 8:3 shows the religious assembly gathered to listen attentively to Ezra's words formed by "the men and the women and those with understanding." Neh. 12:43 explicitly states: "also the women and children rejoiced. And the joy of Jerusalem was heard from afar." Ezra 10:1 again mentions "a very great assembly of men, women, and children from Israel gathered to him [Ezra]." These clarifications are useful, since often biblical texts use collective nouns in a way that makes it difficult to assess to what extent women are meant to be included. For example, 2 Chr. 20:24–25 tells of a large booty obtained by Judah of "livestock in great numbers, goods, clothing, and precious things" (NRSV) taken from the Ammonites and Moabites. Are we to imagine women were taken as booty? That is probable, considering their value as wombs and as workers. Inconsistencies in jargon like this have allowed feminist scholars to open a breach against hegemonic assumptions about what women could do in public life in ancient Israel. Although the official cult in Jerusalem was run by male priests and Levites, there is mention of male and female singers, Heman's children (1 Chr. 25:5–6), and of men and women who sang Josiah's praises, thus setting in parallel singers and female prophets (2 Chr. 35:25). And Hulda, the prophet validating Josiah's reform (2 Chr. 34:22), proves there was recognized female temple personnel, aside from the groups vaguely mentioned in the Bible as performers of abominations, soothsayers, diviners, or *qĕdēšôt*.

Summarizing our case study, the only historical material about the reconstruction of the community around Jerusalem and its temple in the postexilic period is strongly biased against contending groups, led by some prominent men and women such as Noadiah (and, judging from Miriam's leprosy in Numbers 12, prophetic credentials, particularly by women, were an issue in the postexilic communities). The homogenizing project led by Ezra and Nehemiah left out many people from every social stratum, including priests and other leaders, as well as Samaritans. In terms of gender, a particular target was those identified as female outsiders. While men were forced to expel their wives and children, nothing is said of Judahite women married to men from Ashdod, Ammon, and other nations. Were they also compelled to divorce them or had they already been erased from the community? They are simply erased from the community's memory. Were we not reading against the grain and with access to extrabiblical sources, we would have a very limited view of women's worth. And when the Bible ignores or belittles a particular group, some of its readers may feel justified to do likewise.

14.7 WOMEN AND RELIGIOUS PRACTICE

Women were part and parcel of Israel's religious community, even though no traces of a particular moment in which they ritually joined the community have survived (cf. circumcision for males). Would every daughter be automatically included just by birth? Would they be included by marriage? What would happen to those who did not marry or married a non-Israelite? These questions make it hard to imagine that there would be no initiation ceremony. Religious life in recognized sanctuaries, the main interest of large portions of the Hebrew Bible and of much scholarship, is but one aspect of a people's religious life and probably not the most immediate one for many women. There are, however, some clues that women were part of sanctuary-related systems as well as active in domestic settings.

First, some female prophets are named in the historical books. Of these, Hulda was undoubtedly related to the Jerusalem sanctuary; otherwise, her voice (a female voice) would not have sufficed to endorse Josiah's reform. Deborah seems to have enjoyed considerable authority but no sanctuary is mentioned. Her office was under a palm tree, where she performed as judge over the people (Judg. 4:5).

Second, 1 Samuel mentions several evil doings for which Eli's sons would die. Among these, "they lay with the women assembled at the entrance of the tent of meeting" (2:22). The verb translated "assembled" indicates a group of people formed with a purpose, such as an army for war (Isa. 29:8). Since the indication that there were women formed at the entrance of the place of worship is tangential, we are left with no further information on their role, but it would seem to indicate some kind of personnel of the sanctuary.

Third, in the Hebrew Bible the nouns *qādēš*, *qĕdēšâ*, and their plurals appear almost thirty times, but only the occurrences in Gen. 38:21–22, Hos. 4:14, and Deut. 23:17 are feminine. The latter is important for our purposes: "There will be no *qĕdēšâ* amongst the daughters of Israel, there will be no *qādēš* amongst the sons of Israel." Discussion of this law and its relationship or lack thereof to the law on prostitution goes beyond our argument here (see García Bachmann 2013: 295–307). At any rate, the need to have a prohibition against Israel's children becoming *qĕdēšîm* or *qĕdēšôt* indicates their very existence. It is true nothing relates them directly to the temple in the historical books, but one should at least consider that possibility. From 2 Kgs. 23:7 we learn of the women weaving houses for the goddess Asherah at the *qĕdēšîm*'s houses, which were within the Jerusalem temple. The first verses of this chapter report Josiah's reform, following Hulda's confirmation of the book found at the temple. Indeed, we have a witness that within the most official sanctuary in Judah there were houses for the consecrated men called *qĕdēšîm*, whom the Deuteronomists (that is to say, those in favor of Josiah's reform) rejected. And within these houses or perhaps headquarters, the women had a particular task, that of weaving some kind of "houses" for Asherah. The fact that they worked within the Jerusalem temple indicates they belonged to the sanctuary, being perhaps slaves, or perhaps women of a higher status. Since this would have been a wonderful chance for the Deuteronomists to shed a negative light on women whose religious affiliation was for them dubious, it is strange that they would not mention *qĕdēšôt*.[1] This third example is an instance of women's involvement with forms of worship that were, at best, ignored and, at worst, persecuted by some priests, prophets, and kings, while supported by others.[2]

Religious life occurred in domestic or family settings, as well. We hear more about these contexts in the books that portray Israel's origins (Genesis to Judges), but their continuity through and beyond the monarchy has been shown especially by archaeological discoveries. Here again, our sources are, at best, tangential. Yet, they allow us to state that there were religious activities (prayers, incantations, vows) beyond the Levitical male cult in which women felt more at home. Other types of religious practitioners mentioned in the historical books include *'ōbôt*, necromancers, from "(wine) skin," and *'iddĕ'ōnîm*, from the verb "to know." These roots indicate that their negative connotation belongs to a particular theology, not to their profession. And since we are left only with theology that antagonizes such practices, we do not find fair descriptions (Lev. 19:31; Deut. 18:11). One exemplary story in this regard is Saul's consultation of a "mistress in necromancy" at Endor (consulted secretly, since Saul himself had banned them; 1 Sam. 28). The story shows a woman capable of conveying Samuel's spirit to speak to Saul and of offering a proper sacrifice (Tamarkin Reis 1997).

Because of rituals outside the sanctuaries and perhaps also because they were in charge of beginning and end of life (including practical knowledge on herbs for conception, contraception, healing, and killing), throughout the centuries women have often been associated with sorcery and other suspicious—to the established priesthood—activities. As long as women in biblical texts are considered men's source of sexual and religious danger, religious asymmetry against, contempt for, and fear of women will remain. One example occurs in Joshua 22. There is a controversy, where the "sin" is having built a sanctuary to Yhwh in Transjordan. The tribes from Cisjordan strengthen their accusation by reference to the sin of Peor. "Peor" appears ten times in the Bible, nine of which refer to the people (or the men?) "ZNH-ing"—having sexual relations (NRSV) or profaning themselves (JPS) with the women of Moab (Num. 25:1), thus worshipping Baal-Peor and enraging Yhwh. "Women and unbelievers / foreigners are paralleled as a seductive threat to Israelite purity" (Carden 2006: 164).

14.8 WOMEN AND LABOR

Our last item of exploration of women and the historical books is labor, where women, like men, should be evaluated by their contributions and not their gender, body, or sexuality.

Although obvious, it is good to remember that the Hebrew Bible is not a treatise or a legal code on work. Female workers are not protagonists, although sometimes they are central in a story because of their usefulness. Queens and other occupations relating to politics were already mentioned. A particular guild largely unnoticed in that scenario is the advisor. Wisdom made two main contributions—the practical skill (for instance in weaving) and the ability to assess correctly a situation and behave so as not to endanger a person or the community. Some stories concern formal and informal counselors, male and female. Ahithophel the Gilonite advised Absalom publicly to rape his father's concubines in order to claim his kingdom (2 Sam. 16:20). And Amnon's cousin Jonadab, "a very crafty man," made for him the plan to have Tamar come to his bedside (2 Sam. 13:3–5). Likewise, Rehoboam is reported to have asked David's advisors and his own friends for council when the northern tribes came to him (1 Kgs. 12). Complementing them, there are two wise women called upon to advise David in one case and his general Joab in the other, who successfully avoid more bloodshed (2 Sam. 14; 20). Notably, Abigail, depicted as clever and beautiful, also counsels David and prevents him from murder (1 Sam. 25).

It is usually stated that women stayed in the domestic sphere and men interacted with other families. And though there is some truth in that affirmation, it needs class and racial lenses, for the types of work, settings, and degree to which women were compelled to perform tasks varied between, for example, slaves, midwives, prostitutes, cooks, queen mothers, prophets, diviners, or judges. One vexing issue about work in general and female work in particular is how little we can actually know. For instance, 1 Sam. 8:13 mentions cooks, perfumers, and bakers as occupations imposed on young women taken for the king's service in the palace. On the other hand, Neh. 3:8 mentions one of the wall repairers, "Hananiah, one of the perfumers," and 1 Chr. 9:30 attributes to priests the task of preparing oil for the sanctuary. Were it not for Samuel's warning, we would never learn about female perfumers. Were they exceptional or are most texts blind to a variety of female workers? One possible explanation for the divergence between the three texts is their respective realms, court and sanctuary. Again, 2 Sam. 6:16 (and parallel 1 Chr. 13:8) attributes to David leadership in dancing and leaping in celebration of the ark's coming to Jerusalem. These actions are attributed to him despite customary practice by women of leading processions. Another example of professions usually performed by women but attributed to a man in the historical books is weaving the curtains for the temple. Solomon did not weave the hangings nor cast the columns; he had them done for him, of course (2 Chr. 3:14). One could argue that keeping his name is justified because he commissioned those works. On the other hand, Exod. 35:25–27 records the construction of the tent of meeting in the wilderness and recognizes this practical dimension of female wisdom. The account of Solomon's completion of the temple could have recognized work by the women but the narrative prefers him over anonymous female workers.

Largely unnoticed goes also the information concerning the descendants of *hassōphereth* (lit., "the female scribe") in 1 Esdr. 2:55//Neh. 7:57 (which most translations leave as personal name). There is ample possibility that there was "a guild whose ancestor was a female scribe, especially since the presence of female scribes in Babylon (whence this group came) is well attested" (Eskenazi 2001: 92). Given also mention of a female messenger in Isa. 40:9, it should not come as a surprise that some women from the upper classes, perhaps priests' daughters, learned to read and write and could act on behalf of queens and other important women. To complicate our grasp of gender issues in the Bible, a certain Sheerah built Lower and Upper Beth-horon and Uzzen-sheerah (1 Chr. 7:24), an exacting job in physical terms.[3]

In the light of all this evidence, how does a focus on women figures help readers better interpret the historical books? There are at least two possible outcomes. First, it is apparent that women filled a broader range of roles than acknowledged by traditional scholarship. These include leadership roles as queens, queen mothers, prophets, judges, and counselors; religious roles as prophets, judges, necromancers, diviners, *qĕdēšôt*, and other occupations; service roles as cooks, perfumers, prostitutes, childcare providers, and every type of slave. Only by seeking women do we find women. And by finding women we see a more complete picture of the biblical world than an androcentric focus allows. The picture should be deepened with particular questions about children, gender groups unidentified as male or female, foreigners, people with special physical or mental conditions, animals, and other groups forgotten in hegemonic readings.

Second, a focus on various women's roles in the historical books lays bare our iniquities and calls us to repentance. In particular, issues of violence and gender bias must be faced and denounced. Failure to do so contributes to a distorted image of women, men, and God formed in readers by these biases. While texts like Gen. 1:26–28 and Gal. 3:28 proclaim the equal dignity of men and women because of a common origin in God, other texts clearly put women in a secondary role, especially when it comes to control of their own bodies. So women in some texts are barred from access to the official cult and to political rule. Other texts not only limit female participation, but contribute to a biased ideology in which women are dangerous—especially religiously and sexually—to men. Contemporary societies and churches carry on their shoulders a dark legacy of neglect, at best, and downright victimization of women, at worst. But scripture—including the historical books—can also open the way for human rights observance, ecological care, economic justice, gender dignity, and hope for all those who suffer marginalization and victimization.

Notes

1. Traditional translations of these cult officers as "sacred prostitute," "sodomite," and "harlot" are misleading, since the root indicates a consecrated person. There are convincing reasons to consider wrong any sexual connotation of the terms, but even accepting traditional translations would not work against my argument that they were part of the official religion.
2. It is recorded of Maacah, for example, that she paid her support of Asherah with her position as *gĕbîrâ* during her son Asa's reform (1 Kgs. 15:13).
3. Wacker (1999: 148–49) wonders whether this is positive information in the light of the prohibition of rebuilding Jericho.

Bibliography

Ackerman, Susan. 1998. *Warrior, Dancer, Seductress, Queen: Women in Judges and Biblical Israel.* New Haven, CT: Yale University Press.

Ben Zvi, Ehud. 2014. "Othering, Selfing, 'Boundarying' and 'Cross-Boundarying' as Interwoven with Socially Shared Memories: Some Observations." In Diana Edelman and Ehud Ben Zvi, eds.,

Imagining the Other and Constructing Israelite Identity in the Early Second Temple Period. LHBOTS 456. London: Bloomsbury T&T Clark), 20–40.

Boer, Roland. 2006. "1 and 2 Chronicles." In Deryn Guest, Robert Goss, Mona West, and Thomas Bohache, eds., *The Queer Bible Commentary*. London: SCM, 251–67.

Brenner, Athalya, ed. 1994. *A Feminist Companion to Samuel and Kings*. FCB 5. Sheffield: Sheffield Academic Press.

Brenner, Athalya, ed. 2000. *Samuel and Kings*. FCB, 2nd series 7. Sheffield: Sheffield Academic Press.

Camp, Claudia V. 1992. "1 and 2 Kings." In Carol A. Newsom and Sharon H. Ringe, eds., *The Women's Bible Commentary*. Louisville, KY: Westminster John Knox, 96–109.

Carden, Michael. 2006. "Joshua." In Deryn Guest, Robert Goss, Mona West, and Thomas Bohache, eds., *The Queer Bible Commentary*. London: SCM, 144–66.

Cook Steike, Elisabeth. 2013-14. "La feminización del 'otro' en Esdras 9–10. Una lectura desde las masculinidades y la interseccionalidad." *Vida y Pensamiento* 33.2 and 34.1: 211–44.

Cottrill, Amy C. 2012. "Joshua." In Carol A. Newsom, Sharon H. Ringe, and Jacqueline E. Lapsley, eds., *Women's Bible Commentary*. Revised and updated 3rd Anniversary Edition. Louisville, KY: Westminster John Knox, 103–12.

Davidson, Steed Vernyl. 2013. "Gazing (at) Native Women: Rahab and Jael in Imperializing and Postcolonial Discourses." In Roland Boer, ed., *Postcolonialism and the Hebrew Bible: The Next Step*. SemeiaSt 70. Atlanta: Society of Biblical Literature, 69–92.

Eskenazi, Tamara Cohn. 2001. "Hassophereth / sophereth." In Carol L. Meyers and Toni Craven, eds., *Women in Scripture: A Dictionary of Named and Unnamed Women in the Bible, the Apocryphal/ Deuterocanonical Books, and the New Testament*. Grand Rapids: Eerdmans, 91–92.

Eskenazi, Tamara Cohn. 1992. "Ezra-Nehemiah." In Carol A. Newsom and Sharon H. Ringe, eds., *The Women's Bible Commentary*. Louisville, KY: Westminster John Knox, 116–23.

Exum, J. Cheryl. 1999. "Das Buch der Richter. Verschlüsselte Botschften für Frauen." In Luise Schottroff and Marie-Theres Wacker, eds., *Kompendium feministische Bibelauslegung*. Gütersloh/ Chr. Kaiser: Gütersloher Verlaghaus, 90–103.

Fewell, Danna Nolan. 1992. "Joshua." In Carol A. Newsom and Sharon H. Ringe, eds., *The Women's Bible Commentary*. Louisville, KY: Westminster John Knox, 63–66.

Fewell, Danna Nolan. 1992. "Judges." In Carol A. Newsom and Sharon H. Ringe, eds., *The Women's Bible Commentary*. Louisville, KY: Westminster John Knox, 67–77.

García Bachmann, Mercedes L. 2013. *Women at Work in the Deuteronomistic History*. SBL International Voices in Biblical Studies. Atlanta: SBL.

Guest, Deryn. 2006. "Judges." In Deryn Guest, Robert Goss, Mona West, and Thomas Bohache, eds., *The Queer Bible Commentary*. London: SCM, 167–89.

Hackett, Jo Ann. 2012. "1 and 2 Samuel." In Carol A. Newsom, Sharon H. Ringe, and Jacqueline E. Lapsley, eds., *Women's Bible Commentary*. Revised and updated 3rd Anniversary edition. Louisville, KY: Westminster John Knox, 150–63 (e-book paging).

Howard, Cameron, B. R. 2012. "1 and 2 Kings." In Carol A. Newsom, Sharon H. Ringe, and Jacqueline E. Lapsley, eds., *Women's Bible Commentary*. Revised and updated 3rd Anniversary edition. Louisville, KY: Westminster John Knox, 164–79 (e-book paging).

Johnson, Willa M. 2011. *The Holy Seed Has Been Defiled: The Interethnic Marriage Dilemma in Ezra 9–10*. HBM 33. Sheffield: Sheffield Phoenix.

Jonker, Louis. 2016. "'My Wife Must Not Live in King David's Palace' (2 Chr 8:11): A Contribution to the Diachronic Study of Intermarriage Traditions in the Hebrew Bible." *JBL* 135: 35–47.

Karrer, Christiane. 1999. "Die Bücher Esra und Nehemia. Die Wiederkehr der Anderen." In Luise Schottroff and Marie-Theres Wacker, eds., *Kompendium feministische Bibelauslegung*. Gütersloh/ Chr. Kaiser: Gütersloher Verlaghaus, 156–68.

Labahn, Antje and Ehud Ben Zvi. 2003. "Observations on Women in the Genealogies of 1 Chronicles 1–9." *Bib* 84: 457–78.

Laffey, Alice L. 1992. "1 and 2 Chronicles." In Carol A. Newsom and Sharon H. Ringe, eds., *The Women's Bible Commentary*. Louisville, KY: Westminster John Knox, 110–15.

Lee, Kyung Sook. 1999. "Die Königsbücher. Frauen-Bilder ohne Frauen-Wirklichkeit." In Luise Schottroff and Marie-Theres Wacker, eds., *Kompendium feministische Bibelauslegung*. Gütersloh/Chr. Kaiser: Gütersloher Verlaghaus, 130–45.

Lefkovitz, Lori Hope. 2010. *In Scripture: The First Stories of Jewish Sexual Identities*. Lanham: Rowman and Littlefield Publishers.

Marsman, Hennie J. 2003. *Women in Ugarit and Israel: Their Social and Religious Position in the Context of the Ancient Near East*. Brill: Leiden.

Mitchell, Christine. 2012. "1 and 2 Chronicles." In Carol A. Newsom, Sharon H. Ringe, and Jacqueline E. Lapsley, eds., *Women's Bible Commentary*. Revised and updated 3rd anniversary ed. Louisville, KY: Westminster John Knox, 184–90 (e-book paging).

Müllner, Ilse. 1999. "Die Samuelbücher. Frauen im Zentrum der Geschichte Istaels." In Luise Schottroff and Marie-Theres Wacker, eds., *Kompendium feministische Bibelauslegung*. Gütersloh/Chr. Kaiser: Gütersloher Verlaghaus, 114–29.

Ngan, Lai Ling Elizabeth. 2013. "Class Privilege in Patriarchal Society: Women in First and Second Samuel." In Susanne Scholz, ed., *Feminist Interpretation of the Hebrew Bible in Retrospect*, I: *Biblical Books*. Recent Research in Biblical Studies 5. Sheffield: Sheffield Phoenix, 110–34.

Parker, Julie Faith. 2013. "Queens and Other Female Characters: Feminist Interpretations of First and Second Kings." In Susanne Scholz, ed., *Feminist Interpretation of the Hebrew Bible in Retrospect*, I: *Biblical Books*. Recent Research in Biblical Studies 5. Sheffield: Sheffield Phoenix, 135–49.

Scholz, Susanne. 2012. "Judges." In Carol A. Newsom, Sharon H. Ringe, and Jacqueline E. Lapsley, eds., *Women's Bible Commentary*. Revised and updated 3rd Anniversary edition. Louisville, KY: Westminster John Knox, 113–27 (e-book paging).

Stanley, Ron. 2006. "Ezra-Nehemiah." In Deryn Guest, Robert Goss, Mona West, and Thomas Bohache, eds., *The Queer Bible Commentary*. London: SCM, 268–77.

Stone, Ken. 2006a. "1 and 2 Kings." In Deryn Guest, Robert Goss, Mona West, and Thomas Bohache, eds., *The Queer Bible Commentary*. London: SCM, 222–50.

Stone, Ken. 2006. "1 and 2 Samuel." In Deryn Guest, Robert Goss, Mona West, and Thomas Bohache, eds., *The Queer Bible Commentary*. London: SCM, 195–221.

Stratton, Beverly J. 2013. "Consider, Take Counsel, and Speak: Re(Membering) Women in the Books of Joshua and Judges." In Susanne Scholz, ed., *Feminist Interpretation of the Hebrew Bible in Retrospect*, I: *Biblical Books*. Recent Research in Biblical Studies 5. Sheffield: Sheffield Phoenix, 80–109.

Tamarkin Reis, Pamela. 1997. "Eating the Blood: Saul and the Witch of Endor." *JSOT* 73: 3–23.

Trible, Phyllis. 1984. *Texts of Terror: Literary Feminist Readings of Biblical Narratives*. Minneapolis: Fortress.

Ulrich, Kerstin. 1999. "Das Buch Josua. Tradition und Gerechtigkeit—Vom Erbteil der Frauen." In Luise Schottroff and Marie-Theres Wacker, eds., *Kompendium feministische Bibelauslegung*. Gütersloh/Chr. Kaiser: Gütersloher Verlaghaus, 80–89.

Wacker, Marie-Theres. 1999. "Die Bücher Chronik. Im Vorhof der Frauen." In Luise Schottroff and Marie-Theres Wacker, eds., *Kompendium feministische Bibelauslegung*. Gütersloh/Chr. Kaiser: Gütersloher Verlaghaus, 146–55.

Yee, Gale A, ed. 2007. *Judges and Method: New Approaches in Biblical Studies*. Minneapolis: Fortress.

Yee, Gale A. and Athalya Brenner, eds. 2013. *Joshua and Judges*. Minneapolis: Fortress.

CHAPTER 15

EXOGAMY AND DIVORCE IN EZRA AND NEHEMIAH

HERBERT R. MARBURY

READ as part of the corpus of Historical Books, Ezra and Nehemiah narrate an account of the return and the restoration, the culmination of ancient Israel's story. The books conclude in a dramatic climax. The putting away of foreign wives cleanses Israel, assures that the "holy seed" (זֶרַע הַקֹּדֶשׁ) remains pure, and that "those who remain" (גּוֹלָה)—true Israel—survive.

In this reading, return and restoration frame a historical understanding of the admonitions against exogamy and the mass divorces of Ezra 9–10 and Nehemiah 10 and 13. Such a frame depends upon several taken for granted hermeneutical decisions. First, "Historical Books" is a Christian theological category and carries a different meaning than the Jewish category, *Ketuvim* or "Writings." Second, the category organizes the literature to tell a particular story of the nation of Israel, which begins with the possession of the land in Joshua and deploys Ezra and Nehemiah to tell a story of return and restoration. Third, such a reading sees an almost seamless interweaving between biblical history, ancient Israel's history, and our own world. By "biblical history," I mean a story that coheres only within the biblical narrative. That story begins with the creation of the heavens and the earth in Genesis 1, recounts the flood, the migration of Abraham, the exodus from Egypt, the conquest of the land, and an exile.[1] The story is contained within and refers to a "biblical world," that is a time and space constructed by the writers with its own laws about the natural and the supernatural. By ancient Israel's history, I mean a second historical world constructed generally by modern scholars through accepted methods of historiography such as historical anthropology, archaeology, socio-historical criticism in biblical studies, and other agreed upon modes of inquiry.[2] The two worlds are not coterminous, but both worlds intersect with a third, the reader's world, where the category, historical books, takes its theological meaning framed by a *heilsgeschictliche* story.

Scholarly inquiry about the divorces themselves arises implicitly in debates over the dating of the reforms, challenges to the historicity of Ezra and Nehemiah, and in questions about Ezra's or Nehemiah's priority. Each challenge questions the intersection between a "historical" world and a biblical one. In doing so, they test the limits of a return-restoration reading of the mass divorces. These debates contend over the historical ground upon which to make any claim about the divorces. By ground, I mean the evidentiary basis to make claims for historicity.

Challenges to more traditional views of the historicity of Ezra and Nehemiah began early. In 1785, J. D. Michaelis identified Xerxes (485–465 BCE) rather than Artaxerxes Longimanus

I (465–424 BCE) as the emperor named Artashasta in Ezra 7. Subsequently, he dated Ezra's reform in Jerusalem to 479 BCE instead of the consensus dating of 458 BCE In 1787, his student J. G. Eichorn's monumental introduction to the Old Testament returned to the traditional dating. Later debates took the dating of Ezra and Nehemiah forward and located them during the reign of Artaxerxes II in 397 BCE and 384 BCE respectively.[3]

These questions emerged again among Joseph Halévy, A. Kuenen, and A. van Hoonacker, and between W. H. Kosters and J. Wellhausen in the late eighteenth century. In a series of articles beginning in 1881, Halévy argued that Ezra was not the founder of Judaism as the contemporaneous consensus held.[4] Rather, Ezra was a minor figure who only attempted reforms after Nehemiah. Kuenen's (1886) response reaffirmed Ezra as the bringer of the Law and the founder of Judaism. In 1890, Albin van Hoonacker responded with the results of his inquiry into the Ezra-Nehemiah problem, and established one of the most influential positions of that and the next era. He argued that the two figures are reversed chronologically in the biblical text so that Nehemiah arrived first in Jerusalem in 445 BCE in the twentieth year of Artaxerxes I (Neh. 2:1) and that Ezra arrived in 397 BCE in the seventh year of Artaxerxes II (Ezra 7:8). Hoonacker's position of Nehemiah priority held sway in scholarly circles until well into the twentieth century.

Kosters (1895) raised even more severe challenges to the traditional views of Ezra and Nehemiah. He accepted Nehemiah priority and argued that no "return" occurred, nor was the Second Temple constructed under Cyrus's reign. Rather, Nehemiah arrived in Jerusalem in 445 before Ezra and returned to Babylon to dispatch Ezra in 433 BCE. Wellhausen (1895) challenged Kosters's hypothesis. His study emends Ezra 7:7–8 to read the twenty-seventh year rather than the seventh year and argues that Ezra worked in Jerusalem between Nehemiah's missions. The last major nineteenth-century contribution to these historical questions was the most radical. In 1896, in response to Wellhausen and Kosters, C. C. Torrey argued that both the so-called "Ezra memoir" and Ezra himself were literary fictions.[5] For Torrey, the Chronicler was responsible for Ezra's creation. While his work was criticized by W. F. Albright (1946) and his student, J. Bright (1959: 324), there has yet to be an adequate rebuttal of Torrey's argument. In the 1990s, a group of critical historians of the so-called Copenhagen School took up Torrey's doubt about scholars' confidence in interweaving the biblical world and the world of ancient Israel with the world of the reader. Their work demonstrates a radical skepticism about any intersection between the two worlds.[6]

More recent treatments have turned to the text's rhetoric generally in one of three ways. They take up the divorce rhetoric as oriented toward creating a theocratic community, as oriented toward reinforcing cultural cohesion and affirming ethnic identity, or as a direct response to imperial pressures. Examples of the first position include studies by M. Noth, K. Koch, D. Clines, J. Maxwell Miller and J. Hayes, and L. Grabbe.[7] These studies hold that the rhetoric's focus is on religious purity, Mosaic law, and priestly ritual, and is oriented toward creating a theocratic community. In other words, Nehemiah came to Jerusalem because the cult was in disarray, the community in Jerusalem had neglected the temple, the wall was in ruins, and most importantly, the holy seed had defiled itself by mixing with the "peoples of the lands" by practicing exogamy. The divorces were a necessary part of the work of the restoration. They were an attempt to restructure the community according to Deuteronomy 6. G. Ahlström (1994: 889) summarizes this position clearly, "Ezra fulfilled his most important task: Yahweh's people, the *gola* party, had been firmly established.... Ezra's mission was to establish a theocratic society."

The second position sees the rhetoric as constructing ethnic and religious identity along certain cultural boundaries. Employing later anthropological methods, J. Blenkinsopp (1998: 173–77, 363–64), T. C. Eskenazi and Eleanore P. Judd (1994), and D. L. Smith-Christopher (1989; 1991; 1994; 1996) argue that the rhetoric promotes a unified religious and ethnic identity.[8] They conclude that the divorces are attempts to solidify cultural and ethnic solidarity amid the diverse populations seeking ascendancy. Smith-Christopher focuses on the background for the sociology of the exilic community. He argues that several experiences of the *golah* or "returnees," including the survival of a military defeat by Babylon and the subsequent deportation and religious humiliation, shape the community's identity. The sociology of the exilic and postexilic periods is shaped by this common identity. Their ample numbers gave them the means to become a cohesive community; the divorces are one means by which they achieved that cohesion.[9]

Eskenazi and Judd (1994: 273–75) focus on the identity of the *'am ha'arets*. They examine ethnicity, intermarriage, and the conditions necessary for its occurrence as a way of understanding what meaning(s) intermarriage may have held in Yehud. They offer four alternative interpretations as to the women in the exogamous marriages: (1) Judahite or Israelite women who were of no particular ethnic origin but were not exiled and the ensuing conflict over religious purity or Jewishness may perhaps have masked a conflict over land rights; (2) the women could have been Ammonites, Moabites, or members of other ethnic groups present in the Persian Empire; (3) they could have been Judahite or Israelite women whose family practices were different from the *golah*; and (4) Judahite or Israelite women who were not deported to Babylon and who, according to Ezra, could not be ritually acceptable marriage partners.

The third approach holds that the exigencies of imperial rule motivate the divorce rhetoric. Studies by J. Berquist (1995: 110–19) and K. Hoglund (1992: 201–40) extend P. Frei's theory that the Persian Empire exercised extensive control over Yehud.[10] They argue that the interests of the Persian Empire underlie the rhetoric's intent.

These three positions are similar to debates of the earlier era. Each tests the limits of the scholar's historical world at its intersection with the biblical world. Unlike earlier debates that raised questions based on literary analyses of the text, these more recent inquiries attempt to retrieve a historical world through social-scientific methods. "Re-constructed" historical worlds, rather than texts alone, become the means by which they understand the return and restoration, and ultimately, the divorce rhetoric within the historical books. In these reconstructed worlds, no differently than in our world, the divorce rhetoric takes on multiple meanings.

15.1 Reconstructing Yehud: Context for the Exogamous Marriages and Divorces

Whether internally or externally motivated, whether oriented toward the creation of a theocratic community, cultural identity formation, or imperial concerns, the intent and motivation of the divorce rhetoric depend upon their historical context. Size, demography, and economy are primary factors that shape the social world of Yehud under Persian dominion. Taken together, these factors belie traditional understandings of a mass return, and thus a restoration.

For a century, studies based on evaluations of the archaeological evidence have generally agreed on Yehud's small size. In an early study, Albright (1946) estimated the population at 20,000 persons. His conclusion has been followed by most scholars through the better portion of the twenty-first century. Later studies conclude similar figures. C. E. Carter's study (1999: 201–202) took up a review of available archaeological surveys and excavations and estimated a population of 13,350 in the early Persian period that grew to 20,650 by the later Persian period.[11] O. Lipschits's study (2003: 355–64) envisions a larger territory of Yehud than does Carter but only increases the estimate to 30,125. Given the size of Yehud, only about 1,500 people would have lived in Jerusalem. Of that group about 200–600 people (1–3 percent) would be counted among the literate, governing, or ruling classes.[12] Despite variations in the actual estimates, there is agreement that Yehud's population increased steadily from the early Persian period through the Hellenistic period.[13] Lipschits attributes the increase to normal internal processes of the province, while B. Becking (2006) attributes the rise in population to Persian stimulated trade.[14] Both argue that the archaeological data does not support a mass return to Jerusalem.

Absent the return and restoration as framing devices, reading the divorce rhetoric as a part of the historical books raises the question of the intersection between the biblical world and the scholar's reconstructed world and asks, "What meanings arise now?" and "What meanings remain plausible?" In particular, it takes into account the exigencies of imperial rule. In fact, in the aftermath of the Babylonian destruction, it is the Persian Empire that creates the political and economic entity that is Yehud. Its posture toward Yehud would have been no different than that toward Babylon and Egypt. Since authorial intent is foreclosed, such an approach turns to the intentionality of the rhetoric itself as it fulfills the interests of the priesthood, the imperial authorities, and the community. In the social world of Yehud, the meanings of the divorce rhetoric are multivalent and correspond to the interests of at least these three groups.

15.2 THE DIVORCES AND PERSIAN IDEOLOGICAL ENGAGEMENT OF TEMPLE COMMUNITIES

Persian ideological engagement of temple communities took the form of a network of exchanges. In Babylon, the Persians instructed priestly elites to compose new religious traditions celebrating Cyrus's activity. The Cyrus cylinder, one example, collapses a two-year military campaign that led to the city's conquest into an almost bloodless event in 539 BCE. The literature portrays the Persian king as a devotee of Marduk, the Babylonian national deity. In fact, Cyrus claims that Marduk ordered him to attack the city of Babylon and charged him to free its citizens and to restore worship at the deity's temple.[15] Such propaganda legitimated Persian rule. In return, the Persians restored the regular function of the temple in Babylon, thus appeasing its priesthood. In Egypt, Cambyses and Darius I replicated Cyrus's engagement in Babylon. As had the priesthood of Marduk, the priesthood of the sanctuary of Neith, which had been neglected by Psammeticus III, capitulated to Persian rule. The Persian crown instructed Udjahorresne, the Egyptian priest and naval officer, to create for them titles that represent Persian kings as legitimate descendants of the Saite pharaohs. They name Cambyses "King of Upper and Lower Egypt" and Darius I "Great Chief of Every Land, Great Ruler of Egypt."[16] In return, they elevate Udjahorressne to "Chief Physician," giving him prestige in the new imperial order. In both Egypt and Babylon, Persians raided temples, deposed priesthoods, and used public slaughter to punish non-compliant temples or those that fomented rebellion among the local populations.[17]

The Persian presence in Yehud was similar to that in Egypt and Babylon. It created new social forces, loyalties, identities, and power arrangements. In particular, it authorized and funded a new temple, which ensured the ascendancy of the priesthood that occupied it.[18] Unlike the powerful temple systems in Babylon and Egypt, the priesthood in Yehud was smaller, newer, and more vulnerable to the vicissitudes of imperial will. Nonetheless, they vest Cyrus with divine legitimation in their own religious tradition. Similar to Cyrus's appearance in Babylonian religious tradition, he is also written into Isa. 45:1 as Yhwh's messiah.

Understanding these identities and loyalties is important for reading the divorces.[19] In particular, understanding ethnicity in Yehud is a prerequisite for interrogating the "foreignness" of wives in the exogamous marriages. However, identifying ethnic composition is complicated by a lack of agreement on categories, by a lack of evidence for markers of ethnic difference in the archaeological record, and by the use of ethnic designations that speak to modern concerns rather than those of the Jerusalem community. More fruitful than looking to ethnicity in terms of markers such as common descent and common language among others, scholars such as Berquist (2006) turn to a dynamic understanding of ethnicity as a social force. Two designations that scholars have used that arise from the literature of Ezra-Nehemiah itself are *bene ha-golah*, "children of the exile," and *'am ha'arets*, "people of the land."[20] Ethnicity as an identity-forming force continually shapes a group's social, political, and economic interests in one direction over another. In Yehud, two among many other identity-forming forces contested with each other: the first, the Yehudite, includes those cultural, religious, political, and economic claims oriented toward the interests, claims, and self-understandings of the local populations of Yehud with Jerusalem at its center; and the second, the Persian, includes those cultural, religious, political, and economic claims oriented toward affirming imperial control.[21] *Bene ha-golah*, as a self-referential term, refers to a Yehudite identity, while *'am ha'arets* refers to an identity formed toward other interests and loyalties that the Jerusalem community (more specifically, the writers of the text) perceived to be antithetical to its own.

Yehudite identity supported allegiance to certain groups such as those in power in Jerusalem, systems such as the temple economy, ideologies such as the practice of Yahwism, and hierarchies such as the priesthood. At various levels, this identity resisted the ultimate authority of the temple system in favor of the Yahwistic practices of the Second Temple community. Persian and Yehudite identities worked within the matrix of other political, ethnic, family, and religious loyalties. As Jerusalem developed politically and economically from the Persian to the Hellenistic periods, so also did the influence of socio-cultural structures (e.g., the Second Temple) for Yehudite identity formation. Any "ethnic" difference between the two is directly related to the various identity-forming processes, whether imperial or Yehudite.[22]

The Persian imperial system had clear interests and its policies created incentives for fulfilling them. It offered internal stability and protection from external disruption. At the same time, it required certain behaviors, ideologies, positions, and loyalties that infringed upon Yahwism. Persian imperial postures reveal a clue to the geo-political order even without specific material witness to imperial policy in Yehud. By releasing formerly subjected groups from neo-Babylonian repression with the charge to "return" to a homeland and with imperial backing to reclaim their aristocratic status, the Persians created loyal subjects in Jerusalem and elsewhere who would help them establish a Persian presence in remote regions of the empire. In other words, not only did the Persians want the "returnees" to attain and maintain power in this western province of the empire, the returnees themselves saw this as an opportunity to gain a measure of power and affluence that they may not have enjoyed in Babylon.[23] Nonetheless, even with the imperial imprimatur, any arriving group found itself pitted against several wealthier and more established groups.

15.3 READING THE DIVORCES IN EZRA 9–10: NEGOTIATING PERSIAN POWER AND CONSTRUCTING CULTURAL COHESION

The divorce rhetoric both counters and accedes to imperial interests. Ezra 9–10 display this double signification. An imperial political signification reflects the political reality of Persian rule, while a cultic signification offers a counter-narrative.[24]

Three rhetorical moves constitute this political signification. The first constructs the Jerusalem community as constituted by guilt so egregious that they have no moral standing ground but must accept their station under Persian rule. With Ezra's three symbolic acts, the rhetoric sets a dramatic stage.[25] Ezra finally speaks in 9:6 and notes to the audience, "our iniquities have risen above our heads." In Ezra 9:7, the rhetoric proceeds with the guilt motif but with added temporal and spatial dimension. Beginning with the phrase "From the days of our ancestors...," the guilt that was local and referred only to present instances of exogamy becomes transhistorical. The rhetoric claims that from their ancestral beginnings until the present, they have been in "great guilt." Their past indebts them to Yhwh for a history of transgressions so great that their "guilt has expanded to the heavens." The indictment leaves no escape. Punctuated with language of culpability—"guilt" (9:6), "great guilt" (9:7), "iniquity" (9:6, 7), and "unfaithfulness" (9:4)—the rhetoric forecloses on any reprieve from the weight of the guilt. The first move of the rhetoric concludes by directing the proper response to the charge: the people tremble (9:4).

The second move shifts from indictment to punishment. Ezra interprets their situation by referring to the Babylonian destruction, "We," "our kings," and "our priests" "have been given into the hands of the Kings of the lands" (9:7).[26] The rhetoric names the entire community, both the leaders and the people. The verse closes by recalling the temporal dimension of the guilt, "to this day," the *terminus ad quem* to "from the days of our ancestors."

Finally, in Ezra 9:8–9a the rhetorical strategy progresses to communicate imperial expectations—namely, acceptance of their subjugated state and cooperation with imperial rule. The rhetoric recasts their subjugation as "favor." The "favor" is two-fold. First, it refers to their survival as an escaped remnant, that is, "true Israel" over other groups. Second, "favor" refers to the Persian land-grant, most likely tenure to land held by the Second Temple and other aristocrats.[27] In the rhetoric, it is "a stake [lit. tent peg] in this holy place" at the western frontier of the empire.

Just as the rhetoric articulated the proper response to the indictment in 9:4a, "the people trembled," it conveys the people's expected response to what it casts in 9:8–9 as Yhwh's favor. They should accept their lot and view it as an act of Yhwh to "lighten our eyes and sustain us in our enslavement." Moreover, they should cooperate with the Persian program of populating the empire's western frontier and trade routes along the *via maris* with loyal groups. Verse 8 closes and verse 9 opens by reiterating Persian dominion in explicit terms as enslavement. In response to their enslavement, the rhetoric commends to the *golah* the task of constructing a temple in Jerusalem, which it casts as the "house of our God." Both the Persian interest in establishing a loyal urban center in Yehud and the priesthood's interest in encouraging cooperation are apparent.

From the perspective of the Persian authorities, Ezra 9–10 affirm imperial rule, but read as counter-narrative, the rhetoric simultaneously works to undermine Persian authority and supplant it with Yhwh's sovereignty. The same rhetoric both supports and subverts repression.[28] As counter-narrative, the rhetoric uses symbols, personalities, and traditions from ancient Israel's history to disassociate the temple from its imperial origins and ground it in Yhwh's sovereignty. The temple, authorized and funded by the Persians, functioned similarly to other temples in the imperial system as a financial and administrative center. The traditions of David's and Solomon's election by Yhwh legitimated understandings of the Solomonic temple, but the Second Temple was a Persian building project. It symbolized Persian dominion just as other examples of Persian construction throughout the empire. For the Yahwistic community in Jerusalem, an imperially legitimated temple was insufficient. Using symbolic resources—namely, the ability to mediate the power and work of the deity—the rhetoric re-imagines the social world in a way that legitimates priestly authority over imperial dominion.

Ezra's activity in chapter 9 culminates in chapter 10 at the temple. Throughout Ezra's petition and admonition, he does not refer to the temple as a Persian center, but as the "House of God" (9:9; 10:1, 9) When the rhetoric portrays Ezra as carrying out the reforms, it places a priest, not a Persian official as his legitimator. Shecaniah, whose name means "Yhwh dwells," vests Ezra with the authority to carry out a social reordering of the elites in the Persian province. As he admonishes against the exogamous marriages, Ezra repeatedly signifies the marriages as an offense against Yhwh, not the Persian authorities (9:4–6, 8–10, 13–15). In the same way, the Jerusalem community takes its legitimation from historical tradition. The rhetoric's political implications are oriented toward the empire, but its cultic symbolism holds other meanings for the Jerusalem community. These meanings reinterpret the nature of the temple to counter the reality of imperial rule.

For example, Ezra 9:1 begins with deuteronomic rhetoric by invoking the names of the traditional enemies of preexilic Israel, namely the Canaanites, Hittites, Perrizites, Jebusites, Ammonites, Moabites, Egyptians, and Amorites. Deuteronomy raises them as warnings to a group about to enter Canaan and the speeches admonish them not to mix with, but to destroy them. By extension, the rhetoric in Ezra casts his audience as ancient Israel entering the land under Joshua's leadership. These groups are no longer present, but by recalling them the rhetoric establishes a historical connection between the Jerusalem community under Persian dominion and preexilic Israel. Their ancestors failed to heed Moses's admonitions and were exiled. Ezra 9:14 promises that same fate if the marriages are not dissolved. In this way, the rhetoric connects the community in Yehud to the community constructed by their literary traditions, namely, preexilic Israel.

15.4 Imperial Tribute and Community Wealth: Divorces in Nehemiah 10 and 13

Marriage in the ancient world, like divorce, held economic consequences. Its primary functions were procreation along with protection and the orderly transfer of wealth. In this regard, endogomous marriages preserved wealth while exogamous marriages diminished wealth for the Jerusalem community in the imperial system.

Persia's economic relationship to the Second Temple also took the form of a network of exchanges no different than in Babylon and Egypt. In Babylon, the crown supplied the temple at the Eanna at Uruk with tenure to land and enslaved persons.[29] These were not gifts, but investments. In return, the crown expected the temple to use the natural and human resources to produce economic surpluses, which the crown required as a tax or a return on its investment. Persian kings required the temple to pay taxes in kind such as livestock, barley, wine, beer, spices, oil, butter, milk, provisions for state officials, and laborers for royal estates, or in silver. It was not unusual for these taxes to cause temples severe economic hardship or to be forced into debt.[30] In Egypt, the vast temple economies were excellent sources for taxation. The Persians required them to staff and supply the residences of local Persian authorities with lavish material gifts or in-kind support.[31]

Such a policy would have placed great hardship on Yehud and its temple, the center of a relatively small, poor province. Nonetheless, efforts to supply the temple by sending goods from the periphery to the urban center in Jerusalem are evident. As it was under the Babylonians, Persian Yehud operated under a foreign tributary mode of production.[32] Evidence for Yehud's economic developments is scant, but Carter (1999: 250) has shown that by the mid-fifth century, Jerusalem had become the center of several agricultural installations and small villages whose products met the consumption needs of its urban elite. Its wine presses, storage facilities, and olive presses constituted a chain of production of goods as tribute from small villages to Jerusalem. The clear flow of goods and resources from the peasantry to the urban elite attests to differentiation in Yehud's economy. Seals, jewelry, and storage containers not of Yehudite origin evidence the urban elites' participation in the larger imperial economy, particularly in trade with other provinces and Greece.[33] Imperial seals, either as symbols of taxation or the authentication of certain vessels whose contents met the requirements for tribute, indicate the existence of commerce.[34]

Despite its size, Yehud's economy showed evidence of robust participation within the imperial system. Between Jerusalem and outlying areas, the material evidence shows a chain of production of goods that were consumed by the urban elite and traded with other subjects within the imperial system. The presence of imperial seals is evidence that the province's economic activity had developed sufficiently to be taxed by Persian authorities.

From this perspective, since priests also benefited from temple receipts, both the interests of the Jerusalem priesthood and the empire work in tandem. The temple's symbolism for the Jerusalem community notwithstanding, for the Persians it would have been expected to meet a tax burden as would any other temple. Such a requirement would place greater hardship on the temple in Yehud than on larger temples and more affluent provinces such as the ones in Babylon and Memphis. But to meet such a burden, the Jerusalem temple would need to ensure that its devotees maintained tenure to arable land and willingly "tithed" from its produce. In this instance, exogamous marriages diminished the community's wealth by alienating its land tenure.

Similar to Ezra 9, Nehemiah 9 recalls a litany of salvation history beginning with creation and culminating with oppression under Persian rule (9:35–38). In 10:1, the rhetoric calls the people to respond to the repression by agreeing to two provisions of a contract. The first reiterates the admonition not to engage in exogamous marriage. The second calls the community to give silver and in-kind gifts including produce (v.36), livestock (v.37), and wine and oil (v.38) to the temple. These are the same items of tribute that the Persians required of temples throughout the empire. They serve both to meet the temple's obligation to the imperial authorities and to maintain priestly elites in Jerusalem. In Nehemiah 13, the rhetoric is more emphatic. Nehemiah is concerned that the sons of the exogamous marriages no longer speak the language of Judah. Without such a cultural connection they may not continue to support the temple and heritage family land. Absent the community's support, the temple would lose its viability.[35] Nehemiah's urgency in excoriating, beating, and pulling the hair of those in violation of the admonitions reflects this concern.

15.5 Conclusion

When read through the category "historical books," the admonitions against exogamy and the rhetoric of the mass divorces possess a singular meaning. They narrate the return and restoration of the Second Temple community. Recent studies, however, demonstrate that the evidence belies a return, and thus a restoration. Without these as framing devices, the divorce rhetoric possesses a multivalent character and takes on new meanings within the social matrix of Yehud.

In the small province of Yehud, the Second Temple priesthood had few political resources with which to maintain the stability and cohesion of the small Second Temple community, but they made use of the symbolic resources available to any priesthood. In the divorce rhetoric, they recast their lot under Persian dominion as an instance of the deity's favor, and they encourage the community to participate in building the urban center. They also marshaled the deity's anger toward those who refuse to comply. They invoke historical traditions as a way of legitimizing the Second Temple as the "House of God" and not simply a part of the imperial administrative apparatus.

In this regard, in the social world of the small province, return and restoration themselves take on new meanings. By definition, the terms invoke a past existence in the land—a past that the *golah* never experienced. This past, which includes stories of a Solomonic temple, legitimates the new temple as its successor. Similarly, return and restoration legitimate this new community's claim to land in Yehud. They become important concrete and chronological frames to the community's identity. So the divorces, even within the category of historical books, are not diminished by historical research, but are opened to novel meanings. The biblical world and the scholar's world of ancient Israel intersect in new ways and make new claims upon our own world.

Notes

1. Davies 1992: 21–23.
2. Ibid., 16–17.
3. See, e.g., de Saulcy 1868.
4. Halévy 1881; 1885.
5. See Torrey 1896: 238–48, esp. 241.
6. See Lemche 1998 and Davies 1992: 148.
7. See Wellhausen 1895. Martin Noth (1958: 331–32) believed that Ezra's mission attempted to give the religious community in Judah "a new and binding organization since the old tribal federation and its organizations had dissolved...." Klaus Koch (1974) understood Ezra's mission as a means of establishing religious law. For him the divorce rhetoric functioned to make a distinction among the people between the sacred and the profane. David Clines (1984) holds a similar position. J. Maxwell Miller and John H. Hayes (1986: 472) claim that the separatism signified a religious purity. Lester L. Grabbe (1998: 143–50) argues from literary and historical perspectives that the rhetoric indicated a concern for piety and is based on Mosaic Law.
8. Smith-Christopher takes up both archaeological and textual evidence for a sociological and anthropological analysis for the Babylonian and Persian periods. He limits his textual considerations to "biblical texts whose chronological locations in the exilic period have been determined with a reasonable amount of scholarly consensus" (1991: 73).
9. Smith 1991: 76–77. The use of Jeremiah and 2 Kings makes it clear that Smith assumes that those exiled were the same as or at least the descendants of those who returned. While this is often assumed, it is not universally accepted. See, for instance, Davies 1992 and Berquist 1995.
10. Frei and Koch 1996. Frei argues that the empire authorized the Torah.
11. Carter 1999: 201–202.
12. See Lenski 1984: 266–84 and Kautsky 1997: 79–83.
13. B. Becking (2006) has argued convincingly based on literary analysis and archaeological data that the mass return should be described as historical myth. Rather, the evidence shows continuity in the population of the land of Judah during the neo-Babylonian and early Persian periods. The later Persian period shows an increase in population. In an earlier study, Robert Carroll (1992) arrived a similar conclusion based on textual analysis.
14. Both the evidence for remaining settlements in Judah after the Babylonian destruction and the evidence for a gradual increase in population over the course of more than a century belie historical understandings of an exile of all Israel and a mass return.
15. See Marbury 2012: 37–40.

16. Ibid., 42.
17. Ibid., 60–61.
18. For a thorough interrogation of the complexities of identifying the priesthood that might have occupied the temple, see Hunt 2006.
19. See Berquist 2006.
20. These terms are emic designations and apprehend their referents without the surplus of meaning that comes with modern categories. See Carroll 1992: 79–91; Berquist 2006. Ernst Würthwein (1950) argues convincingly for "the people of the land" as landed gentry. But see Fried's (2006: 130) claim that while the referent of the term has generally signified a landed aristocracy, in Ezra 4:4 the term refers to Persian officials.
21. See Berquist 2006:22. Identities are constructed at the nexus of social forces and group perceptions as imagined possibilities only, not as concrete and fixed quantities.
22. See Marbury 2012: 32.
23. Extant records show that former Judahites were relegated in many cases to agricultural labor. See Wunsch 2011: 117. Many of the exiles in Babylon were unable to maintain their former social and economic standing for lack of education or because of the Babylonians' suspicions of their loyalties. Consequently, many were reduced to the status of peasant farmers. See Lemche 1995: 180.
24. Foucault's (2003: 72) counter history is the history of the repressed whose story challenges the sovereign. In the divorce rhetoric, the Second Temple priesthood's resistance to imperial authority appears as a counter history.
25. Ezra rends his cloak, pulls hair from his head and beard, and sits appalled (Ezra 9:3).
26. J. Meyers (1965: 75) argues this phrase refers to the kings of Persia. He cites Clay 1912: 28, n. 6. The first common plural speaks from the perspective of an in-group who identify themselves as "true Israel" and who legitimate their economic and political claims with that understanding (see Becking 2006).
27. See Dandamaev 1974; Hoglund 1992: 238.
28. For a discussion the polyvalent nature of the rhetoric of Ezra-Nehemiah, see Marbury 2012: 304.
29. See ibid., 85.
30. Ibid., 83.
31. Ibid., 37–40.
32. See Gottwald 1992: 84; Yee 1995: 150.
33. See Carter 1999: 257.
34. Carter bases his analysis reports on the number and types of seals from ten sites: Jerusalem, Bethel, Tel en-Nasbeh, Ramat Rahel, Jericho, En-Gedi, Horvat Zimri, El-Jib, Mosah, and Har Adar. Carter divides these into anepigraphic (with either animal or artistic motifs) and epigraphic (with either *Yehud, Moshah,* or *Phw'*). See ibid., 259–68.
35. See Marbury 2012: 305.

Bibliography

Ahlström, Gösta. 1994. *The History of Ancient Palestine*. Minneapolis: Fortress Press.

Albright, William Foxwell. 1946. *From Stone Age to Christianity: Monotheism and the Historical Process*. Baltimore: Johns Hopkins University Press.

Becking, Bob. 2006. "'We All Returned as One!': Critical Notes on the Myth of the Mass Return." In Oded Lipschits and Manfried Oeming, eds., *Judah and Judeans in the Persian Period*. Winona Lake, IN: Eisenbrauns, 3–18.

Berquist, Jon. 1995. *Judaism in Persia's Shadow: A Social and Historical Approach*. Minneapolis: Fortress.

Berquist, Jon L. 2006. "Constructions of Identity in Postcolonial Yehud." In Oded Lipschits and Manfried Oeming, eds., *Judah and Judeans in the Persian Period*. Winona Lake, IN: Eisenbrauns, 53–66.
Blenkinsopp, Joseph. 1998. *Ezra-Nehemiah*. OTL. Philadelphia: Westminster.
Bright, John. 1959. *The History of Israel*. Philadelphia: Westminster.
Carroll, Robert P. 1992. "The Myth of the Empty Land." *Semeia* 59: 79–91.
Carter, Charles E. 1999. *The Emergence of Yehud in the Persian Period: A Social and Demographic Study*. Sheffield: Sheffield Academic Press.
Clay, A. T. 1912. *Business Documents of Murashû*. Publications of the Babylonian Section. Vol. 2. Philadelphia: University of Pennsylvania Press.
Clines, David J. A. 1984. *Ezra, Nehemiah, Esther: Based on the Revised Standard Version*. NCB. Grand Rapids: Eerdmans.
Dandamaev, M. A. 1974. "The Domain-Lands of Achaemenes in Babylonia." *Altorientalische Forschungen* 1: 123ff.
Davies, Philip R. 1992. *In Search of "Ancient Israel."* JSOTSup 148. Sheffield: Sheffield Academic Press.
Eichorn, Johann Gottfried. 1787. *Einleitung in das Alte Testament*. Leipzig: Weidmanns Erben und Reich.
Eskenazi, T. C. and Eleanore P. Judd. 1994. "Marriage to a Stranger in Ezra 9–10." In T. C. Eskenazi and Kent H. Richards, eds., *Second Temple Studies 2: Temple and Community in the Persian Period*. Sheffield: Sheffield Academic Press, 266–85.
Foucault, Michel. 2003. *"Society Must Be Defended": Lectures at the College De France*. Translated by David Macey. Edited by Mauro Bertani and Alessandro Fontana. New York: Picador.
Frei, Peter and Klaus Koch. 1996. *Reichsidee Und Reichorganisation Im Perserreich*. 2nd ed. OBO 55. Fribourg: Universitätverlag.
Fried, Lisbeth S. 2006. "The 'Am Ha'ares in Ezra 4:4 and Persian Imperial Administration." In Oded Lipschits and Manfried Oeming, eds., *Judah and Judeans in the Persian Period*. Winona Lake, IN: Eisenbrauns, 123–46.
Gottwald, Norman K. 1992. "Sociology." In D. N. Freedman, ed., *Anchor Bible Dictionary*, vol. 6. New York: Doubleday, 79–89.
Grabbe, Lester L. 1998. *Ezra-Nehemiah*. New York: Routledge.
Halévy, Joseph. 1881. "Esdras Et Le Code Sacerdotal." *Revue de l'Histoire des Religions* IV: 22–45.
Halévy, Joseph. 1985. "Esdras a-T-Il Promulgue Une Loi Nouvelle?" *Revue de l'Histoire des Religions* XII: 26–58.
Hoglund, Kenneth. 1992. *Achaemenid Administration in Syria-Palestine and the Missions of Ezra and Nehemiah*. SBLDS 125. Atlanta: Scholars Press.
Hoonacker, Albin van. 1890. "Néhémie Et Esdras." *Le Muséon* IX: 151–84, 317–51, 389–401.
Hunt, Alice. 2006. *Missing Priests: The Zadokites in Tradition and History*. Library of Biblical Studies 452. New York: T&T Clark.
Kautsky, John H. 1997. *The Politics of Aristocratic Empires*. 2nd ed. New Brunswick, NJ: Transaction.
Koch, Klaus. 1974. "Ezra and the Origins of Judaism." *Journal of Semetic Studies* 19: 173–97.
Kosters, W. H. 1895. *Die Wiederherstellung Israels in Der Persischen Perioden* [Het herstel van Israel in het perzische tijdvak]. Translated by A. Basedow. Heidelberg: Hörning.
Kuenen, Abraham. 1886. "L'oevre d'Esdras." *Revue de l'Histoire des Religions* XIII: 334–58.
Lemche, Neils Peter. 1995. *Ancient Israel: A New History of Israelite Society*. Sheffield: Sheffield Academic Press.
Lemche, Neils Peter. 1998. *The Israelites in History and Tradition*. LAI. Louisville, KY: Westminster John Knox.
Lenski, G. E. 1984. *Power and Privilege: A Theory of Social Stratification*. Chapel Hill: University of North Carolina Press.

Lipschits, Oded. 2003. "Demographic Changes in Judah between the Seventh and the Fifth Centuries BCE." In Oded Lipschits and Joseph Blenkinsopp, eds., *Judah and Judeans in the Neo-Babylonian Period*. Winona Lake, IN: Eisenbrauns, 323–76.

Magdalene, F. R. and Cornelia Wunsch. 2011. "Slavery between Judah and Babylon: The Exilic Experience." In Laura Culbertson, ed., *Slaves and Households in the Ancient Near East*. OIS 7. Chicago: University of Chicago Press, 113–34.

Marbury, Herbert R. 2012. *Imperial Dominion and Priestly Genius: Coercion, Accomodation, and Resistance in the Divorce Rhetoric of Ezra-Nehemiah*. Uppland, CA: Sopher.

Meyers, J. 1965. *Ezra Nehemiah*. New York: Doubleday.

Michaelis, J. D. 1785. *Üebersetzung Des Alten Testaments Mit Anmerkungun für Ungelehrte*. Göttingen: J. C. Dieterich.

Miller, J. Maxwell and John H. Hayes. 1986. *A History of Ancient Israel and Judah*. 1st ed. Philadelphia: Westminster.

Noth, Martin. 1958. *The History of Israel*. New York: Harper and Brothers.

Saulcy, Felicien Joseph Caignart de. 1868. *Étude Chronologique Des Livres D' Esdras Et De Néhémie*. Paris: A. Levy.

Smith, Daniel L. 1989. *The Religion of the Landless: A Social Context of the Babylonian Exile*. Bloomington, IN: Meyer-Stone Books.

Smith, Daniel L. 1991. "The Politics of Ezra: Sociological Indicators of Postexilic Judaean Society." In Philip R. Davies, ed., *Second Temple Studies I: Persian Period*. JSOTSup 117. Sheffield: Sheffield Academic Press, 73–97.

Smith-Christopher, Daniel L. 1994. "The Mixed Marriage Crisis in Ezra 9–10 and Nehemiah 13: A Study of the Sociology of the Post-Exilic Judaean Community." In T. C. Eskenazi and Kent H. Richards, eds., *Second Temple Studies 2: Temple and Community in the Persian Period*. JSOTSup 175. Sheffield: Sheffield Academic Press, 243–65.

Smith-Christopher, Daniel L. 1996. "Between Ezra and Isaiah: Exclusion, Transformation, and Inclusion of the 'Foreigner' in Post-Exilic Biblical Theology." In Mark B. Brett, ed., *Ethnicity and the Bible*. New York: Brill, 117–42.

Torrey, C. C. 1896. *The Composition and Historical Value of Ezra-Nehemiah*. BZAW 2. Gießen: J. Ricker.

Wellhausen, Julius. 1895. *Die Rükkehr der Juden aus dem Babylonischen Exil*. Nachrichten von der Königlichen Gesellschaft der Wissenschaften zu Göttengen. Göttengen: Philologisch-historische Klasse.

Würthwein, Ernst. 1950. "Amos Studien," *ZAW* 12, nos. 1–2: 10–52.

Yee, Gale A. 1995. "Ideological Criticism: Judges 17–21 and the Dismembered Body." In Gale A. Yee, ed., *Judges and Method: New Approaches in Biblical Studies*. Minneapolis: Fortress, 146–70.

CHAPTER 16

YAHWISTIC RELIGION IN THE ASSYRIAN AND BABYLONIAN PERIODS

RICHARD S. HESS

For the purposes of this article the term *religion* refers to: (1) the service and worship of God or the supernatural; (2) commitment or devotion to religious faith or observance; and (3) a personal set or institutionalized system of religious attitudes, beliefs, and practices.[1] The subject of a specifically *Israelite* religion for present purposes is best defined by temporal and geographical boundaries. Although not mentioned in the biblical texts, the Assyrian king Shalmaneser III mentions fighting King Ahab of Israel as part of a coalition at Qarqar in 853 BCE (COS 2.113A: 263). King Jehu of Israel is also mentioned as paying tribute to this Assyrian ruler in the following decade (COS 2.113F: 270). From the middle of the ninth century BCE, therefore, the Assyrian period, followed by the Babylonian period, extends to the end of the Babylonian Empire in 539 BCE. The end of the Northern Kingdom of Israel (ca. 720 BCE) and of the Southern Kingdom of Judah (ca. 586 BCE) provide important *termini ad quem*. Geographically, the present study focuses on the countries of Israel and Judah, bordered on the north by Tyre and Damascus, on the east by Ammon and Moab, on the south by Edom and the Gulf of Aqaba, and on the southwest and west by Egypt (and its influence in the Sinai peninsula) and the Philistine cities.

In what follows, I consider evidence for religion in this region and time period by reviewing five major sources: biblical, extrabiblical epigraphic, archaeological, iconographic, and onomastic. While even within these groupings there is debate about different types or genres and their interpretation, the five categories themselves provide challenges when attempting to compare and evaluate the evidence between them. It seems best, therefore, to look at the evidence separately in each of these categories before addressing comparisons. Still further, space limitations require selectivity when it comes to the evidence presented and how much analysis and evaluation can be done.[2]

16.1 THE BIBLICAL SOURCES

The parts of the Historical Books of the Old Testament that have *prima facie* relevance for the period described here include 1 Kgs. 16:28–2 Kgs. 25:30 and 2 Chr. 17:1–2 Chr. 36:21. At the beginning of this period King Ahab of Israel (ca. 875/874–854 BCE) married Jezebel, princess of Tyre.[3] This led to the promotion of the state worship of Baal and the installation of four hundred and fifty prophets of Baal (1 Kgs. 18:22). Elijah appears as a prophet of God who predicts drought for the land of Israel, heals and restores to life, and provides food (1 Kgs. 17:1–24). He confronts the prophets of Baal on Mount Carmel and defeats them in a contest between Baal and Yhwh (1 Kgs. 18:20–40). The prophets of Baal are put to death but there is no mention of the fate of the four hundred prophets of Asherah who are also mentioned in the same story (1 Kgs. 18:19).

Many years earlier the first king of the Northern Kingdom of Israel, Jeroboam I, had established the worship of gold calf images at Dan and Bethel (1 Kgs. 12:28–32). These continued under Ahab and his son and successor, Ahaziah. It required no more than nominal assent for the kings to participate in this worship. First Kgs. 19:18 and 2 Kgs. 10:18–23 indicate that the official worship of Baal included bowing towards and kissing the image, and a priesthood distinguished by special garb. Ahab's "asherah," whether that was an image depicting the goddess or some other religious object, remained untouched by Jehu (ca. 841–814/813 BCE), despite his extirpation of the cult of Baal (2 Kgs. 13:6; see Hess 2007b: 250). After injuring himself, Ahaziah consulted Baal-Zebub, god of the Philistine city of Ekron, to determine his fate.

In Judah, the texts of 1 Kgs. 11:5–7 and 2 Kgs. 23:13 suggest that the "high places" (Hebrew *bāmôt*) set up by King Solomon continued in use until Josiah's reform in the late seventh century BCE. These included places of worship for Astarte of Sidon, Chemosh of Moab, and Milkom of Ammon. In addition, the temple of Solomon (1 Kings 6–9) remained present and in use for much of the time until its destruction in 586 BCE. King Jehoshaphat of Judah (ca. 871/870–849/848 BCE) avoided the "high places" that had been erected earlier throughout Judah and used for the worship of various deities. He also drove out religious officials known as the *qĕdēšîm*, a title used at thirteenth-century BCE Ugarit (*qdšm*), which lay just north of Canaan (1 Kgs. 22:46–47 [Heb. 47–48]; Hess 2007b: 251). These latter *qĕdēšîm* may not have been Judeans (Zevit 2001: 462–63).

Jehoshaphat's son Jehoram (ca. 849/848–842 BCE) succeeded him as king. He followed the religious practices of Ahab in the north (2 Kgs. 8:18 = 2 Chr. 21:6). Athaliah, Jehoram's widow and daughter of Ahab, succeeded her husband and continued the religious practices of her parents. In ca. 835 BCE coup brought about Athaliah's death and the coronation of young Joash, sole surviving member of the dynasty of David after the queen's attempt to eliminate that dynasty (2 Kgs. 11:1–21; 2 Chr. 23:1–15). A covenant was made between Judah and Joash and Yhwh, and another covenant between the king and the people of the land. The people destroyed the temple of Baal along with its images, and they put its priest to death (2 Kgs. 11:17–18 = 2 Chr. 23:16–17). There followed a series of Judean kings who are described as doing what was right before Yhwh (Joash/Jehoash, Amaziah, Uzziah/Azariah, and Jotham), reigning from ca. 835 until ca. 735/730 BCE.

Jotham's successor, Ahaz (ca. 735/734 or 731/730 – ca. 715 BCE), introduced a new altar in the temple, removed the great "Sea" (*yām*) and altered some of the temple architecture (see 2 Kgs. 16:10–18; 2 Chr. 28:1–4). He also seems to have constructed high places in the cities of Judah (2 Chr. 28:24–25) and to have passed his son through the fire (2 Kgs. 16:3), which is likely an indication of child sacrifice (Hess 2007b: 252).

When he became sole ruler, the reforms of King Hezekiah of Judah (ca. 716/715–687/686 BCE) removed the high places and the standing stones that were used in worship to deities, as well as the Nehushtan serpent that was worshipped (2 Kgs. 18:1–4). He cleaned out, rebuilt, and re-dedicated the temple of Yhwh with renewed worship of Yhwh (2 Chr. 29:1–36; 31:1–21); he also celebrated the Passover (2 Chr. 30:1–27). When the Assyrian king attacked Judah and threatened the destruction of Jerusalem and the temple, Hezekiah prayed to Yhwh. This led to a great deliverance of Jerusalem and the death of the Assyrian king in his own god's temple (2 Kgs. 18:13–19:37; 2 Chr. 32:1–23). Hezekiah's son and successor, Manasseh (ca. 687/686–ca. 642 BCE), rebuilt the high places, erected altars for Baal, and placed an image of Asherah in the temple of Yhwh along with places for women to sew her garments (2 Kgs. 21:2–7; 23:4–10; 2 Chr. 33:1–9; 34:3–7; see Smith 2003: 113–14 for reflections on the Asherah symbol). Like Ahaz, he burned his son in the fire and practiced various forms of divination. The prohibitions of Deut. 18:10–12 resemble the practice of Manasseh in 2 Kgs. 21:6. Practices of divination and the ghosts and shades produced by such rituals are found in the mention of certain terms like *'ôbôt* and *yiddĕ'ōnîm* (Isa. 8:19; 19:3; 29:4).

The brief reign of Amon was followed by Josiah's (ca. 640–609 BCE). Josiah's reforms, which the text of Kings centers around the discovery of "the book of the law" (ca. 622 BCE), reversed the policies of Manasseh and extended into the area of the former Northern Kingdom, leading to the promise of the female prophet Huldah that Josiah would not see God's judgment during his lifetime (2 Kgs. 22:18–20 = 2 Chr. 34:29–32). Josiah's reforms in 2 Kgs. 23:4–15 provide a summary of the religious life in Judah (and to the north) in the latter half of the seventh century BCE. Josiah removed from the temple objects made for Baal, Asherah, and the host of heaven (v. 4). He also stopped the work of the *kĕmārîm*, cultic officials who burned incense on the high places around Jerusalem and elsewhere in Judah. The *kĕmārîm* worshipped Baal, the sun, the moon, the constellations, and the hosts of heaven (v. 5). Josiah removed the Asherah pole from the temple of Jerusalem (v. 6) and destroyed the house of the religious officials (*qĕdāšîm*, see above) in the temple of Yhwh where the women weavers worked for Asherah (v. 7). He did away with the high places throughout Judah and brought the priests to Jerusalem (vv. 8–9). Josiah also ended the human sacrifice to Molek in the Valley of Ben Hinnom by doing away with the Topheth there (v. 10). He removed the horses and chariots that had been dedicated to the sun and stood at near the entrance to the temple (v. 11). Josiah desecrated the high places that Solomon had built centuries before for Ashtoreth, Chemosh, and Molek (v. 13). The altar at Bethel where Jeroboam I had situated the gold calf and where he had caused the Northern Kingdom of Israel to worship was torn down. Josiah burned the high place and the Asherah pole, and ground all of it to dust (v. 14). While the tomb of the prophet who had come from Judah to speak against Jeroboam I was left untouched (see 1 Kgs. 13:1–32), all the graves of the prophets of Bethel were opened and their bones burned on the altar there (vv. 15–18). Josiah continued his reform as far north as the region of Samaria, where he removed all the high places, killed all the priests associated with high places, and burned their bones on the altar. Josiah also celebrated the Passover, to an extent greater than Hezekiah and not seen since the time of the prophet Samuel (2 Kgs. 23:21–23 = 2 Chr. 35:1, 18–19).

The eighth-century kings of the Northern Kingdom had continued the policies of their predecessors. The most politically successful of these was Jeroboam II (coregent, ca. 793/792–782/781 BCE; sole ruler, ca. 782/781–753 BCE). He continued the religious policies of his predecessors (2 Kgs. 14:23–29). These practices were the subject of prophetic ire in eighth-century Israel, especially as reflected in the books of Amos and Hosea. The continuation of these condemned practices in the north lead to the Assyrian invasion of Israel and its destruction ca. 722 BCE. The deportation that followed, along with the resettlement of the area with adherents to non-Yahwistic religions, as well as the continued representation of the old priesthood established by Jeroboam I, brought further condemnation and the sober evaluation of all these developments in 2 Kings 17—which was also a clear warning to Judah.

Following the untimely death of Josiah in 609 BCE, succeeding kings in Judah turned from their immediate predecessor's practices and followed policies not unlike Manasseh's (2 Kgs. 23:31–24:20; 2 Chr. 36:1–13); a fact confirmed by the prophecies of Jeremiah. In 587 and 586 BCE, the Babylonian army laid siege to Jerusalem, destroyed its defenses and the temple of Yhwh, and took its king and many of its people captive to Babylon (2 Kgs. 25:1–21). Judah became a province of Babylon with its own governor, who however, was soon murdered, leaving the remainder of the leadership to flee to Egypt (2 Kgs. 25:22–26). An earlier successor to Josiah, Jehoiachin, had been deported to Babylon where he was elevated from prison and raised to a position of honor at the table of the Babylonian king (2 Kgs. 25:27–30).

As supporting written sources for the Historical Books, we can consider the prophetic books that claim to date from this time. The chief prophetic books are Isaiah (especially chs. 1–39) and Jeremiah. From these we learn that prophets of Judah received visions (e.g., Isa. 6:1–13); performed symbolic acts that they used to proclaim their messages (e.g., Isa. 20:1–6); announced judgments against nations (Jeremiah 46–51) and individuals that included punishments of death (Jer. 28:16–17), predicted the future (Isa. 41:21–29), and indicted the wealthy (Isa. 3:16–24; 5:8–10) and authorities (Isa. 10:1–4) such as the king (Jer. 13:18) and the priests with their cult (Isa. 28:7–13). These prophets were frequently persecuted (Jer. 20:1–2). Though they appeared in the royal court and in the temple—along with locations removed from both of these—the biblical prophets distinguished themselves from many of the prophets related to royal courts, the so-called "court prophets." These latter could be found at eighteenth-century BCE Mari, in the neo-Assyrian empire, and in Israel and Judah (see 1 Kgs. 18–19; 22:10–23; 2 Kgs. 10:19; 2 Chr. 18:1–22; Jer. 23:9–31; 50:36), as well as elsewhere (see Nissinen 2003). For Isaiah, Jeremiah, and other writing prophets (as well as Elijah and Elisha), the major difference from court prophets lies in their confrontation with royalty and power centers in the state, and their indictment and judgment of the same.

Hosea wrote and prophesied against the Northern Kingdom of Israel in the mid-eighth century BCE. He addressed a variety of interpretations regarding Yhwh and religion in Israel (Hess 2007b: 255–56). Offerings and festivals to Baal and groups of baals were celebrated (Hos. 2:13–17 [Heb 15–19]); men practiced this worship with female participants (*qĕdēšîm* and *zōnôt*) who functioned as prostitutes; calf images were connected with deities at Beth Aven and paid as tribute to Assyria (Hos. 10:5–8). Hosea 13:1–2 connects the adoration of a silver calf image with Baal and with death. This may point to Israel's earlier participation at Baal Peor (Hos. 9:10) and to Baal's death and resurrection as remembered in myths from the thirteenth-century BCE. West Semitic city of Ugarit (Day 2000: 120).

Amos prophesied at a time close to that of Hosea. According to the book of Amos, there were multiple altars for various deities in Israel with fathers and sons visiting prostitutes there (Amos 2:7–8). A meal with much music, drinking, and food is condemned due to its use for exploitation of the poor (Amos 6:3–10). As in Jer. 16:5–9, this feast seems to describe a *marzē(a)ḥ*, a feast that has associations at Ugarit and elsewhere with religious contact with deities and with the dead (see Hess 2007b: 110, 256).

The prophet Micah wrote a few decades later and addressed his words to the Northern Kingdom of Israel and to the Southern Kingdom of Judah. In the north, Samaria worshipped images of various sorts and paid prostitutes fees (Mic. 1:6–7). Mic. 5:10–14 (Heb. 9–13) looks forward to a time without witchcraft, images, and asherah poles.

Child sacrifice is assumed in Mic. 6:6–7 and seems to have continued throughout this period (see Ezek. 16:20–21, 36; 23:37–39; Hess 2007b: 257). Not only does Kings associate this practice with several rulers, it is also mentioned in Ps. 106:37 as something that took place in Israel. Jeremiah 19:4–6; 32:35; and Ezek. 20:25–31; 23:37–39 are texts that attest to the practice of child sacrifice and the prophetic critique of it. Finally, in the catalogue of peoples resettled in Samaria after 722 BCE, 2 Kgs. 17:31 includes mention of the Sepharvites, who are said to have burned their children in fire as sacrifices to their gods.

Egypt, Mesopotamia, and Israel/Judah planted and dedicated gardens to their deities. In the summer special gardens were dedicated to a deity known as Adonis in Greek (in Semitic, this name means "[my] lord"). Evidence for this is found in Isa. 17:10–11 where the epithet *nʿmn*, "pleasant (one)," that is often used for this deity also appears (see Mettinger 2001: 125–28, 146–54, 211). Adonis is a god who left the world during the dry summer season, but returns in the winter when the rains come back. He should be identified with Tammuz for whom the women wail in Ezek. 8:14, and was originally Dumuzi in Sumerian myths from the third millennium BCE. In these stories, the deity goes to the underworld and thereby brings on the dry season, only to return at the beginning of the wet (winter) season. Also known as Baal in Ugarit in the thirteenth century, by the early centuries of the common era this deity was remembered as resurrecting each year with the return of the rains and the vegetation cycle. His officiants worshipped gold, silver, and other images (Isa. 2:6–11). Many other descriptions of similar dying-and-rising cult practices may be alluded to throughout the book of Isaiah (Hess 2007b: 259–60). Isa. 57:5–13 describes an array of religious rituals, and Isa. 65:3–11 and 66:17 outline offerings of pig's blood with pork dinners and three-day old meat (cf. Lev. 7:18; 19:17). Such rituals may be associated with Adonis and with underworld (chthonic) cults and fertility deities. Alternatively, Smith (2001: 120–29) has argued that Baal is not a dying and rising god but a "disappearing god" who returns without rising from death.

Jeremiah is a prophet whose messages appear at the end of the history of Judah. At the time people are said to be worshipping wood and stone (Jer. 2:27–28); this may refer to Baal and Asherah (though with their characteristic symbols reversed). People are also said to have placed despicable things in the temple of Yhwh (Jer. 7:30–32) and to have burned incense on altars to Baal. Some texts identify a cult to the Queen of Heaven, probably the

West Semitic goddess Astarte (Jer. 7:17–18; 44:3, 15–19; Hess 2007b: 99). This cult involved baking cakes, pouring libations, and burning incense. Like the rooftop installations that Josiah removed from the palace, Jer. 19:12–13 and 32:29 describe the burning of incense and pouring of libations on roofs to worship astral deities and other divinities.

The book of Ezekiel is set in the exilic period, but ch. 8 provides a tour of non-Yahwistic cultic practices in the temple before the fall of Jerusalem (see Hess 2007b: 263–64). Ezekiel portrays the worship of various images of deities there, along with rituals for Tammuz and the worship of the sun. Ezekiel. 14:3–4, 7–8 refer to these images as *gillûlîm*. This term is used elsewhere for "dung balls," so it is clearly derogatory in tone. Ezekiel 16 was mentioned earlier in relation to child sacrifice. In this case, the cultic act is done with reference to symbols of male deities. Ezekiel. 43:7–9 describes offerings made to royal ancestors and may also describe prostitution.

While the religion found in the biblical texts outlined above has been described as widespread and nationalistic (see Hess 2007b: 266–68; Albertz and Schmitt 2012: 387–429; Niditch 2015), religious practices in the smaller sphere of the immediate family also occurred. Amos 6:10 records how the oldest living member of the family, the *dōd*, represented the family in their cult. While there may have been annual sacrifices for the family (1 Sam. 1:18), feasts such as the Passover seem to have had the family as a focus from the beginning (see Exodus 12). The biblical text also describes Sabbath observance (Jer. 17:21–27), male circumcision (Gen. 17:23–27), the naming of children, and prayers of various sorts as important religious acts. Deut. 26:14 and its rejection of food offerings for the dead prohibits presenting these sorts of sacrifices at family tombs. The prohibition itself suggests that practices of this type were occurring. There has been much discussion of images known as *tĕrāpîm*, which may also relate to the realm of family religion (see, e.g., 2 Kgs. 23:24). The absence of explicit biblical equations of these figures with deceased ancestors has led Johnston (2002: 188) to deny this association. On the other hand, van der Toorn (1996: 218–25) has argued in favor of the connection, noting the relationship of *tĕrāpîm* and deceased ancestors in West Semitic contexts.

16.2 Extrabiblical Texts

Among extrabiblical written texts, an important work is Eusebius of Caesarea's *Preparation for the Gospel*. This text uses Philo of Byblos and Philo's own citations of a priest from many centuries earlier, who referred to the creation of the gods and the worship of deities who were originally human beings and who invented or did something of great value for their nation or for humanity as a whole (i.e., a kind of euhumeristic account of religion; see Hess 2007b: 269).

Of greater interest and use are the inscriptions found in and around the land of Israel that have something to do with religious matters (Hess 2007b: 274–90). The ninth century sees the earliest extrabiblical inscriptions form the region that address matters related to religion. Foremost is the Mesha inscription of King Mesha of Moab. This text recounts his battles with the Northern Kingdom of Israel during the reigns of Omri and Ahab, as well as his royal building projects. There are victories over Israelite towns that include the capture of an "altar hearth(?)" of Yhwh. This is the first extrabiblical and undisputed mention of the divine name Yhwh. This is the only deity that Mesha mentions in relation to Israel and the only one he knows as a god associated with that nation.

At the north Sinai site of Kuntillet ʿAjrud, which was perhaps something like a caravansary dating from the late ninth or early eighth century BCE, a room with votive offerings that included inscriptions was discovered (Meshel 2012; LeMon and Strawn 2013; Naʾaman 2013; Ornan 2016; Aḥituv 2008: 313–29). These texts mention the deities Yhwh, El, Baal, and perhaps Asherah. Different orthographic styles in these inscriptions imply different authors. Baal appears by himself in the texts. He occurs in descriptions related to warfare. The name of El may either describe a general title for a deity or the name of a god who is also known as the chief of the pantheon in the mythology of thirteenth-century BCE Ugarit. Of all the divine names, Yhwh occurs most often. Sometimes Yhwh appears alone and the name is written in a shortened form as also occurs in Hebrew poetry of the Bible. Sometimes his name occurs with Asherah. Yhwh is associated with Teman (the southern desert) and Samaria. A blessing formula that occurs several times at the site is, "I bless you to [or by] Yhwh (of Teman/Samaria) and to [or by] (his) Asherah." Asherah, a goddess who is a partner with the chief Canaanite god El according to Ugaritic mythology, here seems to be associated with Yhwh as the chief Israelite deity.

From approximately the same time period as the Kuntillet ʿAjrud finds, the Jordan Valley site of Tell Deir Alla yielded collections of plaster fragments that originally formed a text on the walls of what may have been a cult center (Aḥituv 2008: 433–65). Neither the religion of this center nor the language represented by the inscription can be easily identified. The texts describe a vision of "Balaam son of Beor," also known from the biblical book of Numbers, in which natural aspects of the world seem to be turned upside down. There is reference to a group called the Shaddayin. These are a group of spirits or deities who may be related to El Shaddai, a title for God that occurs in Genesis and Job.

From ca. 800 BCE a small pomegranate-shaped ivory contains an inscription that could be reconstructed as, "Belonging to the Temple of Yhwh, holy to the priests" (Hess 2007b: 276–78). Debate continues about the dating of the inscription on the pomegranate and especially the patina that covers the letters. If authentic, the inscription would be the only text from the temple of Yhwh in Jerusalem before 586 BCE.

Like the writings at Kuntillet ʿAjrud, texts inscribed on the walls of Khirbet el-Qom in southern Judah also mention Yhwh and Asherah (Aḥituv 2008: 220–33). Eastward from Khirbet el-Qom along the west coast of the Dead Sea, a cave overlooking Ein Gedi contains an inscription dated to ca. 700 BCE. The text identifies Yhwh as blessed and as the ruler of nations. The epithet, "my lord," appears. Approximately contemporary with this text there are several texts from the Judean burial site at Khirbet Beit Lei (about five miles east of Lachish). These describe Yhwh as sovereign over Jerusalem and probably Judah. A possible interpretation of one of the prayers asks that Yhwh absolve, and presumably the object is the author.

Ostraca are pieces of pottery that have been reused in order to compose notes and letters. The Judean fortresses of Lachish to the west and Arad to the south have yielded dozens of these ostraca, mostly dating from the period before the Babylonian conquest of the land in 586 BCE (Aḥituv 2008: 56–154). Many of these texts provide records of official correspondence between the forts and military leaders in Jerusalem. Just as with correspondence we might write today, these ostraca contain standard literary forms, such as introductions. An example of such a greeting is, "May Yhwh cause you to hear peaceful and good news." Regularly and exclusively, Yhwh is the only deity who receives mention. In lines 7–9 of

Lachish ostracon 5 an additional religious reference occurs: "May Yhwh show you a successful harvest today." On the basis of these texts, it seems clear that, in the final decades of the independent Judean state, military leaders recognized only one deity as lord over the harvest and the nation's agricultural production.

A few miles east of Lachish one finds the burial cave of Khirbet Beit Lei. From ca. 700 BCE several inscriptions have been recovered and studied (Aḥituv 2008: 233–36). While there is disagreement regarding the precise readings of these texts, there is general agreement that they describe Yhwh's control of Jerusalem as its sovereign deity.

Southwest of Jerusalem during this period lay the burial cave at Ketef Hinnom (Barkay et al. 2004; Aḥituv 2008: 49–55). In 1979, two small silver scrolls were discovered in excavations of tombs dating from the decades before the destruction of the city. These scrolls preserve parts of the blessing of Aaron as found in Num. 6:24-26. The texts also mention the Hebrew terms for "covenant" (bĕrît) and "covenantal love/faithfulness" (ḥesed) and express hope of salvation from "the evil." God is described as helper, rock, and the one who rebukes "the evil."

From this brief survey it is apparent that more deities appear in earlier inscriptions. Asherah, Baal, El, and the Shaddayin appear in addition to Yhwh in the eighth-century BCE evidence connected with both the north and the south. Even here, however, Yhwh is a dominant figure and at times the only deity mentioned. This latter situation is the one that obtains in the only foreign inscription to mention a deity in Israel, the ninth-century Mesha of Moab stela. In this text, Yhwh's name appears as the only deity connected with Israel, and he is associated with a cult object. After 722 BCE and the end of the Northern Kingdom of Israel, Yhwh alone receives exclusive mention in the south, in the inscriptions from Judah. There he is associated with the idea of covenant, with ḥesed, with blessing, and with sovereignty over Jerusalem and possibly Judah and other nations. He rebukes and absolves from evil, provides deliverance, is pictured as a rock, and gives the land its fertility.

16.3 ARCHAEOLOGY

Archaeological remains from the period under study address religion in three general areas: architecture, altars, and objects. The first two are exemplified by two key sites, Tel Dan in the north and Tel Arad in the south. Beginning with Dan (see Biran 1994), at the main Iron Age gate area, both outside in the plaza and within the walls of the town, there are standing stones, often associated with the special veneration of divine figures. These appear in small groups. At the highest point on the Tel was the cult site proper; its development is attributed to Jeroboam I and it remained in use up until and even after the Assyrian conquest of Dan ca. 734 BCE. The construction includes a large raised area with a monumental series of stairs (added in the eighth century) that approached it from the south. There is a nearby three-room structure with a stone altar, ash pit, and some iron shovels that were also found there. The stone "horn" that remains from a large horned altar was itself twenty inches high. This may have stood on the platform that may have measured twenty feet square and resembled the one described in Ezekiel 43 (King and Stager 2001: 328-30). By the eighth century the platform was 62 feet by 26 feet, and could easily have accommodated the gold calf attributed to Jeroboam I (see 1 Kgs. 12:26–30).

At the southern end of the country, Tel Arad preserves a Judean fort that was active throughout the period under consideration (see Herzog 2002). The ostraca from the gate area have already been noted. A significant part of this fort contains the remains of a regional cult center. Although the specifics of the chronology and the archaeological strata are debated, it is likely that the three-room sanctuary here was active for most of the ninth and eighth centuries BCE. For much of this time an altar of field stones stood in the outer courtyard. With its plastered top and flint slab for the burned offering to rest upon, the fieldstone altar reflected a religious practice possibly connected with Exod. 20:24–26. The niche (the third "room") within the inner room contained two standing stones and two incense altars, possibly reflecting the worship of two deities.

At the nearby site of Beersheba a large horned altar had been disassembled and reused as part of a wall. This construction suggests a cult center here, as well. Many horned altars were also found at Tel Miqne (biblical Ekron) from the seventh century BCE. Located within the areas where some one hundred olive oil production installations were placed, this suggests a connection between the industry and the worship of deities. Six miles south of Arad at Qitmit and Ein-Hazeva are indications of cults dedicated to the Edomite god Qos from the late seventh or early sixth century BCE. This suggests the presence of Edomite incursions at the end of the period of Judah's independence.

About four and a half miles west of Jerusalem is the site of Tel Moẓa. The excavators have uncovered there the remains of a large building from the ninth century BCE (Iron Age IIA) which they identify as a temple (Kisilevitz 2015). They also found fragments of horse and rider figurines as well as other small items associated with the cult. If this is a temple it would be a remarkable find, given its location, in close proximity to Jerusalem, and its date, in the early period of the monarchy. Biblical associations with high places (cf., e.g., 1 Kgs. 3:4–5) may echo the archaeological picture found here.

Burials represent a separate category within the context of the archaeology of religion. Bloch-Smith (1992; 2002) has demonstrated continuity among major kinds of burials in and around Israel and Judah during the Iron Age. The bench tomb type gains ascendancy at Jerusalem and throughout Judah. From the late eighth century BCE there is no parallel in terms of the prominence of this type of tomb, which is used almost exclusively in Jerusalem (Bloch-Smith 1992: 137, 142). More than other types of tombs, this one emphasizes the burial together of families and of generations. After the body of the most recent burial had decomposed on the stone bench in the tomb, the bones were collected and deposited alongside the bones of other deceased family members in recesses in the tombs.

16.4 Iconography

The significance of the drawings on the large pot sherds found at Kuntillet ʿAjrud, dating to the ninth century, is debated. The two standing figures and one seated lyre player that appear alongside the blessing formula to Yhwh and "his Asherah" may or may not represent figures connected with those two deities (LeMon and Strawn 2013; Naʾaman 2013; Ornan 2016). There is, however, general agreement that the two who are standing appear as the Egyptian deity Bes, a ubiquitous figure who is often found in apotropaic contexts. The nearby image of a tree may represent the goddess Asherah, a symbol of Yhwh, or be an altogether unrelated and isolated image. Because there is no explicit connection between these images and the written texts, and because many other images of people and of animals occur on the sherds that also contain inscriptions of blessings, it is difficult to know if there is an intentional connection between the pictures and the texts.

In Israel, seal impressions and other sources of images reveal Phoenician influence and themes related to subjects like ostriches and caprids (Keel and Uehlinger 1998: 177–281). In some cases, these animals could be images of worshippers (see Ps. 42:2). The images of the bull in Samaria and of the lion in Judah, along with those of the sun disk, could represent symbols of power and strength, and have associations with deities (cf. the calf images already referred to in the biblical text at Dan and Bethel). This could also be true of the ivories that reflect Egyptian imagery in the north, including possible evocation of deities such as Horus, Re, Isis, and Osiris. In these ivories one finds numerous animal depictions and especially the sphinx, which is composed of aspects of a human, a lion, and an eagle, and that may represent powers of intelligence, strength, and speed as in the image of Yhwh's throne in Ezek. 1:10 and the guardian cherubs around his ark in the Jerusalem temple.

A youthful figure with four wings appears occasionally at Hazor, Gezer, and elsewhere; some have seen this as representing Baal. Along with the sun disk and the lotus in the north, these symbols of regeneration and fertility may point to a deity with similar attributes. At the end of the eighth century BCE and throughout the seventh century, the Assyrian symbols of the lunar disk and crescent moon become popular in the region, and were connected with worship of the lunar deity. Nevertheless, in Judah there is an absence of representations of a male deity. On the seal impressions of the burnt archive in Jerusalem (ca. 587 BCE), there are few images. Rosettes may represent solar imagery associated with Yhwh (see Ps. 84:11 [Heb. 12]).

Many small clay figurines occur in the eighth and seventh centuries in and around Israel and Judah. For example, there are now about five hundred figures of horses, often with riders, which are found in groups. Are these related to the "host of heaven" (2 Kgs. 23:5; Job 38:7; Ps. 33:6; Isa. 40:26) where the disk on some of horses' heads could be an image of a divine sun (2 Kgs. 23:11)? The answer to this question is uncertain.

In the final century of Judah's existence many hundreds of pillar-based figurines occur throughout the land, in both cultic and domestic contexts (Darby 2014). Virtually limited to the region of Judah, these clay figurines occur in several different forms, from a schematic "pinched" face to a more artistic representation of the facial features. Their simple design from inexpensive clay materials does not support the interpretation that they represented a goddess. It is unclear if these figures were minor deities, votive objects, or symbols of prayers for birth and lactation; similarly uncertain is whether they were used by females alone or by both genders.

16.5 Onomastics

There are hundreds of personal names attested in Israel and Judah from this period, both within the Bible and outside of it. These Hebrew personal names often appear with a reference to the name of a deity that forms a part of their construction. As such, these names are frequently designated as "theophoric." Sometimes the personal name is shortened by omission of the divine name. At other times the divine name is substituted by a kinship element, especially *'āb*, the word for "father" (e.g., Ahab). In some cases, an ambiguous term is used, such as *'ēl* (e.g., Nathaniel) which can refer to the specific deity who leads the West Semitic pantheon, El, or to the generic title, "god," which can be used of any deity, including Yhwh.

Ran Zadok (2015) finds that about 43 percent of the personal names from Judah and Israel bear a form of Yhwh's name. This is true of the 101 individual personal names from Mesopotamia and from Syria that Zadok identifies as Israelite and Judean and that are attested in the period under consideration. It is also true of some 163 individuals from the northern and Southern Kingdoms before the fall of Samaria (in the north) and before 701 BCE in the south. All of these names occur in sources outside the Bible. The most extensive study that includes both biblical and extrabiblical names from the ninth through early sixth centuries BCE attests to the overwhelming dominance of Yhwh in theophoric names where the deity can be identified (Albertz and Schmitt 2012). Although not differentiated chronologically, this same study does note the presence of other deities in some of the personal names. The one other divine name that gains any prominence is Baal, which occurs only in names from the Samaria ostraca from Israel during the first half of the eighth century BCE. Even at Samaria, however, the number of Yahwistic names is twice that of Baal names (Zadok 2015: 162).

A study of this and several other major collections of Israelite and Judean personal names (Hess 2007a) has found that the there is a significant development from the north to the south and in Judah itself as time moves forward. By 586 BCE, the burnt archive in Jerusalem attests to the exclusive use of Yhwh in theophoric names. This exclusivity is found only in Judah and is not the case in surrounding nations, such as Ammon, where there is significant attestation of personal names where many deities are represented and where the traditional chief god appears in about six of more than one hundred fifty names with divine elements. Even in the earlier periods of Israel and Judah, the dominance of Yhwh in the personal names has no comparison in contrast to the appearance of national deities at Ammon and elsewhere in their onomastica. A significant and unique religious understanding of Yhwh, therefore, must have played a part in the naming practices of Israelites and Judeans—a practice that does not occur in the onomastic profiles of contemporary and contiguous nations.

16.6 Conclusions

Throughout the period under consideration the Historical Books of the Bible (and other biblical compositions) concur with the extrabiblical written sources at Kuntillet ʿAjrud, Khirbet el-Qom, and possibly the double altars at Tel Arad and some of the drawings at Kuntillet ʿAjrud, as well as a few of the personal names, in attesting to the worship of more than one deity. In addition to the dominance of Yhwh, we find Baal and Asherah as deities who were venerated. Yhwh may thus have been seen by some as the leader of a pantheon of deities, such as the Shaddayin of the Deir ʿAlla texts or of the horse and rider figurines.

Moreover, several biblical texts, especially those mentioning the practice of human sacrifice among the kings of Israel and Judah, worship prior to the reforms of Josiah (2 Kgs. 22–23), and various prophetic texts (e.g., Isaiah 57, 65, 66; Ezekiel 8), explicitly mention worship of deities apart from Yhwh. While some of these texts may have been composed at a time later than the period considered here, their connection with practices and myths attested in the Ugaritic texts and elsewhere suggests some measure of continuity with these extrabiblical expressions of worship and with other deities known from the Iron Age.

At the same time, there was a strong tradition in Israel and especially Judah that recognized a distinctive and at times exclusive role for Yhwh. The Mesha stela designates Yhwh alone as the divinity worshipped in Israel. In addition, several biblical texts (such as those concerning Elijah and Elisha), the descriptions of the reigns of Hezekiah and Josiah, other extrabiblical sources (e.g., the Arad and Lachish letters and the Khirbet Beit Lei and Ein Gedi inscriptions), and the unique and overwhelming attestation of Yhwh in the theophoric elements of the onomastica, all point to a tradition of Yahwistic religious practice that continued throughout the history of Israel and Judah. This tradition practiced the worship of Yhwh alone, apart from any other deity.

The texts, archaeology, iconography, and onomastics attest to a variety of religious practices in Israel and Judah, much of which remain uncertain as to precise nature and purpose. Nevertheless, the attestations of strands of religious practices that included the worship of other deities, of Yhwh as head of a pantheon (with Asherah as his consort?), and of Yhwh alone appear to have existed side-by-side throughout the Assyrian and Babylonian periods in Israel and in Judah.

NOTES

1. See w.merriam-webster.com/dictionary/religion (accessed July 8, 2016).
2. For a comprehensive treatment, see Hess 2007b.
3. For this and all other dates, see Thiele 1983; Hess 2014: 19–21.

BIBLIOGRAPHY

Aḥituv, Shmuel. 2008. *Echoes from the Past: Hebrew and Cognate Inscriptions from the Biblical Period*. Jerusalem: Carta.

Albertz, Rainer and Rüdiger Schmitt. 2012. *Family and Household Religion in Ancient Israel and the Levant*. Winona Lake, IN: Eisenbrauns.

Barkay, Gabriel et al. 2004. "The Amulets from Ketef Hinnom: A New Edition and Evaluation." *BASOR* 334: 41–71.

Biran, Avraham. 1994. *Biblical Dan*. Jerusalem: Israel Exploration Society and Hebrew Union College/Jewish Institute of Religion.

Bloch-Smith, Elizbeth. 1992. *Judahite Burial Practices and Beliefs about the Dead*. JSOTSup 123. Sheffield: JSOT.

Bloch-Smith, Elizbeth. 2002. "Life in Judah from the Perspective of the Dead." *NEA* 65: 120–30.

Darby, Erin. 2014. *Interpreting Judean Pillar Figurines: Gender and Empire in Judean Apotropaic Ritual*. FAT II/69. Tübingen: Mohr Siebeck.

Day, John. 2000. *Yahweh and the Gods and Goddesses of Canaan.* JSOTSup 265. Sheffield: Sheffield Academic.

Gitin, Seymour. 2002. "The Four-Horned Altar and Sacred Space." Barry M. Gittlen, ed., *Sacred Time, Sacred Place: Archaeology and the Religion of Israel.* Winona Lake, IN: Eisenbrauns, 95–123.

Herzog, Ze'ev. 2002. "The Fortress Mound at Tel Arad." *TA* 29: 3–109.

Hess, Richard S. 2007a. "Aspects of Israelite Personal Names and Pre-Exilic Israelite Religion." In M. Lubetski, ed., *New Seals and Inscriptions, Hebrew, Idumean and Cuneiform.* HBM 8. Sheffield: Sheffield Phoenix, 301–13.

Hess, Richard S. 2007b. *Israelite Religions: An Archaeological and Biblical Survey.* Grand Rapids: Baker.

Hess, Richard S. 2014. "Introduction. Foundations for a History of Israel." In Bill T. Arnold and Richard S. Hess, eds., *Ancient Israel's History: An Introduction to Issues and Sources.* Grand Rapids: Baker Academic, 1–22.

Johnston, Philip S. 2002. *Shades of Sheol: Death and Afterlife in the Old Testament.* Downers Grove: InterVarsity.

Keel, Othmar and Christoph Uehlinger. 1998. *Gods, Goddesses, and Images of God in Ancient Israel.* Philadelphia: Fortress.

King, Philip J., and Lawrence E. Stager. 2001. *Life in Biblical Israel.* LAI. Louisville, KY: Westminster John Knox.

Kisilevitz, Shua. 2015. "The Iron IIA Judahite Temple at Tel Moẓa." *TA* 42: 147–64.

LeMon, Joel M. and Brent A. Strawn. 2013. "Once More, Yhwh and Company at Kuntillet ʿAjrud." *Maarav* 20: 83–114.

Meshel, Ze'ev. 2012. *Kuntillet ʿAjrud (Ḥorvat Teman): An Iron Age II Religious Site on the Judah-Sinai Border.* Jerusalem: Israel Exploration Society.

Mettinger, Tryggve N. D. 2001. *The Riddle of Resurrection: "Dying and Rising Gods" in the Ancient Near East.* CBOT 50. Stockholm: Almqvist & Wiksell.

Na'aman, Nadav. 2013. "A New Look at Kuntillet ʿAjrud and Its Inscriptions." *Maarav* 20: 39–51.

Niditch, Susan. 2015. *The Responsive Self: Personal Religion in Biblical Literature of the Neo-Babylonian Periods.* AYBRL. New Haven: Yale University.

Nissinen, Martti. 2003. *Prophets and Prophecy in the Ancient Near East.* SBLWAW 12. Atlanta: SBL.

Ornan, Tallay. 2016. "Sketches and Final Works of Art: The Drawings and Wall Paintings of Kuntillet ʿAjrud Revisited." *Tel Aviv* 43: 3–26.

Smith, Mark S. 2003. *The Early History of God: Yahweh and the Other Deities of Ancient Israel.* 2nd ed. Grand Rapids: Eerdmans.

Smith, Mark S. 2001. *The Origins of Biblical Monotheism.* Oxford: Oxford University Press.

Thiele, Edwin Richard. 1983. *The Mysterious Numbers of the Hebrew Kings: A Reconstruction of the Chronology of the Kingdoms of Israel and Judah.* 3rd ed. Grand Rapids: Eerdmans.

Van der Toorn, Karel. 1996. *Family Religion in Babylonia, Syria & Israel: Continuity & Change in the Forms of Religious Life.* SHCANE 7. Leiden: Brill.

Zadok, Ran. 2015. "Israelites and Judaeans in the Neo-Assyrian Documentation (732–602 BCE): An Overview of the Sources and a Socio-Historical Assessment." *BASOR* 374: 159–89.

Zevit, Ziony. 2001. *The Religions of Ancient Israel: A Synthesis of Parallactic Approaches.* New York: Continuum.

CHAPTER 17

YAHWISTIC RELIGION IN THE PERSIAN PERIOD

MELODY D. KNOWLES

> "You'll have no part with us in building a house for our God. We alone will build, for the LORD, the God of Israel, and Persia's King Cyrus commanded us."
>
> (Ezra 4:3; all translations are the author's)

ZERUBABBEL's rebuff to his fellow Yahwists who offered to rebuild the Jerusalem temple in this portrayal of the early days of the Persian period from Ezra 4:3 highlights key values at play in the production and practice of post-exilic religion—all of which affect the composition and interpretation of the Hebrew Bible's historical books. As the ancient community rewrote and retold their narratives about the past, they were also renegotiating core components of their religion. Even as they "rebuilt" what was, effectively, a new temple, they were also "rebuilding" a new past for themselves in their new context. After the partial return of the nation to the land, "Israel" was now a contested identity claimed by distinct and sometimes rival groups: the returned *golah* ("exile") community, those who remained in various parts of the diaspora, and the "people of the land" who never left. Likewise, assumptions about God's relation to Jerusalem had implications for religious practice and identity both within and outside this confined geography. Where should God have a "house"? And who should be allowed to build it? And what would this "house" in Jerusalem mean for Yahwists worshipping outside of the city or the land? Finally, in this new political context, when God's punishment enacted by the Babylonians had transformed into the possibility of restoration under the Persians, how would divine-human relations be reordered and represented in the language of prayer?

Although the text quoted above has Zerubbabel speaking alone, he was also speaking from one social group to another, with assumptions about the tradition in play, and from a particular geographic location. Anyone who wishes to understand the practice of religion by Yahwists in the Persian period must necessarily consider the juncture of the individual within society and environment, as well as the constant renegotiation with past tradition. In an effort to cover this broad territory within the limits of this essay, I will examine the topic via specific religious enactments that permit access into the various construals of time and place (*pilgrimage* and *pilgrimage festivals*), distinctive and regulated cultic activity (*sacrifice*), and revisions of theological expectations (*the words and postures of prayer*).

As evidence for these various enactments, I will utilize both biblical texts and archaeological finds from the Persian period. For various reasons, using either locus is not entirely straightforward. For example, how accurate is the current scholarly consensus for the identification of the post-exilic strand of the Priestly source in the Torah (P)?[1] And how representative is P for portraying the enacted religious practices of the majority of Yahwists during this time? Or how has the archaeological record been misinterpreted by scholars overly eager to shoehorn finds into pre-extant frameworks of "the biblical world"? Given these issues, in this essay I will be clear about sources and nuanced with conclusions. Core texts from the Hebrew Bible employed in this study include Haggai, Zechariah, Isaiah 56–66, P, 1–2 Chronicles, Ezra, Nehemiah, and Book V of Psalter (i.e., Pss. 107–50). I will also include archaeological evidence such as ancient letters, inscriptions, objects, and building remains in order to produce a clearer picture of the religious practices of this period.

17.1 Pilgrimage and Festivals

The "where" and "when" of religious practice is distinctly manifested in pilgrimage and pilgrimage festivals. Communities express the geographic and calendric profile of their beliefs through annual celebrations at specific places.[2] Prior to the Persian period, legislation in Exod. 23:17, 34:23, and Deut. 16:16 decreed that every male appear "before Yhwh" three times a year for the festivals of Weeks, Tabernacles, and Passover/Unleavened Bread. The biblical text includes some early evidence of regular visits to cult places for festival celebrations, but pilgrimage to Jerusalem did not flourish until the Hasmonean period.[3] Thus, the Persian period is a significant environment for this emerging practice, and there is considerable divergence as norms develop.

Geographically, Yahwism was largely confined to the territories of Israel and Judah in the preexilic period, and the Jerusalem temple was the central shrine after the defeat of the northern kingdom in 722 BCE. The later Babylonian destruction of Jerusalem and the forced migrations of the exile resulted in significant changes, and Cyrus's permission to resettle and rebuild did not simply reconstitute the preexilic past. Indeed, many Persian-period Yahwists remained in Mesopotamia, with traditional geographical attachments signaled by giving new settlements names like "Judahtown" (*Āl-Yāḥūdāia/Āl-Yāḥūdu*) (see Pearce and Wunsch 2014).[4] The city of Jerusalem itself was only sparsely populated during this time.[5]

It is significant that in this context of ongoing diaspora (even once resettlement in Yehud was possible), the archaeological record reveals the existence of temples for the worship of Yhwh *outside* of Jerusalem. Yahwists who migrated to the military colony of Elephantine in Egypt maintained their own temple through the late fifth century.[6] Excavations at Gerizim in the province of Samaria reveal a building built at end of the fifth or beginning of the fourth century, with a plan resembling Ezekiel's description of the Jerusalem temple. Inscriptions on the walls indicate that it was known as "the House of Yhwh" (Magen, Haggai, and Tsfania 2004). There may have also been an additional temple at Lachish.[7]

These factors are critical for properly assessing the claims made for Jerusalem in the biblical text. Yahwists throughout the empire were reformulating their theology and religious practice in the context of rival communities and competing constructions for the worship of Yhwh. So even as the texts describe the reconstitution of Jerusalem's cultic hegemony via the festival calendar, they also witness to the possibilities in play and advocate for their own perspective.

The books of Haggai and Zechariah attest to this diversity of geographic ideology. The people are accused of a lack of concern about rebuilding the temple (Hag. 1:2: "These people say, 'The time hasn't come, the time to rebuild the LORD's house'"). Yet Haggai insists that God wants construction to begin immediately: "Thus says the LORD of hosts...'Rebuild the temple so that I may enjoy it and that I may be honored'" (Hag. 1:7-8). The prophet Zechariah also declares that God has "returned to Jerusalem" and the temple will be rebuilt (Zech. 1:16). The return of exiles from Babylon to Jerusalem (Zech. 6:9-11) inaugurates a movement of future pilgrims (including Gentiles) who will come to worship in at the central shrine: "Many people and mighty nations will come to seek the LORD of hosts in Jerusalem" (Zech. 8:22; cf. 6:15; 8:7-8).

Similarly, Third or Trito-Isaiah (Isaiah 56-66) incorporates eschatology into pilgrimage, although with assumptions and goals that are different than the presentations in Haggai and Zechariah. At points, strands within the text downplay the role of Jerusalem and its temple: "Thus says the LORD: 'Heaven is my throne and the earth is my footstool; what is the house that you would build for me, and what is my resting place?'" (Isa. 66:1). Yet other portions clearly promote the return of the people to city as the future ideal, accompanied by faithful converts (Isa. 56:6-7) and the wealth of the nations: "Your sons will come from far away, and your daughters on caregivers' hips...the nation's wealth will come to you...they will be accepted on my altar" (Isa. 60:4-7; cf. vv. 8-22).

In addition to the presentation in the prophetic texts, pilgrimage and festival observance are also part of this period's narrative representation of the past. Even though the timeframe moves from eschatological expectation to the past, texts like Chronicles, Ezra, and Nehemiah highlight the significance of pilgrimage to Jerusalem even as they exhibit diverse attitudes and purposes for the practice.

The Chronicler accentuates the role of pilgrimage as a religious act that has aspirational political import—namely, the unity of the nation. Although the author holds that the ultimate goal is the permanent residence of the entire nation in the land so that they can worship Yhwh in Jerusalem, pilgrimage to the city is championed as a foretaste of this future *desideratum*. At key points in the narrative, the author considerably develops the accounts of the Passover festivals from the Kings source into significant features of particular reigns. Thus, in the account of Hezekiah's rule, the author inserts a lengthy description of the king's Passover that is not present in the source material (2 Chronicles 30), and substantially enlarges the account of Josiah's Passover (2 Kings 21-23 = 2 Chr. 35:1-19). To emphasize the significance of the celebrations, both accounts record that a very large number of animals were sacrificed (19,000 in 2 Chr. 30:24 and 41,400 in 2 Chronicles 35), and that participants came from both the north and the south (2 Chr. 30:11, 25; 35:19). In the text of Chronicles, such festivals function as strategic venues for aspirational enactments of the future unification of the nation.

In representing the later return to the land after the declaration of Cyrus, the books of Ezra and Nehemiah also employ the celebration of festivals in Jerusalem to describe cultic ideals and mark significant junctures in the nation's history. In Ezra, the initial rededication of the altar in Jerusalem occurs in the context of the festival of Booths (Ezra 3:1-4), a celebration that initiates the re-establishment of regular sacrifice in the land (Ezra 3:5–6). The next major moment in the community's life, the dedication of the re-built Temple, is also commemorated with a festival—that of Passover and Unleavened Bread (Ezra 6:19–22).[8] Bracketing these celebrations are two accounts of the return from Babylon in Ezra 1–2 and 7–8, accounts that are themselves described via pilgrimage imagery: waves of people journey to Jerusalem accompanied by cultic vessels and cultic personnel to deliver offerings and to sacrifice (see Knowles 2004). In Nehemiah, the festival of Booths marks the arrival of Ezra in Jerusalem (Neh. 8:13–18).[9] Throughout the two books, therefore, pilgrimage festivals structure the narrative even as they form the community. Within these two texts, celebrating the ancient festivals in Jerusalem is properly the first act upon return to the land, and the celebration inaugurates the festival calendar for the future.

Similar to the prophetic texts, the book of Ezra also indicates that initial resistance to the act of rebuilding the Jerusalem temple was properly overcome. Although Zerubbabel and his colleagues initiate the project, completion is purportedly delayed by "the people of the land" and other "adversaries" (Ezra 4:1–5). A careful reading of the text reveals that the rebuilding took over twenty years in fits and starts (ca. 539–515 BCE), but this rather leisurely timeline is obscured by a barrage of documentation from throughout the empire. Official correspondence concerning the temple building project is quoted verbatim and read publically (1:2–4; 4:11–16; 17–22; 5:7–17), and the documents themselves refer to searches for other documents (4:19). At points, the larger empire is involved in producing texts about the temple, including Samaria and the larger province Beyond the River (4:7–10; 5:6), as well as several generations of the royal court in Persia (1:2–4; 4:17; 5:13; 6:1–3). The book of Ezra indicates that the delay in building is not due to malaise or a theological misunderstanding of the significance of the Jerusalem temple. Even as the building project floundered after enemy opposition, the empire agitated for its eventual success so that the proper worship of Yhwh in the Jerusalem temple could re-commence.

Outside of the narrative texts, the poetry of the Psalms also highlights and enshrines the practice of pilgrimage to the Jerusalem temple during this period. Within Book V of the Psalter, the "Psalms of Ascents" (Psalms 120–34) include a preponderance of pilgrimage themes (see Knowles 2006: 94–96; more generally Crow 1996). These include a call to the shrine (Pss. 122:1; 132:7; 134:7) as well as an emphasis on Yhwh's connection to Jerusalem (Pss. 122:1, 9; 132; 134:1), agricultural and biological fertility (Psalms 126, 127, 128), and the pursuit of justice (Ps. 122:5). Although it strains the evidence to construe Psalms 120–34 as some sort of cultic-liturgical manual used at the various stages of departure and arrival (see Seybold 1978; Mannati 1979), the texts clearly embrace the concerns of pilgrims and promote the practice as well.

Even as texts such as Psalms 120–34 and the book of Chronicles clearly promote pilgrimage to Jerusalem for festival celebrations, other texts manifest a development of some festivals into decentralized, domestic rites. In earlier traditions, festivals such as Passover and Unleavened Bread are celebrated in the central temple with Levites doing the sacrificing (e.g., Exod. 23:14–17; 34:18–26; Deut. 16:1–17). Later versions, however, describe it as a household ritual, with sacrifice by the laity (Exod. 12:1–28, esp. vv. 3–4, 14–28; see Knohl 1995: 19–45; Johnstone 2003).

As a physical enactment involving both time and space, pilgrimage festivals are an elucidatory feature of religious thought and practice. For Persian-period Yahwists, they are also illustrative of ongoing debate. At times, the rebuilding of the Jerusalem temple and subsequent pilgrimage to the site is heralded as a core tenant of piety and proper worship (Chronicles, Ezra, Nehemiah, Psalms 120–34). Yet the delay in rebuilding as well as full-out opposition (Haggai, Zechariah, Ezra) indicate competing trends for parts of the community. The existence of temples for the worship of Yhwh outside of Jerusalem support this conclusion as well, as does the domestication of key festivals such as Passover. Thus, even as the community reformulated itself in the Persian period, different groups enacted different ritual geographies and calendars.

17.2 Sacrifice

Even as pilgrimage enacts a certain "where" of religious practice, so too does relegating distinctive religious acts to certain areas. In the Persian period, different groups of Yahwists variously linked the sacrifice of animals and incense to specific geographies. As with pilgrimage, texts and archaeological evidence show diversity in the practice of sacrifice as well as development over time. Although some groups wanted to relegate all sacrifice to the Jerusalem temple area, others manifested greater geographical openness.

In the Chronicler's account, sacrifice is properly enacted in the central temple by the Levites: "Aaron and his sons sacrifice on the altar for entirely burned offerings and on the altar for incense…" (1 Chr. 6:49; cf. 2 Chr. 2:4).[10] To promulgate this conviction, the author both expands and suppresses accounts of sacrifice in his reuse of the source text Samuel-Kings. The text contains comparatively fewer notices of sacrifice *outside* Jerusalem, and more *within* the city when compared to Samuel-Kings. Examples of such additions include God's announcement that "I have chosen this place [i.e., the temple] as a house of sacrifice" (2 Chr. 7:12), a designation that is unique in the entire biblical text. The lengthy description of sacrifices at the Passover celebrations of Hezekiah in 2 Chronicles 30 has no parallel in the book of Kings, and (as already mentioned) the account of Josiah's Passover is significantly expanded in 2 Chronicles 35 (2 Kgs. 23:21–23 = 2 Chr. 35:1–19). Examples of the Chronicler's suppression of sacrifice outside the city include the delay (by four generations) of recording the building of a high place for worship and sacrifice outside of Jerusalem from the reign of Rehoboam in Kings to that of Jehoram in 2 Chronicles (1 Kgs. 14:22–24; 2 Chr. 21:11). In addition, the Chronicler does not include the explicit notices of sacrifice at high places in reigns of Joash, Amaziah, and Azariah. Repeatedly, the author insists that the only sanctioned sacrifice was in the central cult in Jerusalem, a cultic hegemony summarized by Sennacherib's description of Hezekiah's reforms: "You must worship and burn incense before only one altar" (2 Chr. 32:12).

Other biblical texts highlight the proper performance of sacrifice within Jerusalem, and condemn the practice outside the city. Third Isaiah censures those who "sacrifice in gardens and offer grain offerings on platforms" (Isa. 65:3). In the books of Ezra and Nehemiah, sacrifice is only enacted within Jerusalem (Ezra 3:3–6; 6:16–18; 8:35; Neh. 12:43–47).

Such geographical exclusivity was not the only attitude adopted by Yahwists during this time, however. Texts and archeological excavations indicate an openness to the use of incense in worship outside of Jerusalem, although the sacrifice of animals is more circumscribed. In Mal. 1:11, for example, God seems to welcome the unrestricted use of incense: "From the rising of the sun to its setting my name is great among the nations, and in every place incense is offered to my name." In addition, small incense altars have been found in Persian-period strata within Yehud and the surrounding regions (see Knowles 2006: 56–59, 67–70). In the province of Samaria, several were found in the capital city, and two bronze incense burners (*thymiateria*) were found in and around tombs at Shechem (Reisner, Fisher, and Lyon 1924: 1:333; 2: pl. 80:a–c; Crowfoot, Crowfoot, and Kenyon 1957: 466, 468, fig. 199.2; Stern 1980). Within Yehud, twelve were found in tombs at Gezer, and an additional one, likely dating to this period, was found at Tell en Naṣbeh.[11] An additional example, inscribed with the Yahwistic name of Mahalyah, was found at Lachish (Aharoni et al. 1975: 5–7).

If one accepts the Persian-period date for the "solar shrine" at Lachish, then the floor drains in the inner most room may indicate the practice of animal sacrifice.[12] In addition, sacrifice at Mount Gerizim is indicated by an inscription referring to "the house of sacrifice" as well as a large amount of (mostly burned) animal bones and ash (see Magen, Haggai, and Tsfania 2004: 1.9 and inscription 199).

The texts from Elephantine in Egypt also illustrate developing protocols for sacrifice in this period. When the temple dedicated to Yhwh at the site was burned down by a rival religious group in 410 BCE, the community wrote to the Jerusalem temple establishment asking for help to rebuild. After three years without a response, they wrote to the governors of Yehud and Samaria. In this later letter, the Elephantine community related that their earlier worship in their local temple included the sacrifice of animals, grain, and incense (*TAD* A4.7.21–22 and A4.8.21, pp. 68, 72). In response, the political authorities instructed that worship continue as it had "formerly," but specifically mention only the sacrifice of grain and incense (*TAD* A4.9.9–10, p. 76). In a later document, members of the community explicitly say that they will disallow the sacrifice of animals in their worship in Elephantine—only incense and grain will be offered in the rebuilt worship space (*TAD* A4.10.10–11, p. 78).

Much like the practice of pilgrimage, Yahwistic sacrifice manifests different and emerging attitudes throughout the Persian period. Similar to Zerubbabel's remark that spoke of clear religious and geographic boundaries within the context of differing assumptions (Ezra 4:3), the texts and artifacts witness to a mix of conventions. Although the Chronicler promotes the relegation of all sacrifice to the city of Jerusalem, other Yahwists enact different attitudes concerning what is permitted outside of Jerusalem.

17.3 PRAYER

At the heart of religion and worship is the practice of prayer. In the textual record from the Persian period, there is a discernable trend that presents characters as religious actors with a rich prayer life. In the biblical narratives, individuals such as Nehemiah and Ezra, speaking in first-person voice, are portrayed as having an individual connection to the deity and turn to God frequently with petitions or praise: "Remember me, my God, concerning this..." (Neh. 13:14; also 4:4; 5:19; 6:9, 14; 13:22, 30; see Niditch 2015). Prayer, however, does not only relate to the individual or interior realm. As the narratives depict both private and corporate prayer, the representation of divine-human relations in texts designed to be read by others are acts of public theology. As the community navigated a distinct political situation, prayer in this period manifests both innovation as well as adherence to traditional forms and assumptions.

Many of the prayers begin to incorporate previously extant sacred texts and traditions into standard forms. For example, the interpretation of authoritative texts in the context of addressing God is a hallmark of this period.[13] Long prayers retell the history of God and the people, often by directly quoting or alluding to earlier texts. In Chronicles, David's song of praise on the occasion of the ark's installation in the tent is a medley of Psalms 96, 105, and 106 (1 Chr. 16:8–36), and Solomon concludes his prayer at the temple's dedication with a close paraphrase of Psalm 132 (2 Chr. 6:41–42).

Such reuse of prior texts often occurs in a devotional genre that emerges during this period: the penitential prayer. This form is related to communal laments such as Psalms 44, 74, and 79, but includes a greater emphasis on historical recital and confession and a diminished role or total absence of the concluding vow of confidence/confidence of being heard. These public prayers (often presented in the context of a national religious festival) include a lengthy confession of the community's sins that connect present failings to a larger story of the nation's sinful past in order to encourage both right action and divine forgiveness.[14]

Examples of this form include Isa. 63:7–64:11 [ET 63:7–64:12], where the ancestor's sins are recounted within a larger story of God's acts of mercy and vengeance: "They rebelled... God fought against them.... Then they remembered earlier times when [God] rescued the people...." Strikingly, the community's sins are attributed to God's own hand: "Why do you lead us astray, LORD, from your ways? Why do you harden our heart so we don't fear you?" (Isa. 63:17). The passage concludes with unresolved questions aimed to spur God to action: "After all this, will you hold back, LORD? Will you keep silent and torment us so terribly?" (64:12). The prayer in Ezra 9:6–15 likewise links the current situation of the community to a national story of sin and neglect of God's law: "From the days of our ancestors to this day we have been deep in guilt" (v. 7). But instead of a request to God for either forgiveness or action, the prayer concludes with an exhortation that the people make a confession and separate themselves from the peoples of the land as well as their foreign wives (10:11). The communal prayer in Neh. 9:5–37 contains similar elements, incorporating texts from Exodus.[15] Reciting God's acts of creation, including the choice of Abram and the events at the Red Sea and Mount Sinai (9:5–15), the prayer confesses the repeated faithlessness of the people: "But our ancestors acted arrogantly.... But they were disobedient.... But they again started doing evil against you... but they acted arrogantly... but they wouldn't listen" (9:16–31). The prayer concludes by connecting the people's past faithlessness and God's mercy to the present day: "You have acted faithfully, and we have done wrong. Our kings, our officials, our priests, and our ancestors haven't kept your Instruction" (9:33–34). In response to this faithlessness, the prayer concludes not with a request for mercy, but rather a covenant. As in Ezra 9, the penitential prayer ends with a pledge "to follow the Instruction from God" (Neh. 10:28), namely to avoid intermarriage, economic transactions on the Sabbath and planting crops in the seventh year, as well as promising regular offerings for the support of the temple (Neh. 10:30–39).[16]

In the shadow of the exile, the recorded prayers of the community link God's people throughout time in a "solidarity of guilt" (Bautch 2003: 72) The canon of memory narrows to a few set events: creation, the choice of Abraham, exodus, wilderness, and settlement in the land. These stories function not as sites for celebration but rather theaters of rebellion.[17] The ancestors are remembered for their sins and represented in the most unflattering light. In the prayer in Nehemiah 9, they are twice accused of "acting arrogantly" (vv. 16, 17)—a relatively rare verb in the biblical text that had just been applied to the misdeeds of the Egyptians only a few verses before (v. 10). In these penitential prayers the bond between the members of the present community and the ancestors is as much transgression as it is biology: "From the days of our ancestors to this day we've been deep in guilt" (Ezra 9:7).

Alongside the actual words uttered and moral universe presumed, prayers in this period were sometimes uttered alongside specific physical objects and in specific postures. The posture of prayer signals humility, supplication, and/or mourning—physical attitudes carried over from earlier practice. At points, prayer is accompanied by bowing down (1 Chr. 29:20; the stance for greeting a king in 1 Chr. 21:21), falling on one's face (1 Chr. 21:16), or kneeling with hands upraised to the sky (2 Chr. 6:13; Ezra 9:5). Confession of sins is associated with weeping (Ezra 10:1), fasting (Neh. 1:4; Zech. 7:5), wearing sackcloth and putting earth on the head (Neh. 9:1), or shaving and tearing the hair and beard (Ezra 9:3)—acts related to mourning (see Job 1:20; 2:12; Josh. 7:6), repentance (see Jonah 3:5, 8), and humiliation (see 1 Chr. 19:4–5).

During this period the concern that the praying body orient itself towards Jerusalem also becomes more prominent. As the place chosen by God (1 Chronicles 21), the faithful embody this divine election. In Solomon's prayer at the dedication of the temple, the Chronicler retains the thrice-repeated direction that those outside of the city direct their prayers towards Jerusalem: "pray toward this house...toward the city that you have chosen...toward their land" (2 Chr. 6:32–39 = 1 Kgs. 8:41–50). The text of Daniel also has the protagonist praying in a room with windows opened towards Jerusalem (Dan. 6:11 [ET 6:10]), and he asserts that "I turned my face to my Lord God" in prayer (Dan. 9:3). Although the archaeological evidence is not conclusive, it is likely that the temple at Elephantine also faced Jerusalem.[18] This concern for the direction of prayer is late manifested in the orientation of synagogues towards Jerusalem.[19]

There is also evidence that worship in this period sometimes involved the use of physical objects in both the public and private cults. Small terra cotta figurines of male and female forms (some riding horses) have been found throughout the Galilee and coastal regions. Their religious use is indicated by the special care taken in their discard—often they were deliberately broken and buried together in a designated pit.[20] At this point, none have been found in Yehud, although some biblical texts mention the non-sanctioned use of *asherot* and signs or altars for Baal (e.g., see the "symbol" in Isa. 57:8; see also 2 Chr. 33:3).

In addition to such figurines, people of this period also continued to use apotropaic objects and protective practices to ward off evil.[21] Similar to archaeological discoveries throughout the ancient world, images of the grotesque figure Bes as well as beads made of colored glass or faience with a dot in the center (the "evil eye") were found in homes, shrines, and graves in Persian-period Yehud and Samaria (Stern 1976; Blakely and Horton 1986). Prayers in the Bible may also evidence "reflexes of apotropaic formulae," including this one from Book V of the Psalter:

> Guard me, O LORD, from the power of the wicked;
> Save me from the lawless ones.

> (Ps. 140:5 [ET 140:4])[22]

In addition, there may be references to the "evil eye" in texts such as Prov. 6:20–22; 23:6–8; Eccl. 4:4–8 and Sir. 34:12–13 (Miller 1970; Wazana 2007; Spieckermann 2009).

In the performance of prayer, the extant texts and physical objects from the Persian period portray a community keen to maintain contact with God. As the various groups responded to their present in prayer, they maintained aspects of their tradition even as they innovated new forms of devotion.

17.4 CONCLUSION

As Yahwists renegotiated their tradition in the context of loss and renewal in the Persian period, they brought their inherited understandings of worship, theology, and religious personhood into a socio-political context very different from that of their forebears. Whether in Egypt, Mesopotamia, Samaria, and Yehud, Yahwists throughout the empire reformulated their theology and religious practice. Even as the ritual norms and narratives of the ancestors continued to hold sway, they were interpreted differently by groups of Yahwists in different locales. Thus, while some Yahwists continued to pray while bowing down or kneeling, others began to adopt the genre of penitential prayer. As some continued to offer up to Yhwh sacrifices of incense, others relegated animal sacrifice to Jerusalem alone. And as some advocated for pilgrimage to Jerusalem as the norm, others worshiped at different cult sites. Beyond the geographically specific practices that were often unique to a certain locale, it can be said more generally that post-exilic piety and practice both reflected and influenced core understandings of personhood, communal identity, the experience of time, and the construal of space. Reading the extant texts from this period adequately requires an openness to the likelihood of competing practices and confessions that were in play among different communities of loyal Yahwists.

NOTES

1. For discussions of the contents and dates for P, see, e.g., Knohl 1995; Römer 2008; Shectman and Baden 2009.
2. It is interesting to note the emergence of personal names related to the noun "festival" (ḥg) during this time, including the prophet Haggai in the Bible (Hag. 1:1, 3, etc.; Ezra 5:1; 6:14), as well as related names in the Yahwistic community of "Judahtown" in Babylon that are found in Pearce and Wunsch 2014: ᵐḫa-ga-a the son of Mataniā (a Yahwistic name; text 37:4 dated to 512 BCE) and ᵐḫa-ag-ga-a in text 29:19 (508 BCE) and text 30:5, 8, 10 (507 BCE). See also names such as ḥaggah found at Murashû in Nippur ca. 450–400 BCE listed in Coogan 1976: 23.
3. For the earlier history of pilgrimage, see Merrill 1973–74. For later manifestations, see Safrai 1981, and, more fully, Knowles 2006: 77–103.
4. Additional evidence concerning Yahwists in Mesopotamia in the sixth–fifth centuries comes from the Musashû archive. See Stolper 1985; Stolper and Donbaz 1997; and Joannès and Lemaire 1999: 16–34.
5. For a summary analysis as well as different reconstructions, see Ussishkin 2006: 147–66; and 2012.
6. For the texts found at Elephantine, see Porten and Yardeni 1986–99.

7. Designating the "Solar Shrine" at Lachish as Yahwistic is on the basis of architectural similarities with the temple at Arad, as well as the Yahwistic name inscribed on an incense altar: "Ya'ush son of Mahalyah." See Aharoni et al. 1975: 5–7.
8. For more on the Passover celebration within Ezra, see Becking 1999: 256–75, especially his claim that Ezra 3–6 is best summarized by the title "the abolition of the non-celebration of the Passover festival" (270).
9. It may be that the celebration was not limited to Jerusalem only, although this certainly fits the preponderance of the evidence. According to Neh. 8:17–18, Ezra read the law *to the celebrants*, a point which assumes a community gathered together in one place. And in Neh. 8:15–16, the people went out and "brought" branches (hiphil of *bw'*), another detail suggesting a central location. Finally, given that all the specific places named (i.e., the courts at the house of God, the square at the Water Gate, and the square at the Gate of Ephraim) are in the city, it is likely that the other places without a specific address (i.e., roofs of houses and courts) are in the city as well.
10. In the Chronicler's account, other sites for worship and sacrifice such as Gibeon (1 Chr. 21:29; 2 Chronicles 1) are legitimate only before the Jerusalem temple is built.
11. For the finds at Gezer, see Macalister 1912: 2.442–45, figs. 524–26; 3.225.9; 1.357–58, fig. 185 (tomb 147); 1.358; 3.107.2 (tomb 153); 1.363 (tomb 156); 1.371; and 3.114.1a–d (tomb 176). For the find at Naṣbeh, see Zorn 1993.
12. The Persian period date is argued by Starkey 1937: 171–79; Stern 1982: 61–63; and Ussishkin 2004: 1.95–97. For the floor-drains themselves, see Tufnell 1953: 141 and pl. 121.
13. As Werline (1998: 108) puts it, "prayer and the interpretation of authoritative texts have become the method for understanding and responding to Israel's sins and the people's recurring political crises." See also Newman 1999.
14. For studies of both the genre as well as the ceremonial context, see Boda 1999; and Bautch 2003.
15. For a detailed study of the sources and allusions in Nehemiah 9, see Pröbstl 1997; Boda 1999: 89–187; Newman 1999: 77, 79, 88–92.
16. For a discussion of Zechariah's sermons as additional examples of penitential prayers, see Boda 2005: 49–69.
17. This is in contrast to non-penitential recitals found in texts such as Pss. 44:1–8 and 74:12–15.
18. As argued by Porten 1961: 38–42.
19. For a helpful chart indicating those synagogues in the Diaspora with the Torah shrine orientated toward Jerusalem, see Hachlili 1998: 27.
20. For an overview of the finds, see Kletter 1996; Stern 2001: 490–507.
21. For a recent study, see Elliott 2015.
22. See also Psalm 91 and Ps. 12:7–9 [ET: 2:7–8], as well as the article by Smoak 2010: 421–32, esp. 427.

Bibliography

Aharoni, Yohanan, et al. 1975. *Investigations at Lachish: The Sanctuary and the Residency*. Lachish V. Publications of the Institute of Archaeology 4. Tel Aviv: Gateway Publishers.
Bautch, Richard J. 2003. *Developments in Genre between Post-Exilic Penitential Prayers and the Psalms of Communal Lament*. AcadBib 7. Atlanta: SBL Press.
Becking, Bob. 1999. "Continuity and Community: The Belief System in the Book of Ezra." In Bob Becking and Marjo C. A. Korpel, eds., *The Crisis of Israelite Religion: Transformations of Religious Tradition in Exilic and Post-Exilic Times*. OTS 42. Leiden: Brill, 256–75.
Blakely, Jeffery F. and Fred L. Horton, Jr. 1986. "South Palestinian Bes Vessels of the Persian Period." *Levant* 18: 111–19.
Boda, Mark. 1999. *Praying the Tradition: The Origin and Use of Tradition in Nehemiah 9*. BZAW 277. Berlin: de Gruyter.

Boda, Mark J. 2005. "Zechariah: Master Mason or Penitential Prophet?" In Rainer Albertz and Bob Becking, eds., *Yahwism after the Exile: Perspectives on Israelite Religion in the Persian Era*. STR 5. Assen: Royal van Gorcum, 49–69.

Coogan, Michael David. 1976. *West Semitic Personal Names in the Murashû Documents*. HSM. Cambridge, MA: Scholars Press.

Crow, Loren D. 1996. *Songs of Ascents (Psalms 120–134): Their Place in Israelite History and Religion*. SBLDS 148. Atlanta: Scholars Press.

Crowfoot, J. W., G. M. Crowfoot, and Kathleen M. Kenyon. 1957. *The Objects from Samaria*. London: Palestine Exploration Fund.

Elliott, John H. 2015. *Beware the Evil Eye: The Evil Eye in the Bible and the Ancient World*. Vol. 1: *Introduction, Mesopotamia, and Egypt*. Eugene, OR: Cascade.

Hachlili, Rachel. 1998. *Ancient Jewish Art and Archaeology in the Diaspora*. HdO 35. Leiden: Brill.

Joannès, F. and A. Lemaire. 1999. "Trois tablets cuneiform è onomastique ouestsémitique (collection Sh. Moussaieff [Pls, I–II])." *Transeu* 17: 16–34.

Johnstone, William. 2003. "The Revision of Festivals in Exodus 1–24 in the Persian Period and the Preservation of Jewish Identity in the Diaspora." In Rainer Albertz and Bob Becking, eds., *Yahwism after the Exile: Perspectives on Israelite Religion in the Persian Era*. Assen: Royal van Gorcum, 99–114.

Kletter, Raz. 1996. *The Judean Pillar-Figurines and the Archaeology of Asherah*. Oxford: Tempus Reparatum.

Knohl, Israel. 1995. *Sanctuary of Silence: The Priestly Torah and the Holiness School*. Minneapolis: Augsburg Fortress.

Knowles, Melody D. 2004. "Pilgrimage Imagery in the Returns in Ezra." *JBL* 123: 57–74.

Knowles, Melody D. 2006. *Centrality Practiced: Jerusalem in the Religious Practice of Yehud and the Diaspora in the Persian Period*. SBLABS 16. Atlanta: SBL.

Macalister, R. A. Stewart. 1912. *The Excavations of Gezer*. 3 vols. London: J. Murray.

Magen, Yitzhak, Misgav Haggai, and Levana Tsfania. 2004. *Mount Gerizim Excavations*. 2 vols. Judea and Samaria Publications. Jerusalem: Israel Antiquities Authority.

Mannati, Marina. 1979. "Les Psaumes Graduels constituent-ils genre littéraire distinct à l'intérieur du psautier biblique?" *Sem* 29: 85–100.

Merrill, Arthur L. 1973–74. "Pilgrimage in the Old Testament: A Study in Cult and Tradition." *Ecumenical Institute for Advanced Study Theological Studies: Yearbook*: 45–62.

Miller, Patrick D. 1970. "Apotropaic Imagery in Proverbs 6:20–22." *JNES* 29: 129–30.

Newman, Judith H. 1999. *Praying by the Book: The Scripturalization of Prayer in Second Temple Judaism*. EJL 14. Atlanta: Scholars Press.

Niditch, Susan. 2015. *The Responsive Self: Personal Religion in Biblical Literature of the Neo-Babylonian and Persian Periods*. AYBRL. New Haven, CT: Yale University Press.

Pearce, Laurie E. and Cornelia Wunsch. 2014. *Documents of Judean Exiles and West Semites in Babylonia in the Collection of David Sofer*. CUSAS 28. Bethesda: CDL.

Porten, Bezalel. 1961. "The Structure and Orientation of the Jewish Temple at Elephantine: A Revised Plan of the Jewish District." *JAOS* 81: 38–42.

Porten, Bezalel and Ada Yardeni, eds. 1986–99. *Textbook of Aramaic Documents from Ancient Egypt*. 4 vols. Jerusalem: Hebrew University.

Pröbstl, V. 1997. *Nehemia 9, Psalm 106 und Psalm 136 und die Rezeption des Pentateuchs*. Göttingen: Cuvillier.

Reisner, George Andrew, Clarence Stanley Fisher, and David Gordon Lyon. 1924. *Harvard Excavations at Samaria: 1908–1910*. 2 vols. Cambridge, MA: Harvard University Press.

Römer, Thomas, ed. 2008. *The Books of Leviticus and Numbers*. Leuven: Peeters.

Safrai, Shmuel. 1981. *Die Wallfahrt im Zeitalter des Zweiten Tempels*. Translated by Dafna Mach. Forschungen zum jüdisch-christlichen Dialog 3. Neukirchen-Vluyn: Neukirchener Verlag.

Seybold, Klaus. 1978. *Die Wallfahrtspsalmen: Studien zur Entstehungsgeschichte von Psalm 120–134*. BTS 3. Neukirchen-Vluyn: Neukirchener Verlag.

Shectman, Sarah and Joel S. Baden, eds. 2009. *The Strata of the Priestly Writings: Contemporary Debate and Future Directions*. Zurich: Theologischer Verlag Zurich.
Smoak, Jeremy D. 2010. "Amuletic Inscriptions and the Background of Yhwh as Guardian and Protector in Psalm 12." *VT* 60: 421–32.
Spieckermann, Hermann. 2009. "'Yhwh Bless You and Keep You': The Relation of History of Israelite Religion and Old Testament Theology Reconsidered." *SJOT* 23: 165–82.
Starkey, J. L. 1937. "Lachish as Illustrating Bible History." *PEQ* 69: 171–79.
Stern, Ephraim. 1976. "Bes Vases from Palestine and Syria." *IEJ* 26: 183–87.
Stern, Ephraim. 1980. "Achaemenian Tombs from Shechem." *Levant* 12: 90–111, pls. 13–15.
Stern, Ephraim. 1982. *Material Culture of the Land of the Bible in the Persian Period, 538–332 BC*. Warminster: Aris & Phillips.
Stern, Ephraim. 2001. *Archaeology of the Land of the Bible*. Vol. 2: *The Assyrian, Babylonian, and Persian Periods (732–332 BCE)*. New York: Doubleday.
Stolper, Matthew and Veysel Donbaz, 1997. *Istanbul Murashû Texts*. Leiden: Nederlands Historisch-Archaeologisch Instituut te Istanbul.
Stolper, Matthew W. 1985. *Entrepreneurs and Empire: The Murashû Archive, the Murashû Firm, and Persian Rule in Babylonia*. Leiden: Nederlands Historisch-Archaeologisch Instituut te Istanbul.
Tufnell, Olga. 1953. *Lachish III (Tell Ed-Duweir): The Iron Age*. Oxford: Oxford University Press.
Ussishkin, David. 2004. *The Renewed Archaeological Excavations at Lachish (1973–1994)*. Vols. 1–5. Publications of the Institute of Archaeology 22. Tel Aviv: Emery and Claire Yass Publications in Archaeology.
Ussishkin, David. 2006. "The Borders and *De Facto* Size of Jerusalem in the Persian Period." In Oded Lipschits and Manfred Oeming, eds., *Judah and the Judeans in the Persian Period*. Winona Lake, IN: Eisenbrauns, 147–66.
Ussishkin, David. 2012. "On Nehemiah's City Wall and the Size of Jerusalem during the Persian Period: An Archaeologist's View." In Isaac Kalimi, ed., *New Perspectives on Ezra-Nehemiah: History and Historiography, Text, Literature, and Interpretation*. Winona Lake, IN: Eisenbrauns, 101–30.
Wazana, Nili. 2007. "A Case of the Evil Eye: Qohelet 4:4–8." *JBL* 126: 685–702.
Werline, Rodney A. 1998. *Penitential Prayer in Second Temple Judaism: The Development of a Religious Institution*. SBLEJL. Atlanta: Scholars Press.
Zorn, Jeffrey Ralph. 1993. "Tell en-Nasbeh: A Reevaluation of the Architecture and Stratigraphy of the Early Bronze Age, Iron Age and Later Periods." 4 vols. Ph.D. diss., University of California at Berkeley.

CHAPTER 18

A THEOLOGICAL COMPARISON OF THE DEUTERONOMISTIC HISTORY AND CHRONICLES

MATTHEW J. LYNCH

In the postexilic period, something remarkable happened within the Hebrew scribal world. A historian broke rank with the tradition of supplementing, editing, and revising the existing historical record of the Israelite kingdom, deciding instead that a new type of historical record was needed. The people's circumstances had changed so significantly that the story needed to be retold. This historian retold that story by using large chunks of that earlier historical record while augmenting that with other pieces of the Law and Prophets. Just as Deuteronomy took the existing non-P laws and recast them in a totally new mold, so the Chronicler took the Deuteronomistic History (DtrH) and recast it in a new priestly and psalmic mold. Despite the borrowings and reuse, this new historical work stood on its own.

Scholars have examined the differences between DtrH and Chronicles in terms of their differing historiographies, their distinct Hebrew styles, and their varying ideologies. Theological examinations of the two works have been far fewer by comparison. In their introduction to recent research on DtrH published in 2000, Thomas Römer, Albert de Pury, and Jean-Daniel Macchi observed the need for a comparative study of the theologies animating DtrH and Chronicles (2000: 137–38), but none has yet been offered. The one exception, which preceded Römer, de Pury, and Macchi's remark, was Sara Japhet's groundbreaking *The Ideology of the Book of Chronicles* (1989; reprint 2009). Though this work obviously focuses on Chronicles, Japhet pays attention to differences with Samuel-Kings. It is worth reviewing Japhet's work to set the stage for the present essay that will attempt to provide a theological comparison of Chronicles and DtrH.

18.1 SARA JAPHET

The first 250 pages of Japhet's book address Chronicles conception of God and "God-in-relation" to Israel via election and worship. Japhet builds on insights gained from Julius Wellhausen's *Prolegomena*, Gerhard von Rad's *Das Geschichtsbild des chronistischen Werkes* (1930), and Martin Noth's *Überlieferungsgeschichtlichen Studien* (1943), each of which also examined the distinctive ideological emphases of DtrH and Chronicles.

Von Rad and Noth explored the unique ways that DtrH and Chronicles constructed their histories, including what each distinct work contributes thematically. After their work, the Chronicler's distinctive ideology finally became worthy of study in its own right (Japhet 2009: 2). Von Rad and Noth presupposed the fundamental unity of Chronicles and Ezra-Nehemiah, however—an assumption that no longer holds sway (despite some significant continuities) among biblical scholars—and so Japhet was the first to systematically explore the distinctive ideology of Chronicles per se, and not simply as that is considered when understood as part of a unified work known as the "Chronicler's History" (Chronicles-Ezra-Nehemiah).

Japhet begins with a study of unique divine names in Chronicles. For instance, Chronicles uses the epithet "God of the fathers" twenty-seven times, though it never occurs in parallel texts from Samuel-Kings. It also uses "God of Israel" thirty times when it appears only eight times in its sources (Japhet 2009: 15–16). One might be hesitant to draw sweeping theological conclusions from the appearance of such names, especially since we know that Chronicles draws from a range of Pentateuchal texts, not just DtrH. Nonetheless, the intentional inclusion of these names in parallel passages highlights the Chronicler's concerns to (a) connect postexilic society to pre-Monarchic Israel and (b) emphasize the unity of "all Israel" (Williamson 1977: 82).

Japhet finds Chonicles relatively uninterested in advancing the "monotheistic idea." While the book does include monotheistic affirmations, it also retains several texts that "only" assert Yhwh's incomparability "above all gods" (1 Chr. 16:25–26; 17:20; 2 Chr. 2:4; 6:14). To this observation she adds that the book offers no polemics against other religions and exhibits no interest in reforming the world, qualities that she deems intrinsic to monotheism. Japhet thus parts company with her own teacher, Yehezkel Kaufmann, who believed that the whole Hebrew Bible had a monotheistic shape. Japhet's point, in contrast, is that monotheism is simply not a determining factor in the book's conception of God.

For Japhet, the book's theological convictions shape its stories, not about God, but about the temple. In contrast to DtrH, where kings were evaluated primarily in terms of whether they were idolaters and how they treated the high places, Chronicles focuses on the kings' reverence for the temple. Here Japhet offers some of her most creative and insightful work. Idolatry "interfered with the orderly running of Yhwh worship in the Temple" (Japhet 2009: 165). When the people worshipped illicit divine objects, Chronicles claims that they had "abandoned the temple of the LORD, the God of their ancestors, and worshiped Asherah poles and idols" (2 Chr. 24:18). Whereas in the book of Kings idolatry impacted Israel's relationship with God, in Chronicles, it actually shut down temple worship.

There was a "causal relationship between the two transgressions" of idolatry and disregard for the temple (Japhet 2009: 210).

Japhet's monograph, together with her commentary on Chronicles, brought the study of the book into a new era. If von Rad and Noth gave Chronicles-Ezra-Nehemiah a distinct voice, Japhet distinguished the Chronicler's voice within the trio. Her attention to the book's unique theological contribution allowed interpreters to see Chronicles in sharp relief, and it complemented the kind of work done to distinguish P from D in Pentateuchal scholarship. Further, since Chronicles bears such a strong Priestly imprint, it follows as a continuation of Japhet's work that the book's theology should be compared more explicitly to the Deuteronomistic History.

Beyond Japhet's book, only a few articles have compared the distinct theologies undergirding DtrH and Chronicles. Ehud Ben Zvi (2009) explored various points of contact between the conceptual world of DtrH and Chronicles. His interest lies outside the theological focus of the present essay, though his approach and some of his insights are relevant. Ben Zvi points out that scholars can, and do, overemphasize the differences between these works; furthermore, some comparative studies flatten the diversity *within* each work.

Ben Zvi points to the oft-cited contrast between the Deuteronomist's conception of "delayed judgment" and the Chronicler's concept of "immediate retribution" to illustrate his point. In point of fact, as he shows, the details fail to uphold this contrast. For instance, according to the book of Kings, Manasseh's sin is the primary reason that the Judean Kingdom fell (2 Kgs. 21:10–16), but that judgment was delayed in its effect because of Josiah's reforms. Chronicles lacks the prophecy of the Northern Kingdom's destruction because of Manasseh, and instead recounts the king's "conversion." He receives long life because of his repentant life. Even so, Ben Zvi is able to point to examples of deferred punishment and cumulative sin in Chronicles (e.g., Huldah's prophecy in 2 Chr. 34:22–28; cf. 2 Kgs. 22:14–20), even as DtrH contains instances of immediate judgment (David's sin with Bathsheba) (see Ben Zvi 2009: 62–64).

In the final analysis, Ben Zvi argues that the themes of listening to God's "word" and following God's "teaching" form an important conceptual bridge between the two works. These twin themes stand "at the ideological core of much of the Hebrew Bible, cutting across literary genres and linguistic choices" (2009: 73). However, Ben Zvi's emphasis on this continuity leads him to the debatable claim that in *both* DtrH and Chronicles the scroll-finding narrative in 2 Kings 22 and 2 Chronicles 34 "communicates to the readers the symbolic priority of the written authoritative text over the temple" (2009: 75). It is difficult to sustain that claim for Chronicles, however, since it concludes with a call for the exiles to "go up" to help restore the Temple.

In sum, twenty-seven years after its initial publication, Japhet's work remains the only substantial theological comparison of DtrH and Chronicles, but even her book is not a full-blown comparison. Apart from her discussion of the divine name, Japhet's work focused very little on the book's distinctive (or not-distinctive) portrait of Israel's God. It is perhaps because she dismissed the book's contribution to the "monotheistic idea" that Japhet did not pursue that line of inquiry. To that end the claim of Römer, de Pury, and Macchi—that we need a theological comparison of these two bodies of literature in the Hebrew Bible—still rings true.

18.2 COMPARATIVE CHALLENGES

Japhet and Ben Zvi's studies highlight the possibility and problem of theological comparison between Chronicles and DtrH. On the one hand, the works differ markedly in content and literary shape. For instance, DtrH contains whole swathes of literature not replicated in Chronicles (e.g., Joshua-Judges; Elijah and Elisha cycles); while Chronicles contains large chunks of text not included in DtrH (1 Chronicles 1–9; various psalmic insets). The two works also address different concerns. DtrH seems focused on explaining the eventual fall of the Judean Kingdom (and its political climax under Josiah) while Chronicles addresses postexilic challenges. On the other hand, the two works are remarkably similar, especially when we compare Samuel-Kings with Chronicles. Chronicles reproduces large portions of Samuel-Kings verbatim, and repeats still other portions without significant difference.

We also see the challenge of coherence within each work, especially within DtrH. How can one compare adequately two bodies of literature that seem to lack coherence within themselves? The exercise quickly becomes artificial, depending on which theory of DtrH one adopts. For instance, if one adopts the idea that the DtrH is a loose collection of books only secondarily woven together, one cannot expect much theological consistency, though perhaps the editorial process has created consistency on some matters (e.g., political, social, historical). Then too, in light of the recent theories by Auld and Person that DtrH and Chronicles derive from a common *Grundschrift*, and in light of German theories of significant postexilic redaction of DtrH, we might have to reckon with the possibility of contemporaneous development within the two bodies of literature.

A full-scale theological comparison of DtrH and Chronicles might take the major themes animating each work and look at them from the perspective of the other. Each work may offer a unique perspective, that is, on divine presence, prophecy, kingship, the temple, and so on. Yet in order to maintain a specifically theological focus I have selected the theme of monotheism, or divine supremacy, since this was the one issue that diverted Japhet's attention from the prospect of finding a unique divine profile within each work.

18.3 MONOTHEISM IN SAMUEL-KINGS AND CHRONICLES

The term "monotheism" is a useful designation for explaining the wide-ranging tendency to distinguish Yhwh in absolute terms.[1] Monotheism is thus a broad category, one that cannot be isolated from (a) the specific rhetorical circumstances that give rise to monotheistic assertions or (b) the specific impact on the relationship between Israel and God that results from monotheistic claims. Monotheistic rhetoric took on different shapes in the postexilic period (Smith 2001: 167–78), a point not recognized enough, especially in those studies that suggest a linear development toward one kind of monotheistic belief. In truth, however, the diversity of monotheistic expression allows us to observe two distinct theological expressions of monotheism within contiguous bodies of literature. The material that

Chronicles holds in common with its sources only sharpens our ability to discern how DtrH and Chronicles conceived of Israel's deity.

I will examine five passages from Samuel-Kings for this comparative study—four of these derive from Pakkala's study on monotheism in DtrH (2007),[2] in which he finds only four monotheistic texts in all of Samuel-Kings; to his four I add 2 Kgs. 5:1–19 as a fifth. Despite Pakkala's problematic developmental schema, in which he posits a sharp contrast between "nationalistic" monotheism in DtrH and "universalistic" monotheism in Deutero-Isaiah, his study provides a useful point of departure in the present comparison with Chronicles. Though the texts Pakkala examines appear in passages he deems secondary (redactional) and late, the texts still merit attention because they allow us to examine how similar conceptions of divinity took expression in each work; we can subsequently step back to ask how those expressions fit into the larger theological *Tendenz* of each piece of literature. The intent, therefore, is not to examine the *revision* of Samuel-Kings in Chronicles, but to compare the configurations of divine preeminence within these two works. I have arranged the comparison according to three categories: (1) the relationship between monotheism and the nation, (2) the relationship between divine supremacy and the temple, and (3) monotheism and the land.

18.4 THE NATION AND MONOTHEISM

18.4.1 Samuel-Kings

According to Pakkala, the defining feature of monotheism in DtrH is its "nationalism":

> Although other gods are assumed to be non-existent, the other nations are not invited to join the Israelites in their worship of Yahweh. One would expect that monotheism undermines nationalism, but this does not seem to be the case. The Israel-centered approach of the nomists continues in monotheism. (2007: 175)

Pakkala claims that such nationalism finds expression in all but one monotheistic text in DtrH (2 Kgs. 19:15–19), and that it includes such ideas as Israel's unique election (2 Sam. 7:24; cf. Deut. 4:37; 7:7–9) and Yhwh's deeds on behalf of Israel (2 Sam. 7:23). According to these texts, Yhwh's sole divinity serves his unique relationship with Israel, and not humanity more generally.

Pakkala rightly notes that monotheistic expressions were bound up in Israel's self-identity as a unique nation. Samuel draws an analogy between Yhwh's sole divinity and Israel's absolute uniqueness (כי אין כמוך ואין אלהים זולתך...ומי כעמך כישראל גוי אחד בארץ) "For there is none like you, and no God except you ... and who is like your people, like Israel, a nation unique upon the earth." 2 Sam. 7:22–23//1 Chr. 17:20–21), though it does not correlate the two entriely. For Samuel, it was through Yhwh's salvific deeds for Israel that Yhwh proved himself as the supreme deity. Yhwh "earned his reputation" by delivering Israel from Egypt and from "nations and their gods." Israel thus received its unique status as גוי אחד ("unique nation") on the basis of its relationship to Yhwh (Brueggemann 1998: 17).

The idea that Israel reflects Yhwh's uniqueness also appears in the book of Deuteronomy, where Moses celebrates Israel's unique (1) possession of law and wisdom (Deut. 4:7–8), (2) its uniquely terrifying encounter with Yhwh at Sinai (4:33), and (3) chiefly, the unprecedented wonders performed on its behalf during the exodus (4:34, 37–38) (Brueggemann 1998: 18). Because of these deeds, Israel would come to realize that "Yhwh alone is God, there is none except him [יהוה הוא האלהים אין עוד מלבדו]" (4:35). They would see that "Yhwh is the true God in heaven above and on the earth below. There is none other" (יהוה הוא האלהים בשמים ממעל ועל־הארץ מתחת אין עוד; 4:39).

According to Pakkala (2007: 163–64), Deut. 4:32–40 is among the latest texts in the Hebrew Bible on the basis of its references to exile and return in the preceding section (vv. 25–30), the reference to an existing Torah (v. 44), and the fact that its perspective on heavenly deities differs from that found in earlier parts of the chapter (cf. vv. 15–20). In Deuteronomy 4, obedience to the law is a proper response to Yhwh's sole divinity. This passage thus reflects an effort to sum up the *basis* for Israel's recognition of Yhwh's sole divinity (Yhwh's unique acts), and the proper *response* via covenant obedience.

Yhwh's power as deliverer also forms the basis for claims about his sole divinity in Solomon's temple dedication prayer and blessing. Solomon frames his temple prayer (1 Kgs. 8:22–53) with parallel reflections on Yhwh's uniqueness (v. 23), and by extension, the uniqueness of Israel because of the exodus (v. 53). Solomon then prays that Yhwh would respond to Israel's pleas for deliverance, leading the nations to recognize that "Yhwh alone is God, there is no other" (יהוה הוא האלהים אין עוד; 1 Kgs. 8:59–60).[3] As in Deut. 4:32–40, the rhetorical goal of confronting the people with Yhwh's sole divinity is to inspire obedience to divine laws and commands (1 Kgs. 8:61), but to also to shape expectations around future acts of deliverance.

One such act occurs during the time of Hezekiah. Echoing Solomon's words of appeal, Hezekiah asks Yhwh to deliver them from Sennacherib's power "so that all the earth's kingdoms may know that you alone are God, O Yhwh" (וידעו כל־ממלכות הארץ כי אתה יהוה אלהים לבדך; 2 Kgs. 19:19). This text also has no parallel in Chronicles. Chronicles appears to conflate the two accounts in 2 Kings (2 Kgs. 19:9b–35; 18:17–19:9a, 36–37; cf. 2 Chr. 32:1–22). In a second and likely later account of Sennacherib's siege (2 Kgs. 19:15–19), Kings recounts Hezekiah's prayer of appeal to Yhwh when confined to Jerusalem by the besieging army (Pakkala 2007: 169–70). Hezekiah affirms Yhwh's supremacy on the basis of his deeds in the past and the future, and affirms that "you alone are God [אתה־הוא האלהים לבדך]" of all the kingdoms of the earth. You made the heavens and the earth" (19:15). Continuing with the theme of creation, Hezekiah also acknowledges that the "gods" destroyed by the Assyrians were really "non-gods, indeed, the work of human hands" (לא אלהים המה כי אם־מעשה ידי־אדם; v. 18; cf. Deut. 4:28).

The second motivation for Hezekiah's monotheistic prayer is eschatological recognition by the nations. He prays for Yhwh to save *so that* "all the earth's kingdoms will know that surely you alone are Yhwh God" (כי אתה יהוה אלהים לבדך; 19:19). In contrast to Deuteronomy 4 and 1 Kings 8, there is no emphasis on obedience to divine law, a topic ill-suited to this context. Rather, Hezekiah simply affirms that Yhwh's deliverance would lead to the recognition that Yhwh alone is God.

It is noteworthy that in these three texts from Samuel-Kings (2 Sam. 7:22–23; 1 Kgs. 8:22–53, 59–60; 2 Kgs. 19:15, 19), and in three texts from Deuteronomy (4:34–35; 7:8–9; 32:36–39),

Yhwh demonstrates his sole divinity by delivering Israel from situations of distress.[4] Thus, in five of the six monotheistic passages in the DtrH studied by Pakkala, plus one additional text that he does not treat (Deut 32:36-39), the biblical authors connect Yhwh's supreme uniqueness to his one-of-a-kind acts of national salvation.

The national dimensions of DtrH's monotheism are analogous to those observed by MacDonald (2003a: 215) in Deuteronomy itself where:

> it is... claimed that 'Yhwh is God,' or 'god of gods.' This claim to be a unique divinity is based not on creation, or Yhwh's role in parceling out the nations to other gods, but on Yhwh's faithfulness, mercy and jealousy demonstrated by his election of Israel. In his particular actions for his people, Yhwh shows that he is God. We might say... that Yhwh's claim to be God is not primarily an ontological claim, but more a soteriological one (though such a claim carries with it ontological implications).

In a later study, MacDonald (2009) observes a similar soteriological logic in Deutero-Isaiah. For example, Yhwh demonstrates his sole divinity by the fact that "none can deliver from my hand" (Isa. 43:11-13), and in Isa. 45:22 Yhwh says, "Turn to me and be saved, all the ends of the earth, for I am God and none other." MacDonald concludes that "the monotheism of Second Isaiah is soteriologically, not ontologically, orientated" (2009: 59). Deutero-Isaiah does not express Israel's incomparability using explicit formulas like 2 Sam. 7:22-23, yet it nonetheless asserts that Yhwh specially created, delivered, and formed his people, and that those actions formed the basis for claims about Yhwh's sole divinity (Holter 1995; MacDonald 2009: 53).

In sum, the few monotheistic texts from Samuel-Kings: (1) express Yhwh's sole divinity in terms of his unique acts of national deliverance, and (2) predicate Israel's unique identity among the nations on that defining experience. Moreover, these texts connect the expression of Yhwh's utter uniqueness to a larger rhetorical goal of convincing Israel that Yhwh *alone* was, and will be, responsible for Israel's future deliverance.[5] Israel, accordingly, ought not appeal to any other deity for aid. Finally, (3) two passages extend the implications of national uniqueness to the king (2 Sam. 7:22-29//1 Chr. 17:20-21; 1 Kgs. 8:23-26//2 Chr. 6:14-17) and one passage to Zion (2 Kgs. 19:15, 19). This latter emphasis, not discussed above, is, in the end, a theological correlate to the preceding. Just as Yhwh demonstrated his sole divinity by delivering Israel from Egypt, so he confirmed his reputation by establishing the Davidic throne (2 Sam. 7:22-29; 1 Kgs. 8:23-26) and delivering Zion from the Assyrians (2 Kgs. 19:15, 19). In sum, Yhwh's sole divinity is not an abstract theological claim, but instead, a rhetorical urging premised on Yhwh's unparalleled acts for Israel. To say "you alone are God" is, in no small measure, to assert that *only Yhwh saves*.

18.4.2 Chronicles

Chronicles shares with its sources the idea that Yhwh's exhibited his sole divinity through acts of deliverance for Israel, and that Israel reflected Yhwh's uniqueness (1 Chr. 17:20-21//2 Sam. 7:22-29; 2 Chr. 6:14-17//1 Kgs. 8:23-26). Chronicles also shares the idea that the uniqueness of the nation found expression in a king who embodied in himself Yhwh's election of the people. Chronicles even extends the notion of royal uniqueness when depicting the king as occupant of the divine throne and ruler over the divine kingdom (1 Chr. 29:23).

But Chronicles differs from Samuel-Kings insofar as it configures monotheism in ways that not only augment the unique identity of the king and nation, but also of the *temple*. Chronicles emphasizes more than Kings that the temple was a witness to Yhwh's supreme uniqueness. While Kings refers to the temple as a "lofty residence" (זבל; 1 Kgs. 8:13; 2 Chr. 6:2), it lacks Chronicles's emphasis on the temple's ability to communicate divine attributes. For Chronicles, the temple was a showcase for Yhwh's greatness. In Solomon's dialogue with Huram of Tyre, he states that "the temple I am about to build will be *great* [גדול], for *great* [גדול] is our God *beyond all the gods* [מכל-האלהים]" (2 Chr. 2:4 [5]). In Chronicles, Yhwh exhibits his supremacy *through* the temple.

The Chronicler's claims about the temple's supremacy likely derive from two primary sources. First, the postexilic context in which the Chronicler wrote lent the temple greater prominence as a rallying point for a nation and scattered people without a king, standing army, or political autonomy. The rebuilt temple was the community's primary link to the great God of the past. Second, the book of Psalms had an obvious impact on the book of Chronicles, shaping its author's view of Israelite history. We can see this by returning to 2 Chr. 2:4, which clearly echoes the language of 1 Chr. 16:25//Ps. 96:4, that "Yhwh is *great*" (גדול) and praised "*beyond all gods*" (על כל-אלהים). Like 2 Chr. 2:4, 1 Chronicles 16 celebrates Yhwh's cultic grandeur (Lynch 2014: 104), and it uses the words of the psalter to do so.

Just a few verses later in 2 Chronicles 2, Solomon evokes 1 Chr. 16:24//Ps. 96:3, which calls the people to proclaim Yhwh's "wonders" (נפלאת) throughout the nations: "The temple that I am about to build will be great [גדול] and *wonderful* [√פלא]" (2 Chr. 2:8; cf. 3:5). In the Chronicler's reconstruction the temple was a fitting vehicle for communicating Yhwh's supremacy.

The congruence between the temple's "greatness" and divine "greatness" in this passage runs even deeper. In addition to evoking 1 Chronicles 16 (and Psalm 96), 2 Chr. 2:4 also recalls the idol polemic in Psalm 135. Note the similarity in language here:

Ps. 135:5 (Yhwh)	2 Chr. 2:4 (Temple & Yhwh)
כי אני ידעתי כי־גדול יהוה ואדנינו מכל־אלהים	והבית אשר־אני בונה גדול כי־גדול אלהינו מכל־האלהים
For I am certain that Yhwh is great and (great is) our Lord beyond all gods.	The temple that I am going to build will be great for great is our God beyond all the gods.

The language overlaps considerably, and it is likely that 2 Chr. 2:4 reflects direct influence from the psalm.[6] The most notable feature in Chronicles is how it replaces the divine name from Psalm 135 with a reference to the temple (הבית). Yhwh's *house* not only gains in status, it actually becomes a primary way to express Yhwh's supremacy over the other gods (see further below).

18.5 MONOTHEISM AND DIVINE PRESENCE IN THE TEMPLE

In his study on monotheism in DtrH, Pakkala also posits an connection between the destruction of Israel's first temple and the emergence of monotheism. According to him

(2007: 173), Yhwh's physical representation was destroyed with the first temple, leading the Deuteronomists to the conclusion that only Yhwh's *name* resided in the temple while his *body* remained in heaven, a realm over which he ruled the nations (Deut. 4:36; Deuteronomy 12; 1 Kings 8).

Pakkala's understanding is problematic because Yhwh's "name" and presence are not necessarily contrasted in the Hebrew Bible, generally, or in the specific passages Pakkala cites.[7] However, in at least one text, DtrH contrasts Yhwh's "name" with his physical presence in the temple (1 Kings 8), and points toward a different configuration of divine-institutional supremacy than what one finds in Chronicles. In the outer frame of Solomon's prayer, Solomon seems to contrast Yhwh's heavenly dwelling, from which he hears and sees, with the earthly locus of his "name" (1 Kgs. 8:27–30; 44–45, 48–49).[8] In addition to Yhwh's bodily absence from the temple, there is also a sense of the temple's diminishment embedded in the narrative progression of Solomon's prayer of 1 Kgs. 8:22–53, as Israel and foreigners pray "toward" the temple (vv. 38, 42, 44, 48) but Yhwh hears "from heaven" (vv. 30, 32, 34, 36, 39, 43, 45, 49) in a series of distressing situations that alienate Israel from the temple.[9] One gains a sense of increasing distance by following the location and orientation of the seven petitions within Solomon's prayer:

Location of Petition		Orientation of Petition
8:31–32	at the temple	"before your altar at this temple…"
8:33–34	at the temple	"to you [אליך] at this temple…" Yet "return them to the land…"
8:35–36	in the land	"toward this place…"
8:37–40	in the land	"toward this place…"
8:41–43	in(to) the land (immigrant)	"toward this temple…"
8:44–45	out of the land (temporarily at war)	"toward the city…and toward this temple"
8:46–51	out of the land (in exile)	"toward their land… toward the city… toward the temple"

As the petitions move from the temple to the land (more generically) and then to foreign lands, the orientation of the petitions become more general: from "toward the temple," to "toward the city…and toward this temple," to, finally, "toward their land…toward the city…[and] toward the temple." Even so, according to the logic of this prayer, the international availability of Yhwh works to Israel's benefit, because Yhwh can hear and respond to prayers from anywhere. While Solomon's prayer does not undermine the temple or the possibility of Yhwh's presence therein, it does seem to set up a system of appeal and deliverance that functions even in the event of the temple's *absence* (even if that is only due to *geographical distance*). Indeed, the cultic functions of the temple are completely ignored despite the prayer's emphasis on sin and forgiveness, and nothing mentioned in the prayer is said to take place *in* the temple itself (Fretheim 1999: 50). In fact, Solomon's prayer places little emphasis on Israel's presence in the land, an established priesthood, or a ritual calendar in connection with the temple. The temple possesses an orienting, though not necessarily a socially organizing, role in this prayer.

In anticipation of Israel's exile, Solomon links Yhwh's incomparability and sole divinity with Yhwh's *uncontainability*, and, hence, international availability: "The heavens, even the heavens' heavens" could not contain Yhwh, "how much less this temple" (1 Kgs. 8:27).[10] Yhwh is incomparable *because* his presence could not be contained in one place—not in heaven and certainly not in the temple. This claim creates a tension between the temple's uniqueness as a place for Yhwh's name, on the one hand, and, on the other, the quality that defined Yhwh's uniqueness—namely, his uncontainability (1 Kgs. 8:23, 27-30; 59-60). The temple was less suited than the heavens to manifest Yhwh's uniqueness (hence the use of "heaven" as Yhwh's domain in the prayer). Even so, the temple facilitated communication between petitioners in any location and Yhwh in heaven. Prayers *toward* the temple (and eventually the city or land) could reach heaven—Yhwh's true dwelling place—and catalyze deliverance to prove Yhwh's sole divinity before a watching world.[11]

Solomon's prayer thus depicts a temple that pointed away from itself toward Yhwh's cosmic abode, thereby alleviating the tension it created with Yhwh's transcendence. The prayer draws upon aspects of divine uniqueness without reference to the temple's cultic identity, and instead expresses the temple's ability to orient and serve a scattered people through the dynamics of prayer itself. While the narrative frame of Solomon's prayer does report cultic sacrifices (1 Kgs 8:1-6; 62-66), the absence of any institutionalization of sacrifice, and the omission of cultic elements from the prayer, are notable contrasts to the emphases found in Chronicles's version of the temple's founding (2 Chronicles 6; see below). In the final form of 1 Kings 8, as in 2 Chronicles 6, statements of divine transcendence and divine presence coexist (see esp. 1 Kgs. 8:13//2 Chr. 6:2). Solomon's words in 1 Kgs. 8:23a affirm Yhwh's incomparability in both domains: "Yhwh, God of Israel, there is none like you, a God in heaven *above* and on earth *below*."[12]

Chronicles also insists that the temple mediated Yhwh's transcendent power for those in distress. Not only does Chronicles reproduce most of 1 Kings 8 in 2 Chronicles 6 (but cf. 6:41-42), it also uses Solomon's prayer as a template for another temple prayer later in the book (2 Chr. 20:6-12). Moreover, Chronicles shares, and even develops, the paradox of divine limitlessness and Yhwh's presence in the temple (2 Chr. 6:18//1 Kgs. 8:27; cf. 1 Chr. 29:15 and 2 Chr. 2:5 [6], without parallel).

Despite these similarities, Chronicles links divine supremacy more strongly to divine *presence* in the temple. At the conclusion of Solomon's prayer, the Chronicler inserts a quotation of Ps. 132:1, 8-9 (2 Chr. 6:41-42). Though Chronicles faithfully preserves most of Solomon's prayer (1 Kgs. 8:12-50 in 2 Chr 6:14-40), the use of Psalm 132 directs Solomon's prayer explicitly toward Yhwh's presence:

> So now, Yhwh God, arise to your resting place, you and the ark of your might. May your priests, Yhwh God, be clothed in salvation, and your loyal ones rejoice in your goodness. Yhwh God, do not neglect your anointed ones. Remember (your) steadfast loyalty for David[13] your servant. (2 Chr. 6:41-42)

This quotation follows immediately from the seventh of Solomon's requests, in which he sets out a course of appeal and deliverance for Israel in exile. Significantly, Chronicles's quotation of Psalm 132 stands in for 1 Kgs. 8:51-53, where Solomon prays that God would respond to Israel's pleas for deliverance. Chronicles thus substitutes *a celebration of divine presence* for Kings's *appeal for deliverance*, as if its response were already heeded. Thus, whereas Kings's version of Solomon's prayer depicts a series of appeals that telescopes out and away from the temple, Chronicles's version comes full circle, back to the entrance of

Yhwh, his ark, and the priesthood into the temple (2 Chr 6:41–42). Immediately following Solomon's prayer, Chronicles reports that Yhwh answered with "fire from heaven" as his glory filled the temple (2 Chr. 7:1). This is to say that, in addition to answering prayers of the exiles "from heaven" (2 Chr. 6:21, 23, 25, 30, 33, 35, 39; 7:14), Yhwh also affirms the temple cult "from heaven," and the people respond with worship at the temple:

> When all the Israelites saw the descent of the fire, and the glory of Yhwh upon the house, they fell prostrate on the ground and worshipped, giving thanks to Yhwh: "Surely he is good, his mercy endures." (2 Chr. 7:3)

As is clear from a comparison of 2 Chr. 6:41–42 and 7:3, the people's response acknowledges Yhwh's faithfulness in responding to Solomon's final appeal. Solomon had asked Yhwh to remember his "steadfast love for David" (חסדי דויד; 6:42), and the people praise Yhwh because his "mercy endures" (לעולם חסדו; 7:3). As Riley argues, Chronicles may have included portions of Psalm 132 in order to demonstrate what the "prayer of this place" was to look like (Riley 1993: 91). The "prayer of this place" became a prayer of praise for Yhwh's triumphant cultic presence (2 Chr. 6:41), and an appeal for ongoing faithfulness to the Davidic covenant (2 Chr. 6:42). Chronicles thus directs the temple's purposes back toward cult and king—though the emphasis, in Chronicles, is decidedly on the cult.

The structure of Solomon's temple prayer in Chronicles reflects these twin concerns for divine presence and the Davidic covenant. At the beginning of the prayer, he affirms that "there is none like you a God in the heavens and on the earth, one who keeps the covenant and loyalty to your servants to walk before you with all their heart" (v. 14). Then at the end of the prayer, he quotes from Psalm 132, and asks God to "arise to your resting place, you and the ark of your might," invoking the divine presence theme. He continues with an appeal that Yhwh not "neglect your anointed ones. Remember (your) steadfast loyalty for David your servant" (vv. 41–42). Remarkably, God's presence and loyalty to his "servants" are the qualities for which Solomon had appealed in the omitted section from 1 Kgs. 8:54–61. That loyalty and presence would show that the nations would know that Yhwh is God, and "no other" (1 Kgs. 8:60). It is as if Chronicles's additional material in the prayer answers Solomon's appeal from 1 Kgs. 8:54–61.

In v. 14, Yhwh is incomparable in terms of his location in heaven and earth, and his loyalty to the covenant. The body of the prayer (vv. 15–40) emphasizes Yhwh's presence in heaven. Then, Solomon calls upon Yhwh to demonstrate his incomparability by entering the temple and by maintaining his loyalty to the covenant (vv. 41–42). Yhwh does so (7:1–2) and the people respond in thanksgiving (7:3). Verses 41–42 thereby demonstrate *how* Yhwh is incomparable: He is present in Jerusalem and faithful to the Davidic covenant. These are also the divine qualities to which Solomon appeals in the omitted section from 1 Kgs. 8:54–61. In other words, the Chronicler's additions in 2 Chr. 6:41–42 and 7:1–3 showcase Yhwh *demonstrating* loyalty and presence while Kings has Solomon *asking* God to demonstrate them. Yhwh's cultic presence, in Chronicles, is precisely an indicator of his ongoing commitment to the Davidic covenant. This was surely a point of great significance for the Chronicler's postexilic audience.

Further evidence for the congruence between Yhwh's cultic presence and his supremacy emerges in 2 Chronicles 20. This chapter recounts Yhwh's sweeping victory over a

Transjordanian coalition during the reign of Jehoshaphat. This story is not found in Kings, and here again Chronicles employs language from Solomon's temple prayer to pattern Jehoshaphat's prayer in 2 Chr. 20:6–12.[14] Jehoshaphat appeals to Yhwh as "the God who is in heaven," refers to the "sanctuary for your name," and recalls the conditions of "sword... plague or famine" that would necessitate temple-oriented appeals. Thus far, the prayer looks like a straightforward application of Solomon's prayer as envisioned in 1 Kings 8, where the temple stood as a conduit for human-to-heaven communication. Jehoshaphat's prayer and its surrounding narrative register several changes to the perspective of 1 Kings 8, however, which result in a more prominent role for the physical temple and cult.

First, Jehoshaphat appeals to Yhwh as "the God who is in heaven," who rules "over all the kingdoms of the nations" (2 Chr. 20:6), and against whom "there is no one to oppose you [אין עמך להתיצב]." Chronicles emphasizes Yhwh's transcendence and incomparability (אין עמך) but then draws attention to Yhwh's presence in the temple:

נעמד לפני הבית הזה ולפניך כי שמך בבית הזה

[If] we stand before *this house*, that is, *before you, for your name is in this house*. (2 Chr. 20:9)

Noticeably, this text presupposes an explicit connection between *Yhwh's house, name*, and *presence*. Even though Jehoshaphat affirms (v. 6) that Yhwh is the supreme king "in heaven" and over all nations, Yhwh is also uniquely present in the Jerusalem temple. After Jehoshaphat's appeal, a Levitical prophet assures the people of victory. In response, Jehoshaphat and all the people fall down in worship לפני יהוה ("before Yhwh") at the temple. In short, the Jehoshaphat narrative draws together (a) divine supremacy, (b) divine presence *in* the temple, and (c) an appeal and worship *at* the temple. Yhwh's heavenly dwelling and preeminent kingship stand congruent with his physical presence in the temple.

18.6 The Geography of Monotheism

18.6.1 Samuel-Kings

In several instances, Kings extrapolates from specifically regional, Israelite displays of divine power to make the case that Yhwh is the sole divinity. Two episodes express this clearly. 1 Kings 18:21–40 recounts Elijah's contest with the prophets of Baal. A significant component of Elijah's contest is its geographical location on Mount Carmel, which stood in a contested region between Phoenecia and Israel. This region was claimed for the Israelite Yhwh and Phoenecian Baal.[15]

Kings sets the contest in a time of famine, and therefore the burden of proof fell upon both deities to demonstrate their ability to control the region's weather, which impacted crop production. There is also a wider frame of reference to the contest, however: the contest took place not just to determine Baal's or Yhwh's *regional* supremacy, but rather to demonstrate which deity was האלהים, "the God," without further qualification (v. 24). While it may not be clear from an outsider's perspective why a regional contest would prove sole divinity, the text presupposes that this was, in fact, the case. So it is that Yhwh's ability to demonstrate power over Baal's putative domain (the storm) would prove his sole divinity. Accordingly, Elijah prays for Yhwh to respond in order to reveal that "you, Yhwh, are the true God" (כי־אתה יהוה האלהים; 1 Kgs. 18:37). When Baal remains silent and Yhwh answers with fire from heaven to consume Elijah's sacrifice, the people respond with acclamation, just as Elijah had prayed: "Yhwh is the true God! Yhwh is the true God!" (יהוה הוא האלהים יהוה הוא האלהים; v. 39). In conjunction with this demonstration of power upon the altar, Yhwh then immediately brings heavy rain to the region to demonstrate his power upon the earth.

Elsewhere, Kings records an account of God healing the Aramean general Naaman through the prophetic ministry of Elisha and the intervention of a captured Israelite girl (2 Kgs. 5:1–19). As with the story of Elijah, this story is set in Israel. In response to his miraculous healing in the Jordan River, Naaman exclaims, "Now I know for certain that there is no God anywhere on earth except in Israel" (הנה־נא ידעתי כי אין אלהים בכל־הארץ כי אם־בישראל; v. 15b).[16] Naaman, too, also infers Yhwh's international supremacy on the basis of a regional display of power, coupled with Naaman's inability to find healing outside of Israel along with the helpful intervention of his Israelite servant. Naaman's words echo Elisha's "regional" declaration in v. 8 that Naaman would "realize that there is a prophet in Israel" (וידע כי יש נביא בישראל), but extends its implications much further. As with the Mount Carmel episode, Yhwh's demonstration of power in one region forms the basis of a claim about Yhwh's absolute supremacy.[17] One must stress, however, that recognition of Yhwh's ultimacy does not diminish Yhwh's more particular relationship to a particular area in these stories. In fact, after making his "monotheistic" exclamation, Naaman asks for two mule loads of soil *from Israel* on which to offer sacrifices to Yhwh, vowing to sacrifice to Yhwh only (5:17). In other words, Naaman validates the special position of Israel vis-à-vis the nations even while recognizing the international supremacy of Israel's God. Yhwh was *in* Israel as *the only* deity.

The Elijah and Elisha stories exhibit several common features that are also found in other monotheistic passages in Samuel-Kings. First, they accentuate Israel's unique relationship to Yhwh via his prophets. Elijah prays for it to be known that "you are God in Israel" and that "I am your servant" (1 Kgs. 18:36). Similarly, Elisha quips that Naaman would realize "that there is a prophet in Israel" (2 Kgs 5:8). Second, both episodes take place in the North,[18] and the Elisha story goes so far as to emphasize the uniqueness of Israel's soil. Naaman underscores the geographical point by exclaiming that there is no God on earth "except in Israel" (2 Kgs. 5:15). The "particularist" emphases on Yhwh (vs. another individual deity like Baal) and Yhwh's special relationship with Israel's land pose no stumbling block to drawing large, wide-scale conclusions about Yhwh's (and Israel's) unique position among the nations.

18.6.2 Chronicles

Yhwh also displays his mighty power outside the land in Chronicles, primarily in military encounters (e.g., 2 Chronicles 20). It is noteworthy, however, that Chronicles excludes the possibility that the North had an alternative or competing Yhwh's cult after the division of the kingdoms. There was only ever *one* legitimate cult, and it was in Jerusalem (se 2 Chr. 13:4–12). Chronicles's omission of Elijah's contest with the prophets of Baal and Naaman's healing are therefore part of a general rejection of the North as a place that might manifest legitimate aspects of the cult of Yhwh (contrast Person 2010).

Chronicles redraws the theological map seen in 1 Kings 18–19, 2 Kings 5, and elsewhere, in which true Yahwism existed (albeit under strain) in the North. Moreover, there is evidence that Chronicles transposes stories that occur in the North to apply them to Judah. Yhwh's cult existed only in Judah, after all, and with but two exceptions in Chronicles, the cult was always centralized in the hands of the Levites and priests (2 Chr. 1:3; 33:17). Chronicles revises its sources on several occasions to foreground the unified control that the Levites held on the true Yhwh cult.[19] Still further, according to the Chronicler, from the moment the kingdom split in two all those loyal to Yhwh, including priests and Levites, fled south (2 Chr. 11:13–14, 16).

King Abijah's speech against the North continues this theme: "As for us [in the South], Yhwh is our God, and we did not forsake him.... God is with us as our leader" (2 Chr. 13:10a, 12a). Though Manasseh is exiled to Babylon, and even repents there "in his distress" (2 Chr. 33:12)—another evocation of Solomon's prayer (1 Kgs. 8:37)—he recognizes Yhwh as the "true God" only when he is reestablished as king in Jerusalem (33:13). In short, Chronicles's claims about Yhwh's supremacy and sole divinity accompany its logical correlate: the establishment of the Jerusalem cult and the return of Yhwh's presence.

18.7 Summary and Conclusion

18.7.1 Samuel-Kings

Monotheism in Samuel-Kings draws upon and supports several significant aspects of Israel's self-identity and experience, including the memory of the exodus and of the Davidic covenant, Zion's deliverance from Sennacherib, and various displays of power in Israel. That these are not all unified expressions should come as no surprise, given the diverse material collected by the Deuteronomists, and given the several redactions that Samuel-Kings seems to have sustained.

Nevertheless, several aspects of monotheism in Samuel-Kings recur. (1) Monotheistic language *rhetorically* underscores Israel's distinct national identity, especially as it was formed during its deliverance from Egypt. (2) Samuel-Kings employs several *modes of monotheizing*. The most prominent of these modes is a salvific one: Yhwh has demonstrate or will demonstrate his sole divinity in past or future acts of salvation. These texts also base claims about Yhwh's sole divinity on his covenant with David (2 Sam. 7:22–29), on acts of healing (2 Kgs. 5:1–19), and on God's rule over creation (2 Kgs. 19:15). (3) Kings also deploys monotheistic claims to explain how the exile (and destruction of the temple) do not diminish Yhwh's supremacy. On the contrary, Yhwh remains cosmic ruler supreme. So it is that the mode of *monotheistic configuration between the supreme deity and his temple* "stretches" to allow Israel to experience Yhwh's deliverance outside the land. (4) Accordingly, Yhwh's supremacy finds expressions in Northern Israel and outside the land.

18.7.2 Chronicles

Only two of the five monotheistic texts from Samuel-Kings appear in Chronicles (1 Chr. 17:20–27//2 Sam. 7:22–29; 2 Chr. 32:19//2 Kgs. 19:15–19), and only one (1 Chr. 17:20–27//2 Sam. 7:22–29) leaves the preexisting monotheistic rhetoric of the Samuel-Kings source intact. 2 Chronicles 32 omits the monotheistic content of Hezekiah's prayer as recorded in Kings, including his exclamation, "you alone are God over all the earth's kingdoms" (אתה־הוא האלהים לבדך לכל ממלכות הארץ) and his petition that "all the earth's kingdoms may know that you alone are God" (וידעו כל־ממלכות הארץ כי אתה יהוה אלהים לבדך; 2 Kgs. 19:15, 19). If monotheism becomes a defining feature of early Judaism, as it does and as Pakkala concedes, why would Chronicles not draw upon and expand all preexisting source evidence to that effect? Pakkala's explanation is that "there was no reason to emphasize the point at such a late stage of Israel's religion, because the Jewish community now already generally accepted that only Yahweh is God" (Pakkala 2007: 170). His claim here sounds much like Japhet's made much earlier. Pakkala argues that Chronicles refrains from including Solomon's blessing recorded in 1 Kgs. 8:54–61 because Yhwh's sole divinity was "self-evident" (Pakkala 2007: 171). But Pakkala does not account for the *addition* of texts in Chronicles that explicitly espouse a one-God theology, including the prominent Yhwh-kingship psalm that is included in 1 Chronicles 16 (see also, e.g., 2 Chr. 13:9; 15:3; 33:13). Moreover, on the basis of historical evidence from Elephantine, and literary and material cultural evidence from Yehud, we cannot assume that monotheism had simply "won the day" for Judaism in the postexilic period (see Lynch 2014: 66–67; Frevel, Psychny, and Cornelius 2014). There was still a case to be made for Yhwh's supreme divinity.

A full analysis of DtrH and Chronicles would permit a more precise and nuanced theological comparison between the two bodies of literature than what I have been able to offer here. Even so, working solely with Pakkala's monotheistic texts—with the addition of one more (2 Kgs. 5:15)—as a sample set, one may observe that a predominant premise for monotheizing in Samuel-Kings is Yhwh's salvific response to appeals for deliverance. Israel finds itself in distress and then appeals to Yhwh, who proves his sole divinity by delivering Israel from its peril. The predominant monotheistic configuration in these texts is that of Yhwh with Israel as elect and exalted partner. Yhwh's victories against overwhelming odds—Egyptians, Assyrians, Babylonians—attest to his unrivaled power, and by virtue of these victories' unique relationship to God, they attest to Israel's status as a unique nation. In addition, the exaltation of Yhwh's king, Yhwh's prophets, and Yhwh's city (Zion) also figure in the Deuteronomistic presentations. Like Chronicles, therefore, Samuel-Kings exhibits tendencies to focus on particular individuals or institutions as congeners of the supreme God.

Despite some similarities, Chronicles's configuration of monotheism differs from Samuel-Kings in important ways—ways that suggest an intentional theology of divine supremacy. For Chronicles, the temple cult was the primary center around which all else orbited, including the monarch. Chronicles also makes the temple and priesthood Yhwh's exalted partners, directing much of its narrative toward bolstering these institutions as expressions of divine power and exaltation. These institutions mediate Yhwh's divine supremacy, and as such, are worthy of Israel's unswerving devotion. Chronicles is quite nation-focused like Samuel-Kings, but in a manner that is far more focused on bolstering the temple and its cult, the enduring institutions in postexilic society, and on exalting the

Davidic king as a contributor to those institutions. Moreover, Chronicles emphasizes, far more than Samuel-Kings, that the power, majesty, and preeminence of Yhwh were periodically manifested in the temple, priesthood, and Davidic king.

Samuel-Kings and Chronicles offer different—not necessarily competing—visions of divine supremacy, each suited to its particular milieu. Despite the complex redactional history of DtrH, the inclusion of monotheistic texts fits its general rhetorical purpose—namely, to account for the rise and fall of the Israelite and Judean kingdoms, to provide hope for the future, and to offer a way of relating to the past even while in exile. Chronicles is not interested in explaining the demise of Israel and Judah, but, instead, in rebuilding Israel's identity in the postexilic period. More specifically, Chronicles aims to offer a vision of life for postexilic society that is organized around those institutions that manifest Yhwh's historic supremacy over the cosmos and that recapture the lost glory of Israel.

These broad purposes distinguish the two works, accounting for their different configurations of monotheism, even though lines of continuity obviously exist and can be readily discerned. In the end, DtrH looks to *recapture* the glory of the past through deliverance from exile, which would demonstrate God's loyalty to the covenant. Chronicles, for its part, also looks to Yhwh for deliverance (see, e.g., 1 Chr. 16:35; 2 Chr. 6:40–42), but directs its focus on the rank and file worship of the priests and Israelites around the temple. *That* is the goal of God's deliverance, and that is the experience of divine power and supremacy that Israel's institutions facilitated.

Notes

1. I will refrain here from explaining my definition and use of the term monotheism, by which I mean "categorical uniqueness" or "supreme uniqueness." I have discussed this more in my book on Chronicles (Lynch 2014:20–31).
2. Pakkala identifies only six monotheistic texts in the entire Deuteronomistic corpus (a view I do not share), only four of which derive from Samuel-Kings: Deut. 4:32–40; 7:7–11; 2 Sam. 7:22–29; 1 Kgs. 8:54–61; 18:21–40 and 2 Kgs. 19:15–19. He does not treat Deut. 32:36–42 and 2 Kgs. 5:1–19, and I will include the latter in my analysis of Samuel-Kings.
3. As in Israel's exodus from Egypt (2 Sam. 7:24).
4. Pakkala (1999) connects these texts in Deut and the DtrH as part of a single "nomistic" redactional layer.
5. Accordingly, expressions like אין מלבדו, אין עוד, communicate primarily that Yhwh *acts* alone, and not necessarily that he *exists* alone. Seen in this light, the phrase "there is no one like me" (46:9) is only a shade away from the phrase "there is none other" (45:22), with the latter emphasizing Yhwh's unique capacity to deliver Israel.
6. See Lynch (2019). The verse comparison chart also derives from the same article.
7. e.g., 1 Kgs. 8:12–13; cf. Ps. 11:4a, "But Yhwh is in his holy temple. Yhwh, his throne is in heaven." See esp. Richter 2002. Those that argue for שם ("name") as a marker of Yhwh's physical presence include de Vaux 1967; McBride 1969; McConville and Millar 1994: 111–16; Wilson 1995; Keller 1996; and McCarter 2009. For the contrasting position, Weinfeld 1992: 192–94; Sommer 2009: 65, 241 n. 73. Gerhard von Rad argued earlier for a somewhat mediating position wherein Yhwh's שם in Deut. constituted a quasi-hypostasis, yet still avoided the "crude" idea that Yhwh was fully present at the shrine (1953: 38–39).
8. See MacDonald (forthcoming).

9. Note also the "pilgrimage pattern" implicit in Solomon's thrice-yearly sacrifices (9:25; cf. 2 Chr. 8:13–14 where Solomon organizes "daily" sacrifices).
10. 1 Kgs. 8:28–30 proceeds to emphasize the temple's role as a place of prayer *for deliverance*, while 2 Chr. 2:3 and 5 [4, 6] emphasizes the temple's *ongoing cultic* functions.
11. Even if several monotheistic passages were missing from Chr's *Urtext*, this doesn't negate the comparison or the point that DtrH is marked by the experience of exile.
12. MacDonald (2003b: 115–17) argues that 1 Kgs. 8:23, which reads יהוה אין כמוך אלהים בשמים ממעל ועל הארץ מתחת, should be translated this way in accordance with a repunctuation of the MT.
13. On the objective genitive construction of חסדי דויד, see Williamson 1978. For an argument in favor of a subjective-genitive construction, see Dillard 1987: 51–52.
14. Especially 1 Kgs. 8:9; cf. also 1 Kgs. 8:37, 44//2 Chr. 6:28, 34. On Solomon's prayer as a "charter" for subsequent history in Chronicles, see Dillard 1987: 52–53.
15. Note Elijah's words on Mount Carmel in 1 Kgs. 18:36, "Let it be known that you are God *in Israel*," and the reference in v. 30 to a pre-existing "altar to Yhwh" at the site. That Elijah needed to "repair" Yhwh's altar may attest to a regional struggle between the two deities on Mount Carmel, or an *apologia* for the altar's inclusion in the land.
16. Pakkala omits 2 Kgs. 5:15b from his list of monotheistic passages in DtrH, even though it fits his criterion that monotheistic texts possess an "explicit denial of the existence of other gods" (2007: 163). Note the similarity in language between 2 Kgs. 5:18 and Elijah's words in 1 Kgs. 18:36, "Let it be known today that you are God in Israel."
17. A point expressed well by the contrasting account of Elijah at Horeb in 1 Kings 19.
18. On the importance of crossing borders in the Elijah and Elisha narratives, see Fleming 1932; Hutton 2009: 24–26.
19. e.g., in 1 Chronicles 16; 21:29; and 2 Chronicles 1 in order to explain the sacrifices of David and Solomon at Gibeon. Cf. 2 Chr. 32:17; 33:17. See discussion in Japhet 1993: 389, 528.

Bibliography

Ben Zvi, Ehud. 2009. "Are There Any Bridges Out There? How Wide Was the Conceptual Gap between the Deuteronomistic History and Chronicles?" In Gary N. Knoppers and Kenneth A. Ristau, eds., *Community Identity in Judean Historiography: Biblical and Comparative Perspectives*. Winona Lake, IN: Eisenbrauns, 2009, 57–86.

Brueggemann, Walter. 1998. "'Exodus' in the Plural (Amos 9:7)." In W. Brueggemann, C. Guthrie, and G. W. Stroup, eds., *Many Voices, One God: Being Faithful in a Pluralistic World*. Louisville, KY: Westminster John Knox, 7–26.

De Pury, Albert, Thomas Romer, and Jean-Daniel Macchi, eds. 2000. *Israel Constructs Its History: Deuteronomistic Historiography in Recent Research*. JSOTSup 306. Sheffield: Sheffield Academic Press.

de Vaux, Roland. 1967. "Le lieu que Yahvé a choisi y pour établir son nom." In F. Maas, ed., *Das Ferne und Nahe Wort*. BZAW 105. Berlin: de Gruyter, 219–28.

Dillard, R. B. 1987. *2 Chronicles*. Word Biblical Commentary 15. Waco, TX: Word Books.

Fleming, James. 1932. "Was There Monotheism in Israel before Amos?" *Anglican Theological Review* 14/2: 130–42.

Fretheim, Terence. 1999. *First and Second Kings*. Interpretation. Louisville, KY: Westminster John Knox.

Frevel, Christian, Katharina Psychny, and Izak Cornelius, eds. 2014. *A "Religious Revolution" in Yehûd?: The Material Culture of the Perisan Period as a Test Case*. OBO 267. Göttingen/Fribourg: Vandenhoeck & Ruprecht/Academic.

Holter, Knut. 1995. *Second Isaiah's Idol Fabrication Passages*. BBET 28. Frankfurt am Main: Peter Lang.

Hutton, Jeremy M. 2009. *The Transjordanian Palimpsest: The Overwritten Texts of Personal Exile and Transformation in the Deuteronomistic History.* BZAW 396. Berlin/New York: de Gruyter.

Japhet, Sara. 2009. *The Ideology of the Book of Chronicles and Its Place in Biblical Thought.* Translated by Anna Barber; Winona Lake, IN: Eisenbrauns. (Originally published in 1989).

Japhet, Sara. 1993. *I & II Chronicles.* OTL. Louisville, KY: Westminster John Knox.

Keller, M. 1996. *Untersuchungen zur deuteronomisch-deuteronomistischen Namenstheologie.* BBB 105. Weinheim: Beltz Athenäum Verlag.

Lynch, Matthew. 2014. *Monotheism and Institutions in Chronicles: Temple, Priesthood, and Kingship in Post-Exilic Perspective.* FAT 2/64. Tübingen: Mohr Siebeck.

Lynch, Matthew. 2019. "Divine Supremacy and the Temple: 2 Chronicles 2 and the Fifth Book of Psalms." Pages 323–324 in *Psalmen und Chronik.* Edited by Friedhelm Hartenstein and Thomas Willi. Tübingen: MohrSiebeck, 2019.

MacDonald, Nathan. 2003a. *Deuteronomy and the Meaning of "Monotheism."* Forschungen zum Alten Testament 2/1. Tübingen: Mohr Siebeck.

MacDonald, Nathan. 2003b. "1 Kings VIII 23: A Case of Repunctuation?" *VT* 53: 115–17.

MacDonald, Nathan. 2009. "Monotheism and Isaiah." In H. G. M. Williamson and D. G. Firth, eds., *Interpreting Isaiah: Issues and Approaches.* Leicester: Apollos, 43–61.

MacDonald, Nathan. forthcoming. *The Many Faces of Monotheism.*

McBride, S. Dean. 1969. "Deuteronomic Name Theology." Ph.D. diss., Harvard University.

McCarter, Kyle. 2009. "Aspects of the Religion of the Israelite Monarchy: Biblical and Epigraphic Data." In P. D. Miller, P. D. Hanson, and S. D. McBride, eds., *Ancient Israelite Religion: Essays in Honor of Frank Moore Cross.* Minneapolis: Fortress Press, 137–55. (Originally published in 1987.)

McConville, Gordon and J. G. Millar. 1994. *Time and Place in Deuteronomy.* Sheffield: Sheffield Academic Press.

Pakkala, Juha. 1999. *Intolerant Monolatry in the Deuteronomistic History.* PFES 76. Göttingen: Vandenhoeck & Ruprecht.

Pakkala, Juha. 2007. "The Monotheism of the Deuteronomistic History." *SJOT* 21: 159–78.

Person, Jr., Raymond F. 2010. *The Deuteronomic History and the Book of Chronicles: Scribal Works in an Oral World.* SBL AIL 6. Atlanta: SBL Press.

Richter, Sandra L. 2002. *The Deuteronomistic History and the Name Theology: lᵉšakkēn šᵉmô šām in the Bible and the Ancient Near East.* BZAW 318. Berlin: de Gruyter, 2002.

Riley, W. 1993. *King and Cultus in Chronicles: Worship and the Reinterpretation of History.* JSOTSup 160. Sheffield: JSOT Press.

Smith, Mark S. 2001. *The Origins of Biblical Monotheism.* Oxford: Oxford University Press.

Sommer, Benjamin D. 2009. *The Bodies of God and the World of Ancient Israel.* New York: Cambridge University Press.

Von Rad, Gerhard. 1953. *Studies in Deuteronomy.* London: SCM Press.

Weinfeld, Moshe. 1992. *Deuteronomy and the Deuteronomic School.* Oxford: Clarendon Press.

Williamson, H. G. M. 1977. *Israel in the Books of Chronicles.* Cambridge: Cambridge University Press.

Williamson, H. G. M. 1978. "'The Sure Mercies of David': Subjective or Objective Genitive?" *Journal of Semitic Studies* 23.1: 31–49.

Wilson, Ian. 1995. *Out of the Midst of the Fire: Divine Presence in Deuteronomy.* SBLDS 151. Atlanta: Scholars Press.

CHAPTER 19

DIVINE AND HUMAN VIOLENCE IN THE HISTORICAL BOOKS

DOUGLAS S. EARL

PRIOR to the 1990s the Old Testament historical books were seldom characterized in terms of violence.[1] For instance, in the *Summa Theologiae*, Thomas Aquinas did not consider the issue of violence in relation to biblical narratives. Likewise, with regard to Joshua, a narrative frequently characterized in terms of violence today, ancient interpreters did not use the concept of violence in its interpretation, even though they were aware of moral difficulties. For example, Augustine considered whether Joshua's campaign summary (Josh. 11:14) reflects horrible cruelty, and concluded not. God ordered the campaign so we judge wrongly if we consider it a great evil (see *Questions on Joshua* 16 in Franke 2005: 67), a view reflected by Calvin (e.g., on Josh. 10:18; see 1949: 157–58), and recently Wright (2008).[2]

Origen took a different approach. He was alert to Joshua's moral difficulties, although unlike contemporary readers he seldom characterized them in terms of violence. However, in Homily 12 on Josh. 10:20–26 he makes a passing reference to violence, although the discussion is framed in terms of cruelty (see Homily on Joshua 12:3 in Bruce 2002: 123–24).[3] Origen's approach to the moral difficulty differs from the Gnostics here, who used it to repudiate the narrative, and the later Augustinian tradition, where perceived moral difficulties indicate human finitude. For Origen the moral difficulty at the literal level is real but a cue to locate the text's significance otherwise—spiritually, through intertextual canonical reading. Whilst Origen would no doubt agree with the Augustinian tradition regarding human finitude and God being the measure of all things, he takes Christ as portrayed in the New Testament as the foundation for our knowledge of God and as measure of all, including moral judgments. Origen takes as problematic what Augustine would not, through appeal to the revelation of God as most perspicuous in Christ rather than in the literal sense of Old Testament narrative. Yet Origen rejects the Marcionite hermeneutic, and will not repudiate the witness of scripture, understanding scripture to witness to God, but not literally as in Marcionite and Augustinian traditions.

Origen's moral concerns and spiritual reading had faded from view by the modern era, during which concerns with moral difficulties, and violence in particular, were seldom articulated. An exception is Thomas Morgan, who explicitly contrasts "violence" associated with the Mosaic and conquest traditions with the Abrahamic and Pauline traditions (1739: 105-14). However, such characterization had little lasting impact. To take paradigmatic examples from nineteenth-century German and English scholarship, neither Wellhausen (1885 [1882]) nor Driver (1891) discuss the historical books in terms of violence; in the mid-twentieth century, von Rad (1975 [1957]) does not either. Works in the late modern era are concerned mostly with historical-critical issues rather than ethical issues (e.g., Soggin 1972 [1970]; Boling and Wright 1982). "Violence" is not in view, even in revisionary works where one might expect it to be (Bainton 1960; Gottwald 1979).

There was a watershed in the 1990s with the appearance of various works characterizing the historical books in terms of violence, often to motivate repudiation of certain narratives and associated traditions or theologies (e.g., Rowlett 1996; Prior 1997; Schwartz 1997). The significance of this novel characterization, and the moral response evoked, cannot be overestimated. Such characterization seemed obvious within the rapidly changing cultural context of the era and so went largely unjustified. Various biblical scholars appropriated such works and their conclusions (e.g., Coote 1998: 577-78; Mbuwayesango 2004), whilst secularists and atheists such as Richard Dawkins characterized the biblical traditions in terms of violence to repudiate Christianity (2006: 247). An ever-growing flurry of literature has resulted to address so-called "biblical violence". The concept's use now seems obvious and unavoidable, often leading to moral responses encouraging the repudiation of biblical traditions in greater or smaller part. Alternatively, more questioning responses have developed, either by appealing to traditional resources, or to the nature of the literature and putative context of its composition—namely, Israel suffering oppression from powerful nations—so as to help justify the symbolism adopted and stories promoted (e.g., Collins 2004; McDonald 2004; Moberly 2007; Creach 2013; Zehnder and Hagelia 2013).

Much literature since the 1990s takes as a starting point the characterization of the historical books in terms of violence. I will develop a different approach, paying close attention to the nature of the concept of violence (hereafter, "violence"), considering its applicability to interpretation of the historical books. Indeed, for the historical books (unlike the prophetic literature) "violence" is an interpretative lens that the reader supplies. Arguably, its adoption has analogies with Christian theological reading of the books in that interests of the reader of another context are taken as an illuminative interpretative lens. In the historical books there are only two occurrences of the closest Hebrew semantic equivalent to our term *violence*, i.e., חמס: Judg. 9:24, referring to violence done to the seventy sons of Jerubbaal, and 1 Chr. 12:17 [Eng.], where David claims his hands are free from violence. The paradigmatic use of חמס is perhaps Gen. 6:11, characterizing the earth prior to the flood. It has strongly negative connotations, rendered in the LXX here, as elsewhere, as ἀδικία. חמס is construed in terms of sin or unrighteousness, characterizing action to be repudiated (e.g., Amos 3:10; cf. Swart and van Dam 1997). It is unsurprising then that the concept(s), or semantic equivalents,[4] are absent both from the historical books and their interpretation as a characterization of God or faithful Israel. More surprising is their absence in characterizing Israel's foes or unfaithful Israel, as in the prophetic literature. Of course, actions may be portrayed so as to evoke their interpretation in terms of violence, but this already is to envisage the reader as bringing important presuppositions. "Violence" is an interpretation that readers impose, having a certain ideological charge. It might be a good interpretation, but it is not given explicitly by the text.

There is a tendency to speak of violence and apply the concept uncritically, as if its meaning, application, and moral implications are clear. Mark Vorobej (2016) suggests that definitions of violence can be categorized in terms of the position adopted on the issues of harm, agency, victimhood, instrumentality, and normativity.[5] Dictionary definitions, e.g., "The deliberate exercise of force against a person, property, etc." (*OED* 2014) offer starting points, but are contested. For instance, Krug et al. include psychological aspects and references to maldevelopment and deprivation (2002: 5). Moreover, intuitively and conventionally, violence is distinguished from general use of force in the sense that it is regarded as unlawful or illegitimate (Gilbert 1995): it is a pejorative term. The definition ought to distinguish between the actions of a violent mob, and police using reasonable force to quell the mob.[6]

Let us now consider the usage and grammar of the concept and the intuitions that we wish to capture to illuminate the concept's meaning and significance.[7] Blumenthal suggests that, given Webster's dictionary definition of violence as "the exertion of physical force so as to injure," it is curious that in a survey of attitudes towards violence "only 35 percent of American men define 'police shooting looters' as violence" (1972: 1301). This is less curious if we recognize that in ordinary usage intuitively violence is understood pejoratively: "'violence' ought to be used to pick out those acts that society has a special interest in strongly condemning or at least strongly discouraging." That is, definitions without reference to moral motivations or context are inadequate (Vorobej 2016: 10–12). This is not unproblematic. For instance, the use of force by the police by oppressive governments is often likely to be assessed differently than in Western democracies. Actions promoted in one society may be viewed perjoratively, as violent, by another (Krug et al. 2002: 5).[8] But this simply reflects the nature of ethical and moral concepts (cf. Wittgenstein 2001: §77). Rules for the application of "violence" may be blurry and contextual, with borderline cases. Provisionally then, let us define as violent any action conducted by a person or group with the intent of causing harm or damage by force, either physically or psychologically, to another person, group, or object in a way that is widely regarded as illegitimate or immoral, and violence as the exercise of such action.

Furthermore, there are different contexts or so-called language-games within which "violence" is applied as a description. In particular, different rules govern its application with regard to literature or film (generally fictional perhaps), as against news reports, testimony, or everyday experience in which the above definition is in view. In literature and film, context, including setting, its nature as familiar or fantastic, intention, date of production, anticipated audience, and public expectation, as well as the manner of presentation or mode of portrayal, are factors in the concept's application in a way that they are not otherwise. In film, violence is graded, often via the level of gore portrayed rather than in terms of, for instance, the number of intentional killings.[9] For example, the 1977 Star Wars movie features, among numerous killings, the intentional destruction of Alderaan, an inhabited, civilized planet by the Death Star. Yet the film carries the British Board of Film Classification rating "Universal—Suitable for all." The criterion for this classification in terms of violence is that any violence is "very mild." Outside the context of film or literature, it would be ridiculous to call an inhabited planet's destruction a "very mild" act of violence. Whilst application of the label "violence" to events depicted in film and literature is related to its application in news reports, testimonies, or experience, its rules and grammar are different. The criteria for its application to literature or film, especially in cases where the intention of the work is not historical documentary, are much more stringent. Destruction, harm, or injury might be necessary conditions for application of the label, but not sufficient. Perhaps it is gore, or mode of portrayal, which are largely determinative. So there is then a question of whether the historical books are best compared with literature and film or, for instance, news report, historical documentary, or legal testimony as regards the applicability of the label "violence." I discuss this question of genre elsewhere (Earl 2010; 2017), concluding that the historical books are best compared with literature, or even myth, as understood in contemporary anthropology rather than in its earlier pejorative sense.[10] Indeed, the conclusion that the historical books do not present factual historical report in the modern sense resonates with the majority view in Old Testament scholarship that emerged during the twentieth century. In this case, the bar should be set high for application of "violence" to the so-called historical books, itself perhaps a misleading epithet for the texts if "historical" is taken in the modern sense.

Moreover, as we've seen, the grammar associated with "violence" in traditional religious contexts is associated with sin, but this is not in view in the grammar of "violence" in contemporary societies in which the concept of sin has generally been lost from view. This observation, coupled with the idea that actions described as violent are implicitly condemned in everyday as well as biblical or theological usage, explains the avoidance of the term in traditional Christian interpretation: it would seem odd for Christians to characterize their foundational texts in pejorative terms. Any application of "violence" to the historical books will, for the Christian reader, need to be more carefully nuanced than for a secularist reader for whom repudiation in some sense is often in view.

This raises the question of whether the applicability of the concept of violence to particular cases is clear even where there is agreement on its definition and the language-game in view. It is, I presume, uncontroversial to describe a parent beating their child for a minor misdemeanour as violence, evoking outrage and repudiation. An inappropriate level of force is used, causing harm. But consider a parent who smacks their child, scolding them for jumping into the road. Until recently, such an action would be described using the concept of discipline, understood in the context of love and the desire for the education, protection, and good of the child, and not their harm, even if short-term hurt results. There may be borderline cases. But this has become contested. Smacking a child is, for some, morally wrong. It ought to be repudiated, understood as an act of violence within the context of abuse. So even if there is agreement about the definition of violence and the context of application, its application to particular cases may be disputed, owing to disagreement about what constitutes either harm or legitimate force. Such dispute in application may lead to changes in usage, and ultimately to a different understanding of what is meant by "violence." Its application is often rhetorical, ideological, and political. The potential difficulty with broadened application is that we are led to see less in that important distinctions are elided, such as contrasts between loving and abusive parents. Conversely, it may be argued that broadened application unveils similarities previously obscured through language or tradition. The point is that the contested applicability of the concept often reflects clashes of ideologies or worldviews.

The parent-child example is relevant to the historical books, being used metaphorically to provide an interpretative framework, on the texts' own terms, for Israel's self-understanding as loved and yet disciplined by Yhwh for its own good. Readers are encouraged to interpret Yhwh as the loving parent who disciplines, blesses, and protects his beloved child, and not the capricious, aggressive abuser acting violently. So on their own terms, interpretation of the historical books is perhaps best framed initially in terms of the loving parent-child relationship (cf. Deut. 7:7–8) rather than in terms of violence and xenophobia. This is not to say that this cannot be contested, but to say it is a better perspective from which to start. As with the contemporary parent-child example, disagreements are to be expected owing to conflicting worldviews, with what was once a positively valenced metaphor now contested.

I now consider the concept of violence with regard to three further philosophical issues. First, the observation that "violence" is associated with evoking a sense that what is thus described ought to be morally repudiated. We should note Anscombe's (1958) caution regarding the notion of the "moral ought," a notion that perhaps has "no reasonable sense outside a law conception of ethics" associated with the idea of a divine legislator. "It would be a great improvement if, instead of 'morally wrong', one always named a genus such as 'untruthful', 'unchaste', 'unjust'. We should no longer ask whether doing something was 'wrong', passing directly from some description of an action to this notion; we should ask whether, e.g., it was unjust; and the answer would sometimes be clear at once" (Anscombe 1958: 8–9). So with regard to the historical books, perhaps particular actions are best considered simply in terms of the descriptions given rather than the more abstract and ideologically laden concept of violence supplied by the reader, especially if we understand its application to involve contested judgments involving a problematic "moral ought."

Secondly, does, or in what sense, or how does the application of the label "violence" involve appeal to a putative "moral ought"? Does the application of "violence" primarily involve rational judgment in relation to a supposed "moral wrong," or does it have more emotive aspects associated with evoking outrage, implicitly but rhetorically calling for a repudiation of an action, person, society, or perhaps narrative? James Kirwan (2015) develops a distinction between moral responses and moral judgments to clarify their conflation or confusion. Moral responses are associated with emotions, being involuntary and irrational in that they are prior to reflection and desiring of action. Moral judgments differ. Whilst moral responses are implicit in motivating, moral judgments are a matter of logic. Moral responses happen to us whereas moral judgments are things we do— consciously and rationally derived pronouncements through reason. Moral judgments bleed back into moral responses, however, so they are associated. Moreover, there are two paths to moral judgments: appeal to a feeling already in place so as to elicit a moral response, or, to lay out the principles and logic as if there were moral facts. Conflation of response and judgment allows moral responses to be passed off as moral judgments, so that what is felt or evoked as an emotional response is taken to reflect a metaphysical judgment. Analyzed in these terms of Kirwan's, the natural home for the label and concept of "violence" is the arena of moral responses rather than moral judgments. Application of the concept apparently brings the force of a "moral ought" in the sense that it evokes an emotional moral response that the action described as violent ought to be repudiated. No ultimate metaphysical judgment is in fact made, but it seems like such a judgment has been made.[11] So in these terms, Origen's and Augustine's readings of Joshua 10–11 share the same initial moral response, but Augustine uses a moral judgment to block that response (upon which a theology is built), whilst Origen uses a different moral judgment to develop a hermeneutic incorporating the moral response. The Marcionites, and contemporary readers repudiating the narrative, effectively conflate a moral response with a moral judgment to repudiate and to block appropriation of the text, characterized by use of the term "violence."

Thirdly, let us consider the sense in which application of "violence" is a rhetorical, manipulative, and ideological or political act. This might be developed in terms of Foucauldian discourse analysis by considering power relationships as expressed through the use of language, or alternatively in Orwellian terms of the manipulation of society through changes in language and language use. Who controls the label "violence," its use, and its application? How and why is it used, and by whom? Application of the concept is not innocent and disinterested, often reflecting an emotional manipulation (a moral response) masquerading as a metaphysical judgment (a moral judgment). Contested application involves the confrontation of worldviews or ideologies, such as in the parent-child example. So we should consider what interests are at work, and when the conceptualization of an action as violent is illuminative and helps us to see more and better understand, and when it diminishes our understanding, so that we see less in the promotion of an ideology. When is it illuminative to dissolve conceptual differences, and when it is helpful to reinforce them?

In summary then, the application of the concept of violence evokes, or perhaps manipulates, a moral response of revulsion or outrage towards what is described as violent to lead to its repudiation, seemingly with the force of a moral judgment with metaphysical justification, in that apparently there is a "moral ought" in the repudiation of what is described. Its application may reflect either a desire to reinforce or to change a worldview (cf. Vorobej 2016: 9). The application of "violence" to literature or film has a different grammar than that of its application to experience, testimony, record, or report. There are more stringent criteria, in particular as associated with gore in the mode of portrayal, and the sense of repudiation is perhaps less severe. If successful, the application of "violence" passes off a moral response as a moral judgment, which might be a good judgment or a poor judgment. Violence is a pejorative term, lacking specificity, and it is not innocent or disinterested, but rhetorical, political, and ideological in application.

The avoidance of explicit application of "violence" to characterize Yhwh or faithful Israelites within the historical books and their traditional interpretation reflects an instinct of trust, value, respect, and appreciation of the traditions of which they are a part coupled with a desire for their appropriation in positively shaping a worldview, in contradistinction to an instinct of suspicion, disavowal, and repudiation as adopted by the secularist. Decisions on the application of "violence" in a general sense, which should be contested by the Christian reader, reflect a conflict of worldviews regarding what is life-enhancing rather than life-diminishing. Dilemmas faced since the 1990s by those wishing to respect, cherish, or appropriate the biblical traditions stem from accepting the initial characterization of the historical books in terms of violence. In this characterization, an initial step that looks quite innocent and goes largely unchallenged, the conjuring trick is already made (cf. Wittgenstein 2001: §308). It smuggles in a stance towards the narratives and associated traditions that is already caught up with evoking a pejorative response to and judgment of them. Unknowingly, a lens associated with the ideological assumptions of those seeking to repudiate the biblical traditions, to greater or lesser extents, is adopted. The concept of violence, as a general characterization or interpretative perspective, is unlikely to help the sympathetic reader's interpretation. To be clear, I am not saying that the historical books do not present moral difficulties. Rather, one should be very cautious or suspicious in the application of "violence," at least as a first move. It will bring greater clarity to say that the historical books narrate wars, killings, the destruction of villages, property, etc. as our starting point for interpretation, considering specific narratives on a case-by-case basis, adopting the descriptions given.

However, one should ask whether the historical books have, in fact, in some significant way, motivated violence so that they ought to be associated with violence and repudiated. This reflects an established strategy, modelled by Fiske and Rai (2015: 51–52, 111–27):[12] (1) to characterize certain biblical texts in terms of violence; (2) to suppose portrayals of God and paradigmatic figures such as Joshua then offer idealized ethical models, read literally, to promote violence; and (3) to claim that such texts have indeed motivated violent atrocities. Any right-minded person ought then to repudiate the texts and the tradition(s) of which they are a part. This strategy began by characterizing certain biblical texts in terms of violence, which is then reinforced by the claim that they have in fact inspired violence, further urging their repudiation by shifting the language-game for application of "violence" from literature to testimony, record, and experience. Rhetorically, this is a powerful strategy to disable appropriation of the biblical traditions.

Let us analyze this strategy. First, I am questioning the initial step of the conceptualization of certain narratives in terms of "violence", which evokes a pejorative moral response with associated moral judgment smuggled in. Secondly, it is not at all clear that "tales of exemplary violence of deities and heroes" are such, or were composed to provide "models for humans to emulate" (Fiske and Rai 2005: 111), either in biblical texts or indeed more generally in foundational stories that shape the worldviews of societies. Thirdly, do texts such as Joshua motivate people to commit atrocities as a main pattern rather than as aberrations? There are two questions here: whether Fiske and Rai's claim is true generally that foundational stories of societies (let us call them "myths" without pejorative connotation) offer ethical paradigms in the straightforward sense suggested— an anthropological question; and whether in particular the main pattern of Joshua's appropriation is to be understood in terms of inciting violence. The answer seems negative in both cases.

With regard to the first question, in Victor Turner's anthropological analysis of myth he suggests that myths are liminal phenomena that do not describe what ought to be done or offer models for behaviour. Rather, myths have existential significance that may be understood in terms of symbol (1968: 577). Elsewhere Turner develops the sense in which myths form the basis for enactment in everyday life (1982: 7–19, 122). Whilst they can be composed to incite violence, narratives, qua myth, do not offer paradigms for behaviour straightforwardly. It is perhaps an encultured human instinct to recognize this, as in the case of the grammar of violence in relation to literature and film. Different rules and criteria operate with regard to the application of "violence" to myth, literature, and film than to didactic literature, news reports, historical documentary, legal testimony, and everyday experience, with it being recognized that their significance or mode of appropriation differ. Historical narratives (generally, not just biblical) are perhaps borderline cases, with some functioning more like or indeed as literature or myth, whilst others function more like news report, didactic material, or documentary. How one then forms judgments, applies the label "violence," and appropriates such narratives will differ on a case-by-case basis, with something like a basic encultured human instinct coupled with the tradition of which the narrative is a part offering a guide.[13] Indeed, Turner does not suggest that myths play no part in shaping the attitudes, beliefs, and ethics of a society, for this is their function. Various approaches to myth, such as symbolic and neo-structuralist, analyze their significance, appropriation, and enactment (e.g., Kunin 2004; see Earl 2010 for discussion). Origen's spiritual reading of Joshua can be understood in these terms, reading "spiritual" for "symbolic" in his interpretation. Moral difficulties at the literal level invite construal of Joshua's significance and its enactment in spiritual or symbolic terms.[14]

On the second question, what of the claim that texts such as Joshua have, in fact, been appropriated, as part of the pattern, to commit atrocities? I have argued elsewhere (Earl 2013) that it was not texts such as Joshua that were used to preach the Crusades (one of the instances paradigmatically cited) or that formed the basis for the self-understanding of crusaders, but rather gospel texts speaking of love and sacrifice. Crusaders went, self-sacrificially out of love, to aid their fellow Christians suffering violence. Claims that the historical books have incited violence are overstated. Readers (especially situated in appropriate traditions) are better able to distinguish between literature or myth and didactic texts or historical record, and better able to form responsible judgments regarding their appropriation than Fiske and Rai (2015), Warrior (2001), or Collins (2016) suggest. Perhaps what is at issue is what counts as main patterns or trajectories as opposed to aberrant cases in which the text is demonstrably badly interpreted and misused—i.e., whether there are "enough prominent exceptions . . . to render the text highly problematic" (Collins 2016: 294). The observation that the cited cases are overstated—rather few and localized—suggests that the problematic usages are best considered aberrant misuses.[15] Indeed, the "great majority of Christians and Jews have not taken [Joshua] as warrant [for genocide]" (Collins 2016: 294).

Joshua does of course pose a difficulty, perhaps especially for Christian readers with a vocation to love, owing to the portrait of apparently divinely sanctioned conquest and killing on a grand scale, even if gore is avoided. Might one read Joshua responsibly, so as to draw upon both Origen's insights and insights from contemporary study of myth and symbol, and locate its significance in these terms? As I argue elsewhere (Earl 2010), Joshua is a "fantastic" (i.e., rivers splitting, walls sinking, sun stopping) fictional, symbolic narrative that shapes a worldview (i.e., it is a myth) set in the context of conquest. As such, it is appropriate to seek to construe its significance along the lines Turner suggests. If the overall symbolic sense (or perhaps *Sache*) is unproblematic (i.e., if Joshua is not really about promoting killing or conquest), and given that the narrative is not generally taken as a mandate for violence, comparison with the BBFC guidelines suggests that the criteria for application of the label "violence" to Joshua ought to be fairly demanding. It is fantastic literature set in the distant past with little gore and no expectation of literal enactment. Joshua is composed to shape Israel's conception of its identity in relation to the covenant and other nations by using but nuancing Deuteronomy 7. The story of Rahab (Joshua 2–6) evokes welcome acceptance of the paradigmatic other who nonetheless expresses and enacts faithfulness to Yhwh. Alternatively, Achan's story evokes repudiation towards a paradigmatic Israelite who is unfaithful to the covenant and self-seeking (Joshua 6–7). The hostile kings (Joshua 10) symbolize hostility toward Israel from powerful, violent nations who are to be repudiated and avoided, whilst the story of the Gibeonites (Joshua 9) indicates that there are borderline cases. The organizing symbolic concept is חרם, reflecting a command to (at the literal level) "destroy completely" (Deut. 7:1–5).[16] The different characters represent different responses to חרם, symbolizing responses to Yhwh. Jericho's complete destruction (Joshua 6) is required by the logic of the plot, serving a literary function. The significance of Rahab's rescue and Achan's disobedience would be obscured otherwise. The narrative is set in a prototypical past, drawn into its audience's context by Joshua 23–24, which form a hermeneutical guide and indicate that Joshua's appropriation or enactment is understood in terms of covenant faithfulness and avoidance of idolatry. Although set in the context of mythological conquest, the book's message is that Israel's identity is constituted by those faithful to the covenant—positively exemplified by Joshua and Rahab, negatively by Achan and the hostile kings. This reflects a nuancing of Israel's self-understanding as expressed in Deuteronomy, where identity was more understood in ethnic terms. Indeed, Joshua does not encourage the promotion of self-serving interests in socio-political terms through warfare or violence (Josh. 5:13–15). Joshua's message is generally one that Christian readers would wish to appropriate (subject to recontextualization) rather than repudiate. Approaching Joshua with a prior characterization of violence may encourage one to see less, obscuring rather than illuminating its interpretation. The concept of violence seems unhelpful for its interpretation. This is not to say that dissonances and difficulties do not remain. We cannot simply or entirely discard the literal sense and what it might evoke for a contemporary reader, an issue to which I shall return below.

While violence may be an unhelpful characterization of the historical books that Christian interpreters ought to resist, let us consider now how the concept might illuminate particular narratives, aiding interpretation in that it captures the sort of response that a good reading ought to evoke in a way that has not been recognized traditionally. The traditional avoidance of the concept may stem from a certain construal of what it means to cherish and respect scripture, especially when particular characters are taken to model response to God, whether in a literal or symbolic sense. As the more ambiguous portraits of figures such as David have come into focus, appeal to the concept of violence in certain narratives may illuminate their interpretation. Close reading of some texts may suggest that their authors sought to evoke jarring moral responses to encourage the repudiation of something that the narrative reflects. For example, Van Seters (2009) has argued that the story of David in 1–2 Samuel should be understood as the result of an early deuteronomistic unswervingly positive portrayal of David, promoting the Davidic monarchy, that was rewritten with jarring interjections (such as the story of David and Bathsheba) to cast the Davidic monarchy in an ambivalent light. This suggests reading Samuel with a questioning stance towards some of David's actions, some of which might be interpreted well in terms of violence, offering interpretative possibilities not recognized traditionally given the instinct to view David positively.[17] This highlights the need to avoid flat-footed readings of biblical narratives that overlook subtle and sometimes ambiguous characterizations that may well have been developed to evoke a sense of violence regarding the actions of certain figures, and to be cautious against taking at face-value pious language and claims. Read in its final form, whilst an overall positive construal of David may supply the appropriate framework for interpretation, individual stories point up the often ambiguous behavior of those called by Yhwh, and the ease with which divine calling becomes self-serving and a self-justification for violence (Earl 2017).

The book of Judges is understood well by considering how the reader is encouraged to be outraged by and take a stance against much of what is presented. The refrain, "In those days there was no king in Israel; all the people did what was right in their own eyes" (Judg. 21:25) provides a hermeneutical guide to the book's rhetorical strategy: the combination of these factors diagnoses the violent behavior and society narrated.[18] Characterization of its narratives in terms of violence encourages the audience to repudiate idolatry, remain faithful to the covenant, and to adopt appropriate leadership to ensure this. For the theologically sympathetic reader, there is no real difficulty here as regards violence and applying the concept to certain stories in the book. Judges shows that the result of idolatry, unfaithfulness, and inappropriate leadership is pervasive violence, as contrasted with peace and rest when Israel behaves faithfully under appropriate leadership (cf. Josh. 14:15; 21:44–45). This message would presumably be sharply contested by the secularist. For the secularist, the problem of violence in many societies is understood to stem precisely from religion and its promotion. So this reading of Judges exacerbates the problem as the secularist sees it. There are then two aspects to the issue of violence as related to Judges. There can be agreement that its narratives can be characterized in terms of violence as a helpful interpretative move, crystallizing the stance a good reader should take. The sharp disagreement concerns the diagnosis of such violence and how violence is avoided, reflecting a clash of worldviews. For the theological interpreter reading "with the grain," the solution to violence is faithfulness to Yhwh coupled with appropriate leadership. This promotes peace and rest.[19] For the secularist, the diagnosis Judges offers is simply understood to promote further violence, with the book's message understood pejoratively.

Prior theological or ideological commitments influence whether we construe what is portrayed in a narrative, or the worldview or message promoted overall by a narrative, in terms of violence. These often differ, as we have just seen. What is often at issue concerns what we understand it to be to promote human good and well-being, as contrasted with what is life-diminishing or harmful. For instance, whether one sees Christianity as life-giving or merely a potentially divisive lifestyle choice—or, more specifically for instance, whether one sees idolatry (however understood) as a pressing issue and as an ultimately harmful or destructive way of life or simply a matter of lifestyle choice—will influence how one might regard "violence" to be applicable to the historical books in the many narratives dealing with idolatry. Josiah's reforms offer a paradigmatic case. Josiah tears down the high places given to idolatry and slaughters their priests (2 Kgs. 23:19–20). Here, the moral response that the author seeks to evoke seems clear, involving rejoicing in a good, faithful king who eradicates idolatry and encourages faithfulness to the covenant as life-enhancing and life-restoring to Israel. It is less clear though what behavior or enactment the author would encourage for the narrative's anticipated audience than in the case of Joshua. In symbolic terms, Josiah might be understood as personally undoing the foundational sin of Jeroboam (Nelson 1987: 258), as wiping the slate clean perhaps, with the symbolism evoking the sense of radical contamination that idolatry brings.

If 2 Kings 23 is construed as literature, or indeed myth in Turner's sense, rather than historical record or paradigm understood in literal terms, then the bar ought to be set high for the application of "violence" to the story. There is little gore here, even if Josiah's actions would widely be understood, if performed in a contemporary context, as violent. Second Kings 23 has greater resonances with contemporary experience and is less "fantastic" than Joshua, even if it is symbolic. So whilst 1–2 Kings does have "fantastic" elements, such as the stories of Elijah and Elisha, the books have more historical and perhaps familiar resonances too in some reading contexts. This suggests that 2 Kings 23 is a borderline case in considering the application of the concept of violence, since its genre and its message—in terms of the expectations of what form of appropriation a good reader is encouraged to take—are less clear.

One aspect in considering the application (or not) of the concept of violence here is diagnosed by the moral response the interpreter seeks as regards the promotion or avoidance of idolatry. A secularist would characterize 2 Kings 23 as violent, since portrait and message are understood pejoratively and converge, but it is less clear what a Christian reader might say. Symbolically, the story evokes a strongly negative view of idolatry, promoting its radical avoidance and indeed appropriate forms of leadership to encourage this. Broadly speaking, this is not something that the Christian would wish to repudiate. But it needs careful recontextualization in a Christian context,[20] where the struggle against idolatry is voluntarily embraced and in a sense internalized and spiritualized (although having physical and material consequences), as reflected in the New Testament and, for example, in Origen's homilies. Idolatry is clearly understood as life-diminishing and harmful, and is always to be avoided. Christians promote such a message in society for its good, but response is voluntary and not coerced or enforced. So the conflict with idolatry for the Christian takes a different form from that evoked by 2 Kings 23 as understood in the context of the Old Testament, especially if its significance is construed in realistic rather than symbolic terms. Construed symbolically or spiritually, Josiah's actions may be understood positively and promoted in this sense in a Christian context. However, understood literally or realistically, especially if envisaged in a contemporary setting, Josiah's actions would be repudiated and described as violent by Christians and secularists alike. Thus a number of Christians might characterize 2 Kings 23 in terms of violence, understanding it realistically, expecting its anticipated appropriation was along such lines. But this application of the label of "violence" is not unproblematic, as in broad-brush terms it implicitly reflects the repudiation of a foundational narrative that encourages the repudiation of idolatry by a king who restored Israel to faithful worship of Yhwh. Thus whether "violence" is or is not used in relation to the narrative, clarity is required regarding how the narrative is understood and what is being encouraged or repudiated.

So there are various borderline cases where it is unclear whether the concept of violence is applicable or helpful for the Christian in interpreting certain narratives, although perhaps consideration of the issues involved in relation to the concept may be helpful in bringing clarity. Perhaps Christians might promote an understanding of the historical books as myth (in the non-pejorative anthropological sense), for this is, de facto, often how their Christian significance is outworked. In this case, the bar may be high for application of the label "violence" to potentially realistic narratives in which literal description and symbolic message come apart, and clarifications about repudiation need not arise.

However, dissonances remain even after interpretation of the historical books as literature, fiction, or myth, after Origen's spiritual reading, or after the appreciation of the nature of myth more generally. Even if the significance of such narratives is not construed in literal terms, as record or as making propositional claims about God or what is commanded, the text of Joshua, for instance, still in some sense evokes a picture of God as commanding killing on a mass scale and Joshua conducting it (Joshua 10–11). Likewise, the story of Josiah evokes a picture of slaughter and destruction. Or, in David's story, the poignant image of God taking the life of a baby, or at least allowing a baby to die, remains (2 Sam. 12:13–23). Whilst one might suppose that the significance of each of these ought not be construed factually, it is difficult and perhaps undesirable to detach completely a symbolic or spiritual interpretation from the literal depiction. It is involvement and familiarity with the literal sense that evokes the metaphorical or symbolic (Ricoeur 1969). So interpretative and theological work remains, although as we have seen the concept of violence is so bound up with repudiation and clashes of ideology that often it may not be a good way to conceptualize the dissonances and difficulties for the Christian reader. Its application too readily encourages repudiation of the texts and traditions and too easily evokes a vision of God as an abusive rather than loving parent, or our forebears as a violent mob. So it is not mere semantics. Origen was able to point up the moral difficulties without the concept of violence.

Jagged edges and dissonances ought to remain even if "violence" is a poor way to characterize the dissonances. Dissonances remain since, first, perhaps some of the imagery and symbolism permeating the historical books is unproblematic and indeed evocatively valuable if appropriated in certain ways in some reading contexts but perhaps not others. The resonance, value, and potency of symbols and their moral valence varies from context to context. With regard to violence and its portrayal, Brueggemann suggests, "In a situation of victimization, one is not so worried about violence in the power of one's rescuer" (1994: 803). This issue is developed at length by Volf, who, whilst resisting appeal to God to justify violence concludes that God uses violence (1996: 300–301). But I have argued that "violence" is probably not the right concept here, having pejorative force. Rather, it is preferable to use the Bible's own imagery and symbolism: the picture of God's wrath kindled in response to violence, or the metaphor of God as a "warrior" or "man of war" (Exod. 15:3). The significance and applicability of this image are movingly developed with reference to Israel's experiential context in *Mekhilta Shirata* 4 (see Neusner 1988). Creach suggests, "many objections to God as warrior are bourgeois. From a perspective of power and wealth, it is easy to seek after a God who appears respectable, calm, and non-plussed by the rampant oppression in the world" (2013: 71).

Alternatively, some societies may be blind to what others take to be ethically problematic symbols or stories. (I take this blindness in a neutral rather than pejorative sense.) Were comparable theological narratives written today, different imagery might sometimes be used. But this is not to say that the traditional, cherished narratives passed down to us ought to be discarded, disowned or rewritten. Indeed, secondly, we should exercise humility with regard to the historic construction of Judaeo-Christian (and indeed much western) identity through scripture, in that as it relates to a "cultural memory," it is precisely through the preservation of traditional, historical, and symbolic resources (however problematic or not) that Christian identity is preserved from generation to generation (cf. Hervieu-Léger 2000: 166–76; Assmann 2006: 27–29). Thirdly, we ought to expect dissonances and jaggedness to remain in our response to the historical books owing to the otherness of God. This does, of course, form the (sometimes problematic) basis for dealing with morally difficult texts in the trajectory of Augustine and Calvin. Nonetheless, it captures an important theological insight regarding epistemic and creaturely humility. One ought not to expect God, and those following God's vocation, to be constrained by some Kantian categorical imperative or postmodern ideology or sensitivity. For instance, suffering arising inescapably from a Christian vocation may appear morally ambiguous and perhaps mysterious, from Christ to his contemporary disciple, perhaps being nearly but not quite appropriately described in terms of violence. The challenge we face is that it is often difficult to distinguish between dissonances owing to differences in cultural context and expectations and dissonances arising from the otherness of God. Perhaps the best that we can do was more or less sketched out by Origen, who, from a hermeneutic of trust founded in Christ, never sought to domesticate God, or to disown or rewrite the biblical narratives when moral difficulties arose in the context of the rule of faith, but took them as cues to understand their significance in a different way, however morally demanding and unexpected.

Notes

1. I shall focus on the issue in a Christian context, although much here applies also to Jewish concerns. I am grateful for comments by Walter Moberly and Richard Briggs on a draft of this essay.
2. The killing of Canaan's inhabitants is often justified as divine punishment for sin (cf. Deut. 12:29–32).
3. The concept's use here was probably occasioned by dialogue with the Marcionite tradition and an association of the text with Matt. 11:12.
4. e.g. violence, *violentus*, βιά, and cognates.
5. The literature and approaches are diverse: see, e.g., Lawrence and Karim 2007. There are tendencies (which we cannot discuss here) particularly in Continental philosophy and anthropology to mystify or reify violence and understand it as pervasive, especially in societal structure. However, the term's natural home involves description or interpretation of intentional actions, so reification language appears inappropriate; structural approaches may be best understood as dependent upon but tangential to the approach developed here. See Volf 1996 for theological reflection incorporating such perspectives.
6. For Fiske and Rai (2015), within a society some forms of violence are virtuous. It seems preferable to maintain the intuition that understands violence pejoratively.
7. Metaphorical usage (e.g., of storms) will not be considered.
8. The difficulty in avoiding reference to moral motivations is that the actions of the violent mob and the police are not distinguished by using the concept of violence. However, there is a question of what constitutes appropriate use of force, and by whom, even if the use of force is morally motivated for it to be considered legitimate. The threshold of appropriate use of force by the police is subject to continual scrutiny for instance since perceptions change. It is likely that more people would consider "police shooting looters" as violence today than in the study published in 1972.
9. See British Board of Film Classification Guidelines (2014); Monk-Turner et al. 2004.
10. This is not to say that there is never any historical basis to the narratives, but rather that it is patchy and not the locus of the significance of the narratives.
11. This analysis does not depend on the non-existence or existence of moral facts. The point is that moral responses (having affectual, cultural, or ideological character) are presented *as if they are* or *seem to be* normative or metaphysical judgments, whether or not there is, in fact, such a warrant.

12. See also Prior 1997 or Dawkins 2006. The strategy might be traced to Bainton (1960), writing before the concept of violence was explicitly adopted. The concept's application has reinforced the rhetoric.
13. I take it that narratives and myths are understood within the context of a tradition of use.
14. See Williams 1977 and Origen, *On First Principles* 4.2.9 (trans: Butterworth 1973).
15. See Greenberg 1995 on identifying the misuse of the Bible *as* misuse rather than pattern in contemporary Middle Eastern political contexts.
16. Note the hyperbolic or metaphorical sense even here in the injunction not to intermarry after complete annihilation (7:3–4).
17. e.g. Van Seters's discussion of 1 Samuel 30 (2009: 205–206).
18. See McDonald 2004: 143–73 for a reading of Judges along these lines.
19. Of course, this requires suitable recontextualization for the Christian reader.
20. See Earl 2009 and Murray's (2007) discussion of Nicholas Lash's view of theology as the critique of idolatry.

BIBLIOGRAPHY

Anscombe, G. E. M. 1958. "Modern Moral Philosophy." *Philosophy* 53: 1–19.
Assmann, J. 2006. *Religion and Cultural Memory*. Stanford: Stanford University Press.
Bainton, R. H. 1960. *Christian Attitudes to War and Peace: A Historical Survey and Critical Re-evaluation*. Nashville: Abingdon.
Blumenthal, M. D. 1972. "Predicting Attitudes toward Violence." *Science* (New Series) 176 no. 4041: 1296–1303.
Boling, R. G. and G. E. Wright. 1982. *Joshua: A New Translation with Notes and Commentary*. AB 6. New York: Doubleday.
Bruce, B. J., trans. 2002. Origen, *Homilies on Joshua*. FC 105. Washington, D.C.: The Catholic University of America Press.
Brueggemann, W. 1994. "The Book of Exodus." In L. E. Keck, ed., *The New Interpreter's Bible* Volume 1. Nashville: Abingdon, 675–981.
Butterworth, G. W., trans. 1973. *Origen: On First Principles*. Gloucester: Peter Smith.
Calvin, J. 1949. *Commentaries on the Book of Joshua by John Calvin*. Grand Rapids: Eerdmans.
Collins, J. J. 2004. *Does the Bible Justify Violence?* Facets. Minneapolis: Fortress Press.
Collins, J. J. 2016. "The Friends of Job and the Task of Biblical Theology." *Interpretation* 70.3: 288–300.
Coote, R. B. 1998. "The Book of Joshua." In L. E. Keck, ed., *The New Interpreter's Bible*, Volume 2. Nashville: Abingdon, 555–719.
Creach, J. F. D. 2013. *Violence in Scripture*. Interpretation: Resources for the Use of Scripture in the Church. Louisville, KY: Westminster John Knox.
Dawkins, R. 2006. *The God Delusion*. London: Bantam Press.
Driver, S. R. 1891. *Introduction to the Literature of the Old Testament*. Edinburgh: T&T Clark.
Earl, D. S. 2009. "The Christian Significance of Deuteronomy 7." *JTI* 3.1: 41–62.
Earl, D. S. 2010. *Reading Joshua as Christian Scripture*. JTISup 2. Winona Lake, IN: Eisenbrauns.
Earl, D. S. 2013. "Joshua and the Crusades." In H. Thomas, J. Evans, and P. Copan, eds., *Holy War in the Bible: Christian Morality and an Old Testament Problem*. Downers Grove, IL: IVP Academic, 19–43.
Earl, D. S. 2017. *Reading Old Testament Narrative as Christian Scripture*. JTISup 17. Winona Lake, IN: Eisenbrauns.
Fiske, A. P. and T. S. Rai. 2015. *Virtuous Violence*. Cambridge: Cambridge University Press.
Franke, J. R. 2005. *Ancient Christian Commentary on Scripture: Old Testament IV*. Downers Grove, IL: InterVarsity.

Gilbert, P. 1995. "Violence, Political." In T. Honderich, ed., *The Oxford Companion to Philosophy*. Oxford: Oxford University Press, 900.

Gottwald, N. K. 1979. *The Tribes of Yahweh: A Sociology of the Religion of Liberated Israel, 1250–1050 BCE*. Maryknoll: Orbis Books.

Greenberg, M. 1995. "On the Political Use of the Bible in Modern Israel: An Engaged Critique." In D. P. Wright, D. N. Freedman, and A. Hurwitz, eds., *Pomegranates and Golden Bells: Studies in Biblical, Jewish, and Near Eastern Ritual, Law, and Literature in Honor of Jacob Milgrom*. Winona Lake, IN: Eisenbrauns, 461–71.

Hervieu-Léger, D. 2000. *Religion as a Chain of Memory*. New Brunswick: Rutgers.

Kirwan, J. 2015. "Moral Responses and Moral Judgments." Paper presented at the Durham Philosophy Research Seminar. October 22, 2015.

Krug, E. G., L. L. Dahlberg, J. A. Mercy, A. B. Zwi, and R. Lozano. 2002. *World Report on Violence and Health*. Geneva: World Health Organization.

Kunin, S. D. 2004. *We Think What We Eat: Neo-structuralist Analysis of Israelite Food Rules and Other Cultural and Textual Practices*. JSOTSup 412. London: T&T Clark.

Lawrence, B. B. and A. Karim, eds. 2007. *On Violence: A Reader*. Durham, NC: Duke University Press.

Mbuwayesango, D. 2004. "Joshua." In D. Patte, ed., *Global Bible Commentary*. Nashville: Abingdon, 64–73.

McDonald, P. M. 2004. *God and Violence: Biblical Resources for Living in a Small World*. Scottdale: Herald.

Moberly, R. W. L. 2007. "Is Monotheism Bad for You? Some Reflections on God, the Bible, and Life in the Light of Regina Schwartz's 'The Curse of Cain,'" In R. P. Gordon, ed., *The God of Israel: Studies of an Inimitable Deity*. Cambridge: Cambridge University Press, 94–112.

Monk-Turner, E., P. Ciba, M. Cunningham, P. G. McIntire, M. Pollard, and R. Turner. 2004. "A Content Analysis of Violence in American War Movies." *Analysis of Social Issues and Public Policy* 4.1: 1–11.

Morgan, T. 1739. *The Moral Philosopher*, Volume 2: *Being a Farther Vindication of Moral Truth and Reason*. London.

Murray, P. D. 2007. "Theology 'Under the Lash': Theology as Idolatry-Critique in the Work of Nicholas Lash." in S. C. Barton, ed., *Idolatry: False Worship in the Bible, Early Judaism and Christianity*. London: T&T Clark, 246–66.

Nelson, R. D. 1987. *First and Second Kings*. Interpretation. Louisville, KY: Westminster John Knox.

Neusner, J., trans. 1988. *Mekhilta According to Rabbi Ishmael: An Analytic Translation*. Brown Judaica Studies 148. Atalanta: Scholars Press.

Oxford English Dictionary. 2014. Online edition. www.oed.com. Oxford: Oxford University Press.

Prior, M. 1997. *The Bible and Colonialism: A Moral Critique*. Sheffield: Sheffield Academic.

Rad, G. von. 1975. *Old Testament Theology*, Volume I: *The Theology of Israel's Historical Traditions*. London: SCM (orig. 1957).

Ricoeur, P. 1969. *The Symbolism of Evil*. Boston: Beacon.

Rowlett, L. L. 1996. *Joshua and the Rhetoric of Violence: A New Historicist Analysis*. JSOTSup 226. Sheffield: Sheffield Academic.

Schwartz, R. M. 1997. *The Curse of Cain: The Violent Legacy of Monotheism*. Chicago: Chicago University Press.

Soggin, J. A. 1972. *Joshua*. OTL. London: SCM.

Swart, I. and C. van Dam. 1997. "חמס." In W. A. Van Gemeren, ed., *New International Dictionary of Old Testament Theology and Exegesis*, Volume 2. Carlisle: Paternoster, 177–80.

Turner, V. 1968. "Myth and Symbol." In D. L. Sills, ed., *International Encyclopedia of the Social Sciences*, Volume 10. Michigan: Macmillan and The Free Press, 576–81.

Turner, V. 1982. *From Ritual to Theatre: The Human Seriousness of Play*. New York: PAJ.

Van Seters, J. 2009. *The Biblical Saga of King David*. Winona Lake, IN: Eisenbrauns.

Volf, M. 1996. *Exclusion and Embrace: A Theological Exploration of Identity, Otherness, and Reconciliation.* Nashville: Abingdon Press.

Vorobej, M. 2016. *The Concept of Violence.* New York: Routledge.

Warrior, R. A. 2001. "Canaanites, Cowboys and Indians: Deliverance, Conquest, and Liberation Theology Today." in D. Jobling et al., eds., *The Postmodern Bible Reader.* Oxford: Blackwell, 188–94.

Wellhausen, J. 1885. *Prolegomena to the History of Israel.* Edinburgh: Adam and Charles Black.

Williams, R. B. 1977. "Origen's Interpretation of the Old Testament and Lévi-Strauss' Interpretation of Myth." In A. L. Merrill and T. W. Overholt, eds., *Scripture in History and Theology: Essays in Honor of J. Coert Rylaarsdam.* PTMS 17. Pittsburgh: Pickwick, 279–99.

Wittgenstein, L. 2001. *Philosophical Investigations.* 3rd ed. Oxford: Blackwell.

Wright, C. J. H. 2008. *The God I Don't Understand: Reflections on Tough Questions of Faith.* Grand Rapids: Zondervan.

Zehnder, M. and H. Hagelia. 2013. *Encountering Violence in the Bible.* Sheffield: Sheffield Phoenix.

PART III

APPROACHES: COMPOSITION, SYNTHESIS, THEORY

CHAPTER 20

THE SO-CALLED DEUTERONOMISTIC HISTORY AND ITS THEORIES OF COMPOSITION

THOMAS RÖMER

THE term and the theory of the "Deuteronomistic History" has existed since the publication of a book written by the German scholar Martin Noth and published in 1943 under the title *Überlieferungsgeschichtliche Studien*, which can be roughly translated by "Studies in the Transmission of Traditions." The first part of the book was devoted to the composition and redaction of the book of Deuteronomy and the Former Prophets (Joshua, Judges, Samuel, and Kings), and the second part to an analysis of the books of Chronicles and Ezra-Nehemiah. In the first part of the book (which was later translated into English in 1981), Noth considered the book of Deuteronomy as having been conceived as the introduction to the Former Prophets. These books betray a style and a theology that can be found in the book of Deuteronomy. Therefore Noth speaks—in parallel to the books of Chronicles, Ezra, and Nehemiah, which scholars called the "chronistisches Geschichtswerk" (the "Chronicler's History")—of a "deuteronomistisches Geschichtswerk" ("Deuteronomistic History"). Before presenting Noth's theory, its modification, as well as the current debate, let us briefly recall the observations that led to the idea of a "Deuteronomistic History."

20.1 THE PREHISTORY OF THE THEORY OF THE DEUTERONOMISTIC HISTORY

In the context of the establishment of the documentary hypothesis in the nineteenth century, as advocated by Abraham Kuenen (1886) and Julius Wellhausen (1899), the book of Deuteronomy did always present a special case. Deuteronomy was the only book of the Pentateuch in which the Pentateuchal documents (Yahwist, Elohist, and Priestly Code) did not occur or only in an extremely sparse way (especially in the account of Moses's death in Deut. 34). The so-called "D" source was therefore considered to be limited to the book of Deuteronomy. Contrary to the other documents, D could not be found in the books of Genesis, Exodus, Leviticus, and Numbers except in a very limited way that did not allow the reconstruction of a coherent source. There were advocates of a "deuteronomistic" redaction in the other books, especially the Anglican bishop John William Colenso (1862–79), who tried to demonstrate the presence of redactional inserts into the books of Genesis, Exodus, Leviticus, Numbers, and Joshua. These inserts were due to an exilic "Deuteronomist," who revised the older documents of the Hexateuch. Since the end of the eighteenth century, critical scholarship had indeed very broadly adopted the idea of an original Hexateuch, since—so the argument went—the documents of the Pentateuch needed a fulfillment of the promises made to the patriarchs by telling the story of the conquest of the land. Therefore J, E, and P were also sought and found in the book of Joshua. In the discussion about the formation of the Hexateuch, the book of Deuteronomy was however largely neglected and sometimes even considered as a late insertion into the Hexateuchal narrative shared by the documents or sources of the other books. The fact that Deuteronomy is closely related to the book of Joshua did not attract much attention. The crossing of the Jordan and the conquest of the land are indeed very often mentioned in Deuteronomy and these passages clearly create a link between the books of Deuteronomy and Joshua.

In the beginning of the nineteenth century Wilhelm M. L. de Wette explained this link by the fact that Joshua is a late "deuteronomistic" book in style and theology that depends on the book of Deuteronomy (1806: 137). Heinrich Ewald, in his *History of Israel* (German original: 1843–59, English translation: 1867–86), adopted a similar view by attributing the books of Deuteronomy and Joshua to a deuteronomistic reworking of the Hexateuch, which occurred in two stages. Ewald also realized that the books of Judges, Samuel, and Kings equally underwent deuteronomistic revisions. However, because of the idea of the existence of a Hexateuch, Ewald postulated that these redactors should be distinguished from those that wrote major parts of the books of Deuteronomy and Joshua. Ewald distinguished two main deuteronomistic redactions of the books of Judges, Samuel, and Kings (to which he added the book of Ruth, according to the Greek canon): a deuteronomistic edition during the reign of king Josiah in the seventh century BCE and a Deuteronomist, writing during the exilic (Babylonian) time, whose aim was to explain the reasons for the destruction of Jerusalem and the Babylonian exile. This idea of multiple deuteronomistic revisions was then adopted by Kuenen and Wellhausen. In his *Composition of the Hexateuch and the Historical Books of the Ancient Testament* (1963), Wellhausen admits deuteronomistic editions of the books of Judges, Samuel, and Kings, but he is not much interested to resolve the questions whether these books have been revised by the same deuteronomistic redactors or whether one should postulate different redactors for each book. For the book of Kings he finds two major deuteronomistic revisions: the first occurred under the reign of Josiah, and the second during the time of the Babylonian exile.

At the beginning of the twentieth century, the existence of deuteronomistic redactions in the Former Prophets was thus widely acknowledged. But there was not much interest in explaining and analyzing more precisely the aim of those revisions. The theory of an "old" Hexateuch also prevented many scholars from investigating the stylistic and theological links between the books of Deuteronomy and Joshua on the one hand, and the books of

Judges, Samuel, and Kings on the other. One of the first to challenge the idea that the Pentateuchal sources ended in the book of Joshua was Noth's teacher Albrecht Alt, who demonstrated in several publications (1925; 1927; 1936) that the conquest narratives in Joshua 1–12 are based on an independent Benjaminite collection and cannot be attributed to J and E. The boundaries list in Joshua 13–19, which was often considered to be part of P, was according to Alt from the time of the monarchy and had nothing to do with the Priestly document. Noth adopted this position; first in his commentary on the book of Joshua published in 1938 and then five years later in his *Überlieferungsgeschichtliche Studien*.

20.2 THE INVENTION OF THE DEUTERONOMISTIC HISTORY

Noth opens his investigation with the statement that all the historical traditions of the Hebrew Bible are contained in three large compilations: "These great compilations are the Pentateuch and the historical works of the Deuteronomist and of the Chronicler" (1991: 8).[1] Interestingly, Noth does not explain the term "Deuteronomistic History." He underlines the significance of the Deuteronomist's work as Israel's first history, and compares the Deuteronomist to "those Hellenistic and Roman historians who use older accounts, mostly unacknowledged, to write a history not of their own time but the more or less distant past" (p. 26). Contrary to the Chronicler's history, the work of the Deuteronomist must however "be 'discovered' as a literary entity and unity" (p. 15). Noth does not wish to investigate which passages inside the books of Deuteronomy to Kings are "deuteronomistic." Those texts have been identified, so he claims, for a long time. The real question for Noth is to understand the purpose of those deuteronomistic texts. Former generations were not much interested in describing the aim of the deuteronomistic (Dtr.) redactor or redactors, and this is exactly the task that Noth wants to undertake. He is convinced that the Deuteronomist composed through his own texts, by which he framed and interpreted older traditions, a literary unit.

There is indeed much evidence that the Deuteronomistic History is a coherent literary unit. First of all, Noth observes that "at all the important points in the course of the history, Dtr. brings forward the leading personages with a speech..., which looks forward and backward in an attempt to interpret the course of events" (p. 18). "Elsewhere the summarizing reflections upon history...are presented by Dtr. himself...because there were not suitable historical figures to make the speeches" (p. 19). Noth identifies the following speeches: Joshua 1, 12, and 23 delimit the time of the conquest; Judg. 2:11–3:6 introduces the deuteronomistic interpretation of the time of the Judges, which is concluded by Samuel's farewell speech in 1 Samuel 12; Solomon's speech after the construction of the Jerusalem temple (1 King 8) concludes the account of the origins of the monarchy and introduces the parallel histories of the Northern (Israel) and Southern (Judah) kingdoms; and 2 Kings 17 concludes this period by explaining the reasons for the fall of Samaria. These speeches strongly support the idea that the Deuteronomistic History "was conceived as a unified and self contained whole" (p. 20). Noth certainly admits that after the Deuteronomist had finished his work, later redactors added texts like Joshua 24 and Judg. 2:1–5 that interrupt the deuteronomistic transition from Joshua 23 to the introduction of the time of

Judges in Judg. 2:6–3:6*. But he is not interested in exploring the reasons for those additions. His aim is to explore the reasons that pushed the Deuteronomist to write his history. The *terminus a quo* for his composition is 562 BCE because the Babylonian king Amel-Marduk, who released the Judean king Jehoiachin from his Babylonian prison (an event that is mentioned in the last chapter of Kings), only reigned during this year. The Deuteronomist framed also the book of Deuteronomy in order to transform it into the opening of his historical account. Deuteronomy is constructed as a long farewell speech in which Moses recapitulates earlier events from the time of the sojourn in the wilderness and also foresees the coming events, especially the destruction of Jerusalem and the Babylonian Exile. Therefore, one can understand Moses's speech in Deuteronomy as the prototype of all the following speeches that structure the Deuteronomistic History (p. 31). Noth then investigates the deuteronomistic presentation of the different periods: the Mosaic period, the time of the conquest, the period of the Judges, the first three kings (Saul, David, Solomon), and the period of the two kingdoms until the destruction of Samaria and Jerusalem.

In constructing his history, the Deuteronomist acted like an "honest broker" (p. 128) and did not alter the older traditions he incorporated, even if their ideology did not fit his own ideas. Through this respect towards the older traditions, the Deuteronomistic History also constitutes a source for the history of Israel and Judah in the first half of the first millennium BCE (p. 121). But above all, the aim of the Deuteronomist is to explain the reasons for the destruction of the Israelite and Judean monarchies. These reasons are the disobedience of the people and most of its kings who did not respect the divine law concealed in the book of Deuteronomy and to which Israel was bound by a covenant. For the Deuteronomist, this law required the exclusive worship of Yhwh in the temple of Jerusalem, the only legitimate cultic place. However, the Deuteronomist is not interested in cultic matters (p. 138) but in the observance of the divine law. The curses that conclude the deuteronomic law (destruction, deportation; Deut. 28) have become a reality at the time the Deuteronomist writes his history. His goal was to explain the catastrophe, and he had no hope for a better future. The few texts in Deuteronomy and Kings that envisage a return and a restoration are later additions to the original work (p. 144).

The Deuteronomist was, according to Noth, an independent author, who was not commissioned by any particular individual or group (p. 145). He possibly wrote in Palestine, perhaps in Mizpah, the place where the Babylonians established the governor of the land. He was therefore "one of those who stayed in the land" (p. 145, n. 1).

20.3 THE INITIAL RECEPTION OF NOTH'S THEORY

The first edition of Noth's work was not widely known, and his work gained notoriety only after the second edition that appeared in 1957. Many scholars then agreed with Noth's hypothesis and the term "Deuteronomistic History" found its entry into many textbooks. Noth's ideas also found a confirmation in the work of Alfred Jepsen on the sources of the books of Kings. This work had been written already in 1939 but its publication had been delayed until 1953 because of the Second World War (see Jepsen 1956). Jepsen distinguished three major redactional layers in the books of Kings: (1) a Synchronic Chronicle from the beginning of the sixth century BCE that synchronized the reigns of the Israelite and Judean kings until the reign of Hezekiah and that a redactor combined with a Judean annalistic source; (2) a redaction in Palestine around 550 BCE that integrated many prophetic traditions into the books of kings, and (3) a last revision in the early postexilic time defending Levitical interests. In his foreword to the first edition of his book, Jepsen emphasized the compatibility of his results with Noth's hypothesis and the proximity of his second "prophetic" redactor with Noth's Deuteronomist. Like Noth, Jepsen underscored the idea that this second redactor wanted to show that the fall of Judah and Jerusalem was due to the people's apostasy. But differently than Noth, he focused on the importance of the prophetic text and traditions in the books of Kings, a topic that became important in one of the later modifications of Noth's hypothesis.

In Europe, and especially in German scholarship, the reactions to Noth's idea were generally positive, although many of his followers introduced some different views on the Deuteronomistic History. Noth had portrayed his Deuteronomist as an author who expressed a very pessimistic view of Israel's history and who had no hope for any future. Consequently, he did not pay attention to texts that could be read in a different way. Gerhard von Rad (1958) pointed out that the oracle to David in 2 Samuel 7 and the release of Jehoiachin from prison in Babylonia (2 Kgs. 25:27–30) should be understood as an indication that the Davidic dynasty did not come to an end in 587 BCE. According to von Rad, the Deuteronomist had almost messianic expectations. Hans Walter Wolff disagreed on this point, and pointed out that the main concern of the Deuteronomistic History was not the idea of an unconditional restoration of the Judean monarchy, but much more an appeal to return (*šwb*), which according to Wolff is one of the main foci of the "kerygma" of the Deuteronomist (1975: 90–98). But Wolff also observed that in some texts, especially in Deuteronomy, this return is announced in unconditional language, with a terminology that one finds also in the salvation oracles in the book of Jeremiah (see especially Deut. 4:29–31; 28:45–68; 30:1–10). Wolff saw here the possibility of a later redactor who tried to combine the theology of the first Deuteronomist with ideas of return and salvation from the book of Jeremiah (1975: 96). Contrary to Noth, who saw the Deuteronomist as a single and independent author, Wolff speaks of a deuteronomistic "circle" and prepares the way for the idea of a deuteronomistic "school," or of a multi-layered deuteronomistic edition, a theory that will be the base of the two major modifications that Noth's theory underwent.

20.4 THE TWO MAJOR MODIFICATIONS OF NOTH'S THEORY

20.4.1 Josianic and Exilic Editions of the Deuteronomistic History

In 1968 Frank M. Cross published an article, "The Structure of the Deuteronomic History," which was reprinted five years later under the title, "The Themes of the Book of Kings and the

Structure of the Deuteronomistic History." He pointed out that the book of Kings is characterized by two major themes. The first is the "sin of Jeroboam," that is, the building of Yahwistic sanctuaries in Dan and Bethel outside of Yhwh's chosen place Jerusalem. Consequently, all northern kings are accused of having continued the sin of the founder of the northern kingdom. Because of this sin, Yhwh finally destroyed Samaria, as stated in the deuteronomistic comment in 2 Kings 17. The second theme starts with Yhwh's oracle to David in 2 Samuel 7, where he promises him an eternal dynasty. Both themes are set in contrast: "David in Kings is the symbol of fidelity, Jeroboam is the symbol of infidelity" (1973: 282). Both themes converge in the account of Josiah's reform in 2 Kgs. 22:1–23:25. Josiah destroys the sanctuary at Bethel and brings the sin of Jeroboam to a definitive end; he is also presented as a new David, restoring the kingdom of his ancestor and centralizing the cult in Jerusalem according to the law of the sanctuary in Deuteronomy 12. Accordingly, the Deuteronomistic History "may be described as a propaganda work of the Josianic reformation" (p. 284).

Consequently, for Cross, the first edition of the Deuteronomistic History was written during the lifetime of Josiah and ended with Josiah's praise in 2 Kgs. 23:25. Cross's first edition of the Deuteronomistic History reveals a very different ideology from the one that Noth attributed to his Deuteronomist. The explanation of the exile is, according to Cross, the work of a second, exilic edition of the Deuteronomistic History. A second Deuteronomist (Dtr^2) updated the Josianic edition after the fall of Judah by adding 2 Kgs. 22:36–25:30 and "retouched or overwrote the Deuteronomistic work...to reshape the history, with a minimum of reworking, into a document relevant to exiles for whom the bright expectations of the Josianic era were hopelessly past" (p. 285). Dtr^2 added especially the theme of the sin of Manasseh in 2 Kgs. 21:1–15, which parallels for Judah the theme of Jeroboam's sin and provides an explanation for the downfall of Jerusalem. He also inserted other short passages, which clearly presuppose the events of 587 BCE, such as Deut. 28:3–7, 63–68; Josh. 23:11–13,15–16; 1 Kgs. 6:11–13; 8:46–53; 9:4–9, and others. This theory of a twofold edition is a revival of ideas of Kuenen and Wellhausen (although Cross does not quote them) combined with Noth's idea of a comprehensive historiographical work running from Deuteronomy to Kings. However, Cross confined his demonstration of a Josianic edition of the Deuteronomistic History to the books of Samuel-Kings. Several students of Cross developed the idea of a two-fold edition of the Deuteronomistic History, attributing more texts to Dtr^2 than Cross had done. Richard Nelson added in his doctoral dissertation (published 1981a) several idiomatic expressions that were typical for the second, exilic Deuteronomist, and considered texts such as Judg. 2:1–5; 6:7–10, 2 Kgs. 17:7–20, 24–28, 34b–40, and others as stemming from Dtr^2. Richard E. Friedman (1981), Andrew D. H. Mayes (1983), Gary Knoppers (1993), and many others came to similar conclusions. Cross's model became dominant in Anglo-Saxon scholarship and still is the most popular model on the Deuteronomistic History used by scholars and teachers.

20.4.2 Multiple, Exilic, and Postexilic Strata of the Deuteronomistic History

Noth himself had been aware of later additions to the Deuteronomistic History, but he did not pay attention to them. One of Noth's first critics Otto Eissfeldt, who called Noth "the father of the Deuteronomistic History" (1965: 265) insisted on the diversity of the "Deuteronomistic" texts, which manifest too many differences to be ascribed to a single author or redactor (e.g., the various and contradictory attempts in Judg. 2:11–3:6 to explain why some of the autochthonous people remained in the land, whereas other deuteronomistic texts such as Josh. 21:34–45 insist on the total expulsion of the former inhabitants of the land).

Rudolf Smend, a former research assistant of Martin Noth, took up this observation but tried to reconcile it with Noth's idea of a Deuteronomistic History. Smend's article (German 1971; English 2000) started with an analysis of the divine speech to Joshua in Josh. 1:1–9. Smend observed that the first part of this speech resembles a divine oracle to a military chief who is about to start his campaign. This speech seems to end in verse 6. Verse 7 contains a repetition of the foregoing exhortation ("be strong and do not fear"), but the perspective changes: now Joshua is admonished to keep and remember the Law of Moses day and night. Apparently, verses 7–9 are an addition in deuteronomistic style in order to transform the military speech into a discourse about the observance of the Law. Similar deuteronomistic additions can be found in Josh. 13:1–6; 23, Judg. 2:20–21, 23, and elsewhere, starting in Deut. 1:5 until the last chapter of Kings. Smend invented the siglum DtrN (Deuteronomistic Nomist) for the redactor or redactors (he tended toward a plurality of nomistic redactors) in contrast to the first edition of the Deuteronomistic History (DtrH), which he, like Noth, considered as having been composed during the Babylonian period. A student of Smend, Walter Dietrich added to DtrH and DtrN a "DtrP," a prophetic Deuteronomist (1972), who only intervened in the books of Samuel and Kings. This redactor inserted into the Deuteronomistic History prophetic stories and oracles and provided each one with a note about its accomplishment (1 Kgs. 14:7–13; 1 Kgs. 15:19; 2 Kgs. 21:10–14; 2 Kgs. 24:2, etc.). Timo Veijola developed the idea of a threefold edition of the Deuteronomistic History in the Babylonian and early Persian period in two monographs (1975 and 1977). This model allowed for an explanation of the contradictory statements about kingship in the books of Samuel and Kings. According to Veijola, DtrH (the first Deuteronomist) regarded the monarchy still in a positive way (see 1 Sam. 9–10), DtrP had a very critical position towards monarchy (see 1 Sam. 12), whereas DtrN, while still hostile against the institution of monarchy, tried to whitewash David and Solomon, the founders of the Israelite monarchy (1 Sam. 8:6–22; 1 Kgs. 1:35–37; 2:3–4a). The so-called "Göttingen school" hypothesis was quickly adopted by many European scholars and also some North American scholars (e.g., Ralph Klein 1979).

20.5 Noth's Single Redaction Model Maintained

Some scholars maintained Noth's model of a single Deuteronomist who wrote his history shortly after the destruction of Jerusalem. For example, John Van Seters presented the Deuteronomist as a historian comparable the the Greek historians Herodotus and Thucydides. Contrary to Noth, who thought that the Deuteronomist had integrated older texts into his work, which he sometimes did not revise at all, Van Seters considered the

Deuteronomist above all as an author, who certainly knew some older traditions but used and rewrote them in a very free manner (1983). The ideological contradictions, especially in the books of Samuel and Kings, should not be explained by the integration of older sources, but by later post-deuteronomistic additions. This is, according to Van Seters, the case for the so-called "Court History" in 2 Samuel 2–4, 9–20 and 1 Kings 1–2, which depicts a very weak and dubious David, a picture that does not fit at all with the story of David's rise in the first book of Samuel (2000). The Court History is therefore a late addition from the end of the Babylonian period, a purely fictional, anti-Davidic addition to the work of the Deuteronomist, written in order to counter expectations about the restoration of the Davidic dynasty.

Steven McKenzie (French 1996, English 2000) likewise considers the Deuteronomistic History to be the work of one author (see also Blum 1990; Krause 2015) who wrote shortly after the events of 587 in Mizpah[2] (as also argued by Noth). Contrary to Noth, McKenzie assumes that the Deuteronomist expected a continuation of the Davidic dynasty after the Exile and the destruction of the palace and the temple of Jerusalem.[3] As for the prophetic material of the book of Kings, McKenzie holds (with others) that these stories have been added later into the Deuteronomistic History, an idea which can be compared to the later "prophetic Deuteronomist" of the Göttingen school.

20.6 THE QUESTION OF DEUTERONOMISTIC TEXTS IN THE BOOKS OF GENESIS TO NUMBERS AND THEIR RELATION TO THE DEUTERONOMISTIC HISTORY

In Noth's theory, the book of Deuteronomy was originally the introduction of the Deuteronomistic History *via negationis*. He stated: "there is no sign of 'Deuteronomistic editing' in Genesis–Numbers" (1991: 28). This view has become less obvious, however, especially in European scholarship in which the Documentary Hypothesis is no longer considered a fitting model to describe the formation of the Pentateuch. Scholars such as Erhard Blum (1990) and Rainer Albertz (1992) consider the Pentateuch to be the result of a compromise between a deuteronomistic group and a priestly group, whose compositions had been combined (together with other texts) during the Persian period in order to form the Pentateuch. The most deuteronomistic texts can be found in the Moses and Exodus story.[4] The question then arises about the relation between the deuteronomistic texts in the first books of the Pentateuch and those of the so-called Deuteronomistic History. Most scholars advocating the idea of a larger deuteronomistic composition would argue that the deuteronomistic texts in the Tetrateuch (a designation for the first four books of the Torah) would have been composed after the Deuteronomistic History in Deuteronomy–Kings in order to create a new prologue to this history.[5]

20.7 THE DISSOLUTION OF THE COHERENCE OF THE DEUTERONOMISTIC HISTORY

Contrary to the positions of Noth, Van Seters, McKenzie, and others, there is a trend to focus on the many layers that are detectable inside the books of Deuteronomy to Kings. Already Smend (German 1971, English 2000) indicated that his early postexilic DtrN should be understood as a symbol for a complex redactional process in many stages ($DtrN^1$, $DtrN^2$, $DtrN^3$, etc.). Other followers of the Göttingen model added new sigla and increased the strata inside the Deuteronomistic History. Lohfink (1991) invented a "DtrL" (Deuteronomistische Landeroberungserzählung), a deuteronomistic editor of the conquest stories in Joshua 2–12, who, in the time of Josiah, was the first to combine on a literary level the books of Deuteronomy and Joshua. He also postulated a "DtrÜ" (a "Überarbeiter"), a late Deuteronomist who revised the whole Deuteronomistic History after "DtrN." Lohfink's "DtrÜ" comes close to Kaiser's "DtrS" ("S" standing for "spät," late), covering several late additions and redactions of the Deuteronomistic History (1992: 85). Veijola (1996) found in his commentary on the book of Deuteronomy a "DtrB" (a "bundestheologischer Deuteronomist," a Deuteronomist who introduced in the early Persian period the texts that understand the relation between Yhwh and Israel in terms of a covenant). This inflation of new sigla and layers challenges the idea of a coherent deuteronomistic composition, since it is no longer clear how these numerous layers can be reconstructed in a comprehensive way and how they can be related to each other. It is therefore not astonishing that there is a trend in recent European but also North American scholarship to deny the existence of a Deuteronomistic History.

20.8 THE REJECTION OF THE THEORY OF A DEUTERONOMISTIC HISTORY

Over the last three decades, several scholars, especially in Europe, have rejected Noth's theory on the basis of several observations and arguments. The opponents of Noth's idea insist on the old observation of Eissfeldt (1964) and others that the deuteronomistic texts in the books of the Former Prophets are extremely different from one to another and cannot be assigned to one or two coherent deuteronomistic editions. The deuteronomistic texts in Judges (especially Judg. 2:5–3:6) suggest a cyclic conception of history, while Samuel and Kings clearly present a linear story. The presence of deuteronomistic texts in Judges and Samuel is much more discrete than in the books of Joshua or Kings. Therefore Westermann, who already in 1994 challenged the idea of a Deuteronomistic History, argued that each book of the Former Prophet has a very different history of transmission and composition. It has also been observed that the idea of cult centralization plays a major role in Deuteronomy and Kings but does not appear in Joshua, Judges, and Samuel, where other Yahwistic sanctuaries seem acceptable. Therefore Knauf (French 1996, English 2000), Noll

(2007), and others consider Noth's theory as a major error in biblical scholarship. Auld (1999), Aurelius (2003), and others have adapted an idea of Ernst Würthwein from 1994 who claimed that the so-called Deuteronomistic History should be limited to the books of Kings or Samuel-Kings. They also underline the fact that the importance of the Davidic dynasty in the book of Kings is incompatible with the book of Deuteronomy, which is not interested in kingship at all. The only text in that book that mentions the king, Deut. 17:14–20, limits his power and shows a theology that contradicts the importance of David and his dynasty in the book of Kings.[6] Should one therefore consider Noth's theory as another error of critical biblical scholarship and go back to the position of Ewald, Wellhausen, and others, who noted an important number of deuteronomistic additions and revisions in the Former Prophets but did not recognize any coherence or comprehensive theology in those additions?

20.9 A Deuteronomistic Library instead of a Deuteronomistic History

The present state of research about the theory of the Deuteronomistic History reveals at least four scholarly positions: (1) the theory of one single Deuteronomist; (2) the theory of a Josianic and an exilic edition of the Deuteronomistic History (the "Cross school"); (3) the theory of three major strata of the Deuteronomistic History that originated in the Babylonian period and were completed in the early Persian period (the "Smend school"); and (4) the rejection of the the theory of a comprehensive deuteronomistic work encompassing the books of Deuteronomy to Kings. The positions (2) and (3) are followed by a majority of scholars. Anglo-Saxon scholars largely follow the model of Cross, whereas most Europeans use the model of Smend. There has been little debate between both schools, and few have asked the question whether the insights of both theories could be combined.

Some attempts have been made in this direction. Mark O'Brien (1989) thinks that the Deuteronomistic History originated in the seventh century BCE, but was then edited by three major redactions during the time of the Babylonian exile. Iain W. Provan (1988) analyzes the theme of the "high places" (*bamôt*) in Kings and concludes that there was in fact a first deuteronomistic edition of the books of Samuel and Kings in the Josianic period, which ended with the abolition of the high places by Hezekiah. The authors of this deuteronomistic edition knew a preexilic version of Deuteronomy but did not include the book in their history: "the first DH, although influenced by Dtn laws,... was simply a history of the monarchy from Saul to Hezekiah, with its necessary prologue in 1 Samuel 1–8.... Noth's DH seems best understood as an exilic expansion of an early work as to include an account of giving of the law, the conquest of the land, the period of the judges and the exile" (Provan 1988: 169–70). These approaches, which tend to combine different insights from different "schools," are promising. We should therefore try to take into account the arguments of each of the four positions presented above. In the humanities, hypotheses are rarely completely wrong or completely right. In elaborating a theory about the formation of the books of Deuteronomy to Kings one should therefore try to integrate as many of the above observations as possible.

We may agree with the opponents of Noth's theory that the deuteronomistic passages in the books of Deuteronomy to Kings present themselves in terms of frequency, use of language, and theological themes often in different manners. The supporters of a three-layer-model take this observation into account, by insisting on the necessity of literary and ideological differentiation inside the Deuteronomistic History. Contrary to those who claim that there are no deuteronomistic themes and expressions that bind together the books of Deuteronomy to Kings it can be shown that those themes do indeed exist. The warning against following "other gods" (*'ĕlōhîm 'ăḥērîm*) is a standard expression occurring in all books of the Deuteronomistic History, but is almost lacking in the Tetrateuch.[7] Direct allusions to the exile occur in the Tetrateuch only in Lev. 26:27–33. In the books of Deuteronomy to Kings, Israel's loss of the land and deportation are clearly addressed and appear in almost all of the structuring discourses of the Deuteronomistic History. In regard to these speeches, it can also be observed that the book of Deuteronomy is composed as a lengthy discourse of Moses, providing the pattern for the major comments and farewell speeches in the Former Prophets (see especially Josh. 23 and 1 Sam. 12, which are equally speeches at the end of the life of their protagonists).

The advocates of a Josianic Deuteronomistic History have to be approved as far as certain texts and ideas are better understood in the seventh century BCE than in the exilic period. The parallels between the original edition of Deuteronomy and the loyalty oath of Esarhaddon from 672 BCE make it quite plausible that Deuteronomy was written by scribes who knew this treaty, probably under the reign of Josiah (Otto 1999; Steymans 2003).[8] There are also indications that the conquest accounts in the first part of the book of Joshua may have been composed in reaction to Assyrian military propaganda with which they show many parallels (Younger 1990). It has even been argued that Joshua is constructed as a forerunner of Josiah (Nelson 1981b). There is also much evidence for a seventh-century BCE edition of the books of Samuel and Kings. The frequent use of the formula "until this day" (Childs 1963) refers in some cases clearly to a preexilic situation (Geoghegan 2006), as for instance the remark about the Ark of the Covenant that is placed in the temple of Jerusalem "until this day," which clearly presupposes the existence of the First temple, because there was no such an Ark in the Second temple. The presentation of Josiah as a "new David" also makes better sense in a seventh-century edition. The idea of Cross that 2 Kgs. 23:25 was the ending of the Josianic edition can be bolstered by the observation (not made by Cross) that this concluding verse has a literary parallel in Deut. 6:5:

> 2 Kgs. 23:25: "Before him (= Josiah) there was no king like him, who turned to Yhwh with all his heart, with all his soul, and with all his might (*mě'ōd*)."
>
> Deut. 6:5 "You shall love Yhwh your God with all your heart, and with all your soul, and with all your might (*mě'ōd*)."

In the whole Hebrew Bible, it is only in these two passages that the adverb *mě'ōd* is used as a substantive. In regard to this intertextuality, Josiah was the only one who accomplished the exhortation of Deut. 6:5 literally. And if Deut. 6:4–5 was the original opening of Deuteronomy, as often assumed, we would have a very nice frame holding together a Josianic edition of a collection comprising the scrolls of Deuteronomy, Joshua, Samuel, and Kings. There is little evidence that the book of Judges was already part of this edition, so that we should think more of several scrolls that were kept on the same shelf of a library (Römer 2005): Deuteronomy, Joshua, and Samuel-Kings. It is very possible that this seventh-century BCE library also contained a scroll with the story of Moses and the Exodus in which there are elements that support a date in the neo-Assyrian period (Otto 2000). It has often been observed that the story of Moses's birth and exposition (Exod. 2) contains close parallels to Sargon's birth story, copies of which circulated under Sargon II at the end of the eighth century BCE (Gerhards 2006). The first compilation gathered in the deuteronomistic library in the palace or temple of Jerusalem can indeed be understood, as suggested by Cross, as propaganda literature, in order to legitimate the Judean dynasty and Jerusalem, which after the fall of Samaria considered themselves as chosen by Yhwh. It became crisis literature only after the fall of Jerusalem and the deportation of the upper class to Babylon.

Noth's idea that the Deuteronomistic History was the work of one individual writer who had no link to any religious or political institutions is certainly anachronistic because almost all writings of the Hebrew Bible are to be considered as literature of tradition and have passed through the hands of many copyists and editors who stored the writings in temple or sanctuary "libraries." In this perspective, the deuteronomistic collection was edited and elaborated for at least a century, and there is evidence that enables us to distinguish three major strata of redaction: a first edition under Josiah, a new edition during the Babylonian period (when the book of Judges and probably also the book of Jeremiah were added into the deuteronomistic library), and finally a last revision in the early Persian period before the Deuteronomistic History was broken up and the book of Deuteronomy became the final book of the Pentateuch.

20.9.1 Arguments for a Three-fold Edition of the Deuteronomistic Library

In many of the major deuteronomistic speeches or discourses in the books of Deuteronomy to Kings one can quite easily distinguish three layers that correspond to the three historical periods mentioned above.

20.9.1.1 *Deuteronomy 12*

Let us start with the centralization law in Deut. 12:2–18. This text admonishes the addressees several times to sacrifice only at the place (*maqôm*) that Yhwh has chosen (vv. 4–7, 11–12, 13–14). This commandment is always preceded by a negative statement: vv. 2–4: not to imitate the way of the nations; vv. 8–10: not to act as "today"; v. 13: not to offer holocausts in other sanctuaries. Furthermore, each sequence ends with a call to rejoice (vv. 7, 12, and 18). These observations allow us to distinguish three units: vv. 2–7; 8–12; 13–18. The oldest text can be found in 12:13–18,[9] later enlarged first by vv. 8–12 (with v. 28) and finally by vv. 2–7 (with 29–31). Each of these units reflects one of the three historical contexts of the editing of the so-called Deuteronomistic History.

20.9.1.2 *Deuteronomy 12:13–18*

The original centralization law presumes the existence of the temple of Jerusalem. Those verses were part of the first edition of Deuteronomy and followed perhaps directly the introduction in Deut. 6:4–5. This passage does not seem to presuppose the fiction of Deuteronomy as a speech of Moses, and it assumes the addressees live in the land. The *maqôm* points to the temple of Jerusalem and the unique tribe, which Yhwh will choose, refers to Judah (see similarly 1 Kgs. 8:16; Ps. 78:67–68). This theology of election is perfectly conceivable in the context of the so-called Josianic reform.

20.9.1.3 Deuteronomy 12:8–12

These verses presume the historical fiction of Deuteronomy as a Mosaic speech and the identification of the addressees as the generation of the conquest (12:9–10). After describing in v. 8 the present as a time of disorder, v. 9 states that the addressees have not yet come to the "rest" that Yhwh will provide. This verse points forward to Solomon's speech in 1 Kgs. 8:56: "Blessed be Yhwh, who has given rest (*menuḥâ*) to the people Israel." The theme of "rest" appears in several deuteronomistic texts (see, among others, Josh. 23:1; 2 Sam. 7:1, 11; 1 Kgs. 5:18). For the exilic edition of the Deuteronomistic History, the construction of the temple appears as the fulfillment of the promise of rest given in Deut. 12:10, whereas the exile appears as a time of restlessness and despair (Deut. 28:65: "And among these nations you shall find no rest").

20.9.1.4 Deuteronomy 12:2–7

This last development of Deuteronomy 12, to which belong also verses 29–31, is marked by a segregationist attitude towards the "other nations," comparable to Deut. 7:1–6, 22–26, and 9:1–6. This aggressive attitude suggests ideological and temporal proximity to the books of Ezra and Nehemiah. The order to destroy the altars of the nations (Deut. 12:3) foreshadows 2 Kgs. 23:15, where this expression occurs for the last time in the deuteronomistic corpus (see also Exod. 34:13; Deut. 7:5; Judg. 2:2; 6:30–31; 2 Kgs. 23:12). The relation between Deut. 12:3 and 2 Kgs. 23:15 could indicate, in the context of the early Persian period, a polemical attitude against Samaritan and diaspora sanctuaries.

20.9.1.5 Joshua 11:23; 21:42–45; and 23

These passages contain three different endings of the book of Joshua. Joshua 11:23 sounds very much like a conclusion; it refers to Yhwh's initial speech to Joshua in Josh. 1:1–9* with respect to the conquest of the land (1:2) and the distribution of the land as a *naḥalāh*. This verse suggests that the distribution of the land has already taken place. It is therefore possible that the concluding remark in 11:23 reflects a stage of the formation of Joshua in which the list material in chs. 13–19 did not yet exist (Nelson 1997: 164). If Josh. 11:23 was the original deuteronomistic conclusion of the book (Kratz 2000: 207; Becker 2006: 151), it was probably followed by the report of Joshua's death in Judg. 2:8–9 (or Josh. 24:29–30).

Joshua 21:42–45 insists on the fact that all divine promises have been fulfilled. Yhwh has given the whole land to Israel, which has defeated all the former inhabitants. In some verses of Joshua 23 however, Joshua states that there are still people remaining in the land with which Israel should not interact, whereas other verses (v. 9) insist also on the fact that Yhwh has expelled all nations. This indicates that the exilic deuteronomistic ending of Joshua (Josh.

21:43–45; Josh. 23:1–2*, 3, 9, 11, 14b–16a) was reworked by an early Persian-period redaction with a similar segregationist ideology as in Deut. 12:2–7 (23:4–8, 10, 14b–15).[10]

20.9.1.6 1 Kings 8

Solomon's speech(es) for the dedication of the Jerusalem temple also betray traces of a triple editing during the Josianic, Babylonian, and Persian periods. The oldest part of Solomon's speech can be detected in 1 Kgs. 8:14–21, which refers back to 2 Samuel 7 and links Yhwh's choice of David and the choice of the temple in Jerusalem. The quite triumphant tone of 1 Kgs. 8:14–21* makes perfect sense in the context of the Josianic period. This tone changes with regard to the king and temple in the central prayer that follows.

The exilic deuteronomistic redactor added 1 Kgs. 8:22–40, 46–51, 54–57. First, one can observe that in this exilic edition the deportation is foreseen and the temple has become a *qibla*, a direction toward which the exiles should pray (1 Kgs. 8:48, see also Dan. 6:11). The prayer occasions in vv. 33–40 and 46–51[11] also correspond to the curses of Deuteronomy 28:[12] defeat (1 Kgs. 8:33; Deut. 28:25), no rain (1 Kgs. 8:35; Deut. 28:25), famine, plague, blight, mildew, locusts or caterpillars, enemies (1 Kgs. 8:37; Deut. 28:21–22, 38, 55), deportation and exile (1 Kgs. 8:46; Deut. 28:64–65). In this exilic revision, Solomon insists on the fact that Yhwh fulfilled all his promises. The deportation and the exile are entirely Israel's fault.

The last revision of Solomon's prayer occurs in 8:52–53 and 57–61. In this revision, the temple disappears and is replaced by Yhwh's commandments. This passage also insists on the opposition between Israel, chosen by Yhwh, and the other people (vv. 59–60). These verses relate to the last deuteronomistic layer of Deut. 12:2–7.

20.9.1.7 2 Kings 17:1–23

In the deuteronomistic comment on the fall of Samaria, one can also distinguish three strata. In 2 Kgs. 17:1–6*, 18, 21–23aα.b, the decline of the northern kingdom is explained as the consequence of the failure of the kings of Israel to conform to the deuteronomistic idea of centralization and their worship of other gods. The affirmation of 2 Kgs. 17:18 that now only the tribe of Judah is left fits well with the time of Josiah, and with the affirmation of Deut. 12:14, that there is only one tribe which is chosen by Yhwh. The comment on the fall of Israel in 2 Kgs. 17 was revised during the Babylonian period and new passages were added: 17:7–8a and 19, which parallel the misdeeds of the Israelites with the misdeeds of the Judeans (cf. 1 Kgs. 14:23–24) and announce the coming destruction of Judah.

Verses 12–17 and 20 belong to deuteronomistic revisions from the Persian period. One of the main accusations is now, again, that Israel did not segregate from the surrounding nations. Second Kgs. 17:15b ("they followed the nations that were around them, concerning whom Yhwh had commanded them that they should not do as they did") presents itself as a quotation from Deut. 12:4 and 31 and can therefore be attributed to the same redactional level.

20.9.1.8 The Endings of the Three Editions of the Deuteronomistic History

The different perspectives of the successive editions of Deuteronomistic History are also reflected in their respective endings. First, 2 Kgs. 23:25a is the conclusion of the Josianic edition of the deuteronomistic work. As noted above, Josiah is here celebrated as the new David and the only king who totally accomplished the theological program of Deut. 6:4–5. Second, 2 Kgs. 25:21, "So Judah was exiled away from their land," is constructed in parallel to 2 Kgs. 17:23b and was probably the closing remark of the exilic Deuteronomistic History. The exile appears as the conclusion of the whole history, creating at the same time the myth of an "empty land," suggesting that "all Israel" had been deported, which is in contradiction to the historical facts and other biblical accounts (Barstad 1996). This exilic perspective suggests that the Deuteronomists writing in the Babylonian period found themselves among the exiles. The present conclusion of the book of Kings in 2 Kgs. 25:27–30 has been understood by von Rad and others as a text that expresses hope for the restoration of the Davidic dynasty. It should be noted, however, that King Jehoiachin stays in Babylon "all the days of his life." His coming out of prison, changing of clothes, and receiving a place "second to the king" reminds readers of the fate of the diaspora heroes Joseph, Mordecai, and Daniel. The stories in Genesis 37–50, the book of Esther, and Daniel 1–6 insist on the fact that the land of deportation has become a land where Jews can live and manage interesting careers. As the conclusion of the Persian period edition of the Deuteronomistic History, the destiny of Jehoiachin symbolizes the transformation of exile into diaspora (Clements 2007).

20.10 The "End" of the Deuteronomistic History

Around 400–350 BCE when the Pentateuch was compiled, the pentateuchal editors decided to construct the Pentateuch as a biography of Moses, covering his whole life from his birth (Exod. 2) to his death (Deut. 34). In this context, the book of Deuteronomy was transformed to become the conclusion to the Pentateuch. This redaction added the epitaph in 34:10–12: "never again a prophet like Moses arose in Israel, a prophet whom Yhwh knew face to face...." These verses indicate that the following history contained in Joshua to Kings is not to be understood on the same level. In a way, the books of Joshua to Kings became "deutero-canonical books" in regard to the Torah. They were gathered together with prophetic scrolls and their prophetic character strengthened by the integration of prophetic stories (Elijah and Elisha) in the book of Kings. The Deuteronomistic History had disappeared—until it was rediscovered by Martin Noth.

Notes

1. All quotations are from the second edition of the English translation (Noth 1991).
2. In his 1991 book, *The Trouble with Kingship*, McKenzie still defended a Josianic Deuteronomist.
3. A similar position has recently been advocated in Rückl 2016.
4. According to Blum (2006), his "D-composition" started in Exodus 1.

5. Van Seters (1992) adopts a similar view because he considers his "Yahwist" in Genesis through Joshua as later than the Deuteronomist. The aim of the Yahwist was to write a "Prologue to History." Schmitt (1997) defends the idea of a "late Deuteronomistic History" covering the Enneateuch.
6. In recent scholarship, this passage is often considered as a post-deuteronomistic insert (Achenbach 2009; Römer 2013; Rückl 2016).
7. Only in Exod. 20:3 (Deut. 5:7); 22:13; 34:14 (singular).
8. These parallels are acknowledged by most scholars. There is, however, a trend taking up an old idea of Hölscher (1922), who argued that the first edition of Deuteronomy was written during the Babylonain exile. Cf. for instance, Pakkala 2009. Their main argument is that Deuteronomy is not interested in the question of kingship. One may respond to this that the structure of Deuteronomy may indeed reflect the importance of the high state officers, who according to 2 Kings 22 were at the origin of the "Josianic reform." The copy of Esarhaddon's vassal treaty found recently in the temple of Tell Tayinat (see Lauinger 2012) makes it very plausible that there was also a copy of this treaty in the temple of Jerusalem (Steymans 2013).
9. This section is mainly formulated in the second person singular, contrary to the two other sections.
10. For more details see Römer 2009a.
11. Verses 41–45 are probably an isolated later edition.
12. Burney 1920: 112–15.

Bibliography

Achenbach, Reinhard. 2009. "Das sogenannte Königsgesetz in Deuteronomium 17,14–20." *ZABR* 15: 216–33.
Albertz, Rainer. 1992. *Religionsgeschichte Israels in alttestamentlicher Zeit*. Grundrisse zum Alten Testament 8. Bd 2. Göttingen: Vandenhoeck & Ruprecht. English translation: *A History of Israelite Religion in the Old Testament Period*, Volume 2: *From the Exile to the Maccabees*. OTL. Louisville, KY: Westminster John Knox.
Alt, Albrecht. 1925. "Judas Gaue unter Josia." *Palästina Jahrbuch* 21: 110–17 (= 1953. *Kleine Schriften zur Geschichte des Volkes Israel II*, Munich: C. H. Beck, 276–88).
Alt, Albrecht. 1927. "Das System der Stammesgrenzen im Buche Josua." *ZAW* 54: 59–81 (= 1953. *Kleine Schriften zur Geschichte des Volkes Israel I*. Munich: C. H. Beck, 191–215).
Alt, Albrecht. 1936. "Josua." In Paul Volz et al., eds., *Werden und Wesen des Alten Testaments*. BZAW 66. Berlin: Töpelmann, 13–29 (= 1953. *Kleine Schriften zur Geschichte des Volkes Israel I*. Munich: C. H. Beck, 176–92).
Auld, A. Graeme. 1999. "The Deuteronomists and the Former Prophets, or What Makes the Former Prophets Deuteronomistic?" In Linda S. Schearing and Steven L. McKenzie, eds., *Those Elusive Deuteronomists: The Phenomenon of Pan-Deuteronomism*. JSOTSup 268. Sheffield: Sheffield Academic Press, 116–26 (= 2004. *Samuel at the Threshold: Selected Works of Graeme Auld*. SOTSMS. Hants and Burlington, VT: Ashgate, 185–91).
Aurelius, Erik. 2003. *Zukunft jenseits des Gerichts. Eine redaktionsgeschichtliche Studie zum Enneateuch*. BZAW 319. Berlin and New York: de Gruyter.
Barstad, Hans M. 1996. *The Myth of the Empty Land: A Study in the History and Archaeology of Judah during the "Exilic" Period*. Symbolae Osloenses. Oslo: Scandinavian University Press.
Becker, Uwe. 2006. "Endredaktionelle Kontextvernetzungen des Josua-Buches." In Markus Witte et al., eds., *Die deuteronomistischen Geschichtswerke. Redaktions- und religionsgeschichtliche Perspektiven zur "Deuteronomismus"-Diskussion in Tora und Vorderen Propheten*. BZAW 365. Berlin and New York: de Gruyter, 139–61.

Ben Zvi, Ehud. 2010. "On the Term *Deuteronomistic* in Relation to Joshua-Kings in the Persian Period." In Kurt L. Noll and Brooks Schramm, eds., *Raising Up a Faithful Exegete: Essays in Honor of Richard D. Nelson*. Winona Lake, IN: Eisenbrauns, 61–71.

Blum, Erhard. 1990. *Studien zur Komposition des Pentateuch*. BZAW 189. Berlin and New York: de Gruyter.

Blum, Erhard. 2006. "The Literary Connection between the Books of Genesis and Exodus and the End of the Book of Joshua." In Thomas B. Dozeman and Konrad Schmid, eds., *A Farewell to the Yahwist? The Composition of the Pentateuch in Recent European Interpretation*. SBL Symposium Series 34. Atlanta: SBL, 89–106.

Burney, Charles Fox. 1920. *Notes on the Hebrew Text of the Book of Kings*. Oxford: Clarendon.

Childs, Brevard S. 1963. "A Study of the Formula, 'Until This Day'." *JBL* 82: 279–92.

Clements, Ronald E. 2007. "A Royal Privilege: Dining in the Presence of the Great King." In Robert Rezetko et al., eds., *Reflection and Refraction: Studies in Biblical Historiography in Honour of A. Graeme Auld*. VTSup 113. Leiden and Boston: Brill, 49–66.

Colenso, John William. 1862–79. *The Pentateuch and Book of Joshua Critically Examined*. London: Longman, Roberts & Green.

Cross, F. M. 1973. "The Themes of the Book of Kings and the Structure of the Deuteronomistic History." In *Canaanite Myth and Hebrew Epic: Essays in the History of the Religion of Israel*. Cambridge, MA: Harvard University Press, 274–89.

de Wette, Wilhelm Martin Leberecht. 1806. *Beiträge zur Einleitung in das Alte Testament I*. Halle: Schimmelpfennig und Compagnie.

Dietrich, Walter. 1972. *Prophetie und Geschichte*. FRLANT 108. Göttingen: Vandenhoeck & Ruprecht.

Dutcher-Walls, Patricia. 1991. "The Social Location of the Deuteronomists: A Sociological Study of Factory Politics in Late Pre-Exilic Judah." *JSOT* 52: 77–94.

Eissfeldt, Otto. 1964. *Einleitung in das Alte Testament*. Neue Theologische Grundrisse. Tübingen: J. C. B. Mohr. English translation: 1965. *The Old Testament: An Introduction*. New York: Harper & Row.

Ewald, Heinrich. 1843–59. *Geschichte des Volkes Israel bis Christus*. 6 vols. Göttingen: Dieterich. English translation: 1867–86. *History of Israel*. London: Longmans, Green and Co.

Friedman, Richard E. 1981. *The Exile and Biblical Narrative: The Formation of the Deuteronomistic and Priestly Works*. HSM 22. Chico, CA: Scholars Press.

Geoghegan, Jeffrey C. 2006. *The Time, Place and Purpose of the Deuteronomistic History: The Evidence of "Until This Day."* Brown Judaic Studies 347. Providence, RI: Brown University.

Gerhards, Meik. 2006. *Die Aussetzungsgeschichte des Mose. Literar- und traditionsgeschichtliche Untersuchungen zu einem Schlüsseltext des nichtpriesterlichen Tetrateuch*. WMANT 109. Neukirchen-Vluyn: Neukirchener Verlag.

Hoffmann, Yair. 1994. "The Conception of 'Other Gods' in Deuteronomistic Literature." In Ilai Alon et al., eds., *Concepts of the Other in Near Eastern Religions*. Israel Oriental Studies XIV. Leiden, New York, and Cologne: Brill, 103–18.

Hölscher, Gustav. 1922. "Komposition und Ursprung des Deuteronomiums." *ZAW* 40: 161–225.

Hutton, Jeremy M. 2009. *The Transjordanian Palimpsest: The Overwritten Texts of Personal Exile and Transformation in the Deuteronomistic History*. BZAW 396. Berlin and New York: de Gruyter.

Jepsen, Alfred. 1956. *Die Quellen des Königsbuches*. 2nd ed. Halle: Niemeyer.

Kaiser, Otto. 1992. *Grundriß der Einleitung in die kanonischen und deuterokanonischen Schriften des Alten Testaments*. Band 1: *Die erzählenden Werke*. Gütersloh: Gerd Mohn.

Klein, Ralph W. 1979. *Israel in Exile: A Theological Interpretation*. 2nd ed. OBT. Philadelphia: Fortress.

Knauf, Ernst Axel. 1996. "L'historiographie deutéronomiste' (DtrG) existe-t-elle?" In Albert de Pury et al., eds., *Israël construit son histoire. L'historiographie deutéronomiste à la lumière des recherches récentes*. Le Monde de la Bible 34. Geneva: Labor et Fides, 409–18. English translation: 2000. "Does 'Deuteronomistic Historiography' (DtrH) Exist?" In Albert de Pury et al., eds., *Israel Constructs*

Its History: Deuteronomistic Historiography in Recent Research. JSOTSup 306. Sheffield: Sheffield Academic Press, 388–98.

Knoppers, Gary N. 1993. *Two Nations under God: The Deuteronomistic History of Solomon and the Dual Monarchies*. 2 vols. HSM 52. Atlanta: Scholars Press.

Kratz, Reinhard G. 2000. *Die Komposition der erzählenden Bücher des Alten Testaments. Grundwissen der Bibelkritik*. UTB 2157. Göttingen: Vandenhoeck & Ruprecht. English translation: 2005. *The Composition of the Narrative Books of the Old Testament*. London and New York: T&T Clark—Continuum.

Krause, Joachim J. 2015. "The Book of the Torah in Joshua 1 and 23 and in the Deuteronomistic History." *ZAW* 127: 412–28.

Kuenen, Abraham. 1861–65. *Historisch-critisch onderzoek naar het antstaan en de verzameling van de boeken des Ouden Verbonds*. Amsterdam: S. L. van Looy. English translation: 1886. *An Historico-Critical Inquiry into the Origin and Composition of the Hexateuch*. London: Macmillan and Co.

Lauinger, Jacob. 2012. "Esarhaddon's Succession Treaty at Tell Tayinat: Text and Commentary." *JCS* 64: 87–123.

Lohfink, Norbert. 1991. "Kerygmata des Deuteronomistischen Geschichtswerks." In *Studien zum Deuteronomium und zur deuteronomistischen Literatur II*. SBA.AT 12. Stuttgart: Katholisches Bibelwerk, 125–42.

Lohfink, Norbert. 1999. "Was There a Deuteronomistic Movement?" In Linda S. Schearing and Steven L. Mckenzie, eds., *Those Elusive Deuteronomists: The Phenomenon of Pan-Deuteronomism*. JSOTSup 268. Sheffield: Sheffield Academic Press, 36–66.

Mayes, Andrew D. H. 1983. *The Story of Israel between Settlement and Exile: A Redactional Study of the Deuteronomistic History*. London: SCM Press.

McKenzie, Steven L. 1991. *The Trouble with Kings: The Composition of the Books of Kings in the Deuteronomistic History*. VTSup 42. Leiden: Brill.

McKenzie, Steven L. 1996. "Cette royauté qui fait problème." In Albert de Pury et al., eds., *Israël construit son histoire. L'historiographie deutéronomiste à la lumière des recherches récentes*. Le Monde de la Bible 34. Geneva: Labor et Fides, 267–95. English translation: 2000. "The Trouble with Kingship." In Albert de Pury et al., eds., *Israel Constructs Its History: Deuteronomistic Historiography in Recent Research*. JSOTSup 306. Sheffield: Sheffield Academic Press, 286–314.

Nelson, R. D. 1981a. *The Double Redaction of the Deuteronomistic History*. JSOTSup 18. Sheffield: JSOT Press.

Nelson, Richard D. 1981b. "Josiah in the Book of Joshua." *JBL* 104: 531–40.

Nelson, Richard D. 1997. *Joshua: A Commentary*. OTL. Louisville, KY: Westminster John Knox.

Nentel, Jochen. 2000. *Trägerschaft und Intentionen des deuteronomistischen Geschichtswerks. Untersuchungen zu den Reflexionsreden Jos 1; 23; 24; 1 Sam 12 und 1 Kön 8*. BZAW 297. Berlin and New York: de Gruyter.

Nihan, Christophe. 2012. "'Deutéronomiste' et 'deutéronomisme': Quelques remarques de méthode en lien avec le débat actuel." In Martti Nissinen, ed., *Congress Volume Helsinki 2010*. VTSup 148. Leiden: Brill, 409–41.

Noll, Kurt L. 2007. "Deuteronomistic History or Deuteronomistic Debate? (A Thought Experiment)." *JSOT* 31: 311–45.

Noth, Martin. 1938. *Das Buch Josua*. HAT I/6. Tübingen: J. C. B. Mohr (P. Siebeck).

Noth, Martin. 1967. *Überlieferungsgeschichtliche Studien. Die sammelnden und bearbeitenden Geschichtswerke im Alten Testament*. 3rd ed. Darmstadt: Wissenschaftliche Buchgesellschaft. English translation: 1991. *The Deuteronomistic History*. 2nd ed. JSOTSup 15. Sheffield: Sheffield Academic Press.

O'Brien, M. A. 1989. *The Deuteronomistic History Hypothesis: A Reassessment*. OBO 92. Freiburg (CH) and Göttingen: Universitätsverlag—Vandenhoeck & Ruprecht.

Otto, Eckart. 1999. *Das Deuteronomium. Politische Theologie und Rechtsreform in Juda und Assyrien*. BZAW 284. Berlin and New York: de Gruyter.

Otto, Eckart. 2000. "Mose und das Gesetz. Die Mose-Figur als Gegenentwurf Politischer Theologie zur neuassyrischen Königsideologie im 7.Jh. v. Chr." In Eckart Otto, ed., *Mose, Ägypten und das Alte Testament*. SBS 189. Stuttgart: Katholisches Bibelwerk, 42–83.

Pakkala, Juha. 2009. "The Date of the Oldest Edition of Deuteronomy." *ZAW* 121: 388–401.

Person, Jr., Raymond F. 2002. *The Deuteronomic School: History, Social Setting, and Literature*. SBL 2. Atlanta: SBL.

Provan, Iain W. 1988. *Hezekiah and the Book of Kings: A Contribution to the Debate about the Composition of the Deuteronomistic History*. BZAW 172. Berlin and New York: de Gruyter.

Römer, Thomas. 2005. *The So-Called Deuteronomistic History: A Sociological, Historical and Literary Introduction*. London and New York: T&T Clark—Continuum.

Römer, Thomas. 2009a. "Redaction Criticism: 1 Kings 8 and the Deuteronomists." In Joel M. LeMon and Kent Harold Richards, eds., *Method Matters: Essays on the Interpretation of the Hebrew Bible in Honor of David L. Petersen*. SBL Resources for Biblical Study 56. Atlanta: SBL, 63–76.

Römer, Thomas. 2009b. "The Formation of the Book of Jeremiah as a Supplement to the So-Called Deuteronomistic History." In Diana V. Edelman and Ehud Ben Zvi, eds., *The Production of Prophecy: Constructing Prophecy and Prophets in Yehud*. BibleWorld. London and Oakville, CT: Equinox, 168–83.

Römer, Thomas. 2010. "Book-Endings in Joshua and the Question of the So-Called Deuteronomistic History." In Kurt L. Noll and Brooks Schramm, eds., *Raising Up a Faithful Exegete: Essays in Honor of Richard D. Nelson*. Winona Lake, IN: Eisenbrauns, 85–99.

Römer, Thomas. 2013. "La loi du roi en Deutéronome 17 et ses fonctions." In Olivier Artus, ed., *Loi et justice dans la littérature du Proche-Orient ancien*. BZABR 20. Wiesbaden: Harrassowitz, 99–111.

Römer, Thomas. 2015. "From Deuteronomistic History to Nebiim and Torah." In Innocent Himbaza, ed., *Making the Biblical Text: Textual Studies in the Hebrew and Greek Bible*. OBO 275. Fribourg and Göttingen: Academic Press—Vandenhoeck & Ruprecht, 1–18.

Rückl, Jan. 2016. *A Sure House: Studies on the Dynastic Promise to David in the Books of Samuel and Kings*. OBO 281. Fribourg and Göttingen: Academic Press—Vandenhoeck & Ruprecht.

Schmitt, Hans-Christoph. 1997. "Das spätdeuteronomistische Geschichtswerk Gen I–2 Regum XXV und seine theologische Intention." In J. A. Emerton, ed., *Congress Volume Cambridge 1995*. VTSup 66. Leiden, New York, and Cologne: Brill, 261–79 (= 2001. *Theologie in Prophetie und Pentateuch. Gesammelte Aufsätze*. BZAW 310. Berlin and New York: de Gruyter, 277–94).

Smend, Rudolf. 1971. "Das Gesetz und die Völker. Ein Beitrag zur deuteronomistischen Redaktionsgeschichte." In H. W. Wolff, ed., *Probleme biblischer Theologie. Festschrift für Gerhard von Rad*. Munich: Kaiser, 494–509. English translation: 2000. "The Law and the Nations: A Contribution to Deuteronomistic Tradition History." In Gary N. Knoppers and J. Gordon McConville, eds., *Reconsidering Israel and Judah: Recent Studies on the Deuteronomistic History*. Sources for Biblical and Theological Study 8. Winona Lake, IN: Eisenbrauns, 95–110.

Steymans, Hans Ulrich. 2003. "Die neuassyrische Vertragsrhetorik der 'Vassal Treaties of Esarhaddon' und das Deuteronomium." In Georg Braulik, ed., *Das Deuteronomium*. Österreichische Biblische Studien 23. Frankfurt am Main et al.: Peter Lang, 89–152.

Steymans, Hans Ulrich. 2013. "Deuteronomy 28 and Tell Tayinat." *Verbum et Ecclesia* 34 (online: http://verbumetecclesia.org.za): 13 p.

Thompson, Richard Jude. 2013. *Terror of the Radiance: Aššur Covenant to Yhwh Covenant*. OBO 258. Fribourg and Göttingen: Academic Press—Vandenhoeck & Ruprecht.

Van Seters, John. 1983. *In Search of History: History in the Ancient World and the Origin of Biblical History*. New Haven, CT and London: Yale University Press.

Van Seters, John. 1992. *Prologue to History: The Yahwist as Historian in Genesis*. Zürich: Theologischer Verlag.

Van Seters, John. 2000. "The Court History and DtrH: Conflicting Perspectives on the House of David." In Albert de Pury and Thomas Römer, eds., *Die sogenannte Thronfolgegeschichte Davids*.

Neue Einsichten und Anfragen. OBO 176. Freiburg (CH) and Göttingen: Universitätsverlag—Vandenhoeck & Ruprecht, 70–93.

Veijola, Timo. 1975. *Die ewige Dynastie. David und die Entstehung seiner Dynastie nach der deuteronomistischen Darstellung.* AASFSerB 193. Helsinki: Suomalainen Tiedeakatemia.

Veijola, Timo. 1977. *Das Königtum in der Beurteilung der deuteronomistischen Historiographie.* AASFSerB. 198. Helsinki: Suomalainen Tiedeakatemia.

Veijola, Timo. 1996. "Bundestheologische Redaktion im Deuteronomium." In Timo Veijola, ed., *Das Deuteronomium und seine Querbeziehungen.* PFES 62. Helsinki and Göttingen: Finnische Exegetische Gesllschaft—Vandenhoeck & Ruprecht, 242–76.

von Rad, Gerhard. 1958. "Die deuteronomistische Geschichtstheologie in den Königsbüchern." In *Gesammelte Studien zum Alten Testament.* TB 8. Munich: Chr. Kaiser, 189–204. English translation: 1953. "The Deuteronomistic Theology of History in the Books of Kings." In *Studies in Deuteronomy.* SBT 9. London: SCM Press, 74–91.

Wellhausen, Julius. 1963. *Die Composition des Hexateuchs und der historischen Bücher des Alten Testaments.* Reprint from the edition of 1899. Berlin: de Gruyter.

Westermann, Claus. 1994. *Die Geschichtsbücher des Alten Testaments. Gab es ein deuteronomistisches Geschichtswerk?* Gütersloh: Chr. Kaiser.

Wolff, Hans Walter. 1961. "Das Kerygma des deuteronomistischen Geschichtswerks." *ZAW* 171–86. English translation: 1975. "The Kerygma of the Deuteronomic Historical Work." In Walter Brueggemann and Hans Walter Wolff, eds., *The Vitality of Old Testament Traditions.* Atlanta: John Knox, 83–100.

Würthwein, Ernst. 1994. "Erwägungen zum sog. deuteronomistischen Geschichtswerk. Eine Skizze." In *Studien zum deuteronomistischen Geschichtswerk.* BZAW 227. Berlin—New York: de Gruyter, 1–11.

Younger Jr., K. Lawson. 1990. *Ancient Conquest Accounts: A Study in Ancient Near Eastern and Biblical History Writing.* JSOTSup 98. Sheffield: JSOT Press.

CHAPTER 21

READING THE HISTORICAL BOOKS AS PART OF THE PRIMARY HISTORY

RICHARD S. BRIGGS

21.1 Prologue: Echoes of Scripture across the Primary History

GEARING up for the narration of the story of Abram/Abraham and the nation that will come from him, Genesis 11 tells the story of Yhwh scattering the builders of a heaven-assailing tower. "Therefore it was called Babel (*bābel*)," says v. 9. This word that occurs well over two hundred times in the Old Testament is almost always translated "Babylon" in English translations, apart from here (and Gen. 10:10), and once it starts reappearing in 2 Kings 17–25, Babylon (*bābel*) forms the climactic context for the whole primary narrative, ending with the victory of the Babylonians—at least from the perspective of 2 Kings—and a dispiriting end to the story of Abraham's descendants. They, like their tower-building forebears, are scattered across the earth, with the verb for "scattering" from Genesis 11 (*pûṣ*; Gen. 11:4, 8, 9) reoccurring, for example, in 2 Kgs. 25:5. English translations of *bābel* notwithstanding, readers are unlikely to miss the link. How the link was crafted and what its effects may be are two different questions, but one way or the other (or both), Genesis 11 and 2 Kings 25 connect across the canon.

The Genesis prologue (chs. 1–11) has notoriously little uptake in the rest of the Old Testament, and especially in Genesis–2 Kings. What about other, perhaps more embedded, links across the law and the prophets? At the moment of the giving of the law, with Moses on Mount Sinai, Aaron finds himself presiding over the creation of a golden calf as a focal point of the worship of other "gods" (Exodus 32). It is an archetypal incident of the people rejecting God, as Aaron pronounces: "These are your gods, O Israel, who brought you up out of the land of Egypt" (Exod. 32:4). It also results in a certain *déjà vu* for the reader arriving at 1 Kings 12, who reads that Jeroboam, the newly installed king of the seceding

Northern Kingdom, sets up a Northern worship alternative in Shechem with two calves of gold, stating: "Here are your gods, O Israel, who brought you up out of the land of Egypt" (1 Kgs. 12:28). Does 1 Kings 12 recapitulate the founding sin of the golden calf, or does the author of Exodus craft the Sinai narrative to point towards Jeroboam's leading the people in rejection of God? Again, either way, the intertextual echoes are unmissable.

As for the prophets, the strange incident of Elijah and the so-called "still small voice" (1 Kgs. 19:12, KJV) is part of a poignant narrative of the spectacular successes of 1 Kings 18 being followed by a paradigmatic long dark night of the prophetic soul. This story, near the beginning of the emergence of major named prophets in the narratives of Kings, sees Elijah running to Mount Horeb (1 Kgs. 19:8), which is clearly the same place as "Mount Sinai," and encountering God's presence there in strikingly non-dramatic, though no less mysterious, terms: not in the wind (*rûaḥ*), not in the earthquake, not even in the fire (*'ēš*, such as had hosted the divine presence appearing to Moses in Exod. 3:2), but in "a sound of sheer silence" (*qôl dĕmāmâ daqqâ*; "a voice, a thin whisper"). On Mount Sinai God spoke, and Moses received the law. On Mount Horeb, God is present, but with no new revelation for Elijah, other than that of God's own presence. The ensuing narrative effectively sees God telling Elijah to go back and get on with his work. Are we to think that the prophets are secure in—and commissioned by—the prior word of *tôrâ*? Was that part of the agenda of the authors of Exodus and/or Kings, or does such a conclusion emerge solely out of the experience of reading the Torah and the Historical Books in their current sequence?

These examples of interpretive resonance or, in the felicitous term impressed upon biblical scholars by Richard B. Hays (1989), "echoes" between the Pentateuch and the Historical Books may serve to push the reader towards the question: what is at stake in reading the Historical Books as part of a longer complex of texts running from Genesis through 2 Kings? It is to this broader, more systematic, inquiry that the present essay is addressed.

21.2 PUTTING THE HISTORICAL BOOKS IN CONTEXT

Bible readers old and new have long been trained in understanding the importance of context for good Bible reading: but which context? Several candidates for significant reading contexts are readily apparent for most biblical texts. One may rightly be concerned with the *context of the author*, and the original intended function of the text, perhaps in both pre-literary and prior literary forms as well. The *context of the finished text* in whatever collection has preserved and transmitted it is clearly also important. On another level, the *contexts of readers* often exert rather more pressure on interpretive proposals than those readers always realize, as may be the case, for example, with earlier scholarly readings of the Historical Books in terms of grand narratives of national identity, rise and fall, or the significance of great (and not so great) leaders. Such readings could arguably tell us as much about nineteenth- and twentieth-century perspectives on historiography as about the biblical authors' and editors' intentions.

The *literary context* of the text may seem the simplest of these levels on which to establish some basic parameters, but with the Historical Books this context resists straightforward clarification. On a macro-level, the very existence of the competing labels "Old Testament" and "Hebrew Bible" points to a conflict of contexts, although this particular conflict still admits of considerable overlap in interpretive interests. More subtle is the difference between taking these texts as "the Historical Books" or "the Former Prophets," with those labels' alternate emphases on historical accounting, on the one hand, or the presentation of a divinely orchestrated (prophetic) purpose, on the other. These are not mutually exclusive emphases, to be sure, but the orientation to which they predispose the reader is clearly different in each case. Most significant for our purposes, there is the further difference between approaches that read these books as a continuation of the canon beyond the opening Pentateuch/Torah, and those that read them as a distinct history, mostly understood in modern times as allied to and governed by the perspectives of Deuteronomy, and therefore called "the Deuteronomistic history" (Noth 1991).

All of these options merit attention, and also set the context within which the concerns of the present study may best be situated, in an exploration of the strengths and weaknesses of one particular reading context: that of reading the Historical Books as part of the primary history. Before exploring some examples of how this might make a difference to the interpretation of Joshua–2 Kings, it will be helpful to offer a brief discussion of the various reading commitments that are at work when one speaks of a primary history in the first place.

21.3 THE PRIMARY HISTORY: ANGLES OF APPROACH

The "primary history" is a name given by David Noel Freedman to the literary entity that runs from the beginning of Genesis to the end of Kings. He introduced the language of "primary history" more or less by fiat in a series of articles (Freedman 1963; 1976; 1990), and the label is perhaps unfortunate in its simple annexation of the word "history" to such a varied literary corpus. Nevertheless, the term has gained some currency and offers readers possibilities for thinking about the Historical Books and their intertextual resonances.

In the Jewish canon, the primary history amounts to nine books: the Torah combined with the Former Prophets. Freedman thus also called this complex the "Enneateuch," to contrast with (and perhaps to some extent to bypass) prevailing scholarly options about the most helpful way to frame the interpretive context of the Pentateuch. Gerhard von Rad (1966) spoke of a Hexateuch, since it was the book of Joshua that to some degree narrated a fulfilment of the story of Israel begun under Abraham and Moses. Other scholars were occupied with a Tetrateuch, in particular Martin Noth, as a result of separating out the book of Deuteronomy in order to attach it to the Deuteronomistic history, and thus leaving a four-book corpus as its predecessor. But Freedman posited a nine-book primary history that settled relatively early into a fixed canonical form. Each of these suggested contexts—Freedman's, von Rad's, and Noth's—operates with different historical hypotheses and has different implications for reading (Dozeman et al., 2011).

In practice, Freedman's idea can be taken as just one option among many, given the range of contexts available to readers. It is clear that Freedman himself saw it as a privileged account, whereby the location of the Historical Books as completing the Pentateuch was held to be key to assessing these books' purpose. Freedman's own view developed into a theory of careful overall synthetic editing of the Hebrew Bible, pre-Daniel, towards the end of the time of Nehemiah in the Persian period (Freedman 1991). The result was a remarkable literary unity, which he sought to demonstrate by counting words and other structural criteria across four canonical sections: the Torah, the Former and then Latter Prophets, and the Writings (without Daniel). This historically rooted attempt to privilege a primary history has gained little support, however. Likewise, Freedman's attempt to uncover the "nine commandments" and their transgressions, distributed as keys to the Enneateuch (Freedman 2000) seems ingenious but overly speculative as a historical proposal.

On the other hand, the congruence between Freedman's primary history and the shape of the Jewish and Christian canons results in the usefulness of the label for literary and/or canonical purposes in describing approaches to these texts that take seriously the location of the Historical Books as successors to the Pentateuch. Thus David J. A. Clines (1990: 85–105) recasts the primary history as a literary corpus to be held in strange canonical tension with a "secondary history," which was once called "the Chronicler's history." He suggests that readers are then at liberty to let the Old Testament's juxtaposition of these two overarching narrative accounts serve to trouble and undermine each other with regard to their respective intentions to tell the whole story, since a different way of telling the story exists immediately alongside. Clines offers a self-consciously literary account, studiously ignoring historical matters pertaining to the production of these histories, but highlighting a range of reading possibilities.

Attempts to integrate some aspects of literary and historical factors in reading the Pentateuch followed by the Historical Books can tend towards canonical approaches, whereby complexities in the text are recognized as pointing towards redactional processes lying behind the text, but in which a good deal of the interpreter's attention is focused on the nature and purposes of the resultant final (canonical) text. A good example of thoughtful theological probing of the Historical Books in this literary-canonical manner is offered by Rolf Rendtorff (2005: 94–162). He draws out the contrast between the Pentateuch's focus on history "brought about by God or... viewed and presented directly in its relationship to God" and the Historical Books' apparently "secular" approach, which seems to overlap with the modern category of a "history of Israel," except that prophetic interaction and the frequent theological evaluation of kings consistently draws the reader back towards the Pentateuchal approach (2005: 677). And yet, a properly canonical approach wants to draw the reader beyond the primary history (a term Rendtorff himself does not use) towards even wider canonical contexts, and thus although there are overlaps here, a canonical reading carries more wide-ranging theological commitments than an approach that simply postulates a primary history.

In some ways, working with the Historical Books as part of the primary history is a project both like and unlike the more often trod critical path of reading them as part of the Deuteronomistic history. In this latter approach, one seeks to categorize the narrative emphases under the rubric of Deuteronomistic theology, typically with emphases on the failure that brought about judgment (Noth), occasionally balanced by a recognition of divine grace and perseverance with Israel (von Rad), and then, sometimes, an attempt to match different Deuteronomistic evaluations to two (or more) redactions (Cross 1973: 274–89).[1] One difference, however, is that it is the broader canvas of the whole Pentateuch that is in view as the preceding text if one is reading the primary history, rather than just Deuteronomy (or D, for scholars persuaded that this Pentateuchal source is not identical with the finished fifth book of the canon). One can see immediately how this invites a reading of the Historical Books that interacts more fully with creation, exodus, or priesthood, to name just a few of the obvious thematic emphases of the first three Pentateuchal books. Similarly, the classic Wellhausenian tendency to downplay law as a late decline of an otherwise vibrant faith tradition may be revisited and challenged by locating the Historical Books as part of a primary history, since the shape of the primary history sees law as an early and orienting perspective through which to read all that follows, regardless of whether it was early or late historically. Even so, all of these elements in a reading of the primary history have certain hermeneutical elements in parallel with the project of reading the Historical Books as part of a Deuteronomistic history insofar as they locate Joshua–Kings within a larger framework, and lead to questions pertaining to how the import of one text (D or the Pentateuch, depending) reframes the interpretation of another (the Historical Books).

The other major difference between focusing on a primary history and a Deuteronomistic history concerns the extent to which one is invested in questions of discerning the historical direction of influence. Despite Freedman's own historical theories, an emphasis on the primary history lends itself naturally to reframing questions of influence as questions of intertextuality. On this view, one need not resolve the often imponderable complexities of discerning which text came first, and which one followed up with conscious citation or echo. Rather the question is reformulated into the recognition that readers of the texts are free to discern echoes between one text and another, both equally present to the reader at one and the same time. I turn now to consider some examples of how this helps to reframe the interpretation of the Historical Books in their interplay with corresponding Pentateuchal texts.

21.4 Intertextual Readings in the Primary History

I will examine first a case where a text from Deuteronomy is significant with respect to the Historical Books, to see how the relevant interpretive issues are recast. Then, I will consider a case where texts from the wider Pentateuch can develop the interpretation of the Historical Books. Kings and priests offer us the two focal themes for these two cases.

21.4.1 Israel's Kings

The classic passage in Deut. 17:14–20 anticipates Israel's problems with a king once they are in the land. Verse 15 permits them to appoint a king "whom Yhwh your God will choose," one of their own people. Four proscriptions follow: the king in question is not to acquire many horses for himself nor "return the people to Egypt" for more horses (which is a strikingly resonant way to proscribe horse-collecting); neither may he acquire many wives or amass silver and gold. The many wives, in particular, will turn his heart away (17:17). The positive requirement is to make a copy of the *tôrâ* ("law/instruction"), so that the king will fear Yhwh and that his descendants will reign over Israel.

This passage stands out in Deuteronomy as the only law that mentions an Israelite king. It is perhaps located in chapter 17 because of some preceding passages about the consulting of "judges and officials" (*šōpĕtîm* and *šōmĕrîm*) to adjudicate disputes (16:18), and, in particular, the levitical priests and presiding judge (17:9) for more difficult cases. Even so, the law of the king stands out from the rest of the Pentateuch as a reflection on later Israelite polity and concerns.

Other references to a king in Israel in the Pentateuch are few, but not non-existent. In Deuteronomy one should note the curse upon a future wayward people and "the king they have set over them" in 28:36; and the oblique reference to a "king in Jeshurun," as part of Moses's final blessing (33:5). Otherwise, such passing mentions as there are consist only of, first, the promise in Genesis of descendents who will be kings, which is repeated with variations in Gen. 17:6, 16; 35:11; second, two verses in Balaam's oracles, where Num. 24:7 foresees a great king for Israel, though the previous oracle, in 23:21, has Yhwh as king over Israel; and third, marginally, the reference in Exod. 19:6 to a priestly kingdom, though the emphasis there falls more on the priestly aspect than imagining whether or not this kingdom requires a human king. There are of course many other mentions of multiple kings in the Pentateuch, but that is part of the point: Israel is surrounded by nations with kings, and engages frequently with them, beginning with Lot's entanglements in Genesis 14, through the troubles with Pharaoh king of Egypt and the kings of Moab, Bashan, and elsewhere. Israel at this time is different, however: it has no king.

It is a standard observation that Deuteronomy 17 appears to be legislating after the fact for the chaos caused by Solomon's turn to many wives (1 Kings 11), who "turned his heart away" (11:9), along with his excessive importing of horses from, among other places, Egypt (10:28), and amassing vast quantities of silver and gold (particularly in 1 Kings 10). All of this tallies so neatly with Deuteronomy 17 that it makes sense to see the Torah passage as intending to address Solomon's own failings, with Deut. 17:18–20 arguably reflecting a later and more positive portrait of Josiah vis-à-vis the book of the law (2 Kings 22–23). But historicizing approaches to the relevant texts (such as with the Deuteronomistic history) quickly seem to exhaust the significance of the material: Deuteronomy 17 is explained by virtue of its historical relocation to the monarchy, while the narratives about Solomon are read not as part of the post-history of Deuteronomy 17 but as the trigger for it. It is of course possible to read Deuteronomy 17 as pre-dating Kings if one assumes that the author(s) of Kings then crafted the material to reflect badly in specific ways on Solomon's failings (and, perhaps, Josiah's successes), thereby creating the remarkable correlation with all the things Deuteronomy had been worried about. An intertextual reading, however, need not invest in this or indeed any other historical reconstruction while retaining what is most interesting in both those approaches.

Thus, on the one hand, for the reader of the primary history, 1 Kings 11 does operate in the shadow of Deuteronomy 17. The relocation of an historically prior narrative (Solomon's kingship) to sit under the echoes of Deuteronomy 17 implies a dual theological emphasis.

First, the word of the Lord is to be understood as preceding the human exploits that it addresses. God is the initiator of judgment upon extravagant kingship, rather than being the one who reacts to it. Clearly this was not sufficiently well perceived in the midst of Solomonic excess, and so the piecing together of the primary history testifies to a slow realization that this kind of kingship is not what will serve either God or the interests of Israel. The text is then written to make this God's priority, for the benefit of all who come afterwards and read. In other words, the primary history constructs a theological understanding of what is at stake in such royal behavior, rather than simply reporting how it appeared. Second, self-aggrandizement is to be understood as proceeding necessarily from a heart that is not set on obedience (to echo an idiom for Deuteronomy's persistent requirement). Solomon needed a good deal of gold in the building projects outlined in 1 Kings 6–10, much of it for the temple. The narrative reads as if he could not discern the point at which the acquiring of gold ceased to be in service to obedience and became a habit that served only himself. Should he have known better? The locating of Deuteronomy 17 in advance of his exploits suggests that Solomon's behavior, no less than others, flowed out of the heart, and was therefore not innocent, which of course would also be very hard to prove on the ground in the midst of the events transpiring at that time.

On the other hand, Deuteronomy 17 now precedes the whole narrative of Judges 17–21 (with its four-times repeated refrain "there was no king in Israel") and 1 Samuel with its controverted attitudes to kingship. In 1 Samuel in particular, divine enthusiasm for the appointment of a king is, to say the least, equivocal. Where does the idea of having a king come from for Israel? Presumably from their wide-ranging experience of the surrounding nations having kings, who were typically perceived as responsible for organizing their military and economic successes (cf. 1 Sam. 8:5). The primary history suggests, however, that kingship was God's idea initially, or perhaps in the abstract—hence the initiative of Deuteronomy 17—but that the particular instantiation of Israel's asking for a king in 1 Samuel 8 is driven by the wrong reasons; hence, it is a rejection of God (see 1 Sam. 8:7). That kingship in itself can be both positive and negative—for God's people under God—is thus not just the way it happens to work out, as witnessed in 1–2 Kings, but is part of the focus of the (primary history) text, taken on its own literary-canonical terms. Such a reading may rightly be pursued with regard to 1 Samuel (as per Chapman 2016), but it may also draw upon and in turn illuminate the whole primary history within which readers encounter 1 Samuel.

21.4.2 Israel's Priests

Our understanding of the historical development of Israelite priesthood struggles over the twin obstacles of lack of information and inherent tensions in what information exists. Indeed, it may represent one of the most intractable issues in our ability to reconstruct the history of Israelite religion. Attention to the canonical witness of the primary history is not a shortcut to historical information, therefore, but focuses on how the matter is presented to the reader of these texts. In the case of kingship, already discussed above, the modern scholarly way in to the issue notices that the Torah contains regulations that pertain to a much later context. With priesthood, the entry point is reversed: given the emphasis on priests and priestly ministry in the Torah, it is strange to turn to the Historical Books and find Israel's story proceeding with relatively little focus on this issue. Again, we start with some of the data and then explore the interpretive implications.

Priests are of course at the heart of the concerns of Leviticus, but a careful reading of the Pentateuch as the beginning of the primary history yields the following observations. The core inaugural text on priests is Exodus 28–29, with a scattering of further references in subsequent chapters of Exodus that make good sense as being consequent upon Exodus 28–29. The mention of the "priestly kingdom" in Exod. 19:6, for example, was noted earlier. A well-known interpretive crux concerns the double reference to priests in the regulations about ascending the mountain at Exod. 19:22, 24, long before the institution of the priesthood. This is doubtless an anachronism, either by way of deliberate retrospective renaming or by dislocation of textual elements (see Houtman 1993–2002: 2.458). Earlier in the book of Exodus there are three references to Midianite priests (2:16; 3:1; 18:1). Leviticus is the central scriptural text about priests, with most passages describing aspects of their roles and responsibilities, memorably summarized in Lev. 10:10. Leviticus 8–10 relates the implementation of their consecration as anticipated in Exodus 29. Some readings of Leviticus delineate an originally separate "Holiness Code" in chapters 17–26, in which the requirements of holiness, still under the purview of the priests, extend into many matters of everyday life. Numbers has a similar way of expecting the priests to be involved in a range of duties, and presupposes that they are in place and acting to fulfill the mandates of the Exodus and Leviticus texts. Some aspects of this arrangement persist into Deuteronomy, though the profile of priests is lower. There are fourteen mentions of priests in Deuteronomy, but none in the opening eleven chapters. In five of these fourteen instances the phrase "levitical priests" is used (17:9, 18; 18:1; 24:8; 27:9), which occurs nowhere else in the Torah (and only six times elsewhere in the entire Old Testament). This phrasing seems to imply some form of demarcation from other, non-Levitical priests, which in turn reflects later concerns lying behind these sections of Deuteronomy. For completeness, we may also note that Genesis contains half a dozen references to Egyptian priests in the Joseph narrative, and the sole, mysterious instance of Melchizedek, the priest of "God most high" (*'ēl 'elyôn*; Gen. 14:18). In the case of the priesthood, therefore, the pre-Sinai narrative of the primary history offers something of a parallel to the Israelite experience with kingship: it was seen as part of a foreign system before it was adopted in Israel.

The Historical Books witness to a range of degrees of engagement with priesthood. In Joshua the priests carry the ark, lead Israel in procession, and the Levites, in particular, are excluded from land allocation (Josh. 18:7) because of what is assumed to be the significance of the role of priesthood. Judges conspicuously lacks mention of priests until the stories of chapters 17–21, and even then what is described is limited to localized priests failing to offer anything like the model to which the Torah aspired. In Samuel and Kings the interaction with priesthood "becomes fatefully entwined with the story of kingship" (McConville 1999: 80, arguing that this theme reaches a climax with 2 Kings 11–12 and the religious reforms under Joash). Although coverage of the priests is wide-ranging through Kings, and although there are reasons why some aspects of priestly responsibility are less likely to be of concern given that the narratives operate far more widely than a narrow cultic focus, a reader of the primary history will nevertheless notice that the template for priests offered in the Torah does not play out in the Historical Books quite as one might have anticipated. 1

Samuel 3's scenario of Samuel sleeping in the presence of the ark of God is a particularly acute example in light of Leviticus's emphases on the requirements of holiness to approach the presence of God, e.g., the warnings of Lev. 16:2.

It is a well-known feature of Pentateuchal studies that the late dating for P and a limited appreciation for priesthood as compared to other forms of religious and spiritual life were two sides of the same coin for Wellhausen and many who followed after him. If priesthood indicates the decay of lively faith (a view not uncommon among low-Protestant interpretive traditions to this day), then its demotion as "late" allows a *non*-Priestly narrative to emerge from Genesis all the way through to Kings. How might reading the primary history as it now stands resist such a construction?

The formal elements of religious observance that characterize Exodus 25–40 and Leviticus are opaque to many modern readers. Matters of priesthood take their place with regulations concerning sacrifice and the construction of a tabernacle as strange forms of ritual. But the abiding concern of this complex of texts is clearly to create the holy conditions within which the God of Israel may dwell with the people of Israel. It is one thing to disbelieve such a claim, as perhaps many modern readers may do, but it is another to miss it as the claim that the text makes. By contrast, the roles of priests in Samuel–Kings might be characterized as "temple functionaries," attending to the proper performance of worship services, and involved in playing their parts in the apparatus of court and state business, as observed above. The core claims of the nature of priestly identity and purpose are muted in the Historical Books to the extent that they appear at all.

To illustrate this, it is instructive to reflect on the distribution of the uses of forms of the word "holy"/"holiness" (*qādôš*/*qōdeš*) in the Historical Books. This recurrent term in Leviticus (and the later sections of Exodus, as well as some prescriptive sections of Numbers) is used less often in Deuteronomy, where it is broadened out to refer to the whole people of Israel (Deut. 7:6; 14:2, 21; 26:19; 28:9), not just the priests. When a reader moves on to the Historical Books, however, something striking happens. The terms themselves are relatively rare apart from in the narrative of the building and dedication of the temple in 1 Kings. But most significantly, the terms are almost always found on the lips of characters in the narrative who are *not* priests, including cases when those characters are in interaction with priests. In other words, it is no longer the priests themselves who impress upon Israel (or its kings) the need to understand and practice holiness, and insofar as the idea of holiness is kept alive in the text it is done so by others.

References to holiness or being holy are made by the mysterious "commander of the army of Yhwh" in Josh. 5:15; by Joshua himself in Josh. 6:19 and 24:19; by Hannah in 1 Sam 2:2; by the people of Beth-shemesh in 1 Sam 6:20; by David and the priest Ahimelech in the exchange in 1 Samuel 21 about David's men needing bread (in which the priest does mention holy bread twice, though the text reads as if it is David who really understands the significance of the situation, not Ahimelech); and then, as noted above, several times in the temple narratives of 1 Kings 6–8 in a range of settings of speakers and narrator, in cases where priests are certainly involved (albeit in a manner that fits exactly the notion of their being temple functionaries handling items designated as holy) in a building project attributing the initiative to Solomon (and likewise twice in 1 Kgs. 15:15, translated as "votive gifts" in NRSV); by the Shunammite woman in 2 Kgs. 4:9;

by King Jehoash (addressing priests) in 2 Kgs. 12:4 (ET: 12:3), then reported by the narrator in 12:19 (ET 12:18); and finally by the prophet Isaiah in 2 Kgs. 19:22. In all of this, Ahimelech's reference to "holy bread" is the only time a priest mentions or initiates any kind of reference to the holy, and this takes place in a narrative that does not reflect well on the priestly initiative.

This is a truly striking pattern, even if one goes on to the appropriate nuancing that a full study of holiness in the Historical Books would require.[2] To be clear, the point is not that the priests would not have understood themselves as engaged in holy activity, or even as guardians of the holy objects that were in use in temple activity and most of all in service to a holy God. Nor can one simply conclude that the broader connotations of holiness are necessarily absent at all points in the text when the specific vocabulary is not used, though one has to say that the authors almost seem to have gone out of their way to avoid having priests utilize the vocabulary whereas others are allowed to keep it alive. One could also suggest that it is simply rare to have any direct speech from priests in the texts of the Historical Books, and this is true; but the point is that there are a handful of cases where anyone's direct speech foregrounds holiness, and none of them comes from the mouths of priests. This is not a claim about an authorial intention to portray matters this way, which could not be known even if it is true, but it is an accurate observation about textual emphases.

Priests and priesthood are widely studied in modern academic biblical studies, and of course large sections of the Pentateuch are ascribed to P; indeed, as many current hypotheses have it, the fundamental demarcation of Pentateuchal material is between "priestly" and "non-priestly" strata. Yet strangely all of this interpretive labor frequently does not attend to the conceptualities of the priesthood in a way that takes seriously its own Pentateuchal emphasis on engaging with the reality of a holy God.

With respect to the interpretation of the Historical Books, what might one conclude on the basis of all this? Reading these books as part of the primary history, do they testify to a loss of priestly nerve? Does the reduction of priesthood to a kind of maintenance of certain rituals indicate part of the problem of Israel's history in these books? Do the books offer a critique of priesthood by having foreigners and prophets and kings keep alive the conceptuality of holiness instead? Certainly modern critical study, in which the Pentateuch has to all intents and purposes been separated from the Historical Books, has struggled to recognize much merit in the Pentateuchal formulation of a holiness agenda for the reading of the Historical Books; and when scholars have cross-compared sideways from the Deuteronomistic history to the work of the Chronicler, which is more hospitable to these emphases, they have tended to operate in the shadow of Wellhausen's famous opinion: "See what Chronicles has made out of David! . . . [H]is clearly cut figure has become a feeble holy picture, seen through a cloud of incense" (1878: 182). A reader of the primary history is unlikely to think of conjoining the adjectives "feeble" and "holy" as they make their way through Leviticus, and thus enters the Historical Books from a fundamentally different horizon than Wellhausen. The point about a synthetic reading of the primary history is thus that one looks for the shaping influence of this agenda in the unfolding text, rather than pondering the historical question of what the priesthood was actually perceived to be during the era of the monarchy.

21.5 THEME(S) IN THE HISTORICAL BOOKS WHEN READING FROM THE PRIMARY HISTORY

What is the theme of the Historical Books, and what difference does it make to ask this question in the context of the primary history? Given that these books are considered under different genre headings in Jewish and Christian tradition, as prophets or histories, it is unlikely that there would only be one answer to the question of theme(s). The most an interpreter could hope for is that any statements of theme(s) are defensible readings of the text, with the evident possibility that multiple and not necessarily mutually sympathetic readings are possible. In fact such big picture attempts to read coherent themes over long stretches of Old Testament narrative remain relatively rare in scholarly circles, and even then sometimes end up emphasizing the multiplicity of interpretive angles possible (see Polzin 1980; 1989; 1993).

The four books of the Former Prophets seem in certain ways to form a simple pattern of two pairs: a book emphasizing unifying initiative followed by a book that records diversifying or disintegrating trends. Thus Joshua (titled with a singular individual's name) presses the reader to celebrate the settling of the one promised land and unifying renewal of the covenant, while Judges (with its impersonal, plural title) appears to imagine local leaders in various localities pursuing independent agendas. Samuel (once again taking its title from the name of a singular individual) presses the reader to celebrate, eventually, the installation of a unifying king in one central location, along with a promise of dynastic security, while Kings (with its impersonal, plural title) has multiple kings in a split kingdom, disintegrating towards exile. The book that fits least well into such a schema is Samuel, which despite its undeniably positive elements also includes indications that kingship is not ideal, and shows David's family fracturing through the conflicts among his sons. Thus, in a manner that we shall consider further below, Konrad Schmid connects the Historical Books with the Pentateuch and locates the key turning point at Judges: "the most elementary organizing theme in Genesis–2 Kings is the division of the material into one large history of salvation section and one large history of judgment section, each connected with the theme of the land," moving from "possession and division of the land" to "loss of land," with Judges forming "a somewhat neutral transition between the two" (2010: 19–20).

The fact that the Historical Books end with exile, or "loss of land," indicates that any overarching theme must incorporate some degree of judgment and decline (Clines 1990: 93–98), as indeed has been the case with most articulations of the significance of a Deuteronomistic history. One way to lighten the darkness of such readings, aside from von Rad's (1953: 84–91) focus on the Davidic promise and subsequent persistent grace (cf. 2 Samuel 7 and other such passages), has been to explore the positive narratives of Josiah (2 Kings 22–23) as an initial, possibly original, ending to the story, followed by a second post-Josianic redaction of the whole, as proposed by Cross (1973), and in various nuanced alternatives ever since. The move towards a broader conception of the primary history offers some interpretive options here. Indeed, the standard view that the "book of the law" in 2 Kings 22 is Deuteronomy in some form has been challenged in those readings willing to look for other resonances between the rhetorical contexts of 2 Kings and the wider Pentateuch (such as Monroe 2011, who thinks that some form of the so-called "Holiness Code" is in view).

In a significant study, David J. A. Clines (1997) offered a broad-brush and engaging attempt to think in synthetic terms about "the theme of the Pentateuch." His conclusion, that the theme was "the partial fulfilment—which implies also the partial non-fulfilment— of the promise to or blessing of the patriarchs" (1997: 30), expounded across three main elements (*posterity* in Genesis 12–50; *divine-human relationship* in Exodus–Leviticus; and *land* in Numbers–Deuteronomy), found its purchase in reading Gen. 12:1–3 as a key focal text to determine what followed. He also offered suggestive readings of the "prefatory theme" of Genesis 1–11, arguing that while it might in itself have a negative theme regarding human destruction of God's good gifts in creation, it was pulled in a more positive direction in the context of the Pentateuch as a whole: "No matter how drastic human sin becomes...God's grace never fails" (1997: 83). Interestingly, Clines seemed to understand that the location of Genesis 1–11 before his selected theme statement made it unreasonable to expect those chapters to fit neatly into the theme of the finished whole. He did, however, point to one particular study of Walter Brueggemann (1968) that hypothesized Genesis 1–11 to be the work of a Yahwist in the court of King David, telling stories that correlated primal episodes of theological significance with specific failings of David's sons. While Clines rightly notes that this seems unwarrantedly specific as a historical hypothesis about authorship (since other options are equally plausible), one could recast Brueggemann's proposal as a literary observation about intertextual resonance, if and when Genesis 1–11 is read as the prelude to the whole primary history (see McBride 2000). The result of such an approach would be a reading of aspects of the David story in mutual dialogue with emphases in Genesis, specifically with regard to reflection upon the nature and incidence of sin in both the primeval history and the succession narratives.

A feature of his discussion over which Clines does not linger is the ambiguity about sin and judgment that he notes in Genesis 1–11. He sees Genesis 1–11 in itself as patient of (indeed "utterly ambiguous" regarding) two contrasting views: a negative one concerning persistent and spreading human sin and a positive one concerning divine grace delivering from judgment—neither of which, he says, is obviously inappropriate. The oddity of his appeal to "utter ambiguity" here is that something like these two views are classically held together in much Christian thinking under the rubric of the doctrine of "original sin." One need not be invested in the full-scale Augustinian conceptuality of such doctrinal formulations to understand that at least one mainstream option regarding "original sin" has been to see it as affirming at one and the same time the two claims that Clines observes: there is persistent and spreading human sin (usually held to be a result of some originary fall), and yet in spite of this God remains gracious towards humankind. More subtle versions of this view recognize that, rather like Genesis 3 itself, the doctrine does not seek to explain sin, so much as characterize human existence this way, with the anti-moralistic result that a sober accounting of human endeavor requires recognition of both persistent failure in the face of grace and persistent grace in the face of failure (McFarland 2010).

Attempts to understand the theme(s) of the Historical Books thus might do well to consider the kind of approach Clines takes to the Pentateuch, and extend it to the broad sweep of the primary history. The first section of the present study did just that with the example of the *bābel* narrative. How might other striking opening statements in Genesis 1–11 shed light on what follows through to the end of Kings?

When Freedman asked this question, he saw the loss of Eden in Genesis 3 as prefiguring the loss of the land in the expulsion of exile in 2 Kings 25 (Freedman 1993: 13; 2000: 5–6). He is not unique in such a view, given that many people writing on Genesis 1–3 date it later than the rest of the Deuteronomistic history, and therefore have been inclined to look for such resonances (see, e.g., Van Seters 1992: 107–34). Certainly there are resonant parallels between the earth (*'ereṣ*) as living-space in Genesis 1 and 2, throughout Genesis 1–11 and the rest of Genesis, and the land (*'ereṣ*) of Israel-Judah, as the living-space for God's people, in Joshua–Kings. The resonance fades a little when one specifies that it is the garden within the land that is lost in Genesis 3, whereas it is the land as a whole that is lost in 2 Kings 17 and 25.

Some read the opening of Genesis as symbolic of the construction of sacred space in the manner of a temple cosmology (e.g. Walton 2011). Although such a reading might then work well as an interesting intertext for the fall of Jerusalem at the other end of the primary history, it must be said that Genesis 1–3 does not obviously present itself as locating the earth or the creation in a temple setting: temple and sacred-space categories seem to have to be supplied by the reader from elsewhere. There is also rather little take-up of such an emphasis through the rest of the primary history, and thus this reading is less relevant to the present enquiry.

A more interesting reflection is whether the theme of "original sin," however that label is parsed, is sustained through the primary history. The argument for a positive answer in the case of the Pentateuch is made by Gary Anderson (2001), who offers a reading of P as the redactor of various emphases in J's narratives. He provides a compelling account of the repeated pattern of divine provision and immediate failure: "'immediacy' may be the best way to define 'original sin' in its Old Testament context. As soon as Israel receives the benefaction of her election, she offers not praise and gratitude but rebellion" (2001: 26). Anderson focuses on the golden calf narrative (Exodus 32), showcasing idolatry at the immediate moment of receiving the law; the "strange fire" (*'ēš zārâ*) offered by Nadab and Abihu (Lev 10:1), demonstrating failure at the immediate moment of instituting the sacrificial system; and, presumably dependent upon these accounts, especially the Exodus one, Adam and Eve's eating of the fruit in Gen. 3, representing failure at the immediate moment of being installed in God's creation. This theme surely continues through the Historical Books, too. Anderson restricts his discussion of this point to a couple of examples from Kings: the contrast between the completion of Solomon's monarchy and the promises to Jeroboam (1 Kings 11) followed by the split of the kingdoms; and the establishment of Solomon himself on the throne (1 Kings 2) followed in the very next verse (3:1) by a statement about his marriage alliance with Pharaoh king of Egypt. There is almost no space for deliberation: the narrative moves directly from gracious provision to human failure. Clearly, the parallels observed earlier between Exodus 32 and 1 Kings 12 also fit well in this understanding.

One could offer a profitable reading of the Historical Books in the context of the whole primary history attentive to this dynamic. Note how Joshua 6 ends with the capturing of Jericho and the notice that "Yhwh was with Joshua," while Joshua 7 opens with "the Israelites broke faith" in the sin of Achan.[3] Arguably a positively construed narrative climax in the book of Judges is Samson's final killing of the Philistines at the end of chapter 16, followed immediately by the grim narratives of the epilogue(s) to that book. This dynamic may also be relevant to discerning the puzzling logic surrounding the failure or rejection of Saul's kingship (1 Samuel 13 and 15) after the extended focus on installing him as the chosen king. Finally, the strange, parabolic narrative of the man of God in 1 Kings 13 narrates him as going straight from pronouncing judgment on Jeroboam, to his own failure, in admittedly testing circumstances, to be obedient to the word of Yhwh given to him. If this narrative is rightly read as symbolic of the perspective of the rest of the Kings' account (as strikingly argued by Karl Barth, defended in Bosworth 2002), then this may serve further to support the value of extending the view offered by Anderson—and hinted at but not followed through by Clines—that the logic of "original sin" is substantively present in one way or another at regular points in the whole primary history.[4]

The prospects may become brighter for further "primary history readings" that shed light on the Historical Books if current scholarly turmoil over the nature, extent, or even existence of the Deuteronomistic history persuades more readers to look to larger or just different sections of the canonical text to discern various patterns and themes. Character studies are one area where wider perspectives sometimes surface more naturally, such as in Marti J. Steussy's negotiation of the differing portraits of David in the primary history, the Chronicler's work, and Psalms (1999). But direct attempts to redraw interpretive paradigms around a primary history are rarer (though see the engaging brief work of Brodie 2000).

A strong example of the kind of revisioning that follows such a move is Konrad Schmid's study, mentioned earlier, *Genesis and the Moses Story* (2010). The substantive agenda of this book is to explore how the "ancestor story" and the "Moses/Exodus" story represent two alternative foundation narratives, merged in the final canonical account. Part of the rationale for this inquiry is a reconsideration of the merits of the Deuteronomistic history theory, and Schmid argues instead that the more significant breaks in the primary history are the ones that separate Genesis from Exodus, and Joshua from Judges. Along the way he reconsiders how and why Genesis–2 Kings stands as a single continuous text, and what sorts of markers one might look for in assessing its component parts (2010: 16–35, 50–70). Schmid's own approach is governed by strong, indeed theological (see 2010: 350–53), convictions about the need to ground interpretive conclusions in hypotheses about original historical contexts. His resultant literary observations about the finished text are also theological: Genesis emphasizes promise (with "an inclusive and irenic theology") while Exodus and following texts, in Deuteronomistic perspective, emphasize obedience to the will of God ("an exclusive and aggressive theology"). The juxtaposition of these sets of narratives does not indicate that promise wins out over obedience, "[r]ather, the two perspectives now exist alongside one another" in Genesis–2 Kings, though how "remains [an] open" question. (2010: 265–67).

The theological convictions that drive Schmid to his conclusions about the importance of historical delineation of traditions will by no means persuade all readers; but the readings of the finished texts that they produce are open to all for further scrutiny and development. That the Historical Books are thereby cast into broader interpretive (and theological) settings, however, is clear, and suggests that, *mirabile dictu*, there may have been wisdom in the final canonical shape of the primary history after all. It seems plausible to suggest that fresh attention to large-scale readings of biblical texts will allow the Historical Books to be read in fresh, literarily, theologically, and historically productive and sensitive ways.

Notes

1. Römer 2005 offers a lucid summary of all these approaches and more.
2. In his genre-by-genre study of holiness in Old Testament traditions, Gammie (1989: 116–24) spends little time on the historical books, noting mainly their difference on this topic, as Deuteronomistic history, from Deuteronomy; but he does note that the emphasis on holiness is basically "attenuated" in the historical books.
3. On a less significant level, it is an oddity that Josh. 2:1, Joshua's commission to the spies to view the land, is followed in Josh. 2:2 by "so they went and entered the house of a prostitute."
4. Theological accounts would normally go on to argue that this is because it is everywhere present in human endeavor.

Bibliography

Anderson, Gary A. 2001. "Biblical Origins and the Problem of the Fall." *Pro Ecclesia* 10: 17–30.
Bosworth, David. 2002. "Revisiting Karl Barth's Exegesis of 1 Kings 13." *BibInt* 10: 360–83.
Brodie, Thomas L. 2000. *The Crucial Bridge: The Elijah-Elisha Narrative as an Interpretive Synthesis of Genesis-Kings and a Literary Model for the Gospels*. Collegeville, MN: Liturgical Press.
Brueggemann, Walter. 1968. "David and His Theologian." *CBQ* 30: 156–81.
Chapman, Stephen B. 2016. *1 Samuel as Christian Scripture: A Theological Commentary*. Grand Rapids: Eerdmans.
Clines, David J. A. 1990. *What Does Eve Do to Help? And Other Readerly Questions to the Old Testament*. JSOTSup 94. Sheffield: JSOT Press.
Clines, David J. A. 1997. *The Theme of the Pentateuch*. JSOTSup 10. Sheffield: Sheffield Academic Press. (1st ed. 1978.)
Cross, Frank Moore. 1973. *Canaanite Myth and Hebrew Epic. Essays in the History of the Religion of Israel*. Cambridge, MA: Harvard University Press.
Dozeman, Thomas B., Thomas Römer, and Konrad Schmid, eds. 2011. *Pentateuch, Hexateuch, or Enneateuch? Identifying Literary Works in Genesis through Kings*. AIL 8. Atlanta: SBL.
Freedman, David Noel. 1963. "The Law and the Prophets." In G. W. Anderson et al., eds., *Congress Volume: Bonn 1962*. VTSup 9. Leiden: Brill, 250–65.
Freedman, David Noel. 1976. "Canon of the OT." In *IDBSup*. Nashville: Abingdon, 130–36.
Freedman, David Noel. 1990. "The Formation of the Canon of the Old Testament." In Erwin B. Firmage, Bernard G. Weiss, and John W. Welch, eds., *Religion and Law: Biblical-Judaic and Islamic Perspectives*. Winona Lake, IN: Eisenbrauns, 315–31.
Freedman, David Noel. 1991. *The Unity of the Hebrew Bible*. Ann Arbor: University of Michigan Press.
Freedman, David Noel. 2000. *The Nine Commandments: Uncovering a Hidden Pattern of Crime and Punishment in the Hebrew Bible*. New York: Doubleday.
Gammie, John G. 1989. *Holiness in Israel*. OBT. Minneapolis: Fortress Press.
Hays, Richard B. 1989. *Echoes of Scripture in the Letters of Paul*. New Haven, CT and London: Yale University Press, 1989.
Houtman, Cornelis. 1993–2002. *Exodus*. HCOT. 4 vols. Leuven: Peeters.
McBride, S. Dean Jr. 2000. "Divine Protocol: Genesis 1:1–2:3 as Prologue to the Pentateuch." In William P. Brown and S. Dean McBride, Jr, eds., *God Who Creates. Essays in Honor of W. Sibley Towner*. Grand Rapids: Eerdmans, 3–41.
McConville, J. G. 1999. "Priesthood in Joshua to Kings." *VT* 49: 73–87.
McFarland, Ian A. 2010. *In Adam's Fall: A Meditation on the Christian Doctrine of Original Sin*. Challenges to Contemporary Theology. Chichester: Wiley-Blackwell.

Monroe, Lauren A. S. 2011. *Josiah's Reform and the Dynamics of Defilement. Israelite Rites of Violence and the Making of a Biblical Text*. New York: Oxford University Press.
Noth, Martin. 1991. *The Deuteronomistic History*. 2nd ed. JSOTSup 15. Sheffield: Sheffield Academic Press. (1st ed., 1981; German original, 1943.)
Polzin, Robert. 1980. *Moses and the Deuteronomist: A Literary Study of the Deuteronomic History*, Part One. New York: Seabury Press.
Polzin, Robert. 1989. *Samuel and the Deuteronomist: A Literary Study of the Deuteronomic History*, Part Two. San Francisco: Harper & Row.
Polzin, Robert. 1993. *David and the Deuteronomist: A Literary Study of the Deuteronomic History*, Part Three. Bloomington: Indiana University Press.
von Rad, Gerhard. 1966. "The Form Critical Problem of the Hexateuch." In von Rad, ed., *The Problem of the Hexateuch and Other Essays*. Translated by E. W. Trueman Dicken. Edinburgh: Oliver & Boyd, 1–78.
von Rad, Gerhard. 1953. *Studies in Deuteronomy*. SBT 9. London: SCM Press.
Römer, Thomas. 2005. *The So-Called Deuteronomistic History. A Sociological, Historical and Literary Introduction*. London: T&T Clark.
Rendtorff, Rolf. 2005. *The Canonical Hebrew Bible: A Theology of the Old Testament*. Leiden: Deo Publishing.
Schmid, Konrad. 2010. *Genesis and the Moses Story: Israel's Dual Origins in the Hebrew Bible*. Siphrut: Literature and Theology of the Hebrew Scriptures 3. Winona Lake, IN: Eisenbrauns.
Steussy, Marti J. 1999. *David: Biblical Portraits of Power*. Studies on Personalities of the Old Testament. Columbia, SC: University of South Carolina Press.
Van Seters, John. 1992. *Prologue to History: The Yahwist as Historian in Genesis*. Zurich: Theologischer Verlag Zurich.
Walton, John. 2011. *Genesis 1 as Ancient Cosmology*. Winona Lake, IN: Eisenbrauns.
Wellhausen, Julius. 2003. *Prolegomena to the History of Israel*. Translated by J. S. Black and A. Menzies. Reprint ed. Eugene, OR: Wipf and Stock. (German original, 1878.)

CHAPTER 22

SYNCHRONIC READINGS OF JOSHUA-KINGS

SERGE FROLOV

22.1 INTRODUCTION

MODERN biblical exegesis began with, and for most of its history held fast to, the premise that the text of the Hebrew Bible, including that of the historical books, is not of a piece. Rather, it is an assemblage of larger or smaller elements that came into being at different times, under different circumstances, and in pursuit of different, sometimes even mutually incompatible agendas. The creator of the final version was no more than a compiler and/or final editor. Predictably, in more than one case these developments have brought about what can only be described as exegetical excesses. To cite two examples having to do with Joshua-Kings, Ivar Hylander's 1932 dissertation argued that 1 Samuel 1–15 developed out of as many as four initially unrelated traditions after passing through the hands of as many as four redactors; and much more recently, Philippe Guillaume (2004) discovered as many as seven redactional layers in Judges. In Joshua-Kings, the tendency towards fragmentation was at least dampened somewhat by the dominance, since the mid-twentieth century, of Martin Noth's highly economical deuteronomistic hypothesis that envisioned a single redactor of Deuteronomy-Kings (Noth 1957: 1–110). Yet, even Noth's successors did not avoid the overall disintegrative trend, postulating two or even three Deuteronomists.

With all this in mind, a pushback against the prevailing tendency towards fragmentation was almost inevitable; if anything, it is surprising that it took until the 1980s—in other words, almost two hundred years of lockstep march in one direction—to materialize. Likewise, it is hardly accidental that several of the very first books affirming or assuming the unity of the biblical text—David Gunn's 1978 *The Story of King David* and 1980 *The Fate of King Saul*, Robert Polzin's 1980 *Moses and the Deuteronomist*, Robert Alter's 1981 *The Art of Biblical Narrative*, and the first installment of Jan Fokkelman's *Art and Poetry in the Books of Samuel*, also published in 1981—were either fully or to a substantial extent devoted to (parts of) Joshua-Kings. The same is true, importantly, of Meir Sternberg's 1985 *The Poetics of Biblical Narrative*, which was quickly recognized, in terms of both theory and praxis, as a classic of the approach discussed in the present chapter. Within two decades, all parts of Joshua-Kings were closely examined with little, if any, recourse to sources, traditions, or redactional layers. Suffice it to mention, in addition to the titles listed above, the publications of Daniel Hawk on Joshua (2000), Barry Webb (1987) and Tammy Schneider (2000) on Judges, Lyle Eslinger (1985), Moshe Garsiel (1985), V. Philips Long (1989), and Robert Polzin (1989) on Samuel, and Burke Long (1984; 1991) on Kings.

The new approach has been variously called "holistic," "integrated," "synthetic," "literary," and "synchronic." However, the first four terms are somewhat unsuitable, each in its own way. "Integrated" and "synthetic" are misleading in that they presuppose a process of creating a whole out of disjointed pieces, whereas it is precisely the departure point of the readings that are usually classified under this heading that the biblical text *is* a unity which the preceding modern scholarship has unnecessarily, perhaps even illegitimately, broken into sources, traditions, or redactional layers. At best, these designations are applicable to the relatively small minority of studies whose aim is to prove that this or that piece of the Hebrew Bible is coherent enough to eliminate the need for any examination of the trajectory whereby it may have come into being. "Holistic" is presumptuous: any reading of the Hebrew Bible—or, for that matter, of any other composition—is reductive by definition for the simple reason that no human being can produce, and put to paper in an even marginally manageable way, an interpretation that covers all possible angles on the text while fully accounting for all of its details and features. "Literary" is confusing because historically, especially in the nineteenth century, source criticism—which in many respects is the polar opposite of the interpretive paradigm that the term is meant to reference today—was known as "literary criticism." "Synchronic" also carries the potential for confusion because in linguistics the term is used in a somewhat different sense than in biblical studies (see Frolov 2004: 8 n. 16 and references there). However, since here we deal with two different fields, this will be the term of choice in the present chapter. For its purposes, the readings described as synchronic are those that deny or ignore the text's evolution over time—which is the main subject of diachronic analysis.

The approach discussed here can also be described as text-oriented, in the sense that it follows New Criticism in literary studies (and its German counterpart, *Werkinterpretation*) as well as Wolfgang Iser's (1978) version of reader-response criticism in seeing the text as possessing an inherent meaning—or, more precisely, a range of meanings that may be broad but is not infinite, being circumscribed by the properties of the interpreted fragment, such as its lexics, grammar, syntax, literary structure, plot development, and the like. A distinction is to be made therefore between this approach and the reader-oriented paradigms, which also tend to examine the text synchronically but postulate, in the vein of post-structuralism and Stanley Fish's (1986) reader-response criticism, that its meaning comes strictly from the reader, based on his or her identity (feminist, womanist, and mujerista criticism, queer and transgender criticism) or agenda (postcolonial, ecological, liberationist criticism).

Text-oriented synchronic studies have been massively instrumental in exploring issues that diachronic scholarship has seldom, if ever, touched upon (except, perhaps, for some form critics). These issues include characterization, the interplay of differing and often conflicting perspectives of the narrator and the *dramatis personae*, the role of tension, suspense, ambiguity, and gaps in the narrative, the trajectories of the plot and breaks in them, the patterns of repetition, the employment of type-scenes, the relationship between ideology and aesthetics, and the like.[1] At the same time, it can be argued that the paradigm's main objective—to stop and roll back fragmentation of the Bible's fabric—has not been fully met for two interconnected reasons.

First, in trying to counteract the disintegrative tendencies of modern diachronic exegesis, synchronically minded interpreters have not consistently addressed the root cause of these tendencies—the perception that the biblical text, replete as it is with discrepancies, rough transitions, sudden terminological shifts, and repetitions, cannot possibly be the work of a single hand. At most, a few publications have sought to prove that certain fragments, such as 1 Samuel 1–12 in the cases of Eslinger (1985) and Wénin (1988) or 1 Samuel 9–11, 13–15 in Long's (1989), are in fact coherent enough to render diachronic examination unnecessary. However, such piecemeal approach is not particularly promising, in part because it would take forever to subject the entire Joshua-Kings—to say nothing of the Hebrew Bible as a whole—to such a scrutiny, but mainly because coherence or lack thereof is in the eye of the beholder. It is hardly accidental that after a relatively short wave of such publications, mostly in the late 1980s, they almost ceased to appear. What is more, diachronic concepts have continued to seep into synchronic exegesis. Two examples lying at the opposite ends of its short history would suffice. Polzin (1980; 1989; 1993) follows Noth's essentially redaction-critical hypothesis (1957) in designating the author of Deuteronomy-Kings a Deuteronomist, and Webb's recent commentary on Judges adopts an age-old reconstruction of the book's formation (incorporated by Noth and further detailed by Wolfgang Richter [1970]) when maintaining that it "was developed from a cycle of stories depicting the exploits of hero figures from Israel's heroic age" (2012: 60).

Second, while decrying diachronic fragmentation of the biblical text, synchronically minded exegetes have inadvertently contributed to the process by focusing on relatively limited pieces—a few chapters in most cases, a single book at best—and rarely if ever asking whether they qualify as literary units and if they do, whether they belong with a larger whole. For instance, the first volume of Fokkelman's grand study of Samuel (1981) also covers, without much explanation, 1 Kings 1–2. If a canonical book is a literary entity, would it not be more consistent to stop at 2 Samuel 24? And if it is not, maybe 1 Samuel 1 is not the best place to start?[2] Likewise, Long's monograph (1989) examines 1 Samuel 13–15 and, separately, chs. 9–11. What are the criteria for singling out these particular texts? How about ch. 12? And even if the two pieces are indeed units of some kind, what about their broader contexts—Samuel as a whole, Joshua-Kings, perchance even the entire Genesis-Kings?

With these vulnerabilities in mind, the present chapter will continue with a sustained critique of the diachronic paradigm, designed to demonstrate—using examples from Joshua-Kings—that no matter how troubled and convoluted the biblical text might look, reading it synchronically is the only viable option. Next to follow is a sample synchronic examination of Joshua-Kings. In order to avoid falling into the fragmentation trap, it will begin by positioning the entire four-book sequence vis-à-vis the rest of the Hebrew Bible. The next step will be to establish the internal literary structure of this sequence. Finally, the chapter will concentrate on one of the relatively small units isolated at the previous stage, reading it both in its own right and in the context of the larger literary structures of which it is a part.

22.2 Is There a Diachronic Option?

In the fourteenth century, Franciscan friar William of Ockham suggested a heuristic principle known as "Ockham's razor" (or *lex parsimoniae*) that is usually formulated "Plurality must never be posed without necessity" or "Entities must not be multiplied without necessity." In other words, an assumption is redundant if a phenomenon can be adequately explained without it. When sufficiently thought through, the ramifications of this principle are nothing short of devastating for diachronic biblical exegesis.

Sources, traditions, and redactional layers posited by diachronic criticism are assumptions par excellence: there is not a single explicit indication of their existence in the received Joshua-Kings, nor is any of them represented in the extant manuscripts. Of course, in and of itself that is not sufficient reason to pronounce them figments of imagination. If the state of the canonical biblical text cannot be explained by more economical means, diachronic hypotheticals may present themselves as viable options. But is it ever the case?

As already mentioned, modern exegetes have long pointed to inconsistencies, lack of continuity, repetitions, and the like as evidence of the text's diachronic development; indeed, not a few have vehemently argued that any other solution would be unscientific (e.g., Dolansky 2014). Yet, there is no compelling reason why such features could not be introduced, or at least tolerated, by a single author for rhetorical or aesthetic purposes—as admitted by Edenburg (2016: 10–11) despite her diachronic preferences. Indeed, a negative of this kind would be exceedingly difficult, if not altogether impossible, to prove. On the one hand, it is of no consequence that today the editorial board of a scholarly journal would not look kindly upon an article that is written the way the Bible is (which, one might suspect, is what sits at the back of many interpreters' minds when they assess the coherence of the biblical text). On the other, the Bible itself is proof enough that the features in question could be considered tolerable if not welcome: if someone, at some point did not believe that they are, we would not have them in the canonical version(s). In addition, blatant inconsistencies—to say nothing of rough transitions and repetitions—can be found in modern writings that indubitably did not undergo any kind of diachronic evolution.[3] There is consequently no need to postulate multiple authors or redactors in order to account for the present condition of the biblical text. Under such circumstances, all these assumptions fall prey to Ockham's razor.

A case in point is Judges 4 and 5. The two pieces may seem to contradict each other on several issues—the number of tribes that participated in the campaign led by Deborah and Barak, the manner of Sisera's assassination by Jael, and the site of the decisive battle. Accordingly, it has almost become a truism of modern scholarship that the latter chapter—the so-called Song of Deborah—is one of the oldest fragments in the Hebrew Bible whereas the former is a much later account, possibly created in an attempt to make sense of the vague poetic description (e.g., Ackroyd 1952; Halpern 1988: 76–97; Kawashima 2004: 17–34). However, upon close scrutiny the alleged tensions prove much smaller than they are usually taken to be (Frolov 2013: 139–41). At the same time, Lawson Younger (1991) has demonstrated that much greater discrepancies can be found in Mesopotamian and Egyptian inscriptions reporting the same event in prose and then in poetry. Apparently, for the scribes, or scribal guilds, that produced these inscriptions such considerations as conventions of the genre or aesthetics of variation trumped consistency.

All the aforesaid does not mean that the most economical reading of the Hebrew Bible would always be synchronic. In more than a few cases, the Bible itself creates a diachronic perspective. The most obvious example is the prophetic books, whose superscriptions explicitly ascribe them to different individuals, many of whom are explicitly said to have lived decades, sometimes centuries apart. It would consequently be a default, Ockham-compliant approach to consider these books as representing different perspectives conditioned by the historical circumstances of the presumed authors. That, however, is emphatically not the case with Joshua-Kings, which contains no explicit signals of being a product of more than one hand. As a matter of fact, the same is true of the Enneateuch (Genesis-Kings) as a whole—with consequences that will be discussed below, in section 22.3.

Another major issue with the diachronic approach is the relative unlikelihood of the text's evolution envisioned by it. With the perceived imperfection of the canonical version as its starting point, any diachronic project can be considered successful only if it yields a perfect, unproblematic pre-canonical formulation. That, however, makes it necessary to explain why someone chose to ruin this perfection, by either making incongruous additions (redaction criticism) or incongruously combining several perfect pieces (source criticism). In text-critical studies, the principle *lectio difficilor potior* has always been considered paramount, on the reasonable assumption that a scribe deliberately amending a text can be expected to seek a smoother, easier formulation, not a bumpier, more difficult one. Why would it be any different in so-called higher criticism? Of course, a redactor or compiler may be inept, but since the same is true of an author, this line of reasoning ends up completely obviating the need for diachronic conjectures—not to mention that exegetically any verdict of ineptness is a dead end.

A textbook example of this difficulty is 1 Samuel 16–18. According to 1 Sam. 16:15–23, David joined Saul's court at the king's request personally addressed to David's father (see especially v. 19). However, in 17:12–31 David arrives in Saul's camp from his native Bethlehem, and in 17:55–58, Saul repeatedly asks whose son he is. Various diachronic explanations of this apparent inconsistency have been proposed, mostly positing two independent accounts of David's early court career, one (the longer "source A") starting with him being employed as a court musician and another (the shorter "source B") with his day-saving appearance on the battlefield (e.g., Lust 1986; Tov 1986).[4] Proponents of such solutions never pause to think, however, why a hypothetical compiler or redactor would mar the immaculately coherent narrative sequence of "source A" by inserting 17:12–31, 55–58 (plus bits and pieces in ch. 18). What could be so important about David going to war with provisions for his brothers (and having a tiff with one of them) rather than simply accompanying Saul? With this consideration in mind, even tentative synchronic readings appear preferable (such as that of Gooding 1986).

Admittedly, it is possible to imagine a situation in which a scribe would feel compelled to revise a text even at the expense of its coherence. Thus, the present writer has argued elsewhere that 1 Samuel 1–8 can (albeit does not necessarily have to) be viewed as an interpolation made with a view to counteracting the predominantly pro-monarchic tendency of Judges and 1 Samuel 9–12—and of Joshua-Kings as a whole (Frolov 2004: 176–94). For a politically engaged postexilic litteratus, faced with the seemingly established reality of kingless restoration sponsored by an imperial power, this may look like a good reason to disturb the placidity of the conjectured original text. However, the hypothesis stumbles on a simple question: why could not the same scribe overwrite this text rather than resorting to a rough interpolation—or, push coming to shove, follow the example of Chronicles (created around the same time) in producing his own text, one better reflective of the changed circumstances? Any diachronic reconstruction assumes, by its very nature, that redactors or compilers could not or would not revise the texts received from their predecessors but felt free to combine these texts or to add to them. Yet, there is no evidence of such a stage in the Bible's formation, and in any case, judging by the liberties that some intertestamental works (Jubilees, for example) and especially Qumran documents take with biblical books, this stage must be dated very late, no earlier than the turn of the eras.[5]

Finally, even apart from the issues discussed above, diachronic exegesis is vulnerable at its core because ultimately it is rooted in the interpreter's admission of inability to comprehend the existing biblical text—or at least a certain feature or aspect thereof. In other words, the point of departure for any diachronic exercise is failure. That alone renders it untenable even as an ad hoc solution in the absence of a plausible (and exegetically profitable) synchronic reading. Failure rarely breeds success, and by starting with the assumption that the received Hebrew Bible—or a certain element thereof—is essentially meaningless, diachronic exegesis forfeits any chance of endowing it with meaning at the end of the road. At best, it can try to explain—not without major difficulties noted above—how the biblical text came into being. For the vast majority of those who are interested in it, be their motivation religious or secular, this is a matter of secondary, if any, importance. When it comes to understanding what the Bible may be trying to say, synchronic reading is the only viable option. And although fragmentation of the biblical text may look like a plausible way of dealing with its complexities, in fact it is not.

22.3 THE MACROCOSM: READING JOSHUA-KINGS SYNCHRONICALLY

A synchronic examination of a text should properly start with a determination of its literary status. Does it constitute a self-contained unit and if it does, is this unit a part of a larger whole (or, perhaps, several larger structures) and what is its internal layout? In other words, what, if anything, is it contained in and what does it contain? Our synchronic reading of Joshua-Kings will begin with asking these questions because, as noted above, failure to do so constitutes a major weakness of many synchronic studies, one that opens a back door to fragmentation that is a hallmark of diachronic exegesis.

In the Tanak, the consonantal sequence that begins with ויהי אחרי מות משה in what we know as Josh. 1:1 and ends with כל ימי חיו in 2 Kgs. 25:30 is divided into four books, while Christian canons have two additional divisions roughly in the middle of Samuel and Kings and also place Ruth between Judges and Samuel. Yet, there is hardly any reflection of these divisions in the text proper. First, none of the books displays a superscription—not even Ruth. On the contrary, in two cases—Judg. 1:1 and 2 Sam. 1:1—the incipient book is explicitly characterized as a continuation of the preceding one through a reference relating all that is recounted in the former to the last event reported in the latter (respectively, "And it came to pass after Joshua's death" and "And it came to pass after Saul's death"). In another two, the plot effortlessly spills across the divide. First Kings 1–2 concludes David's biography that begins in 1 Samuel and in particular the account of the violent culling of his potential successors that begins in 2 Samuel. In a similar way, 2 Kings 1–2 completes the cycle of Elijah stories stretching all the way from 1 Kings 17.[6]

The transition from Judges to 1 Samuel may appear discontinuous, in that the latter introduces a whole set of new characters whose storylines seem at first to have nothing to do with anything reported in the former and the (relatively) serene atmosphere of 1 Samuel 1–3 presents a sharp contrast to the orgy of violence in Judges 19–21. Nevertheless, in fact the two books are tightly connected to each other. The opening of 1 Samuel—ויהי איש אחד מן־הרמתים צופים "and there was a certain man from Ramataim-zophim"—closely resembles Judg. 13:2; 17:1, 7; 19:1, as well as 1 Sam. 9:1, each of which introduces a new protagonist; the sequence is not just highly distinctive but also unique because the formula does not appear elsewhere in the Hebrew Bible (see Richter 1970: 14–15; Frolov 2004: 50–52). Moreover, in 1 Samuel 7 the book's titular character in effect completes Samson's mission in Judges 13–16 by ridding Israel of the Philistine threat (already Judg. 13:5 anticipates that someone other than Samson will achieve it). The title "judge" in application not only to Samuel (1 Sam. 7:6) but also to Eli (1 Sam. 4:18), as well as verbal parallels between 1 Sam. 7:4 and Judg. 10:6 (two of just four verses in the Hebrew Bible mentioning both Baal and Astarte) serve as additional links. The former observation also militates against seeing Ruth as an organic part of the Joshua-Kings continuum despite the fact that its setting fits, especially in view of Ruth 4:17–22. With judges featured on both sides of the Judges–Samuel divide, it would be redundant to specify that the events of Ruth took place "when judges ruled" (1:1) if the book were indeed intended for the place it occupies in Christian canons. Accordingly, it will be henceforth excluded from consideration.

It should also be noted that Joshua-Kings is relatively homogeneous in generic terms. All four (or six) books are dominated by narrative. Its shape and especially its pace may change dramatically but these shifts do not seem to be associated with boundaries between canonical books: thus, Judg. 1:1–26 resembles Joshua 10–11 rather than the rest of Judges, and 1 Kings 1–2 stands in this respect much closer to 2 Samuel 9–20 than to most of Kings. In terms of other genres, the block of lists in Joshua 12–21 stands out, and while Judges and Samuel contain some poetry (Judg. 5:2–31; 1 Sam. 2:1–10; 2 Sam. 1:18–27; 22:2b–51) there is none in Joshua or Kings. However, almost all of these distinctive fragments are uniformly subordinated to narrative. Poetic pieces are opened by *verba dicendi*, which essentially turns their recitation into one of the reported events (Judg. 5:1; 1 Sam. 2:1a; 2 Sam. 1:18a; 22:1–2a), and most lists are introduced by *wayyiqtol* verbs such as ויהי "and it was" or ויצא "and it [the lot] came out," in other words, represented as results of recounted actions.

If Joshua-Kings is a continuum, is it open or closed? In this respect, there is a drastic contrast between the beginning and the end. Just like Judges and 2 Samuel, Joshua begins not with a superscription of any kind but rather with a reference to the last event reported in the book that precedes it in all canons, Deuteronomy. That alone indicates that the narrative sequence stretches without a slightest break across what Jewish and to a lesser extent Christian tradition sees as a divide between two separate corpora—the Torah and the Former Prophets in the former, the Pentateuch and the Historical Books in the latter.

Between Joshua assuming leadership in Deut. 34:9 and his receiving first instructions from the deity in Josh. 1:1–9 lies only a thirty-eight-word encomium to Moses in Deut. 34:10–12. In generic terms, the main difference between Genesis-Deuteronomy and Joshua-Kings lies in the fact that the former is heavy on commandments while the latter contains none. Still, since there are very few commandments in Genesis-Exodus 19 (in terms of volume, more than a third of Genesis-Deuteronomy) and especially since they are invariably presented as pronouncements of Yhwh or Moses—in other words, subordinated to narrative—this is not a sufficient reason to draw a major boundary between Deuteronomy and Joshua.

At the opposite end of the continuum, its plot comes to a complete halt in 2 Kgs. 25:30. The book that follows in the Jewish tradition, Isaiah, begins with a superscription that not only sharply distinguishes it from the preceding text but also explicitly moves the clock almost two centuries back (Isa. 1:1). In addition, the generic difference between it and Joshua-Kings could not be greater (contra Römer 2011). As far as Christian canons are concerned, Chronicles obviously does not qualify as a sequel to Joshua-Kings, as it essentially goes over the same ground as Genesis-Kings but initially in a very different way, as far as both content and form are concerned, with all the accounts prior to Saul's death replaced by genealogies (1 Chr. 1–9). When the Hebrew Bible finally does move—in Ezra—beyond the chronological point reached by Joshua-Kings, it does so by building not on it but on Chronicles (as suggested by the unique catchline 2 Chr. 36:22–23 = Ezra 1:1–3aβ^1).

Joshua-Kings is thus not a literary entity in its own right but rather a part of a larger (macro-)unit—Genesis-Kings, or the Enneateuch. In this unit, it plays a major structural role. I have argued elsewhere that "the macrostructure of the biblical text is defined, in the first instance, by explicit authorial signals, such as superscriptions…recurrent formulae…and summaries" (Frolov 2013: 5). Out of these, only the recurrent formulae are consistently present in the Enneateuch; there is no formulaic pattern encompassing the entire macro-unit but more localized patterns cover most of it between them. In Joshua-Kings, they are highly noticeable. First, there are the five formulae (see especially Greenspahn 1986: 386–89) that define the cycles of apostasy, oppression, repentance, and deliverance unfolding in Judges and stretching, as will be explained below, well into 1 Samuel. Second, there are regnal formulae that begin sparsely in Samuel (the first of them occurs in 1 Sam. 13:1) and become much denser in Kings; these are often paired with regnal summaries (e.g., 1 Sam. 14:47–52). In the balance of the Enneateuch, Genesis is punctuated by תולדות formulae (from 2:4 through 37:2) and Exodus 16—Deuteronomy by highly precise date references, usually to the year, month, and date after the exodus from Egypt (from Exod. 16:1 through Deut. 1:3). Consistently, all the patterns are preceded by stretches of text that are not covered by them but in subject-matter terms prepare for them: the תולדות formulae by Gen. 1:1–2:3 (which is itself densely formulaic but in a different way), the date references by Exodus 1–15, the cycle formulae by Deut. 34:1–Judg. 1:26, and the regnal formulae by 1 Samuel 8–12.[7]

Out of these breaks, Deut. 34:1–Judg. 1:26 is by far the largest, potentially suggesting a major literary boundary. The text's syntactic layout points in the same direction. Standard biblical Hebrew uses *wayyiqtol* verbs to recount events of the past; a chain of such verbs functions, accordingly, as the master sequence of the Enneateuch. This chain is regularly disrupted, and thereby structured, by intrusions of other verbal forms (other than in subordinate clauses and quoted speech). Among the disruptions in question, none is greater than that created by Deut. 1:1–5 and especially by the nominal and, even more importantly, asyndetic (אלה הדברים) formulation of v. 1: since the fragment refers, as noted above, to all the farewell discourses of Moses, it identifies almost all of Deuteronomy (ch. 34 being the only exception) as an enormous digression. The book also straddles a major subject-matter shift: Israel is landless in Genesis-Deuteronomy and landed in Joshua-Kings.[8] Finally, its combination of commandments and sermons constitutes an ideal transition from Genesis-Numbers that contains commandments but no sermons to Joshua-Kings featuring some sermons but no commandments.

The structure emerging from the above considerations is as follows:

Narrative presentation of events from the creation of the world to Jehoiachin's exaltation	Gen. 1:1–2 Kgs. 25:30
I. Landless Israel	Gen. 1:1–Num. 36:13
1. The Origins	Gen. 1:1–50:26
a. Prelude	Gen. 1:1–2:3
b. Origins proper (תולדות)	Gen. 2:4–50:26
2. The Commandments	Exod. 1:1–Num. 36:13
a. Prelude (Exodus)	Exod. 1:1–15:27
b. Commandments proper (date formulae)	Exod. 16:1–Num. 36:13
Intermission: recapitulation and paraenesis	Deut. 1:1–33:29
II. Landed Israel	Deut. 34:1–2 Kgs. 25:30
1. The Judges	Deut. 34:1–1 Sam. 7:17
a. Prelude	Deut. 34:1–Judg. 1:26
b. Judges proper (cycle formulae)	Judg. 1:27–1 Sam. 7:17
2. The Kings	1 Sam. 8:1–2 Kgs. 25:30
a. Prelude	1 Sam. 8:1–12:25
b. Kings proper (regnal formulae and summaries)	1 Sam. 13:1–2 Kgs. 25:30

Joshua-Kings constitutes, together with Deuteronomy 34, one of two main parts of the Hebrew Bible's largest macro-unit—the Enneateuch. Centrally positioned in this macro-unit is Moses's farewell instruction and admonition—his Torah. In this sense, the four books can indeed be described as Deuteronomistic history—with an all-important caveat that Genesis-Numbers also qualifies as such. Internally, Joshua-Kings is likewise bipartite (Deuteronomy 34–1 Samuel 7 + 1 Samuel 8–2 Kings 25), with 1 Samuel 8–12 serving as a strategically important link between the two segments. As will be shown in the next section, the notion of the Torah's centrality is also operative in the latter unit.

22.4 The Microcosm: Reading 1 Samuel 8–12 Synchronically

Between them, these five chapters are a knot of well-known, nay notorious, *cruces interpretum*. First, the text's attitude towards the monarchy is, or at least appears to be, highly inconsistent. In 8:7–8; 10:18–19; 12:12, 17, 19–20 the people are scolded in no uncertain terms for their request to be ruled by a king; indeed, on the first of these occasions this request is described as being in line with "everything they have done from the day [Yhwh] brought them up from Egypt and to this day in abandoning [Yhwh] and serving other gods" (v. 8a). At the same time, in 9:16 the monarch is appointed as Israel's savior, in a divine response to its distress, in 10:27 those refusing to recognize him as such are characterized as "worthless people," and 12:14, 21–25 creates the impression that kingship can work if the people remain observant (which could hardly be the case if the institution was another kind of idolatry).

Similarly inconsistent is Israel's status vis-à-vis its nemesis, the Philistines. In ch. 8, the request for a king does not mention any external threats, in a good agreement with ch. 7, according to which "Yhwh's hand was upon the Philistines all the days of Samuel" (v. 13b). Yet, in 9:16 it is from their hand that Israel has to be saved, and the casual mention of Philistines near Gibeah in 10:5 (cf. 13:3) indicates that the situation is now worse than in 1 Samuel 4–6 and probably Judges 13–16 as well: the country is under military occupation.[9]

It is common in synchronic exegesis to stress that much of the anti-monarchic rhetoric in the piece seems to come from Samuel who is anything but a disinterested party and whose stance is not necessarily shared by the narrator (e.g., Eslinger 1985: 259–62). Indeed, the prophet seems hell-bent on sabotaging the regime change. While in 8:9 the deity commands him to disclose to the people only the "custom of the king"—in other words, the monarchy's socioeconomic cost—according to the next verse, Samuel tells them "*all* the words of Yhwh," presumably including those describing the much graver theological implications of their request (vv. 7–8). In 8:22, he dismisses the people without appointing a king despite the deity's explicit order to do so (v. 21). It is only when the designated monarch bumps into him in the street and Yhwh specifically points him out (9:15–17) that Samuel launches the investiture. And later, in chs. 13 and 15, he can be seen as contributing to Saul's stumbles if not setting him up (e.g., Gunn 1980: 65–67). Is he genuinely concerned about the institution or simply unhappy about being sidelined as a leader? Given that by appointing his sons as judges (8:1) he essentially tried to found his own dynasty, the latter possibility presents itself as plausible at the very least.

At the same time, there is little doubt that Yhwh shares Samuel's sentiments about kingship. The strongest anti-monarchic statement in the discussed fragment—indeed, in the Hebrew Bible as a whole if not in the entire corpus of ancient Near Eastern literature—comes from the deity's mouth (8:7–8). Samuel just echoes it in 12:12, 17, 20 and especially in 10:18–19 (note the verb מאס in both 8:7 and 10:19). Moreover, the Philistines' surprising resurgence in ch. 9 can be cogently explained by the deity's displeasure, to put it mildly, with the people's request for a king. In Judges, oppression by foreign powers consistently comes in response to Israel's abandonment of Yhwh and worship of other gods (2:11–15; 3:7–8; 10:6–7). In 1 Sam. 8:7–8, Yhwh tells Samuel that the request for a king is tantamount to both; in terms of Judges it is only logical that foreign occupation ensues in the next chapter. The people's crying (צעקה) to the deity, referred to in 9:16, perfectly fits into the same pattern (cf. Judg. 3:9, 15; 4:3; 6:7; 10:10). In this sense, 1 Samuel 8–12 launches a new cycle of apostasy, oppression, repentance, and deliverance.

The deity's attitude would seem to stand in no small degree of tension not only with 9:15–17, where Saul is appointed as a king precisely to deliver the people from the Philistines (an equivalent of making Baal a judge), but also, and much more importantly, to the directives of the Torah. Deuteronomy 17 not only permits Israel to appoint a king once they take over the land and settle there but actually insists on it: the absolute-infinitive-with-finite-verb formulation שום תשים endows the otherwise casuistic commandment of vv. 14–15a with apodictic force. In 1 Samuel 8, the people do everything by the book—the Book of Deuteronomy: the land is under their control (after the Philistines' defeat in ch. 7) and they do not insist on having a foreigner as a king (cf. Deut. 17:15b) or giving him too much economic and political clout (cf. Deut. 17:16–17). They even include in their request a quote from Deuteronomy with regard to having a king "like all the nations" (compare Deut. 17:14b and 1 Sam. 8:5b). Yet, the deity immediately characterizes their request as rejection and another kind of idolatry—concepts that are nowhere to be found not only in the Torah but also in the entire Enneateuch apart from 1 Samuel 8–12 and Judg. 8:23. The latter occurrence is of primary importance in making sense of what is going on in the former piece.

With the Enneateuch read synchronically—as it should be given its status as a literary macro-unit—it is difficult to deny that between Deuteronomy 17 and 1 Samuel 8 the deity starts having second thoughts about the monarchy. Moreover, it appears likely that this happened due to Gideon's implication—not only uncalled-for but also unprepared by anything in the Torah—that when a king reigns in Israel Yhwh does not ("I will not rule over you, nor will my son rule over you; Yhwh will rule over you").[10] In other words, Yhwh was introduced to the idea of being Israel's only rightful sovereign, and found it appealing.

Of course, the very notion that the deity may undergo a change of mind, much less do it under (one might say, corrupting) human influence, may be theologically unpalatable to many. This is probably one of the deepest-seated reasons why even synchronically minded exegetes have missed the trajectory (one might say, character development) traced in the previous paragraph. Yet, it would be epistemically incorrect to derive biblical theology deductively from normative theology; rather, normative theology of the communities that consider the Hebrew Bible their sacred scripture can (although does not necessarily have to) be inductively derived from biblical theology as uncovered by exegesis. In fact, the Hebrew Bible offers multiple examples of Yhwh being influenced by humans, such as Abraham in Gen. 18:23–32 or Moses in Num. 14:11–20, and even sketchy supernatural figures, such as Satan in Job 1–2.

What is truly remarkable in 1 Samuel 8–12 is not the apparent shift in the deity's political philosophy but rather the outcome of this shift. First, despite feeling undeservedly rejected yet again by the people, Yhwh unambiguously orders Samuel, not once but twice (8:9, 22), to grant their request for a king. Even if the purpose is malicious—letting Israel shoot itself in the foot—the analogy with foreign worship that the deity draws in v. 8 still proves hollow: it is difficult to imagine Yhwh commanding veneration of Baal or Astarte, even by way of operant conditioning. The difference stems from the fragment's broader context: while the Torah categorically and on multiple occasions forbids serving other gods, it permits and even encourages the monarchy (see above).

Second, and even more strikingly, after placing Israel under Philistine occupation as though the people had indeed committed idolatry, Yhwh, as already mentioned, responds to their outcry by appointing a king—in other words, the alleged object of their idolatry—as the deliverer. The cycle thus fizzles—or, rather, proves illusory—even before the oppressor is confronted, and a new structural pattern, governed by regnal formulae and summaries, logically sets in as soon as the unit ends. Both Yhwh and Samuel may still gripe and grumble (in unison in 12:16–20) but there is not a peep about doing away with the monarchy, and ultimately the institution not only survives the rejection of its founder,

Saul, but also becomes permanent at the deity's initiative (2 Samuel 7). Gideon's headlong proclamation of Yhwh's kingship does cost Israel dearly, but it does not have lasting consequences.

The overall political stance of 1 Samuel 8–12 is thus consistent not only with Deuteronomy 17 but also with the strong pro-monarchic, especially pro-Davidic, bend elsewhere in Joshua-Kings and particularly in Judges.[11] With that, the last vestige of the alleged antimonarchic strand in the second half of the Enneateuch disappears without a trace. While certain characters, including the one known as Yhwh, may have misgivings about the institution, the authorial position is unswervingly in its favor. Accordingly, biblical messianic tradition inherited (in different hypostases) by Judaism and Christianity is rooted in more than just one out of two alternative worldviews; the entire tide of the enneateuchal narrative builds towards it.

At the same time, the unit goes much deeper than that by demonstrating that the Torah trumps divine whims: if it says that Israel should have a king as soon as it feels the urge, that cannot be changed even if Yhwh has second thoughts.[12] The deity remains bound by the conditions of the covenant no matter what. Again, this may sound theologically beyond the pale, but at least the Jewish tradition would seem to concur. In the famous "oven of Akhnai" scene from the Talmud, the majority of sages overrules R. Eliezer in a halakhic dispute, although his position is supported by miracles and even by a heavenly voice; their response to the divine intervention is, "[the Torah] is not in heaven" (see Deut. 30:12). Yhwh's reaction? Smiling and saying, "My children have defeated me. My children have defeated me" (*Bava Mezi'a* 59b).

To be sure, the interpretation presented here by no means exhausts the possible synchronic ways of reading Joshua-Kings as a whole and 1 Samuel 8–12 in particular. At the same time, it does demonstrate that synchronic analysis is not just fully capable of satisfactorily resolving even the most vexing problems presented by the biblical text. In the process, it also uncovers layers of meaning that diachronic approaches are more likely to obscure than to reveal.

Notes

1. Sternberg, as made clear already by the title of his *magnum opus* (1985), places most of these issues under the rubric of "poetics."
2. Contrary to Eslinger's facile decision to do precisely that, quoting Lewis Carroll's "Begin at the beginning" (1985: 51).
3. In one Jules Verne novel, a sailor is left as a punishment on an uninhabited island in March 1865; after spending twelve years in isolation, the same sailor is rescued in another novel by the same author in October 1866. Baruch-Benedictus Spinoza, the grandfather of diachronic criticism, was therefore wasting his breath when he tried to prove that the Enneateuch was assembled out of disparate documents by demonstrating that the 480 years figure in 1 Kgs. 6:1 does not match the sum of other chronological references between the exodus from Egypt and the construction of the Temple (Spinoza 2007: 133–35).
4. The reconstruction of the purported two sources is based to a large extent on the absence of 17:12–31 and several smaller pieces of chs. 17 and 18 in *Codex Vaticanus* of the Septuagint.
5. In particular, "source B" allegedly underlying 1 Samuel 17–18 is neither well rounded nor continuous in any of the existing reconstructions, presupposing a cutting and pasting process of some kind.

6. Admittedly, the cycle is not continuous, and in particular, the last chapter of 1 Kings belongs to it only by virtue of Ahab's death reported in it (1 Kgs. 22:34–38) fulfilling Elijah's prophecy (21:19). Still, the fact that Elijah is introduced in 1 Kings and dies in 2 Kings tells volumes about continuity between the two books. Moreover, the same is true of Elisha.
7. The תולדות formula in Gen. 37:2 can be reasonably applied to the rest of Genesis but not to Exodus, and the date in Deut. 1:3 is specifically that of Moses's discourses, which end in Deuteronomy 33. Judges 1:27–3:6 serves as a prologue to the cycles of apostasy, oppression, repentance, and deliverance (see Frolov 2013: 28–29), and, as argued above, the cycle that begins in Judges 13 actually ends only in 1 Samuel 7 (note echoes of the "crying" formula in 1 Sam. 7:8–9 and the "subjugation" formula in v. 13).
8. In Genesis, Israel's ancestors live in the land promised to them by the deity but do not possess it.
9. Indeed, many enigmatic details of 1 Samuel 9–10 are comprehensively accounted for by the fact that the investiture of Israel's first king had to be kept secret from the occupiers (see Frolov 2007a).
10. On Gideon's systemic theological ignorance, see Frolov 2013: 184–85.
11. On this trend as formative in Joshua-Kings, see Frolov 2007b: 176–78; on Judges in this respect, see Sweeney 1997; Frolov 2013, especially 193–99.
12. On Judges 9 as another demonstration that Deuteronomy 17 is not to be trifled with, see Frolov 2013: 196–97.

Bibliography

Ackroyd, Peter R. 1952. "The Composition of the Song of Deborah." *VT* 2(2): 160–62.
Alter, Robert. 1981. *The Art of Biblical Narrative*. New York: Basic Books.
Dolansky, Shawna. 2014. "Deuteronomy 34: The Death of Moses, Not Source Criticism." *JBL* 133.3: 669–76.
Edenburg, Cynthia. 2016. *Dismembering the Whole: Composition and Purpose of Judges 19–21*. AIL 24. Atlanta: SBL.
Eslinger, Lyle M. 1985. *Kingship of God in Crisis: A Close Reading of 1 Samuel 1–12*. Sheffield: Almond.
Fish, Stanley. 1986. "Is There a Text in This Class?" In Hazard Adams and Leroy Searle, eds., *Critical Theory Since 1965*. Tallahassee: Florida State University Press.
Fokkelman, Jan. 1981. *Narrative Art and Poetry in the Books of Samuel: A Full Interpretation Based on Stylistic and Structural Analyses*. Vol. I: *King David (II Sam. 9–20 and I Kings 1–2)*. Assen: Van Gorcum.
Frolov, Serge. 2004. *The Turn of the Cycle: 1 Samuel 1–8 in Synchronic and Diachronic Perspectives*. Berlin: de Gruyter.
Frolov, Serge. 2007a. "The Semiotics of Covert Action in 1 Samuel 9–10." *JSOT* 31.4: 429–50.
Frolov, Serge. 2007b. "Evil-Merodach and the Deuteronomist: The Sociohistorical Setting of Dtr in the Light of 2 Kgs 25,27–30." *Bib* 88.2: 176–78.
Frolov, Serge. 2013. *Judges*. FOTL 6B. Grand Rapids: Eerdmans.
Garsiel, Moshe. 1985. *The First Book of Samuel: A Literary Study of Comparative Structures, Analogies and Parallels*. Ramat-Gan: Revivim.
Gooding, David W. 1986. "An Approach to the Literary and Textual Problems in the David-Goliath Story: 1 Sam 16–18." In Dominique Barthélemy, ed., *The Story of David and Goliath: Textual and Literary Criticism*. Fribourg: Éditions universitaires; Göttingen: Vandenhoeck & Ruprecht, 55–86.
Greenspahn, Frederick E. 1986. "The Theology of the Framework in Judges." *VT* 36.4: 386–89.
Guillaume, Philippe. 2004. *Waiting for Josiah: The Judges*. London: T&T Clark.
Gunn, David. 1978. *The Story of King David: Genre and Interpretation*. Sheffield: JSOT.
Gunn, David. 1980. *The Fate of King Saul: An Interpretation of a Biblical Story*. Sheffield: JSOT.

Halpern, Baruch. 1988. *The First Historians: The Hebrew Bible and History*. San Francisco: Harper & Row.

Hawk, L. Daniel. 2000. *Joshua*. Berit Olam. Collegeville, MN: Liturgical Press.

Hylander, Ivar. 1932. *Der literarische Samuel-Saul-Komplex (I. Sam. 1–15): traditionsgeschichtlich untersucht*. Uppsala: Almqvist & Wiksell; Leipzig: Harrassowitz.

Iser, Wolfgang. 1978. *The Act of Reading: A Theory of Aesthetic Response*. Baltimore: Johns Hopkins University Press.

Kawashima, Robert S. 2004. *Biblical Narrative and the Death of the Rhapsode*. Bloomington: Indiana University Press.

Long, Burke O. 1984. *1 Kings with an Introduction to Historical Literature*. FOTL 9. Grand Rapids: Eerdmans.

Long, Burke O. 1991. *2 Kings*. FOTL 10. Grand Rapids: Eerdmans.

Long, V. Philips. 1989. *The Reign and Rejection of King Saul: A Case for Literary and Theological Coherence*. Atlanta: Scholars Press.

Lust, Johan. 1986. "The Story of David and Goliath in Hebrew and Greek." In Dominique Barthélemy, ed., *The Story of David and Goliath: Textual and Literary Criticism*. Fribourg: Éditions universitaires; Göttingen: Vandenhoeck & Ruprecht, 5–18.

Noth, Martin. 1957. *Überlieferungsgeschichtliche Studien: Die sammelnden und bearbeitenden Geschichtswerke im Alten Testament*. Tübingen: Max Niemeyer.

Polzin, Robert. 1980. *Moses and the Deuteronomist: A Literary Study of the Deuteronomic History*. Part One: *Deuteronomy, Joshua, Judges*. New York: Seabury.

Polzin, Robert. 1989. *Samuel and the Deuteronomist: A Literary Study of the Deuteronomic History*. Part Two: *1 Samuel*. San Francisco: Harper & Row.

Polzin, Robert. 1993. *David and the Deuteronomist: A Literary Study of the Deuteronomic History*. Part Three: *2 Samuel*. Bloomington: Indiana University Press.

Richter, Wolfgang. 1970. *Die sogenannten vorprophetischen Berufungsberichte: Eine literaturwissenschaftliche Studie zu 1 Sam 9, 1–10, 16, Ex 3f und Ri 6, 11b–17*. Göttingen: Vandenhoeck & Ruprecht.

Römer, Thomas. 2011. "How Many Books (*teuchs*): Pentateuch, Hexateuch, Deuteronomistic History, or Enneateuch?" In Thomas B. Dozeman, Thomas Römer, and Konrad Schmid, eds., *Pentateuch, Hexateuch, or Enneateuch? Identifying Literary Works in Genesis through Kings*. AIL 8. Atlanta: SBL, 25–42.

Schneider, Tammi J. 2000. *Judges*. Berit Olam. Collegeville, MN: Liturgical Press.

Spinoza, Benedict de. 2007. *Theological-Political Treatise*. Cambridge: Cambridge University Press.

Sternberg, Meir. 1985. *The Poetics of Biblical Narrative: Ideological Literature and the Drama of Reading*. Bloomington: Indiana University Press.

Sweeney, Marvin A. 1997. "Davidic Polemics in the Book of Judges." *VT* 47.4: 517–29.

Tov, Emanuel. 1986. "The Nature of the Differences between the MT and the LXX in 1 Sam. 17–18." In Dominique Barthélemy, ed., *The Story of David and Goliath: Textual and Literary Criticism*. Fribourg: Éditions universitaires; Göttingen: Vandenhoeck & Ruprecht, 19–46.

Webb, Barry G. 1987. *The Book of Judges: An Integrated Reading*. Sheffield: Sheffield Academic Press.

Webb, Barry G. 2012. *The Book of Judges*. NICOT. Grand Rapids: Eerdmans.

Wénin, André. 1988. *Samuel et l'instauration de la monarchie (1 S 1–12): Une recherche littéraire sur le personage*. Frankfurt am Main: Peter Lang.

Younger, K. Lawson. 1991. "Heads! Tails! Or the Whole Coin?! Contextual Method and Intertextual Analysis: Judges 4 and 5." In K. Lawson Younger, William W. Hallo, and Bernard F. Batto, eds., *The Biblical Canon in Comparative Perspective*. Lewiston: Mellen, 109–35.

CHAPTER 23

THE RISE AND FALL OF THE SO-CALLED CHRONICLER'S HISTORY AND THE CURRENT STUDY OF THE COMPOSITION OF CHRONICLES, EZRA, AND NEHEMIAH

RALPH W. KLEIN

ACCORDING to the Chronicler's History hypothesis, most of 1 and 2 Chronicles, Ezra, and Nehemiah come from a single author. In the words of Otto Eissfeldt:

> The work of the Chronicler originally... comprised not only the two books of Chronicles, but also the books of Ezra and Nehemiah, and thus presented the history of the kingdom of Judah... from Adam to its re-founding by Nehemiah and Ezra. The books of Ezra and Nehemiah are seen to be the conclusion of the work not only by the similarity of language and of thought—love of the Temple and its cultus, and in particular of the Levites and singers—but especially by the fact that it relates the restoration of those treasures whose loss is related in II Chron. xxxvi, 1–21. In addition, the conclusion of II Chron. (xxxvi, 22–23) agrees almost word for word with the opening of Ezra (i. 1–3), so that the point at which the division was made is clearly recognizable.
> (Eissfeldt 1965: 530; cf. Zunz 1832: 13–36; Movers 1834: 14 holds that Chronicles was completed before Ezra)

A number of scholars conclude that the Nehemiah Memoir was combined with 1–2 Chronicles and Ezra secondarily creating a gap between the work of Ezra in Ezra 7–10 and his reading and interpretation of the Torah in Nehemiah 8.[1] Conclusions like these have been vigorously discussed in the secondary literature and deserve careful reconsideration.

23.1 ARGUMENTS FOR AND AGAINST COMMON AUTHORSHIP OF CHRONICLES, EZRA, AND NEHEMIAH

Joseph Blenkinsopp (1988: 47–54) argues for the Chronicler's History hypothesis because Chronicles and Ezra-Nehemiah share the same religious interests and ideology. He notes that preparations for building the First and the Second Temple are described in parallel ways (cf. 1 Chr. 22:2, 4, 15 and 2 Chr. 2:9, 15–16 with Ezra 3:7). In both instances, the altar is set up before the temple is built (see 1 Chr. 21:18–22:1; Ezra 3:2). Both temples are endowed by the heads of ancestral houses (1 Chr. 26:26; Ezra 2:68). In both Chronicles and Ezra-Nehemiah there is great interest in the sacred vessels (1 Chr. 28:13–19; 2 Chr. 5:1; Ezra 1:7; 7:19; 8:25–30, 33–34). The order of sacrifices (2 Chr. 2:3; 8:13; Ezra 3:4–6) and the enumeration of sacrificial materials (1 Chr. 29:21; 2 Chr. 29:21, 32; Ezra 6:9, 17; 7:17–18, 22; 8:35–36) are practically identical. Similarly, the descriptions of liturgical music and of musical instruments and who are to play them correspond closely (1 Chr. 15:19; 16:5–6; 25:1, 6; 2 Chr. 5:12–13; Ezra 3:10; Neh. 12:35). Blenkinsopp also notes that after Hezekiah's and Josiah's reforms there is a celebration of Passover (2 Chr. 30; 35:1–19). In Ezra, the renewal of cult also concludes with the celebration of Passover (Ezra 6:19–22).

But these arguments are not conclusive: in my judgment, they reflect a common liturgical tradition rather than offering proof of identical authorship. If we think of "authorship" in a broad sense of a scribal school sharing the same goals, language, and religious outlook on the past, the identity of a singular, author might not be within our grasp (cf. Blenkinsopp 1988: 47–54; 2009: 163–66). The controversy over mixed marriage in Ezra 9–10 is in sharp contrast to the attitude toward mixed marriage in Chronicles (see below) and is among the factors that speaks strongly in favor of separate authorship according to many authors.

23.1.1 Linguistic Arguments

The contemporary discussion of the linguistic evidence for and against the unity of authorship in the Chronicler's History was initiated by Sara Japhet (1968: 330–71). She concluded that linguistic forms found respectively in Chronicles or Ezra-Nehemiah stand in opposition to one another and are mutually exclusive. She also argued that technical terms and stylistic peculiarities unique to each of the two books strengthen the argument against unity of authorship. Publications by Throntveit (1982) and Williamson (1977: 37–59) raised serious questions about the force of her arguments but agreed with her that Chronicles and Ezra-Nehemiah do not come from one author. Basing himself on long lists of vocabulary compiled by Driver (1960 [1897]: 535–40) and Curtis and Madsen (1910: 27–36), Williamson recognized that the list in Driver was designed to demonstrate the peculiarities and mannerisms in Chronicles, Ezra, and Nehemiah, not to show unity of authorship. Similarly, Curtis and Madsen note that many of the words in their list appear in only one of the books. Williamson found only six expressions from these long lists that favor unity of authorship, but serious questions can be raised about four of these six items. The best example for unity of authorship is the particular Hebrew construction ʻ*ad lĕ-* before a substantive but it is found only fifteen times in Chronicles and four times in Ezra. David Talshir (1988), too, called many of Japhet's linguistic conclusions into question, demonstrating that there is no necessary linguistic opposition between the two books, and that the linguistic affinity between them is extremely high. He pointed out that evidence from the Nehemiah Memoir cited by Japhet is irrelevant to this discussion since by common consensus the author of the Nehemiah Memoir is different from the author of the other parts of Ezra and Nehemiah. Still further, the authors of Chronicles and of Ezra-Nehemiah were consistent in the use of short forms for the 2nd- and 3rd-person imperfect consecutive verbal forms but used the long forms for the 1st-person consecutive forms. With regard to theophoric names Japhet had concluded that Ezra-Nehemiah uniformly used the long form (*-yāhû*) while Chronicles uses both the long form and the short form (*-yâ*). But Talshir argued that the author of Ezra-Nehemiah cited names according to the contemporary short form in post-exilic times while the author of Chronicles tried to preserve the classical long form, especially when citing sources (as in material taken from Samuel-Kings) or when recalling famous figures from preexilic history. After reviewing the use of technical terms, syntax, and idioms and other vocabulary, Talshir concluded that the author of the Nehemiah Memoir is someone other than the writer of Chronicles and Ezra-Nehemiah although the works do show similar provenance. He also determined that the similarity in both grammar and vocabulary between Chronicles and of the other parts of Ezra-Nehemiah were noteworthy. They may not prove single authorship, but did argue for proximity in time and place of composition for the two works. In short, linguistic evidence does not prove separate authorship for Chronicles and Ezra-Nehemiah, and in Talshir's opinion should lead to serious consideration of single authorship on other grounds. Robert Polzin, too, thought there was an extremely strong case for similarity in authorship on the basis of linguistic evidence (1976: 71), but Throntveit revised that conclusion as follows: there is an extremely strong case for similarity *in language*—not, that is, necessarily in authorship—between Chronicles and Ezra-Nehemiah (1982: 215). These arguments for unity of authorship based on similarities of language become more tenuous if VanderKam (1992) is right that Ezra and Nehemiah are two separately authored works, with each having its distinctive point of view.

23.1.2 The Overlap between 2 Chr. 36:22–23 and Ezra 1:1–3a

2 Chronicles ends as Ezra begins with an overlapping citation of the edict of Cyrus that authorized the Jews to return to the Holy Land from Babylon and to rebuild the temple. The text in Ezra is longer by one and one half verses.

Those who hold to the unified authorship of Chronicles and Ezra-Nehemiah argue that when the books were separated, for whatever reason (as they now are in the canon), an overlap was created that pointed to the original connection between the two works. In the scholarly edition of the Hebrew Bible, *Biblia Hebraica Stuttgartensia*, Ezra and Nehemiah are printed right before Chronicles, the last book in the canon. In Codex Leningradensis, however, Chronicles is the first book in the Writings and Ezra-Nehemiah is the last, which makes some kind of connecting point between the two books quite helpful. Menahem

Haran (1985) cited the custom in documents from Mesopotamia of writing catch lines that connected two segments of a literary work, but there is no other use of such a technique in the Hebrew Bible. If Ezra-Nehemiah was completed before Chronicles, the overlap could have been created in Chronicles to indicate where the story told in Chronicles continues. The shortened form of the edict in the last verse in the Hebrew Bible ("Whoever is among you from all his people, may his God be with him and let him go up!"; 2 Chr. 36:23) may imply an invitation in a later historical context for Jews to return to Jerusalem and the land even after the destruction of Jerusalem in 70 CE (see Klein 2012: 547; Kalimi 2005: 155–56). The longer version in Ezra ("Whoever is among you from all his people, may his God be with him and let him go up to Jerusalem which is in Judah and build the house of Yhwh the God of Israel he is the God who is in Jerusalem"; Ezra 1:3) ties the expression more clearly to the sixth-century BCE context. The overlap of the last verses in Chronicles and the first verses in Ezra has been explained as pointing to the original unity of the Chronicler's history or to the original separation between Chronicles and Ezra-Nehemiah, but the explanations for this overlap are educated guesses at best. Williamson even proposes to end Chronicles after 2 Chr. 36:21, making the overlap in Chronicles completely secondary (1977: 9–10).

23.1.3 The Witness of 1 Esdras

The apocryphal book of 1 Esdras is a somewhat free Greek translation, probably coming from the second century BCE, that includes a translation of 2 Chronicles 35–36, Ezra 1–10, and Nehemiah 8. It also includes a separate narrative that has no biblical parallel, which involves a debate among three youths about what is the strongest thing in the world (1 Esdr. 3:1–5:6). This additional passage is placed after the equivalent of Ezra 1:1–11 and 4:6–24a (= 1 Esdr. 2:1–25 [ET 2:1–30]). Some scholars have taken 1 Esdras as a translation of an earlier form of 1 and 2 Chronicles, Ezra, and Nehemiah 8 to which the Nehemiah Memoir had not yet been added—forming one version of the hypothetical Chronicler's History.

Frank Moore Cross posited three editions of the Chronicler's History, largely due to his analysis of 1 Esdras (1975: 4–18). Despite this multi-stage theory of the text's development, Cross advocated for the Chronicler's History hypothesis throughout.[2] The first edition, Chr_1, was dated by Cross between the founding of the Second Temple in 520 BCE and its completion in 515 BCE. It contained 1 Chronicles 10–2 Chronicles 34 plus the Hebrew text lying behind 1 Esdr. 1:1–5:62 (ET 1:1–5:65)—that is, 2 Chronicles 35–36 and Ezra 1:1–3:13—with the story of the three youths in 1 Esdr. 3:1–5:6 (original to the Chronicler's History, according to Cross) included after Ezra 1:1–11//1 Esdr. 2:1–14 (ET 2:1–15) and Ezra 4:16–24//1 Esdr. 2:15–25 (ET 2:16–30). Ezra 2:1–3:13//1 Esdr. 5:7–62 (ET 5:7–65) was placed after the story of the three youths.

Cross believed that the order of the pericopae in 1 Esdras was older than the canonical order and historically superior. This edition (Chr_1) was designed to support the restoration of the kingdom in early postexilic times under the leadership of Zerubbabel. Ending the Chronicler's History with Ezra 3:13 in Chr_1 was based on a suggestion by David Noel Freedman (1961).

The second edition of the Chronicler's History, Chr_2, contained 1 Chronicles 10–2 Chronicles 34 plus the Semitic text lying behind 1 Esdras (2 Chronicles 35–36, Ezra 1:1–11,

4:6–24a, the story of the three youths in 1 Esdr. 3:1–5:6, and Ezra 2:1–4:5//1 Esdr. 5:7–70 [ET 5:7–73]), the Aramaic materials in Ezra 5:1–6:18//1 Esdr. 6:1–7:9, the Hebrew of Ezra 6:19–22//1 Esdr. 7:10–14, plus the Ezra narrative in Ezra 7:1–10:44//1 Esdr. 8:1–9:36). Ezra 10:44 (= 1 Esdr. 9:36) was followed immediately by Neh. 7:72a–8:12 (= 1 Esdr. 9:37–55) where Ezra reads the Torah to the people. Along with many other scholars, Cross believed that the ending of Nehemiah 8 (vv. 13–18) had been lost by a textual accident in 1 Esdras. In Chr$_2$, Zerubbabel was still given the exalted title "servant of the Lord" (1 Esdr. 6:26 [ET 6:27]), which may be contrasted with Ezra 6:7 (MT) where both his name and title are lost. Cross attributes this change to the editor of Chr$_3$ (see below), but it seems more likely that "Zerubbabel the servant of the Lord" is a secondary expansion in 1 Esdras (cf. Z. Talshir 2001: 359). Chr$_2$ was dated by Cross to about 450 BCE, after Ezra's mission which he dated to 458 BCE.

The final edition, Chr$_3$, consisted of 1 Chronicles 1–9 (the genealogical introduction to Chronicles) plus the *Vorlage* of Chr$_2$ plus the Nehemiah Memoir. The addition of the Nehemiah Memoir broke the connection between Ezra 10 and Nehemiah 8. According to Cross it was this edition that also eliminated the story of the three youths in 1 Esdr. 3:1–5:6. Furthermore, according to Cross, Zerubbabel's royalist/messianic movement was snuffed out and his end was ignominious or pathetic. Chr$_3$ was dated by Cross to 400 BCE or slightly later.

Cross's study shows how dominant the Chronicler's History hypothesis was in the not-so-distant past. Cross held, correctly in my judgment, that an earlier form of the wording of 2 Chronicles 35–36, Ezra 1–10, and Nehemiah 8 could be reconstructed on the basis of 1 Esdras and Esdras B (see Klein 1966). He erred in assigning the story of the three youths to the original form of the Chronicler's History that was later removed rather than reckoning that the addition of the story was a secondary change introduced by the redactors or translators of 1 Esdras (see further below). Cross also did not recognize that the text of 1 Esdras does not presuppose that Nehemiah 8 followed immediately after Ezra 10 (see below).

23.1.4 The Book Called 1 Esdras

Is the book of 1 Esdras a fragment of the putative Chronicler's History that once included an additional sixty-three chapters (1 Chronicles 1–29 and 2 Chronicles 1–34) at its beginning? Williamson (1977: 19–21) based on 1 Esdr. 1:21–22 (ET 1:23–24), a passage not included in MT, argues that 1 Esdras once began with a translation of 2 Chronicles 34 (the beginning of Josiah's reign), but van der Kooij (1991b), basing himself on the same verses in 1 Esdras, argued that 1 Esdras never included anything earlier than 2 Chronicles 35. Z. Talshir (2011: 111) notes that many have considered this starting point a strange redactional decision. She cites as a possible parallel how the Chronicler began his narrative of the monarchy with the last chapter of Saul's reign (1 Chronicles 10//1 Samuel 31). In Talshir's opinion, the location of Josiah's Passover right at the beginning of 1 Esdras proves that it is a secondary work in comparison with the canonical book of Chronicles.

I would add the following arguments to this position (see Klein 2011: 225–35). 2 Chronicles 35 presented a number of theological difficulties to the author of 1 Esdras, who, as a result, began his document by addressing those difficulties. In attempting to explain why the exemplary king Josiah was killed in battle at an early age, 2 Chr. 35:22 had faulted Josiah for not listening to the words of Neco from the mouth of God. But readers might well ask themselves whether God had made himself known to Josiah on this important issue only through a Gentile king. 1 Esdras solves that problem by saying that Josiah did not heed the words of Jeremiah the prophet from the mouth of God (1 Esdr. 1:26 [ET 1:28]). Instead of King Josiah being severely wounded (2 Chr. 35:23), the translator of 1 Esdr. 1:28 (ET 1:30) has the king cry out "I am very weak." After his servants remove him from the battle, Josiah climbs up into his second chariot under his own power and, arriving in Jerusalem, he dies. The net result is that in 1 Esdras, Josiah is not explicitly wounded by Neco, and in fact he is gathered to his grave in peace as Huldah had prophesied (cf. 2 Kgs. 22:20//2 Chr. 34:28). The two additional verses in 1 Esdr. 1:21–22, not included in 2 Chronicles 35, were probably added to the text of the Hebrew version of 1 Esdras (Z. Talshir 2001: 38) and indicate that ancient readers of Chronicles were also not satisfied with the transition between the laudatory account of Josiah's Passover and the immediately following account of the king's death at the hands of Neco. The supplementary verses in 1 Esdras state that Josiah was not among the sinners of his day, but that Josiah was instead grieved by the sinful behavior of his contemporaries (see van der Kooij 1991b). The impiety of Israel in Josiah's time contrasts explicitly with the piety of Josiah in 1 Esdr. 1:21 (ET 1:23). For these reasons, 2 Chronicles 35 seemed like an appropriate place to begin 1 Esdras.

The present text of 1 Esdr. 9:55 ends awkwardly in mid-sentence with the words "And they came together," based on Neh. 8:13a. By common agreement, something is missing at the end of the book. An exception to this judgment is offered by van der Kooij (1991a). But is it only a translation of the rest of Nehemiah 8 (vv. 13b–18) that is missing, or is it a translation of Neh. 8:13b–18 and some or all of Neh. 9:1–13:31? If the latter is the case, an additional five (or more) chapters have been lost at the end of the supposed Chronicler's History in 1 Esdras.

Another question is whether the Chronicler's History originally contained a Semitic equivalent for 1 Esdr. 3:1–5:6 that was later dropped in the canonical book of Ezra, as Cross proposed, or if the story of the three guardsmen was added to an earlier form of Ezra that then required the transfer of Ezra 2:1–4:5 (1 Esdr. 5:7–70) to a position after the story of the three guardsmen. The three guardsmen in the story debate what was the strongest thing in the world: wine (1 Esdr. 3:17b–24), the king (1 Esdr. 4:1–12), or women and truth (1 Esdr. 4:13–41). The third argument won the day and the wise speaker of this argument is identified as Zerubbabel in 1 Esdr. 4:13. Z. Talshir (2011: 112–19) has argued persuasively that this information about the importance of Zerubbabel provides the reason for the inclusion of 1 Esdr. 3:1–5:6 because the Hebrew text of Ezra 1 had not provided an appropriate introduction to the character Zerubbabel, who is first mentioned in Ezra 2:2 with a listing of ten other early and unimportant leaders (Z. Talshir). The pericope concerning the three guardsmen takes the reader to the second year of Darius whereas Ezra 1 takes place in the first year of Cyrus. Hence the equivalent of Ezra 2:1–4:5 (1 Esdr. 5:7–70) was placed after the story of the three guardsmen where its dating to the second year of Darius makes more sense. The present text of 1 Esdras leaves the equivalent of Ezra 4:6–24 at its original position (1 Esdr. 2:15–25 [ET 2:16–30]). Since the inclusion of the story of the three guardsmen required major redactional repositioning of Ezra 2:1–4:5, there is no need to attribute its content/inclusion or its different placement of Ezra 2:1–4:5 to the original text of the Chronicler's History. In Z. Talshir's opinion (2011: 113), 1 Esdras in its present form, with the story of the three youths as its distinctive mark, is a composition based upon textual material well known from the canonical version of Chronicles, Ezra, and Nehemiah. Talshir concludes, "The 1 Esdras text is certainly secondary in comparison with the MT since the correspondence with Artaxerxes is clearly concerned with the building of the city and the walls [Ezra 4:12], not the temple" (2011: 125).[3]

One of the major puzzles of the canonical Ezra-Nehemiah is why Ezra's reading of the Torah is located in Nehemiah 8 whereas Ezra has not appeared at all in Nehemiah 1–7 after his involvement with the issue of intermarriage in Ezra 9–10. This is usually explained, not with complete satisfaction, to the secondary combination of the Nehemiah Memoir with the Ezra materials. In 1 Esdras a translation for Neh. 8:1–13a (= 1 Esdr. 9:37–54) comes almost immediately after the mixed marriage pericope in 1 Esdr. 8:65–9:36. Is that its "original" position in the supposed Chronicler's History? Some have thought so, but Williamson (1977: 34–35) and Z. Talshir (2011: 125–27) have noted that 1 Esdr. 9:37 is in fact a translation of Neh. 7:72 (ET 7:73), which is the final verse in the list of returnees in Neh. 7:6–72 (ET 7:7–73; cf. Ezra 2:70) indicating that the translator or redactor of 1 Esdras knew the location of Ezra's reading of the Torah in the same awkward position as in Nehemiah 8 (MT), widely separated from Ezra 10.

Here, then, are the arguments against the position that 1 Esdras witnesses to an original unity of Chronicles and Ezra-Nehemiah in a "Chronicler's History":

1. There is no reason to think 1 Esdras began earlier than with a translation of 2 Chronicles 35.
2. The addition of the narrative of the three youth is the *raison d'être* for 1 Esdras. Schenker (1991; 2011), Böhler (1997; 2003), and Cross (1975) are incorrect in arguing that the arrangement of materials in 1 Esdras is older than the arrangement in the canonical Ezra.
3. There is no way to know how long the original ending of 1 Esdras was, but the different possibilities are not relevant to the discussion about the supposed Chronicler's History.
4. 1 Esdras knew the sequence of Nehemiah 7 → 8, but 1 Esdras does not presuppose the existence of a form of the Chronicler's History prior to the time when the Nehemiah Memoir had been added.
5. The alternate arrangement of the equivalent for Ezra 2:1–4:25 is the result of including the story of the three youths.

23.2 Ideological/Theological Differences between Chronicles and Ezra-Nehemiah

Numerous differences exist in terms of theology or ideology between Chronicles and Ezra-Nehemiah. These have frequently been discussed with reference to the question of a "Chronicler's History."

23.2.1 Mixed Marriages

The book of Ezra-Nehemiah is strongly critical of mixed marriages, whether these are marriages with women of other nations; with women who are not part of the *Golah* group (Ezra 9–10); or women of Ashdod, Ammon, and Moab (Neh. 13:26). The last-mentioned passage insists that it was foreign women who made Solomon sin. Chronicles, however, never criticizes mixed marriages, and in its idealized depiction of Solomon it omits entirely 1 Kgs. 11:1–13, which narrates Solomon's numerous marriages with foreign women who are blamed with turning Solomon's heart after other gods. Ezra-Nehemiah is dealing with a contemporary problem confronting the postexilic community while Chronicles seems unperturbed by the mixed marriages of earlier times and almost never offers a word of rebuke about mixed marriages. Note, for example, the following unions recorded in Chronicles: the patriarch Judah marries a Canaanite woman Bath-shua (1 Chr. 2:3); David's sister Abigail bore a son to Jether the Ishmaelite (1 Chr. 2:17); the Judahite Sheshan gave his daughter to an Egyptian slave (1 Chr. 2:34–35); David was married to Maacah the daughter of Talmai the king of Geshur (1 Chr. 3:2); the Judahite Mered married Bithiah daughter of Pharaoh (1 Chr. 4:17); some of the descendants of Shelah married into Moab (1 Chr. 4:22); Manasseh the son of Joseph had an Aramean concubine (1 Chr. 7:14); the Benjaminite Shaharaim had sons in the country of Moab, presumably through a Moabite wife (1 Chr. 8:8); King Huram sends Huram-abi, the son of a Danite woman and a Tyrian father to work on the temple (2 Chr. 2:13 [ET 2:14]); Solomon was married to Pharaoh's daughter (2 Chr. 8:11); Rehoboam's mother was Naamah the Ammonite, a wife of Solomon (2 Chr. 12:13). An apparent exception to the Chronicler's acceptance of foreign marriages concerns the marriage alliance Jehoshaphat made with the house of Ahab (2 Chr. 18:1; 19:2; 22:3), but in this case, the wife in question was an Israelite. The issue here, then, may not be about marriage at all, since the Chronicler routinely criticizes reliance on alliances.

23.2.2 The Early History of Israel

Chronicles focuses on the patriarch Jacob, whom it calls by the name "Israel" twelve times. The only two references to the name "Jacob" occur in 1 Chr. 16:13, 17 where the Chronicler is quoting Ps. 105:6, 10. In 1 Chr. 16:13, instead of Abraham and Jacob in the *Vorlage*, the Chronicler reads Israel and Jacob. In the poetic parallelism of 1 Chr. 16:17, the Chronicler refers to Jacob and Israel as in Ps. 105:10. In the genealogy at the beginning of the book, the beginning of the people as the elect of God occurs not with Abraham but with Israel (1 Chr. 2:1–2). Chapters 2–8 give details of the descendants of the sons of Israel. The exalted role of Jacob/Israel is not paralleled in Ezra.

In Chronicles, the exodus tends to be down-played or de-emphasized. In Solomon's prayer at the dedication of the temple in 1 Kgs. 8:21, the king refers to the covenant Yhwh made with the ancestors when he brought them out of the land of Egypt. That becomes the covenant Yhwh made with the Israelites in 2 Chr. 6:11. The Chronicler does not include an equivalent for the second mention of the exodus in 1 Kings 8 (v. 53), but in 2 Chr. 6:41–42 he includes quotations from Pss 132:8–10 and 132:1, which contain dynastic promises to David and report David's efforts on behalf of the ark. Nehemiah bases his appeal to Yhwh on the exodus in Neh. 1:10, and the confession in Nehemiah 9 refers to the election of Abraham (vv. 7–8). The exodus and related events, including the conquest, are central throughout Neh. 9:9–25. On the basis of the mention of the exodus in 1 Chr. 17:21; 2 Chr. 6:5; and 7:22, along with an allusion to it in 2 Chr. 20:7–11, Knoppers (2003: 81) concluded that there is no major tension between Chronicles and Ezra-Nehemiah on this issue.

23.2.3 The Fall of the Northern Kingdom and the Positive Attitude toward Notherners

Chronicles does not include the fall of the Northern Kingdom from 2 Kings 17 and presupposes that the north is inhabited by genuine Israelites after the Assyrian conquest (2 Chr. 30:5–11, 18, 25; cf. generally Braun 1977: 59–62). The only reference to the exile of the northern tribes in Chronicles mentions only the two and one half Transjordanian tribes in 1 Chr. 5:26 at the time of Tiglath-pileser. In Ezra 4 there are references to the resettlement of the land in the time of Esarhaddon (v. 2) and the time of "Osnappar" (v. 10), apparently a reference to Ashurbanipal. Zerubbabel sharply rejects the offer of the northerners connected to Esarhaddon to participate in the temple project (Ezra 4:3).

The Chronicler, by way of contrast, has a genuinely positive attitude toward the north. During the reign of Rehoboam, priests and Levites from the north took their stand with him and walked in the way of David and Solomon. Those who had set their hearts to seek Yhwh came to Jerusalem from all the tribes of Israel to sacrifice to God (2 Chr. 11:13–17). Asa took cities in hill country of Ephraim and his reforming activities included those cities. People from Ephraim, Manasseh, and Simeon joined with Judah and Jerusalem to enter a covenant to seek Yhwh (2 Chr. 15:8–15). Jehoshaphat established garrisons in the cities of Ephraim which his father Asa had taken (2 Chr. 17:2), and he traveled to the hill country of Ephraim to bring people back to Yhwh the God of their ancestors (2 Chr. 19:4). During the reign of Ahaz, 200,000 Judean women and children were brought to Samaria with the intent of enslaving them. The prophet Oded criticized the north for the severity of its attacks against Judah, and certain Ephraimites condemned the northerners for bringing the captives to Samaria. The northerners clothed the captives who were naked, gave them sandals, provided them with food and drink, anointed them, and carried all the weak among the captives and brought them in safety to Jericho (2 Chr. 28:8–15).[4]

The Chronicler reports that Hezekiah sent messengers to all Israel from Beersheba to Dan to come to Jerusalem to celebrate the Passover (2 Chr. 30:1). The messengers went to Ephraim and Manasseh and as far as Zebulun. While some northerners mocked the messengers, a few from the tribes of Asher, Manasseh, and Zebulun humbled themselves and came to Jerusalem. Hezekiah prayed for those northerners who had not ritually prepared themselves to celebrate the Passover, and Yhwh forgave these people. Northerners also participated when the Passover was extended for a week (2 Chr. 30:5–25). Hezekiah's destruction of illegitimate cultic sites included those in Ephraim and Manasseh (2 Chr. 31:1). Josiah's reforming activities extended to Manasseh, Ephraim, and Naphtali (2 Chr. 34:6–7). When Josiah inquired of Huldah, he asked also about those who were left in Israel (2 Chr. 34:21). Monies for the repair of the temple came from Manasseh and Ephraim (2 Chr. 34:9). Josiah made all who were in the territory of Israel serve Yhwh their God (2 Chr. 34:33).

These interactions of Judeans and their kings with the north are a far cry from the hostility toward the north demonstrated in Ezra 4:1–4 and the prohibition of intermarriage with the peoples of the land which is found in Neh. 10:31 (ET 10:30).

23.2.4 Immediate Retribution

Chronicles is noted for its doctrine of retribution, in which a king is rewarded or punished for good deeds or errors within his own lifetime. There is virtually no trace of this doctrine in Ezra-Nehemiah, except for Ezra 9:8, 9, 15, and Neh. 9:31, 33, and 36, which refer to God's righteousness in inflicting punishment. The vocabulary of 2 Chr. 7:14 and its promise of rewards for those who repent does not hold programmatic significance in Ezra-Nehemiah, as it does in Chronicles (Klein 2012: 111).

23.2.5 The Netinim and the Sons of Solomon's Servants

These groups are mentioned throughout Ezra-Nehemiah, but they are absent from Chronicles except for an incidental mention of the Netinim in 1 Chr. 9:2, which is borrowed from Neh. 11:3. The Chronicler considered the gatekeepers (1 Chr. 9:17–18) and the singers to be Levites (2 Chr. 5:12), though they have not attained this status in Ezra-Nehemiah (Ezra 7:24; Neh. 11:19; 13:10). Nehemiah 11 is later than Nehemiah 7//Ezra 2 since the singers are included among the Levites (Neh. 11:15–17), although the gatekeepers have not yet attained Levitical status in this passage (11:19).

23.2.6 Israel

In Chronicles, "Israel" is described as made up of all of the twelve tribes, and the Chronicler uses the term "remnant" to refer to those in the north, or in both kingdoms, after the fall of Samaria (2 Chr. 30:6; 34:9, 21; Williamson 1977: 125–26). Ezra, on the other hand, distinguishes sharply between the "holy seed" and the other peoples of the lands (Ezra 9:2), and "Israel" consists of Judah and Benjamin—that is, the postexilic community.

23.2.7 Greater Emphasis on the Davidic Monarchy in Chronicles

Chronicles is dominated by David and the covenant Yhwh made with him (1 Chr. 17:1–15; 2 Chr. 7:18; 13:5; 21:7; 23:3), while David plays a minor role in Ezra-Nehemiah and no mention is made of the covenant with him. Abijah's sermon in 2 Chronicles 13 insists on the eternal character of the Davidic rule. Ezra-Nehemiah, on the other hand, insists on the importance of the Sinai covenant and the promise to Israel's ancestors, and makes no reference to the Davidic ancestry of Zerubbabel (1 Chr. 3:19; Hag. 2:23). Scholars are divided on whether there is a messianic hope in Chronicles; there surely is none in Ezra-Nehemiah. David is primarily a cult founder in Ezra-Nehemiah, he is much more than that in Chronicles. He is a successful warrior (1 Chronicles 14, 18–20), a recipient of dynastic promises (1 Chronicles 17), a repentant sinner (1 Chronicles 21), and a skilled administrator (1 Chronicles 22–29). Knoppers concluded: "Even when one accounts for differences in sources and coverage, one must acknowledge a difference in how each work construes David's significance" (2003: 82).

23.3 SEPARATE WORKS BUT COMMON THEMES

The substantive differences in theology, purpose, and perspective discussed above have convinced scholars such as myself that Chronicles and Ezra-Nehemiah are separate works, each of which needs to be interpreted in its own right. The differences should not be overplayed to the total exclusion of important commonalities, however. Chronicles and Ezra-Nehemiah advocate for the primacy of Jerusalem, the exclusive status of the Jerusalem Temple, the importance of supporting the priests and the Levites, and the critical role that Judah, Levi, and Benjamin have in maintaining the legacy of Israel (Knoppers 2003: 89). Despite these shared interests it remains unlikely that just one individual was responsible for both works.

Even so, it seems clear that the account of the building of the Second Temple in the early chapters of Ezra is modeled after the building of the First Temple as portrayed in Chronicles. It is unclear whether the connections between Ezra and Chronicles at this point are due to the work of the author of Ezra or an editorial attempt by a later hand to bring the story of the return into conformity with Chronicles. Chronicles mentions Jeremiah in telling the story of the end of Judah (2 Chr. 36:12), and the decree of Cyrus allowing Jews to return home is said to be the fulfillment of the word of Yhwh from the mouth of Jeremiah (2 Chr. 36:21–22; Ezra 1:1; Knoppers 2003: 77). Chronicles tells how the temple furnishings were all sent into Babylon (2 Chr. 36:7, 10, 18–19), but the book of Ezra notes that these furnishings were returned (Ezra 1:7–11). The first chapters of Ezra underscore the continuity between the preparations for building the Second Temple and the preparations for building the First Temple (Knoppers 2003: 78). Knoppers asserts that "[t]he resonance between the opening chapters of Ezra and Chronicles seems patent" (2003: 80). But, the question remains, and stands unanswered, if it was the original author of Ezra who modelled himself on the account of Chronicles at this point, or if the similarity is the achievement of a subsequent redactor (see Knoppers 2003: 78).

23.4 CONCLUSION

While Chronicles and Ezra-Nehemiah share a number of common themes, such as an interest in genealogy, the importance of the Jerusalemite temple cult, and the supporting of priests and Levites, these books were not written by one person. Although uncertainty remains, the writer or redactor of Ezra 1–6 seems to have modeled his account of the Second Temple on the account of the First Temple in Chronicles. Several arguments employed in earlier versions of a Chronicler's History hypothesis have lost their power. The language of these books is very similar, but there is not enough evidence from this dataset alone to prove unity or disunity of authorship. The short overlap between 2 Chronicles 36 and Ezra 1 is similarly inconclusive. 1 Esdras is now clearly seen as a secondary arrangement of materials from the canonical 1–2 Chronicles and Ezra-Nehemiah and is not an earlier draft of the Chronicler's history.

The theological or ideological differences between Chronicles and Ezra-Nehemiah are striking and decisive at this point. These differences start with the far more positive view of marriage with outsiders in Chronicles than in Ezra-Nehemiah where there is a strong polemic against such unions. Chronicles has a much broader and more inclusive concept of the Israelite community than does Ezra-Nehemiah, especially with Chronicles' positive attitude toward North Israel and northerners in general. The high role of Jacob/Israel in Chronicles is not followed in Ezra-Nehemiah where Israel is primarily limited to the *Golah* group. Immediate retribution within a person's lifetime is repeatedly affirmed in Chronicles, but is absent from Ezra-Nehemiah. The Davidic covenant so central to Chronicles is absent from Ezra-Nehemiah, and David is much more than a cult founder in Chronicles. In light of these differences, Chronicles, Ezra, and Nehemiah are distinct works and there should be no more serious consideration of a Chronicler's History hypothesis.

Notes

1. Blenkinsopp (1988: 46) assigns the following verses to the Nehemiah Memoir: 1:1–2:20; 3:33–7:5; 12:31–43; 13:4–31; other scholars differ on some details of which verses belong to the Nehemiah Memoir.
2. In what follows I have changed the verse numbers in Cross's citations of 1 Esdras to agree with the critical edition of Hanhart (1974) and noted where necessary the alternate verse numbers in English versions.
3. 1 Esdras mistakenly adds the temple on two occasions: 1 Esdras 2:17–18 (ET 2:18, 20).
4. This story may form the background for the parable of the Good Samaritan in Luke 10:29–37 (see Klein 2012: 501).

Bibliography

Böhler, Dieter. 1997. *Die heilige Stadt in Esdras α und Esra-Nehemia: Zwei Konzeptionen der Wiederherstellung Israels*. OBO 158. Fribourg: Universitätsverlag and Göttingen: Vandenhoeck & Ruprecht.

Böhler, Dieter. 2003. "On the Relationship between Textual and Literary Criticism: The Two Recensions of the Book of Ezra: Ezra-Neh (MT) and 1 Esdras (LXX)." In Adrian Schenker, ed., *The Earliest Text of the Hebrew Bible: The Relationship between the Masoretic Text and the Hebrew Base of the Septuagint Reconsidered*. SBLSCS 52. Atlanta: SBL, 35–50.

Braun, Roddy L. 1977. "A Reconsideration of the Chronicler's Attitude toward the North." *JBL* 96: 59–62.

Braun, Roddy L. 1979. "Chronicles, Ezra, and Nehemiah: Theology and Literary History." In J. A. Emerton, ed., *Studies in the Historical Books of the Old Testament*. VTSup 30. Leiden: Brill, 52–64.

Braun, Roddy L. 1986. *I Chronicles*. WBC 14. Waco, TX: Word.
Cross, Frank Moore. 1975. "A Reconstruction of the Judean Restoration." *JBL* 94: 4–18.
Curtis, Edward Lewis and Albert Alonzo Madsen. 1970. *A Critical and Exegetical Commentary on the Books of Chronicles*. ICC. New York: Scribner's.
Dirksen, Pieter B. 2005. *1 Chronicles*. HCOT. Translated by Anthony P. Runia. Leuven: Peeters.
Driver, Samuel R. 1960. *An Introduction to the Literature of the Old Testament*. New York: Meridian Books. (Original 1897.)
Eissfeldt, Otto. 1965. *The Old Testament: An Introduction*. Translated by Peter R. Ackroyd. New York: Harper and Row.
Freedman, David Noel. 1961. "The Chronicler's Purpose." *CBQ* 23: 436–42.
Fried, Lisbeth S., ed. 2011. *Was 1 Esdras First? An Investigation into the Priority and Nature of 1 Esdras*. Atlanta: SBL.
Gelston, Anthony. 1996. "The End of Chronicles." *SJOT* 10: 53–59.
Hanhart, Robert, ed. 1974. *Esdrae liber I*. Septuaginta VIII, 1. Göttingen: Vandenhoeck & Ruprecht.
Haran, Menahem. 1985. "Book-Size and the Device of Catch-Lines in the Biblical Canon." *JJS* 36: 1–11.
Japhet, Sara. 1968. "The Supposed Common Authorship of Chronicles and Ezra-Nehemiah Investigated Anew." *VT* 18: 330–71.
Japhet, Sara. 1993. *I and II Chronicles: A Commentary*. OTL. Louisville, KY: Westminster John Knox.
Kalimi, Isaac. 2005. *An Ancient Israelite Historian: Studies in the Chronicler, His Time, Place and Writing*. Studia Semitica Neerlandica. Assen: Royal Van Gorcum.
Klein, Ralph W. 1966. "Studies in the Greek Texts of the Chronicler." Th.D. dissertation, Harvard University.
Klein, Ralph W. 2004. *1 Chronicles*. Hermeneia. Minneapolis: Fortress Press.
Klein, Ralph W. 2011. "The Rendering of 2 Chronicles 35–36 in 1 Esdras." In Lisbeth S. Fried, ed., *Was 1 Esdras First? An Investigation into the Priority and Nature of 1 Esdras*. Atlanta: SBL, 225–36.
Klein, Ralph W. 2012. *2 Chronicles*. Minneapolis: Fortress Press.
Knoppers, Gary N. 2003. *1 Chronicles 1–9*. AB 12. New York: Doubleday.
Kooij, Arie van der. 1991a. "On the Ending of the Book of 1 Esdras." In C. E. Cos, ed., *LXX: VII Congress of the International Organization for Septuagint and Cognate Studies*. SCS 31. Atlanta: Scholars Press, 37–49.
Kooij, Arie van der. 1991b. "Zur Frage des Anfangs des 1. Esrabuches." *ZAW* 103: 239–52.
Mosis, Rudolf. 1973, *Untersuchungen zur Theologie des chronistischen Geschichtswerks*. Freiburger theololgische Studien 92. Freiburg: Herder.
Movers, F. C. 1834. *Kritische Untersuchungen über die biblische Chronik*. Bonn: T. Habicht.
Newsome, J. D. 1975. "Towards a New Understanding of the Chronicler and His Purpose." *JBL* 94: 201–17.
Noth, Martin. 1957, *Überlieferungs-Geschichtliche Studien*. 2nd ed. Tübingen: Max Niemeyer.
Pakkala, Juha. 2011. "Why 1 Esdras Is Probably Not an Early Version of the Ezra-Nehemiah Tradition." In Lisbeth S. Fried, ed., *Was 1 Esdras First? An Investigation into the Priority and Nature of 1 Esdras*. Atlanta: SBL, 93–107.
Pohlmann, K.-F. 1991. "Zur Frage von Korrespondenzen und Divergenzen zwischen den Chronikbüchern und dem Esra/Nehemia-Buch." In J. A. Emerton, ed., *Congress Volume Leuven 1989*. VTSup 43. Leiden: Brill, 314–30.
Polzin, Robert. 1976. *Late Biblical Hebrew: Toward an Historical Typology of Biblical Hebrew Prose*. HSM 12. Missoula, MT: Scholars Press.
Schenker, Adrian. 1991. "La Relation d'Esdras A' au texte massorétique d'Esdras-Néhémie." In Gerard J. Norton and Stephen Pisano, eds., *Tradition of the Text: Studies Offered to Dominique Barthélemy in Celebration of His 70th Birthday*. OBO 109. Freiburg: Universitätsverlag and Göttingen: Vandenhoeck & Ruprecht, 218–49.
Schenker, Adrian. 2011. "The Relationship between Ezra-Nehemiah and 1 Esdras." In Lisbeth S. Fried, ed., *Was 1 Esdras First? An Investigation into the Priority and Nature of 1 Esdras*. Atlanta: SBL, 45–58.

Talshir, David. 1988. "A Reinvestigation of the Linguistic Relationship between Chronicles and Ezra-Nehemiah." *VT* 38: 165–93.

Talshir, Zipora. 1999. *1 Esdras. From Origin to Translation*. SBLSCS 47. Atlanta: SBL.

Talshir, Zipora. 2001. *1 Esdras. A Text Critical Commentary*. SBLSCS 50. Atlanta: SBS.

Talshir, Zipora. 2011. "Ancient Composition Patterns Mirrored in 1 Esdras and the Priority of Canonical Composition Type." In Lisbeth S. Fried, ed., *Was 1 Esdras First? An Investigation into the Priority and Nature of 1 Esdras*. Atlanta: SBL, 109–29.

Throntveit, Mark A. 1982. "Linguistic Analysis and the Question of Authorship in Chronicles, Ezra and Nehemiah." *VT* 32: 201–16.

VanderKam, James C. 1991. "Ezra-Nehemiah or Ezra and Nehemiah?" In Eugene C. Ulrich et al., eds., *Priests, Prophets, and Scribes: Essays on the Formation and Heritage of Second Temple Judaism in Honour of Joseph Blenkinsopp*. JSOTSup 149. Sheffield: JSOT Press, 55–75.

Welten, Peter. 1973. *Geschichte und Geschichtsdarstellung in den Chronikbüchern*. WMANT 42. Neukirchen: Neukirchener Verlag.

Willi, Thomas. 1972. *Die Chronik als Auslegung: Untwersuchungen zur literarischen Gestalten der historischen Überlieferung Israels*. FRLANT. Göttingen: Vandenhoeck & Ruprecht.

Williamson, H. G. M. 1977. *Israel in the Books of Chronicles*. Cambridge: Cambridge University Press.

Williamson, H. G. M. 1982. *1 and 2 Chronicles*. NCB Commentary. Grand Rapids: Eerdmans.

Zunz, Leopold. 1832. *Die gottesdienstliche Vorträge der Juden historisch entwickelt*. Berlin: Asher.

CHAPTER 24

1 ESDRAS: STRUCTURE, COMPOSITION, AND SIGNIFICANCE

KRISTIN DE TROYER

When reading the so-called apocryphal book of 1 Esdras[1] and comparing it with its nominal twin, the canonical book of Ezra-Nehemiah,[2] the parallels are obvious: the two compositions look very much alike. 1 Esdras parallels the contents of the entire book of Ezra and chapter 8 of the book of Nehemiah. In its first chapter, 1 Esdras has also text in common with 2 Chronicles 35–36. In 1 Esdras, however, there is a two chapter long "supplement," called "the story of Darius' bodyguards" (Nickelsburg 1983: 131–35) or "the story of the youths" (Z. Talshir 1999: 58–109). This story does not have a parallel in the Hebrew or Greek Bible.

The question as to how the books of Ezra-Nehemiah and 1 Esdras relate to each other seems, therefore, an important question to pursue. Moreover, as 1 Esdras also has elements in common with the book of Chronicles, 1 Esdras also needs to be studied in relationship to that composition. How does 1 Esdras relate to the "canonical" biblical texts? More precisely, how does 1 Esdras relate to the Historical Books? And finally, how does a book like 1 Esdras help Biblical scholars to understand the phenomenon of the Historical Books?

24.1 Two Hypotheses in Previous Scholarship

A short summary of 1 Esdras research demonstrates a wide variety of opinions on questions like these.[3] The history can be reduced to a set of debates: first, is 1 Esdras dependent on Ezra-Nehemiah or did 1 Esdras exist before the Books of Ezra-Nehemiah? Second, what is the relationship between Chronicles and 1 Esdras and did the Chronicler also write 1 Esdras?

In 1970, Pohlmann nicely summarized the debate, grouping the main options into two categories: fragment hypothesis (*Fragmentenhypothese*) and compilation hypothesis (*Kompilationshypothese*) (see also Pohlmann 1980; 1991). Scholars favoring the former claim that 1 Esdras is a fragment of a larger work that contained all of Chronicles, and Ezra-Nehemiah and that 1 Esdras offers an earlier redaction than the biblical, canonical text. According to this hypothesis, therefore, 1 Esdras was written by the Chronicler. Those who defend the compilation hypothesis state that the author of 1 Esdras knew the canonical books of Chronicles and Ezra-Nehemiah and compiled this composition using material from these books. In this latter view, therefore, 1 Esdras is no longer a witness to the older book of Ezra-Nehemiah and Chronicles, but is itself derived from these books. Whereas Michaelis (1783) is the earliest representative of the fragment hypothesis, Bertholdt (1813: 1005–13) is the earliest of the defenders of the compilation hypothesis—both *avant-la-lettre* of course. Since Pohlmann's study, these categories have been used in the 1 Esdras debate and the two hypotheses continue to be defended and debated.[4]

24.2 THE LONG ADDITION: THE STORY OF THE THREE YOUTHS/BODYGUARDS

Research on whether or not 1 Esdras is dependent on Chronicles and Ezra-Nehemiah must engage the presence of the long "supplement" found in 1 Esdras 3–5. As Torrey noted, this episode is "of some length which interrupts the Biblical account and is not found elsewhere" (1946: 43). This episode is the Story of the Three Youths or Bodyguards. In this story, the three men compete in an intellectual competition: each presents what they think is the strongest thing. They invite King Darius to decide which statement seems the wisest and to give the winner rich gifts and great honors of victory, superb attire and goodies, and to seat the winner next to the king and be called Kinsman of Darius (1 Esdr. 3:5–7). The three bodyguards write their statements and put them under the pillow of Darius (1 Esdr. 3:8). The first bodyguard says "wine is the strongest" (1 Esdr. 3:10); the second argues that "the king is strongest" (1 Esdr. 3:11); the third contender seems to have a two-part answer: "women are strongest, but above all things truth is victor" (1 Esdr. 3:12). The king finds the statements and has the three young men called in to explain their positions. The first one does a fine job explaining his thoughts (1 Esdr. 3:17b–24); the second, too, is equally impressive (1 Esdr. 4:1–12). Then the third gets his turn to explain his arguments (1 Esdr. 4:13–41). At the end of his speech, the king makes his decision, choosing the third bodyguard as the winner (1 Esdr. 4:42). The story continues with an extra request on behalf of the third bodyguard (1 Esdr. 4:43–46)—"to build Jerusalem"—with the king granting it (1 Esdr. 4:47–57). Then the third bodyguard, now identified as Zerubbabel, says a prayer of thanks (1 Esdr. 4:58–63).

24.3 THE ORIGIN AND FUNCTION OF THE STORY

Scholarly opinion regarding this story varies. The pendulum swings from Torrey to Z. Talshir (with the title of the story changing as well): Torrey (1970: 20, 30) argued that the story of the three "bodyguards" was inserted into the original story and strongly changed it, while Z. Talshir (1999: 6) argued that 1 Esdras was composed to provide a framework for the story of these three "youths."

Other options exist. Pohlmann (1980: 382) holds the opinion that the story was inserted into the Greek translation of 1 Esdras by an interpolator. Laato however, declares that it was a compiler who added the story (1992: 311). Williamson (1996: 212) seems to hit the nail on the head by stating that defenders of the fragment hypothesis have no alternative than to explain the story as inserted by an interpolator to the parallel story of Chronicles and Ezra-Nehemiah. Böhler (1997: 69) summarizes those scholars who have defended the interpolation idea: it is "a special, later literary development" in 1 Esdras.[5]

With her view on the story, Z. Talshir modifies the compilation hypothesis in her own way: "I Esd is neither a 'fragment' surviving from a mostly lost book, nor, strictly speaking, a compilation of chosen units from the canonical books, but rather, a section deliberately cut out from Chr-Ezr-Neh, to form a framework for the Story of the Youths" (1999: 6). She continues: "The Book of I Esd was created for the purpose of retelling the history of the Restoration in such a way that it revolved around the Story of the Three Youths and its hero Zerubbabel" (ibid.).

Laato (1992) sees a clue to the origin of 1 Esdras in its stress on the Davidic dynasty and its positive view of the twelve tribes of Israel. "This feature," he states, "might also explain why the later editor wanted to compile 1 Esdr" (1992: 311; cf. Eskenazi 1988: 44–56). Blenkinsopp notes that 1 Esdras "appears to elevate Zerubbabel and Ezra as the founding fathers at the expense of Nehemiah" (1988: 57).

In a previous work on 1 Esdras, and specifically on the so-called insertion, I have argued for two levels in the insertion (De Troyer 2015): the original story about the three youths defending what they think is the strongest in the empire (wine, the king, or women) and a secondary element (truth)—inserted in the mouth of the third man—so as to introduce and connect this account with the story about Zerubbabel and his plan to rebuild the Temple. It is clear, after all, that the speech of the third bodyguard (1 Esdr. 4:13–41) consists of two sections: a section on "women" (1 Esdr. 4:13–32) and a section on "truth" (1 Esdr. 4:33b–41). As Bird notes: "The third discourse is obviously a synthetic construction developed from pre-existing materials about the strength of women with the addition of truth tacked on at the end very creatively albeit intrusively" (2012: 166). In between the two sections is a first response of the king (1 Esdr. 4:33a). There are signs, therefore, that the speech of the third bodyguard consists of an original section on "women" and an added piece on "truth." The bit about "truth" is thus an instance of editorial expansion. The following arguments demonstrate the point:

1. The introduction of the third speaker signals that the text has been updated. The third speaker is first referred to as "the third who had spoken of women and truth began to speak" (1 Esdr. 4:13)—this is very much like the introductions of the first (3:17) and the second speaker (4:1)—but then the text adds: "And this was Zerubbabel" (4:13b).[6]
2. Similarly, with regard to the third speaker's topic, there is an indication that the text was revised and expanded: whereas both the first and the second speaker have talked about only one theme, the third speaker addresses two: "women and truth."[7]
3. Moreover, in the first reference to the topic of the third discourse, the sentence could have ended with "women are strongest," but it continues with an exception

("but"; Greek *hyper de*) and a vague reference to "all things" (Greek *panta*) instead of "women" (3:12): "but above all things truth is victor" (NRSV).
4. Next, in the elaboration of the argument, it is clear that the text has two parts: 1 Esdr. 4:14–32 deals with "women" and 4:33b–41 deals with "truth."
5. Even the transitional verse (4:33a) could be seen as the conclusion of the first part, with 4:42ff as the continuation of 4:33a: "Then the kings and the nobles looked at one another..." (4:33a) "then the king said..." (4:42).[8]
6. Finally, the inserted text about truth (4:33b–42) itself refers to the three topics of wine, the king, and women (4:37), which again indicates that these topics were the original three, with truth added secondarily.

The function of the added material is clear: it introduces not only the topic of truth, but also Zerubbabel. The latter figure is the textual link between the reworked and expanded story of the three bodyguards and the story of the building of the Temple, which is recounted in 1 Esdras and its source, the Book of Ezra-Nehemiah.

24.4 THE LANGUAGE OF 1 ESDRAS

Only very few scholars mention the possibility that 1 Esdras is a rewritten Greek text (see Keil 1873; Carrez 1994; Thackeray 1898–1904). The majority of scholars hold the opinion that 1 Esdras is a translation from a Hebrew/Aramaic original. The proof for a Semitic original seems to be provided by Torrey in his seminal *Ezra Studies* (1970: 23–25). Zimmerman (1963/64) offered additional proof. Z. Talshir notes that "scholarly opinion rarely goes beyond a general impression of the subject, and all of it takes its cue from Torrey" (1999: 81; cf., e.g., Pohlmann 1980: 382 n. 23). Reading Torrey's work, I found a distinct view on the original language of the Ezra materials. Torrey starts from the Aramaic documents found in Ezra 4–6, and then acknowledges a Hebrew editor, the Chronicler. The result of the latter's work is a Hebrew-Aramaic story (Torrey 1970: 35, 115, 140–62, 208–51; see also 1946: 48). In her own work, Z. Talshir consistently retroverts the Greek text of 1 Esdras into a Hebrew-Aramaic *Vorlage* (the text underlying the translation). Talshir is the first to analyze the translation character of the story. Her work shows that "the kind of language which it reflects indeed sways the pendulum over to Aramaic" as the original language (1999: 83). Other scholars also refer to a Hebrew/Aramaic original of 1 Esdras. Note, for instance, Grabbe's opinion: "The book of 1 Esdras is not just similar or parallel to the Hebrew Ezra and Nehemiah but, except for 1 Esdras 3–4, clearly was translated from a Hebrew text almost the same as 2 Chronicles 35–36, Ezra 1–10, and Nehemiah 8" (1998: 80).

Some scholars, like Pohlmann (1980: 378) for instance, are hesitant, thinking it too difficult to reconstruct a Hebrew/Aramaic original from what seems a rather free translation. Yet other scholars have a more optimistic view when it comes to retroversion, however. Böhler acknowledges the difficulties, stating that, although the equivalents chosen by the translator will not make retroversion easy, they do allow comparison with the original words of the Masoretic Text (MT), since the translation of 1 Esdras is, while not slavishly stereotypical, nevertheless striking and precise (1997: 39). Böhler concludes that the translation is both faithful and good (1997: 52).

Hanhart has compared 1 Esdras and the LXX of Ezra-Nehemiah (= 2 Esdras). After a careful analysis he concludes:

> The comparison of the two translations makes it clear that one cannot prove any direct literary dependence. The dependence of the two texts... is only then possible if one accepts a common Hebrew Aramaic *Vorlage*, at times different from the Massoretic text. Moreover, presuming independence, one has to take into account the (characteristics of the) pre-existing traditions of translating texts, in which the translators were rooted.
>
> (1974b: 17; my translation)

Hence, Hanhart keeps the option of a *Vorlage* that differed from the current Hebrew text of Ezra-Nehemiah open, stressing the different translation techniques of the two Greek translators (see also Hanhart 1993; 1999). Böhler also pleads for the possibility of a distinct Semitic *Vorlage*, suggesting that the *Vorlage* of 1 Esdras reflects a text that must not be simply identified as proto-masoretic (1997: 35).

In her 1999 monograph, Z. Talshir deals extensively with the *Vorlage* of 1 Esdras in comparison to 2 Chronicles 35–36, Ezra 1–10, and Nehemiah 8. She defends her reconstruction of the *Vorlage* as follows: "while I Esd's *Vorlage* is indeed hidden under the heavy veil of quite eccentric translation, it remains an acceptable witness to the history of the text" (1999: 114). Talshir sets out to investigate the translator's technique and to consider his tendencies and peculiarities as opposed to possible variants in his text. She does so to make the *Vorlage* more accessible (1999: 114–15). This *Vorlage* is clearly at variance with the MT and so Talshir suggests that it must have departed from the main text at an early stage and undergone a substantial process of transmission. The *Vorlage* was subsequently changed by the reviser who created 1 Esdras. She notes that it is "complicated to distinguish between the changes that already existed in the version used by the reviser and those introduced by him, or between possible changes which entered the text in the course of transmission" (1999: 179). Talshir also points to the difficulty in distinguishing between "variations that go back to the translator and variants in the *Vorlage*" (1999: 179).

Here again, the "supplementary" story of the three youths makes research into the original language of 1 Esdras more complicated. Torrey claimed it was written in Aramaic: "This bit of 'Wisdom Literature' will be treated separately. Its original language was Aramaic, as has been abundantly proven" (1946: 44). Z. Talshir, in collaboration with D. Talshir, focused on the original language of the and to show "that it is translation-Greek" (1999: 83). Importantly, Hanhart points to the story of the three youths fact that 1 Esdras' Greek is very consistent. It does not change in passages that do have a Hebrew or an Aramaic counterpart or that have no attested Semitic *Vorlage* (1974b: 12). Hanhart, whose judgment I trust, also questions a Semitic *Vorlage* for 1 Esdr. 3:1–5:6, "the existence of which remains debated" (1974b: 12; my translation).

24.5 1 Esdras as History

What to make of 1 Esdras as history? First of all, many scholars seem to not distinguish between literary and historical chronology. There are for instance, those who uphold the order of events in Ezra, such as Noth (1960: 300–16), Cross (1975: 5–6) and Soggin (1984: 261–80), and who consider that depiction of events as historically correct. Williamson (1983), on the other hand, has convincingly demonstrated that Ezra 1–6 was composed at the end of the literary development of the books of Ezra-Nehemiah, and that it is therefore difficult to use it as proof for a historical sequence of events. Pohlmann defends the literary originality of 1 Esdras. At the same time, he considers Ezra 1–6 to represent the historical sequence of events (see Pohlmann 1970: 149). In my judgment, one cannot conclude anything about the historical reality behind the texts—if there is such a reality—if one has not first established the literary development and relation between the texts (see, e.g., Japhet 1994: 201–208).

Hanhart has studied the chronological sequence of events and the opposition to the rebuilding of the temple (1995). As the (translated) title of his study reveals ("An Unknown Text of the Greek Ezra Tradition"), Hanhart analyses an unknown piece of Ezra text. Before dealing with the extract from the Greek Ezra tradition that he discovered in a tenth-century manuscript of "The rest of the words of Jeremiah," Hanhart explains the opposition to the city/temple building and its conclusion in Ezra 4:24 as follows. The author associated the opposition against the building of the temple under Cyrus and Darius with the opposition against the building of the city and its walls under Artaxerxes. Both texts, the text about the rebuilding of the city and the one about the temple, mention, at the beginning, "the enemies of Judah and Benjamin." According to Hanhart, the entire period of the Second Temple is characterized by the opposition of the enemies of Judah and Benjamin. The author stressed the continuous opposition and therefore wrote in Ezra 4:24: "then, also—under Darius—was the work on the temple stopped" (Hanhart 1995: 115–16). The author only wanted to refer to the opposition against the building of the city walls for reasons of comparison; the verse does not imply that the city walls were already built. In a literary report, one can compare two events, given the fact that both reports were written much later than the actual events happened—if they happened at all.

I have studied the time indication "in the second year of Darius" in the books of Ezra-Nehemiah, 1 Esdras, and relevant other biblical books. I concluded that "the second year of Darius" functions in 1 Esdras to give a maybe slightly better chronological sequence of events in comparison with especially the book of Ezra. The study of the use of this expression in 1 Esdras within the larger context of the book also demonstrates how the author of 1 Esdras rewrote what he or she had in front of him/her (De Troyer 2011).

24.6 A Rewritten Text?

After studying the text of 1 Esdras, my judgment is that the compilation theory better explains the difficulties of the text. 1 Esdras is dependent on the MT of 2 Chronicles 35–36 and the MT of Ezra-Nehemiah (and some other texts). The differences between the texts of 1 Esdras and its sources (the story of Josiah, the additional verses in 1:21–22, the reorganization of the letters to and from King Artaxerxes, the insertion of the Three Youths Story, the addition of Nehemiah 8 at the end of the story, and the omission of the Nehemiah story) can be explained as deliberate redactional rewritings. These changes happened not on the Greek level, however, but on the Aramaic/Hebrew level. The author of the *Vorlage* of 1 Esdras has interpreted and rewritten the Hebrew text of Ezra-Nehemiah and some others. The differences are not due to a translator or to a different Hebrew *Vorlage*, but to the editor who reworked the MT texts into a new story.

For instance, whereas the additional verses in 1 Esdras 1 can be traced back to the Hebrew texts of 2 Kings 24, the translator can be credited for minor changes reflecting parallels in the Greek text. The Three Youths Story can be explained through its emphasis on Zerubbabel. In this "supplement," Zerubbabel wins a wisdom contest and is granted permission to go to Jerusalem and rebuild the Temple. The figure of Zerubbabel receives more attention in 1 Esdras than in Ezra-Nehemiah. Zerubbabel can be seen in the line of Solomon, who was gifted with wisdom and who built the Temple. That Zerubbabel is from Davidic lineage is mentioned in a phrase of 1 Esdras that does not occur in its parallel text in Ezra-Nehemiah—namely, 1 Esdr. 5:5. The story clearly puts Zerubbabel forward as the wise leader who is responsible for the building of the second Temple. The "positioning" of this story also influenced the organization and composition of the larger context in which the opposition to the building of the Temple is depicted. In comparison to Ezra-Nehemiah, there is a reorganization of the correspondence between "an opposing group" and King Artaxerxes. In my opinion, a small detail explains this reorganization. The pericope about the letters ends with the famous line: "And the building of the temple in Jerusalem stopped until the second year of the reign of King Darius of the Persians" (1 Esdr. 2:30b; NRSV). Then, the story of the three youths follows. This story is situated, therefore, at the court of King Darius. I am of the opinion that the "insertion" of the three bodyguards story begged for the reorganization of the text, more precisely for a mentioning of King Darius just before this narrative. By pasting the letter-pericope just before the story of King Darius, the pericope made way for the story about King Darius. As already noted, Zerubbabel plays a larger role in 1 Esdras than in Ezra-Nehemiah. I conclude that the insertion of the story of the three youths, the working into the text of the element of "truth" and "Zerubbabel," and finally, the reorganization of the text happened at the same time.

In my opinion, the Three Youths Story serves three goals. First, it explains how the work of building the Temple was resumed in the second year of King Darius. Second, it offers an alternative explanation about how Darius gave permission to rebuild the Temple. Third and finally, it depicts Zerubbabel as the winner of the contest and hence, as the one who received permission to go and rebuild. The "insertion" of the Three Youths Story, thus, is not really an insertion at all, but part of a larger rewriting of the entire story. Moreover, as the majority of scholars have accepted an Aramaic *Vorlage* for the three youths story, I believe the "(non-)insertion," its adaptation to turn it into a story about Zerubbabel, and the reorganization to have taken place at the level of the Semitic *Vorlage* of 1 Esdras. That there could have been a document containing both Hebrew and Aramaic texts, is proven by the simple existence of the books of Daniel and Ezra that contain both languages. I also acknowledge that the translator of the Hebrew-Aramaic *Vorlage* was responsible for some of the differences between the Semitic *Vorlage* and the Greek translation. The name of the province (see, for instance, 2:16: in Coelesyria and Phoenicia; see also 2:23) is a good example of the translator's hand.

If I have to situate this understanding of 1 Esdras within the broader context of the Ezra-Nehemiah research, I would point to the important contribution of Williamson (1985).

Williamson argues for a rather late addition of Ezra 1–6, intended to fill out the gap left between the exiles returning from Babylon and the restoration of the temple community. Williamson writes that the author of these chapters "is concerned to trace lines of continuity between the restored community and the Israel of pre-exilic times, between the second and the first temples, and so on" (1985: xxxiv). This author also justifies "the rejection of the offer of northern participants in the restoration itself" (ibid.). Not only is Ezra 1–6 a literary creation aimed at legitimizing the community and its temple, Ezra 7–10 is also a literary creation aimed at offering a perfect counterpart for the figure of Nehemiah: Ezra. I believe Garbini's intuition to be right when he writes that the person Ezra is a "purely literary creation" (1988: 154).

I therefore see the literary development of the book of Ezra-Nehemiah as follows. First, Nehemiah covered two topics: the rebuilding of the city and the restoration of the Law. The person of Ezra was then created, stressing his mission to restore the Law (Ezra 7–10). Finally, the story about the rebuilding of the temple was added (Ezra 1–6). By now, it should be obvious to the reader that I consider both the book of Ezra-Nehemiah and 1 Esdras as literary creations, not historical reports. Originally, the figure of Ezra was created as a better image of Nehemiah. The temple story was created as to parallel and outweigh the city story.

Schenker and Böhler have pointed to the difference in sequence of events between the two books. The order of events in Ezra-Nehemiah is different from the one in 1 Esdras. In Ezra-Nehemiah, the altar is built first, then the temple, and finally, in the book of Nehemiah, the city. In 1 Esdras the order is reversed. That text offers the following sequence: first, the city is restored, then the altar is erected, and finally the temple is built. Neither story can be used for a historical account of the history of the Second Temple, for both stories have been written with an agenda in mind. In 1 Esdras, the author explains why the work on the temple was first initiated, then stopped, and finally resumed. The author presumes that there was already a city. The author of Ezra-Nehemiah, on the other hand, creates the impression that the first thing that the Jews had on their mind when returning from exile was precisely the restoration of the temple. I do not wish to press beyond the literary reports offered by both stories. My own sense, however, is that the returning Jews first built the city, an altar, and after that, the temple.

The Hebrew-Aramaic text of 1 Esdras not only offers a different sequence of events, it also offers a different view on leadership. 1 Esdras is truly an alternative version. Precisely these differences in perspective have led to two different stories. First, the addition of and stress on the piety of King Josiah and the impiety of his people in 1 Esdras is more than just an addition; it offers the clue to understanding this book's perspective. It opens a window into the question as to why this text was created. In my opinion, the author of 1 Esdras emphasizes that Ezra, the (fictitious) leader of the Second Temple community must be seen in the line of Josiah, not as mere counterpart to Nehemiah. The importance of Josiah explains the addition of 1 Esdras 1, and especially verses 21–22. Moreover, the importance of the pious king Josiah explains the omission of the character Nehemiah, who was but a good governor. The author of 1 Esdras must have known the Nehemiah material (see Williamson 1996). Hence, the author of 1 Esdras deliberately omitted the Nehemiah material from his story.

At this point I would like to bring in the evidence of Nehemiah 8, which is placed at the end of 1 Esdras. This material in 1 Esdras was taken from the book of Nehemiah. It was, however, not inserted at its—most probably—original place, that is, between Ezra 8 and 9. The insertion of this chapter at the end of 1 Esdras proves that its author knew the biblical book of Ezra-Nehemiah, but that the author refused to make a reference to Nehemiah, and instead opted for an association with King Josiah. There is yet another important parallel between Ezra and Josiah that should be noted: Ezra continues the commitment to the law as expressed by Josiah. Finally, Ezra continues and improves the mission of Josiah. The author of 1 Esdras stresses that although the king was pious, the people were not. The text speaks "concerning those who sinned and acted wickedly toward the Lord" (1:24; NRSV). The text thus opposes the pious king and his impious subjects. Ezra turns these impious subjects into a godly people. At the end of the story of 1 Esdras, Ezra reads the Law. "The multitude answered: 'Amen.' They lifted up their hands, and fell to the ground and worshipped the Lord" (9:47; NRSV). The last thing that Ezra does is to proclaim a feast: "This day is holy to the Lord" (9:50; NRSV). Ezra therefore finishes the work that King Josiah started. The people finally become followers of the Law. Then, the people celebrate "for they were inspired by the word and brought together" (9:55; NRSV). Whereas the text ends rather abruptly ("they were brought together"), Van der Kooij maintains that 1 Esdras 9:55 was truly intended to be the last sentence of the book (see Van der Kooij 1991a). The insertion of Ezra's reading of the law brings things full circle. In a real sense, the people at the end of 1 Esdras are truly ready to celebrate Passover.

In sum, the book of 1 Esdras was written to emphasize the connection between Ezra and Josiah. The Second Temple community not only continues the community of the First Temple, but its leaders also continue the emphasis on the Law as started by King Josiah. Still further, Ezra succeeds in his mission: might he have surpassed even the great King Josiah? At the very least, Ezra revives and revises Josiah. The Three Youths Story is present to explain how the building of the temple was continued after some years and was elaborated in order to ensure that Zerubbabel takes center posittion. Zerubbabel revives and revises King Solomon and resembles him in his wisdom.

24.7 Conclusion

In light of the preceding discussion, we may say that the author of the *Vorlage* of 1 Esdras compiled this book using 2 Chronicles 35–36, Ezra-Nehemiah, and 2 Kings 22–23 (and its parallels). The author inserted the Three Youths Story, reorganized the letters, added Nehemiah 8 (Ezra reading the Law), and offered an editorial perspective in 1 Esdr. 1:21–22. By these means, the author created 1 Esdras as we now have it and, in doing so, offered an alternative story of MT Ezra-Nehemiah. In this alternative story, Zerubbabel continues the work of Solomon. Ezra continues, improves and completes the work of Josiah. Ezra stresses the importance of the Law, reforms the community, and celebrates Passover. His story ends with the celebration of a Holy Day. The new community is established and celebrates its completion.

A final word about the sort of author that created in 1 Esdras. In 1 Esdras we may see an editor/author at work who made use of available material, adding, where necessary, new material that fitted the larger agenda of the book. This author did something that is evident in many other texts, including ones found in the New Testament where, for instance, Matthew and Luke make use of Mark and Q, while still using additional material to round out their respective Gospels.

Notes

1. In Greek Bibles, this book comes first, hence 1 Esdras, but in the Vulgate, it is counted after Ezra and Nehemiah, hence 3 Esdras, a label that is still used frequently in German scholarship.
2. Up to the time of the early church writer Jerome, Ezra-Nehemiah was considered one book. After Jerome, who split the book into two sections, it became known as the Book of Ezra and the Book of Nehemiah.
3. For a more detailed analysis of 1 Esdras in comparison with the canonical books, see De Troyer 2002.
4. See further De Troyer 2002; also the essays by Klein, Schweitzer, and Fried in the present volume.
5. See further Böhler 1997: 67–72. He cites Z. Talshir in support of this position but in point of fact, she defends the *opposite* side of the scholarly spectrum. According to her, the raison d'être of 1 Esdras is precisely the story of the three youths (see above).
6. As Z. Talshir states: "In a previous literary version of the story, the winner may have been anonymous or identified as someone else" (2001: 187). See also Coggins's remark: "It is probable that in the original form of the debate this speech, like the first two, was anonymous, and was complete in itself without the elaboration concerning truth which now follows" (in Coggins and Knibb 1979: 29). Torrey, on the other hand, considered the entire story a Zerubbabel legend (1970: 23–25; cf. 1946: 50).
7. Torrey (1946: 49) notes: "This seems hardly fair; the agreement was that each should name 'one thing,' ἕνα λόγον. Why should this contestant have two strings to his bow?" Z. Talshir (2001: 187) opines that "[t]he story might have had a different form that did not include the fourth speech" (about truth).
8. Coggins also considers this part of the original ending: "It is probably that the original form of the story is here broken off; we should expect this reaction of *the king and the chief men* to lead to their decision, probably the awarding of the prize to the third speaker. Instead, a further speech follows" (in Coggins and Knibb 1979: 30; his emphasis).

Bibliography

Bertholdt, Leonhard. 1813. *Historisch-kritische Einleitung in sämmtliche kanonische und apocryphische Schriften des alten und neuen Testaments*, Part III. Erlangen: J. J. Palm.
Bird, Michael F. 2012. *1 Esdras*. Leiden: Brill.
Blenkinsopp, Joseph. 1988. *Ezra-Nehemiah*. OTL. Louisville, KY: Westminster John Knox.
Böhler, Dieter. 1997. *Die heilige Stadt in Esdras α und Esra-Nehemiah: Zwei Konzeptionen der Wiederherstellung Israels*. OBO 158. Freiburg: Universitätsverlag.
Carrez, Maurice. 1994. "1. Esdras Septante." *RHPR* 74: 13–42.
Clines, David J. A. 1984. *Ezra, Nehemiah, Esther*. NCB. Grand Rapids: Eerdmans.
Coggins, Richard J. and Michael A. Knibb. 1979. *The First and Second Books of Esdras*. Cambridge: Cambridge University Press.
Cross, Frank Moore. 1975. "A Reconstruction of the Judean Restoration." *JBL* 94: 4–18.
De Troyer, Kristin. 2002. "Zerubbabel and Ezra: A Revived and Revised Solomon and Josiah? A Survey of Current 1 Esdras Research." *Currents of Biblical Research* 1: 30–61.

De Troyer, Kristin. 2002. "4Q550 in the Context of the Darius Traditions: The Need for Integration of Tools." In J. Cook, ed., *Proceedings of the Sixth International Conference on Bible and Computers: The Bible from Alpha to Byte*. Leiden: Brill.

De Troyer, Kristin. 2011. "The Second Year of Darius—The Key to the Relation between 1 Esdras and Ezra-Nehemiah." In Lisbeth S. Fried, ed., *Was 1 Esdras First? An Investigation into the Priority and Nature of 1 Esdras*. SBL AIL 7. Atlanta: SBL, 73–81.

De Troyer, Kristin. 2015. "'A Man Leaves His Own Father': On Relationships in 1 Esdras." *Biblische Notizen* 164: 35–50.

Eskenazi, Tamara Cohn. 1986. "The Chronicler and the Composition of 1 Esdras." *CBQ* 48: 39–61.

Eskenazi, Tamara Cohn. 1988. *In an Age of Prose: A Literary Approach to Ezra-Nehemiah*. SBLMS 36. Atlanta: Scholars Press.

Eskenazi, Tamara Cohn. 1993. "Current Perspectives on Ezra-Nehemiah and the Persian Period." *Currents in Research: Biblical Studies* 1: 59–86.

Eskenazi, Tamara and Kent Harold Richards, eds. 1994. *Second Temple Studies*, Vol. 2: *The Temple Community in the Persian Period*. JSOTSup 175. Sheffield: Sheffield Academic Press.

Garbini, Giovanni. 1988. *History and Ideology in Ancient Israel*. London: SCM.

Grabbe, Lester. 1998. *Ezra-Nehemiah*. Old Testament Readings. London: Routledge.

Hanhart, Robert. 1974a. *Esdrae liber I*. Septuaginta VIII/1. Göttingen: Vandenhoeck & Ruprecht.

Hanhart, Robert. 1974b. *Text und Textgeschichte des 1. Esrabuches*. Göttingen: Vandenhoeck & Ruprecht.

Hanhart, Robert. 1993. "Ursprünglicher Septuagintatext und lukianische Rezension des 2. Esrabuches im Verhältnis zur Textform der Vetus Latina." In Robert Gryson, ed., *Philologia Sacra: Biblische und patristische Studien für Hermann J. Frede und Walter Thiele zu ihrem siebzigsten Geburtstag*, Band I: *Altes und neues Testament*. Freiburg: Herder, 90–119.

Hanhart, Robert. 1995. "Ein unbekannter Text zur griechischen Esra-Überlieferung." In Robert Hanhart, ed., *Lothar Perlit zum 65. Geburtstag am 2. Mai 1995*. Göttingen: Vandenhoeck & Ruprecht, 111–32.

Hanhart, Robert. 1998. "Zur griechischen und lateinischen Textgeschichte des 1. und 2. Esrabuches in ihrem Verhältnis zueinander." In Jean-Marie Auwers and Andre Wénin, eds., *Lectures et relectures de la Bible: Festschrift P.-M. Bogaert*. Leuven: University Press and Peeters, 145–63.

Japhet, Sara. 1994. "Composition and Chronology in the Book Ezra-Nehemiah." In Tamara Eskenazi and Kent Harold Richards, eds., *Second Temple Studies*, Vol. 2: *The Temple Community in the Persian Period*. JSOTSup 175. Sheffield: Sheffield Academic Press, 189–216.

Keil, Carl Friedrich. 1873. *The Books of Ezra, Nehemiah, and Esther*. Edinburgh: T&T Clark.

Kooij, Arie, van der. 1991a. "On the Ending of the Book of 1 Esdras." In Claude Cox, ed., *VII Congress of the IOSCS-Leuven 1989*. SCS 31. Atlanta: Scholars Press, 31–49.

Kooij, Arie, van der. 1991b. "Zur Frage des Anfangs des 1. Esrabuches." *ZAW* 103: 239–52.

Laato, Antti. 1992. *Josiah and David Redivivus: The Historical Josiah and the Messianic Expectations of Exilic and Postexilic Times*. Stockholm: Almqvist & Wiksell International.

Michaelis, Johannes D. 1783. *Deutsche Übersetzung des Alten Testaments, mit Anmerkungen für Ungelehrte*, Vol. 13: *Esra, Nehemia, Esther*. Göttingen: Ruprecht.

Myers, Jacob M. 1974. *I and II Esdras*. AB 42. Garden City: Doubleday.

Nickelsburg, George W. E. 1983. "The Bible Rewritten and Expanded." In Michael E. Stone, ed., *Jewish Writings of the Second Temple Period: Apocrypha, Pseudepigrapha, Qumran Sectarian Writings, Philo, Josephus*. Assen: Van Gorcum and Philadelphia: Fortress, 89–156.

Noth, Martin. 1960. *The History of Israel*. New York: Harper and Row.

Pohlmann, Karl-Friedrich. 1970. *Studien zum dritten Esra. Ein Beitrag zur Frage nach dem ursprünglichen Schluß des chronistischen Geschichtswerks*. FRLANT 104. Göttingen: Vandenhoeck & Ruprecht.

Pohlmann, Karl-Friedrich. 1980. *3. Esra-Buch*. Gütersloh: Gütersloher Verlaghaus-Gerd Mohn.

Pohlmann, Karl-Friedrich. 1991. "Zur Frage von Korrespondenzen und Divergenzen zwischen den Chronikbüchern und dem Ezra/Nehemia-Buch." In John A. Emerton, ed., *Congress Volume: Leuven 1989*. VTSup 43. Leiden: Brill, 314–30.

Schenker, Adrian. 1991. "La relation d'Esdras A' au texte massorétique d'Esdras-Néhémie." In G. J. Norton and S. Pisano, eds., *Tradition of the Text: Studies Offered to Dominique Barthélemy in Celebration of His 70th Birthday*. OBO 109. Fribourg: Universitätsverlag, 218–48.

Soggin, J. Alberto. 1984. *A History of Israel: From the Beginnings to the Bar Kochba Revolt, AD 135*. London: SCM.

Talshir, Zipora. 1999. *I Esdras: From Origin to Translation*. SCS 47. Atlanta: SBL.

Talshir, Zipora. 2001. *1 Esdras: A Text Critical Commentary*. SCS 50. Atlanta: SBL.

Thackeray, Henry, St. J. 1898–1904. "1 Esdras." In J. Hastings, ed., *Dictionary of the Bible*, Vol. I. New York: Scribner, 758–63.

Torrey, Charles C. 1945. "A Revised View of 1 Esdras." In Louis Ginzberg, *Jubilee Volume on the Occasion of His Seventieth Birthday*. New York: The American Academy for Jewish Research, 395–410.

Torrey, Charles C. 1946. *The Apocryphal Literature: A Brief Introduction*. 2nd ed. New Haven, CT: Yale University Press.

Torrey, Charles C. 1970. *Ezra Studies*. Reprint ed. New York: Ktav. (Original 1910.)

Walde, B. 1913. *Die Esrabücher der Septuaginta*. Freiburg: Herder.

Williamson, H. G. M. 1983. "The Composition of Ezra i-vi." *JTS* 34: 1–30.

Williamson, H. G. M. 1985. *Ezra, Nehemiah*. WBC 16. Waco, TX: Word.

Williamson, H. G. M. 1996. "The Problem with 1 Esdras." In J. Barton and D. J. Reimer, eds., *After the Exile: Essays in Honour of Rex Mason*. Macon, GA: Mercer University Press and Kampen: Kok Pharos, 201–16.

Zimmermann, Frank. 1963/64. "The Story of the Three Guardsmen." *JQR* 54: 179–200.

CHAPTER 25

SYNTHETIC AND LITERARY READINGS OF CHRONICLES AND EZRA-NEHEMIAH

STEVEN J. SCHWEITZER

WITHIN the field of biblical studies, the book of Chronicles has long been linked closely with the book of Ezra-Nehemiah (commonly understood and counted as one book in Jewish interpretation). Several factors can be identified in explaining this long-standing association. While Chronicles presents one version of Israel's history stretching *prima facie* from Adam (1 Chr. 1:1) to Cyrus (2 Chr. 36:22–23), Ezra-Nehemiah continues the story of the returned community at the time of Cyrus (Ezra 1:1) throughout the Persian period. When read sequentially, the books seem to present a continuous narrative. Jewish interpretation included a claim to common authorship for these books: they were written by Ezra and completed by Nehemiah (*b. B. Bat.* 15a). Such a view of common authorship, or at least a common redactor, was typical among biblical scholars throughout the nineteenth and most of the twentieth centuries, with the anonymous individual or group responsible being termed "the Chronicler." Arguments for considering Chronicles-Ezra-Nehemiah as a single authorial or editorial unit included: similarity of style and characteristic language; compositional technique; the doublet of the Edict of Cyrus in 2 Chr. 36:22–23 and Ezra 1:1–3a; the Greek text of 1 Esdras, which contains material from 2 Chronicles 35–36, Ezra 1–10, and Nehemiah 8 (Fried 2011); and common themes and emphases. This changed after the influential studies by Japhet (1968) and Williamson (1977: 5–70; 1983), which argued persuasively that Chronicles should be understood as distinct from Ezra-Nehemiah. Of course, these more recent studies have been challenged (Blenkinsopp, 1988: 47–54), defended, and refined since, but the result has been a clear shift among scholars, away from the consensus of common authorship or single, final redaction toward viewing each composition on its own terms (Knoppers 2003: 72–100). The term "the Chronicler" is now commonly applied to the author or editor of Chronicles alone, independent of the book of Ezra-Nehemiah. Scholars will also use this term, "the Chronicler," to signify both a single author or editor or a group of individuals working together (as a "scribal school" or "scribal guild") to create the book of Chronicles. As noted below, while multiple redactional layers from multiple hands were once commonly affirmed, more recent analyses have affirmed the literary unity of the whole with limited redactional activity.

As scholars began to view Chronicles as distinct from Ezra-Nehemiah, new investigations into the literary nature and theological perspectives of each separate work were undertaken. While previous scholarship had spoken of a "Chronicler's History" that reflected a unified Chronicles-Ezra-Nehemiah both in literary and theological terms (Noth 1987), this reevaluation has resulted in an appreciation of each book as its own work. The books do share some common concerns (for example, the temple and its personnel or genealogies), but other issues of ideology are more dissimilar than compatible (for example, the inclusion of foreigners or the relationship with the North/Samaria). It is difficult, if not impossible, to imagine a single author or editor could be responsible for the final versions of both books in their present forms. Recognition of the integrity of each book is at least partially responsible for renewed interest in these biblical books.

In addition, recent scholarly attention on the postexilic period, especially the Persian and early Hellenistic periods, has benefited the study of Chronicles and Ezra-Nehemiah. These centuries were often ignored or dismissed as minimally important for the development of the Hebrew Bible or were even viewed as being deficient theologically by earlier scholars. The landscape has shifted dramatically. With new discoveries and publications of texts (such as the Dead Sea Scrolls and Elephantine Papyri) and archaeological sites (such as Ramat Rachel and various Persian archives), numerous studies on the many compositions, biblical and extrabiblical, composed and editing during these centuries have been produced in an effort to reevaluate commonly held positions in the light of new data. Studies in Chronicles and Ezra-Nehemiah are experiencing something of a renaissance, with an explosion of new research, publications, and commentaries in recent decades.

The following discussion will focus on key developments in several areas of research into these books, emphasizing synthetic and literary approaches, many of which are a direct result of the shifts and new data mentioned above.

25.1 Narrative Unity and Redaction in the Final Forms of Chronicles and Ezra-Nehemiah

Especially when associated with Ezra-Nehemiah, literary approaches to the book of Chronicles tended to emphasize multiple redactional layers (Freedman 1961; Cross 1975), positing large sections of text—mostly in the form of various lists—added to an original narrative. In this view, the entire genealogical introduction (1 Chronicles 1–9) and the lists of temple personnel (1 Chronicles 23–27) were understood as later additions largely unconnected to or poorly integrated with the narrative. In addition, differences between details in these lists (such as the age of the Levites or the heads of families) or between the lists and the narratives were typically explained by subsequent editing meant to connect such details to the practices of the editor's own day that had since changed. However, a deeper appreciation for how these two sections function within the overall purpose of the book is now evident among scholars. The current tendency among Chronicles scholars is to assess the book as a unified whole without positing multiple editorial hands and layers (Klein 2006: 11–13).

This is particularly true of the genealogies in 1 Chronicles 1–9. Once labeled as riddled with "rank textual growth" (Noth 1987: 36) and dismissed, recent treatments of these genealogies emphasize how these lists function on their own as a coherent unit and how they prepare the reader for many of the themes that will follow in the narrative such as: inclusion of foreigners, importance of the temple personnel (especially the Levites), retribution, the Davidic-Solomonic dynasty, and prayer and seeking God. Rather than simply preserving history out of antiquarianism, the Chronicler uses this extended introduction to convey the "fundamental structure of the book" so that the genealogies "*are* the book" in terms of its major themes (J. W. Wright 1999: 154; emphasis original). Building on classic treatments by biblical scholars (Johnson 1969; Wilson 1977), interpreters of Chronicles have also found great insight in examinations of genealogies from the Greek world (Knoppers 2003: 245–65). Many of the techniques, structuring devices, use of narrative asides, and other features of the Chronicler's genealogies have strong parallels in genealogies from Greek sources. The idea that the genealogies are designed to reflect the relationship of the Chronicler's present or an imagined future moves the discussion of these names beyond questions of historicity or preservation of sources. Such an idea raises questions about identity formation as evidenced by how the Chronicler has both used sources and created connections among the individuals and groups represented by those names (Schweitzer 2007: 31–75).

Appreciation for the literary character of Chronicles extends well beyond finding links between the genealogies and the remainder of the narrative, however. Taking seriously the text as a whole, scholars have identified structural devices, repetitive terms and patterns, and intertextual links that demonstrate the quality and richness of the Chronicler's work as a literary masterpiece that employed techniques consistent with other writing during this same period, especially in Hellenistic historiography. This appreciation of the Chronicler as a skilled scribe who was able to create a complex and theologically sophisticated retelling of Israel's history has allowed reassessments of prior conclusions that too simplistically flattened the book's message. For example, while many scholars would assert the Chronicler's promotion of immediate retribution is mechanistic and fairly rigid in its application (following Japhet 2009: 120–55), others have become much more cautious in claiming the absolute consistency of that pattern across the entire book without exception (Kelly 2003; Klein 2006: 46–47; Ristau 2009: 242–47; J. W. Wright 2013). As Chronicles scholarship is able to stand on its own, without needing to account for Ezra-Nehemiah as part of a unified work, and without relegating large sections or conflicted internal details to secondary hands, more nuanced views of the book's overall message in *its final form* can be articulated while still recognizing the complexity of the extended, unified narrative.

The separation of Chronicles from Ezra-Nehemiah has not only benefited the former, but also the latter. Ezra-Nehemiah can be better assessed on its own, without recourse to Chronicles and its unique features. While Chronicles scholarship has more recently tended to emphasize the unity of the book without complicated redactional schema, a trend among Ezra-Nehemiah scholars seems quite the opposite. A few advocates in the 1990s argued that Ezra and Nehemiah were originally separate books (Becking 1998; VanderKam 1992;

Kraemer 1993); about a decade later, Ezra-Nehemiah's compositional history saw new analyses, positing conflicting redactional processes that resulted in the final form of the book (Pakkala 2004; J. L. Wright 2004). Scholars engaging these new proposals and dealing with text-critical issues raised by the MT, LXX, and Dead Sea Scrolls as they relate to Ezra-Nehemiah have revisited long-standing assumptions and conclusions about the nature of the book, its unity and disunity, and its presentation of theology and history particularly in light of Persian imperial policies (Boda and Redditt 2008; Kalimi 2012; Burt 2014; Fried 2015a; 2015b; Fulton 2015). The result has been a deeper appreciation for the unique perspectives of this composition as well as the literary character of its final form and its constituent parts. As with Chronicles, Ezra-Nehemiah is enjoying a resurgence of scholarship attentive to its complexity.

25.2 THE FUNCTION OF SOURCES IN CHRONICLES AND EZRA-NEHEMIAH

It is obvious that the author(s) and editor(s) of both Chronicles and Ezra-Nehemiah have made extensive use of sources in the compilation of the books. There has been much discussion about what sources were used, if they actually existed or are scholarly constructs, and the literary techniques by which they were incorporated into these compositions. Sometimes the sources in question are specified within the text itself (1 Chr. 9:1; 27:24; 29:30; 2 Chr. 9:29; 12:15; 13:22; 16:11; 20:34; 24:27; 25:26; 26:22; 27:7; 28:26; 32:32; 33:18–19; 35:26–27; 36:8) while at other times the sources are putative: presumably used but without explicit citation. In the latter case, readers are aware of the inclusion of sources only because those texts exist independently of Chronicles and Ezra-Nehemiah or have been reconstructed by scholars.

A summary of the identifiable "biblical" sources used in Chronicles include:

- Genesis (especially the genealogies in chs. 5, 10, 11, 25, 36, 46; the Abrahamic covenant in ch. 17; the near sacrifice of Isaac in ch. 22; the reference to Reuben's sin and the names of the twelve sons of Israel in ch. 35; the narrative concerning Judah and Tamar in ch. 38; the blessing of Ephraim and Manasseh in ch. 48; and possibly the blessing of Jacob in ch. 49);
- Exodus and Numbers (large portions of both books);
- Deuteronomy (esp. ch. 16);
- Joshua (especially the settlement lists in chs. 13, 15–17, 19, 21; and the narrative about Achan in ch. 7);
- Judges (especially the narrative about Ehud in ch. 3; and possibly the references to Joshua in chs. 1–2);
- Ruth (probably the Davidic genealogy in Ruth 4:17b–22, although it is possible that Ruth is using 1 Chronicles);
- Samuel (especially 1 Samuel 31; 2 Samuel 5–10, 13, 23–24; Chronicles also evidences knowledge of other details of Samuel throughout the entire book);

- Kings (especially 1 Kings 3–10; 11:26–43; 12:10–24; 14:21–15:24; 22; 2 Kgs. 8:16–29; 9:27–29; chs. 11–12; 14:1–22; 15:1–7, 32–38; ch. 16; 18:1–8, 13–37; 20:20–21; 21:1–23:3; 23:21–23; 23:28–24:20; 25:1–21; and a familiarity with many other details in the book such as what is found in 2 Kgs. 20:1–11, 12–19);
- Ezra-Nehemiah (especially Nehemiah 11; Ezra 2//Nehemiah 7; and other traditions about the Levites; perhaps also Ezra 1:1–3a; it is unlikely that Chronicles knew Ezra-Nehemiah in its final form);
- Psalms (esp. Pss. 96, 105, 106, 136:1, 132:8–10, and possibly 39:13 [ET 12]);
- Isaiah (esp. Isa. 7:9; perhaps some of the Hezekiah narratives in Isaiah 36–39);
- Haggai (perhaps the references to Joshua the priest);
- Zechariah (esp. Zech. 4:10; perhaps the references to Joshua the priest).

This list indicates the scope of the Chronicler's "biblical" sources, which draws heavily from the books of the Torah and Samuel-Kings along with smaller portions from the Psalms and allusions to the prophetic literature (Schweitzer 2011). The Chronicler employs a variety of approaches to these sources that can be quickly summarized under four categories: replication, omission, addition, and rearrangement. These types of changes can occur within long passages, on the one hand, or by means of individual words, on the other—or anywhere along the spectrum in between (Japhet 1993:14–23; Knoppers 2003: 66–71, 118–28; Kalimi 2005; Klein 2006: 30–44). In addition to material maintained without adjustment, the Chronicler made changes to the sources when incorporating them into the book; these changes suggest something about the theological and ideological perspectives that the Chronicler wanted to emphasize or reframe by means of rewriting and redactional use of sources. Careful attention to the differences between the text reflected in Chronicles and its sources demonstrates a certain consistency in the Chronicler's *Tendenz* that is conveyed through the text. In this way, both synchronic and diachronic literary approaches are valuable in assessing the Chronicler's presentation: the text of Chronicles must be assessed on its own as an independent writing, but it must also be analyzed in relationship to the sources that it is using. Both approaches reveal insights into the Chronicler's message and methods, and both are beneficial to the study of Chronicles.

In addition to "biblical" sources, the Chronicler also names a number of other sources in the book that cannot be identified with known "biblical" texts. They can be grouped into three categories: (1) royal records (1 Chr. 9:1; 27:24; 2 Chr. 16:11; 25:26; 27:7; 28:26; 35:26–27; 36:8); (2) prophetic writings written by a prophet (1 Chr. 29:30; 2 Chr. 9:29; 12:15; 13:22; 24:27; 26:22); (3) prophetic writings contained within royal records (2 Chr. 20:34; 32:32; 33:18–19). Beside these named sources, it is very likely that the Chronicler had access to additional sources though these go unspecified in the text. Such sources would likely have included a variety of lists or genealogical information that lie behind much of the presentation in 1 Chronicles 1–9 and 23–27 including military muster lists, preexilic genealogies, and priestly and Levitical genealogies. In these instances, the Chronicler does not indicate that any preexisting written material was consulted and incorporated, but it nevertheless appears that sources have been used—in other words, these are unlikely to be pure creations by the Chronicler. The authenticity and historicity of these sources—both the acknowledged and unacknowledged—is the subject of much debate. Also unclear is the extent to which the Chronicler refers to actual sources or to "imagined" ones, and scholarly opinion ranges dramatically.

The book of Ezra-Nehemiah contains a number of different sources. Scholars have typically identified the following (Williamson 1985: xxiii–xxxv):

- several decrees and letters from Persian kings (Ezra 1:1–4; 4:17–22; 6:3–5; 6:6–12; 7:12–26—all except the first composed in Aramaic, the administrative language of Persia);
- letters written to the Persian kings (Ezra 4:6–16; 5:6–17);
- the so-called Nehemiah Memoir (first person accounts throughout Neh. 1:1–7:5; 12:31–43; 13:4–31);
- a resettlement list (Ezra 2//Nehemiah 7) and other lists of names (Ezra 8:1–14; 10:18–44; Neh. 10:1–27; 11:3–36; 12:1–26);
- the so-called Ezra Memoir, although its exact parameters are vigorously debated by scholars (accounts in first and third person connected with Ezra in Ezra 7–10 and Nehemiah 8).

Additionally, two extended prayers are included in Ezra 9:5–15 and Neh. 9:6–37, which may have existed independently before they were incorporated into the narrative.

The extent of sources within Ezra-Nehemiah is significant. As already noted, numerous redactional processes have been proposed to explain how these complex and disparate materials were integrated into one book. The majority of scholars agree that some form of the material of Ezra 1–6 was likely collected on its own and later added to the remainder of the material in Ezra 7–Nehemiah 13. The lists in Nehemiah 11 and 12 were likely late additions (Fried 2015a: 4; Fulton 2015), but the compositional history of Ezra 7–Nehemiah 13 is heavily debated.

Two texts in particular have drawn attention based on both literary and chronological concerns: (1) Ezra's reading of the Torah in Nehemiah 8 and (2) the apparent chronological misplacement of the events in Nehemiah 5, which fit thematically and logically better with the circumstances recounted in Nehemiah 13.

1. The sudden appearance of Ezra in Nehemiah 8—he is otherwise absent throughout Nehemiah 1–7 and 10–13—and the textual witness of 1 Esdras, which includes Nehemiah 8 immediately after Ezra 10, has suggested to some scholars that Nehemiah 8 was originally independent or somehow linked with Ezra 7–10 before being relocated to its present position (see Pakkala 2004). Other scholars have argued that the chapter is original to its current placement (J. L. Wright, 2004).
2. Nehemiah 5:14 explicitly includes reference to Nehemiah's twelve years as governor until the thirty-second year of Artaxerxes, a statement after the events being presented in the chapter. The final verse (5:19) also includes a prayer of remembrance for good, something found otherwise only in Nehemiah 13, which also contains reference to the same year of Artaxerxes. Similar socio-economic concerns and religious practices appear in both chapters. While these considerations are not conclusive with regard to the possibility that all of chapter 5 is misplaced chronologically (Williamson 1985: 234–36), the thematic and linguistic links between the two chapters are strong and require explanation from a literary perspective (Burt 2014).

The difficulty in discerning how the editor(s) of Ezra-Nehemiah used sources in the composition of the book is further complicated by the fact that most of the identified sources are no longer extant for comparison. The various letters and lists appear only in

Ezra-Nehemiah, with few exceptions: the edict of Cyrus (Ezra 1:1–3) is repeated in 2 Chr. 36:22–23, and the lists in Nehemiah 11 overlap with those in 1 Chronicles 9. It is clear that "biblical" sources are also alluded to or referenced in Ezra-Nehemiah:

- the prophets Haggai and Zechariah are mentioned in Ezra 5:1–2; 6:14;
- the celebrations of Passover and Unleavened Bread (see Exod. 12:43–49; Lev. 23:4–8; Num. 27:16–25; Deut. 16:1–8) are mentioned in Ezra 6:19–22, although it is unclear which Pentateuchal text may have been the primary source;
- stereotypical and repeated language from Deuteronomy is found, for example, in Neh. 1:7–9;
- the command to observe the festival of Sukkoth for eight days (Lev. 23:33–43; Num. 29:12–38) is found in Neh. 8:13–18;
- the two penitential prayers in Ezra 9 and Nehemiah 9 contain numerous allusions to key events in Israel's history, in summary fashion;
- Solomon's foreign wives (1 Kgs. 11:1–8) are mentioned in Neh 13:26–27;
- Deut. 23:3–5 is cited in Neh. 13:1–3.

Both Chronicles and Ezra-Nehemiah benefit from comparative literary analyses, addressing the literary relationship of texts and the use of one text by another in creating something new. While sources in both books can be identified, there remain opportunities to explore how each uses these sources and the various intertextual connections between books. As appreciation for the literary sophistication of both Chronicles and Ezra-Nehemiah continues to grow, new treatments of these issues will undoubtedly reveal additional insights.

One word of caution seems appropriate at this point: analyses that explore literary relationships must take into account the various textual traditions found in ancient witnesses, especially the MT, the LXX, and the Dead Sea Scrolls. Prior scholarship may, at times, have too quickly argued that changes present in Chronicles or Ezra-Nehemiah are due to an intentional adjustment by the author or editor without recognizing that an alternative reading is present in another manuscript tradition(s) and so may not have originated with the author(s) or editor(s) of these books. That is, the author(s) or editor(s) may have been following another textual tradition(s) instead of introducing the change due to some sort of (presumed) ideological agenda. The need to adjudicate the evidence from textual variants and alternative readings is vital to any claim about redactional activity on the part of the author(s) or editor(s) of these books (McKenzie 1984; Knoppers 2003: 52–71; Klein 2006: 26–30; Fried 2015a: 5–7; Fulton 2015). Greater attention to these textual traditions permits scholars to make more nuanced claims about the message and methods of these ancient writings (see Fried in this volume).

25.3 Mixed Marriage, Foreigners, Samari(t)ans, and Identity Formation in Chronicles and in Ezra-Nehemiah

A series of related topics that distinguish Chronicles from Ezra-Nehemiah are their respective views of intermarriage, the inclusion or exclusion of foreigners, the attitude toward the Northern Kingdom and those in Samaria, and the concern and basis for identity formation within each composition. This distinction can be demonstrated with a few examples from Chronicles: the numerous foreigners included in the Chronicler's genealogies, and especially the Judahite line (1 Chronicles 2–4), without a hint of condemnation; the repeated invitations to the Northern tribes to participate in the religious festivals made by the reforming kings from Judah and that were accepted by some Northerners (2 Chr. 11:13–17; 15:9–15; 30:1–11, 18–20; 35:18); and the presentation of "all Israel" as extending beyond the narrowly defined unit of the returnees or those in the Persian province of Yehud. In contrast, Ezra-Nehemiah reflects the marginalization and removal of foreign wives and children (Ezra 9–10) and the similar exclusion of foreign women and those of foreign descent (Neh. 13:1–3, 23–27); the rejection of the North or Samari(t)ans (a term often used to note how the identity of those living in and descended from the North [the "Samarians"] becomes blurred in these texts with the latter group known as the Samaritans) to participate in the rebuilding projects (Ezra 4:1–5); the continued conflict between Sanballat and Nehemiah (Neh. 2:10, 19–20; 4:1–23; 6:1–19; 13:28–29); and further separation from foreigners both in terms of marriage and commerce on the Sabbath (Neh. 9:1–3; 10:28–31; 13:15–22, 30).

In the Chronicler's genealogies, foreigners are integrated into the lineage of Israel both by explicit intermarriage and by the subtle incorporation of foreigners without direct statements of marriage (1 Chr. 2:3, 17, 34–35, 55; 3:2; 4:17–18; 4:21–22; 7:14). The Chronicler does not shy away from identifying such ancestors as foreigners, nor is this practice condemned; instead, the Chronicler seems to make special points about these individuals such that Israel cannot exist without them as part of their past (Knoppers 2001a; 2001b). This acceptance of foreigners within the community through marriage mirrors the desired inclusion of Israelites from the North who would once again join the community in Jerusalem through worship at the temple. The repeated inclusion of these individuals and the apparent hope for restoration with the North can be understood as the Chronicler's desire for restoration with the Samari(t)an community of his own day, whom he still regards as part of Israel (Japhet 2009: 241–74; Knoppers 2013: 71–101). While the Chronicler did not affirm the worship practices of the Samari(t)an community of his day, he nonetheless recognized them as part of "all Israel," which he hoped would one day be restored and reunited around a single temple (the Jerusalem one, of course), just as in the days of Hezekiah (2 Chronicles 30).

The Chronicler's characteristic use of the term "all Israel" to define those recognized as belonging to the community has been a particular focus of scholarly attention (Williamson 1977; Japhet 2009: 209–74; Jonker 2016). The scope of the referents for the phrase is wide, and reflects the Chronicler's desire for the constitution of his postexilic community, as noted by many scholars (Jonker 2016: 282). The concept is used to form the identity of this imagined community. As a function of identity formation, it is used as an attempt at self-definition, typically through the construction of "boundary markers." However, as demonstrated by numerous scholars, the term has a certain degree of fluidity and expansiveness, so that the boundaries for "all Israel" reflect openness rather than a rigidity that excludes certain groups from the community. In Chronicles, "Israel" therefore includes the biological descendants of the eponymous ancestor Jacob/Israel, but it also includes those foreigners who have intermarried into that lineage. "Israel" is not only those from the southern tribes, but from the North as well. "Israel" thus includes not only the subgroup of tribes who returned from the Babylonian exile, but also those who did not return from the Babylonian exile or from the Assyrian deportation as well as those who never went into exile. In sum, "Israel" is not confined to only those who reside in the land of Israel. "Israel" also is not limited to one specific time; "Israel" continues to exist across the centuries despite historical changes: there is no one moment in time when "Israel" exists in an ideal form as the parameters of "Israel" are constantly shifting. Finally, in addition to land and biology, "Israel" has a religious component, so that all those who worship the God of Israel are understood to belong to this community, regardless of ancestry or location.

"Israel" in Chronicles is thus defined in genealogical, social, political, and religious terms. Inclusion in "Israel" is articulated in ways that are trans-temporal, trans-spatial, trans-political, and trans-biological (Schweitzer 2007: 53–60). Ultimately, the concept of "all Israel" is used to create "an understanding of their coherence primarily as a religious community. Those who seek Yahweh are considered to be part of All-Israel" (Jonker 2016: 191). With worship at its center (Graham 1999; Endres 2001), the Chronicler envisions a community that is not defined primarily by ethnicity, in contrast to Ezra-Nehemiah.

Ezra-Nehemiah presents a community in and around Jerusalem whose boundaries and identity markers are renegotiated with the arrival of multiple groups of returnees from the Babylonian exile during the Persian period. Whereas Chronicles witnesses a more tolerant, even supportive, view of intermarriage, those responsible for Ezra-Nehemiah rejected that and other associations with perceived foreigners as threats to the community. The "intermarriage crisis" reflected in Ezra 9–10 and repeated in Nehemiah 13 results in group redefinition. This "watershed" moment in Israel's history has received extensive investigation, with scholars drawing on a variety of methodological approaches from various disciplines (anthropology, sociology, postcolonial studies, literary approaches) to assist in understand the nature of the events recorded (Janzen 2002; Frevel 2011; Southwood 2012; Eskenazi 2014). As with the genealogies of Chronicles, comparative evidence from the Greek world has been particularly insightful (Fried 2015b).

The application of these methods (and sources) have raised questions about the status and identity of these women as truly "foreign" (Eskenazi and Judd 1994). Comparative anthropological and sociological research suggests that the women labeled as "foreign" may have been people who had never gone into exile, but remained in the land. That is to say that these women were possibly (likely) ethnically Israelite but are regarded as outsiders and "othered" by use of the label "foreigner" (Eskenazi and Judd 1994). Whether this is the case or not remains uncertain, but the text clearly presents them as foreigners and as a threat to the holiness of the community, so that they must be "sent away"—that is, divorced. The initial complaint about the practice of intermarriage is that the "holy seed has mixed itself" (Ezra 9:2)—a claim that invokes purity language and that requires separation (Fried 2015a: 365–66). Separation was deemed essential because of the close connection between intermarriage and idolatry (Deut. 7:1–6), with the punishment for idolatrous activities being exile (see Deut. 28:41, 63–64; Ezra 9:14–15; Neh. 13:25–27). For those responsible for Ezra-Nehemiah, especially situated around groups recently returning from the experience of exile, such a threat cannot be taken lightly. The practice of endogamy (marriage within one's own recognized community, tribe, or clan group) is, therefore, the desired position of the book, even while it also witnesses to the practice of exogamy (marriage outside of one's own recognized community, tribe, or clan group) among the community in and around Jerusalem during this period.

Securing the community against a perceived threat from foreigners extends beyond intermarriage to trade with foreigners on the Sabbath in Neh. 13:15–22. Many questions have been raised about the recurrence of intermarriage concerns during the time of Nehemiah's absence as governor (at least, that is the implication of the text) in Neh. 13:23–27 and its relationship to Ezra 9–10. However one understands that relationship, Nehemiah 13 notes the issue of spoken language as a factor in determining identity (vv. 23–24) and includes observance of Sabbath—specifically avoiding trade with outsiders on that day—as a distinctive marker for the community. It is worth noting that trade with foreigners generally is not decried, only trade *on the Sabbath*, the observance of which is now also tied into identity.

It is clear that, in Ezra-Nehemiah, a community is attempting to define itself and does so by using ethnicity and spoken language, purity terminology, and socio-economic and religious practices. This approach and the ability of the community, especially its leadership, to enforce such policies, should be seen in the light of comparative sociological studies. These studies emphasize the low status of the community—as a small group that sees itself under threat and struggling for power, rather than as an elite, empowered, authoritative group with stability and privilege (see, e.g., Smith-Christopher 1994). Such a social location may help make the concern with "foreigners" and exogamous intermarriage in Ezra-Nehemiah more understandable to modern readers, even if it remains unpalatable.

The dynamics around intermarriage in Ezra-Nehemiah are mirrored by the conflict with the Samari(t)ans and especially between Sanballat and Nehemiah. In contrast to Chronicles, Ezra-Nehemiah takes a position of hostility and rejection toward the community to the north, which had its own leadership and temple. Archaeological evidence now supports the existence of a temple at Mount Gerizim during the Persian period prior to the time of Alexander the Great (Knoppers 2013: 120–34), so one does not need to consider the account of Ezra-Nehemiah as a projection of a subsequent conflict from the Hellenistic period back into the past. Instead, the tension evidenced by Ezra-Nehemiah can be legitimately understood in light of its literary and historical context in the Persian period (Knoppers, 2013: 135–68).

With Chronicles and Ezra-Nehemiah, different understandings of who should constitute the community known as "Israel" are constructed and the boundary markers are quite different. As other biblical and extrabiblical books engage in similar themes and the issue of identity remains a contemporary concern in our own time, topics related to mixed marriages, foreigners, and identity formation will continue to garner significant scholarly attention (see Garcia-Bachmann, Marbury, and Howard in this volume).

25.4 Utopian Readings of Chronicles and Ezra-Nehemiah

One literary approach that brings together many of the aspects discussed in the previous sections is the use of utopian literary theory to read the books of Chronicles and Ezra-

Nehemiah. An initial investigation in select chapters of Chronicles by Boer in 1999 was expanded and refined by Schweitzer (2007; 2016)—together these works provide the methodology and first interpretative ventures from this perspective (see further Schweitzer and Uhlenbruch 2016; for discussion, including critique, see Cataldo 2010; Blenkinsopp 2011; Klein 2012: 2-4; Wilson 2015; Jonker 2016: 36-42).

Schweitzer's utopian approach begins with the recognition that texts that construct societies do not necessarily reflect historical reality but may instead present alternative realities. Many of the visions of the future in the biblical prophetic literature could be understood in this manner (Ben Zvi 2006), but the same approach can be applied to non-prophetic, historiographic texts. While Chronicles has often been understood in critical scholarship as a text which reflects the realities of the postexilic period for the purpose of maintaining a status quo of the society during the Second Temple period—a view based more on assumptions about the nature of the book than evidence (see Schweitzer 2007: 12; 2009)—a utopian reading suggests that the book conveys a critique of the status quo by projecting a desired future into the past. Drawing comparisons to More's *Utopia* written in 1516 (the "good place" that is "no place"), Schweitzer argues that utopian readings of Chronicles reveal more about the problems and ideological struggles of the period during which Chronicles was composed rather than the historical situation of the author(s) or editor(s) (2007: 14-30).

Schweitzer (2007) applies a utopian reading to three dominant themes in Chronicles: genealogies and identity, the Davidic dynasty and politics, and the temple (especially its presentation of the Levites), emphasizing the way in which the Chronicler shapes the narrative to highlight positive features that can be a source of hope for his community in creating a future that is different from its present—specifically by anchoring "desired changes solidly in the hallowed past" (30). The Chronicler's history is thus not really about the past, but about the future that might yet be if the community would only implement the ideals presented in the book. Instead of being composed to explain the exile and the factors that caused it (a primary concern for the Deuteronomistic History), Chronicles recasts the past to move his community forward in the hope of something better, beyond the trauma of the exile and toward a community that can be, act, and remain faithful (Schweitzer 2016).

The idea that the Chronicler's history is more about the future than the past and oriented toward hope is not new among scholars of Chronicles (Schweitzer 2007: 30; Japhet 2009: 384-93), but a utopian reading explores the construction of an alternative reality rather than assuming it reflects historical reality. The result of such a shift emphasizes the imagined and constructed nature of the depiction of reality in the book, illuminating the degree to which various themes are utilized to reinforce and promulgate such a vision. Rather than historical reconstruction, a utopian reading reveals ideological assertions and the means of establishing the world created as reflected within the text. Scholars debate which aspects of the book are historical and which are future possibilities. More often, they have tended to suppose historical depictions, but this is based on assumptions rather than evidence. Elsewhere, I have attempted to illustrate how the book can be read quite differently by changing such assumptions (see Schweitzer 2007).

The same shift of perspective can be applied to Ezra-Nehemiah with similar results (Cataldo, 2010; 2016; Ben Zvi 2016). Ezra-Nehemiah expresses concern over those who would threaten the utopian ideals of the community and so attempts to limit or remove those threats. The degree to which this depiction reflects historical reality or an imagined possibility is difficult to support with evidence, as is also the case with Chronicles. A utopian reading privileges the latter option, however, suggesting that the narrative records a desired history ("what should have happened") according to those who agree with its perspectives. A utopian reading asks questions like: What if the texts about intermarriage are not historical, but ideological, reflecting a contrast to the reality in which the author(s) or editor(s) found himself? How should this change the way scholars approach the depictions of the community in this book? Finally, as utopia and its related concept of dystopia are relative terms dependent on context and the parameters of the society at hand, the question of "Utopia for whom? Dystopia for whom?" must always be asked and answered, revealing those who benefit from and are harmed by the ideology being advocated. These are questions of power and how it is wielded. In Ezra-Nehemiah, those at the margins (women, children, foreigners) are without power and are under threat.

In ways like these, utopian readings of Chronicles and Ezra-Nehemiah can contribute to more nuanced arguments about the ideologies of these books and the contexts in which they were composed and/or edited. As Jonker states, "With reference to Chronicles... utopian theory can potentially help us to be more specific in our interpretations of the book to indicate how the Chronicler made use of traditions about the past in order to urge an audience (or various audiences) towards a specific vision for the future that functions in the specific present (of the Chronicler)" (2016: 42). The same sentiment holds true for utopian readings of Ezra-Nehemiah. Further investigations using this approach will refine interpretations and open up new questions.

Bibliography

Becking, Bob. 1998. "Ezra's Re-Enactment of the Exile." In Lester Grabbe, ed., *Leading Captivity Captive: 'The Exile' as History and Ideology*. JSOTSup 278. Sheffield: Sheffield Academic, 40–61.

Ben Zvi, E., ed. 2006. *Utopia and Dystopia in Prophetic Literature*. Göttingen: Vandenhoeck & Ruprecht.

Ben Zvi, Ehud. 2016. "Re-Negotiating a Putative Utopia and the Stories of the Rejection of Foreign Wives in Ezra-Nehemiah." In S. Schweitzer and F. Uhlenbruch, eds., *Worlds that Could Not Be: Constructing Utopia in Chronicles, Ezra and Nehemiah*. LHBOTS 620. London: T&T Clark, 105–28.

Ben Zvi, E., and Edelman, D., eds. 2011. *What Was Authoritative for Chronicles?*. Winona Lake, IN: Eisenbrauns.

Blenkinsopp, J. 1988. *Ezra-Nehemiah*. OTL. Louisville, KY: Westminster John Knox.

Blenkinsopp, J. 2011. "Ideology and Utopia in 1–2 Chronicles." In E. Ben Zvi and D. Edelman, eds., *What Was Authoritative for Chronicles?*. Winona Lake, IN: Eisenbrauns, 89–103.

Boda, M. J., and Redditt, P. L., eds. 2008. *Unity and Disunity in Ezra-Nehemiah: Redaction, Rhetoric, and Reader*. Sheffield: Sheffield Phoenix.

Boer, R. 1999. "Utopian Politics in 2 Chronicles 10–13." In M. P. Graham and S. L. McKenzie, eds., *The Chronicler as Author: Studies in Text and Texture*. JSOTSup 263. Sheffield: Sheffield Academic, 360–94.

Burt, S. 2014. *The Courtier and the Governor: Transformations of Genre in the Nehemiah Memoir* 17. Göttingen: Vandenhoeck & Ruprecht.

Cataldo, J. 2010. "Whispered Utopia: Dreams, Agenda, and Theocratic Aspirations in Yehud." *SJOT* 24: 53–70.

Cataldo, J. 2016. "Utopia in Agony: The Role of Prejudice in Ezra-Nehemiah's Ideal for Restoration." In S. Schweitzer and F. Uhlenbruch, eds., *Worlds That Could Not Be: Constructing Utopia in Chronicles, Ezra and Nehemiah*. LHBOTS 620. London: T&T Clark, 144–68.

Cross, F. M. 1975. "A Reconstruction of the Judean Restoration." *JBL* 94: 4–18.

Endres, J. C. 2001 "Joyful Worship in Second Temple Judaism." In Lamontte M. Luker, ed., *Passion, Vitality, and Foment: The Dynamics of Second Temple Judaism*. Harrisburg, PA: Trinity Press International, 155–88.

Eskenazi, T. C. 2014. "Imagining the Other in the Construction of Judahite Identity in Ezra-Nehemiah." In E. Ben Zvi and D. Edelman, eds., *Imagining the Other and Constructing Israelite Identity in the Early Second Temple Period*. LHBOTS 456. London: Bloomsbury, 230–56.

Eskenazi, T. C. and E. P. Judd. 1994. "Marriage to a Stranger in Ezra 9–10." In T. C. Eskenazi and K. H. Richards, eds., *Second Temple Studies*, Vol. 2: *Temple Community in the Persian Period*. JSOTS 175. Sheffield: Sheffield Academic, 266–85.

Freedman, D. N. 1961. "The Chronicler's Purpose." *CBQ* 23: 436–42.

Frevel, C., ed. 2011. *Mixed Marriages: Intermarriages and Group Identity in the Second Temple Period*. LHBOTS 547. London: T&T Clark.

Fried, L. S., ed. 2011. *Was 1 Esdras First? An Investigation into the Priority and Nature of 1 Esdras*. Atlanta: SBL.

Fried, L. S. 2015a. *Ezra: A Commentary*. Sheffield: Sheffield Phoenix.

Fried, L. S. 2015b. "No King in Judah? Mass Divorce in Judah and in Athens." In J. M. Silverman and C. Waerzeggers, eds., *Political Memory in and after the Persian Empire*. Atlanta: SBL, 381–401.

Fulton, D. N. 2015. *Reconsidering Nehemiah's Judah: The Case of MT and LXX Nehemiah 11–12*. Tübingen: Mohr Siebeck.

Graham, M. P. 1999. "Setting the Heart to Seek God: Worship in 2 Chronicles 30.1–31.1." In M. P. Graham, R. R. Marrs, and S. L. McKenzie, eds., *Worship and the Hebrew Bible*. JSOTSup 284. Sheffield: Sheffield Academic, 124–41.

Graham, M. P., and McKenzie, eds. 1999. *The Chronicler as Author: Studies in Text and Texture*. JSOTSup 263. Sheffield: Sheffield Academic.

Graham, M. P., S. L. McKenzie, S. L., and G. N. Knoppers, eds. 2003. *The Chronicler as Theologian*. JSOTSup 371. London: T&T Clark.

Graham, M. P., K. G. Hoglund, and S. L. McKenzie, eds. 1997. *The Chronicler as Historian*. JSOTSup 238. Sheffield: Sheffield Academic.

Janzen, D. 2002. *Witch-hunts, Purity and Social Boundaries: The Expulsion of the Foreign Women in Ezra 9–10*. JSOTSup 350. Sheffield: Sheffield Academic.

Japhet, S. 1968. "The Supposed Common Authorship of Chronicles and Ezra-Nehemiah Investigated Anew." *VT* 18: 332–71.

Japhet, S. 1993. *I & II Chronicles*. OTL. Louisville, KY: Westminster John Knox.

Japhet, S. 2006. *From the Rivers of Babylon to the Highlands of Judah*. Winona Lake, IN: Eisenbrauns.

Japhet, S. 2009. *The Ideology of the Book of Chronicles and Its Place in Biblical Thought*. Reprint ed. Winona Lake, IN: Eisenbrauns.

Johnson, M. D. 1969. *The Purpose of the Biblical Genealogies: With Special Reference to the Setting of the Genealogies of Jesus*. Cambridge: Cambridge University Press.

Jonker, L. C. 2016. *Defining All-Israel in Chronicles*. Tübingen: Mohr Siebeck.

Kalimi, I. 2005. *The Reshaping of Ancient Israelite History in Chronicles*. Winona Lake, IN: Eisenbrauns.

Kalimi, I., ed. 2012. *New Perspectives on Ezra-Nehemiah: History and Historiography, Text, Literature, and Interpretation*. Winona Lake, IN: Eisenbrauns.

Kelly, Brian E. 2003. "'Retribution' Revisited: Covenant, Grace and Restoration." In M. P. Graham, S. L. McKenzie, and G. N. Knoppers, eds. *The Chronicler as Theologian*. JSOTSup 371. London: T&T Clark, 206–27.

Klein, R. 2006. *1 Chronicles*. Hermeneia. Minneapolis: Fortress.

Klein, R. 2012. *2 Chronicles*. Hermeneia. Minneapolis: Fortress.
Knoppers, G. N. 2001a. "'Great among His Brothers,' But Who Is He? Heterogeneity in the Composition of Judah." *JHS* 3.4: online: www.jhsonline.org.
Knoppers, G. N. 2001b. "Intermarriage, Social Complexity, and Ethnic Diversity in the Genealogy of Judah." *JBL* 120: 15–30.
Knoppers, G. N. 2003. *1 Chronicles 1–9*. AB 12. Garden City, NY: Doubleday.
Knoppers, G. N. 2013. *Jews and Samaritans: The Origins and History of Their Early Relations*. Oxford: Oxford University Press.
Kraemer, D. C. 1993. "On the Relationship of the Books of Ezra and Nehemiah." *JSOT* 59: 73–92.
McKenzie, S. L. 1984. *The Chronicler's Use of the Deuteronomistic History*. HSM 33. Atlanta: Scholars Press.
Noth, M. 1987. *The Chronicler's History*. JSOTSup 50. Sheffield: Sheffield Academic.
Pakkala, J. 2004. *Ezra the Scribe: The Development of Ezra 7–10 and Nehemiah 8*. BZAW 347. Berlin: de Gruyter.
Ristau, K. A. 2009. "Reading and Rereading Josiah: The Chronicler's Representation of Josiah for the Postexilic Community." In G. N. Knoppers and K. A. Ristau, eds., *Community Identity in Judean Historiography: Biblical and Comparative Perspectives*. Winona Lake, IN: Eisenbrauns, 219–47.
Schweitzer, S. J. 2007. *Reading Utopia in Chronicles*. LHBOTS 442. London: T&T Clark.
Schweitzer, S. J. 2009. "A Response." *JHS* 9: online: www.jhsonline.org.
Schweitzer, S. J. 2011. "Judging a Book by Its Citations: Sources and Authority in Chronicles." In E. Ben Zvi and D. Edelman, eds., *What Was Authoritative for Chronicles?*, Winona Lake, IN: Eisenbrauns, 37–65.
Schweitzer, S. J. 2016. "Exile, Empire, and Prophecy: Reframing Utopian Concerns in Chronicles." In S. Schweitzer and F. Uhlenbruch, eds., *Worlds That Could Not Be: Constructing Utopia in Chronicles, Ezra and Nehemiah*. LHBOTS 620. London: T&T Clark, 81–104.
Schweitzer, S. J., and Uhlenbruch, F., eds. 2016. *Worlds That Could Not Be: Constructing Utopia in Chronicles, Ezra and Nehemiah*. LHBOTS 620. London: T&T Clark.
Smith-Christopher, D. L. 1994. "The Mixed Marriage Crisis in Ezra 9–10 and Nehemiah 13: A Study of the Sociology of Post-Exilic Judaean Community." In T. C. Eskenazi and K. H. Richards, eds., *Second Temple Studies*, Vol. 2: *Temple Community in the Persian Period*. JSOTSup 175. Sheffield: Sheffield Academic, 243–65.
Southwood, K. E. 2012. *Ethnicity and the Mixed Marriage Crisis in Ezra 9–10*. Oxford: Oxford University Press.
VanderKam, J. 1992. "Ezra-Nehemiah or Ezra and Nehemiah?" In E. Ulrich et al., eds., *Priests, Prophets and Scribes*. Sheffield: Sheffield Academic, 55–75.
Wilson, I. D. 2015. "Chronicles and Utopia: Likely Bedfellows?" In I. D. Wilson and D. V. Edelman, eds., *History, Memory, Hebrew Scriptures*. Winona Lake, IN: Eisenbrauns, 151–65.
Wilson, R. R. 1977. *Genealogy and History in the Biblical World*. YNER 7. New Haven, CT: Yale University Press.
Williamson, H. G. M. 1977. *Israel in the Book of Chronicles*. Cambridge: Cambridge University Press.
Williamson, H. G. M. 1983. "The Composition of Ezra i-vi." *JTS* 34: 1–30.
Williamson, H. G. M. 1985. *Ezra-Nehemiah*. WBC 16. Waco, TX: Word.
Wright, John W. 1999. "The Fabula of the Book of Chronicles." In M. P. Graham and S. L. McKenzie, eds., *The Chronicler as Author: Studies in Text and Texture*. JSOTSup 263. Sheffield: Sheffield Academic, 136–55.
Wright, Jacob L. 2004. *Rebuilding Identity: The Nehemiah-Memoir and Its Earliest Readers*. BZAW 348. Berlin: de Gruyter.
Wright, John W. 2013. "Divine Retribution in Herodotus and the Book of Chronicles." In P. Evans and T. Williams, eds., *Chronicling the Chronicler: The Book of Chronicles and Early Second Temple Historiography*. Winona Lake, IN: Eisenbrauns, 195–214.

CHAPTER 26

THE ROLE OF ORALITY AND TEXTUALITY, FOLKLORE AND SCRIBALISM IN THE HISTORICAL BOOKS

SUSAN NIDITCH

The border shared by oral-compositional sensibilities and written libretto is beautifully exemplified by the Historical Books of the Hebrew Bible. Some of the pieces in this corpus such as Judges 5 are characterized by formulaic language, a mark of oral composition, and actually imagine settings for extemporaneous performance. The Historical Books, moreover, offer numerous examples of narrative variants, alternate versions of comparable content, another indication of oral traditional style. On the other hand, the Historical Books frequently allude to written documents and seem to valorize letters, decrees, chronicles, and examples of monumental writing. This interplay between oral and written is in no way limited to the Historical Books and is characteristic of the anthology of works preserved in the Hebrew Bible. The Historical Books, however, are especially informative about the written end of the continuum and revealing of attitudes to writing even while preserving oral style material. These works suggest much about the value placed upon oral-style and writing by authors set in particular contexts, the better to appreciate the composers behinds these works and key aspects of their worldviews. Reflecting upon scribal elites, their relationship to writing, and their attitudes to oral and written media relates to the recollection and creation of history itself and to the processes of cultural construction.

26.1 FOLKLORISTS ON THE ORAL, THE WRITTEN, AND HISTORY

Folklorists have long been interested in the relationship between orally composed literature, written texts that in style and content are suggestive of oral tradition, and history. History is approached by folklorists with varying emphases. While some scholars seek to verify actual events of the past with the help of preserved oral accounts and written forms of folk tradition, others eschew the possibility of such reconstruction of events and rather point to social and cultural dimensions revealed by folklore and to the intellectual trends to which they point. In his study of history, folklore, and oral tradition as they relate to early modern England, D. R. Woolf, for example, both asks if "oral" or "folk" sources provide a window on what actually happened in the past or if they are more accurately a valuable source for the "preservation of perceptions" (1988: 35). The folklorist Richard M. Dorson reviews scholars' concerns about the "accuracy" of media such as ballads and oral tradition as they relate to history, but quoting Lucy Maynard Salmon also points to folklorists' attention to the "'unconscious record' offered by the legend of the times and civilization in which it circulated," reflecting "communal myth that gives their world meaning." He notes moreover that the "popular prejudices and stereotypes nourished by oral tradition have affected the course of history" (1964: 221, 224, 228). Working with African tradition, Jan Vansina asks about "the validity of oral traditions as sources for history" (1971: 443). Vansina explores limitations, definitions of history that allow for the inclusion of "lore of the past," and differences between oral and written sources. Vansina asks whether it is indeed possible "to reconstruct" an "original tradition from variants" (p. 448; see also p. 455) and points to the possibility of corroborating folk versions of events by means of "independent tradition" (p. 458).

Another thread in studies of orality and historicity builds on the work of classicists concerning the relationship between performed speech acts and the composition of history. The biblical scholar Raymond Person suggests that ancient historiography including that preserved in the Hebrew Bible "was typically read aloud" and existed in multiforms—hence the existence of lengthy doublets in 2 Samuel–2 Kings and 1 and 2 Chronicles (2016: 73). While proof that such works are rooted in oral performance is elusive, the inclusion of both works in the biblical canon does speak to a quality of oral cultures in the written Bible, that is, the valorization of variants and multiforms. What we can say with certainty is that biblical writers do portray characters delivering historiographically rich speeches, for example Josh. 24:1–13, Judg. 11:12–27, and Neh. 9:6–37. The nature and quality of the historicity of such historiographic content is, of course, another matter, as noted by Dorson (1964) and the others discussed above.

It comes as no surprise to biblicists that a good deal of attention has been given to questions about historicity itself. Can these oral and oral-style traditions preserve actual information about the past? Conclusions drawn often suggest that indeed some specific information can be gleaned concerning leaders, or battles, or other key events but that such troves of material (which would include all of the Historical Books) are more informative about the aesthetics, concerns, and attitudes of authors set in particular cultural settings.

The study of the relationship between epic and history by John Miles Foley (2010), a creative scholar of early and oral literatures, moves in several of the directions that interest this essay concerning the sort of history offered by the Historical Books, the nature of the content included and how is it shaped, and the cultural and social tensions that are implicit. We begin with some observations concerning oral and written.

26.2 Texture, Text, Context: Variation and Imagined Life-settings

In a recent study, Peter Friedlander (2015) compares oral and manuscript traditions of a particular Indian genre, the Kabīr song, and points to types of variation characteristic of each. Several of his interests are relevant to our study of oral and written in the Historical Books. He attends to changes over time in each kind of tradition, oral and written, aware that neither is static or fixed, and emphasizes that differences in oral and written versions of the Kabīr tradition hold information about the audiences who receive them. He notes, "there is a constant interweaving between oral and written traditions of the Kabīr songs" (p. 196). Friedlander, a contemporary folklorist, has the option of experiencing current performances of this centuries-old song tradition, whereas we have only the written preserved texts of ancient Levantine traditions. Nevertheless his emphases on diachronic developments, multiplicity, audience or reception context, and the interplay between oral and written at every stage of the tradition's development are relevant to the present study as well.

Matters of texture in the Israelite corpus are especially important in assessing oral and writerly sensibilities reflected in the vocabulary and patterns of language of literature in the Historical Books. Terminology of singing, recounting, speaking, and saying with the use of ethnic genre designations such as *māšāl* and *šîr*, and verbs including especially '*mr, dbr*, "to say" and "to speak," point to performance, immediacy, and verbal interaction, whereas references to *ktb*, "to write," and to *sēper*, "a document," suggest writerly sensibilities, the work of scribes. The present study of oral and written in the Historical Books begins with a close look at the ancient song in Judges 5 and its narrative parallel in Judges 4.

The very fact that the story of the battle with Sisera at the Wadi of Kishon and the powerful vignette involving the woman warrior Jael is found in two versions, preserved side by side, points again to an oral-traditional mentality that places value upon the multiplicity and variation reflected in the libretto of scripture. Texturally, Judges 4, like much of the book of Judges, is characterized by unperiodic enjambment so that the thought is complete at the end of the line, and an adding style impressionistically layers image upon image as the tale unfolds (Lord 1968: 54; Cross 1998: 142–43). This compositional modality is typical of oral-style literatures world-wide (Polak 1998). Oral-style composition in the Hebrew Bible, however, evidences a variety of registers. The style of Judges 5 is more densely parallelistic than its narrative variant in Judges 4 and more recognizable to modern readers as poetic. Judges 5 provides an excellent case study in the oral-traditional end of the spectrum as it emerges in the Historical Books and points to the valorization of a kind of literature that is preserved or composed according to traditional patterns and expectations.

The very inclusion of Judges 5 in the telling of a history of early Israel testifies to the vibrancy of traditional forms in the process of national self-expression and cultural construction within historiographic contexts.

The vocabulary of Judges 5 emphasizes speech acts: "telling" in 5:1; "listening" and "lending an ear" in the parallelistic formula of 5:3; "recounting" in 5:11; and the language of song, sound, and music in 5:1, 3, 11, 12. The root "to sing" may well be a marker of an ethnic genre which refers to a poem set to music or perhaps a "lyric" (Mowinckel 1935). Within the šîr, or "song," are various types that range widely in theme and content from epic account to praise song to lament. Closest to our example from Judges is Exodus 15 (see 15:1, 20–21), and perhaps Num. 21:17–19. Numbers 21:17–19 is framed as a celebratory song followed by a brief geographic annal, tracing the footsteps of a migratory Israel. Preceding this piece is another border text that is described as "said in the document (sēper) of the wars of Yhwh." Nuances of oral recitation and written text combine, for the document "says" or "declares" ('mr).

As a composition, Judges 5, while clearly preserved in writing, reveals engagement at the oral end of the spectrum. In addition to the vocabulary discussed above that points to speech acts, the scene in vv. 10–11 has listeners or readers imagine an occasion for oral performance of this song, where people meet between the waterholes and tell a tale of victory, possibly accompanied by musical instruments, if the translation "tambourines" is correct (Niditch 2008: 72). The narrative itself is rich in epic themes of battle in which the divine and human realms interact, warrior prowess is emphasized, and individual players such as Sisera and Jael provide important cameo scenes. Judges 5, moreover, presents this sort of imagery and content within formula patterns found elsewhere in the tradition.

The formula as defined by the great scholars of early and oral literatures, Albert B. Lord and his teacher Milman Parry, is a group of words used throughout a tradition or within one piece of traditional literature to convey a particular idea or image (see Lord 1968: 30). As Lord has noted, some formulas share the same words in a full-throated variety of repetition but equally important are recurring formula patterns whereby different terms that are equivalent place-holders fill out a shared and culturally recognizable syntactic and semantic pattern (p. 44). This process works especially well in ancient northwest Semitic works in which terms that are parallel in meaning are so important to the construction of bicola and tricola. Formula patterns allow for variation, flexibility, and creativity in the hands of a talented composer and evoke the process of extemporaneous composition. I have discussed at some length the formula pattern related to the description of epic heroes (tribe+location+tenting/dwelling) found in the catalog of warriors in Judg. 5:16–18 and elsewhere in the preserved tradition, e.g., Gen. 16:12; 49:13 (see Niditch 2015: 98). Another excellent example that points to the texture of traditional literature incorporated into the history of Israel is provided by formulaic language at Judg. 5:4–5, found also at Ps. 68:8–9 (Eng. 68:7–8). This formulaic description captures the essence of the divine warrior, marching forward to battle in an earth-transforming, storm-producing way. The examples from Judges 5 and Psalm 68 point to traditional variation within the parameters of formula patterns (e.g., the deity may be called "God" or "Yhwh," he may march from the "open country of Edom" or from the "wilderness") and to formulas that share precisely the same words. In terms of its formulaic texture, its content rich in epic motifs of battle and victory, and assumed bardic context, Judges 5 is thus rich in qualities of the oral traditional song.

Another recurring and important term associated with a traditional literary form that appears frequently in the Historical Books is the *māšāl*. The ethnic genre signaled by this term is rooted in the meaning "to compare" and is a kind of "oblique and artful communication that sets up an analogy between the communication (a saying, an icon, a narrative, a symbolic action, or another form) and the real-life setting of the listeners" or imagined listeners (Niditch 1993: 86). Often translated in English as proverbs, parables, or fables, *měšālîm* are found throughout the Historical Books.

Solomon's divinely inspired gifts as a leader include the capacity to compose *šîrîm* and to create *měšālîm* (1 Kgs. 5:12 [Eng. 4:32]), and notice that the verb *dbr*, "to speak" is used in connection with Solomon's composition of *šîrîm*. Placing of proverbs in the mouths of kings (1 Kgs. 20:11), the attribution of a parable to a disenfranchised prince (Josh. 9:7), or the use of a proverb as local observers' commentary on the first king, Saul (1 Sam. 10:11–12; 19:20–24) all point to writers' awareness of the cultural importance of this means of communication for messaging and portray their characters as employing *měšālîm*. As the controllers of their historical tales, these writers use the *māšāl* to project and shape worldview. Whether the term *māšāl* is used explicitly to describe the interaction as in the comments concerning Saul or the communication event is a *māšāl* by virtue of its content, structure, and context, as in the case of Jotham's tale about the trees (Judg. 9:7–15), the form is an integral component of narration, meaning, and message in the Historical Books, revealing of the authors' identity and the audience at whom they aim a particular version of the past.

Jotham's *māšāl* about the selection of a king for the trees, like the song in Judges 5, is described as oral performance. Jotham stands on the height of Mount Gerizim and "raises his voice and cries out" (Judg. 9:7). The parable of the trees is characterized by traditional style repetition in syntax: three plantings are offered kingship and refuse it as beneath them. Only the bramble accepts. The author conveys the message that the king is not a fruitful olive tree or vine or fig tree, but a "bramble," a worthless, troublesome plant who will nevertheless have power to punish and destroy the supposed cronies who appoint him if they display any sign of disloyalty. Parallels are thus made between Abimelech, the would-be king, and the bramble, underscoring the negative portrayal of this murderous son of Gideon who seeks kingly status illegitimately by killing his brothers, the seventy sons of Gideon (Judg. 9:16–21). More broadly, however, the parable may serve as an observation on the value of kingship itself, for Gideon, a hero judge of old, had refused this role when offered by the people (Judg. 8:22–23). The author may be anti-monarchic in his political orientation. At the very least he warns about the dangers of monarchic rule, aware that many kings have been political and moral failures in Israel. His use of this parable points to the way in which reciprocity and loyalty in this form of governance is fragile at best, as the subsequent course of events as narrated indicates (Judg. 9:22–55). The parable thus enables the composer to present a view of polity and history and identifies his or her orientation.

The inclusion of the *šîr* of Judges 5 and the *māšāl* of Judges 9 in the early history of Israel, as well as the use of *měšālîm* in portrayals of interactions between other characters in narration about the monarchy, raise questions about the nature of that history and about the orientation to the past found in Historical Books.

Even apart from definable genres and terminology associated with them, Israelite history-telling like that of so many pre-modern cultural traditions is highly anecdotal, formulaic in patterns of content, and characterized by various forms of repetition, the quintessential characteristic of traditional-style literature. In his discussion of epic and history, Foley describes such material as "traditional history" (2010: 349). The runner who comes from the battle to report its outcome to Eli evidences a predictable and recurring pattern of events, expressed in formulaic language, preserved in several places in the tradition (see Gunn 1974: 513–18). Action by the servants of the injured king Ahaziah, who seeks to locate the prophet Elijah in order to hear about his prospects for healing, is repeated three times (2 Kgs. 1:9–13), and the outcome the last time is underscored because of variation from the previous repetitions. What affect do these traditional forms have on receivers of the history, what attitude to history do they convey? This sort of historical narration may not trace the course of actual events regarding the progress of a battle with the Philistines and death of Eli's sons that mark the end of his leadership or regarding the death of Ahaziah. Nevertheless, these tales indicate what is important to their writers who are set in particular socio-historical settings. In the case of Eli, the traditional motif of the runner reinforces a message about the inevitability of a divinely sent prediction. The topos of the runner and his actions is not merely a means of conveying a war report, heightening drama as events race to their end, but underscores belief in Yhwh's control of all events. The recurring effort by Ahaziah to bring Elijah to him reinforces the latter's power and again the divinely controlled inevitability of the king's demise. History thus expressed is a rich culture-defining medium. Emphasizing narrative and political dimensions, Assyriologist Piotr Michalowski famously coined the phrase "history as charter" (1983), a concept emphasized as well by John Miles Foley (2010: 355–56) who also employs the language of charter. The very aesthetic of these traditional narrations is significant to consider in evaluating and interpreting the Historical Books. In this context, the ground-breaking work of Hayden White (1978; 1987) is most relevant.

26.3 HISTORY AND HISTORIOGRAPHY

Building on the work of R. G. Collingwood, White explores the narrative dimensions of history-telling, suggesting that the "authority of history" lies in "the authority of reality itself" and that "the historical account endows this reality with form and thereby makes it desirable by the imposition upon its processes of the formal coherency that only stories possess" (1987: 20). The story is critical and the interpretation of history that emerges in story is informed by plot structure, involving a particular aesthetic and emotive quality (White 1978: 67, 70, 72, 82); by a paradigm of explanation or a cognitive quality (pp. 67, 72); and by a moral or ideological, ethically engaged dimension (p. 67; see also Brettler 1998: 1–10, 18–19).

The Historical Books do cohere by means of a narrative arc, a plot-line that traces an evolution from the conquest to the judges to the early monarchy to the united monarchy, the monarchies of Israel and Judah, and the exile. The sweep of that history in and of itself is a source of self-definition and identity, reflecting and shaping Israel. Within that greater narrative arc however are numerous smaller stories, episodes, and scenes that have their own form and integrity. The aesthetic and emotive quality of each of these contributions will differ, as noted in the discussion of texture, narrative formulicity, and ethnic genre above. The traditional qualities of pieces such as Judges 5 and 9 are significant. Familiar, culturally shared forms and the formulaic language in which imagery and content take shape reflect and affect attitudes in and of themselves, by dint of those very forms, repetitions, and turns of phrase. Works such as Judges 5 and 9 now set in a broader history lead audiences to think about the culture and identity that they share. They offer a communal myth in the sense of value-laden, meaning-rich, recurring narrative. Judges 5, for example, a victory song with epic nuances, evokes ethnic pride, a sense of victory that not only informs views of the past but influences views of a future aided by God. These "emplotted" narrative pieces also relate to a larger paradigm for the interpretation of history. Throughout Joshua–2 Kings and into Ezra and Nehemiah is a view of the way history works.

Israelite historians explain patterns of events within the contours of the covenantal relationship with the deity Yhwh, a particular sort of paradigm. When Israel follows the ways of Yhwh (however that is precisely defined) they succeed and all goes well in international status, economic well-being, and political stability. When they fail to follow covenant by worshiping other deities or by engaging in various forms of inner Israelite ethical transgression, they are defeated in war, exiled, and suffer drought, plague, and deprivation. Importantly, however, the works that contribute to a bigger plot, the larger arc of Israelite history, and that share an important paradigm explaining why history goes a certain way, admit of different and sometimes conflicting ideologies. Indeed these seeming discrepancies in attitudes regarding the monarchy or the centralization of ritual in Jerusalem reveal debates and tensions that are characteristic of ancient Israelite culture and essential to understanding it historically. In this sense, the very process of redaction or harmonization is extremely revealing if we seek to understand the Israelites' concerns. The tensions are not always resolved. The Chronicler neatly edits somewhat in the style of modern authors or propagandists to emphasize David's nobility and the people's devotion to the temple, revealing the Chronicler's own goals, orientation, and cultural setting, but the Deuteronomic Historian retains bumpy contradictions and rough edges thereby allowing readers to appreciate the debates about king and temple that are critical to understanding Israelite social and cultural history.

As noted above, Judges 9 serves as a warning about kings and to some extent this ambivalence about the benefits and legitimacy of monarchy carries through tales of the kings to follow. On the other hand, some (but not all) tales of David unabashedly glorify the kingly role. In this category is the tale of the dragon-slayer pattern whereby the lad David, a youngest son and inexperienced warrior, defeats the well-armed, formidable enemy leader Goliath (1 Samuel 16). The combat, a cameo scene in the larger war, has the combatants taunt one another in traditional style ("Am I a dog that you come to me with sticks" [1 Sam. 16:43]). David's defeat of Goliath proves him worthy of kingship, and the tale of his first victory provides propaganda in defense of the institution of the monarchy itself in which the talented and worthy rise to the top, divinely chosen. Other contributors to this volume will discuss the pro-Davidic tendenz of the extant biblical history of the northern and southern kings and questions concerning sources, verisimilitude, and possible origins of the underlying paradigm, mentioned above, in conservative northern circles. What I emphasize is the revealing tensions in the material while noting—to reprise language of Hayden White—that the story-line, the paradigm, and these various ideologies as expressed reveal the appreciation of traditional speech and modes of expression.

And yet it should come as no surprise, given that all this material is preserved and handed down in writing, that the written medium is also a self-confessed, self-consciously important tool in the construction and transmission of history and the cultural identity that it informs. It is to references to writing (the use of *ktb*, "to write," the related *miktab* "letter," and *sēper* "document" or "scroll") that we turn and to various questions concerning the relationships between oral and written media. How are writing and orality pictured as interacting in biblical accounts of Israelite and Judean history? Can one posit developments in attitudes to the oral and the written or writers who emphasize one mode of communication rather than the other? Do these modes of communication relate to trends in intellectual history that affect the imagining of history itself? What is the significance of receiving an edited, multi-layered, anthological composition prepared by scribes for the creation of and attitudes towards a national history?

26.4 References to Writing and Interplay with the Oral

The interplay between the written and the oral is pervasive in the Hebrew Scriptures. In Deuteronomy 31–32, for example, the people are commanded to "write down" this *šîr*, a performative genre, to "teach it," and "to put it in their mouths" (Deut. 31:19; see also Exod. 17:14). Moses "writes" the song at Deuteronomy 31:22 but "recites" it at 31:30 and 32:44. Brian Britt points to the alternation in Deuteronomy 31–34 between prophetic speech acts/events and texts "to be written, recited, and learned" as they relate to the portrayal of Moses (2004: 173). Clearly the preserved tradition reflects a belief in the importance and value of oral sharing and recitation but also a respect for writing down, archiving, and preserving (see also Num. 21:14). Reference to such interplay is found as well in the Historical Books. Indeed 1 and 2 Chronicles not only make reference to "songs" but also to the training of singers as official participants in the institutional temple apparatus, linked to the scribal culture itself (1 Chr. 6:16; 15:16; 25:7). The tradition is richly characterized by references to oral and written modes, but the case can be made that the biblical writers who get the last word portray the "later" period as using more writing, more reliant on writing.

References to communications written down on monuments or upon documents (terminology of *ktb* and *sēper*) are common in the Hebrew Bible as a whole, juxtaposed with texts said to be "song" or characteristic in style and content of oral-traditional media (e.g., Exod. 17:14; 24:7; 39:30; Num. 21:14; 5:23). The tales of the early chieftain leaders of the people in Joshua and Judges, as well as tales of the early monarchy, similarly include references to documents and often juxtapose references to writing with images of oral recitation or media: (1) monumental writing by Joshua (Josh. 8:32; see also 24:26–27) concerning words written in the book or document of the torah of God (24:26) and the stone as witness who "heard" all that the deity had said (24:27); (2) the writing down of a list of the elders of Succoth for Gideon (Judg. 8:14); (3) Samuel's oral declaration concerning the role of the king and his writing it down in a document (1 Sam. 10:25); (4) reference to a composition that seems to be entitled "The Bow" (2 Sam. 1:18), a lament over Jonathan and Saul attributed to David, orally taught and performed, and yet said to be preserved in the

Book of Yashar (see also 2 Chr. 35:25 discussed below); (5) David's sending of a lettre caché in a battle context to dispose of Uriah, his lover's husband (2 Sam. 11:14, 15). I mention these examples from Joshua, Judges, 1 and 2 Samuel because in part what interests me, allowing for complexities of date, authorship, and redaction history of the material, is the way in which ancient historiographers who got the last word portray early times preceding the supposed advent of a full bureaucracy versus the subsequent situation. The ancient historiographers whose work is preserved in the Hebrew Bible portray changes in attitudes to writing over the course of Israelite and Judean political history as they tell of the united monarchy, the two kingdoms, and the periods following the conquests by Assyria, Babylonia, and especially Persia.

26.5 Records, Archives, Letters, and Momigliano

References to archives, records, and letters are more numerous in the ancient historiographers' portrayal of the full-blown monarchies both in 1 and 2 Kings and in 1 and 2 Chronicles, especially in comparison to tales of the chieftain leaders in Judges, a work that has only one reference to writing in a battle context (Judg. 8:14). The books of 1 and 2 Kings include frequent use of the tag "the rest of the acts of so and so are written in the books of the acts (or chronicles) of the kings of Judah (or the kings Israel)" (e.g., 1 Kgs. 11:41 [Book of the Acts of Solomon]; 15:7, 23, 31; 16:5, 14, 20, 27; 22:46; 2 Kgs. 8:23; 12:20; 15:11). The implication is that written records are kept, the trusted historiographer has had access to these reliable sources concerning Northern and Southern Kingdoms, the history he has recounted is backed up by their existence, and the bureaucracy is in order.

Relevant in this context is the tale about the finding of a written document of the law during the reign of Josiah (2 Kgs. 22:8–20). It surfaces during repairs to the temple under this reforming king. The implication is that written archives were preserved as in other neighboring cultures, but that this document had been lost. The contents of the document are read out loud to the king and relate to a divine message, as confirmed by the prophet Huldah (2 Kgs. 22:15–20). Once again, oral and written sensibilities intertwine. This interplay between written and oral sensibilities is emphasized as well in the Persian period ritual scenes of Nehemiah 8 featuring the scribe leader Ezra and his Levite assistants who translate a written torah out loud and find within the text a reminder about celebration of the festival of booths. The written is shared orally and a written text is thus justification for ritual action (Niditch 1996: 106).

Like the Deuteronomic History, Chronicles makes reference to archives but with some interesting nuances. The books of 1 and 2 Chronicles suggest, for example, that there existed a book of the kings of Israel *and* Judah, a seemingly somewhat more encyclopedic collection including the records of north and south, gathering together northern and southern traditions (see, e.g., 2 Chr. 16:11; 27:7; 28:26; 35:27; 36:8), a holistic view which suits the worldview of the Chronicler (see Newsome 1975; Japhet 1989). The Chronicler also makes reference to collections not mentioned in deuteronomic texts: written collections of the prophetic words of the figures Samuel the "seer," Nathan the "prophet," and Gad the "visionary" (1 Chr. 29:29), of the prophet Shemiah and the visionary Iddo (2 Chr. 12:15); the midrash (commentary, study, exposition) of the prophet Iddo (2 Chr. 13:22); and an intriguing reference to the midrash or commentary on the book of the kings (2 Chr. 24:27).

While one would not want to impose later Rabbinic meanings of midrash onto texts from Chronicles, nevertheless, the terminology of midrash suggests an exposition on a set, even canonical, collection of material that elaborates upon it or literally searches further into it. Such exposition or commentary may also sit on the border of re-oralization and intertextuality, suggesting issues in written and oral media discussed above that involve the interplay between the two communicative modalities from stylistic and process-related perspectives. Midrash is a derivative genre related both to oral composition and to scribalism.

The lament for Josiah produced by male and female singers is also said to be written down in a collection called "The Laments." (2 Chr. 35:25). It is important to emphasize that the author of 1 and 2 Chronicles does appear to re-use, edit, and add to a set tradition preserved in the Deuteronomic History. The precise parallels between shared material seem to suggest that the Chronicler did have available an earlier set and written or memorized tradition (Niditch 1996: 127–29; contrast Person 2010: 18, 84, 159–61). And so several ideas emerge from a consideration of oral-traditionality and scribalism as these categories relate to an appreciation of the Historical Books. Authors do portray the courts of Israel and Judah, as well as postexilic forms of leadership, as employing writing in various ways, but writing always intertwines with the oral as for example when texts are read out loud. On the other hand, the Persian-period works of the Chronicler, Ezra-Nehemiah, and Esther seem to extend and deepen such references to and interests in written sensibilities.

In one of his many seminal lectures, Arnaldo Momigliano suggests that both postexilic historiography found in the Hebrew Bible and Greek historiography of the fifth century BCE reveal "similar reactions to the common background of the Persian period" (1977: 26). Momigliano points to various phenomena that characterize this Persian- influenced historiography: (1) the use of "narrative in the first person" (pp. 27–28); (2) the use of letters; and (3) references to documents and archives (p. 31). This style of historiography "reflect(s) conditions of a political organization in which documents had assumed particular importance" and importantly this is true even if the letters quoted are not genuine and the archives fictional (p. 32).

Particularly striking in Persian-period historical works is the use of letters. To be sure, archaeologists have unearthed material evidence of actual official correspondence, for example the Arad letters—twenty-one documents on ostraca that date to the early sixth century BCE—and the Lachish letters—texts that deal primarily with military matters and that date to the period before the Babylonian destruction of 587/586 BCE (see Niditch 1996: 52). Dennis Pardee (1982) takes note of the formulaic quality of these letters, touching upon the border shared by the oral and the written. Pardee also suggests that many earlier letters may have been lost and that the small number preserved has to do with the staying power of the material on which they were written. Ostraca survive whereas papyri disintegrate in the climates of Israel and Judah and so, Pardee argues, many examples from the period of the monarchy have been lost.

In assessing the written preserved corpus of the Hebrew Bible it is important to note that, as Momigliano suggests, Persian-period literature seems to make more reference to written correspondence than earlier corpora. We have already alluded to references in 1 and 2 Chronicles to apparent collections of material and such references are significant whether or not the corpora existed, for such references in the historiographic narrative point to assumptions about archives, kept and available to later historians. The Chronicler also includes references to the use of written communication, not found in the comparable location in the Deuteronomic History: a letter to King Jehoram from the prophet Elijah (2 Chr. 21:12); a reference to written directives prepared by David and Solomon (2 Chr. 35:4); and Hezekiah's letter to the northern Israelites of Ephraim and Manasseh concerning a pilgrimage to the temple in Jerusalem for Passover (2 Chr. 30:1, 6).

All of these passages suggest that the written message has lasting power, a communiqué, for example, from the great first kings of Israel that is available for consultation and to reinforce behavior by Josiah centuries later (2 Chr. 35:4). Jeremiah's sending of a scroll whose message survives the burning of the scroll by the angry king Jehoiakim who rejects its words of condemnation and doom seems to valorize the power of the oral and the secondary nature of written messages (see Niditch 1996: 104–105). Elijah's letter to Jehoram qua letter, however, has enormous power and seems to denote the status of its prophetic sender, his wisdom and leadership, and the seriousness of the message. The power of written words to help bring about what they predict is on the other hand rooted in a world of incantations and material religion and speaks to the perceived power of the written in an essentially oral world where ordinary people do not have easy access to complex communication in writing. As Momigliano suggests, however, the Persian-period work of the Chronicler does allude to written communication employed by the elites for important communicative purposes. Similarly, Hezekiah's letter portrays a kingdom in which the central government makes use of couriers. Written letters are a means of unifying or attempting to unify northern and southern portions of the Israelite community, a way in which monarchs communicate to their subjects or would-be subjects. No such letter sending is found in the deuteronomistic account of Josiah's similar effort to centralize Passover worship and perhaps speaks to the sensibilities of the Persian period as opposed to attitudes of writers of a few centuries earlier, depending upon our dating of 1 Kgs. 23:21–23. The reference to Hezekiah's letter, in fact, uses vocabulary for "letter" found frequently in late biblical material: 'igeret, a term found also in Neh. 2:7, 8, 9; 6:5, 17, 18. This term for letter appears as well in Esth. 9:26, 29.

Also important to mention is the reference in 2 Chr. 36:22–23 to a written edict from Cyrus allowing for the rebuilding of the temple, found also in Ezra 1:2–4. Notice that the written edict is delivered by a herald, information again on the border of oral and written communication. This evidence does not allow one to pass judgment on the historicity of the particular written edict as depicted, as if the authors had an actual text before their eyes or committed to memory, but indicates that the historiographer believes that Persian monarchs produced edicts that sound like what is here written. As Piotr Michalowski has written about the Sumerian king list, it is "not a reflection of real events but is, rather, a depiction of an *idea* of reality" (1983: 243). Given that the return happens, an edict permitting it must have been written and would have been framed this way.

The presence of letters and references to written sources is a matter of worldview and modes of doing historiography. Written media and means of communication are overtly valorized in portrayals of the monarchies. The elites of the court are expected to use letters and to consult and create archival material. Inclusion of references to such written media suggests that doing historiography involves their use and access to such media. The authors of the Historical Books in fact suggest a transition in respect to writing between portrayals of the period of the judges in the biblical book of Judges to the period of the monarchy. In Judges, the verb "to write" appears only once when the chieftain Gideon asks a young man to jot down a list of officials and elders whom he will later punish, a passage that I believe has been misunderstood as an example of literacy on the part of the young and untutored at an early period in Israel. Those who have the final word in producing the arc of narration that runs from Joshua through 2 Kings do, however, picture kings producing archives or records. The authors of later historiographic texts from the Persian period, who produced 1 and 2 Chronicles, Ezra, and Nehemiah (and we might include the tale of Esther in this context) are even more fulsome in their portrayal of the ways in which writing is used to communicate by the elites, whether prophets or especially rulers and their bureaucracy.

I write in terms of portrayals, for the interplay between oral and written, the appreciation for variants, and the respect for the power of the oral world continues even to the close of the biblical period, as does evidence of the interplay of the two media. Folk forms such as proverbs, the presence of repetition and variation, traits of oral-traditional style, allusions to writing on monuments, references to the writing down of songs/epics are all found both in portrayals of early and later history. The paradigm of blessing and judgment unifies the whole, while ideological tensions, debates, and implicit anxieties about essential historical issues involving polity, group identity, and other matters remain perhaps purposefully unresolved and unharmonized, at least in deuteronomistic material. In these tensions are critical revelations about Israelite social history, about the matters that concern historiographers. They wrestle with providing a governing, unifying, self-defining mythology while allowing for difference and change. In this sense, the Historical Books offer genuine reflection on Israelite history. If, however, one asks how the various contributors to the tradition view the use of writing in history and so portray it, and what impression is created by the redacted whole, the conclusion is that biblical historiographers do show increasing emphasis on scribalism and place more fully oral worlds in the "past." Of course, the most oral-traditional of biblical texts ultimately have been preserved by scribal elites, and we need to acknowledge that the supposed products of these elites such as archives, letters, or decrees are all creatively imagined or assumed by the writers whether or not they actually existed as described.

Bibliography

Brettler, Marc Zvi. 1998. *The Creation of History in Ancient Israel*. New York: Routledge.
Britt, Brian. 2004. *Rewriting Moses: The Narrative Eclipse of the Text*. JSOTSup 402. London and New York: T&T Clark.
Cross, Frank Moore. 1998. *From Epic to Canon: History and Literature in Ancient Israel*. Baltimore: Johns Hopkins University Press.
Dorson, Richard M. 1964. "Oral Tradition and Written History." *Journal of the Folklore Institute* 1: 220–34.
Foley, John Miles. 2010. "Traditional History in South Slavic Oral Epic." In David Konstan and Kurt A. Raaflaub, eds., *Epic and History*. Chichester: Wiley-Blackwell, 347–61.

Friedlander, Peter. 2015. "Kabīr: Oral to Manuscript Transitions." *Oral Tradition* 29: 187–202.
Gunn, David. 1974. "'The Battle Report': Oral or Scribal Convention?" *JBL* 93: 513–18.
Japhet, Sara. 1989. *The Ideology of the Book of Chronicles and Its Place in Biblical Thought*. Frankfort am Main: Peter Lang.
Lord, A. B. 1968. *The Singer of Tales*. New York: Atheneum.
Michalowski, Piotr. 1983. "History as Charter: Some Observations on the Sumerian King List." *JAOS* 103: 237–48.
Momigliano, Arnaldo. 1977. *Essays in Ancient and Modern Historiography*. Middletown, CT: Wesleyan University Press.
Mowinckel, Sigmund. 1935. "Hat es ein israelitisches Nationalepos gegeben?" *ZAW* 53: 130–52.
Newsome, J. D. 1975. "Toward an Understanding of the Chronicler and His Purposes." *JBL* 94: 201–17.
Niditch, Susan. 1993. *Folklore and the Hebrew Bible*. Minneapolis: Fortress Press.
Niditch, Susan. 1996. *Oral World and Written Word: Ancient Israelite Literature*. Louisville, KY: Westminster John Knox Press.
Niditch, Susan. 2005. "The Challenge of Israelite Epic." In John Miles Foley, ed., *A Companion to Ancient Epic*. Oxford: Blackwell, 277–87.
Niditch, Susan. 2008. *Judges: A Commentary*. OTL. Louisville, KY: Westminster John Knox Press.
Niditch, Susan. 2015. "Folklore and Israelite Tradition: Appreciation and Application." In Susan Niditch, ed., *The Wiley Blackwell Companion to Ancient Israel*. Chichester: Wiley Blackwell, 87–102.
Pardee, Dennis. 1982. *Handbook of Ancient Hebrew Letters*. SBL Sources for Biblical Study 15. Chico, CA: Scholars Press.
Person, Raymond. 2010. *The Deuteronomic History and the Book of Chronicles: Scribal Works in an Oral World*. SBL AIL 6. Atlanta: SBL.
Person, Raymond. 2016. "Biblical Historiography as Traditional History." In Danna Nolan Fewell, ed., *Oxford Handbook of Biblical Narrative*. Oxford: Oxford University Press, 73–83.
Polak, Frank H. 1998. "The Oral of the Written: Syntax, Stylistics and the Development of Biblical Prose Narrative." *JANES* 26: 59–105.
Schmidt, Brian B., ed. 2015. *Contextualizing Israel's Sacred Writings: Ancient Literacy, Orality, and Literary Production*. SBL AIL 22. Atlanta: SBL.
Vansina, Jan. 1971. "Once Upon a Time: Oral Traditions as History in Africa." *Daedalus* 100: 442–68.
White, Hayden. 1978. *Tropics of Discourse: Essays in Cultural Criticism*. Baltimore and London: Johns Hopkins Press.
White, Hayden. 1987. *The Content of the Form: Narrative Discourse and Historical Representation*. Baltimore and London: Johns Hopkins.
Woolf, D. R. 1988. "The Common Voice: History, Folklore, and Oral Tradition in Early Modern England." *Past and Present* 120: 26–52.

CHAPTER 27

FEMINIST AND POSTCOLONIAL READINGS OF THE HISTORICAL BOOKS

CAMERON B. R. HOWARD

27.1 THE DESTABILIZING POWER OF FOREIGN WOMEN IN JOSHUA AND KINGS

FEMINIST and postcolonial approaches to the study of the Hebrew Bible share commitments to amplifying the voices of the marginalized, both within the text of the Bible and among its readership. They unmask structures of power lurking in biblical texts and in the dominant interpretations of those texts, and they identify ways the Bible has been used to justify, perpetuate, or resist oppression throughout history, from the biblical era into the modern world.

The Historical Books of the Hebrew Bible provide provocative material for critics bearing these commitments. Parts of the book of Joshua depict the Israelites as a deadly colonizing force conquering the land of Canaan. Violence against women, most graphically portrayed in the rape and dismemberment of the Levite's concubine in Judges 19, serves as indicator of ever-increasing social depravity in the pre-monarchic era. David's seizure of Bathsheba and orchestration of Uriah's death in the book of Samuel illustrate the appetites of kings and their particular dangers for women. In the book of Kings, Solomon is praised for his international political savvy, yet criticized for his many marriages to non-Israelites. In the restoration era depicted in Ezra-Nehemiah, questions of how to maintain Judean identity under Persian imperial rule come to a head in the issue of intermarriage with foreign women, which is deemed such a threat to post-exilic Judean society that men are forced to send away their wives and children of foreign descent. The book of Chronicles is conspicuous in its focus inward on Israel and the nearly non-existent references to women. Christine Mitchell has shown how Chronicles "overwrites, effaces, and erases women," even in its presentation of procreation and birth (Mitchell 2012: 184–91; citation from 186).

Shadows of these difficult texts continue to loom over the modern era. European colonizers of the Americas likened themselves to ancient Israel, entering a new Promised Land and claiming a divine mandate to possess it.[1] "Jezebel," the name of the infamous wife of King Ahab of Israel (1 Kgs. 16:31), has become an epithet in popular culture to imply a woman is devious, manipulative, and sexually promiscuous.[2] In some communities, control over women and even violence against them find justification in biblical texts (Seibert 2012).

Within both feminist and postcolonial scholarship, critics differ about whether these texts can ever be "recovered" or "rehabilitated" for liberation, theologically or otherwise. There is certainly a strong interpretive tradition throughout history that draws on the Bible as a source of resistance to oppression. Postcolonial biblical scholarship's emphasis on "vernacular hermeneutics," including contextual (and often non-"academic") readings from indigenous communities and the developing world, has been particularly helpful in highlighting these redeployments of the Bible as a tool for liberation.[3] Even so, a "hermeneutics of suspicion" reigns for both deconstructive and reconstructive projects in much of both postcolonial and feminist biblical criticism, pushing back against centuries of interpretation that have exploited the Bible to rule over others.

Feminist and postcolonial readings of the Historical Books coalesce particularly starkly in the trope of the "foreign woman," which runs like Rahab's crimson cord through this portion of the Hebrew Bible canon. At once desired and reviled, seductive yet dangerous, foreign women are associated with foreign gods, and they are blamed for introducing those deities to Israelite men, turning their loyalties away from exclusive worship of Yhwh, the God of Israel. Each of the Historical Books exhibits, in its own way, anxiety about foreign women. Though sometimes foreignness is generalized as simply not-Israelite, the Historical Books are especially concerned with women from the peoples in and around Canaan. These are nations named in the book of Deuteronomy as those with whom marriage is forbidden when the Israelites cross into the Promised Land:

> When the LORD your God brings you into the land that you are about to enter and occupy, and he clears away many nations before you—the Hittites, the Girgashites, the Amorites, the Canaanites, the Perizzites, the Hivites, and the Jebusites, seven nations mightier and more numerous than you—and when the LORD your God gives them over to you and you defeat them, then you must utterly destroy them. Make no covenant with them and show them no mercy. Do not intermarry with them, giving your daughters to their sons or taking their daughters for your sons, for that would turn away your children from following me, to serve other gods. Then the anger of the LORD would be kindled against you, and he would destroy you quickly. (Deut. 7:1–4, NRSV)

In fact, the texts' preoccupation with the dangers of foreign women may be yet another important datum in the argument that the books of Joshua, Judges, Samuel, and Kings comprise a "Deuteronomistic History" that shares the theological concerns of the book of Deuteronomy. There are certainly close echoes of the Deuteronomic prohibition across the four subsequent texts. Yet through the lenses of feminism and postcolonialism, this thematic overlap must be regarded not only as a stylistic choice or indicator of shared authorship, but also as a persistent and consequential ideological orientation.

After introducing some of the orienting questions of feminist and postcolonial approaches, I will suggest some possibilities for using these approaches to understand the trope of the foreign woman in two of the Historical Books: Joshua and Kings. These two books recount Israel's pre-monarchic and monarchic eras, respectively; yet, like all of the Historical Books of the Hebrew Bible, they were produced in the exilic or postexilic era, when Israel labored under foreign rule, first by the Babylonians and then by the Persians (Römer 2007). In this way, the books bear traces of ancient Israel as both colonizer and colonized—the force behind a conquest, yet also a people who experience exile and occupation. As Steed Davidson notes, "To the extent that we agree that the Hebrew Bible stands as a product of empire while also being produced in the midst of empire, then the seemingly contradictory discourses of imperialism and anti-imperialism will emerge in the same text, and vexingly so, at the wrong times and places" (Davidson 2013: 69). Most urgent for this essay is the fact that all of the Historical Books of the Hebrew Bible share a broadly "imperial" background, thus making them especially open to postcolonial investigation. The nature and direction of that imperialism are precisely the kinds of questions this essay will begin to explore.

The goal of this essay is not to suggest one particular, "correct" reading; in fact, both feminist and postcolonial critics push readers to think expansively about the possibilities of meaning for any text, showing how claims to any one, "right" reading have often fueled the oppression of those against whom the reading is used. Nor should postcolonialism or feminism be considered "methods" for reading biblical texts; instead, they are ideologically oriented "approaches" or "criticisms" that can exercise multiple methods, including the tools of literary theory, narratology, historical analysis, and the social sciences.[4] Though not unconcerned with questions of redaction, many feminist readings make primary use of narratological and other synchronically oriented methods. Historical-critical questions about the Historical Books can be of particular import for postcolonial readings, which are interested in how texts intersect with specific political realities. Sociological analysis has proved particularly useful for both postcolonial and feminist priorities, since that mode of inquiry engages systems of oppression and often falls at the intersection of literary and historical issues. The readings of biblical texts in the present essay are primarily synchronic, driven by literary methods, but also engage historical-critical and sociological insights as appropriate.

27.2 Feminist Approaches

Feminist criticism of biblical texts is often described as an "identity-based" approach; that is, it recognizes that every interpreter reads from a particular social location, and it reads through the lens of women's experiences. In this regard feminist criticism has been instrumental in dismantling the assumption that there is a scientific, purely objective way of reading the Bible, pointing out instead that appeals to objectivity often assume a male reader as the norm. Not every interpretation by a woman is necessarily a feminist reading, and not every feminist reading must be conducted by a woman. Nevertheless, feminist biblical scholarship attends to the experiences of women as literary characters, as historical figures, and as readers of the Bible.

Feminist readings have brought to the fore the Bible's female characters and voices—both where they are present and where they are absent. For the Historical Books, this has meant focusing on women like Rahab, Debra, Tamar, Bathsheba, and Jezebel, whose stories figure prominently in Joshua-Kings. Women who remain unnamed in the narratives, such as the Levite's concubine (Judges 19) or the widow at Zarephath (1 Kings 17), have also received sustained attention. A focus on the Bible's female characters has necessarily highlighted the prevalence of violence against women—and particularly sexual violence against women—in its stories. In addition to engaging the experiences of individual women, feminist criticism also identifies social structures that perpetuate the subjugation of women, giving particular attention to the ways that the Bible both reflects ancient patriarchal systems and has been used to promote patriarchy in the modern world. The related fields of gender studies, queer theory, and masculinity studies continue to challenge feminist readers to consider the implications of gender performance beyond a strict male-female binary.

Feminist scholarship has also opened up new avenues of inquiry into Israelite life at the level of the household. Whereas much of the content of the Historical Books focuses on public spaces within ancient Israel, Israel's largely male leadership, and its macro-history, feminist approaches have turned to the spaces where women's presence would have been more regular and their authority more pronounced. At the same time, in its assertion that imperial structures influence every aspect of life in a colonized region, postcolonial theory is nudging feminist criticism to "zoom out," bringing renewed attention to the ways these "private" and "public"—or "macro" and "micro"—spheres affect each other in more nuanced ways, particularly through power structures mediated by ethnic and class differences.[5]

Like the broader first- and second-wave feminist movements, the enterprise of feminist biblical scholarship has been criticized for assuming that women's experience is monolithic. As Gale Yee writes, "Privileging gender blinds one to the fact that sexism interlocks with other social forms of oppression and exploitation, which are then encoded in the biblical text" (Yee 2003: 7; cf. Dube 2000: 111–12). Like womanist, mujerista, and Asian-feminist approaches, postcolonial criticism has highlighted the ways in which race, ethnicity, and class intersect with gender identity to shape all women's experiences, and therefore also their readings of the Bible. Musa Dube, whose work has been instrumental in charting the intersections of feminist and postcolonial biblical scholarship, points out that in its monodimensional advocacy based on Western women's experiences, feminism has colluded with the forces of imperialism: "The failure of Western feminists to recognize and to subvert imperialist cultural strategies of subjugation means that their advocacy for women's liberation has firmly retained the right of the West to dominate and exploit non-Western nations" (Dube 2000: 26). Dube cautions against the temptation to substitute "patriarchy" as a catch-all term for oppression, when imperialism and patriarchy work together to "doubly colonize" many women (Dube 2000: 111ff.).

At the same time, the nationalistic decolonizing movements of the twentieth century were often themselves highly gender-exclusive programs: "the new postcolonial nation is historically a male-constructed space, narrated into modern self-consciousness by male leaders, activists and writers, in which women are more often than not cast as symbols or totems, as the bearers of tradition" (Boehmer 2005: 22). Visions of national liberation have normed the male postcolonial subject and ignored the particular ways women act in and experience both imperialism and decolonization. Thus, feminism and postcolonialism offer constructive challenges to each other, working toward critical perspectives that recognize the intersections of identities, the multivalence of oppression, and the social and political systems that perpetuate injustice. Ultimately, however, they share deep connections. R. S. Sugirtharajah, a prominent and pioneering voice in postcolonial biblical scholarship, describes these connections: "What unites feminist and postcolonial critique is their mutual resistance to any form of oppression—be it patriarchy or colonialism. In their strategies of resistance, both feminist and postcolonial critics are of one accord. They seek to uncover subjugation of both men and women in colonial texts, and the modes of resistance of the subjugated, and expose the use of gender in both colonial discourse and social reality" (2002: 28–29).

27.3 Postcolonial Approaches

Like feminist criticism, postcolonialism also has its roots in identity-based critique. Postcolonial studies as a discipline in the Western academy arose out of the global twentieth-century movement of decolonization. As former colonies of European nations began to achieve independence, the voices of novelists, poets, and critics from those colonized nations became amplified "as creative literature and as a resistance discourse" (Sugirtharajah 2002: 11). Postcolonial studies then grew to become a broad-based critical approach. Like feminist theory, postcolonial studies were initially concentrated in the field of literary criticism and were subsequently deployed by biblical scholars.

At the heart of postcolonial theory is the assertion that the political power structure of empire affects all areas of life for both colonizer and colonized, include all cultural output. Sustaining every empire is the organizational principle of "extraction": the central imperial power extracts natural, economic, and human resources from its peripheral territories, using those resources to maintain its power and perpetuate its growth.[6] Traditionally an "empire" has been understood as a nation-state that expands its territory and influence via military force, using violence or the threat of violence as the primary means of growing and maintaining its power. As European colonial projects of the modern era have dissolved, however, critics have pointed to other ways that "empire" manifests itself today, including the influence of multinational corporations and other global economic forces.

Postcolonial theory has given rise to a host of new and re-purposed terms that characterize its discourse, such as mimicry, ambivalence, hybridity, subaltern, decolonization, and nationalism, to name only a few key ideas.[7] However, because postcolonial theory usually takes as its starting point the circumstances of modern European colonialism, biblical scholars attempting to deploy the concepts of postcolonial theory to analyze biblical texts and the ancient world run into some significant incongruities, despite the generalizability that the word "theory" might imply. For example, the ruling strategies of the British Empire, which provide an historical touchstone for many postcolonial theorists, differed strikingly from those of the ancient Near Eastern empires. The British Empire considered British culture the height of civilization, and part of its imperial program was an attempt to impose British practices—from worshiping the Christian God to taking afternoon tea—as a "civilizing" influence on the nations it conquered. Bhabha calls this phenomenon "mimicry," but notes that mimicry is always characterized by "ambivalence," the way in which the colonized is "almost the same, but not quite" (2004: 122). In other words, the colonized subjects could never *really* be British, never be the same as the colonizer, even though the colonizer also wanted to make the colonized in his own image. After all, full realization of the British identity might mean assuming the role of conqueror, or desiring British freedoms, which would then undermine the very project of British imperialism.

This kind of historical mimicry—assimilating colonized subjects into an "almost-the-same-but-not-quite" identification with the colonizer—was never a noticeable part of ancient imperial strategy in the biblical era, and so analogous representational strategies in biblical literature are more difficult to pinpoint. The Persian Empire, for example, which ruled Judah during the production of many of the Hebrew Bible's texts, encouraged the imperially supervised flourishing of local culture and religion, a strategy that both won "hearts and minds" and facilitated the establishment and oversight of economic centers for well-organized extraction of taxes and tribute. On the level of historical analysis, then, "mimicry" does not always translate easily into biblical studies. Scholars must be attuned to both the possibilities and the limitations of using modern theory's most popular categories. At the same time, precisely because of the differences, postcolonial theory can move biblical studies in previously unimagined directions. Postcolonialism has become a particularly vital critical lens for the history of interpretation. Colonial expectations have often been reproduced by Western scholars in their readings of biblical texts. Biblical interpretations, like the biblical texts themselves, are cultural products of imperial contexts and should themselves be analyzed with a postcolonial approach.

Postcolonial theory makes frequent use of the dichotomy of colonizer versus colonized. The prevalence of these organizing categories raises the question: does ancient Israel represent an example of colonizer or colonized? From an historical, geo-political perspective, the answer must be *colonized*. By the time Israel was established as a dynastic entity, it was beholden to tribute relationships with the larger imperial entities surrounding it, including Egypt and Assyria. Even at the height of the period of monarchic rule, ancient Israel was never itself a sprawling empire like its neighbors. The fall of Samaria to the neo-Assyrian Empire, and the subsequent fall of Jerusalem to Babylon, mark specific moments in which Israel and Judah lost control of their kingdoms, so that both land and governance were controlled by foreign powers. Even with the repatriation of Judean exiles under the Persian Empire, control of Judah and its people still remained with the Persian kings and his satrapal appointees. When the defeat of Persia by Alexander ushered in the Hellenistic age, power simply transferred from one imperial entity to another.

While the historical record paints Israel in the role of the colonized, many textual representations give a very different picture. In the conquest of Canaan described in the book of Joshua, Israel enters the land "to take possession of the land that the LORD your God gives you to possess" (Josh. 1:11 NRSV). In many cases this taking possession is done by warfare, including the "devotion to destruction" (or "ban"; Hebrew: *herem*) of everything—living and non-living, captors and treasure—in the defeated city. For example, after the city of Jericho falls, "Then they devoted to destruction by the edge of the sword all in the city, both men and women, young and old, oxen, sheep, and donkeys" (Josh. 6:21). Entrance into the land is accompanied by annihilation of its indigenous peoples; ancient Israel is depicted as a ruthless—and successful—colonizer.

In the ongoing narrative of the Enneateuch, the conquest account is the culmination of the liberation of the Hebrews from slavery in Egypt; having been freed from Pharaoh's servitude, they are empowered by God to take possession of Canaan and establish their own society there. In the course of forty years within the arc of the story, the Hebrews are transformed from a downtrodden group of refugees miraculously escaping oppression to a formidable fighting force invading and occupying an inhabited land. The subjects of the Egyptian empire become colonizers themselves.[8] Robert Allen Warrior has argued that the exodus event, the central narrative of liberation and the defeat of oppression in the Hebrew Bible, must not be interpreted separately from the subsequent conquest narrative, which calls for the annihilation of the indigenuous Canaanites: "Yahweh the deliverer became Yahweh the conqueror" (Warrior 1991: 289).

Although the narrative itself may be compelling, the descriptions of the conquest offered in Joshua do not align with the ancient historical reality. Archaeological evidence suggests that the Israelites emerged gradually as a distinct people among the Canaanites, rather than entering the land all at once as a foreign invading force. Even the biblical text itself offers up an alternative view of the conquest's aftermath. Joshua 11:16 asserts, "So Joshua took this whole land: the highlands, the whole arid southern plain, the whole land of Goshen, the lowlands, the desert plain, and both the highlands and the lowlands of Israel" (CEB). Yet already at Josh. 13:1, the extent of the conquest is contradicted: "Now Joshua had reached old age. The LORD said to him, 'You have reached old age, but much of the land remains to be taken over'" (CEB). Similarly, Judges 1 describes a host of peoples who were not totally driven out of the land. L. Daniel Hawk argues that the stories of indigenous survivors interwoven with the battle narratives in Joshua provide a counterpoint to the book's dominant narrative of exclusion (Hawk 2012). What could explain the discrepancy between the text's striking account of imperial victory and the subsequent textual details—as well as historical reality—that undercut it?

Further complicating the postcolonial analysis of biblical texts is the discrepancy between the eras they depict and the possible eras in which they were written and edited. This temporal distance particularly affects the Historical Books, precisely because of their genre designation. The agenda-driven nature of these books, as well as the differences between today's understanding of "history" and that of the ancient world, is well established. Even so, the texts still provide an historical and cultural portal into some part of Israel's past. But which part? For example, do the books of the Deuteronomistic History (Joshua-Kings) comment on life in ancient Israel during Assyrian domination, the imperial situation of the eighth and seventh centuries BCE?[9] Or do they instead, as Noth's long-held thesis proposed, reflect the concerns of a sixth-century exilic author? Or, since they likely did not reach their final form until the Persian period, are their main ideas commentary on life under Achaemenid rule (Römer 2007: 169–83)? Contemplating the historical, social, and political imperial contexts addressed by biblical texts requires negotiating priorities between the setting, the (initial) composition, and the (subsequent) editing. Often, though, as is the case with this essay, postcolonial interpretation does not hinge on particular historical details, but rather the larger orienting conception of empire. In showing the similarities between characteristics of both ancient and modern empires and their texts, postcolonial biblical studies can inform the broader field of postcolonial theory, even as it is also informed by it.

27.4 THE FOREIGN WOMAN IN JOSHUA

Reading the story of the conquest of Canaan in Joshua 3–13 through the work of postcolonial theorist Frantz Fanon allows one to understand the Joshua account as a violent fantasy of the colonized. One of the foundational theorists for postcolonial studies, Fanon was a Martinique-born psychiatrist who worked in Algeria during its struggle for independence from France. He joined Algeria's National Liberation Front soon after the Algerian Revolution began in 1954. In his book *The Wretched of the Earth*, Fanon describes the colonial world as "Manichean," divided starkly between the abundance and safety of the colonizer's life, and the scarcity and violence that characterize life for the colonized. This bifurcated world instigates a neurosis for the colonized, who desires everything the colonizer has, and for the colonizer, who is aware of the colonized person's desire and thus lives in perpetual fear of the colonized, causing the colonizers to double down on their oppressive tactics.

Fanon asserts that the only cure for these colonial neuroses, and the only way that the inherently violent system of colonialism can be overthrown, is the "cathartic" violence of decolonization. He writes:

> The violence which governed the ordering of the colonial world, which tirelessly punctuated the destruction of the indigenous social fabric, and demolished unchecked the systems of reference of the country's economy, lifestyles, and modes of dress, the same violence will be vindicated and appropriated when, taking history into their own hands, the colonized swarm into the forbidden cities. To blow the colonial world to smithereens is henceforth a clear image within the grasp and imagination of every colonized subject. To dislocate the colonial world does not mean that once the borders have been eliminated there will be a right of way between the two sectors. To destroy the colonial world means nothing less than demolishing the colonist's sector, burying it deep within the earth or banishing it from the territory.
>
> (Fanon 2004: 5–6)

In Fanon's view, the undoing of the colonizer's totalizing violence—and the resolution of the desires and fears of colonizer and colonized alike—requires the complete demolition of the world of the colonizer, replacing it and filling it with formerly colonized peoples.[10] As a prescription for decolonization, Fanon's vision is both controversial and troubling, inasmuch as it proposes violence as an antidote to violence. As a description and diagnosis of imperial realities, however, it can be a helpful lens for making sense of the similarly troubling violence described in the book of Joshua, as well as teasing out the imperial and anti-imperial threads in the book.

When the Israelites cross over the Jordan River (Josh. 3), they cross from the sector of the ones colonized to the sector of the ones colonizing, enacting the swarm, dislocation, and demolition that Fanon describes. Every time they utterly destroy every person or every living thing in a Canaanite city (e.g., Josh. 10:28–42), they are essentially "blow[ing] the colonial world to smithereens" (Fanon 2004: 5). Joshua 5:1 relates that the Amorite and Canaanite kings were rendered spiritless, breathless, and had failing hearts upon hearing of Israel's crossing. In the kings' fears, one can almost hear the whisper of Fanon's colonizers: "They want to take our place" (Fanon 2004: 5). Yet, the Amorite and Canaanite kings are not the Babylonian kings and the Persian kings. This is not an account of decolonizing violence directed at the ancient Israelites' colonizers; instead, the Canaanites are those who, in the scope of the narrative, experience colonization by the Israelites. Is the book of Joshua creating a colonial world, or destroying one?

When the scribes behind this story "take history into their own hands," in Fanon's phrase, they do so not with action toward the future, but rather by reimagining the past. Rediscovering the past is, in fact, part of Fanon's vision for decolonization, though he presents that process as one of recovering rather than of fabrication of ancient traditions (Fanon 2004: 147–49). During the process of decolonization, asserts Fanon, the colonized intellectual will experience a nationalist awakening that differentiates his work from the colonialist bourgeoisie he initially mimics, embracing instead the distinctive cultural modes of his home nation. In the new past envisioned in Joshua, the colonized subject's desire to possess converges with a longing for catharsis that is achieved by appropriating and redirecting imperial violence back onto the colonizer. In other words, the desire to be the colonizer collides with the desire to destroy the colonizer. The Canaanites represent the possessors of the Israelites' land; thus, they stand in the colonizers' role, and, therefore, in the way. At the same time, they represent the colonized subject upon whom the colonizer (here, Israel) enacts its violent takeover. Imperial and anti-imperial discourses intertwine in the text, as Davidson has said, "and vexingly so" (Davidson 2013: 69). Nonetheless, by highlighting the concepts of desire and neurosis, Fanon's work helps to show how a sixth-century (or later) text by a subjugated Israel could produce such a striking, yet fractured picture of ancient Israelite imperial domination.

Adding a feminist lens to this reading of Joshua reveals some of the limitations of using Fanon's postcolonial theory to interpret the book. *The Wretched of the Earth* only rarely engages questions of gender directly.[11] The conflict between colonizer and colonized described within it is assumed to be between male agents, and the desire is imagined in male (and largely heteronormative) terms: "The gaze that the colonized subject casts at the colonist's sector is a look of lust, a look of envy. Dreams of possession. Every type of possession: of sitting at the colonist's table and sleeping in his bed, preferably with his wife" (Fanon 2004: 5). The colonizing agents addressed by the divine mandate in the book of Joshua are also understood to be male, as the admonition not to marry Canaanite women underscores (Deut. 7:3). Though there are occasionally more inclusive descriptions of the people of Israel, the default Israelite in Joshua is the circumcised male warrior (see Josh. 5:2–7).

In the emerging body of postcolonial feminist interpretations of the Bible, the character Rahab has received some of the most sustained attention. Amid texts that give blanket warnings against the dangers of women belonging to entire ethnic groups, Rahab stands out as a Canaanite woman who, rather than being a hindrance to the Israelites' quest, facilitates their colonial moment. Despite the repeated admonitions not to marry Canaanite women, the text does not bat a metaphorical eye when the Israelite spies spend the night with one (Josh. 2:1). What makes Rahab different?

The text emphasizes Rahab's Yahwistic piety and fidelity to Israel, rather than commitments to her own people or gods. After lying to officials from the king of Jericho and sending them on a fruitless pursuit (Josh. 2:3–7), Rahab delivers a speech proclaiming the greatness of Yhwh, the God of the Israelites, and negotiates for her life and the life of her family from the Israelites in the conflict to come (Josh. 2:8–14). The spies agree to the bargain, and they follow through on their promise, removing Rahab and her family from her house and placing them outside Israel's camp before burning down the city (Josh. 6:22–25). The spies place a condition on the agreement—that Rahab hang a crimson cord from her window during the invasion—in a move that sets up Rahab's deliverance as an echo of the Passover narrative (Hawk 2000: 49–50). Steed Davidson asserts that Rahab's own speech in the story marks her as a Yahwist, but that the narrator's presentation of Rahab—including repeatedly referring to her as a prostitute (6:17, 22, 25) and settling her family outside the camp (6:23)—continues to mark her otherness (Davidson 2013: 81; also Hawk 2000: 104).

For Dube, Rahab represents the colonizer's fantasies about colonized women, as well as about the land itself, as part of a "type-scene of land possession" (Dube 2000: 77, 119). As a prostitute, Rahab metonymically stands in for the land, available to any man for the taking.[12] Therefore, she functions in Joshua 2 not only in the part of the foreign woman, but also as representative of the foreign land to be conquered. Some feminist critics have highlighted Rahab's agency, her courage, and other admirable characteristics, in an attempt to show her resistance against the forces that oppress her. Dube counters these readings with the reminder that Rahab is "doubly colonized" (Dube 2000: 80); she faces not only patriarchy, but also the forces of imperialism:

> Far from undercutting the interests of the Israelites, Rahab embodies their interests. She does not resist their acts, aims, and dreams; she advances the promise. To regard her as a dependable, courageous woman when she can only do this by being party to the annihilation of her own city and people—a sellout—is to overlook that Rahab, like her dead people, is... culturally and politically dead.   (Dube 2000: 80)

Drawing on Fanon's thought, Davidson also affirms Dube's observation that Rahab's agency necessarily involves betrayal of her own people. To be sure, Rahab's actions result in the survival of her family in the face of death, and in later tradition she is often regarded as a hero. Nevertheless, as Davidson emphasizes, "The postcolonial response requires destabilizing the power of the text, in this case the Bible, as the final arbiter of reality, especially the reality of the native context" (Davidson 2013: 88). Postcolonialism points readers to Rahab's identity as an indigenous Canaanite woman facing the conquest of her land and the extermination of her people. Rather than automatically assuming the perspective of the text, which represents Rahab as eager to side with an invading army, postcolonial readings consider how the text may—or may not—serve imperializing interests.

27.5 THE FOREIGN WOMAN IN 1 AND 2 KINGS

The opening chapters of 1 Kings describe the ascendance of Solomon to the throne in Israel and give an account of his reign. By many measures Solomon is an ideal king: he demonstrates wisdom, he amasses wealth, and the nations of the world stand in awe of him. In fact, 1 Kgs. 4:20–21 (Hebrew 4:20–5:1) describes a prosperous, contented nation at home, and imperial control over a significant territory abroad: "Judah and Israel were as numerous as the sand by the sea; they ate and drank and were happy. Solomon was sovereign over all the kingdoms from the Euphrates to the land of the Philistines, even to the border of Egypt; they brought tribute and served Solomon all the days of his life" (NRSV). While the size of ancient Israel was never near the size of the territories commanded by neighboring nations like Egypt and Assyria, the text again nostalgically represents Israel as an imperial power, despite a dire warning from Samuel about the many ways kings "take"—that is, extract—resources and labor, even from their own people (1 Sam. 8:1–22). Security, too, purportedly characterized Solomon's reign: "During Solomon's lifetime Judah and Israel lived in safety, from Dan even to Beer-sheba, all of them under their vines and fig trees" (1 Kgs. 4:25, NRSV). The colonizing violence imagined in Joshua has given way to a peaceful stasis. Life under Solomon is life in Fanon's colonist's "sated, sluggish sector" (Fanon 2004: 5).

This description of Israel's contentment under Solomon's international power seems to answer the longing for monarchic governance "like other nations" that prompts the people to ask Samuel to appoint a king (1 Sam. 8:4). Yet this memory of a Solomonic golden age—exaggerated and nostalgic, to be sure, but perhaps with a bit more grounding in historical reality than the Joshua account—pronounces judgment on Solomon even as it revels in his greatness:

> King Solomon loved many foreign women along with the daughter of Pharaoh: Moabite, Ammonite, Edomite, Sidonian, and Hittite women, from the nations concerning which the LORD had said to the Israelites, "You shall not enter into marriage with them, neither shall they with you; for they will surely incline your heart to follow their gods." Solomon clung to these in love. (1 Kgs 11:1–2, NRSV)

The strategy of making marriage alliances, which brings the wealth of many nations into Solomon's kingdom, is precisely the tactic that will divide Israel and, ultimately, bring about its complete downfall. Solomon's glory, a metonym for ancient Israel's imperial aspirations, is concomitant with his downfall; the two cannot be separated. To use the language of postcolonial criticism, the book of Kings's characterization of Solomon is steeped in hybridity.

"Hybridity" is a watchword in postcolonial theory, made famous by the work of Homi Bhabha in his book *The Location of Culture*. It is a term that has acquired a life of its own, and is sometimes used broadly in postcolonial criticism to refer simply to a meeting and mixing of cultures. In Bhabha's understanding, hybridity has a more narrow significance (2004: 145–74).[13] Hybridity, like the closely related concept of "mimicry," is grounded in modern European imperialism and cannot always be neatly overlaid onto the ancient biblical context. Nonetheless, it offers some ideas that prove generative for the current study. In brief, hybridity is a destabilizing force inherent in the encounter between the colonizer and colonized in colonial discourse. The colonizer's texts—not only its strategies and practices—seek to produce an identity for the colonizer fully distinct from the colonized, and yet by engaging the colonized, any "pure" identity for the colonizer is compromised. Thus, in the encounter with the colonized, colonialism's aspirations toward superiority-through-difference contain the seeds of its own undoing.[14] King Solomon's imperial identity, which depends upon his ability to construct relationships with tribute-paying nations via marriage alliances, is itself destabilized by the encounter with those foreign women.[15]

As subsequent kings take the throne in the separate kingdoms of Israel and Judah, the problem of the foreign woman persists, epitomized in the character of Jezebel. If Rahab represents the foreign woman of the colonizer's dreams, Jezebel is the foreign woman of his nightmares. As the Sidonian wife of Ahab, she epitomizes the Historical Books' anxiety about Canaanite women. She murders the prophets of Yhwh. She unrepentantly worships her own gods rather than turning to her husband's God, and there is no indication she is unfaithful in her marriage. In fact, by underscoring her devotion to Baal and to her husband, the text reinforces just how faithful a person Jezebel is. As Wilda C. Gafney writes, "It is a painful irony that the biblical authors castigate the Israelites for failing to model this kind of fidelity" (Gafney 2017: 242). The excess Solomon showed in taking a thousand wives and concubines is echoed in the extravagance of Jezebel's employment of 450 prophets of Baal and 400 prophets of Asherah (1 Kgs. 18:19). She shows no desire to be possessed; on the contrary, her seizure of Naboth's vineyard shows Jezebel, rather than her Israelite husband-king, as the one who extracts resources (Howard 2012). Like Solomon's own foreign wives, Jezebel enables Ahab to realize his identity as imperial extractor. She makes him an effective king, and yet she simultaneously makes him a failed king. Again, the same mechanism that defines empire also undermines it. When Jehu succeeds at having Jezebel thrown down from her window to her death, horses trample her body until she is nothing but skull, feet, and palms (2 Kgs. 9:35). It is as if Jehu attempts what Joshua's invading army failed to do in the first place: wipe this Canaanite woman off the face of the earth. Once again, the attempt at establishing hegemonic identities backfires; in her graphic death, Jezebel is not erased from ancient Israelite history, but rather remains ineffaceably written on its story.

Both feminist and postcolonial lenses push back against the text's thoroughly negative evaluation of Jezebel. Suspicious of the motivations of narrators, authors, and redactors, these approaches do not automatically side with the perspective of the text. They consider the intersections of Jezebel's identities as a woman and a non-Israelite (Sidonian), and how those crossings are negotiated in imperial contexts. The goal is not necessarily to recover Jezebel's worth for modern readers, nor to justify the text's animosities by recourse to its exilic or post-exilic imperial realities, but rather to expose the dynamics of fear and desire, power and powerlessness, and imperialism and anti-imperialism that the text harbors. In her religious fidelity and her royal agency, Jezebel embodies characteristics that ancient Israel desires. However, in the otherness as a foreign woman with foreign gods, she represents that which ancient Israel fears and spurns. The collision of these dynamics yields a textual representation that seeks Jezebel's erasure but cannot accomplish it.

27.6 Conclusion

Postcolonial and feminist readings of the Historical Books should be understood as working neither in opposition nor in separate silos, but in tandem. Each approach expands the interpretive possibilities of the other, unearthing new layers of meaning. Postcolonial criticism charts the imperial relationships at work both within and behind the biblical texts, and it asserts that every aspect of culture—including the Bible—is affected by those imperial relationships. Feminist criticism considers power structures through the lens of gender, identifying ways women read and are read in biblical texts.

This essay has turned to Joshua and Kings as examples from the Historical Books where the dangers of the "foreign woman" are emphasized in order to suggest ways feminist and postcolonial approaches can illuminate the foreign woman trope. All of these observations highlight the layers of complexity inherent in the text's questions about identity and power. Drawing on the foundational postcolonial work of Fanon, I have suggested that the conquest narrative in Joshua is more than a colonizing text: it also reflects the violent fantasies of the colonized. Beyond the broad-based "pro-monarchic" or "anti-monarchic" sentiments expressed in the Deuteronomistic History, ambivalence about monarchy in 1 and 2 Kings reflects the postcolonial notion of "hybridity," in which the longing to define Israelite kingship over and against foreign women is what ultimately destabilizes monarchic (read: imperial) identity.

The comparable interests of feminist criticism and postcolonialism highlight the intersections of imperial status, gender, and ethnicity. This essay has showcased representations of two foreign women from the Historical Books: Rahab, whose loyalty to Yhwh and negotiations with the Israelite spies save the life of her family, and Jezebel, the wife of the Israelite king who refuses to give up her Canaanite gods. The desires and fears of the (presumptively male) colonizer collide in each character's representation. Rahab becomes enough like an Israelite to be "safe," but her survival comes at the cost of assimilating to her people's invaders. At the same time, her presence as a foreigner living in Israel counters some of Joshua's other imperializing claims about the total elimination of the Canaanites from the land (Hawk 2012). Jezebel, on the other hand, helps to realize the Israelite desire to have an extractor-king, and yet she is also understood as a toxic figure who facilitates the downfall of the kingdom.

When the Historical Books attempt to define Israelite identity over and against the Canaanites, they turn to the concept of the "foreign woman" to help construct that identity; yet that strategy, as Rahab and Jezebel's characterizations show, undermines the purity of the very identity being constructed. The destabilizing phenomenon demonstrated by postcolonial theorists reflecting on modern empires is also present in ancient biblical contexts, and in some ways is magnified by the contrast between ancient Israel's experiences under empire and the portraits of Israel as colonizer that dot the Historical Books. This circumstance underscores the continuities between ancient and modern imperial systems of representation, making the confluence of feminist and postcolonial studies a perennially fruitful critical perspective for biblical interpretation.

Notes

1. A flagship example of this analogy is in John Winthrop's 1630 sermon "A Modell of Christian Charity," in which he not only famously invokes the Matthean image of a "city on a hill," but also paraphrases Moses's speech in Deuteronomy 30, thus aligning the establishment of New England with the Israelites' entrance into Canaan: "But if our heartes shall turne away soe that wee will not obey, but shall be seduced, and worship ... other Gods, our pleasures, and proffitts, and serve them; it is propounded unto us this day, wee shall surely perishe out of the good Land whither wee passe over this vast Sea to possesse it" (Winthrop 1998: 41). For more on the use of the Bible in the European settlement of the Americas, see Noll 2016.

2. Wilda C. Gafney (2017: 240) points out that "Jezebel" is already a slur in Rev. 2:20.
3. For a discussion of vernacular hermeneutics, see Sugirtharajah 2001.
4. See the discussion on theory vs. criticism in Sugirtharajah 2002: 12–14.
5. For a critique of feminist criticism's focus on individual women at the expense of larger economic concerns, see Roland Boer 2005.
6. See Berquist 2006; also Boer 2015. While not using the term to define empires exclusively or even in particular, Boer names "extractive economic patterns" as an alternative model to "allocative economic patterns" within ancient Israel's "sacred economy."
7. For a salient overview of many of the "major considerations" and key terms in postcolonial biblical studies, see Perdue and Carter 2014, 5–35.
8. The distinction between "imperialism" and "colonialism" can be felt here. The extraction of human resources that characterizes the Hebrews' forced labor in Egypt, particularly from people of a different ethnicity or nationality, is a hallmark of *imperialism*; however, *colonialism* is not at play there, since that extraction is happening in Egypt itself, without an invading or occupying force in the Israelites' homeland. Recently some theorists have begun to use the term *settler colonialism* to describe the particular way that "the Israelites, especially towards the end of Genesis–Joshua, become an autonomous collective that claims both a special sovereign charge and a regenerative capacity" (Pitkänen 2015: 10).
9. Crowell 2013 reads the foreign-woman trope as reflective of Israel and Judah's experiences under Assyrian domination.
10. It must be noted that Fanon's diagnosis of the desire to *replace* the colonizer is by no means an endorsement of becoming *like* the colonizer. See discussion in Davidson 2013.
11. Despite a paucity of direct references to issues of sex and gender, the psychoanalysis that Fanon practices is built upon questions of the representation of sexuality and sexual difference. See Gwen Bergner, "Who Is That Masked Woman? or, The Role of Gender in Fanon's *Black Skin, White Masks*," PMLA 110 (1995): 75–88.
12. For more on "hypersexualization" as part of the characterization of foreign women in the Deuteronomistic History, see Crowell 2013.
13. In its inherent ambivalence, hybridity is closely related to Bhabha's idea of mimicry, described above.
14. A somewhat analogous destabilization is captured by Deut. 25:19 and may be instructive here: "Therefore when the LORD your God has given you rest from all your enemies on every hand, in the land that the LORD your God is giving you as an inheritance to possess, you shall blot out the remembrance of Amalek from under heaven; do not forget." By writing down and not forgetting the command to blot out the remembrance of Amalek, Amalek's remembrance is secured! The attempt at hegemony over Amalek's memory is destabilized—even undone—by the acknowledgment of it.
15. For more on mimicry and hybridity in the historical books, see Crowell 2013.

BIBLIOGRAPHY

Bergner, Gwen. 1995. "Who Is That Masked Woman? Or, the Role of Gender in Fanon's *Black Skin, White Masks*," PMLA 110.1: 75–88.
Berquist, Jon L. 2006. "Postcolonialism and Imperial Motives." In R. S. Sugirtharajah, ed., *The Postcolonial Biblical Reader*. Malden, MA: Blackwell, 78–95.
Bhabha, Homi. 2004. *The Location of Culture*. New York: Routledge.
Boehmer, Elleke. 2005. *Stories of Women: Gender and Narrative in the Postcolonial Nation*. Manchester: Manchester University Press.

Boer, Roland. 2005. "On the Absence of Feminist Criticism of Ezra-Nehemiah." In Caroline Vander Stichele and Todd Penner, eds., *Her Master's Tools? Feminist and Postcolonial Engagements of Historical-Critical Discourse*. Global Perspectives on Biblical Scholarship 9. Atlanta: SBL, 233–52.

Boer, Roland. 2015. *The Sacred Economy of Ancient Israel*. LAI. Louisville, KY: Westminster John Knox.

Crowell, Bradley. 2013. "Good Girl, Bad Girl: Women of the Deuteronomistic History in Postcolonial Perspective." *BibInt* 21: 1–18.

Davidson, Steed Vernyl. 2013. "Gazing (at) Native Women: Rahab and Jael in Imperializing and Postcolonial Discourses." In Roland Boer, ed., *Postcolonialism and the Hebrew Bible: The Next Step*. SemeiaSt 70. Atlanta: SBL, 69–92.

Dube, Musa. 2000. *Postcolonial Feminist Interpretation*. St. Louis: Chalice.

Fanon, Frantz. 2004. *The Wretched of the Earth*. Translated by Richard Philcox. New York: Grove Press.

Gafney, Wilda C. 2017. *Womanist Midrash: A Reintroduction to the Women of the Torah and the Throne*. Louisville, KY: Westminster John Knox.

Hawk, L. Daniel. 2000. *Joshua*. Berit Olam. Collegeville, MN: The Liturgical Press.

Hawk, L. Daniel. 2012. "The Truth about Conquest: Joshua as Narrative, History, and Scripture." *Interpretation* 66.2: 129–40.

Howard, Cameron. 2012. "1 and 2 Kings." In Carol A. Newsom, Sharon H. Ringe, and Jacqueline E. Lapsley, eds., *Women's Bible Commentary*. 3rd ed. Louisville, KY: Westminster John Knox, 164–79.

Mitchell, Christine. 2012. "1 and 2 Chronicles." In Carol A. Newsom, Sharon H. Ringe, and Jacqueline E. Lapsley, eds., *Women's Bible Commentary*. 3rd ed. Louisville, KY: Westminster John Knox, 184–91.

Noll, Mark A. 2016. *In the Beginning Was the Word: The Bible in American Public Life, 1492–1783*. Oxford: Oxford University Press.

Perdue, Leo G. and Warren Carter. 2015. *Israel and Empire: A Postcolonial History of Israel and Early Judaism*. London: Bloomsbury.

Pitkänen, Pekka. 2015. "Reading Genesis-Joshua as a Unified Document from an Early Date: A Settler Colonial Perspective." *Biblical Theology Bulletin* 45.1: 3–31.

Römer, Thomas. 2007. *The So-Called Deuteronomistic History: A Sociological, Historical and Literary Introduction*. London: T&T Clark.

Seibert, Eric A. 2012. *The Violence of Scripture: Overcoming the Old Testament's Troubling Legacy*. Minneapolis: Fortress.

Sugirtharajah, R. S. 2001. *The Bible and the Third World: Precolonial, Colonial and Postcolonial Encounters*. Cambridge: Cambridge University Press.

Sugirtharajah, R. S. 2002. *Postcolonial Criticism and Biblical Interpretation*. Oxford: Oxford University Press.

Warrior, Robert Allen. 1991. "Canaanites, Cowboys, and Indians." In R. S. Sugirtharajah, ed., *Voices from the Margin: Interpreting the Bible in the Third World*. Maryknoll: Orbis, 287–95.

Winthrop, John. 1998. "A Modell of Christian Charity." In Conrad Cherry, ed., *God's New Israel: Religious Interpretations of American Destiny*. Chapel Hill: University of North Carolina Press, 37–41.

Yee, Gale. 2003. *Poor Banished Children of Eve: Woman as Evil in the Hebrew Bible*. Minneapolis: Fortress.

CHAPTER 28

THE DEUTERONOMISTIC HISTORY AS LITERATURE OF TRAUMA

DAVID JANZEN

28.1 THE STUDY OF TRAUMA

TRAUMA, deriving from the Greek word for "wound," is studied in many fields, including psychology, literary criticism, sociology, history, philosophy, law, and, in the twenty-first century, biblical studies, especially within the field of Hebrew Bible. Trauma is perhaps best known outside the academic world as associated with Posttraumatic Stress Disorder, or PTSD. The fifth edition of the *Diagnostic and Statistical Manual of Mental Disorders* (more commonly known as DSM-5) states that PTSD is caused by direct experience or witnessing of a traumatic event or events, such as warfare, physical or sexual assault, torture, or being a prisoner of war. PTSD is manifested through intrusive symptoms such as recurrent and involuntary memories of the event, distressing dreams related to it, and dissociative reactions like flashbacks in which it appears as if the traumatic events are recurring. These dissociative states can last from seconds to days in length, and can even involve "a complete loss of awareness of present surroundings." PTSD is also manifested through, among other things, numbing symptoms, in which victims try to avoid memories, thoughts, and feelings associated with the traumatic event, or are even unable to remember aspects of it (American Psychiatric Association 2013: 271–75). In our present study, of course, we have a literary rather than a psychological interest in trauma since we are examining a writing, but the canonical approaches to the study of trauma in literature are rooted in the ways in which psychoanalysis has dealt with it, and it is helpful for us to begin there.

To start with a work cited frequently in literary studies of trauma, Sigmund Freud's *Beyond the Pleasure Principle*, originally published in 1920, resulted in part from Freud's observation following World War I that soldiers' dreams repetitively returned to violent events, much like those of survivors of horrific accidents. These dreams, writes Freud, with their repetitiveness and literal representation of the violence, are very unlike non-traumatic ones that serve healing functions, and Freud refers to these patients as "fixated" to their trauma (Freud 1966–74: 18:12–14). He thus notices here one example of the intrusive symptoms of PTSD that DSM-5 would later describe, and Freud concludes that the events encountered by victims of trauma were so horrifying, so far outside the realm of everyday experience, that they were utterly unprepared for them. Because they were psychologically overwhelmed, they did not truly experience the trauma; the trauma was thus repressed and returned belatedly through dreams and other intrusive symptoms as the victims tried to control and know what they did not fully experience (18:30–33). This dissociation means that survivors encounter trauma as something foreign yet immediately present to their psychological lives.

The psychologist Pierre Janet, a contemporary of Freud, drew similar conclusions. Janet describes memory as the telling of an autobiographical story in which new experiences are synthesized in light of one's sense of self. He observes that as one's sense of self changes in light of new experiences, older memories change as a result, but he notes that his traumatized patients do not assimilate their trauma in this way. Trauma does not become part of one's life narrative—not being experienced, it cannot be truly understood and so cannot be associated into a self-narrative. So traumatic memories, Janet concludes, do not act like normal memories (Janet 1925: 1.660–63), just as Freud noticed that traumatic dreams are not at all like normal dreams. As a result, Janet writes, trauma is not actually remembered but reproduced through intrusive symptoms like flashbacks. Traumatic memories are not memories at all in our usual understanding of the term because they are completely dissociated from one's sense of self, intruding rather than being integrated into it.

Much more recent biomedical investigations of trauma support these conclusions. While in a psychologically healthy person the conscious memory system of the hippocampus and the unconscious memory system of the amygdala are well integrated and create autobiographical memory, traumatic memories are not stored this way. They are commonly retained as images, sounds, and bodily sensations, unlike normal memories. During the sorts of events that produce trauma, stress-related chemicals are released that impair the functioning of the hippocampus that cannot then properly encode the memories of the event. As a result, traumatic memories remain the same over time and are not under voluntary control, seeming like foreign bodies that stand over against the self. Memory tracts established under conditions of severe stress become the preferred neural pathways when later conditions of stress occur, which is why victims repetitively and compulsively relive traumatic memories when they later find themselves in even mildly stressful situations (van der Kolk and van der Hart 1995; Stien and Kendall 2004: 90–96).

Because trauma is not fully experienced and does not exist in the normal memory system, it is also not known by the survivor. Overwhelmed by violence far beyond their capacity to make sense of the world, victims have no way to categorize it; trauma simply does not fit into their understandings of the world or their selves (van Alphen 1999: 24–26). Traumatic knowledge, it would seem, "is as close to nescience as to knowledge" (Hartman 1995: 537). Most Holocaust survivors, for example, "know" trauma only in a fragmented, decontextualized way such as in isolated thoughts or sensations with no clear connection to their self-understandings, and thus this "knowledge" is not meaningful (Auerhahn and Laub 1998: 29–30). And because trauma involuntarily and literally repeats in these isolated sensations, dreams, flashbacks, and other intrusive ways, it freezes time, continually interrupting the present with a past that seems very real and yet cannot be understood. Trauma is thus not amenable to narrative, either that of the victim's autobiographical sense of self or literary narratives. Narratives need a sense of chronology to function, and stories are based on events experienced and known by characters. Trauma, really, is anti-narrative. Narrative creates order out of chaos, placing different events at different points in time to form a story, precisely what trauma does not allow (see Luckhurst 2008: 84–86). As Shoshana Felman puts it, testimony to trauma "seems to be composed of bits and pieces of a memory that has been overwhelmed by occurrences that have not settled into understanding or remembrance, acts that cannot be constructed as knowledge or assimilated into full cognition, events in excess of our frames of reference" (Felman and Laub 1992: 5). The result, then, is that trauma survivors themselves frequently doubt the veracity of their experiences. Primo Levi writes that, upon arrival at Auschwitz, "We looked at each other without a word. It was all incomprehensible and mad..." (Levi 1996: 26). As the epigraph for *None of Us Will Return*, the first book of her Holocaust trilogy, Charlotte Delbo writes, "Today I am not sure that what I wrote is true. I am certain that it is truthful" (Delbo 1995: 1). Simon Srebnik, one of the two survivors of Chelmno, where four hundred thousand Jews were murdered, said in an interview at the camp, "It was terrible. No one can describe it. No one can recreate what happened here. Impossible? And no one can understand it. Even I, here, now.... I can't believe I'm here. No, I just can't believe it" (Lanzmann 1995: 3). The whole first part of Elie Wiesel's *Night* is a testimony to the inability of the Holocaust's victims to believe: they do not believe the first witnesses who tell them of what the Nazis are already doing to the Jews; they do not believe the Germans will reach their small Hungarian town; once the Nazis arrive, they do not believe that they will do anything very terrible to them. "Was he [Hitler] going to wipe out a whole people? Could he exterminate a population scattered throughout so many countries? So many millions! What methods could he use? And in the middle of the twentieth century!" (Wiesel 1981: 18–19).

Trauma resists narrative not only because it defies experience, knowledge, and belief, but because language itself fails at the threshold of trauma. There is an obvious reason for this which Jean Améry, a victim of Auschwitz and of torture by the SS, explains:

> It would be totally senseless to try to describe here the pain that was inflicted on me. Was it "like a red-hot iron in my shoulders," and was another "like a dull wooden stake that had been driven into the back of my head"? One comparison would only stand for the other, and in the end we would be hoaxed by turn on the hopeless merry-go-round of figurative speech. The pain was what it was. Beyond that there is nothing to say. Qualities of feeling are as incomparable as they are indescribable. They mark the limit of the capacity of language to communicate.   (Améry 1980: 33)

As Levi puts it, words like "hunger," "fear," and "pain" cannot possibly mean the same things to Holocaust survivors as they do to those who have not experienced this kind of trauma; a whole new language would be necessary to explain the camps (Levi 1996: 129). So if trauma cannot be narrativized or communicated, it is no wonder that Wiesel, perhaps the best known Holocaust writer, says that words cannot express the Holocaust and that he himself does not understand it (Wiesel 1978). Simply to recount historical events—and there are plenty of them in the works of the authors just cited, not to mention in the writings of many, many other survivors—is not to know or explain trauma, it is simply to know facts around it. And so Raul Hilberg, a Holocaust historian, expresses concern that readers of his works might mistakenly believe that they have encountered the true Holocaust in his academic writing (Hilberg 1988: 25). Objective historiography is narrative, precisely what trauma resists, and Hilberg realizes that his histories cannot contain or represent trauma, and so to that extent are unable to represent the full truth of the Holocaust.

Literature of trauma may or may not be written by trauma survivors, but reflects a traumatic event—Holocaust testimonies are obvious examples—and tends to be characterized by literary reflections of psychological trauma. Because traumatic intrusions literally repeat the trauma in traumatic memories, dreams, fugue states, and so on, literature of trauma is marked by this repetition. Since trauma survivors relive (rather than remember) the trauma, the traumatic past is always present in victims' lives, stripping the present of its reality and so shattering chronology. This is how Delbo puts it as she reflects on her post-Auschwitz experience:

> I was unable to get reaccustomed to myself. How could I reaccustom myself to a self which had become so detached from me I was not sure I ever existed? My former life? Had I had a former life? My life afterwards? Was I alive to have an afterwards, to know what afterwards meant? I was floating in a present devoid of reality.   (Delbo 1995: 237)

Literature of trauma is thus also marked by temporal disjuncture, as the traumatic past intrudes into and displaces the present. Because trauma is not experienced and thus not known, the trauma itself is not part of the survivor's life narrative, and narratives of trauma inevitably fragment, as Delbo says her self has, as memories of the trauma intrude into the narrative of the writing.

The temptation, then, is to say nothing, and trauma tends to silence. Listeners generally do not want to be exposed to trauma testimony, which is very difficult to hear. Since even the survivors are not in a position to be able to believe it, listeners are equally unable to imagine an "antiworld" so utterly different from their own that even ethical agency does not exist (Langer 1995: 4-6). Agency is absent insofar as trauma controls the victim, but also insofar as at the encounter with trauma the victim was absolutely helpless and could not act. There is no ethical system that makes sense in this context, since morality depends upon agency (1995: 29-30, 32). There is a tendency on the part of non-survivors to create narratives that overwrite trauma with narratives of morality and heroism, creating a subjectivity the victim did not have, and so to view trauma through the lenses of familiar and comfortable national narratives and myths (Tal 1996: 115-16). Even therapists of Vietnam War veterans tried to impose the narrative of the successful warrior on their trauma patients, thereby erasing the trauma with an heroic national myth (1996: 150-53).

The study of trauma in sociology tends to focus precisely on those narratives that erase trauma, and thus is generally a very different kind of investigation than that within literary criticism, which developed out of the study of trauma in psychoanalysis. Sociology approaches trauma not as that which is not known but as something imbued with meaning by the group. The sociologist Jeffrey Alexander writes that trauma is something constructed by a society in order to help create a sense of meaning and identity for the group. Looking to some kind of catastrophe in the past the society believes has happened, trauma from Alexander's perspective defines injury, establishes a victim, and attributes responsibility, even though there may be no actual historical referent for the trauma the group has constructed (Alexander 2004). Vamik Volkan strives to draw some connection between psychological and sociological approaches, arguing that the trauma inflicted on a society can be inherited by many succeeding generations. Although Volkan refers to this as "chosen trauma," he sees it as based in an unconscious definition of identity through transgenerational transmission of trauma. Nonetheless, he ultimately describes trauma as something experienced and also consciously chosen and reawakened in order to bind a community together (Volkan 1997: 36–49). For Arthur Neal, collective trauma also results from events that actually occurred and that radically challenge a society's understanding of the world. The group, writes Neal, needs to restore order to this shaken worldview, and it will respond by making sense of it, thus locating a cause for trauma that allows the nation to regain some of the control it feels it has lost (Neal 1998: 13–15). Over time, traumas become absorbed into national self-understanding, and may be understood as negative events or heroic responses to adversity (1998: 201–204). For Ron Eyerman, cultural trauma is something that a group negotiates and articulates in order to repair a break in the social fabric caused by a horrifying event, such as slavery for African Americans (Eyerman 2001: 3–4). Following the lead of the Durkheimian Maurice Halbwachs, Eyerman writes that individual memory is really a function of group memory because individuals are inevitably members of groups, and collective memory is an interpretation of the past constructed to benefit the society and to help its members make sense of reality (2001: 5–10). So for Eyerman and other sociologists, traumatic memory truly is like normal memory and it is something that can provide identity to a people and thus something that can be known, something constructed to benefit society.

These two approaches, that of literary criticism, which developed out of the psychoanalytical study of trauma, and the sociological, are not easily reconcilable. Literary criticism generally begins with the concept of trauma as what is not known, whereas sociology tends to see trauma as an experience constructed by the group that makes trauma understandable and meaningful to its members. And while literary theorists can also refer to collective trauma, for some scholars the relationship they describe between individual and collective trauma is far from clear (e.g., Kansteiner 2004: 207–209; Visser 2011: 276–77). However, postcolonial theorists who have interacted with trauma theory argue that traditional accounts of trauma have failed to recognize that trauma can result from the sort of everyday violence and threat of violence common in the colonial context (e.g., Novak 2008: 37; Rothberg 2009: 87–96). "Insidious trauma" refers to trauma caused by oppression that persists over time, like that experienced by those subject to colonial rule, and can result in trauma just like the "punctual trauma" of prolonged exposure to combat and the like (Brown 1995). In a context of continual oppression and terror produced by colonial rule, we would expect trauma to be widespread throughout a society for at least as many generations as such rule lasts.

28.2 A Sociological Reading of Trauma in the Deuteronomistic History

Scholars who use some version of trauma theory in their study of the Hebrew Bible tend to prefer approaches more at home in the presuppositions of sociological readings of trauma than of literary ones. In these studies, one is less likely to read of trauma as that which is not fully known and cannot be communicated, and more likely to encounter claims that biblical writings are responding to trauma by constructing meaning and symbolic worlds for Judeans traumatized by invasion, destruction, and exile. This may be a result of a desire to locate therapeutic value within biblical texts, but at any rate we will begin our discussion of the Deuteronomistic History (Dtr) with this approach, asking in what ways the work might act to restore meaning and reconstruct a coherent worldview for a society traumatized by a sixteen-month siege that culminated with famine, the slaughter and rape that would have inevitably accompanied Jerusalem's fall, forced migration, and the colonial experience of exile.

Destruction and exile bookend Dtr, appearing at its culmination in 2 Kings 25 and foreshadowed throughout Deuteronomy, where Israel is repetitively warned that their actions could lead to destruction and exile (4:25–28; 7:1–10; 8:11–20; 9:12–14; 11:16–17; etc.) and is provided with a gruesome and detailed description of what this will be like (28:15–68). This is clearly the trauma toward which the work as a whole moves and which it explains to its readers. Judah in exile was a traumatized community, and Dtr appears to address the trauma they have suffered. The text certainly imbues the catastrophe suffered by the exiles with meaning and explanation: destruction and exile and all their concomitant horrors are explained as punishment devised by a just God for an evil nation. Dtr most immediately explains the exiles' trauma as the result of "the sins of Manasseh" that "he caused Judah also to sin" (2 Kgs. 21:10–16; 23:26–27; 24:3–4). On the one hand, it seems as if the king is responsible for the apostasy that the people committed and that resulted in the trauma they experienced. The use of the verb ḥāṭā' in the hiphil to describe the king's leadership in the nation's sin is a common explanation of apostasy in Kings (1 Kgs. 14:15–16; 15:26, 34; 16:13, 19, 26; etc.). Nonetheless, the sin of foreign worship leading to destruction is one to which Israel is consistently drawn even without royal leadership in Dtr. Judges is largely structured by a repetitive cycle in which Israel's apostasy consistently leads to foreign invasion as punishment, and Deut. 9:4–7 describes the people as "stubborn" and "rebellious," stating that God's gift of the land is not due to their righteousness but to the wickedness of the Canaanite nations who will be destroyed in the conquest. Israel commits the sin of idolatry at Horeb, at the nation's very genesis, sparking a divine desire to destroy this stubborn and corrupt people practically at the moment they emerge out of Egypt (9:8–14). If Manasseh is immediately responsible for leading Judah to commit the sin that results in the trauma of destruction and exile, this is merely leadership in the direction that the people themselves tend. Manasseh may receive Dtr's censure, but Deuteronomy and Judges portray a people who would have acted the same way even without him.

If blaming the victim hardly seems like the kind of cultural construction of exile that will repair a break in the social fabric, we can note that guilt is something widespread among trauma survivors (Lifton 1991: 489–99), perhaps because feeling a sense of ethical agency, even a negative one, gives them a belated sense of control over a situation in which they were utterly helpless. Potentially, then, this sort of explanation helps to restore meaning to the traumatized community in exile, helps to repair, as Ronnie Janoff-Bulman puts it, the assumptions of the goodness and justness of the world that were shattered in trauma (Janoff-Bulman 1992: 49–69), and gives them hope that they have the ability to reverse the disaster they have survived, since their own actions have caused it.

The worldview behind Dtr's explanation of the trauma—what we might call the trauma's meaning in this sociological reading—assumes that God controls history and is able to reward as well as punish. The universe is not chaotic and devoid of meaning in this narrative; the moral universe is a just one in which God reacts to Israel's actions. Indeed, God often inclines to mercy, consistently releasing Israel from merited punishment in Judges despite the people's failure to repent, and is willing to delay punishment even when it is merited, thus allowing more generations to live on the land than would otherwise have been the case. This is certainly true in Kings, where God promises to destroy the North for committing "the sins of Jeroboam, which he sinned and which he caused Israel to commit" (1 Kgs. 14:16); although all the Northern kings that follow continue to cause Israel to sin as Jeroboam did, God waits two centuries before removing the people from the land. So in this meaningful world there is a future for the exiles, for repentance and continued adherence to the covenant will be met with divine mercy and guarantee a return to and prosperity in the land (Deut. 30:1–10).

28.3 A Literary Reading of Trauma in the Deuteronomistic History

While this sort of narrative may benefit the group, or at least its leadership, it does not actually address the exiles' psychological trauma. If we move away from the sociological understanding of trauma as constructed meaning to the idea of trauma in literary criticism as the overwhelming event not experienced or known, then it would seem that Dtr's narrative has simply overwritten or erased the exiles' trauma. Trauma is anti-narrative, and Dtr is a totalizing narrative, drawing in all the information and explanation the author or tradents believed necessary in order to explain the past. Dominick LaCapra describes a totalizing historical narrative as one that presents itself as explaining everything, and that involves a sovereign—like God—who does not make mistakes, certainly not judicial ones (LaCapra 1994: 190–91). A fetishistic narrative, he writes, is much like this, marginalizing trauma and presenting the historian's own values as realized in history (1994: 192–93), which is a fair description of Dtr. Whatever Dtr may do in regard to collective trauma, the work does not deal with or attempt to work through the psychological trauma suffered by the exiles. There are no victims of trauma in the work, only criminals justly punished. Like a legal trial that needs to be aware of all relevant evidence, Dtr also (from its supporters' standpoint) renders a true verdict about the past. This, however, must be done at the expense of trauma, which is erased by a narrative that cannot comprehend it. In a literary reading of trauma theory, the Deuteronomistic History hardly seems to be literature of trauma at all. It is still possible to pursue a literary reading of trauma in Dtr, however, in the sense that we can look for gaps in the narrative that challenge its totalizing self-presentation. In trauma, writes Felman, "language is in process and in trial, it does not possess itself as a conclusion, as the constatation of a verdict or the self-transparency of knowledge" (Felman and Laub 1992: 5). If there are any traces of trauma in Dtr, they will be traces of absence, deconstructing the narrative's totalizing impulses and throwing its explanations and meanings into unresolved doubt. Trauma does not, in this reading, offer a counter-narrative that produces verdicts about the language and meaning it puts on trial, for trauma leaves only ambiguity and a lack of certainty.

An important aspect of Dtr's narrative is its foundation in the belief of God's justice; little of the narrative's meaning holds if God is not just, for then moral chaos would reign and the exiles' suffering would have no meaning. Yet trauma deconstructs this tenet at numerous points. For example, the summary of the explanation of the destruction of the North in 2 Kgs. 17:7–23 condemns the North with sins that the narrative ascribes only to Judah and its kings, such as the worship of the host of heaven and the passing of one's own children through fire (17:16–17; cf. 16:3; 21:3, 5, 6), or sins that the narrative mainly attributes to Judeans, such as worship at high places and pillars (17:9–11). At this extremely important point of narrative explanation, where the destruction of the North for cultic sin points toward a similar fate for Judah, one might expect an absolutely clear presentation of the evidence against the North that reveals unwavering divine justice in its destruction. But, given the previous witness of Dtr's narrative, some, although certainly not most, of this seems like false evidence, and God's justice is thus called into question (Janzen 2012: 229–30). The same issue arises in the very first story of the Dtr, the narrative of the refusal of the first generation of Israel to enter Canaan because, following the report of a spy mission into the land, they do not trust that God is able to defeat the inhabitants (Deut. 1:1–2:15). Here, punishment falls not only on the people for their failure to trust but on Moses as well, even though he had voiced his complete confidence in God's power (1:29–31). Caleb, who exhibits the same trust as Moses, is rewarded with entrance into the land (1:36), but Moses, like the rest of his generation, will die outside of it (1:37), again undermining the narrative's presentation of God as just judge (Janzen 2012: 79–81). And, to take just one more example, the ambiguity of God's justice is raised again in the story of the idol at Horeb (Deut. 9:8–10:11), the first story of apostasy that Dtr describes at length. Here, Moses dissuades God from destroying Israel for the sin (9:13–14) by appealing not to God's justice or even mercy but to God's vanity, claiming that this destruction would lead the nations to conclude that God simply lacked the power to bring Israel into the land (Janzen 2012: 77–78).

These gaps in Dtr's overall presentation of God's justice do not in themselves create a rival narrative. One could read 2 Kings 17 as suggesting the North committed all of the same sins as Judah, but that Dtr's narrative has simply failed to provide stories of northerners involved in each category of sin to which the explanation of the North's destruction refers. One could attribute God's prohibition of Moses's entrance into the land as punishment for allowing the spy mission to proceed in the first place, even though such a rationale is absent from the narrative and even though Joshua's authorization of a similar mission in Josh. 2:1 goes unpunished. And one could understand Deut. 9:8–10:11 as suggesting that Moses's actions of repentance in destroying the idolatrous calf, actions later imitated by Josiah's reforms in 2 Kgs. 23:6, 11, 15–16, are the true reason God decided not to destroy Israel, even though the narrative does not make this connection. These stories provide ambiguities, gaps, and absences of clear narrative explanation, not clear counter claims. Yet they are important absences, for, from the author's or tradents' standpoint, it assumedly matters whether or not God is aware of or cares about which sins the people have or have not committed. The explanation of the destruction and exile of the North in 2 Kings 17 reads like a foreshadowing of the fate Dtr's readers have undergone, and so at a point where we might expect the narrative to be absolutely clear that failure to keep the law leads to destruction—that this part of God's moral structuring of the world applies to Israel and Judah alike—we encounter instead an absence of clear explanation that throws the narrative into question, even if this deconstruction does not provide a verdict that contradicts that of Dtr's narrative. It assumedly matters as well that God be seen to have clear and just reasons for deciding who will die outside of the land as punishment—the potential fate of exilic readers—and who has exhibited enough trust in God to enter it. It assumedly matters that God responds to Israel's actions on the just basis of the law and covenant laid out in Deuteronomy and that God cannot be flattered or goaded into ignoring the covenant's moral basis. But what we find instead in these stories is the presence of trauma in ambiguity, in the absence of clear narrative explanation. In none of them is there a clear contradiction of the narrative's claims, but the foundations of the narrative's ethical worldview that explains trauma and its meaning are thrown into an unresolved trial in each case. There is no verdict in any of them because trauma is present as an absence of a totalizing narrative that accounts for and explains all relevant aspects of the past.

Trauma intrudes into Dtr's narrative in other ways. At first glance, the chronology of the narrative consists of a simple forward movement, beginning with Moses's speeches in the Transjordan and ending with the exile. Yet there are subtle breaks in this chronology, glimpses of the readers' traumatic past that is repeated over and over. The trauma of invasion and foreign rule continuously repeats in Judges, suggesting that there is one time only, trauma time, not a linear progression, and that Israel has always suffered the exiles' trauma (Janzen 2012: 129–34). Moses, addressing the generation of Israelites about to cross the Jordan, the descendants of those who left Egypt but died in the wilderness as punishment for their lack of trust (Deut. 2:14–15), speaks to them as if they were their parents, as if they were the ones who rebelled against God (1:22–40) and who are now in graves outside of the land, an uncanny repetition of the exiles' own trauma that makes it appear that every generation of Israel, guilty or not, suffers what the first and last generations of Israel do (Janzen 2012: 84–86). In fact, Deuteronomy 29 seems to conflate the generation of Israel addressed by Moses in Moab with the exiles themselves. Here, Moses refers to divine punishment of those within the Moab generation who turn to foreign worship: "the LORD will single them out from all the tribes of Israel for calamity" (29:17–20 [18–21]). Yet somehow this punishment of individuals or families within Israel results in a devastation of the land which rivals that of Sodom and Gomorrah, a punishment in which God will "cast them into another land, as is now the case" (29:21–27 [22–28]). The "now" of the Moab generation has become the "now" of the exiles, a "now" in which Israel repeats the exiles' trauma over and over (Janzen 2012: 88–89).

Trauma's disruption of Dtr's chronology can end up deconstructing the work's narrative truths. When it can seem as if all the generations of Israel live the exiles' trauma, then it can seem as if the innocent suffer as the guilty do, as is the case when Moses addresses the generation in Moab as if they had committed their parents' sin and received their punishment. And it is not only Moses who at times fails to distinguish between the different generations of Israel, for God sometimes appears to do likewise, thereby casting divine justice into question. For example, in Judg. 2:1–5 God condemns Israel for making a covenant with the Canaanites. Given the time frame established in Judg. 1:1, the generation of Israel in question would appear to be that of the post-conquest generation which follows the time of Joshua, and yet the only covenant with Canaanites to which the narrative refers takes place under Joshua's leadership in Joshua 9*. The narrative suggests, but does not claim, that the post-conquest generation is being wrongly accused, although it is certainly possible to read Judges 1–2 as implying that the post-conquest generation themselves made covenants with the Canaanites to which the narrative does not refer. Thus, the narrative is again brought into unresolved trial, but still not refuted through a counter-narrative (Janzen 2012: 130–32). And the very fact that 2 Kings 17 suggests, but does not claim, that the North suffers for Judah's sin could be seen as raising the same unresolved problem as to whether or not God can tell the difference between different generations of Israel. From the standpoint of Dtr's explanation of the exiles' trauma, this is not a minor issue; Moses may claim in Deut. 7:10 that God "repays in their own person those who reject him," but the exiles suffer for "the sins of Manasseh," a king who died in peace after a long reign two full generations before the destruction of Jerusalem. Does Dtr suggest that the exiles suffered for sins they did not commit? Trauma time does not simply disrupt Dtr's chronology, suggesting that the people relive the same trauma generation after generation, it deconstructs the narrative's understanding of a just and divinely mandated moral order.

28.4 The Deuteronomistic History's Repression of Trauma

A sociological reading of trauma in Dtr can make the work seem therapeutic: meaning is constructed through explanation, thereby restoring a comforting view of a just cosmos to the exiles. The difficulty with this sort of conclusion, however, is that the narrative erases the psychological trauma of the exiles. An explanation that blames the victim has little interest in healing individuals' psychic trauma—imagine, for example, blaming rape victims (and there surely would have been some among the exiles) for the traumas they have suffered. There may well have been some group within the Judean elite who hoped to benefit from a restored sense of unity within the community, but whatever the author or tradents may have been aiming to do with the narrative, it does not appear that the work's goals were dominated by therapeutic interests.

Therapists who work with trauma survivors aim to act as listeners who accept the truth of the victims' testimonies so that they can see their own witness as true, and so that they can eventually create a narrative in which the trauma is known by a self that can retain some perspective and distance from the traumatic events (Auerhahn and Laub 1998: 33). By creating a testimony that others and then oneself can accept and believe, trauma can be integrated into a sense of self (Martínez-Alfaro 2014: 189–90); trauma is then not something endured and relived as it repeats and controls the self, but part of a narrative created through choice (Brison 1999: 46–47). This is not something that is possible for all trauma survivors (Felman and Laub 1992: 78–79). Nor, to be fair, will this kind of integration even be desirable in all cases. For Judeans in exile and in the colonial context of the postexilic period, perhaps the numbing effects of trauma that free victims from terrifying feelings were more adaptive than attempts to recall and integrate it (cf. Herman 1992: 42–45; and Craps 2014: 51–57).

There is a real difference between a history writing and a trauma testimony. The goal of the first is to present the past in what the author understands as an objective manner, not to provide a therapeutic forum for traumatic anti-narrative. The author or tradents of Dtr did not need to write a history; he or she or they could have chosen instead to produce something like Lamentations, a work that allows the traumatized to give testimony. Histories, however, need not work to repress and silence trauma as Dtr does. Historians cannot simply adopt the voice of the victim if they are to remain objective, but writing with empathy creates, as LaCapra puts it, "empathetic unsettlement" that is attentive to the voices of the victims and allows their testimony to upset the narrative (LaCapra 2001: 37–42). This approach will steer the narrative away from a simplistic and redemptive closure that overwrites and thus denies the trauma (Friedlander 1993: 130–33) as Dtr does. Nonetheless, despite the author's (and/or tradents') best attempts to provide readers with a totalizing narrative of history that represses trauma, trauma appears as narrative absence, deconstructing narrative claims and putting them on unresolved trial. Dtr has silenced trauma, and so trauma can only return in the work as explanatory silence. Empathetic unsettlement is not something that the Dtr provides in and of itself; in the end it appears to have been created as a totalizing and fetishistic narrative. The empathetic unsettlement LaCapra describes is possible only once Dtr is read intertextually with a work like Lamentations.

Bibliography

Alexander, Jeffrey C. 2004. "Toward a Theory of Cultural Trauma." In Jeffrey C. Alexander, ed., *Cultural Trauma and Collective Identity*. Berkeley, CA: University of California Press, 1–30.

Alphen, Erich van. 1999. "Symptoms of Discursivity: Experience, Memory, and Trauma." In Mieke Bal, Jonathan Crewe, and Leo Spitzer, eds., *Acts of Memory: Cultural Recall in the Present*. Hanover, NH: University Press of New England, 24–38.

American Psychiatric Association. 2013. *Diagnostic and Statistical Manual of Mental Disorders*. 5th ed. Washington, D.C.: American Psychiatric Publishing.

Améry, Jean. 1980. *At the Mind's Limits: Contemplations by a Survivor on Auschwitz and Its Realities*. Translated by Sidney Rosenfeld and Stella P. Rosenfeld. Bloomington, IN: Indiana University Press.

Auerhahn, Nanette C. and Dori Laub. 1998. "Intergenerational Memory of the Holocaust." In Yael Danieli, ed., *International Handbook of Multigenerational Legacies of Trauma*. New York: Plenum Press, 21–41.

Brison, Susan J. 1999. "Trauma Narratives and the Remaking of the Self." In Mieke Bal, Jonathan Crewe, and Leo Spitzer, eds., *Acts of Memory: Cultural Recall in the Present*. Hanover, NH: University Press of New England, 39–54.

Brown, Laura S. 1995. "Not Outside the Range: One Feminist Perspective on Psychic Trauma." In Cathy Caruth, ed., *Trauma: Explorations in Memory*. Baltimore: The Johns Hopkins University Press, 100–12.

Caruth, Cathy. 1996. *Unclaimed Experience: Trauma, Narrative, and History*. Baltimore: The Johns Hopkins University Press.

Craps, Stef. 2014. "Beyond Eurocentrism: Trauma Theory in the Global Age." In Gert Beulens, Sam Durrant, and Robert Eaglestone, eds., *The Future of Trauma Theory: Contemporary Literary and Cultural Criticism*. London: Routledge, 45–61.

Delbo, Charlotte. 1995. *Auschwitz and After*. Translated by Rosette C. Lamont. New Haven, CT: Yale University Press.

Eyerman, Ron. 2001. *Cultural Trauma: Slavery and the Formation of African American Identity*. Cambridge: Cambridge University Press.

Felman, Shoshana and Dori Laub. 1992. *Testimony: Crises of Witnessing in Literature, Psychoanalysis, and History*. New York: Routledge.

Freud, Sigmund. 1966-74. *The Standard Edition of the Complete Psychological Works of Sigmund Freud*. Translated by James Strachey. 24 vols. London: The Hogarth Press.

Friedlander, Saul. 1993. *Memory, History, and the Extermination of the Jews of Europe*. Bloomington, IN: Indiana University Press.

Hartman, Geoffrey H. 1995. "On Traumatic Knowledge and Literary Studies." *New Literary History* 26: 537-63.

Herman, Judith Lewis. 1992. *Trauma and Recovery*. New York: Basic Books.

Hilberg, Raul. 1988. "I Was Not There." In Berel Lang, ed., *Writing and the Holocaust*. New York: Holmes & Meier, 17-25.

Janet, Pierre. 1925. *Psychological Healing: A Historical and Clinical Study*. Translated by Eden Paul and Cedar Paul. 2 vols. London: George Allen & Unwin.

Janoff-Bulman, Ronnie. 1992. *Shattered Assumptions: Towards a New Psychology of Trauma*. New York: The Free Press.

Janzen, David. 2012. *The Violent Gift: Trauma's Subversion of the Deuteronomistic History's Narrative*. LHBOTS 561. New York: T&T Clark.

Kansteiner, Wulf. 2004. "Genealogy of a Category Mistake: A Critical Intellectual History of the Cultural Trauma Metaphor." *Rethinking History* 8: 192-221.

Kolk, Basel A. van der and Onno van der Hart. 1995. "The Intrusive Past: The Flexibility of Memory and the Engraving of Trauma." In Cathy Caruth, ed., *Trauma: Explorations in Memory*. Baltimore: The Johns Hopkins University Press, 158-82.

LaCapra, Dominick. 1994. *Representing the Holocaust: History, Theory, Trauma*. Ithaca, NY: Cornell University Press.

LaCapra, Dominick. 2001. *Writing History, Writing Trauma*. Baltimore: The Johns Hopkins University Press.

Langer, Lawrence L. 1995. *Admitting the Holocaust: Collected Essays*. Oxford: Oxford University Press.

Lanzmann, Claude. 1995. *Shoah: The Complete Text of the Acclaimed Holocaust Film*. New York: Da Capo Press.

Levi, Primo. 1996. *If This Is a Man/The Truce*. Translated by Stuart Woolf. London: Vintage.

Lifton, Robert Jay. 1991. *Death in Life: Survivors of Hiroshima*. Chapel Hill, NC: The University of North Carolina Press.

Luckhurst, Roger. 2008. *The Trauma Question*. London: Routledge.

Martínez-Alfaro, María Jesús. 2014. "Fugal Repetition and the Re-enactments of Trauma: Holocaust Representation in Paul Celan's 'Deathfugue' and Cynthia Ozick's *The Shawl*." In Marita Nadal and Mónica Calvo, eds., *Trauma in Contemporary Literature: Narrative and Representation*. New York: Routledge, 178-93.

Neal, Arthur G. 1998. *National Trauma and Collective Memory: Major Events in the American Century*. Armonk, NY: M. E. Sharpe.

Novak, Amy. 2008. "Who Speaks? Who Listens? The Problem of Address in Two Nigerian Trauma Novels." *Studies in the Novel* 40: 31-51.

Rothberg, Michael. 2009. *Multidirectional Memory: Remembering the Holocaust in an Age of Decolonization*. Stanford: Stanford University Press.

Stien, Phyllis T. and Joshua C. Kendall. 2004. *Psychological Trauma and the Developing Brain: Neurologically Based Interventions for Troubled Children*. New York: The Haworth Maltreatment and Trauma Press.

Tal, Kalí. 1996. *Worlds of Hurt: Reading the Literatures of Trauma*. Cambridge: Cambridge University Press.

Visser, Irene. 2011. "Trauma Theory and Postcolonial Literary Studies." *Journal of Postcolonial Writing* 47: 270–82.
Volkan, Vamik. 1997. *Bloodlines: From Ethnic Pride to Ethnic Terrorism*. New York: Farrar, Strauss, and Giroux.
Wiesel, Elie. 1978. "Why I Write." In Alvin H. Rosenfeld and Irving Greenberg, eds., *Confronting the Holocaust: The Impact of Elie Wiesel*. Bloomington, IN: Indiana University Press, 200–206.
Wiesel, Elie. 1981. *Night*. Translated by Stella Rodway. Harmondsworth: Penguin Books.

PART IV
RECEPTION: LITERATURE, TRADITIONS, FIGURES

CHAPTER 29

JOSHUA IN RECEPTION HISTORY

ZEV I. FARBER

29.1 Reception of Joshua's Character in the Bible

The reception history of Joshua begins in the biblical text itself. Like many biblical books, the book of Joshua was not written by one author in one period, and the expansions of Joshua's story both within the book of Joshua as well as in the Pentateuch reflect the later authors' reception of his story and their reworking or expansion of it to fit their own historiographical conceptions or rhetorical needs.

Joshua's character goes through three very substantial developments from the early source material to the biblical text as we have it. Joshua likely began as a local Ephraimite military leader, similar to figures like Gideon or Jephthah. At some point, Joshua goes from being an Israelite military leader to *the first* Israelite military leader in the Cisjordan, and thus the single link in the chain between the period of the exodus and wilderness wandering, on one hand, and the settlement of the land of Canaan, on the other. This likely came as a part of Israelite mnemohistory's adoption of the Egypt and wilderness accounts as universal Israelite experiences, thus necessitating a "conquest of the Cisjordan" as a discrete event, with Joshua as the leader.

This conquering Joshua was painted in monarchic colors, if not described as an actual king, in the conquest account of Joshua 10, which mimics royal Assyrian conquest accounts, as well as in the assumption of Joshua's absolute authority over all Israel. Moreover, being the conqueror of the land, in turn, brought up the issue of land division, something with which the book of Numbers and the book of Joshua credit him.

Joshua's connection to the exodus and wilderness wandering had just as great an effect on his persona. As the leader who would receive the mantel from Moses himself, Joshua became Moses's protégé in the wilderness. This led to Joshua's explicit connection to Torah study, since a student of Moses must be infused with Torah. It also led to descriptions of Joshua as a prophet of Yhwh and as a miracle worker.[1]

All of the above images are part of Joshua's reception inside the biblical text. Later reception history often connected itself to one or another of these images based on the needs of the receiving community and/or the interest of the author writing about this important biblical figure.

29.2 The Challenge of Post-Biblical Reception

Some of the images used of Joshua that are found in the Bible are in tension with each other, or, at least, are not overlapping in the portraits they paint. A warrior is something different from a Torah scholar, or a lad who spends his early years cloistered with the deity in the Tent of Meeting. This is not to say that a warrior cannot be Torah scholar or a godly youth, only that each image could survive without the other just fine, and that they are somewhat different in hue.

Thus, it is not surprising that later works featuring Joshua will, at times, build their respective portraits around only one or two of the biblical images, jettisoning the verses and presentations that do not fit with what the author is trying to get across. This is a core challenge when studying the reception history of a venerated figure. On one hand, a pious author wishes to show continuity between his work and the revered ancient figure. On the other hand, a successful religious work wants to show relevance, and it is likely that what may have been meaningful and relevant to one society is no longer so with another. Any given author must figure out how to properly strike this balance.

In what follows, I will look at a number of presentations of Joshua. Each has its own nuances, but to simplify matters, we will divide the presentations into two general categories. In the first, Joshua is seen primarily as a leader, especially as a military leader. In the second, Joshua is viewed primarily as a religious figure, especially as the purveyor of Moses's Torah.

29.2.1 Joshua as Warrior and Political Leader

A large swath of Joshua's activities in the Bible are military, and his military accomplishments can be broadly included under the rubric of Joshua as leader and grouped with other examples of him exercising political leadership, including in the division of the land for settlement.

29.2.1.1 *Defender of Israel: Ben Sira (Second Century BCE)*

As part of his survey of Israelite leaders from Joshua to Simon the Just (Sirach 46–50), Ben Sira offers an encomium to Joshua (46:1–10) that begins by referring to him with the epithet "mighty warrior" (גיבור החיל). Joshua is further described as one who took vengeance on God's enemies and who gave the land as an inheritance to Israel. Ben Sira includes physical descriptions of Joshua's military pose, spear in hand, taken from the description of him in the battle over Ai, and refers to him as someone against whom no one could stand. Even the miracles that Ben Sira mentions, namely the stopping of the sun and the hailstones, are wartime miracles.

With these miracles, God supports Joshua during battle in response to Joshua's plea for help. Despite the aggressive nature of the imagery, Ben Sira subtly inverts the positions of invader and invaded in his description of Joshua's battles by describing the Canaanites as having attacked Joshua and even God (depending on how one translates 46:6). Perhaps Ben Sira found the image of a powerful defender of Israel more palatable then a powerful conqueror of Canaanites.

29.2.1.2 *Military Statesman: Josephus (First Century CE)*

Another ancient source that emphasizes Joshua's martial character is Josephus, in his *Antiquities of the Jews*. Josephus is influenced by Greek and Roman images of statesmen-philosophers, and his version of Joshua appears in this likeness more than in a classically biblical image. Josephus tells us that Joshua trained in military strategy and tactics under "General" (Greek *strategos*) Moses, and cuts his teeth in the battle with Amalek, for which he and Moses stayed up all night planning (*Ant.* 3.49–52).

After Moses's death and the people's mourning, Josephus transitions immediately to the story of Joshua sending the spies, eliminating God's speech encouraging Joshua (*Ant.* 5.1–2). This could simply be part of Josephus's understandable need to abridge the biblical account, but it serves to present a Joshua ready and waiting for military action.

Another difference between the biblical account and Josephus comes in Joshua's reaction to the first failure at Ai. Whereas Joshua panics in the biblical text and needs God's direct interference in order to regain his stability (Josh. 7:7–15), in *Antiquities* (*Ant.* 5.38–43), he calmly analyzes the problem and moves to a solution. Keeping calm during a crisis is the epitome of a Greek statesman-general.

This description of Joshua fits Josephus's view of Joshua as a leader. In addition to the many motivational speeches Josephus composes on Joshua's behalf, Josephus makes the transition from war to the division of land, perhaps the stickiest point in the biblical text, Joshua's idea and not God's. Josephus explains the reason for the shift as tactical: the Canaanites have pockets of fortified positions and it would be best to ignore them for now and start occupying the rest of the land. This contrasts with the much less flattering biblical presentation (Joshua 13), in which God commands Joshua to begin the division of the land because Joshua is now elderly and has not completed his work.

Josephus summarizes Joshua's life with the following:

> He was a man not falling short in sagacity, nor unacquainted with setting out his thoughts clearly to the masses, rather [he was] topmost in both of these. In both works and hazards he was of stout heart and greatly adventurous. He held sway with great skill over matters of peace, at all times adapting himself to the good. (*Ant.* 5.118)[2]

Nothing in this description contradicts the biblical image of Joshua, and yet it is at some remove from the biblical portrayal. Joshua, in Josephus, is an ideal Hellenistic military statesman.

29.2.1.3 *Ambivalence about Joshua as a Warrior and King: Mekhilta of Rabbi Ishmael (Third Century* CE*)*

Although not the dominant image in rabbinic literature, the Mekhilta of Rabbi Ishmael (*Parashat be-Shalaḥ, Masekhta de-Amalek* 2) pictures Joshua as a king, anointed on the day he defeated the Amalekites. This same work, however, offers a negative spin on this same image, relating that when Moses sent Joshua to fight with Amalek, he criticized Joshua for hiding under the cloud of glory and "saving his head for a crown" (*Masekhta de-Amalek* 1; author's translation).

The *Mekhilta* also expands on the image of Joshua's power and military prowess, painting him as particularly aggressive in battle, decapitating his most powerful enemies. The same text, however, also describes him as showing mercy by not desecrating the bodies.

29.2.1.4 *Joshua the Warrior and Giant Killer: Tarikh al-Ṭabari (Ninth–Tenth Centuries* CE*)*

The Persian Muslim scholar Abū Jaʿfar Muḥammad ibn Jarīr al-Ṭabarī wrote a chronicle recounting the history of Israel, the Arabs, and the Persians from creation until 915 CE called, *A History of the Prophets and Kings* (popularly referred to as *Tarikh al-Ṭabari*). In Book 3 of this work, al-Ṭabari tells his version of the story of Joshua. Since al-Ṭabari used multiple sources of information for his chronicle, including Muslim, Jewish, and Christian traditions, his description is neither linear nor uniform. Nevertheless, his presentation focuses on Joshua as a warrior, especially the tradition of Joshua defeating giants—a theme already present in the biblical account (see Josh. 11:21–22).

Joshua's first act as leader in the *Tarikh* is to attack Jericho and destroy the giants therein (Al-Ṭabari, 1991: 88). The Bible makes no mention of Jericho having giants, but al-Ṭabari seems to work with the assumption that all the natives of Canaan were giants, ostensibly based on his understanding of the spy story in Numbers with its claim that the spies felt like grasshoppers in comparison with the people they saw there (Num. 13:33).

Mixing the battle of Jericho with the battle against the southern coalition, al-Ṭabari has Joshua stop the sun for an hour while the Israelites attack the giants and destroy them. After the battle, Joshua offers sacrifices but they are not accepted. He immediately realizes that someone took some of the spoils of war, and when he finds the person, he burns the culprit and the stolen goods in a sacrifice to God.

Al-Ṭabari then tells another version of the Jericho story, then the Ai story, then war with the king of Jerusalem, whom Joshua reduces to beggary. He then quickly tells the story of the war with the five kings, and the execution of these kings who were hiding in a cave. Then he covers Joshua's conquest of the rest of the cities of the Cisjordan in a sentence, and Joshua's division of the land in half a sentence before ending with Joshua's death.

In short, Joshua from beginning to end is a warrior and conqueror for al-Ṭabari. Joshua stands out because of his battling of giants, his multiple conquests, the vast amounts of enemies he slaughtered, and his ability to use miracles against his foes.

29.2.1.5 *The Regal King Joshua: Samaritan Book of Joshua (Fourteenth Century* CE*)*

The Samaritan community does not have a canonical book of Joshua, though they do hold him in high esteem. Eventually, a non-canonical book of Joshua was written in Arabic during the medieval period, which (re)tells the story of Joshua and the conquest. Samaritan Joshua (*SJ*) offers multiple images of its protagonist, but its dominant and distinctive image is as a king.

The scene retelling Joshua's assumption of power after Moses's death is an inauguration scene, complete with flags, banners, and explicit use of the term "king" (*malik*). Joshua wears a purple robe and a crown, and he sits on a throne.

Joshua's reign is characterized by his military exploits. In that sense, *SJ* follows the overall contours of the biblical account in Joshua 1–12. *SJ* begins, however, with a preamble describing the war against Midian. In the biblical text (Numbers 33), Joshua is never mentioned with regard to this battle, but in *SJ* he plays a crucial role. In a scene reminiscent of Josephus's treatment, Joshua asks to take part in the Midianite battle so that he can learn tactics and gain experience from the master, Moses.

One method *SJ* employs to heighten Joshua's majesty and fearsomeness is having secondary characters describe him to other characters in the text. So, for example, pretending to be natives on the way back from a scouting excursion, the Israelite spies report that they saw Joshua and describe the encounter as follows:

> This man was a colossus. His speech shatters [people's] spirits and his words cleave hearts.... No sooner had we stood before him when he announced our names and our lineage and our country, as well as when we began our journey and the spots where we went—and he was correct about everything he said about us.... And we know his name is Joshua son of Nun, and that he put to flight the Amalekites and is the killer of Sihon and the destroyer of Og, and the annihilator of the kings of Midian and Moab.   (*SJ*, 13)[3]

This speech may have been designed to strike fear, but as the reader finds out in a later chapter, if anything the spies were underreporting Joshua's fearsomeness. After the completion of the conquest, Israel is challenged in battle by a new enemy: Shaubak, king of Persia, an account unique to *SJ*. This enemy has a powerful army of sorcerers and giants, and Shaubak's opening salvo is in a letter to Joshua in which he refers to him as "a murdering wolf" and derides him for having had no mercy, even killing women and children during his conquest (a claim that is true according to the biblical text).

Joshua receives this letter on Pentecost, and tells the people nothing about it, so as not to ruin the festivities. This detail underscores Joshua's presence of mind and self-control, essential characteristics for a good leader. After the holiday, Joshua calls in the messengers who delivered the letter to receive his response, in which Joshua includes the following description of himself:

> I do not boast to be a giant, or the disciple of a giant, or the child of a giant. I boast that I am a disciple of the Speaker of God [Moses], physically and spiritually, and the child of the Friend of God [Abraham], foundation of the prophets and the pure branch. I boast in the myriads of the holy who march with my army. I am not a giant but the master of giants is with me, and my height from the ground is five royal cubits. There is no armor in my dress, likewise for mail and helmets; rather my dress is a gown colored of azure and purple and scarlet, and a royal crown is upon my head, and the name of my Lord is written upon the crown. I ride a white colt, whose cloth is purple and whose saddle is of pure gold.   (*SJ*, ch. 29)

The presentation of Joshua in this passage combines three elements. He underlines his ties to God and to God's chosen representatives on earth; he emphasizes his royal attire and prestige; and he makes it known that, though not a giant proper, he is enormous: about eight feet (2.5 meters) tall. This description, combined with the messengers' report about Joshua, Elazar, and the Israelite army has a strong effect on Shaubak's troops, bringing many of them to tears.

Surprisingly, Joshua is not the hero of the Shaubak story. In fact, Joshua is captured in the ensuing battle by wizardry and must be saved by the vassal king he had appointed over the Transjordan, Nabih (biblical Nobah). To get Nabih to bring his army and rescue him, Joshua writes him a letter and sends it to Nabih tied to the leg of a dove. In it, Joshua, though clearly frightened, keeps his presence of mind and rhetorical skill:

> Get up right now, do not sleep! If you are sleeping—awaken; and if you are awake—sit up; and if you are sitting—stand; and if you are standing—walk; and if you are walking—hurry!
> (*SJ* ch. 36)

Once Joshua is rescued, he rejoins the great battle and even calls up the powers of the wind to blow back the powerful thunderbolts of Japhet's son as well as the arrows and spears of the enemies' other giants. (In *SJ*, Japhet's son, i.e., Noah's grandson, is an evil giant with magical powers, still alive in the time of Joshua and fighting on the side of Shaubak.) In short, Joshua in *SJ* is a king, a warrior, and even a wizard all rolled into one.

29.2.1.6 *The Conqueror of Israel: Ben Gurion's Zionist Narrative (1958)*

That the early leaders of the embattled *Yishuv* (the Jewish community in Palestine) and, after 1948, the nascent State of Israel, would look to Joshua as precedent and inspiration is not surprising. One pointed example of this is the study group that the first Prime Minister of Israel, David Ben Gurion, convened in his home in 1958. The idea was that the presentations would be academically sound, and the findings and eventual write up would demonstrate the utility of the Zionist project for understanding the Bible accurately. The inaugural biblical book chosen for the group was the book of Joshua.

The choice of Joshua was not random. Ben Gurion saw Joshua as a symbol of "actualized Zionism" and once declared that no one had better interpreted Joshua than the Israeli defense forces in 1948.[4] In fact, Moshe Dayan, an important Israel general, compared himself to Joshua explicitly.[5] Ben Gurion further felt that the use of a biblical figure such as Joshua as a symbol would garner more international sympathy and support for the Zionist project.

Each week a different speaker presented an analysis of a given aspect of the book, and this was followed by discussion and debate, all of which is recorded in the final publication. Many of the speakers were reputable biblical scholars, others were academically minded Israeli politicians, such as the Prime Minister himself, the President (Yitzhak Ben-Zvi), and the head of the Jewish Agency (Zalman Shazar).

Many of the talks focused on the historicity of the battle accounts, from different perspectives. The study group was functioning at a time when the ascending view in academia, especially among American and Israeli scholars, was that of the American archaeologist, William Foxwell Albright, who believed that conquest account was more or less supported by archaeology and should be treated as historical. In fact, one of the speakers was Yigael Yadin, an Israeli archaeologist whose work was fully in line with Albright's understanding. Since Yadin was also the military head of operations during the War of Independence, and one of the key strategists behind the Israeli victory in 1948, one could easily imagine him as an instantiation of Joshua in the eyes of some of his contemporaries.

Significantly, both Yadin and another archaeologist, Yohanan Aharoni, emphasized the importance of settlement in their respective talks: for Yadin, settlement was the completion of conquest; for Aharoni, it was in lieu of conquest.[6] Such interpretations cannot be divorced from the speakers' circumstances; it would be unrealistic to imagine that the participants in this study group would be able to entirely divorce their analyses of what the Israelites faced in the period of conquest from the reality of the Israeli experience that they themselves faced.

After defeating the invading armies in 1948 and receiving recognition from the United Nations, Israel needed to settle the land more extensively. In addition, after the Jews living in Muslim dominated countries were forcibly evicted from their homes in the wake of the War of Independence and relocated to Israel, the Israeli government had a serious refugee problem that required massive resources to resettle these people in their new land. Yadin and Aharoni were likely reading Joshua 13–19 with this in mind, especially since this part of Joshua, unlike chs. 6–12, assume a large native Canaanite population still living in the land—a reality comparable to the one Israelis encountered with Palestinian natives now under their control.

Rachel Havrelock has pointed out that Aharoni's description of the archaeological picture of the Israelite settlement is highly reminiscent of the kibbutz movement in the pre-state *Yishuv* days. According to Aharoni, the Israelites enter and settle an area that is not being used, and this is where they build their houses and plant their farms. It is only later in the process, once the Israelites are already established, that altercations and eventually battles come about between the Israelites, who mostly occupy the hill country, and the Canaanite city-states, mostly in the lowlands.

The final talk, David Ben Gurion's "The Antiquity of Israel on Its Land," sets the tone for the entire project. Ben Gurion argues that the entirety of the exodus and wilderness wandering accounts, including slavery, the departure from Egypt, and the Sinai experience, only happened to the Joseph tribes. When Joshua returns with this group, he brings along with him the new Mosaic Law and the covenant with Yhwh. With this, he organizes all the Israelites, those who are returning and those who were already there, and leads them in a war to establish Israelite dominance on the land.

Setting aside the question of whether such a theory has any historical merit, its significance is found in the underlying point: Israel has always been on its land. Some left and then returned, but the land was always filled with Israelites from the time of the patriarchs. Perhaps even more significant for Ben Gurion, Joshua is the leader of the returning Israelites—in modern Israeli parlance, the *Olim Chadasim*—and he becomes the leader of all the Israelites, both native born and newly returning. It seems unlikely that David Ben Gurion, the duly elected leader of Israel and Israelis (including the native born) did not have in the back of his mind that he himself was an immigrant, and that before 1906 (i.e., until he was 20 years old), he was David Grün of Plonsk, Poland.

29.2.2 Religious Figure

In the Bible, Joshua is Moses's servant and successor. He communicates with God directly in the Tent of Meeting, is told to deliberate on Torah day and night, sets up an altar for God in the new land, circumcises the men, holds a Passover celebration, performs miracles, and exhorts the people to be loyal to Yhwh. These various points gave ample room for later interpreters to present him as an important religious figure.

29.2.2.1 A Prophet of the Pesher Style: Apocryphon of Joshua (Second–First Centuries BCE)

The *Apocryphon of Joshua* only survives in fragments and thus it is impossible to offer a reading of Joshua's image in this work in general. Nevertheless, the surviving fragments include scenes in which Joshua prophesies the future. In one fragment, Joshua predicts how someone will rebuild Jericho and how he and his sons will die, tying the curse in Josh. 6:26 to the story of Hiel and his sons in 1 Kgs. 16:34.

In another fragment, Joshua prophesies the birth of David, even mentioning his father's name. He further predicts the conquest of Jerusalem and describes the preparations David will make for the building of the Temple in matter reminiscent of Chronicles. Thus, the *Apocryphon of Joshua* bears some relationship to the *pesher* style of interpretation, a hermeneutic approach to the Bible popular in the Qumran community, in which a biblical passage or prophecy is interpreted as directly relevant to later times. Although it is not a classic *pesher*, since it does not relate the passages in Joshua to the interpreter's time, it participates in the genre of *pesher* insofar as it turns Joshua into someone who offers his generation specific information about the future, something that Joshua does not do in the biblical book.

29.2.2.2 A Philosopher Companion for Moses: Philo (Early First Century CE)

Some Greco-Roman period sources focus on Joshua only as Moses's apprentice and successor. These sources are not really interested in Joshua, but see his role as accentuating that of Moses. Philo (ca. 25 BCE–50 CE), for example, describes a number of scenes in which Joshua interacts with Moses, all of which focus on Moses's state of mind. This is likely because Philo deals primarily, and almost exclusively, with the Pentateuch in his many works.

Philo describes the relationship between Moses and Joshua in terms reminiscent of David and Jonathan, as a "heavenly and unmixed love from which all virtue is derived" (*Virt.* 55). The image of philosophical friendship was an important *topos* in Greek culture, and Philo even offers an example of a philosophical dialogue between Moses and Joshua in his allegorical interpretation of their conversation upon hearing the noise from the camp in the golden calf story.

Philo describes Moses's joy when God picks Joshua to be his successor, due to Joshua's being "his most excellent pupil and the imitator of his amiable and excellent disposition" (*Virt.* 66). Similarly, in his explanation for Moses changing Joshua's name, Philo writes,

"Joshua means 'the salvation of the Lord' being the name of the most excellent possible character" (*Mut.* 122). In short, Joshua is generically "excellent" but only interesting insofar as he mirrors and continues Moses's legacy.

29.2.2.3 Religious Poet and Builder of Altars: Biblical Antiquities of Pseudo-Philo (First or Second Century CE)

In rewriting the biblical narrative from Adam to Saul, the *Biblical Antiquities* of Pseudo-Philo dedicates five chapters to Joshua. *Biblical Antiquities* follows the basic contours of the biblical storyline but only in broad strokes. Despite the ample space given to the Joshua account, *Biblical Antiquities* has only one half-verse about Joshua doing battle or conquering and just one half-verse about Joshua dividing land among the tribes. This may be contrasted with the biblical account, which devotes no less than six chapters to battle (Joshua 6–8, 10–12) and seven chapters (Joshua 13–19) to divvying up the land; the difference in emphasis is clear.

The account of Joshua in *Biblical Antiquities* begins with his near collapse upon the news of Moses's death. God has to tell Joshua to calm down, stop crying, and take his position as leader. He even commands Joshua to put on Moses's old clothes so that he can become a new man. Although this opening presentation of Joshua isn't negative per se, since there is merit in mourning the death of Moses and understanding the depth of that loss, it is not quite positive either, since leaders are meant to lead, not collapse, in the face of difficult circumstances. That said, this negatively tinged opening is exceptional in *Biblical Antiquities*, since its overall portrayal of Joshua is decidedly positive. Joshua's most conspicuous role in *Biblical Antiquities* is as a speechmaker and songwriter. His speechmaking begins earlier than his role as a leader. When the scouts discourage the people from entering the land with their report, Joshua poetically and sarcastically retorts:

> Just as sturdy iron can overcome stars, or just as weapons can vanquish flashes of lightening, or just as the will of man can extinguish thunder, thus can this people oppose God.
> (*L.A.B.* 15.2; author's translation)

Upon assuming the mantel of leadership, Joshua delivers a severe speech that warns Israel that the consequences of sin will be God abandoning them. In an inversion of Moses's petition to God in Exod 32:11–13, Joshua tells the people that neither worry about what the gentiles will say nor even the promise to the Patriarchs will protect them from divine abandonment if they disobey God.

Another major speech comes as Joshua solves the crisis of the Transjordanian altar by delivering a fire and brimstone oration. Most significantly, Joshua relies on the threat of God's anger as well as the emphasis on what is proper worship according to the Torah. But he does not threaten military action—another example of how Joshua is transformed into an almost entirely religious icon in *Biblical Antiquities*.

Two more speeches appear in the work, perhaps meant to reflect the two final speeches in the biblical book (Joshua 23–24). The first is the longest and most intricate of Joshua's speeches in *Biblical Antiquities*, in which he describes Israel's history, emphasizing themes such as Abraham's piety and the revelation at Sinai. His final speech, right before his death, is terse and pessimistic in tone. Joshua dies believing the Israelites will fail and be punished, mimicking the attitude in the song of Moses (and Joshua!) in Deuteronomy 32.

Joshua's other major role in *Biblical Antiquities* is as the establisher of holy sites. He erects a stone altar in Gilgal and plasters the Torah on stones on Mount Ebal, where he offers peace-offerings, sings songs of praise, and dances with the ark—all activities usually associated with priests and Levites. Finally, he sets up a semi-permanent worship site in Shiloh, and establishes a yearly holiday (whether at Shiloh or Gilgal is unclear).

29.2.2.4 *A Frightened Student and Keeper of a Secret Scroll: Assumptio Mosis (First–Second Centuries CE)*

Assumptio Mosis (The Assumption of Moses) offers an account of Moses's final conversation with Joshua. Most of the work is an eschatological prediction that Moses has written down and wishes Joshua to save for the Jews to read at the end of days. The beginning and end of the work (as it now stands; the manuscript is cut off and so the true ending is lost) are a conversation between Moses and Joshua, in which Moses tells Joshua that he will soon die and informs him of his role to bear this scroll with its eschatological prediction. Moses informs Joshua of his need to be strong and to keep Torah, which reflects the spirit of the Deuteronomistic account found in Deuteronomy 31 and Joshua 1.

The surprising element in *Assumptio Mosis* is Joshua's reaction; he panics. He collapses at Moses's feet, tears his clothes, and proceeds to deliver a fear-driven rant that lasts for thirteen verses. Some of his fears are strange, such as the claim that no one will succeed in burying Moses, but most have to do with his new responsibilities: Joshua is afraid that he will not succeed in providing the Israelites with enough food and water; he is afraid that God will not listen to his entreaties;[7] and he is afraid that he will not be able to defeat the Amorites in battle.

This last fear is particularly not in keeping with Joshua's image in the Bible. Since when is Joshua, the defeater of Amalek, the brave and loyal spy, and the conqueror of Canaan, afraid of war? This unusual depiction underlines the key philosophical claim of *Assumptio Mosis*: humans have no power in this world. Everything is in God's hands. Since Moses was exceedingly pious, God made him successful, but if Joshua is not as pious as Moses—and he believes he is not—then he may fail. This image of leadership is par for the course in a book whose messianic figure (Taxo) saves the world by starving himself and his sons to death in a hunger strike against the wicked gentiles. In a book dedicated to the concept of passive resistance, Joshua the fearless conqueror has no real place.

29.2.2.5 *The Joshua-Jesus Typology: Early Christian Interpretations (Second–Fourth Centuries CE)*

In Greek, Joshua and Jesus have the same name. This fact would have been obvious to any Greek-speaking Jew or early Christian, and may even have been implied in the New Testament accounts of Jesus at the Jordan River, or in possible allusions to Joshua in Hebrews 3–4 (see Whitfield 2010). Nevertheless, the correlation makes its first explicit appearance in the *Epistle of Barnabas* (late first or early second century CE), which offers an allegorical interpretation of the Amalek account of Exodus 17. *Barnabas* 12 states that the Israelites won because of the figural appearance of Jesus on the battlefield: Moses stretched out his arms as Christ did on the cross, and Joshua shares Jesus's name.

From observations like this, a Joshua-Jesus typology was created and was a dominant force in early Jewish-Christian polemics. A developed version of the typology is a key part of Justin Martyr's (103–65 CE) *Dialogue with Trypho*. In addition to the use of the typology to explain the Amalek story, Justin Martyr makes a number of other connections. He is particularly interested in Num 13:16 (LXX text), the scene in which Moses changes Joshua's name from *Ausei* (Hosea) to *Iesus* (Joshua). He ties this to the claim God makes in Exod. 23:21, where God states that a messenger will be sent "who will bear my name." Justin states (paragraphs 75, 106, 113) that the messenger, whose role it was to conquer Canaan, is none other than Joshua, and God's name (i.e., the name "Jesus") was upon him. Justin also picks up on the description of Joshua circumcising the people a second time, interpreting this as an allegory for the spiritual circumcision that Jesus will offer the world in the future.

Another Church Father who made extensive use of this typology, also in polemical fashion, was Tertullian (ca. 160–225 CE) in his *Adversus Iudaeos*. Although making a number of the same arguments as Justin, Tertullian emphasizes the larger argument of the typology. Joshua was Moses's successor. Moses gave Israel the law and Joshua gave them the Promised Land. This foreshadows the relationship between Jesus and Torah. The Jews had the law, but Jesus is the successor to the law and will bring the "wandering people"—that is, the gentiles—to the "Promised Land"—that is, salvation and eternal life.

A third Church Father who made use of this typology in anti-Jewish polemic was Zeno of Verona (ca. 300–80 CE), who literally taunts his (imagined) Jewish opponents with the "fact" that Joshua was meant to foreshadow Jesus, and that the Jews should realize the need to circumcise their hearts in Christ (as per Tertullian's understanding of Joshua's circumcision of the Israelites for a second time), but that they are too stubbornly "Pharisaic" to accept it (*Sermons* 1.13).

Despite its early utility as a polemical argument against Jews, the Joshua-Jesus typology comes into its own as an intra-Christian concept in Origen's (ca. 185–250 CE) *Homilies on Joshua*. In his first homily, Origen offers an allegorical interpretation of Joshua the person. Like Justin and Tertullian, Origen is interested in Joshua's name, but since he is preaching to a Christian audience, and not polemicizing with an imagined Jewish one, he is free to interpret New Testament passages as well. Thus, he reads the reference in Phil. 2:9–10, regarding Jesus's name being "above all names," as a reference to the name Joshua/Jesus (as opposed to the name "Christ" or "Lord" which seems to have been the letter's intent). Since the name is so special, it can be no coincidence that Moses's successor Joshua bore it and that Moses specifically renamed him with it.

Reading the Amalek story, Origen finds a different message than Barnabas did. Moses does not lead the army against the enemy because he cannot; he needs Joshua to accomplish this task. In this way, we can see that Joshua was greater than Moses. The same holds true of Moses being unable to deliver the Promised Land to Israel and requiring Joshua to do it instead. In fact, Origen compares the acts of Moses in the Torah to those of Joshua in the Book of Joshua, and finds that Joshua was the greater leader. Perhaps Origen's most poignant allegorical reading is of Josh. 1:1, in which God says to Joshua "Moses, my servant, is dead." Origen comments,

Indeed, the law is dead, and the legal precepts are now defunct.... Therefore, Iesu, my Lord and Savior, took up the headship. (Homily 1 parag. 3)[8]

Eusebius of Caesarea (263–339 CE) adds another verse to support the correlation between Joshua and Jesus. In Exod. 25:40, God tells Moses that he should make everything "according to the form shown you on the mountain." Eusebius argues that God himself, i.e., Jesus, is the form Moses sees on the mountain, and for this reason Moses picks Hosea bin Nun as his successor, and gives him the name "Joshua/Jesus" (*Historia Ecclesiastica* 1.3; *Demonstratio Evangelica* 4.7).

Cyril of Jerusalem (313–86 CE) also discusses the typology in his *Catecheses* (10.11), listing Joshua and Jesus's parallel actions. Joshua crosses the Jordan; Jesus is baptized in the Jordan. Joshua appoints twelve people to divide the land; Jesus has twelve apostles. Joshua saves Rahab the harlot; Jesus offers salvation to harlots. Joshua makes the walls of Jericho fall with a sound (the blast of the shofar); Jesus predicts the Temple will fall with a sound (his voice).

The Syriac-speaking Church Fathers do not make use of the Joshua-Jesus typology. Nevertheless, Aphrahat (270–345 CE) does express interest in parallels between Jesus and Joshua. The comparison appears in a number of his demonstrations, primarily in a polemical context. In his attack against the Jewish practice of physical circumcision (*Demonstrations* 11), he offers no less than eight examples of how Joshua prefigures Jesus. Aphrahat prefers quantity over intricate argumentation, and thus many of his examples seem forced, such as: Joshua erected rocks as testimony and Jesus named Simon "Rock" (*Kephas*). Aphrahat has a similar list of comparisons (*Demonstrations* 21), showing how Joshua and Jesus were both persecuted. Ironically, in order to make this argument, Aphrahat needs to turn the entire conquest of Canaan into an example of Joshua fighting in self-defense, a very creative and against-the-grain reading of that text.

Despite the fact that Aphrahat offers more parallels between Joshua and Jesus than any of the Church Fathers, he makes very little use of the name correlation. In fact, in a number of other demonstrations, Aphrahat makes the same type of comparison between Jesus and other figures (e.g., Moses in *Demonstrations* 12 and 20), such that a reader who was unfamiliar with the earlier patristic typology would not think that Jesus's connection with Joshua was any more significant than his connection with other characters from the Old Testament.

29.2.2.6 *The Rabbi of the Land: Rabbinic Interpretation (Second–Seventh Centuries CE)*

In rabbinic literature, Joshua is a rabbi. He forms an essential link in the chain of the Oral Law's transmission (*m. Abot.* 1.1) and demonstrates his worthiness to replace Moses by giving a lecture in the study house with Moses in the audience (*Sifrei* Numbers 140; *Midrash Tanḥuma*, "VaEthanan," 6). As the first "rabbi" of the land, Joshua commands ten new post-Mosaic laws about the land (*b. Bab. Qam.* 80b–81a), dealing with practical matters such as grazing and fishing rights. He was also the first to enact *periah*, the peeling back the epithelium during circumcision (*b. Yeb.* 71b).

Joshua is also portrayed as a composer of liturgy, specifically the second blessing of the grace after meals, "on the land and sustenance" (*b. Ber.* 48b) and the *Aleinu* prayer (*Sha'arei*

Teshuvah 43, dating to the medieval period). Joshua was so righteous that the manna fell only due to his merits (*Mekhilta of Rabbi Ishmael; Be-Shalaḥ, Masekhta de-Va-Yissa* 3). Appreciating her faith and service, Joshua marries Rahab after the conquest of Jericho (*b. Meg.* 14b).

Joshua is Moses's protégé, even treating him like God (*Abot of Rabbi Nathan* A, ch. 27). He makes a fool of himself nagging Moses to study Torah with him (*Midrash Tannaim*, Deut. 34:9). He serves as Moses's valet, gathering his breakfast (*manna*) in the morning and carrying his washing to the bathhouse for him (*Midrash Tzedaqot* 1.6–7). Joshua even tries to save Moses from dying by praying for him until the angel Samael forces him to stop (*Midrash Peṭirat Moshe*).

Joshua was nevertheless inferior to Moses, who was the greatest prophet. So, Joshua's greatest miracle, the stopping of the sun, was in fact also performed by Moses (*Sifrei Deuteronomy; Parshat Ha'azinu*, 306; *b. Avod. Zar.* 25a). The hailstones that fall on the enemy during Joshua's defense of Gibeon were left over from the hailstorm Moses brought down on the Egyptians (*b. Ber.* 54b). The Gibeonites, who tricked Joshua, had actually tried this trick on Moses first, but with no success (*Midrash Tanḥuma; Nitzavim* 5).

The rabbis illustrate the inferiority of Joshua to Moses graphically by saying that whereas Moses was like the sun, Joshua was like the moon—that is, a lesser light (*Sifrei Numbers, Pinḥas* 140; *b. Bab. Bat.* 75a). Joshua even (unintentionally) once cancelled Torah study, the afternoon sacrifice, and a night of procreation (*b. Eruv.* 63b). During the mourning period for Moses, he forgot hundreds or even thousands of *halakhot* and legal proofs (*b. Tem.* 16a).

29.2.2.7 *The Joshua Generation: United States President Barack Obama (2008)*

The utility and power of Joshua imagery persists. In modern times, the U.S. President Barack Obama made use of the imagery of Joshua taking the Israelites into the Promised Land as part of his campaign for presidency. In Obama's discourse, the previous generation of African Americans, who fought for civil rights, were the Moses Generation. He makes reference to a number of leaders for this generation, such as Rosa Parks, John Lewis, Anne Cooper, and the Reverend Joseph Lowery, but the Moses he seems to envision is the Reverend Martin Luther King, Jr. This generation marched, just as the Israelites marched, and even won many battles, but they did not make it to the Promised Land.

In Obama's usage, the Promised Land stands for full integration into American society, with no barriers even to the highest office. As the first African American candidate for president to be chosen by one of the main American political parties, Obama was poised to break that final barrier, and thus, in his allegory, he was Joshua to King's Moses. In a speech he delivered in Selma, Alabama in 2007, Obama said:

> I'm here because somebody marched. I'm here because you all sacrificed for me. I stand on the shoulders of giants. I thank the Moses generation; but we've got to remember, now, that Joshua still had a job to do. As great as Moses was, despite all that he did, leading a people out of bondage, he didn't cross over the river to see the Promised Land. God told him your job is done. You'll see it. You'll be at the mountain top and you can see what I've promised.... You will see that I've fulfilled that promise but you won't go there. We're going to leave it to the

Joshua generation to make sure it happens. There are still battles that need to be fought; some rivers that need to be crossed.... The previous generation, the Moses generation, pointed the way. They took us 90% of the way there. We still got that 10% in order to cross over to the other side. So the question, I guess, that I have today is what's called of us in this Joshua generation? What do we do in order to fulfill that legacy; to fulfill the obligations and the debt that we owe to those who allowed us to be here today? (March 4, 2007)[9]

Obama's use of Joshua leading the people to the Promised Land to represent Obama's leading of the African-American community into an age of equality highlights the flexibility of Joshua's image in reception history. Whether or not this reading of Joshua, or any of the others surveyed in this piece, can be considered a "good" reading of the text from a critical perspective is questionable; nevertheless, they all attest to the power of his character in the Bible, and its continued ability to speak to people, ancient, medieval, and modern, from biblical times to the present.

29.3 Conclusion

The above survey highlights the paradox of important characters in myth and history. On one hand, each reception demonstrates a continuity with the past, maintaining the importance of a character, who was esteemed by the ancient Israelites and Judeans more than two millennia ago. On the other hand, different societies have different needs and ideals, and thus, although it is always the same Joshua in a broad sense, in another sense, each society has its own Joshua.

Notes

1. The latter point may already have been part of Joshua's story, but it received more emphasis once Joshua became connected to Moses.
2. Author's translation in consultation with Begg 2005.
3. Author's translation in consultation with Anderson and Giles 2005: 67–142.
4. See discussion in Shapira 1997: 645–74.
5. Dayan 1978: 225–26.
6. Aharoni subscribed to Albrecht Alt's hypothesis of slow migration from the Transjordan.
7. This strongly contrasts with 4 Ezra 7: 106–108, which describes Joshua as a prophetic intercessor on behalf of the people, as Abraham and Moses were.
8. Origen 2002: 29.
9. See Peters and Woolley.

Bibliography

Al-Ṭabari, Abū Ja'far Muḥammad ibn Jarīr. 1991. *History of the Prophets and Kings*, Vol. 3: *The Children of Israel*. Translated by William Brinner. Albany: University of New York Press.

Anderson, Robert T. and Terry Giles. 2005. *Tradition Kept: The Literature of the Samaritans.* Peabody: Hendrickson.

Barthelot, Katell. 2010. "The Image of Joshua in Jewish Sources from the Second Temple Period." *Meghillot* 8–9: 97–112. [Hebrew]

Begg, Christopher T. 2005. *Judean Antiquities Books 5–7: Translation and Commentary.* Flavius Josephus: Translation and Commentary 4. Leiden: Brill.

Begg, Christopher T. 2010. "Josephus' and Pseudo-Philo's rewritings of the Book of Joshua." In Ed Noort, ed., *The Book of Joshua*. BETL 250. Leuven: Leuven University Press, 555–88.

Corley, Jeremy. 2010. "Joshua as Warrior in Ben Sira 46:1–10." In Jan Liesen and Pancratius C. Beentjes, eds., *Visions of Peace and Tales of War.* Deuterocanonical and Cognate Literature Yearbook. Berlin: de Gruyter, 207–48.

Daniélou, Jean. 1960. *From Shadows to Reality: Studies in the Biblical Typology of the Fathers.* Translated by Dom Wulstan Hibberd. Westminster: The Newman Press.

Dayan, Moshe. 1978. *Living with the Bible*. Illustrated by Gemma Levine. New York: William Morrow.

De Vos, J. Cornelis. 2010. "Josua und Jesus im Neuen Testament." In Ed Noort, ed., *The Book of Joshua*. BETL 250. Leuven: Leuven University Press, 523–40.

Earl, Douglas S. 2010. *Reading Joshua as Christian Scripture*. JTISup 2. Winona Lake, IN: Eisenbrauns.

Elßner, Thomas R. 2008. *Josua und seine Kriege in jüdischer und christlicher Rezeptionsgeschichte.* TF 37. Stuttgart: W. Kohlhammer.

Farber, Zev I. 2016. *Images of Joshua in the Bible and Their Reception.* BZAW 457. Berlin: de Gruyter.

Feldman, Louis H. 1989. "Josephus's Portrait of Joshua." *HTR* 82: 351–476.

Feldman, Louis H. 2001. "Philo's Interpretation of Joshua." *JSP* 12: 165–68.

Havrelock, Rachel. 2013. "The Joshua Generation: Conquest and the Promised Land." *CRR* 1: 308–26.

Hurtado, Larry W. 2007. "'Jesus' as God's Name, and Jesus as God's Embodied Name in Justin Martyr." In Sara Parvis and Paul Foster, eds., *Justin Martyr and His Worlds*. Minneapolis: Fortress Press, 128–36.

Niessen, Friedrich. 2000. *Eine Samaritanische Version des Buches Yehošua und die Šobak-Erzählung.* TSO 12. Hildesheim: Georg Olms.

Noort, Ed. 2000. "Joshua: The History of Reception and Hermeneutics." In Johannes C. De Moor and Harry F. Van Rooy, ed., *Past, Present, Future: The Deuteronomistic History and the Prophets*. OTS 44. Leiden: Brill, 199–215.

Noort, Ed. 2006. "Der Reißende Wolf—Josua in Überlieferung und Geschichte." In *Congress Volume Leiden 2004*. VTSup 109. Leiden: Brill, 153–73.

Origen. 2002. *Homilies on Joshua*. Translated by Barbara Bruce. Edited by Cynthia White. FC 105. Washington, D.C.: Catholic University of American Press.

Peters, Gerhard and John T. Woolley. *The American Presidency Project*. Online at http://www.presidency.ucsb.edu/ws/?pid=77042.

Rabin, Hayim, Yehuda Elitzur, Hayim Gevaryahu, and Ben Tzion Luria, eds. 1971. *Studies in Tanakh by the Study Group in the House of David Ben-Gurion*. Jerusalem: Kiryat Sefer. [Hebrew]

Reiner, Elchanan. 2012. "From Joshua through Jesus to Simeon bar Yohai: Towards a Typology of Galilean Heroes." In Neta Stahl, ed., *Jesus among the Jews: Representation and Thought*. Routledge Jewish Studies Series. London: Routledge, 94–105.

Remnick, David. 2008. "The Joshua Generation Race and the Campaign of Barack Obama." *The New Yorker*, November 17: 68–83.

Rofé Alexander. 2004. "Joshua Son of Nun in the History of Biblical Tradition." *Tarbiz* 73: 333–64. [Hebrew]

Schaeffer, Francis August. 2004. *Joshua and the Flow of Biblical History*. 2nd ed. Wheaton: Crossway Books.

Shapira, Anita. 1997. "Ben-Gurion and the Bible: The Forging of an Historical Narrative?" *Middle Eastern Studies* 33.4: 645–74.

Whitfield, Bryan. 2010. "The Three Joshuas of Hebrews 3 and 4." *PRS* 37: 21–35.

Yongue, C. D. 1991. *The Works of Philo: Complete and Unabridged*. Peabody, MA: Hendrickson (orig. 1844–55).

CHAPTER 30

DEBORAH IN RECEPTION HISTORY

JOY A. SCHROEDER

JUDGES 4–5 features a remarkable character, the prophet Deborah (also spelled Devorah and Devora) who is a prophet, judge, war leader, singer, and "mother in Israel" (Judg. 5:7). In the Judges 4 prose account of her activities, Deborah judges Israel while seated under a palm tree named for her. In response to Canaanite oppression, she summons the military commander Barak and delivers a word from the LORD. Deborah instructs Barak to lead 10,000 warriors to Mount Tabor and meet the army of the Canaanite general Sisera in battle. When Barak refuses to undertake the venture without her, the prophet retorts that she will join him but the victory will be credited to a woman (Judg. 4:8–9). Deborah announces the day for the attack, which successfully defeats the Canaanites. Sisera flees to the tent of the woman Jael, who promises safety but assassinates him with a tent peg driven through his skull. Judges 5, a victory ode uttered by Deborah and Barak, is an ancient poem recounting the same story in mythic terms. Interpreters generally regard the poem to be much older than the prose text of Judges 4.

In Jewish and Christian reception of Deborah's story, gender concerns are prominent. The same themes recur through the centuries: spiritual equality of male and female; the appropriateness of educating women; questions about women's civil, religious, and military leadership; and domesticity, maternity, and proper female deportment. Interpreters also looked for meaning in Deborah's name ("bee" or "hornet") and epithet ("wife of Lappidoth" or "woman of torches").

30.1 DEBORAH THROUGHOUT TWO MILLENNIA OF LITERATURE, ART, AND MUSIC

Interpreters discussed Deborah in literary, musical, and artistic works found in an astonishingly wide variety of genres and venues. In late antiquity, Jewish sages dealt with

Deborah in midrashic, Talmudic, and other rabbinic texts. In the same period, Christian authors invoked Deborah in letters, sermons, prayers, polemical treatises, and books of church instructions. Medieval Christian clergy wrote about Deborah in commentaries, scholastic treatises, and letters to women. Christian artists depicted Deborah's battle against the Canaanites. Jewish authors compiled commentaries expanding upon earlier rabbinic themes. In the early modern period (1500–1800), women entered into the conversation with their own writings, including polemical treatises against misogyny they saw in male-authored treatises, or in defenses of women's education. Sixteenth-century European Protestant men wrestled with the appropriateness of the queenship of Mary and Elizabeth Tudor. George Frideric Handel (1685-1759) celebrated Deborah's courageousness in the oratorio *Deborah* (1733), written for a London audience.

Gender debates featuring Deborah heated up in the nineteenth century. Christians argued about the appropriateness of women preaching, voting, and holding office. Jewish and Christian women authored commentaries and "scripture biographies," a genre offering literary portraits of biblical characters, sometimes employing novelistic features. Deborah was usually included in these collections of scripture biographies, which imaginatively explored the lives of biblical women, often stressing their wisdom, virtue, and bravery. In the twentieth and twenty-first centuries, Deborah continued to be used in gender debates, in support of or opposition to women's leadership as rabbis, preachers, and civil leaders. Devotional writings and works of fiction helped girls and women reflect on the roles of mother, wife, and career woman. Jewish and Christian feminist scholarship, especially after the 1970s, sought liberating themes in Judges 4–5 and critiqued the patriarchy they found in the biblical text. Interpreters seeking to expand women's roles in synagogue, church, and society found Deborah to be a powerful model and compelling biblical precedent. Their opponents argued that Judges 4–5 did not endorse the expansion of women's public roles.

30.2 DEBORAH THE BEE, WOMAN OF TORCHES

In late antiquity, the name *Devorah* ("bee") provided material for men to reflect on the prophet's character and voice their opinions about women's proper deportment. Greco-Roman literature presented the bee as a model for female behavior: industrious and (as they thought) inclined to remain close to the hive. In the *Jewish Antiquities* (5.200-201), Jewish historian Flavius Josephus (37 – ca. 100 CE) highlighted this connection by informing his audience that "Deborah" means "bee" (*melissa* in the Greek). The Christian monk Jerome (ca. 347–420), defending his instruction of women, spoke of Deborah as gathering and drinking sweet nectar from the scriptures; he omits any mention of the prophet as producer of the scriptural words found in Judges 5 (*Letter* 54.17). Early Christian men found the sweetness of the honey produced by bees to be a fitting description of the gentleness they perceived in Deborah and other godly women. In late antiquity, several Jewish sages recognized her authoritative nature and were more concerned with her hornet-like sting. In the Babylonian Talmud, Rav Nachman is critical of Deborah for summoning Barak rather than traveling to beseech him in person. He said that two names are hateful:

Deborah the hornet and Huldah the weasel, for both haughty women sent messages to their interlocutors (Barak and King Josiah respectively) rather than humbly appearing before the men they addressed (*Megillah* 14b).

Christian interpreters such as Nicholas of Lyra (ca. 1270–1349), in *Literal Postill* on Judges 4, used the bee imagery to argue that Deborah was the symbol of a good bishop, who has both sting and honey, acting stern when necessary and soothing when needed. Occasionally, the bee's productivity was an image used to speak positively of a woman's study and teaching of scripture, as we find in Peter the Venerable's letter to the scholarly nun Heloïse (1098–1164). The abbot compares her to Deborah, praising her for satisfying her nuns with the sweetness of scripture (*Letter* 115). The bee imagery persisted, especially in Christian instruction to women. Puritan preacher Cotton Mather (1663–1728) said that the "good wife" is a Deborah who is industrious within her hive. In the modern period, feminist scholars celebrated Deborah's powerful "sting." Jewish scholar Tikva Frymer-Kensky (2002: 49) wrote: "Like the queen bee, she raises up the swarm for battle, sending out the drones to protect the hive and conquer new territory." Deborah's identity as "hornet" entered into twenty-first-century popular culture through the videogame franchise Mortal Kombat, which features a female character D'Vorah, a warrior who can attack opponents with her stinger and with swarms of wasps released from her hands. The online description of the character explains that she is named after the prophet of Judges 4.[1]

Deborah's designation *'ešet lappîdôt* can mean "woman of torches" or "wife of Lappidoth," a name unattested elsewhere in Hebrew scripture. The Jewish translators of the Septuagint called her *gynē Laphidōth*, which could be interpreted "woman of Lappidoth," perhaps intending to refer to a place name, or "wife of Lappidoth," the meaning chosen by Jerome's Latin Vulgate translation (*uxor Lappidoth*). In rabbinic circles, however, she was called "woman of lamps." In the Babylonian Talmud, the sages explained that she made wicks for the lamps in the sanctuary (*Megillah* 14a). This theme was further developed in the *Tanna děbe Eliyyahu* (*Lore of the School of Elijah*), which dates from the ninth century or earlier. In this text, Deborah instructs her husband to make thick wicks for the sanctuary lamps in Shiloh so that the scholars would have much light by which to study. Thus her husband could share in the scholars' reward in the world to come (*Eliyyahu Rabbah* 48). Many Christian and Jewish feminists in the twentieth and twenty-first centuries embraced the idea that *'ešet lappîdôt* is an epithet. Their Deborah was no tame wick-maker. Rather, she was "fiery woman" or "woman of flames." For these interpreters, Deborah's epithet signifies her fiery nature as a powerful warrior and leader.

30.3 WIFE OF LAPPIDOTH

Ancient Christian commentators holding Deborah up as a model for other women generally emphasized that she was properly submissive to her husband Lappidoth, despite the lack of biblical evidence of wifely submission. The *Apostolic Constitutions* (8.2.8–9), a fourth-century Greek text from Syria, urges female prophets to submit to their husbands the way Deborah deferred to Lappidoth. Some medieval rabbinic sources held that Barak ("lightning") and Lappidoth were the same man due to the fact that both names referred to bright lights (*Eliyyahu Rabbah* 48). Medieval Christian commentators, drawing on Jewish traditions, generally followed suit by conflating Lappidoth and Barak. Thus Deborah's husband Lappidoth is no longer a background figure but—identified as the warrior Barak—was elevated to the status of co-judge. Deborah is thereby given a husband who can match her military exploits.

Several Christian commentators in the nineteenth and twentieth centuries expressed discomfort with the idea of the woman Deborah elevated over her husband. In *Feminine Faces*, a 1942 collection of scripture biographies, Methodist minister Clovis G. Chappell (1882–1972) expressed the opinion that Deborah neglected her duties as wife and homemaker. Numerous women defended Deborah's ability to juggle her public responsibilities with her home life. Victorian-era Jewish novelist Grace Aguilar (1816–47), in her widely read biographical collection *The Women of Israel* (1844), explained that Deborah outranked her husband in public matters yet also attended to domestic duties. A woman's public and private duties could be perfectly compatible. In the late twentieth century, as an increased number of women entered the paid work force, Christian evangelical women wrote devotional materials that employed Deborah as an example of a godly working wife and mother—biblical precedent for married women working outside the home.

Modern fictionalized treatments of Deborah explored her relationship with Lappidoth. Ann Burton's Christian romance novel *Deborah's Story* (2006) described the tender emotions Deborah felt for her love interest "Jeth Lappidoth." In *The Triumph of Deborah* (2008), Israeli novelist Eva Etzioni-Halevy characterizes Deborah's marriage as fraught and conflicted. Jealous of Barak and resentful of Deborah's military duties, Lappidoth divorces her. After several erotic encounters with Barak, Deborah finally reunites with Lappidoth. In a feminist short story, "Of Deborah and Jael," in Sara Maitland's collection *Telling Tales* (1983), Deborah and Jael express female solidarity. The story hints at a lesbian relationship between the two women. After the battle the two warrior women realize that their husbands now fear them and they will never have to endure male touch again.

30.4 A Mother in Israel

In her victory ode, Deborah refers to herself as "a mother in Israel" (Judg. 5:7). In biblical times, this term may have had military connotations, since the poem celebrates Deborah's protective warrior qualities. The other biblical use of the term may refer to the defensive nature of the city Abel-Beth Ma'acah in 2 Sam. 20:19. In his commentary on Judges, Protestant reformer Conrad Pellican (1478–1556) compared Deborah to a heroic mother hen putting herself in harm's way to protect her chicks. Many assumed that she was the mother of biological children, though no offspring are mentioned in the Bible. In *Concerning Widows* (8.45), Bishop Ambrose of Milan (ca. 339–97) said that Barak was Deborah's own son, whom she trained and cheered on in a motherly fashion.

Numerous male and female interpreters regarded the label "mother in Israel" to refer to Deborah's supposed maternal tenderness. Sentimentally rhapsodizing about Deborah's gentle motherhood, some urged women to choose maternity and domesticity over public roles. Nineteenth-century women's rights activists, however, said that "mother love" should be expressed in the public sphere through women's voting and office-holding. Thus Deborah, as "mother in Israel," was regarded as a powerful biblical example of the alignment of women's domestic values with public service. In 1894, Anna Howard Shaw (1847–1919), a Methodist minister who later became president of the National Woman Suffrage Association, delivered an address, "The Fate of Republics," which said that the United States had suffered from "too much fathering" from pilgrim fathers, founding fathers, city fathers, and the like. She said the republic needed more "mothering," exemplified by Deborah the "mother in Israel" who effectively ruled her nation by applying maternal principles such as honesty and resistance to bribery. In nineteenth-century Methodist and African Methodist Episcopal circles, "mother in Israel" was a term of respect for women who exercised leadership roles in Bible studies, women's groups, and congregational activities.

Numerous twentieth-century portrayals of Deborah emphasized her biological motherhood. An illustration by Mariel Wilhoite in *Heroes of the Bible* (1940), a children's book by Olive Beaupré Miller (1883–1968), depicts Deborah addressing Barak. She stands authoritatively beneath the palm tree, left arm upraised, giving instructions to the commander. Behind her, on a blanket at her feet, a baby (who is perhaps a bit forlorn) looks toward its mother. Another child tugs on Deborah's skirt, trying to get her attention. Bernice Hogan's children's novel *Deborah* (1964) depicts its protagonist as a housewife drawn reluctantly into the role of judge and warrior through necessity and circumstances. At the conclusion, Deborah happily agrees with her husband Lappidoth's assertion that she can retire from her career as judge so they can start a family. She will bear children and truly become "a mother of Israel."

Twentieth- and twenty-first-century feminist scholars examined the literary portrayals of motherhood in Judges 4–5, finding patriarchal ideology and irony in the text. For instance, according to J. Cheryl Exum (2007: 70–72), the three female characters mentioned specifically in the text (Deborah, Jael, and Sisera's mother) are maternal figures who are simultaneously life-giving and violent. Deborah protects her children while also sending her sons off to war. Jael offers Sisera milk and a safe lap while planning his murder. Sisera's mother anxiously awaits her son's return while being reassured by her ladies in waiting that Sisera is merely delayed, dividing the spoils, which include captive Israelite women assault victims.

30.5 THE PROPHET AS PUBLIC RELIGIOUS LEADER

Judges 4:4 calls Deborah "a woman, a prophet" (*'iššâ nĕbîâ*). Beginning as early as the second century CE, interpreters wrestled with whether her prophetic role was public or private, and whether women of their own day could regard Deborah as precedent for women's public religious leadership. Through the centuries, the implications of Deborah's prophetic role were vigorously debated in Christian and Jewish conversations about women's religious leadership. Proponents of female religious leadership—especially ministries such as rabbi, priest, pastor, deaconess, and preacher—said that Deborah served as a precedent for women's ministerial roles. Their opponents generally asserted that Deborah offered merely private counsel or represented a divinely authorized exception that did not serve as warrant for other women to imitate. Christian prayers for the ordination of deaconesses included reference to female prophets Miriam, Deborah, Anna, and Huldah (*Apostolic Constitutions* 8.20.1–2).

Rabbinic texts stressed the public setting of Deborah's activity, under the Palm of Deborah (Judg. 4:5). In the Babylonian Talmud, Rav Simeon ben Abishalom stated that she met with men outdoors—rather than inside her house—for the sake of privacy, to avoid scandal (*Megillah* 14a). One opinion found in the *Tanna děbe Eliyyahu* stated that, seated under her palm tree, Deborah instructed multitudes in Torah. Another opinion, found in the same text, expressed more skepticism about the size of Deborah's audience, asserting there were so few faithful people in Israel at that time that her disciples could be seated within the space of half of the shade of a palm tree (*Eliyyahu Rabbah* 50). A number of medieval Jewish texts, such as the *Zohar* (*Vayikra* 19b), explain that the line "Awake, awake, Deborah" (Judg. 5:12) indicated she temporarily lost the prophetic spirit because she had praised herself in the preceding verses. The same text, however, commended Deborah, together with Hannah, for composing praises to God unequaled by the words of men. In the Middle Ages, Kairite Jews, who accept the authority of the Hebrew scriptures but not the rabbinic tradition, included Deborah's name in the list of authentic transmitters of the biblical text, as one of the guarantors of Kairite legitimacy.

The New Prophecy, a Christian sectarian movement, dubbed "Montanism" by its opponents after its male co-founder Montanus, was noted for endorsing women's prophetic leadership. Founded in the middle of the second century CE by Priscilla, Maximilla, and Montanus, the movement encountered severe opposition based, in part, on its support of women's leadership roles. Most New Prophecy writings were destroyed or lost, but the words of their mainstream or "orthodox" Christian opponents suggest that New Prophecy adherents used biblical female prophets such as Deborah as warrant for women's religious leadership. Anti-Montanist polemicists argued vigorously against the view that Deborah exercised public leadership. The Alexandrian exegete Origen of Alexandria (ca. 185–ca. 253) asserted that Deborah offered private advice to Barak, in contrast to the public activity of Isaiah and Jeremiah. An anonymous fourth-century *Dialogue between a Montanist and an Orthodox* explains that Deborah and other authentic biblical female prophets followed St. Paul's injunctions (1 Cor. 11:5), humbly "veiling" themselves metaphorically by not circulating books under their own names—a virtuous practice not shared by Priscilla, Maximilla, and other New Prophecy women who authored books.

Numerous Christian women in the Middle Ages reported visionary experiences, dictating or penning religious texts that circulated in Europe. Though the medieval mystics themselves did not invoke Deborah, their male supporters used the biblical prophet as an example to defend against detractors. In their prefaces to women's works and in their writings about these women, clergymen compared Hildegard of Bingen (ca. 1098–1179), Elisabeth of Schönau (ca. 1128–64), Mechthild of Magdeburg (ca. 1206–82), and Birgitta of Sweden (ca. 1303–73) to Deborah, arguing that the biblical text offered proof that God inspired women as well as men. However, medieval Christian theologians generally argued that Deborah's role was unofficial. Distinguishing between prophecy and the sacrament of ordination, scholastic theologians such as Thomas Aquinas (ca. 1225–75) said Deborah's example did not support women's ordination. In particular, the command in 1 Tim. 2:12, "I do not permit a woman to speak or have authority over a man," prevented women from holding religious office or receiving ordination. As for Deborah's authority, Aquinas said that it was civil rather than religious (*Sentence Commentary*, distinction 25, q. 2, art. 1).

In the early modern period, Quaker co-founder Margaret Askew Fell Fox (1614–1702), imprisoned for her public speaking, wrote a treatise entitled *Women's Speaking Justified, Proved and Allowed of by the Scriptures* (1667). Fell Fox noted that Barak did not silence Deborah when she publicly "preached" by singing her ode in Judges 5.

During America's Second Great Awakening (ca. 1790–1844) and its aftermath, hundreds of Euro-American and African American women preached in churches, rented halls, homes, outdoor worship settings, revivals, and camp meetings. These women, usually from Baptist, Methodist, or African Methodist Episcopal traditions, frequently drew large supportive crowds, but their ministries also encountered opposition. Faced with opponents citing apostolic injunctions to female silence in the religious assembly (1 Tim. 2:12 and 1 Cor. 14:33–35), female preachers were regularly required to defend their public speech. Women preachers and evangelists answered their opponents' challenges with examples of authoritative biblical women such as Miriam, Mary Magdalene, and Huldah. Deborah was usually on their list. Zilpha Elaw (ca. 1790), an African American who preached in the Methodist tradition, lifted up Deborah as an illustration of women's public ministry. Nineteenth-century Euro-American and British women who invoked Deborah in the defense of female preaching included Quaker abolitionist speaker Sarah Moore Grimké (1792–1873), Methodist evangelist Phoebe Worrall Palmer (1807–74), Salvation Army co-founder Catherine Booth (1829–90), and Frances E. Willard (1839–98), a Methodist temperance leader who wrote a book entitled *Woman in the Pulpit* (1889). When Antoinette Brown Blackwell (1825–1921) was ordained as a Congregational minister in 1853, Luther Lee, the Methodist minister who delivered the sermon, specifically mentioned Deborah as precedent for women's ministry.

In the late nineteenth century, female journalist Ray Frank (1861–1948) addressed synagogues publicly and led services in Reform and Orthodox Jewish congregations. She was called "a latter day Deborah" (see Umansky 1997). In a 1922 *responsum* on the topic of women's ordination to the rabbinate, Rabbi Jacob Zallel Lauterbach (1873–1942) said Deborah's example supported the possibility of female religious teachers but that it did not set a precedent for female rabbis. In response, citing the example of female biblical prophets, Rabbi Abrams put himself on record as favoring the ordination of women (see Jacob and Zemer 2001: 201–209). The first female rabbi, Regina Jonas (1902–44), who was ordained in 1935 Berlin and was murdered at Auschwitz, wrote a halachic treatise on the topic of female rabbis. The treatise addressed the argument that Deborah's role was merely a "divine exception" that did not set precedent for women's religious leadership. In her careful survey of rabbinic treatments of Deborah, Jonas concluded that God's appointment of Deborah, who was accepted as judge and prophet by the Israelites, should be regarded as the "highest form of intervention." If God chooses to appoint women and if people were to accept female rabbis (as Jonas predicted they would because of the changes she observed in a modern society that accepted women's expanded roles), then female ordination to the rabbinate was perfectly consistent with rabbinic principles (see Klapheck 2004: 153). Throughout the twentieth and early twenty-first centuries, numerous female rabbis and Jewish feminists found inspiration in the figure of Deborah. In late twentieth-century Europe, female rabbis, cantors, religious leaders, and their supporters formed a feminist network called *Bet Debora* (House of Deborah), which now organizes conferences, publishes the *Bet Debora Journal*, and supports Jewish women's studies.

In the twentieth century, as a growing number of Christian denominations debated the possibility of ordaining women, proponents of women's ordination and public ministry looked to biblical examples. Among those who invoked Deborah were Canadian-born evangelist preacher Aimee Semple McPherson (1890–1944), founder of the International Church of the Foursquare Gospel, and television evangelist and faith healer Kathryn Kuhlman (1907–76). Vashti Murphy McKenzie (b. 1947), the first female bishop in the African Methodist Episcopal church, characterized Deborah as a model of a divinely called woman who had a husband who supported her public ministry. In his book *Bobbed Hair, Bossy Wives, and Women Preachers* (1941), fundamentalist evangelist John Rice, an outspoken opponent of women's preaching, argued that Deborah and other biblical women were never sent to preach publically. Deborah's counsel to Barak, unlike the public preaching of Isaiah and Jeremiah, was brief—able to be recorded in a mere two verses—and delivered privately. Feminist and womanist scholars in the late twentieth and early twenty-first centuries regularly highlighted Deborah's authority as a significant religious leader.

30.6 JUDGE DEBORAH, CIVIL LEADER

Judges 4:4–5 reports that Deborah was judging (*šōpĕṭâ*) Israel and that the Israelites came up to her for judgment (*lammišpāṭ*). In *Midrash Rabbah Ruth* 1.1 (fourth–fifth century CE), Rabbi Huna counts Deborah among the judges. The Aramaic *Targum Jonathan*, an early medieval source, adds details about Deborah's extensive property holdings that included palm trees, gardens, and olive orchards. The text asserts that she supported herself with her own property, suggesting that she was judicially honest and immune to bribery. Jacob ben Asher (ca. 1269–1340), in *Choshen Mishpat*, said Deborah did not deliver forensic opinions but was, instead, an "instructor" of the judges of Israel. Christian canon lawyers such as Gratian of Bologna (d. before 1160) reconciled Deborah's judgeship with canon laws that prohibited women from serving as witnesses in certain cases. Gratian's *Decretum* (chapter 15, question 3) explains that the Old Covenant prior to the coming of Christ was deficient and permitted practices no longer licit during the time of the "perfection of grace" brought through Christ. Thus, in Hebrew Bible times, Deborah could serve as judge. Now, in the time of grace, women are subject to the apostolic commandment that women should not have authority over men, since the woman Eve brought sin into the world (1 Tim. 2:12).

On several occasions medieval Christian men used Deborah's example to praise and exhort women who were secular leaders. In 1064, Peter Damian (1007–72), cardinal bishop of Ostia, wrote a letter to the duchess Adelaide, who ruled lands in northern Italy and Burgundy. He urged her to use her civil authority to curtail clerical marriage and concubinage (Letter 114). Citing the example of Deborah and Barak, a male-female pair of warriors who defeated Sisera, Peter said that a partnership between Adelaide and Cunibert, bishop of Turin, could drive clerical sin from Adelaide's lands. In their arguments against women's ordination, scholastic theologians such as Thomas Aquinas and Bonaventure (ca. 1217-74) asserted that Deborah appropriately held temporal power, just as some women of their own day lawfully ruled in the civil sphere.

In the sixteenth century, debates about Deborah as precedent for women's civil authority became heated when Henry VIII's Roman Catholic daughter Mary Tudor (1516-58) ascended to the English throne in 1553, causing a Protestant nation to return to Catholicism. Protestant leaders argued about the legitimacy of female rule, and the example of Deborah figured prominently. John Calvin (1509-64) reports that Deborah ruled by divine prerogative. Deborah was an extraordinary example, raised up by God as punishment to shame men for their laxity. In his notorious treatise *First Blast of the Trumpet Against the Monstrous Regiment of Women* (1558), Scottish reformer John Knox (ca. 1515-60) said that particular biblical examples do not establish common law. Deborah's leadership was not precedent for current practice any more than Solomon's polygamy was warrant for plural marriage in the sixteenth century. Furthermore, unlike the Roman Catholic Mary Tudor, Deborah was a "godly matron." Finally, Knox argued that Deborah's authority was spiritual rather than temporal.

When Mary Tudor died and her Protestant half-sister Elizabeth (1533-1603) came to the English throne in 1558, the new queen styled herself as a godly "Deborah." Protestant supporters regarded her as a champion, raised up by God to defend their nation against Roman Catholic idolatry, symbolized by the Canaanites. In 1563 Elizabeth published a prayer asking God for strength "so that I, like another Deborah, like another Judith, like another Esther, may free Thy people of Israel from the hand of Thy enemies" (Marcus, Mueller, and Rose 2000: 157). In his commentary on Judges, Protestant biblical scholar Peter Martyr Vermigli (1499-1562) said that Deborah asserted princely authority when she summoned Barak to carry out her military commands. He wrote to Queen Elizabeth in 1558, expressing his support and urging her to "play the role of holy Deborah for our times" by protecting the nation against foreign idolatry and aggression. Vermigli suggested that she find "some godly Barak," a male partner to assist her (Letter 200).

Throughout the century following Elizabeth's death in 1603, Protestant authors continued to equate the English monarch with Deborah as an example of heroic queenship. Roman Catholic authors, in turn, praised Catholic queens and noblewomen in similar terms. In 1647, Jesuit author Pierre Le Moyne (1602-75) published a collection of scriptural biographies, accompanied by beautiful engravings by Charles Audran (1594-1674), entitled *La Gallerie des Femmes Fortes* (*The Gallery of Heroic Women*). Le Moyne's collection opens with a chapter on Deborah and closes with one on Mary Stuart (1542-87), the Roman Catholic "Queen of Scots" executed by Elizabeth. Le Moyne's praise of both women is superlative. Deborah is portrayed as a commanding, eloquent monarch who holds court and administrates the affairs of state under her majestic palm tree.

Deborah was frequently invoked in the nineteenth and twentieth centuries in American battles for abolition, women's suffrage, and expansion of political rights. In 1833, African-American political writer and speaker Maria W. Stewart (1803-79) defended her public speech and political activism by asserting that she was following the example of Deborah who was raised up by God to be a judge in Israel. Euro-American abolitionist Angelina Emily Grimké (1805–79), in her *Appeal to the Christian Women of the South* (1836), urged her readers to emulate Deborah, Miriam, and other biblical women who confronted tyranny and opposed slavery. In *The Woman's Bible* (Part II, 1898), the first overtly feminist biblical commentary, suffragist and women's rights advocate Elizabeth Cady Stanton (1815–1902) objected to the fact that Deborah's role as judge was not acknowledged in the list of heroes celebrated in Heb. 11:32:

> Deborah was a woman of great ability. She was consulted by the children of Israel in all matters of government, of religion and of war. Her judgment seat was under a palm tree, known ever after as "Deborah's Palm." Though she was one of the great judges of Israel for forty years, her name is not on the list, as it should have been, with Gideon, Barak, Samson and Jephthah. Men have always been slow to confer on women the honors which they deserve. (pp. 18–19)

Deborah was portrayed as a powerful national leader in a 1913 women's rights pageant, *Daughters of Dawn: A Lyrical Pageant or Series of Historic Scenes for Presentation with Music and Dancing*, by Bliss Carman and Mary Perry King. In the performance, which included music, interpretive dance, and lantern slideshow illustrations, Deborah's intellectual gifts unite with Barak's brawn, so that man and woman complement each other—the male figure following the wise lead of the female.

In 1918, women of Great Britain received the right to vote and hold seats in Parliament. Commenting on this political development in his *Speakers Bible* (1924), a homiletical aid, Scottish Free Church clergyman James Hastings (1852–1922) said Deborah brought motherly values into the public sphere and was guided by women's "intuition." He considered her public leadership to be an extension of motherhood—something he commends to female readers and listeners. Hastings exhorted women to bring their innate motherly values into politics without sacrificing femininity or neglecting domestic responsibilities.

Judge Deborah was similarly invoked when Israel became a state in 1948. Ben Zion Hai Ouziel (1880–1953), Sephardi Chief Rabbi, used Deborah's public leadership as an argument for women voting, holding public office, and participating in Israeli politics.

In 2008, Alaska governor Sarah Palin (b. 1964) became a United States vice presidential candidate and running mate of Republican presidential contender John McCain. In debates held primarily on the Internet, conservative evangelical Christians argued about whether Palin could properly be compared to Deborah. Supporters such as J. Lee Grady, editor of the Pentecostal magazine *Charisma*, suggested that Palin, herself a Pentecostal, had received spiritual "anointing" like Deborah and thus could bring divinely inspired conservative motherly values to the White House. Other conservative Christians expressed opposition, responding that God's authorization of women leaders like Deborah served as an indictment of the failures of male leadership. Parallel to the dire situation in ancient Israel, Palin's candidacy was proof of the spinelessness and moral bankruptcy of Republican party leadership.

30.7 Warrior and Military Leader

In the biblical text, Deborah provides Barak with military strategy, announces the day of the Israelite attack on the Canaanites, and celebrates the victory with a triumphant ode relishing her enemy's defeat. Through the centuries numerous commentators—male and female—expressed discomfort with her warrior role. Artists, however, eagerly included Deborah in battle scenes and depicted her with armor, helmet, and weapons. Two thirteenth-century French medieval manuscript paintings, in the *Morgan Picture Bible* (folio 12r) and the *St. Louis Psalter* (folio 47v), show Deborah and Barak seated on horses, together with the troops (who are dressed in crusader-era armor) pursuing the fleeing Canaanites. Deborah, dressed like an Amazon in armor and helmet, is armed with sword and shield in a woodcut by Pierre Eskrich (ca. 1530 – ca. 1590) for a Roman Catholic Bible published by Guillaume Rouillé in Lyon in 1556. She wears a plumed helmet and wields an upraised sword in Charles Audran's engraving for LeMoyne's *La Gallerie des Femmes Fortes*.

Several medieval authors invoked Deborah to express support for particular women's military efforts. In *Vita Mathildis*, a tribute to Countess Matilda of Tuscany (1046–1115), the monk Donizo (*fl.* 1115) praised the noblewoman for sending armed forces to rescue the princess Praxides from her abusive husband, Emperor Henry IV (1050–1106). Donizo compared Matilda to Deborah and Jael. In 1429, French writer Christine de Pizan (ca. 1364–ca. 1429) composed a poem entitled "The Miracle of Joan of Arc" to celebrate Joan of Arc's (1412–31) victory at Orleans. De Pizan said the French heroine rivaled notable biblical men and women, including Deborah.

In the early modern era, the printing press offered opportunities for women, in growing numbers, to publish books and pamphlets. Frequently these women's works were refutations of misogynistic pamphlets. Lutheran reformer Argula von Grumbach (1492–ca. 1554) and English poet Amelia Lanyer (1569–1645) each used the image of Deborah and Jael defeating their male enemies as a metaphor for their own written attacks against misogynistic literary enemies. In her treatise *A Practical Problem: Whether the Study of Letters is Fitting for a Christian Woman*, Dutch scholar Anna Maria van Schurman (1607–78) alarmed her contemporaries by suggesting that women should study works of military science. Her interlocutors André Rivet (1572–1651) and Gisbertus Voetius (1589–1676) stressed that Deborah and Jael were extraordinary exceptions not to be emulated in ordinary circumstances, though they allowed that a desperate city under siege might need the help of women to throw rocks at the enemy or carry gunpowder or ammunition to the fighting men.

Nineteenth-century women were generally uncomfortable with Deborah's bellicose praises of Jael, who slaughtered Sisera with her gory tent peg. In their scripture biographies they sometimes explained Deborah's approval of Jael as motivated by indignation against Sisera's intended rape of Israelite women (Judg. 5:30). Harriet Beecher Stowe (1811–95), in her popular collection *Woman in Sacred History* (1873), viewed Deborah as a female defender of women, rightly outraged by the rapacious Sisera. Male and female authors in the late nineteenth and early twentieth centuries said that Deborah's warrior tendencies were best emulated by the assertive women temperance leaders who relentlessly fought for prohibition of alcohol.

In the twentieth and early twenty-first centuries, Deborah was rarely considered in debates about women in combat. An exception is found in a denominational study, the Orthodox Presbyterian Church's 2001 *Report of the Committee on Women in the Military and in Combat*, which concluded that Deborah and Jael served as precedent for non-combatant support roles such as the medical corps. In several American cities, including San Antonio, Texas, and Raleigh, North Carolina, the names "Deborah's House" and "Deborah Center" have been used for support services, such as transitional housing, for female veterans.

Euro-American feminist scholars have generally registered discomfort with the warfare celebrated in the text. However, Guatemalan liberation theologian Julia Esquivel (1987: 22) argued that Deborah's example demonstrates that people "may militarily defend the right to life and the struggle for liberation." Biblical scholar Gale Yee (1993: 106) said that Deborah's stories were similar to the empowering "tales of Chinese swordswomen who fought against tyranny on behalf of their people." Yee also notes that most contemporary women treat Deborah as an example as they struggle on "their personal battle fields" and that "in a paradoxical twist in her warrior image," Deborah has been a model for women's anti-war activism (1993: 125).

In 2007, Don Levine, creator of popular toys such as G.I. Joe, launched "Almighty Warriors," a line of biblical action figures. Marketed alongside the hulking, muscular figures of Noah, Samson, and David, "Deborah the Warrior" is a feminine blonde fashion doll, whose shiny sapphire-blue jumpsuit is accessorized by a delicate pink wrist scarf and a tiny plastic shield.

30.8 AUTHOR AND EDUCATED WOMAN

In Judges 5, Deborah and Barak sing a lengthy song together. Numerous interpreters treated the text as composed solely by Deborah. In his commentary on Judges 5, the Netherlandish monk Denis the Carthusian (1402–71) regarded Deborah as the ode's divinely inspired composer, with Barak merely singing it with her—just as Paul credited Timothy and Silvanus in 1 Thess. 1:1 even though Paul was the epistle's sole author. Early modern women used Deborah's authorship and erudition to defend women's education and justify their own publishing activities. Mexican nun Sor Juana Inés de la Cruz (1648–95) wrote a defense of women's learning, *Response to the Very Illustrious Sor Philothea*, praising the legal expertise of Deborah who issued laws. Similar affirmation of Deborah's legal erudition is found in the work of Bathsua Reginald Makin (ca. 1600—after 1675), who wrote *An Essay to Revive the Ancient Education of Gentlewomen* (1675), an apologia for women's learning and an advertisement for her London academy for young women. Rivkah bat Meir of Prague (d. 1605), who studied Hebrew biblical and rabbinic texts, wrote *Meneket Rivkah* (*Rebecca's Nurse*, published 1609), a Yiddish book that encouraged Jewish women to study religious writings, either by reading books for themselves or by listening to texts read aloud. Bat Meir explained that Deborah's words, "My heart is with Israel's leaders" (Judg. 5:9) meant, "My heart is attached to the scholars of Israel," so that women were encouraged to learn from scholars. When Norwegian hymn writer Dorothe Engelbretsdatter (1634–1710) encountered skeptics who thought her incapable of writing beautiful verses and accused her of plagiarizing texts written by her husband or some other man, she responded with the example of Deborah's composition. Engelbretsdatter called herself "Bergen's Deborah."

Nineteenth-century women frequently regarded Deborah's composition to be inspiration for their own authorship. Irish novelist Lady Sydney Morgan (1783–1859), in *Woman and Her Master* (1840), noted that Deborah's work predated Homer's epics by thirteen centuries. Harriet Beecher Stowe, in *Woman in Sacred History*, argued that the Jewish tradition nurtured poetic gifts in women, as evidenced by the songs of Hannah (1 Sam. 2:1-10), Deborah, and the Virgin Mary (Luke 1:46–55). When nineteenth- and early twentieth-century scholars of higher criticism questioned Deborah's authorship of the ode, generally assuming that the anonymous author must be male, Methodist Protestant minister Lee Anna Starr Lee (1853–1937) objected: "Some redactors are apparently averse to allowing woman any share in the making of the Sacred canon" (1926: 143). Various twentieth- and twenty-first-century feminist scholars have posited female authorship of the ode—or at least the possibility of women contributing to and preserving the text (see Bal 1988: 112).

30.9 CONCLUSION: A POLYVALENT PROPHET

As prophet, judge, war leader, singer, and—as most interpreters supposed—wife and mother, the biblical Deborah provided rich source material for readers' speculations, study, inspiration, and potential disruption of gendered social expectations. Through the centuries, countless interpreters projected their own socially constructed assumptions onto the multi-faceted figure. Deborah has been seen as warrior, preacher, author, tender mother, pious wick-maker of sanctuary lamps, and—in some interpretations—a bad housekeeper or haughty woman who did not know her place. Most often she was held up as an example for women to emulate, even if the qualities for which she was praised (such as domesticity and submissiveness) were not always found in the biblical text. In numerous cases, the fiery biblical figure needed to be tamed or domesticated to fit within the interpreter's framework. Other readers, especially those who sought biblical precedent for women's expanded roles in society, politics, and religious communities, found Deborah's story to be a powerful source of personal inspiration and a compelling scriptural justification for institutional change.

NOTE

1. "D'Vorah," *Mortal Kombat Wiki*, http://mortalkombat.wikia.com/wiki/D'Vorah, accessed October 30, 2016.

Bibliography

Ackerman, Susan. 1998. *Warrior, Dancer, Seductress, Queen: Women in Judges and Biblical Israel*. The Anchor Bible Reference Library. New York: Doubleday.

Aguilar, Grace. 1844. *The Women of Israel, or, Characters and Sketches from the Holy Scriptures and Jewish History, Illustrative of the Past History, Present Duties, and Future Destiny of the Hebrew Females, as Based on the Word of God*. London: Groombridge.

Bal, Mieke. 1988. *Murder and Difference: Gender, Genre, and Scholarship on Sisera's Death*. ISBL. Bloomington: Indiana University Press.

Beecher Stowe, Harriet. 1873. *Woman in Sacred History*. New York: J. B. Ford and Company.

Burton, Ann. 2006. *Deborah's Story*. Women of the Bible. New York: Signet.

Carman, Bliss and Mary Perry King. 1913. *Daughters of Dawn: A Lyrical Pageant or Series of Historic Scenes for Presentation with Music and Dancing*. New York: Mitchell Kennerley.

Conway, Colleen M. 2017. *Sex and Slaughter in the Tent of Jael: A Cultural History of a Biblical Story*. New York: Oxford University Press.

"D'Vorah." *Mortal Kombat Wiki*. http://mortalkombat.wikia.com/wiki/D'Vorah. Accessed October 30, 2016.

Esquivel, Julie. 1987. "Liberation, Theology, and Women." In John S. Pobee and Bärbel von Wartenberg-Potter, eds., *New Eyes for Reading: Biblical and Theological Reflections by Women from the Third World*. Oak Park, IL: Meyer Stone, 21–27.

Etziony-Halevy, Eva. 2008. *The Triumph of Deborah*. New York: Plume.

Exum, J. Cheryl. 2007. "Feminist Criticism: Whose Interests Are Being Served?" In Gale A. Yee, ed., *Judges and Method: New Approaches in Biblical Studies*. Minneapolis: Fortress, 65–90.

Frymer-Kensky, Tikva. 2002. *Reading the Women of the Bible*. New York: Schocken.

Gunn, David M. 2005. *Judges through the Centuries*. Blackwell Bible Commentaries. Malden, MA: Blackwell.

Jacob, Walter and Moshe Zemer, eds. 2001. *Gender Issues in Jewish Law: Essays and Responsa*. Studies in Progressive Halakhah. New York: Berghahn.

Klapheck, Elisa. 2004. *Fräulein Rabbiner Jonas: The Story of the First Woman Rabbi*. San Francisco: Jossey-Bass.

Maitland, Sara. 1983. *Telling Tales*. London: Journeyman.

Marcus, Leah S., Janel Mueller, and Mary Beth Rose, eds. 2000. *Collected Works of Elizabeth I*. Chicago: University of Chicago Press.

Schroeder, Joy A. 2014. *Deborah's Daughters: Gender Politics and Biblical Interpretation*. New York: Oxford University Press.

Stanton, Elizabeth Cady. 1993. *The Woman's Bible*. Reprinted. Boston: Northeastern University Press (orig. New York: European Publishing Company, 1895–98).

Starr, Lee Anna. 1926. *The Bible Status of Woman*. New York: Fleming H. Revell.

Taylor, Marion Ann and Christiana de Groot, eds. 2016. *Women of War, Women of Woe: Joshua and Judges through the Eyes of Nineteenth-Century Female Interpreters*. Grand Rapids: Eerdmans.

Umansky, Ellen. 1997. "Ray Frank (1861–1948)." In Paula E. Hyman and Deborah Dash Moore, eds., *Jewish Women in America: An Historical Encyclopedia*, Vol. 1. New York: Routledge, 467–69.

Yee, Gale A. 1993. "By the Hand of a Woman: The Metaphor of the Woman Warrior in Judges 4." *Sem* 61: 99–132.

CHAPTER 31

SAMSON IN RECEPTION HISTORY

KELLY J. MURPHY

IN the episode "Black Tie" of the American television series "30 Rock," the character Tracy Jordan (played by Tracy Morgan) explains to his co-worker how "there are two types of women in this world: one who gives you strength and one who takes strength from you, like Delilah took strength from Samson in that movie." A quotation from a TV show might seem like a peculiar way to begin, but in many ways the quip epitomizes the long reception history of the biblical Samson. As Jordan's remark "from that movie" clearly illustrates, audiences may not know where to find the original story, but many nevertheless recognize the figure of Samson. "Like Delilah took strength from Samson" also serves as a reminder that the "story of Samson is a story of women" (Exum 1993: 61). The major events in the narrative found in Judges 13–16 involve not only Samson but also the women of the story: an unnamed mother, an unnamed Philistine wife, an unnamed sex-worker, and, perhaps most illustrious of all, the named Delilah. After all, "[j]ust try to imagine the story without them" (Exum 1993: 61). In short, to tell the story of the reception of the figure of Samson requires tracing the hermeneutical paths not only of him, but also of the women, both named and unnamed, whose story it is, too.

31.1 SAMSON IN JUDGES (AND BEYOND)

The narrative of Samson and these women is found in the book of Judges, which explores one version of the history of pre-monarchic Israel, depicting a time when the so-called "judges" (Hebrew *šōpĕṭîm*, from the root *š-p-t*, "to judge") temporarily led various Israelite tribes as they attempted to establish themselves in the Promised Land. Of course, as is regularly observed, the famous characters of the book—figures like Gideon, Jephthah, and Samson—act less like legal adjudicators and more as local rulers or military deliverers who attempt to save the Israelites from their enemies (e.g., Judg. 3:9, 15; 6:14; 8:22; 10:1, 2, 3; 13:5). The stories of these deliverers follow a cyclical pattern: the Israelites turn away from Yhwh → Yhwh gives them into the hands of an enemy nation → the Israelites cry out to their God for help → Yhwh then appoints a deliverer to save them → and the deliverer then brings "rest" to the land (see Judg. 3:11, 30; 5:31; 8:28). Inevitably, the Israelites begin again to "do evil in the eyes of Yhwh" (see Judg. 2:11, 3:7, 12; 4:1; 6:1; 10:6; 13:1) and so the cycle repeats. But, as is also often noted, this pattern begins to break down as the narrative unfolds. This is nowhere clearer than with Samson (see Exum 1990).

The stories of the so-called judges are stories of "unlikely heroes," as Samson, "a Nazirite who does not live up to his promise," exemplifies (Exum 1990: 412). It begins with the expected refrain: "The Israelites again did what was evil in the sight of the LORD, and the LORD gave them into the hand of the Philistines forty years" (Judg. 13:1). Here, however, the Israelites never cry out to Yhwh for help, and, as the narrative winds down, Samson (like Jephthah before him) fails to bring rest to the land. From the outset, Samson is only destined to "begin" to deliver the Israelites from the Philistine threat (see Judg 13:5), and unlike the previous deliverers he never musters an army, but rather spends most of his time with women (though these relationships frequently end with Samson's vengeful exploits against the Philistines). As with the book of Judges more broadly, there are a number of scholarly positions on the history behind the Samson narrative: some scholars argue that Samson is, in fact, a remembered hero from Israel's pre-monarchic days, while others suggest that parts of the story were added to the book of Judges much later, perhaps under the influence of Hellenistic hero-stories.[1] As the narrative now stands, the portrait the text paints of Samson is ambiguous at best. Accordingly, readers throughout the reception history of Samson puzzle over whether he should be considered a hero, one led astray by the lures of foreign women, or a scoundrel, who leads both himself and others into ruin.

For later readers, evaluating Samson is difficult because, despite his questionable behavior (such as his death-by-suicide), the narrator of the book of Judges never outwardly condemns him. Rather, the text reports that Samson was, in the end, respectfully buried in "the tomb of his father Manoah" (Judg. 16:31). The ways that interpreters appraise Samson is, as is often noted, further complicated by the very beginning of his reception history, found in the New Testament, where Heb. 11:32–34 reads:

> And what more should I say? For time would fail me to tell of Gideon, Barak, Samson, Jephthah, of David and Samuel and the prophets—who through faith conquered kingdoms, administered justice, obtained promises, shut the mouths of lions, quenched raging fire, escaped the edge of the sword, won strength out of weakness, became mighty in war, put foreign armies to flight.[2]

The book of Hebrews thus remembers Samson (alongside other figures from the Historical Books of Judges, Samuel, and Kings) as a figure of faith, omitting mention of his violent acts and his revenge-inspired suicide. Moreover, this text from Hebrews begins a long tradition of ignoring the significant role that the women in the story play. Accordingly, later interpreters are caught between the ambiguous depiction of the Nazirite found in the book of Judges and the approbative language applied to him in Heb. 11:32.

As one of the most famous figures from the Historical Books of the Hebrew Bible, rivaled perhaps only by King David, the reception histories of Samson and the women found in Judges 13–16 are extensive. Consequently, the following pages can only briefly outline some of the major questions and concerns voiced by readers through the centuries. Even so, by (re)visiting three significant scenes in the narrative revolving around a mother, a wife, and Delilah, we may appreciate how (re)reading Judges 13–16 through the eyes of its many interpreters reveals that the story of Samson, both in and outside the biblical text, is a story of these women as much as a story about the (in)famous judge. Still further, this hermeneutical investigation will demonstrate how some of our own questions about the Historical Books and its famous figures are reflected in the questions of others, as well as how the context(s) of the many interpreters of the past, no less than the contemporary context(s), shape how one approaches Israel's memories of its earliest history and (anti-)heroes.

31.2 A Mother, Or: "One Would Suppose This Woman...Might Have Had a Name"

The Italian painter Tintoretto's "The Annunciation to Manoah's Wife" (ca. 1555–59) demonstrates how the "story of Samson is a story of women" from its very beginning. In the painting, Samson's mother-to-be takes up most of the canvas on the left, while the divine visitor, a child-like figure, appears on the right. Manoah's wife bows her head toward the angel, seemingly aware that she is in the presence of the divine, while Samson's father, as in the biblical narrative, is absent. Like Tintoretto's painting, Judges 13 opens by focusing on Samson's mother, to whom a divine messenger appears, announcing, "Although you are barren, having borne no children, you shall conceive and bear a son" (Judg. 13:2–5).

Samson's mother has long fascinated later readers, and interpreters often fill in the gaps left unanswered in the biblical text. For example, Josephus, a Jewish historian writing in the first century CE, notes that Manoah's wife was "remarkable for her beauty and pre-eminent among the women of her time," and that Manoah was "madly enamored" with her, but also distressed by their childless marriage (*Ant.* 5.8.2; Josephus 2005: 285). In Josephus's version, when the woman told Manoah that she had been visited by a messenger, "extolling the young man's [i.e., the angel's] comeliness and stature," Manoah was accordingly "driven by these praises to distraction and to conceive the suspicions that such passion arouses" (*Ant.* 5.8.3; Josephus 2005: 287). As in the biblical narrative, Josephus depicts Manoah as slow to realize that he was talking with a divine messenger, and fearful of what might follow the visit, needing to be comforted by his wiser wife (*Ant.* 5.8.3; Josephus 2005: 287). Pseudo-Philo, another Jewish interpreter who also wrote in the first century CE, gives Samson's mother a name, Eluma, describing how she and Manoah each blamed the other for their lack of children (*LAB* 41:1; Harrington 1985: 355). In Philo's account, Eluma prays about her childlessness and the messenger appears, saying, "You are the sterile one who does not bring forth" (*LAB* 42:3; Harrington 1985: 355), while also assuring her she would have a child and that she was to name him Samson (*LAB* 42:3; Harrington 1985: 356).

Such interpretive gap-filling continued in early rabbinic discourse. In one midrash—a form of early Jewish interpretation of biblical texts that sought to fill in the gaps in biblical stories, composed roughly between 200 C.E. and 1000 C.E.—the mother is called Zleponi, because she turned to look at the messenger, a word play on the Hebrew verb *pnh*, "to turn to the side, pay attention to" (*Num. Rab.* 10:5; see *Bava Batra* 91:a). In another her name is

Haẓlel, the "l" doubled because the divine messenger appeared to her "twice; once in the city and once in the field" (*Num. Rab.* 10:5). As in Pseudo-Philo, the rabbis pondered why Manoah and his wife could not bear a child, explaining that the repetition "and his wife was barren, and bore not" (Judg. 13:2) held the answer: each blamed the other (*Num. Rab.* 10:5). Any repetition in the biblical text provided a clue that there was more to be understood; here the emphasis on the wife's barrenness was meant to signal to readers "that there was a quarrel between Manoah and his wife, he saying to her, 'You are barren and this is the reason why you do not bear,' while she said to him, 'You are barren and this is the reason why I have not borne'" (*Num. Rab.* 10.5). For the rabbis, the fact that the messenger appeared to the woman, not to Manoah, resolved this dispute: it was the wife who was barren (*Num. Rab.* 10:5).

While some interpretations focus on Samson's mother, Samson's father also proved puzzling for interpreters. At best Manoah appears to be "outside the loop" (Niditch 2008: 145). The messenger twice appears to the woman, despite Manoah's request for a visit (Judg. 13:3–5, 9–10) and even once they meet, Manoah fails to recognize that he is speaking to a divine, not human, messenger (Judg. 13:6, 8, 17). In particular, many readers paused at Judg. 13:11, "Manoah got up and followed his wife." The Talmud, a collection of early Jewish teachings and commentary on the Torah collected between roughly 200 CE and 500 CE, records Rabbi Nahman's comment, "From the following verse we know that Samson's father, Manoah, was an ignoramus, as it is written: 'And Manoah...went after his wife'" (*b. Ber.* 61a).[3] Not only did Manoah physically follow his wife, and so "reverse the expected order of status in a patriarchal culture" (Niditch 2008: 145), but according to the Talmud he also "followed her words and advice" (*b. Ber.* 61a), a shocking revelation in the androcentric world of the early rabbis. Much later, the Israeli writer David Grossman observes, "The ring and resonance of these words convey the slow, heavy movements of Manoah, whose name means 'rest' and, in more recent Hebrew, also means 'late,' in the sense of 'deceased.' Thus in five words...the narrator sketched a sluggard of sorts who drags after his quick, energetic wife" (Grossman 2006: 25).

Yet certain early Christian interpreters came to radically different conclusions about Manoah (no doubt revealing their own androcentric bias, though in a different manner). For example, in the fourth century CE, the Christian bishop Ambrose assured readers that Manoah's desire for a divine visit was not "out of jealousy for his wife...but rather because he was moved by a desire for a favor from heaven and wished to share the benefit of the heavenly vision" (*Letter* 35; Ambrose 1954: 178). After all, "One depraved by vices of the soul would not have found such favor with the Lord that an angel would return to his house, give the admonition which the fulfilling of the prophecy entailed, be suddenly raised in the form of a glowing flame, and depart" (*Letter* 35; Ambrose 1954: 178).

While early interpreters filled in details or attempted to explain Manoah's secondary role in the narrative, a different line of interpretation asked how the story might guide basic, day-to-day life for its readers. Many female readers would look to Samson's mother as a model for their own lives.[4] For example, Samson's mother became an example for abstaining from alcohol. Elizabeth Cady Stanton, an American suffragist and early leader in the women's rights movement of the 1800s, declares, "The nine months of ante-natal life is the period when the mother can make the deepest impression in forming future character, when she has absolute power for weal or for woe over the immortal being" (1898: 30). The temperance movement of the nineteenth century, with its many female supporters, no doubt looms behind these statements. Stanton also wryly observes, "One would suppose this woman, so honored of God, worthy to converse with angels on the most delicate of her domestic relations, might have had a name to designate her personality instead of being mentioned merely as the wife of Manoah or the mother of Samson" (1898: 30).

After twenty-three verses largely devoted to Samson's mother, the narrative finally introduces Samson. As Susan Niditch, a contemporary biblical scholar, notes, Samson is "named by his mother, another sign of her status in a patrilineal world" (2008: 146; see Judg. 13:24). Samson's name is often understood as being etymologically related to the Hebrew word for sun (*šemeš*), producing definitions such as "Sunny One, Sun Child" (Niditch 2008: 146). Connecting the definition of Samson's name to the sun is an interpretive trajectory that can be traced back as far as the Talmud, where one passage explains, "Samson [*Shimshon*] is called by the name of the Holy One, Blessed Be He," invoking Ps. 84:11, "For the Lord God is a sun and shield" (*b. Sotah* 10a). Josephus understands Samson's name to mean "strong" (*Ant.* 5.8.4; Josephus 2005: 289), perhaps because he "had in mind biblical passages in which the sun symbolizes strength" (Josephus 2005: 289). Pseudo-Philo adds that the divine messenger instructs Samson's mother on what to name the child, explaining, "For this one will be dedicated to your LORD" (*LAB* 42:3; Harrington 1985: 356), conceivably drawing a connection between the Hebrew verb *šmš*, "to serve," and the instructions that Samson was to live as a Nazirite (see Harrington 1985: 356). The eighteenth-century revivalist preacher Jonathan Edwards understood the name typologically: "His name, *Samson*, signifies *little son*, well agreeing with a type of the Messiah, that great Sun of Righteousness so often compared in the prophecies to the sun" (*Types of the Messiah*; Edwards 1993 [1834]: 254). Reading Samson (and his many troubling adventures) as foreshadowing Christ (and therefore, often as allegorical) would become a common theme for many Christian interpreters.

In Judaism, the story that announces Samson's birth and his future status as a Nazirite serves as the *haftarah* for the Torah portion of Num. 4:21–7:89, and so merges the traditions about the Nazirite vow from the book of Numbers with Samson's unusual designation as a Nazirite from birth. The vow taken by Samson's mother left the rabbis pondering over the different kinds of Nazirites: "What is the difference between a permanent Nazirite and a Nazirite like Samson, both of whom remain Nazirites forever?" (*b. Nazir* 4a). For one thing, a life-Nazirite was allowed to thin their hair with a razor, while Samson was not allowed to do so (*b. Nazir* 4a). Moreover, Samson could come into contact with the dead without fault: How else could Samson's encounter with the lion's carcass and use of the jawbone of the donkey be explained? (*b. Nazir* 4b). The difference between Samson and other Nazirites appears to be that his "Nazarite status did not stem from a vow uttered by a human being," but rather from the words of an angelic messenger (b. *Nazir* 4b).

Interpreters were not immune from seeing that despite his status as a Nazirite from birth, Samson's life as it unfolds was full of strange behavior. So Ambrose explains that Samson is worthy of admiration, "not because he gave great evidence of temperance and sobriety from boyhood by abstaining from wine, nor because as a Nazarite he was ever faithful to guard his sacred trust, with locks unshorn, but because from his youth...he worked amazing deeds of strength, perfect beyond the measure of human nature" (*Letter* 35; Ambrose 1954:

177). Yet what exactly might it mean when the text says, "The spirit of the LORD began to stir him in Mahaneh-dan, between Zorah and Eshtaol" (Judg. 13:25)?

A number of accounts of Samson's strength appear in the reception history of the text, answering just this question, including one midrashic tale that held that, "When the Holy Spirit abode with Samson, his hairs became stiff and knocked against another like a bell, and their clang traveled as far as from Zorah to Eshtaol" (*Lev. Rab.* 8:2). Rabbi Samuel b. Nahman noted that Samson was able to knock two mountains together "just as a man takes two stones and knocks them one against the other" (*Num. Rab.* 14:9), while for Rabbi Judah, the verse clues readers in that "when the Holy Spirit rested on Samson, it enabled him to traverse a distance as long as from Zorah to Eshtaol in a single step" (*Num. Rab.* 14:9).[5] Yet even if some early Jewish commentary reflected on Samson's strength with some pride or fondness, a cautionary element also appears: "There have been some who increased their strength to their advantage and others who increased it to their disadvantage. They who increased it to their advantage were David and Judah, and they who increased it to their disadvantage were Samson and Goliath" (*Eccl. Rab.* 1:18).

That Samson might use his famous strength for less than ideal reasons appears in Christian readings of the narrative as well. The early Christian theologian Augustine (354–430 CE) explains that Samson's strength "came from grace," and "belonged to the Spirit of the Lord," but also that "In Samson we have a vessel, in the Spirit we have what fills it. A vessel can be filled and emptied; and every vessel gets its contents from elsewhere" (*Sermon* 364.2; Augustine 1995: 276). Accordingly, if Samson's ensuing behavior is questionable, one might reason that the vessel has been emptied of the Spirit.

31.3 A Wife, Or: "He Made Terrible Choices When It Came to Relationships"

Judges 14, like the opening chapter of the Samson story, also begins by focusing on a female character. In this case, the text opens with Samson's unnamed wife, the second of the women whose stories are so intertwined with the story of Samson that it is impossible to unravel the reception history of one without the other. Yet unlike Samson's mother and his later lover, Delilah, Samson's Philistine wife from Timnah receives relatively scant attention outside of the biblical text, even though many of Samson's most famous actions, such as slaying a lion with his bare hands and killing a thousand Philistines with only a donkey's jawbone, follow as a direct consequence of their relationship. Instead, while women across the ages have sometimes looked to the story of Samson's mother for counsel on their own lives, the stories in Judges 14–15 are most often used to hold up Samson, not his Philistine wife, as an edifying figure—maybe because the text preserves few details about her or, perhaps, because her status as a Philistine woman often renders her as Other and thus as suspect (see, for example, Gafney 2016: 57–61).

In particular, Samson becomes a model for how to (not) behave for young boys and men. For example, in the *NIV Boys Bible: Your Ultimate Manual* (2002), a textbox advises its young readers:

> Samson was called by God, sure, but he made some crazy decisions, such as hanging out with the wrong crowd and marrying someone who didn't share his commitment to the Lord.... He was proud and spoiled. He had muscles, he was called by God and he thought, "Man, I am larger than life." He was strong all right, but he made terrible choices when it came to relationships. Time after time, Samson's temper and poor decisions pushed him *out* of favor with others. A man of God should grow *in* favor with people and with God.
>
> (Osborne 2002: 320)

If the *Boy's Bible* is one illustration of how the figure of Samson is used to instruct young men, it also demonstrates how Samson's story is typically edited for younger audiences. For though the textbox cautions that Samson hung out "with the wrong crowd" and married "someone who didn't share his commitment to the Lord," it ignores one of the key lines from the biblical text that would trouble later readers: "His father and mother did not know that [Samson's desiring the Philistine woman] was from the LORD; for he [the LORD] was seeking a pretext to act against the Philistines" (Judg. 14:4).

While the textbox in the *NIV Boy's Bible* blames Samson for his tumultuous relationships, other interpreters come to different conclusions. For many, the idea that Samson's desire "was from the LORD" was baffling. In one midrashic text, for example, Rabbi Eleazer explains that "the prohibition against intermarriage is recorded in seven places" in the Bible (*Num. Rab.* 9:24). Accordingly, a common interpretive thread connects Samson's tragic fate with this first encounter with the Philistine woman: because Samson gave into the pleasure of seeing her, he fittingly loses his eyesight at the hands of the Philistines (*Num. Rab.* 9:24). Others simply retold the story by omitting the divine drive that spurned Samson's desire. Ambrose wrote that Samson's parents "did not realize that [Samson's] purpose was so set that, if the Philistines refused her to him, he would become very angry, nor that they, if they gave their consent, would be bringing an end to the wrong treatment of the conquered" (*Letter* 35; Ambrose 1954: 179). Much later, Edwards would again turn to typology: "Samson married a Philistine, and all the women that he loved were of that people that were his great enemies, agreeable to those prophecies that represent the Messiah as marrying an alien from the commonwealth of Israel ... and the many prophecies that speak of Christ's calling the Gentiles and his saving sinners" (*Types of the Messiah*; Edwards 1993 [1834]: 255).

Typological readings also helped readers to make sense of the story of Samson and the lion, one of the most legendary scenes depicting his preternatural strength. According to the biblical text, when Samson encounters a lion on the way to Timnah, "The spirit of the LORD rushed on him, and he tore the lion apart barehanded as one might tear apart a kid" (Judg. 14:6). For many Christian interpreters, the lion symbolized Christ's enemies, with Edwards writing that the scene is "agreeable to the prophecies which represent the Messiah destroying his enemies as a strong lion destroying his prey" (*Types of the Messiah*; Edwards 1993 [1834]: 255). For others, like the Christian bishop Caesarius of Arles (470–542 CE), the lion prefigured Christ: "Many of the fathers have spoken a great deal about this lion, beloved brothers, and all of them have said what is fitting and in accord with the facts. Some have said that the lion prefigured Christ our Lord. Truly, this is very appropriate, for to us Christ is a lion in whose mouth we found the food of honey after his death" (*Sermon* 119.1; Caesarius of Arles 1964: 189).[6]

The story of Samson "tearing the lion apart barehanded" is also a favorite in art, including paintings by Lucas Cranach the Elder (1525) and Gustave Dore (1866), Albrecht Dürer's woodcut (ca. 1497–98), and Cristoforor Stati's sculpture (1604–1607). In each, the hero sits on or stands above the lion, hands wrenching open its jaws. Depictions of Samson and the lion also appear on twelfth-century tableman pieces, a precursor to the game of backgammon, while the opposition pieces depict scenes of the Greek Hercules, illustrating yet another strand running throughout the reception of Samson: comparisons between the two strongmen, both of whom are remembered for fighting a lion to death and for being betrayed by women they love. Such comparisons pre-date the game pieces, stretching at least as far back as Eusebius, an early Christian bishop who lived roughly 260–339 CE ("Samson ruled over the Hebrews, who is said to have been irresistible in strength of body, like the famous Hercules among the Greeks" [*Praep. Ev.* 9.10; Eusebius 2002: 518]). Typical observations include those like the famous American abolitionist Harriet Beecher Stowe (1811–96 CE), who remarks on Samson, "The legends of ancient history have their parallels. Hercules, the deliverer, made the scoff and slave of Omphale, and Anthony, become the tool and scorn of Cleopatra, are but repetitions of the same story" (1873: 112). Moreover, Samson is sometimes described as the "Jewish Hercules," from Ebenezer Cobham Brewer's 1899 *The Reader's Handbook of Famous Names in Fiction, Allusions, References, Proverbs, Plots, Stories and Poems* (Brewer 1904 [1899]: 485) to Joseph Telushkin's 1991 *Jewish Literacy* (60). The two even appear side-by-side in film, such as in Petro Francisci's Italian 1964 "sword-and-sandal" film, "Hercules, Samson, and Ulysses."

Samson's defeat of the lion leads directly to Samson's famous riddle, with which he challenges the "thirty companions" brought to celebrate with him at the wedding feast. Samson proposes the following riddle: "'Out of the eater came something to eat. Out of the strong came something sweet" (Judg. 14:14), which the men cannot answer. Puzzled by the idea that the Philistines, enemies of the Israelites, would bring Samson thirty "companions," Josephus writes that they did so "from fear of this young man's strength... ostensibly as companions, in reality as his guardians, lest he should be minded to create any disturbance" (*Ant.* 5.8.6; Josephus 2005: 291). Ambrose uses Samson's riddle as evidence that marrying outside the faith leads to disaster, writing, "Of the many, I shall set forth one, and by the mention of this one it may be clear how dangerous it is to marry a woman who is a stranger [to the faith]. Who more than the Nazarite, Samson, ever was mightier and from the cradle more endowed with strength by the Spirit of God? Yet he was betrayed by a woman and because of her he was unable to stay in God's good favor" (*Letter* 35; Ambrose 1954: 176). In the nineteenth century, Stowe also criticized Samson's wife, noting that his "strength was overcome and made the tool of woman's weakness" (1873: 111).

Caesarius of Arles explains that the answer to the riddle, "What is sweeter than honey? What is stronger than a lion?" signifies Christ's resurrection: "Truly, out of the eater, that is, from death which devours and consumes all things, came forth that food which said, 'I am the bread that has come down from heaven'" (*Sermon* 118.3; Caesarius of Arles 1964: 185; see John 6:41). To explain Samson's crass reply to the Philistines ("If you had not plowed with my heifer, you would not have found out my riddle" [Judg. 14:18]), Caesarius continues, "this heifer is the church which had the secrets of our faith revealed to her by her husband" (*Sermon* 118.3; Caesarius of Arles 1964: 185), illustrating yet again that it is impossible to tell the story of Samson's reception history without tracing the story of the women, too.

Judges 15 continues the story of Samson and, according to the *NIV Boy's Bible*, his "terrible choices when it came to relationships" (Osborne 2002: 320). Again, the story opens with a focus on the unnamed wife, as Samson returns to her only to discover that she has been married to one of his companions (Judg. 15:1–2). In Josephus's retelling, Samson "renounced his nuptials" with his Philistine wife after she revealed to the townspeople the answer to his riddle, after which point she, "scorning him for his wrath, was united to that friend of his who had given her away" (*Ant.* 5.8.6; Josephus 2005: 293). While Josephus omits the conversation with Samson's father-in-law that is the impetus for Samson's subsequent revenge (*Ant.* 5.8.7; Josephus 2005: 293–94), Edwards explains how the father-in-law's offer to give Samson his wife's sister in marriage "is agreeable to what the prophecies represent of the Messiah's coming to the Jews first, when he was offered up as a lamb or kid, making the first offer of the glorious benefits of his sacrifice to them and their rejecting to him, and the calling of the Gentiles and the more glorious and beautiful state of the Gentile church than of the ancient Jewish church" (*Types of the Messiah*; Edwards 1993 [1834]: 257). Such supersessionist readings, which depict the Jews as rejecting Christ, often surface in the typological interpretations of the Samson narrative, again reflecting the contexts (and presuppositions) of some of its readers. According to Caesarius of Arles, the man who married Samson's wife "prefigured all heretics," such as "Donatus, Arius, Manichaeus, and other vessels of error and perdition" (*Sermon* 118.3; Caesarius of Arles 1964: 185), offering yet another glimpse into what worried some early Christian writers.

If Samson's companion, who marries Samson's first wife, stands for the heretics, so too do the foxes in one of the most incredulous scenes of the story, when Samson catches three hundred foxes, ties lit torches to their tails, and turns them loose into the Philistine fields to destroy their crops (Judg. 15:4–8). For many early Christian readers, the story was clearly allegorical. For example, Augustine comments that Samson "could, of course, have set fire to the crops by a much simpler method, if he hadn't been thinking of some hidden meaning in the foxes" (*Sermon* 364.2; Augustine 1995: 277), and later adds, "What's the meaning of the foxes' tails tied together? What can the foxes' tails be, but the backsides of the heretics, whose fronts are smooth and deceptive, their backsides bound, that is condemned, and dragging fire behind them, to consume the crops and works of those who yield to their seductions?" (*Sermon* 364.4; Augustine 1995: 278–79). By the time of the Enlightenment, the French author Voltaire (1694–1778 CE) writes, "I pray you tell me by what trick Samson caught three hundred foxes, tied them together by their tails, and fastened lighted torches to their hind quarters, in order to set fire to the harvests of the Philistines. Foxes are found only in wooded country. There was no forest in this district, and it seems rather difficult to catch three hundred foxes alive and tie them together by their tails" (*Questions of Zapata* 38; Voltaire 1994 [1766]: 56–57).

The Flemish sculptor Giovanni Bologna captures Samson's next rampage in a marble piece entitled "Samson Slaying a Philistine" (ca. 1562), which portrays Samson holding the jawbone of a donkey as he grasps a crouching Philistine man by the hair. In the biblical text, Samson reportedly kills one thousand Philistine men with this jawbone (Judg. 15:15–17), about which Voltaire cast his aspersions: "When it comes to the jaws of asses, you certainly owe me explanations" (*Questions of Zapata* 38; Voltaire 1994 [1766]: 57). After this feat, Samson exclaims, "With the jawbone of a donkey, heaps upon heaps, with the jawbone of a donkey, I have slain a thousand men" (Judg. 16:16). The scene makes Ambrose lament that Samson was not "as controlled in victory as he was strong against the enemy," adding that Samson "neither erected an altar nor sacrificed a victim to God, but, failing to sacrifice and taking glory to himself, he called the place 'the killing of the jawbone' to immortalize his triumph with an everlasting name" (*Letter* 35; Ambrose 1954: 184). For the *NIV Boy's Bible*, the jawbone scene provides yet another real-life lesson for young men: "Just as Samson reached for the jawbone, we need to reach out for our calling, whether it's a computer mouse or a basketball" (Osborne 2002: 322).

When the chapter concludes, Samson forgets his wife, now dead, though it was because of her that his violent rages began. Alone and thirsty, Samson calls out to God, "You have granted this great victory by the hand of your servant. Am I now to die of thirst, and fall into the hands of the uncircumcised?" (Judg. 15:18). Josephus's retelling highlights even more strongly how Samson attributes the victory "to his own valor" (*Ant.* 5.8.9; Josephus 2005: 297), until "seized with a mighty thirst and recognizing that human valor is a thing of naught, he acknowledged that all was attributable to God," and so Samson prays for help. In both the biblical text and Josephus's version, God causes a spring of water to appear for Samson (Judg. 16:19; *Ant.* 5.8.9; Josephus 2005: 297). Much later, John of Damascus, a Byzantine monk born at the end of the seventh century CE, uses this story to support the idea of Christian relics: "For if by the will of God water poured out of the precipitous living rock in the desert, and for the thirsty Samson from the jawbone of an ass, is it unbelievable that fragrant ointment should flow from the relics of the martyrs?" (*Orthodox Faith* 4.15; John of Damascus 1958: 368).

Samson's strength and violence-filled actions following his marriage to the tragically fated Philistine woman from Timnah leaves later readers with much to ponder, and the texts become a source for midrashic gap-filling, moral guidance, and proof-texts for later beliefs. That these chapters are often troubling for many audiences is perhaps why Pseudo-Philo only records, "And when he had begun to grow up and sought to attack the Philistines, he took for himself a wife from the Philistines. The Philistines burned her in the fire, because they had been badly humiliated by Samson" (*LAB* 43:1–2; Harrington 1985: 357), omitting entirely the stories of the riddle, the foxes, and the jawbone. Augustine concludes, "Insofar, you see, as Samson performed feats of strength and wonders, he represented Christ the head of the Church; while insofar as he acted wisely, he bore the likeness of those in the Church who live just lives; where he happened to be taken unawares, and to have acted foolishly, he represented those who are sinners in the Church" (*Sermon* 364.3; Augustine 1995: 277).

Though writers like Josephus and Pseudo-Philo briefly mention the fate of the unnamed wife, her death is largely ignored by both early and later interpreters. One exception is Regina Spektor's 2006 song "Samson," in which Samson's Philistine wife appears to lament, among other things, that history does not remember their story or her love for Samson (see Long and Sawyer 2015: 210). In another example, Wil Gafney names the wife "Yashirah," from the Hebrew for "smooth" or "right" (see Judg. 14:3), seeing her as "good and pleasing in herself, to herself, not dependent on the approval of any man" (2016: 61). "In womanist solidarity with Yahsirah," Gafney "mark[s] and mourn[s] her passing" (2016: 60).

31.4 DELILAH, OR: "SHE OWED HIM NO OBEDIENCE, NO FAITH"

The story of Delilah and the love-struck hero, Samson, which ends with his death, is perhaps the best recognized of all the stories about Samson. Yet there is a third woman in the story before Delilah appears: the unnamed woman of Gaza (Judg. 16:1). Upon leaving Gaza at midnight, Samson famously "took hold of the doors of the city gate and the two posts, pulled them up, bar and all, put them on his shoulders, and carried them to the top of the hill that is in front of Hebron" (Judg. 16:3). One common interpretive trajectory connects Samson's fate to his earlier tryst with the sex-worker at Gaza: so Rabbi Samuel b. Nahman explains that though one might cast disparagements on Samson's first wife, "The intercourse at Timnah was by way of marriage, but his deterioration began at Gaza" (*Num. Rab.* 9:24). Similarly, the Christian bishop Isaac the Syrian, who lived from roughly 613 to 700 CE, writes, "For this reason God departed from him and surrendered him to his enemies" (*Ascetical Homilies* 10; Isaac the Syrian 2011: 194). Alternatively, typological readings stress that this foreshadows Christ's crucifixion and death. As Gregory the Great, who was pope in the late sixth century CE, explains, "Whom, dearly beloved, does Samson foreshadow by his deed but our Redeemer? What does the city of Gaza signify if not the lower world?" (*Forty Gospel Homilies* 21; Gregory the Great 1990: 162).

Many interpreters conflate the unnamed woman at Gaza with Delilah, including both Josephus (*Ant.* 5.8.11; Josephus 2005: 299–301) and Pseudo-Philo, the latter of whom writes that Samson "was led astray after her and took her to himself for a wife" (*LAB* 43:5; Harrington 1985: 357). Pseudo-Philo also adds God's evaluation to his retelling: "Behold now Samson has been led astray through his eyes, and has not remembered the mighty works I did with him; and he has mingled with the daughters of the Philistines.... And now Samson's lust will be a stumbling block for him, and his mingling a ruin, and I will hand him over to his enemies, and they will blind him" (*LAB* 43:5; Harrington 1985: 357).

The opening verses from Neil Sedaka's 1962 song "Run Samson Run" illustrates, yet again, how the reception history of Samson is also the story of the women in its pages (as well as being a narrative that lends itself to [sometimes questionable] counsel). Sedaka warns Samson to run from Delilah while also cautioning his own (male) listeners that all women are, to some extent, akin to Sedaka's understanding of Delilah as a cheater and one who led Samson to his death. Aspersions on Delilah pre-date Sedaka, of course, and are not restricted to men. For example, Stowe wrote, "With the history of this inspired giant is entwined that of a woman whose name has come to stand as a generic term for a class—Delilah!" (1873: 110), and, indeed, the name Delilah has entered the vernacular as synonymous with "seductress" or "treacherous." Yet for the nineteenth-century Clara B. Neyman, while Delilah "abuses—the power which she had gained over Samson by virtue of her beauty and her personal attractions," her story also serves to teach "men as well as... women! Let man overcome the lust of his eyes and prostitution will die a natural death" (1898: 34).

Though the narrative informs readers that Samson "fell in love with a woman in the valley of Sorek, whose name was Delilah" (Judg. 16:4), the text adds nothing more. Readers are left to guess whether Delilah is an Israelite or a Philistine, whether she and Samson are married, and, perhaps most importantly, whether she loves Samson in return. Readers are informed that the lords of the Philistines ask Delilah to find out what gives Samson his strength, so that they might "bind him in order to subdue him" (Judg. 16:5). What follows is a scene made famous by early rabbis and Christian interpreters as well as Hollywood producers and the makers of "30Rock": Delilah repeatedly asks Samson for the secret to his strength and he repeatedly lies to her, until "finally, after she had nagged him with her words day after day, and pestered him, he was tired to death," and so reveals to her that his strength lies in his hair (Judg. 16:16-17). For Josephus and Pseudo-Philo, Samson tells Delilah his secret in no small part because he was drunk (*Ant.* 5.8.11; Josephus 2005: 299-301; *LAB* 43:6; Harrington 1985: 357)—it is that fact that causes him to fall asleep in Delilah's lap.

Exegetes have long puzzled over the meaning of Delilah's name.[7] For the rabbis, it was a hint toward her character, as they connected it to the Hebrew root *d-l-l*, meaning, "to weaken" (*Num. Rab.* 9:24). In fact, "Even if her name had not been Delilah she deserved to be called by such a name. She enfeebled his strength, she enfeebled his actions, she enfeebled his determination" (*Num. Rab.* 9:24). Though it is clear that Delilah does reveal Samson's secret to the Philistine lords, the narrative is ambiguous on several levels. It is Samson who repeatedly lies in the story, while Delilah tells the truth about what she wants to know (Judg. 16:6: "Please tell me what makes your strength so great, and how you could be bound, so that one could subdue you") and what was going to happen (Judg. 16:9, 12, 14, 20: "the Philistines are upon you!"). Accordingly, per Niditch, the scene "strikes many commentators as proof of [Samson's] folly" (Niditch 2008: 169), while Tammi J. Schneider (2000: 222) observes that "Samson was either so naïve as not to see what was happening, or so arrogant and confident in his strength that he had no fear."

For the rabbis, Judg. 16:18 held a key to one ambiguity in the text: How did Delilah know that Samson "had told her his whole secret" with his final answer, especially after all of his lies? The answer: Delilah realized that Samson told the truth because he used God's name in his final reply, "for I have been a Nazirite to God from my mother's womb" (*Num. Rab.* 9:24; see Judg. 16:17). Delilah then let Samson fall asleep on her lap, and "she called a man, and had him shave off the seven locks of his head" (Judg. 16:19), though popular culture often misremembers this detail as Delilah cutting Samson's hair herself. The hair-cutting scene appears regularly in paintings, from Peter Paul Ruben's "Samson and Delilah" (1610) to Anthony van Dyck's similar "Samson and Delilah" (1620), where Delilah watches, seemingly impassive or indifferent, as Samson's hair is shorn. However, in van Dyck's later painting of the same scene (1630), Delilah stretches out her hand to an agonized Samson as Philistine guards pull him away from her, raising a number of interpretive questions: Did Delilah love Samson, too? Or was she a deceitful *femme fatale*? The biblical text remains ambiguous.

John Milton's 1671 *Samson Agonistes*, a poetic drama, focuses on the last hours of Samson's life, when he is already blinded and slaving away in the Philistine mill. Though at the start Samson laments his lot ("O loss of sight, of thee I most complain! Blind among enemies, O worse than chains, Dungeon, or beggary, or decrepit age!" [68-69]), by the end the tragedy depicts a repentant Samson, "All these indignities... these evils I deserve and more, acknowledge them from God inflicted on me justly" (1169-71). Predictably, Delilah, depicted by Milton as Samson's wife, betrays him in the tragedy, and Samson, who dies to save his people, is again portrayed as prefiguring Christ.

Inspired by Milton's work, Handel wrote "Samson," which premiered in 1743, and also centers on the final chapter of the Samson story. The strongman likewise appeared in the French composer Camille Saint-Saëns's 1877 opera *Samson and Delilah*, which begins in Gaza and tells a story of the Philistines using Delilah to capture Samson. Once again, Delilah here causes Samson to share the secret of his strength with her. Of course, songs about Samson and Delilah are not restricted to the realm of classical music or the stage of the opera. In addition to Neil Sedaka's "Run Samson Run," the Grateful Dead are famous for their "Samson and Delilah," which likewise casts aspersions on Delilah.

Samson and Delilah's story also makes for (seemingly endless) movies, a story of love gone wrong, or, perhaps more commonly, the story of the *femme fatale* who tricks a loving man into his ruin. There is a long list of films entitled *Samson and Delilah*, based either entirely or loosely upon the biblical narrative. The most renowned is Cecil B. DeMille's 1949 *Samson and Delilah*. DeMille's film fills gaps in the biblical text in a way similar to early Jewish discourse: all of the female characters in the story are named, from Samson's Philistine-wife-to-be (Semadar) to his mother (Hazelelponit) to Delilah, figured here as Semadar's younger sister. In the film, Delilah devises the plan to defeat Samson by seducing him, but DeMille adds details absent from the biblical narrative. For example, once the Philistines capture Samson, Delilah feels guilty for betraying him and she remains in the temple as Samson pushes the pillars apart, and so dies with Samson and the Philistines. In addition to feature-length films, a number of television episodes have been loosely based on the story (such as the "Samson and Delilah" episode of the series *Terminator: The Sarah Connor Chronicles* and the 1990 "Simpson and Delilah" episode of *The Simpsons*).

Though Delilah is often portrayed negatively, this is not invariably the case.[8] In the nineteenth century Sarah Hale, an American promotor of women's education, wrote the following:

> Delilah conquered Samson, and in the means she employed was far less culpable than he; because she was his paramour, perhaps his victim, and he the heaven-gifted champion of Israel. Read the history as recorded in the Bible, not in Milton's "Samson Agonistes," where the whole is set in a false light. Delilah was not the wife of Samson. She owed him no obedience, no faith. But his strength was consecrated to God—he was the traitor, when he disclosed the secret. See Judges, from chapters xiii. to xvii. (1855: 36)

More recently, a number of feminist biblical interpreters continue this line of thought, and, instead of seeing Delilah as *femme fatale* or archetypal bad girl, read Delilah's story as one of an independent woman who "initiates the action" in the story and "secures for herself financial security" (Fewell 1992: 73–74); or, if Delilah is understood as a Philistine, she may even be "a hero to her own people" (Klein 1993: 42). Others recognize the bind that Delilah might find herself in, especially at the hands of the Philistine men. For example, in Gafney's womanist reading of the Samson story, she writes of Delilah, "I posit Delilah is not playing Samson for sport or money; she is playing for her life and therefore willing to take a life or, in this case, hand over a life" (2016: 67). Such readings seek to see the story from Delilah's perspective and thus pay more attention to the only named woman in Judges 13–16 than the biblical text and many earlier commentators do.

Once the Philistines take Samson away, Delilah exits the biblical story (even if this is often portrayed otherwise in later retellings, such as DeMille's film). The focus turns, finally, to Samson alone, with no female character to accompany him (or to be blamed for his actions). Again, for many, the fact that the Philistines gouged out Samson's eyes made perfect sense: it was his lustful eyes that brought about his downfall (*Num. Rab.* 9:24; *LAB* 43:5; Harrington 1985: 356). Numerous artists capture the brutality of the blinding scene, with Rembrandt's "The Blinding of Samson" (1636) depicting a host of guards struggling to hold down the Israelite hero as one drives a knife into Samson's right eye. While Rembrandt captures the agonizing moment of Samson's disfigurement, Lovis Corinth's 1912 "The Blinded Samson" depicts Samson afterward, with a bloody bandage covering his eyes and his chained hands feeling for the sides of the doorway in which he stands.

For the rabbis, the idea that Samson was "grinding" for the Philistines connoted sexual activity, and so some rabbinic texts record that the Philistine women came to Samson for sex in the hopes that their children would be strong like him (*Num. Rab.* 9:24; *b. Sotah* 10a). As Josephus finishes his retelling of Samson's story, he leaves out the prayer for revenge found in Judg. 16:28, merely noting, "And it is but right to admire the man for his valor, his strength, and the grandeur of his end, as also for the wrath which he cherished to the last against his enemies. That he let himself be ensnared by a woman must be imputed to human nature which succumbs to sins; but testimony is due to him for surpassing excellence in all the rest" (*Ant.* 5.8.12; Josephus 2005: 303). In Pseudo-Philo's version, Samson muses, "Go forth, my soul, and do not be sad; die, my body, and do not weep about yourself" (*LAB* 43:7–8; Harrington 1985: 357). Moreover, Philo increases the number of Philistines that Samson kills alongside himself from the biblical three thousand (Judg. 16:27) to "40,000 men and women" (*LAB* 43:8; Harrington 1985: 357). One midrash notes how "two strong men arose in the world—one in Israel and Goliath among the nations of the world—and both of them were destroyed from the world.... Why? Because their gifts were not from the Holy One, blessed be He, but they snatched it for themselves" (*Num. Rab.* 22:7). Some ancient interpreters rush to defend Samson, even if his death is an act of suicidal revenge. For example, Augustine solves the problem of Samson's death by arguing "Nor is Samson, who crushed both himself and his enemies in the collapse of the house, excused on any other ground than that the Spirit, who had been working miracles through him, secretly commanded him to do this" (*City of God* 1:21; Augustine 2012: 24). Yet later, Grossman (2006: 142–43) notes, "in the echo chamber of our own time and place there is no escaping the thought that Samson was, in a sense, the first suicide-killer."

In his death, as in his life, Samson remains ever complex: is he a hero, who at least begins to defeat the Philistines, or is he a tragic dupe, who ruins the lives of all around him? Though the text ends by recording that he is buried in the tomb of his father, there is no record of peace coming to the land. Moreover, it is only in his death that the story can be told without the women of the narrative.

31.5 CONCLUSION

The hermeneutical paths that branch out from Judges 13–16 offer a glimpse into how the story of Samson is also a "story of women," and that interpreters were often as interested in the named and unnamed women of the story as they were in the hero who the narrative would commonly be named after. A number of shared exegetical techniques appear and reappear in the afterlives of this story, from gap filling, typological readings, and the attempt to solve the problem of seemingly questionable behavior (and the related blaming of the women for any such behavior) to examples of how the text has been looked to for daily guidance and support. Throughout all of these trajectories, common questions resurface, and these questions are sometimes the same that we, as contemporary readers, might have. So, with Stanton, perhaps we might find ourselves observing that Samson's mother "might have had a name to designate her personality instead of being mentioned merely as the wife of Manoah or the mother of Samson," or, with Hale, that, after all, Samson's "strength was consecrated to God—he was the traitor, when he disclosed the secret." And as we trace the hermeneutical paths that stretch from the earliest Jewish and Christian writers to an episode of an American television show, we may also see the various ways that the context(s) of different readers and interpreters influence how they read the story of Samson and the women—from worries over Manichean heretics to Enlightenment skepticism about catching three hundred foxes to a general lack of biblical literacy ("like Samson in that movie"). (Re)reading the story of the reception of the figure of Samson—along with the named and unnamed women of the narrative—informs and deepens our understanding of how many afterlives these three short chapters have had, and reminds us of how deeply the Historical Books like that of the book of Judges have touched the world in which we live.

Notes

1. For more on the compositional history of the Samson narrative, see Niditch 2008 and Gross 2009. For more on theories of the origins and composition of the Deuteronomistic History, see Thomas Römer's article in this volume.
2. Samson is also frequently identified as the otherwise unknown figure of Bedan mentioned in Samuel's farewell speech, "And the Lord sent Jerubbaal and Barak, and Jephthah, and Bedan, and rescued you out of the hand of your enemies on every side; and you lived in safety" (1 Sam. 12:11). According to *Eccl. Rabb.* 1:4, "Jerubbaal is Gideon, Bedan is Samson, while Jephthah is the man of that name." Many English translations of 1 Samuel include Samson in the list, footnoting that the Hebrew reads "Bedan," while some Greek and Syriac manuscripts read Samson.
3. Talmudic translations throughout are from The William Davidson digital edition of the Koren Noé Talmud, found here: https://www.sefaria.org/texts/Talmud.
4. For a fuller treatment of nineteenth-century female biblical interpreters, see Taylor and de Groot 2016. It was through this excellent volume that I discovered many of the nineteenth-century women featured in this essay, and how they used Judg. 13–16 in their own lives (including for the temperance movement).
5. The idea that sometimes the spirit was with Samson ("when" in *Num. Rab.* 14:9) allowed the rabbis to account for some of Samson's more questionable behavior. For more on the "spirit of Yhwh" in the book of Judges, see Levine 2009; MacDonald 2013; Murphy 2015.
6. Judges 14:9 reads, "He scraped it out into his hands, and went on, eating as he went. When he came to his father and mother, he gave some to them, and they ate it. But he did not tell

them that he had taken the honey from the carcass of the lion." The idea that the honey might have come from the mouth of the lion depends on a reading of the Septuagint, which says, "And he did not tell them that he had taken the honey from the mouth of the lion."

7. So Niditch writes, "One possibility, 'loose hair,' would relate both the Samson's status as *Nazir* and to Delilah's undoing the 'plaits of his hair.' A second possibility is 'small, slight.' A charming name for a young girl, the name would also serve to evoke Samson the superman's conquest by a woman. A third possibility, a play on the word for 'night,' suggests mystery and surreptitiousness" (2008: 164 n. e).

8. In short, as Schneider notes, the figure of "Delilah has not fared well in most analyses of this text until more recently" (2000: 218–19).

Bibliography

"30 Rock." Episode no. 1, Season 12, first broadcast February 1, 2007, by NBC. Directed by Don Scardino and written by Kay Cannon and Tina Fey.

Ambrose. 1954. *Letters, 1–91.* FC 26. Translated by Mary Melchior Beyenka. Washington, D.C.: The Catholic University of America Press.

Augustine. 1995. *Sermons.* Vol. 10. Translated by Edmund Hill. Edited by John E. Rotelle. New York: New City Press.

Augustine. 2012. *City of God.* Translated by William S. Babcock. New York: New City Press.

Brewer, Ebenezer Cobham. 1904. *The Reader's Handbook of Famous Names in Fiction, Allusions, References, Proverbs, Plots, Stories and Poems.* Rev. ed. Philadelphia: J. B. Lippincott.

Caesarius of Arles. 1964. *Sermons, Volume 2 (81–116).* Translated by Mary Magdeleine Mueller. FC 47. Washington, D.C.: Catholic University of America Press.

Edwards, Jonathan. 1993 (1834). *Typological Writings.* Vol. 11 of *The Works of Jonathan Edwards.* Edited by Mason I. Lowance and David H. Walters. New Haven, CT: Yale University Press.

Eusebius. 2002. *Preparation for the Gospel, Part 1, Books 1–9.* Translated by Edwin Hamilton Gifford. Eugene, OR: Wipf and Stock.

Exum, J. Cheryl. 1990. "The Centre Cannot Hold: Thematic and Textual Instabilities in Judges." *CBQ* 52: 410–31.

Exum, J. Cheryl. 1993. "Samson's Women." In *Fragmented Women: Feminist (Sub)versions of Biblical Narratives.* Valley Forge: Trinity Press International, 61–93.

Fewell, D. N. 1992. "Judges." In *The Women's Bible Commentary.* Edited by Carol A. Newsom and Sharon H. Ringe. Louisville, KY: Westminster John Knox, 67–77.

Freedman, Harry and Isidore Epstein, eds. 2001. *The Soncino Midrash Rabbah.* Brooklyn, NY: Judaica Press.

Gafney, Wil. 2016. "A Womanist Midrash of Delilah: Don't Hate the Playa Hate the Game." In *Womanist Interpretations of the Bible: Exploring the Discourse.* Edited by Gay L. Byron and Vanessa Lovelace. SemeiaSt 85. Atlanta: SBL Press, 49–72.

Gregory the Great. 1990. *Forty Gospel Homilies.* Translated by David Hurst. CS 123. Kalamazoo, MI: Cistercian.

Gross, Walter. 2009. *Richter.* HThKAT. Freiburg: Herder.

Grossman, David. 2006. *Lion's Honey: The Myth of Samson.* Translated by Stuart Schoffman. New York: Canongate.

Hale, Sarah. 1855. *Women's Record; or, Sketches of all Distinguished Women, from the Creation to A. D. 1854.* New York: Harper and Bros.

Harrington, D. J. 1985. "Pseudo-Philo." In *The Old Testament Pseudepigrapha.* Edited by J. H. Charlesworth. Garden City, NY: Doubleday, 2.297–377.

Isaac the Syrian. 2011. *The Ascetical Homilies of Saint Isaac the Syrian*. Translated by The Holy Transfiguration Monastery. Rev. 2nd ed. Boston, MA: The Holy Transfiguration Monastery.

John of Damascus. 1958. "An Exact Exposition of the Orthodox Faith." In *Writings*. Translated by Frederic H. Chase. FC 37. Washington, D.C.: The Catholic University of America Press, 165–406.

Josephus, Flavius. 2005. *Jewish Antiquities, Books IV–VI* (Josephus Vol. VI). Loeb Classical Library 490. Translated by H. St. J. Thackeray. Cambridge, MA: Harvard University Press.

Klein, L. R. 1993. "The Book of Judges: Paradigm and Deviation in Images of Women." In *A Feminist Companion to Judges*. FCB 4. Edited by A. Brenner. Sheffield: JSOT Press, 55–71.

Levine, Baruch A. 2009. "Religion in the Heroic Spirit: Themes in the Book of Judges." In *Thus Says the Lord: Essays on the Former and Latter Prophets in Honor of Robert R. Wilson*. Edited by John J. Ahn and Stephen Cook. LHBOTS 502. New York: T&T Clark, 27–42.

Long, Siobhán Dowling and John F. A. Sawyer. 2015. *The Bible in Music: A Dictionary of Songs, Works, and More*. New York: Rowman & Littlefield.

MacDonald, Nathan. 2013. "The Spirit of Yhwh: An Overlooked Conceptualization of Divine Presence in the Persian Period." In *Divine Presence and Absence in Exilic and Post-Exilic Judaism*. FAT 2. Edited by Nathan MacDonald and Izaak J. de Hulster. Tübingen: Mohr Siebeck, 95–120.

Milton, John. 1998. *The Complete Poems*. Editor John Lenoard. London: Penguin.

Murphy, Kelly J. 2015. "Masculinity, Moral Agency, and Memory: The Spirit of the Deity in Judges, Samuel, and Beyond." In *JBR* 2: 175–96.

Neyman, Clara B. 1898. "The Book of Judges, Chapter II." In *The Woman's Bible*, Part 2: *Joshua to Revelation*. Edited by Elizabeth Cady Stanton. Boston: Northeastern University Press, 21–23.

Neyman, Clara B. 1898. "The Book of Judges, Chapter III." In *The Woman's Bible*, Part 2: *Joshua to Revelation*. Edited by Elizabeth Cady Stanton. Boston: Northeastern University Press, 34.

Niditch, Susan. 2008. *Judges: A Commentary*. OTL. Louisville, KY: Westminster John Knox.

Osborne, Rick. 2002. *NIV Boys Bible: Your Ultimate Manual*. Grand Rapids: Zonderkidz.

Schneider, Tammi J. 2000. *Judges*. Berit Olam. Collegeville, MN: Liturgical.

Stanton, Elizabeth Cady. 1898a. "The Book of Judges, Chapter II." In *The Woman's Bible*, Part 2: *Joshua to Revelation*. Edited by Elizabeth Cady Stanton. Boston: Northeastern University Press, 18–21, 23–26.

Stanton, Elizabeth Cady. 1898b. "The Book of Judges, Chapter III." In *The Woman's Bible*. Part 2: *Joshua to Revelation*. Edited by Elizabeth Cady Stanton. Boston: Northeastern University Press, 28–30, 32–34.

Steinsaltz, Adin, Tzvi Hersh Weinreb, Shalom Zvi Berger, and Joshua Schreier, eds. 2012. *Koren Talmud Bavli Berakhot*. Jerusalem: Shefa Foundation.

Stowe, Harriet Beecher. 1873. *Woman in Sacred History*. New York: J. B. Ford & Co.

Taylor, Marion Ann and Christiana de Groot, eds. 2016. *Women of War, Women of Woe: Joshua and Judges through the Eyes of Nineteenth-Century Female Biblical Interpreters*. Grand Rapids: William B. Eerdmans.

Telushkin, Joseph. 1991. *Jewish Literacy*. New York: William Morrow.

Voltaire. 1994. *A Treatise on Toleration and Other Essays*. Great Mind Series. Translated by Joseph McCabe. Amherst, NY: Prometheus Books.

CHAPTER 32

SAUL IN RECEPTION HISTORY

BARBARA GREEN

THE biblical narratives of Saul invite interpreters to consider and reshape moments of action and situations of deep emotion. Beloved for their situations of competition as well as love between Saul and David, offering also many opportunities to ponder the intersection of God and human beings, these stories have a rich reception history in Western culture. We will sample various genres into which the biblical Saul story has been received and reinterpreted to suggest a broad diversity of ways to extend the narrative into the lives of later readers. The basic challenges of reception include receiving an older work suitably in a new time period and transposing the literary text into another genre.

32.1 THE SAUL NARRATIVE IN 1–2 SAMUEL

The narrative of Saul in 1–2 Samuel, long by biblical standards (twenty-four chapters), can be summarized into seven main moments allowing adequately for subsequent discussion. The biblical narrative is skillfully articulated with many places of rich undecidability for interpretive exploitation, lending itself to enhancement as well.

First, the elders of Israel ask the prophet Samuel for a king, in place of judges who have ruled Israel with declining success. God, not unambiguously pleased, grants the request, which Samuel communicates to the elders. Whether we are to envision the first king among those who hear the news is not clear. We do not know whether Saul understands that, though the divine answer was affirmative, it came with a warning of the limits of kingship and its negative potential. The Saul story is as much about the office as it is about the man, so this first step where kingship is asked and granted is crucial (1 Sam. 8).

Second, the king must be selected, and Saul is chosen and affirmed, repeatedly and by various players (chs. 9–12): first by God to the prophet Samuel; Saul is then anointed (twice) by Samuel, who is given signs to indicate God's desire for Saul. Saul is chosen by lots and approved by most of the people. Even when he hides, he is found. Though Saul begins as hesitant to accept the responsibility, he is the king.

Third, almost at once Saul does two things that provoke the prophetic announcement that no son of his will succeed him, that his kingship is abrogated. The first of these (chs. 13–14) occurs in a situation of warfare where Saul is accused of violating the directions of his prophet in the matter of sacrifice. Whether or how precisely Saul was at fault is not clear in the text, but Samuel expresses no doubt. The second episode (ch. 15) involves God's charging the king by prophetic directive to place under absolute destruction the people Amalek and all their possessions as punishments for an old attack committed by Amalek when the Israelites were fleeing the Egyptian Pharaoh. Saul's disobedience—his refusal to do as instructed and his persistence in denying his responsibility while blaming others—leads to his termination as king, though Saul begs to save face. He is granted that small favor, since after his "firing," he appears to continues in his position.

A fourth part of his story, beginning at ch. 16 and extending very briefly through ch. 17, involves the arrival of David at Saul's household. Not knowing that, at God's direction, Samuel has anointed David, Saul agrees to a suggestion made by his own servants that a young musician be brought to soothe Saul when he is afflicted with what readers learn is an evil spirit from God. When Saul's fighters are beset by a Philistine giant who challenges single-combat, the boy David, appearing at the camp to provision his brothers, volunteers to fight the giant. Saul arms David to do this deed, but David removes the armor and kills the giant with simpler tools. Saul commandeers David to his household, and Saul's son, Jonathan, offers royal gear to David as had his father. Very briefly Saul seems un-conflicted about the presence of David.

But as early as the return from the battle, a fifth phase begins, when Saul takes offense at his interpretation of the victory song sung and eyes David as wanting the throne. While simultaneously both giving David responsibility and status (David marries Saul's daughter Michal) and undermining him, Saul is shown over the space of chs. 19–26 to escalate his attack on David, such that David moves by degrees from Saul's hurled spear, from his table, from his palace, and from his territory. After ascertaining and demonstrating that Saul cannot be relied upon to overcome hostility for more than a short time, David moves further afield, gathering men and their families to himself and eluding pursuit by Saul, who kills priests suspected of assisting David. Several times Saul comes close to David's hiding place, but pursuit breaks off without harm. As such episodes recur, we see David as the more powerful hunter, positioned to harm Saul. Reflecting on that very point, David withdraws a final time into territory controlled by the Philistines, Saul's nemeses. There David assumes the role of double agent, appearing and claiming to work for Achish of Gath while undertaking his own raids on others.

Sixth, the Philistines muster for a major attack on Saul, who, learning of it, enters the last two moments of his life (chs. 28 and 31 within the set chs. 27–31). Though the narrative grows distracted by demonstrating that David was nowhere near the scene of Saul's death, it provides us with the crucial and moving scenes of Saul's final night and day on earth. Characterized as freshly afraid at the massing Philistines, Saul disguises himself, searching by night the skills of a medium reputedly able to make contact with the dead, forbidden though such action is in biblical law. Saul asks her to raise Samuel from the dead, which she first refuses but then undertakes. The woman recognizes Samuel apparently by his prophet's mantle. Saul, learning (apparently without seeing) that his prophet is present, names the Philistine threat, characterizes God as silent, and begs his prophet for instruction. Samuel answers harshly if truthfully, reminding Saul that his kingship has long since been torn from him and given to David as a consequence of disobedience. As for outcomes, Samuel tells Saul that he will join him among the dead on the next day. Saul's shock at hearing this word topples him in a faint. When Samuel has disappeared, the woman prevails upon Saul to eat a meal she sets before him. Thus strengthened, he goes to his last battle.

Finally, seventh, initially attended by warriors and specifically by Jonathan (and two other sons) who die bravely, Saul eventually fights alone valiantly, attended only by his armor-bearer. The king begs this servant to kill him, lest he be abused by his opponents. The armor-bearer, fearful, refuses, and so Saul falls on his own sword. The bodies of Saul and his sons are stripped, disfigured, and impaled on Philistine walls, from where they are taken by night by men of Jabesh of Gilead, whom Saul had assisted early in his reign. The news of Saul's death is brought to David by an alleged witness, whom David kills. Saul's story ends with David's lament for Saul and Jonathan, the so-called Song of the Bow, arguably the most beautiful poem in the whole Bible.

32.2 Early Re-Telling of the Story: Josephus

The reception and representation closest to the biblical story in both time and genre occurs as what is commonly called the "Rewritten Bible" (Zsengellér 2014). The label calls attention to ways in which Jewish scholars in late biblical and early post-biblical times sought to make the traditional stories accessible to and relevant for audiences needing them reshaped for their own experience, not to replace but to supplement older stories for later generations. These audiences, comprising both Hellenized Jews unfamiliar with Hebrew and Gentiles ignorant of Jewish lore and customs, were helped by the writings of historian Flavius Josephus (ca. 37–100 CE). His reprise of Saul's life is Book 6 of *Antiquities of the Jews*, a work extending from creation until the Roman War (Josephus 1991). Josephus, himself a Jew though adopted into one of the noble Roman families, sought to present both ancient and recent events favorably, not least his own participation in the Jewish/Roman war of 66–72 CE. Josephus's strategies included translating the material from Hebrew into Greek; abridging what was unnecessarily complex; adding detail and opinion to assist understanding; clearing up apparent contradictions; resolving ambiguities and gaps that add richness to the biblical story; setting events to appeal to those who had not heard of them before; eliminating information that might confuse or disedify people about Jewish customs or history—in sum, seeking to uplift all with the Jewish heritage (Avioz 2015).

In Josephus's telling, Samuel himself preferred aristocracy to kingship, but the people demanded a king. God, also disappointed, comforted Samuel over what had happened. Josephus thus cuts the tangle of uncertainties about the choice of kingship, making it less conflicted. As the assembly of elders, slow to disperse after hearing that kingship was to be granted, demanded that the man be produced at once, Josephus says Samuel reassured them that he would reassemble them when he learned the man's identity.

Josephus adds detail to Saul's attributes (a fine mind to a tall body), explains the awkwardness of Saul's ignorance of the ways of prophets (e.g., his not knowing that they did not require payment), and claims that Saul felt belittled by how Samuel addressed him. Josephus explains Saul's early reticence to tell his kin about his recent adventure with Samuel, explaining that even those who love others may feel jealousy when good fortune befalls them. Similarly, when Saul was chosen king by lots but not found when it was time to anoint him, Josephus explains that the first king, humble and modest, hid himself, thinking that those over whom he was to rule should exert themselves to find him, as indeed they did, helped as well by God.

The biblical events comprising the rejection of Saul's dynasty and of the first king himself, filled with events open to multiple interpretations, are smoothed out for Josephus's readers. He resolves biblical uncertainty about Samuel's arrival at the sacrifice clearly in favor of the prophet and against the king. In the same battle, when winning, Saul adjured his fighters not to eat, but Saul's son, Jonathan, not hearing the command, violated it. Josephus names this action of the king unhappy and blameworthy, noting that often in such circumstances people who feel things are proceeding well make foolish choices.

Josephus treats the brief time of Saul's favoring David by making additions to the biblical narrative. Saul, aware of his self-inflicted misery, sought his prophet's presence no more, so that God withdrew his spirit from Saul and gave it to David. This left Saul with demonic disorders, such that he appeared about to choke, to the despair of all his physicians, who recommended the services of a harpist and singer. There David pleased Saul, being the only one able to perform music so that the king's mind was restored.

Josephus moves quickly into the long period where Saul's animosity toward David grew, forcing David from Saul's presence. Saul's lethal feelings in Josephus's tale are occasioned by the women's song celebrating the victory over the Philistines, crediting David over Saul—a viewpoint the biblical text allows to Saul without claiming it as the women's intent. As David was betrothed to Saul's daughter, Michal, Josephus reads David as unaware that Saul did not wish him well—again, a point that the biblical account leaves more ambiguous. When David left Saul's palace for the last time, stopping en route to be assisted by the priest of Nob with bread and sword, the matter is reported to Saul. Josephus then describes the scene at Saul's court in which the king upbraided his kinsmen and courtiers for not assisting him against David, since only the Edomite Doeg (called a Syrian by Josephus) informed him that the priest had inquired for David. This scene is ambiguous in the biblical story and unanticipated in anything Josephus has said. Saul, so fearful that he is unable to accept the honest words of the priest, ordered him slain. Josephus denounces deficiencies of leadership, the barbarity of the crime, and the lack of pity for children or the aged, and critiques Saul for his severe injustice, for his refusal to sense God's wishes, his lack of interest in acquiring evidence of guilt, and his refusal of suitable process to determine the facts of the priest's action. The several scenes of this long section, where Saul and David came face to face, are re-worked to abridge details of topography and language. Josephus cleans up David's colorful language (his references to himself as a dead dog and a flea) while stressing the injustice of Saul's pursuit of David, making David seem more right than Saul.

Josephus treats the last two episodes of Saul's life more sympathetically than his treatments of earlier ones suggest he would. The massing of Philistines drives Saul to fear the outcome. With God silent and Samuel dead, Saul sought out a necromancer. As Josephus narrates the scene, Saul entreats her successfully to assist him, assuring her specifically that he would not tell anyone of her deed. Persuaded, she brings up Samuel without knowing who he is, the method a bit obscure. Josephus simplifies the detail of which participant saw what, but agrees with the biblical text that Samuel had no good news for Saul, telling him bluntly what was to happen the next day. Saul faints from grief, Josephus says, again clarifying a gap in the biblical narrative. The necromancer begs him to eat, slaughtering for his last meal a calf of which she was very fond and for whom she had long cared. Josephus praises her hospitable kindness to Saul, urging readers to imitate her virtues, offering no condemnation of her skill with the dead, as proscribed for Israelites of the time. The next day brings Saul into battle with the Philistines, where Josephus praises Saul's courage, going into battle knowing the dire outcome. Saul's military courage and determination to die honorably are extolled. Josephus avoids the biblical storyline's two versions of the death of Saul, summarizing that Saul died as Samuel had prophesied, primarily for disobedience in the slaying of the Amalekites and for his slaughter of the priests of Nob and their households. Solving a notorious crux in the biblical data about the length of Saul's reign (see 1 Sam. 13:1), Josephus informs us that the reign of Saul was twenty years: eighteen while Samuel lived and two past the prophet's death.

32.3 Music

The transposition of biblical narratives, verbal and ancient, into music of a later era presents a challenge taken up wonderfully by George Frideric Handel (1685–1759), German-born but composing oratorios in London and in English. The oratorio is a musical form originating in the seventeenth century (the baroque period) in Italy. Opera was banned during Lent, so oratorio, as a sort of unstaged opera—biblical texts performed by chorus and soloists, with instrumental accompaniment but without costume, scenery, or action—filled in. Handel, a committed Lutheran, was both eager to explore and present these biblical pieces and also to please his audiences.

Saul, composed in 1738 (though begun earlier and reworked over several years) and performed in 1739, is considered one of Handel's finest works (Burrows and Dunhill 2002), the first with a bass voice lead, longer than any previous oratorio. *In nuce*, the work portrays King Saul's tragic, conflicted, and irrational behavior, as well as the loss of both throne and affections of those he loved. Handel took great pains and considerable expense to have musical instrumentation appropriate to the sounds he wanted to suggest (e.g., kettledrums for battle), aiming as well for what he considered authentic biblical instruments (the tubalcain, timbrel, sackbut). He commissioned a new organ and a glockenspiel for this particular oratorio (Burrows 2012).

Handel's *Saul* concentrates on two main moments of the biblical story. First is the induction of David into the household of Saul after the defeat of Goliath, initiating various conflicts among Saul, David, Merab, Michal, and Jonathan. The second major moment is Saul's learning his fate—that he is about to die in battle and why (his refusal to obey God's orders regarding Amalekites). The oratorio ties these moments together by having King Saul die by the hand of an Amalekite.

The *Saul* libretto follows the biblical material more closely than do some, with the skill of composing fresh and original poetry for the biblical text more highly appreciated at the time than we may suppose (Rooke 2012). The oratorio is not simply a musical edition of a biblical story but a rearrangement to suit composer and audience. Handel explores the deeper feelings and inner lives of the characters (though not to the extent that will happen in later music), notably the conflict within Jonathan over various loyalties and the ignorance of Saul over the cause of his troubles. Though the biblical narrative indeed suggests Jonathan's conflicts of loyalty to feuding people, these are more elaborated in the oratorio, where Jonathan's numerous recitatives allow him to explore them. In the biblical text, Saul has early been informed that and why he lost his kingship shortly after the event that occasioned it, but the oratorio dramatically delays his learning that information until the end of his life.

The oratorio features significant repetition, even delay of plot progression. Lines repeat, even words, allowing hearers to "hear" what is happening in scores challenging to follow, providing time to react word by word as a singer moved through a piece—the ear being slower than the eye. If the recitative, with simpler accompaniment, had as one of its functions to allow the audience to track the thread of the plot, arias, often accompanied by more instrumentation, allowed the character to reflect more generally on what was happening and the audience to appreciate that perspective, with a minor break from following the verbal action so intently. The various shifts in the music also allow variety, space to rest, and opportunity to absorb the implications of the music. The chorus, similar to its role in Greek drama, has the responsibility to sum up, to comment, and to explain what an audience might otherwise have missed.

Scholars offer two contexts for the particular power of the oratorio *Saul*. The first, personal to the composer, is that while working on the oratorio, Handel suffered a palsy of his arm and hand, making it impossible for him to play instruments and eventually to work on the piece. Contemporaries suggest he lapsed into a despondency and thus would have understood something of Saul's experience. At the national level, the oratorio's dealing with themes of kingship gained and lost, contested and aborted, were intense issues for the English public in Handel's day. Feelings were intense on various sides of the killing of Charles I, the choices of James II to return to the religion of his ancestors, and the replacement of James with a monarch whose claim to the throne was questionable. Composers and audiences were accustomed to the Adam/Christ and Saul/David/Christ typology, as well as to the notion of human/divine kingship, and they likely had local and current events of kingship and the legitimacy of regicide firmly in mind while Handel composed and audiences heard *Saul*.

Another composer presenting Saul in music was Modest Mussorgsky (1839–81), whose aim was to develop the national character of Russian music distinctively from Western music. There are two editions of this rather heavy song (A and B), composed for a baritone accompanied by piano, taking up the issue of Saul's awareness of his approaching death. The poem, "King Saul," that underlies the song is based on a text of Lord Byron (Brown 2002) and is translated as follows:

> Oh, leaders, if it has fallen to my lot
> To perish ignominiously in battle before God's people
> Do not falter. Go boldly into battle

....
You who carry my bow and shield:
If my army should succumb to dark terror,
If it falters before the enemy and flees,
Oh do not let me outlive that fateful moment.
Rather, let me die, struck down nobly by your hand!
Oh my son, my heir,
The call to arms has already resounded through the hills
....
Oh my son! Our dreaded hour is upon us.

The words suggest that the king is realistic about what may—does—happen, though also briefly hopeful that the encounter with the enemy may go well. That some flee and all die is known from the biblical text, but the speaker in the poem holds a hope for victory, senses it at hand. The hero's address envisions two persons: Saul instructs his armor-bearer to kill him if his death is imminent, and the king addresses his son and heir as well, who does not succeed his father, dying first. That the father addresses his son suggests a theme from the biblical narrative: Saul's refusal to acknowledge that David, not Jonathan, will rule after him. The Russian's reception of the biblical subtext combined with Byron's poem adds significantly to the emotion connected to losing a battle and a life, a quality more implicit in the biblical text.

32.4 VISUAL ART/PAINTINGS

Graphic artists have loved the Saul story, featuring it in many scenes: old king soothed by the music of the young shepherd boy; the prophet Samuel rebuking Saul; events of Saul's last days (meeting Samuel *redivivus* at Endor, dying on Mount Gilboa).

Saul's most dramatic moment—confronting and being confronted by his old prophet, Samuel, called up from the dead—is portrayed by two artists, Englishman William Blake (1757–1827) and Anglo-American artist Benjamin West (1738–1820).

Blake, poet as well as painter and engraver, was deeply affected by the Bible and reproduced many of its scenes. *The Ghost of Samuel Appearing to Saul* was produced in 1800 and is presently at the National Gallery of Art in Washington, D.C. Done with pen and ink and water color over graphite (12 5/8 x 13 9/16 inches), the work features Samuel looming between the woman of Endor, who has raised him, and King Saul, who has requested it. The medium (on the left) sits on her haunches with one arm wrapped around herself and the other thrust into the air. She seems androgynous, clothed in a rough garment, her hair wild, upper torso bare. King Saul also seems literally taken aback at the arrival of the prophet, resting on one knee and rearing back, hands splayed and mouth agape in apparent shock. Saul's companions, float above him. Samuel is lighter in color than the other two figures, who share tones of darker to lighter reddish gray, as well as emerging full-bodied, as contrasted to their crouched positions. Contrasted also in posture, the prophet is stiff and awkward, arms pressed to his body. Samuel does not look so much angry as surprised by what the woman has done.

West, born in Pennsylvania, was adopted by a patron, introduced to the company of other artists of his era, and eventually made court painter by King George III. West's *Saul and the Witch of Endor*, painted in oil on canvas in the late eighteenth century (approximately 16 x 23 inches), is at the Art Institute of Chicago. Busier than Blake's work, the painting features five figures, three (perhaps more) males who appear startled and one, likely the medium, lying at the feet of the emerging prophet. The white garments and billowing steam or smoke attending the emerging prophet take up nearly half of the work. Though the three standing figures, elaborately dressed in richly hued clothing (gold, russet, blue, brown), show fear by their faces and hands, the face of the prophet is obscured by the hood of his shroud. His hands also are expressive, pointing to something we cannot quite see. Though the biblical text suggests that Saul went to Endor disguised, the elaborate headgear of the figure with the spear (or stick) likely designates the king, as the other males are hatless or wearing armor. The supine figure, if the medium, is hatless. West's painting is dramatic in a way Blake's is not, possibly due to the expressions on the faces (Rowland 2010).

The Dutch artist Rembrandt Harmenszoon van Rijn (1606–69) produced several studies of Saul and David. Rembrandt knew well and was deeply affected by biblical narratives, producing much art from both testaments, all filled with feeling and drama. His work, *David Offering the Head of Goliath to King Saul* (1627), is a busy scene. It is oil on panel (about 10 x 15 inches) now held at the Kunstmuseum in Basel. The work is dominated by a portly Saul, standing, with Samuel bent at his side, peering at what is being offered. To the right of them, the boy David, on one knee, presents the head of Goliath, wrapped in a cloth but with the grinning faced exposed. David's shepherd's bag is visible to us and a sword lies abandoned in the foreground. Saul is elderly and wearing a blue mantle, his expression difficult to read—interest, at least; Samuel appears intent. Two children, carrying Saul's train, whisper together, oblivious to the portentous event, while a spotted dog is braced before the figures, barking. Numerous men and some horses fill the scene from the back, not all attentive to what is happening in front of them, a domed building looming behind them. Saul lays a hand on Samuel, perhaps to restrain or support him. The colors of the clothing are mostly light, with Saul's gold brocade dominating.

Rembrandt's two studies of King Saul with shepherd-musician David playing the harp give us the opportunity to see two works of the same subject with three decades intervening: (1) *David Playing the Harp before Saul*, done ca. 1629 and 1631, oil on oak panel (roughly 24 x 19 inches), at the Städel Museum in Frankfurt; (2) *Saul and David*, dated to 1665, oil on canvas (51.2 x 64.8 inches), at the Royal Picture Gallery Mauritshuis, the Hague. The earlier work seats a large Saul in the center of the work, with a smaller David in the lower left, playing a harp the size of his upper body (instrument and upper body are all that is visible). Saul grasps a long spear in his right hand, his left circled around the arm of his chair. The king is garbed in a gold cape that covers him and is splayed behind and a prominent medallion and chain, with headgear typical of a nobleman. His face is difficult to read: perhaps he is avoiding the music and sight of the harpist. His eyes are not so clearly fixed on the musician—indeed, they are not looking at the same thing. The boy, his hair bound by a thin fillet and his clothing dark, plays with two hands, his head bent over the instrument.

The later work has moved Saul, still dominating, slightly to the left of center and placed David in the lower right hand corner. Saul's clothing is more elaborate, scarlet and gold against a dark background. He holds a fabric to his face, as if blocking the musician from his sight, possibly weeping. Saul's right hand, supporting if not quite holding his spear, is elongated. The expression is less intense, and with only one eye visible, clearly not fixed on David. David, smiling faintly and garbed in similar colors as Saul, watches his hands, plying the strings of his harp. Though together, they seem not to relate, except insofar as we know the story (Schwartz 1991).

32.5 LITERATURE/DRAMA

Two famous modern English writers have produced plays derived from the story of Saul. David Herbert Richards Lawrence (1885–1930) was prolific in the fields of English literature: novels, short stories, letters, poetry, plays, non-fiction, travel books, and translations. Though considered progressive about issues of sexuality (his writings were banned by various authorities), he was politically far to the right. His drama, *David: A Play in Sixteen Scenes*, was published in 1926.

It opens with Saul disobeying God and Samuel regarding the Amalekites, with Saul's daughters taunting King Agag by offering him forbidden booty. Saul hopes to hide his disobedience from the prophet, while Jonathan, knowing his father has displeased prophet and deity, dreads Samuel's approach. The biblical text substantially provides the discourse, culminating in Saul's acknowledging his disobedience but begging a blessing nonetheless. Samuel subsequently anoints David, who takes up residence with Saul. All three of Saul's children are drawn to David. Saul, overhearing them, accuses Michal of witchcraft, a charge she denies. We hear in Saul's talk his conflict with God, whom he both loves and dreads, and we hear David and Jonathan discuss why God has abandoned Saul.

The Goliath scene features David's victory sung and feted—the women's song to welcome the warriors being more explicitly pro-David than is its biblical counterpart. Jonathan, fearful of losing David's love now that he is a hero, exchanges not only weapons but clothing with David, a pledge of their mutual commitment, speaking carefully of their love. Since the king promised a daughter to the giant-slayer, his daughters discuss which of them it shall be, each seeming at the surface unwilling to wed David. Meanwhile, Saul finds fault with David and, contrary to the biblical text, learning that David has been anointed, wants him dead. As David, still Saul's musical healer, sings a psalm and accompanies it on his harp, Saul rants crazily against it, resistant also to reason offered by his loyal men. Saul subsequently careens between jealousy and compunction in regard to David. But when Merab is wed to another, David voices his passion for Michal, his language filled with metaphor and innuendo of desire and fulfillment (arrows shot and water pitchers to be filled). This language also frames the inconsistent demeanor of Saul toward David. Jonathan warns David of danger while Michal helps him escape through a window. Saul is enraged at his daughter's deceit, though Michal is more subservient to her father than in the biblical text.

Saul's last appearance in the drama comprises his interaction with a band of prophets, associated with Samuel, to whom David has fled. Samuel speaks regretfully of Saul's fate, recalling days when he was eager for the things of God. Saul meets his death, or feels its approach, speaking still of David. The king is more pitiful than in the biblical text, his madness more exaggerated, his struggle with God more developed. The choice to end his life early (in terms of the biblical text) seems odd, even abrupt, as though perhaps Lawrence had lost interest or simply stopped.

James Matthew Barrie (1860–1937) was a Scot who spent much of his productive life in England. He is best known for his *Peter Pan* and other material focused on children and fantasy. *The Boy David: A Play in Three Acts* was produced in London in December 1936, at the end of Barrie's life. The first act, featuring David and his mother and brothers, accomplishes Samuel's anointing of David, with brief allusions to Saul. David is shown to be an unlikely choice in the eyes of his family. The second act, taking place near the site where the Philistines have challenged Saul and Israel, provides the primary exposure to Saul's complexity. Jonathan, a boy of about twelve, is approached by a servant of Saul, looking for his master. The two agree that Saul has become irresolute, with both troubled by this change in his demeanor. Saul, appearing next, feels he has been abandoned by the prophet who selected him, and—reviewing briefly the circumstances of his choice—admits he has loved being king and grows angry at the suggestion that his selection was nothing but a punishment for the peoples' demanding a king. Saul owns his disobedience in the slaughter of the Amalekites, but hears from Samuel's messenger ominous words: "...woe to Saul, for a boy will rule in thy place" (1938: 80). Saul assumes Jonathan is meant and questions him about his eagerness to succeed. Saul is suddenly struck unable to know those with whom he has been talking, though he recovers shortly.

Next (still in the second act) comes a unique scene, where the shepherd boy David meets Saul while searching for him. Saul, revealing only his patronym, converses with David about shepherding. David feels the two have much in common. Saul speaks to his new friend enigmatically about his strange "two-ness," feeling like both a man and a roaring lion. Saul's best qualities emerge as he converses with the boy who does not recognize him and who speaks disingenuously and admiringly to Saul about the life of a shepherd. But the Goliath scene intervenes, where David volunteers as challenger, revealing in his talk with Jonathan that he somehow has acquired a token of King Saul. David slays the giant to the happiness of all Saul's men and inherits the giant's tent. In a third scene of this second act, David and Jonathan play there with Goliath's former possessions, like the small boys they are. Saul is angry at Jonathan for spending time with the boy we know is David, bringing forward material from later in the biblical story. When David sees them talking, he recognizes the son of Kish whose full identity Jonathan reveals. David speaks to the king of premonitions he experienced when killing the giant, and their discussion shifts to a woman at Endor who has survived Saul's driving other mediums out of his land. They touch on the topic of prostrating to royals, with Saul asking David how he knows such a thing. David admits he learned the custom when Samuel bowed to him. David plays music for a perturbed and erratic Saul.

In the third act, the action moves back to the home of Jesse, where David, boy-like, converses with his mother before falling asleep. Some of the later biblical events are suggested as night visions (Saul's men tracking an adult David who has fled the court, Saul planning to use a daughter to ensnare David, the king angered as David escapes) from which David awakes in the morning, still a boy, though anointed by the prophet and having slain the giant. The last of the visions involves the woman of Endor and the dead Samuel, speaking of the death of Saul and Jonathan and David's singing of it. The final scene features David and Jonathan, still young, enjoying each other's company. Like Lawrence, Barrie appears to have found the whole biblical story to be too long for a drama, hence the selection and development of key scenes and the rather superficial rush through the rest of them.

32.6 FILM

Three recent movies based on the stories of Israel's first kings show us reception into film. Though typically named for David, they spend considerable time on the overlap between Saul and David.

King David, directed by Bruce Beresford and starring Edward Woodward (as Saul), appeared in 1985. Beginning with the prophet Samuel's rejecting the kingship of Saul for his disobedience regarding Amalekites, it shows Saul's deterioration as he shouts, murmurs about a vision he had (actually comprising Jacob's wrestling with the angel of Gen. 32), weeps when challenged, and shows suspicion of his children and household and eventually of the priests, whom he has killed. The inconsistency of Saul while pursuing David is suggested, though in this interpretation Saul knows from the start that Samuel has anointed David. Omitting the scene at Endor, Saul's alienation from Yhwh is shown before the final battle of Gilboa, as he refuses to offer sacrifices. Only when Jonathan and Saul's assistant, Abner, remain determined to fight alongside him do the other Israelites overcome their misgivings over Saul's breach of piety. In this final battle, Saul is shown brave and skilled, killing many before he takes his own life when he sees his son Jonathan dead. The biblical ambivalence over the manner of Saul's death is suggested by toggling between the battle scene and a runner from Gilboa bringing David the crown and armlet of Saul, only to be killed for his efforts. Needing to be considerably shortened and simplified for the visual medium, the film sometimes has a narrator voice explain what is happening, as it often steps apart from the biblical script for one reason or another.

The Story of David, directed by David Lowell Rich and Alex Segal, starring Anthony Quayle (Saul), was released in 1976. It also spends half its time on the relationship between the two men. Saul is shown as more ill than crazy, afflicted by blinding headaches and eventually by visions and other signs of instability. Attended by the young David as both armor-bearer and musician, the old king's genuine care for the younger man is clear. The rejection of Saul by Samuel is prominent, though the anointing of David is not pictured, only spoken of by the prophet. What unifies Saul's antipathy toward David is the song sung to celebrate David's victory over Goliath. We watch the people acclaim David in song, and we hear Saul review the song, repeating it in his own imagination, singing it under his breath. Gripped by whatever drives him, Saul's persecution of David is rooted in the song. The love between the two men is also strong, as is the impact both Saul and Jonathan have upon David's loyalty. Prone to rearrange the biblical story's details to make for easier following, the movie shows Saul's last meeting with David fraught for both. David's unwillingness to take Saul's life is stressed. The information communicated in the biblical narrative by the Endor scene is alluded to by Saul as a vision in his head. By the time we see the king on Mount Gilboa, he is already dead, the protrusion of his sword suggesting that he fell on it.

Unlike these previous two, *David: The Bible Collection*, spends all its time on Saul and David, reviewing their relationship variously. Part of a set exploring Bible characters, this film (released in 1997), was produced by Robert Markowitz and stars Jonathan Pryce (Saul) and Nathaniel Parker (David). Beginning with Saul's disobedience to prophet and deity with the Amalekites—minimized by the king attempting to explain his decisions to Samuel—Samuel suggests that what will drive Saul to madness is ignorance over the identity of God's next choice for king. Saul goads David to reveal a supposed scene of his anointment, which David never admits. Saul later claims that the young David is the ghost of Saul's boyhood, returning to drive him mad, or that his condition resulted from a fall from his horse. Whatever the root, Saul goes ever stranger, laughing inappropriately, ruling irresponsibly, drinking intemperately—offering too many causes for the royal decline.

This film, unlike the other two, provides a role for Saul's wife, a feature left provocatively undeveloped in the biblical story. Ahinoam is shown angry at her husband for favoring David. Michal, likewise, comes to see David as having driven a wedge between herself and her father, though the persona of David in this film remains utterly loyal to Saul. Though David must flee Saul's presence, he frequently declares his loyalty, never raising a hand against his lord. Jonathan, though deeply concerned for his father and often frustrated at his tactics, also stands by him, at great cost. The film spends considerable time on the scandal of David's sojourn with Philistines, exploring the various possibilities of that biblical datum. David is shown shrewder than his hosts, secretly pleased when they refuse his help to fight Saul at Gilboa—a situation King Saul comes to learn. David is also regretful at being unable to help Saul, and the movie shows David near Gilboa (rather than far removed at Ziklag), even visiting the battle site and calling out for Saul and Jonathan, though they are beyond hearing him. The film thus destroys the distance between the two that marks David as innocent of killing Saul.

In general, perhaps due to genre constraints (though more likely to other factors), the films miss virtually all the subtlety and beauty of the biblical text. Reverting prominently to battle, neighing horses, odd costumes, morbid music, and demented leadership, they miss the subtlety of the story they aim to tell.[1]

Note

1. The author would like to express gratitude to colleagues in art history and music: Kathryn Barush, Leslie D. Ross, Marie Sagues, and Andrea Sheaffer.

Bibliography

Avioz, Michael. 2015. *Josephus' Interpretation of the Books of Samuel*. London: Bloomsbury.
Barrie, James Matthew. 1938. *The Boy David: A Play in Three Acts*. London: Peter Davies.
Brown, David. 2002. *Mussorgsky: His Life and Works*. Oxford and New York: Oxford University Press.
Burrows, Donald. 2012. *Handel*. 2nd ed. Oxford: Oxford University Press.

Burrows, Donald and Rosemary Dunhill. 2002. *Music and Theatre in Handel's World: The Family Papers of James Harris, 1732–1780.* Oxford and New York: Oxford University Press.

Effra, Helmut von and Allen Staley. 1986. *The Paintings of Benjamin West.* New Haven, CT: Yale University Press.

Lawrence, D. H. 2015. *David: A Play in Sixteen Scenes.* Edited by B. K. DeFabris. San Bernardino, CA: Timeless Classics.

Josephus, Flavius. 1991. *The Works of Josephus: Complete and Unabridged.* Translated by William Whiston. Peabody, MA: Hendrickson.

Rooke, Deborah W. 2012. *Handel's Israelite Oratorio Libretti: Sacred Drama and Biblical Exegesis.* Oxford: Oxford University Press.

Rowland, Christopher. 2010. *Blake and the Bible.* New Haven, CT: Yale University Press.

Schwartz, Gary. 1991. *Rembrandt: His Life, His Paintings.* London: Penguin Books.

Zsengellér, József, ed. 2014. *Rewritten Bible after Fifty Years: Texts, Terms, or Techniques? A Last Dialogue with Geza Vermes.* JSJSup 166. Leiden: Brill.

CHAPTER 33

DAVID IN RECEPTION HISTORY

DOMINIK MARKL

DAVID is one of the most complex characters in biblical narrative and the emblematic king of Israel. How do David's special talents, and personal shortcomings relate to his success and failure in politics? Can we trace a "psychology of leadership" in these narratives? This essay will examine links between the character of David and his political leadership in the Bible, and then trace the subsequent political reception of the figure of David. Three sections will be devoted to biblical and three to post-biblical images of David the politician, before I ask, in the conclusion, how David might inspire a contemporary reflection on the relationship between personality and public responsibility.

33.1 PARADIGMATIC KING OF ISRAEL: 1 SAMUEL 16–1 KINGS 2

"The David narratives in the books of Samuel constitute the most powerful and artistic of all the narratives of ancient Israel," wrote Walter Brueggemann (2002: x). Robert Alter even suggested that "the story of David is probably the greatest single narrative representation in antiquity of a human life evolving by slow stages through time, shaped and altered by the pressures of political life, public institutions, family, the impulses of body and spirit, the eventual sad decay of the flesh" (Alter 1999: ix). The outstanding quality of the literary presentation of David's character is generally acknowledged, as is his role as the paradigmatic king of Israel. Although Saul is Israel's first chosen king (1 Sam. 10:24; 12:13), he is eventually rejected by God (13:13–14; 15:23, 26) and subsequently contrasts negatively with the shining figure of David: "YHWH has torn the kingdom of Israel from you this very day, and has given it to a neighbour of yours, who is better than you" (1 Sam. 15:28). It is David who receives the promise of dynastic succession to the throne "forever" in Nathan's Oracle (2 Sam. 7:16).

Although the David story clearly integrates a great diversity of traditions that present heterogeneous images of his personality, these traditions were redactionally composed and integrated into a grand episodic sequence that is—despite some obvious disruptions—held together by numerous narrative threads (Sonnet 2006: 276–82). Such threads are partly created, as will be shown in what follows, by traits in David's character that develop through the long span of his life. The present analysis is thus exclusively interested in the literary representation of David's character (so also Steussy 1999) and not concerned with questions of its relationship to historical reality (see, e.g., McKenzie 2000; Halpern 2001) nor with the narratives' literary growth (see, e.g., Adam 2007; Van Seters 2009).

David's life is presented in two major movements: his ascent to kingship in Jerusalem (1 Samuel 16–2 Samuel 6), and his reign until his resignation and death (2 Samuel 7–1 Kings 2), introduced by Nathan's Oracle. While the first part of his life is marked by remarkable success, the second is increasingly troublesome, ending in frailty and senility. David goes through significant stages in his biography, but some aspects of his character seem to persist across them and develop consistently over his lifetime. I shall here concentrate on five aspects of David's characterization and on how they relate to his performance of his political responsibilities.

33.1.1 Small but Great

Jesse introduces his son David into the narrative as "the little one" (*haqqāṭān*, 1 Sam. 16:11), since he is the youngest among his brothers. Within the narrative of David's anointing, this expression highlights the unexpectedness of the divine choice, but in the larger context of the David story it ironically introduces the personality who is supposed to receive "a great name, like the great ones of the earth" (2 Sam. 7:9). If one ventures to interpret "the little one" psychologically—in terms of David's role in his family—one may perhaps relate it to a certain tension in David's character between humility and bold self-assertion. This tension is highlighted in his eldest brother's accusation of "presumptuousness" in the Goliath story (*zādôn*, 1 Sam. 17:28), where David is indeed portrayed as full of self-confidence. By contrast, he claims to feel unworthy to receive Saul's daughter Merab as his wife, which was the reward promised to the one who would slay Goliath (1 Sam. 17:25–27): "Who am I and who are my kinsfolk, my father's family in Israel, that I should be son-in-law to the king?" (18:18). This question is closely echoed in David's prayer at a decisive turning point in his life: "Who am I, O Lord YHWH, and what is my house, that you have brought me to this point?" (2 Sam. 7:18; translations throughout are based on the NRSV with some modifications). Before advancing to the throne, the "simple" David displays great respect for the role that he is destined to assume—not least by twice sparing Saul (1 Samuel 24 and 26). But even after a long period on the throne, David is willing to accept humiliating treatment from Shimei (2 Sam. 16:5–13). The tensions within the small, but self-assertive, and the great, but humble, David are one aspect of his attractiveness as a literary figure, but perhaps also part of his charisma as a political leader.

33.1.2 Shepherd and Warrior

The second statement that Jesse makes about David is directly related to his political destiny: "he is keeping the sheep" (1 Sam. 16:11). Just as with Moses, called when keeping Jethro's flock (Exod. 3:1), David's early responsibility as a shepherd is a metaphor for his future role (McKenzie 2000: 47–51), made explicit in Nathan's oracle: "I took you from the pasture, from following the sheep to be prince over my people Israel" (2 Sam. 7:8). David's experience as a shepherd is immediately related to two character traits that are essential to his leadership of Israel: his attitude of care and his courage in defending the flock from enemies.

The latter aspect is identified by David himself: "Yhwh, who saved me from the paw of the lion and from the paw of the bear, will save me (*yaṣṣîlēnî*) from the hand of this Philistine" (1 Sam. 17:37). David's courage, strength, and trust in God were learnt by defending the flock from wild animals, and these same qualities enabled him to defeat Goliath. This in itself is a programmatic, proleptic allusion to David's successful warfare throughout his lifetime, summarized in the Song of David (cf. *yaṣṣîlēnî* in 2 Sam. 22:18 and the verbal root *nṣl* in vv. 1, 49). Gifted with bravery, the young David, speaking to the king, is already concerned with the courage of others: "Let no one's heart fail because of him; your servant will go and fight with this Philistine" (1 Sam. 17:32). This concern is conversely perverted when David—now speaking as the king—encourages Joab through a messenger: "Do not let this matter be evil in your eyes, for the sword devours now one and now another" (2 Sam. 11:25).

David's attitude of shepherd-like care is expressed in one of the "appendix" episodes collected at the end of 2 Samuel. When David sees the angel of God punishing the people because of his census, he prays: "I alone have sinned, and I alone have done wickedly; but these sheep, what have they done?" (2 Sam. 24:17). By contrast, Nathan depicts David as a rich owner of flocks and herds who kills the one and only ewe lamb of a poor man to make him aware of his sin against Uriah and Bathsheba (2 Sam. 12:1–6). The narrative highlights that David's sin, committed secretly in private, is specifically outrageous as an act of neglect of his political responsibility. The voice of God announces that the sword and public shame will fall upon David (2 Sam. 12:12); this is later realized in Absalom's usurpation of the throne (2 Samuel 15).

33.1.3 Musician and Poet

A third distinctive trait of David is his musicality. His talent at playing (*n-g-n*) the lyre brings him to Saul's court, and it has a therapeutic effect on Saul, relieving him from his "evil spirit" (1 Sam. 16:16–23). For this purpose, David plays daily at Saul's court (18:10). He sings a song of lamentation after Saul's and Jonathan's deaths (2 Sam. 1:17) and composes a song "for Yhwh" towards the end of his own life (2 Sam. 22:1). At a central turning point of his life, David's musical expressivity is seen in his dance before the "ark of God" (2 Sam. 6:5): he dances "with all his might" (v. 14). David's musical talent had initated his career at the court, but in this instance it casts doubt on his honor in the eyes of Saul's daughter Michal (v. 16). She suggests that the "king of Israel" has "uncovered" himself "before the eyes of his servants' maids" like a "vain fellow" (v. 20). But David defends his expressive liberty on religious grounds: he danced "before Yhwh," he emphasizes twice (v. 21). He claims "I would make myself yet more contemptible than this, and I would be abased in my own eyes," but his liberty could not do any harm to the acknowledgment of his authority: "by the maids of whom you have spoken, by them I shall be held in honor" (v.22). David's confidence in the affection of women relates to another personality trait, as shall be seen in the following.

33.1.4 Lover and Leader

David's life is characterized by intense human relationships, in which he provokes strong emotional reactions. David's attractiveness is programmatically expressed in his name, which is most easily understood as "the beloved" (Hoffmann 1973: esp. 207–12). Saul first "loves" David "greatly" (1 Sam. 16:21), but then becomes "very angry" because of David's success (18:8; cf. Eliab's wrath in 17:28), and later even fears him, becoming his enemy "for all days" (18:29). While Goliath despises and curses David at first sight (17:42–43), Jonathan famously loves David "as his own soul" (18:1; cf. 20:17). Jonathan and Saul become enraged against each other because of their opposing feelings for David (20:30, 34). "All Israel and Judah" loves David for his leadership in war (18:16). Saul's daughter Michal is the first women to love David (18:20). Emotional relationships thus both support and endanger David's early career at Saul's court.

While David is initially shown as causing powerful emotions, he is then increasingly seen being emotional himself, weeping with Jonathan (1 Sam. 20:41), after the supposed deaths of his wives (30:4), and before the impending death of Bathsheba's child (2 Sam. 12:21–22). David's continuing attachment to Jonathan is seen in his lament (2 Sam. 1:23) and in his protection of Jonathan's son Mephibosheth (2 Samuel 9; cf. 21:7). Emotions overcome David in his relationship with his own children. He is enraged by Amnon's crime against Tamar (2 Sam. 13:21), but he weeps about Amnon's death at Absalom's hand (13:36) and mourns for many days (v. 37). Only after several years is David able to give Absalom a kiss of reconciliation (14:33), just before being betrayed by him. Fleeing from Absalom, David ascends the Mount of Olives, weeping (15:30). The most impressive mourning scene, however, occurs after Absalom's deadly defeat. "The king was deeply moved, and went up to the chamber over the gate, and wept; and as he went, he said, 'O my son Absalom, my son, my son Absalom! Would I had died instead of you, O Absalom, my son, my son!'" (19:1). David's mourning is a damaging political embarrassment (vv. 3–5), and he has to give in to Joab's forceful accusation (vv. 6–9).

33.1.5 Pious King

Another prominent character trait of David coincides with a central interest of deuteronomistic historiography—the king's relationship with Yhwh. Divine choice and David's anointment through Samuel aims at establishing a dynasty, as Nathan's Oracle promises (2 Sam. 7:5–16), which is summarized in the final words of David's Song: "Who magnifies the salvation for his king, and shows steadfast love to his anointed, to David and his descendants forever" (2 Sam. 22:51). In a proleptic allusion, Samuel announces that "Yhwh has sought out a man after his own heart" (1 Sam. 13:14). The "spirit of Yhwh" comes upon David through the anointing (1 Sam. 16:13), which David acknowledges in his "last words": "The spirit of Yhwh has spoken through me, his word is upon my tongue" (2 Sam. 23:2).

The young David displays trust in God in battle (1 Sam. 17:37, 45–47). As a king, his prayer in response to Nathan's Oracle expands this trust to the future of his dynasty (2 Sam. 7:18–29). David prays at several other occasions (2 Sam. 12:16; 15:31; 24:10, 17). The Song of David (2 Samuel 22//Psalm 18), a grand theological poem that implies an idealized self-presentation of David, is only loosely integrated into the narrative plot through the superscript, but is connected to the surrounding narratives by several motifs (Watts 1992:

99–109). David shows great respect for Saul's life because he is the "anointed of Yhwh" (1 Sam. 24:7, 11; 26:9, 11, 16, 23; 2 Sam 1:14, 16), an attitude that might explain why David—despite his involvement in countless battles—is conceded a natural death (1 Kgs. 2:10). A probably late redaction ensures that David instructs Solomon to keep the "Torah of Moses" before his death (1 Kgs. 2:3).

33.1.6 A Colorful Character

Many other aspects should be taken into consideration in an attempt to do justice to David's characterization in these narratives: after fleeing from Saul he is depicted as a merciless bandit and liar (1 Samuel 27) and even as Israel's king he does not refrain from brutality in warfare (2 Sam. 8:2). On the other hand, David has a fine ethical conscience in his sparing of Saul (1 Sam. 24:6), which makes even Saul acknowledge his future kingship (v. 21). As a king, David "administered justice and equity to all his people" (2 Sam. 8:15) and he is "like the angel of God" in "hearing good and evil" (14:17). One might call David charismatic, probably helped by the attractiveness of his natural beauty (1 Sam. 16:12, 18); but this is especially seen in his ability to provide leadership even in desperate situations (1 Sam. 22:2) and to gain the favour and approval of the people: "All the people took notice of it [David's fasting after Abner's death], and it pleased them; just as everything the king did pleased all the people" (2 Sam. 3:36). At the same time, one could call David an eccentric—in his ecstatic dance before the ark as also in his acceptance of Shimei's curses (2 Sam. 16:5–13).

Is there any credibility to such a diverse, heterogeneous, and contradictory character? David's colourful image certainly arises in part from the diversity of traditions related to him—the "beloved of the songs of Israel" (2 Sam. 23:1), but it is also a central reason for his continuing attractiveness. As clearly as David does reflect several common aspects of ancient Near Eastern portrayals of kings, he also remains a leader sui generis (Dietrich 2003). David is "a complex person whose motives are often suspect" (Steussy 1999: 82). He is portrayed as an exceptional, charismatic, artistic leader, and a masculine symbol. David, the small and bold boy, the great and humble king, the protective and caring pastor of his flock, deeply failing and profoundly repenting, the sensitive musician and ruthless warrior, the beloved and enraging, the weeping and mourning, the eccentrically dancing and devoutly praying, elected bearer of dynastic promise: it is the richness of his characterization that made David an emblematic leader and ceaselessly attractive for futher reflection on leadership: his own and others'. In Zenger's words, "King David has inspired the biblical tradition as no other figure has" (1998: 263).

33.2 Sweet Singer of Israel or Founder of the Cult? Chronicles and the Psalter

While several traditions of the David narratives in 1 Samuel 16–1 Kings 2 may well go back to preexilic times and thus presuppose the reality of the monarchy, the first major re-writing of the David story, found in the Book of Chronicles (1 Chronicles 11–29), is firmly situated in the time of the Second Temple period (on reasons for a date not before the fourth century BCE see Klein 2006: 13–16). The historical setting of the Chronicler, after the decay of the monarchy with the now absolutely central role of the Temple, partly explains the great shift of emphasis in the idealized portrayal of David found here, since he is predominantly depicted as the founder of the main cultic institutions in Jerusalem (cf. Pomykala 1995: 107–109; Abadie 1999; Steussy 1999: 99–128; Dietrich 2006: 73–84): the temple (1 Chronicles 17; 21–22; 28:1–29:9) and the Levitical and priestly functions (1 Chronicles 15–16; 23–26). The Chronicler has no interest whatsoever in David's emotional relationships. He manages to tell the David story without using the verb "to love," thereby disentangling David from any ambiguous relationships with Jonathan or Bathsheba (cf. 1 Chr. 20:1–3), or other compromising matters such as Absalom's revolt. Instead, he uses the scene of the transfer of the ark to Jerusalem to report David's commissioning of the Asaphites to praise YHWH (16:7). Nathan's oracle and David's prayer are rendered (nearly) at full length (1 Chronicles 17; cf. 2 Samuel 7). David's personal piety is even more emphasized by another prominent prayer of praise before his death (1 Chr. 29:10–19). His last words encourage the assembly of Israel, "Bless YHWH your God!" (29:20).

David's relationship to the psalms may have ancient roots, but the redactional processes of the "Davidization" of the Psalter clearly continued in the Second Temple period (Hossfeld and Zenger 2010). While David appears as commissioning psalmody in Chronicles, he is himself prominently portrayed as a composer of poetic prayers in the Psalter itself by means of its superscriptions. Several collections of psalms are attributed to him (Psalms 3–41; 51–72; 101–103; 108–10; 138–45), which were likely composed and redacted in subsequent stages (cf. Kleer 1996: 78–127). It is especially noteworthy that Psalm 18, a slightly edited version of the Song of David (2 Samuel 22), forms the center for the first collection. Thirteen "biographical" headings relate individual psalms to specific situations in David's life from the books of Samuel (Psalms 3; 7; 18; 34; 51; 52; 54; 56; 57; 59; 60; 63; 142), suggesting that the David psalms should be read like an amplification of his biography that reveals his prayer life. David thus becomes a paradigmatic "figure of integration" (Millard 1994: 230–34) and the praying king par excellence (for detailed discussions, see Auwers 1999; Steussy 1999: 131–88).

Ben Sira's praise of David, composed ca. 195–175 BCE (Sir. 47:1–11), already presupposes this image created in (and by) the Psalter: "In all that he did he gave thanks to God the Most High, with words of glory; with all his heart he loved his Maker and every day he praised him with song" (Sir. 47:8; see Marböck 1995; Kleer 1996: 131–77). The passage suggests that "it is David's twofold talent as hero and composer of song texts that predisposes him for being king" (Zenger 1998: 266).

33.3 THE DAVIDIC MESSIAH OF THE NEW TESTAMENT

Drawing on prophetic and early Jewish traditions (Pomykala 1995), the New Testament portrays Jesus as a descendant of David (Burger 1970). This is probably first attested in Paul's letter to the Romans (1:3: "descended from David according to the flesh") but is also established via use of the title "son of David," found in the address of blind Bartimaeus in Mark (10:47–48, but cf. 12:35–37; Rodríguez Láiz 2016) as well as the genealogies of Matthew (1:1–17; cf. Piotrowski 2016) and Luke (3:23–38; cf. Strauss 1995) and also in the Johannine tradition (John 7:42; Rev. 5:5; 22:16). The political implication of this view is seen in the idea that Jesus bring about "the kingdom of our father David" (Mark 11:10), which is strongly tied to the promise of an eternal dynasty in Nathan's Oracle (Pietsch 2003) and centrally attested in the royal title "Christ" ("the Anointed"; Waschke 2001: 1–104). The Psalms, globally attributed to David, are frequently adduced to corroborate this view (Attridge 2003), specifically the royal Psalms (esp. Psalms 2; 110) and Psalm 22 in the Passion narratives (Sänger and Bons 2007). The typological application of motifs of the Davidic kingdom to Jesus implies the spiritualization of political ideas: "my kingdom is not from this world" (John 18:36). The typological role of David in the New Testament strongly influenced the Christian reception history of the figure of David, even in concretely political contexts.

33.4 DAVIDIC EMPERORS AND HARP-PLAYING KINGS IN LATE ANTIQUITY AND THE MIDDLE AGES

Some of the most ancient visual representations of David that have come down to us show David defeating Goliath on early Christian sarcophagi. A much richer early Jewish and Christian iconography of David may have existed (Wessel 1966: 1145–47), but the fight against Goliath, typologically understood as Christ's triumph over Satan (Wyss 1968: 487; Goldschmidt 1902: 29–30), may also have expressed early Christian sentiments against a hostile Roman Empire. The wall paintings of the synagogue of Dura-Europos (245 CE), which depicted the anointment of David among other scenes from his life, may even have represented a David-Orpheus, taming wild beasts, above the Torah shrine (Zenger 1998: 268–74; on related iconography, see Finney 1978; Herrero de Jáuregui 2010: 115–16, 119–22). In political terms, this scene invokes a Messianic age of peace rather than actual worldly dominion, and may express the religious hope of a Jewish minority at the eastern frontiers of the Roman Empire, which remained unfulfilled in the secular sphere: Dura was destroyed by the Sassanids only a dozen years later (256 CE). Rabbinic portrayals of David as a pious student of the Torah served intra-Jewish political purposes (Cohen 1991). The Rabbinic tradition most likely influenced the image of David in Islam, where he is predominantly seen as an example of piety (Hasson 2001).

The emphasis in the reception of the figure of David clearly changed with the emergence of Christian emperors. Ambrose of Milan dedicated his *Apologia David* to Emperor Theodosius in 390, requiring from him to follow David's example and repent after the massacre of Thessaloniki (Herkommer 2003: 392). Ambrose's keen interest in David in several writings is also expressed in the David cycle carved on the wooden door of his church in Milan, dedicated in 386 (Goldschmidt 1902: 27–28). Marcian (reigned 450–57) was acclaimed Novus David at the Council of Chalcedon in 451 (Ewig 1956: 10–11). An early example of this typology in the visual arts is found in the apse mosaic of the church of St. Catherine at Mount Sinai. Below the figure of Christ in the Transfiguration appears a bust of David in a medallion surrounded by prophets, clearly in the guise of a Byzantine emperor—most likely Justinian (reigned 527–65), the monastery's founder (Leader 2000: 417–18; Müller 2004: 34–35). For the first time in the history of art, David wears a crown (Zahnd 2008: 79). Later Byzantine emperors, especially Herakleios (reigned 610–41) and Basileios I (reigned 867–86), invoked the succession from Saul to David to envision themselves as legitimized usurpers (Ludwig 2003). During the reign of Herakleios (more precisely, between 613 and 630 CE), a set of nine high-quality silver plates was produced (discovered in Cyprus in 1902), depicting scenes from David's early life (1 Samuel 16–18). These plates may have been commissioned by the emperor himself as a gift (Spain 1977: 237; for critical discussion and images see Leader 2000).

While allusions to David were quite sporadic and played a minor role for Byzantine emperors, the identification with David became central for the Carolingians (Zahnd 2008). Pippin the Younger (king of the Franks, 751–68) was portrayed as a new David (Ewig 1956: 44–47), but such identification reached a climax under Charlemagne (Holy Roman Emperor, 800–14; Anton 1968: 420–22; Herkommer 2003: 409–10). It was adopted by several other medieval kings such as Frederick II at his coronation in Jerusalem in 1229 (Herkommer 2003: 399). The representations of David and ruling kings in art are closely related from the ninth to the twelfth centuries (Steger 1961: 121–32). The importance of this symbolism can be seen, for example, in the imperial crown of the Holy Roman Empire (now in Vienna's Hofburg), probably first used at the coronation of Otto II in 967. It shows David in an enamel with a quotation from Ps. 99:4 (Vulgate 98:4): *honor regis iudicium diligit*, "the king's honor loves judgment" (Herkommer 2003: 401). David typology is powerfully represented in the pictorial programme of Reims Cathedral, the coronation church of the French monarchs (Herkommer 2003: 405–408). For the coronation of Charles V of France in 1364, Guillaume de Machaut composed the instrumental piece *Hoquetus David* (Herkommer 2003: 408).

David the psalm-singing musician is seen in close relationship with David the king in the medieval imagination—clearly influenced by the figure of David portrayed in the Psalter. Augustine (cf. Mayer 2003) already interpreted David's musicality as an expression of pious statesmanship: "Now David was a man skilled in songs, who dearly loved musical harmony . . . and by it served his God . . . by the mystical representation of a great thing. For the rational and well-ordered concord of diverse sounds in harmonious variety suggests the compact unity of the well-ordered city" (*De Civ. Dei*, 17:14; trans. Marcus Dods). The image of the harp playing David served as an example of the *princeps literatus* and the noble minnesinger (Steger 1961: 133–38). The king's harp even became a symbol of harmonious reign (Vinay 2005). Rabanus Maurus as well as Dante in his *Divina Commedia* saw David's dance as an expression of humility that exalts the king (Schade 1962–63: 3).

33.5 MICHELANGELO'S GIANT NUDE: DAVID AS A POLITICAL SYMBOL IN EARLY MODERNITY

David had sporadically played a quite prominent role in political theology from late antiquity to late medieval times, but his figure became intensely and colorfully entangled in the political struggles of early modern Europe. David's transformed and emblematic role is monumentally visible in Michelangelo's giant David sculpture (the statue is more than four metres tall minus its base) on the Piazza della Signoria in Florence. The sculpture was commissioned on August 16, 1501, and erected in the city's centre of public administration in May 1504. Its political symbolism "embraced the widest range of interpretive messages," as John Paoletti (2015: 174) observed:

> Biblical history and classical mythology, pagan allegory and biblical caveat, egregious fictions of civic foundation and references to recent history, the ironic depiction of the weak adolescent of the biblical narrative as a heroic marble giant, all turn on issues of the power of the Florentine Signoria to govern wisely and well. The colossal statue was a sign to the people that their city—despite ongoing wars with Pisa, threats from Medici and papal forces from without, and continued controversy about the form that the new republic was taking—was strong and capable of overcoming all adversity.

The new focus on the Bible promoted during the Reformation involved David prominently in theories of the state and of legitimate resistance (Metzger 2003; DeLapp 2014; on the wider context Hill 1993). In the Netherlands, William of Orange was celebrated as a new David, expressed both on the stage and in the song *Het Wilhelmus*, which became the Dutch national anthem (Bloemendal 2008: 296–97; DeLapp 2014: 73–96; on the seventeenth century, see Nitsche 1998: 270–91). In 1572, English Parliament and church representatives strongly advised Elizabeth I to have Mary Stuart executed, illustrating their argument with reference to David's struggles with Saul and Absalom, as the context required (Metzger 2003: 439–41). According to George deForest Lord, the David story may even have been "the central political myth of seventeenth-century England" (Lord 1972: 177), and its political reception culminated in a nearly absurd, satirically overstretched typology applied to King Charles II in John Dryden's *Absalom and Achitophel* (1681; see, with a wealth of comparative material, Metzger 1998).

David is invoked in didactic literature for princes (Fürstenspiegel; Kipfer 2015: 323–30) and his life is used to draw lessons for political theory. Machiavelli adduces David as an example of a successful military leader in his *Principe* and is clearly uninterested in other aspects of the biblical character (Münkler 1995: 113–15). Virgilio Malvezzi (1595–1654) develops political and moral lessons from the biblical king's life in *Il Davide perseguitato*. On David's career from shepherd to king, for example, he comments: "Let Kings learne to take their Ministers sometimes even of the sheepfold. The best men are not alwaies in the greatest Palaces: a lowly Cottage often times incloses a high spirit, and a ragged Rock a very cleere Diamond" (from Robert Ashley's translation, London 1647, quoted after Prescott 2012: 20).

In drama, David is portrayed as an example of political leadership and of moral lessons (Bocian et al. 1989: 87; Nitsche 1998: 292–99; Meyer 2003; Bloemendal 2008). Even in the exegesis of the Psalms, the Renaissance developed a "more politicised tradition" in concretely imagining David in his biographical setting at Saul's court, making the most of the issue of slander addressed in the Psalms and not without speaking to the ambience of contemporary courts (Prescott 1991: esp. 164).

David's musicality did not disappear from reflections at this time. Theories about what influence music might have on melancholy and evil spirits, starting from David's curative performance before Saul, is a long chapter in the (pre-)history of psychiatry (Kümmel

1969). Some aristocrats and monarchs presented themselves not only as lovers of the arts, but even composed music themselves, referring to their biblical exemplar, King David (Kipfer 2015: 232f.). A year before his execution, a harp-strumming Charles I appeared on the frontispiece of the 1648 edition of Malvezzi's *David Persecuted* with the legend "Touch not my Anointed / And do my Prophets no harme. Psal: 105.15" (Prescott 2012: 21–22). Charles's execution could be seen as a signal of the approaching decline of David's immediate prominence in modern politics.

33.6 DAVID INDIVIDUALIZED AND PSYCHOLOGIZED

The medieval and early modern image of David, which had generally presupposed the Bible's authority and its exemplary, normative value—notwithstanding the ambiguities of David's character—came into question in the Enlightenment. "The pressures on King David" began "in the late seventeenth century, with the deeply controversial David entry in Pierre Bayle's *Dictionaire historique et critique*" (Sherwood 2015: 651). The anonymous work *The Life of David: or, the History of the Man after God's Heart* (1761) is ironic and, in fact, portrays a perfidious character (on backgrounds see Metzger 1998: 395). It was used by Voltaire for his *Saul et David* (1767), in which David is portrayed in the words of Abigail as a "barbare débauché" (Engler 2003: 765–66). Subversive readings of David, and the ever-shrinking importance of the monarchies, led to a decline in the traditional topoi of the political David typology. Allusions to David in Charles Dickens's *David Copperfield* (1850; Bar-Yosef 2006) or Thomas Hardy's *The Mayor of Casterbridge* (1886; Moynahan 1975) are predominantly interested in psychological aspects of individual David-like characters. Socially relevant reflections on Davidic themes, however, continued. An example is the increasing interest in the intense friendship between David and Jonathan in the discourse on homoeroticism by writers such as Oscar Wilde in the nineteenth century and continued in the gay movement of the twentieth century (Harding 2013).

David has only occasionally appeared in concrete political reflection in recent decades. Examples of his ambivalent potential have been adduced in the context of the state of Israel (on drama, see Abramson 2004). For the celebrations of the supposed 3,000th anniversary of Jerusalem in 1954, the Koussevitzky Foundation of the Library of Congress commissioned Darius Milhaud to compose his monumental opera *David* (Helen Leneman in Van Seters et al. 2011: 610), giving support to the Zionist cause. The Danish filmmaker Anne Wivel, on the other hand, produced the documentary *David or Goliath* (1988) in the context of the First Intifada, portraying the state of Israel as Goliath, opposed by a Palestinian David (Rhonda Burnette-Bletsch in Davis et al. 2013: 256). The National Museum of Colombia (Bogotà) displays a large-scale series of photographs entitled "David quiebramales" by Miguel Angel Rojas. The photos show a young male nude in a posture similar to Michelangelo's David. It may take a second glance to see that the man's left leg is missing. As a soldier, he had lost it to a mine. Michelangelo's symbol of strength is here transformed into a tragic image of Colombia's civil war and the yearning for it to end.

33.7 AN IMAGE OF POLITICAL LEADERSHIP

Both the biblical portrayal and the political reception of the figure of David raise fascinating questions. One might wonder why the Israelite historiographers presented Israel's paradigmatic king with such a complex biography in Samuel-Kings, not characterizing him simply as a foundational hero, but creating a complex mixture of human talent and failure. From the analysis presented above it may seem possible that this narrative presents—besides many other layers of meaning—a paradigmatic reflection on the relationship between human character and political leadership, integrating both idealistic and realistic aspects. While this human richness is unfolded with a religious emphasis in the image of David in the Psalter, the Chronicler does not seem to have felt quite comfortable with it, presenting instead a strongly idealized David. Based on precursors in the prophetic writings, the New Testament drew on David mainly as a typological predecessor of Jesus Christ, thus setting the tone for a long history of typological applications in the Christian reception of David.

The political reception of the figure of David goes hand in hand with the history of the role of biblical religions in society. Emperors and kings identified with the divinely authorized kingship of David with varying frequency and intensity from late antiquity to modern times. David's various conflicts lent themselves as examples, culminating in their application to concrete political scenarios and political theory, stimulated by the biblical orientation of the Reformation. The decline of Christian monarchs and the criticisms of Enlightenment led to the shrinking of David's importance as a political example, but his private life, with its moral intricacies, has continued to attract interest.

Political appropriations of the David story employed a great variety of hermeneutical strategies, whose exploration would be an intricate endeavor in its own right (cf. Markl 2020). They are alike, by definition, in being interested readings and applications of the biblical figure to their respective times and political situations. We should not end this journey with David through history, therefore, without asking how his image(s) could inspire us to think about the relationship between character and political responsibility today. Among the many possible directions of thought, I offer only one observation. Both the Bible and many threads in the history of reception perceive David the musician as being intimately related to David the politician. David's musical—that is, human and cultural—sensitivity is a key talent that enables him to perceive deeply and communicate effectively. Today, by contrast, politicians often appear on the world stage who go so far as to boast about their lack of cultural and human sensitivity. What politicians need is the "*cultura animi,* that is, a mind so trained and cultivated that it can be trusted to tend and take care" of the world (Arendt 1961: 218–19). At least with regard to his musicality, therefore, one may continue to feel a great sympathy with David the politician over many of his more belated successors.

BIBLIOGRAPHY

Abadie, Philippe. 1999. "La figure de David dans le livre de Chronique." In Desrousseaux and Vermeylen 1999: 157–86.

Abramson, Glenda. 2004. "Israeli Drama and the Bible: Kings on the Stage." *AJS Review* 28: 63–82.
Adam, Klaus-Peter. 2007. *Saul und David in der judäischen Geschichtsschreibung: Studien zu 1 Samuel 16–2 Samuel 5*. FAT 51. Tübingen: Mohr Siebeck.
Alter, Robert. 1999. *The David Story: A Translation with Commentary of 1 and 2 Samuel*. New York: W. W. Norton.
Anton, Hans Hubert. 1968. *Fürstenspiegel und Herrscherethos in der Karolingerzeit*. Bonn: Röhrscheid.
Arendt, Hannah. 1961. "The Crisis in Culture: Its Social and Political Significance." In *Between Past and Future: Six Exercises in Political Thought*. New York: The Viking Press, 197–226.
Attridge, Harold. W. 2003. "Giving Voice to Jesus: Use of the Psalms in the New Testament." In H. W. Attridge and M. E. Fassler, eds., *Psalms in Community: Jewish and Christian Textual, Liturgical, and Artistic Traditions*. SBL Symposium Series 25. Atlanta: SBL, 101–12.
Auwers, Jean-Marie. 1999. "Le David des psaumes et les psaumes de David." In Desrousseaux and Vermeylen 1999: 187–224.
Bar-Yosef, Eitan. 2006. "'It's the Old Story': David and Uriah in II Samuel and David Copperfield." *The Modern Language Review* 101: 957–65.
Bloemendal, Jan. 2008. "König von Gottes Gnaden? Der gute und der böse Monarch auf der frühmodernen Bühne in den Niederlanden bis ca. 1625 anhand der Davidspiele." In C. Meier, B. Ramakers, and H. Beyer, eds., *Akteure und Aktionen: Figuren und Handlungstypen im Drama der frühen Neuzeit*. Symbolische Kommunikation und gesellschaftliche Wertesysteme 23. Münster: Rhema, 289–319.
Bocian, Martin et al. 1989. "David." In *Lexikon der biblischen Personen: Mit ihrem Fortleben in Judentum, Christentum, Islam, Dichtung, Musik und Kunst*. Stuttgart: Alfred Kröner, 83–92.
Burger, Christoph. 1970. *Jesus als Davidssohn: Eine traditionsgeschichtliche Untersuchung*. FRLANT 98. Göttingen: Vandenhoeck und Ruprecht.
Brueggemann, Walter. 2002. *David's Truth in Israel's Imagination and Memory*. 2nd ed. Minneapolis: Fortress.
Cohen, Stuart A. 1991. "The Bible in Intra-Jewish Politics: Early Rabbinic Portraits of King David." *Jewish Political Studies Review* 3: 49–65.
Davis, Michael D. et al. 2013. "David and Goliath, Story of." In *EBR* 6: 243–56.
Déclais, Jean-Louis. 1999. *David raconté par les musulmans*. Paris: Cerf.
DeLapp, Nevada Levi. 2014. *The Reformed David(s) and the Question of Resistance to Tyranny: Reading the Bible in the 16th and 17th Centuries*. LHBOTS 601. London: Bloomsbury.
Desrousseaux, Louis and Jacques Vermeylen, eds. 1999. *Figures de David à travers la Bible: XVIIe congrès de l'ACFEB (Lille, 1er–5 septembre 1997)*. Lectio Divina 177. Paris: Cerf.
Dietrich, Walter, and Hubert Herkommer, eds. 2003. *König David—biblische Schlüsselfigur und europäische Leitgestalt*. Kolloquium der Schweizerischen Akademie der Geistes- und Sozialwissenschaften 19. Freiburg Schweiz: Universitätsverlag/Stuttgart: Kohlhammer.
Dietrich, Walter. 2003. "König David—biblisches Bild eines Herrschers im altorientalischen Kontext." In Dietrich and Herkommer 2003: 3–31.
Dietrich, Walter. 2006. *David, der Herrscher mit der Harfe*. Biblische Gestalten 14. Leipzig: Evangelische Verlagsanstalt.
Engler, Balz. 2003. "David im englischen Drama." In Dietrich and Herkommer 2003: 761–75.
Ewig, Eugen. 1956. "Zum christlichen Königsgedanken im frühen Mittelalter." In *Das Königtum: Seine geistigen und rechtlichen Grundlagen*. Lindau: Jan Thorbecke, 7–73.
Finney, P. C. 1978. "Orpheus—David: A Connection in Iconography between Greco-Roman Judaism and Early Christianity?" *Journal of Jewish Art* 5: 6–15.
Fröhlich, Ida, ed. 2019. *David in Cultural Memory*. Contributions to Biblical Exegesis and Theology 93. Leuven: Peeters.
Frontain, Raymond-Jean and Jan Wojcik, eds. 1980. *The David Myth in Western Literature*. West Lafayette: Purdue University Press.
Goldschmidt, Adolph. 1902. *Die Kirchentür des heiligen Ambrosius in Mailand: Ein Denkmal frühchristlicher Skulptur*. Strassburg: Heitz.

Gosselin, Edward A. 1976. *The King's Progress to Jerusalem: Some Interpretations of David during the Reformation Period and Their Patristic and Medieval Background*. Malibu, CA: Undena Publications.

Halpern, Baruch. 2001. *David's Secret Demons: Messiah, Murderer, Traitor, King*. Grand Rapids: Eerdmans.

Halpern, Baruch et al. 2007. "David." In *EncJud* 5: 444–58.

Harding, James E. 2013. *The Love of David and Jonathan*. Sheffield: Equinox.

Harding, James E. et al. 2013. "David and Jonathan, Story of." In *EBR* 6: 256–70.

Hasson, Isaac. 2001. "David". *Encyclopedia of the Qurān* 1.495–97.

Hennig, John. 1967. "Zur Stellung Davids in der Liturgie." *ALW* 10: 157–64.

Herkommer, Hubert. 2003. "Typus Christi—Typus Regis: König David als politische Legitimationsfigur." In Dietrich and Herkommer 2003: 383–436.

Herrero de Jáuregui, M. 2010. *Orphism and Christianity in Late Antiquity*. Sozomena 7. Göttingen: de Gruyter.

Hill, Christopher. 1993. *The English Bible and the Seventeenth-Century Revolution*. London: Allen Lane.

Hoffmann, Adalbert. 1973. *David: Namensdeutung zur Wesensdeutung*. BWANT 100. Stuttgart: Kohlhammer.

Hossfeld, Frank-Lothar and Erich Zenger. 2010. "Überlegungen zur Davidisierung des Psalters." In U. Dahmen and J. Schnocks, eds., *Juda und Jerusalem in der Seleukidenzeit. Herrschaft—Widerstand—Identität. Festschrift für Heinz-Josef Fabry*. BBB 159. Göttingen: Vandenhoeck & Ruprecht, 9–90.

Hourihane, Colum, ed. 2002. *King David in the Index of Christian Art*. Princeton: University Press.

Kipfer, Sara. 2015. *Der bedrohte David: Eine exegetische und rezeptionsgeschichtliche Studie zu 1 Sam 16–1 Kön 2*. SBR 3. Berlin: de Gruyter.

Kleer, Martin. 1996. *"Der liebliche Sänger der Psalmen Israels": Untersuchungen zu David als Dichter und Beter der Psalmen*. BBB 108. Bodenheim: Philo.

Klein, Ralph W. 2006. *1 Chronicles: A Commentary*. Hermeneia. Minneapolis: Augsburg Fortress.

Kümmel, Werner. 1969. "Melancholie und die Macht der Musik: Die Krankheit des König Sauls in der historischen Diskussion." *Medizinhistorisches Journal* 4: 189–209.

Leader, Ruth E. 2000. "The David Plates Revisited: Transforming the Secular in Early Byzantium." *The Art Bulletin* 82: 407–27.

Leneman, Helen. 2010. *Love, Lust, and Lunacy: The Stories of Saul and David in Music*. Bible in the Modern World 29. Sheffield: Sheffield Phoenix Press.

Lord, George deForest. 1972. "'Absalom and Achitofel' and Dryden's Political Cosmos." In E. Miner, ed., *John Dryden. Writers and their Background*. London: G. Bell and Sons, 156–90.

Ludwig, Claudia. 2003. "David—Christus—Basileus: Erwartungen an eine Herrschergestalt." In Dietrich and Herkommer 2003: 367–82.

Marböck, Johannes. 1995. "Davids Erbe in gewandelter Zeit (Sir 47,1–11)." In *Gottes Weisheit unter uns: Zur Theologie des Buches Sirach*. HBS 6. Freiburg i. Br.: Herder, 124–32.

Markl, Dominik. 2020. "Reception History of the Hebrew Bible/Old Testament." In *Oxford Research Encyclopedia of Religion*. Oxford University Press. doi: http://dx.doi.org/10.1093/acrefore/9780199340378.013.112.

Mayer, Cornelius. 2003. "David." *Augustinus-Lexikon* 2.235–44.

McKenzie, Steven L. 2000. *King David: A Biography*. Oxford: Oxford University Press.

McKinnon, James W. 1995. "David." In *Musik in Geschichte und Gegenwart* 2, 1094–1101.

Metzger, Hans-Dieter. 1998. "David, der Musterkönig. Zur politischen Intention eines religiösen Sinnbilds im England des 17. Jahrhunderts." In B. Mahlmann-Bauer and W. G. Müller, eds., *Staatstheoretische Diskurse im Spiegel der Nationalliteraturen von 1500 bis 1800*. Wolfenbütteler Forschungen 79. Wiesbaden: Harrassowitz, 393–426.

Metzger, Hans-Dieter. 2003. "David und Saul in Staats- und Wiederstandslehren der Frühen Neuzeit." In Dietrich and Herkommer 2003: 437–84.

Meyer, Heinz. 2003. "David poenitens als Exempelfigur des Jesuitentheaters." In N. Miedema and R. Suntrup, eds. *Literatur—Geschichte—Literaturgeschichte: Beiträge zur mediävistischen Literaturwissenschaft*. Frankfurt a. M.: Lang, 841–62.

Millard, Matthias. 1994. *Die Komposition des Psalters: Ein formgeschichtlicher Ansatz*. FAT 9. Tübingen: J. C. B. Mohr (Paul Siebeck).

Moynahan, Julian. 1975. "The Mayor of Casterbridge and the Old Testament's First Book of Samuel: A Study of Some Literary Relationships." In R. Bartel, J. S. Ackerman, and T. S. Warshaw, eds. *Biblical Images in Literature*. Nashville: Abingdon Press, 71–88.

Müller, Andreas. 2004. "Das Verklärungsmosaik im Katharinenkloster: Zur Bedeutungsvielfalt religiöser Bilder." In M. Tamcke, ed., *Blicke gen Osten. Studien zur orientalischen Kirchengeschichte* 30. Münster: Lit, 27–55.

Münkler, Herfried. 1995. "Moses, David und Ahab. Biblische Gestalten in der politischen Theorie der frühen Neuzeit." In J. Ebach and R. Faber, eds., *Bibel und Literatur*. Munich: Wilhem Fink, 113–36.

Nitsche, Stefan Ark. 1998. *David gegen Goliath: Die Geschichte der Geschichten einer Geschichte. Zur fächerübergreifenden Rezeption einer biblischen Story*. ATM 4. Münster: Lit.

Paoletti, John T. 2015. *Michelangelo's* David: *Florentine History and Civic Identity*. New York: Cambridge University Press.

Pietsch, Michael. 2003. *"Dieser ist der Sproß Davids . . . ": Studien zur Rezeptionsgeschichte der Nathanverheißung im alttestamentlichen, zwischentestamentlichen und neutestamentlichen Schrifttum*. WMANT 100. Neukirchen-Vluyn: Neukirchener.

Pioske, Daniel D. et al. 2013. "David." In *EBR* 6: 189–242.

Piotrowski, Nicholas G. 2016. *Matthew's New David at the End of Exile: A Socio-Rhetorical Study of Scriptural Quotations*. SNT 170. Leiden: Brill.

Pomykala, Kenneth E. 1995. *The Davidic Dynasty Tradition in Early Judaism: Its History and Significance for Messianism*. EJL 7. Atlanta: Scholars Press.

Prescott, Anne Lake. 1991. "Evil Tongues at the Court of Saul: The Renaissance David as a Slandered Courtier." *Journal of Medieval and Renaissance Studies* 21: 163–86.

Prescott, Anne Lake. 2012. "The 2011 Josephine Waters Bennett Lecture: From the Sheephook to the Scepter: The Ambiguities of David's Rise to the Throne." *Rennaissance Quarterly* 65: 1–30.

Rodríguez Láiz, Ana. 2016. *El Mesías hijo de David: El mesianismo dinástico en los comienzos del cristianismo*. Estella (Navarra): Verbo Divino.

Salmen, Walter. 1995. *König David: Eine Symbolfigur in der Musik*. Freiburg: Universitäts-Verlag.

Sänger, Dieter and E. Bons, eds. 2007. *Psalm 22 und die Passionsgeschichten der Evangelien*. BThSt 88. Neukirchen-Vluyn: Neukirchener.

Schade, Herbert. 1962/63. "Zum Bild des tanzenden David im frühen Mittelalter." *Stimmen der Zeit* 172: 1–16.

Sherwood, Yvonne. 2015. "Early Modern Davids: From Sin to Critique." In K. Killeen, H. Smith, and R. Willie, eds., *The Oxford Handbook of the Bible in Early Modern England, c. 1530–1700*. Oxford: University Press, 640–58.

Sonnet, Jean-Pierre. 2006. "'Que ne suis-je mort à ta place!' De la cohérence narrative du cycle de David (1 S 16–1 R 2)." In P. Abadie, ed., *Mémoires d'Écriture. Hommage à Pierre Gibert*. Le livre et le rouleau 25. Bruxelles: Lessius, 274–95.

Spain, Suzanne. 1977. "Heraclius, Byzantine Imperial Ideology, and the David Plates." *Speculum* 52: 217–37.

Steger, Hugo. 1961. *David Rex et Propheta: König David als vorbildliche Verkörperung des Herrschers und Dichters im Mittelalter, nach Bilddarstellungen des achten bis zwölften Jahrhunderts*. Nürnberg: Carl.

Steussy, Marti J. 1999. *David: Biblical Portraits of Power*. Columbia, SC: University of South Carolina Press.

Strauss, Mark L. 1995. *The Davidic Messiah in Luke-Acts: The Promise and Its Fulfillment in Lukan Christology*. JSNTSup 110. Sheffield: Academic Press.

Valler, Shulamit. 1994. "David and 'His' Women: Biblical Stories and Talmudic Discussions." In A. Brenner, ed., *Samuel and Kings*. FCB 5. Sheffield: Academic Press, 129–42.

Van Seters, John. 2009. *The Biblical Saga of King David*. Winona Lake, IN: Eisenbrauns.

Van Seters, John et al. 2011. "Bathsheba." In *EBR* 3: 598–613.

Vinay, Dominique. 2005. "Le symbolisme politique de David à la harpe dans le Penser du Royal Mémoire de Guillaume Michel (1518)." *Albineana, Cahiers d'Aubigné* 17: 123–51.

Waschke, Ernst-Joachim. 2001. *Der Gesalbte: Studien zur alttestamentlichen Theologie*. BZAW 306. Berlin: de Gruyter.

Watts, James. 1992. *Psalm and Story: Inset Hymns in Hebrew Narrative*. JSOTSup 139. Sheffield: Academic Press.

Wessel, Klaus. 1966. "David." *Reallexikon zur byzantinischen Kunst* 1: 1145–61.

Wyss, Robert L. 1968. "David." *LCI* 1: 477–90.

Zahnd, Ueli. 2008. "Novus David—Νέος Δαυιδ." *Frühmittelalterliche Studien* 42: 71–87.

Zenger, Erich. 1998. "David as Musician and Poet: Plotted and Painted." In J. C. Exum and S. D. Moore, eds., *Biblical Studies/Cultural Studies*. JSOTSup 266. Sheffield: Sheffield Academic Press, 263–98.

Zingel, Hans Joachim. 1968. *König Davids Harfe in der abendländischen Kunst*. Cologne: Musikverlag Gerig.

CHAPTER 34

SOLOMON IN RECEPTION HISTORY

SARA M. KOENIG

In the Bible, Solomon, the son of David and third king of Israel, is renowned for his wisdom and wealth. He is the celebrated builder of the first temple in Jerusalem and traditionally believed to be the author of Proverbs, Ecclesiastes, and Song of Songs. But the Solomon of 1 Kings also had a thousand wives and concubines, and in his old age, they turned his heart away from God. Consequently, after Solomon's death the United Kingdom of Israel divided into the Southern Kingdom of Judah and the Northern Kingdom of Israel, events which signaled the beginning of the end for both kingdoms. Within the Historical Books of the Hebrew Bible—especially through the lens of the Deuteronomist—Solomon is a pivot between David's orthodox fidelity to Yhwh and the increasingly polytheistic worship of those kings who follow Solomon. Solomon's story in 2 Samuel 12–1 Kings 11 broadly mirrors Israel's story in the Historical Books, starting with a love of God and ending in rejection and punishment.

There is no one single perspective on Solomon in the biblical texts. Not only is he connected with both the Historical Books and the writings, but even within a block of chapters such as 1 Kings 3–11 the complex compositional history of the text suggests multiple perspectives on Solomon: the wise king makes foolish choices about increasing his wives; the temple builder acquires horses from Egypt; the one who loves God worships at the high places. Solomon's image multiplies even further in postbiblical reception: among other things, he communicates with animals, controls demons, fathers the Ethiopian royal dynasty, uses water and astrology to practice divination, and works with the wood of the cross. Such receptions of Solomon come from details or gaps in the text that are like threads that get pulled out and woven into new tapestries of meaning or that are embellished with new materials. Studying Solomon's reception helps readers appreciate how many interpretive possibilities exist for any one section or specific character in the biblical books. Because of the sheer range of Solomon's reception, this chapter cannot be exhaustive. Instead, it will consider how Solomon is amplified, embellished, and appropriated in three main areas from the biblical narrative: his wisdom, his temple building, and his wives and women. These categories are not discrete, as they bleed into one another, but are chosen for their heuristic value.

34.1 Solomon's Wisdom

According to 1 Kings 3, God gave Solomon wisdom after Solomon requested it in a dream, after Solomon succeeded his father David on the throne. Jewish legends, however, say that Solomon's wisdom began to be known when he was only 3 years old (Seymour 1924: 14). Solomon's imprecise self-description, "I am a young lad" in 1 Kgs. 3:7 gets specified in various ways in later literature: Rashi calculated that he was 12 when he became king (Rosenberg and Hochberg 1980: 33), Josephus wrote that he was 14 (Josephus, *Ant.* 5.8, 211), and both Abarbanel and the nineteenth-century commentator Charles S. Robinson placed his age at 19 (Robinson 1889: 256; Rosenberg and Hochberg 1980: 33). Josephus added that, when Solomon judged between the two women in 1 Kgs. 3:16–28 and the people heard Solomon call for a sword, they "privately laughed at the king, as no more than a youth." Only after the mother of the living child spoke up did the people recognize Solomon's wisdom (Josephus *Ant.* 8.2.2). One rabbi disapproved of the ordeal that the mother experienced, describing Solomon's method of judging as fit for a boy, not for a wise ruler. The rabbi said that he would have wound a rope of wool around Solomon's neck to strangle him if the mother had not been filled with compassion (Cohen 1983: 277).

Certain receptions specify and clarify the nature of the divine origins of Solomon's wisdom. For example, some midrashim explained that Solomon knew the identity of the mother of the living child because the holy spirit spoke to Solomon, saying, "She is the mother thereof" (Cohen 1983: 278; Freedman 1983: 797). When Solomon hired Egyptian workers for the temple, the divine spirit also revealed to him that Pharaoh Neco had sent workers who were destined to die before the end of the year. The Pharaoh was told the same thing by his astrologers, so in this account Solomon's divine wisdom is contrasted with those who foretell through astrology. Other receptions of Solomon depict him as an astrologer himself. Solomon presented the ill-fated Egyptian men with shrouds before sending them back to Egypt with the message, "If you are short of shrouds for the needs of your dead, behold here they are with their shrouds; arise and bury them" (Cohen 1983: 204; Slotki 1983: 749; Ginzberg and Stern 2003: 954). Solomon also received his divine wisdom from a holy book of wisdom—the *Sepher Ha-Razim* ("the book of mysteries")—from God and the angels, according to Jewish legends. Certain legends have the book first given to Adam, Enoch, and Noah; Noah learned from the book how to build the ark. Noah gave the book to Shem, from whom it passed to Abraham, Jacob, Levi, Moses, and Joshua before it was given to Solomon, "who learnt all his wisdom from it, and his skill in the healing art, and also his mastery over the demons" (Torijano 2002: 204–205; Ginzberg and Stern 2003: 142). Solomon's control over demons is a special type of his wisdom, which is taken up further below.

Though Solomon's wisdom ultimately came from God, three different humans are credited with teaching Solomon: Nathan, Shimei, and Bathsheba. Nathan is identified as Solomon's teacher in the Zohar (Ginzberg and Stern 2003: 948). The contemporary novelist Geraldine Brooks (2016) also has Nathan teaching Solomon. Brooks's Solomon is similar to the Solomon in Jewish legends: wise long before he takes the throne. She describes him as asking a question "so profound that one could hardly credit that it issued from the mind of a small boy" (Brooks 2016: 242). Nineteenth-century Anglican Alexander Whyte asserted that Solomon's prayer in 1 Kings 8 could not have been composed by Solomon alone, for he was "the greatest castaway in the Bible... so soon to be a scandal and a reprobation," and therefore it must have been written under Nathan's guidance (Whyte 1898: 186). The Talmud (*b. Giṭ.* 59a; *b. Sanh.* 36a) and other Jewish legends identified Shimei as Solomon's teacher. This is the same Shimei who cursed David (2 Sam. 16:5–13), repented (2 Sam. 19:16–23), and was ultimately put to death by Solomon (1 Kgs. 2:8–9; 36–46). While Shimei was alive, Solomon would not marry Pharaoh's daughter, but after Shimei died, Solomon took her as his wife (Ginzberg and Stern 2003: 947). Still other traditions suggest that Solomon's mother, Bathsheba, taught him his wisdom. In part, this idea comes from the connection of Solomon with King Lemuel in Prov. 31:1–9, whose wise mother warned him against giving his strength to women and drinking wine. This biblical text is amplified in midrashim that narrate how Solomon slept late on the day the temple was to be dedicated. The Israelites were grieved because they were unable to perform the service of dedication, but also afraid to wake their royal king, so they told Bathsheba, who "came and woke him up and reproved him" (Israelstam and Slotki 1983: 159–60; Slotki 1983: 352–53). Novelist Francine Rivers has Bathsheba promise God during her pregnancy with Solomon that she will raise up her son "to be a man after Your own heart" by teaching him God's law (2009: 372). Despite Rivers's allusion to the description of David in 1 Sam. 13:14, her novel concludes with Bathsheba aware that her son is not like his father in his fidelity to God.

Rivers' reception of Solomon is just one of many that connect Solomon's wisdom with God's law. The midrash affirms that until "Solomon arose no one was able to understand properly the words of the Torah, but as soon as Solomon arose all began to comprehend the Torah" (Simon 1983a: 9–10). The rabbis had several metaphors to illustrate Solomon's wisdom regarding the Torah: R. Naḥman said the Torah was like a large palace with many doors, and those who entered were unable to find their way back to the entrance until a clever person hung a coil of string on the way to the door so all could travel by means of the string. R. Jose compared the Torah to a big basket of produce without handles, so it could not be lifted and carried until Solomon made handles for it. R. Shila said the Torah was like a deep well full of "cold, sweet, and wholesome water," from which no one could drink until Solomon came, "and joining rope to rope and cord to cord, drew from it and drank, and then all began to draw and drink" (Simon 1983: 9–10).

Other rabbis discussed the eclectic nature of Solomon's wisdom, asserting that Solomon did not only search out words of Torah, "but all that was done under the sun; for instance, how to sweeten mustard, how to sweeten lupines" (Simon 1983: 8) or "how to prepare a hot brew consisting of a third part each of wine, water, and pepper" (Cohen 1983: 39). Solomon's eclectic knowledge also derives from Greek vocabulary in the LXX. Pablo Torijano has argued that *parabolē* ("comparison, proverb") and *ōdē* ("song") in 1 Kgs. 4:32 mean, respectively, "astronomical conjunction" and "spell, charm," which could explain how Solomon's wisdom extended in the first century CE and beyond to subjects like astrology, astronomy, and magic (Torijano 2002: 32–33). The assertion in 1 Kgs. 4:33 (Heb. 5:13) that Solomon would discourse about animals, birds, reptiles, and fish was expanded to mean that Solomon could speak *with* those creatures (Ginzberg and Stern 2003: 957). Rabbi Isaac said "If an ass brayed, he knew what it meant; if a bird chirped, he knew what it meant" (Cohen 1983: 2; Simon 1983a: 13). Legends tell of Solomon judging wisely over—and communicating with—a menagerie of animals, including serpents, swallows, bats, roosters, cows, donkeys, ravens, and nightingales (Seymour 1924: 95–113; Ginzberg and Stern 2003: 951–52). Rudyard Kipling had Solomon speak with butterflies in one of his *Just So Stories*, "The Butterfly Stamped" (Kipling 1907: 225–49). Solomon had a special relationship with certain birds: it was said he had a large eagle he rode back and forth to Tadmor in the wilderness (Cohen 1983: 72; cf. 2 Chr. 8:4), and the hoopoe bird— with feathers on its head that look like a crown—features prominently in the stories about Solomon and the queen of Sheba in Judaism and in Islam (Lassner 1993).

Solomon's wisdom was also displayed in his conversations with various interlocutors. The biblical references to the queen of Sheba's visit in 1 Kgs. 10:1–3 and 2 Chr. 9:1–2 include the note that she attempted to test Solomon with hard questions. In various midrashim and the Targums, her questions are expounded as riddles such as, "Three entered a cave and five came forth," in which case the answer is Lot, his two daughters, and their two children (Ginzberg and Stern 2003: 960). She also gave him tests: for example, she placed a thousand males and females of the same stature and clothing, and asked him to distinguish between them. In one tradition, Solomon brought silver basins before them and commanded them to wash their faces; the females washed their faces with both hands, while the males washed only with the hand on which the water was poured. In another tradition, Solomon placed food before them, and the males ate with bare hands, but the females put on gloves before eating (Seymour 1924: 143, Ginzberg and Stern 2003: 960). Josephus described Hiram of Tyre sending Solomon "sophisms and enigmatical sayings," which Solomon successfully solved (Josephus *Ant.* 8.5.3). Solomonic dialogue literature from the medieval era includes dialogues with Marcolphus—or Marcolf—a carnivalesque and foolish peasant who, with his wife, asked bawdy questions to challenge Solomon (Bradbury and Bradbury 2012). Solomon also dialogues with Saturn, a prince of the Chaldeans. The dialogues with Marcolphus circulated on the continent of Europe, particularly in Germany, while those featuring Saturn are Anglo-Saxon in origin; they also differ in that Marcolphus seemed more interested in perverting Solomon's wisdom than learning from it (Anlezark 2009: 12).

Solomon's wisdom has long been associated with the biblical books of Proverbs, Ecclesiastes, and Song of Songs. Proverbs 1:1. Eccl. 1:1; and Song 1:1 all identify—directly or obliquely—Solomon as the author of those collections, a tradition not seriously questioned until the Enlightenment. The rabbis affirmed that Solomon composed those books after "the holy spirit rested on him" (Simon 1983: 4–5, 7, 9–10), but have different ideas about the order. Rabbi Ḥiyya said Proverbs came first, then Song of Songs, then Ecclesiastes, while Rabbi Jonathan said Solomon first composed Song of Songs, then Proverbs, and last Ecclesiastes, arguing, "When a man is young he composes songs; when he grows older he makes sententious remarks; when he becomes an old man he speaks of the vanity of things" (Simon 1983a: 17). Solomon is also associated with the deuterocanonical Wisdom of Solomon, as well as the Syriac and Greek *Odes of Solomon* and *Psalms of Solomon*, texts dated between the first and third century (Sparks 1984; Harkins 2016). In 2008, the *Odes of Solomon* were adapted into worship music with Solomon's pseudepigraphal name removed; it is merely identified as "The Odes Project" (see https://www.theodesproject.com/). The references in Wisd. 6:22 and 7:15–22 suggest that Solomon is a teacher of special knowledge; in texts such as the *Testament of Solomon* or the *Hygromanteia* (a medieval book of magic spells attributed to Solomon), Solomon is the teacher of secrets (Torijano 2002: 91; see further below).

In 1 Kings 3, God approvingly responded to Solomon's request for wisdom—and not wealth—by granting Solomon wealth along with his wisdom. According to Jewish legend, Solomon acquired his wealth after God commanded the sea to cast up every valuable thing that had been thrown into it (Ginzberg and Stern 2003: 949). Others have sought more concrete sources of Solomon's wealth, albeit in fictional form, such as late nineteenth-century author H. Rider Haggard. Haggard wrote *King Solomon's Mines* about adventurers seeking out—and finding—Solomon's diamond mines in South Africa. Archeologists have attempted to locate Solomon's copper mines in both the southern Jordan and in Israel's Timna Valley (Ben-Yosef 2016). One example of Solomon's wealth, according to Rabbi Ḥama b. Ḥanina, is that his table never lacked anything: "neither roses in summer nor cucumbers in winter; but he enjoyed these the whole year..." (Cohen 1983: 56). Solomon's glorious attire is mentioned in the Sermon on the Mount (Matt. 6:29), and Robert Barrett Browning's poem "Popularity" references the precious shells from Tyre that produced dye for the "hangings for his cedar-house / That, when gold-robed he took the throne / In that abyss of blue, the Spouse / Might swear his presence shone."

Solomon's inimitable throne of ivory overlaid with gold also communicated his great wealth: it was decorated with lions standing beside the arm rests, and twelve more lions were on the six steps leading up to the throne, one standing on each end of the step (1 Kgs. 10:18–20). The midrashim add that, as Solomon ascended each step, a herald would proclaim a warning. One midrash takes the six warnings from Deut. 16:19–17:1: "you shall not judge unfairly," "you shall not show partiality," "you shall not take bribes," "you shall not set up an Asherah," "you shall not set up a pillar," and "you shall not sacrifice an ox or sheep with a defect" (J. Rabbinowitz 1983: 106–107). In Midrash Numbers and Midrash Esther, however, the first three warnings are from Deut. 17:16–17, and not in textual order: on the first step, a herald warns, "he shall not multiply wives" (Deut. 17:17). The second and third warnings, respectively, are "he shall not multiply horses" (Deut. 17:16) and "neither shall he amass silver and gold to excess" (Deut. 17:17) (Simon 1983: 27–28; Slotki 1983: 490). Such frequent warnings highlight Solomon's later forgetfulness and sinfulness. The many wives are the most problematic, as will be discussed below; Solomon's wealth is less obviously negative.

In fact, Solomon's vast wealth was positive when it was read allegorically, as in some midrashim and by certain Christian commentators. Rabbi Ḥiyya b. Nehemiah asserted that the biblical text speaks of Solomon's material wealth only in connection with matters of Torah, adducing Eccl. 2:4–8 as an allegory for Torah teaching and studying. The "great works" were the written words of God, the "houses" were houses of study and synagogues, the "vineyards" were the rows of disciples who sit in tiers like a vineyard, the "gardens and parks" were the Mishnah, and the "trees of all kinds of fruit" were the Talmud and so forth (Cohen 1983: 58–59). In the fourth century, Church Father Ephrem the Syrian (306–73) read the silver in 1 Kgs. 10:27 as signifying the riches of Christ's gospel (1737: 467). But as early as the Deuteronomist, concerns were expressed with Solomon's amassing of gold and silver (Deut. 17:17). Nineteenth-century commentator Frederic Farrar wrote that Solomon's "worldly ostentation demanded from his people sacrifices from which they reaped no satisfaction... the indolent luxury and gilded pomp of his Court could only be maintained by the imposition of taxes which fell with crushing weight on the pauperized people" (Farrar 1831: 149). Walter Brueggemann is similarly critical of Solomon's wealth, stating that the Lord's promises of riches are fulfilled "not by a supernatural, miraculous act but by shrewd, cunning, and powerful acts of state," which include international arms dealing (1 Kgs. 10:26–29), internal taxation (1 Kgs. 4:7–19), and cheap/forced labor (1 Kgs. 5:13–18 [Heb. 5:27–32]; 9:15–23) (Brueggemann 2005: 124). Some interpreters point to the evidence of Solomon's greed in the size of his own palace respective to the temple (Fuller 1876: 286): he took thirteen years to build his house, but only seven to build the temple (see 1 Kgs. 6:38–7:1). However, the midrash explains that he was especially diligent when he was building the Temple, and dallied when he built his own palace (Simon 1983: 3).

34.2 Solomon's Temple Building

Solomon's greatest achievement was building the temple. Midrash Rabbah Esther claims that from the beginning of the world, God appointed Solomon to be "the foremost of builders," while David was "the foremost of singers" (Simon 1983: 10). That Solomon, and not David, built the temple, is emphasized in different ways by different biblical texts. 2 Samuel 7 and 1 Chronicles 17 highlight that God's promise of an eternal dynasty for David is not conditioned on David being the one to build the temple, while 1 Kgs. 5:3 and 1 Chr. 22:8; 28:3 suggest that David's involvement in wars prevented him from building.

The biblical texts also vary in their witness as to Solomon's direct involvement in the building process. According to 1 Chronicles 29 and 2 Chronicles 2, David prepared for the temple by acquiring the necessary provisions, but that account is not paralleled in Kings. Solomon is the subject of the verbs in 1 Kings 6, not only building the edifice, but also constructing temple accessories such as the lampstands, the basin, etc. But 1 Kings 5 explains that Hiram of Tyre furnished the wood for the temple (1 Kgs. 5:1–10 [Heb. 5:15–24]) and that not only Hiram's builders, but Solomon's builders and the Gebalites made preparations of wood and stone for the temple (1 Kgs. 5:18 [Heb. 5:32]). The Gebalites are also mentioned in Ezek. 27:9, and Farrar explained that even in Homer's writings, they were "famed for embroidered robes and skill in workmanship" (Farrar 1831: 77). Hiram—also known as Huram-Abi (2 Chr. 4:16)—is said to be the master architect and the first mason in the tradition of the Freemasons, who trace their origin to the building of the temple. A Masonic document from the seventeenth century affirms, "King Solomon at the building of the Temple of Jerusalem...fformed [sic] Lodges, and gave and Granted their Commissions and Charters to those of or belonging to the science of Masonry" (Hughan 1895: 143). In the earliest Masonic Catechism, the *Edinburgh Register House MS.* from 1696, the answer to the question about the location of the first lodge is, "In the porch of Solomon's Temple" (Horne 1972: 30).

In addition to references where Solomon was helped in the construction of the temple by other people, a rich tradition of reception holds that he built it with the help of supernatural beings. One of these is the Shamir, a worm created "at twilight on the sixth day of creation together with other extraordinary things" which could cut the hardest of diamonds, and was used instead of iron tools (cf. 1 Kgs. 6:7; also Deut. 27:5–6) to cut the stones for the temple. The Shamir had been guarded in paradise until Solomon needed it, and it vanished when the temple was destroyed (*b. Soṭ* 48b; Ginzberg and Stern 2003: 35). Alternate readings understood the Shamir to be a special type of non-living tool. One rabbi said that the stones themselves cried out with a loud voice, broke off the quarry, flew to the site, and laid themselves on the structure (Seymour 1924: 124), but demons are the other beings Solomon used to build the temple, according to a number of sources.

One of those sources is the *Testament of Solomon*, part of the testaments of the twelve patriarchs, a composite Jewish pseudepigraphal work dating between the first and fifth centuries CE. Narrated in Solomon's voice in first person, it tells how the archangel Michael gave him a ring by which he would have power over demons; Solomon used the ring to entrap various demons to help him build the temple. For example, the demon Ornias cut the stones at the temple, the she-demon Oneskelis spun hemp for the ropes used in building, seven female spirits dug the foundations, and so forth (see Sparks 1984: 737–45). Several demons mentioned in the *Testament of Solomon* appear in other Judeo-Christian texts, including Beelzebub (see Mark 3:22, Matt. 12:24–27, Luke 7:15) and Asmodeus (Tobit 3:8, 17). Asmodeus appears in other Jewish legends about Solomon, such as when this "king of demons" wants to show Solomon something new, sticks his finger in the ground, and up comes a two-headed man (Ginzberg and Stern 2003: 950–51). In the Talmud (*b. Giṭ.* 68a–b) Asmodeus, or Ashmedai, is the one who locates the Shamir for Solomon, but he later deposes Solomon on his throne (see further below). The gnostic tractate *Testimony of Truth* discusses how Solomon used demons to build Jerusalem, then imprisoned the demons in water pots in the temple (Torijano 2002: 181).

Solomon's mastery over demons, and not solely in temple building, is well attested in various types and eras of reception. The idea comes from the phrase *šiddâ wěšiddôt* in Eccl. 2:8 which occurs nowhere else in the Hebrew Bible (Seow 1997: 131–32) but which is explained in the Talmud as "male and female demons" (*b. Giṭ.* 68a; Davis 2016: 580). It was popularly believed in the medieval era that the baths referenced in Eccl. 2:8 were heated by demons and that evil spirits haunted baths (Cohen 1983: 57). One Jewish legend described how, on the night of Solomon's birth, the devil heard a voice saying that one would be born who would trouble him and make slaves of his children. The newborn Solomon had "the appearance of dazzling purity," and "the demons were bereft" (Seymour 1924: 13–14; Lassner 1993: 202–203). Solomon's control over demons is also exhibited in various amulets from the third century CE onward, which contain visual or textual references to Solomon, and that were thought to have apotropaic power (Torijano 2002: 72–131). Similar—and replica—amulets are currently available for purchase through websites such as www.kingsolomonamulet.com. Josephus recounts seeing his countryman Eleazar free people possessed by demons: Eleazar put a ring "which had under its seal one of the roots prescribed by Solomon" to the nose of the possessed man. When the man smelled the root, Eleazar drew the demon out through the man's nostrils, and when the man fell down, Eleazar commanded the demon never to return, speaking Solomon's name and reciting incantations composed by Solomon (Josephus *Ant.* 8.46–48). Josephus directly connected this event with Solomon's wisdom and understanding, while the text of the *Hygromanteia* tips more toward emphasizing Solomon's skill as a magician and astronomer. In the *Hygromanteia*, Solomon instructed Rehoboam how to foretell the future by using a basin filled with water to summon demons, and how to learn mastery over planets, the Zodiac, angels, and demons (Torijano 2002: 231–53). Solomon also controls demons in Islamic traditions. *Sura* 27:17 in the Qur'an asserts that Solomon's host included men and jinn, and the Islamic *History of Prophets and Kings* by the ninth-century Muslim historian Abū Ja'far Muḥammad b. Jarīr al-Ṭabarī explains that God compelled the jinn to serve Solomon (al-Ṭabarī 1991: 152–61). Some argue for a connection between Solomon, the immediate son of David, and Jesus as the "Son of David" who casts out demons (Matt. 12:22–29). Even as the gospels, however, refer to the "queen of the south" coming to hear the "wisdom of Solomon," they also clarify "what is here is greater than Solomon" (Matt. 12:42; Luke 11:31; Torijano 2002: 113; Klutz 2006: 88).

Solomon's temple was frequently understood allegorically, as when the Venerable Bede (672–735) asserted, "The house of God which king Solomon built in Jerusalem was made as a figure of the holy universal Church" (Bede 1995: 5). Martin Luther understood the temple as a type of a spiritual person (2016: 294), while Johannes Piscator argued for three typological meanings: Solomon's temple was a type of Christ's body, a type of the church, and a type of each believer's body (Piscator 1646: 265). Each item within the temple was also assigned spiritual significance, though the allegories varied. For example, in John Bunyan's "Solomon's Temple spiritualized," he explained the eighteen-cubit height of the pillars (1 Kgs. 7:5) as symbolic of the "high call" of "the apostles of the Lamb" (1804: 86). Bede, however, read eighteen as a multiple of three and six, with three representing faith in the Trinity and six representing works because the world was made in six days. He explained, "And three is multiplied by six when *the righteous person who lives by faith* acquires knowledge of pious belief by the performance of good works" (Bede 1995: 74–75).

Solomon's temple gets textually described and physically recreated in numerous traditions. The four earliest textual sources are in Kings, Chronicles, Josephus, and the second-century Jewish historian Eupolemus. Josephus multiplies the size of the temple beyond the descriptions in Kings and Chronicles, frequently adding specific numbers that are lacking in those biblical sources and expanding others (Josephus *Ant.* 8.64–89). Some of these expansions may have been influenced by the descriptions of the reimagined temple in Ezek. 40:17, or even by recollections of Herod's temple (Feldman 1976: 79–80). Eupolemus described the foundation and building of Solomon's temple, and, like the Chronicler, emphasized David's role in preparing for the building (Torijano 2002: 35–37). Physical replicas of Solomon's temple were made in Europe in the late seventeenth century: Rabbi Jacob Yehuda Leon's model was exhibited in London, while Gerhard Schott's baroque architectural model produced in Hamburg is still on display in the Hamburg Museum. Models were also made for both the 1939 and 1964 World's Fairs in New York City, and in the 1950s, biblical scholars G. Ernest Wright and Paul Leslie Garber created replicas based on their academic research (Horne 1972: 54–56). The Universal Church of the Kingdom of God in São Paulo, Brazil inaugurated their own version of Solomon's Temple in 2014. It seats ten thousand, is one hundred eighty feet tall, and comes complete with a replica of the Ark inside (see http://sites.universal.org/templodesalomao/). According to 1 Kgs. 6:38 and 8:2, Solomon waited to dedicate the temple almost a year after he completed building it. Jewish commentators explain that the time of dedication corresponded with the month when Abraham was born (Ginzberg and Stern 2003: 966). Other midrashim connect the completion of the temple with Solomon's marriage to Pharaoh's daughter (Israelstam and Slotki 1983: 158; Slotki 1983: 351), the first of a multitude of women who lead to Solomon's downfall.

34.3 SOLOMON'S WIVES AND WOMEN

Solomon's marriage to Pharaoh's daughter—identified by name in tradition as Bithiah—is recorded in 1 Kings 3, before Solomon asks for wisdom, and before Solomon begins to build the temple. Receptions, however, play with the chronology of the event. Rabbi Judan explained that there were two celebrations on the same night: one for the completion of the temple, and the other for Solomon's marriage to Pharaoh's daughter. When God noted the people rejoicing for the wedding, "At that moment it entered His mind to destroy Jerusalem" (Israelstam and Slotki 1983: 158–59). The Talmud specified that God's declaration in Jer. 32:31, that Jerusalem provoked God to wrath and fury, "applied to the time after Solomon married the daughter of Pharaoh" (b. Nid. 70b). Other Jewish texts have an archangel—Gabriel or Michael—planting a reed into the sea on the day of the wedding. Silt and the like slowly accumulated around the reed, making it into an island, and on the day when Jeroboam set up the golden calves, a little hut was built there that was the first dwelling place of Rome (b. Sanh. 21b; Simon 1983: 60).

These three traditions draw a connection between Solomon's marriage and the eventual destruction of Jerusalem and both temples, but other receptions are more sanguine about Solomon's marriage alliances. Nineteenth-century commentator George Matheson argued that "the main motive, which lighted the myriad nuptial torches of Solomon," was Solomon's desire to weaken the memory of Saul's house in Israel by marrying outside of Israel into adjacent lands (Matheson 1902: 296–97). Some note the political wisdom of Solomon's intermarriage: late seventeenth-century commentator Matthew Henry observed how Solomon would receive tax breaks from his pharaonic father-in-law (Henry 1708: 630), while Farrar noted the military and geographical gains (Farrar 1831: 55). Contemporary scholar Claudia Camp discusses the strategic role that the "strange women" play in 1 Kings 3–11, especially Pharaoh's daughter and the queen of Sheba (Camp 2000).

The queen of Sheba is a character with an extensive afterlife of her own. She is identified with the beloved in Song of Songs based on her description as "black and beautiful" (Song 1:5), and she is given various names: "Bilqis" in Arabic texts and "Candace" or "Makeda" in Ethiopian tales. In the Qur'an, she worships the sun, and corresponds with Solomon via a letter carried by the hoopoe bird before she eventually comes to see Solomon in person. At Solomon's palace, she mistakes the highly polished glass floor for a pool of water, and uncovers her legs to wade through the supposed water. When Solomon explains that it is glass, the queen of Sheba acknowledges her mistake and then chooses to submit to Allah and stop worshipping the sun (Sura 27:15–44). Persian art often depicts her standing in water before Solomon, as does the stained glass in King's College Chapel, Cambridge (Ullendorf 1968: 144–45). The queen of Sheba's legs are particularly hairy in some versions of the story, so Solomon commissions demons to prepare a special depilatory before he marries her (Seymour 1924: 146–48; al-Ṭabarī 1991: 162–63). Other variations on the story have her with deformed—webbed—feet, or with the feet or legs of a donkey (Watt 1974: 99). Arabic receptions explained her animal limbs as coming from her jinn mother, as donkeys were culturally associated with the devil (Abdulaali 2012). Similarly, some Jewish legends connect the queen of Sheba with the demonic Lilith, Adam's original wife who refused to serve him (Silberman 1974: 78–82; Lassner 1993: 21–24). Jacob Lassner argues that in many receptions, the queen of Sheba subverts gender ideals (Lassner 1993).

Ethiopian tales give both Solomon and the queen of Sheba some measure of agency. Solomon seduced the virgin queen by giving her highly seasoned meat, and then inviting her to spend the night in his chambers. She agreed on condition that he would swear not to take her by force. His rejoinder was that she must not take anything in his house, but when she woke in the night she was so thirsty that she took and drank a bowl of water he had placed by her bed. After they slept together, Solomon dreamed that the *Shekinah* left Israel and moved to Ethiopia. The queen gave birth nine months and five days later to a son Menelik, the founder of the Ethiopian dynasty (Brooks 2002: 30–33). Article 2 of the 1955 Ethiopian Constitution asserts, "the Imperial dignity shall remain perpetually attached to the line ... [which] descends without interruption from the dynasty of Menelik 1, son of the Queen of Ethiopia, the Queen of Sheba, and King Solomon of Jerusalem" (Ullendorff 1968: 139). When Menelik was grown, he visited his father Solomon, and Solomon sent a group of Israelites back to Ethiopia with Menelik. This group of young men—by the will of God— took the ark out of the temple and carried it with them to Ethiopia (Brooks 2002: 60–63). The queen of Sheba's encounter with Solomon is frequently illustrated in traditional Ethiopian art, in stylized multiple-panel sequences.

Both the queen of Sheba and Solomon appear in twelfth-century legends of the cross. In some versions, she saw the wood and venerated it, while in others, she warned Solomon about how the Messiah would bring about the end of the Jewish kingdom. In those accounts, Solomon buried the wood in an attempt to prevent it being used for the crucifixion, but in the spot where it is buried, the pool of Bethesda welled up and the wood was found in the pool at the time of Christ's passion. Other versions minimized the queen of Sheba's role, and emphasized Solomon's unsuccessful attempts to use the wood to build the temple (Baert 2004: 291–303). Brueggemann (2005: 121) observes that the queen of Sheba articulated the purpose of Solomon's rule as "justice and righteousness" (1 Kgs. 10:9). That pairing, so common in prophetic texts and in psalms, nowhere else refers to Solomon.

Negative assessments of Solomon's many wives are frequently encountered. Even so, it is not surprising, in light of the above, to encounter a variety of positions on Solomon's wrongdoing in this regard. Some rabbis highlighted that Solomon clearly knew the commands in Deut. 12:17 not to multiply wives, and—out of arrogance or overconfidence—ignored it, saying, "Well, I will multiply and still my heart will not turn away" (Lehrman 1983: 103). A thread of interpretations suggest that he was tricked, as when Rabbi Eleazer the son of Rabbi Jose the Galilean explains the reference in Neh. 13:26 (that the foreign women caused Solomon to sin) as meaning that Solomon "used to have intercourse with them when they were menstruous, and they did not tell him" (Simon 1983: 16). In one Jewish legend, Solomon was in love with a Jebusite woman who worshipped Moloch and Raphan, and asked him to pay homage to those gods. Solomon resisted for some time, but finally acquiesced to her request that he take five locusts and crush them in his hands in the name of Moloch. Not unlike Samson devoid of his hair, Solomon was immediately bereft of his strength, wisdom, and God's spirit. He then sank so low that, in order to please her, he built temples to Baal and Raphan (Ginzberg and Stern 1993: 964). A Jewish tradition recorded in the Talmud and midrash has Solomon tricked by the demon king Asmodeus who deposed Solomon. Solomon had told Asmodeus that the demons could not be great if their king was in bondage by a mortal. Asmodeus replied that if Solomon removed Asmodeus's chains, and would lend Asmodeus his magic ring, then Asmodeus would show Solomon his greatness. Solomon did so, and Asmodeus immediately flung Solomon four hundred parasangs (historical Iranian units of distance, equivalent to leagues) from Jerusalem, replacing him on the throne. One clue that the king was not really Solomon was that he always wore stockings; as indicated in the story of the queen of Sheba, demons were thought to have feet of animals. Solomon wandered as a beggar, but eventually returned and reclaimed a ring of power, causing Asmodeus to fly away. The story ends with reference to Song 3:7–8 about Solomon's palanquin, but not as a description of the lover's wealth and might. Rather, the three-score mighty men referenced in those verses are necessary to protect the human Solomon from his fear at night of the demons (*b. Giṭ.* 65b; Slotki 1983: 420).

Still others asserted that Solomon did no wrong with all his wives. In the Talmud, Rabbi Nathan declared that Solomon did not sin: he explained that though 1 Kgs. 11:4 says that Solomon's wives turned away his heart to go after other gods, "he did not go"; and the reference in 1 Kgs. 11:7 meant that Solomon "intended to build a high place for Chemosh, but did not build it" (*b. Šabb.* 56b). The Church Father Isho'dad of Merv (ca. 850) wrote that Solomon himself did not apostatize or worship the idols, but gave his wives freedom to worship; unlike his father David, he did not prevent their worship or convert them (Isho'dad 1963: 110–11). Rabbi Jose b. Ḥalafta declared that when 1 Kgs. 11:2 says that Solomon clung to his wives "in love," it meant "to make them beloved [to God], to bring them near [to God], to convert them and to bring them under the wings of the *Shechinah*" (Simon 1983: 16). But within that same collection of midrash, Rabbi Jose's statement is encompassed by other rabbis' statements to the contrary. It is preceded by Rabbi Hunia's bald assertion, "[Solomon] committed three sins. He acquired too many horses, he took too many wives, he accumulated too much silver and gold..." (Simon 1983: 14–15), and immediately followed with the report that Rabbi Joshua b. Levi, Rabbi Simeon b. Yoḥai, and Rabbi Eleazer the son of Rabbi Jose the Galilean all disagreed with Rabbi Jose b. Ḥalafta (Simon 1983: 16).

Christian commentators in the Enlightenment offered poetic analogies for Solomon's heart being turned away. Henry wrote, "the lustre both of his goodness and his greatness is here sullied and eclipsed, and his sun sets under a cloud" (Henry 1708: 631). Whyte compared Solomon to both a shipwreck and "a blazing lighthouse... set up in the sea of life to warn every man and to teach every man" (Whyte 1898: 182–83). Whyte and Farrar also refer to a proverb "of the east" that said that inside the royal staff on which Solomon leaned there was a secret worm—of pride, sensuality, and selfishness—gnawing on its center (Farrar 1831: 160; Whyte 1898: 193).

In the same way that there are multiple responses to Solomon's wrongdoing, there are a variety of receptions about whether or not he repented, was forgiven, or was granted salvation. In 1675, Puritan Francis Roberts admitted that because Scripture "doth not afford us so evident a Resolution herein... therefore learned men both ancient and modern have been of several opinions herein, and seem much unresolved about this matter" (Roberts 1675: 66). Evidence mustered—for and against Solomon's repentance—comes from debates about the canonicity of Ecclesiastes and Song of Songs, from specific biblical texts, and even from other receptions. Whyte asserted that Solomon never repented, and that was the reason for canonical debates about the books associated with Solomon (Whyte 1898: 191).

Certain rabbis, however, said that after Solomon repented, "the holy spirit rested on him and he composed these three works: Proverbs, Song of Songs, and Ecclesiastes" (Simon 1983: 4–5). Similarly, John Wesley (1703–91) argued that Solomon wrote the book of Ecclesiastes as "a public testimony of his repentance and detestation of those wicked courses to which he had addicted" (Wesley 1975: 1893). Rabbi Simon drew on 2 Sam. 12:13, which records an assurance for pardon for David, and argued, "Just as his father had all his iniquities forgiven...so with him, too" (Simon 1983: 7). Church Father Cyril of Jerusalem (ca. 313–386) read Prov. 24:32 LXX as proof that Solomon repented (Cyril 1969: 103). Job 34:33 was used in a midrashic tale about how the chief Jewish tribunal proposed including Solomon in the list of people who "have no share in the world to come." As they debated, a ghost of David pled on his son's behalf, a fire came forth from the interior of the Holy of Holies, and a heavenly voice quoted Prov. 22:29 and spoke about Solomon's priority in building the temple. The tribunal finally relented—and decided that Solomon would have a share in future life—when the heavenly voice came a second time and quoted Job 34:33 to warn that God would not reward them if they persisted in excluding Solomon (Slotki 1983: 556). In Dante's *Divine Comedy*, Solomon is in paradise, and that reception influenced Italian fourteenth-century artist Orcagna, who has Solomon on the side of paradise in his painting "Last Judgment" in Campo Santo, Pisa (Farrar 1831: 162; Stone 1896: 481). Centuries before Whyte, St. Augustine (354–430) argued that Solomon never repented because the Bible does not directly record it (2007: 365). Augustine's assessment of "Solomon in his [own] time" did not prevent him from receiving Solomon allegorically as a figure of Christ (Augustine 1956: 606); it was not a problem that Solomon be both. Augustine is not the only individual to interpret Solomon in multiple ways. Henry understood Solomon to be both a cautionary tale for all humans who might fall into sin (1708: 633), and also asserted—based on 2 Sam. 12:25—that Solomon "typified Jesus Christ, that blessed Jedidiah, the son of God's love, concerning whom God declared again and again, This is my beloved Son, in whom I am well pleased" (1708: 505).

34.4 Conclusion

If a single person—like Augustine or Henry—could receive Solomon in different ways, it is also true that multiple people read the same material with differing conclusions. For example, in contrast to Henry's typological reading of "Jedediah," Baruch Halpern asserted that the reason why Solomon was also called "Jedidiah," or "beloved of the LORD," was for obvious etymological connections with David "the beloved." Halpern states that this was done as public propaganda to counter suspicions that Solomon might be Uriah's son (2001: 401–403). Many have analyzed the name "Solomon" for its connections with both Jerusalem and peace; Josephus, for example, so emphasized Solomon's peacefulness that he added explanations as an apologetic for Solomon's vengeance toward Joab and Adonijah (Feldman 1976: 75–76). Such focus on Solomon's peacefulness was unusual, given that Josephus typically characterized successful Hellenistic rulers as warriors (Torijano 2002: 107). Brueggemann, however, observed that the *shalom* brought about in Solomon's reign was gained through blood and maintained through power (2005: 51–55). A Muslim perspective is different still: Al-Ṭabarī's Islamic history described Solomon as "a warfaring man, who rarely ceased his constant campaigning. No sooner would he hear about a ruler in some part of the world, but he would go to him to humble him" (1991: 153). Solomon was whitewashed in much European art, such as the painting "The Judgment of Solomon" by the Italian Renaissance master Giorgione, but Solomon was visually depicted as black by painter Jon Onye Lockard (1932–2015) in his "King Solomon and the Queen of Sheba," and by photographer James C. Lewis in his 2014 series "Icons of the Bible." Walter Arthur McCray, pastor and president of the National Black Evangelical Association (NBEA) argued for Bathsheba's probable ethnicity as a Canaanite Hittite, a group descended from Heth, Canaan, and Ham. If Ham was the ancestor of African nations, then the assumption is that the Hittites were black; McCray takes Bathsheba's supposed identity as a black Hittite to mean that Solomon was therefore also black (McCray 1990: 126–27).

Not only is there no single perspective on Solomon in the rich and complicated history of reception, there seems to be no single Solomon, as a person or character, given the wide variety of comparisons made between him and other literary and historical figures. He is evoked in relationship to the Pharaoh of Exodus (Brueggemann 2005: 155), Alexander the Great, Persian kings Chosroes I and Jemshid (Seymour 1924: 9), Francis Bacon (Whyte 1898: 187), and British monarchs Elizabeth I (Matheson 1902: 292) and Edward the Sixth (Farrar 1831: 158). Lord Melbourne evoked Solomon when the young Princess Victoria was told she was now queen of England; Melbourne "opened the Bible and read to the young sovereign the story of Solomon's dream at Gibeon" (Whyte 1898: 184). That Solomon can be amplified, embellished, and appropriated by so many people is a testimony to the generativity of the biblical text, and the inimitable way that it yields multiplicities of receptions over time.

Bibliography

Abdulaali, Wafaa. 2012. "Echoes of a Legendary Queen." *HDB* 40/3–4. Online at: https://bulletin.hds.harvard.edu/articles/summerautumn2012/echoes-legendary-queen (cited August 18, 2017).

Al-Ṭabarī, Abū Jaʿfar Muḥammad b. Jarīr. 1991. *The History of al-Ṭibarī*, Vol. III. Translated by William M. Brinner. Albany: State University of New York Press.

Anlezark, Daniel, ed. 2009. *The Old English Dialogues of Solomon and Saturn*. Cambridge: D. S. Brewer.

Augustine. 2007. *Answer to Faustus, a Manichean*. Translation and notes by Roland Teske. Hyde Park: New City Press.

Augustine. 1956. *Expositions on the Book of Psalms*. NPNF 8. Edited by Philip Schaff. Repr. ed. Grand Rapids: Eerdmans.

Baert, Barbara. 2004. *Heritage of Holy Wood: The Legend of the True Cross in Text and Image*. Leiden: Brill Academic.

Bartlett, John R. 1985. *Jews in the Hellenistic World: Josephus, Aristeas, The Sibylline Oracles, Eupolemus*. CCWJCW 1. Cambridge: Cambridge University Press.

Bede, the Venerable. 1995. *On the Temple*. Translated by Seán Connolly. TTH 21. Liverpool: Liverpool University Press.

Ben-Yosef, Erez. 2016. "Back to Solomon's Era: Results of the First Excavations at 'Slaves' Hill' (Site 34, Timna, Israel)." *BASOR* 376: 169–98.

Bradbury, Nancy Mason and Scott Bradbury, eds. 2012. *The Dialogue of Solomon and Marcolf: A Dual-Language Edition from Latin and Middle English Printed Editions*. Kalamazoo, MI: Medieval Institute Publications.

Brooks, Geraldine. 2016. *A Secret Chord*. New York: Penguin.
Brooks, Miguel F., ed. 2002. *Kebra Negast: The Glory of Kings*. Trenton, NJ: The Red Sea Press, Inc.
Brueggemann, Walter. 2005. *Solomon: Israel's Ironic Icon of Human Achievement*. Columbia, SC: University of South Carolina Press.
Bunyan, John. 1804. *Minor Works Containing: The Water of Life; Solomon's temple Spiritualized; Christ a Complete Saviour; Divine Breathings; and Grace Abounding*. Portsmouth, NH: William & Daniel Treadwell.
Camp, Claudia, V. 2000. *Wise, Strange, and Holy: The Strange Woman and the Making of the Bible*. Sheffield: Sheffield Academic Press.
Cohen, Abraham, trans. 1983. *Midrash Rabbah Ecclesiastes*. 3rd ed. London: The Soncino Press.
Cyril, Bishop of Jerusalem. 1969. *The Works of Saint Cyril of Jerusalem*, Vol. 1. Translated by Leo P. McCauley and Anthony A. Stephenson. Washington, D.C.: Catholic University of America Press.
Davis, Joseph M. 2016. "Solomon and Ashmedai (*b. Gittin* 68a-b), King Hiram, and Procopius: Exegesis and Folklore." *JQR* 106: 577–85.
Ephrem the Syrian. 1737. *Sancti Patris nostri Ephrem Syri Opera omni*, Vol. 1. Edited by J. A. Assemani. Rome.
Farrar, Frederic William. 1831. *Solomon: His Life and Times*. New York: Fleming H. Revell.
Feldman, Louis. 1976. "Josephus as an Apologist to the Greco-Roman World: His Portrait of Solomon." In Elizabeth Schüssler Fiorenza, ed., *Aspects of Religious Propaganda in Judaism and Early Christianity*. Notre Dame: University of Notre Dame Press, 69–98.
Freedman, Harry, trans. 1983. *Midrash Rabbah Genesis*. 3rd ed. London: The Soncino Press.
Fuller, Thomas. 1876. *Good Thoughts in Bad Times and Other Papers*. New York: E. P. Dutton and Company.
Ginzberg, Louis, and David Stern. 2003. *Legends of the Jews*. Philadelphia: Jewish Publication Society.
Halpern, Baruch. 2001. *David's Secret Demons*. Grand Rapids: Eerdmans.
Harkins, Angela Kim. 2016. "The Odes of Solomon as Solomonic Pseudepigrapha." *JSP* 25: 247–73.
Henry, Matthew. 1708. *Commentary on the Whole Bible*, Vol II: *Joshua to Esther*. Old Tappan, NJ: Fleming H. Revell.
Horne, Alexander. 1972. *King Solomon's Temple in the Masonic Tradition*. London: Aquarin Press.
Hughan, William J. 1895. *The Old Charges of British Freemasons: Including a Reproduction of the "Haddon Manuscript," and Particulars of All the Known Manuscript Constitutions from the Fourteenth Century*. London: George Kenning.
Isho'dad of Merv. 1963. *Commentaire d'Isho'dad de Merv sur l'Ancien Testament*, Vol. 3: *Livre des sessions*. Edited by C. van den Eynde. CSCO 230 (Scriptores Syri 97). Louvain: Secrétariat du CSCO.
Israelstam, Jacob and Judah Slotki, trans. 1983. *Midrash Rabbah Leviticus*. 3rd ed. London: The Soncino Press.
Kipling, Rudyard. 1907. *Just So Stories*. New York: Doubleday, Doran & Co.
Klutz, Todd E. 2006. *Rewriting the Testament of Solomon: Tradition, Conflict and Identity in a Late Antique Pseudepigraphon*. LSTS 52. London: T&T Clark.
Lassner, Jacob. 1993. *Demonizing the Queen of Sheba: Boundaries of Gender and Culture in Postbiblical Judaism and Medieval Islam*. Chicago: University of Chicago Press.
Lehrman, S. M., trans. 1983. *Midrash Rabbah Exodus*. 3rd ed. London: The Soncino Press.
Luther, Martin. 2016. "Marginal Gloss on 1 Kings 6:4." In Derek Cooper and Martin J. Lohrmann, *Reformation Commentary on Scripture*, Vol. 5: *1–2 Samuel, 1–2 Kings, 1–2 Chronicles*. Downers Grove, IL: IVP Academic, 294.
Matheson, George. 1902. *The Representative Men of the Bible: From Adam to Job*. New York: Hodder and Stoughton.
McCray, Walter Arthur. 1990. *The Black Presence in the Bible*. Chicago: Black Light Fellowship.

Morgan, Michael A., trans. 1982. *Sepher Ha-Razim: The Book of the Mysteries*. Chico, CA: Scholars Press.

Piscator, Johannes. 1646. *Commentarii in omnes libros Veteris Testamenti*, Vol. 2. Herbornae Nassoviorum.

Rivers, Francine. 2009. *A Lineage of Grace: Five Stories of Unlikely Women Who Changed Eternity*. Carol Stream, IL: Tyndale House.

Roberts, Francis. 1675. *Clavis Bibliorum: The Key of the Bible, Unlocking the Richest Treasury of the Holy Scriptures*. 4th ed. London: J.R. for Peter Parker.

Robinson, Charles S. 1889. *From Samuel to Solomon*. New York: American Tract Society.

Rosenberg, A. J. and Reuven Hochberg, trans. 1980. *Mikraoth Gedaloth Kings 1*. Brooklyn: The Judaica Press.

Seow, C. L. 1997. *Ecclesiastes*. AB 18C. New York: Doubleday.

Seymour, John Drelincourt. 1924. *Tales of King Solomon*. London: Oxford University Press.

Silberman, Lou H. 1974. "The Queen of Sheba in Judaic Tradition." In James B. Pritchard, ed., *Solomon and Sheba*. London: Phaidon Press, 65–84.

Simon, Maurice, trans. 1983. *Midrash Rabbah Esther and Song of Songs*. 3rd ed. London: The Soncino Press.

Slotki, Judah, trans. 1983. *Midrash Rabbah Numbers*. 3rd ed. London: The Soncino Press.

Sparks, H. F. D. 1984. *The Apocryphal Old Testament*. Oxford: Clarendon Press.

Stone, J. M. 1896. "Aspects of the Renaissance." *The Month: An Illustrated Magazine of Literature, Science, and Art* 382: 473–92.

Torijano, Pablo A. 2002. *Solomon the Esoteric King: From King to Magus, Development of a Tradition*. JSJSup 73. Leiden: Brill.

Ullendorff, Edward. 1968. *Ethiopia and the Bible*. London: Oxford University Press.

Watt, W. Montgomery. 1974. "The Queen of Sheba in Islamic Tradition." In James B. Pritchard, ed., *Solomon and Sheba*. London: Phaidon Press, 85–103.

Wesley, John. 1975. *Explanatory Notes upon the Old Testament*, Vol. 3. Reprint ed. Salem, OH: Schmul Publishers.

Whyte, Alexander. 1898. *Biblical Characters*, Vol. 2: *Gideon to Absalom*. New York: Fleming H. Revell.

CHAPTER 35

EZRA AND NEHEMIAH IN RECEPTION HISTORY

ARMIN SIEDLECKI

THE figures of Ezra and Nehemiah are perhaps the most liminal figures in the Hebrew Bible. Their position is one that occupies the boundaries between historiographic divisions (exilic and postexilic periods), geographic regions (Persia and Judah), canonical units (Historical Books and writings), and interpretative paradigms (historical leaders and socio-literary exemplars). As a result, they have commanded less attention in the history of interpretation than other heroes and heroines from the history of ancient Israel and Judah, such as Moses, Joshua, Deborah, or David. At the same time, however, their liminality also accorded them a connecting role between different divisions or categories, which could on occasion give them a surprisingly prominent position, for example in Baruch Spinoza's assertion that the Torah and other parts of the Hebrew Bible were written or edited by Ezra the scribe.[1]

35.1 EARLY INTERPRETATIONS

Given the major role Ezra and Nehemiah are said to have played in the reconstruction of the temple and the city of Jerusalem, there is relatively little mention of them in early Jewish or Christian literature. Neither of the two is mentioned in the New Testament and while there is a tradition in Jewish apocryphal literature associated with the name of Ezra or Esdras, not much is said about them outside of this body of literature. 1 Esdras (Ἔσδρας β), a Greek work (relying on Hebrew and Aramaic sources), which contains materials from 2 Chronicles and from the book of Ezra, as well as Nehemiah 8 (the public reading of the law by Ezra), makes no mention of Nehemiah. It was presumably widely read by Greek-speaking Jews in antiquity. Josephus (*Ant.* 11.1.1–11.5.6.) follows it very closely in his account of Judah's history during the Persian period, which also includes information about Nehemiah. Ben Sira in his catalogue of great Jewish figures remembers Nehemiah for rebuilding the walls of Jerusalem (49:11–13), but ignores Ezra. Perhaps even more curiously, 2 Macc. 1:18–2:15 does not mention Ezra, but speaks of Nehemiah as someone who founded a library and collected books about the kings and prophets of Israel and Judah, activities that would perhaps be more naturally associated with Ezra "the scribe." The source of this tradition is unknown and is at odds with the book of Nehemiah, which has Nehemiah rebuild the walls of Jerusalem, but does not associate him with any priestly or scribal roles. This tradition may reflect an early conflation of the figures of Ezra and Nehemiah. All this suggests that the traditions about both Ezra and Nehemiah were still very much in flux in the first and second centuries BCE, even after the text of the biblical books of Ezra-Nehemiah (as well as the text of 1 Esdras) had long been established.

This relative silence about the figures of Ezra and Nehemiah is related to the historical setting of the two characters, rather than the historical setting for the composition of the books. While many of the canonical books found their current form during or after the time described in Ezra-Nehemiah, almost all of them are set before the Persian period. The most obvious example is Daniel 7–12, which was composed in 167 BCE, but which is set during the Babylonian exile. In other words, the canon of the Hebrew Bible is not delimited by what texts existed by the fifth century BCE, but rather by their historical content. In the words of John Barton:

> If by calling books canonical we mean that they are divinely sanctioned, and so have a high claim on the reader's attention, then the "closure" of the canon must imply that no other books have this status. What is outside the canon is, comparatively, unimportant. A very early manifestation of this tendency can be seen in the "decision" (or unconscious consensus) that only two blocks of narrative material belonged in the first two parts of the canon. The whole of history to the death of Moses has pride of place, being found in the Torah; and then the subsequent history from Joshua to the Exile forms the first half of the Prophets. *There are thus two "ages" in the history of Israel (or of the human race), and narrative accounts of any events that occurred after the second age have less than "canonical" status.* This position is modified by the work of the Chronicler and by the authors of Ezra and Nehemiah (who may or may not have belonged to the same school), who continue the post-exilic history into the Persian period. But, as Josephus rightly says in *Contra Apionem* 1.37–43, "From Artaxerxes to our own times the complete history has been written, but has not been deemed of equal credit with the earlier records." Josephus says that this is "because of the failure of the exact succession of prophets"; but that is his own interpretation, and has no "official" status. The fact he is interpreting, however, is indeed a fact. *Jewish historiography dealing with the period after Ezra and Nehemiah never became canonical, whereas entirely fictitious accounts of events allegedly before them often did: Daniel, for example, in the Hebrew Bible, Judith and Tobit in the Greek.*[2]

At the same time, however, we may note a certain proliferation of apocalyptic texts associated with the name of Ezra during the Roman period. The Latin Vulgate contains a book called 4 Esdras by Jerome and typically identified as 2 Esdras in the Apocrypha of English Bibles, a work which includes at least three separate later compositions. The largest of these (2 Esdras 3–14) is a late first-century CE Jewish apocalyptic text typically called 4 Ezra in modern scholarship. This text is preceded by a third-century CE Christian apocalypse usually called 5 Ezra (2 Esdras 1–2), introduced as "the second book of the prophet Ezra the son of Seraiah, son of Azariah, son of Hilkiah, son of Shallum, son of Zadok, son of Ahitub" (2 Esdras 1:1, RSV) and comprising a vision of the son of God and the rejection by

God of the Jewish people. The final two chapters—sometimes called 6 Ezra (2 Esdras 15–16)—represent another apocalypse of distinct compositional origin.³

In 2 Esdras 14:37–48, Ezra (also named Salathiel in 2 Esdras 3–14) dictates ninety-four books to five scribes over a period of forty days.

> And when the forty days were ended, the Most High spoke to me, saying, "Make public the twenty-four books that you wrote first and let the worthy and the unworthy read them; but keep the seventy that were written last, in order to give them to the wise among your people. For in them is the spring of understanding, the fountain of wisdom, and the river of knowledge." (2 Esdras 14:45–47, RSV)

The twenty-four books correspond to the books of the Hebrew Bible, while the remaining seventy books are secret and apocryphal revelations, but the entire passage evokes a comparison between Ezra and Moses, including the numbers five (number of scribes and number of books in the Pentateuch) and forty (days of dictation and years in the wilderness). However, as Fulton following Feldman observes, "unlike Moses, to whom God dictates the law, Ezra provides the dictation to the five scribes."⁴

The ambivalence of Ezra and Nehemiah in the process of canonization is remarkable, as both figures are among the chronologically final figures described in the Hebrew Bible and among the first to be associated with the study and interpretation of scripture. They stand, so to speak, with one foot in the biblical canon and with one foot outside of it. In particular Ezra, the "scribe skilled in the Torah of Moses," was perceived as the subject of the biblical text that bears his name, but also—and perhaps foremost—as the transmitter, interpreter, and even author of scripture, as his association with later apocalyptic traditions suggests. In Judaism, this view persisted in the post-biblical period and beyond, with Ezra gaining in significance and Nehemiah's role diminishing, especially after the destruction of the second temple in 70 CE and the final loss of political independence. Ezra's status as scribe and sage was seen as the more important ideal than Nehemiah's political leadership.⁵ There is little in terms of rabbinic commentary on Ezra-Nehemiah, no midrashic collection and fewer references than to most other canonical books. On the other hand, the Talmud notes that "Ezra would have been worthy to receive the Torah had Moses not preceded him" (tSan > tSanh (2x) and bSan > bSanh; QohR 1:4),⁶ according him a higher status in terms of his priestly office.

Ezra-Nehemiah also did not attract much attention during the Middle Ages. In Christianity, medieval exegesis was dominated by the hermeneutical quadriga, the four-fold sense of scriptural meaning: literal, allegorical, moral, and anagogical (spiritual), which finds its counterpart in the Jewish *PaRDeS*: *Peshat* (the literal meaning), *Remez* (allegorical meaning), *Derash* (comparative, midrashic meaning), and *Sod* (secret meaning). In Christianity, the only complete commentary on Ezra-Nehemiah is by Bede, whose reading is intent on exposing "something deeper and more sacred in the marrow of the spiritual sense, since ... it designates the Lord himself and his temple and city, which we are."⁷ Bede's commentary also constituted much of the basis for the Ezra-Nehemiah portion of the *Glossa Ordinaria* and therefore played a normative role in the medieval Christian reading of the book. As it was almost exclusively allegorical and anagogical in its orientation, Ezra and Nehemiah themselves largely disappeared as literary or historical characters, pointing to the larger heavenly reality promised by the book. Jewish exegesis on the other hand tended to focus on the literal sense, clarifying historical details or linguistic problems associated with the Aramaic portions of the books of Ezra (4:8–6:18; 7:12–26). The image of Ezra, which continued to overshadow that of Nehemiah, basically followed earlier Rabbinic views in comparing Ezra to Moses and Aaron and characterizing him as a priest and teacher, actively involved in the writing, transmission, and interpretation of scripture.

35.2 Historical-Critical Considerations

Spinoza's idea of Ezra's authorship and redaction of significant portions of the Hebrew Bible follows from his assertion that the Pentateuch could not have been written by Moses.[8] Although he invoked Abraham Ibn Ezra (1089–1164) as the first to suggest a non-Mosaic origin of the Torah, this idea is typically seen as an early factor in the development of historical-critical scholarship and a hallmark of modern biblical studies since the eighteenth century. It is connected to the characterization of Ezra as a "scribe skilled in the Torah of Moses." His theory did not find many followers, but the textual evidence he presented to disprove Mosaic authorship laid the foundation for source criticism and the idea propagated by Jean Astruc (1684–1766) that the Pentateuch and other biblical books were made up of different compositional sources that were later redacted into a coherent whole.[9] This naturally raises the questions of the authorship of the books of Ezra and Nehemiah and to what extent Ezra and Nehemiah were themselves involved in the writing of the texts that became the books that bear their name. Nehemiah's involvement has often been assumed, since most of the book of Nehemiah is written in the form of a first-person report, which has come to be known as the Nehemiah Memoir.[10] Regarding the reason for this composition, Sigmund Mowinckel has pointed to similarities with royal inscriptions, commemorating a ruler's achievements.[11] Others have noted possible generic connections between the first-person style of the Nehemiah story and certain Psalms, in which an accused person seeks to vindicate himself before his enemies.[12] However, many agree that the closest parallel to this text is found in "late Egyptian autobiographical votive texts addressed to a deity and deposited in the temple. These are clearly apologetic and deal with the difficulties encountered and overcome in the pursuit of the author's political and religious goals. In Nehemiah's case these goals were the rebuilding of the wall and securing the defenses of Jerusalem; its repopulation; the rectification of social abuses; the support and smooth functioning of the cult; the preservation of the community's identity threatened by foreign admixture; and, in general, its regulation by law."[13]

The role of Ezra as author is somewhat more complex, since the book incorporates several different compositional sources. Much of the book of Ezra is written in the third-person and follows the style of an historical narrative, but also includes a roster of returning exiles (ch. 2), a royal decree (1:1–4; 6:3–5), and diplomatic correspondence (4:11b–16, 17–22; 5:7b–17; 6:3–12; 7:11–26). Ezra himself does not appear in the book until ch. 7 and Ezra 1–6 is typically thought to be based on a different compositional source from Ezra 7–10. Furthermore, the text is itself reflected in various compositions associated with the name Ezra. In the Septuagint, Ezra and Nehemiah are presented as one book, called Ἔσδρας Β′ (Esdras

B'). In addition, the Greek text of the Hebrew Bible contains a work called Ἔσδρας A' or I Esdras, which begins with the last two chapters of 2 Chronicles (2 Chronicles 35–36 = I Esdras 1), followed by the textual material associated with the figure of Ezra in the Masoretic Ezra-Nehemiah, albeit in a different order. The work is also called Greek Esdras and sometimes 3 Esdras, as in the Latin (Vulgate) tradition, which labels the Masoretic Ezra as 1 Esdras and Nehemiah as 2 Esdras. In addition, I Esdras 2:30b–5:6 contains textual material not found in the Masoretic tradition. Compositional primacy is generally given to Ezra-Nehemiah (Ἔσδρας B'), but there is debate about whether I Esdras is a deliberate revision of the Hebrew text[14] or represents an independent composition drawing on some of the same source materials as the Masoretic text.[15]

The overlap of 2 Chronicles and the book of Ezra (two verses; 2 Chr. 36:22–23 = Ezra 1:1–3) and even more of 2 Chronicles and 1 Esdras (two chapters; 2 Chr. 35–36 = I Esdras 1) among other factors have led to the speculation that these works have a common compositional origin. Already the Talmud (b.B.Bat. 15a) had suggested that Ezra was essentially the author of Ezra-Nehemiah and of Chronicles. A somewhat different interpretation was formulated by Leopold Zunz in the late nineteenth century, which also posited a common author behind both works, although he did not identify this author with the historical figure of Ezra, but rather with the anonymous designation of Chronicler.[16] This view subsequently became dominant in historical-critical scholarship and was questioned only in the latter part of the twentieth century. Following the work of Japhet and Williamson,[17] the idea of a common origin was generally abandoned and Ezra-Nehemiah was seen a separate and earlier text than Chronicles, although Blenkinsopp has suggested that a more nuanced view of a common authorship may be maintained "if we understand Chronistic authorship in the broad sense of a scribal school sharing the same goals, language, and religious outlook on the past."[18]

Aside from source-critical considerations, historicity was the other chief issue of historical-critical scholarship that dominated the nineteenth and twentieth centuries. In the virtual absence of contemporary witnesses outside the biblical text and only a few mentions by ancient authors, the biblical books themselves were taken as the chief source of information for the historical Ezra and Nehemiah. George Rawlinson's observation made in the late nineteenth century is perhaps characteristic in this regard: "The lives of Ezra and Nehemiah are known to us, almost wholly, from the Books that bear their names."[19] The questions that dominated the endeavor to reconstruct the historical figures of Ezra and Nehemiah were (1) the sequence of their missions and the dates of their activity, (2) the nature of their offices within the postexilic community and their relationship to the Persian court, and (3) their actions and the impact of their actions on Second Temple period Judaism. Both Ezra and Nehemiah are associated with the reign of Artaxerxes (אַרְתַּחְשַׁסְתְּא Ezra 7:1, Neh. 2:1), but it is unclear whether this refers to Artaxerxes I (465–423) or Artaxerxes II (404–359). The two characters appear to act largely independent of each other, but the book's internal chronology is inconsistent, since the story of Nehemiah is interrupted by the reappearance of Ezra in Nehemiah 8 and because both Ezra and Nehemiah deal with a crisis of mixed marriages in Judah, raising the question of whether this refers to the same historical event which subsequently became associated with both Ezra and Nehemiah independently or if there were two separate mixed marriage crises during the early Persian period. An initial reading of the text suggests that Ezra came to Jerusalem in the seventh year of Artaxerxes (I? 458 BCE; Ezra 7:7–8), and Nehemiah in the twentieth year of Artaxerxes (I? 445 BCE; Neh. 1:1; 2:1; 5:14), staying for a duration of twelve years (433 BCE), with both characters present at the public reading of the law by Ezra in 445 (Neh. 8:9). However, outside of Neh. 8:9 and 12:26, the two figures are never mentioned together. Furthermore, since Ezra was specifically commissioned by the Persian king to instruct the people of Yehud in the law of the God of heaven as well as the law of the king (Ezra 7:25–26), it is implausible that he should have waited thirteen years (from 458 to the arrival of Nehemiah in 445) to perform a public reading of the law as presented in Ezra 8, especially given the urgency with which Ezra generally approaches other matters of religious importance. A relatively common solution to this problem was to posit that the activity of Ezra should not be seen as stretching over a period of thirteen years, but that the public reading of the law occurred in 458 BCE, well before Nehemiah arrived on the scene, and that Ezra's attempt at dissolving mixed marriages (Ezra 9) was largely unsuccessful and therefore repeated by Nehemiah (Neh. 13).[20]

Ezra's role among the Jewish exiles and his office within the early postexilic community in Jerusalem are not clearly defined by the biblical text. Instead, he is introduced with a lengthy genealogy (Ezra 7:1–5), going back to Aaron, emphasizing his priestly legitimacy and authority. Added to this is his designation as a "scribe skilled in the law of Moses, which Yhwh the God of Israel had given." While he does not act as a priest in the book of Ezra, his expertise in legal matters constitutes the basis for his commission by Artaxerxes as he is charged to judge the people in Avar-Nahara (עֲבַר נַהֲרָה the province "Beyond the River"), to teach the laws of his God to those who do not know it, and to enforce both the law of [his] God and the law of the king (Ezra 7:26). While the reference to the familiarity of the scribe with the law was one of the chief reasons why Spinoza had argued for Ezra's authorship of the Torah and of other parts of the Bible, it is not entirely clear which "canon" or collection of laws is referred to here. The traditional assumption was that it referred to "the Pentateuch as a whole in more or less its present form."[21] Other suggestions regarding the nature and extent of Ezra's law include the Priestly code or the book of Deuteronomy, while more recent studies have been hesitant to try to identify a specific body of legislation.

Nehemiah is first introduced as cup-bearer (Neh. 1:11b) to the king. There is a tradition that identifies him as a eunuch in the royal court, based on the presence of a royal consort in Neh. 2:6 during his audience with the king and on the evidence of some Septuagint manuscripts.[22] This tradition is occasionally invoked in the interpretation of Neh. 6:11 ("should one like me enter the temple?") to argue that Nehemiah was prohibited from entering the sanctuary because he was a eunuch and that the plot by his enemies to lure him to the temple was not a veiled attempt to kill him, but to get him to break the law. While the evidence for this interpretation is tenuous, it adds an interesting dimension to the contrast between Nehemiah's commission by the king—which occurs in a private context as suggested by the presence of a royal consort—and Ezra's commission, which was described in terms of an official, diplomatic document.

The context of Nehemiah's commission notwithstanding, Nehemiah was sent to Jerusalem in an official capacity and Neh. 5:14 identifies him as "governor in the land of Yehud" (the Persian province of Judah). Although no specific authorization is given in the text, the rebuilding of the walls of Jerusalem are typically seen as one of Nehemiah's chief activities during his governorship (Neh. 2:11–4:23; 7:15–19). In addition, Nehemiah addresses questions of injustice and economic exploitation (Neh. 5), the repopulation of Jerusalem (Neh. 11), enforcing the observation of the Sabbath (13:15–22), and the dissolution of mixed marriages (13:23–30), a problem also addressed in the book of Ezra (Ezra 9–10). Throughout his tenure as governor, Nehemiah is opposed by neighboring leaders, in particular, Sanballat the Horonite, Tobiah the Ammonite, and Geshem the Arab.

For much of the nineteenth and twentieth centuries, Ezra and Nehemiah were seen as the chief architects of Judean reconstruction following the Babylonian exile, and the books of Ezra and Nehemiah were seen as the prime sources for this reconstruction, provided they were viewed through the lens of classical historical-critical scholarship. One notable exception to this trend was the work of C. C. Torrey, who had questioned the historical significance of the exile and the subsequent reconstruction during the Persian period, even denying the historical existence of such figures as Ezra.[23] He posited that population movements from Palestine to Mesopotamia began before the destruction of the temple in 587 BCE and continued into the Persian period and beyond, and that the idea of exile and return, as well as the theological position accorded to it, was the result of the Chronicler's fictitious propaganda against the Samaritan community north of Jerusalem and its rival sanctuary at Mount Gerizim.[24] Nevertheless, Torrey's ideas were almost categorically rejected by biblical scholars, prompting Carroll to observe that "[i]f there is a consensus among biblical scholars in this area it seems to take the form of adopting a profoundly anti-Torrey position."[25] It was not until the final decade of the twentieth century that many of the questions that dominated historical-critical scholarship receded to the background. Due to the re-evaluation of the historical reliability of the biblical sources, along with the rise of literary and sociological approaches to the text, compositional and ideological structures have become the focus of attention, as has the development of the postexilic community as a whole rather than the historical reconstruction of the book's characters. Characteristic of this shift was Lester Grabbe's call that "we should cease to write the history of Judah in the first part of the Persian period by lightly paraphrasing the book of Ezra with the occasional Elephantine papyrus tossed in plus a spoonful or two of Olmstead for leavening."[26]

35.3 Sociological, Anthropological, and Literary Impulses

As Persian-period studies began to proliferate in the past few decades, Spinoza's claim that Ezra was author of the Torah and of other parts of the Hebrew Bible perhaps finds some modified resonance in the more recent idea that the Hebrew Bible is largely a product of the Persian period. It is not the individual authorship by Ezra that is being considered, but rather the idea that the community that provides the setting for Ezra and Nehemiah and the interaction of that community with the larger Persian Empire gave rise to the current form of the Pentateuch and to much of the Hebrew Bible as we know it. An early example of this idea is Peter Frei's theory of Persian imperial authorization,[27] which argued that the codification of regional laws, such as the Torah, within the Achaemenid Empire contributed to the political consolidation of Persian power over its conquered territories. While the specifics of Frei's argument have been called into question,[28] the idea that much of the Hebrew Bible's literature in its current form has its origin during the Persian period has gained increasing support, especially since the last decade of the twentieth century.[29]

The kind of research that is conducted on Persian-period texts tends to be deliberately conscious of ideological factors and often utilizes sociological insights and methods. As a result, historical questions are formulated somewhat differently than they were by previous generations. While more recent studies do not deny the relevance of such issues as the authenticity of the commission of Ezra (Ezra 7:11–26) or the specific relationship between Ezra and Nehemiah and their historical sequence, they do not generally emphasize them. In general, there has been an overall shift away from concerns with individuals like Ezra or Nehemiah, their achievements, or even the historical origin of specific conflicts, towards social structures or constitutive elements in the religious and political infrastructure of the Persian province of Yehud. "Temple" and "Community" are two central key terms and frequent deliberate focal points for biblical studies in the Persian period. Other topics in Ezra-Nehemiah that lend themselves to social-scientific and ideological readings include the distribution of land, the relationship between the province of Yehud and the larger Persian Empire, and the dissolution of mixed marriages, which is related in two separate stories connected with Ezra and Nehemiah respectively.

The questions posed by social-scientific analyses of the text either have an historical bend or a literary-ideological orientation, largely corresponding to diachronic or synchronic readings respectively. Socio-historical approaches are diachronic insofar as they are concerned with trying to reconstruct the community that is described in the text and that gave rise to the text. Literary analyses on the other hand are synchronic and focus on textual structures, characterization, and ideological subtexts. Literary studies of Ezra-Nehemiah with a primarily aesthetic concern, such as the narratological criticism that Genesis or the Deuteronomistic History attracted in the latter part of the twentieth century, are relatively rare. One notable exception is offered by Tamara Eskenazi, whose analysis focused on issues of thematic structuring and characterization. Especially with regard to the latter, she offered some significant insights about the figures of Ezra and Nehemiah as literary characters. Rather than describing Ezra and Nehemiah as grand heroic figures, she suggests that the text actually paints a somewhat "anti-heroic" picture. "Ezra is decidedly a model figure. What he exemplifies, however, is a shift from grand and heroic exploits of the individual to another mode of effective leadership in which autocratic tactics are abnegated. One might indeed say that, in contemporary fashion, Ezra-Nehemiah develops Ezra as a protagonist who is an anti-hero."[30] Furthermore, in her reading, Nehemiah functions as a negative foil to Ezra, largely because he embraces the same autocratic tactics of leadership rejected by Ezra: "Ezra is pictured as a self-effacing teacher of Torah who diligently includes others as coworkers, delegates authority, and teaches his people to function well without him... Nehemiah, on the other hand, persistently asserts himself, amasses power, issues unilateral directives, and places himself as the indispensable center."[31]

35.4 Conclusions

Ezra and Nehemiah did not leave a large footprint on the history of interpretation. For the most part, biblical interpreters did not go far beyond what is said about them in the books that bear their names as they represent the religious and political leadership of the early postexilic community. However, in the case of Ezra the scribe, teacher, and priest, the implicit comparison with Moses and Aaron did provide the potential for interpretative trajectories that have found expression in his association with early Jewish apocalyptic literature and in his assumed authorship of some of portions of the larger biblical text. The place of Ezra and Nehemiah in the history of interpretation must be understood within the context of their own liminality and ambiguity. They belong at the same time to Persia and to Yehud/Judah. They are between exile and home. They represent continuity and new beginning. Ezra in particular is both subject and author, part of Scripture and also a teacher and transmitter of Scripture. This ambivalence is characteristic of the way Ezra and Nehemiah have been received and understood in the history of interpretation, and it makes them at the same time elusive, but also highly compelling characters.

Notes

1. Spinoza 1670: d.VIII.
2. Barton 1996: 78–79 (emphasis mine).
3. Cf. Metzger 1983: 517.
4. Pakkala et al. 2014: 631.
5. Ibid., 632.
6. Ibid., 633.
7. Bede 2006.
8. Cf. Harvey 2010: 42.
9. Astruc 1753.
10. For a comprehensive discussion of the Nehemiah Memoir, its compositional history, and its early reception, see Wright 2004.
11. Mowinckel 1923.
12. Kellermann 1967.
13. Blenkinsopp 1988: 46–47.
14. e.g. ibid., 70–71.
15. e.g. Grabbe 2004: 83.
16. Zunz 1832: 13–16; Movers 1834.
17. Japhet 1968; Williamson 1977.
18. Blenkinsopp 2009: 164.
19. Rawlinson 1890: iii.
20. See Smith 1971: 120–25. An alternative theory is offered by Kellermann, who places Ezra's arrival in Jerusalem in 398 BCE during the reign of Artaxerxes II; see Kellermann 1968.
21. Clines 1984: 182.
22. LXX Vaticanus has εὐνοῦχος (eunouchos = eunuch) for מַשְׁקֶה in Neh. 1:11b, while LXX Alexandrinus reads οἰνοχόος (oinochos = wine-bearer).
23. Torrey 1910.
24. Ibid., 321–33.
25. Carroll 1998: 73.
26. Grabbe 1991: 105.
27. Frei 1984.
28. Rütterswörden 1995; Wiesehöfer 1995.
29. Hoglund 1992; Berquist 1995; Siedlecki 2010.
30. Eskenazi 1988: 62.
31. Ibid.

Bibliography

Astruc, Jean. 1753. *Conjectures sur les memoires originaux, dont il paroit que Moyse s'est servi pour composer le livre de la Genese.* Paris: P. Guillaume Cavelier.

Barton, John. 1996. "The Significance of a Fixed Canon of the Hebrew Bible." In Magne Sæbø, C. Brekelmans, Menahem Haran, Michael A. Fishbane, Jean Louis Ska, and Peter Machinist, eds., *Hebrew Bible, Old Testament: The History of Its Interpretation.* Göttingen: Vandenhoeck & Ruprecht.

Bede. 2006. *On Ezra and Nehemiah; Translated with an Introduction and Notes by Scott Degregorio.* Translated by Scott DeGregorio. Liverpool: Liverpool University Press.

Berquist, Jon L. 1995. *Judaism in Persia's Shadow: A Social and Historical Approach.* Minneapolis: Fortress.

Blenkinsopp, Joseph. 1988. *Ezra-Nehemiah.* Philadelphia: Westminster.

Blenkinsopp, Joseph L. 2009. *Judaism, the First Phase: The Place of Ezra and Nehemiah in the Origins of Judaism.* Grand Rapids: Eerdmans.

Carroll, Robert P. 1998. "Exile! What Exile? Deportation and the Discourses of Diaspora." In Lester L. Grabbe, ed., *Leading Captivity Captive: "The Exile" as History and Ideology.* Sheffield: Sheffield Academic Press, 62–79.

Clines, David J. A. 1984. *Ezra, Nehemiah, Esther.* Grand Rapids: Eerdmans.

Eskenazi, Tamara Cohn. 1988. *In an Age of Prose: A Literary Approach to Ezra-Nehemiah.* Atlanta: Scholars.

Frei, Peter. 1984. "Zentralgewalt und Lokalautonomie im Achaemenidenreich." In Peter Frei and Klaus Koch, eds., *Reichsidee und Reichsorganisation im Perserreich.* Göttingen: Vandenhoeck & Ruprecht, 7–43.

Grabbe, Lester L. 1991. "Reconstructing History from the Book of Ezra." In Philip R. Davies, ed., *Second Temple Studies,* vol. 1: *Persian Period.* Sheffield: JSOT Press, 98–107.

Grabbe, Lester L. 2004. *A History of the Jews and Judaism in the Second Temple Period.* LSTS. Vol. 1. London and New York: T&T Clark.

Harvey, Warren Zev. 2010. "Spinoza on Ibn Ezra's 'Secret of the Twelve.'" In Michael A. Rosenthal and Yitzhak Y. Melamed, eds., *Spinoza's "Theological-Political Treatise": A Critical Guide.* Cambridge: Cambridge University Press, 41–55.

Hoglund, Kenneth G. 1992. *Achaemenid Imperial Administration in Syria-Palestine and the Missions of Ezra and Nehemiah.* SBLDS. Atlanta: Scholars.

Japhet, Sara. 1968. "The Supposed Common Authorship of Chronicles and Ezra-Nehemiah Investigated Anew." *VT* 18: 330–71.

Kellermann, Ulrich. 1968. "Erwägungen zum Problem der Esradatierung." *Zeitschrift für die alttestamentliche Wissenschaft* 80: 55–87.

Kellermann, Ulrich. 1967. *Nehemiah: Quellen, Überlieferung und Geschichte.* Berlin: Töpelmann.

Metzger, Bruce M. 1983. "The Fourth Book of Ezra." In James H. Charlesworth, ed., *The Old Testament Pseudepigrapha.* Garden City, NY: Doubleday, 517–59.

Movers, Franz C. 1834. *Kritische Untersuchungen über die biblische Chronik.* Bonn: Habicht.

Mowinckel, Sigmund. 1923. "Die Vorderasiatischen Königs- Und Fürsteninschriften." In Emil Balla, ed., *Euxaristhrion: Studien zur Religion und Literatur Des Alten und Neuen Testaments: Hermann Gunkel zum 60. Geburtstage, Dem 23. Mai 1922.* Göttingen: Vandenhoeck & Ruprecht, 278–322.

Pakkala, Julia, Sebastian Fuhrmann, Deirdre N. Fulton, Eran Viezel, David Zucker, Bernard McGinn, Andrew Rippin, et al. 2014. "Ezra (Book and Person)." In Hans-Josef Klauck, ed., *Encyclopedia of the Bible and Its Reception.* Berlin and Boston: de Gruyter, 626–41.

Rawlinson, George. 1890. *Ezra and Nehamiah: Their Lives and Times.* London: James Nisbet & Co.

Rüttersworden, Udo. 1995. "Die Persische Reichsautorisation: Fact or Fiction?" *Zeitschrift für Altorientalische und Biblische Rechtsgeschichte* 1: 47–61.

Siedlecki, Armin. 2010. "Persian Period Studies Have Come of Age." In Louis C. Jonker, ed., *Historiography and Identity (Re)Formulation in Second Temple Historiographical Literature*. New York: T&T Clark, 123–31.
Smith, Morton. 1971. *Palestinian Parties and Politics That Shaped the Old Testament*. New York: Columbia University Press.
Spinoza, Baruch. 1670. *Tractatus Theologico-Politicus*. Amsterdam: Jan Rieuwertsz.
Torrey, Charles C. 1910. *Ezra Studies*. Chicago: University of Chicago Press.
Wiesehöfer, Josef. 1995. "'Reichsgesetz' oder 'Einzelfallgerechtigkeit': Bemerkungen zu P. Frei's These von der Achaemenidischen 'Reichsautorisation.'" *Zeitschrift für Altorientalische und Biblische Rechtsgeschichte* 1: 36–46.
Williamson, H. G. M. 1977. *Israel in the Books of Chronicles*. Cambridge: Cambridge University Press.
Wright, Jacob L. 2004. *Rebuilding Identity: The Nehemiah-Memoir and Its Earliest Readers*. Berlin: de Gruyter.
Zunz, Leopold. 1832. *Die gottesdienstlichen Vorträge der Juden, historisch entwickelt. Ein Beitrag zur alterthumskunde und biblischen Kritik, zur Literatur- und Religionsgeschichte*. Berlin: A. Asher.

CHAPTER 36

THE HISTORICAL BOOKS IN THE NEW TESTAMENT

STEVE MOYISE

36.1 INTRODUCTION

No text is an island. Rather, it exists within a web or matrix of other texts, broadly conceived as a system of signs. The meaning of a text is not confined to its originating moment but changes when new texts come along and reposition it. As Mikhail Bakhtin said, "The word lives, as it were, on the boundary between its own context and another, alien context" (1991: 284). Readers must therefore make choices. Certain contexts are privileged (Deuteronomist; Chronicler; Hebrew canon; Christian Bible), while others are set aside. For example, those writing from a "Christian theology" perspective (e.g., see the volumes in the Brazos Theological Commentary on the Bible) assume that the promise of a Davidic dynasty in 2 Sam. 7:12–14 was fulfilled in Jesus Christ. This then has implications for interpreting other texts: Solomon's failure is partially explained by being led astray by foreign wives (1 Kgs. 11:4) but more fundamentally, it was because he was not the "son of David" intended by the promise. On the other hand, historical study over the last couple of centuries has made it an axiom that interpretations such as these are distortions of the original meaning and must be firmly set aside. Between these two extremes lies the relatively recent discipline of "reception history" (Lieb, Mason, and Roberts 2011). As the editors of the Blackwell Bible Commentaries series put it, the aim is to "draw on all the insights of modern research to illustrate the rich interpretative potential of each biblical book" (preface to all the volumes). For some readers, to speak of "choices" may sound too arbitrary and perhaps a reference to "commitments" would be better. The point is that meaning is not something that is simply excavated from texts; the reader must contribute something in order to have a "dialogue with the text and with the texts within the text" (Ruiz 1989: 520).

It is clear that the Historical Books of the Hebrew Bible were not as important to the New Testament authors as the Torah, Latter Prophets, and Psalms. The fifth edition of the United Bible Society's *Greek New Testament* lists only six quotations from the Historical Books (1 Sam. 13:14; 2 Sam. 7:8; 7:14; 22:50; 1 Kgs. 19:10/14; 19:18), compared with fifty-eight for Psalms, fifty-five for Isaiah, and thirty-six for Deuteronomy (the most quoted books in the NT, as indeed they are among the Dead Sea Scrolls). Nevertheless, a significant number of allusions are listed: Joshua (nineteen); Judges (nine); 1 Samuel (twenty-three); 2 Samuel (nineteen); 1 Kings (thirty-three); 2 Kings (twenty-two); 1 Chronicles (twenty); 2 Chronicles (twenty-eight); Ezra (five); Nehemiah (five). David is mentioned fifty-three times by name, followed by Elijah (twenty-nine) and Solomon (ten), and there are cameo roles for people like Rahab (Heb. 11:31; Jas. 2:25) and Elisha (Luke 4:27). Key events are mentioned, such as the fall of Jericho (Heb. 11:30), Elijah's prayer for rain (Jas. 5:18; cf. Rev. 11:6), and the building of the temple (Acts 7:45–47). The angelic announcement of Samson's birth lies behind the similar announcement of Jesus's birth (Judg. 13:3/Luke 1:31), and the multiplication of loaves by Elisha (2 Kgs. 4:43–44) has influenced the story of the feeding of the five thousand (Matt. 14:19–20). Of particular significance is the promise of a Davidic dynasty (2 Sam. 7:12–14), quoted or alluded to in Luke 1:32–33; John 7:42; Acts 2:30; 13:23; 2 Cor. 6:18; Heb. 1:5; 12:7; and Rev. 21:7.

The examination below follows these broad categories and divides the chapter into two sections: (§36.2) historical summaries; (§36.3) key people or events.

36.2 Historical Summaries

There are three historical summaries in the NT, two in Acts (7:2–53 by Stephen; 13:16–41 by Paul) and one from the author of Hebrews (Heb. 11:4–40). There are also two genealogies of Jesus (Matt. 1:2–17; Luke 3:23–38), which draw on the lists found in Chronicles (and Ruth). These have always attracted controversy since Matthew says the grandfather of Jesus was called Jacob, while Luke says he was Heli and offers a completely different set of ancestors until they agree on Zerubbabel, son of Shealtiel/Salathiel (see Ezra 3:2). Many solutions have been offered (e.g., legal adoption, levirate marriage) but none have proved convincing. Perhaps what is most surprising, given that the early church believed that membership of the people of God was not determined by Jewish heritage (Rom. 10:12), is that two of the four Gospel writers felt the need to provide Jesus with a suitable genealogy. This has brought a renewed interest in the purpose of biblical genealogies (Johnson 2002; Hood 2011).

36.2.1 The Genealogies of Jesus and Chronicles

John Nolland (2005: 70) thinks that the book of Ruth provided Matthew with the ten names between Judah and David and the formula "X fathered Y" (Gk: *egennēsen*), which he then supplemented by taking 16 names from 1 Chronicles 3. There are several points of interest. First, Salmon is said to have fathered Boaz "by Rahab" (Matt. 1:5). This cannot be the Rahab from the conquest narratives but is almost certainly intended to evoke that figure (see below). Second, the mention of Perez's brother Zerah, even though the line does not go through him, corresponds to 1 Chr. 2:4. Matthew also follows Chronicles in reminding readers of the sordid story that led to his birth (Genesis 38) by mentioning his mother Tamar. On the other hand, Chronicles is silent about the story of David and Bathsheba but

Matt. 1:6 speaks of "Solomon by the wife of Uriah." The mention of Rahab, Tamar, and (by implication) Bathsheba is noteworthy, though there is debate as to whether the emphasis is on their gender, ethnicity, or poor treatment by men. The debate also invites reflection on their role in the narratives of the Historical Books. Third, a fourth woman is mentioned by Matthew (Ruth), who is said to be the mother of Obed (as in Ruth 4:17), though Chronicles is silent on this. Gundry (1994: 15) thinks this confirms that ethnicity is the common denominator because her Moabite background is stressed in the text (1:1, 2, 6; 2:6; 4:3). However, since the fifth woman to be mentioned (Mary) is clearly a Jew, it may be that God's freedom in election is what ties them together. Fourth, the NRSV follows the earliest codices (Sinaiticus/Vaticanus) in printing "Asaph the father of Jehoshaphat" and "Amos the father of Josiah", instead of the "Asa" and "Amon" of Kings and Chronicles. This could simply be a slip but Gundry (1994: 15–16) thinks it is a deliberate attempt to evoke great figures from Israel's past (as also with "Jacob the father of Joseph the husband of Mary" in Matt. 1:16). On the other hand, translations such as the NIV and REB follow the Byzantium manuscripts and print "Asa" and "Amon" in agreement with Chronicles. Fifth, there is only one name (Uzziah) between Joram and Jotham, whereas 1 Chr. 3:11–12 has Ahaziah, Joash, Amaziah, and Azariah. Since Uzziah was the throne name of Azariah (2 Chr. 26:1), it seems likely that Matthew deliberately omitted three of the names to preserve his stated pattern of fourteen generations each between Abraham and David, David to the exile, and the exile to Jesus (Matt. 1:17). Finally, calling Zerubbabel's father Salathiel (LXX spelling) links him with the great restoration figure mentioned in postexilic texts (Hag. 1:12; Ezra 3:2; Neh. 12:1), but 1 Chr. 3:19 says that Pedaiah was his father. Is this simply Matthew's error or is there something more complicated going on between Chronicles and Ezra?

Luke shares the Chronicler's concern to take the genealogy back to Adam (but in reverse order) rather than beginning with Abraham, and he agrees with most of the names, with the exception of Admin and Arni (Luke 3:33) instead of Ram (Matt.–Aram) between Hezron and Amminidab (he also follows the LXX of Gen. 10:24 by inserting Cainan between Shelah and Arphaxad). However, his major change is that he takes the genealogy not through the kingly line of Solomon but through Nathan his brother. This line is of no interest to the Chronicler, who does not even name his sons (there is a fleeting reference in Zech. 12:12). Luke thus continues with a set of names that are otherwise unattested, though some have significant biblical connotations (Eliakim, Joseph, Judah, Levi), until he joins up with the postexilic Shealtiel and Zerubbabel—only to depart once again from Matthew. Levirite marriage is a possible solution to some of these conundrums but it is overwhelmingly clear that theological concerns govern both genealogies, as they do in Chronicles. This makes it possible (some would say probable) that small details (e.g. Asa/Asaph), often thought to be mistakes, might have held some significance for the authors/editors of all three works. It should also be noted that Sparks (2008) has argued that the emphasis on Jesus as the "son of David" in the Gospel genealogies has misled scholars into thinking that the Davidic dynasty is the focus of the genealogies in Chronicles. He thinks 1 Chronicles 1–9 is arranged as a chiasm with 1 Chr. 6:33–38 (cult officials) at the centre. Although the Chronicler clearly has a special interest in David, Solomon, and Hezekiah, the book as a whole "indicates that the kings are presented primarily in their relationship to, and their actions for or against the cult, the cultic place and the cultic officials" (2008: 365).

36.2.2 Stephen's Speech (Acts 7:2–53)

Stephen's speech takes the form of a defense against the accusation that he preaches against the "holy place and the law" (Acts 6:13). After recounting key events in the lives of Abraham, Joseph, and Moses, he speaks of how the "tent of testimony" was brought into the land and remained until the time of David, who "asked that he might find a dwelling place (*skēnōma*) for the house of Jacob" (Acts 7:46, quoting Ps. 132:5). Stephen continues: "But (*de*) it was Solomon who built a house (*oikos*) for him. Yet (*alla*) the Most High does not dwell in houses made with human hands" (Acts 7:47–48a). Albert Hogeterp takes this as a complete rejection of the temple: "Stephen's polemic implies an unparalleled contrast between the 'days of David' which were still characterised by a tent of witness and Solomon's building of a house for God" (2013: 150). Similarly, Todd Penner refers to what has just been said in Acts 7:41 ("And they made a calf in those days, and offered a sacrifice to the idol and rejoiced *in the works of their hands*") and concludes that for Stephen, the building of the temple "represents the culminating act of impiety" (2004: 317).

However, the Greek particles *de* and *alla* do not always carry adversative force in the NT and Gregory Beale thinks the point is not that Solomon committed a sin in building a fixed structure, but it was not a "sufficient fulfilment" (2004: 217) of the promise: Jesus Christ is now the locus of God's presence. On the other hand, 1 Kgs. 8:27 and 2 Chr. 2:6 make it quite clear that Solomon (as they present him) did not think God could be contained in the heavens, let alone a building, and Scott Hahn suggests that we are invited to see this as one of the "dialectical tensions within Israel's history" (2012: 10), along with the establishment of the monarchy.

36.2.3 Paul's Speech (Acts 13:16–41)

Paul's speech/sermon focuses on God's choice of the patriarchs and then the testimony about David: "I have found David, son of Jesse, to be a man after my heart, who will carry out all my wishes" (Acts 13:22). This draws on 1 Sam. 13:14 ("the LORD has sought out a man after his own heart"), but the first-person speech and the verb "to find" also suggest influence from Ps. 89:20 ("I have found my servant David"), with "son of Jesse" (1 Chr. 10:14; 29:26; Ps. 72:20) replacing "servant". The phrase "carry out all my wishes" appears to be drawn from the LXX of Isa. 44:28 (concerning Cyrus), but the Targum of 1 Sam. 13:14 replaces "a man after my heart" with "a man doing my will," which might have contributed to the connection between the two texts (so Wilcox 1965: 21–24).

Unlike Stephen's speech, Paul does not make capital out of Israel's failures but he does speak of God removing (*methistēmi*) Saul. This is arguably weaker than the *exoudeneō* of 1 Sam. 15:23, 26; and 16:1, which means "despise" or "treat with contempt." This brief account ignores the fact that Saul continued to reign until his death (1 Chr. 10:14). It is also of interest that Saul's reign is reckoned as forty years (Josephus *Ant.* 10:143 has twenty), a possible answer to the missing words in the MT of 1 Sam. 13:1.

36.2.4 Hebrews 11

Hebrews 11 differs from the two main historical summaries in that it focuses on individuals who were "commended for their faith," even though they "did not receive what was promised" (Heb. 11:40). This is seldom mentioned in the actual accounts and is probably a deduction from the author's belief that "without faith it is impossible to please God" (11:6). Thus it was by faith that "the walls of Jericho fell" and "Rahab the prostitute did not perish with those who were disobedient, because she had received the spies in peace" (11:30–31). Historical critics have traditionally viewed this as simply the author's tendentious use of sources in order to prove his point, but there are more constructive ways of viewing it. For example, Ellingworth (1993: 621) notes that the Greek word used in Josh. 6:18 for the "ban" (Heb. *ḥerem*) is *anathema*, which could imply moral criticism and hence the inhabitants' "disobedience" might have a basis in the text (albeit the LXX). More generally, the fact that Hebrew Bible narratives do not specifically mention "faith" does not mean that it was absent; it may simply have been assumed.

The author of Hebrews then notes that time would fail him to mention "Gideon, Barak, Samson, Jephthah, of David and Samuel and the prophets" (11:32). The characters are not mentioned in their biblical order and are perhaps to be read in pairs, with the superior (Gideon/Samson/David) mentioned first. The rest of the exploits could refer to a variety of individuals. Defeating lions could be a reference to Daniel, Samson, or David, and the phrase, "Women received their dead by resurrection" (11:35) most likely refers to either the widow of Zarephath (1 Kgs. 17:17–25) or the Shunammite woman (2 Kgs. 4:18–37). Although in one sense, the phrase "by resurrection" (*ex anastaseōs*) is simply a way of describing what happens in the stories, the use of *anastasis* invites a reading that links the stories with the developing concept of resurrection in later Jewish texts (e.g. Dan. 12:2), as well as Christianity.

36.3 KEY PEOPLE

36.3.1 David

Although David is mentioned by name fifty-three times in the NT, the majority of these occur in the claim that Jesus is a "son of David" (Matt. 1:20; 9:27; 15:22; 20:30), or more specifically, "*the* son of David" (Matt. 1:1; 12:23; 21:9, 15; 22:42)—that is, the Messiah (*christos*—anointed one). In Luke's nativity story, the angel tells Mary that God will give to Jesus "the throne of his ancestor David. He will reign over the house of Jacob for ever, and of his kingdom there will be no end" (1:32b–33). A little further on, Zechariah prophesies that God has "raised up a mighty saviour for us in the house of his servant David" (1:69). A Christian theology approach will naturally see such texts as providing the key to interpreting 2 Sam. 7:12–14, especially the phrase, "I will establish the throne of his kingdom *forever*." However, it should also be noted that scholars such as Richard Horsley (1993) have used the Hebrew Bible background to argue for a more "political" view of Jesus.

Thus the relationship between the texts is more "dialogical" than simply one text having mastery over the other.

There is debate as to whether Jesus's birth in Bethlehem triggered memories of David's birth place—unusually called the "city of David" in Luke 2:4, 11 but "the village where David lived" in John 7:42—or whether the prophecy of Mic. 5:2 (quoted in Matt. 2:6) gave rise to the stories. There is nothing intrinsically improbable about Jesus being born in Bethlehem but the attempts to support it by Matthew and Luke look decidedly suspicious. For example, Luke tells us that Joseph had to go to Bethlehem because "a decree went out from Emperor Augustus that all the world should be registered" (2:1) and that this happened "while Quirinius was governor of Syria" (2:2). We have no evidence of such a census and most scholars regard its stated purpose as illogical (censuses were for the purpose of taxation and so it was where you worked that was important). Matthew tells us that the magi were directed to Bethlehem by a star, but when questioned by Herod (2:4) they apparently knew all along that it had to be Bethlehem because of the prophecy of Mic. 5:2 (Moyise 2013: 45–56).

David is particularly remembered in the NT for speaking through the Spirit (Matt. 22:43; Acts 1:16; 4:25) and as the author of a number of psalms (notably Psalms 2 and 110). In the Historical Books, it is Solomon who is particularly remembered for this skill (1 Kgs. 4:32), although David is portrayed as a talented musician (1 Sam. 16:23). The one story from the Historical Books that is specifically recounted occurs in a dispute between Jesus and the Pharisees regarding the Sabbath. Jesus has apparently allowed his disciples to "pluck heads of grain" while walking through the grain fields (Mark 2:23), which the Pharisees regard as unlawful. Jesus defends their actions by referring to the incident where David ate the "bread of the presence" because the priest Ahimelech had no ordinary bread available (1 Sam. 21:1–6). Ahimelech's reasoning was that this was acceptable providing David's men had "kept themselves from women" (21:4). It is unclear what Jesus's precise reasoning is here. Ultimately, he can decide what does or does not break the Sabbath because he is "lord even of the Sabbath" (Mark 2:28). Perhaps Jesus's particular point (as told by Mark) is that like David's soldiers, they are on a mission from God and so are to be regarded as in a state of purity. The lack of clarity in Mark invites mutual reflection with the story in 1 Samuel.

36.3.2 Elijah

The complex editing of 1 Kings makes it difficult to form a coherent view of Elijah, though some literary critics have attempted it (e.g. Cohn 1982). As the text stands, Elijah boldly declares to Ahab that it will only rain at his command (17:1), takes on 450 prophets of Baal in a contest to see whose god will answer prayer (18:18–46), and then flees for his life when Jezebel vows to kill him (19:3). Despite the success indicated by 18:39 ("When all the people saw it, they fell on their faces and said, 'The LORD indeed is God; the LORD indeed is God.'"), he twice declares that he is the only Israelite to have remained faithful (19:10, 14) and asks God to end his life (19:4).

The NT is particularly interested in two aspects of this portrait: his ability to stop and start the rain and his (misguided) belief that he is the only faithful Israelite left. The first is cited by three NT authors. In the book of James, it is used to illustrate the principle that the "prayer of the righteous is powerful and effective" (5:16). The emphasis falls on the quality of Elijah's faith, for although he was a "human being like us... he prayed fervently that it might not rain, and for three years and six months it did not rain.... Then he prayed again, and the heaven gave rain and the earth yielded its harvest" (5:17–18). The reference to being a "human being like us" (*homoiopathēs*) is clearly rhetorical, suggesting that there is no reason why his readers should not pray likewise, but perhaps there is also a nod towards Elijah's subsequent frailties. The Greek word (which appears only in 4 Macc. 12:13 and Wis. 7:3 in the LXX and only here and in Acts 14:15 in the NT) means "same nature", but the KJV rendered it "subject to like passions," and more recently, the NJB has "as frail as ourselves."

Very different is Luke's reference, where the emphasis falls entirely on God. After a visit to the synagogue in Nazareth, Jesus utters what appears to be a popular proverb: "Truly I tell you, no prophet is accepted in the prophet's home town" (4:24). He then says: "But the truth is, there were many widows in Israel in the time of Elijah, when the heaven was shut up for three years and six months, and there was a severe famine over all the land; yet Elijah was sent to none of them except to a widow at Zarephath in Sidon" (4:25–26). The emphasis is not on Elijah's prayer but on God (note the passives: "was shut up"; "was sent") and in particular, on God's concern for those outside of Israel. This is confirmed by the following reference to Elisha: "There were also many lepers in Israel in the time of the prophet Elisha, and none of them was cleansed except Naaman the Syrian" (4:27). Christian interpreters are apt to pit the "universalism" of the NT against the "particularism" of the Hebrew Bible, but these references suggest a more nuanced view. Like Kings and Chronicles, the subject matter of the Gospels is primarily about Jews, making the reference to Naaman and the widow of Zarephath stand out. Chronicles is easily seen as "fiercely nationalistic" but as Hahn points out, "Israel is asked to understand itself in light of the world's beginnings and in light of the history of the world's peoples" (2012: 22). A study of the relationship between Jews and non-Jews in both sets of writings could be mutually illuminating.

Additionally, in the book of Revelation, John records a vision of two witnesses who will prophesy for 1,260 days and "if anyone wants to harm them, fire pours from their mouth" and they "have authority to shut the sky, so that no rain may fall during the days of their prophesying" (11:5–6). Elijah is not named in the text but it is clearly alluding to him. Like James, the focus is on a human attribute, but it is his authority rather than his faith that is uppermost. It is also of interest that all three passages refer specifically to "three years and six months" (or the equivalent in days), whereas 1 Kgs. 18:1 speaks only of "in the third year of the drought." It would appear that by NT times this was an established tradition, perhaps drawn from the half-week of Dan. 7:25 (almost certainly in the case of Revelation).

The second point of interest among NT texts is Elijah's misguided belief that he is the only Israelite that has remained faithful. In Romans 11, Paul is seeking to refute the suggestion that the inclusion of the Gentiles implies that God has rejected his people. He begins by citing his own background as an "Israelite, a descendant of Abraham, a member of the tribe of Benjamin" (11:1). This sounds like Paul is citing himself as evidence that God has not rejected his people, but as James Dunn (1988: 637) notes, this would be somewhat trite. It is more likely that Paul is reminding his readers of his credentials to offer authoritative interpretations of Scripture and perhaps also to pave the way for a comparison between himself and Elijah. He begins by asking whether they know the scripture where Elijah "pleads with God against Israel" (11:2) and then quotes from 1 Kgs. 19:10 in the form, "Lord, they have killed your prophets, they have demolished your altars, I alone am left, and they are seeking my life" (11:3). The complaint is repeated in 1 Kgs. 19:14 but the LXX uses a different verb for "demolished," and so Paul probably has 19:10 in mind though he abbreviates and changes it. What is of interest here is Paul's interpretation that Elijah's plea is "against (*kata*) Israel." Elijah is certainly citing their faults (despite the repentance of 1 Kgs. 18:39!) but is he asking God to judge them? Perhaps Paul took the words "and they are seeking my life" as a reference to the Israelites, though the context (1 Kgs. 19:2) firmly places the blame on Jezebel.

The story continues in 1 Kgs. 19:15–18 with Elijah commanded to anoint Hazael king of Aram and Jehu king of Israel (along with the prophet Elisha) and then a future slaughter is predicted in which anyone who "escapes from the sword of Hazael, Jehu shall kill; and whoever escapes from the sword of Jehu, Elisha shall kill" (19:17). However, the next verse shows that this is not as final as it sounds: "Yet I will leave seven thousand in Israel, all the knees that have not bowed to Baal, and every mouth that has not kissed him" (19:18). Paul cites this in Rom. 11:4: "But what is the divine reply to him? 'I have kept for myself (*katelipon*—aorist) seven thousand who have not bowed (*ekampsan*—aorist) the knee to Baal'" (11:4–5). The change of tense from "I will leave" to "I have kept" (the LXX has the strange "you have kept") is perhaps no more than Paul looking back from a distance but the effect is to heighten Elijah's misconception. He thinks he is the only faithful Israelite alive but in fact there are seven thousand who have remained faithful. It is interesting that Paul can use the idea of a remnant to emphasize both "numerical diminishment" (Rom. 9:27–28) and "the continuing fidelity of God" (Byrne 1996: 330).

The idea that Paul sees his situation as in some ways parallel to that of Elijah is further attested in Gal. 1:13–17. Here Paul talks of his exceedingly great zeal (*perissoterōs zēlōtēs*) that led him to try and destroy the church (1:13). As N. T. Wright (1996: 683–92) argues, any first-century Jew would immediately connect this "zeal" with the Phineas/Elijah tradition, but the specific reference to travelling to Arabia and then back to Damascus (1:17) clearly points to Elijah (1 Kgs. 19:8, 15). Thus Wright (1996: 687) says: "Saul, having taken the Elijah of 1 Kings 18 as his role model in his persecuting zeal, took the Elijah of 1 Kings 19 as his role model when confronted, after his zealous triumph, with a totally new reality that made him question his whole life and mission to date." Not all would agree with this interpretation of Paul (e.g. Stevens 2016), but it does raise interesting questions for our understanding of 1 Kings 18–19. Are we to understand a change in Elijah's zeal after his experience at Horeb?

The complexity of the portrait of Elijah in 1–2 Kings is also indicated by the fact that both John the Baptist and Jesus can be likened to him (Zetterholm 2010: 575–85). The identity of John is linked more closely with the interpretation of Malachi than 1–2 Kings, though some find the description of his clothing in Mark 1:6 ("Now John was clothed with camel's hair, with a leather belt around his waist") reminiscent of the description of Elijah in 2 Kgs. 1:8 ("A hairy man, with a leather belt around his waist"). However, according to Luke 4:25–26, Jesus specifically links his own ministry with that of Elijah, and his refusal to allow a would-be disciple to say farewell to his family using plough imagery is surely an allusion to Elisha's request in 1 Kgs. 19:20–21. The bringing to life of the widow's only son in Luke 7:11–15 is reminiscent of 1 Kgs. 17:17–24 (and 2 Kgs. 4:32–37), and Thomas Brodie (2004) finds numerous other parallels. Some of these are rather fanciful (see Kloppenborg and Verheyden 2014), but they open interpretive possibilities that might not otherwise have been considered.

36.3.3 Solomon

We have already noted the reference to Solomon in Stephen's speech in Acts 7 in connection with the building of the temple. There are two further references to him in the Gospels. The first is an illustration of God's care for the world, asserting that not even "Solomon in all his glory" was clothed like the "lilies of the field" (Matt. 6:28–29). This may simply be a rhetorical point but perhaps contains a criticism of Solomon's wealth, which ultimately led to his downfall (through the possession of so many wives). It is interesting that in the same context, we are told that the weight of gold that came to Solomon annually was 666 talents (1 Kgs. 10:14), a number representing supreme evil for the author of the book of Revelation (Rev. 13:18).

The second reference to Solomon is used as a judgment on the scribes and Pharisees who insist on seeing signs, whereas the "queen of the South ... came from the ends of the earth to listen to the wisdom of Solomon, and see, something greater than Solomon is here!" (Matt. 12:42; Luke 11:31). Some scholars have suggested that this latter reference might also refer to Jesus's exorcistic activity, since we know from Josephus (*Ant.* 8.42–47) that the later portrait of Solomon as an exorcist was current in the first century (Rodríguez 2010: 194). Other scholars, however, find the differences far more significant and think it unlikely that the Gospel writers had such traditions in mind (so Nyström 2016: 69–92). Given that the central claim is that "something greater than Solomon is here," it seems likely that for the sake of argument, Jesus is simply assuming the common view of Solomon's greatness (facilitated by the Chronicler) rather than the much more ambiguous view of Kings.

36.3.4 Queen of Sheba

Both Matthew and Luke pair the saying about the queen of the South with a saying about the people of Nineveh also rising up at the judgment "because they repented at the proclamation of Jonah" (Matt. 12:41; Luke 11:32). This suggests that the focus of the saying is not on Solomon but the attentiveness and commitment of the queen herself. This is, of course, the story of the visit of the queen of Sheba in 1 Kgs. 10:1–13/2 Chr. 9:1–12. Kim Huat Tan (2016: 54–57) thinks the designation "queen of the South" (otherwise only found in *T. Sol.* 19:3; 21:1, which may be Christian additions) is deliberate and mirrors the location of Nineveh in the North. He thinks the effect is to change the emphasis from wealth to universality, also indicated by the expression "from the ends of the earth." The parallel with Nineveh might suggest that Jesus is aware of the negative assessment of her found in later Jewish literature (*T. Sol*; *Tg. Sheni of Esther*; *Tg. Job*) and perhaps views her visit to Solomon as something of a conversion, as in Islamic tradition (see Lassner 1993). More generally, like the references to Naaman and the widow of Zarephath, it points to a hope for non-Jews in a text that is primarily about Jews.

36.3.5 Rahab

Along with the mention of a Rahab as the mother of Boaz in Matthew's genealogy, there are two further references in the NT. As we have seen, the author of Hebrews uses her as one of his "cloud of witnesses." Joshua does not specifically mention that her actions were the result of faith, but it is a reasonable deduction from Josh. 2:11 ("The LORD your God is indeed God in heaven above and on earth below"). Interestingly, in keeping with the purposes of James, he cites her as an example of good works rather than faith: "Likewise, was not Rahab the prostitute justified by works when she welcomed the messengers and sent them out by another road" (Jas. 2:25). Both texts highlight her hospitality, and this is perhaps what connects her with Abraham and perhaps also why James changed "spies" to "messengers."

36.3.6 Elisha

We have already noted Elisha's healing of Naaman the Syrian, and it is also probable that the feeding miracles in the Gospels have been influenced by 2 Kgs. 4:42–44, where Elisha feeds a crowd of one hundred people with twenty barley loaves. Note the following parallels in the stories: (1) a man/boy has a small number of loaves; (2) Elisha/Jesus commands that the loaves be used to feed a large crowd; (3) the question is raised as to how such a small quantity can feed so many; (4) the command is reiterated and the people are fed; (5) there is some left over. It is also clear that the feeding stories in the Gospels evoke the last supper narrative (taking... giving thanks... blessing... distributing), and this could invite a sacramental understanding of the Elisha feeding. It was not just a one-off miracle but symbolized God's provision, as in the wilderness wanderings.

36.3.7 Jezebel

The name "Jezebel" only occurs once in the NT and is the name given by the author of the book of Revelation to a false prophet in the church at Thyatira: "But I have this against you: you tolerate that woman Jezebel, who calls herself a prophet and is teaching and beguiling my servants to practice fornication and to eat food sacrificed to idols" (Rev. 2:20). Now it is possible that this irritating (to John) prophetess happened to be called Jezebel but most commentators regard it as a deliberate attempt to discredit her by linking her with the "Phoenician wife of Ahab who programmatically led the northern kingdom into Baal worship and sorcery" (Osborne 2002: 155). John accuses her of "beguiling my servants to practice fornication" but in the light of the Hebrew Bible allusion (cf. 2 Kgs. 9:22), this is probably a reference to apostasy. Thus the insult only works if the reader imports some of the connotations from the Hebrew Bible.

36.3.8 The Births of Samson and Samuel

It is not surprising that the birth of Jesus is told in a manner that evokes a number of Hebrew Bible texts. After all, the Gospel writers had to show that the revelation of God's plan in Jesus was in continuity with the promises made to Israel. What is surprising is that the announcement to Mary in Luke 1:31 ("And now, you will conceive in your womb and bear a son") and her consequent song of joy in Luke 1:46–52 ("My soul magnifies the Lord, and my spirit rejoices in God my Saviour.... He has brought down the powerful from their thrones, and lifted up the lowly") evoke the announcement to Samson's mother in Judg. 13:5 ("for you shall conceive and bear a son") and Hannah's prayer in 1 Sam. 2:1, 8 ("My heart exults in the LORD; my strength is exalted in my God .... He raises up the poor from the dust; he lifts the needy from the ash heap"). What links the two Hebrew Bible passages is the nazirite vow of Num. 6:2 (cf. Judg. 13:5; 1 Sam. 1:11), and Matt. 2:23 applies a wordplay to link this with the place where Jesus was raised—*Nazaraios* (Menken 2004: 161–77). However, it is not Jesus who exhibits such ascetic qualities in the Gospels but John the Baptist (Luke 7:33–34), whose mother (Elizabeth) shares the misery of childlessness with Hannah (Luke 1:25/1 Sam. 1:10–11). Further, the incident of the boy Jesus considering the temple as his true home (Luke 2:41–52) echoes the story of Samuel (Murphy 2010: 16–17). Thus a complex intertextuality exists between the various miraculous births in the Hebrew Bible (including the famous Isa. 7:14 text quoted in Matt. 1:23), inviting mutual interpretation.

36.3.9 Megiddo

There is an altogether different type of allusion in Rev. 16:16, which describes an apocalyptic battle at "Harmagedon" (16:16). Since the author specifically tells his readers that this is a Hebrew word, they are probably to infer that "Har" means "mountain," leaving the "magedon" as a possible allusion to "Megiddo," where King Josiah died (2 Kgs. 23:30). If this is the case, then it was probably prompted by the reference to mourning "in the plain of Megiddo" in Zech. 12:11.

36.4 Conclusion

Though the NT authors were more interested in the Torah, Latter Prophets, and Psalms, the use of the Historical Books does have a number of points of interest. The references to David, Solomon, and the temple, as well as Elijah, Elisha, and Rahab, invite reflection on those narratives. The ongoing struggle to understand the genealogies in Matthew and Luke continues to spark interest in the genealogies of Chronicles. Some of the interest in the NT use of the Historical Books stems from a Christian theology approach and a whole commentary series (Brazos Theological Commentary on the Bible) is dedicated to it. For others, the interest is in a more general reception history (see Blackwell Bible Commentaries), where later interpretations represent something of the "semantic potential" of the text. This chapter has demonstrated some of the insights that follow from such approaches.

Bibliography

Bakhtin, Mikhail M. 1991. *The Dialogic Imagination*. Austin: University of Texas Press.
Beale, Gregory K. 2004. *The Temple and the Church's Mission: A Biblical Theology of the Dwelling Place of God*. Downer's Grove, IL: IVP Academic.
Brodie, Thomas L. 2004. *The Birthing of the New Testament: The Intertextual Development of the New Testament Writings*. Sheffield: Sheffield Phoenix Press.
Byrne, Brendan. 1996. *Romans*. Sacra Pagina. Collegeville, MN: Liturgical.
Cohn, Robert L. 1982. "The Literary Logic of 1 Kings 17–19." *JBL* 101: 333–50.
Dunn, James D. G. 1988. *Romans 9–16*. WBC 38. Dallas: Word.

Ellingworth, Paul. 1993. *The Epistle to the Hebrews: A Commentary on the Greek Text*. Grand Rapids: Eerdmans/Carlisle: Paternoster.

Gundry, Robert H. 1994. *Matthew: A Commentary on His Handbook for a Mixed Church under Persecution*. 2nd ed. Grand Rapids: Eerdmans.

Hahn, Scott W. 2012. *The Kingdom of God as Liturgical Empire: A Theological Commentary on 1-2 Chronicles*. Grand Rapids: Baker Academic.

Hogeterp, Albert I. A. 2013. "King Solomon in the New Testament and Jewish Tradition." In J. Verheyden, ed., *The Figure of Solomon in Jewish, Christian and Islamic Tradition: King, Sage and Architect*. Leiden: Brill, 143-64.

Hood, Jason B. 2011. *The Messiah, His Brothers and the Nations: Matthew 1.1-17*. LNTS. London: T&T Clark.

Horsley, Richard A. 1993. *The Liberation of Christmas: The Infancy Narratives in Social Context*. New York: Continuum.

Johnson, Marshall D. 2002. *The Purpose of the Biblical Genealogies with Special Reference to the Setting of the Genealogies of Jesus*. 2nd ed. Eugene, OR: Wipf and Stock.

Kloppenborg, John S. and Joseph Verheyden, eds. 2014. *The Elijah-Elisha Narrative in the Composition of Luke*. LNTS. London: Bloomsbury.

Lassner, Jacob. 1993. *Demonizing the Queen of Sheba: Boundaries of Gender and Culture in Postbiblical Judaism and Medieval Islam*. Chicago: The University of Chicago Press.

Lieb, Michael, Emma Mason, and Jonathan Roberts, eds. 2011. *The Oxford Handbook of the Reception History of the Bible*. Oxford: Oxford University Press.

Menken, Maarten J. J. 2004. *Matthew's Bible: The Old Testament Text of the Evangelist*. Leuven: Leuven University Press/Peeters.

Moyise, Steve. 2013. *Was the Birth of Jesus According to Scripture?* London: SPCK. Eugene, OR: Wipf and Stock.

Murphy, Francesca Aran. 2010. *1 Samuel*. Brazos Theological Commentary on the Bible. Grand Rapids: Brazos Press.

Nolland, John. 2005. *The Gospel of Matthew*. The New International Greek Testament Commentary. Grand Rapids: Eerdmans.

Nyström, Jennifer. 2016. "Jesus' Exorcistic Identity Reconsidered: The Demise of a Solomonic Typology." In Tobias Hägerland, ed., *Jesus and the Scriptures*. Library of New Testament Studies. London: Bloomsbury T&T Clark, 69-92.

Osborne, Grant R. 2002. *Revelation*. Baker Exegetical Commentary on the New Testament. Grand Rapids: Baker Academic.

Penner, Todd. 2004. *In Praise of Christian Origins: Stephen and the Hellenists in Lukan Apologetic Historiography*. Emory Studies in Early Christianity. New York: T&T Clark.

Rodríguez, Rafael. 2010. *Structuring Early Christian Memory: Jesus in Tradition, Performance, and Text*. Library of New Testament Studies. London: T&T Clark.

Ruiz, Jean-Pierre. 1989. *Ezekiel in the Apocalypse: The Transformation of Prophetic Language in Revelation 16:17-19:10*. Frankfurt: Peter Lang.

Sparks, James T. 2008. *The Chronicler's Genealogies: Towards an Understanding of 1 Chronicles 1-9*. AcadBib. Atlanta: SBL.

Stevens, Chris S. 2016. "Paul, the Expected Eschatological Phinehas-Elijah Prophet Law-Giver." In Stanley E. Porter and David I. Yoon, eds., *Paul and Gnosis*. Pauline Studies 9. Leiden: Brill, 80-104.

Tan, Kim Huat. 2016. "The Queen of Sheba and the Jesus Traditions." In Tobias Hägerland, ed., *Jesus and the Scriptures*. Library of New Testament Studies. London: Bloomsbury: T&T Clark, 48-68.

Wilcox, Max. 1965. *The Semitisms of Acts*. Oxford: Clarendon Press.

Wright, N. T. 1996. "Paul, Arabia, and Elijah (Galatians 1:17)." *JBL* 115: 683-92.

Zetterholm, Magnus. 2010. "The Books of Kings in the New Testament and the Apostolic Fathers." In A. Lemaire and B. Halpern, eds., *The Book of Kings: Sources, Composition, Historiography and Reception*. VTSup 129. Leiden: Brill, 561-84.

Ancient Sources Index

Hebrew Bible/Old Testament
Genesis
1:1–2 Kgs 25:30 347
1:1–Num 36:13 347
1:1–50:26 347
1–11 323, 334, 335
1–3 335
1 228, 335
1:1–2:3 346, 347
1:26–28 225
2:4–50:26 347
2:4–37:2 346
2 335
3 334, 335
3:20 220
4:25–5:11 220
5 382
6:11 285
10 382
10:10 323
10:24 539
11 323, 382
11:4 323
11:8 323
11:9 323
12–50 334
12:1–3 334
12:7 176
13:7 82
13:14–17 191
14:18 330
15:7 176
16:12 396
17 382
17:6 328
17:7–8 79
17:8 176
17:16 328
17:23–27 246
18:23–32 349
22 382
23:7–9 191
25 382
32 493
32:28 79
35 382

35:11 328
36 382
37–50 79, 317
37:2 351
38 382, 538
38:21–22 222
39:17 102
46 382
48 382
49 382
49:13 396

Exodus
1:1–Num 36:13 347
1:1–15:27 347
1–15 346
1 317
1:15 102
2 314, 317
2:6–7 102
2:16 330
3:1 330, 498
3:2 324
3:8 176
12 246
12:1–28 257
12:3–4 257
12:14–28 257
12:38 88
12:43–49 385
15 216, 396
15:1 396
15:3 295
15:20–21 396
16:1–Deut 1:3 346
16 346
17 447
17:14 400
18:1 330
19 346
19:6 328, 330
19:22 330
19:24 330
20:3 318
20:24–26 249
22:13 318

Exodus (Continued)
23:14–17 257
23:17 255
23:21 447
24:7 400
25–40 331
25 185
25:40 448
28–29 330
28:21–29 185
29 330
30:12–13 185
32 323, 335
32:4 323
32:11–13 445
34:13 315
34:14 318
34:18–26 257
34:23 255
35:4 185
35:20–29 185
35:25–27 224
36:3–7 185
39:30 400

Leviticus
7:18 245
8–10 330
10:1 335
10:10 330
16:2 331
16:3 55
17–26 330
19:17 245
19:31 223
23:4–8 385
23:33–43 385
26:27–33 313

Numbers
4:21–7:89 470
5:23 400
6:2 547
6:24–26 248
12 222
13 192
13:16 447
13:33 440
14:11–36 349
14:24 192
21:14 400
21:17–19 396
23:9 83
23:21 328
24:7 328
25:1 223
27 217
27:4 216

27:7 217
27:16–25 385
27:18–20 203
29:12–38 385
32:1–24 192
32:12 192
33 441
36 216, 217

Deuteronomy
1:1–33:29 347
1:1–2:15 428
1:1 347
1:1–5 347
1:3 351
1:5 309
1:22–40 429
1:29–31 428
1:36 192, 428
1:37 428
2:14–15 429
3:12–20 192
4 271
4:7–8 271
4:15–20 271
4:25–30 271
4:25–28 426
4:28 271
4:29–31 307
4:32–40 271, 281
4:33 271
4:34–35 271
4:34 271
4:35 271
4:36 274
4:37–38 271
4:37 270
4:39 271
4:44 271
5:7 318
6 229
6:4–5 313, 315, 317
6:5 313
7 291
7:1–10 426
7:1–6 315, 387
7:1–5 292
7:1–4 407
7:3–4 297
7:4 414
7:5 315
7:6 331
7:7–11 281
7:7–9 270
7:7–8 288
7:8–9 271
7:10 430
7:22–26 315

8:11–20 426
9:1–6 315
9:4–7 426
9:8–10:11 428
9:8–14 426
9:12–14 426
9:13–14 428
11:16–17 426
12 159, 274, 314, 315
12:2–18 314
12:2–7 314, 315, 316
12:2–4 314
12:3 315
12:4–7 314
12:4 316
12:8–12 314, 315
12:8–10 314
12:8 315
12:9–10 315
12:9 315
12:10 315
12:11–12 314
12:13–18 314
12:13–14 314
12:13 314
12:14 316
12:17 520
12:28 314
12:29–32 296
12:29–31 314, 315
14:2 331
14:21 331
16 382
16:1–17 257
16:1–8 385
16:16 255
16:18 328
16:19–17:1 515
17 328, 329, 348, 349, 350, 351
17:9 328, 330
17:14–20 100, 197, 312, 327
17:14–15a 349
17:14b 349
17:15–20 188
17:15 197, 327
17:15b 349
17:16–17 196, 349, 515
17:16 515
17:17 328, 515
17:18–20 328
17:18 196
17:19–20 196
18 330
18:1 330
18:11 223
18:10–12 243
20:16 82

20:18 82
21:10–14 216
23:3–5 385
23:4–8 316
23:10 316
23:14b–15 316
23:17 222
24:8 330
25:19 419
26:14 246
26:19 331
27:5–6 516
27:9 330
28–30 202
28 306, 316
28:3–7 308
28:9 331
28:15–68 426
28:21–22 316
28:25 316
28:36 328
28:38 316
28:41 387
28:45–68 307
28:63–68 308
28:63–64 387
28:64–65 316
28:65 315
29 429
29:17–20 [18–21] 429
29:21–27 [22–28] 429
30 418
30:1–10 307, 427
30:12 350
31–34 400
31–32 400
31 446
31:19 400
31:20 176
31:22 400
31:30 400
32 446
32:36–39 271, 272
32:36–42 281
32:44 400
33 351
33:5 328
34–1 Sam 7 347
34:1–2 Kgs 25:30 347
34:1–1 Sam 7:17 347
34:1–Judg 1:26 346, 347
34 81, 304, 317, 347
34:9 203, 346, 449
34:10–12 317, 346

Joshua
1–12 81, 305, 441
1–5 82

Joshua (Continued)
1 18, 305, 446
1:1–9 309, 315, 346
1:1 344, 447
1:2–3 176
1:2 315
1:6 309
1:7–9 309
1:7 309
1:11 411
2–6 291
2 216, 217, 415
2:1 337, 414, 428
2:2 337
2:3–7 414
2:3 216
2:8–14 414
2:9–10 16
2:11 546
3–13 413
3 413
4:12 192
5:1–9 217
5:1 413
5:2–7 414
5:5 16
5:6 176
5:13–15 292
5:15 331
6–12 443
6–8 445
6–7 291
6 82, 83, 292, 335
6:17 415
6:18 541
6:19 331
6:21 411
6:22–25 415
6:22 415
6:23 415
6:25 216, 415
6:26 444
7–9 82
7–8 83
7 217, 335, 382
7:6 261
7:7–15 439
7:16–18 177
7:26 13
8:29 13
8:32 400
9–10 83
9 292, 430
9:1–2 16
9:3–23 192
9:7 397
10–12 445

10–11 288, 295, 345
10 82, 291, 437
10:1–2 16
10:12–13 13
10:18 284
10:20–26 284
10:28–42 413
11 82
11:1 16
11:10 82
11:16–23 84
11:16 412
11:21–22 440
11:23 315
12–21 345
12 305
13–22 217
13–21 82
13–19 305, 315, 443, 445
13 382, 439
13:1–6 309
13:1 412
13:23 309
14:6–14 192
14:15 293
15–19 14
15–17 382
15:9 52
15:16–17 217
15:20–62 14
17–21 330
17:3 217
17:14–18 192
17:18 192
18:7 330
18:21–28 14
18:21–24 14
19 382
19:49–50 192
20 14
20:1 203
20:6 185
21 382
21:34–45 309
21:42–45 315
21:43–45 315–316
21:44–45 293
22–24 82
22 223
22:3 192
23–24 292, 445
23 9, 18, 305, 313, 315
23:1–2 316
23:1 315
23:3 316
23:9 315, 316
23:11–13 308

23:11 316
23:14b–16a 316
23:15–16 308
24 202, 305
24:1–13 394
24:2 204
24:15 193
24:16–18 192
24:19 331
24:26–27 400
24:26 400
24:27 400
24:29–30 315
24:29 203
24:30 13
24:32 13

Judges
1–16 478
1–2 382, 430
1 14, 217, 412
1:1–26 345
1:1–5 13
1:1 344, 429
1:15 13
1:27–1 Sam 7:17 347
1:27–23:6 351
2:1–5 305, 308, 429
2:1 466
2:2 315
2:5–3:6 311
2:6–3:6 306
2:8–9 315
2:11–3:6 305, 309
2:11 467
2:20–21 309
2:22 222
2:23 309
3–16 96
3 84, 382
3:7–11 195
3:7 467
3:9 348, 466
3:11 467
3:12–30 195
3:12 567
3:15 348, 466
3:30 467
4–5 84, 195, 216, 342, 452, 453, 456
4 395, 452, 454
4:1 467
4:3 348
4:4–5 459
4:4 456
4:5–6 194
4:5 222, 457
4:8–9 452
5 13, 84, 215, 216, 393, 395, 396, 397, 399, 452, 458, 463

5:1 345, 396
5:2–31 345
5:3 396
5:4–5 396
5:6 195
5:7 452, 455
5:9 463
5:10–11 396
5:11 396
5:12 396, 457
5:16–18 396
5:30 216, 462
5:31 467
6–8 84, 198
6:1 467
6:6 195
6:7–10 18, 204, 308
6:7 348
6:11–24 13
6:14 466
6:30–31 315
7:1 13
7:4–7 13
7:25 13
8–9 197
8:2 13–14
8:14 400, 401
8:21 14
8:22–23 96, 397
8:22 466
8:23 349
8:27 197
8:28 467
8:32 13
9 84, 96, 351, 397, 399
9:7–20 14
9:7–15 188, 397
9:7 397
9:8–15 96
9:15 197
9:16–21 397
9:22–55 397
9:24 285
10:1–5 14, 96
10:1 466
10:2 466
10:3 466
10:6–12:6 195
10:6 345, 467
10:10 348
10:11–14 18
11–12 84
11:12–27 394
11:34 216
11:40 216
12:1–6 195
12:7–15 14

Judges (Continued)
12:7 13
12:8–15 96
13–16 84, 195, 345, 348, 466, 467, 479
13 351, 468
13:1 467
13:2–5 468
13:2 345, 469
13:3–5 469
13:3 538
13:5 466, 546, 547
13:6 469
13:8 469
13:9–10 469
13:11 469
13:17 469
13:24 470
13:25 471
14–16 97
14–15 471
14 471
14:4 472
14:6 472
14:9 480
14:14 473
14:18 474
15 474
15:1–2 474
15:4–45 474
15:15–17 475
15:18 475
15:19 13
16 336
16:1 476
16:3 476
16:4 476
16:5 477
16:6 477
16:8 479
16:9 477
16:12 477
16:14 477
16:16–17 477
16:16 475
16:17 477
16:18 420
16:19 475, 477
16:20 477
16:21 215
16:31 13, 467
17–21 97, 329
17–18 84
17:1 345
17:6 97, 194
17:7 345
17:16 177
18:1 97, 194
18:27–28 18
19–21 84, 204, 215, 345
19 406, 409
19:1 97, 194, 345
19:25 97
20:8 194
20:46 195
21:21 216
21:25 177, 188, 194, 293

Ruth
1:1 177, 345, 539
1:2 539
1:6 539
2:6 539
4:3 539
4:17–22 345
4:17 539
4:17b–22 382

1 Samuel
1–15 339
1–12 341
1–8 312, 343
1–3 345
1–2 215, 217
1 97, 98, 341
1:1 209
1:3 55
1:10–11 547
1:11 547
1:18 246
1:23 53
1:24 55
1:25 55
2–4 97
2:1–10 216, 345, 464
2:1 546
2:1a 345
2:2 331
2:7 546
2:11–15 348
2:11 55
2:22 52
2:27–36 18, 205
3 204, 330–331
3:7–8 348
4:1–7:2 16
4–6 348
4:9 214
4:15 52
4:18 345
4:21 215
6:20 331
7 102, 345, 348, 349, 351
7:4 345
7:6 345
7:8–9 351

ANCIENT SOURCES INDEX 555

7:13 351
7:13b 348
7:15 97
8–2 Kgs 25 347
8:1–2 Kgs 25:30 347
8–12 205, 346, 347, 348, 349, 350
8:1–12:25 347
8 98, 197, 202, 205, 329, 348, 349, 483
8:1–22 416
8:1–3 195
8:1 348
8:4 416
8:5 195, 329
8:5b 349
8:6–22 309
8:7 329, 348
8:7–8 347, 348
8:8a 348
8:9 348, 349
8:11–17 98, 100, 179, 188, 196
8:13 224
8:18 196
8:19–20 196
8:21 348
8:22 348, 349
9–1 Kgs 2 98
9–12 343, 483
9–11 341
9–10 309, 351
9:1–10:16 98, 205
9 348
9:1 102, 345
9:2 98
9:15–9:17 348
9:16 348
9:21 98, 102
10–11 54
10 54, 102
10:2 13
10:3–4 102
10:5 348
10:6–7 348
10:11–12 14, 397
10:17–27 98, 205
10:18–19 347, 348
10:19 348
10:20 102
10:21–22 98
10:23 98
10:24 496
10:25 102, 196, 400
10:27 102, 348
11 98, 102, 103
11:4 13
11:5 102
11:6–8 98
11:12–14 102

12 9, 18, 205, 305, 309, 313, 342
12:11 480
12:12 347, 348
12:13 496
12:14–15 196
12:14 348
12:16–20 349
12:17 347, 348
12:20 347, 348
12:21–25 348
13:1–2 Kgs 25:30 347
13–15 341
13–14 98, 205, 484
13 336, 348
13:1 103, 346, 487, 540
13:3 348
13:4–7 102
13:7–15 98
13:13–14 496
13:14 513, 537, 540
13:17–18 102
13:19–22 102
14:2 13
14:4–5 13
14:11 102
14:47–52 98, 346
14:52 103
15 98, 205, 336, 348, 484
15:23 496, 540
15:26 496, 540
15:28 496
16–1 Kgs 2 500
16–2 Sam 4 96
16–2 Sam 5 99, 105
16–2 Sam 6 497
16–31 205
16–18 343, 503
16 98, 205, 399, 484
16:1–13 99, 102
16:1 540
16:11 497
16:12 500
16:13 499
16:15–23 343
16:16–23 498
16:18 500
16:19 16, 343
16:21 499
16:23 542
16:43 399
17–18 51, 350
17 350, 484
17:4 53
17:12–31 343, 350
17:25–27 497
17:28 497, 499
17:32 498

1 Samuel (Continued)
- 17:37 498, 499
- 17:42–43 499
- 17:45–47 499
- 17:55–58 343
- 18 343, 350
- 18:1–4 103
- 18:1 499
- 18:6–10 216
- 18:8 499
- 18:10 498
- 18:16 499
- 18:18 497
- 18:20 499
- 18:29 499
- 19–26 484
- 19:24 14
- 20 99, 103
- 20:17 499
- 20:23 53
- 20:25 102
- 20:30 499
- 20:32 55
- 20:34 499
- 20:41 499
- 21 331
- 21:1–6 542
- 21:4 542
- 21:8 103
- 22:1–2 104
- 22:2 500
- 22:6 13
- 22:7 102, 103
- 23:1–29 13
- 23:1 102
- 23:14–18 103
- 24 99, 497
- 24:6 500
- 24:7 500
- 24:11 500
- 24:21 500
- 25 99, 224
- 26 99, 497
- 26:1 13
- 26:3 13
- 26:9 500
- 26:11 500
- 26:16 500
- 26:23 500
- 27–31 484
- 27 99, 104, 500
- 28 205, 223, 484
- 30 297
- 30:4 499
- 30:26–30 104
- 31 96, 103, 218, 357, 382, 484
- 31:11–13 13, 103

2 Samuel
- 1–8 205
- 1 99, 104
- 1:1 344
- 1:14 500
- 1:16 500
- 1:17 498
- 1:18–27 13, 345
- 1:18 400
- 1:18a 345
- 1:19–27 216
- 1:23 499
- 2–4 103, 310
- 2:9 103
- 2:12–32 13
- 3 104
- 3:7 218
- 3:10 104
- 3:32 13
- 3:33 216
- 3:36 500
- 4 104
- 4:2–3 103
- 4:12 13
- 5–10 382
- 5:1–3 54
- 5:2 16
- 5:4–5 54
- 5:4 105
- 5:6–10 54
- 5:6–9 104
- 5:8 14
- 6 96, 99, 104, 205
- 6:1–19 16
- 6:2 52
- 6:5 498
- 6:14 498
- 6:16 224, 498
- 6:20 498
- 6:21 498
- 6:22 498
- 6:23 17
- 7–1 Kgs 2 497
- 7 18, 96, 99, 209, 307, 316, 333, 350, 501, 516
- 7:1 315
- 7:5–16 499
- 7:8 498, 537
- 7:9 497
- 7:11 315
- 7:12–16 209
- 7:12–14 537, 538, 541
- 7:14 537
- 7:16 209, 496
- 7:18–29 499
- 7:18 497
- 7:22–29 272, 279, 280, 281
- 7:22–23 270, 271, 272

7:23 270
7:24 270, 281
8 96, 99
8:2 500
8:7 52
8:15 500
8:16–18 14, 104
9–20 16, 205, 310, 345
9 98, 99, 499
9:7 103
9:9 103
9:13 17
10–12 205
10 99
11–1 Kgs 2 99
11–20 96
11–12 99
11 104, 218
11:14 401
11:15 401
11:25 498
11:26 218
11:27b 196
12–1 Kgs 11 511
12 104, 209
12:1–6 498
12:10 218
12:12 498
12:13–23 295
12:13 522
12:16 499
12:21–22 499
12:24 17, 218
12:25 522
12:26–31 99
13–20 99
13 104, 218, 382
13:3–5 224
13:21 499
13:36 499
13:37 499
14 99, 224
14:17 500
14:33 499
15–20 104
15 498
15:30 499
15:31 499
16:1–14 98
16:5–13 497, 500, 513
16:6 58
16:20 224
16:21 217
16:22 218
17 99
17:11 104
18 99

18:18 13
19 104
19:1 499
19:3–5 499
19:6–9 499
19:16–23 513
19:17–31 98
20 216, 224
20:19 455
20:23–26 14, 104
21–24 16, 99
21 218
21:2 103
21:7 499
21:12–14 13
21:14 16
21:15–22 14, 104
22:1–23:7 216
22 501
22:1–2a 345
22:1 498
22:2b–51 345
22:18 498
22:49 498
22:50 537
22:51 499
23–24 382
23:1 500
23:2 499
23:8–38 104
23:8–39 14
24 13, 96, 210, 341
24:10 499
24:15 104
24:17 498, 499
24:24 184
24:25 16

1 Kings
1–11 99
1–2 16, 96, 99, 100, 205, 218, 310, 341, 345
1:1–2:11 56
1 210
1:6 18
1:8 98
1:35–37 309
2–11 60
2 99, 335
2:1–4 209
2:3–4a 309
2:3 500
2:8–9 513
2:8–3:9 98
2:10 500
2:11 54, 105
2:12–21:29 56–57
2:12 17
2:35a–o 60

1 Kings (Continued)
2:35c 60
2:35f 60
2:35g 60
2:35h 60
2:36–46 98, 513
2:46–47 58
2:46 17, 100
2:46a–l 60
2:46d 61
2:46g 60
3–11 17, 511, 519
3–10 60, 383
3 100, 215, 512, 515, 519
3:1 335
3:1a 60
3:1b 60
3:4–15 100
3:4–5 249
3:7 512
3:13b 58–59
3:14 58–59
3:16–28 17, 100, 512
4 100
4:1–19 105
4:2–6 14, 15
4:7–19 14, 178, 516
4:7 181
4:13 57
4:20–21 [Heb. 4:20–5:1] 415–416
4:20 60
4:25 416
4:32 513, 542
4:33 [Heb. 5:13] 513
5 100, 516
5:1–10 [Heb. 5:15–24] 516
5:1a 60
5:2–4 60
5:3 516
5:4 58
5:5 60, 104
5:6 60
5:8 60
5:12 [ET 4:32] 397
5:13–18 [Heb. 5:27–32] 516
5:14 60
5:15–9:14 60
5:15–32 174, 181
5:18 315, 516
5:27–32 181
5:31–32a 60
6–10 329
6–9 242
6–8 331
6–7 100, 105
6 57, 516
6:1 60, 80, 350

6:1b 60
6:5 57
6:7 516
6:10 57
6:11–14 57–58, 60
6:11–13 308
6:15 57
6:18–19 57
6:37–38a 60
6:38–7:1 516
6:38 518
6:38b 60
7:1–12 60
7:1–2 276
7:2–8 15
7:3 276
7:5 518
7:30–32 57
7:38 57
7:51 60
8 9, 18, 100, 271, 274, 275, 277, 305, 316, 360, 513
8:1–6 61, 275
8:2 518
8:9 282
8:12–13 13, 281
8:12–50 275
8:13 273, 275
8:14–21 316
8:14 276
8:15–40 276
8:15–26 209
8:16 56, 58, 315
8:21 360
8:22–53 271, 274
8:22–40 316
8:23–26 272
8:23 271, 275, 282
8:23a 275
8:27–30 274, 275
8:27 275, 540
8:28–30 282
8:29 59
8:30 274
8:31–32 274
8:32 274
8:33–34 274
8:33–40 316
8:33 316
8:34 274
8:35–36 274
8:35 316
8:36 274
8:37–40 274
8:37 279, 282, 316
8:38 274
8:39 274
8:41–50 261

8:41–45 318
8:41–43 274
8:41–42 58–59, 276
8:42 274
8:43 274
8:44–45 274
8:44 274, 282
8:45 274
8:46–53 308
8:46–51 274, 316
8:46 316
8:48–49 274
8:48 274, 316
8:49 274
8:51–53 275
8:52–53 316
8:53 271, 360
8:54–61 276, 280, 281
8:54–57 316
8:56 315
8:57–61 316
8:59–60 271, 275, 316
8:60 276
8:61 271
8:62–63 181
8:62–66 275
8:65 57
9–10 100
9 181
9:1–9 209
9:1–6 100
9:4–9 308
9:9 60
9:15–23 516
9:15–22 60
9:15 178
9:15b 61
9:16–18 61
9:17–19 105
9:23 60
9:24a 60
9:24b 60
9:25 60, 281
10 181, 328
10:1–13 17, 545
10:1–3 514
10:8 219
10:9 520
10:10–11 181
10:13 181
10:14 545
10:18–20 515
10:22 60
10:26–29 516
10:26 60
10:27 515
10:28 328

11 96, 100, 105, 328, 335
11:1–13 360
11:1–8 385
11:1–2 416
11:2 521
11:4 521, 537
11:5–7 242
11:7 521
11:9 328
11:26–43 383
11:26–40 210
11:26–39 206
11:29–39 13
11:40–14:22 60
11:41 13, 17, 100, 401
11:42 105
12 105, 224, 323, 324, 335
12:1–24 206
12:10–24 383
12:21–24 13, 206, 210
12:24a–z 60
12:24a 60
12:24g–n 57
12:25 15
12:26–30 248
12:28–32 242
12:28 324
12:4 18
13 13, 206, 336
13:1–32 243
13:1–10 181
13:1–3 18
13:15–18 243
13:30–31 13
14:1–20 57
14:1–18 13
14:1–3 181
14:7–13 309
14:15–16 426
14:16 427
14:19 13, 15, 29
14:21–15:24 383
14:21 59
14:22–24 258
14:23–24 316
14:25–28 15, 17, 210
14:25–26 52
14:26 15
14:29 13, 29
15:1–8 210
15:5–6 59
15:7 59, 401
15:9–24 210
15:13 219, 225
15:15 331
15:17 15
15:18 15

1 Kings (Continued)
15:19 309
15:22 15
15:23 15, 210, 401
15:26 426
15:29 60
15:31 401
15:34 426
16–2 Kgs 21 29
16 219
16:1–14 206
16:1–4 210
16:2–4 60
16:5 15, 401
16:11–12 60
16:12 60
16:13 426
16:14 401
16:19 426
16:20 15, 401
16:21–28 17
16:21–22 61
16:24 15
16:26 426
16:27 15, 401
16:28–2 Kgs 25:30 242
16:29–22:20 20
16:29 61
16:31 407
16:34 15, 444
17–2 Kgs 10 17
17–2 Kgs 14 206
17–2 Kgs 13 210
17:1–2 Kgs 8:15 13
17:1–24 242
17 345, 409
17:1 542
17:2–6 207
17:7–16 207
17:8–15 181
17:10–16 13
17:17–24 207, 544
17:17–25 541
18–20 208
18–19 244, 279, 544
18 207, 324, 544
18:1 543
18:18–46 542
18:19 242, 417
18:20–40 242
18:21–40 277, 281
18:22 242
18:24 277
18:30 282
18:36 278, 282
18:37 278
18:39 278, 544

19 282, 544
19:2 544
19:3 542
19:4 542
19:8 324, 544
19:10 537, 542, 543, 544
19:12 324
19:14 537, 542, 544
19:15–18 544
19:15–17 17, 281
19:15 544
19:17 544
19:18 242, 537, 544
19:20–21 544
19:39 542
20 13, 207
20:1–43 13
20:11 14, 397
20:34 181
21 207
21:17–19 196
21:19 351
21:27–29 208
22:1–2 Kgs 25:30 56
22 13, 383
22:1–40 210
22:1–28 13
22:10–23 244
22:32 58
22:34–38 351
22:39 15
22:41 61
22:45 15
22:46–47 [Heb. 47–48] 242
22:46 401
22:52 61
23:21–23 403

2 Kings
1–2 345
1:8 544
1:9–13 398
1:9–15 13
1:17 61
2 207
2:1–25 61
2:13–14 17
2:23–24 13
2:23 56, 58
3 13
3:1 61
3:8 58
3:20 56, 58
4:1–7 181
4:8–13 216
4:9 331
4:18–37 541
4:32–37 544

4:42-44 546
4:43-44 538
5 13, 279
5:1-19 270, 278, 279, 281
5:8-27 181
5:8 278
5:10-14 13
5:15 278, 280
5:15b 278, 282
5:17 278
5:18 282
6 13
6:24-7:20 13
6:24-25 181
6:26-31 217
6:26-33 17
7
8:1-15 13
8:1-6 216
8:4 13
8:7-15 14
8:7-11 181
8:16-29 383
8:18 242
8:23 401
9 21
9:22 546
9:27-29 383
9:35 417
9:37 58
10 219
10:18-23 242
10:19 244
10:34 15
11-12 330, 383
11:1-21 242
11:1 113
11:14-18 121
11:17-18 242
12 211
12:2 219
12:4 [ET v. 3] 332
12:18-19 [ET vv. 17-18] 15
12:19 [ET v. 18] 15, 332
12:20 401
13:6 242
13:7 [ET v. 6] 15
13:8 15
13:12 15
13:14-21 61
13:20-21 13
13:25 21
14 21
14:1-22 383
14:1-18 206
14:14 16
14:15 15

14:22 15
14:23-29 207, 244
14:25 21
14:28 15
14:28b 22
15:1-7 383
15:10 15
15:11 401
15:14 15
15:15 15
15:19-20 15, 22
15:25 15
15:29-30 22
15:30 15, 22
15:32-38 383
16 383
16:3 243, 428
16:5 23
16:6-9 15
16:8 16
16:10-18 243
16:10 23
17-25 323
17 18, 159, 202, 207, 244, 305, 316, 335, 361, 428, 430
17:1-23 316
17:1-6 316
17:2 56-58
17:3 109, 110
17:4 18, 109, 110
17:5-6 15, 23, 111
17:5 110
17:6 23, 110, 111
17:7-23 428
17:7-20 308
17:7-8a 316
17:9-11 428
17:12-17 316
17:15b 316
17:16-17 428
17:18 316
17:19 316
17:21-23aα.b 316
17:21 245
17:23b 317
17:24-28 308
17:24-27 23
17:24 23, 111
17:34b-40 308
18-20 13, 207, 208, 211
18-19 115, 124
18:1-8 383
18:1-4 243
18:1 113
18:2 113
18:3-8 113
18:3 113
18:4 113

2 Kings (Continued)
18:7 114, 120
18:8 118
18:9 110
18:9–12 15
18:9–10 23, 112, 113
18:10 110
18:11 23
18:13–19:37 243
18:13–37 383
18:13–16 23, 112, 115
18:13–15 15
18:13 112, 115
18:14 23, 116
18:15 16
18:17–19:36 24
18:17–19:9a 271
18:17–19a 116
18:17 112, 116
18:19–35 117
18:20–21 115
18:32 117
18:36–37 271
19 115, 117
19:8 112, 117
19:9 116, 117
19:9b–35 271
19:14 117
19:15–19 270, 271, 280, 281
19:15 271, 272, 279
19:17 116
19:19 271, 272
19:22 332
19:32 116
19:35 116, 117
19:36–37 116
19:36 24
19:37 14, 25, 26
20 61, 115
20:1–11 383
20:4 61
20:5 61
20:6 61, 112
20:8 61
20:9 61
20:10 61
20:12–19 17, 208, 383
20:12–15 181
20:12 114
20:20–21 383
20:20 15, 114
21–23 256
21 119
21:1–23:3 383
21:1–18 25, 208
21:1–15 308
21:1–9 118

21:2–9 59
21:2–7 243
21:3 428
21:5 428
21:6 243, 428
21:10–16 268, 426
21:10–15 18
21:10–14 309
21:10 208
21:17 15
21:23–24 121
21:23 15
22–23 121, 252, 282, 333, 375
22:1–23:30 208
22:1–23:25 308
22 268, 318, 334
22:3 121
22:8–20 401
22:11–20 208
22:14–20 212, 268
22:15–20 18, 401
22:18–20 243
22:20 358
22:36–25:30 308
23 293, 294
23:4–15 243
23:4–10 243
23:4 243
23:5 243, 250
23:6 243, 428
23:7 222, 243
23:8–9 243
23:10 243
23:11 243, 250, 428
23:12 121, 315
23:13 242, 243
23:14 243
23:15–20 121
23:15–18 206
23:15–16 428
23:15 122, 315
23:16–18 13
23:19–20 293
23:19 122
23:21–23 244, 258, 383
23:24 246
23:25 308, 313
23:25a 316
23:26–27 18, 120, 426
23:27 18
23:28–24:20 383
23:29–30 212
23:29 123
23:30–34 123
23:30 547
23:31–24:20 244
24–25 152

24 373
24:2 309
24:3–4 18, 426
24:3 120
24:10–17 15, 26
24:13 16
24:14 152
25 61, 161, 181, 323, 335, 426
25:1–21 27, 244, 383
25:5 323
25:21 317
25:22–26 244
25:27–30 27, 244, 307, 317
25:30 344, 346

1 Chronicles
1–29 357
1–9 16, 269, 346, 357, 380, 381, 383, 539
1:1–5 220
1:1 379
1:11 220
1:13 220
1:18 220
2–8 360
2–4 386
2:1–2 360
2:3 360, 386
2:4 538
2:17 360, 386
2:34–35 360, 386
2:34 220
2:55 386
3 538
3:2 360, 386
3:11–12 539
3:19 362, 539
4:17–18 386
4:17 360
4:21–22 386
4:22 360
5:1 16
5:25–26 16
5:26 22, 361
6:1–15 209
6:12–13 209
6:16 400
6:31–48 16
6:33–38 539
6:49 258
7:14 360, 386
7:24 225
8:8 360
9 385
9:1 382, 282
9:2 362
9:17–18 362
9:17–34 16
9:30 224

10–2 Chr 34 356
10 95, 357
10:13–14 16, 96
10:14 540
11–29 95, 501
11:3–4 54
11:18–21 221
12:17 285
13 96
13:6 52
13:8 224
14 362
15–16 501
15 96
15:16 400
15:19 354
16 273, 280, 282
16:5–6 354
16:7 501
16:8–36 260
16:13 360
16:17 360
16:24 273
16:25–26 267
16:25 273
16:35 281
17 96, 209, 363, 501, 516
17:1–15 362
17:1–14 209
17:10b–14 209
17:14 209
17:16–27 17
17:20–27 280
17:20–21 270, 272
17:20 267
17:21–22 501
17:21 361
18–20 362
18 96
18:8 52
19:4–5 261
20:1–3 501
21–29 96
21 96, 210, 261, 363
21:16 261
21:18–22:1 354
21:21 261
21:25 184
21:29 263, 282
22–29 363
22:2 354
22:4 354
22:5–19 221
22:7–16 18
22:8 516
22:15 354
23–27 380, 383

1 Chronicles (Continued)
    23–26 501
    25:1 354
    25:5–6 221
    25:6 354
    25:7 400
    26:6 354
    27:24 382, 383
    28:1–29:9 501
    28:1–8 209, 210
    28:2–21 18
    28:3 516
    28:13–19 354
    29 210, 516
    29:1–5 18
    29:6–9 184
    29:7 184
    29:10–19 17, 18, 501
    29:15 275
    29:20 221, 261, 501
    29:23 272
    29:26 540
    29:29 209, 210, 402
    29:30 382, 383
2 Chronicles
    1–34 357
    1–9 95
    1 96, 263, 282
    1:3 279
    2–7 96
    2 273, 516
    2:3 282, 354
    2:4 258, 267
    2:4 [ET v. 5] 273
    2:5 [ET v. 6] 275, 282
    2:6 540
    2:8 273
    2:9 354
    2:13 [ET v. 14] 360
    2:15–16 354
    3:5 273
    3:14 224
    4:16 516
    5:1 354
    5:2–7 61
    5:12–13 354
    5:12 362
    6 275
    6:2 273, 275
    6:3–17 209
    6:5–6 56, 58
    6:5 361
    6:11 360
    6:13 261
    6:14–40 275
    6:14–17 272
    6:14 267, 276
    6:18 275
    6:20 59
    6:21 276
    6:23 276
    6:25 276
    6:28 282
    6:30 276
    6:32–39 261
    6:33 276
    6:34 282
    6:35 276
    6:39 276
    6:40–42 281
    6:41–42 260, 275, 276, 360
    6:41 276
    6:42 276
    7:1–7:3 276
    7:1 276
    7:3 276
    7:12 258
    7:14 276, 362
    7:17–22 210
    7:18 362
    7:22 361
    8:4 61, 514
    8:11 219, 360
    8:13–14 281
    9 96
    9:1–12 545
    9:1–2 514
    9:7 219
    9:29 210, 382, 383
    10:15 210
    11:5–12 16
    11:13–17 361, 386
    11:13–14 279
    11:16 279
    12:1–12 210
    12:13 360
    12:15 210, 382, 383, 402
    13 362
    13:4–12 17, 18, 279
    13:5 362
    13:9 55, 280
    13:10a 279
    13:12a 279
    13:22 210, 382, 383, 402
    14–15 210
    15:1–7 210
    15:3 280
    15:8–15 210, 361
    15:9–15 386
    16:7–10 210
    16:11 382, 383, 401
    16:12 210
    17:1–36:21 242
    17:2 361

18 210
18:1–22 244
18:1 360
18:31 58
19:1–3 210
19:2 360
19:4 361
20 277, 278
20:1–30 211
20:2–6 115
20:6–12 275, 277
20:6 277
20:7–11 361
20:9 277
20:24–25 221
20:34 382, 383
20:35–37 211
21 211
21:6 242
21:7 362
21:11 258
21:12 403
22:3 219, 360
23:1–15 242
23:3 362
23:16–17 242
24:17–27 211
24:18 267
24:27 382, 383, 402
25:5–13 211
25:14–28 211
25:26 382, 383
26:1–15 211
26:1 539
26:16–23 211
26:22 382, 383
27:7 382, 383, 401
28 211
28:1–4 243
28:8–15 361
28:8 217
28:9–21 211
28:24–25 243
28:26 382, 383, 401
29–31 113
29:1–36 243
29:21 354
29:25 210
29:32 354
30 256, 354, 386
30:1–27 243
30:1–11 386
30:1 361, 403
30:5–25 361
30:5–11 361
30:6–9 17, 18
30:6 362, 403

30:11 256
30:18–20 386
30:18 361
30:24 256
30:25 256, 361
31:1–21 243
31:1 361
32 115, 280
32:1–23 24, 243
32:1–22 271
32:2 114
32:3–4 114
32:4 121
32:5 114
32:6 114
32:12 258
32:17 282
32:19 280
32:20 211
32:30 16
32:32 211, 382, 383
33 119
33:1–20 25, 26
33:1–9 243
33:3 261
33:4–5 121
33:11 26, 119
33:12–13 119
33:12 279
33:13 279, 280
33:15 121
33:14–16 119
33:17 279, 282
33:18–19 382, 383
33:24 121
34–35 121
34 268, 357
34:3–7 243
34:6–7 361
34:6 122
34:8 121
34:9 122, 361, 362
34:21 361, 362
34:22–28 212, 268
34:22 221
34:28 358
34:29–32 243
34:33 121, 361
35–36 67, 356, 357, 367, 370, 371, 372, 375, 379, 530
35 256, 258, 357, 358, 359
35:1–19 256, 258, 354
35:1 244
35:4 403
35:17–18 122
35:18–19 244
35:18 386
35:19 256

2 Chronicles (Continued)

35:20–27 123
35:20–25 209
35:20–24 212
35:20 16
35:22 357
35:23 358
35:25 212, 216, 220, 221, 401, 402
35:26–27 382, 383
35:27 401
36 147, 161, 364
36:1–13 244
36:7 363
36:8 382, 383, 401
36:9–10 26
36:11–21 27
36:11–13 212
36:12 363
36:14–21 212
36:14 209
36:20–21 152
36:21–22 363
36:21 356
36:22–23 208, 212, 346, 355, 379, 385, 403, 530
36:23 66, 356

Ezra

1–10 356, 357, 370, 371, 379
1–6 64, 70, 71, 75, 208, 363, 372, 374, 384, 529
1–4 71
1:1–3:13 356
1–2 257
1 358
1:1–11 356
1:1–4 384, 529
1:1–3 385, 530
1:1–3a 355, 379, 383
1:1–3aβ¹ 346
1:1 379
1:2–4 16, 150, 257, 403
1:3 147, 356
1:7–11 363
1:7 354
1:9–11 16
2:1–4:5 357, 358, 359
2:1–3:13 356
2 69, 153, 362, 383, 384, 529
2:1–70 16
2:2 358
2:63 72
2:68 354
2:69 184
2:70 359
3–6 263
3 69
3:1–4 256
3:1 69, 70
3:2 354, 538, 539
3:3–6 258
3:5–6 257
3:7 354
3:10 354
3:11 64
3:12 72
3:13 356
4–5 156
4 152, 361
4:1–5 257, 386
4:1–4 362
4:2–6 65
4:2 26, 361
4:3 254, 259, 361
4:4 238
4:6–24 358
4:6–24a 356, 357
4:6–23 16
4:6–16 384
4:6 16
4:7–23 16
4:7–11 26
4:7–10 257
4:8–6:18 529
4:9–11 65
4:10 361
4:11–16 75, 257
4:11b–22 71
4:11b–16 529
4:12 359
4:16–24 356
4:17–22 257, 384, 529
4:17 184, 257
4:19 257
4:24 372
5:1–6:18 357
5:1–2 385
5:1 262
5:6–17 16, 384
5:6 257
5:7–17 257
5:7b–17 71, 529
5:13 257
5:17–6:5 65
6:1–3 257
6:1–2 12
6:3–12 529
6:3–5 16, 384, 529
6:6–12 16, 71, 384
6:7 357
6:9 354
6:14 262, 385
6:15–18 64
6:16–18 258
6:17 354
6:19–22 257, 354, 357, 385
7–Neh 13 384

7–10 64, 68, 71, 74, 353, 374, 384, 529
7:1–10:44 357
7–8 74, 257
7 64, 229, 529
7:1–10 70, 74, 75
7:1–5 531
7:1 530
7:7–8 229, 530
7:8 74, 229
7:9 74
7:10 68, 74, 75
7:11–26 533
7:11–16 529
7:12–26 16, 71, 384, 529
7:14 74
7:17–18 354
7:19 354
7:22 354
7:24 362
7:25–10:44 75
7:25–26 531
7:25 74
7:26 39, 531
7:27–10:44 74
7:28–10:44 75
7:28 75
8 74, 531
8:1–14 16, 384
8:15 75
8:25–30 354
8:26–27 16
8:27 184
8:31 74
8:33–34 354
8:35–36 354
8:35 258
9–10 64, 215, 228, 233, 234, 354, 359, 360, 385, 386, 387, 388, 532
9 18, 74, 75, 234, 236, 260, 531
9:1–2 221
9:1 235
9:2 151, 362, 387
9:3 238, 261
9:4–6 234
9:4a 234
9:4 74, 233
9:5–15 384
9:5 261
9:6–15 260
9:6 233
9:7 233, 260, 261
9:8–9 234
9:8–9a 234
9:8–10 234
9:8 234, 362
9:9 234, 362
9:10–11 74

9:13–15 234
9:14–15 387
9:14 235
9:15 362
10 64, 74, 151, 357, 359, 384
10:1 75, 221, 234, 261
10:7 75
10:9 74, 75, 234
10:11 260
10:16 74
10:17 74
10:18–44 384
10:18–43 16
10:44 357
11 363

Nehemiah
1–7 17, 359, 384
1:1–7:5 284
1:1–2:20 364
1:1–2 68
1:1 74, 531
1:2 151
1:4 261
1:7–9 385
1:10 361
1:11b 531, 534
2–6 64
2 70
2:1 74, 229, 530, 531
2:6 531
2:7 403
2:8 403
2:9 403
2:10 386
2:11–4:23 531
2:19–20 386
3 71
3:1–32 16
3:8 224
3:32 67
4–6 70
4:1–23 386
4:4 259
5 384, 531
5:1–18 184
5:14 384, 531
5:15 154
5:17 154
5:19 259, 384
6:1–19 386
6:5 403
6:9 259
6:11 531
6:14 220, 259
6:15 70, 71, 74, 75
6:17 403
6:18 403

Nehemiah (Continued)
  7 69, 153, 359, 362, 383, 384
  7:6-72 [ET 7:7-73] 359
  7:7-72a 16
  7:15-19 531
  7:57 224
  7:65 72
  7:70-8:18 74
  7:70-7:72 184
  7:72-8:1 69
  7:72 [ET 7:73] 359
  7:73-8:1 70
  8-10 64, 71
  8 64, 65, 68, 69, 70, 71, 73, 74, 75, 150, 156, 353, 356, 357, 358, 359, 367, 370, 371, 372, 374, 375, 379, 384, 401, 526, 530
  8:1-13a 359
  8:1-12 73
  8:1 74
  8:2 74
  8:3 150, 221
  8:8 150
  8:9 73, 150, 531
  8:13-18 257, 357, 385
  8:13b-18 358
  8:13 74
  8:15-16 263
  8:17-18 263
  9:1-13:31 358
  9 18, 71, 236, 261, 263, 361, 385
  9:1-3 386
  9:1 74, 261
  9:5-37 260
  9:5-15 260
  9:6-37 384, 394
  9:7-8 361
  9:9-25 361
  9:10 261
  9:16-31 260
  9:16 261
  9:17 261
  9:31 362
  9:33 362
  9:34 260
  9:35-38 236
  9:36 362
  9:38-10:27 16
  10-13 384
  10 71, 228
  10:1-39 [ET 9:38-10:39] 71
  10:1-27 384
  10:1-2 [ET 9:38-10:1] 73
  10:1 236
  10:2 73
  10:28-31 386
  10:28 260
  10:30-39 260

  10:31 [ET 10:30] 362
  10:36 236
  10:37 236
  10:38 236
  11 362, 383, 384, 385, 531
  11:1-2 17
  11:3-36 384
  11:13 362
  11:15-17 362
  11:19 362
  11:25-36 70
  11:25-26 16
  11:3-24 16
  12 384
  12:1-26 16, 384
  12:1 539
  12:22 68
  12:26 531
  12:27-43 64, 70, 71, 74
  12:31-43 17, 364, 384
  12:33 70
  12:35 354
  12:36 70
  12:37 70
  12:38 70
  12:40 70
  12:43-47 258
  12:43 221
  13 64, 151, 159, 215, 228, 384, 386, 388, 531
  13:1-3 385, 386
  13:4-31 17, 364, 384
  13:4-22 184
  13:10 362
  13:14 259
  13:15-22 386, 388, 531
  13:22 259
  13:23-30 532
  13:23-27 386, 388
  13:23-24 221, 388
  13:25-27 387
  13:26-27 385
  13:26 360, 520
  13:28-29 386
  13:28 155
  13:30 259, 386

Esther
  2:23 12
  6:1-2 12
  6:8-11 43
  9:26 403
  9:29 403

Job
  1-2 349
  1:20 261
  2:12 261

34:33 522
38:7 250

Psalms
2 502, 542
3–41 501
3 501
7 501
11:4a 281
12:7–9 263
18 501
22 502
33:6 250
34 501
39:13 [ET 12] 383
42:2 250
44 260
44:1–8 263
51–72 501
51 501
52 501
54 501
56 501
57 501
59 501
60 501
63 501
68 396
68:8–9 [ET 68:7–8] 396
72:20 540
74 260
74:12–15 263
78:67–68 315
79 260
84:11 250, 470
89:20 540
91 263
96 260, 273, 383
96:3 273
96:4 273
99:4 188
99:4 [Vulgate 98:4] 503
101–103 501
105 260, 383
105:6 360
105:10 360
105:14 188
105:15 505
106 260, 383
106:37 245
107–150 255
108–110 501
110 502, 542
120–134 257, 258
122:1 257
122:9 257
126 257
127 257
128 257
132 257, 260, 275, 276
132:1 275, 360
132:5 540
132:8–10 360, 383
132:8–9 275
134:1 257
134:7 257
135 273
135:5 273
136:1 383
138–45 501
140:5 261
142 501

Proverbs
1:1 514
6:20–22 262
14:35 188
16:12–14 188
22:29 522
23:6–8 262
24:32 [LXX] 522
31:1–9 513

Ecclesiastes
1:1 514
2:4–8 515
2:8 517
4:4–8 262

Song of Solomon
1:1 514
1:5 519
3:7–8 521

Isaiah
1–39 244
1:1 346
2:6–11 245
3:16–24 244
5:8–10 244
6:1–13 244
7–9 208
7 112
7:1–9 23
7:8 26
7:9 383
7:14 547
8 61
8:7–8 61
8:9 243
10:1–4 244
10:26 13
10:29 13
17:10–11 245
19:3 243
20 112
20:1–6 244
20:1 111

Isaiah (Continued)
  20:2 111
  20:3–6 111
  29:4 243
  29:8 222
  30:6–7 115
  36–39 24, 207, 208, 211, 383
  36–37 115
  37:38 25, 26
  40:9 224
  41:21–29 244
  40:26 250
  42 162
  43:11–13 272
  44:28 [LXX] 540
  45:1 155, 232
  45:22 272, 281
  46:9 281
  56–66 148, 255, 256
  56:6–7 256
  57 252
  57:5–13 245
  57:8 261
  60 162
  60:4–7 256
  60:8–22 256
  63:7–64:11 [ET 63:7–64:12] 260
  63:12 260
  63:17 260
  65 252
  65:3–11 245
  65:3–4 258
  66 252
  66:1–2 256
  66:17 245

Jeremiah
  2:27–28 245
  7:17–18 246
  7:30–32 245
  9:16 216
  13:18 244
  16:5–9 245
  17:21–27 246
  19:4–6 245
  19:12–13 246
  20:1–2 244
  22:24–27 26
  23:9–31 244
  28:16–17 244
  29 183
  32:29 246
  32:35 245
  39:1–10 27
  39:3 28
  44:3 246
  44:15–19 246
  46–51 244

  50:36 244
  52 61, 252
  52:2–3 61
  52:7 61
  52:15 61
  52:18–19 61
  52:27 61

Lamentations
  5:1–8 152

Ezekiel
  8 252
  8:14 245
  14:3–4 246
  14:7–8 246
  16:20–21 245
  16:36 245
  20:25–31 245
  23:37–39 245
  27:9 516
  37 149
  37:1–13 64
  40:17 518
  43 248
  43:7–9 246

Daniel
  1–6 317
  6:11 261, 316
  7–12 526
  7:25 543
  9:3 261
  12:2 541

Hosea
  2:13–17 [Heb. 15–19] 244
  4:14 222
  9:10 245
  10:5–8 245
  13:1–2 245

Amos
  2:7–8 245
  3:10 285
  5:15 97
  6:3–10 245
  6:10 246

Jonah
  3:5 261
  3:8 261

Micah
  1:6–7 245
  5:2 542
  5:10–14 245
  6:6–7 245

Haggai
  1:1 262
  1:2 256

1:3 262
1:7–8 256
1:12 539
2:23 69, 362

Zechariah
1:16 256
4:10 383
6:9–11 256
6:15 256
7:15 261
8:7–8 256
8:22 256
12 162
12:11 547
12:12 539

Malachi
1:1 259

New Testament
Matthew
1:1–17 502
1:1 541
1:2–17 538
1:5 538
1:6 539
1:16 539
1:17 539
1:20 541
1:23 547
2:6 542
2:23 547
6:28–29 545
6:29 515
9:27 542
11:12 296
12:22–29 518
12:23 541
12:24–27 517
12:41 545
12:42 518, 545
14:19–20 538
15:22 541
20:30 541
21:9 541
21:15 541
22:42 541
22:43 542

Mark
1:6 544
2:23 542
2:28 542
3:22 517
10:47–48 502
11:10 502
12:35–37 502

Luke
1:25 547
1:31 538, 546
1:32–33 538
1:32b–33 541
1:46–55 464
1:48 546
1:69 541
2:1 542
2:2 542
2:4 542
2:11 542
2:41–52 547
3:23–38 502, 538
3:33 539
4:24 542
4:25–26 542, 544
4:27 538, 542
7:15 517
7:33–34 547
10:29–37 364
11:31 518, 545
11:32 545

John
6:41 473
7:42 502, 538, 542
18:36 502

Acts
1:16 542
2:30 538
4:25 542
6:13 540
7 545
7:2–53 538, 540
7:41 540
7:45–47 538
7:46 540
7:47–48a 540
13:16–41 538, 540
13:22 540
13:23 538
14:15 543

Romans
1:3 501
9:27–28 544
10:12 538
11 543
11:1 543
11:2 543
11:3 544
11:4–5 544

1 Corinthians
11:5 457
14:33–35 458

2 Corinthians
  6:18 538
Galatians
  1:13–17 544
  1:13 544
  1:17 544
  3:28 225
Philippians
  2:9–10 447
1 Thessalonians
  1:1 463
1 Timothy
  2:12 457, 458, 459
Hebrews
  1:5 538
  3–4 446
  11 541
  11:4–40 538
  11:6 541
  11:30–31 541
  11:30 538
  11:31 538
  11:32–33 467
  11:32 461, 467, 541
  11:35 541
  11:40 541
  12:7 538
James
  2:25 538, 546
  5:16 542
  5:17–18 543
  5:18 538
Revelation
  2:20 419, 546
  5:5 502
  11:5–6 543
  11:6 538
  13:18 545
  16:16 547
  21:7 538
  22:16 502

Old Testament Apocrypha
Tobit
  1:2 110
  1:13 110
  1:15 110
  1:21–22 26
  3:8 517
  3:17 517
Wisdom of Solomon
  6:22 514
  7:3 543
  7:15–22 514

Sirach (Ben Sira)
  34:12–13 262
  46–50 438
  46:1–10 438
  46:6 439
  47:1–11 501
  47:8 501
  44–49 69
  49:11–13 526
  49:11 69
  49:12–13 67
  49:12 70
  49:13 70
2 Maccabees
  1:18–2:15 526
  1:18 67
  1:20–36 68
  6:2 160
1 Esdras
  1–9:36 74
  1:1–5:62 [ET 1:1–5:65] 356
  1 75, 374, 530
  1:21–22 357–358, 372, 374, 375
  1:21 [ET 1:23] 358
  1:24 375
  1:26 [ET 1:28] 358
  1:28 [ET 1:30] 358
  2:1–25 [ET 2:1–30] 356
  2:1–15 71
  2:1–14 [ET 2:1–15] 356
  2:15–25 [ET 2:16–30] 356, 358
  2:16–30 71
  2:16 373
  2:17–29 71
  2:17–18 [ET 2:18, 20] 364
  2:23 373
  2:30b–5:6 530
  2:30b 373
  3–5 368
  3–4 370
  3 68
  3:1–5:6 356, 357, 358, 371
  3:1–5:3 71
  3:5–7 368
  3:7 68
  3:8 368
  3:11 368
  3:12 368, 369
  3:17 369
  3:17b–24 358, 368
  4:1–12 358, 368
  4:1 369
  4:13–41 358, 368, 369
  4:13–32 369
  4:13 358, 369
  4:13b 369

4:14–32 370
4:33a 369, 370
4:33b–42 370
4:33b–41 369, 370
4:37 370
4:42 368, 370
4:43–46 368
4:47–57 368
4:58–63 368
5:4–46 71
5:5 373
5:7–70 357–358
5:7–62 [ET 5:7–65] 356
5:40 72, 73
5:47–65 71
5:60 72
5:66–73 71, 72
5:66–70 65
5:73 72
6:1–7:9 357
6:8–22 71
6:20–25 65
6:24–34 71
6:26 [ET 6:27] 357
7:10–14 357
8:1–9:36 357
8:6 74
8:9–24 71
8:61 74
8:65–9:36 359
8:82 74
9 74
9:5 74
9:16 74
9:17 74
9:36 357
9:37–55 71, 73, 74, 357
9:37–54 359
9:37 359
9:47 375
9:49 73
9:50 375
9:55 358, 375

2 Esdras
1–2 527
1:1 527
2:63 72
3–14 527, 528
11–23 65
13:40 110
14:37–48 528
14:45–47 528
15–16 528
18:9 73

4 Maccabees
12:13 543

Old Testament Pseudepigrapha
4 Ezra
7:106–108 450
Testament of Solomon
19:3 545
21:1 545

Dead Sea Scrolls
4QKgs 56
4QSam^a 51–56, 62
4QSam^b 53–54, 62
4QSam^c 54, 62
5QKgs 55
6QpapKgs 56

Ancient Near Eastern Texts and Inscriptions
ANET
  ANET 233–34 17
  ANET 246 120
  ANET 271–72 10
  ANET 272–74 10
  ANET 272 114
  ANET 277–81 10
  ANET 284 110
  ANET 286 112
  ANET 287 111, 115
  ANET 288 112, 115, 116, 117
  ANET 291 119
  ANET 293 119
  ANET 294 119
  ANET 296 120
  ANET 298–300 120
  ANET 301–07 11
  ANET 302 119
  ANET 312–15 11
  ANET 315–16 12
  ANET 320–21 11
  ANET 321 12
  ANET 557–60 11
  ANET 560–62 11
  ANET 564–66 10
  ANET 646–51 11
  ANET 654–55 11
  ANET 655–66 11
ARTA
  No. 001 44
BaAr
  6:1 136
Babylonian Chronicle
  ii 12–23 114
COS
  COS 1.37D 10
  COS 1.72–77 9

COS (Continued)
  COS 1.104 10
  COS 1.134 10
  COS 1.135 10
  COS 1.136 10
  COS 1.137 11
  COS 1.138 11
  COS 1.147 11
  COS 1.148 11
  COS 2.1 17
  COS 2.23 11
  COS 2.25 10
  COS 2.28 12
  COS 2.30 11
  COS 2.35 11
  COS 2.39 11
  COS 2.113A–F 10
  COS 2.113A 241
  COS 2.113F 241
  COS 2.118A 110
  COS 2.118C 110
  COS 2.118D 110
  COS 2.118E 110
  COS 2.119A 117
  COS 2.119B 117
  COS 2.119E 116
  COS 2.124 12
  COS 2.295–96 111
  COS 3.43M 12
CUSAS
  28:1 136
  28:10 139
  28:37 139
  28:40 139
  28:41 139
  28:42 139
  28:52 139
  28:53 139
  28:71 139
  28:103 139
RIMA
  3A.0.102.2 20, 21
  3A.0.102.10 21
  3A.0.102.12 21
  3A.0.102.88 21
  3A.0.104.7 21
  3A.0.104.8 21
  3A.0.105.1 22
RINAP
  1 13/31 30
  1 14/15 22
  1 21/22 22
  1 35 22
  1 42 22
  1 44 22
  1 47 23
  1 49 22
  3 4 24
  4 1 25
  4 5 25
SAA
  1 110 24
  2 2 22
  9 1.8 25
  9 3.3 25
  15 280 23
  16 63 23
TAD
  A4.7.21–22 259
  A4.8.21 259
  A4.9.9–10 259
  A4.10.10s–11 259

Classical Sources
Herodotus, Histories
  1.125 34
  2.141 117
  2.157 123
  2.159.2 124
  3.97 38
  5.21 40
  5.52–54 41
  6.41 40
  8.90 12
  8.91 41

Josephus
  Ant. 3.49–52 439
  Ant. 5.1–2 439
  Ant. 5.8 512
  Ant. 5.8.2 468
  Ant. 5.8.3 468
  Ant. 5.8.4 470
  Ant. 5.8.6 473, 474
  Ant. 5.8.7 474
  Ant. 5.8.9 475
  Ant. 5.8.11 476, 477
  Ant. 5.8.12 479
  Ant. 5.38–43 439
  Ant. 5.118 439
  Ant. 5.200–201 453
  Ant. 6 485
  Ant. 6.67–69 54
  Ant. 6.171 53
  Ant. 7.54 54
  Ant. 7.61 54
  Ant. 7.65 54
  Ant. 7.104–106 52
  Ant. 8.2.2 512
  Ant. 8.42–47 545
  Ant. 8.46–48 517
  Ant. 8.5.3 514
  Ant. 8.64–69 518

Ant. 8.70 57
Ant. 10.143 540
Ant. 11.1.1–11.5.6 526
Ant. 11.1–158 68
Ant. 11.1–8i 36
Ant. 11.158 68
Contra Apionem 1.37–43 527
Vita 417-18 51

Plutarch
  Artaxerxes 3 43

Philo
  Mut. 122 445
  Virt. 55 444
  Virt. 66 444

Pseudo-Philo
  L.A.B. 15.2 445
  L.A.B. 41.1 468
  L.A.B. 42:3 468, 470
  L.A.B. 43:1–2 475
  L.A.B. 43:5 476, 479
  L.A.B. 43:6 477
  L.A.B. 43:7–8 479
  L.A.B. 43:8 479

Xenophon
  Anabasis 1.9 44
  Anabasis 7.8 41
  Cyropaedia 8.617–18 41
  Hellenica 4.1.607 40

Rabbinic and Other Jewish Literature

Abot of Rabbi Nathan
  A, Ch. 27 449

Babylonian Talmud
  Avod. Zar. 25a 449
  B. Bat. 14b 66, 67
  B. Bat. 15a 67, 379, 530
  B. Bat. 75a 449
  B. Bat. 91:a 468
  Bab. Qam. 80b–81a 448
  Ber. 48b 448
  Ber. 54b 449
  Ber. 61a 469
  Eruv. 63b 449
  Git. 59a 513
  Git. 65b 521
  Git. 68a–b 517
  Git. 68a 517
  Meg. 14a 454, 457
  Meg. 14b 449, 454
  Nazir 4a 470
  Nazir 4b 470
  Nid. 70b 519
  Sanh 21b 519, 528
  Sanh. 36a 513
  Sotah 10a 470, 479
  Sotah 48b 516
  Šabb. 56b 521
  Tem. 16a 449
  Yeb. 71b 448

Ecclesiastes/Qoheleth Rabbah
  1:4 480, 528
  1:18 471

Eliyyahu Rabbah
  48 454
  50 457

Leviticus Rabbah
  8:2 471

Mekhilta of Rabbi Ishmael
  Be-Shalah, Masekhta de-Va-Yissa 3 449
  Parashat be-Shalah, Masekhta de-Amalek 1 440
  Parashat be-Shalah, Masekhta de-Amalek 2 440

Midrash
  Midrash Peṭirat Moshe 449
  Midrash Tanḥuma 448–449
  Midrash Tannaim 449
  Midrash Tzedaqot 1.6–1.7 449

Mishnah
  Abot. 1.1 448

Numbers Rabbah
  9:24 472, 476, 477, 479
  10:5 468, 469
  14:9 471, 480
  22:7 479

Ruth Rabbah
  1.1. 459

Sha'arei Teshuvah
  43 448–449

Sifrei
  Sifrei Deuteronomy 449
  Sifrei Numbers 448–449

Tosefta
  Sanh 4:7 528

Zohar
  Vayikra 19b 457

Christian Literature

Ambrose
  Concerning Widows 8.45 455
  Letter 35 469, 470, 472, 473, 475

Aphrahat
  Demonstrations 11 448
  Demonstrations 12 448
  Demonstrations 20 448
  Demonstrations 21 448

Apostolic Constitutions
  Apostolic Constitutions 8.2.8–9 454
  Apostolic Constitutions 8.20.1–2 457

Augustine
  De Civ. Dei 1:21 479
  De Civ. Dei 17:14 503
  Sermon 364.2 471, 474
  Sermon 364.3 474
  Sermon 364.4 474

Caesarius of Arles
  Sermon 118.3 473, 474
  Sermon 119.1 473

Cyril of Jerusalem
  Catecheses 10.11 448

Epistle of Barnabas
  12 447

Eusebius
  Demonstratio Evangelica 4.7 448
  Historia Ecclesiastica 1.3 448
  Praep. Ev. 9:10 473

Gratian
  Decretum Ch. 15, q. 3 459

Gregory the Great
  Forty Gospel Homilies 476

Isaac the Syrian
  Ascetical Homilies 10 476

Jerome
  Letter 54.17 453

John of Damascus
  Orthodox Faith 4.15 475

Justin Martyr
  Dialogue with Trypho ¶ 75 447
  Dialogue with Trypho ¶ 106 447
  Dialogue with Trypho ¶ 113 447

Origen
  On First Principles 4.2.9 296
  Homily 1 ¶ 3 448

Peter the Venerable
  Letter 115 454

Peter Damian
  Letter 114 459

Peter Martyr Vermigli
  Letter 200 460

Thomas Aquinas
  Sentence Commentary, distinction 25, q. 2, art. 1 458

Zeno of Verona
  Sermons 1.13 447

Qur'an

Sura 27:15–44 519
Sura 27:17 517

Author Index

Abadie, P. 106, 501, 506, 509
Abdulaali, W. 519, 523
Abegg, M., Jr. 62
Abraham, K. 28, 30, 132, 138–139, 141, 162–163
Abramson, G. 505–506
Abusch, T. 156, 163
Achenbach, R. 318
Achtemeier, P.J. 163
Ackerman, J.S. 509
Ackerman, S. 225, 465
Ackroyd, P.R. 120, 124, 342, 351
Adam, K.-P. 497, 507
Adams, H. 351
Adams, M.J. 92
Adams, S.L. 185
Aejmelaeus, A. 62
Aguilar, G. 455, 465
Aharoni, Y. 84, 122, 124, 212–213, 263, 443, 450
Ahituv, S. 247–248, 252
Ahlström, G. 229, 238
Ahn, J.J. 141, 482
al-Ṭabari, A. 440, 450, 518–519, 523
Albert, J. 165
Albertz, R. 123–124, 130–131, 133, 141, 148, 150, 163–165, 167, 169, 246, 251–252, 264, 310, 318
Albright, W.F. 83, 87, 90, 124, 229, 231, 238, 442–443
Alexander, J.C. 424–425, 431
Alon, I. 319
Alphen, E. van 422, 431
Alster, B. 32
Alstola, T. 27–28, 30
Alt, A. 84–85, 87, 90, 106, 305, 318, 450
Alter, R. 83, 90, 339, 351, 496, 507
Altmann, P. 163, 175, 185
Álvarez-Mon, J. 34, 45–46
Améry, J. 423, 431
Ames, F.R. 130, 143–144
Amit, Y. 18, 108, 129
Anderson, G.A. 335–337
Anderson, G.W. 337
Anderson, R.T. 450–451
Anlezark, D. 514, 523
Anscombe, G.E.M. 288, 297
Anton, H.H. 503, 507
Arendt, H. 506–507
Arnold, B.T. 124, 126, 128, 253
Artus, O. 321

Arubas, B. 153, 167
Aruz, J. 46
Askin, L. 69, 76
Assmann, J. 295, 297
Astruc, J. 529, 534–535
Attridge, H.W. 502, 507
Aucker, W.B. 164
Auerhahn, N.C. 422, 430–431
Augustin, M. 166
Auld, A.G. 269, 312, 318
Aurelius, E. 312, 318
Ausloos, H. 62–63
Auwers, J.-M. 377, 501, 507
Avi-Yonah, M. 127
Avigad, N. 38, 45, 110, 124
Avioz, M. 485, 494
Avishur, Y. 169
Avitz-Singer, L. 153, 164
Azzoni, A. 36, 45

Baden, J.S. 262, 265
Baert, B. 520, 523
Bagg, A. 22, 30
Bahat, D. 121, 124
Bainton, R.H. 285, 296–297
Baker, D.W. 126
Baker, H. 46, 132, 143, 146
Bakhtin, M.M. 537, 547
Bal, M. 431, 464–465
Balla, E. 535
Balzaretti, C. 66, 76
Bar-Yosef, E. 505, 507
Bar-Yosef, O. 86, 90
Barag, D. 163
Barkay, G. 248, 252
Barmash, P. 159, 163
Barnard, H. 93
Barrick, W.B. 111, 124
Barrie, J.M. 492–494
Barstad, H.M. 132, 141, 152, 163, 317–318
Bartel, R. 509
Barth, F. 134, 137, 141
Barth, K. 336
Barthélemy, D. 351–352
Barthelot, K. 451
Bartlett, J.R. 523
Barton, J. 92, 141, 145, 149, 163, 378, 534–535

AUTHOR INDEX

Barton, S.C. 298
Batten, L.W. 67, 76
Batto, B.F. 352
Bautch, R.J. 260, 263
Beale, G.K. 540, 547
Beaulieu, P.-A. 133, 136, 141–142
Becker, U. 315, 318
Becking, B. 23, 30, 68, 76, 112, 118, 125, 148, 158–159, 163, 168, 231, 237–238, 263–264, 381, 390
Bedford, P.R. 152, 163
Beentjes, P.C. 451
Begg, C.T. 450–451
Beit-Arieh, I. 125
Ben Zvi, E. 32, 129, 132–133, 142–144, 199, 220, 225–226, 268–269, 282, 319, 321, 389–392
Ben-Tor, A. 83, 90
Ben-Yosef, E. 515, 523
Benech, C. 46
Benveniste, É. 73, 76
Berger, S.Z. 482
Bergner, G. 419
Berlejung, A. 32, 146
Berman, J. 151, 163, 190, 198
Berquist, J.L. 130–131, 133, 142, 149, 151, 163, 168, 230, 232, 237–239, 419, 534–535
Bertholdt, L. 368, 376
Betlyon, J.W. 38, 45, 148, 153, 163
Bettles, E. 47
Beulens, G. 431
Beyer, H. 507
Bezzel, H. 107
Bhabha, H. 411, 416, 419
Bienkowski, P. 88, 90
Bietak, M. 90
Biggs, R.D. 125
Biran, A. 248, 252
Bird, M.F. 369, 376
Blakely, J.F. 261, 263
Blenkinsopp, J. 67, 74, 76, 141, 147, 150, 153, 163, 166–167, 169, 230, 239, 354, 364, 369, 376, 379–390, 530, 534–535
Bloch-Smith, E. 249, 252
Bloch, Y. 28, 30, 132, 134, 136, 138, 140, 142
Bloemendal, J. 504, 507
Blum, E. 310, 317, 319
Blumenthal, M.D. 286, 297
Boardman, J. 46–47, 155, 163
Bocian, M. 504, 507
Boda, M.J. 76, 147, 163, 263–264, 382, 390
Boehmer, E. 409, 419
Boer, R. 175, 185, 220, 226, 389–390, 419–420
Bohache, T. 226–227
Böhler, D. 72, 76, 359, 364, 369–371, 374, 376
Boling, R.G. 285, 297
Bonfiglio, R. 162–163
Bons, E. 502, 509
Borger, R. 25, 30

Bosworth, D. 336–337
Boucharlat, R. 36, 45, 46, 154, 163
Boyarin, D. 151, 163
Bradbury, N.M. 514, 523
Bradbury, S. 514, 523
Brams, S.J. 193, 198
Braulik, G. 321
Braun, R.L. 361, 364–365
Bream, H.H. 127
Brekelmans, C. 535
Brenner, A. 107, 226, 227, 482, 509
Brett, M.B. 240
Brettler, M.Z. 18, 107, 198, 398, 404
Brewer, E.C. 473, 481
Briant, P. 34–43, 45, 47–48, 63, 147–148, 154–155, 163
Bright, J. 83, 90–91, 119, 122, 125, 229, 239
Brinkman, J.A. 114, 120, 125
Brison, S.J. 430–431
Britt, B. 400, 404
Brodie, T.L. 336–337, 544, 547
Brooks, G. 512, 524
Brooks, M.F. 520, 524
Broshi, M. 118, 125
Brosius, M. 43, 45, 168
Brown, B.A. 135, 142
Brown, D. 488, 494
Brown, L.S. 425, 431
Brown, S.C. 34, 45
Brown, W.P. 337
Bruce, B.J. 284, 297
Brueggemann, W. 270–271, 282, 295, 297, 322, 334, 337, 496, 507, 515–516, 520, 522–524
Buber, M. 198
Bunyan, J. 518, 524
Burger, C. 501, 507
Burney, C.F. 318–319
Burrows, D. 487, 494, 495
Burt, S. 382, 384, 390
Burton, A. 455, 465
Butterworth, G.W. 297
Busto Saiz, J.R. 62
Byrne, B. 544, 547
Byron, G.L. 481

Cagni, L. 137, 142
Callieri, P. 36, 45
Calvin, J. 284, 297
Calvo, M. 432
Cameron, A. 36, 48
Cameron, G.G. 45
Camp, C.V. 226, 519, 524
Campbell, A.F. 203, 205, 213
Campbell, E., Jr. 125
Carden, M. 223, 226
Carman, B. 461, 465
Carrez, M. 370, 376
Carroll, R.P. 78, 237–239, 532, 534–535

Carter, C.E. 231, 235, 237–239
Carter, E. 34, 45
Carter, W. 419–420
Caruth, C. 431
Cataldo, J. 389–391
Chan, M.J. 27, 30
Chapman, S.B. 329, 337
Charlesworth, J.H. 481, 535
Chauveau, M. 36, 45, 48
Chavalas, M.W. 124, 129
Cherry, C. 420
Childs, B.S. 115, 125, 313, 319
Ciba, P. 298
Clay, A.T. 139, 142, 238–239
Clements, R.E. 199, 317, 319
Cline, E.H. 87, 91, 133, 142
Clines, D.J.A. 74, 76, 229, 237, 239, 326, 333–334, 337, 376, 534–535
Cogan, M. 24–25, 30, 112–113, 119, 125, 127, 157, 161, 163
Coggins, R.J. 376
Cohen, A. 512–515, 517, 524
Cohen, R. 31
Cohen, S.A. 502, 507
Cohn, R.L. 542, 547
Colenso, J.W. 319
Collins, J.J. 285, 291, 297
Collon, D. 135, 142
Comaroff, J. 155, 164
Comaroff, J.L. 155, 164
Conway, C.M. 465
Coogan, M.D. 91, 93, 125, 262, 264
Cook Steike, E. 226
Cook, J.M. 147, 164, 377
Cook, S. 482
Cooper, D. 524
Coote, R.B. 179, 185, 198, 285, 297
Copan, P. 297
Corley, J. 451
Cornelius, I. 160, 164, 166, 282
Cos, C.E. 365
Cottrill, A.C. 226
Cox, C. 377
Craps, S. 430, 431
Craven, T. 226
Creach, J.F.D. 285, 295, 297
Crewe, J. 431
Cross, F.M., Jr. 51, 62, 122, 125, 164, 202–203, 213, 307–308, 312–314, 319, 327, 333, 337, 356–357, 359, 364–365, 372, 376, 380, 391, 395, 404
Crow, L.D. 257, 264
Crowell, B. 419–420
Crowfoot, G.M. 259, 264
Crowfoot, J.W. 259, 264
Culbertson, L. 144, 240
Cunningham, M. 298
Curtis, E.L. 67, 76, 354, 365
Curtis, J. 46

Da Riva, R. 133, 142
Dahlberg, L.L. 298
Dahmen, U. 508
Dalley, S. 24, 30, 125
Dam, C. van 285, 298
Dandamaev, M.A. 38, 46, 137, 142, 238–239
Danieli, Y. 431
Daniélou, J. 451
Darby, E. 250, 252
Davidson, S.V. 226, 408, 414–415, 419–420
Davies, P.R. 18, 78, 86–87, 91, 114, 128, 151, 153, 163–164, 166, 237, 239–240, 535
Davies, S. 47
Davis, J.M. 517, 524
Davis, M.D. 505, 507
Dawkins, R. 285, 296, 297
Day, J. 125, 245, 253
Dayan, M. 450, 451
Déclais, J.-L. 507
DeLapp, N.L. 504, 507
Delbo, C. 423–424, 432
Desrousseaux, L. 506–507
Deutsch, R. 169
Dever, W.G. 80, 83, 85, 87–91
Dhorme, É. 137, 142
Dietrich, W. 107, 202, 213, 309, 319, 500–501, 507–508
Dillard, R.B. 282
Dirksen, P.B. 365
Dolansky, S. 342, 351
Donbaz, V. 28, 30, 262, 265
Dorson, R.M. 394, 404
Dozeman, T.B. 91, 148, 164, 319, 325, 337, 352
Driver, S.R. 67, 76, 285, 297, 354, 365
Dube, M. 409, 415, 420
Dunhill, R. 487, 495
Dunn, J.D.G. 543, 547
Durand, J.-M. 145
Durrant, S. 431
Dušek, J. 36, 38, 46, 160, 164
Dusinberre, E. 36, 46, 155, 164
Dutcher-Walls, P. 319

Eaglestone, R. 431
Earl, D.S. 287, 291, 293, 297, 451
Ebach, J. 509
Ebeling, E. 41, 46
Echols, C.L. 84, 91
Edelman, D.V. 149, 164, 166, 199, 225, 321, 390–392
Edenburg, C. 107, 342, 351
Edwards, I.E.S. 125
Edwards, J. 470, 472, 474, 481
Ehrlich, C.S. 107
Eichmann, R. 133, 142
Eichorn, J.G. 229, 239
Eissfeldt, O. 308, 311, 319, 353, 365
Elayi, J. 38, 46, 145
Elazar, D.J. 198

Elitzur, Y. 451
Ellingworth, P. 541, 548
Elliott, J.H. 263–264
Elßner, T.R. 451
Emerton, J.A. 19, 132, 142, 321, 364–365, 378
Endres, J.C. 387, 391
Engler, B. 505, 507
Eph'al, I. 36, 46, 117, 125, 127, 137, 142, 164
Epstein, I. 481
Erickson, C.L. 89, 91
Eshel, H. 160, 164
Eskenazi, T.C. 64, 76, 224, 226, 230, 239–240, 369, 377, 387, 391–392, 533–535
Eslinger, L.M. 340, 341, 348, 350–351
Esquivel, J. 463, 465
Etziony-Halevy, E. 455, 465
Evans, C.A. 91
Evans, C.D. 120, 125
Evans, J. 297
Evans, P.S. 116, 125, 392
Ewald, H. 304, 312, 319
Ewig, E. 502, 507
Exum, J.C. 125, 226, 456, 465–467, 481, 510
Eyerman, R. 425, 432

Faber, R. 509
Fales, F.M. 128, 135, 137, 142–143
Fanon, F. 413–416, 418–420
Fantalkin, A. 153, 164
Farber, Z.I. 451
Farrar, F.W. 515, 516, 519, 521–524
Fassberg, S.E. 19
Fassler, M.E. 507
Faust, A. 89, 91, 152, 164, 182, 185
Feldman, L.H. 451, 518, 522, 524
Feldman, M. 142
Felman, S. 423, 427, 430, 432
Fernández Marcos, N. 62
Fewell, D.N. 217, 226, 405, 478, 481
Finkelstein, I. 68, 70, 76, 85, 87–91, 93, 106–107, 113–115, 117–118, 122–123, 125, 129, 153, 164, 179, 185
Finley, M. 185
Finney, P.C. 502, 507
Fiorenza, E.S. 524
Firmage, E.B. 337
Firth, D.G. 283
Fischer, B. 92
Fish, S. 340, 351
Fishbane, M.A. 535
Fisher, C.S. 259, 264
Fiske, A.P. 290–291, 296–297
Fitzpatrick-McKinley, A. 148, 154–156, 164
Fleming, D.E. 153, 164
Fleming, J. 282
Flint, P.W. 62
Fokkelman, J.P. 107, 339, 341, 351
Foley, J.M. 395, 398, 404

Foster, K.P. 154, 165
Foster, P. 451
Foucault, M. 238–239
Frahm, E. 30
Francfort, H.-P. 36, 46
Franke, J.R. 284, 297
Fredriksen, P. 157, 165
Freedman, D.N. 66–67, 76, 93, 239, 297, 325–327, 335, 337, 356, 365, 380, 391
Freedman, H. 481, 512, 524
Freedman, H. 524
Frei, P. 39, 46, 156, 165, 230, 237, 239, 532, 534–535
Frerichs, E.S. 93
Fretheim, T. 274, 282
Freud, S. 421–422, 432
Frevel, C. 139, 143, 166, 280, 282, 387, 391
Fried, L.S. 68–73, 75–78, 133, 143, 152, 155, 165, 238–239, 365–366, 376–377, 379, 382, 384–385, 387, 391
Friedlander, P. 395, 405
Friedlander, S. 431, 432
Friedman, R.E. 165, 308, 319
Frolov, S. 340, 342–343, 345–346, 351
Frontain, R.-J. 507
Frood, E. 92
Frymer-Kensky, T. 454, 465
Fuchs, A. 23, 30
Fuhrmann, S. 535
Fuller, T. 516, 524
Fulton, D.N. 68, 70, 77, 144, 382, 384–385, 391, 528, 535

Gabbay, U. 33, 140, 143, 146, 157, 162, 165, 168
Gadd, C.J. 125
Gadot, Y. 92, 152–153, 165, 167
Gafney, W.C. 417, 419–420, 471, 478, 481
Galil, G. 31, 107
Gallagher, W.R. 24, 31, 113–116, 118, 125
Gammie, J.G. 337
Ganzert, J. 163
Garbini, G. 374, 377
García Bachmann, M.L. 215, 222, 226, 388
Garrison, M.B. 34, 43, 45, 46
Garsiel, M. 340, 351
Garstang, J. 90
Gasche, H. 37, 46
Gasquet, F.A. 66, 77
Gelston, A. 365
Genz, H. 92
Geoghegan, J.C. 313, 319
Geraty, L.T. 80, 91
Gerhards, M. 314, 319
Gesche, P. 139, 143
Gevaryahu, H. 451
Gilbert, P. 286, 297
Giles, T. 450, 451
Gillaume, P. 164
Gilmour, R. 19, 107
Ginsberg, H.L. 122, 125

Ginzberg, L. 378, 512–518, 520, 524
Gitin, S. 91, 253
Glassner, J.-J. 19
Gnuse, R.K. 148, 165
Goldschmidt, A. 502, 507
Gondet, S. 36, 46
Gooding, D.W. 343, 351
Gordon, R.P. 298
Goss, R. 226–227
Gosselin, E.A. 507
Gottwald, N.K. 87, 91, 175, 185, 198, 238–239, 285, 297
Grabbe, L.L. 29, 31, 76, 80, 90–91, 107, 112, 116–118, 124–129, 144, 148, 151–156, 165, 213, 229, 237, 239, 370, 377, 390, 532, 534–535
Graf, D. 41, 46
Graham, M.P. 107, 387, 390–392
Granerød, G. 148, 157–158, 165
Grayson, A.K. 19–26, 31, 110, 126
Green, A.R.W. 200
Greenberg, I. 433
Greenberg, M. 140, 143, 297
Greenspahn, F.E. 346, 351
Greer, J.S. 82, 92
Grelot, P. 36–37, 46
Groneberg, B. 47
Groot, C. de 465, 480, 482
Gropp, D. 160, 165
Grosby, S. 134, 143
Gross, W. 480–481
Grossman, D. 469, 479, 481
Grotius, H. 191, 198
Gryson, R. 377
Guest, D. 226–227
Guillaume, P. 339, 351
Gundry, R.H. 539, 548
Gunn, D.M. 107, 339, 348, 351, 398, 405, 465
Gunneweg, A.H.J. 69, 77
Güterbock, H. 19
Guthrie, C. 282

Hachlili, R. 263–264
Hackens, T. 163
Hackett, J.A. 84, 91, 114, 126, 226
Haerinck, E. 37, 46
Hagelia, H. 285, 299
Hägerland, T. 548
Haggai, M. 255, 259, 264
Hahn, S.W. 540, 543, 548
Hale, S. 478, 480–481
Halévy, J. 229, 237, 239
Hallo, W.W. 125, 126, 352
Hallock, R.T. 36, 41, 46
Halpern, B. 87, 91, 107, 113, 126, 165, 203, 213, 342, 352, 497, 508, 522, 524, 548
Hammond, N.G.L. 46, 47, 125
Handy, L.K. 107
Hanhart, R. 65, 66, 77, 364–365, 371–372, 377

Hanson, P.D. 283
Haran, M. 67, 77, 355–356, 365, 535
Harding, J.E. 505, 508
Harkins, A.K. 514, 524
Harmatta, J. 46
Harper, P. 36, 46
Harrington, D.J. 481
Hart, O. van der 422, 432
Hartman, G.H. 422, 432
Harvey, P.B., Jr. 68, 77
Harvey, W.Z. 534–535
Hasel, M.G. 86, 90–91
Hasson, I. 502, 508
Hastings, J. 378
Hausleiter, A. 133, 142–143
Havrelock, R. 443, 451
Hawk, L.D. 340, 352, 412, 415, 418, 420
Hayes, J.H. 110, 112–113, 119, 121–122, 126–127, 229, 237, 240
Hays, R.B. 324, 337
Hazony, Y. 190, 198
Heim, R.D. 127
Heinz, M. 142
Hendel, R. 81, 91
Henkelman, W.F.M. 36, 38–39, 42, 45–47, 49, 78, 143
Hennig, J. 508
Henry, M. 519, 521–522, 524
Hentschel, G. 107
Herkommer, H. 502–503, 507–508
Herman, J.L. 430, 432
Herr, L.G. 39, 47, 85, 91
Herrenschmidt, C. 48
Herrero de Jáuregui, M. 502, 508
Hervieu-Léger, D. 295, 298
Herzog, Z. 113, 126, 249, 253
Hess, R.S. 91, 93, 122, 126, 242–247, 251–253
Hilberg, R. 423–424, 432
Hill, C. 504, 508
Himbaza, I. 321
Hobbes, T. 191, 198
Hobbs, T.R. 121, 126
Hobson, D.W. 126
Hochberg, R. 512, 525
Hoffmann, A. 499, 508
Hoffmann, Y. 319
Hoffmeier, J.K. 80, 92
Hoffner, H.A. 19
Hogeterp, A.I.A. 540, 548
Hoglund, K. 153, 230, 238–239, 391, 534–535
Holmgren, F.C. 64, 77
Hölscher, G. 318–319
Holter, K. 272, 282
Honderich, T. 297
Hood, J.B. 538, 548
Hooker, P.K. 121, 126
Hoonacker, A. van 229, 240

Hornblower, S. 40, 47, 49
Horne, A. 516, 518, 524
Horowitz, W. 23, 25, 31
Horsley, R.A. 541, 548
Horton, F.L., Jr. 261, 263
Hossfeld, F.-L. 501, 508
Hourihane, C. 508
Houtman, C. 330, 337
Howard, C.B.R. 226, 388, 417, 420
Hübner, U.H. 30
Huffmon, H.B. 200
Hughan, W.J. 516, 524
Hugo, P. 62, 63, 107
Hulster, I. de 157, 163–164, 482
Hunt, A. 238–239
Hurowitz, V. 126
Hurtado, L.W. 165, 451
Hurvitz, A. 19, 93, 297
Hutton, J.M. 282, 319
Hylander, I. 339, 352
Hyman, P.E. 465

Iser, W. 340, 352
Isho'dad 521
Israelstam, J. 513, 518–519, 524

Jacob, W. 458, 465
Jacobs, B. 46, 78
Jacobs, M.R. 212–213
Janet, P. 422, 432
Janoff-Bulman, R. 426, 432
Janzen, D. 387, 391, 428–430, 432
Japhet, S. 67, 77, 107, 150–151, 165, 208, 212–213, 266–269, 282–283, 354–355, 365, 372, 377, 379, 381, 383, 386, 389, 391, 401, 405, 530, 534–535
Jean, É. 92
Jenkins, A.K. 112, 126
Jepsen, A. 306, 307, 319
Ji, C.-H.C. 157, 159, 165
Joannès, F. 28, 31, 47, 134, 143, 262, 264
Jobling, D. 298
Johnson, M.D. 381, 391, 538, 548
Johnson, W.M. 226
Johnston, P.S. 246, 253
Johnstone, W. 257, 264
Jones, C.E. 47, 49, 143
Jonker, L.C. 164, 166, 219, 226, 386, 387, 389–391, 536
Judd, E.P. 230, 239, 387, 391
Jursa, M. 27, 31, 46, 130, 132–134, 136, 138, 143, 146

Kaiser, O. 311, 319
Kalimi, I. 30, 32, 78, 265, 356, 365, 382–383, 391
Kalvelagen, D. 142
Kansteiner, W. 425, 432
Karim, A. 296, 298
Karrer, C. 226
Katchadourian, L. 155, 165

Katz, D. 142
Katz, H. 185
Kautsky, J.H. 237, 239
Kawashima, R.S. 342, 352
Keck, L.E. 297
Keel, O. 162, 250, 253
Keil, C.F. 370, 377
Kelle, B.E. 106, 108, 110, 122, 124, 126, 128, 130, 143–144, 212–213
Kellens, J. 43, 45, 47
Keller, M. 281, 283
Kellermann, U. 534–535
Kelly, B.E. 120, 121, 126, 381, 391
Kendall, J.C. 422, 432
Kent, R.G. 36, 42, 43, 47
Kenyon, K.M. 90, 121, 126, 259, 264
Kerr, R.M. 77
Kessler, R. 107
Keulen, P.S.F. van 120, 126
Khan, D. 30, 117, 126
Khatchadourian, L. 165
Khazanov, A.M. 86, 90
Killebrew, A.E. 80–81, 85, 86, 88–90, 92, 108
Killen, K. 509
King, M.P. 461, 465
King, P.J. 248, 253
Kipfer, S. 107, 504–505, 508
Kipling, R. 514, 524
Kirwan, J. 288, 298
Kisilevitz, S. 249, 253
Kitchen, K.A. 109, 116, 126
Klapheck, E. 458, 465
Klauck, H.-J. 535
Kleer, M. 501, 508
Klein, L.R. 478, 482
Klein, R.W. 208, 212–213, 309, 319, 356–357, 362, 364–365, 376, 381, 383, 385, 389, 391–392, 501, 508
Kletter, R. 263–264
Klingbeil, G.A. 91, 93
Klinkott, H. 37, 47
Kloner, A. 158, 165
Kloppenborg, J.S. 544, 548
Klutz, T.E. 518, 524
Knapp, A. 25, 31
Knauf, E.A. 24, 30–31, 115, 117, 126, 153, 165, 311, 319
Knibb, M.A. 376
Knohl, I. 257, 262, 264
Knoppers, G.N. 82, 133–134, 143–145, 147–151, 159, 160–161, 164–169, 208, 212–213, 282, 308, 320–321, 361, 363, 365, 379, 381, 383, 385–386, 388, 391–392
Knowles, M. 153, 158, 166, 257, 259, 262, 264
Knust, J.W. 77
Koch, H. 48
Koch, K. 46, 229, 237, 239, 535
Kochavi, M. 84
Kofoed, J.B. 19
Köhbach, M. 144

Kolk, B.A. van der 422, 432
Konstan, D. 404
Kooij, A. van der 116, 126, 357-358, 365, 375, 377
Koroglu, K. 92
Korpel, M.C.A. 168, 263
Kosters, W.H. 229, 239
Kozuh, M. 47, 49, 143
Kraemer, D.C. 68, 77, 382, 392
Kratz, R.G. 107, 158, 166, 315, 320
Krause, J.J. 310, 320
Krebernik, M. 146
Kreuzer, S. 63
Krug, E.G. 286, 298
Kuan, J.K. 110, 126
Kuenen, A. 229, 239, 303-304, 308, 320
Kuhrt, A. 35-36, 38-41, 45-48, 119, 121, 126, 132, 143, 155, 166, 168
Kümmel, W. 504-505, 508
Kunin, S.D. 291, 298

Laato, A. 360, 377
Labahn, A. 220, 226
LaCapra, D. 427, 431-432
Laffey, A.L. 221, 226
Lambert, W.G. 132, 143
Landsberger, B. 114, 129
Lanfranchi, G. 34, 47
Lang, B. 432
Lange, A. 62-63
Langer, L.L. 424, 432
Langgut, D. 153, 167
Lanzmann, C. 423, 432
Lapsley, J.E. 226-227, 420
Lassner, J. 514, 517, 520, 524, 545, 548
Laub, D. 422-423, 427, 430-432
Lauinger, J. 318, 320
Lawrence, B.B. 296, 298
Lawrence, D.H. 491-493, 495
Leader, R.E. 503, 508
Lecoq, P. 36, 47
Lee, K.J. 107
Lee, K.S. 219, 227
Lefkovitz, L.H. 227
Lehrman, S.M. 520, 524
Leichty, E. 25, 31
Leith, M.J.W. 155, 157, 159-160, 166
Lemaire, A. 28, 31, 36, 39, 47, 73, 77, 122, 127, 134, 139, 143, 148, 158, 166, 262, 264, 548
Lemche, N.P. 80, 86, 92, 237-239
Lemmelijn, B. 62, 63
LeMon, J.M. 247, 249, 253, 321
Leneman, H. 505, 508
Lenfant, D. 35, 47
Lenski, G.E. 237, 239
Leonard-Fleckman, M. 106-107
Lesko, L.H. 93
Leuchter, M. 199

Levi, P. 423, 432
Levin, C. 32, 132-133, 142-144
Levin, Y. 145, 164
Levine, B.A. 480, 482
Levine, L.D. 48
Levinson, B.M. 148-149, 166-168, 190, 199
Levinson, J. 165
Levy, T.E. 80, 90-92
Lewis, D.M. 46-47, 49
Lichtheim, M. 85, 92
Lieb, M. 537, 548
Lieberman, S. 125
Liesen, J. 451
Lifton, R.J. 426, 432
Lim, T.H. 164
Lincoln, B. 155, 162, 166
Lipiński, E. 21, 31
Lipschits, O. 27, 31, 76, 92, 129, 132, 141, 144-145, 150-154, 157, 163-167, 169, 231, 238-239, 265
Liss, H. 134, 144
Locke, J. 191, 199
Lohfink, N. 311, 320
Lohr, J.N. 91
Lohrmann, M.J. 524
Long, B.O. 340, 352
Long, S.D. 475, 482
Long, V.P. 126, 340-341, 352
Loprieno, A. 81, 92
Lord, A.B. 395-396, 405
Lord, G.D. 504, 508
Lorderbaum, M. 199
Loretz, O. 22, 31
Lovelace, V. 481
Lozano, R. 298
Lubetski, M. 30, 141, 143, 253
Lucas, R., Jr. 189, 198
Luckhurst, R. 423, 432
Ludwig, C. 503, 508
Luker, L.M. 391
Luria, B.T. 451
Lust, J. 343, 352
Luther, M. 518, 524
Luukko, M. 23, 31
Lynch, M. 273, 280-281, 283
Lyon, D.G. 259, 264

Maas, F. 282
Macalister, R.A.S. 263-264
Macchi, J.-D. 266, 268, 282
MacDonald, N. 272, 281-283, 480, 482
Machinist, P. 108, 535
Mackenzie, D.N. 48
Madsen, A.A. 67, 76, 354, 365
Maeir, A.M. 77, 92
Magdalene, F.R. 132, 144, 240
Magen, Y. 160, 164, 167, 255, 259, 264
Magness, J. 77

Mahlmann-Bauer, B. 508
Maitland, S. 455, 465
Malamat, A. 121–122, 127
Mannati, M. 257, 264
Marböck, J. 501, 508
Marbury, H.R. 237–238, 240, 388
Marcus, D. 65–66, 77
Marcus, L.S. 460, 465
Marrs, R.R. 391
Marsman, H.J. 227
Marti, L. 145
Martin, C. 36, 47–48
Martínez-Alfaro, M.J. 430, 432
Marzahn, J. 135–136, 145
Mason, E. 537, 548
Matheson, G. 519, 523–524
Mathiesen, I. 40, 47
Matthews, C.R. 92
Matthews, V.H. 84, 92, 122, 127
Mayer, C. 280, 503, 508
Mayer, W. 22, 24, 31, 112, 115–116, 127
Mayes, A.D.H. 19, 308, 320
Mazar, A. 106, 108, 128, 179, 185
Mazar, M. 91
Mbuwayesango, D. 285, 298
McBride, S.D. 281, 283, 334, 337
McCarter, P.K., Jr. 62, 281, 283
McCarthy, D.J. 199
McConville, J.G. 82–83, 92, 281, 283, 321, 330, 337
McCray, W.A. 523, 524
McDonald, P.M. 285, 297–298
McFarland, I.A. 334, 337
McGinn, B. 535
McInerney, J. 92, 145
McIntire, P.G. 298
McKay, J.W. 119–120, 127
McKenzie, S.L. 108, 167, 208, 213, 310–311, 317–318, 320, 385, 390–392, 497–498, 508
McKinnon, J.W. 508
Meier, C. 507
Melamed, Y.Y. 535
Mendenhall, G.E. 87, 92, 199
Menken, Maarten J.J. 547–548
Mercy, J.A. 298
Merrill, A.L. 262, 264, 299
Meshel, Z. 247, 253
Mettinger, T. 199, 245, 253
Metzger, B.M. 534–535
Metzger, H. 36, 47
Metzger, H.-D. 504, 508
Meyer, H. 504, 508
Meyers, C.L. 147, 167, 178, 185, 226
Meyers, E.M. 126, 147, 167
Meyers, J. 238, 240
Michaelis, J.D. 228, 240, 368, 377
Michalowski, P. 398, 403, 405
Micheel, R. 212–213

Middlemas, J.A. 131–132, 141, 144
Miedema, N. 508
Milgrom, J. 127
Millar, J.G. 281, 283
Millard, A.R. 22, 31, 116, 127
Millard, M. 501, 508
Miller, G.P. 190, 199
Miller, J.M. 112–113, 119, 121–122, 127, 229, 237, 240
Miller, M.L. 132–133, 143–144
Miller, P.D. 262, 264, 283
Miller, R.D. II 77
Milton, J. 477–478
Min, K.-J. 68, 77
Miner, E. 508
Miroschedji, P. de 34, 47, 92
Mitchell, C. 162, 220, 227, 406, 420
Moberly, R.W.L. 285, 298
Momigliano, A.D. 36, 47, 402–403, 405
Monk-Turner, E. 296, 298
Monroe, L.A.S. 334, 338
Moor, J.C. de 451
Moore, C.A. 127
Moore, D.D. 465
Moore, M.B. 106, 108, 110, 126, 128, 212–213
Moore, S.D. 510
Moreno Hernández, A. 62
Morgan, M.A. 525
Morgan, T. 284, 298
Morgenstern, M. 199
Morris, E. 80, 90, 92
Mosis, R. 120, 127, 365
Movers, F.C. 353, 365, 534–535
Mowinckel, S. 396, 405, 529, 534–535
Moyise, S. 542, 548
Moynahan, J. 505, 509
Muddiman, J. 92
Mueller, J. 460, 465
Muilenberg, J. 199
Müller, A. 503, 509
Müller, R. 108
Müller, W.G. 508
Müllner, I. 216, 227
Münkler, H. 504, 509
Murphy, C.M. 185
Murphy, F.A. 547–548
Murphy, K.J. 480, 482
Murray, P.D. 297–298
Myers, J.M. 377

Na'aman, N. 21, 23, 30–31, 81, 83, 88, 90–91, 93, 108, 113–114, 117, 121, 123, 125, 127, 247, 249, 253
Nadal, M. 432
Nam, R. 175, 185
Naveh, J. 36, 46–47, 122, 127
Neal, A.G. 425, 432
Nelson, R.D. 19, 93, 204, 213, 293, 298, 308, 313, 315, 320

Nentel, J. 320
Neumann, H. 146
Neusner, J. 295, 298
Newman, J.H. 263, 264
Newsom, C.A. 226–227, 420, 481
Newsome, J.D. 365, 401, 405
Neyman, C.B. 476, 482
Ngan, L.L.E. 227
Nickelsburg, G.W.E. 367, 377
Niditch, S. 84, 93, 246, 253, 259, 264, 396–397, 401–403, 405, 469–470, 477, 480–482
Niehr, H. 160, 167
Niemann, H.M. 166
Niessen, F. 451
Nihan, C. 153, 159, 167, 320
Nissinen, M. 25, 31, 213, 244, 253
Nitsche, S.A. 504, 509
Noll, K.L. 311, 319–321
Noll, M.A. 418, 420
Nolland, J. 538, 548
Noort, E. 451
North, R.G. 120, 127
Norton, G.J. 77, 365, 378
Noth, M. 82, 84, 93, 108, 119, 127, 176, 185, 201–203, 205, 208, 213, 229, 237, 240, 267–268, 303, 305–313, 317, 320, 325–326, 338–339, 341, 352, 365, 372, 377, 380–381, 392, 412
Notley, R.S. 128
Novak, A. 425, 432
Novotny, J. 24, 31, 76
Nyström, J. 545, 548

O'Brien, M.A. 203, 205, 213, 312, 320
Oded, B. 23, 32, 120, 127, 152, 167
Oelsner, J. 132, 137, 144
Oeming, M. 134, 144–145, 150, 153, 163, 165, 167, 238–239, 265
Ofer, A. 118, 128
Olmo Lete, G. del 142
Olmstead, A.T. 128
Orlin, E. 77
Orlinsky, H.M. 57, 62
Ornan, T. 247, 249, 253
Osborne, G.R. 546, 548
Osborne, R. 472, 474–475, 482
Oshima, T. 23, 25, 31
Ostwald, M. 46–47, 49
Otto, E. 313–314, 320–321
Overholt, T.W. 299

Pakkala, J. 26, 27, 32, 69, 74, 77, 270–274, 280–283, 318, 321, 365, 382, 384, 392, 534–535
Pangle, T.L. 189, 199
Paoletti, J.T. 504, 509
Pardee, D. 402, 405
Park, S.J. 110, 128
Parker, B.J. 133, 144

Parker, J.F. 227
Parker, S.B. 19
Parkinson, W.A. 89, 93
Parpola, A. 114, 129
Parpola, S. 22–25, 30, 32, 114, 128
Parry, D.W. 62
Parvis, S. 451
Patte, D. 298
Pearce, L.E. 26, 28–29, 32, 130–133, 136–137, 144, 148, 161, 167, 183, 186, 255, 262, 264
Pearson, D. 93
Pedersén, O. 27, 32
Penner, T. 420, 540, 548
Perdue, L.G. 419–420
Perrot, J. 36, 38, 46–47
Person, R.F. 116, 128, 212–213, 269, 279, 283, 321, 394, 402, 405
Peters, G. 450–451
Petersen, D.L. 209, 213
Pietsch, M. 502, 509
Pioske, D.D. 509
Piotrowski, N.G. 502, 509
Piquer Otero, A. 62
Pisano, S. 77, 365, 378
Piscator, J. 518, 525
Pitkänen, P. 419–420
Piwowar, A. 70, 77
Pobee, J.S. 465
Pohlmann, K.-F. 365, 367–370, 372, 377, 378
Polak, F.H. 395, 405
Polanyi, K. 174, 186
Pollard, M. 298
Polzin, R. 333, 338–341, 352, 355, 365
Pomykala, K.E. 501, 509
Porten, B. 36, 38, 41, 47–48, 167, 262–264
Porter, J.R. 199
Porter, S.E. 548
Posener, G. 36, 38, 48
Potts, D. 34, 48
Pregil, M.E. 77
Prescott, A.L. 504–505, 509
Prior, M. 285, 296, 298
Pritchard, J.B. 525
Pröbstl, V. 263–264
Propp, W.H.C. 80, 90–92
Provan, I.W. 312, 321
Psychny, K. 166, 280, 282
Pummer, R. 159–160, 167
Purvis, J.D. 159, 167
Pury, A. de 266, 268, 282, 319–321

Raaflaub, K.A. 48, 404
Rabbinowitz, J. 515
Rabin, H. 451
Rad, G. von 267–268, 281, 283, 285, 298, 307, 322, 325, 327, 333, 338
Rai, T.S. 290–291, 296, 297

Rainey, A.F. 84–85, 93, 113, 128
Ramakers, B. 507
Rawlinson, G. 530, 534–535
Rawls, J. 191, 193, 199
Ray, P.J., Jr. 91, 93
Redditt, P.L. 76, 147, 163, 382, 390
Redford, D.B. 80–81, 86, 93, 110, 115–116, 128
Redmount, C. 80–81, 93
Reimer, D.J. 378
Reiner, E. 451
Reisner, G.A. 259, 264
Remnick, D. 451
Rendsburg, G. 199
Rendtorff, R. 75, 77, 326, 338
Rezetko, R. 164, 319
Richards, K.H. 239–240, 321, 377, 391–392
Richardson, S. 30, 32
Richter, S.L. 281, 283
Richter, W. 341, 345, 352
Ricoeur, P. 295, 298
Riley, W. 276, 283
Ringe, S.H. 226–227, 420, 481
Rippin, A. 535
Ristau, K.A. 134, 143, 282, 381, 392
Rivers, F. 513, 525
Roaf, M. 47
Roberts, F. 521, 525
Roberts, J. 537, 548
Robinson, C.S. 512, 525
Rochberg-Halton, F. 48
Rodríguez Láiz, A. 502, 509
Rodríguez, R. 545, 548
Rofé, A. 451
Rogerson, J. 114, 128
Rollinger, R. 47, 142
Rollston, C.A. 139, 144
Römer, T.C. 212–213, 262, 264, 266, 268, 282, 314, 318, 321, 337–338, 346, 352, 408, 412, 420
Rooke, D.W. 488, 495
Root, M.C. 34, 43, 46, 48, 155, 167
Rose, M.B. 460, 465
Rosenbaum, J. 128
Rosenberg, A.J. 512, 525
Rosenberg, J. 199
Rosenfeld, A.H. 433
Rosenthal, M.A. 535
Roth, M.T. 138, 145
Rothberg, M. 425, 432
Rothenbusch, R. 64, 77
Rousseau, J.-J. 191, 199
Rowland, C. 490, 495
Rowlett, L.L. 285, 298
Rückl, J. 317–318, 321
Rudolph, W. 67, 70, 74, 77
Ruiz, J.-P. 537, 548
Rüttersworden, U. 534–535

Sæbø, M. 108, 535
Safrai, S. 262, 264
Saidel, B.A. 88, 93
Saley, R.J. 62
Salmen, W. 509
Sancisi-Weerdenburg, H. 34, 42–43, 45–46, 48
Sanders, S.L. 141, 145
Sänger, D. 502, 509
Sass, B. 135–136, 145
Sasson, J. 141
Satlow, M.L. 77
Saulcy, F.J.C. 237, 240
Sawyer, J.F.A. 475, 482
Schade, H. 503, 509
Schaeffer, F.A. 451
Schaudig, H. 133, 142–143
Schearing, L.S. 318, 320
Schenker, A. 62, 63, 72, 76–78, 359, 364–365, 374, 378
Scherer, A. 108
Schiffman, L.H. 77, 166
Schipper, B.U. 123, 128
Schloen, J.D. 91, 168
Schmid, K. 164, 319, 333, 336–338, 352
Schmidt, B.B. 144, 149, 168, 405
Schmidt, E.F. 36, 42, 48
Schmitt, H.-C. 318, 321
Schmitt, R. 36, 42, 43, 48, 246, 251–252
Schmitz, P.C. 77
Schnegg, K. 142
Schneider, T.J. 80, 90–92, 340, 352, 477, 481–482
Schniedewind, W.M. 139–140, 145, 212–213
Schnocks, J. 508
Schökel, L.A. 127
Scholz, S. 227
Schottroff, L. 226–227
Schramm, B. 319, 321
Schreier, J. 482
Schroeder, J.A. 465
Schulte, L. 155–156, 167
Schwartz, B.J. 164
Schwartz, G. 491, 495
Schwartz, R.M. 285, 298
Schweitzer, S.J. 376, 381, 383, 387, 389–392
Searle, L. 351
Secunda, S. 33, 140, 143, 146, 157, 162, 165, 168
Segal, J.B. 36, 48
Seibert, E.A. 407, 420
Seitz, C.R. 115, 128
Seow, C.L. 517, 525
Seybold, K. 257, 264
Seymour, J.D. 512, 514, 517, 519, 523, 525
Shaked, S. 36, 47, 48
Shapira, A. 450–451
Shectman, S. 262, 265
Sherman, P. 199
Sherwood, Y. 505, 509
Siapkas, J. 134, 145

Siedlecki, A. 534, 536
Silberman, L.H. 520, 525
Silberman, N.A. 106–107, 113–115, 117–118, 122, 123, 125
Sills, D.L. 298
Silverman, J.M. 391
Simon, M. 513–516, 519–522, 525
Ska, J.-L. 108, 148, 168, 535
Slotki, J. 512–513, 515, 518–519, 521–522, 524–525
Smend, R. 202, 213, 309, 311–312, 321
Smith-Christopher, D.L. 230, 237, 240, 388, 392
Smith, D.L. 237, 240
Smith, H. 509
Smith, H.S. 36, 47, 48
Smith, M. 534, 536
Smith, M.S. 86, 93, 148, 168, 243, 245, 253, 269, 283
Smoak, J.D. 263, 265
Soggin, J.A. 122, 128, 285, 298, 372, 378
Soldt, W. 142
Sollberger, E. 125
Sommer, B.D. 281, 283
Sonnet, J.-P. 497, 509
Southwood, K.E. 134, 138, 139, 145, 387, 392
Spain, S. 503, 509
Spalinger, A. 128
Sparks, H.F.D. 514, 517, 525
Sparks, J.T. 539, 548
Sparks, K.L. 134, 145
Spieckermann, H. 46, 119, 128, 262, 265
Spina, F.A. 200
Spinoza, B. 350, 352, 526, 529–532, 534, 536
Spitzer, L. 431
Stade, B. 115, 128
Stager, L.E. 86, 90, 93, 125, 248, 253
Stahl, N. 451
Staley, A. 495
Stanley, R. 227
Stanton, E.C. 461, 465, 469–470, 480, 482
Starkey, J.L. 128, 263, 265
Starr, L.A. 464–465
Stavrakopoulou, F. 120, 128, 141, 145
Steen, E. van der 88, 90
Steger, H. 503, 509
Steinsaltz, A. 482
Stern, D. 512–518, 520, 524
Stern, E. 149–150, 168
Stern, E. 36, 48, 91, 117–118, 124, 128, 148, 153, 168, 259, 261, 263, 265
Stern, I. 137, 145, 158, 165
Sternberg, M. 339, 350, 352
Steussy, M.J. 336, 338, 497, 500–501, 509
Stevens, C.S. 544, 548
Steymans, H.U. 313, 318, 321
Stien, P.T. 422, 432
Stökl, J. 38, 48, 140–141, 144, 145, 163, 165, 167, 169
Stolper, M.W. 28, 30, 32, 34, 36–37, 40–41, 45, 47–49, 78, 132, 145, 161–162, 168, 262, 265
Stone, J.M. 522, 525

Stone, K. 215, 217, 227
Stone, M.E. 377
Stowe, H.B. 462, 464, 465, 473, 476, 482
Stratton, B.J. 227
Strauss, L. 190, 199
Strauss, M.L. 502, 509
Strawn, B.A. 117, 124, 128, 162–163, 168, 247, 249, 253
Streck, M.P. 32, 146
Strecker, G. 165
Stronach, D. 36, 49, 154, 168
Stroup, G.W. 282
Sugirtharajah, R.S. 410, 419–420
Sumner, W. 34, 42, 49
Suntrup, R. 508
Swart, I. 285, 298
Sweeney, M.A. 119–121, 124, 128, 203–205, 207–208, 212–213, 351–352
Szuchman, J. 86, 93

Tadmor, H. 19, 22–23, 30, 32, 110, 112, 114, 116, 125, 128–129
Tal, K. 424, 432
Tal, O. 153, 164
Tallon, F. 46
Talmon, S. 199
Talshir, D. 67, 78, 355, 365, 371
Talshir, Z. 62, 65, 67, 78, 357–359, 365, 367–371, 376, 378
Tamarkin Reis, P. 223, 227
Tamcke, M. 509
Tan, K.H. 545, 548
Tatum, L. 118, 129
Tavernier, J. 73
Taylor, M.A. 465, 480, 482
Telushkin, J. 473, 482
Thackeray, H. St. J. 370, 378
Thames, J.T., Jr. 152, 168
Thiele, E.R. 112, 129, 252, 253
Thomas, H. 297
Thompson, R.J. 321
Throntveit, M.A. 354–355, 366
Thureau-Dangin, F. 72, 78
Tilia, A.B. 36, 49
Timm, S. 137, 145
Tinney, S. 139, 145
Tolini, G. 134, 137–138, 145
Torijano Morales, P.A. 62–63, 512–514, 517–518, 522, 525
Torrey, C.C. 67, 73–74, 78, 229, 237, 240, 368, 370–371, 376, 378, 532, 534, 536
Tov, E. 62–63, 166, 343, 352
Trebolle Barerra, J. 54, 56, 62–63
Trible, P. 227
Troyer, K. de 62, 369, 372, 376, 377
Tsfania, L. 255, 259, 264
Tufnell, O. 263, 265
Tuplin, C. 73, 78
Turner, R. 298
Turner, V. 290–291, 293, 298

Uehlinger, C. 24–25, 32, 112, 122, 129, 155, 168, 250, 253
Uhlenbruch, F. 389–392
Ulf, C. 142
Ullendorff, E. 519–520, 525
Ulrich, E.C. 62–63, 65, 78, 366, 392
Ulrich, K. 227
Umansky, E. 458, 465
Ussishkin, D. 24, 32, 113, 115–116, 129, 262–263, 265

Valkama, K. 27, 32
Vallat, F. 37, 49
Valler, S. 509
Van Buylaere, G. 23, 31
Van der Spek, R.J. 39, 49
Van der Toorn, K. 149, 167–168, 246, 253
Van Gemeren, W.A. 298
Van Rooy, H.F. 451
Van Seters, J. 19, 83, 93, 108, 292, 297–298, 309–311, 318, 321, 335, 338, 497, 505, 509
Vander Stichele, C. 420
Vanderhooft, D. 133, 139–140, 145, 150, 154, 167, 203, 213
VanderKam, J.C. 68, 75, 78, 166, 355, 366, 381, 392
Vansina, J. 394, 405
Vattel, E. de 191, 198
Vaughn, A.G. 108, 113, 129
Vaux, R. de 281–282
Veijola, T. 108, 309, 311, 322
Veldhuis, N. 139, 146
Verheyden, J. 544, 548
Vermeylen, J. 108, 506–507
Vidal, J. 142
Viezel, E. 535
Vinay, D. 503, 510
Visser, I. 425, 433
Vogt, E. 114, 129
Volf, M. 295–296, 298
Volkan, V. 425, 433
Voltaire. 474–475, 482, 505
Volz, P. 318
Effra, H. von 495
Vorobej, M. 286, 289, 298
Vos, J.C. de 451

Wacker, M.-T. 225–227
Waerzeggers, C. 38, 48, 49, 132–134, 140–141, 144–146, 163, 165, 167–169, 391
Wälchi, S. 108
Walde, B. 378
Wallerstein, I. 133, 146, 175, 181, 186
Walters, S.D. 55, 63
Walton, J. 335, 338
Walzer, M. 189, 199
Warrior, R.A. 291, 298, 412, 420
Warshaw, T.S. 509
Wartenberg-Potter, B. von 465
Waschke, E.-J. 502, 510
Wasmuth, M. 38, 49

Watanbe, K. 22, 32
Waters, M. 49, 147, 168
Watt, W.M. 519, 525
Watts, J.W. 39, 49, 148, 156, 165, 168, 499, 510
Wazana, N. 262, 265
Webb, B.G. 340–341, 352
Webb, P. 136, 146
Weber, M. 175, 186
Weidner, E.F. 27, 32, 131, 146
Weinberg, J.P. 108
Weinfeld, M. 19, 31, 125, 281, 283
Weinreb, H. 482
Weippert, H. 118, 129
Weippert, M. 21, 32, 85, 245
Weiss, B.G. 337
Welch, J.W. 337
Wellhausen, J. 120, 129, 229, 237, 240, 267, 285, 298, 303–304, 308, 312, 322, 327, 331–332, 338
Wells, B. 199
Welten, P. 366
Wendrich, W. 92, 93
Wenham, G.J. 126
Wénin, A. 341, 352, 377
Werline, R.A. 263, 265
Wesley, J. 522, 525
Wessel, K. 502, 510
West, M. 226, 227
Westbrook, R. 31, 199
Westermann, C. 311, 322
Wette, W.M.L. de 304, 319
White, C. 451
White, H. 398–399, 405
White, J.B. 125
White, M.C. 107
Whitelam, K.W. 87, 93, 179, 185, 199–200
Whitfield, B. 446, 451
Whyte, A. 512–513, 521–523, 525
Wiesehöfer, J. 49, 147, 168, 534, 536
Wiesel, E. 423, 433
Wilcox, M. 540, 548
Wildavsky, A. 200
Willi, T. 108, 366
Williams, R.B. 296, 299
Williams, S.N. 82, 83, 92
Williams, T. 392
Williamson, H.G.M. 32, 67, 69, 74, 78, 120, 124, 128, 129, 147, 151–152, 168, 267, 282–283, 354, 356–357, 359, 362, 366, 369, 372–374, 378–379, 384, 386, 392, 530, 534, 536
Willie, R. 509
Wilson, I.D. 281, 283, 389, 392
Wilson, R.R. 200, 381, 392
Winckler, H. 24, 32
Winitzer, A. 140, 146, 157, 168
Winthrop, J. 418, 420
Witte, M. 318
Wittfogel, K. 175, 186
Wittgenstein, L. 286, 289, 299

Wojcik, J. 507
Wolak, A.J. 139, 146
Wolff, H.W. 213, 307, 321, 322
Wolfram, H. 88, 93
Wolpe, D. 108
Wolschke-Bulmahn, J. 163
Woods, C. 47, 49, 143
Woolf, D.R. 394, 405
Woolley, J.T. 450–451
Wright, C.J.H. 284, 299
Wright, D.P. 93, 297
Wright, G.E. 83, 285, 297
Wright, J.L. 74, 78, 108, 130, 143–144, 150, 169, 382, 384, 392, 534, 536
Wright, J.W. 78, 381, 392
Wright, N.T. 544, 548
Wunsch, C. 28–29, 32, 130–132, 137–138, 144, 146, 148, 161, 167, 183, 186, 238, 240, 255, 262, 264
Würthwein, E. 238, 240, 312, 322
Wuttman, M. 42, 49
Wyatt, N. 142
Wyss, R.L. 502, 510

Yadin, Y. 83, 93, 129, 443
Yamada, S. 22–23, 30, 32
Yardeni, A. 36, 41, 48, 167, 262, 264
Yee, G.A. 227, 238, 240, 409, 420, 463, 465

Yerushalmi, D. 162
Yongue, C.D. 451
Yoon, D.I. 548
Young, R.A. 24, 33
Young, T.C.
Younger, K.L., Jr. 21–24, 32, 83, 93, 110–111, 114, 129, 161, 169, 313, 322, 342, 352
Yurco, F.J. 86, 93

Zadok, R. 23, 28, 31, 33, 73, 78, 132, 134–135, 146, 157, 161, 169, 251, 253
Zahnd, U. 503, 510
Zehnder, M. 285, 299
Zemer, M. 458, 465
Zenger, E. 500–502, 508, 510
Zertal, A. 83–84, 93, 159, 169
Zetterholm, M. 544, 548
Zevit, Z. 122, 129, 242, 253
Zimmermann, F. 370, 378
Zingel, H.J. 510
Zohar, N.J. 199
Zorn, J.R. 263, 265
Zsengellér, J. 485, 495
Zucker, D. 535
Zuckerman, S. 87, 90, 93
Zunz, L. 67, 78, 353, 366, 530, 534, 536
Zwi, A.B. 298